REPORT OF THE
ABORIGINAL JUSTICE INQUIRY
OF MANITOBA

VOLUME 1:
THE JUSTICE SYSTEM
AND
ABORIGINAL PEOPLE

Associate Chief Justice
A.C. HAMILTON
Commissioner

Associate Chief Judge
C. M. SINCLAIR
Commissioner

PUBLIC INQUIRY INTO THE ADMINISTRATION
OF JUSTICE AND ABORIGINAL PEOPLE

Canadian Cataloguing in Publication Data

Manitoba. Public Inquiry into the Administration of
Justice and Aboriginal People
    Report of the Aboriginal Justice Inquiry of Manitoba

Commissioners: A.C. Hamilton, C.M. Sinclair.
Cover Title.

A summarized version of Volume 1 of this report exists on videocassette, available in English, Cree, Ojibway, Dene, Dakota, and Island Lake dialect.

Includes bibliographical references.

Contents:
vol. 1. The justice system and Aboriginal people.
vol. 2. The deaths of Helen Betty Osborne and John Joseph Harper.

ISBN 0–7711–0882–6

1. Justice, Administration of—Manitoba. 2. Discrimination in criminal justice administration—Manitoba. 3. Race discrimination—Manitoba. 4. Indians of North America—Manitoba—Legal status, laws, etc.. 5. Métis—Manitoba—Legal status, laws, etc. 6. Osborne, Helen Betty, 1952–1971. 7. Harper, John Joseph, 1951–1988.

I. Hamilton, A. C. II. Sinclair, C. M. III. Title. IV. Title: The justice system and Aboriginal people. V. Title: The deaths of Helen Betty Osborne and John Joseph Harper.

KEM529.5.C75 A75 1991   345.7127'05'08997   C91–092658–1

Printing: D. W. Friesen and Sons Ltd., Altona

 This Report is printed on recycled paper
using vegetable based inks.

The report is available from:

Queen's Printer
Lower Level – 200 Vaughan Street
Winnipeg, Manitoba
R3C 1T5
(204) 945–3101 fax (204) 945–7172

Cover and page design: Doowah Design Inc., Winnipeg

Logo Design: Keiron Flamand

The logo includes the Anglo-Canadian symbol for justice – the balance scales, which weigh evidence without favour to either side; the traditional Métis sash; eagle feathers, symbolic of strength and vision; which are attached to a traditional plains Indian shield, symbolic of protection, one of the functions of justice.

The circle, symbolic of the drum, which is important to Aboriginal peoples dominates the logo. Part of the symbolism of the drum is to represent the heartbeat of Mother Earth and closeness to nature. The circle is also symbolic of harmony and balance.

PUBLIC INQUIRY INTO THE ADMINISTRATION OF JUSTICE AND ABORIGINAL PEOPLE
5th floor-175 Carlton Street, Winnipeg, Manitoba R3C 3H9
ph. 945-5799, or 1-800-282-8069 (within Manitoba), or Fax Number 945-4246
Commissioners: Associate Chief Justice A.C. Hamilton, Associate Chief Judge C.M. Sinclair

August 12, 1991

The Honourable James C. McCrae
Minister of Justice
Room 104 Legislative Building
Winnipeg, Manitoba
R3C 0V8

Dear Mr. Minister:

We, the Commissioners appointed to investigate, report and
make recommendations respecting the relationship between the
administration of justice and Aboriginal peoples of Manitoba,
and to investigate all aspects of the deaths of Helen Betty Osborne
and J. J. Harper, hereby submit our Report.

Yours respectfully,

Associate Chief Justice A. C. Hamilton,
Commissioner

Associate Chief Judge C. M. Sinclair,
Commissioner

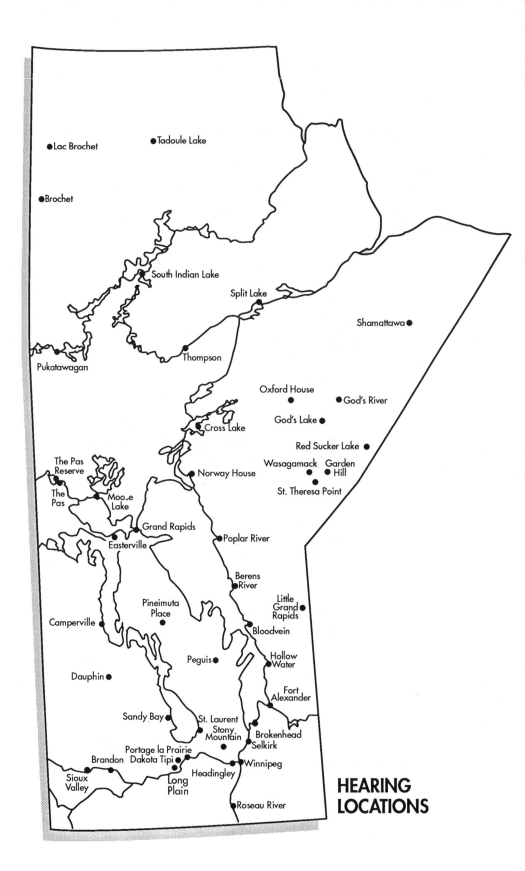

●Lac Brochet   ●Tadoule Lake

●Brochet

●South Indian Lake

Split Lake ●

Shamattawa ●

●Pukatawagan

Thompson ●

Oxford House ●

●God's River

God's Lake ●

●Cross Lake

Red Sucker Lake ●

Wasagamack ●   Garden Hill ●

The Pas Reserve ●

●Norway House

St. Theresa Point ●

The Pas ●

Moose Lake ●

●Grand Rapids

●Easterville

●Poplar River

Berens River ●

Pineimuta Place ●

Little Grand Rapids ●

Camperville ●

Bloodvein ●

Peguis ●

Hollow Water ●

Dauphin ●

Fort Alexander ●

Sandy Bay ●

St. Laurent ●

Stony Mountain ●

Brokenhead ●

Selkirk ●

Portage la Prairie ●

Brandon ●   Dakota Tipi ●

Winnipeg ●

Sioux Valley ●

Long Plain ●

Headingley ●

Roseau River ●

HEARING LOCATIONS

TABLE OF CONTENTS

7. ABORIGINAL JUSTICE SYSTEMS

8. COURT REFORM

CHAPTER 1

———

THE INQUIRY AND THE ISSUES

In law, with law, and through law, Canada has imposed a colonial system of government and justice upon our people without due regard to our treaty and Aboriginal rights. We respect law that is fair and just, but we cannot be faulted for denouncing those laws that degrade our humanity and rights as distinct peoples.

Ovide Mercredi
Berens River

Introduction

The justice system has failed Manitoba's Aboriginal people on a massive scale. It has been insensitive and inaccessible, and has arrested and imprisoned Aboriginal people in grossly disproportionate numbers. Aboriginal people who are arrested are more likely than non-Aboriginal people to be denied bail, spend more time in pre-trial detention and spend less time with their lawyers, and, if convicted, are more likely to be incarcerated.

It is not merely that the justice system has failed Aboriginal people; justice also has been denied to them. For more than a century the rights of Aboriginal people have been ignored and eroded. The result of this denial has been injustice of the most profound kind. Poverty and powerlessness have been the Canadian legacy to a people who once governed their own affairs in full self-sufficiency.

This denial of social justice has deep historical roots, and to fully understand the current problems we must look to their sources. We attempt to provide some of that context in the first part of this report. The mandate of this Inquiry is to examine the relationship between Aboriginal people and the justice system, and to suggest ways it might be improved. In this report we make many recommendations about how existing institutions of justice—the police, the courts, the jails—can be improved. But far more important than these reforms is our conclusion that the relationship between Aboriginal people and the rest of society must be transformed fundamentally. This transformation must be based on justice in its broadest sense. It must recognize that social and economic inequity is unacceptable and that only through a full recognition of Aboriginal rights—including the right to self-government—can the symptomatic problems of over-incarceration and disaffection be redressed.

The problems are daunting and our proposals are far-reaching. But we believe that in the interests of justice, the process of transformation must begin immediately.

The Creation of the Inquiry

The Aboriginal Justice Inquiry was created in response to two specific incidents in late 1987 and early 1988.

The first of these was the November 1987 trial of two men for the 1971 murder of Helen Betty Osborne in The Pas, Manitoba. While the trial established that four men were present when the young Aboriginal woman was killed, only one of them ultimately was convicted of any crime. Following the trial, allegations were made that the identity of the four individuals who had been present at the killing was known widely in the local community shortly after the murder. Both the chief of The Pas Indian Band and the mayor of The Pas called for a judicial inquiry that would examine that and other questions related to the murder, including why it had taken 16 years to bring the case to trial.

On March 9, 1988 J.J. Harper, executive director of the Island Lake Tribal Council, died following an encounter with a City of Winnipeg police officer. The following day the police department exonerated the officer involved. Others, particularly those in the province's Aboriginal community, believed that there were many questions which had been left unanswered by the police department's internal investigation. In this case as well, numerous individuals requested the creation of a judicial inquiry.

These two incidents were seen by many as troubling examples of the manner in which Manitoba's justice system was failing Aboriginal people. The evidence of this failure has been apparent and abundant. While Aboriginal people comprise 11.8% of Manitoba's population, they represent at least 50% of the province's prison population. Recidivism is common and there are few signs that rehabilitation programs are producing the desired result. Court services in Aboriginal communities are limited and occasional, beset by delay and misunderstanding. Aboriginal relations with police forces in all parts of the province are marked by mutual suspicion. Aboriginal criticism of the justice system generally has been harsh and pervasive. The need for change was becoming increasingly apparent.

On April 13, 1988 the Manitoba government created the Public Inquiry into the Administration of Justice and Aboriginal People, which we refer to as the Aboriginal Justice Inquiry, by Order-in-Council. The Order-in-Council was replaced later by a statute, subsection 3(1) of which provides:

> The commissioners shall investigate, report and make recommendations to the Minister of Justice on the relationship between the administration of justice and aboriginal peoples of Manitoba, guided by but not limited to the terms of reference set out in the Schedule.

The Schedule provides:

> The purpose of the commission is to inquire into, and make findings about, the state of conditions with respect to aboriginal people in the justice system in Manitoba and produce a final report for the Minister of Justice with conclusions, options and recommendations.

> The commission's deliberations are to include consideration of all aspects of the cases of J.J. Harper and Helen Betty Osborne, and the commission may make any additional recommendations that it deems appropriate with respect to those cases, including a recommendation that there be further consideration of particular matters or further inquiry into any aspect of either case.

Scope of inquiry

The scope of the commission is to include all components of the justice system, that is, policing, courts and correctional services. The commission is to consider whether and the extent to which aboriginal and non-aboriginal persons are treated differently by the justice system and whether there are specific adverse effects, including possible systemic discrimination against aboriginal people, in the justice system. The commission is to consider the manner in which the justice system now operates and whether there are alternative methods of dealing with aboriginal persons involved with the law. For example, the commission may review the following issues:

Policing:

– policing issues in relation to aboriginal people;

– deployment of personnel and accessibility of policing services;

– arrest and charging procedures;

– cultural sensitization for police officers and affirmative action programs;

– the conduct and training of wildlife officers relating to aboriginal people.

Access to and adequacy of legal counsel:

– eligibility and access to Legal Aid;

– access in remote communities.

Court processes:

– use of bail and custody;

– prosecutorial discretion and plea bargaining;

– role of court communicators;

– effect of time delays from arrest to trial;

– family proceedings;

– Youth Court;

– child welfare proceedings.

Court dispositions:

– comparative types of dispositions among aboriginal and non-aboriginal people;

– use of custodial sentences;

– availability of sentencing alternatives.

Post sentencing:

– differential success of aboriginal and non-aboriginal groups on probation;

– availability and use of fine option program;

– prison experiences, such as temporary absences and parole;

– use of half-way houses;

– re-integration to communities and reserves.

Other:

– awareness and knowledge of justice system by aboriginal people;

– communication between justice system personnel and aboriginal people;

– employment of aboriginal people in justice system.

The Work of the Inquiry

It was decided from the outset that the Inquiry would employ a variety of approaches. For the Osborne and Harper matters, we needed to examine the specific details and the conduct of particular individuals. These individuals might have their personal interests affected by this examination. As a result, we decided to proceed in a formal way, ensuring that all interested parties were represented by counsel, that all witnesses could be cross-examined, that their rights would be respected and that all testimony was given under oath.

The Inquiry faced a number of legal challenges launched by the Winnipeg Police Association. In 1989 the work of the Inquiry was delayed when one of these challenges led the Manitoba Court of Appeal to rule that Orders-in-Council establishing the Inquiry were invalid because they were passed in English only. The Inquiry was re-established subsequently by an *Act to Establish and Validate the Public Inquiry into the Administration of Justice and Aboriginal People.*

For the general questions about how the justice system dealt with Aboriginal people, we decided it was critical to hear directly from Aboriginal people. In order to do this, we travelled to the Aboriginal communities of this province: from Roseau River in the South to Tadoule Lake in the North, from Little Grand Rapids and Shamattawa in the East to The Pas and Sioux Valley in the West. Our Inquiry visited over 36 Aboriginal communities, approximately 20 of which were accessible only by winter roads and air travel. We also held hearings in seven other Manitoba communities, including extensive hearings in the city of Winnipeg. We held hearings in five provincial correctional institutions.

Non-Aboriginal persons also were encouraged to make presentations and many, including representatives of various governments, police forces and social agencies, did so. All the presentations we heard were crucial in coming to an understanding of the problems and in shaping our findings and recommendations.

All the community hearings were open to the public. Those who appeared before us were invited to express any and all of their concerns with the justice system. They were not required to submit written presentations, were not examined by Commission counsel, were not cross-examined and were not required to testify under oath.

We took this approach after considerable deliberation. We believed that Aboriginal people already were alienated from, and intimidated by, the formal court system. We wanted to utilize a process that would encourage frank and open expressions of opinion.

In these hearings we did not attempt to make determinations of "fact" about individual incidents and injustices that were related to us. Our primary concern was to learn how the legal system was working, what people felt about the system and if people were being well served by it. Approximately 1,000 people made presentations at our community hearings. These presentations have been transcribed and indexed, and form a permanent record of the proceedings.

In addition to the hearings, we conducted research projects covering a wide range of subjects. Some of the research was done by our own research staff, including a survey of inmates at seven correctional institutions, a survey of Crown and defence lawyers, and a survey of members of the judiciary. We also commissioned experts in various areas to prepare background papers for us. We combined this information with our own experience and the presentations made to us during community hearings to come to the conclusions we have reached.

To expand our understanding further, we visited a number of tribal courts in the United States, conducted a symposium on tribal courts and sponsored a conference of Aboriginal elders. In total, we received more than 1,200 presentations and exhibits, held 123 days of hearings, travelled more than 18,000 kilometres in Manitoba alone and accumulated approximately 21,000 pages of transcripts (including exhibits but not including research papers, library materials or written presentations). The communities we visited and the names of those who made presentations are listed in the Appendices. To those people, we owe a great debt of appreciation for their efforts and contributions.

During the community hearings, tribal court symposium and elders' conference, we had an opportunity to learn how Aboriginal people feel about Manitoba's justice system. In the dozens of communities and jails we visited, we heard Aboriginal people speak eloquently about their experiences with the various institutions of justice. Those experiences are overwhelmingly negative. Hundreds of presenters told us that the justice system is foreign, insensitive and often oppressive.

Whether they live in remote northern communities or in the city of Winnipeg, Aboriginal people spoke of their alienation from a justice system which arrests them, convicts them and incarcerates them in disproportionate numbers.

> We feel that we are victims of an alien system in law that has been imposed on us as Indian people, and that the devastating and tragic results are borne out in the negative statistics of our people involved in a Canadian system today.
>
> Chief Louis Stevenson
> Peguis

> Anyone in the justice system knows that Lady Justice is not blind in the case of Aboriginal people. She has one eye open. She has one eye open for us and dispenses justice unevenly and often very harshly. Her garment is rent. She does not give us equality. She gives us subjugation. She makes us second class citizens in our own land.
>
> Chief Allan Ross
> Norway House

They spoke of policing which is at times unresponsive and at times over-zealous, usually insensitive and often abusive. They spoke of a system of laws and courts which ignores significant cultural factors, and subjects them to incomprehensible proceedings and inordinate delays in the disposition of their cases. They spoke of a penal system which is harsh and unproductive. They spoke of parole procedures which delay their release from the penal system. They spoke of child welfare and youth justice systems which isolate young people from their families and their communities. They spoke too of historic wrongs, of betrayals and injustice, and of a vision for restoring social harmony to their communities.

We wish to offer special acknowledgement to the presenters who appeared before us. Their presentations were often disturbing and often poignant. They told us more about the state of the justice system and its effects on Aboriginal people than we could ever hope to have learned by any other means. Their words and their concerns provide the compass for our discussion of the issues.

Aboriginal Peoples in Manitoba

Definitions

In this report we have accepted the terms as found in the *Constitution Act, 1982*. The Aboriginal people of Canada include the Indian, Metis and Inuit people. That does, however, lead us inevitably to a consideration of what or who are Indians, Metis or Inuit. For our purposes, when we refer to Indians, we will be talking about the Aboriginal people who are entitled to be registered as Indians pursuant to the *Indian Act* of Canada. (S.C. 1985 c. 1–6) Metis people are those Aboriginal people of mixed blood, Aboriginal-white ancestry who are, and who consider themselves as being, neither Indian nor Inuit, or who regard themselves as Metis. Inuit people are those Aboriginal people who were known formerly as Eskimos.

Status Indians are those people recognized as Indians under the *Indian Act* and are entitled to be registered as such in the Indian Register maintained by the Department of Indian Affairs in Ottawa. That is why they are referred to sometimes as "registered" Indians.

"Non-status Indian" is a term which has been applied to people of Indian ancestry who are not, for one reason or another, registered under the *Indian Act*.

Manitoba's Aboriginal Population

There are a number of distinct nations or tribal groupings of Aboriginal people in Manitoba. Most of these peoples were present in Manitoba many centuries before Europeans arrived. The Aboriginal people of Manitoba are the Chipewyan (or Dene) in the northernmost parts of the province, the Cree in the North (with the Swampy Cree in the northwest and the Oji-Cree of Island Lake in the northeast), the Ojibway (or Saulteaux) in the central and eastern regions, the Dakota (or Sioux) in the South and western regions, and the Metis throughout the province. Each of these groups has a distinct history, culture, economy, language and political organization. In addition, by virtue of treaties, the Constitution and the *Manitoba Act*, Aboriginal peoples have a legal status that is unique among all other Canadians.

Because many Aboriginal people boycotted the 1986 census, it is difficult to reach an accurate determination of how many Aboriginal people there are in Manitoba. Although there are other sources to turn to, such as the Department of Indian Affairs and

Northern Development, the Department of Northern Affairs and the Manitoba Metis Federation, problems exist with the assumptions on which the reports of each of these agencies are based.

We engaged a statistical analysis firm to review various studies and produce an estimate for our Inquiry.[1] On this basis we have estimated the Aboriginal population of Manitoba in 1991 to be 130,000 and the non-Aboriginal population to be 969,300, of a total Manitoba population of 1,099,300. This means that Aboriginal people represent 11.8% of Manitoba's population. By contrast, the 1986 census estimates that only 85,000 Aboriginal people live in Manitoba (or 8.1% of the total population).

According to these estimates, there are 77,000 registered (status) Indians in Manitoba, 47,000 Metis and 6,000 non-status Indians. We estimate there are 49,000 Aboriginal persons living on reserves and 81,500 Aboriginal persons living off reserves. This means that 37% of Aboriginal people live on reserves and 63% live off reserves. Approximately 63% of status Indians in Manitoba live on reserves, which is one of the highest proportions of on-reserve residencies in Canada.

We estimate that 41,000 Aboriginal people (or 36% of the province's Aboriginal population) live in the North, where they constitute 61% of that region's population of 76,517.

In southern Manitoba, excluding the city of Winnipeg, we estimate that there are 42,500 Aboriginal people (or 33% of the province's Aboriginal population). They constitute 10.7% of that region's population of 396,500.

We estimate that 41,000 Aboriginal people (or 31% of the province's Aboriginal population) live in the city of Winnipeg. They constitute 6.5% of Winnipeg's population of 626,232.

Manitoba's status Indians are organized in bands or, as they have come to refer to themselves, First Nations. Most First Nations have lands reserved exclusively for them under the *Indian Act*. There are 61 First Nations in Manitoba. Because some bands have more than one land reserve, these 61 First Nations live on a total of 102 land reserves. There are a number of claims still outstanding about the designation of reserves.

Manitoba First Nations generally are small, with approximately 40 of them having populations of less than 1,000, and approximately 25 with populations of less than 500.[2] Of all the regions in Canada, Manitoba has the highest proportion of its band population living in remote areas; for nine or 10 months a year, approximately 20 Aboriginal communities are accessible only by air. On the other hand, Manitoba has the lowest proportion of bands in urban locations in Canada.[3] This is in sharp contrast to Manitoba's non-Aboriginal population, more than half of whom live in one central location: Winnipeg.

The 1986 census reported that 28% of all Manitoba's Indian population had an Aboriginal language as the first language spoken as a child and still understood the language. It was reported that 84% of reserve residents retained their Aboriginal languages in the homes, compared to 34% of off-reserve residents. Nationally, 18.5% of Canada's Indians are reported by the census as having retained their mother tongue.[4]

The Socio-Economic Status of Aboriginal People

Aboriginal people face greater socio-economic problems than does any other segment of Canadian society. Because official statistics generally report only for status Indians, these are the figures we present. We believe the conditions of all Aboriginal people in Manitoba have strong similarities, although there are some significant differences between life on and off reserves.

Aboriginal people living on Manitoba reserves experience the most crowded housing conditions in Canada.[5] The majority of homes on reserves are heated by cook stoves and space heaters. Less than half of on-reserve homes in Manitoba have indoor plumbing.[6]

Indians are twice as likely as other Manitobans to have less than a grade nine education, three times less likely to complete high school and six times less likely to receive a university degree.[7] The unemployment rate for Indian people is four times higher than for non-Indian people.[8] These statistics greatly underestimate the true state of Aboriginal unemployment, since they only consider those persons actively looking for work. Because there is so little employment available, many Aboriginal people do not "actively look" for what is not there and, therefore, are not calculated in the official unemployment rate. Manitoba's Indian population has among the highest rates of welfare dependency in Canada, at close to 80% for reserve residents.[9]

The people who appeared before us did not fail to pass judgment on these social inequalities.

> When I look around me and see it is there, the human misery that afflicts my people, the agony of hunger etched on our children's faces, the blank look in the eyes of our young people, the despair of adults growing old before their time, the bewilderment of old people cast aside. All of these afflictions are a reality with my people. All of these afflictions are consequences of the racial prejudice and discrimination that my people must contend with on a day to day basis.
>
> John Letandre
> Winnipeg

> We have nothing. And I think that's the greatest injustice in this country.
>
> Brian Cromarty
> Norway House

The Indian death rate for persons between 25 and 44 years of age is five times the non-Indian rate. The average age of death for Indian men is 25 years younger than for non-Indian men. The average age of death for Indian women is 28 years younger than for non-Indian women. Tuberculosis, known as a disease of poverty, occurs seven times more frequently in Manitoba's Indian population.[10]

As we noted earlier, a similar picture is presented when one examines the province's prison population. In 1965, 22% of prisoners at Stony Mountain federal penitentiary were Aboriginal. In 1984 this proportion was 33%.[11] In 1989 the superintendent of the institution told our Inquiry the figure was now 40%.[12]

The situation is even worse in provincial jails. In 1983, 37% of all admissions to the Headingley Correctional Institution were Aboriginal.[13] In 1989 the Manitoba Department of Justice told the Inquiry that 47% of Headingley's population were Aboriginal. In fact, the department told the Inquiry that 55% of the total provincial jail population were Aboriginal.[14]

We visited most of the province's jails, witnessed dehumanizing conditions and heard inmates talk about the cultural isolation they experienced behind bars.

> If more ceremonies were made available to the inmates, such as the Shaking Tent, the Firestick Ceremony, the Yu-wipi, a lot of the psychological problems, psychiatric problems, mental problems, spiritual problems could be rectified while the person is incarcerated here.
>
> Stony Mountain inmate

Many presenters spoke of the severity and the ineffectiveness of the corrections system, and demanded that the whole conception of sentencing be changed to meet the needs of Aboriginal offenders.

> [W]hen Christopher Columbus landed in this sacred isle, there were none of our people in prisons. It seems to me that a violent people need prisons to control themselves, but we don't need that.
>
> We have become the victims of a very vicious system which intends to keep itself going, but as long as I live I will speak against that obscenity.
>
> Art Solomon
> Winnipeg

Jail figures and projections are even worse for Aboriginal youth and Aboriginal women. Sixty-one per cent of all admissions to the Manitoba Youth Centre and the Agassiz Youth Centre in 1989 were Aboriginal. On October 1, 1990, 64% of the Manitoba Youth Centre's population and 78% of Agassiz's population were Aboriginal youths. At the Portage jail for women, 67% of all admissions in 1989 were Aboriginal.

Aboriginal over-representation extends into the child welfare system, as well. For 1989–90, 32% of the children in care in Manitoba were registered Indians. This percentage undoubtedly would be higher if Metis and non-status Indian children were included.

> I was separated from my biological family when I was two years old by the welfare.... I was taken for the reason that the welfare thought that they could rule the native children but in my mind they went too far by stepping in and thinking that they were doing the best for me. In the long-run they have ruined my life and childhood.
>
> Lori Ann Thompson
> Camperville

As disturbing as these figures are, they may worsen. In 1971 more than half of Manitoba's Indian population were under 15 years of age. This compared to 22% in the non-Indian population.[15] Further, the Indian birth rate was twice as high as the non-Indian birth rate, and this too is expected to continue as more Aboriginal youth enter their child-bearing years.[16]

As well as the relative ages of Aboriginal people in Manitoba compared to non-Aboriginal people, the large proportion of Aboriginal people living in rural areas, particularly on reserves, is another way in which Aboriginal circumstances are very different. Further, Aboriginal socio-economic problems are of an entirely greater magnitude than those of any other segment of Canadian society.

Aboriginal People and the Justice System in Manitoba

Manitoba's justice system is founded on laws written in the English and French languages. It is a complex system whose practitioners must undergo years of training. It has many specialized terms, so that even a person relatively well conversant in English or French likely will not understand the subtleties of the law and legal proceedings.

The justice system operates through a complicated mix of governments, agencies and individuals. The federal government is responsible for Indians and reserves, the *Criminal Code,* the *Young Offenders Act,* penitentiaries (for the most serious offenders), the National Parole Board, the RCMP, the *Divorce Act* among other statutes, and appointments to Court of Queen's Bench and the Court of Appeal.

The provincial government is responsible for the prosecution of offences, administration of courts, the *Child and Family Services Act,* hunting and fishing laws and other legislation, correctional institutions (for less serious offenders), probation services, child welfare agencies, regulation of the police (other than the RCMP) and appointments to the Provincial Court of Manitoba. Municipalities are responsible for choosing the police service they want and contributing a portion of the cost, and for municipal by-laws. First Nation governments are responsible for band by-laws and the provision of a very wide array of services on reserves. First Nation responsibilities are considerably different from those of municipal governments.

Numerous agencies, many funded by governments, provide services in the justice system, including Legal Aid Manitoba, agencies to assist offenders, agencies to assist victims, and so on. In addition, private individuals, particularly lawyers, make their livelihoods helping people use the justice system.

It is a costly system. By our estimate, taking into account Manitoba's share of federal expenditures on justice, the Manitoba Department of Justice, municipal police forces, conservation officers, the child welfare system, and non-government agencies and expenditures, approximately half a billion dollars are spent each year on justice in Manitoba. With Manitoba's Aboriginal population representing 12% of the total population of the province and more than 50% of the jail population, it is clear an enormous amount of money is being spent dealing with Aboriginal people.[17]

It is for many Manitobans an awe-inspiring and revered system, one which links them to a centuries-old struggle for the right of people to be ruled by laws. To Aboriginal people it appears in a very different light.

One of the most powerful symbols of European-based cultures is the scales of justice. This portrays the goals and obligations of all who work within the Canadian justice system. It proclaims that each person's right, each point of view, is to be accorded fair and equitable weight. Justice respects, protects, and offers redress to restore that balance of fairness and equity.

Yet the overwhelming evidence coming before you from our people is that the fairness and equity of the Canadian justice system do not apply to us. In relation to Canadian First Nations, the system is profoundly unbalanced. More often than not, we do not experience, nor do we see, justice being done; nor do our families and neighbours; nor did our parents and grandparents. This Inquiry cannot fail to note, like a sinew, or thread, linking the testimony of our people, not so much anger as profound disillusion; a hardening, a deepening, an increasing, loss of respect for the Canadian justice system.

> Grand Chief David Courchene
> Winnipeg

The police forces of Manitoba are the first point of contact with the justice system for most Aboriginal people. The relationship is clearly an uneasy one. We heard many complaints about insensitivity and abuse.

I believe the present justice system is not fair to native people. Police and some courts are harder on native people. They think that we are big alcoholics and should be killed. As a result, police brutalize Indians when they are drunk or sober.... Police verbally abuse natives. They call us down and say that we are good for nothing, worthless bums.

> Lonnie Hiebert
> Winnipeg

And after about how many months it was [after my brother's suicide], the RCMP officer then went to my mother's place with a bag of bloody clothes and handed the clothes to my mother. "Here, Mrs. Brightnose, here are your son's clothes." He reached into his pocket—"Oh, I almost forgot something, here's the bullets that he used."

> Jeff Brightnose
> Cross Lake

The courts also were accused of insensitivity. In particular, residents of remote Aboriginal communities complained about the circuit court system which administers justice on a periodic, fly-in basis. Many people who spoke to us felt that court personnel did not understand community problems and had no comprehension of cultural differences.

> We didn't make the laws, although we have to live with them. There is no understanding of the cultural differences, the value system of people, and the values of their families, the values of their children, the values of things in life. There's no understanding of that in a lot of the communities by the enforcers, by the law, by the judges that make sentences. The only thing they know is that the person is coming up on the docket and he has to be charged according to the letters or the figures or statistics, whatever they have. That's the only understanding they have.
>
> Ed Campbell
> The Pas

The related problems of unfamiliar language and unfamiliar concepts of justice pose serious problems to those who come before courts.

> Perhaps, no one has ever thought of this, but how terrifying it must be for the Aboriginal person not to speak the language of the court system. This is like the old educational system, where our children were forced to a school that is totally alienated from them.
>
> Rebecca Ross
> Cross Lake

The Report

The result of all the efforts of the Inquiry is this report. This volume begins by placing the position of Aboriginal people and the Canadian justice system in an historical context, laying special emphasis on Aboriginal concepts of justice and the development of Aboriginal and treaty rights. We examine the roots of Aboriginal over-representation in the province's correctional institutions, looking at both the causes of criminal behaviour and the role of systemic discrimination in the justice system. We then discuss proposals for a separate Aboriginal justice system, placing the concept in the context of the right of Aboriginal self-government and already existing Aboriginal courts in other jurisdictions.

Other sections of this volume examine the existing justice system and the ways in which it adversely affects Aboriginal people. We look at the role of the police and the courts, the appropriateness of current sentencing practices and the level of employment of Aboriginal people throughout the justice system. Of particular concern to us are the nature of court services throughout the province and issues of family violence and child welfare; each of these matters is dealt with in a separate chapter. We end with a discussion of how our recommendations can be implemented.

The second volume of the report deals specifically with the cases of Helen Betty Osborne and J.J. Harper. Both these cases are reviewed in detail in that volume and specific recommendations are made on each case.

In addition to the written reports, we have produced a video presentation of the major points of the general report. This video has been produced in English, Cree, Ojibway, Island Lake dialect, Dakota and Dene. We decided to produce a video so that the report could be more accessible to the majority of Aboriginal persons, particularly in their own languages.

CHAPTER 2

ABORIGINAL CONCEPTS OF JUSTICE

Introduction

When the white man first seen us, when they first said, "Well, there's some-thing wrong with these people here. They don't have no religion. They have no judicial system. We have to do something for these people." I guess that must have been what they thought because they totally screwed up what we already had.

They introduced new religion and there was nothing wrong with our old reli-gion. They just didn't understand it. We had our own ways of teaching our children, like the Elders and everything. There was nothing wrong with that way of teaching children. They just didn't understand it.

The same thing with our judicial system. We had that judicial system and the white people, when they came here, they didn't see that. They said, "These guys have nothing. We have to introduce all these different things to them so they can be one of us." That's exactly the problem that we have.

Chief Philip Michel
Brochet

Aboriginal peoples have always had governments, laws and some means of resolving disputes within their communities. North American Aboriginal societies were dynamic cultures that adapted constantly to meet changing circumstances. Aboriginal people were influenced by their relations with one another in migrations, warfare, conquest, and in commercial and/or political unions.

They had vast, complicated, intertribal trading systems that covered the continent. They developed sophisticated external relationships between and among tribes that cemented these commercial and political relations. Later, with the coming of Europeans, they extended similar trade and diplomatic relations to various countries in Europe.

Aboriginal peoples have persisted for thousands of years as distinct cultural entities. They never have been conquered in war. They were allies. They have never surrendered their original right to govern themselves in accordance with their customs and cultures. Although successive federal governments have tried to interfere with or diminish that right, and to replace it with their concepts of "Aboriginal" government, they have done so without much success.

More importantly, successive federal governments and religious organizations in Canada have tried to interfere with, and even destroy, the cultures of Aboriginal people and to supplant them with European cultures and values, again without much success. At best, this amounts to discrimination. At worst, it is cultural genocide.

The daily, systemic cultural discrimination inflicted upon Aboriginal people by the justice system, however unintentional, demeans and diminishes the importance and relevance of their cultures, languages and beliefs. At the very least, as one Aboriginal language interpreter told our Inquiry, Aboriginal people have a right to understand what is happening to them.

> I was appalled to learn that a man had been hired [as an interpreter] who does not speak any native Aboriginal language at all and it still exists. And again, I ask these questions; how has this man been able to interpret for an Aboriginal person who cannot speak or understand English? How many Aboriginal people have been denied the right to defend themselves because this man is not capable of understanding and interpreting their testimony? How many Aboriginal people have been convicted because this man was unable to translate a Crown attorney's questions accurately so that they understand what they were being asked; therefore, unknowingly, and perhaps falsely, incriminating themselves? And how many Aboriginal people have pleaded guilty out the sheer futility of what seems to be a hopeless situation?
>
> Barbara Whitford
> Portage la Prairie

"What is certain for Aboriginal people," that same person added, is that what "they have managed to retain to a considerable degree, in all this turmoil, is their distinct identity." In fact, despite attempts to eradicate Aboriginal cultures, cultural distinctiveness remains a hallmark of Aboriginal life.

In this chapter, we discuss Aboriginal and non-Aboriginal concepts of justice, in brief. We discuss how they are similar and how they are different. We try to explain how they work and how their purposes and processes differ.

Aboriginal People and the Role of the Elders

To understand an Aboriginal community, one must appreciate first the role that the elders play within it. The prominent position accorded to elders is a striking feature of Aboriginal societies. They have been largely responsible for retaining much of the knowledge of Aboriginal cultural traditions about which we heard so much in the course of our hearings.

Elders—both men and women—are the "teachers" and, in some cases, are the "healers"—that is, the "medicine people"—of the tribe. The role of elders within Aboriginal communities sometimes varied, but generally consisted of helping the people, individually and collectively, to gain knowledge of the history, traditions, customs, values and beliefs of the tribe, and to assist them to maintain their well-being and good health. They were respected for their wisdom and for their experience, and for the fact that, having lived a long life, they were able to advise the people on what to do in difficult situations, as a result of that experience. In some tribal authorities today, councils of elders exist, with the right to advise tribal officials and tribal governments on various matters of interest to the tribe.

Elders have long been considered the ones who bridge between the ancient traditions and beliefs of the people and the modern-day influences that come into play in the day-to-day lives of Aboriginal men and women. This was so even in past times when there were only Aboriginal people on this continent.

"Medicine men" and "medicine women" were not necessarily elders in the sense that they were not necessarily people who had lived a long life. They were people who had been traditionally trained from their youth in the natural medicines and plants of the forests and fields, including training in their benefits and how they were to be used to heal the body's ailments. In addition, they also received training in the treatment of the person's spiritual and mental needs.

Although the role of elders and healers came under strong attack as a result of government policy, elders still have a place of prominence within Aboriginal communities and there still are people within Aboriginal communities with knowledge and training in the traditions of Aboriginal healing. The role of both elders and healers within Aboriginal societies is still very important and many Aboriginal people still go to them for advice, assistance and treatment, sometimes even in conjunction with treatment they may be receiving from medically trained professionals.

That is because, in almost all Aboriginal belief systems, each person has three aspects which make up his or her whole being. Those are the body, the mind and the spirit. It is said that for Aboriginal people to heal from whatever ails them, all aspects of their being need to be treated—not just one. In that respect, the Aboriginal belief is in the holistic treatment of the person. Aboriginal healers, when called upon to minister to a sick person, do not only administer medicines to the body, but also conduct spiritual ceremonies for the spirit and counsel the person to help clear his or her mind of the effects of the sickness.

In Aboriginal beliefs, if only the body is treated, then healing cannot take place properly. If the body becomes ill, then the spirit and mind also are affected. In the same way, it is believed that before the body becomes sick, there are often signs of the impending sickness apparent in the mental or spiritual status of the person. Preventive steps thus can be taken by addressing the person's spiritual needs early on. Keeping the spirit strong was seen as practising preventive medicine. Elders, and people who know of traditional ways of healing, are considered very important and are respected highly by Aboriginal people.

Some Aboriginal elders believe that Aboriginal people who are ill must have all three aspects healed fully in the Aboriginal way. Some have said that if an Aboriginal person goes to a non-Aboriginal doctor, then that person cannot be healed properly in the traditional way, since traditional healing methods and modern medicine do not mix. Others believe that if medical doctors are treating the person's body, then traditional Aboriginal healers can and must attend to the treatment of the person's mind and spirit. In the same way, if the person is receiving psychiatric treatment from a psychiatrist, then his or her physical and spiritual needs still can be met through traditional healing methods. In this way, elders believe that there is always room for traditional methods of healing to take place.

In the case of Aboriginal inmates, elders believe that healing is required for them, even though there may not be any direct, harmful physical effects from incarceration, because they believe that there are harmful effects upon an individual's mind and spirit from being locked up.

Many Aboriginal people believe that as well, particularly some of the Aboriginal inmates from whom we heard. Some institutional officials are just beginning to recognize the potential importance that Aboriginal elders and healers can have within their institutions.

It is apparent that Aboriginal elders will continue to play a very important role in the future of Aboriginal societies. Understanding the role which they play is important to appreciate why events evolve as they do within Aboriginal communities, because the elders wield great influence.

Aboriginal and Non-Aboriginal Peoples: Two Worldviews

Aboriginal peoples do not adhere to a single life philosophy, religious belief or moral code. Indeed, there are and have been considerable differences among tribes. The Aboriginal peoples of North America, for the most part, hold fundamental life philosophies different from those of the dominant European-Canadian society. These differences in worldviews between European-Canadians and Aboriginal people are broad enough and general enough to make most European-Canadian institutions incompatible with the moral and ethical value systems of Aboriginal Canadians.

At a fundamental cultural level, the difference between Aboriginal and Western traditions is a difference in the perception of one's relationship with the universe and the Creator. For instance, in the Judeo-Christian tradition:

[Mankind was told to] fill the earth and subdue it, rule over the fish in the sea, the birds of heaven, and every living thing that moves upon the earth.[1]

In contrast, Ojibway thought believes that man does not hold "dominion" over the earth and all its creatures. In fact, man is the least important entity in creation.

Creation came about from the union of the Maker and the Physical World. Out of this union came the natural children, the Plants, nurtured from the Physical World, Earth, their Mother. To follow were Animalkind, the two-legged, the four-legged, the winged, those who swim and those who crawl, all dependent on the Plant World and Mother Earth for succour. Finally, last in the order came Humankind, the most dependent and least necessary of all the orders.[2]

The differences between these two worldviews account, in large part, for the differences in the philosophy, purposes and practices of legal and justice systems. Each worldview is the basis for the customs, manners and behaviour that are considered culturally appropriate. One's individual or cultural understanding of humanity's place in creation, and the appropriate behaviour that understanding dictates, pervade and shape all aspects of life.

Psychological and anthropological profiles of Ojibway, Dakota, Apache, Navajo and Cheyenne subjects have identified recurring personality characteristics which seem to be culturally induced and which are so universal that they could be equated with "primary Native values."[3]

The seven traditional values of the Ojibway, or Anishnabe, are wisdom, love, respect, bravery, honesty, humility and truth.[4] A study of the psychological and behavioural patterns of the Sioux identifies several central values for the Dakota people: conformity with the group and harmony within it; concentration on the present; ability to make personal decisions; reluctance to show emotions; reverence for nature even while using it; and constant awareness of God.[5] The four great virtues of the Oglala Dakota, taught in the Sundance, are bravery, generosity, fortitude and integrity.[6] Apache beliefs and values can be stated as: respect for the autonomy of the individual; non-interference; desire for harmony in interpersonal relations; respect for individual freedom; and cooperation and sharing.[7]

The basic values of Cheyenne culture are: respect for the spirit world; desire for harmony and well-being in interpersonal relationships; desire for harmony and balance with nature; bravery and mastery of self; generosity, sharing and cooperation; individual freedom and autonomy consistent with cooperation and collective well-being; and humility and respect in all relationships.[8]

None of these values would be found inadequate or inappropriate by the dominant Canadian society; the same or similar values exist within most of the world's cultural traditions. However, European-Canadian society has developed conventions which allow some traditional ethical and moral values to be separated, at least temporarily, from everyday life. Aboriginal North Americans tend not to do so.

An obvious example is the ease with which a member of the dominant society can plead not guilty to a charge for which that person, in fact, is responsible. In the Western tradition, the plea is not seen as dishonest; it is understood as a conventional response to an accusation, based on the doctrine that people are not required to incriminate themselves and that it is up to the prosecution to prove guilt. In Aboriginal societies, to deny a true allegation is seen as dishonest, and such a denial is a repudiation of fundamental and highly valued standards of behaviour. As well, the European concept of "guilty/not guilty" runs counter to most Aboriginal philosophy, so much so that Aboriginal societies have no words for "guilty" or "not guilty" in their languages because they have not developed these concepts.

The Meaning of Justice

At the most basic level of understanding, justice is understood differently by Aboriginal people. The dominant society tries to control actions it considers potentially or actually harmful to society as a whole, to individuals or to the wrongdoers themselves by interdiction, enforcement or apprehension, in order to prevent or punish harmful or deviant behaviour. The emphasis is on the punishment of the deviant as a means of making that person conform, or as a means of protecting other members of society.

The purpose of a justice system in an Aboriginal society is to restore the peace and equilibrium within the community, and to reconcile the accused with his or her own conscience and with the individual or family who has been wronged. This is a primary difference. It is a difference that significantly challenges the appropriateness of the present legal and justice system for Aboriginal people in the resolution of conflict, the reconciliation and the maintenance of community harmony and good order.[9]

Aboriginal Concepts of Law

There were and are Aboriginal laws. There were and continue to be Aboriginal governments with lawmaking powers and with provisions to enforce those laws. There were and are Aboriginal constitutions that are the supreme "law of laws" for some Aboriginal peoples and their nations.

Examples of such indigenous governments and their laws exist around the world. In the United States, tribal governments have long been recognized by U.S. courts as "domestic, dependent nations" with the inherent power to enact such laws as they deem necessary. We have described how these laws are interpreted and enforced in our chapter on Aboriginal justice systems.

No society can exist without law. Laws grow from the customs, traditions and rules of a society of people. They exist to inform people what that particular society considers to be acceptable and unacceptable.

Many non-Aboriginal writers in the past have regarded Aboriginal societies through the stereotypes and cultural biases they held at that particular time, or that they accepted as "true" from the time of the original account. These histories, for the most part, still comprise most of the history courses taught in Canadian schools, from elementary school to university. One such writer was Diamond Jenness, whose books were and still are referred to widely in many schools and universities as authoritative accounts of Aboriginal societies.

In the absence of chiefs and of any legislative or executive body within the tribes and bands, law and order depended solely on the strength of public opinion. There were no written laws, of course; merely rules and injunctions handed down by word of mouth from an immemorial antiquity, and more temporary taboos operative during the lifetime of an individual. Persuasion and physical force were the only methods of arbitrating disputes, social outlawry or physical violence the only means of punishing infractions of the moral code or offences against the welfare of the band or tribe....

Fear of the blood-feud was a powerful restraint on murder, and social disapproval, more keenly felt in small communities than in large, checked the commission of many lesser crimes. Strangers, however, even people of a neighbouring tribe, might be robbed or killed with impunity; they had no rights, unless they married into a band or placed themselves under the protection of some powerful family.[10]

Such attitudes about Aboriginal people and the stereotypes they promote continue to persist, regardless of how much one might hope they would be out of favour or distasteful in today's society. But they seem embedded firmly in Western culture. They spring from centuries-old theories, philosophies and policies that form a worldview through which Western man has perceived and interpreted other cultures.

Recently, however, more and more historians are seeking to divest historical accounts of past stereotyping and cultural bias in order to present a more realistic, more accurate and, perhaps, more fair version of history. This more recent account of Aboriginal society in Canada describes almost the same situation as does the previous author, but from a more neutral viewpoint:

Europeans' pronouncements that Indians had no government were contradicted by their practice of dealing with Indian chiefs through the protocol of diplomacy with sovereign states. The bulk of evidence about Indian communities implies structures of political association irreconcilable with assumptions of anarchy. From anthropology comes the root conception of "kinship state", a community of families and clans in which some of the ordering functions of society are performed by the kin groups individually while others are assigned to officers and councillors chosen cooperatively.

In this structure, as European observers were quick to notice, there was no law in the European sense, and no specialized apparatus of law enforcement. Binding decisions were made by legitimate officers, however, and before the intervention of Europeans eroded the chiefs' authority there were forceful sanctions for both occasional decisions and enduring customs. In a community where every man bore arms no need existed for a corps of specialized police; any man could be appointed to act guard or do executioner's duty. Early seventeenth-century observers reported that the paramount chiefs of the tribes sometimes inflicted corporal punishment upon criminals with their own hands.

Families also bore responsibility for protecting kinsfolk, and the accompanying threat of vengeance sanctioned by custom proved an effective deterrent to potential wrongdoers. Such sanctions in their social context were more effectual than European procedures of criminal justice; Adriaen Van der Donck wonderingly noticed "how uncommon" crimes were among the Hudson River Indians. "With us," he continued, "a watchful police is supported, and crimes are more frequent than among them." Not recognizing the sanctioning functions performed by means that he had himself described, he was baffled to understand how there could be so little crime "where there is no regard paid to the administration of justice." A lawyer himself, Van der Donck could recognize due process only when it appeared in the forms to which he had been trained. That fault was shared by other Europeans contemporary with himself and in following generations.[11]

Regardless of whether the laws of Aboriginal societies conformed to the preconceptions of Europeans, there were laws and a system of sanctions that allowed Aboriginal people to function in a coherent and orderly fashion. Aboriginal people could hardly be characterized, as Jenness implied, as living in anarchy or having a system of "social outlawry."

Indian tribes were internally more peaceful than European nations partly because of the kin-oriented sanctions pervading Indian villages, as distinct from the greater impersonality of European social relationships, and partly because Indian custom defined and punished fewer crimes than European law....

The same customary sanctions were notably tolerant of many sorts of behaviour that Europeans classed as crime, especially regarding deviant sexual and religious conduct. There was no crime of fornication or "unnatural vice" among Indians, nor was there any heresy as that was defined by European law. All sex relations except rare cases of rape were personal matters outside the jurisdiction of sachem and council, and religious belief was totally personal.... Indians knew nothing of the whole class of offences called by European lawyers "crimes without victims". When one considers the floggings, jailings, hangings, torture and burnings inflicted by European states for the multitude of crimes that did not even exist in Indian society, one becomes painfully aware that an incalculably great proportion of European violence against persons was inflicted by the very agencies whose ostensible function was to reduce violence.[12]

This does not imply that Aboriginal societies were free of crime or criminal activity. There were laws against certain types of behaviour and, inevitably, as with all laws, they would be broken. However, the types of behaviours that were considered objectionable or aberrant might have been different from those identified by European societies. The manner in which Aboriginal people imposed sanctions was different too. This was to be expected, after all, since they sprang from a whole different world which had evolved entirely different societies from those in Europe.

Social control rested in kinship. Among native cultures the means of control was in the close contacts of their members. The sanctions of ridicule, avoidance and shame were effective means to check those deviants who fell into behavioural lapses. Internal, unofficial communication was the process.[13]

These types of sanctions suited most misbehaviours within a small, tightly knit group of people who often were family members. However, some crimes required more serious sanctions than mere scolding or ridicule. As in European societies, some crimes required the complete removal of the criminal from society. In most Aboriginal societies, this meant banishment. In such close, family-oriented societies, where survival depended upon communal cooperation, such sanctions were considered a humane alternative to death, no matter how traumatic they may have been to the offender.

However, there were other behaviours that Aboriginal societies recognized as crimes. Again, the reasons why Aboriginal people considered such behaviour criminal differed from the reasons perceived by European societies. So did the manner in which Aboriginal people sought to resolve such disruptions to their societies. These differences were frequently looked upon with a certain amount of disdain by Europeans who often interpreted the actions of Aboriginal people through their own cultural values and biases.

> The French were frequently critical of the Huron for the lenient attitude they took towards thieves. The simplicity and relative impermanence of Huron possessions, and the sharing of goods and housing among extended families, probably made ownership intrinsically a matter of less concern to them than it was to Europeans (Herman 1956; Stites 1905). More importantly, however, because of the semi-public nature of Huron dwellings and the lack of any formal policing in their villages, there was little that could be done to protect movable possessions against theft. The main concern of the Huron was therefore to minimize the disruptive consequences of quarrels that might arise from such actions.

> This was done by defining theft very narrowly, as the taking of goods forcibly from an individual or from inside a longhouse without permission. In theory, a person was entitled to carry off anything he found lying about unattended. In order to protect their valuables, both from fire and thieves, the Huron either carried them around with them or hid them in caches dug into the soil beneath their houses. The Huron did not fine or penalize a thief, nor did they permit a man from whom goods had been stolen to reclaim them without first inquiring how someone else had come to possess them. A refusal to answer constituted an admission of guilt. If a man could prove who had robbed him, he and his relatives were socially sanctioned to go to the thief's longhouse and carry off everything on which they could lay their hands. Hence, relatives of a person who had stolen very little might find themselves bruised and despoiled. Again, pressure was put on kin groups to enforce good behaviour among their members.[14]

Treason and the practice of witchcraft, or the use of "bad medicine" in order to inflict injury upon another, also were treated as serious crimes. Treason was seen as the betrayal of the family group, or clan, and as such almost always required the death penalty. Witchcraft was a much more difficult activity to prove and it was handled in a more delicate manner. The person using witchcraft might have to pay some form of compensation. If, however, the person refused to compensate the complainant, the offender might face a death penalty. But these were extreme situations.

There was one other serious category of crime. The manner in which it was handled within Aboriginal societies shows the philosophy underlying the way in which Aboriginal people viewed law and justice.

> In theory, murder placed an absolute obligation upon the kinsmen of the dead man to seek revenge by clamouring for the slaying of either the murderer or someone closely related to him. The obligation fell particularly upon the clansmen of the murdered person, that is, upon his sisters, mother's brothers, and sisters' sons.... Depending on the degree of relationship between the murderer and the murdered man, a killing might give rise to a prolonged blood feud between the clan segments, villages, tribes, or even confederacies to which they belonged. Thus blood feuds varied in scale from family quarrels to major wars. The Huron were well aware that no tribal organization and no confederacy could survive if internal blood feuds went unchecked. One of the basic functions of the confederacy was to eliminate such feuds among its members; indeed, between Huron, they were regarded as a more reprehensible crime than murder itself.[15]

Instead of bloody and disruptive feuds within the society, Aboriginal people settled upon a system of atonement and reparation by the offender to the victim. The payment would be borne by all members of the offender's clan or family and it would be shared by all members of the victim's clan or family. Only if such payment were refused did the clan have the right to resort to violence or arms.

The amount of the compensation could vary. The compensation for a crime against a chief or an elder, for example, was greater than that paid to a person of lower rank. The compensation for a crime against a woman was greater than that against a man. Since the penalty would be paid by the offender's clan as a whole, and not merely by the individual offender, repeat offenders could expect to receive less and less support from their clan for their crimes. In this way, the clan or family, through peer pressure, would regulate behaviour within itself and exert influence throughout the society.

By making criminal activity a collective responsibility of a tribe, village or a clan, Aboriginal people were able to impose law and order without resorting to capital punishment or other harsh forms of sanctions. The philosophy in Aboriginal society was for all parties to acknowledge the crime, allow for some process of atonement, and install a system of reparation or compensation in order to restore harmony to the community.

But even more to the point, Europeans and Aboriginal people viewed the same crime of murder in different ways. The two groups perceived the other's system of justice as inconsistent, incoherent and incomprehensible.

Of crimes common to both societies, murder requires special notice. It was conceived of differently by Indian and European and was therefore punished by different processes. In Europe murder was an offence against the state; among Indians it was an offence against the family of the victim. European law demanded the murderer's life as atonement to the state; Indian custom made his life forfeit to his victim's family. In Europe, the state apprehended the murderer; among Indians it was the family's obligation to do so. European observers tagged the Indian custom "revenge" and blathered much about the savagery revealed by it. Yet, as compared to the state's relentlessness, the tribe provided an institution carefully and precisely designed to stanch the flow of blood. The obligation of blood for blood could be commuted into a payment of valuable goods by the murderer's own kin-folk to the relatives of his victim. This custom (which had been known centuries earlier in Anglo-Saxon England as *wergild*) was a widespread stabilizer of Indian societies, forestalling the development of obligatory revenge into exterminating feuds. Although the term feud has been used freely by the condemners of savage society, Marian W. Smith has been unable to find the phenomena properly denoted by it. "True feud," she remarks, "in its threat of continued violence between particular groups, is surprisingly rare in the New World."

Europeans understood the *wergild* custom and used it themselves in their dealings with Indians, but only unilaterally. Europeans would pay blood money to avert Indian revenge for the killing of an Indian, but Indians were not permitted to buy absolution for the killing of a European. In the latter case the Europeans demanded the person of the accused Indian for trial in a European court. In the event of nonapprehension of the suspected culprit, mass retribution might be visited upon his village or tribe. The savagery of revenge, therefore, was simply a semantic function of its identification with an Indian; European revenge was civilized justice.[16]

The underlying philosophy in Aboriginal societies in dealing with crime was the resolution of disputes, the healing of wounds and the restoration of social harmony. It might mean an expression of regret for the injury done by the offender or by members of the offender's clan. It might mean the presentation of gifts or payment of some kind. It might even mean the forfeiture of the offender's life. But the matter was considered finished once the offence was recognized and dealt with by both the offender and the offended. Atonement and the restoration of harmony were the goals—not punishment.

It is this strong, even central, cultural imperative to prevent or deter violent acts of revenge or retribution that runs through all these accounts. Aboriginal societies felt it important that offenders atone for their acts to the aggrieved person and the victim's family or clan. European society demanded the state punish the offender. In the Aboriginal justice system, once the atonement had been made and the offence recognized, the matter was forgotten and harmony within the community was considered restored. In the European justice system, the offender "pays his debt" to society, usually by going to jail. Rarely is there atonement to the person or persons injured. There is little restoration of harmony within the community.

This form of Aboriginal justice exists, to some extent, in Aboriginal communities to this day. Here is an example of one person's experience:

In March 1987 the city of Whitehorse hosted The Third Annual Northern Conference. It was convened to examine the delivery and impact of justice services in remote Indian and Inuit communities.... One of the sessions explored mediation techniques to see if they might be more appropriate than our adversarial courts. Three participants were selected to form a panel to mediate a fictitious dispute between a young lad and the owner of a store which had been broken into. One of the panel members was Charlie Fisher, an Elder from the Islington Reserve at Whitedog, and Ontario's first Native Justice of the Peace....

He began by getting rid of the chairs, then the long table which had separated the three panelists from the disputants. Everyone sat in a circle, as equals. He then required two further participants to act as Elders "representing" the two disputants. As he continued, it became clear that it was not only the physical format or cast of participants which differed, but also its process and its very function.

The boy and the store owner never spoke, not even to the panel. There was no discussion whatever about the break-in itself, about the theft and damage, about how each party felt about the other, or about what each might do to set matters straight. Further, the panel would not impose restitution, punishment or any consequence at all. They would not even discuss the issue of consequences.

Once those in attendance understood what was NOT going to take place, there was only one question left: "why, then, is there a panel at all?"

Charlie Fisher then defined the purpose of that traditional forum. It was used to rid themselves of what he called "bad feelings". Each would be "counselled" by his representative Elder, privately, until his spirit was "cleansed" and made whole again. At convocations of the panel the representing Elder could signify that such "cleansing" had been achieved by touching the peace pipe. The panel would convene as often as necessary until both Elders so signified. At that point, the peace pipe could be lit and passed to all. As far as the community was concerned, that would be the end of the matter. Whether the two disputants privately arranged recompense of some sort was entirely up to them. Both had been "restored to the community and to themselves" the moment the pipe was passed.[17]

The author, Rupert Ross, is a Crown attorney in northern Ontario. He describes the non-Aboriginal participants as "perplexed" by the demonstration they had just witnessed. There was no "fact-finding," no allocation of blame or responsibility and "no discussion (much less imposition) of consequences." Perhaps, his group surmised, there was little need to do so in such small, tightly knit Aboriginal communities where public opinion carried so much weight. Or maybe a system that doesn't rely on punishment also doesn't need "fact-finding" to ensure an innocent person is not punished by mistake.

In the end, the author concluded that "such explanations are superficial in the extreme." The real answer may lie deep within the "basic ethics" of the traditional culture itself.

Aboriginal Culture

In trying to describe Aboriginal cultures to non-Aboriginal Canadians, it is important to recognize the difficulty of such a task. Imagine trying to describe Canadian culture to a non-Canadian. Canadian society is not homogeneous; there are many peoples, many cultures and languages, and many regions. Similarly, Aboriginal people are many peoples, cultures and languages in many regions.

Furthermore, any attempt at description will tend to be an over-simplification and will carry the risk of a certain amount of stereotyping. Once that is understood, it is important to realize how culture can influence one's cultural characteristic, cultural "ethic" or "rule of behaviour." A cultural "ethic" or "rule of behaviour" may be described as a behavioural characteristic or quality that is so ingrained, so prevalent, within an identifiable or specific group of people as to become almost a trait. Again, we warn about the risk of stereotyping.

Aboriginal people, it is important to stress, are not all the same. For instance, the Cree in northern Quebec have a completely different language, culture and society than the Mohawk only a few hundred miles away in southern Quebec. The Cree are patriarchal, which means they trace their lineage, families and clans through the male parent. The Mohawk, on the other hand, are matriarchal and determine their heritage through the female parent. The Cree are a hunting, trapping and fishing society. The Mohawk are an agricultural people. Although both peoples live in the province of Quebec, they are, perhaps, as different from one another in language, culture and social characteristics as the Spanish are from the Norwegians in Europe.

In Manitoba, similar cultural differences exist between the Ojibway and the Chipewyan and between the Dakota and the Metis, and even within a tribe of people, such as the Cree. For example, there are subtle differences in social characteristics between the Swampy Cree of northwestern Manitoba and the plains Cree in Saskatchewan.

Yet, it may be argued, all these peoples share certain characteristics, as well. These similar characteristics are examples of Aboriginal ethics or rules of behaviour. Aboriginal ethics and rules of behaviour are "present in some form in all tribes of North America," according to Dr. Clare Brant, a Mohawk psychiatrist who has studied and written in this area.[18]

According to Dr. Brant, Aboriginal ethics become most pronounced when contrasted to the behaviours considered "normal" by most Canadians. These behaviours are sometimes explained by non-Aboriginal Canadians in terms of popular stereotypes about Aboriginal people, or worse. From his own profession, he gives this example:

> Many general psychiatrists see Native children and adolescents in assessments, and often find them passive, difficult to assess, and not forthcoming. This behaviour, which affects the individual Native child's attitude and performance in an assessment situation, is understandable in view of the child's cultural background. The psychiatrist may, at times, misinterpret the behaviour as resistance, passive-aggression, opposition, depression, or withdrawal. The general psychiatrist's failure to recognize the derivatives of the individual child's cultural heritage as they affect his behaviour in a clinical situation may result in unperceived errors in diagnosis, in formulation, and in treatment. For example, overuse of antidepressants and the all too frequent diagnosis of personality disorders may occur. This may turn what is intended to be a helpful encounter into one that is not useful or even traumatic for the patient. Such encounters will no doubt also be frustrating for the clinician.[19]

Dr. Brant's description of the misunderstandings between doctor and Aboriginal patient is similar to the cultural miscues our Inquiry has heard about for Aboriginal people in the justice system. They often result from a lack of knowledge about Aboriginal people and their cultures. Such misunderstandings can be just as disastrous for an Aboriginal person in the justice system as in the medical system.

> When [Aboriginal people] refuse to follow the exhortations of our rules, we judge them as deficient in rule-obedience or, worse still, rule-less. In our ignorance, we have failed to admit the possibility that there might be rules other than ours to which they regularly display allegiance, an allegiance all the more striking because it is exercised in defiance of our insistent pressures to the contrary.[20]

Cultural Imperatives

A cultural imperative, or rule of behaviour, is a cultural value that dictates the actions and reactions of Aboriginal people to given situations. For instance, in general, Aboriginal people are non-confrontational. Aboriginal people usually will seek to resolve disputes or to make their opinions known to others in ways that avoid direct confrontation. Confrontation violates one of several Aboriginal cultural rules of behaviour that deem the preservation of harmony paramount, rather than personal satisfaction or gain.

While such cultural differences between Aboriginal people and non-Aboriginal people have been noticed and remarked upon by various non-Aboriginal writers for hundreds of years, few people have tried to explore and explain these differences in terms understandable to the general population. Instead, these differences have been explained away in terms of handy stereotypes and vague generalizations, to the detriment of real understanding. The justice system has been no less insensitive and ignorant of these differences than other sectors of society.

Although there is an awakening to the fact that the over-representation of Native people in the jails of Canada may result from cultural conflicts between the Canadian legal system and the Native people, there is still a lack of acceptance by the legal system of the conceptual conflicts faced by Aboriginal people coming before the courts.[21]

According to Brant, there are at least 10 distinct Aboriginal cultural ethics or rules of behaviour, and perhaps there are even more. He categorizes them under three main headings. Brant calls the first category of Aboriginal behaviours "conflict suppression." The second he calls "projection of conflict" and the third is "humiliating superego."

The individual and group survival of this continent's Aboriginal Plains, Bush and Woodlands people required harmonious interpersonal relationships and cooperation among members of a group. It was not possible for an individual to survive alone in the harsh natural environment but in order to survive as a group, individuals, living cheek by jowl throughout their lives, had to be continuously cooperative and friendly.[22]

Brant believes there are four major ethics or rules of behaviour and four lesser ones in the broad category of "conflict suppression" that continue to influence the lives of Aboriginal people today. He says they grew out of the need of extended families, clans, villages or tribes to maintain harmony and ensure survival of the group.

Ethic of Non-Interference

One of the most important is the ethic of non-interference. It "promotes positive interpersonal relationships by discouraging coercion of any kind, be it physical, verbal or psychological." It stems from a high degree of respect for every individual's independence and regards interference or restriction of a person's personal freedom as "undesirable behaviour."[23]

The ethic of non-interference is one of the most widely accepted principles of behaviour among Native people. It even extends to adult relationships with children and manifests itself as permissiveness. A Native child may be allowed at the age of six, for example, to make the decision on whether or not he goes to school even though he is required to do so by law. The child may be allowed to decide whether or not he will do his homework, have his assignments done on time, and even visit the dentist. Native parents will be reluctant to force the child into doing anything he does not choose to do.[24]

This ethic is one of the most difficult for non-Aboriginal people to understand because it often conflicts with their conceptions of "accepted" practice. In European-Canadian society, for instance, children are told what to do, when to do it and what will happen if they do not do it. Advice is offered freely and regularly, whether it is welcomed or not. Children are expected to conform, rather than to experiment, and to learn by rote, rather than by innovation.

The importance of the ethic of non-interference helps to explain the use of stories in Aboriginal societies. If advice is given, it is usually in the form of a story. It lays out a situation with options. The advice is contained in the story and the listener is free to understand it as he or she wants to, and to act or to not act on that advice accordingly.

This rule of behaviour is still strongly evident in Aboriginal communities. Where it once was necessary to ensure the survival of a group, this ethic continues to be functional to maintain harmony within the community. It demands people show respect for other people's personal privacy. It promotes individual self-reliance and responsibility with assurances that others will not intercede or interfere in the individual's personal affairs. Finally, it encourages people to make decisions, and accept responsibility for those decisions, starting at an early age.

The Rule of Non-Competitiveness

The second ethic Brant describes is the rule of non-competitiveness. It exists to suppress internal conflict within a group by "averting intragroup rivalry." It also acts to prevent the embarrassment "that a less able member of the group might feel" while involved in a group activity. Brant says this ethic often is misinterpreted by many European-Canadians as an inability to compete. However, he says, success or attainment of goals for Aboriginal people stress a more cooperative approach, as opposed to the imposition of one person's will upon the group, or the attainment of personal success at the expense of group needs.[25]

Emotional Restraint

One of Brant's theories concerns the ethic he has called the "exercise of emotional restraint." It is a complement to, and an extension of, the ethics of non-interference and non-competitiveness. It too developed out of a need to control outbursts of emotions that might cause disruption in tightly knit groups or families. However, he warns, it is a double-edged sword.

> On the positive side, it promotes self-control and discourages the expression of strong or violent feelings. However, emotions such as joyfulness and enthusiasm are suppressed along with anger and impulses to destructiveness.[26]

Brant says this ethic may be "problematic" for Aboriginal people in today's society when "repressed hostility," against distant government bureaucracy, for instance, "often explodes into the open under the influence of alcohol and inappropriately visited upon by innocent bystanders such as a spouse, child or casual acquaintance." It may also lead to problems in dealing with grief from separation or loss. He quotes one study in which "Forty-four percent of the Native people who consulted a psychiatrist ... were suffering from grief reaction of one kind or another."[27]

Sharing

Sharing is another rule of behaviour exhibited by many Aboriginal peoples. In some instances, it was institutionalized in ceremonies to ensure that no one became too rich or powerful and, conversely, that no one became too poor or too powerless. Such ceremonies included the Potlatch of the West Coast and the Sundance of Manitoba. However, it was, and remains, a daily feature of Aboriginal societies in a less formal fashion.

> In Aboriginal times, when this principle originated among Native peoples, group survival was more important than individual prosperity; consequently, individuals were expected to take no more than they needed from nature and to share it freely with others. Of course, this is somewhat akin to the central principle of Marxism and Christianity. Native people however, regard it neither as a political ideology nor as a religious requirement. It was and still is simply a part of the Native way of life. Although the main function was to help ensure group survival in the face of the ever present threat of starvation, it also serves as a form of conflict suppression by reducing the likelihood of greed, envy, arrogance and pride within the tribe.[28]

These four major Aboriginal ethics or rules of behaviour (non-interference, non-competitiveness, emotional restraint and sharing) form the basis of daily relations within Aboriginal communities. But they work with four supplementary ethics: a concept of time, the expression of gratitude and approval, social protocols, and the teaching and rearing of children.

Conflicts Arising from Aboriginal Cultural Imperatives

Aboriginal people have developed their own views and customs, or rules of behaviour, that are sometimes in conflict with those of the dominant society. For example, Aboriginal people have a very different concept of time from that of most other Canadians. It is referred to jokingly by Aboriginal people as "Indian time" or "Metis time." But it is simply an acknowledgement that events will take place when it is the proper time, after the required social protocols have been followed, or as long as they do not interfere with other duties or activities.

> [T]he Native person has an intuitive, personal and flexible concept of time. It may have had its origin in an age when the activities of Native people were regulated by the seasons—by the sun, the migratory patterns of birds and animals, and a changing food supply.... Today, the Native concept of time seems less a principle for living with nature and more of a manifestation of the need for harmonious interpersonal relationships. For example, Tom, Dick and Harry may not make it to an 8 pm meeting because they have other responsibilities they are unable to leave because the time is not right. If they have a particular interest in the matter under discussion, the meeting will not be started until they arrive or until some message is received that they are not coming. To start without them might offend these esteemed members of the community.... In another, more social context, it might be rude and inconsiderate to start a dance at a wedding celebration without all the brothers and sisters of the bride and groom being able to take part in the first waltz.[29]

To illustrate the relevance in the justice system of such cultural differences between Aboriginal and non-Aboriginal people, here is an example provided by a Micmac court worker in Nova Scotia:

> Now time is usually divided in the Micmac world according to the positioning of the sun. Now if you are a Micmac person being examined or cross-examined on the witness stand, the lawyer might say, "Well, did you see this happen at seven o'clock in the morning?" And the Native person would answer to me, "Yes, no he would say, "Wej kwap niaq" which means the sun has just risen. And so I would turn around and I would give that statement to whoever was asking the questions. And then the Prosecutor not being satisfied with this answer, would say, "yeh, but ... was it seven o'clock in the morning?" And the Native person would say, "Well, you know the sun had risen." And simply because seven o'clock in the morning in the summer and seven o'clock in the winter are different in the sense that the sun rises at different times. So he would find difficulty in answering—answering the question. And sometimes he would eventually say, "Yes, it was seven o'clock in the morning" just to get out of that situation.[30]

Other Rules of Behaviour

There are rules governing nearly every form of social behaviour. There is a rule dictating the proper way to commend another or express appreciation so as not to embarrass that particular person or demean the less-than-adequate accomplishment of another person. There are rules governing proper etiquette or social protocol. "Native society has highly structured and demanding rules of social behaviour. There are rules about everything. Many, however, are specific to individual villages, clans, tribes and bands, a fact that can cause problems, given the ethic of non-interference."[31]

There is even a rule that defines the proper method of teaching Aboriginal young people or children. Unlike European-Canadians, Aboriginal people teach their young people through example. They allow the children to set their own goals and to learn that which the children feel is important or worthwhile. This method also respects the other rules of behaviour restricting interference and avoiding conflict. This method of teaching has often been misinterpreted or misunderstood by European-Canadians as a sign of poor parenting.

However, it conveys information about the proper behaviour to the young person while it promotes self-reliance and responsibility. It also engenders respect for the rules of society while it reinforces the importance of role models, parents and other people doing the teaching—the elders in the community.

Brant surmises these ethics or rules of behaviour are reinforced within Aboriginal society by two other factors. The first is "the projection of conflict," or the removal of blame to the outside, away from the immediate family or clan and towards some unseen and distant villain. This villain might take the shape of a witch or a monster and originally was used to discipline people by implied threat. "Anger provoked them, so children were taught from a very early age never to engage in angry behaviour. Anger was considered not only unworthy and unwise, but dangerous as well."[32]

The second factor is the use of teasing, shaming and ridicule as a means of social control to discourage unwelcome behaviour and encourage the maintenance of harmony. On one hand, the use of such humiliation encouraged closeness and kept young people attached to the group, promoting group unity and survival. On the other hand, it drove the more reckless, bold or rebellious away from the group which, again, promoted stability within the group. It also emphasized the use of peer pressure to reinforce the rules of society upon the individual.

Again, we stress that these theories of human behaviour are, as Brant himself warns, "far from complete." They may lend themselves to oversimplification and stereotyping. Brant recognizes this danger and presents them not as confirmed fact, but as theories to encourage debate and to "promote the further demystification of Native behaviour." We do so as well. We present them to illustrate the vast differences in worldviews and in psychological behaviours between Aboriginal and non-Aboriginal peoples.

We do, however, believe that Dr. Brant's work is valuable as a tool for understanding how the cultural values of Aboriginal people determine their actions in certain situations. This is an understanding that even many Aboriginal people lack. Brant's findings become even more critical when one considers the impact that non-Aboriginal systems of government, policies and programs have had upon Aboriginal people, due to this lack of knowledge. To a large extent, this same knowledge has determined the manner in which Aboriginal people have reacted to government injustices.

In addition, the suppression of the rights of Aboriginal people to perform certain ceremonies and to adhere to their cultural imperatives has contributed to the social disruption in their communities. This disruption has interfered with the ability of Aboriginal people to deal with the various pressures confronting them. It also has denied them culturally appropriate ways of maintaining harmony and limiting social disruption.

Aboriginal cultures have, and continue to practise, ceremonies which encourage the controlled release of emotions in an appropriate manner. There are "grieving" ceremonies in which Aboriginal people are encouraged to deal with loss and separation. The "shaking tent" and "sweat lodge" ceremonies were used in this manner to "purify" or rid a person of latent hostilities and anger.

Sports, games and social functions allowed individuals to express anger, competitiveness or happiness in socially acceptable ways. There were "healing" circles in which the most deeply felt hurts were explored and dealt with within the context of traditional teachings. There were elders who counselled and advised individuals and the tribe on how to resolve disputes and relieve tensions.

What has been suppressed by laws and other religions in the past are these traditional mechanisms by which Aboriginal people have dealt with personal problems and pressures. Many of these ceremonies were outlawed by governments until very recently. These ceremonies are still dismissed or debased by some people, even today. The disruption of Aboriginal societies, for the most part, has not interfered greatly with such rules of behaviour, but it has interfered greatly with the means by which Aboriginal people maintained personal balance and well-being.

Cultural Imperatives and Systemic Discrimination

> Until we realize that [Aboriginal people] are not simply "primitive versions of us" but a people with a highly developed, formal, complex and wholly *foreign* set of cultural imperatives, we will continue to misinterpret their acts, misperceive their problems, and then impose mistaken and potentially harmful "remedies."[33] [Emphasis in original]

It is exactly this misunderstanding that is at the heart of systemic discrimination. The justice system assumes much about the people who appear before it. The system assumes all persons will use the same reasoning when protecting their interests, when choosing their pleas, when conducting their defences, when confronting their accusers, when responding to detailed questions, and when showing respect and remorse to the court. It also assumes that punishment will affect all persons in the same manner.

When the justice system of the dominant society is applied to Aboriginal individuals and communities, many of its principles are at odds with the life philosophies which govern the behaviour of Aboriginal people. The value systems of most Aboriginal societies hold in high esteem the interrelated principles of individual autonomy and freedom, consistent with the preservation of relationships and community harmony, respect for other human (and non-human) beings, reluctance to criticize or interfere with others, and avoidance of confrontation and adversarial positions.

Methods and processes for solving disputes in Aboriginal societies have developed, of course, out of the basic value systems of the people. Belief in the inherent decency and wisdom of each individual person implies that any person will have useful opinions in any given situation, and should be listened to respectfully. Aboriginal methods of dispute resolution, therefore, allow for any interested party to volunteer an opinion or make a comment. The "truth" of an incident is arrived at through hearing many descriptions of the event and of related, perhaps extenuating, circumstances.

Impossible though it is to arrive at "the whole truth" in any circumstance, as Aboriginal people are aware, they believe that more of the truth can be determined when everyone is free to contribute information, as opposed to a system where only a chosen number are called to testify on subjects carefully chosen by adversarial counsel, where certain topics or information are inadmissible, and where questions can be asked in ways that dictate the answers.

Because the purpose of law in Aboriginal society is to restore harmony within the community, not only the accused has to be considered. Other people who have been or might be affected by the offence, particularly the victim, have to be considered in the matter of "sentencing" and disposition.

In the Ojibway concept of order, when a person is wronged it is understood that the wrongdoer must repair the order and harmony of the community by undoing the wrong. In most cases, the responsibility is placed on the wrongdoer to compensate the wronged persons. This concept of order makes the individual responsible for the maintenance of harmony within the society. Restitution to the victim or victims is, therefore, a primary consideration.

The person wronged, bereaved or impoverished is entitled to some form of restitution. In the eyes of the community, sentencing the offender to incarceration or, worse still, placing him or her on probation, is tantamount to relieving the offender completely of any responsibility for a just restitution of the wrong. It is viewed by Aboriginal people as a total vindication of the wrongdoer and an abdication of duty by the justice system.

The accused also may have dependants who are involved in some way. Aboriginal people believe care has to be taken so that actions to control the offender do not bring hardship to others. The administration of justice in Aboriginal societies is relationship-centred and attempts to take into account the consequences of dispositions on individuals and the community, as well as on the offender.

The differences between Aboriginal processes and the processes of the Canadian justice system are profound. The Canadian justice system, like other justice systems in the European tradition, is adversarial. When an accusation has been made against an individual, legal advisers representing plaintiff and defendant confront one another before an impartial judge or jury. Witnesses are called to testify for or against the accused; that is, to criticize or explain the actions of another. Guilt or innocence are decided on the basis of the argument that takes place between legal representatives. Retribution is demanded if the person accused is considered guilty.

The concepts of adversarialism, accusation, confrontation, guilt, argument, criticism and retribution are alien to the Aboriginal value system, although perhaps not totally unknown to Aboriginal peoples. In the context of Aboriginal value systems, adversarialism and confrontation are antagonistic to the high value placed on harmony and the peaceful coexistence of all living beings, both human and non-human, with one another and with nature. Criticism of others is at odds with the principles of non-interference and individual autonomy and freedom. The idea that guilt and innocence can be decided on the basis of argument is incompatible with a firmly rooted belief in honesty and integrity that does not permit lying. Retribution as an end in itself, and as an aim of society, becomes a meaningless notion in a value system which requires the reconciliation of an offender with the community and restitution for victims.

The same contradictions between Aboriginal values and the dominant justice system result in a heavy burden being placed on Aboriginal accused, plaintiffs and witnesses who enter into the "white" justice system. Accusation and criticism (giving adverse testimony), while required in the Canadian justice system, are precluded in an Aboriginal value system which makes every effort to avoid criticism and confrontation. "Refusal or reluctance to testify, or when testifying, to give anything but the barest and most emotionless recital of events" appears to be the result of deeply rooted cultural behaviour in which "giving testimony face to face with the accused is simply wrong ... [and] where in fact every effort seems to have been made to avoid such direct confrontation."[34] In Aboriginal societies, it may be ethically wrong to say hostile, critical, implicitly angry things about someone in his or her presence, precisely what our adversarial trial rules require.

Plea-making is another area where the mechanics of the Canadian justice system are in conflict with Aboriginal cultural values. Aboriginal individuals who, in fact, have committed the deeds with which they are charged are often reluctant or unable to plead not guilty because that plea is, to them, a denial of the truth and contrary to a basic tenet of their culture.

Some people have pointed out to our Inquiry that many Aboriginal people have trouble comprehending the "white" concept of guilt or innocence before a court, in terms of their own culture. There is no such concept in Aboriginal culture and so there are no words in their vocabulary for "guilty" or "not guilty." This example comes from the Royal Commission on the Donald Marshall, Jr., Prosecution in Nova Scotia.

Q   I was starting to ask you if you could explain to us the ... meaning of the word "guilty" in Micmac.

Francis: There really is no such word as "guilty" in the Micmac language. There is a word for "blame". So an Indian person who's not as knowledgeable let's say in the English language if he were asked if he were guilty or not, he would take that to mean, "Are you being blamed or not?" and that's one of the reasons I found that Native people were pleading guilty is because they suspect that the question was, "Is it true that you're being blamed?" and the Native person would of course say, "Yes." In other words, but the real question being, "Are you guilty or not guilty?" and the answer of course would be "Yes, I plead guilty," thinking that's blame. What they neglected to say was, "Yes, I'm guilty that I'm being blamed but I didn't do it."[35]

Similar problems with language exist between Aboriginal people and the justice system in Manitoba. We had this exchange with Art Wambidee, a court worker from the Sioux Valley First Nation:

Q   You mentioned as well problems in interpreting some of the words that are used in court. That issue was raised with us before by people in the north talking about the Cree language, that there is no concept for "guilty" or "innocent". It doesn't translate into one word. Is that the same thing with your language?

Art Wambidee: It's the same thing, yes.

Q   How would you, if you had to interpret "guilty" or "not guilty" for someone in your language? How would you interpret that? What would you make them try to understand?

A   Well, I guess that I'd sort of interpret it, "Did you do that, or didn't you?"

A final example is the implicit expectation on the part of lawyers, judges and juries that people standing accused before them should show remorse and a desire for rehabilitation. However, Aboriginal cultural imperatives demand that they accept, without emotion, what comes to them. Aboriginal people, therefore, might react contrary to the expectations of people involved in the justice system. In the Aboriginal person's powerlessness, he or she simply may wait passively, with head respectfully bowed, to receive the judgment of the court. This attitude has been carried over into Aboriginal behaviour within the justice system.

In his effort to honour those pleading his case, he makes every attempt to agree to their requests, (to) give answers that please, and not to argue or appear adversarial.[36]

Judges and juries can hardly be impartial when they misinterpret the words, demeanour and body language of individuals. Witnesses who refuse to testify, and people accused of crimes who refuse to plead and who show no emotion, are judged differently from those who react in ways expected by the system. Their culturally induced responses are misunderstood, sometimes as contempt, and may result in an unfair or inappropriate hearing and in inappropriate sentencing. To require people to act in ways contrary to their most basic beliefs and their ingrained rules of behaviour not only is an infringement of their rights—it is a deeply discriminatory act.

Language Issues

Lawyers, court communicators, family court workers, juvenile workers, Aboriginal community members and other concerned people stressed to our Inquiry the pervasiveness of language problems for Aboriginal people at every stage of Manitoba's system of justice.

These issues are not merely of language; they go to the heart of our society's obligation to ensure that people understand their legal rights and obligations, the nature of any charges against them and any legal proceedings affecting their rights. The right of all people to the use of a familiar language, preferably their first language, is not always met. Canadian courts do not automatically provide interpreters for Aboriginal people, nor do enforcement and corrections agencies. An even more fundamental question, beyond this immediate and pressing omission, is whether Aboriginal people understand the concepts behind the language used in the legal system, even when interpreters and translators are used.

Understanding Words

On a mechanical level, there are obvious problems when the police, lawyers and the courts conduct business in a language that is not the mother language, nor even perhaps the second language, of the people involved. Translation and interpreter services often are not available. When offered, they may be inadequate or even prejudicial.

On the philosophical level, there is the serious question of whether the legal terms of the dominant society can be translated into Aboriginal languages. Even if that can be done, does the translation actually convey the same concept to Aboriginal people in their mother tongue as it does to European-language speakers?

Mechanical language problems have been identified at every step of the legal process. When individuals are approached by police under what police officers consider suspicious circumstances, they often cannot explain what may be, in fact, innocent situations. They may not understand the reasons for their arrests or the explanations of their rights. Remarks and explanations made in inadequate or broken English or French during arrest, transportation and booking have been misunderstood by arresting officers and used to incriminate some Aboriginal people. As northern paralegal Sylvia Grier told us, "Police reports were not accurate because of an inability of Aboriginal speakers to explain the circumstances to the police."

Aboriginal people who do not speak a dominant language cannot ask to use a telephone or request a public defender, or even ask for help to do so, if there are no translation services provided while they are booked. Translation is not readily available during consultations between the people accused and their lawyers. In the courtroom, according to Chief Philip Michel of Brochet, "by-standers are often sworn in to act as interpreters ... [with] no guarantee of proper communication or unbiased translation."

It is obvious that defendants who do not speak English or French, or who do not speak the relevant language well, will be at a disadvantage during courtroom proceedings. It is not so obvious that many Aboriginal people who do speak a dominant language may have a command of that language which enables them to function in most areas of life, but which is not adequate for dealing with formal courtroom language. This problem is not restricted to Aboriginal peoples. Many lifelong, fluent and highly articulate anglophones and francophones cannot deal with "legalese."

It is also apparent to observers that many people do not realize that they are missing or misunderstanding parts of the proceedings. As we learned from our hearings, many are reluctant to admit a language deficiency in public.

A fundamental right of all Canadians in the justice system ought to be the right to use a known language, preferably their mother tongue. Obvious as this may seem, and in spite of the fact that the *Charter of Rights and Freedoms* enshrines a person's right to an interpreter, there is no program to ensure that Aboriginal people have access to an interpreter in court, nor are they told they have a right to one. Although there are a number of court communicators working in our courts, their mandate is "to assist Native Peoples in the development of a better understanding of their rights, interests, privileges, and responsibilities in relation to the criminal justice system. It is the role of the Court Communicator to assist Native Peoples through the process and attempt to bridge any gaps which may exist."[37] In other words, their job is to interpret cultures, not languages, and their training prepares them mainly to interpret the customs of the dominant society to Aboriginal peoples—not the other way around.

Court communicators in the Manitoba program may provide interpreting services, but only unofficially, "due to a lack of other available resources."[38] Interpreting is not part of their role. Local people are frequently hired as court interpreters, but many people see their services as inadequate because they are untrained, not properly qualified, and can give no guarantee of impartiality or neutrality.

Apparently, the only interpreter/translator training program in use in Canada is the one in the Northwest Territories. The program consists of a course and materials prepared for freelance and government interpreters. It is designed to help them understand existing court procedures, language and protocol.

However, translation problems are described within the context of English. The material does not deal with the differing concepts of Aboriginal and dominant society approaches to law and justice. Many of the inadequacies of the Legal Interpreter's Handbook, the manual prepared for court communicators in the Northwest Territories, are the result of ethnocentricity and cultural misunderstanding by the authors.

The Manitoba *Native Court Interpreter's Manual* has been judged by some Cree scholars and linguists to be an adequate beginning to the process of translating legal language into Aboriginal languages. However,

> ... problems encountered with the Court Manual and with the process of translating and verifying the words requested were all the result of the difficulty of creating a vocabulary for which there is no cultural concept in the language. The vocabulary has to be developed and agreed upon, then taught to the people it will impinge upon.[39]

Understanding Legal Concepts

There are really two types of misunderstandings that arise from the translation of terms from one language into another. The first is easier to understand: some words simply do not translate directly into an Aboriginal language. Much more difficult and, therefore, more prone to misunderstandings, is the attempt to convey the concepts implied by technical legal words.

Take the word "truth," for example. "Truth" is a key concept in the Canadian legal system and, as such, is considered definite and definable. One swears "to tell the truth, the whole truth and nothing but the truth." There are well-defined sanctions for people whom the court determines are not telling the "truth" or are committing perjury.

On the other hand, the Ojibway understanding of "truth" incorporates the concept that "absolute truth" is unknowable.

> When an Ojibway says "niwii-debwe", that means he is going to tell "what is right as he knows it". A standard expression is "I don't know if what I tell you is the truth. I can only tell you what I know."[40]

> It is as a philosophical proposition that in saying a speaker casts his words and his voice as far as his perception and his vocabulary will enable him or her, that it is a denial that there is such a thing as absolute truth; the best and most the speaker can achieve and a listener expect is the highest degree of accuracy. Somehow that one expression, "w'dab-ahae", sets the limits to a single statement as well as setting limits to truth and the scope and exercise of speech.[41]

Truth and knowledge, to an Ojibway, are always relative. Individuals can say only what they have observed or experienced, and are prepared to doubt whether they have done so accurately and correctly. Culturally ingrained habits of respect for others and for other people's opinions, of doubt concerning one's own rightness and righteousness, of willingness to be corrected, and of unwillingness to set oneself up as an authority or expert, account for the readiness with which Aboriginal witnesses appear to change their testimony.

An Aboriginal person challenged by someone perceived to be wiser, more powerful or more knowledgeable may agree readily that perhaps the other person is right. The Aboriginal person, in certain circumstances, is open to suggestions that he or she may have misunderstood, misperceived or misheard the events that are under examination.

The proceedings of the Royal Commission on the Donald Marshall, Jr., Prosecution contain an example of the Aboriginal understanding of the relativity of truth.

Q   What about the questioning process, the questioning of a witness in the Courtroom, of a Micmac witness?

Francis: That was another area in which I found to be just devastating towards Native people who attempted to defend themselves in that—in almost all cases a Native person who was not that familiar with the English language would work so hard to try to satisfy the person who was asking the questions. If for instance, either a lawyer or a prosecuting lawyer was asking the questions to a native person on the witness stand and was not satisfied with the answer that he or she received, would continue to ask the question by checking a word here or there and asking the same question and the native person would change the answer from, let's say a "no" to a "yes" or a "yes" to a "no." ... simply because he felt that whatever he was doing, he wasn't doing it right and he would attempt to satisfy the person asking the questions.

Q   Regardless of the truth?

Francis: Regardless of the truth.[42]

The exchange, odd though it sounds to anglophone ears, illustrates the point that the lawyer or prosecuting lawyer was searching for "absolute truth," a concept the witness' culture does not accept.

From the time of his or her arrest until sentencing, the "truth," as revealed by the Aboriginal individual, will be relative to his or her perceptions of the situation. This could very well mean many different versions of the "truth": one during police interrogation, one in conversation with lawyer or lawyers, the one known widely in the Aboriginal community and, finally, the one given under cross-examination in court. In the Indian view, at no point would he or she be accused of lying. All the versions would be deemed reasonable in view of what might have happened, and no one would deem it necessary to judge one version more right than the others.

Other concepts embedded in Aboriginal culture and expressed through Aboriginal languages would be interpreted somewhat differently in English. Concepts of time and space, for example, are much less precise in Aboriginal languages, while they are exactly measured and divided into uniform units in English. More specifically, words describing time or distance in Aboriginal languages would tend to be vague, such as "near," "too heavy" or "after sundown," as compared to "three feet," "110 pounds" and "a quarter after 11" in English.

The inability to name an exact time, or estimate a distance or a weight with precision, is due in large part to the irrelevance of these concepts to Aboriginal life. In a courtroom, the persistence of a lawyer in trying to elicit a precise response results in the witness becoming convinced that the lawyer is asking for verification of his or her own point of view.

The Aboriginal witness, when confronted by a question whether the distance was 10, 20 or one foot, is stumped. The information is of no interest to the witness but appears to be of considerable importance to the lawyer. The lawyer is in a position of authority and, therefore, is to be honoured by concurrence with his or her point of view, whatever it might be. So the Aboriginal witness will try to reassure the lawyer that the information is correct.[43]

Many Aboriginal people are just as vague when it comes to such things as house numbers. An individual knows where home is in terms of how to get there, but may not bother to remember the house number. This very circumstance has resulted in many people being recorded mistakenly by the police as having "no fixed address," thus affecting their prospects for bail or consideration during sentencing.

New Concepts—Old Words

Some words can be translated directly from an Aboriginal language into the English language, but they may not convey the same concept. Some concepts are totally foreign to Aboriginal thought and so new words or phrases have to be invented to approximate the meaning. Former court interpreter Barbara Whitford gave this example:

Q   What about other phrases that you may have some difficulty or that an interpreter or a person who speaks, say, only Ojibway, would have difficulty understanding an English legal concept. Probation is an example....

Barbara Whitford: Actually, you have posed a very difficult question, as it just happened for me this afternoon and I was unable to be able to say to that woman, in my language, the question that you just asked.

Q   The question about probation?

A   I could come back and tell you. I need to think about that. I need to seek an older person, perhaps my mother, who might have that language. Are you understanding what I am saying?

Q   Yes. So, you don't have a way of explaining it. You couldn't explain probation....

A   Not right off the bat. As I'm sitting here, no, I cannot answer that, no.

Because most concepts of the dominant justice system differ from those of Aboriginal societies, words used to describe the concepts in an Aboriginal language have had to be newly coined or invented, or explained with words that actually have different meanings. The way that Art Wambidee translates "probation" for an offender is, "it will mean that he's dragging a rope behind him." Barbara Whitford gave us other examples:

Q   It has often been said that in Aboriginal languages, Ojibway and Cree and others, that there is no single word that captures what a lawyer is.

Barbara Whitford: Right.

Q If you were asked to interpret a lawyer, the word lawyer, how would you explain that?

A Well, I have a word for that, for lawyer.

Q What is that word?

A (Indian name for lawyer).

Q And what does that translate back in English meaning?

A Someone who defends you.

Q How about judge; do you have a word for judge?

A I was sitting there this afternoon contemplating that. No, not right offhand, I don't. But it is along the same lines as what I just said, the person who makes the decision regarding.

Many words used in Aboriginal languages to describe the concepts of the Canadian legal system carry connotations which they may or may not have in English. The Cree term for "arrested" (literally, he or she was "caught") implies a presumption of guilt, as does the Cree word for "accused."

Even if legal proceedings were carried out entirely in Aboriginal languages, there would be problems describing concepts which are wholly Western. In European languages, for instance, "to appeal" is to act in a particular way, but in Ojibway the relevant word is an abstraction which means the "science of appealing," or the "art of appealing." It cannot be used to describe an act. For the word in Ojibway to be given the added meaning of action would be to violate Ojibway grammatical structures and the manner of thought which underlies them.[44]

Other words have been translated literally from English into Aboriginal languages. The English word "bail," for instance, has been translated into Ojibway and means bail as in "bailing a boat." The Ojibway word itself is unclear until it is put into context. To use the single Ojibway word for "bail," as we use the English word in a courtroom context, would require widespread consultation and acceptance about the word or phrase among Ojibway speakers. Unlike English, Ojibway does not have a body of words with double meanings (homonyms) whose individual meanings are dependent on context.[45] The imposed introduction of a homonymic element would be another violation of Ojibway grammar and the worldview it expresses.

Many Ojibway words are imprecise, or perhaps it would be better to say that many words do not describe in detail. For instance, there is no way to distinguish between a defence lawyer and a Crown attorney in a short phrase. To explain the difference between these two kinds of lawyers would require a detailed explanation of the workings of the court in order for an Ojibway-only speaker to understand the concepts.

Finally, the English language and lifestyle are not threatened in North America, nor is change feared. Aboriginal people, on the other hand, are justifiably concerned about the erosion of their cultures and languages, and are understandably less open to incorporating "foreign" concepts and elements into their languages.

A basic problem in using Aboriginal languages in the legal system is that until recently they did not exist in print. Some Aboriginal languages still have not been put into written form. This makes the standardization of words and their meanings difficult, if not impossible, in some cases. The same word in the same language can imply different meanings from community to community and from regional dialect to regional dialect.

If it is determined that Aboriginal languages are going to be used in the courts, then language development activities have to proceed to build a corpus of Aboriginal language terms which are universally understood and accepted with that language group.[46]

Conclusion

Law has a special meaning to Aboriginal people. The "law," to Aboriginal people, means rules that they must live by and it reflects their traditional culture and values. For instance, the Ojibway worldview is expressed through their language and through the Law of the Orders, which instructs people about the right way to live. The standards of conduct which arise from the Law of the Orders are not codified, but are understood and passed on from generation to generation. Correct conduct is concerned with "appropriate behaviour, what is forbidden, and the responsibility ensuing from each."[47] The laws include relationships among human beings as well as the correct relationship with other orders: plants, animals and the physical world. The laws are taught through "legends" and other oral traditions.

Broadly speaking, Aboriginal people share many values with other peoples around the world. Yet, despite these similarities, Aboriginal cultures are vastly different from other cultures in Canada and throughout the world. They are unique and have no other place of origin. Despite this distinctiveness, Aboriginal cultures and ways of life have been assumed by the dominant society to be without value or purpose. Past policies deemed it best that these cultures be stamped out altogether. Failing that, it was decided that Aboriginal cultures would have to melt into the mainstream in the hope they would assimilate and disappear.

Aboriginal cultures and the values they represent have not disappeared. Instead, they have adapted to new times and new situations. They remain vibrant and dynamic today. The rules of behaviour and the cultural imperatives of Aboriginal society continue to determine how an Aboriginal person views the surrounding world, and they influence that person's actions and reactions with other individuals and with society as a whole.

So do the laws, customs and traditions that have been defined by that culture. They define the concepts of justice in Aboriginal cultures. These laws respect the cultural imperatives that restrict interference and encourage restraint. Their primary purpose is to discourage disruption and to restore harmony when it occurs. They developed in other times and for other circumstances, but they remain powerful and relevant in Aboriginal society today.

We cannot continue to ignore the cultures of Aboriginal people and the laws, customs and values they generate. We cannot keep denying their very existence. To do so would be to compound past mistakes that have precipitated horrific consequences for Aboriginal people. If the justice system in Manitoba is to earn the respect of Aboriginal people, it must first recognize and respect their cultures, their values and their laws.

CHAPTER 3

──────

AN HISTORICAL OVERVIEW

Introduction

We recognize that Canadians know relatively little about Aboriginal history and culture. Few Manitobans have had the opportunity to learn about their fellow citizens of Aboriginal background. In order that they might come to terms with our analysis of the present crisis and our recommendations for dealing with it, we invite all Manitobans to join us in reviewing that history.

Until very recently, the books that Manitobans and Canadians studied in high schools and universities were appallingly deficient in their treatment of Aboriginal history. A 1971 study of 88 books that most frequently appeared on Canadian history courses concluded that Indians were treated as part of the background to a European story.[1] Sometimes, Indians were discussed in the introductory chapter on the environment and then relegated to a minor role. They might be enemies, as in the case of the Iroquois in New France, or allies, including Joseph Brant in the American Revolution and Tecumseh in the War of 1812, but rarely were they treated as human beings, let alone political strategists or caring parents or any of the other roles reserved for non-Aboriginal historical figures. This blindness must not continue. Manitoba's Aboriginal people are playing an increasingly important role in every aspect of the province's life. It is incumbent upon all Manitobans to ensure that the errors of their ancestors are corrected and that the history of their fellow citizens of Aboriginal descent is better understood so Aboriginal people are able to occupy a position in society which recognizes their contribution to the development of our community.

Manitoba's Aboriginal people have known three different justice regimes. The first, a product of custom, negotiation and experience, developed before the arrival of Europeans during the centuries in which only Aboriginal people inhabited this part of the Americas. The second, which commenced with the arrival of Europeans in the 17th century, did not end Aboriginal law, but merely added English, Scottish and French complements in parallel with it. The third began with Manitoba's entry into Confederation in 1870. Although it has remained essentially unchanged to the present, this third regime has had a devastating impact on Manitoba's Aboriginal people during the last four decades.

We do not know a great deal about Aboriginal customary law as it developed and was applied in the first era before the arrival of Europeans. With the assistance of research in other parts of Canada and the world, and after consultation with Aboriginal elders, however, we believe we are able to understand its character and role in Aboriginal society before European contact.

Aboriginal customary law changed little in the second era, which extended from about 1660 to 1870. Nevertheless, the arrival of European peoples did place constraints upon Aboriginal customary activity and did introduce a different legal atmosphere.

The third justice regime commenced with the entry of Manitoba into Canada in 1870. The rapid development of a Europe-oriented society required accommodations by Aboriginal people. It left them with less freedom to live according to their own laws and customs. Treaties, the *Indian Act,* criminal law, school regulations, church pressures and government control over the harvesting of natural resources were aspects of a new and pervasive Canadian legal system that increasingly interfered with Aboriginal life. In this era, the Canadian government sowed the seeds that have returned as a bitter harvest during our generation.

Dramatic change occurred during the third regime, but it became a social crisis for Aboriginal people in the decades after World War II. Manitoba's Aboriginal citizens have not been alone in having to adjust to the impact of governmental authority. Indeed, increased government regulations have affected us all. But Aboriginal people have experienced greater changes than have other Canadians. The legal and economic status of Aboriginal people, the economic foundation of their traditional life and the cultural attributes that were regarded as essential to their continued survival had been under attack since 1870, but since 1950 those attacks have intensified and the results have been devastating.

Law in the Pre-Contact Aboriginal Community

Law in an Aboriginal community was found in unwritten conventions before the arrival of Europeans. Although these rules were never codified, we observe that there were consistent patterns in the treatment of such matters as relations with other nations, family problems, and disputes about behaviour and property. These patterns became part of Aboriginal oral tradition and were passed from generation to generation. One can easily speak about these patterns in terms of "law" and "justice." Aboriginal people have resided in this part of the globe for thousands of years, or hundreds of generations. Aboriginal legends speak of the original peoples being on this land from the time of its creation. In essence, they have lived here from time immemorial. Archeological evidence of hearths at the forks of the Red and Assiniboine rivers, of garden plots at Lockport near Selkirk on the Red River, of rock paintings in the Whiteshell and of bison jumps in the Assiniboine River valley near Brandon are merely the best known of the physical evidence of this long occupation. As this evidence accumulates, scholars have sketched a picture of hunting-based and agriculture-based societies, of trade and of material culture that demonstrates how effectively they adapted to their environment. The social structures of these communities, however, their politics, diplomacy and family relations, are less evident. It is much more difficult to create a picture of the society in which these people lived their lives. Our brief description of the customary law that prevailed in these Aboriginal communities, drawn from oral histories of the people and written accounts of early contacts, will suffice to underline our conclusion that a separate and distinct legal system existed in pre-contact Aboriginal history.

We appreciate that it is difficult to define Aboriginal or "customary" or "traditional" law. In its broadest application, customary law includes three different subjects: specific rules that prescribe proper behaviour in a community; observable regularities in everyday human behaviour; and definable approaches to instances of dispute.[2] However, it is difficult to be precise about what constitutes a law or a legal system in an Aboriginal world that does not employ such fixed concepts. A few illustrations should demonstrate, however, how a legal "system" operated in pre-contact Aboriginal Manitoba and why such cultural bases must be a part of our thinking in today's Manitoba.

Our understanding of how traditional Ojibway and Cree cultural practices related to justice is similar to that published by Michael Coyle in a recent article.[3] Ojibway and Cree decision making involved the participation and consent of the community at large. Behaviour was regulated by ostracism, shame and compensation for the victim's loss, even if only symbolic compensation were possible. Elders undertook the regular teaching of community values and warned offenders on behalf of the community. They publicly banished individuals who persisted in disturbing the peace. Elders might undertake to mediate dangerous disputes and to reconcile offenders with victims. In cases of grave threats or such serious offences as murder, physical punishment and even execution of the offender might be undertaken either by the community or by those who had been wronged. In all instances the sanction of tribal elders was necessary.

A murder in the Eagle Hills in 1775–76 illustrates the practice. According to Matthew Cocking, the Hudson's Bay Company trader at Cumberland House, who had heard the story from "Pedler Henry," a quarrel had occurred among the Beaver Indians of the Eagle Hills (probably Crees in the area northwest of present-day Saskatoon). Cocking's report is worth close attention:

> That no account has been recieved [sic] from the Beaver Indians, only from the reports of others they are not expected to come down even in the Summer, on account of a Quarrel having happened between them and some others last Winter. That an Indian was shot by another the first of this Winter at the upper Settlement, the Indian killed having murdered his Wife last

Summer was the reason of the other's taking the same revenge, the Woman being his Sister: Tis supposed that the affair will stop here....[4]

Cocking's choice of words is significant. A man had "murdered" his wife. As a matter of "revenge," that man was "shot" by the woman's brother. Note that this act of retaliation is not described as murder and that the traders assume the "Quarrel" had been settled.

These traditional methods of social control served the same purpose as our modern criminal justice system. Fur trader Daniel Harmon discovered when he visited southern Manitoba in the early 19th century that:

It is a common thing among all the Natives, for an offender to offer property in satisfaction for an injury, and when this is accepted by the injured party, contention between them entirely ceases. Even murder is, sometimes, in this way atoned for; but not commonly. In ordinary cases, nothing but the death of the murderer, or of some of his near relatives, will satisfy the desire for revenge.[5]

The insistence upon retaliation deterred the public and the individual offender from repeating the offence and it might have helped in the rehabilitation of the wrongdoer.

The role of elders, and their regular use of shame and expulsion in Ojibway, Assiniboine and Cree societies, illustrate how "force," defined broadly to include such mild sanctions, was used in these cultures. The Roman Catholic missionary, Father de Smet, described how Assiniboine Indians in Manitoba and adjoining lands disciplined offenders in the hunt:

Their guns, their bows, and arrows are broken, their lodges cut in pieces, their dogs killed, all their provisions and their hides are taken from them. If they are bold enough to resist this penalty, they are beaten with bows, sticks, and clubs....[6]

Although their culture showed evidence of both Aboriginal and European origins, the Metis of Manitoba conducted their buffalo hunts in a fashion that reinforces de Smet's observations. Alexander Ross, a leading citizen of Red River, recorded the rules of a hunt in the 1840s:

1. No buffalo to be run on the Sabbath-day.

2. No party to fork off, lag behind, or go before, without permission.

3. No person or party to run buffalo before the general order.

4. Every captain with his men, in turn, to patrol the camp, and keep guard.

5. For the first trespass against these laws, the offender to have his saddle and bridle cut up.

6. For the second offence, the coat to be taken off the offender's back, and be cut up.

7. For the third offence, the offender to be flogged.

8. Any person convicted of theft, even to the value of a sinew, to be brought to the middle of the camp, and the crier to call out his or her name three times, adding the word 'Thief,' at each time.[7]

Another example from an Aboriginal culture also will illustrate the application of force. In the early 1980s, the Gitksan and Wet'suwet'en Indians of British Columbia embarked upon a project to record their traditional laws. In this process, they decided to reword the definition of enforcement offered by the pioneer legal anthropologist, E. Adamson Hoebel, to fit their customary usage.[8] Their new definition of law added ostracism and shame as mechanisms of enforcement, just as Cree and Ojibway cultures might do. Their final statement read:

A social norm is legal if its neglect or infraction is regularly met, in threat or in fact, by the application of physical force, ostracism or shame by an individual or group possessing a socially recognized privilege of so acting.[9]

We conclude that Aboriginal enforcement mechanisms, although not codified in today's sense, served the same purpose in Manitoba's pre-contact Aboriginal societies as did the justice system of the European societies of that time. Crime and punishment became part of each Aboriginal group's oral record, preserved by elders in story and legend. A British Columbia illustration will clarify the process. When the Gitksan-Wet'suwet'en Tribal Council began its project to record traditional laws, the elders had trouble understanding what researchers sought under the title of "law." Eventually, the word was translated as *ada'awk*, which means "history" in literal translation. In those societies, each of the major social units, called a "house," has its own history which is passed down from one chief to the next. It establishes continuity from past to present, asserts a claim to resources and territory, and recounts the story of its relations with other houses. Each member of the house must act in conformity with the principles of the *ada'awk*; thus, for the Gitksan and Wet'suwet'en, principles of historical record are principles of behaviour and can be translated as "law."[10] This perspective was expressed by Delgam Uukw, a Gitksan chief, to the British Columbia Supreme Court:

By following the law, the power flows from the land to the people through the Chief; by using the wealth of the territory, the House feasts its Chief so he can properly fulfill the law. This cycle has been repeated on my land for thousands of years. The histories of my House are always being added to. My presence in this courtroom today will add to my House's power, as it adds to the power of the other Gitksan and Wet'suwet'en Chiefs who will appear here or who will witness the proceedings. All of our roles, including yours, will be remembered in the histories that will be told by my grandchildren. Through the witnessing of all the histories, century after century, we have exercised our jurisdiction.[11]

As in British Columbia, so in Manitoba: each Aboriginal group had its history and its codes of behaviour.

Unwritten law, including negotiation, mediation and summary review of a disagreement, is often a part of daily life and yet not subject to all the requirements of a formal court hearing. We must remind Manitobans that all justice systems depend upon public awareness of their role and function in order to be effective:

> [Justice systems rely upon] publicity whereby norms and leadership are reaffirmed and litigation derives its therapeutic value. The law is held in the hearts and minds of the people and, because such knowledge is unevenly distributed throughout society, moots [informal hearings] constitute public forums that provide frequent opportunities for the law to be restated or to be modified.[12]

The existence of social norms, the use of force and ostracism to enforce them, and the existence of a group—the elders—accustomed to asserting the integrity of such rules underlay the Aboriginal approach to justice before Europeans arrived in this part of the world. As we shall see, these customary practices survive to this day in the outlook of Aboriginal people.

Aboriginal and European Legal Regimes during the Era of Peaceful Co-Existence, 1660–1870

The arrival of Europeans in the northern half of North America in the 17th century set events in motion that changed the context of Aboriginal law, although not the customs and laws themselves. We regard this period as the beginning of a second justice regime in Manitoba.

Aboriginal people and European newcomers lived in peace in Manitoba for more than 200 years, from about 1660 to the mid-19th century. They established mutually satisfactory economic relations while dwelling in essentially separate worlds. In the view of the Aboriginal people, the Europeans dwelt on the rim of an Aboriginal universe. As the English missionary, John West, discovered to his surprise, the Aboriginal people in the area around the forks of the Red and Assiniboine rivers "consider themselves the standard of excellence. In their fancied superior knowledge they are often heard to remark, when conversing with a European, 'You are almost as clever as an Indian.'"[13]

Seen from the European perspective, from within the palisades of a trading post or from the middle of a trading canoe, Aboriginal people were crucial indeed to all activities in the region, at least until the early decades of the 19th century. Food, trade, diplomacy, even marriage and family matters often were controlled by the Aboriginal inhabitants of this land. Europeans, far from dictating the course of events, negotiated to secure their own means of existence. This balance shifted as the decades passed, however, and by the early 19th century Europeans in eastern North America were sufficiently numerous to have established rules that favoured their interests there. In the West, it was slightly different. From the early 1600s to 1870, the Aboriginal people of prairie Canada lived within a society defined by traditional Aboriginal laws, while Europeans in the region increasingly demanded a justice system for themselves akin to those in Britain and Europe.

The customary seasonal cycle of resource-harvesting continued among Manitoba's Aboriginal people after the introduction of the European fur trade. Small family-based bands dispersed during the depths of winter to hunt game and gather furs in the boreal forest. They congregated on the edges of lakes or on the plains in the spring and summer, when food was plentiful and the weather was warm, to attend to tribal matters and religious affairs. Intertribal trade fuelled the exchange at English and French fur trade posts. European traders simply fit into the accustomed annual cycle when they exchanged European goods for furs and food.

Trade did not result in Aboriginal dependence on Europeans. One Mandan chief, commenting on the members of the Lewis and Clark expedition who travelled through his land (south of present-day Winnipeg) in the early 19th century, said that there were "only two sensible men among them, the Worker of Iron and the Maker of Guns," and concluded that there was so little strength among the rest that his "young men on horseback would do for them as they would do for so many wolves."[14]

The arrival of increasing numbers of traders after France ceded its interest in Canada to British rule in 1763 was part of a significant change in Aboriginal circumstances in the western interior. Increasingly, trading posts were erected near Indian hunting territories. Europeans assumed direct control of the fur and goods exchange, thus eliminating Aboriginal middlemen. Europeans took Aboriginal women as partners and became members of mixed-race families. They also contributed to the growing trade in guns and horses that altered the Aboriginal diplomatic and military balance in the interior of the continent. European diseases devastated a number of Aboriginal communities during the next century. Despite great changes, however, Aboriginal cultures continued as they had for centuries. As Archbishop Taché commented in 1868 about the Aboriginal peoples of this land, "all of them ... retain their original social customs."[15]

Aboriginal Status and International Law

If Aboriginal customary law was unchanged in this era, the European legal context of North American society was revised drastically. Two aspects of this change affected the Aboriginal people of Canada's western interior. First, the application of principles of international law and sovereignty affected Aboriginal tenure. Second, local legal arrangements by fur trading companies and, later, by the settlement at Red River also had an impact upon Manitoba's justice system.

The Aboriginal people of Manitoba had no doubts about their control over their lives or their right to occupy this portion of the earth. Their sovereignty resided in and emanated from the land itself. This was not true of Europeans. They were the newcomers, the invaders, and they required justification in their own legal system for their incursions. This justification came from a variety of European legal conventions and approaches. The relevant international law, treaties and the evolution of legal concepts of Aboriginal rights will be reviewed in Chapter 5.

"Discovery," the planting of flags and the declaration of territorial claims did not establish European ownership of Canada.[16] Instead, early European writers on international law, of whom Vitoria and Vattel are best known, acknowledged that Aboriginal nations had status in international society. This status could be subverted, it is true, either through negotiation or conquest. In fact, land in every part of the globe during the era of European expansion was acquired either by cession or conquest. Acquisitions of either type would have been sanctioned by contemporary legal concepts. But in the absence of either, it is apparent that international law did not hold that Aboriginal sovereignty merely melted or disappeared at the whim of the Europeans.

We do not wish to suggest that, in all cases, Aboriginal nations retained international sovereignty after their territory had been "acquired" or claimed by Imperial powers. But we do conclude that Aboriginal nations had the right to be treated under the domestic law of the colonizing nation in a way that respected either their status in international law, or the treaty or cession commitments that they had negotiated, or both. Elsewhere we point out that Aboriginal nations, at least in Manitoba, have not been so treated.

Aboriginal communities in Canada exercised a sovereign right to govern themselves, in law as well as practice, before European colonization of this land and, to the extent that they did not surrender their right to do so, thereafter. As James Crawford has explained:

> [I]nternational law accepted 'tribes or peoples having a social and political organization' as entities entitled to govern their own affairs and possessing authority over their territory; where these entities exercised a degree of independent governmental authority sufficient for the general maintenance of order, they could be regarded as States in international law, and thus as sovereign ... it does not matter whether particular groups were fully independent, or were to some degree subject to the control or direction of another group: collectively the Indian tribes exercised the full range of governmental powers. Applying these tests there can be no doubt that Aboriginal peoples in North America exercised a sovereign right to govern themselves before European contact, and until the acquisition of sovereignty and the assumption of control over their lands by the European colonizers.[17]

In western Canada, this sovereign right continued and was respected throughout the era of the second justice regime.

The crucial agreements shaping British-Aboriginal arrangements after the fall of New France to British control were the *Royal Proclamation of 1763* and the various treaties signed in the next few decades. The Proclamation was part of Britain's assumption of control over New France. It was precipitated by a political crisis, an Aboriginal siege at Detroit led by Chief Pontiac. The Proclamation forbade white settlement beyond a "proclamation line" and it confirmed principles by which Aboriginal-European relations should be conducted. Britain declared that the Crown must formally extinguish Indian rights, that the Crown *alone* could undertake such obligations, that private interests could not extinguish Aboriginal claims to land, and that negotiations for the surrender of Aboriginal title must occur at an open assembly with the full consent of all the people. It should be underlined that, in legal terms, the *Royal Proclamation* did not establish Aboriginal rights in North America; rather, as James Crawford has written and the Supreme Court of Canada has stated, it assumed their existence.[18] Moreover, it did not create a treaty tradition; rather, it confirmed a practice that had begun in the eastern colonies in previous generations. It was logical and natural that the British government would extend this practice to another North American colony.

The Application of European Law in Manitoba before 1870

The new justice regime in Manitoba after 1660 also was evident in the daily give and take of trade, marriage, property claims, disputes over personal goods, and the struggles between employer and employee that we now call labour-management relations. In the Manitoba historical record, we have discovered cases in which both European and Aboriginal people accepted the need for adaptation of their inherited legal practices. We also have reviewed incidents where they employed legal principles unique to one culture or the other. Several examples will illustrate these different circumstances.

The emergence of new marriage and family conventions in the 18th and early 19th centuries demonstrates the extraordinary nature of the Manitoba legal "frontier." As historian Sylvia Van Kirk has explained, intermarriage between fur traders and Indian or Metis women was fundamental to the growth of a fur trade society:

> [T]he norm for sexual relationships in fur-trade society was not casual, promiscuous encounters but the development of marital unions which gave rise to distinct family units ... fur-trade society developed its own marriage rite, marriage *à la façon du pays*, which combined both Indian and European marriage customs. In this, the fur-trade society of Western Canada appears to have been exceptional. In most other areas of the world, sexual contact between European men and native women had usually been illicit in nature and essentially peripheral to the white man's trading or colonizing ventures. In the Canadian West, however, alliances with Indian women were the central social aspect of the fur traders progress across the country.[19]

These aspects of the second justice regime represented a merger of two cultures, not the dominance of one over another. Fur traders offered substantial presents to the parents of their brides; Aboriginal families, in their turn, accepted political and economic responsibility for their new allies. Each had cemented an "alliance," a social as well as a personal tie, in the process. And when, near the end of this era, some fur traders raised problems by threatening to abandon their families, the Hudson's Bay Company even instituted a law requiring that they "make such provision for their [families'] future maintenance, more particularly for that of the children, as circumstances may reasonably warrant and the means of the individual permit."[20]

Both Europeans and Aboriginal people seemed to believe that serious crimes such as murder demanded immediate and equivalent retaliation. One of the most striking examples of this identity of outlook occurred at Cumberland House in 1796.[21] The North West Company employees at that post suspected two recently arrived Swampy Cree men of having killed one of their company colleagues at Isle à la Crosse. The Nor'Westers shot one of the two Crees as he attempted to evade their "arrest," and then bound the other and threw him beside the corpse in an attempt to win a confession. Although this failed, "they then made him confess everything with the rope about his Neck, which he did, and informed him of every one who was accomplices with him—he said that he was the Sole cause of the Death of the Canadian, and seemed perfectly satisfied that he deserved this ignominious Death." He was hanged immediately. The two bodies were dragged outside the stockade and left as a lesson to others. Men at the nearby Hudson's Bay Company post interred the bodies on the following day. According to a trader, the local Indians appeared "very much terrified and shocked, never seeing a [sic] hearing of the like before." He suggested the execution would act as a deterrent. There is no record of Indian retaliation for the Cumberland House "executions" of 1796, but, as historian Paul Thistle comments, swift retaliation by the victims' relatives would have been the rule just a few years earlier. In 1777, for example, Indians killed three Canadian traders to avenge harsh treatment. The Cumberland House deaths demonstrate that, although the Europeans perhaps were prepared to delay briefly in order to secure a confession, they did not shrink from murder in order to intimidate Aboriginal people in the vicinity.

"Rough justice" existed in many forms. On several occasions, North West Company traders beat Indian hunters whom they suspected of trading with the competition.[22] On the other hand, a Nor'Wester who had stolen an Indian's property, including his canoe and all his winter supplies, escaped without penalty through the generosity of his victim. This may well have been an example of the kind of tactics employed by Aboriginal people to exert control over a relationship—in this case, a trading relationship. When some Indians attempted to raid a trading post in 1823, they were given "a good drubbing for their trouble" by the Hudson's Bay Company staff. The Indians then vented their frustration on a company cow by cutting off part of its tail.[23]

None of these incidents of conflict should be seen as evidence of a consistent pattern of law enforcement. Instead, as one might conclude from Paul Thistle's detailed study of the Cumberland House district, the Indians lived according to their rules, and the fur traders by theirs within the context of company discipline. Moments of disagreement in Indian-European relations sometimes were resolved by force, sometimes not.

The crucial European issue was "jurisdiction." Thus, the fall of New France caused some legal confusion because the new administration of Canada, according to Britain's *Royal Proclamation of 1763*, specifically excluded the so-called "Indian Territory" west of the province of Quebec. Within two years, a law was passed (the first of several in the next few decades) to provide for the arrest of offenders in Indian Territory and their transport to the nearest British colony for trial.[24] Whether the HBC Charter or the laws of Canada prevailed in the West during the next century is unclear. When confronted by serious wrongdoing by one of their fellows, Europeans were likely to resort to their accustomed legal systems. Thus, when one fur trader was shot by another in a quarrel over furs in 1802, the survivor (who claimed he fired in self-defence) and a witness travelled all the way from the North-West to Montreal in order to secure a trial in the courts of Lower Canada.[25] However, under the Hudson's Bay Company Charter of 1670, the company itself could enact laws for the "good government" of its territory and could judge company personnel "in all causes whether civil or criminal, according to the laws of this Kingdom." Thus, at least for the HBC and its employees, the law of the western interior was the English law of 1670 and its subsequent development. Because it made no allowance for Aboriginal authority or for such competitors in the fur trade as the French or the Nor'Westers, the HBC rule was ambiguous and uncertain. The *Canada Jurisdiction Act* of 1803 was supposed to clear up these contradictions by giving the courts of Lower Canada jurisdiction over criminal offences committed in an undefined zone described as "the Indian Territory." The Nor'Westers argued that this included Rupert's Land but the Hudson's Bay Company insisted that its Charter took precedence there. The 1803 Act too was a failure.

The death in 1816 of 20 of Selkirk's colonists and of the colony governor, Robert Semple, at the hands of Cuthbert Grant and his Metis soldiers, who were allegedly under orders from the North West Company, raised a public outcry in Britain and Canada for intervention and for settlement of the jurisdictional question. Although the problems of the fur trade soon were regulated, the question of legal jurisdiction was not. Instead, the Hudson's Bay Company introduced laws and courts that applied to the European inhabitants of this territory, and especially to the growing settlement at the Red River (under the title of Assiniboia), while the rest of the western interior was left in a kind of legal limbo until 1870.[26] Within this "vacuum," it need hardly be added, Aboriginal law prevailed as it had done for centuries. Only Europeans perceived an absence or ambiguity in the law.

The introduction of a Hudson's Bay Company-sponsored legal authority after 1821 inaugurated an interesting and unusual era of experimentation in European-Aboriginal judicial relations. The courts in the district known as Assiniboia (approximately southern Manitoba) developed slowly between the 1820s and the 1860s. At first, Indians in the district were not subject to this jurisdiction, at least not completely. Thus, a murder of one Indian by another in 1824 produced a trial and a reprimand from the governor, but no punishment. After the reorganization of the colony's local government in 1835, however, a regular police and judicial system was set in place and all residents of the community, including Indians, became subject to this jurisdiction as far as "British" residents were concerned. What Aboriginal people thought of this assertion of authority has not been determined. A resolution of the council declared in 1837 that "the evidence of an Indian be considered valid and be admitted as such in all Courts of this settlement," implying that Indian testimony had not been accepted before.[27] Local magistrates, several of whom were Metis, presided over the district courts. A higher court, the General Quarterly Court of Assiniboia, was instituted as well and it too had a number of Metis magistrates. In short, a distinctively Manitoban mix of European and Aboriginal legal cultures was evolving in Red River, this most unusual settlement, in the decades around mid-century. Non-Aboriginal people established the context—the institutions and the laws of this society—but a substantial number of Aboriginal people, almost all of whom were Metis, participated in its working.

Inevitably, enforcement was a problem in a world where armed Metis horsemen constituted the single most powerful military force. As long as the Hudson's Bay Company could count on Imperial troops for support, as in 1846–48 and 1857–61, its rule was secure. But when left to its own devices, the company could not control the settlement, let alone the entire western interior. The first casualty of this weakness was the company's very monopoly over trade, the crucial economic gift of the Charter of 1670. The monopoly fell by default in the trial of the Metis trader, Guillaume Sayer, in 1849. Sayer was prosecuted in a company court and found guilty of trading illegally for furs. But the HBC did not have the strength in armed might to enable the court to impose a punishment. Its failure to exact a penalty permitted the armed Metis on the courthouse steps to exult that trade was free, *"Le commerce est libre."*

Laws concerning bounties for wolves and the placing of flags over holes cut in the river ice (to warn horse and rider) could be enforced without much difficulty in the Red River Settlement. However, the big legal and political issues—sovereignty, property rights, language and religion—became increasingly difficult as the pace of economic development quickened. After Confederation in 1867, news that the territory would cease to be ruled by the Hudson's Bay Company began to circulate in 1868, but neither the British nor Canadian governments discussed the matter with the residents of the North-West. Then, in 1869, "Canadians" arrived from the East and the rumours increased.

Confederation brought a significant shift in British-Aboriginal relations. Constitutional and governmental powers were divided between the federal government and the four provinces that were replacing previous colonies. Some issues of national import were allocated to the exclusive jurisdiction of the Crown. One of these issues was described in section 91(24) of the then *British North America Act*, 1867, as "Indians, and Lands reserved for the Indians." This section not only conveyed law-making power in this area exclusively to the Government of Canada, but it also empowered the federal government to honour the existing treaty obligations of the Imperial Crown and to negotiate new ones. At the same time, the original four provinces received most of the natural resources through section 109, which stated:

> All Lands, Mines, Minerals and Royalties belonging to the several Provinces of Canada, Nova Scotia, and New Brunswick at the Union,... shall belong to the several Provinces of Ontario, Quebec, Nova Scotia, and New Brunswick in which the same are situate or arise, subject to any Trusts existing in respect thereof, and to any Interest other than that of the Province in the same.

In addition, the provinces were granted jurisdiction over public lands and local matters. This left both levels of government with authority over land. The new Parliament passed its first legislation regarding Indians within a year of its creation, which was inspired primarily by colonial statutes in Upper and Lower Canada.[28] Still, fundamental questions of law remained unanswered.

When Louis Riel and his Metis allies challenged the Canadian government's survey and barred the entry of the Canadian governor, William McDougall, in the autumn of 1869, they merely were demonstrating what had become evident in the preceding generation: without the presence of troops in Red River, Hudson's Bay Company law depended on the consent of Rupert's Land residents. That consent was no longer forthcoming.

The late dean of Manitoba's historians, W.L. Morton, described the Metis action of 1869–70 as a "resistance," not a rebellion. His interpretation declared that a power vacuum existed in the Red River Settlement. British, Canadian and HBC claims to sovereignty over this territory had ceased to have any force. Riel had stepped into the void and established a legitimate "provisional government."[29]

Appealing to the "law of nations" and the "rights of man," Riel's Declaration of Metis Independence of 8 December 1869 launched an eight-month government at Red River, drawn from the French- and English-speaking parishes of the settlement. It was a Metis government; that is, it was run by French- and English-speaking inhabitants of mixed European and Aboriginal heritage.

Although the exact legal status of the bargaining process between Canada and Manitoba is a matter of debate, it cannot be denied that the provisional government negotiated the terms by which Manitoba entered the Canadian confederation. Its delegates secured some important gains and sustained reverses. In the end, a relationship of trust and legal obligation was established between two distinct entities.

Louis Riel described the legislation which sealed the bargain, the *Manitoba Act, 1870*, as a "treaty," in order to convey his view that the deal had the character of an arrangement between nations.

Prime Minister John A. Macdonald, on the other hand, regarded it as a domestic rearrangement, a transfer of responsibility within the British household. The existence of Manitoba was a political necessity, part of the price paid to acquire once and for all an extraordinary land and an ocean-to-ocean future for the new nation. The views of the two men were never reconciled, even to this day.

In the legislation arranging for its assumption of control over the North-West, Canada made several promises concerning Aboriginal people. First, it agreed to accept responsibility for any compensation offered to Indians for land lost to incoming settlers. Second, it accepted the obligation of protecting Indian interests in the new order. Third, it promised 1.4 million acres to be divided among "the children of the half-breed heads of families" as a step "towards the extinguishment of the Indian Title." Fourth, it accepted a number of clauses that were sought by the Metis or their representatives as the means of their self-preservation, including provincial status itself, the use of French in courts and Legislature, an Upper House (that is, a bicameral Legislature) on the Quebec model, and a guarantee concerning denominational schools.[30] In each case, the promises were of considerable importance to the Aboriginal people. Moreover, the fact that the *Manitoba Act* was passed by the Canadian Parliament and then re-enacted by the Imperial Parliament in 1871 ensured it a status greater than that of ordinary legislation.[31]

Two hundred years of relative peace and cooperation between Aboriginal and European peoples had been distinguished by continuity within each community and two sets of legal assumptions. Manitoba's justice system between 1660 and 1870 consisted of two distinct bodies of rules, penalties and enforcement mechanisms. This flexibility ended with the creation of the Canadian province of Manitoba on July 15, 1870.

The Justice Regime under Canadian Rule, 1870–1950

The third justice regime extends from the time of Manitoba's entry into Confederation in 1870 to the present. We will divide our discussion into two parts, one dealing with the period from 1870 to 1950, and the other with the most recent 40 years.

The third justice regime differed drastically in official character from its predecessor. Indeed, all the rules changed for Manitoba's Aboriginal inhabitants. After Canada assumed responsibility for the West, its administrators actually attempted to take control of the lives of Aboriginal people. Their approach relied on three key steps: first, the signing of the treaties which transferred vast tracts of land to the government; second, the passage of the *Indian Act* which granted absolute power over Indian people to a federal department and its agents (both the treaties and the *Indian Act* were in place by the end of the 1870s); and, third, the direction of the Metis, separated from Indians by these administrative and legal decisions, onto a different path in 1870. Within two decades Aboriginal people had been pushed aside by incoming settlers. They remained in a backwater, neglected by Ottawa and offered little support by the province.

Early federal statutes were consolidated and revamped when the first *Indian Act* was enacted in 1876. The Act advanced the policy of seeking to assimilate Aboriginal people, severing their spiritual connection with the land, encouraging a shift in their economy and undermining their traditional government. Indians were encouraged or compelled to "enfranchise" (a term used to reflect that people were acquiring the vote, or "franchise," through losing their Indian status) if they obtained a university or professional education, left the reserve for prolonged periods, sought to send their children to public rather than residential schools, or if Indian women married men who were not registered Indians. When the *Indian Act* became the legal device to impose these changes, the Indian agent was the local messenger for the Department of Indian Affairs to implement its policies. The *Indian Act* even went so far as to define a "person" as "an individual other than an Indian."

The Canadian prairies entered a global economy in the last half of the 19th century. Within one generation, the price and production of farm products became crucial matters for prairie dwellers. Newcomers set the rules in local politics. Aboriginal people were governed by legislation originating in Ottawa or Manitoba and by exceptionally powerful local bureaucrats. The two communities, Aboriginal and white, reserve and town, had few points of political intersection.

How had this revolution happened? The virtual extinction of the buffalo was pivotal. Suddenly, between 1870 and 1882, the foundation of the plains economy for millennia—a foundation of greater relative importance than oil or electricity in our day—was no more. Moreover, the context of life always had been established by the land itself. Now, private property, cultivation, cattle grazing and railways would change forever the place of the land in Aboriginal life. In earlier days, Aboriginal people understood that government and its laws flowed from daily life itself; henceforth, however, an alien and distant institution would determine the rules of Aboriginal existence. The dualism of the pre-1870 justice system had officially ceased. As part of the new Canada, prairie Aboriginal people were to be governed by Canadian law. Their own institutions of law and justice came under severe and constant attack.

Aboriginal people themselves acknowledged the development of a new order, although their vision of their future clearly differed from that which Canada had for them. Where possible, especially in northern Manitoba, they worked within their own justice system as they had for centuries. But in the South, especially as the years passed, the new administration increasingly prevailed. In all parts of the province and in the North-West Territories, both Aboriginal and non-Aboriginal people recognized the importance of establishing an understanding between the two societies. Treaties were the foundation of the new order. The key documents for Manitoba, Treaties 1 through 6, were signed between 1871 and 1876. Treaty 10 followed, as did adhesions of individuals and groups.

Although they were based upon the principles elaborated in the *Royal Proclamation of 1763*, the prairie treaties also reflected the concerns of the new Canadian government to control the pace of development and to ensure peaceful occupation. They guaranteed reserves to the Indians where Indian people believed they would be free from European incursion. They also guaranteed the payment of annuities, the right to hunt and fish in traditional use areas, and transitional economic assistance, including schools and equipment. In exchange, Canada would assume absolute sovereignty over other land.

There is much debate about the character and purpose of these treaties. Were they real-estate transactions, once-and-for-all purchases that had no further implications beyond the words on the page and the transfer of "ownership"? Or were they alliances, ongoing relationships that would have to be renewed and reviewed as circumstances changed? Because these documents are of such crucial importance, we consider their implications in Chapter 5.

The numbered treaties of the 1870s are very "British" legal documents. They deal in specifics, in clauses discussing a plough or a school, not in general statements of principle about sovereignty and continuing responsibilities. Nonetheless, they do arise from presumptions that were the basis for the treaties negotiated before Confederation and from the *Royal Proclamation*. The difference in effect, however, lies in the existence of the single most important factor in Aboriginal life since European contact, the *Indian Act*. Significantly, this exceptional piece of legislation is not mentioned in the treaties.

Earlier treaties had assumed Aboriginal self-government. After 1874, however, when federal Indian legislation was declared to be in force in Manitoba, Canadian authorities argued that when Aboriginal people in the West signed the treaties, they had bargained away not only their lands, but also their powers over local affairs. Thus, the treaties were not what they seemed, nor indeed what the Indians had accepted in the 1871 and 1873 negotiations. By an act of the federal Parliament, unilaterally conceived and drafted without Indian knowledge, Ottawa drastically altered the circumstances of Aboriginal life.

The history of Canada's Indian legislation goes back to Britain's paternal and patronizing concern for the disadvantaged of the world, and for the victims of its own rapid industrialization in the 18th and early 19th centuries. The rise of Christian evangelism in England and of humanitarian campaigns occurred during those decades of social crisis. Idealism and social concern impelled political reformers to ban child labour, to form lobby groups to abolish the African slave trade and to form Christian missionary societies to convert Aboriginal people throughout the British Empire. Canada, like India, Africa, Australia and New Zealand, was a target of this attention.

The change in England's outlook toward cultures that differed from its own produced changes in Canadian Indian policy in the 1850s. A relationship that had been remarkable for its interdependence and cooperation foundered on the growth of Canadian "civilizing" forces. It also foundered on Indian resistance to the "civilizers." Ontario's Indians, for example, insisted upon common land ownership as the basis for a continuing distinct culture. Canadian officials insisted that proper industry and morality could accrue only to land-owning, enfranchised, assimilated Indians—that is, *former* Indians. Canada's *Gradual Civilization Act* of 1857 was the first of many laws designed to extinguish Aboriginal cultures, to "break them to pieces" as one Aboriginal leader declared.[32]

The newly confederated Canada turned to the issue of Indian affairs in 1869. Having failed to make headway in their "civilizing" campaign in the preceding decade, officials of the Indian Affairs bureaucracy urged the abolition of Aboriginal self-government and were successful. The 1869 *Act for the Gradual Enfranchisement of Indians* provided for the possibility of band elections under the supervision of the Superintendent-General for Indian Affairs.[33] By amendments passed seven years later, in 1876, the elected band council could make no laws without confirmation by Canada's Governor in Council.[34] Henceforth, the federal government would control life on Indian reserves and promote measures that were designed to assimilate Indians into European-Canadian society. Traditional means of selecting Aboriginal leaders, which were built on consensus and were very flexible, thus could be bypassed or overruled.

Federal legislation on Indians was imposed on Manitoba in 1874. The policy of enfranchisement and assimilation did not change, despite numerous minor revisions to the Act, from that day to the present.

The new justice system, as represented by the *Indian Act* and supplementary legislation, soon was being employed to prevent Aboriginal people from expressing their traditional beliefs, from pursuing their traditional economy and from asserting their political rights as individuals or as members of Canadian society. In every aspect of life, from criminal law to education and religious expression, from hunting to agriculture, from voting to the use of lawyers, Aboriginal people ran into regulations that restricted their freedom. Traditional systems of government were replaced by a restricted and illusory form of democracy in which only adult men had a voice and a vote. All real power rested with the Indian agent, who supervised the voting, chaired the meetings, kept the official records, decided when, where and if the chief and council would meet, and controlled the council's agenda. All Indian agents were granted considerable power by 1881, by being appointed automatically as justices of the peace through *An Act to amend "The Indian Act, 1880."* (S.C. 1881, c. 17, s. 12) Each agent had full authority to conduct trials anywhere in the country involving Indians charged with violating the *Indian Act* or with certain crimes under the *Criminal Code*. As a result, the Indian agent could direct the police to prosecute "troublemakers" and then sit in judgment. The agents effectively had power over all aspects of daily life.

The role of elders and the extended family as teachers of the young was destroyed. Residential schools were established by the Department of Indian Affairs in conjunction with religious denominations. Children were forcibly removed from their families and transported far away for most of the year to attend schools where English was the sole language of instruction and children were punished for speaking their own language. Far from simply "civilizing" Indians, as had been the apparent purpose of government policy in the first half of the 19th century, the new system actually utilized aggressive, coercive methods to bring about Aboriginal assimilation.

Government officials clearly represented the values and circumstances of their times. They were neither stupid nor incompetent. The culture in which they dwelt was imbued with racist assumptions and presumptions that were not considered abhorrent to anyone in Canadian society except to the Indians. Officials acted in the belief that they could not leave any group of Canadians without the benefits of Christianity and the values of industrialized England. This is why a policy that seems to us shortsighted and odious could command widespread assent in the Canadian community of the time.

Government officials and missionaries saw the disasters that could result from Aboriginal exposure to the worst sort of white environment. This was part of the thinking behind their idea that Christianity and "civilization" must be delivered together. In some parts of the country, although less often in Manitoba, trading posts degenerated into dirty, disease-ridden, violent settlements. Commenting on one of the less savoury posts, Fort Simpson in northern British Columbia, William Duncan, Church of England missionary, condemned the idea that mere "civilization" without the Gospel would convince Aboriginal people to adopt Canadian ways:

> I think this instance [Fort Simpson] alone to the contrary is sufficient to explode such an absurdity. No, civilization apart from Christianity has no vitality—how then can it impart life? It is the fuel without the fire, how then can it radiate heat? Civilization appeals to the eye and to the hands, but not to the heart. It may move the muscles but it cannot reach the hidden springs of life.[35]

These government and church policies, however well intended, reduced an autonomous and secure people to the status of children in the eyes of the law, and thus robbed the Aboriginal community of the very rights that were said to be at the heart of the British system of government. Aboriginal people, in their turn, employed numerous strategies of resistance. It is no wonder that such fundamental disagreements produced social crisis.

The purpose of government policy was to remake Indians into "good Canadians." In the words of a prairie newspaper, in its review of Aboriginal exhibits at an agricultural fair, it would make "the Red Man White in all but colour."[36]

This purpose required that Aboriginal distinctiveness be destroyed. Any significant political resistance to Canadian Aboriginal policy would be met with the full force of the state and the law.

The most dramatic episode in this story is the 1885 uprising in the North-West Territories. We have all heard about the hanging of Louis Riel after his trial in Regina. We have heard little or nothing about the other trials during the summer of 1885. We think of the uprising as an Aboriginal—Metis and Indian—protest but ignore the details of the Indian diplomatic and military campaign during 1883–85 to establish larger, contiguous reserves and to throw off the shackles of the *Indian Act*. According to court statistics, in addition to two whites (one acquitted, one found insane) and 46 Metis (28 released without trial, 11 released upon a recognizance of $400 to attend trial but later dismissed, and seven found guilty), there were 81 Indians arrested and placed in the holding cells after the 1885 uprising. The courts eventually sentenced 44 Indians to jail terms, most for "treason-felony." The Cree chief Poundmaker, one of those charged, was "convicted on evidence that, in any ordinary trial would have ensured his acquittal without the jury leaving the box," according to an experienced legal observer.[37] He received a three-year sentence.

Big Bear, who also was charged with treason-felony and given a three-year term, had been one of the leaders who opposed violence. He repeated this defence to the court before his sentencing, saying in part, according to a newspaper report:

> The time would come when the Indians of the North-West would prove of signal service to the Great Grandmother, and he appealed again to the court for pity and help to the remainder of his tribe. In conclusion, he would say that whenever he spoke stiff to the Indian agents, he did so in order to get his rights. The North-West belonged to him, but he, perhaps, would never live to see it again. He asked the court to publish his speech broadcast. He was old and ugly, but he had tried to be good. In conclusion he made a powerful appeal for the children and helpless of his tribe.[38]

Most of the Indians were sent to Manitoba's Stony Mountain prison. Their hair was cut off (Poundmaker and others had long braids) either during their trials or when they arrived in Manitoba in the autumn of 1885, and they were allotted various tasks. Big Bear was employed as a carpenter, then in the barns and as a servant or "chore-boy" for the steward's wife in her home next to the prison. He was said to be devastated. He reportedly accepted conversion to Christianity in the summer of 1886. Twenty-nine other Indian inmates were alleged to have done so in February of that year, but this may have been linked to the federal cabinet's decision to release many of those Indian prisoners—but not Big Bear—in March and April. The report of Big Bear's conversion came when he was very weak and one might well imagine the depth of despair that could lead him to renounce his lifelong beliefs.

The government wanted no martyrs. One Arrow, unable to move without assistance and broken-hearted that he had been ignored when the first group of parolees was selected, was released in April, but he never left the St. Boniface bed to which he was moved and he died within two weeks of his liberation. When Big Bear too fell ill in January 1888, the federal cabinet approved his release. He died within the year.

A huge gallows was erected in Battleford in the late autumn of 1885. Eleven days after Riel's hanging, on November 27, hoods were placed over prisoners' heads and ropes were adjusted, and while they sang their death songs eight Indians were executed. The trials, the imprisonments and the hangings spoke of a new order.

The character of that new order was discussed years later by Joe Dion, a grand-nephew of Big Bear:

> The rebellion of 1885 ended up absolutely nothing gained by anybody ... only a deep rooted feeling of distrust on both sides was the unfortunate result of the clash. Throughout the years this feeling of distrust has diminished but very little and may never be completely lived down. True, we were at fault. We broke our treaty with the whites, but only after we learned that honesty with them was as thin as the paper on which our X had been drawn for us.[39]

Indian people viewed Canadian honesty as "thin" because of what they inferred from the treaties and because of what they understood their relationship to be with government and the Crown. Their judgment also arose from what actually was done under the cover of the *Indian Act* by Canadian governments and officials. The use of Canadian law to control Aboriginal education and religion illustrates the depth of the cultural divide between the two communities, and the basis for the Aboriginal perspective.

European and Aboriginal people long have recognized that schools were influential cultural institutions. Canadians have waged historic struggles over their control, not least in Manitoba where "schools questions" were debated keenly in the 1890s and again during World War I, as well as in recent decades.

In the treaty discussions of the 1870s, Indian negotiators had sought and obtained promises from the government that schools would be provided on their reserves. By choosing to ask for schools and to send their children to them, they were making a profound decision. Indian leaders were accepting the need to adapt to, and to make their way into, the European-Canadian cultural milieu. They were not, however, agreeing to become European-Canadians or to cease to be Aboriginal peoples. They saw, however, the need to make an economic transition and to learn the arts of communication associated with writing, print and the telegraph.

The fact that Aboriginal people voluntarily made this choice is important. Government records contain numerous Aboriginal requests for schools. As Dan Kennedy, later an Assiniboine chief, recalled, he was told at the age of 12 that he must learn "the whiteman's magic art of writing, 'the talking paper.'"[40] Despite their wish to learn these communication skills, many Aboriginal people did not want lessons in the Christian religion. As soon as possible, they believed, their own people would become teachers. As they had done in the past, they wished to control the values that were being communicated to their children.

Even those Aboriginal parents who chose to send their children to schools would not have expected that the curriculum included a great deal more than reading, writing and arithmetic; or that the children might be taught to hate their former culture and to reject their families. This statement in the Annual Report of the Department of Indian Affairs in 1889 would not have been well received by Aboriginal people, particularly by those who negotiated the treaties:

> The boarding school dissociates the Indian child from the deleterious home influences to which he would otherwise be subjected. It reclaims him from the uncivilized state in which he has been brought up. It brings him into contact from day to day with all that tends to effect a change in his views and habits of life. By precept and example he is taught to endeavour to excel in what will be most useful to him.[41]

Manitoba's Aboriginal people may have wanted one type of school, but they soon were compelled to attend another. In 1894 the federal government passed legislation that provided for the arrest and conveyance to school of truant children, and for fines or jail terms for parents who resisted. Indian agents were given the power to commit children under 16 to such schools and to keep them there until they were 18. The Province of Manitoba did not introduce compulsory schooling for non-Indians until 1916, 22 years later. As a way of ensuring that the most compelling cultural messages were delivered to the children, and of keeping government costs to a minimum, the government increasingly relied on church missionary societies, particularly of the Methodist, Presbyterian, Anglican and Roman Catholic churches, to operate residential schools. Canadian people are only beginning in the 1990s to comprehend how harsh, how demeaning, how exploitive were these institutions. The form and content of this education bore no resemblance to that desired by Aboriginal parents.

The economic crisis associated with the near-extinction of buffalo, the political struggles caused by the *Indian Act* and the conflicts over educational policy all caused tension and conflict in Aboriginal communities. These anxieties were made worse, in the view of Aboriginal elders, by the growing struggle between government and Indian over Aboriginal religious expression. For many elders, the freedom to worship in traditional ways was crucial to Aboriginal cultural survival. However, the Canadian government made it a crime to practise traditional prairie and British Columbia Aboriginal religious ceremonies, including the Thirst Dance, the Sundance and the Potlatch. The law that introduced the religious prohibition was an 1884 amendment to the *Indian Act* and banned "give-away ceremonies." Another amendment in 1895 prohibited "wounding or mutilation" ceremonies (associated with Plains Indian rituals by uncomprehending non-Aboriginal observers). Yet another amendment in 1906, revised slightly in 1914, forbade dancing of every description and made it a criminal offence for Indian people to participate in festivals, pageants or stampedes in western Canada without government consent. Indian people even were prohibited from wearing traditional Indian costume without government consent. The rules were only eliminated in the *Indian Act* amendments of 1951.[42]

The story of government and church opposition to the religious ceremonies, and of Aboriginal resistance, has been documented with precision.[43] We have been impressed by the consistency and patience shown by Aboriginal leaders as they fought to retain the right to worship in their own way. Their letters to the Department of Indian Affairs deplored the moral dilemma in which they had been placed: obey either the secular law of Canada or the law of their God. An example of these many letters is one from Joe Ma-ma-Gway-See in 1908 that defended the Aboriginal right to hold a Sundance: "The law you make is of this world and we follow the law of God. If you stop everything we do we may as well go without the law of God.... I am afraid of your trying to stop sun dances according to the law of God. I have never seen him but it is in his command to us and you are trying to stop it...."[44]

The Aboriginal leaders understood full well the legal implications of the government ban. One of the great traditional chiefs of that generation of negotiators, Thunderchild of the Plains Cree, explained his case in his own language to Reverend Edward Ahenakew, also a Cree, who then translated it:

> Can things go well in a land where freedom of worship is a lie, a hollow boast? To each nation is given the light by which it knows God, and each finds its own way to express the longing to serve Him. It is astounding to me that a man should be stopped from trying in his own way to express his need or his thankfulness to God. If a nation does not do what is right according to its own understanding, its power is worthless.
>
> I have listened to the talk of the white men's clergy, and it is the same in principle as the talk of our Old Men, whose wisdom came not from books but from life and from God's earth. Why has the white man no respect for the religion that was given to us, when we respect the faith of other nations?
>
> ... The white men have offered us two forms of their religion—the Roman Catholic and the Protestant—but we in our Indian lands had our own religion. Why is that not accepted too? It is the worship of one God, and it was the strength of our people for centuries.
>
> I do not want to fight the white man's religion. I believe in freedom of worship, and though I am not a Christian, I have never forgotten God. What is it that has helped me and will help my grandchildren but belief in God?[45]

Other laws and regulations also had an effect on religious expression. The government imposed a "pass system" which disrupted religious ceremonies by preventing extended families dispersed on different reserves from meeting together. The pass system had been discussed by government officials in 1884–85 in response to the diplomatic campaigns for Aboriginal solidarity led by Big Bear and other Saskatchewan chiefs. It was imposed by a local agent without senior government approval in 1885.

As well as a means of restricting religious ceremonies, the pass system was used to control or prevent parent-child meetings at residential schools and to undercut political activities. Indian people were not allowed to leave the reserve to hunt, fish or trap, to seek employment, or to visit their children in residential schools without first obtaining an official pass from the local Indian agent. Withheld passes could result in severe hardship, and the threat to do so was one powerful force in inducing parents to agree to permit their children to be taken away for schooling.

The *Criminal Code* in 1892 made it possible to charge with an indictable offence any person "who induces, incites, or stirs up any three or more Indians, non-treaty Indians or half-breeds" to meet together to make demands upon civil servants in a riotous or disorderly manner. This clear violation of the fundamental principle of freedom of association enjoyed by Canadians significantly prevented the development of Aboriginal political organizations and minimalized the pressure on the federal government to honour its obligations. Any efforts by Indian people to pursue justice through Canadian courts about their grievances were blocked effectively as well by the *Indian Act*, which made it an offence to raise money to commence claims against the Crown and made it illegal for a lawyer to receive fees to represent an Indian or band for this purpose without the consent of the Superintendent General from 1927 to 1951. (*An Act to amend the Indian Act*, S.C. 1926–27, c. 32, s. 149A)

Although the pass system was enforced fairly strictly by the North-West Mounted Police in the 1880s, neither Indians nor police accepted the legality of the prohibition for long. It was a makeshift policy, intended to control and monitor people's movements, and would have been thrown out of any court. It is striking, however, that no less an authority than Sir John A. Macdonald recognized its illegality and yet thought the introduction of the system was "in the highest degree desirable." The prime minister made the damning admission that "no punishment for breaking bounds can be inflicted & in case of resistance on the grounds of Treaty rights should not be insisted on."[46] Despite aggressive attempts by the Indian Affairs staff to enforce the restrictions, the pass system fell into disuse by the opening decades of the 20th century.

The intended destruction of Aboriginal culture was associated, in the government's view, with the image of a new type of Aboriginal Canadian, one much like his or her non-Aboriginal Canadian counterparts, one who worked and thought and spoke in the country's common cultural "language." Proper economic behaviour was to be part of this language. In southern Manitoba, the destruction of the buffalo ensured that agriculture would be an important part of the Aboriginal economic transition.

For too long, Canadian scholars have perpetuated the idea that Aboriginal culture was hostile to field crops and animal-raising. This is simply not true. Aboriginal people in northern Ontario and the prairie provinces had seized the opportunity earlier to become farmers for the obvious reason that they faced an economic crisis. Unfortunately, a combination of climatic reverses, inconsistent government financial support and disastrous federal policy decisions destroyed the hope of Aboriginal agriculture.[47]

The legal system itself played a large part in this tragedy. The law was used to forbid Indian sales of produce off the reserve without the approval of the Indian agent. It later prevented Indians from mortgaging reserve lands in order to purchase farm implements. Such controls undermined the very initiative that the government claimed was its goal. Aboriginal people, according to the expressed intent of Indian Affairs officials, could not be permitted to develop their agricultural operations beyond "peasant farming." The *Indian Act* contained the following provision from 1876 until 1951:

No Indian or non-treaty Indian, resident in the Province of Manitoba, the Northwest Territories or the District of Keewatin [later changed to "the Province of Manitoba, Saskatchewan or Alberta"] shall be held capable of having acquired or of acquiring a homestead ... to a quarter section, or any portion of land....[48]

As a policy declaration put it, the government should

... restrict the area cultivated by each Indian to within such limits as will enable him to carry on his operations by the application of his own personal labour and the employment of such simple implements as he would likely be able to command if entirely thrown upon his own resources, rather than to encourage farming on a scale to necessitate the employment of expensive labour-saving machinery.[49]

Indians would have to walk their fields with hoe and scythe before they could purchase binders and reapers. Yet, free grants of "homestead" land were distributed widely to newcomers by the federal government under the *Dominion Lands Act*, which even advertised such grants abroad to attract European immigrants. By the end of the 19th century, Aboriginal hopes for agriculture had been dashed. Residents on the reserves had been reduced to garden-plot and subsistence farmers.

The relative weakness of reserve agriculture created a new crisis when prairie settlement began to boom in the late 1890s. The demand for farmlands, when combined with European-Canadian cultural values concerning the "proper use" of land, posed new threats to the Aboriginal reserves. As local pressure on the Prairies increased, laws were revised to permit, first, rental of reserve lands to white farmers and, second, sale of these lands by the Indian Affairs department to local farmers. Although this story will take years to unravel, one scholar estimates that half the land allocated to reserves in southern Saskatchewan, 270,000 of 520,000 acres, was sold between 1896 and 1928.[50]

Every Manitoban should be told at least one chapter in the provincial story of Aboriginal land surrenders. The most striking case concerns the historic Aboriginal settlement situated along the Red River between Lower Fort Garry and Lake Winnipeg. The Indian settlement in this area had been recognized in the Selkirk treaty of 1817 and was led shrewdly for nearly half a century by one of the signatories of that treaty, Chief Peguis. Under the title of the St. Peter's Settlement, a large tract of land was set aside as the home of nearly 2,000 Aboriginal people in the Stone Fort Treaty, known as Treaty 1, in 1871. However, the pressures for "development" of this prime agricultural land, and the uncertain status of many of the riverbank lots that had been granted years before to Peguis and later sold to non-Indians, produced seemingly endless legal disputes in the late 19th century. None of this was exceptional. The eventual solution was, however, nothing short of disgraceful.

The federal government appointed a Royal Commission headed by the Chief Justice of the Manitoba Court of Appeal, Hector Howell, in 1906 to investigate the disputes. Rather than investigate, Howell suggested that the solution to the problem was simply to move the Indians. A series of rigged meetings of questionable legality followed. The appalling campaign for surrender of the reserve, led by men who wished to speculate in forthcoming land sales, was abetted by insider trading in lands by government officials, bribe payments to Indians and a coerced vote by St. Peter's residents that could never be called fair or honest.

Having been cheated out of the land that had been theirs for more than a century, the St. Peter's Indians waged a campaign for its restoration. Eventually, a provincial Royal Commission reviewed the circumstances of the surrender and concluded in 1912 that "the Surrender was not only voidable but void, could not be ratified and was not so ratified."[51] Nonetheless, the federal government chose not to intervene. Instead, it confirmed the allocation of a new reserve on the Fisher River (the present Peguis Reserve) and enacted the *St. Peter's Reserve Act* in 1916 to validate legal titles to land on the old reserve.[52] Despite the protests of the St. Peter's band, the case was closed, at least as far as the government was concerned.

The St. Peter's case is not unique. Manitoba chiefs contended in 1978 that at least 25 bands in the province had not received their full land allotment under the terms of their treaties.[53] In addition, a number of other unusual cases—like the St. Peter's surrender—demonstrated that the economic base of the Aboriginal people had shrunk in the century since the original treaty agreements were negotiated. Many of these surrenders seem to have been marked by "moralistic, self-righteous, and dictatorial" actions by government officials and the wrongful extinguishment of Aboriginal land claims, as one historian concluded after investigating the disappearance of the Turtle Mountain Dakota reserve.[54]

Political Responses

Aboriginal people did not accept these impositions, infringements and betrayals without protest. Their political representatives spoke out many times against injustices. However, just as law could be used to forbid a religious ceremony or an economic initiative, so it could crush a movement of political resistance. The Canadian government effectively weakened Aboriginal spokespeople throughout the period of the third justice regime.

The government first used the treaties to undermine Aboriginal sovereignty. Chiefs who had been independent in the pre-1870 era were regarded as agents of the federal administration in the new order. Alexander Morris, a Lieutenant-Governor of Manitoba in the 1870s, suggested to the government that the chiefs "should be strongly impressed with the belief that they are officers of the Crown, and that it is their duty to see that the Indians of their tribes obey the provisions of the treaties." He argued that it would be advantageous to the government "to possess so large a number of Indian officials, duly recognized as such, and who can be inspired with a proper sense of their responsibility to the Government."[55]

After the passage of the *Indian Act* in 1876, the government had much greater power over Aboriginal political activity. It controlled, first, the decision over who could be admitted to membership in the political community: an Indian was someone designated by federal law as an Indian. It also controlled the process by which leaders were selected. Traditional chiefs could be removed. The Indian agent, a government appointee, regulated and chaired the meetings of band councils and the elections of chiefs and councillors. He was given the powers of a stipendiary magistrate or police magistrate in respect to the *Indian Act* and to some criminal offences. Moreover, the agent could suspend Indians who, in his view, had conducted their family relations badly. Finally, the agent could control the band's economic planning and its funds.

The assumption of the original *Indian Act* was that, as they gained experience with European-Canadian life, Indians would want to leave their bands and join the larger society. The formal transfer from "Indian" to "Canadian" status would occur when they acquired the franchise. However, very few Indians followed this path. In 1920, as a result, the Act was amended to give the federal cabinet power to take away Indian status from an Indian family head (and his family) and to make his enfranchisement compulsory. This clause was repealed in 1922, reinstated in 1933 and finally dropped in 1951. It illustrated that the destruction of Indian culture and the control of political decisions remained at the heart of federal government policy in the 20th century. As the department's deputy minister, Duncan Campbell Scott, wrote: "Our object is to continue until there is not a single Indian in Canada that has not been absorbed into the body politic, and there is no Indian question, and no Indian Department."[56]

Manitoba Indians continued to reject outright the assimilative goals of the federal government. In 1947 the Indian Association of Manitoba, led by Tommy Prince, a decorated war veteran from the Brokenhead Band, among others, called for the repeal of the *Indian Act* and a return by both parties to the original treaties.[57] The key Aboriginal political goal continued to be the restoration of self-government. The secretary of the Fort Alexander Catholic Association told the joint committee reviewing the *Indian Act* that, "Much self-reliance and an urge to progress would ensue if more and more power was left to the council for management of the local affairs with the friendly cooperation of the Indian agent."[58]

The Metis

The Metis, despite their Aboriginal origins, were separated from Indians by the numbered treaties and the *Indian Act*. Their history subsequently followed a very different course. Metis struggles over land in the Red River Valley during the 1870s produced disagreements that have been raised again in today's courts. Certainly, there never has been a secure settlement of differences between Metis people and the larger Manitoba society.

The definition of the term "Metis" is complicated. At the simplest level, it applies to children of mixed European and Aboriginal parentage. In the 19th century, it also might have meant that an individual occupied a position as an economic or cultural intermediary between the two societies. Thus, mixed-race people who lived and hunted with Indians, or who accepted a plot of land in St. Peter's Mission on the Red River, might well be seen as Indians but, if they served as translator or freighter and lived in trade- and farm-based settlements, they would be regarded as Metis.

Language also played a role in the attributions of identity. This meant not only Aboriginal and European language usage, but also whether one employed in daily life the various European-Aboriginal language combinations known as Bungi and Michif.

Religion too could distinguish Indian from Metis, just as it separated English-speaking Protestant "country-born" households from French-speaking Roman Catholic "Metis" families. After the 1870s, former Indians who had lost their status under the *Indian Act* (which was the case for many people, including Indian women who married European-Canadian or "non-status" men until the Act was changed in 1985) also complicated the Metis category.

Eventually, perhaps at some point in the early 20th century, history and family networks, group consciousness and political forces combined to select those who wished to maintain a Metis identity. From that time, some Canadians have identified themselves as Metis. This has acquired political significance since the 1982 revision of the Constitution of Canada, which recognized "Metis" as a distinct category of Aboriginal person.[59]

It will be apparent that the history of the families themselves has been crucial in the evolution of a Metis consciousness. In Manitoba, the Metis rallied in the early 20th century to tell their story because they believed the histories then available, mainly by English-Canadians, did not do them justice. After much work and many delays, Auguste Henri de Tremaudan's *Histoire de la nation metisse dans l'ouest canadien* was published in 1936.[60] In their foreword to the work, the Historical Committee of L'Union Nationale Metisse Saint-Joseph de Manitoba explained their purpose:

> The Metis owed to themselves, and to those who have gone before, a chronicle that will inspire in the new generation of French-Canadian Metis a pride in their ancestry and their past. The knowledge of these facts will enable them to hold their heads high and say, "This is our land. It has the right to our love, loyalty and life. For it, our fathers suffered and triumphed. By it, they marked the path of our national future."[61]

The history of Manitoba's Metis people has been marked by conflict and neglect. In the 1870s, Winnipeg was likened to an armed camp that denied peaceable access to French-speaking citizens of mixed race.[62] As Lt. Governor Archibald commented in 1871, the Metis were concerned

> ... not so much, I believe by the dread about their land allotment as by the persistent ill-usage of such of them as have ventured from time to time into Winnipeg from the disbanded volunteers and newcomers who fill the town. Many of them actually have been so beaten and outraged that they feel as if they were living in a state of slavery. They say that the bitter hatred of these people is a yoke so intolerable that they would gladly escape it by any sacrifice.[63]

Because a court case continues concerning the allocation of lands a century ago, we do not wish to comment directly on that matter. Nonetheless, the legacy of bitterness must not be minimized.

A 1959 government report by Jean H. Lagasse, *A Study of the Population of Indian Ancestry Living In Manitoba*,[64] concluded that heredity (some degree of Indian ancestry) and a way of life (associated with poverty and with proximity to Indian communities) still distinguished a group of Manitobans as Metis. It argued that Metis were an important, sizeable component of the provincial population (nearly 24,000) and that it would be

> ... helpful to re-establish the solidarity of the Metis as an ethnic group. It would link the people of the fringe settlements with a past of which they could be proud. It would give them a group with which they could feel at home and through that group a place in modern society. Some Metis parents told the research office that they had never revealed their Metis background to their children."[65]

The main recommendations of the study were based on the conclusions that Metis, like Indians, had a lower standard of living than other Canadians and that new policies were necessary to address their problems.[66] Some of these concerns still apply today, 32 years later.

Crisis in Aboriginal Relationships with the Justice System, 1950–1990

Aboriginal people sustained serious blows in the 80 years after Confederation. They lost not only their traditional economy, but also, thanks to an extraordinary series of official interventions, their political and religious autonomy. Although some bands managed to avoid the long arm of Canadian bureaucracy, most felt the increasing pressure brought about by changes in their legal status. The third justice regime, in our view, introduced a series of tragic mistakes in Canadian-Aboriginal policy.

The third justice regime continued to operate after World War II, but its effects were dramatically different. We are suggesting that the official rules did not change, but that the reality of contact and enforcement, as opposed to the theory, did supplant Aboriginal law in this period. Canada's laws and police impinged increasingly on the daily life of Manitoba's Aboriginal people after 1950 and the consequence has been disastrous for the Aboriginal community.

Manitoba was merely a tiny part of an integrated international economy and trading community in the decades after 1945. Like citizens all over the world, Manitobans were required to adjust to the new patterns of trade and technology. Farms and country towns could hold their children no longer. The proportion of the population able to work in agriculture declined steadily. At the same time, Winnipeg grew in population. As the global competition for economic growth increased, entrepreneurs and government turned to the northern lands of the province—to the rivers and forests and mineral wealth—for resources that might provide additional revenue and jobs. Wildlife legislation was applied extensively to Aboriginal people for the first time. Even food harvesting activities became subject to strict controls on seasons and catch limits. Each of these trends had an impact on Manitoba's Aboriginal population.

The Treatment of Indian Veterans

Indian veterans returned from the war to find that all the rights they had possessed while in the service disappeared after they returned to their reserves. The laws applicable to Indians stated that they could not vote, could not enter licensed establishments or participate in real decision making within their communities.

Indian veterans indicated to us that they did not receive the benefits available to veterans after both world wars and the Korean conflict, and stated that the legislation that governed their rights was discriminatory in content and application. The controversy centres on the *Soldier Settlement Act* [67] and the *Veterans' Land Act*,[68] both of which were intended to direct the settlement of returning soldiers to western rural areas and to increase agricultural production.

The *Soldier Settlement Act* made provision for either a grant of free land or the lease of land and loans to purchase land, livestock and equipment, plus instruction in agricultural methods. The Minister of the Interior made Dominion lands available free to veterans, or the Soldier Settlement Board purchased land on behalf of the veterans.

The Indian Affairs department administered the *Soldier Settlement Act* to Indian veterans settling on and off the reserve as a result of an amendment to the *Indian Act*.[69] The actual distribution of benefits to Aboriginal veterans appears not to have occurred because:

- Indian veterans who settled on the reserve "received" what they already were entitled to under the *Indian Act*.[70]

- Indian veterans who settled off the reserve were prohibited by a section of the *Indian Act* from acquiring homesteads off the reserve.[71]

A regulation under the *Veterans' Land Act* in 1945[72] authorized Indian Affairs to administer the veteran's grant of $2,320 to Indian veterans who settled on the reserve. The local Indian agent provided information and authorized grants for the purchase of a building or for building improvements. A grant to purchase household and fur trapping equipment could not exceed $250 and $850, respectively, with the remaining amount to be used for the purchase of land, farm equipment or livestock. The money also could be used towards the acquisition of occupation rights to land located within a reserve.

Although Aboriginal veterans apparently were eligible for *Veterans' Land Act* benefits off the reserve, it is uncertain whether they did receive land and other benefits. The *Indian Act* continued to prohibit the acquisition of parcels of land or "homesteads." As well, the Indian veteran who settled off the reserve automatically lost benefits under the *Indian Act* and could become enfranchised.

The Indian Affairs branch and its agents administered the *Veterans' Land Act* on behalf of Veterans' Affairs. In effect, the local Indian agents had total control of the program in that they provided information to veterans and also awarded benefits. The actual number of applications made by Aboriginal veterans, the number refused and the reasons for refusal are unknown. A New Brunswick/Nova Scotia study indicated that local Indian agents were the "weak link" in the administration of benefits to Aboriginal veterans.[73]

The topic of Indian veterans' entitlement is important and should be acknowledged. A detailed study of the federal statutes and regulations, and their implementation, is needed to determine the exact points of unequal treatment of Aboriginal veterans. We have not done so. However, we are able to conclude the following:

- Indian veterans do not appear to have received benefits off the reserve, and if they left the reserve, they lost status and benefits under the *Indian Act.*

- Indian veterans who remained on the reserve were entitled already to land under the *Indian Act,* and yet, it appears that the reserve land allocated to Indian veterans was treated as though it had been granted under the *Soldier Settlement Act* or the *Veterans' Land Act.*

- The transfer of the ownership of land to or by Indians on or off reserves created jurisdictional problems because of the contradictory provisions of the *Veterans' Land Act* and *Indian Act.*

- The Department of Indian Affairs poorly administered *Veterans' Land Act* benefits for Aboriginal veterans who settled on the reserve.

Post-War Change

Enforcement of Canadian law among Aboriginal Manitobans became increasingly important in the decades after World War II. Although the statistics are notoriously unreliable, the Superintendent (later Commissioner) of Penitentiaries did report annually to Parliament on the numbers of inmates in federal correctional institutions. In our brief survey of the Manitoba incarcerations, we discovered that the proportion of "Indians" and of "Indian half-breeds," and of the various other equivalent designations that appeared in the reports for 1900, 1913, 1932–33, 1934–35 and annually until the 1949–50 report, in the Manitoba penitentiary populaton reflected no more than the Aboriginal proportion of the Manitoba population in this period.[74] The Aboriginal proportion of the Manitoba penitentiary population increased in an extraordinary fashion during the decades after 1950. We estimate that more than 55% of all jail admissions in 1989 were Aboriginal, whereas the Aboriginal proportion of the provincial population was just under 12%. We believe that policing agreements with the Royal Canadian Mounted Police play a part in this story because they introduced consistent enforcement of Canadian law to communities where, until that time, Aboriginal law still operated. We also recognize that construction of highways and the use of automobiles added an important new cause for police activity. The Bracken Report of 1955, which led to the wider availability of alcoholic beverages in the province, accelerated the trend to greater Aboriginal involvement in the justice system. So too, as we shall see, did closer supervision of, and amendments to, social and family legislation.

Northern Manitoba especially was affected by the changes after World War II. The single ribbon of rail from The Pas to Churchill was completed in 1929, but the railway was just the precursor of the highway and airplane, and the hydro-electric and mine developments that have transformed the northern part of the province since 1945. We urge Manitobans to keep in mind how recent is the economic revolution in northern Manitoba. Major projects associated with Thompson, Lynn Lake, Sherridon, Jenpeg, Grand Rapids and Leaf Rapids occurred after 1945. It is only 65 years, one lifetime, since Manitoba bush pilots carried pigeons with them—to send messages in case a mechanical failure forced them to land on an isolated northern lake. The cultural adaptations appropriate to the new circumstances in northern Manitoba, whatever the merit of the projects themselves, cannot occur overnight.

Many Canadians, Aboriginal and non-Aboriginal, challenged the constitutional and political arrangements governing Indian and Metis people during this era. Although the *Indian Act* was revised in 1951, its underlying philosophy was not changed. By the 1960s, the long-standing opposition in the Aboriginal community to its provisions was reinforced by public recognition that the Act was no longer defensible. The government's treaty promises, made in the 1870s, also returned to the public agenda.

The Franchise

The most important barrier to fall was the vote. Manitoba's Aboriginal people, at least the hundreds who lived within the boundaries of the "postage stamp province" in 1870–71, including the inhabitants of the large community in St. Peter's parish, possessed the right to vote in the provincial election of 1870. Like their fellow Manitobans, they only had to be "householders," meaning "master or chief of a household." A statute of 1871 introduced a formal property qualification (a voter must own property worth $100 one year before the election or, in the case of tenants, pay a yearly rental of at least $20), but Aboriginal people retained the franchise.[75]

Prime Minister Macdonald's administration finally passed a federal franchise law in 1885. It permitted certain Indians to vote by providing that the word "person" meant a male person including an Indian but disqualifying

> ... Indians in Manitoba, British Columbia, Keewatin and the North-West Territories, and any Indian on any reserve elsewhere in Canada who is not in possession and occupation of a separate and distinct tract of land in such reserve, and whose improvements on such separate tract are not of the value of at least one hundred and fifty dollars, and who is not otherwise possessed of the qualifications entitling him to be registered on the list of voters under this Act.[76]

In 1886 the Manitoba government revised its *Election Act* to disqualify Indians or persons of Indian blood receiving an annuity from the Crown.[77] Both exclusions should be placed in the context of the 1885 uprising in what is now Saskatchewan. Nonetheless, the removal of a fundamental right of citizenship was a profound blow to Aboriginal membership in the Canadian community. A generation later, in 1931, Manitoba followed the Ontario example and amended this legislation to permit Indians who had served in the British or Canadian armed forces, or in the forces of a British possession, or the forces of a British ally during the Great War, to vote in provincial elections.[78]

Finally, in 1952 Manitoba returned the provincial franchise to Aboriginal people.[79] Only in 1960, 75 years after the first legislation, did the federal government return the franchise in national elections to Manitoba's (and the nation's) Indian people.[80] The relationship between the vote and Aboriginal political action in the 1960s and 1970s should be a salutary reminder of the importance of this pivotal expression of sovereignty—or at least of some measure of control over one's life—in public affairs.

Although the *Indian Act* was revised after extensive hearings in 1951, the revisions did not answer the Aboriginal requests for greater self-government. While some of the Act's worst aspects were eliminated, the power of Indian agents remained. Indian agents still exercised complete control over band councils, served as justices of the peace and regulated virtually all aspects of daily life. One important change was the inclusion of a provision (formerly section 87 and now section 88) that made provincial laws applicable to Aboriginal people on reserves. While this was subject to certain limitations, such as federal laws, treaties and by-laws, the clear intent was to involve provincial governments more actively in daily life and to reduce the unique legal status that reserves had enjoyed previously.

One of the by-products of this initiative was the sudden arrival of the child welfare system, delivered by social workers applying urban, middle-class standards. Thousands of Aboriginal children were taken from their families across the country as being in need of protection. This experience, referred to as the "Sixties Scoop," had a profound and very destructive effect on many Aboriginal communities.[81] Combined with the residential school system, it meant that generations of children were not raised within their families or communities, thereby never learning their traditional culture or patterns of parenting.

Aboriginal Political Campaigns after 1969

The rapidly changing context of Canadian politics and increasing pressure from Aboriginal organizations forced the government to review its Indian policies again in the 1960s. The result was the White Paper of 1969, entitled *Statement of the Government of Canada on Indian Policy*. Influenced by Prime Minister Trudeau and developed after three years of consultation, the government articulated a position in direct conflict with the advice received. This statement of policy opposed continuation of a distinct Indian status and of treaties between Canada and Aboriginal people. Treaties were regarded as anachronisms to be discarded, and Aboriginal rights and Aboriginal title were dismissed as irrelevant and without legal foundation. The new policy would repeal the *Indian Act* and transform reserves into communities no different from their non-Aboriginal neighbours. The ideal being set out was equality under the law. (We discuss different interpretations of "equality" in Chapter 4.) Three centuries of legal and customary arrangements would have been abrogated in one legislative stroke.

The White Paper provoked condemnation from Aboriginal groups across the country and soon was dropped. If the policy proposals died, the Aboriginal political response did not. The national Indian campaign against the White Paper developed into a movement and an organization. The rallying points included self-government and Aboriginal rights, but at the centre of the discussions were land claims, treaties and the Aboriginal relationship with the Crown.

A consequence of the federal government's disastrous failure in launching the White Paper was that, in the following years, Ottawa was much more interested in seeking the opinions of Aboriginal people. It dropped its proposal to repeal the *Indian Act*. It funded separate regional and national organizations for Indians, Inuit and Metis peoples, and it began to devolve administrative responsibility upon local chiefs and councils. Local band agents, some of whom had been evicted from reserves in the 1960s, withdrew to district and regional offices. In their place, an Aboriginal civil service and Aboriginal programs began to emerge on the reserves.

In 1973, the Supreme Court delivered its historic decision on the land claim of the Nishga of northern British Columbia.[82] Although the appeal was lost, six justices of Canada's highest court concluded that Aboriginal title existed under Canadian law.

The federal government, searching for a policy in the aftermath of the White Paper, announced in August 1973 that it would negotiate the settlement of Aboriginal title land claims, henceforth known as "comprehensive claims," in northern Quebec, British Columbia, the Yukon and Northwest Territories. The existing policy concerning treaty and reserve land claims would be continued under the rubric of "specific claims." In addition, southern Quebec and Atlantic Canada, where treaties but not land surrenders were at issue, were placed in a third, undefined category. Thus, as in the rest of Canada, so in Manitoba: Aboriginal concerns about unfulfilled promises slowly were being addressed. The issue now became one of administrative lethargy. How long would the process take?

The national campaign to patriate the Constitution also drove Aboriginal politics. By promising constitutional renewal after the Quebec referendum of 1980, Prime Minister Trudeau implicitly raised the issue of treaty and Aboriginal rights. Aboriginal organizations seized an opportunity to entrench these rights beyond the reach of future governments, and to win respect for their claims and status in the nation's constitution. Indian, Inuit and Metis national leaders cooperated in the presentation of a joint case and, in January 1981, the Joint Parliamentary Committee and the federal cabinet agreed to include a clause in the draft constitution concerning recognition of Aboriginal and treaty rights. A year of intense lobbying followed. In the end, a diluted version of the Aboriginal and treaty rights clause became part of the constitution that was proclaimed on April 17, 1982.

Patriation of the Constitution was a turning point for Canadian-Aboriginal people. Section 35 recognized and affirmed the "existing aboriginal and treaty rights of the aboriginal peoples of Canada." Under this section, Aboriginal peoples were defined as "the Indian, Inuit and Metis peoples." (s. 35(2)) Another section shielded those rights, as well as other rights and freedoms of the Aboriginal peoples, from challenge under the *Charter of Rights and Freedoms*. (s. 25) A third section promised a First Ministers' Conference on Aboriginal constitutional matters before April 17, 1983. (s. 37) That conference, in turn, agreed that both sections 25 and 35 of the *Constitution Act, 1982* would be amended to protect the rights contained within past and future land claims settlements as treaty rights. It also decided to amend section 35 to guarantee sexual equality among Aboriginal men and women in the enjoyment of their rights. The conference declared too that none of the provisions of the *Constitution Acts* of 1867 and 1982 expressly referring to Aboriginal peoples could be amended without prior consultation between legislators and Aboriginal peoples at a First Ministers' Conference. Finally, having listed issues of mutual concern but being unable to agree on a definition of Aboriginal and treaty rights, the conference decided to meet at least three more times.

The amendments to the Constitution were passed by all provincial legislatures, except that of Quebec, and by the Parliament of Canada, and were proclaimed in force in June 1984. In that year, and again in 1985 and 1987, Canadians watched the dramatic First Ministers' Conferences with Aboriginal leaders. In the full glare of the television lights and with the advantage of national media attention, these meetings generated public awareness of Aboriginal issues and focussed debate on the constitutional recognition of an Aboriginal right to self-government. One measure of the gains made by Aboriginal people in this period was the boldness of the report of the House of Commons Special Committee on Indian Self-Government in 1983, which endorsed an official recognition of Aboriginal rights to self-government.[83] Although progress has been slow in the intervening years, the need for, and the public willingness to support, new departures in Aboriginal policy are clear.

The Constitution was only one of the areas in which Aboriginal status was debated in the decades after 1950. Judicial rulings on hunting and fishing rights and on land claims produced more than a little anger among Manitoba Indians as they seemingly won, then lost, then regained treaty-protected rights. Their claims to land under the treaty promises of a century ago similarly were delayed in government offices as if they were part of an administrative game. Particular resources, like wild rice, that had been part of Aboriginal life for centuries, also became subject to provincial regulations, and thus seemingly were taken out of Aboriginal control and placed in the hands of distant bureaucrats whose priorities might differ from those of the people who had once "owned" the natural product. We discuss these issues in detail in Chapter 5.

The Department of Indian Affairs managed its "wards" aggressively in the decades after World War II. Henceforth, it seemed, housing and economic development on the reserve, education in both the reserve and urban settings, the use of "Friendship Centres" to stimulate Aboriginal migration to the cities, and family-centred matters including income support and adoption, in particular, would require an army of civil servants, on the one hand, and Aboriginal acquiescence, on the other. Child justice and family welfare issues entered the public sphere during these decades. Family crises propelled children into courts and expanded the size of welfare agency case files. Too often, family members were separated. Too often, as the Manitoba people have learned in recent years, Aboriginal children were sent out of the community and out of the country. Too often, as is indicated by the commonplace observation that over half the children at the Manitoba Youth Centre are Aboriginal, children ended up in custody. Again, we will address some of these matters in Chapters 14 and 15.

Aboriginal Dislocation

The experience of the band at Tadoule Lake will illustrate how law and government administration can affect an Aboriginal group in our own time. This group of about 300 Dene people hunt and fish in the territory west of Churchill. Although their life is far from easy, the community members believe it is preferable to the alternatives they have seen. During our visit to this settlement in January 1989, we were greeted with wonderful hospitality, were driven around the area behind dog teams, and heard the moving and courageous story of the band's experience during Manitoba's third justice regime.

The band had been living near the Hudson's Bay Company's Duck Lake trading post in 1956, trapping furs and hunting caribou in the region as it had done for years. Fur prices declined, the company decided to close the post, and the services that the band had received, from supplementary food to medical assistance and emergency radio transmissions, stopped. Government officials visited the band and informed it that, in the circumstances, it would have to move to Churchill. The band members said they did not want to move and asked the officials to assist them to stay in their traditional area. The officials cited the annual costs and declined. Several months later, without further discussion, airplanes arrived and all the people were taken to Churchill where, as elder Thomas Duck told our Inquiry, they were "just dumped out on the beach ... and people were living ... in tents and then finally they were hauled to another location by boat in fall ... [when] little shacks, 12 x 16 or 12 x 14 one room shacks" were erected for them. That was in 1956.

Fifteen years of social devastation followed. In the 1970s, a substantial proportion of the community decided to return to traditional life and eventually established the Tadoule Lake settlement. Band councillor Albert Thorassie told us that his people:

> [B]ear the wounds and carry the physical and psychological scars for those tormenting years ... it continues to haunt us in ways unimaginable to outsiders. We lost one whole generation of people who would now be the backbone of our community ... through violent deaths from freezing, hit and run ... homicide, suicide and alcohol-related incidents.... We find it hard to this day to rebuild from the destruction and chaos of those years.... We find it hard to re-grasp the drum and ... to sing and play the hand game, because during those years in Churchill ... the only thing we knew was alcohol and violence and all the disgusting things that go with it.
>
> In the past, a Sayisi Dene was respected and feared by all Athapaskan people and other tribes, because of our great numbers and fearlessness and our abilities to live in a beautiful but harsh environment.
>
> Today, we are just fragments of a great tribe, beaten and down, but not out. And we are not giving up. We long to hear our drum beating again, our heart that stopped beating for so long....

We have so much to tell the world regarding the injustices that ... were imposed by society and by the federal government without our people's consent....

If the Tadoule Lake experience were unique, we in the South might be inclined to regret the matter and turn our attention to other issues. But it is not unique. Moose Lake, Chemawawin, Grand Rapids, South Indian Lake, Brochet all have equally compelling stories. The northern experience has been repeated time after time from 1869 to the present. Economic opportunity is assessed; development is launched; the environment is altered drastically. European-Canadians take resources and Aboriginal Canadians suffer the consequences.

Chief Esau Turner of the Swampy Cree Tribal Council described the Grand Rapids and Saskatchewan Power projects in exactly these terms when he addressed our Inquiry:

[H]uge changes have been imposed on native people.... Economic activity has come into our area which has changed our way of life, but has rarely given us a substitute in terms of jobs and ownership of that economic activity. Lost, too, in the changes were many traditions and values that kept our culture strong and our communities united. The taking of land, the imposition of another economic system and replacement of our social systems with systems of laws and government from outside meant the decline in local customs, local responsibility and local ways of life. The changes to the economy and the systems that have developed around native people have taught dependency rather than independence.... In abdicating responsibility we have fallen into many problems. Alcohol, welfare and Indian Affairs threatened to replace our culture, our independence and our strength as a people.... What we want to stress is that self-government means the ability to have local decision-making regarding matters which affect the lives of our people ... the ability to develop independence ... the ability to reinforce culture, customs and traditions....

Conclusion

Manitoba's Aboriginal people have known three justice regimes. During two of those regimes, they exercised control over their lives. In the third, this control was taken from them. It was done in a manner that clearly crossed the lines of fairness. We deplore the injustice which was done to Aboriginal people during this regime. By treating Aboriginal people in a condescending manner, by smothering their political and cultural expressions, as well as by failing to deal in a forthright and respectful manner with legitimate Aboriginal claims, Canadian government policy has done all Canadians a disservice. The loss of Aboriginal self-determination is obvious. The loss of identity and self-respect by the Aboriginal youth of our nation is lamentable.

These considerations must be kept in mind to fully appreciate the nature of the problems which we will now begin to address.

Chapter 4

Aboriginal Over-Representation

Introduction

As we noted earlier, Aboriginal people constitute approximately 12% of the Manitoba population. Yet, Aboriginal people account for over one-half of the 1,600 people incarcerated on any given day of the year in Manitoba's correctional institutions.

This is a shocking fact. Why, in a society where justice is supposed to be blind, are the inmates of our prisons selected so overwhelmingly from a single ethnic group? Two answers suggest themselves immediately: either Aboriginal people commit a disproportionate number of crimes, or they are the victims of a discriminatory justice system. We believe that both answers are correct, but not in the simplistic sense that some people might interpret them. We do not believe, for instance, that there is anything about Aboriginal people or their culture that predisposes them to criminal behaviour. Instead, we believe that the causes of Aboriginal criminal behaviour are rooted in a long history of discrimination and social inequality that has impoverished Aboriginal people and consigned them to the margins of Manitoban society.

Since racism exists throughout Manitoban and Canadian society, we have found that overt racism also exists in the administration of Manitoba's justice system. As in society generally, overt racism must be confronted and condemned when discovered. There is no room in the administration of justice for those who are racist, because the power that rests in the justice system is enormous.

However, for Aboriginal people a more serious problem exists. We find that a system that seeks to provide justice on the principle that all Canadians share common values and experiences cannot help but discriminate against Aboriginal people, who come to the system with cultural values and experiences that differ substantially from those of the dominant society.

Cultural oppression, social inequality, the loss of self-government and systemic discrimination, which are the legacy of the Canadian government's treatment of Aboriginal people, are intertwined and interdependent factors, and in very few cases is it possible to draw a simple and direct correlation between any one of them and the events which lead an individual Aboriginal person to commit a crime or to become incarcerated. We believe that the overall weight of the evidence makes it clear that these factors are crucial in explaining the reasons why Aboriginal people are over-represented in Manitoba's jails.

It is also important to recognize that while this over-representation is the most graphic and disturbing example of the adverse impacts these factors have on Aboriginal people, it is not an isolated problem. Aboriginal over-representation is the end point of a series of decisions made by those with decision-making power in the justice system. An examination of each of these decisions suggests that the way that decisions are made within the justice system discriminates against Aboriginal people at virtually every point. We discuss how that happens in this chapter. We begin, however, by pointing out a number of the disproportionate and adverse impacts that characterize the dealings of Aboriginal people in the justice system.

- More than half of the inmates of Manitoba's jails are Aboriginal.

- Aboriginal accused are more likely to be denied bail.

- Aboriginal people spend more time in pre-trial detention than do non-Aboriginal people.

- Aboriginal accused are more likely to be charged with multiple offences than are non-Aboriginal accused.

- Lawyers spend less time with their Aboriginal clients than with non-Aboriginal clients.

- Aboriginal offenders are more than twice as likely as non-Aboriginal people to be incarcerated.

The over-representation of Aboriginal people occurs at virtually every step of the judicial process, from the charging of individuals to their sentencing.

In subsequent chapters we address each of these issues and make specific proposals as to how these impacts can be reduced or eliminated. Just as the causes of these impacts are complex and interrelated, our proposals are also multifacetted and attempt to deal with both the legacy of cultural oppression of Aboriginal people and the systemic discrimination that exists within the system.

Aboriginal Criminal Behaviour

As we stated in the introduction to this chapter, we believe that the fact that large numbers of Manitoba's Aboriginal people come into conflict with the law stems from a mixture of discrimination on the part of the justice system and actual criminal behaviour on the part of Aboriginal people. In this section we examine the available statistics relating to Aboriginal crime rates and then examine the causes of criminal behaviour among Aboriginal people.

One might expect the police, courts and jails to be rich sources of information for such a discussion. However, these agencies simply do not keep meaningful statistics, especially ones that compare the experiences of Aboriginal and non-Aboriginal persons. This makes it extremely difficult to understand why Aboriginal people are so over-represented, or to propose meaningful reforms. Almost everything that is "known" about the system is based on personal observation or occasional, limited attempts to gather information.

Crime rates are indeed higher in Aboriginal communities. Why this is so is what we want to explore. Whether the system responds appropriately is another, equally significant issue.

The problem is magnified because of difficulties in defining "crime," and because different societies have different concepts of crime. For example, many Aboriginal peoples continue to exercise their rights to hunt and fish, although they risk prosecution under provincial and federal laws for doing so. In addition, society's "criminals" are part of a larger group, some of which escape detection or conviction. We know next to nothing about the group that does not get caught or convicted.

Aboriginal Crime Rates

National crime rates for Indian bands are available from the Department of Indian Affairs. According to the department, the national crime rate is 92.7 per 1,000 population, while the crime rate for Indian bands is 165.6 per 1,000 population (1.8 times the national rate). Nationally, the violent crime rate is 9.0 per 1,000, while for Indian bands the violent crime rate is 33.1 per 1,000 (3.67 times the national rate). Departmental figures also make it clear that members of Indian bands are far more likely to be the victims of violent crime than other Canadians.[1]

The 1989–90 crime rate for areas of Manitoba policed by the RCMP, excluding reserves, was 10,025 offences for every 100,000 persons. The rate on reserves was 15,053 offences for every 100,000 persons, or 1.5 times greater. Another way of viewing this information is that approximately 17.5% of the offences occurred on reserves, while the reserve population was approximately 12.3% of the total population policed by the RCMP (according to Statistics Canada figures).[2]

Our analysis of information provided from a study of Provincial Court data[3] shows that on the reserves surveyed, 35% of crime fell into a group of four offences: common assault, break and enter, theft under $1,000 and public mischief. Aboriginal persons were charged with fewer property offences, and more offences against the person and provincial statute violations, than non-Aboriginal persons.

These trends were also found by criminologists Mary Hyde and Carol LaPrairie, whose study showed that Aboriginal crime was quite different from non-Aboriginal crime. For Aboriginal people, their study found more violent offences, fewer property offences, more social disorder offences, higher overall rates of crime, and a strong relationship between alcohol abuse and crime. Almost conspicuously absent were crimes for profit, such as drug trafficking, prostitution, fraud and armed robberies. Although there were more violent offences than non-Aboriginal people committed, the majority of crimes committed were petty offences.[4]

Hyde and LaPrairie found that a very high proportion of Aboriginal violent crimes were directed against family members—a minimum of 41.4%. The actual figure may be much higher, because in another 50.2% of the files they studied, the relationship between attacker and victim is not known. It is known, however, that violent offences most frequently take place in private residences.[5]

It would be both unfair and inaccurate to stereotype all reserves as having a high crime rate. While some reserves have very high rates, other reserves have crime rates that are much lower than the provincial average.

The reserves that the Provincial Court data reported on had a considerably higher crime rate than other reserves in Manitoba, and at the same time had higher average incomes than other reserves. The reserves in the Provincial Court database had crime rates of 9,233 offences for every 10,000 persons aged 15 years or older, compared to a rate of 4,480 for every 10,000 persons aged 15 years or older on all other reserves in Manitoba. These reserves had more than twice the crime of other reserves (or were more likely to bring crime to the attention of the police). On the other hand, the median household incomes were $15,528 for the reserves examined by the Provincial Court study and $9,756 for non-Provincial Court study reserves.

It is important to note also that the statistics say nothing about Aboriginal crime off-reserve. In Manitoba, the majority of the Aboriginal population live off reserves (in large part because the Metis population almost entirely does not live on Indian reserves).

In conclusion, we believe that there is a higher rate of crime among Aboriginal people, but we also believe that over-policing and systemic discrimination within the justice system contribute greatly to it.

Studies of Canadian prison admissions indicate that alcohol abuse is a factor in many of the crimes committed by Aboriginal people. These include violation of liquor laws, crimes committed while the offender was under the influence of alcohol and offences committed to obtain additional alcohol supplies.[6] Despite this strong correlation, we do not believe alcohol abuse should be viewed as a "cause" of Aboriginal crime. Rather, we believe that Aboriginal alcohol abuse arises from the same conditions which have created high Aboriginal crime rates.

Criminological Theories

An entire field of study, criminology, is devoted to determining causes of crime, and a great deal of academic attention has been directed toward explaining Aboriginal over-representation in the criminal justice system. Theories about the causes of crime generally fail to explain crime satisfactorily, in part because there is so little information about crime, police and the courts, and in part because there is so much confusion about correlations, causes and crime.

When it comes to explaining disproportionate crime rates, there can be many different conclusions, often based on widely different interpretations of the same data. Many of the theoretical differences are based on the ideologies of their proponents. Some criminologists tend to downplay social explanations for crime, preferring to attribute criminality to purely individual factors. Others rely almost completely on social explanations of deviance.

Often, the theories merely describe conditions in which crime frequently occurs, without trying to explain why it occurs. Many theories do try to explain what the causative factor is, but they rarely explain why the factor affects some persons and not others.[7] Many theories overlap and describe the same conflicts within society, using a variety of different labels. Many of the theories are plausible, but few are completely persuasive or satisfactory. The interaction of human motivation and social forces resists neatly compartmentalized explanations or solutions. Even a quick review of some of the theoretical approaches demonstrates the variety of explanations which can be brought to bear.

Some theories are of no use at all in explaining the complex interaction of factors causing crime. One such theory relates to genetic causes of crime. There may well be certain biological or genetic conditions which affect a particular individual's ability to make rational choices and to behave in socially accepted ways. The notion that these individual problems occur across entire races or ethnic groups has no basis in fact. Crime is universal and its causes are not related to race or ethnicity.

One school of thought is called functionalist theory, which suggests that because crime exists in all societies, it must have a function. The function suggested is that crime is required by societies to help define normalcy, to make some behaviours more attractive and to induce greater social cohesion.[8] The superiority theory suggests that humans are conditioned to strive for superiority and, therefore, some people turn to crime as a means of achieving superiority.[9] Strain theory suggests that people whose ambitions are severely frustrated will experience anger, which will lead to rebellion against the real or perceived causes of those frustrations.[10]

Conflict theory suggests that when a person is influenced strongly by two conflicting cultures, the attachment to the rules of either one is weakened and can produce deviant behaviour.[11] Social disorganization theory explains deviance as a side effect of rapidly changing society—industrialization, urbanization, rapid technological change, and so on.[12] Ecological theory identifies conditions in which crime flourishes, focussing mostly on physical conditions such as high density population, poverty, mixed use (i.e., residential and industrial), transience (homeless people, renters) and dilapidation.[13] A specific condition that has been studied is crowded housing. Overcrowding has numerous consequences which may lead to interpersonal conflicts by itself, or simply add to the various stresses with which individuals must cope.[14]

Differential association theory provides that crime is learned by associating with others who have already rejected conduct norms and have committed themselves to deviance as a way to satisfy their desires.[15] Criminality may be learned through films and other media.[16] Another theory holds that persons will be more likely to conform when they stand to benefit by conforming.[17] Other theories suggest that childhood exposure to violence and victimization in turn leads to violence. More than a dozen studies were done between 1978 and 1986 that offer evidence that violence begets violence.[18]

The Social Roots of Crime

If you accept our assertion that much of the root cause of Indian peoples' disproportionate conflict with the justice system lies in their poverty and marginal position in Canadian society, then what do you think is going to happen in the next 10 or 20 years, if radical changes do not occur?

Ovide Mercredi
Berens River

It is difficult not to concur with Ovide Mercredi's assertion that the root causes of Aboriginal over-representation in the criminal justice system can be found in the poverty and marginalization of Aboriginal people. The Canadian justice system is, at its heart, a system of individual responsibility, where sanctions are levelled at specific individuals for specific actions which can be demonstrated, in a court of law, to have taken place, but it is also clear that there are social roots to criminal behaviour. It is extremely difficult not to conclude that there exists a significant relationship between social inequality and criminal behaviour.

To the extent that poverty does play a causative role in crime, it is not at all clear exactly how the causation process operates. To begin with, the majority of poor persons, of whatever race or circumstance, are not criminals. Further, the incidence of crime does not coincide consistently with income or employment levels. However, we cannot ignore the fact that Aboriginal people occupy the bottom rung on Canada's socio-economic ladder and simultaneously are vastly over-represented in our prisons. Our survey of inmates, for example, reveals that only 30% of Aboriginal respondents were employed full time prior to their most recent arrests.

A variety of international studies point to the link between poverty and criminal behaviour. A British study concluded that working-class boys were twice as likely to become delinquents if they came from low-income families.[19] A Danish study that examined the lives of people born in Copenhagen between 1941 and 1952 discovered that those children who had grown up in low-income families and lived in slum areas had a rate of imprisonment that was four times higher than all children born in the city during that period.[20] Similar American studies have concluded that youths from lower socio-economic backgrounds are more likely to commit more, and more serious, crimes than youths from more privileged backgrounds.[21]

Some theories argue that it is not simply having few material things that plays a causative role, it is a question of being poor *compared* to others in the society; i.e., a sense of being hindered from attaining what others in society are able to attain. This point has particular relevance to Aboriginal people, given the unjust and repressive treatment they have received at the hands of the Canadian government. A recent study found that inequality was a better predictor of homicides than was poverty alone. This was true of economic inequality and even more true of racial inequality. This study concluded that:

> [W]hat most predictably generates violent crime is not the simple absence of material goods, but rather the deeper attitudes of hopelessness and alienation produced by inequalities that are perceived as unjust.... Violence results "not so much from lack of advantage as from being taken advantage of."[22]

One criminologist gives the example of Third World countries with low crime rates, and suggests that this can be explained by "a strong and encompassing community life that offers meaningful work and family roles in the midst of material deprivation."[23] A study in rural India found that strong family relationships are important deterrents to interpersonal violence "because they provide a fundamental sense of belonging to a larger supportive community and because they provide the setting in which informal social sanctions against aggression and crime can operate effectively."[24]

Hyde and LaPrairie conducted a study of crime on 25 Indian reserves in Quebec. The study used four categories of Indian communities. It found that the communities that assimilated the least, that were the most remote and had the lowest incomes, had the least crime (below the national average), while the communities that were closest to urban centres and that had the greatest integration, the highest incomes and formal education, had the highest rates of property crime and the second highest rates of violent crime among the four community types.[25]

Aboriginal crime does not fit easily into any one of these various theories, perhaps because it appears to fit easily into all of them. From our review of the information available to us, including the nature of the crimes committed by Aboriginal people, and after hearing the hundreds of submissions presented to us in the course of our hearings, we believe that the relatively higher rates of crime among Aboriginal people are a result of the despair, dependency, anger, frustration and sense of injustice prevalent in Aboriginal communities, stemming from the cultural and community breakdown that has occurred over the past century.

The Socio-Economic Situation of Aboriginal People

So we find ourselves in the fertile breeding grounds of crime: high unemployment, lack of educational opportunities, substandard housing, inadequate health care, tradition, hunting, fishing and trapping rights being violated, a shortage of recreation facilities, and being subject to the law and which many times we don't understand, laws which do not fit with our culture, values and traditions.

Chief Dennis Shorting
Little Saskatchewan Band

It is these substandard living conditions, unfair and unequal opportunities, unequal education, chronic high unemployment, and inadequate housing which generates the frustration and anger that leads to offences and criminal activity.

Chief Louis Stevenson
Assembly of Manitoba Chiefs

In Manitoba, Aboriginal people undoubtedly are the poorest of the poor. Low incomes, unemployment, poor health care, inadequate levels of education, crowded and substandard housing conditions—all are characteristic of Aboriginal life in Canada. It is crucial to recognize that the social condition of Aboriginal people is a direct result of the discriminatory and repressive policies that successive European and Canadian governments have directed towards Aboriginal people. The assault on Aboriginal self-government and culture that we outlined in the previous chapter served to impoverish and subordinate Aboriginal people. The overview of Aboriginal socio-economic conditions that we present now should be seen as the adverse impact of the European civilization of North America.

Poverty

An analysis of the 1986 census data provides a disturbing overview of the depth of Aboriginal poverty. The reported average income of persons with "total Aboriginal origins" in Manitoba is $10,672, compared to the average income of $16,796 for the province as a whole. There were 21.8% of status Indians who reported no income, compared to 11.5% of the total Manitoba population.[26]

Aboriginal people experience poverty more frequently than do non-Aboriginal people. According to a study conducted by Winnipeg's Social Planning Council, more than one-half of Aboriginal households exist below the poverty line, compared to about 20% of non-Aboriginal households.[27]

This is part of a disturbing trend. Between 1981 and 1986, every Aboriginal group experienced an increase in the proportion of the population relying on government transfer payments as the major source of income.[28]

Unemployment

Unemployment rates are notoriously subject to wide interpretation because the statistics only count as "unemployed" those persons actively searching for work. If a person is not looking for work, and this could be for any number of reasons, including the obvious one for many reserve residents that there are simply no jobs to be had, then the person is not considered "unemployed" in official statistics.

Even with this underestimation of the true level of employment, the Indian unemployment rate is four times the non-Indian rate. According to the 1986 census, the labour force participation rate for Indians on reserves (those employed or included in unemployment statistics) averaged 53%, compared to 66.6% for non-Indian persons. The unemployment rate for Manitoba's Indian population was 26.3%, compared to 7.6% for the total provincial population.[29] We believe that the actual rate of unemployment among Aboriginal people in some communities is two to three times higher than that.

While the statistics reveal there is a positive relationship between employment and education, the employment benefits of an education are far less evident for Indian persons. According to 1981 figures, those Indians with high school education had unemployment rates three times higher than non-Indian persons with high school education. Non-Indian persons without high school had much lower unemployment rates than Indians without high school education. [30]

Age, Birth and Families

Indian people have a much different age distribution than the general population in Manitoba. In 1971, 51% of the Indian population were under 15 years of age. For 1991, this is estimated to have declined to 38%. The corresponding 1991 figure for non-Indian people was 22%.[31] Because there continues to be a high number of Aboriginal youth entering their child-bearing years, it is expected the Aboriginal birth rate will continue to remain higher than the provincial rate for some time.[32]

Indian families are more likely to be single-parent families, especially off-reserve, where 36% are single-parent families, compared to the provincial and reserve average, both at 18%.[33]

One important factor to take into account when considering over-representation is that young people are represented disproportionately in crime in all cultures. Thus, at least some of the Aboriginal over-representation is simply a reflection of the different age structure in their population.

Health and Death

The Indian death rate for persons between 25 and 44 years of age is five times higher than the non-Indian rate. For Indian men, the average age at death is 25 years younger than for non-Indian men. For Indian women, it is 28 years younger.[34]

Infant mortality rates also are higher, as are dietary problems.[35] The suicide rate for Indian persons is more than double the non-Indian rate.[36]

Housing

In 1981 on-reserve residents in Manitoba lived in the most crowded housing conditions in Canada.[37] This was the situation before the passage of Bill C-31, which reinstated thousands of Indians to their status, a proportion of whom have returned to their reserves. In addition, there has been a decade of high birth rates since then. The average Aboriginal household has twice as many people as non-Indian households.[38]

Indian housing is of inferior condition. Their homes are three times more likely to be in need of major repair. Only 40% of Indian homes have central heating, compared to 82% for non-Indian homes. Only 44% of Indian dwellings on-reserve, and 34% of Manitoba's total Indian population, have indoor plumbing. This is well below the national average for Indian homes of 82%, and the non-Indian average of 94%.[39]

Indian people rent accommodations and change residences more frequently than non-Indian people. This is especially true for off-reserve Indian people. Non-Indian families were two and a half times more likely than off-reserve Indian households to live at their present address for six years or more (48% vs. 18%). Seven of 10 non-Indian households lived at their present address for three years or more, compared to only 35% of off-reserve Indian households.[40]

Education

According to the 1986 census, 34.2% of Manitoba's Indian population over the age of 15 had less than grade nine education, compared to 18.2% of the total provincial population.[41]

Aboriginal education has suffered from a long history of being primarily a tool of cultural assimilation. Aboriginal students, particularly on-reserve, are being instructed in a second language. Only recently has Aboriginal education attempted to prepare Aboriginal students for skilled employment or post-secondary education.

Even today, Aboriginal education is culturally biased. The materials and subjects used for teaching are largely designed for and by non-Aboriginal persons, with little or no regard for the cultures, histories and realities of Aboriginal life. Although residential schools have disappeared, it is still the case in many reserves that children must leave the community to attend high school, resulting in the absence of family support and parental involvement in the education system.

The Justice System and Aboriginal Poverty

We can trace an unbroken record of injustice back through generations, to our grandfathers and our grandmothers, our great-grandfathers and to those before them. We can trace them back to the time when a label was put on our people, legitimate victim. Other people learned that they could victimize us and nothing would happen because the laws, your laws, did not protect us.

Rufus Prince
Long Plain

From the perspective of Aboriginal people, the justice system has contributed to Aboriginal poverty by failing to provide them with the means to fight the oppressive conditions imposed upon them. It has not assisted Aboriginal peoples in defending their claim to their lands or in enforcing their treaty promises. In fact, at one time it was illegal for lawyers to represent Aboriginal persons without the consent of the federal government or for Aboriginal people to raise money to press their land claims. The loss of Aboriginal land is a clear contributor to poverty.

Nor has the justice system assisted Aboriginal peoples in defending their freedoms of belief, religion and association. The law forced Aboriginal parents, under threat of prosecution from the justice system, to send their children to residential schools. The justice system also failed to protect Aboriginal families from the child welfare practices of the 1960s and 1970s, which continue to create problems off reserves today. The separation of families, the oppression of culture and language, and the lack of Aboriginal control over decisions within their communities have contributed to inadequate education and to community breakdown, which in turn lead to poverty, as community resources are underdeveloped.

Stress

Another link between poverty and crime focusses on how the various social conditions associated with poverty contribute to stress. A recent study shows that while stress factors may increase one by one, the proportion of people unable to cope with stress multiplies with each additional stress—some social scientists refer to this as a "compound interest effect."[42] Most people can deal well with one or two and even three major stresses at once, but after a point, more and more people lose the ability to cope. Their manner of ceasing to function varies: some withdraw into passivity or illness, while others act out violently against themselves or others.[43]

There is a wide array of stresses affecting Aboriginal people. One of the stresses is poverty, with its related effects. Other stresses are just as important, and perhaps more important, than poverty. Primary among these are the cultural conflicts and frustrations faced by Aboriginal people. They are confronted with acts of discrimination on a regular basis. Aboriginal people are the objects of education, health care, child welfare and justice systems that have historically denied the value of Aboriginal beliefs and practices. Aboriginal people have been denied the opportunity to make decisions to control their own lives and communities. Aboriginal people have been forced to conform to foreign systems without being fully accepted or respected by those systems. At the same time, Aboriginal people have had their own cultures attacked and denigrated. All these factors have created enormous stresses and frustration.

Lisa Hobbs Birnie, a former member of the National Parole Board, offers this description of Aboriginal crime:

> The native crime that I saw seemed to spring out of spontaneous rage and fury, as if the heart and mind had been one long-smouldering fire that had finally been ignited into an explosion. The planning, the conspiracies, the calculated risk, the cool and deliberate scheming that characterize so many white crimes are usually absent from the average native pattern. In fact, many native crimes occur in bars, or at parties, or in the middle of the street, and often in the middle of the day when all the world is around to see. There is nothing hidden about them. The offender has no hope of avoiding detection, no hope of getting away with it. There is in much native crime a terrible element of self-destruction, a certitude of punishment to follow, a hopeless despair, and a loathing of self. No one who felt his or her life was worth living would act in this way.[44]

Conclusion

In concluding our discussion of the roots of Aboriginal crime, we wish to stress the links between the anger and frustration created by Aboriginal poverty and criminal behaviour. The poverty experienced by Aboriginal people has a number of unique—and oppressive—aspects. The avenues through which Aboriginal people might be able to escape from their current social conditions, such as the justice system, the education system, economic development in their communities and the institutions of local government, are perceived by Aboriginal people to be under the control of external governments.

As we stated at the outset of this chapter, the over-representation of Aboriginal people in the province's criminal justice system is not related solely to high Aboriginal crime rates. We believe that Aboriginal over-representation also arises because the current justice system, in many ways, is culturally inappropriate and discriminatory in its treatment of Aboriginal people. There can be no question that the poor are vastly over-represented in the criminal justice system. Since Aboriginal people are vastly over-represented among the poor, any discrimination felt by poor people has a disproportionate impact on Aboriginal people.

What constitutes criminal conduct and how it is punished are also related in part to economic considerations. The criminal law has made illegal some acts that are linked directly to poverty, such as vagrancy, public intoxication and stealing, and incarcerates those who are unable to pay fines, or holds in custody those who cannot post bail. There are other discrimantory barriers facing Aboriginal people as well, including cultural ones. We will now discuss the role discrimination plays in the over-representation of Aboriginal people in the criminal justice system.

Systemic Discrimination in the Justice System

Overview

Prejudice, racism and discrimination have existed since the beginning of human history. They are particularly likely to develop when there is close association of separate groups of people, especially if they have different cultures, religions or skin colours. Canada has a long and tragic history of discrimination and racism.

Racism in Canada is not confined to any particular group. Racist government policies authorized slavery in Canada until 1834; created segregated schools for blacks and Indians; prohibited Chinese persons from certain kinds of jobs or activities; expropriated property and confined Japanese-Canadians to internment camps during World War II; permitted the expulsion of the Acadians from the Maritimes; virtually prohibited the entry of Jewish refugees into Canada during the Holocaust; discriminated against Indians, Chinese, Japanese, East Indians and others with regards to voting rights; and established racist immigration classifications and quotas.[45]

Aboriginal peoples have experienced the most entrenched racial discrimination of any group in Canada. Discrimination against Aboriginal people has been a central policy of Canadian governments since Confederation.

Thus a policy devised in the 1830's was reiterated, elaborated, and carried forward to Confederation. Almost intact it has served up to this day as the guiding star for administrators of Indian affairs. Probably in no other sphere has such continuity or consistency of clarity of policy prevailed; probably in no other area has there been such a marked failure to realize ultimate objectives.[46]

The discrimination against Aboriginal people by our governments and permitted by the general Canadian population represents a monumental symbol of intolerance. Government policies have been singularly aimed, for over a century, at reducing the differences that exist between Aboriginal life and the mainstream of Canadian society, in the hope that Aboriginal peoples would disappear as distinct societies. The extent to which Aboriginal peoples have retained their distinctiveness is a testimonial to their strength and endurance as peoples.

In the previous section we concluded that Aboriginal communities are experiencing more crime than other communities. We reviewed the causes for this and concluded that much of this crime results from conditions that are the legacy of past policies of oppression and discrimination. Conditions have been created in Aboriginal communities to which some individuals will respond by acting in deviant ways.

Here, we discuss discrimination that is related directly to the current operation of the justice system, discrimination that affects individuals who may not be guilty of the charges made against them, or discrimination that imposes greater hardships on Aboriginal offenders than on others.

The Law and Discrimination

Racism, prejudice and discrimination are widely used terms in our society, and are generally well understood. However, each term has its own interpretation difficulties. "Prejudice" is a word with origins from Latin, and means literally to "pre-judge." Typically, prejudice means forming negative opinions about persons because of specific attributes, such as skin colour, religion, physical handicap, or other attributes. Discrimination is doing something or failing to do something because of prejudice.

Racism is a form of discrimination. Usually, the term "race" in this context is meant to refer not only to skin colour, but also to religion, language or country of origin. Precise definitions of race are elusive, and serve only to make unjustifiably broad generalizations about groups of people who have considerable differences among them. However, racism is a fact. There are many people who form negative opinions and act on those opinions because of what they think a person's race is.

The 1948 *Universal Declaration of Human Rights* of the United Nations declares:

All are equal before the law and are entitled without any discrimination to equal protection of the law. All are entitled to equal protection against any discrimination in violation of this Declaration and against any incitement to such discrimination. (Art. 7)

[Article 2 provides every right in the Declaration is for the benefit of] everyone ... without distinctions of any kind, such as race, colour, sex, language, religion, political or other opinion, national or social origin, property, birth or other status.

The United Nation's International Covenant on Civil and Political Rights provides:

26. All persons are equal before the law and are entitled without any discrimination to the equal protection of the law. In this respect, the law shall prohibit any discrimination and guarantee to all persons equal and effective protection against discrimination on any ground such as race, colour, sex, language, religion, political or other opinion, national or social origin, property, birth or other status.

27. In those states in which ethnic, religious or linguistic minorities exist, persons belonging to such minorities shall not be denied the right, in community with the other members of their group, to enjoy their own culture, to profess and practice their own religion, or to use their own language.

The International Covenant on Economic, Social and Cultural Rights and the Optional Protocol to the International Covenant on Civil and Political Rights, combined with the two documents quoted above, are known collectively as the International Bill of Human Rights. In total, there are approximately 60 international documents proclaiming the importance of human rights, including the 1965 Convention on the Elimination of All Forms of Racial Discrimination.

Canada has ratified the latter Convention as well as the International Bill of Human Rights. It also proclaimed its acceptance of these principles domestically in 1960, through the passage of the Canadian *Bill of Rights*. This proved to be largely ineffective in advancing the primacy of human rights, in part because it was an ordinary statute and not part of an entrenched constitution. In 1982, the new *Constitution Act* included the *Charter of Rights and Freedoms*. One of its provisions dealt with equality. It did not come into force until 1985, to allow governments time to prepare for this new standard of judging legislation. Section 15 states:

15 (1) Every individual is equal before and under the law and has the right to the equal protection and equal benefit of the law without discrimination and, in particular, without discrimination based on race, national or ethnic origin, colour, religion, sex, age or mental or physical disability.

(2) Subsection (1) does not preclude any law, program or activity that has as its object the amelioration of conditions of disadvantaged individuals or groups including those that are disadvantaged because of race, national or ethnic origin, colour, religion, sex, age or mental or physical disability.

In addition, each province has its own human rights legislation. One of the more recent and comprehensive is the 1987 Manitoba *Human Rights Code*, which states:

9 (1) In this Code, "discrimination" means

(a) differential treatment of an individual on the basis of the individual's actual or presumed membership in or association with some class or group of persons, rather than on the basis of personal merit; or

(b) differential treatment of an individual or group on the basis of any characteristic referred to in subsection (2); or

(c) differential treatment of an individual or group on the basis of the individual's or group's actual or presumed association with another individual or group whose identity or membership is determined by any characteristic referred to in subsection (2); or

(d) *failure to make reasonable accommodation for the special needs of any individual or group, if those special needs are based upon any characteristic found in subsection* (2).[Our emphasis]

The applicable characteristics for the purposes of clauses 1(b) to (d) include "ancestry, including colour and perceived race," "nationality," "ethnic background," "religion or creed" and "political activity," among others. Subsection 9(3) provides:

(3) In this Code, "discrimination" includes any act or omission that *results* in discrimination within the meaning of subsection (1), *regardless of the form that the act or omission takes and regardless of whether the person responsible for the act or omission intended to discriminate.* [Our emphasis]

The *Human Rights Code* prohibits discrimination in various areas of human activity, such as in housing, public contracts and employment practices. An exception is permitted in employment if the discrimination is based upon bona fide and reasonable requirements or qualifications for the position. (s. 14)

The Supreme Court of Canada now has had the opportunity to comment on discrimination several times since the passage of the *Charter of Rights and Freedoms*, and it is important to understand how the court views discrimination.

[D]iscrimination may be described as a distinction, whether intentional or not but based on grounds relating to personal characteristics of the individual or group, which has the effect of imposing burdens, obligations or disadvantages on such individual or group not imposed upon others, or which withholds or limits access to opportunities, benefits and advantages available to other members of society. Distinctions based on personal characteristics attributed to an individual solely on the basis of association with a group will rarely escape the charge of discrimination, while those based on an individual's merits and capacities will rarely be so classed.[47]

Systemic Discrimination

Two common terms used when discussing discrimination are "overt" and "systemic." Generally, "overt" discrimination is discrimination which is open and deliberate, and intended to be discriminatory. The term "systemic" discrimination is used where the application of a standard or criterion, or the use of a "standard practice," creates an adverse impact upon an identifiable group that is not consciously intended.

What section 9(3) of the Manitoba *Human Rights Code* makes explicit for Manitoba, the Supreme Court in *Andrews* makes clear for the whole country: discrimination does not necessarily require intent, but can be established upon proof of adverse impact. Mr. Justice McIntyre adopted this leading statement from the *Report of the Federal Royal Commission on Equality in Employment*:

> It is not a question of whether this discrimination is motivated by an intentional desire to obstruct someone's potential, or whether it is the accidental by-product of innocently motivated practices or systems. If the barrier is affecting certain groups in a disproportionately negative way, it is a signal that the practices that lead to this adverse impact may be discriminatory.[48]

A good example of systemic discrimination, which has recently been acknowledged and remedied, at least partly, involves height and weight restrictions employed by many police departments in past years for their recruits. Although these standards are neither racially nor gender based, their imposition had the effect of eliminating most women and many visible minorities. Criteria which appear to be neutral in this situation had an adverse impact upon those particular groups. While one could not argue with the wish of police forces to have members who could withstand the physical demands of the work, it was universally recognized that there were better ways of achieving that goal.

In principle, the justice system applies apparently neutral laws and policies to all Manitobans in an equal manner. In reality, those laws and policies are developed by leaders of a society that is culturally distinct from (and to some extent antagonistic to) Aboriginal societies. As a result, there are wide differences in services available across the province and for specific groups. There exist numerous laws and practices that discriminate in a systemic manner against Aboriginal people. To give but a few examples, translation services are inadequate, court sittings in Aboriginal communities are infrequent, and the law discriminates against low-income people in the granting of bail and imprisonment for non-payment of fines.

Of equal importance is the manner in which the decision-maker applies the law to the individual. "Is this a dangerous person?" and "Is this a person who can be trusted?" are important, yet inherently subjective, questions. Such questions are necessarily influenced by one's own culture and one's own perception of other cultures.

A significant part of the problem is the inherent biases of those with decision-making or discretionary authority in the justice system. Unconscious attitudes and perceptions are applied when making decisions. Many opportunities for subjective decision making exist within the justice system and there are few checks on the subjective criteria being used to make those decisions. We believe that part of the problem is that while Aboriginal people are the objects of such discretion within the justice system, they do not "benefit" from discretionary decision making, and that even the well-intentioned exercise of discretion can lead to inappropriate results because of cultural or value differences. Winnipeg lawyer Greg Rodin, in a presentation on behalf of B'nai Brith, made this point:

> It is plain to us, however, that native people are victims of discrimination of the most insidious kind; the kind which rarely can be remedied through our legal processes because it is often subtle and well camouflaged.

> The real source of this discrimination is the well-meaning individual who does not consider himself a bigot but who, without realizing it, adheres to stereotypical views concerning natives. When these individuals hold positions of authority in our institutions, the result is institutional discrimination against native people and perpetuation of injustice and lack of equal opportunity.

However one understands discrimination, it is clear that Aboriginal people have been subject to it. They clearly have been the victims of the openly hostile bigot and they also have been victims of discrimination that is unintended, but is rooted in policy and law.

The Evidence

The best evidence of systemic discrimination lies in the adverse impacts that the system has on Aboriginal people.

Over-Incarceration

The over-representation of Aboriginal people in our prisons has been getting significantly worse over the past 25 years. Prior to the Second World War, Aboriginal prison populations were no greater than Aboriginal representation in the population. By 1965, however, 22% of the inmates at the Stony Mountain penitentiary were Aboriginal. In the subsequent years this trend has continued and accelerated.

In 1984 Aboriginal people accounted for 33%[49] of the population at Stony Mountain federal penitentiary and by 1989 they accounted for 46% of the penitentiary population. In 1983 Aboriginal people accounted for 37%[50] of the population of the Headingley Correctional Institution; by 1989 they accounted for 41% of the institution's population. In 1989 Aboriginal people accounted for 67% of the inmate population at the Portage Correctional Institution for women. The Aboriginal population in institutions for young people in 1989 was 61%.

The Aboriginal population of all provincial correctional institutions in 1989 was 57%. The Aboriginal population of all correctional institutions in Manitoba (both federally and provincially administered) in 1989 was 56% (according to figures provided by the Manitoba Department of Justice and the Correctional Services of Canada).

Thus, Aboriginal people, depending on their age and sex, are present in the jails up to five times more than their presence in the general population. Moreover, "the full extent of the problem is not known because statistics underestimate the extent of Aboriginal representation in the ... correctional system."[51]

Over-Charging of Aboriginal People

According to our analysis of the Provincial Court study statistics, 22% of Aboriginal persons appearing in Provincial Court faced four or more charges, compared to only 13% of non-Aboriginal persons. At the other end of the scale, while 50% of non-Aboriginal charged persons faced only one charge, this was true for only 37% of the Aboriginal persons.

The data showed that Aboriginal persons who were charged faced 2.72 charges per person, compared to 2.19 for non-Aboriginal persons (almost 25% more charges per Aboriginal person).

The Denial of Bail and Pre-Trial Detention

Studies of Provincial Court data reveal that:

- Aboriginal charged persons were 1.34 times more likely (55% versus 41% of non-Aboriginal charged persons) to be held in pre-trial detention.

- Of adult males between the ages of 18 and 34, Aboriginal persons spent approximately 1.5 times longer in pre-trial detention.

- Aboriginal charged women aged 18–34 were 2.4 times (48% compared to 20% of non-Aboriginal charged women) more likely to be held in pre-trial detention.

- In Winnipeg, Aboriginal detained persons spent more than twice as long in pre-trial detention as non-Aboriginal persons. Of persons held in pre-trial detention but subsequently released on bail, Aboriginal persons spent more time in custody before release.

- Aboriginal youth in pre-trial detention were detained an average of 29.3 days, compared to 10.8 days for non-Aboriginal youth.

Less Time with Lawyers

Our survey of inmates revealed that Aboriginal inmates spend considerably less time with their lawyers. In fact, Aboriginal accused are more likely than non-Aboriginal accused to appear in court without a lawyer. While 61% of Aboriginal respondents saw their lawyers three or fewer times, 63% of non-Aboriginal respondents saw their lawyers four or more times. Forty-eight per cent of the Aboriginal respondents spent less than an hour in total with their lawyers, compared to 46% of non-Aboriginal inmates who saw their lawyers for three or more hours. The lack of time spent with a lawyer can have significant consequences for how an accused is dealt with in the system, because the lawyer may be less informed about the circumstances of the offence, the potential defences and the resources available as alternatives to detention.

Sentencing and Guilty Pleas

According to our analysis of Provincial Court study data, Aboriginal persons pleaded guilty in 60% of the cases, compared to 50% for non-Aboriginal persons.

Our analysis of the data also reveals that approximately 25% of Aboriginal persons received sentences that involved some degree of incarceration, compared to approximately 10% of non-Aboriginal persons, or 2.5 times more for Aboriginal persons.

In the sentencing of males between 18 and 34 years of age, Manitoba courts handed sentences involving some degree of incarceration to 29.5% of the Aboriginal offenders and 10.9% of the non-Aboriginal offenders. In the sentencing of females between 18 and 34 years of age, Manitoba courts handed sentences involving some degree of incarceration to 19.2% of the Aboriginal offenders and 3.7% of the non-Aboriginal offenders.

Our analysis showed that 79% of Aboriginal offenders received a "full sentence" (one in which the most serious charge is not reduced or where the sentence is not a discharge or suspended sentence), compared to 65% of non-Aboriginal offenders. Forty-two per cent of Aboriginal accused received "minimum sentences" (absolute and conditional discharges, suspended sentences and reprimands), while 58% of non-Aboriginal accused received such sentences. However, the data revealed no difference between Aboriginal and non-Aboriginal persons in the number of previous convictions, so the prior criminal record does not explain this discrepancy.

These statistics are dramatic. There is something inherently wrong with a system which takes such harsh measures against an identifiable minority. It is also improbable that systemic discrimination has not played a major role in bringing this state of affairs into being.

Discriminatory Factors

There are a variety of systemically discriminatory factors at play which are likely to be present at most steps of the criminal law process and which lead to adverse impacts on Aboriginal people. These include the economic disadvantages that Aboriginal people experience, the impact of the poor quality of educational service provided to Aboriginal people, cultural differences between Aboriginal and non-Aboriginal people in their approach to the law, the lack of Aboriginal people employed in the justice system and the level of service that the justice system provides to Aboriginal people. We shall examine these factors in turn and then look at their impact on the various steps in the judicial process.

Economic Disadvantage

Many judges take employment into account when considering what an appropriate sentence might be. Employment can be interpreted by some as an indication of trustworthiness or as an indication that the individual would not risk his or her job by getting into more trouble. Judges also may want to ensure employment is continued, out of a concern for the economic dependants of the accused.

Employment can be important in deciding whether to release a person on bail or whether to impose a jail sentence. Employment potential or plans can be used as a reason to release a person on parole. Since Aboriginal people have less access to employment, this factor has a disproportionately negative impact on Aboriginal people.

Educational and Language Factors

Given the poor quality of educational services provided to Aboriginal people, any justice system program that relies on educational credentials to enable persons to benefit from the program will result in disproportionately less benefit for Aboriginal persons, due to literacy problems.

The presumption that ignorance of the law is no excuse has a disproportionate impact on Aboriginal people, who are less likely to be able to read the law, to have access to libraries or government offices for legal information, and are less likely to learn about the law in school. Since Aboriginal concepts of the law are also different, it is unfair to presume that Aboriginal people *should* know what non-Aboriginal law deems to be wrong behaviour.

The justice system does virtually nothing to reach Aboriginal people in their first languages. It does not produce pamphlets or even signs in Aboriginal syllabics; it does not produce information videos in Aboriginal languages; it does not permit persons who speak only their Aboriginal language to sit on juries; and it does not provide for translation to the public who attend court in their communities. Any translation provided is for the benefit of the accused and the court party only. The accused's family, the victim (when not testifying), the chief and council, and any other spectators must rely on English, even when all persons concerned in a particular incident are more comfortable using the local Aboriginal language.

The justice system does make a token effort to accommodate Aboriginal languages for the accused through the Court Communicator program, which recently has been converted to an Aboriginal Court Worker program and is undergoing a re-examination of its goals. Court communicators are not widely available to assist persons, spend even less time with accused persons than lawyers and are unavailable particularly in urban centres. Even when communicators are present, their effectiveness is limited since their instruction is minimal and has not included training in legal terminology or translation problems. Court communicators are not trained interpreters, although they have been relied upon in that way from time to time.

Cultural Factors

Our earlier chapter on Aboriginal concepts of justice outlined the ways in which differing cultural views of justice and justice systems can lead to systemic discrimination against Aboriginal people within the Canadian justice system.

To briefly recap the findings of that chapter, systemic discrimination based on cultural factors can arise from differing concepts of crime and justice, conceptual misunderstandings and communication difficulties. Different cultures can have differing concepts of crime. There can also exist different concepts as to the purpose of a legal system. Aboriginal cultures seek to promote individual autonomy and personal freedom, while protecting community harmony and preserving personal relationships. These values are in conflict with the Canadian justice system, which stresses confrontation, a restriction of those issues which can be addressed by the courts, and the use of adversarial counsel, and makes extensive use of punitive rather than restitutive sanctions. The point was made by Harvey Blacksmith in his testimony at Cross Lake:

> The way the law is run is complicated and frustrating. It's a clash between two completely different races, different opinions, different thoughts, feelings and so on.

The clashing values lead to a variety of conceptual misunderstandings. In the Canadian legal system, guilt is a technically defined term; for example, to be guilty of certain crimes a person must not only have committed an act, he or she must have had a criminal intent. It is quite proper for people who have committed certain acts to plead not guilty and, indeed, to be acquitted. It should not be seen as surprising that this intricate definition of guilt and innocence does not translate easily into other cultures and languages. As a result, an Aboriginal person might feel compelled to plead guilty to a charge if he or she had committed the act, even if that person had not had a criminal intent, or had some technical defence.

In addition, many Aboriginal languages simply do not have words which are equivalent to the language of the Canadian judicial system. Words such as "arrest," "bail" and "probation," to name only a few, resist easy and clear translation. Those translations which do exist often give the terms a coloured or loaded meaning. Also, Aboriginal cultures may place less significance on measured distance, time and location than do non-Aboriginal cultures—leading to difficulties when Aboriginal witnesses are questioned as to when something happened or where something happened.

The 1986 census reported 28% of all Manitoba's Aboriginal population had an Aboriginal language as the first language spoken as a child and still understood. For persons identified in the census as "North American Indian only," the proportion with an Aboriginal language as a mother tongue was reported at 52%.[52] It was reported that 84% of residents on-reserve retained their Aboriginal mother language in the home, compared to only 31% off-reserve.[53]

The fact is that one of the most frequent complaints we heard during the hearings was that Aboriginal people did not understand the court process and did not understand their options at various stages in the process.

> A probation officer came across a certain client who had gone through the system three times. Three times he had failed to do his community service order. [The] probation officer found that the boy didn't understand English. [He] spoke to the boy in Saulteaux and explained to him what his community service obligations were and within a week the boy had done them.
>
> Ron Richard
> Manitoba Metis Federation

Most of the time when a native person is charged, they don't always fully understand what is said, or understand the charge. They don't understand what the judge is saying, and it's these people that plead guilty.

Joan Soulier
South Indian Lake

As important as it is to understand what is going on in court, it is more important to understand one's rights when dealing with the police. Statements made to the police are the primary tool of the prosecution to convince persons to plead guilty, and are the primary evidence for the prosecution in trials. While the police must advise accused persons of their rights to remain silent and to consult a lawyer, it is not at all clear that these rights are being fully understood. An ability to communicate in English is no assurance of an ability to understand fine distinctions and interpretations of legal terms. There are no court communicators available at the police interview stage, which is arguably more important than having them present in court.

Level of Service Provided

Generally, the justice system is designed for a population that is highly urbanized, literate in English or in French, and has a basic understanding of how to take advantage of existing support services.

The justice system serves Winnipeg best, and then the other large non-Aboriginal centres. Remote reserves in the North are the absolutely last priority of the justice system. Getting protection from police and obtaining access to courts, justice services, lawyers and jails are all the more difficult for Aboriginal people because these services involve added cost and travel.

Approximately 37% of Manitoba's Aboriginal population live on reserves (62% of registered Indians). We estimate that 36% of Manitoba's Aboriginal population live in the north of the province, compared to only three per cent of the rest of the population. We estimate that a further 31% of Manitoba's Aboriginal population live in the city of Winnipeg, compared to 60% of Manitoba's non-Aboriginal population.[54]

A lack of facilities, resources and services in Aboriginal communities becomes another factor in the poor treatment of Aboriginal people. Decisions not to release a person on bail, probation or parole sometimes stem from the fact that needed supervision or counselling services do not exist in the person's home community.[55]

The Under-Employment of Aboriginal People in the Justice System

According to the Province's affirmative action statistics, as of April 4, 1991, only 3.16% or 36 of the Department of Justice's 1,141 employees (excluding corrections) were Aboriginal. Of these 36, 12 were court communicators (which are positions only available to Aboriginal persons), two were human rights officers, two were sheriffs and one was an accountant. There is only one judge, and no one in management positions within the department, no lawyers, and no policy and research officers.

In the correctional field, the numbers are somewhat better, with 6.43% or 77 Aboriginal employees out of 1,197 total employees. Of these 77 people, 48 are correctional officers and 27 are counsellors (including probation officers).

This under-employment represents a clear systemic bias against Aboriginal people. We also believe the exclusion of Aboriginal people from decision-making positions within the justice system virtually guarantees that none of the discretionary decisions made by system personnel will be culturally appropriate to Aboriginal people.

Where Discrimination Occurs in the Justice System

The factors that we have considered above come into play at a variety of points in the justice system and help to bring about the adverse impacts that we have identified earlier. In this section we identify the major points of discrimination in the criminal justice system. Subsequent chapters will provide detailed analyses of these issues and propose a variety of reforms.

The Selection of Who Is to be Policed

Differences in crime statistics between Aboriginal and non-Aboriginal people result, at least in part, from the manner in which the behaviour of Aboriginal people becomes categorized and stigmatized. This may happen because, to a certain extent, police tend to view the world in terms of "respectable" people and "criminal" types. Criminal types are thought to exhibit certain characteristics which provide cues to the officer to initiate action. Thus, the police may tend to stop a higher proportion of people who are visibly different from the dominant society, including Aboriginal people, for minor offences, simply because they believe that such people may tend to commit more serious crimes. Members of groups that are perceived to be a danger to the public order are given much less latitude in their behaviour before the police take action. An example might be a group of Aboriginal youth who gather in a park. Because it is believed that their presence may be a precursor to more deviant action, they are subjected to controlling activities by the police.

Some studies of the causal relationship between poverty and crime have focussed on the attention which police forces and legislators give to the activities of the poor, while upper-class conduct, such as tax evasion, conflicts of interest, unsafe working conditions, polluting, etc., go relatively unregulated and unenforced. "Crime and delinquency are 'found' among the poor because that is where they are sought."[56]

Many who appeared before us complained about being stopped on the street or on a country road and questioned about their activities. We heard complaints that Aboriginal people are charged with offences more often than their non-Aboriginal counterparts. They may also be charged with a multiplicity of offences arising out of the same incident. Many charges are never proceeded with, and appear to have been unnecessary. We believe that many Aboriginal people are arrested and held in custody, where a non-Aboriginal person in the same circumstances either might not be arrested at all, or might not be held.

Pre-Trial Detention

Judges traditionally consider factors such as employment, mobility, family ties, whether the accused is employed, whether the accused has a fixed address and the accused's links with the community when determining whether to grant bail. Because of their disadvantaged position, the impact on Aboriginal people is negative.

Legal Representation

Because of their low incomes, Aboriginal people are not as able as non-Aboriginal people to obtain legal representation. Legal Aid rejects more than 6,500 applications per year, and has rules that severely limit the availability of Legal Aid services for civil and family cases and for certain "minor" criminal cases—even though any criminal conviction results in a criminal record with its consequent negative influence. Further, Legal Aid financial guidelines mean that the "working poor," who earn too much to qualify for Legal Aid but cannot afford a lawyer, go without representation.

The Hearing Process

Accused persons usually face a variety of court hearings before the charges against them are disposed of. As we noted above, the court procedures are often quite culturally foreign to Aboriginal people. Not only may certain terms and concepts be unfamiliar to them, but Aboriginal people may feel that, out of respect to the officers of the court, they should provide the answers which they believe the officials are expecting.

But the court system itself discriminates against Aboriginal people in its rules and procedures. The court system involves several court hearings. When the period of time between court hearings is a minimum of one month, as in the case of circuit court, even a simple matter can take several months to resolve. This delay has a negative impact on the entire Aboriginal community—victims, witnesses and their family members, as well as the accused. We were told that people often plead guilty simply to bring this prolonged period of anxiety to an end.

The circuit courts do not provide separate adult, youth and family court sittings, something which is unheard of in the city of Winnipeg.

In addition, the Court of Queen's Bench, the only court in Manitoba which holds jury trials, does not hold any trials in Aboriginal communities. As a result, Aboriginal people accused of serious crimes are rarely tried by juries comprised of members of their home community.

Sentencing

Another factor in Aboriginal incarceration is the employment and income status of the accused. Our survey of lawyers found that 79% (67 of 85) felt that the employment and income status of the accused was important or very important to the sentencing judge.

Some studies report that pre-trial detention contributes to more convictions and harsher sentences, as the sentencing judge already knows that the police and, in many cases, another judge have found the offender should be in jail.[57] The high rates of Aboriginal pre-trial detention thus may contribute to incarceration rates.

It is often said that pleading guilty is a mitigating factor in sentencing, being an indication that the offender accepts responsibility for the crime and is remorseful. If that is true, Aboriginal persons do not appear to benefit as much as they should, because they are pleading guilty more often than non-Aboriginal persons, but are being sentenced more harshly.

It is also said that Aboriginal persons receive harsher treatment in the justice system because they commit more crimes, have longer criminal records, face a greater number of charges or face more serious charges. Our analysis of Provincial Court data shows that, while Aboriginal offenders are incarcerated 2.5 times as much as non-Aboriginal offenders, on average Aboriginal and non-Aboriginal accused had the same number of previous convictions, Aboriginal accused faced 1.24 times as many charges, and 1.35 times as many Aboriginal accused faced more than one charge.

On the other hand, the available data indicate that Aboriginal persons are more likely to commit offences against the person. Reserves are experiencing as much as six times the rate of offences against the person as non-reserve areas.

There are other indications, however, that seriousness of the offence is not an adequate explanation for Aboriginal incarceration rates. The Provincial Court data indicate that for "common offences" (mischief, wilful damage, theft of less than $1,000 and common assault), Aboriginal men aged 18–34 were more likely to receive sentences of incarceration and the sentences they received tended to be longer than those given to non-Aboriginal men in the same age category. Aboriginal women aged 18–34 were more likely than non-Aboriginal women to receive sentences of incarceration, but sentences were not significantly different from those given to non-Aboriginal women in the same age category.

In addition, Aboriginal persons consistently have represented approximately 60% of total fine defaulters admitted to jails, even though Aboriginal offenders had fewer outstanding fines.[58]

For these reasons we conclude the number of charges and the seriousness of charges do not adequately account for Aboriginal rates of incarceration.

Conclusion

Historically, the justice system has discriminated against Aboriginal people by providing legal sanction for their oppression. This oppression of previous generations forced Aboriginal people into their current state of social and economic distress. Now, a seemingly neutral justice system discriminates against current generations of Aboriginal people by applying laws which have an adverse impact on people of lower socio-economic status. This is no less racial discrimination; it is merely "laundered" racial discrimination. It is untenable to say that discrimination which builds upon the effects of racial discrimination is not racial discrimination itself. Past injustices cannot be ignored or built upon.

Whatever legal niceties may be made as to how to classify the discrimination that is going on, whether it offends the *Charter* or not, the point is that Aboriginal people are

experiencing adverse impacts. The justice system should be trying to find ways to alleviate these adverse impacts.

A century of paternalism and duplicity in government policies has had disastrous
consequences. Canada's original citizens have lost much of their land and livelihood,
family life has been ruptured, and community leadership and cohesion have broken
down. These policies have left many Aboriginal people not only impoverished, but also
dependent and demoralized. These government policies must also be held ultimately
responsible for a good portion of the high rates of Aboriginal crime, which are the almost
inevitable result of social breakdown and poverty.

The conclusion that Aboriginal over-representation in criminal behaviour has
deep social and historical roots is not unique to Canada. Another country dealing with
the same issues is Australia. The 1991 Royal Commission into Aboriginal Deaths in Custody investigated 99 deaths of Aboriginal persons while in jail. Many of the comments of
the Australian Royal Commission apply equally to Canadian-Aboriginal relations.

> From that history many things flow which are of central importance to the issue
> of Aboriginal over-representation in custody. The first is the deliberate and sys-
> tematic disempowerment of Aboriginal people starting with dispossession
> from their land and proceeding to almost every aspect of their life....
>
> Every turn in the policy of government and the practice of the non-Aboriginal
> community was postulated on the inferiority of the Aboriginal people; the origi-
> nal expropriation of their land was based on the idea that the land was not
> occupied and the people uncivilised; the protection policy was based on the
> view that Aboriginal people could not achieve a place in the non-Aboriginal
> society and that they must be protected against themselves while the race died
> out; the assimilationist policy assumed that their culture and way of life is without
> value and that we confer a favour on them by assimilating them into our ways;
> even to the point of taking their children and removing them from family....[59]

We believe it is clear that the social situation of Aboriginal people is a direct result
of a history of social, economic and cultural repression, all carried out under a cloak of
legality. This is a disturbing picture. But it also makes it clear that the high crime rates
that characterize Aboriginal communities are not a natural phenomenon, but a direct
result of government policies.

To change this situation will require a real commitment to ending social inequality in Canadian society, something to which no government in Canada has committed
itself to date. This will be a far-reaching endeavour and involve much more than the justice system as it is understood currently. It will require governments to commit themselves to economic and social policies that will allow Aboriginal citizens to participate
fully in Canadian life. In the case of Aboriginal people, it will also involve a significant
redistribution of political and economic power as governments honour the historical
commitments made to Aboriginal people through treaties and other formal agreements.

Despite the magnitude of the problems, there is much the justice system can do to assist in reducing the degree to which Aboriginal people come into conflict with the law. It can reduce the ways in which it discriminates against Aboriginal people and the ways in which it adds to Aboriginal alienation.

More importantly, it can give to Aboriginal people the opportunity to direct their own lives and communities through significant involvement within the existing system and by assisting them in the development of their own justice systems.

Such a development would increase the level of fairness and equality for Aboriginal people in the system. As Rosalie Abella, the commissioner of the 1984 federal Commission on Equality in Employment, has stated, "Equality is evolutionary, in process as well as in substance, it is cumulative, it is contextual, and it is persistent."[60] She describes equality this way:

> Equality is, at the very least, freedom from adverse discrimination. But what constitutes adverse discrimination changes with time, with information, with experience and with insight. What we tolerated as a society 100, 50 or even 10 years ago is no longer necessarily tolerable. Equality is thus a process—a process of constant and flexible examination, of vigilant introspection, and of aggressive open-mindedness.... If in this ongoing process we are not always sure what "equality" means, most of us have a good understanding of what is "fair". And what is happening today in Canada to women, native people, disabled persons and many racial and ethnic minorities is not fair.
>
> It is not fair that many people in these groups have restricted employment opportunities, limited access to decision-making processes that critically affect them, little public visibility as contributing Canadians, and a circumscribed range of options generally. It may be understandable, given history, culture, economics, and even human nature, but by no standards is it fair.[61]

Chief Justice Dickson, on behalf of the majority of the Supreme Court of Canada, said, "The interests of true equality may well require differentiation in treatment."[62] In *Andrews v. Law Society of British Columbia,* at 299, Mr. Justice McIntyre said:

> It must be recognized ... that every difference in treatment between individuals under the law will not necessarily result in inequality and, as well, that identical treatment may frequently produce serious inequality.

Madame Justice Wilson, writing for the Supreme Court of Canada in *R. v. Turpin et al.* (1989), 69 C.R. (3d) 97, at 126–28, says:

> In concluding that s. 15 is not violated in this case, I realize that I am rejecting the proposition accepted by several Courts of Appeal in Canada that it is a fundamental principle under s. 15 of the Charter that the criminal law apply equally throughout the country.... I do not think ... that this can be stated in terms of "fundamental principle" and in bald and absolute form for the purposes of s. 15. In my view, s. 15 mandates a case by case analysis.

It is important that a concept of equality be developed that respects differences more fully and that understands how different cultures may have different concepts of equality. Rosalie Abella expanded on the importance of accommodating differences as a part of equality.

> Sometimes equality means treating people the same, despite their differences, and sometimes it means treating them as equals by accommodating their differences.

> Formerly, we thought that equality only meant sameness and that treating persons as equals meant treating everyone the same. We now know that to treat everyone the same may be to offend the notion of equality. Ignoring differences may mean ignoring legitimate needs. Equality means nothing if it does not mean that we are of equal worth regardless of differences in gender, race, ethnicity, or disability. The projected, mythical, and attributed meaning of these differences cannot be permitted to exclude full participation.

> Ignoring differences and refusing to accommodate them is a denial of equal access and opportunity. It is discrimination. To reduce discrimination, we must create and maintain barrier-free environments so that individuals can have genuine access free from arbitrary obstructions to demonstrate and exercise fully their potential. This may mean treating some people differently by removing the obstacles to equality of opportunity they alone face for no demonstrably justifiable reason....[63]

> Discriminatory distinctions are only those which are unreasonably exclusionary, which are not objectively justifiable by standards of necessity, safety or civility, as opposed to standards of preference, economic exigency or tradition. This includes too the concept of reasonable accommodation imported from human rights jurisprudence; namely, *is there an alternative available which is equally conducive to the achievement of the law's or program's purpose which has a lesser adverse impact?* [64] [Our emphasis]

The notion of differing concepts of equality was well presented to the Royal Commission on Bilingualism and Biculturalism by an unidentified Quebec lawyer:

> When they speak of equality, English Canadians mean equality of individual civil rights, that is of persons considered individually, while when we French Canadians speak of equality we do not mean civil rights at all, we mean collective national rights, we mean the rights of the French Canadian nation to develop in accordance with its own characteristics.[65]

This raises the important question of how we view individuals, and especially how we view their relationship to their group identity. Professor Sarah Salter, in a thoughtful paper entitled "Inherent Bias in Liberal Thought,"[66] argues that the equality with which we are most familiar is based on a concept where the individual identifies himself or herself as a person *separate* from others. Equality, therefore, means dealing with separate, autonomous individuals. Professor Salter argues that we must also acknowledge the concept of "extended identity," where individuals identify themselves *with* others.

Those whose identity is based on notions of autonomy place higher value on property or power as a means to secure the autonomy, whereas those whose identity is based on notions of extended identity place greater emphasis on relationships.

It is clear that the idea of extended identity applies to the Aboriginal experience. Aboriginal people identify themselves in relation to their group. Whatever harms the group, harms the identification of persons within the group. Aboriginal people place very great emphasis on the interdependence of all things.

One often hears the question of rights discussed as a conflict between individual and collective rights. For Aboriginal people and others who have a philosophy of extended identity, there is no conflict—the individual and the group are connected so closely that a choice cannot be made between them. The interests of both the individual and the group must be pursued.

One expression of an Aboriginal view of equality is found in the 1988 *Report of the Task Force on Aboriginal Peoples in Federal Corrections*:

> Many Aboriginal nations recognize four sacred colours: black, red, white and yellow. These colours may be seen as representing the four primary peoples of mankind. As with all other creations, the four peoples have their own place in the Sacred Circle.
>
> To maintain the Creator's design of balance and harmony within Creation, each people must recognize their own place in the Circle and recognize that, while different, they must treat each other equally. If one people were to try to become the same as another, the result would be imbalance and disharmony. Disservice is done to the Creator if the differences of the four peoples are not recognized and honoured. The Sacred Circle would lose its harmony if the four peoples were not treated equally. Because of many Aboriginal peoples' deep roots in their own culture, the delivery of service to those individuals must take their spiritual and cultural background into account, including such values as art, language, family and community. Aboriginal-specific programs and services are thus warranted whenever they are required to ensure the same opportunity of results.[67]

Equality and fairness must, in the future, be the hallmarks of Canadian society's treatment of Aboriginal people. This will involve addressing the legacy of centuries of oppression and exploitation that has marked Canadian policy to the present day. The justice system has been a central instrument of the destructive policies of the past. We believe it can play a positive role in the future in helping to make reasonable accommodation for Aboriginal peoples as it deals with individuals who come into conflict with the law, and with the larger Aboriginal community as that community takes control of its own justice system.

CHAPTER 5

ABORIGINAL AND TREATY RIGHTS

[T]he earth does not belong to man; man belongs to the earth. This we know. All things are connected like the blood which unites one family. All things are connected. Whatever befalls the earth befalls the sons of the earth. Man did not weave the web of life; he is merely a strand in it. Whatever he does to the web, he does to himself.

> Chief Seattle, 1854
> Aboriginal Worldview

Man is the measure of all things.

> Protagoras, Greek Philosopher
> (458–410 B.C.)
> European Worldview

Introduction

When Europeans came to the Americas they were considered outsiders but, in accordance with the Aboriginal view, were permitted to share in the land and its resources. Elders have told us that, in the eyes of the Creator, the Europeans as outsiders could not enjoy the same rights as the original inhabitants. Whatever rights the Europeans wanted had to be sought from those who were placed upon the land first by the Creator. It is a belief common to many Aboriginal societies that the Creator placed Aboriginal people upon this land first for a reason, and that, as the first ones on the land, they were placed in a special relationship to it. In the worldview of Aboriginal people, the Europeans were visitors and, as such, were bound to respect the obligations of that status.

For Aboriginal peoples, the land was part of their identity as a people. The earth was their Mother, the animals were their spiritual kin and all were part of the greater whole, which was life. Their culture was grounded in nature. Time was marked by the changing seasons and the rising and setting of the sun, rather than by numbers, and their existence was marked by an acceptance of and respect for their natural surroundings and their place in the scheme of things. The thinking of Aboriginal peoples was cyclical, rather than linear like that of the Europeans. Everything was thought of in terms of its relation to the whole, not as individual bits of information to be compared to one another. Aboriginal philosophy was holistic, and did not lend itself readily to dichotomies or categories as did European philosophy. So, for Aboriginal people, their rights were—and still are—seen in broad, conceptual terms.

The most fundamental of those rights is the right to their identity as Aboriginal people. Since that identity was derived largely from the land they used and occupied before the arrival of the Europeans, they believe they had—and still have—certain rights in regard to the land, including continuing habitation and use of the land, whether it be for hunting, fishing, trapping, gathering food and medicines, or for any other traditional pursuits.

This right to identity also implies the further right to self-determination, for it is through self-determination that a people preserves their collective identity. The right to self-determination can take several forms. It includes, among many other things, the authority to retain one's culture in the face of threatened assimilation, the right of a child to be raised in his or her own language and culture, and the right to choose between an Aboriginal and a non-Aboriginal way of life. This latter right is violated if the traditional economy of an Aboriginal group is disrupted severely or damaged by the encroachments of a civilization that exploits or abuses natural resources on a large scale, such as a hydroelectric project, a pipeline or a strip mine. Further, the right to self-determination implies the right to take charge of one's own affairs so as to ensure effectively that Aboriginal identity and culture will be respected in the political sphere. These are the Aboriginal rights of the indigenous people of Canada.

Like Aboriginal rights, treaty rights are also understood by Aboriginal peoples in broad, conceptual terms. Unlike Aboriginal rights, however, treaty rights are more susceptible to the restrictive interpretations of the federal and provincial governments. Governments have claimed that treaty rights are limited to written promises made to Aboriginal groups by the Crown in specific treaties. In return for these promises, First Nations in Manitoba are purported to have agreed to "yield up" the land they traditionally used and occupied, and to move to reserves in order to make room for the expanding white settlements.

The signing of the post-Confederation numbered treaties in Manitoba was a solemn affair, resulting from negotiation through a bilateral, consensual process. Indian tribes in Manitoba had been using the formality of the treaty-making process for many generations prior to the arrival of the Europeans and, to those tribes, the solemnity of the occasion marked the new relationship. The representatives of the Crown were well aware of the importance of the process to the Indian tribes and, as some writers have pointed out, took advantage of that sense of importance. To a large extent, Indian tribes negotiated for what they could, but were faced with negotiators whose mandate was to obtain signatures upon the treaty documents by whatever means necessary. Their view of the importance of the treaty differed considerably from the Indians'.

The European objectives were to exercise complete control over the land, and to make it safe for settlement and for the development of its resources. In negotiating the treaties, the newcomers sought to provide the minimum in benefits in return for peace and control of the land.

Nevertheless, many provisions in the treaties were included at the insistence of the Aboriginal groups. Many verbal promises, not included in the written versions of the treaties, were made to reassure the Indian representatives about the exact nature of the agreements. The promises, both written and oral, were to be good "as long as the sun shines, the grass grows, and the rivers flow." These promises are just as important as the written words defining treaty rights.

Aboriginal people consider the treaties to be agreements made between sovereign nations. Aboriginal signatories agreed to give up only their rights to certain tracts of land, not their right to govern their own lives and affairs. While Europeans considered the treaties as transfers of title to land, Aboriginal nations perceived them merely to be agreements to share the land, as they did with the animals and other groups. Aboriginal peoples perceived the treaties as agreements only to share the land because the concept of legal title to land, as the Europeans understood it, was foreign to their culture. Clearly, however, Aboriginal people did have a strong concept of territory—individual occupation of specific parcels of land was an acknowledged part of almost all Aboriginal societies. However, land was not something which an individual could divide, transfer, surrender, destroy or own to the exclusion of all others. The land was there to be shared, as it was the source of all life.

Today, Aboriginal peoples believe their treaty rights have become a series of broken promises. Time and time again during our hearings, people spoke eloquently about their understanding of the treaties and their frustrations at the manner of their treatment. Aboriginal people in Manitoba firmly believe that despite, or perhaps more properly, because of the treaties they entered into with the Crown, they were to have been allowed to retain part of their land, to retain their identities, their cultures, their languages, their religions and their traditional ways of life, including their laws and their systems of government. Those things have been denied to them.

Even the manner in which the reserve land was set aside for the various First Nation signatories has been a source of frustration. Instead of reserves being viewed by government as land for which Aboriginal people retain their original title, the government has persisted in the view that land was surrendered to the Crown, which then "gave it back" to Aboriginal people.

Aboriginal people were to have been partners in the new arrangement, with an equal say in defining their ongoing relationship with the Crown. They have been denied that.

The various promises made under treaties were explained to and understood by Indians in broad, conceptual terms, and were to include a commitment to the economic development of reserves and to the education of the members of their community, and a respect for the tribe's traditional form of government. The treaties, according to the understanding of Aboriginal peoples, were arrangements between two groups who had agreed to share the land and respect each other's autonomy. Aboriginal people wanted to choose and direct how Western influences would affect them, but they never got the chance.

Today, the treaties are still important to Aboriginal peoples because they represent a state of affairs that was abrogated arbitrarily and unilaterally by one party: the government. That is why Aboriginal peoples insist that the Crown respect the "spirit" and "intent" of the treaties, and not just the precise written "terms."

In the courts, in Parliament and in land claims negotiations, the messages from the non-Aboriginal side of the process have been mixed. In 1852 the Upper Canada Court of Queen's Bench rejected the notion of Indian rights, arguing that "the common law is not part savage and part civilized."[1] In 1964, in a Supreme Court of Canada decision dealing with the important issue of whether Indian hunting rights were nullified by the general provisions of the *Migratory Birds Convention Act*, the court was more intrigued by the issue of whether there had to be proof that the duck in question was wild rather than tame.[2] With respect to the issue concerning the validity of hunting rights guaranteed by treaty, the court ruled those rights invalid in two sentences by relying upon the Court of Appeal's earlier judgment in the case, in which Parliament was viewed as possessing the authority to breach treaties if it intentionally chose to do so.

In the 1970s a remarkable shift in judicial attitudes began. The Supreme Court of Canada began to demonstrate its change in thinking when six of seven judges declared that Aboriginal title to land was recognized by the common law.[3] The most dramatic example is a 1984 Supreme Court decision which affirmed an Indian band's title to reserve land on the basis of the pre-contact Indian legal order.[4] In a case the following year, the Supreme Court also held that it was no longer acceptable to be bound by the biases and prejudices of another era, and that "treaties and statutes relating to Indians should be liberally construed and doubtful expressions resolved in favour of the Indians...."[5]

These recent pronouncements from the Supreme Court are clearly inconsistent with the traditionally hostile judgments of the past. They have been followed by a number of other decisions over the past five years that have further expanded the importance to be given to Aboriginal and treaty rights at law. Nevertheless, many questions and uncertainties remain regarding the content of these rights, their effect on existing legislation and the scope of Crown obligations to Aboriginal people.

If the courts have been unclear, then Parliament and non-Aboriginal political leaders have been equally so. The long-standing question as to the exact nature and extent of Aboriginal and treaty rights has yet to be resolved through legislation, or agreement, while legislation dealing adequately with the issue of Aboriginal self-government has been nearly nonexistent.

The expectations raised by four First Ministers' Conferences in the mid-1980s and the House of Commons Special Committee Report of 1983 on Indian self-government have yet to yield the promised and needed constitutional and legislative reforms.

The proper method of land claims settlements, as well, has yet to be determined. In the Yukon and Northwest Territories, negotiations have been dragging on since 1973; in British Columbia they have barely begun; on the Prairies, agreements-in-principle to resolve outstanding treaty land entitlements either have not been reached or are yet to be implemented. In Manitoba a 1984 agreement-in-principle between treaty entitlement chiefs and the provincial and federal governments to resolve outstanding treaty land entitlements was never ratified by the federal government.

The absence of clarity or significant initiatives on the part of both the federal and provincial governments has resulted in frustration, anger and conflict. This has cast a dark cloud over the relationship between Aboriginal people and government, not only in Manitoba but throughout Canada. As we will indicate in greater detail below, rectifying the historic injustices, while extending proper respect and substance to Aboriginal and treaty rights, is vital for the well-being of all Canadians. Clearly, restoring honour to the Crown, while rebuilding Aboriginal communities, is needed.

Aboriginal-Crown Relations

The relationship between Aboriginal peoples and the newcomers has been of great importance to both sides since the earliest days of contact between European explorers and the original inhabitants of this land. Representatives of European monarchs arriving on this continent found Indian nations with highly sophisticated economies, governments, cultures, legal regimes, religions and trading relations. Recent evidence suggests that there were as many as eight million indigenous people throughout what is now Canada and the United States in the early 17th century, with approximately three million residing in what was to become Canada.

The Indian nations of the eastern seaboard welcomed the newcomers, assisted them to survive in a foreign land and offered to share the resources of their territory with them. Formal treaties defining a system of peaceful co-existence and respect for each group's separate identity were negotiated in the early 1600s. This pattern of utilizing treaties to determine the nature of the European-Aboriginal relationship was proposed by each side, as it reflected the approach previously used both in North America and in Europe.

The British Crown adopted this practice (already implemented by the Dutch and other European nations at least as early as 1664) by negotiating the Two Row Wampum Treaty with the Iroquois Confederacy. At the core of this treaty was the concept of peaceful co-existence. The British were to travel on the river of life in their large ship containing their laws, religious beliefs, customs, traditions and ways of life. Travelling alongside, but separate in their canoe, were the Iroquois, who carried with them the Great Law of

Peace and their traditions, customs, spiritual beliefs and way of life. Each nation would enjoy the bounty of the lands and waters but would continue to govern its own affairs as independent nations.

Great Britain, for a time, did pursue a policy of respecting the land and harvesting rights, as well as the autonomy of Indian nations. Not only was this in keeping with emerging standards of international law, enunciated by Francisco de Vitoria, Bartolome de las Casas, Grotius and others, but it also reflected self-interest. Britain wished to maximize commercial trade with Indian nations, particularly regarding furs, which was fostered by developing a positive relationship.

In addition, the numbers and military superiority of the Aboriginal inhabitants meant that peace and friendship were an astute policy to pursue. Furthermore, the British government was in competition with other Europeans, especially the French. Thus, Indian allies were vital to British ambitions. As a result, the treaty-making process, coupled with respect for Aboriginal land rights and sovereignty, quickly became the cornerstone of official British policy. Numerous treaties were negotiated with various Indian nations along the east coast throughout the 1700s, including several with the Micmac and Malecite nations of what has become Atlantic Canada. This policy was codified in a sense through the *Royal Proclamation* of October 7, 1763, which was promulgated after the British victory over France and the Treaty of Paris of 1763. The *Royal Proclamation* was designed to determine both the future of the newly acquired colonies of Quebec, Florida and Grenada, as well as relations with Indian nations.

The *Royal Proclamation* officially declared that the Indian nations who remained within the borders of any of the British colonies were not to be "molested" in their possession of traditional territories. The 1763 Proclamation of King George III put it this way:

> And Whereas it is just and reasonable, and essential to our Interest, and the Security of our Colonies, that the several Nations or Tribes of Indians with whom We are connected, and who live under our Protection, should not be molested or disturbed in the Possession of such Parts of our Dominions and Territories as, not having been ceded to or purchased by Us, are reserved to them, or any of them, as their Hunting Grounds.[6]

If the Indian nations chose to surrender any or all of their lands within the new and existing colonies, then this could occur by treaty, with the specific process described in the Proclamation. It is interesting to note that the major elements of the treaty process outlined by the *Royal Proclamation* (such as requiring a public meeting in the presence of Crown representatives and allowing only the Crown, rather than private individuals, to make treaties) are still reflected in the *Indian Act* surrender requirements and the general land claims process. Those Aboriginal people residing outside these colonies were to be left untouched by settlers and local colonial governments, according to the Proclamation.

While much has transpired since 1763 in the Aboriginal-Crown relationship, the essential elements of the *Royal Proclamation* remain. The Proclamation has become one of the founding constitutional documents of Canada and has clear implications for Manitoba. It is appended as a schedule to the *Constitution Act, 1982* and expressly referred to in section 25(a) as part of the Aboriginal rights shielded from any negative effects of the *Charter of Rights and Freedoms*.

This treaty-making process, which the Proclamation enshrined, was used to acquire land for settlement throughout most of modern-day Ontario from the beginnings of Upper Canada until the Williams Treaty of 1923. (An adhesion to Treaty 9 dates even later.)

Such treaty making was used in what became Manitoba, beginning with Lord Selkirk's treaty in 1811 and followed by the numbered treaties, starting with Treaties 1 and 2 in 1871.

However, treaty making for Aboriginal people was not started by the *Royal Proclamation*, for the evidence is clear that Aboriginal people were making treaties among themselves long before the arrival of the Europeans and for some time after their arrival, prior to the Proclamation.

While some have argued that the terms of the *Royal Proclamation of 1763* are limited to certain geographically defined areas of North America, and that the area formerly covered by the Crown grant to the Hudson's Bay Company is not included, we think that such an interpretation misses the point. The *Royal Proclamation* did not create Aboriginal title and it is clear that it is not the only legal recognition of Aboriginal rights. Part of the importance of the Proclamation is the process which it identified as the means by which Aboriginal title was to be addressed. It was a clear recognition that the rights of Aboriginal peoples were to be "purchased" fairly through treaties and not simply to be ignored.

Aboriginal title has been part of our common law since settlement. Imperial, colonial, federal and provincial governments have never attempted to legislatively define either Aboriginal title or Aboriginal rights. The Crown has never sought to expressly extinguish Aboriginal title. The one exception to this appears to be the case of the Metis, to whom 1.4 million acres were to be granted in exchange for their "Indian title" under the *Manitoba Act*, 1870. Neither the judiciary nor governments has delineated a clear perspective regarding the meaning and status to be attributed to the rights of the original owners of Manitoba. For this reason, uncertainty remains today as to the full extent of outstanding Aboriginal and treaty rights in this province.

Two fundamentally different perspectives exist. For their part, Aboriginal people still believe that they have an obligation to protect and nurture the land and all living things. They regard themselves as stewards or caretakers of their traditional territory, with a continuing right to use the land and share in its bounty. They further believe that they have maintained the authority to govern their own affairs.

Treaties are still seen by them as solemn agreements between sovereign nations, designed to confirm their Aboriginal rights and supplement them with express commitments from the Crown. In return, the Aboriginal nations agreed to share their land with the Crown for the benefit of its subjects, by allowing the Crown to make land available for settlement. Other lands were reserved for exclusive Aboriginal use under Aboriginal control.

Federal and provincial governments, on the other hand, have tended to view the relationship in a rather different light. The Crown wished to acquire land free from Aboriginal title so that it could resell it to immigrants seeking a new start. The Crown wished to populate its new colonies rapidly and extensively. Governments believed that Aboriginal peoples would eventually disappear. They sought to foster this process through policies of assimilation. Governments clearly thought that Aboriginal rights would decline in importance, and the treaties in Ontario and the Prairies were designed to allow that transition to occur at an appropriate pace. The treaties themselves were drafted to reflect an absolute surrender of Aboriginal title to land, while contrary assurances of an ongoing, respectful relationship were being given by Crown negotiators. While the Crown's representatives were making promises during treaty negotiations that Aboriginal people would not be disturbed in their way of life, the federal government was developing a policy designed to achieve the opposite.

Over time, the federal and provincial governments came increasingly to the view that the treaties and Aboriginal rights were relics of the past that could be ignored with impunity. Once the governments had achieved title over the land, the treaties had no significance to them.

What little significance the treaties did retain for the federal and provincial governments was largely a result of court decisions and the reluctant acceptance that they were still important in the eyes of Aboriginal people. However, the effect of the treaties was restricted as much as possible. The nation-to-nation relationship that had been the cornerstone of dealings between the Crown and Aboriginal peoples for three centuries was transformed thoroughly during the 20th century, after most of the Manitoba treaties had been signed.

As we have discussed in our chapter on the history of the relationship between Aboriginal people and the justice system in Manitoba, much of the century which followed the signing of the treaties was marked by the cultural repression and impoverishment of Aboriginal people. Indian agents tightly controlled the economic and political affairs of Aboriginal communities. The process of reasserting sovereignty has been a slow and often painful one for Aboriginal people. Gradual gains such as enhanced civil rights were offset by setbacks such as the disastrous child welfare policies of the 1960s and 1970s. Ironically, it was a government policy document, advocating the extinguishment of rights and the assimilation of cultures, which provided the spark to reignite Aboriginal self-determination. The 1969 federal White Paper galvanized response and resulted in a new political cohesion of Indian groups.

The Devolution of Indian Affairs

Another of the repercussions of the rejection of the White Paper was the acceleration of the removal of the individual Indian agents. Although Indian bands began evicting agents in 1965, the vast majority remained under the tight control of the local agents as the 1970s began. This changed rapidly as the Department of Indian Affairs withdrew its officials to district and regional offices, thereby allowing chiefs and councils to run their own meetings and set their own priorities. Bands began to establish their own civil services and to operate their own programs on reserves. The process of devolving control over the delivery of community services has continued over the past 20 years. It is extremely important to realize that local Indian governments have only been functioning with any level of authority for little more than two decades.

The *Calder* Case and Land Claims

The White Paper of 1969 committed the federal government to respond to historic grievances based on a failure to fulfil treaty promises to land and on illegal losses of reserve land or band funds over the years. Dr. Lloyd Barber was appointed as the Indian Claims Commissioner and he quickly discovered that there were numerous outstanding claims involving a massive amount of land and money. The federal government responded by creating a branch within the Department of Indian Affairs to fund claimant groups in their attempts to document the historical basis of claims. Federal officials were appointed to negotiate resolution of the grievances.

Assertion of rights based on Aboriginal title to land continued to be rejected by both federal and provincial governments until the Supreme Court of Canada delivered its judgment in *Calder v. Attorney General of British Columbia,* [1973] S.C.R. 313. This landmark case was brought by the Nishga of northern British Columbia, who argued that they had possessed Aboriginal title to their traditional territory since time immemorial and had never surrendered or lost their rights to the land. Six of the seven judges who examined these issues agreed that Aboriginal title was a valid legal concept recognized by Canadian common law. They were divided equally, however, as to whether colonial legislation in British Columbia had effectively extinguished the Aboriginal title of the Nishga. Mr. Justice Judson, on behalf of two others, concluded that this pre-Confederation legislation dealing with Crown land generally was sufficiently inconsistent with the continued existence of Aboriginal title so as to extinguish it. Mr. Justice Hall's decision, concurred with by two others, disagreed, as he declared that Aboriginal title could be terminated only by legislation that explicitly stated this effect in clear and plain language. The seventh judge rejected the Nishga's appeal on procedural grounds.

Although the Nishga lost, the fact that six Supreme Court of Canada judges concluded that Aboriginal title still existed as part of the common law forced the federal government to develop a new position. Indian Affairs minister Jean Chretien announced a new federal policy in August of 1973, expressing a willingness to negotiate the settlement of Aboriginal title land claims, which it called "comprehensive claims," in northern Quebec, both territories and British Columbia. The existing policy of resolving treaty and reserve land claims was sustained under the label "specific claims." Southern Quebec and Atlantic Canada were placed in a third and undefined category, and were described incorrectly as entirely non-treaty areas.

Further litigation over the balance of the decade helped clarify the continued existence of Aboriginal title for the Dene in the Mackenzie Valley despite Treaties 8 and 11,[7] for the Cree in northern Quebec,[8] and for the Inuit in the eastern Arctic.[9] Litigation in Manitoba, sparked by hydro-electric development, helped to encourage the parties to ultimately negotiate the Northern Flood Agreement (NFA).

Major claims began to be filed with the federal government almost immediately after it proclaimed its policy shift in 1973. Negotiations were commenced shortly thereafter, but only the impetus of massive resource development projects resulted in the conclusion and implementation of two major land claims settlements, through the James Bay and Northern Quebec Agreement of 1975 (and a small adhesion for the Naskapi through the Northeastern Quebec Agreement of 1978) and the Inuvialuit Agreement of 1984 in the Beaufort Sea region. Negotiations elsewhere have dragged on for years while many other Aboriginal groups wait in line for their claims even to be addressed, as the federal government restricted the number of claims under negotiation to six at any one time until September 1990. Eighteen claims are pending in British Columbia alone.

The Aboriginal title claims process has been limited to First Nations and the Inuit, except in the Yukon and the Northwest Territories, where the Metis and non-status Indians are included. As a result, claims of Metis and unofficial Indian communities are not accepted, leaving the Metis in Manitoba without a negotiation process by which to pursue their land claims. In addition, the federal government is of the view that the land surrender treaties effectively extinguished Aboriginal title in Ontario and the Prairies, with the result that no comprehensive claims can be submitted by First Nations in these four provinces. The federal government also continues to refuse to address Aboriginal title claims in southern Quebec and in Atlantic Canada (except for Labrador).

Constitutional Reform

Another dramatic initiative that affected Aboriginal people was Prime Minister Pierre Trudeau's desire to patriate the Canadian Constitution, along with a "made-in-Canada" amending formula and an entrenched bill of rights. This venture came as response to the pledge of constitutional renewal made during the federal government's campaign against sovereignty-association in the Quebec referendum of 1980. Aboriginal groups were very concerned about how this could violate the treaty commitments reached with the Crown and feared that Canadian control over the Constitution could result in further damage to their rights, or a repeal of federal responsibility altogether. On the other hand, Aboriginal organizations saw the negotiation of new portions of the Constitution as an excellent opportunity to protect their unique Aboriginal and treaty rights from attack by antagonistic federal or provincial governments in the future. At the same time, the possibility was created to achieve proper respect for these rights in the supreme law of the land, so as to overturn years of court decisions that had upheld legislative interference with hunting and fishing rights.

After a coordinated initiative involving all Indian, Inuit and Metis national leaders, the federal cabinet and the Joint Parliamentary Committee agreed in January of 1981 to include a clause in the draft constitution that would recognize Aboriginal and treaty rights. This provision was dropped in November of that year at the insistence of several premiers, as part of the price of obtaining their support for a revised constitutional package. Although the affirmation of these historic rights was deleted, Trudeau replaced it with a clause requiring a constitutional conference to be convened by the prime minister, involving premiers, territorial leaders and representatives of the Indian, Inuit and Metis peoples. As a result of intense lobbying from Aboriginal people and thousands of non-Aboriginal Canadians, the first ministers back-pedalled somewhat and restored the Aboriginal and treaty rights provision, albeit in a watered-down form.

The *Charter of Rights and Freedoms*, proclaimed on April 17, 1982, was a turning point in Canadian history in many ways. As a result of the *Charter*, limitations were imposed upon the power of Parliament and the provinces to pass laws within their jurisdictions. Our courts were invested for the first time with the authority to scrutinize legislation passed and otherwise valid to determine if the overriding rights of Canadians described within the *Constitution Act, 1982* had been violated. The judiciary now had the obligation to strike down any law breaching a fundamental freedom that could not be justified as "a reasonable limit prescribed by law in a free and democratic society" by virtue of section 1 of the *Charter*.

The position of Aboriginal people, both within Canadian law and Canadian society, was changed dramatically by the new Constitution. When the negotiation process was complete, the supreme law of the land included three provisions dealing with Aboriginal peoples. The most important of the three is section 35, which recognized and affirmed the "existing aboriginal and treaty rights of the aboriginal peoples of Canada." Under this provision, Aboriginal peoples are defined as including "the Indian, Inuit and Metis peoples." (section 35(2)) Section 35 is outside the *Charter*, and therefore is not subject to limitations as allowed by section 1 of the *Charter*. The second provision, included in the *Charter*, shields the unique rights and freedoms of the Aboriginal peoples from challenge under any of the other provisions of the *Charter of Rights and Freedoms*. Section 25 states:

> 25. The guarantee in this Charter of certain rights and freedoms shall not be construed so as to abrogate or derogate from any aboriginal, treaty or other rights or freedoms that pertain to the aboriginal peoples of Canada including
>
> (a) any rights or freedoms that have been recognized by the Royal Proclamation of October 7, 1763; and
>
> (b) any rights or freedoms that now exist by way of land claims agreements or may be so acquired.

The final provision (section 37) promised a First Ministers' Conference on Aboriginal constitutional matters before April 17, 1983. Prime Minister Trudeau called that conference into session in early 1983 and consensus was reached on some matters. It was agreed that both sections 25 and 35 of the *Constitution Act, 1982* would be amended to include the rights contained within past and future land claims settlements as treaty rights. Secondly, it was decided to amend section 35 to guarantee sexual equality among Aboriginal men and women in the enjoyment of these unique rights. It was accepted further that none of the provisions in the *Constitution Acts* of 1867 and 1982 that expressly referred to Aboriginal peoples should be amended at any time without first consulting with Aboriginal peoples through a First Ministers' Conference. Since the first ministers and Aboriginal leaders could only articulate a long list of issues of mutual concern in a protocol, rather than provide a definition or identification of the scope of Aboriginal and treaty rights, they decided to meet on at least three more occasions.

Amendments to the Constitution were passed by all provincial legislatures, except Quebec's, and by the Parliament of Canada, with the effect that they were proclaimed in force in June 1984. Sections 25 and 35 were revised to extend similar treatment as treaties to both previous and future land claims agreements. A new provision was added to guarantee Aboriginal and treaty rights equally to male and female Aboriginal persons. Another section (section 35.1) requires the prime minister to convene a First Ministers' Conference if amendments to sections 25, 35, 35.1 or 91(24) are ever under consideration in the future. The section 37 meeting process also was extended until April 17, 1987.

First Ministers' Conferences were held before the television cameras in 1984, 1985 and, finally, in 1987, resulting in a striking degree of national attention being devoted to Aboriginal issues. The focal point for discussion rapidly became the issue of the right of Aboriginal peoples to govern themselves, and the constitutional recognition of that right. The debate centred on whether the extension of this right should be subject to the complete control of both federal and provincial governments, or if the right simply should be stated within the Constitution and the elaboration of its implications be left to future negotiations.

While some limited flexibility in positions was evident and several parties attempted to fashion a compromise, the chasm between the two dominant views was too broad to be bridged. Fundamentally, this reflected two deeply felt and divergent views of the Aboriginal-Crown relationship. Aboriginal people asserted that they have the inherent right to govern their own affairs and have never surrendered this right. Thus, the issue from their perspective relates solely to regaining acceptance by general society of the ability and authority of Aboriginal people to determine their own future. Implementing this acceptance then gives rise to discussions regarding the interrelationship of the federal, provincial and Aboriginal governments.

The prime minister and most premiers took the position that Aboriginal people did not have any existing right to self-determination. They believed that Aboriginal people could obtain such a right only through the extension of delegated powers under Canadian legislation or by way of constitutional change.

The excitement and hopes of Aboriginal people during the First Ministers' Conferences have long since subsided. Since there was no agreement on an amendment on Aboriginal self-government, or regarding ongoing mechanisms for debating and adjudicating Aboriginal issues, the previous situation has largely returned, but with significant public support for Aboriginal positions.

The federal government relies exclusively on direct negotiations to resolve claims. Negotiation is the only alternative to expensive litigation, which few Aboriginal groups can afford or desire, given its adversarial nature and their lack of faith in the legal system. While both a Special Parliamentary Committee on Indian Self-Government in 1983 and the Canadian Bar Association in 1988 recommended the establishment of new institutions to deal with the settlement of claims, improvements have yet to be implemented. The settlement process is protracted, legalistic and distanced from the claimants.

The International Origins of Aboriginal and Treaty Rights

Introduction

One of the primary issues with which Canadian society has to come to grips is the historical legacy of its acquisition of Aboriginal lands. We are not talking here about the questionability of the treaties, for that is quite another matter. The issue involves how Canadian and American legal systems have addressed the nature and form of the Aboriginal legal interest in the land now within Canada and the United States, and of the legal techniques used to assert dominion over lands which enjoyed some degree of legal protection in international law. The failure of the legal system to deal adequately with the issue is reflected in the following judicial statement:

> "[T]he exclusive right of the United States to extinguish" Indian title has never been doubted. And whether it be done by treaty, by the sword, by purchase, by the exercise of complete dominion adverse to the right of occupancy, or otherwise, its justness is not open to inquiry in the courts.[10]

The attitude which this reflects has prevailed for a considerable period of time and has led to a feeling of considerable distrust on the part of the Aboriginal community. The community is generally reluctant to call upon the courts to help it resolve some very serious legal issues with the Canadian government, but particularly where Aboriginal lands are concerned.

Despite the desire of various governments to confine the question of Aboriginal issues to a domestic context, certain fundamental Aboriginal rights have been recognized in international law and practice since the 15th century.

The Basic Features of International Law

International law, unlike municipal or domestic law, does not have a legislative body to promulgate binding principles. International law is limited further by the fact that there is no one tribunal with jurisdiction to resolve all international disputes. The role of the primary existing tribunal, the International Court of Justice, is restricted to resolving only those disputes jointly referred to it by recognized nation states.

The existence and nature of an international rule of law is not always easy to determine in the absence of a legislative body. The accepted sources of international law are set out in the *Statute of the International Court of Justice*. In ascertaining the law in a given dispute, the court first looks to see if there is an applicable treaty (an international convention) between the parties. Where none exists, the court then looks to international custom, as evidenced by state practice. In order for a practice to be a binding custom, it must be both uniform and obligatory, rather than a matter of convenience. If the court is unable to apply an international treaty or custom, Article 38.1 provides for subsidiary means of determining "rules of law." These include reference to judicial decisions and the work of scholars.

The decisions of international courts and tribunals are not binding except between the parties in respect of the particular case. The decisions of municipal courts (i.e., courts of each nation) also are not binding in international disputes. Rules of law derived from treaties take precedence over rules of law derived from custom, and general principles of domestic law are subordinate to both. Canadian courts can and do apply rules of international law, provided they do not conflict with statutes or some fundamental constitutional principle.

In *R. v. Sioui,* [1990] 1 S.C.R 1025, the Supreme Court of Canada clearly reiterated prior statements that international law need not be referred to in order to resolve matters arising from Indian treaties. The existence and validity of an Indian treaty are not dependent upon its meeting the test of an international treaty cognizable at international law. However, that does not mean that international law is irrelevant where Aboriginal rights are concerned. On the contrary, we believe that international law has evolved over the years a number of principles which are useful when considering the contemporary Aboriginal situation in Canada and in concluding what is the most appropriate course of action to take in the future.

The Roots of Aboriginal Rights in International Law

Aboriginal rights became an issue for Europeans in the 16th century with the Age of Discovery. Various European nations engaged in competition with each other to expand their influence throughout the world and to control world trade, justifying their drive to do so as part of their obligation to spread Christianity. The severity of the competition among nations naturally led to strained relations and sometimes to outright war among the various competitors, with the result that international "understandings" were developed in order to control the outbreak of hostilities and to enforce alliances. These understandings eventually evolved into a body of law in the form of principles of international or extraterritorial conduct deemed acceptable to "civilized" nations. The individuals most responsible for the development of this body of principles addressed their minds to the way that the "discoverers" were dealing with the indigenous people already in occupation of the territories which they "discovered."

The "fathers" of contemporary international law were, thus, the "fathers" of Aboriginal rights theory. Aboriginal law originated, and is grasped best, as a branch of international law, with the basic concepts of modern doctrine being hammered out by Francisco de Vitoria, Bartolome de las Casas and other Spanish theological jurists of the 16th and 17th centuries.

In a 16th century treatise, *De Indis et de Jure Belli Reflectiones,* Vitoria outlined the basic concepts of Aboriginal rights. At the University of Salamanca, Vitoria lectured extensively on the subject of the Aboriginal people of North America. He dealt with the Aboriginal population being "discovered" by the Spanish adventurers, and the respective rights and duties of each. Reports of military abuses, enslavement and massacres of these newly discovered people had reached Spain. There were heated debates about the matter, resulting in both the Crown of Spain and the Papacy issuing a series of *cedulas* and "papal bulls" decrying such abuses and attempting to ensure that certain basic rights were recognized. These measures proved ineffective, however, because the central authorities were unable to control the outposts in the New World, and were unwilling to impose trade embargoes and forego the riches of exploitation.

Although Vitoria's influence on international law is derived primarily from his impact on later scholars, he is recognized as one of the most important thinkers of his time, and his work had a measurable influence on the policies and attitudes of those in power. In his concept of the law of nations, Vitoria asserted that all people had certain inherent rights, including possession of a spirit or soul and the capacity for salvation. According to Vitoria, Indians could not be deprived of their possessions unless the Spaniards could advance a just cause for doing so. Simply stating that Indians were not Christians did not suffice, nor did stating that Indians were of unsound mind.

Vitoria also dealt with the title to land being advanced by the Spaniards. He unequivocally rejected the concept of basing title on the status of the Spanish emperor as the "Lord of the World." He also stated that title could not be based merely on the Indians' rejection of the supremacy of the Pope. With reference to title based on claims that Spain was the first European nation to "discover" the New World, Vitoria dismissed that proposition outright, saying the land "discovered" already had an owner from a public and private point of view: the Indians. The most that discovery could do was to grant priority to the discovering state vis-a-vis other potential colonizers in pursuing trade with or land purchases from the indigenous nation. Likewise, papal grants could not substantiate title, but merely allocate priority rights among Catholic nations.

In *Reflectiones,* Vitoria also outlined the nature of what constituted legitimate contact with the Indian nations. If the Indians were hostile after the Spaniards had demonstrated their "friendly" intentions, only then were the Spaniards legitimately allowed to use force, and even then it had to be measured to inflict the least amount of damage. Vitoria concluded this work on a practical note, stating that commerce with the Indians was permitted, and that the Spanish Crown was bound by law and expediency to maintain its administration of the lands in question, as there were already many Aboriginal converts. The Spanish Crown accepted the validity of the principles articulated by Vitoria, although it perverted their intent through devising the *requirimientos,* in which the king's offer of friendship was read aloud in Spanish in a deserted locale. The failure of the Indians to accept the offer authorized the military to attack.

One century later, Hugo Grotius, a Dutch scholar much influenced by Vitoria, published a treatise on Aboriginal rights entitled *De Jure Praedae Commentarius.* Grotius adopted many of Vitoria's concepts and beliefs. Expanding on Vitoria's belief that the Spaniards were entitled by the law of nations to travel and reside among the Indians, Grotius stated that the Spaniards would have just grounds for waging war with the Indians if they were prevented by the latter from carrying on the practice of commerce or conversion.

Grotius, however, agreed with Vitoria's belief that Indians could not be deprived of their property or possessions unless there was just cause, and that mere paganism did not constitute a just cause. Grotius also agreed that the Indians should be converted only through peaceful means and that any Indians enslaved under the pretext of conversion should be released. Grotius further reiterated Vitoria's belief that the emperor did not have the right to convert the new provinces to his own use and that any pretext used in favour of such a practice was unjust. The principles enunciated a century earlier in regard to Spain's dealings in the New World were accepted by Grotius, and he seems simply to have applied them specifically to matters of Dutch interest.

Samuel Pufendorf, a contemporary of Grotius, criticized both Grotius and Vitoria in his renowned work, *De Jure Naturae et Gentium*. The Indians, Pufendorf argued, were under no obligation to receive visiting foreigners, as was the case with other nations. As the "property holders," the Indians had the right to consider and determine the purpose and length of the visit, as well as the number of visitors. Even when the Indians granted the visitors certain trade and commercial privileges, they also had the right to revoke such privileges. It was untenable to suggest, Pufendorf argued, that the Indians were forced to welcome such visitors, especially when to do so would be at their own peril.

The work of these three scholars, the founding fathers of international law, is significant because all three recognized the importance and existence of certain fundamental Aboriginal rights in international law. Their views were largely adopted, albeit with several important modifications, by Emmerich Vattel, writing in the mid-18th century. It is his description of Aboriginal rights to land and sovereignty that became influential among American jurists in the following century.

The Use of Doctrines of International Law

Since the beginning of the Age of Discovery, European states have engaged relentlessly in the process of divesting indigenous peoples of their lands, and have sought to justify and legitimate this practice through the use of the doctrines of discovery, occupation, adverse possession, conquest and cession. On the whole, domestic courts have either ignored or generally misapplied and misinterpreted these doctrines in their discussions of "Aboriginal title," thereby upholding the status quo of Aboriginal dispossession.

The starting point in determining what rights Aboriginal people had at international law when they first were in contact with Europeans requires an examination of the legal provisions applicable to those nations which asserted authority over North America after contact. We will examine in turn each of the rationales for European claims to sovereignty and underlying title to the discovered territories.

The Doctrine of Discovery

The doctrine of discovery has been—and still is—rigorously advanced by various authors, jurists, legal scholars, nation states and domestic courts as the foundation upon which English, Canadian or American sovereignty in North America is based. The basic premise is that the first state to "discover" an uninhabited region with no other claims to it automatically acquires territorial sovereignty. Originally, the doctrine was limited to *terra nullius*—literally, a barren and deserted area—as reflected by the noted English scholar of the common law, Blackstone, writing in his *Commentaries*. The concept of *terra nullius* was expanded later, without justification, to include any area devoid of "civilized" society. In order to reflect colonial desires, the New World was said by some courts to fall within this expanded definition.

The traditional doctrine of discovery has never been recognized as vesting a valid claim or title to a "discovered" territory. Since Vitoria's vehement rejection of the doctrine in the 16th century, such a claim has been seen only as establishing an initial and incomplete title to the territory in question. This traditional interpretation has been ratified and affirmed in decisions from international courts in this century.[11] While there is some debate among academics about this claim's validity,[12] the dominant view clearly is in favour of the traditional elaboration of this doctrine.[13]

Although the doctrine of discovery has been advanced occasionally by European powers since the "discovery" of the New World, such a claim was based more upon expediency than international law. The validity of the claim is dependent upon the status of the territory as *terra nullius*—an uninhabited land. Because Indians already occupied the land at the arrival of the Europeans, Vitoria unequivocally rejected such a title when it was asserted in the New World. Although there were many attempts to found claims based on discovery, the doctrine, by itself, was not considered sufficient to establish a valid claim, and does not appear to have been accepted officially by the competing states themselves, unless the discoverer was able to demonstrate an actual and effective governmental presence.

In *Johnson v. M'Intosh*, 21 U.S. (8 Wheat.) 543 (1823), however, the United States Supreme Court applied the doctrine of discovery in order to justify American sovereignty over the land included in what is now the United States of America. The court held that:

- The principle of discovery was acknowledged by all Europeans because it was in their interests to do so.

- The nation making the "discovery" had "the sole right of acquiring the soil and establishing settlements on it."

- The rule regulated the relations among the competing interests of European powers.

- The original inhabitants had the right to retain possession of their land, but were without any powers of alienation other than to the "discoverers" who had obtained exclusive title by virtue of making the "discovery."

When one considers both the international legal reality of the time and state practice, this decision appears to be more an effort to justify the taking of Indian territory that had already occurred than a serious analysis and application of the principles demanded by international law. Quite simply, the concept that Aboriginal inhabitants could only alienate their interest in the land to the "discoverer" was a legal fiction, because that concept did not originally exist in international law. In the *Island of Palmas* case (1928), 2 R.I.A.A. 829, the doctrine of discovery, as a means to justify the taking of Aboriginal lands, was considered and rejected definitively in just such a situation by the Permanent Court of Arbitration.

The Doctrine of Occupation

It has been argued by some that if discovery was seen to vest only an imperfect title, then discovery plus occupation completed the claim. There was, however, a traditional requirement that the land so discovered and occupied had to be a *terra nullius*. At one time, an area devoid of "civilized" society was alleged by some scholars to fall within the scope of such a requirement.[14] The more accurate historical interpretation, which is reflected by the modern jurisprudence in international law, precludes the requirement's application to any region with an indigenous population that is organized socially and politically.

According to the *Island of Palmas* case, a claim based on discovery was incomplete until accompanied by "the effective occupation of the region claimed to be discovered." The term "effective occupation" incorporates the notion of "uninterrupted and permanent possession." Based on such a rule and interpretation, it would appear that the only ones capable of successfully advancing a claim based on discovery and occupation may be the Aboriginal peoples themselves, because they are the ones who could argue best that they first discovered and occupied the vacant territory many thousands of years ago.

There was much debate about the definition of *terra nullius* for some time. Although the term was commonly accepted as meaning "uninhabited," some decisions have held that certain tribal lands could be said to fall within the scope of "uninhabited" if the peoples of the area exhibited an unwillingness to exploit the land in a "civilized" fashion. Such decisions, like many of the European policies of dealing with indigenous peoples, were largely the result of expediency and ethnocentrism. The present state of international law, as expressed by the International Court of Justice in the *Western Sahara Case*, precludes a region from being termed "uninhabited" if nomadic or resident tribes with a degree of social and political organization are present in the area. The issue then becomes, in individual cases, whether a specific indigenous group meets the test by exhibiting a sufficient degree of internal organization to be recognized as a distinct society, so as to effectively occupy the land and administer it as its own.[15]

It appears from the Canadian case law that probably every Aboriginal group would meet this test. The standard is not similarity to European civilization, and no particular level of "sophistication" is required.[16] International law merely requires that the society was organized sufficiently to meet the needs of its members and was recognizable by others as a legal entity that inhabited the territory with a settled system of government. This test has been articulated by one of the leading scholars of the 20th century on this subject:

> [I]n order that an area shall not be territorium nullius it would appear ... to be necessary and sufficient that it be inhabited by a political society, that is, by a considerable number of persons who are permanently united by habitual obedience to a certain and common superior, or whose conduct in regard to their mutual relations habitually conforms to recognised standards.[17]

It should be noted that the colonizing nations themselves applied this test in the 18th and 19th centuries, with the Indian treaties demonstrating its practical application. The *Western Sahara Case*'s adoption of it in 1975 indicates that it reflects current international law. This test, however, should not be confused with international law requirements established for recognition as a nation state, which include additional criteria.

The Doctrine of Adverse Possession

The doctrine of adverse possession has frequently been linked to the above two doctrines to consolidate a valid claim to territory. Adverse possession basically posits that you can acquire title to part of another state's land if you openly occupy it for an extended period of time and the original owner acquiesces to your presence. In order for such a claim to be valid, there must be a *de facto* exercise of sovereignty which is peaceful and unchallenged. This doctrine is similar to one that exists within the Canadian domestic law by virtue of provincial and territorial legislation (the relevant *Limitations Act*, which establishes a 10- or 20-year rule among private parties and 60 years versus the Crown) or through reception of English law (regarding federal Crown land).

It would take little effort to discover in Canadian or Manitoban history sufficient examples of Aboriginal resistance to European occupation of the land to refute the application of this doctrine. Significant European occupation of lands in Manitoba did not occur until the Selkirk Settlement of 1811. That settlement came about as a direct result of Aboriginal consent being negotiated with Indian Chief Peguis by Lord Selkirk prior to the arrival and occupation of the land by the European settlers. The Hudson's Bay Company, which constituted the only significant European presence prior to that era, acknowledged in its practices the Indian sovereignty in the territory, and deliberately did not interfere with Indian control over their territory. In fact, various instructions sent to the trading post managers in North America by the senior officials of the company always emphasized the importance of not interfering in the internal affairs of the Indians, and in ensuring that wherever trading posts were established, the "Indian title" was purchased. When the company transferred its interest in the territory to Canada, it specifically required that the new Dominion negotiate land surrenders with the Indians, and in 1872 the Canadian government began to do so. Those earlier negotiations between the company and the Indians, as well as the later treaties between the Dominion and the First Nations, enabled the land to be settled by Europeans with Indian consent, as the latter agreed to share their territory.

To the extent that they reflect only a surrender of exclusive Indian title to much of the land, the treaties also amount to a confirmation of the Indian right to retain all other aspects of their Aboriginal title (i.e., their "other" Aboriginal rights), since only the land rights were surrendered.

What is clear, however, is that Canadian sovereignty in western Canada is dependent to a large degree upon the validity of the treaties in those areas covered by them.

The Doctrine of Conquest

With respect to its traditional interpretation, the doctrine of conquest allowed using force or waging war only if a nation's security or rights were threatened. Under traditional international law, a country was no more justified in exploiting another through force than was a private individual. Conquest gave the victorious nation the full right to colonize the vanquished nation and change its legal regime. These rights usually were described in the peace treaty that ended the war. The doctrine of conquest only operated, however, if the conquered territory actually was annexed and possessed by the conqueror. In terms of the indigenous lands in North America, these criteria normally were not met as no state of war was declared, although hostilities were not infrequent.[18]

The present interpretation of the doctrine of conquest was outlined by the Permanent Court of International Justice in the *Status of Eastern Greenland Case* (1933), 3 W.C.R. 148 at 171. According to this decision:

> [The doctrine of conquest] only operates as a cause of lack of sovereignty when there is a war between two states and by reason of the defeat of one of them sovereignty over territory passes from the loser to the victorious state.

The doctrine of conquest frequently has been confused with the doctrine of discovery. Both are also the cause of further confusion, as they have international and domestic law purposes. At international law, conquest can cause the vanquished to lose sovereignty when the conqueror chooses to annex part or all of the territory of the loser. As has been indicated already, discovery *per se* can justify only the acquisition of sovereignty over uninhabited territories, and even then mere discovery without actual occupation is insufficient.

These two doctrines are also used for an entirely different purpose: determining what law comes to be applied within the newly acquired territory as opposed to the international law standards governing the legitimacy of the process of acquisition itself. The common law distinguishes among settled, ceded and conquered colonies for the purposes of defining precisely when and on what terms the common law becomes the basic foundational law of the colony. This function is embraced within the English doctrine of reception of laws. It is quite possible, therefore, for a territory to be treated as being acquired at international law by conquest or cession (treaty), and then for the common law to be applied on the basis that the land is treated as a settled colony.

Canada, in fact, is treated largely as a settled colony under the reception of laws doctrine, with the common law being "received" by each colony as it stood on the date the first local colonial statute was passed. The sole example of using the conquest theory for domestic purposes relates to the colony of New France, in which King George III imposed the common law through the *Royal Proclamation of 1763*. French civil law was restored in non-criminal matters through the *Quebec Act* of 1774.

It is clear from our history that conquest was rarely, if ever, relevant in the acquisition of sovereignty over Aboriginal peoples and title to their lands. While this was argued forcefully by the Province of Nova Scotia and a variety of other governments in the *Simon* case, the Supreme Court of Canada decisively rejected its application in relation to the Micmac treaties of 1725 and 1752. The court further stated in *R. v. Simon*, [1985] 2 S.C.R. 387 that the conquest doctrine could apply in Canada only if a declaration of war had been proclaimed previously by the Crown, and there was no evidence of this ever occurring in Aboriginal-Crown relations.

The Doctrine of Cession

From the discussion thus far, it would appear that the consent of indigenous peoples is a necessary precondition to the legitimate acquisition of their territory, except where war has been officially declared and the conquest doctrine applies. The signing of valid treaties would fulfil the requirement for consent but, as mentioned elsewhere, the exact legal nature and effect of the Indian treaties are plagued by uncertainty. In some instances, Aboriginal groups voluntarily surrendered their Aboriginal title, but in other instances fraud, undue influence and misunderstanding would seem to invalidate the arrangement.

The history of Indian treaties is filled with injustice and dishonesty, if not in the negotiations themselves, then certainly in the implementation and interpretation of the treaties. To begin with, the Indians' understanding of the treaties rarely coincided with that of the Europeans. Indian people generally believed that they were only signing an arrangement to share the land with the newcomers, not, as some government officials later asserted, that they were agreeing to an abject surrender of their land and sovereignty. To the Indians, the treaties were intended to ensure that all people had access to the traditional territory of the Indian nations. This meant to them that they would continue to use their land as before and that mutually exclusive uses would not occur on a large scale. Clearly, they could not know or realize that such treaties would be relied upon later to exclude them from areas they had inhabited traditionally or to restrict them to the small parcels set aside as their reserves. If they had been told that that was to be the case, there is much doubt that they ever would have agreed. In fact, there is considerable evidence that many of the assurances given during the treaty negotiations were deliberately ignored by governments. The Indian nations of Manitoba were told that the various treaties confirmed their continued rights to use the land as they always had and that the Crown would guarantee this for as long as the lands and waters existed. Including guarantees of their hunting and fishing rights demonstrated that their traditional economies were to be protected. This required their ability to use their traditional territory.

The precise legal nature and effect of Indian treaties in North America are uncertain under international law, but the validity of many of the treaties could be easily questioned and rendered uncertain at common law, in light of both the questionable tactics used by the Crown's representatives in inducing Aboriginal groups to sign and the failure of the Crown to honour its obligations.

The Application of International Law
to Aboriginal Peoples in Canada

When Europeans first came here, their main objective was commerce. When France and England engaged in their fierce competition for the exploitation of Canada for its furs, Aboriginal people were enlisted in the service of one side or the other, as they played a vital role as military allies and essential trading partners.

Early European settlements in Canada were insignificant in size until the late 1700s and almost nonexistent in Manitoba until well into the 19th century. Their precarious and vulnerable position in a harsh, unknown country necessitated the cultivation of friendly relations with the Aboriginal people. As the fur trade became larger and colonists undertook farming, these settlements began to expand in size and in numbers. Relations between the two groups began to change. Exploitation of the natural resources of the country for economic gain eventually evolved into a desire to gain total dominion.

The transformation in the relationship between settlers and Aboriginal people accelerated first with the defeat of France by England and then through the arrival in eastern Canada of thousands of United Empire Loyalists fleeing the United States after the American Revolution. Britain needed large tracts of land to accommodate the new arrivals and also needed Indian allies to oppose American ambitions for expansion. This necessitated a policy of continuing to cultivate friendly relations with Indian nations and the focussing of this policy on western portions of what later became central Ontario, while acquiring land by treaty in southeastern Ontario for settlers. The Aboriginal peoples in northern and further western regions (from Lake Huron to the Pacific Ocean) became the new suppliers of furs and trading partners.

This relationship in the West, and particularly in Manitoba, began to change in the 19th century. First came Lord Selkirk's desire to establish a new colony for British immigrants in 1811. This objective was tolerated by the Indian nations because it did not disrupt the fur trade significantly and did not involve much of their territory. The desire for a lumber industry later sparked Imperial interest in acquiring title to the remainder of the Great Lakes area in 1850, and the Hudson's Bay Company purchased portions of Vancouver Island during the next few years. After its creation in 1867, the new government of Canada sought to assert its dominion over a vast territory of what is now western Ontario and the Prairies. It turned to the treaty process to obtain ready access to Indian lands. For the Metis, the government, through the *Manitoba Act,* 1870, attempted to extinguish title in exchange for promises of individual land grants.

The Indian leaders of Manitoba were not told that the Crown intended to restrict them to reserves while the balance of their traditional territory was to be allocated to benefit the newcomers. Instead, Alexander Morris, the Crown representative, offered reassurances that life would remain largely unchanged. Yet, within a few years, by the mid-1870s, the Crown had established what it needed—a written record of a passive conveyance of land that would reflect the "truth" to the public, while the oral version of the negotiations would be remembered only by the Indian nations.

At the same time, the federal and Manitoba governments were passing general land legislation that took no cognizance of the presence of Aboriginal peoples. The new federal government of Sir John A. Macdonald followed a policy of largely ignoring the special status of Aboriginal peoples after the treaties were signed. Assimilation into the dominant society was the agenda of the day, with little recognition given to the assurances made during treaty negotiations. Provincial legislation and regulations were used extensively to facilitate the sale of land rights belonging to Metis children, who were the sole recipients of those rights under section 31 of the *Manitoba Act,* 1870.

Proper respect for the principles of international law by Canadian governments would have protected Aboriginal people from the treatment they received during the treaty-making era and subsequently. The colonization of the "New World" essentially involved the assertion of territorial and jurisdictional sovereignty by the European governments. In order for each one to legitimate its claims in the eyes of its European competitors, it was necessary for the colonizer to demonstrate a valid legal claim or title to the territory in question. In order to do so, however, reliance had to be placed on international law, yet that law contained principles concerning Aboriginal people which made it clear that the Aboriginal interest in the land could not be ignored. The manner in which legal title was asserted as against the Aboriginal people in subsequent domestic court decisions is clouded by the obvious lack of attention to those principles.

Thus, the traditional international law doctrines of discovery, occupation, adverse possession, conquest and cession bore little resemblance to the way in which they came to be applied in American, English and Canadian case law. The most critical redefinition of international law by the judiciary occurred in its use of the doctrine of discovery to justify European claims.

The Fiction of Discovery in Canadian and American Law

As indicated earlier, the United States Supreme Court viewed title to all the land in the New World as being rooted in the doctrine of discovery. This doctrine, according to Chief Justice Marshall, acted as an ordering principle for the European colonization of North America.[19] He asserted that it essentially held that the "discovering" nation acquired the sole right before all other European nations to extinguish Indian title to the soil and to establish settlements on it. The doctrine of discovery, he felt, also served to define the new relationship between the colonists and the indigenous populations. The Aboriginal people, Marshall reasoned, still had the right to occupy the soil, but their general powers of alienation had become restricted as the "discovering" nation had gained the "underlying" title to the land. In addition, European territorial sovereignty expanded to accommodate this new reality. The Indians became enveloped within this new European territory, and subject to European sovereignty. It is as though a blanket of European title was cast over the land, covering all those upon whom it fell. The Europeans had acquired the right to extinguish Indian title however they pleased, and this principle was said to be unquestionable. There was, however, literally no basis in international law for the assertion of such a principle.

Marshall's use of the discovery doctrine was clearly inconsistent with the traditional doctrines of territorial acquisition under international law. Nevertheless, it was affirmed by various English decisions, and tacitly accepted by leading Canadian cases such as *St. Catherine's Milling & Lumber Co. v. R.* (1888), 14 A.C. 46 (P.C.) and *Calder.* Like a thread, it runs through Canadian jurisprudence and is now the accepted justification for the expropriation of the underlying title to Aboriginal lands in both the United States and Canada.

Marshall's legal fiction, enunciated through several landmark decisions—*Johnson v. M'Intosh; Cherokee Nation v. Georgia*, 30 U.S. (5 Pet.) 1 (1831); and *Worcester v. Georgia*, 31 U.S. (6 Pet.) 515 (1832)—was never meant to explain the historic or cultural reality involved in the European expropriation of the New World. His aim was to ratify what had been done and to forge a new compromise that would give at least some recognition to the rights of First Nations while not challenging the foundations of a new country. While his undue concern for expediency rather than justice may be criticized, his court is no more deserving of reproach than the later courts that affirmed him. It can be said that at least he reflected an age in which slavery was legal, women had few rights, the franchise was limited and overt racism was common.

Other Rationales Supporting Colonization

The exact nature of the legal status of Aboriginal peoples in relation to the colonizing European powers has yet to be resolved in international law. Although this has been a legitimate concern of international law since its advent, conflicting notions of "sovereignty" and "dependency" have clouded the issue. International law has not remained constant over the years. Instead, principles have often been revamped to reflect prevailing attitudes and the colonial ambitions of European powers. The movement toward decolonization after World War II has sparked a renewed concern to reconsider the content of international law.

Sovereignty

Although the concept of sovereignty has different meanings and is prone to ambiguity, its most common application in the realm of international, as opposed to domestic, law is derived by linking the two notions of "independence" and "statehood." Since the state is the fundamental unit of international law, a fully sovereign state is an independent one. With respect to international considerations, this independence can exist only as a matter of law, such that a state is capable of creating a voluntary position of dependence through its treaty-making powers. Thus, under international law, treaty making is a consensual process by which the respective rights and status of each nation are altered, with the sovereignty of each being unaffected unless the matter is addressed specifically within the treaty.

Bilateral international treaties entered into by Britain, like treaties in general, include two major types:

1. Treaties that bring both states under the same law and serve as an entrenched instrument under domestic law.

2. Treaties that establish military protection.

The 1707 *Act of Union* between Scotland and England is an example of the first type of treaty. Under this treaty, both countries are said to enjoy "fundamental and essential conditions," and in all other respects the constitutional status of England and Scotland has merged, with the latter retaining its civil law regime. By contrast, Wales and Ireland were said to have been "conquered," and have been subject traditionally to parliamentary control without the benefit of a treaty to provide basic constitutional limits. The Migratory Birds Convention between Mexico, the U.S.A. and Great Britain (on behalf of Canada) is a variation of this form of treaty.

The use of the second type of treaty reflects an ancient principle of the law of nations. A leading 18th century jurist, Emmerich Vattel, has described such a treaty as one in which sovereign states unite in an unequal alliance. In order to provide for its safety, the weaker state places itself under the protection of the stronger and agrees in return to perform services to obtain that protection. In terms of the law of nations, the weaker state is still regarded as sovereign.

In *Worcester v. Georgia,* the United States Supreme Court adopted Vattel's interpretation of such treaties and applied it to describe the relations between the First Nations of America and the United States, in light of a distinction drawn one year earlier in *Cherokee Nation v. Georgia.* In that case, the court maintained that there was a cardinal difference between the Indian treaties and treaties involving other nations, because the Indians and the United States resided within the same boundaries. Although the First Nations were acknowledged to have the unquestionable right to occupy the lands in their possession, they were characterized in *Worcester* as "domestic dependent nations," rather than as foreign ones. They were declared to have lost their independence simply by virtue of the presence and numerical superiority of the colonizers. Nevertheless, the First Nations retained internal or residual sovereignty. This approach certainly ran counter to the prevailing principles of international law established earlier by Vitoria, Grotius and Pufendorf.

Treaties

Although the existence of treaties between Aboriginal peoples and Europeans is itself a compelling indication that Aboriginal peoples once were sovereign, the only things widely accepted about their legal status are that the treaties create binding legal obligations between the parties and that certain rules of construction favourable to the Aboriginal party apply in their interpretation.

Mr. Justice Lamer (as he was then) delivered a unanimous decision of the Supreme Court of Canada in which he declared that the Huron Nation was an independent sovereign state when it negotiated a treaty with the British Crown's representative in 1760. (R. v. Sioui, [1990] 1 S.C.R. 1025) The court implied that a similar status existed for all Indian nations.

In terms of international law, the word "treaty" is defined as "an international agreement concluded between States in written form and governed by international law, whether embodied in a single instrument or in two or more related instruments and whatever its particular designation."[20]

In the *Cayuga Indians Case* (1926), 6 R.I.A.A. 173, a tribunal of the International Court of Justice held that the treaties in question did not bind the federal government.

Instead, they constituted a contract between the State of New York and the Cayugas, with the United States being free from liability should the State of New York fail to perform its promises. In the *Island of Palmas* case the Permanent Court of Arbitration disposed of the matter in similar fashion, as did the courts of England in the relatively recent case of *R. v. The Secretary of State for Foreign and Commonwealth Affairs, Ex parte: The Indian Association of Alberta, Union of New Brunswick Indians, Union of Nova Scotia Indians*, [1981] 4 C.L.N.R. 86 (Eng. C.A.).

Despite the pronouncements of these courts, there has been persuasive and strong resistance to this interpretation. The legal status of a treaty between a European state and a non-European one has been the source of much controversy in international legal circles, particularly since World War II. With respect to treaties between England and indigenous peoples, the facts of each case determine whether the treaty extinguished the independence of the indigenous nation, or created rights and obligations between the two signatories, recognizable at international law.

By contrast, the idea that such treaties could create international legal relations and rights has been viewed as undesirable by Canadian and British courts (e.g., *St. Catherine's Milling* and *Simon*). This view had been articulated earlier, in an 1837 report on Aboriginal peoples by a Select Committee of the British House of Commons on Aborigines. The committee had rationalized its conclusion on the basis of the often disparate bargaining powers of each party.

In 1832, the Marshall court of the United States, in *Worcester v. Georgia*, gave credence to the international aspect of Indian treaties by stating that the use of the words "nation" and "treaty" by the Crown and later by the United States government, with respect to the American-Indian dealings, was intentional and, to a certain extent, placed the Indians in a similar category as the signatories of other American international treaties. This position was echoed in a judgment by the Privy Council. In *Re Southern Rhodesia*, [1919] A.C. 211, it was held that the British government's repeated reference to an African king's sovereignty over his kingdom automatically made him sovereign in the eyes of international law.

There is no clear consensus on whether treaties with indigenous peoples constitute treaties in international law. The view that would allow for the greatest fairness and equity in each case is the one that most closely captures the historical, sociological and legal intentions of both parties in making the treaty.

Guardianship

The concept of guardianship is the product of the ethnocentric assumption that European civilization is superior to the civilizations of indigenous peoples. The concept of sovereignty normally implicit in the treaty-making process clearly was undermined by the European belief in the existence of a measurable distinction between the "civilized" and the "uncivilized" nations of the world. The application of this belief led to indigenous peoples being treated as "children" or wards of the state, rather than as sovereign nations. The European adoption of a patriarchal role was justified glibly by their perceived need for Europeans to look after the protection and welfare of this "unfortunate race."

The doctrine of guardianship dates back to Vitoria, who paradoxically premised his theory of Aboriginal rights in part on the belief that the newly "discovered" Indians were less mature and intelligent than their advanced and learned "discoverers." To avoid dire consequences, the Indian people needed to be protected from abuses by the "superior" European powers. This attitude was mirrored by zealous missionaries who sought to rescue the Indian from the grasp of "savagery" and "paganism." Over the course of time, the concept of guardianship became official colonial policy in the New World, and became an accepted theory in international law by Europeans in the late 19th century to justify their wholesale colonization of most of the world.

Despite the professed positive aims of this doctrine, the inescapable conclusion is that it worked to the severe disadvantage of indigenous peoples. The concept of guardianship was used to justify the destruction of Aboriginal cultural institutions, and enabled the colonists to deny the intrinsic worth and validity of anything Aboriginal.

Aboriginal Nationhood Status Today

In the realm of classic international law, indigenous peoples were designated as the objects, rather than the subjects, of international law. Although only nation states recognized by Europeans traditionally have been afforded a legal personality in the international arena, the exact legal status of indigenous peoples has yet to be resolved.

From time to time the question arises as to whether indigenous people ever have enjoyed or still enjoy aspects of sovereignty recognized at international law. The development of international law over the years clearly suggests that the question could be resolved in their favour. In Article 1 of the Montevideo Convention (1933), the criteria for internationally recognized statehood are said to be:

- a permanent population;

- a defined territory;

- a government; and

- the capacity to enter into relations with other states.

Aboriginal peoples also have been pointing with greater frequency over the past 20 years to other important, modern international conventions. The International Covenant on Civil and Political Rights and the International Covenant on Economic, Social and Cultural Rights both state in Article 1 that "[a]ll peoples have the right of self-determination." The *Charter of the United Nations* also refers in Article 1(2) to "respect for the principle of equal rights and self-determination of peoples" as one of its primary purposes. Canada is a signatory to all three documents and, therefore, is required by international law to adhere to their terms. Numerous other resolutions of the U.N. contain similar language, although the precise scope of the term "peoples" is not defined.

Aboriginal groups in the United States and Canada, in their bid for the recognition of their right to self-determination, frequently have emphasized the relevance of these international instruments to their situation. They have asserted that their right under international law to cede various aspects of their sovereignty to another state was never exercised insofar as Canada was concerned.

International law has been advancing very rapidly over the past decade in addressing the specific concerns of indigenous peoples who do not yet form recognized nation states. The International Labour Organization (ILO) recently overhauled its Indigenous and Tribal Populations Convention No. 107 and Recommendation No. 104 from 1957. Convention No. 169 was passed by the ILO in June 1989 to remove the paternalistic language of its predecessor and to expand the borders of indigenous rights that it recognizes and seeks to advance. This convention now has come into force as an international standard, although Canada has yet to decide whether it will ratify Convention No. 169. The convention recognizes indigenous rights to land and to establish unique institutions to protect and promote economic, social, cultural and legal advancement. The issue of ratification of this convention should be explored by the federal and provincial governments in consultation with Aboriginal people, without delay.

The U.N. Human Rights Commission established a Working Group on Indigenous Populations in 1982. That group has been meeting almost every summer to consider the need for further international law standards. Currently, it is circulating the second draft of a declaration on the rights of indigenous peoples for comment by member states and indigenous organizations. The working group intends to propose a declaration for adoption by the U.N. General Assembly in the near future. The Organization of American States, of which Canada is now a full member, is drafting a declaration specific to the Aboriginal peoples of the Americas, which it hopes to conclude next year in recognition of the 500th anniversary of contact.

At present, indigenous peoples throughout the world are attempting to rectify the imbalance of the past. Given the evolving recognition of their unique position within the historical and international context, it is clearly conceivable that their attempts will prove successful.

Conclusion

If the status of indigenous peoples under international law from the early 1800s has been unclear until recently, it must be remembered that Europeans were responsible for the content and direction of that law. It also must be realized that domestic courts have misinterpreted and misapplied the principles of international law.

Where, then, does all this lead us? In our opinion, it points inexorably to the conclusion that Aboriginal people have not been dealt with fairly in the manner by which their lands have been taken from them. It is clear that the treaty negotiations occurred in settings where unequal bargaining positions prevailed. The issues reflected in the written versions of the treaties do not conform to the Aboriginal understandings of those same treaties. A clear example of that is the manner in which the right to self-government of the Aboriginal people has been undermined, not by the treaty documents themselves, but by the way in which the provisions of the treaties, particularly the land surrender provisions, have been interpreted by the various government administrations over the years.

Federal and provincial governments have generally approached the treaties as documents justifying their right to intrude greatly in the lives of Indian people. They have considered treaties as containing limited promises that could be overridden when desired. These governments have also adopted the view that Aboriginal people have no rights except as expressly contained in the written treaty documents or otherwise given by valid legislation.

The Aboriginal people have approached the treaties as ones in which covenants were made between the Crown and Aboriginal nations. In their view, the Crown acquired only those rights expressly specified in the treaties, while all others, including the right to self-government, were retained by the Aboriginal nations. When confronted with the question of establishing to the satisfaction of this Inquiry how Aboriginal people lost their right to continue to govern themselves, the Deputy Minister of Justice, John Tait, stated:

> I know of no piece of legislation that articulates in a specific line that there was a right [to self-government] and that the right was taken away....

During the course of negotiating the matter of treaty and Aboriginal rights in the constitutional talks of a few years ago, the various governments of this country essentially admitted that the Aboriginal people had the right to govern themselves, but failed to agree with the Aboriginal leaders in attendance on the nature and extent of that right. The latter fact is not surprising, considering that Aboriginal people want the explicit constitutional recognition of their right to continue to govern themselves to be as clear as possible, whereas the provincial and federal governments wanted this right to be as dependent upon their control and consent as possible.

We believe that there is no longer an issue as to whether Aboriginal people have the right to govern themselves in accordance with their customs and traditions. It is clear, we believe, that they have that right. It also is clear that there is little agreement on how far that right extends into existing federal and provincial jurisdictions. It is regrettable that this vital concern has been addressed in terms of whether our first ministers are willing to "give" power and on what conditions. Instead, we believe that the way in which this should be addressed is to question how and to what extent Aboriginal people lost their original right to self-determination. Those who assert that the right is already limited are the ones who should bear the onus of proving this contention. Their inability to do so would mean that the right still continues in force.

In our view, Aboriginal people have not lost the right to govern their own affairs. This right to self-determination precedes colonization and has never been voluntarily surrendered. There is no evidence that Aboriginal people were ever conquered so as to be susceptible to the victor's unilateral domination. None of the treaty negotiations in Manitoba indicates any intention by the Aboriginal leadership to surrender their governmental authority. Further, international law today clearly recognizes the right of peoples to determine their own future.

It is possible today to assert that Aboriginal people enjoy an ongoing right to self-determination which is not subject to federal or provincial interference. That position is confirmed by section 35 of the Constitution.

It is our assessment that Aboriginal rights to self-determination must be acknowledged openly and freely by all levels of government.

The law now starts from a presumption in favour of the continued existence of Aboriginal and treaty rights. This reflects a considerable change in Canadian law. Some limitations were accepted by Canada's courts in previous years, but, in our opinion, such tendencies and those past decisions are no longer valid under the law as it now stands. The legal philosophies and the 19th century theories which gave rise to those decisions must now be discarded.

The Evolving Law on Aboriginal and Treaty Rights

Introduction

Aboriginal and treaty rights are both of major relevance in this province. Parts of Manitoba are included in Treaties 1, 2, 3, 4, 5, 6, 9 and 10, which were signed between 1871 and 1930. First Nations which are signatories to Treaties 3 and 9 do not reside in the province. The existence of these treaties, as well as the provision in the *Manitoba Act, 1870* that benefited the Metis, reflected recognition that the Aboriginal peoples possessed title to this territory.

As mentioned earlier, the basic policy of the Imperial and later Canadian governments towards Aboriginal peoples was influenced by expediency, self-interest, respect for the military and trading importance of Aboriginal peoples, colonial demands for land, threats of external competition, perceptions of European superiority, occasional regard for international law and response to practical realities. The Canadian courts played almost no role in this equation until the late 1800s, in stark contrast to the significant jurisprudence that was being articulated in the United States as early as the 1790s. Even the earliest decisions from English courts during the 1700s[21] were ignored by the American courts after Independence and, surprisingly, by Canadian courts, as well. The three most important decisions on Aboriginal title and Indian sovereignty were enunciated in the 1820s and 1830s by the United States Supreme Court: *Johnson v. M'Intosh*, *Cherokee Nation v. Georgia* and *Worcester v. Georgia*.

The first important Canadian case on Aboriginal title did not arise until over 50 years later, and in this case the dispute really was between the federal and Ontario governments (*St. Catherine's Milling & Lumber Co. v. R.*). The corporate litigant was merely caught in the middle of a power struggle between Ottawa and Toronto over who acquired the land, jurisdiction and benefits from the surrender of Aboriginal title through Treaty 3, as the company had received a federal timber licence, causing the Province to sue it for trespass and damages. The Ojibway were not even a party to the lawsuit that was determining their rights and status, nor were they consulted on this vital case. Interestingly, the federal government argued that Aboriginal title was equivalent to fee simple ownership, because it acquired full ownership of the land from the Ojibway through the treaty. This position was rejected by the Canadian courts and then by the Judicial Committee of the Privy Council on appeal, which declared instead that Aboriginal title was a mere "burden" on provincial Crown title that disappeared when the federal government obtained its surrender by treaty.

Aboriginal people only reluctantly began to assert their Aboriginal or treaty rights with any regularity in Canadian courts in the 1950s, and even then it was as defendants in confronting hunting and fishing harvesting charges. Aboriginal peoples did not voluntarily invoke the authority of the Canadian judiciary to define their rights until the ground-breaking case of *Calder v. Attorney General of British Columbia* in 1973.

The continuing hesitation to utilize Canadian courts to address Aboriginal and treaty rights issues may reflect several factors. One of these is that it was illegal for Indians or lawyers to pursue land claims in court, or to collect or receive money for this purpose, under the *Indian Act* from 1927 until its last major overhaul in 1951. The very limited scope given to Aboriginal and treaty rights by the courts, as exemplified by the Privy Council's description of Aboriginal title as merely being "a personal and usufructuary right, dependent upon the good will of the Sovereign,"[22] or the virtually racist language in *R. v. Syliboy*, [1929] 1 D.L.R. 307 (N.S. Co. Ct.), was also very discouraging to potential litigants.

Furthermore, launching major lawsuits, especially ones requiring extensive expert and historical evidence, is an exceedingly expensive undertaking that is well beyond the financial means of almost all Aboriginal groups and individuals. Choosing to argue Aboriginal or treaty rights in a Canadian court is also very risky for Aboriginal people. It removes all control over the future well-being of the group or community from its members and places it largely in the hands of non-Aboriginal judges who have almost no background regarding Aboriginal legal issues, and limited awareness and sensitivity toward the concerns of Aboriginal people. In this context, the stakes are very high indeed when the typical "winner take all" outcome of litigation is combined with the potential for the decision to govern future generations.

These restrictions on the use of litigation help to explain the lack of clarity and certainty in our jurisprudence, especially in comparison with federal Indian law in the U.S. Likewise, legislation has not been utilized to clarify the nature and legal status of Aboriginal and treaty rights. Parliament clearly has legislative jurisdiction pursuant to section 91 (24) of the *Constitution Act, 1867* to enact statutes concerning "Indians, and Lands reserved for the Indians." This has justified federal statutes regarding Indians since 1868 and the *Indian Act* since 1876. These statutes, however, have had nothing whatsoever to say about Aboriginal title and very little effect on treaty rights. The prevailing view, as supported by the Supreme Court of Canada in *Natural Parents v. Superintendent of Child Welfare*, [1976] 1 W.W.R. 699, also has been that provinces have no constitutional authority to legislate explicitly regarding Indians or their lands. Therefore, provincial governments could not resolve the confusion statutorily and Parliament has chosen not to do so.

This general situation has changed significantly over the past few years, through a number of major court decisions and the influence of the new Constitution.

The Legal Authority to Enter into Treaties

The treaty-making process began in early 17th century New England and New York, and continued in Canada, first in the Atlantic provinces during the 1700s and later in Upper Canada after 1763. Negotiating treaties was a response to the reality of a significant number of organized Indian groups living in settled territories. The legal theory that best explains the reasons for treaties is the natural law idea that established communities have rights to the lands they use and occupy. Natural law was the basis of international law, and played a significant role in 17th and 18th century British legal thinking. In the early treaty-making process, the natural rights of Aboriginal peoples were recognized, and the treaty-making process itself was confirmed later in the *Royal Proclamation of 1763*.

When Rupert's Land was transferred to Canada in 1869, Canada assumed the obligation of compensating the Indians for land taken up by settlement. The deed of surrender from the Hudson's Bay Company to the Crown stated the following:

> 14. Any claims of Indians to compensation for lands required for purposes of settlement shall be disposed of by the Canadian Government in communication with the Imperial Government; and the Company shall be relieved of all responsibility in respect of them.[23]

An Imperial Order-in-Council was issued on June 23, 1870, directing that Rupert's Land was to become part of Canada on July 15, 1870. The conditions imposed for this transfer included the one just quoted. The transfer was preceded by a series of Resolutions and Addresses of the Canadian Parliament, in which the commitment was explicitly made that the interests of the First Nations would be protected and that compensation would be provided for any land acquired.

The assumption of this obligation tacitly recognized the belief that the Indians had certain territorial rights at odds with the asserted title of the Crown. Like the *Royal Proclamation of 1763*, the transfer documents did not create Indian rights, because those already existed. The transfer documents merely dealt with who was to compensate, in the event that compensation or treaties were necessary.

Between 1871 and 1922, treaties were negotiated in Rupert's Land and the North-West Territories, with adhesions for various groups continuing up to the 1950s. In cases dealing with federal financial obligations, the question of the legal enforceability of the treaties arose. While some courts upheld treaty provisions on the basis of contract law,[24] other courts declined comment on the legal enforceability of the treaties, simply holding that the treaty provisions in question had been overridden by statute.[25] In fact, the *Indian Act* neither authorized treaty making nor provided that treaties in general had legal force, other than in exempting treaty Indians since 1951 from provincial laws that conflicted with treaties as a result of section 88 of the Act.

The Supreme Court of Canada, in *R. v. Simon*, declared that Indian treaties are in a special class all their own. Chief Justice Dickson stated:

> An Indian treaty is unique; it is an agreement *sui generis* which is neither created nor terminated according to the rules of international law.[26]

While Manitoba Indians are said to derive certain rights through the treaties they signed, the Manitoba treaties, like the other Indian treaties in Canada, gained greater legal status in 1982. Section 35 of the *Constitution Act, 1982* recognized and affirmed existing treaty rights. This effectively precluded any further arbitrary parliamentary interference with those rights, such as had occurred under the previous doctrine of parliamentary supremacy, through which the courts concluded that Parliament legally could do whatever it wished, even if it was unjust and dishonourable to violate solemn treaty commitments.

The Manitoba Treaties

The written versions of Treaties 1 to 6, 9 and 10 all have relevance in Manitoba. The content of the federal government's narrow version of the treaties, which is based upon a strict reading of their terms, may be grouped and summarized as follows.

• **Sovereignty and Allegiance.** The expressed goal of the treaties signed in Manitoba was "peace and goodwill" between the Indians and the Queen. While the treaties did not deal expressly with the transfer of sovereignty over Indians from the Indian tribes to the Crown, all referred to the Indians as subjects. This has been relied upon by the federal government as being recognition of a transfer of allegiance and sovereignty. However, since the treaties were negotiated through the chiefs, the existing political order was also recognized.

• **Surrender of Land.** The stated intention of the treaties was to open up the area for settlement. Under the treaties, the Indians were said to have ceded, released, surrendered and yielded up the land to the Crown forever. The language of the individual treaties reflects the wording used by lawyers, as if these were deeds conveying private interests in land.

• **Reserves.** Most of the Prairie treaties promised reserves on the basis of one square mile per family of five. Treaties 1, 2 and 5, however, were exceptions as they merely promised 160 acres per family of five. The rationale for identifying smaller reserves under these three treaties is unclear.

• **Education.** Treaties 1 to 5 promised schools on reserves. Treaty 9 promised to pay teachers' salaries, but did not expressly link the schools to the reserve system. This latter treaty probably reflects the development of the off-reserve residential school system by the time the treaty first was signed in 1905.

• **Economic Development.** As stated in Treaties 3 and 5, the reserves were established for the purposes of farming. Under the treaties, agricultural assistance in the form of animals, farm implements, ammunition and twine was promised.

• **Ban on Alcohol.** Under Treaties 1 to 5, alcohol was banned from the reserves.

• **Hunting and Fishing Rights on Surrendered Lands.** Although hunting and fishing rights were not included in the written versions of Treaties 1 and 2, they were promised orally and have been written into each of the subsequent Manitoba treaties. Treaties 4 and 9 went further and promised trapping, as well.

• **Annuities.** Annuity payments to the chiefs and band members were provided for under each treaty. In Treaty 5, the annuity payments to the chiefs were referred to as an "annual salary," and these payments sometimes were supplemented by gifts of flags, medals, clothing and buggies.

• **Regulatory or Legislative Authority of Canada**. The Government of Canada reserved for itself certain regulatory authority under the treaties. There was no reference to legislative authority or parliamentary supremacy. Under the treaties, Canada prohibited the presence of alcohol on the reserves and was expected to strictly enforce this regulation. Hunting, fishing and trapping rights were also made subject to federal legislation. Moreover, Treaties 3 to 9 allowed the expropriation of reserve lands without federal legislation, in return for due compensation, if the reserve lands were needed for public works.

The Relationship of Treaties to the *Indian Act*

There are striking differences between the *Indian Act* and the treaties. First, the *Indian Act* was not formulated by the bilateral, consensual process which had characterized the negotiations of the treaties. Second, the *Indian Act* sought to replace the traditional Indian political system by arbitrarily defining a process for the selection of chiefs and councils. And third, the *Indian Act* imposed upon Indian nations an artificial grouping called the "band," and sought to define who was legally entitled to be called an "Indian" in Canada.

The *Indian Act* represented a shift in the way the Canadian government dealt with Indians. It was not designed to create or recognize existing rights, but, instead, essentially represented an attempt by a government bureaucracy to manage the lives of Indians and Indian communities. Thus, almost overnight, Indians went from being recognized as having independent political and territorial rights under the treaty process, to being subject to the concept of unilateral parliamentary supremacy under the *Indian Act*. In Manitoba federal legislation was not brought into force until May 1874, so it was not applicable in the province at the time of the negotiations of Treaties 1, 2 and 3. Arguably, therefore, its provisions were not an issue to resolve during the early stages of the treaty process. It was in force at the time of the later treaties. However, it is clear, as well, that its terms never really were applied or even explained to the more isolated bands included in those later negotiations, until well after the treaties had been negotiated. Thus, Indian people were negotiating treaties under the expectation that they would continue as before to govern their own affairs, while the Crown knew that it would be imposing a legislative regime to suppress traditional authority and transform the lives of Indian people in a way contrary to their wishes.

Problems with the Validity and Text of Treaties

Indian leaders have always maintained the importance of the treaties, and this position has been consistent up to the present date. While commentators have called the treaties flawed and nothing more than legalized theft, Indian leaders generally have taken a different tack.

They have argued for a conceptual interpretation of the treaties, one reflecting their spirit and intent, which is more in line with what the original signatories believed the agreements entailed. To Indian leaders, the treaties are a recognition of Indian sovereignty. As long as the treaties continue in existence—despite their flaws—they serve as a continuing recognition of the Indian right to autonomy and self-government. The treaties represent a permanent relationship between the Crown and Indian people. They reflect solemn undertakings by both sides. The Indian nations pledged to be allies of the Crown forever and to support the Crown, even in times of conflict with other countries. For this reason, Indian people had a very high rate of participation in the armed forces during times of war—even though they were not subject to the conscription laws applicable to others.

The Crown was seen as committing itself to promote the well-being of its Indian allies. It was seen by Indian nations as assuming obligations under the treaties that were to be of a beneficial nature to the Indian signatories and the peoples they represented. This was not seen as including, however, the authority to dictate to Indian people how they would live and how their governments would act.

The various promises made under each treaty have a special significance to Indians. The promise of hunting, fishing and trapping rights is seen as a preservation of the traditional economy of the Indian peoples throughout their entire traditional territory, rather than limited to the reserves. The promise of ploughs and seed is seen as a commitment to economic development. The promise of reserves is viewed as a permanent guarantee of a land base on which Indian communities can flourish without external influence or control. The promise of a "medicine chest" is seen as the provision of free health care services, adequate to the needs of Indian people. The promise of schools is interpreted as a guarantee of free education, sufficient to meet the aspirations for Indian children to acquire those skills and opportunities essential to confront changing circumstances. The confirmation of rights to harvest fish and game is viewed as confirmation of traditional economies and lifestyles. This means that the land will be shared and used by both sides in a manner not mutually exclusive so that wildlife will remain plentiful.

Although Indians have argued for a conceptual interpretation, the courts have been more inclined to debate whether the treaties should be given a literal or liberal interpretation. The decisions over the years have been largely mixed and inconsistent. For example, in one case, the Exchequer Court interpreted the promise of a "medicine chest" to cover all prescription drugs for Treaty 6 bands,[27] but in another case, the Saskatchewan Court of Appeal held that the promise did not even extend to the provision of a doctor's services.[28] Another point of recent disagreement between Indians and the government has been the issue of funding for post-secondary education. While Indian leaders have fought the federal government's new policies which seek to impose drastic limits on funding, the issue has yet to go before the courts.

The Impact of the *Constitution Act, 1982*

The provisions in the new Constitution have already had a dramatic effect on the way in which our courts are now dealing with legal disputes concerning Aboriginal and treaty rights. In order to understand the current state of the law and its likely future development, one must first appreciate the former situation so that the change in the law is more apparent.

Prior to Constitutional Recognition

While the Canadian courts had given some effect to the existence of the Aboriginal peoples' title to their own land, the *St. Catherine's Milling* case indicated that this title survived solely at the pleasure of the Crown. It could be extinguished by conquest, treaty or unilateral Crown action.[29] Subsequent courts readily concluded that Aboriginal rights to land and its natural resources were subject to regulation by both federal and provincial laws of general application, even where these laws never stated on their face that they were intended to override Aboriginal rights. As a result, Aboriginal people were regularly convicted for infringing federal and provincial fish and game legislation.[30] While the courts clearly stated that both First Nations and the Inuit could possess Aboriginal rights (*Calder* and *Baker Lake*), the legal rights of non-status Indians and the Metis appeared more doubtful.[31]

Treaty rights have received slightly better treatment than Aboriginal rights by the Canadian courts. The general thrust of the case law is that these rights were regarded as providing an exemption to the application of provincial legislation to Indians, when there was a conflict between a particular statutory provision and a treaty term.[32] This exemption would not apply, however, when the provincial statute prohibited an activity at all times[33] or when it dealt with public safety.[34] Treaty rights, however, were subject to being overridden by valid federal legislation. Thus, the *Fisheries Act* and the *Migratory Birds Convention Act* were relied upon regularly to restrict the exercise of treaty rights.[35]

The courts shed little light on the content of Aboriginal and treaty rights. Aboriginal title was declared to be part of the common law in recognition of the fact that Aboriginal people had been here for thousands of years before the arrival of Europeans. Therefore, any group that could prove that it had occupied identifiable lands exclusively as a distinct society prior to the advent of British claims would be seen as possessing rights to the land. The precise scope of these rights was not fully articulated, although the courts indicated that they included the activities necessary to sustain the continuation of the group's way of life, such as hunting, fishing and gathering.

The courts were somewhat clearer in describing treaties as including both the written terms and oral promises that were made during the negotiations.[36] The Supreme Court of Canada ultimately resolved the dispute concerning how treaties, as well as statutory provisions regarding Aboriginal peoples, should be interpreted. A treaty is to be given a meaningful interpretation in contemporary society, rather than frozen in time as it might have been exercised on the date it was signed.[37] It is also to be read in a way that does not bring dishonour to the Crown.[38] Possible interpretations that might suggest sharp dealing or trickery are to be rejected.[39]

Treaties, therefore, are to be construed liberally, rather than literally. This means that each treaty should be understood not according to any technical meanings that could be attributed to the words used, but, rather, in their ordinary sense. In particular, they should be interpreted in the manner in which they would have been understood naturally by the Aboriginal signatories, with any doubts resolved in favour of Aboriginal people.[40]

The legal position in Manitoba and the other Prairie provinces, as well as a part of British Columbia, is complicated somewhat by the existence of the Natural Resources Transfer Agreements (NRTA). The Manitoba agreement, like the other three, conveyed the federal government's ownership of Crown land and natural resources to the provincial government, so as to put Manitoba in a position equivalent to those provinces that had existed previously as colonial governments, who acquired full Crown ownership rights when they joined Confederation. The *Constitution Act, 1930* incorporated these Natural Resources Transfer Agreements as constitutional amendments. Within the agreements is a provision designed to protect the continuation of Aboriginal wildlife harvesting rights. The relevant section in the Manitoba agreement (R.S.M. N30, s. 13) is as follows:

> In order to secure to the Indians of the Province the continuance of the supply of game and fish for their support and subsistence, Canada agrees that the laws respecting game in force in the Province from time to time shall apply to the Indians within the boundaries thereof, provided, however that the said Indians shall have the right, which the Province hereby assures to them, of hunting, trapping and fishing game and fish for food at all seasons of the year on all unoccupied Crown lands and on any other lands to which the said Indians may have a right of access.

The Supreme Court of Canada declared the overall purpose of this clause to be "to effect a merger and consolidation of the treaty rights theretofore enjoyed by the Indians but of equal importance was the desire to re-state and reassure to the treaty Indians the continued enjoyment of the right to hunt and fish for food."[41] A considerable amount of litigation has occurred over the last 30 years regarding the scope and precise meaning of each phrase within this provision. The courts have concluded that it only applies to restrict provincial legislation, but not federal statutes. It provides a limited exemption to Indians in terms of where they can harvest free from provincial restraint: on unoccupied Crown land and other places where they have a right of access for wildlife harvesting. This constitutional right also relates solely to food purposes and not commercial ones, even where the commercial aspect is secondary or accidental, as in the sale of a bear hide when the bear was shot in self-defence.[42] The Supreme Court of Canada has declared that certain treaty rights have been absorbed and altered by the Natural Resources Transfer Agreements. In return for acquiring the right of food harvesting throughout the Prairies so as to extend beyond the boundaries of a particular treaty, Indian people are subject to provincial regulation of commercial harvesting practices.[43] It is important to note that this exchange of rights occurred without Indian consultation or consent.

After the New Canadian Constitution

The *Charter of Rights and Freedoms* contains a specific section designed to recognize and preserve these special legal rights from any challenge based on other provisions within the *Charter* itself, including the guarantee of equality in section 15. Section 25, as amended in 1984, states:

> 25. The guarantee in this Charter of certain rights and freedoms shall not be construed so as to abrogate or derogate from any aboriginal, treaty or other rights or freedoms that pertain to the Aboriginal peoples of Canada including
>
> > (a) any rights or freedoms that have been recognized by the Royal Proclamation of October 7, 1763; and

(b) any rights or freedoms that now exist by way of land claims agreements or may be so acquired.

Part II of the *Constitution Act, 1982* contains the substantive recognition of the unique position of the original inhabitants of Canada. It not only includes a positive assertion of legal rights within the Constitution as "the supreme law" of Canada by virtue of section 52, but it also ensures a distinct role in the current constitutional amending formula, to a limited degree. As a result of amendments negotiated during a First Ministers' Conference on Aboriginal Constitutional Matters in 1983, and proclaimed in force in 1984 through the *Constitutional Amendment Proclamation, 1983,* the relevant provisions now read in Part II as follows:

35 (1) The existing aboriginal and treaty rights of the aboriginal peoples of Canada are hereby recognized and affirmed.

(2) In this Act, the "aboriginal peoples of Canada" includes the Indian, Inuit and Metis peoples of Canada.

(3) For greater certainty, in subsection (1) "treaty rights" includes rights that now exist by way of land claims agreements or may be so acquired.

(4) Notwithstanding any other provision of this Act, the aboriginal and treaty rights referred to in subsection (1) are guaranteed equally to male and female persons.

35.1 The government of Canada and the provincial governments are committed to the principle that, before any amendment is made to Class 24 of section 91 of the "Constitution Act, 1867," to section 25 of this Act or to this Part,

(a) a constitutional conference that includes in its agenda an item relating to the proposed amendment, composed of the Prime Minister of Canada and the first ministers of the provinces, will be convened by the Prime Minister of Canada; and

(b) the Prime Minister of Canada will invite representatives of the aboriginal peoples of Canada to participate in the discussions on that item.

Section 35.1, therefore, does guarantee that Aboriginal peoples must be consulted on any future amendments to sections 91(24), 25, 35 and 35.1. It does not prevent amendments to these sections without Aboriginal consent, however, nor does it give Aboriginal people any veto over such proposed changes. It also does not guarantee them a role in other amendments that indirectly might affect them or their rights.

Provisions in the Constitution of Canada are not to be interpreted in the traditional fashion used with regular legislation. The Supreme Court of Canada has declared repeatedly that constitutional interpretation is different from normal interpretation of statutes and private agreements. Constitutional interpretation requires a broad, purposive approach to be used in light of general principles and the purposes underlying the constitutional provisions themselves. This approach is particularly apt in relation to the *Charter of Rights and Freedoms* and section 35. Not only are the Aboriginal provisions part of the Constitution and warrant a liberal interpretation, but their source is unique as they were not drafted solely by legislators. Instead, the wording was agreed to jointly by Aboriginal leaders and first ministers.

The legal impact of section 35 was far from clear when it was first proclaimed. Ensuing cases have clarified some aspects, but the provision is still in a period of legal evolution. Considerable debate has occurred as to the impact of including these provisions, particularly those recognizing and affirming the "existing aboriginal and treaty rights of the aboriginal peoples." The debate centred on two major issues: the precise legal effect of placing Aboriginal and treaty rights in the constitution; and the question of the beneficiaries of any tangible legal benefits of this provision, if it did have any significance. The former issue has dominated attention and could affect all Aboriginal peoples, while the latter has tended to focus upon whether non-status Indians and Metis had any real rights that deserved recognition and affirmation in the first place.

The first few years after patriation were a period of legal uncertainty. Most government lawyers and some others asserted the narrow view that section 35 merely codified the prior state of the law. They argued that the presence of the word "existing" in section 35(1) was intended to confirm the existing legal situation. On this basis, they argued that Aboriginal and treaty rights could still be extinguished or regulated by either explicit or general legislation. They thought that any significant legal change in the status quo required more explicit language through further constitutional amendments. In other words, section 35 was largely an "empty box" that could be filled, if that was seen as politically appropriate, through amendments negotiated via the First Ministers' Conference process mandated by section 37 (and later section 37.1). The initial court decisions on section 35 tended to adopt this view.[44] A few even asserted that section 35 had no legal effect at all.[45]

At the opposite end of the spectrum were Aboriginal leaders and many others who argued that section 35 was specifically intended to transform the status quo. They viewed the First Ministers' Conference process as a means through which the Constitution could be amended so as to be worded more clearly and precisely to eliminate the likelihood of extensive and expensive litigation, and to enable greater public comprehension. They considered section 35 to imply a "full box" of rights, including the right of self-government. Under this theory, all Aboriginal and treaty rights were restored to full flower, free from any federal or provincial restraints. Apart from a few exceptional lower court decisions,[46] the courts have either ignored this position or rejected it.[47]

Between these two extremes were a variety of other interpretations. At the conservative end was the view that all prior alterations and extinguishments of Aboriginal and treaty rights remained effective, but that subsequent extinguishment was no longer possible. New restrictions would be acceptable only if they accorded with previous approaches toward regulating rights.[48] It was also suggested that regulations which had prevented the exercise of these rights before 1982 had the effect of extinguishing the rights so that they were "lost" and unable to be protected by section 35.[49]

Another view was that "existing aboriginal and treaty rights" meant "unextin-guished" rights, so that section 35 does not retroactively annul prior extinguishments of Aboriginal rights so as to restore the rights to their original unimpaired conditions. On the other hand, previous regulations and limitations of Aboriginal and treaty rights did not necessarily mean that the rights had been extinguished, only that they could not be exercised in full, due to the presence of a statute. In such a situation, the rights had been "sleeping" rather than "dead" and could be awakened by section 35.

While the First Ministers' Conference process was underway, some courts pre-ferred to avoid articulating the scope of section 35 in much detail, as judges felt that these issues were being addressed and hoped they would be resolved within this polit-ical forum.[50]

The Supreme Court of Canada indicated through its decision in *Guerin* in Decem-ber 1984 that the new legal approach toward Aboriginal issues was not limited to the interpretation of treaties and the *Indian Act*. In the latter case, the court unanimously rejected federal arguments that the Crown owed no legal obligations to the Musqueam Indian Band concerning the way in which the Department of Indian Affairs handled reserve lands surrendered for lease as a golf course. Although three different judgments were delivered, seven of the eight justices apparently were not impressed by the legal submissions of counsel for the federal government. The court decisively rejected the position that the Crown-Indian relationship was one that could be characterized merely as an unenforceable political trust. Instead, Mr. Justice Dickson, as he was then, on behalf of three colleagues, labelled it a fiduciary obligation flowing from the doctrine of Aboriginal title and the foundations of the Aboriginal-Crown relationship that pre-dated Confederation. In his opinion, certain sections of the *Indian Act* reflected this historic relationship, but the Act was not itself the source. Aboriginal title was a function of long-standing presence, and the duties of the Crown to respect Aboriginal rights stemmed from the unique relationship intentionally formed with Aboriginal peoples by the Crown. He further declared that the federal government was subject to fiduciary duties which had been violated in this instance, resulting in damages being assessed by the trial judge at $10 million plus interest.

The *Guerin* decision did far more than establish a fiduciary obligation in Canadi-an law regarding the manner in which the Crown exercises its discretion in dealing with Indian reserves. Mr. Justice Dickson clearly removed any lingering doubts resulting from the divergent views of the Supreme Court in *Calder*. He further stated that Aboriginal title was neither created by the *Royal Proclamation*, nor limited to its geographical scope. Aboriginal title instead is recognized independently by the common law and is a *sui generis*, or unique interest in land. It is not dependent upon the *Royal Proclamation*, the *Indian Act* or "any other executive order or legislative provision."[51]

The transformation in judicial thinking evident in *Guerin*, as well as the change that it made in Canadian law, did not affect the attitudes of the first minsters. However, this decision has had a considerable impact on developments in the jurisprudence. Although *Guerin* did not address section 35, it was likely influenced by the presence of the new constitutional provisions. The court, really for the first time in Canadian history, placed clear limits on the discretion of the Crown to exercise its jurisdiction over Aboriginal peoples in ways conflicting with Aboriginal interests. Unlimited federal power, which had been the hallmark of the treatment of Aboriginal peoples, now had been tempered by the duty to act as a fiduciary in advancing the interests of First Nations.

Judgments over the last few years have expanded this transformation in the Aboriginal-Crown relationship. The courts have generally chosen to give section 35 a broad, remedial interpretation in relation to both federal and provincial legislation. The judiciary has further widened the scope of both Aboriginal and treaty rights in a fashion that is independent of section 35, yet interrelated to this constitutional provision. This judicial approach also has not been limited to the members of the Supreme Court of Canada.

The changes in the law are most notable in several areas. The fiduciary obligation doctrine first advanced in *Guerin* has been expanded significantly by the Supreme Court in 1990 in *R. v. Sparrow*, [1990] 1 S.C.R. 1075. The fiduciary obligation now applies clearly to all Aboriginal peoples and not just Indian bands. It is also not restricted to reserve lands or *Guerin*-type situations. Furthermore, this duty applies to both the federal and provincial governments under the common law, and the obligation is also incorporated within subsection 35(1) so that it has constitutional protection.

The Supreme Court of Canada in *Sparrow* declared that the nature of this obligation is connected to "the concept of holding the Crown to a high standard of honourable dealing with respect to the Aboriginal peoples of Canada."[52] This results in the imposition of strict standards of trust-like conduct that will be supervised by the courts.

In our opinion, this means that the governments of Canada and Manitoba are under legally enforceable obligations to act on behalf of Aboriginal groups and communities. This general fiduciary obligation means that the Manitoba and federal governments are required by law to place the interests of Aboriginal people first and foremost as a reflection of the special, historic Aboriginal-Crown relationship. The practical inequality that has existed for generations, under which the Crown has had the power to affect the lives and rights of Aboriginal peoples any way it wanted to, now must cease.

The governments of Manitoba and Canada now have had over a year to study the implications of the Supreme Court of Canada's decision in the *Sparrow* case. Neither government has released its official interpretation yet, or declared how it will change its practices to meet the legal obligations it carries in relation to all Indian, Inuit and Metis peoples. We note with interest that the government of Ontario released its new position in the area of wildlife harvesting in May 1991.

It is clear that the federal and provincial governments possess fiduciary obligations for Indian, Inuit and Metis peoples that cannot be avoided. These obligations are now entrenched constitutionally in section 35. The governments of Canada and Manitoba should delay no longer in making this obligation the explicit cornerstone of the new relationship that they should be forging with Aboriginal people.

■ The federal and provincial governments each issue a public statement
within 180 days of the release of our findings describing how each government intends to meet its fiduciary obligation to the Aboriginal people of this province.

In the last few years, the courts have also begun to elaborate upon both the scope
of section 35 in general and its impact upon legislation. The appellate courts of British
Columbia, Ontario and Nova Scotia[53] have led the way in rejecting the earlier narrow
views of the Saskatchewan Court of Appeal.[54] The *Sparrow* decision of the Supreme
Court of Canada now confirms the correctness of the broad, remedial approach in
relation to section 35.

The *Sparrow* case involved a Musqueam Band member who was charged in 1984
for fishing with a drift net longer than permitted by the band food-fishing licence given
under the federal *Fisheries Act*. The Supreme Court of Canada was confronted for the first
time with arguments directly raising the question of the effect of subsection 35(1) on
long-standing federal legislation. Previously, the court had stated on many occasions
that federal law prevailed over Aboriginal fishing rights.[55] The court concluded in
Sparrow that:

> The word "existing" makes it clear that the rights to which s. 35(1) applies are
> those that were in existence when the *Constitution Act, 1982* came into effect. This
> means that extinguished rights are not revived by the *Constitution Act, 1982*.[56]

The court went on, however, to say that this does not mean that the existing Aboriginal right is merely the right as it stood on April 17, 1982, subject to regulation. Instead,
"existing" means "unextinguished," so that Aboriginal rights, even though extensively
regulated before, are protected by subsection 35(1) in their historic, unregulated form as
long as they were regulated only, but not completely terminated. Furthermore, these
rights "must be interpreted flexibly so as to permit their evolution over time"[57] and they
are "'affirmed in a contemporary form rather than in their primeval simplicity and
vigour.'"[58] The court also placed limits on the test for any extinguishment that might
have occurred prior to 1982. The court adopted the "clear and plain language" test that
had been asserted by Mr. Justice Hall in the *Calder* decision, rather than the less rigorous
approach of Mr. Justice Judson. This means that legislation cannot extinguish or infringe
Aboriginal title or Aboriginal rights unless it uses explicit language indicating that the
statute is intended to affect these unique rights negatively. The scheme of restricting
Aboriginal rights, present for almost a century through the *Fisheries Act* and its regulations, was declared to be inadequate to limit or eradicate Aboriginal rights.

In *Sparrow* the court outlined the legal import of subsection 35(1). It must be
given a generous, liberal interpretation so as to be "sensitive to the Aboriginal

perspective itself on the meaning of the rights at stake,"[59] in keeping with the unique Crown-Aboriginal relationship that placed "the honour of the Crown" at issue. Section 35 "also affords Aboriginal peoples constitutional protection against provincial legislative power."[60] This does not mean, however, that:

> [A]ny law or regulation affecting Aboriginal rights will automatically be of no force or effect by the operation of s. 52 of the *Constitution Act, 1982*. Legislation that affects the exercise of Aboriginal rights will nonetheless be valid, if it meets the test for justifying an interference with a right recognized and affirmed under s. 35(1).[61]

The justification standard established by the Supreme Court consists of several components. First, the existence of an Aboriginal right must be demonstrated, along with specific legislative interference of that right. Such interference may range from regulating the exercise of the right or prohibiting it entirely. If *prima facie* infringement of subsection 35(1) is proven, then the onus shifts to the Crown. The Supreme Court declared that this "may place a heavy burden on the Crown" (at 1119), but this was appropriate where the Crown sought to violate a constitutionally protected right through existing legislation.

To justify such an interference, the Crown must establish a "valid legislative objective," which requires more than mere allegations that the law reflects the "public interest" implemented by legislators. Instead, the Crown actually must prove that the legislation is essential to carry out vital purposes and does, in fact, meet such purposes.

The next step in the analysis created by the court is to prove that the method chosen to attain this objective by the Crown respects the "special trust relationship and the responsibility of the government" regarding Aboriginal people.[62] This meant, in the context of the *Sparrow* case, that the court demanded tangible proof that the constitutional priority accorded to Aboriginal rights was being met in fact in the allocation of the natural resource. The Crown, therefore, would have to prove that the first priority status given to the Aboriginal right for fishing for food, social and ceremonial purposes was respected by the legislation while it simultaneously infringed the right. The court also described certain questions that should be addressed as part of this analysis, including whether the least possible infringement has occurred, compensation has been offered if the rights have been expropriated, and the Aboriginal group has been consulted in the development and administration of the law. The court expressly left open the question as to whether commercial fishing was an Aboriginal right, as the issue did not arise in that case, although the judgment noted that the Ontario Court of Appeal in *R. v. Agawa*, [1988] 3 C.N.L.R. 73 had found commercial fishing to be a treaty right, but that it had been regulated validly by the *Fisheries Act*.

The Supreme Court has stated clearly that Aboriginal rights must be given full respect and be "taken seriously" by governments in the exercise of their spheres of authority. Although the *Sparrow* case involved a member of an Indian band, the court judgment was expressly intended to be relevant to all Aboriginal peoples. The thrust of the judgment in *Sparrow* is also not limited to Aboriginal rights, as a number of courts have reached similar results in reference to treaty rights. Aspects of the *Migratory Birds Convention Act* have been ruled to be of no force and effect by the Manitoba Court of Appeal in *R. v. Flett*, [1991] 1 C.N.L.R. 140 (C.A.); affirming [1989] 4 C.N.L.R. 128 (Q.B.); affirming [1987] 5 W.W.R. 115 (Prov. Ct.). Certain fisheries regulations relating to licensing, closures and quotas have received the same result for violating treaty rights[63] or Aboriginal rights.[64]

The Nova Scotia Court of Appeal's decision early in 1990, in *R. v. Denny et al.* (1990), 94 N.S.R. (2d) 253, is also illuminating for its analysis of the interplay between Aboriginal and treaty rights. The Micmac defendants argued they had Aboriginal rights that were protected by 18th century treaties. The court accepted their argument on Aboriginal rights and did not feel it necessary to address the treaty rights issue. The Supreme Court of Canada cited the *Denny* decision at length and with favour in *Sparrow*. The particular relevance for Manitoba from the decision is that, in our opinion, it negates the common perception that treaty beneficiaries cannot also possess additional Aboriginal rights.

The reaction of the Manitoba courts to these issues over the past few years is particularly noteworthy. The most important case has been *Flett*, which involved the application of the *Migratory Birds Convention Act* to treaty rights. As mentioned earlier, the position before the introduction of section 35 was that this Act, through its general language, could override express treaty rights guaranteeing Indians the authority to hunt as they always had,[65] even though the treaty obligations of the Crown preceded the passage of this statute. Counsel for Flett argued before Judge Martin of the Manitoba Provincial Court that the former case law had been rendered irrelevant by the entrenchment of existing treaty rights in subsection 35(1) of the *Constitution Act, 1982*.

Judge Martin concluded that the new Constitution had made a significant change in the law. He rejected provincial arguments that the law remained the same, and stated:

> [S]urely the government intended that rights guaranteed and existing since time immemorial will be recognized, and therefore not abrogated, denigrated or extinguished, without at least consultation and subsequent constitutional enactment.[66]

He went on to acquit Flett on the basis that his treaty right prevailed over the conflicting provisions of the *Migratory Birds Convention Act* and its regulations. The provincial government appealed this decision, which is within its authority. Amazingly, the Department of Natural Resources continued to enforce the legislation as if the decision had never been rendered. As Gene Whitney, Enforcement Coordinator of the Canadian Wildlife Service, told us:

> [I]t was recommended by the Department of Justice that [*Flett*] only being a provincial court decision, nobody is bound by it and they suggest that we continue to [lay charges].

This was completely improper. Canadian criminal law does permit a stay of a trial judgment during the appeal process, but only upon decision by the court hearing the appeal and in very limited circumstances. No stay was sought by the Crown or ordered by any court. The government was simply flouting the law, as it had no authority whatsoever to ignore this decision. Judge Martin's decision was the law and deserved to be both respected and followed unless or until overturned. It brings dishonour to the government and the Crown when court decisions are not respected solely because the government has lost the case and has launched an appeal. Continuing to prosecute Indians on the same basis that had been rejected by Judge Martin after the trial decision in *Flett* imposed great hardship on those charged, and brought the government as well as the legal system in Manitoba into disrepute. This cannot be justified and should never be repeated.

Judge Martin's decision in *Flett* was upheld two years later by Mr. Justice Schwartz of the Manitoba Court of Queen's Bench. Mr. Justice Schwartz relied, as well, upon a decision of Madame Justice Conrad of the Alberta Queen's Bench that had been delivered after the decision of Judge Martin.[67] Both superior courts declared that subsection 35(1) had fundamentally altered the law, resulting in full protection being granted to the proper exercise of treaty rights. While unsafe methods of hunting could be regulated and preservation of a species maintained, the provisions under the Act which restrained hunting seasons and bag limits were of no force or effect regarding unextinguished treaty hunting rights. Section 35 had confirmed and entrenched the original treaty rights unaffected by the *Migratory Birds Convention Act*. This did not repeal or invalidate the Act, but rendered it inoperative when it conflicted with treaty rights.

Again, the Manitoba government chose to appeal and continued to refuse to give full weight to the Queen's Bench decision in the interim. In 1991 the Court of Appeal unanimously refused to grant leave to appeal, in no uncertain terms. The majority of the court also took the unprecedented action of awarding costs against the government in the amount of $15,000, to reimburse the Assembly of First Nations for the expenses it incurred through intervening in the last stage of the judicial process. The court was advised that the Crown had already agreed to substantially cover the costs of *Flett.*

The law is clear in Manitoba. Treaty rights must be respected. Rights under treaties will prevail over inconsistent federal or provincial legislation, except for the very limited circumstances where safety or essential conservation practices are at issue. In the latter case, treaty beneficiaries are still to receive priority in the allocation of the harvest.

The *Flett* case also demonstrates what has been a continuing source of conflict in Aboriginal-Crown relations in this province. We are referring to the regrettable and unlawful tendency of the federal and Manitoba governments to refuse to immediately honour decisions from our courts that reject government policies concerning resource management. We were told time and time again during the hearings that treaty rights were being infringed by conservation officers. Typical of these complaints was that from Rex Ross of the God's River Band:

> What [the conservation officer] did was to go out on the lake, a few hundred yards offshore from God's River. He pulled Alex Yellowback's net and fish from the ice and drove all the way back to the Narrows with it. Why? Because Alex never attached his permit number for domestic fishing to the net.

This raises some serious issues. God's River is part of Treaty #5. It is a treaty between the Government of Canada and ourselves. The treaty clearly says we can use the land and lakes for gathering food for domestic use. In fact, the treaty encourages us to do this by promising to provide equipment for this purpose. What right then, does an employee of the Province of Manitoba have to impose on us any obligations to secure a permit from the province for fishing for domestic use?

The decision of the Supreme Court of Canada in the *Sparrow* case provides another ready example. The Supreme Court delivered its unanimous judgment on May 31, 1990, in which it clearly declared that Aboriginal and treaty rights are entitled to priority in the allocation of fish and game resources. Nevertheless, governments across the land have responded by saying that they must study the decision and analyse its impact upon existing legislation and enforcement policies. While this approach may be readily understandable initially, it does not justify sustaining prior enforcement practices against Aboriginal people in a way that suggests the law has not changed.

Furthermore, governments cannot postpone action by studying the matter indefinitely. The impact of the *Sparrow* case is still under review by the federal government, more than one year later, in terms of its impact on the legislative regime and enforcement policies regarding harvesting of fish and migratory birds by Aboriginal people. The Indian and Metis people of Manitoba still do not know how the federal government will interpret the law. They still do not have any assurance that they will not be charged for exercising their Aboriginal and treaty rights. This naturally increases immeasurably the sense of frustration of Aboriginal people, due to a problem that is clearly contrary to the basic foundations of our legal system, which depends on clarity of the law and respect for the decisions of Canadian courts. Uncertainties created by government must cease immediately.

Although the jurisprudence does not answer every question, the courts recently have given a great deal of guidance. In our view, it is now clear that existing Aboriginal and treaty rights, regarding the specific territory involved, override provincial or federal legislation that infringes these rights.

The test articulated by the Supreme Court of Canada in *Sparrow* now establishes the basis upon which individual legislative provisions are to be assessed to determine their continuing validity. Even where the legislative interference with Aboriginal and treaty rights is able to be justified in the facts of a particular case, there still will be a number of critical issues that must be addressed. The Supreme Court has directed the Crown to do three things. First, the government must consider compensation where the rights are restricted unavoidably. Second, the Crown must consult with Aboriginal people to minimize any negative impact of an infringement of Aboriginal or treaty rights. Finally, the government must monitor the situation regularly to determine if the defensible rationale underlying the specific terms of the infringement that was acceptable in a particular case still exists or has disappeared.

Our courts have established an entirely new approach toward the examination of Aboriginal legal issues, which includes the fiduciary obligation, the content of Aboriginal title, and the scope of Aboriginal and treaty rights. This approach applies to all legislation, whether or not Aboriginal peoples or their unique legal rights are mentioned. The broad thrust of the law covers both federal and provincial legislation because both levels of government owe a fiduciary duty to all Indian, Inuit and Metis people.

It is our conclusion that, insofar as Aboriginal and treaty rights are concerned, the Canadian law has changed fundamentally. While the occasional decision may be completely out of step with this development, our opinion is that the Supreme Court has sent a clear message that Aboriginal and treaty rights must be given new respect by both governments and the courts. The Aboriginal-Crown relationship has been transformed to be more in keeping with its original foundations, but applied in contemporary terms. This significant shift in the law has clear implications for the position of Aboriginal people in Manitoba.

We anticipate that negotiations on constitutional renewal and reform will probably occur in the near future. These discussions may well include efforts to achieve sufficient support for an amendment on self-government, designed to remove uncertainty and confirm that section 35 of the *Constitution Act, 1982* does contain the right of Aboriginal peoples in Canada to govern their own affairs. We are hopeful that this will be successful, as we have concluded that the "aboriginal rights" within subsection 35(1) include the right of self-government. In our opinion, this right to self-government encompasses within it the right to establish and administer a justice system. While we favour such constitutional clarification to reduce conflict, we do not believe that such an amendment is in any way a necessity or precondition before our recommendations can be implemented.

We recommend elsewhere that the governments of Manitoba and Canada recognize the existence of that right and take the actions necessary within their respective authority to provide the opportunity in which Aboriginal justice systems can develop. This is a matter which requires political will at the highest levels. We invite the two governments to demonstrate that will.

Land Rights

Aboriginal people across Canada continue to vigorously assert rights and title to their traditional territories and to the regions they were moved to under pressure from encroaching settlers. Despite the clear recognition of Aboriginal title, and the prior practice of utilizing treaties to regulate Aboriginal-Crown relations concerning land until the late 1800s, there is still a persistent claim from Indian, Inuit and Metis peoples that their land rights have not been respected by either federal or provincial governments. Aboriginal witnesses repeatedly told us about both the rights to land they possess and the longstanding violations of those rights by the Manitoba and federal governments. Similarly, they spoke of how the treaty promises have largely been ignored. Chief Esau Turner, representing the Swampy Cree Tribal Council, told us at our hearing at The Pas:

> The Treaty promised land that would be ours forever. We have not received the land promised to us over 100 years ago.

Chief Jim Tobacco, of the Moose Lake Band, told us of a similar broken promise:

> Our lands were taken at the time of Treaty No. 5, and the treaty promises
> were broken. Our people were moved from the Narrows at North Arm in
> 1893 and promised land, [which] were never provided.... [O]ur way of life,
> our economy, our traditions have been destroyed.

We sympathize with the frustration that was so apparent in the voices of presen-ters as we travelled the province. The Aboriginal people of Manitoba must be commend-ed for the impressive display of patience and restraint they have demonstrated over the years in the face of government inaction.

There should be no controversy today surrounding the issue of treaty land entitle-ment. In fact, treaty land entitlement should not even be an outstanding issue. It is a sub-ject that is so simple and straightforward that it never should have arisen as a source of conflict in the first place.

Under the numbered treaties, the Indian nations of Manitoba were promised explicitly by the Crown that they would retain large tracts of land for their permanent and exclusive use, as partial payment for surrendering their complete title to all other land in the province. Formulas were set out in each treaty for determining how much land would be reserved for the individual Indian bands that participated in the treaty. In Manitoba, Treaties 3, 4, 6, 9 and 10 contained a formula that guaranteed that reserves would be established by the federal government on the basis of one square mile for each family of five. Under Treaties 1, 2 and 5, a far less generous formula of 160 acres per fami-ly of five was used. These simple formulas could have been applied easily, once the actu-al populations of the individual Indian bands were determined. Having then determined the appropriate amount of land, all that remained to be done was for the parties to select the preferred location for the reserve and to have the site surveyed properly. No confirm-ing Order-in-Council was necessary.[68]

As a result of what must be either gross federal incompetence or a deliberate unwillingness on the part of the government to fulfil its solemn commitments, 25 Mani-toba Indian bands still are denied their full land entitlements. The Government of Cana-da could easily have fulfilled this lawful obligation on its own until 1930, when it trans-ferred ownership of all Crown lands and natural resources to the Province of Manitoba through the Natural Resources Transfer Agreement. That transfer unfortunately generat-ed decades of intergovernmental wrangling. Federal-Manitoba conflict is clearly not, however, an acceptable reason for inaction on moral, political and legal commitments of such magnitude. Manitoba treaties provide the foundations for the Crown's acquisition of the territory and its ability to convey good title to individual settlers and corporations.

The Natural Resources Transfer Agreements contained a clause designed to address how the treaty land entitlement issue was to be resolved. Clause 10 of the Alberta and Saskatchewan agreements and clause 11 of the Manitoba agreement provide that the federal transfer of the Crown's interest does not undermine the Indian interest in reserve lands. They also include a mechanism to facilitate the creation of new reserves to fulfil treaty promises. The Manitoba provision, which is identical to those applying in the other two provinces, states:

ABORIGINAL AND TREATY RIGHTS

11. All lands included in Indian reserves within the Province, including those
selected and surveyed but not yet confirmed, as well as those confirmed, shall
continue to be vested in the Crown, and administered by the Government of
Canada for the purposes of Canada, and the Province will from time to time,
upon the request of the Superintendent General of Indian Affairs, set aside, out
of unoccupied Crown lands hereby transferred to its administration, such further areas as the said Superintendent General may, in agreement with the
appropriate Minister of the Province, *select as necessary to enable Canada
to fulfil its obligations under the treaties with the Indians of the Province*,
and such areas shall thereafter be administered by Canada in the same way
in all respects as if they had never passed to the Province under the provisions
hereof. [Our emphasis]

This provision, along with the rest of the NRTA, was made an express amendment to
the original Canadian Constitution of 1867. It is now called the *Constitution Act, 1930* and is
part of "the supreme law of Canada" by virtue of section 52 of the *Constitution Act, 1982*.

Nevertheless, the presence of a mechanism and the existence of a constitutional
obligation have not resulted in the fulfilment of these long-standing promises. We
believe that immediate implementation of these outstanding obligations is required.

Indian Reserves

The purpose and rationale for reserves has varied from time to time and place to
place. Beginning in the 1700s, Quebec reserves were designed to train Aboriginal peoples
in agriculture and Christianity, but in the Maritimes they served as places of refuge from
the gradual expansion of colonists. In the Prairies, the purposes were mixed, serving
both functions and the additional function of being a homeland where Aboriginal peoples could pursue their traditional way of life. Reserves also were created by the Crown as
institutions for economic, social, cultural and political change. Not only were reserves to
aid the assimilationist policies of the federal government, but they also got Aboriginal
peoples out of the way so other land could be "settled" by white immigrants. Indian
reserves have been central to the Indian policies of both the United States and Canada.

Indian witnesses repeatedly told us of the importance of retaining reserves and
improving their conditions. They also spoke directly about the problems caused by current reserves being too small to meet their needs. Roderick Harper, through an
interpreter at Red Sucker Lake, told us:

[W]e wanted to expand [the reserve] ... we needed more lands to live in, and
the excuse that is being told is that the provincial government doesn't want to
relinquish those lands for our children to maintain their own livelihood with.

The Development of Treaty Land Entitlements

While the Manitoba treaties contained a formula for calculating the size of reserves
to be established, this calculation could not be done until the precise population of each
band had been determined.

Despite treaty negotiator and later Lieutenant Governor Alexander Morris' admonitions that "all convenient speed" be used in establishing the reserves, reserve promises were implemented only in part. For some Indian bands, part of the treaty land entitlement was fulfilled, but the other part was put off to a later date. For other Indian bands, their treaty land entitlement was not fulfilled, since they lived in isolated and remote areas and the lack of European immigration into the area made "all convenient speed" unnecessary, at least for the federal government.

The transfer of federal Crown lands to Manitoba in 1930 complicated matters even more, as it brought a new party into the issue: the Manitoba government, with its own set of interests and motivations. Instead of completing the promise of reserve lands by settling all outstanding treaty land entitlements before transferring the land to the Province, the federal government simply inserted clause 11 into the NRTA. This provision, however, did not allow the federal government to select unilaterally which land the Indians would get. Rather, the decision now would have to be made with provincial cooperation.

The Formulas

The original purpose of the formulas in the numbered treaties was to secure an adequate land base for each band's future reserve. The treaty promises to the southern bands of cattle, ploughs, harrows and seed confirm the basic agricultural role which their reserve lands were to serve for them. There was a major problem with the formulas, though. The formula in those treaties only served its purpose if the reserve lands were situated along the fertile belt of the Prairies. If the reserve lands were situated outside the fertile belt, then the agricultural formula was meaningless, because farming would be unable to provide an economic base. Hunting, fishing, gathering and trapping, however, could continue to sustain northern reserves. In order for these activities to serve as the new economic base for reserves above the fertile belt, larger tracts of land were needed than those available under the formulas of the numbered treaties.

It is difficult to understand, therefore, why the treaty land entitlement formula for Treaty 5, which covers almost all of northern Manitoba, is the same as for Treaties 1 and 2 in the province's agricultural south. If there was any justification for this, it must have been that the reserves would be the home for treaty beneficiaries, but that those beneficiaries would continue to have unlimited access to traditional use areas outside the reserves for important economic activities, such as hunting, fishing and trapping. The importance of maintaining and protecting these rights over non-reserve traditional use areas must have been seen in that light. In addition, the necessity of receiving the entire land entitlement under treaties, therefore, takes on added meaning.

One issue which has been the source of contention relates to the date at which the population of the band is to be fixed for purposes of the formula.

Under one settlement agreed to between Canada, the Saskatchewan Indian Nations and the Province of Saskatchewan in 1976, the population of the band as of December 31, 1976 was multiplied by the acreage formula set out in the treaty to arrive at the amount of land to which the band was entitled. If the band had previously received no land from the Crown, then this was the amount to which it was entitled. If the band had received some land but not its full entitlement, then the amount received to date would be deducted from the amount derived from this formula, and the remainder would be what the band was still entitled to. This model has been called the "Saskatchewan Formula." However, it is only one settlement and is not binding on the situation in Manitoba.

The First Nations in Manitoba take the position that the amount of land to which they are entitled is to be determined by using the population of the band at the time the particular parcel of land is set aside. They appear to have some precedent for that position. The Saskatchewan Formula, using populations as of December 31, 1976, is one example where the governments recognized a modern-day population. It appears that the size of many reserves established over the years was based upon the total band membership of the day.

The formula most unfavourable to the interests of treaty Indians waiting for their promised land is the preferred option of the federal and provincial governments. This is the "shortfall on first survey" formula. Under this formula, the population of the band, at the date the first piece of reserve land was surveyed, is multiplied by the acreage per person promised under the treaty to arrive at the treaty land entitlement, less any land they have received from the Crown to date. This proposal is unfavourable because the population of the band at the date of first survey was usually significantly less than the band's current population. The smaller the band population figure used in the formula, the smaller the amount of land the Province and the federal government have to set aside for the First Nations.

The matter has been difficult to resolve through negotiation, in view of the tremendous distance which separates the parties. What is clear is that the governments seem to think they have nothing to lose and everything to gain by waiting. Delay allows greater encroachment to occur on already diminishing Crown lands. Precise figures are difficult to ascertain, but according to the Treaty and Aboriginal Rights Research Centre of Manitoba, when Crown lands and resources were transferred to Manitoba in 1930, 111.7 million acres of unoccupied Crown land were available for selection by the entitlement bands. The total today is less than one-half that figure. Available Crown land will continue to decline.

Treaty entitlement bands have made it clear that they wish to avoid disturbing private landowners. It is, therefore, in the best interests of the First Nations to have the matter resolved quickly, because they cannot be assured that there will be a sufficient amount of quality land available for selection in future years. If currently available land were placed under a moratorium against disposition so as to be kept free from development, then the First Nations would not suffer from the two governments' intransigence. As it is now, they are clearly the losers in the waiting game.

The Province has consistently favoured the "shortfall on first survey" formula. While the Province is concerned with giving up as little land as possible, and the federal government is wringing its hands at this sometimes unpleasant, embarrassing situation, the entitlement chiefs of Manitoba seemed to be concerned solely with resolving the issue as soon as possible. To this end, many offers of compromise have been extended, but whenever settlement appears close, political obstacles or changes of government seem to stall the tripartite negotiations.

The Present State

Although the entitlement issue was mentioned in the Natural Resources Transfer Agreement of 1930, and discussed briefly in the 1950s and 1960s in relation to isolated problems, little was done about resolving this issue until 1975. That year the Minister of Indian Affairs wrote to the three Prairie premiers, urging that outstanding entitlement issues be addressed and settled. Movement first occurred in Saskatchewan. An exchange of letters between the Federation of Saskatchewan Indians, the federal government and the Province of Saskatchewan in 1976 and 1977 led to the establishment of the Saskatchewan Formula. The fixing of the population as of December 31, 1976 was not intended as a significant modification of the entitlement. Rather, it was merely a decision designed to facilitate getting on with a settlement, through specifying an exact date on which population figures could be calculated. It was not expected that the process would get derailed.

In July of 1977, Warren Allmand, then the Minister of Indian Affairs, wrote the premier of Manitoba, suggesting the Saskatchewan Formula as a basis for settling entitlement claims in Manitoba. Later that month, the entitlement chiefs of Manitoba passed a resolution supporting the Saskatchewan Formula, with some adjustment in the date for calculating population. Following this decision, 26 entitlement claims were made to the federal and provincial governments. A new provincial government reverted to the "shortfall on first survey" formula. The federal government, however, rejected the Province's position and restated its support of the Saskatchewan Formula.

In August 1981 John Munro, Minister of Indian Affairs, appointed his parliamentary secretary, Ray Chenier M.P., as his personal representative to negotiate with the bands and the Province. Another new Manitoba government placed the issue under consideration, and the Treaty and Aboriginal Rights Research Centre published a detailed report on the treaty land entitlement issue.

In September 1982 the Province, with the agreement of the entitlement chiefs, appointed Manitoba lawyer Leon Mitchell Q.C. to investigate and report on the issue. His report was completed in January 1983. By this time the federal government had accepted 20 separate claims as being valid and six more were pending. The Mitchell report confirmed that the federal government's historic and traditional position on treaty land entitlement was to use the current-day population of the band, with the population being fixed as of the date of transfer of a particular parcel of land.

Beginning in the spring of 1983 and continuing for over a year, the federal and provincial governments negotiated with the treaty entitlement chiefs to resolve this outstanding obligation.

In August 1984 an agreement-in-principle was signed by the Treaty Land Entitlement Committee of Chiefs, the Province and the federal government. This agreement-in-principle:

- Recognized 23 bands as having outstanding entitlements.

- Accepted the use of the Saskatchewan Formula.

- Provided that future legislation on Indian band membership would not affect entitlement.

- Stipulated that all mineral rights or royalties on existing reserve lands and those to be set aside would go to the bands.

- Gave the Province certain rights for hydro development and rights of "re-acquisition" of 1/20 of future lands for specified purposes.

- Provided for a Treaty Land Entitlement Board of Implementation to facilitate the process, and a supplementary role for a mediator.

But this agreement was not to be. In September 1984 a new federal government was installed and the agreement-in-principle began to fall apart. With this collapse came the withdrawal of the provincial government's moratorium on the disposition of Crown land. This moratorium, established several years earlier, had prevented the transfer of Crown lands adjacent to reserves to third parties without the consent of the band.

By the beginning of 1988, the federal government reversed its position and accepted the "shortfall on first survey" formula for future negotiations. As of June 1989, 13 of the 23 entitlement bands recognized in the 1984 agreement-in-principle tentatively had made land selections within this new formula, on the basis that it would not prejudice their position that they are entitled to more acreage derived from present population figures. Even this latest compromise, however, did not bear fruit and there have been no new developments on this issue since then.

The entitlement chiefs no longer support the 1984 agreement-in-principle because too many years have passed to base a settlement today on band populations that existed in 1976. Indian communities continue to grow as a result of high birth rates and the effect of rectifying past discrimination through restoration of Indian status to thousands of people through Bill C-31. The federal government is currently reviewing its policy in this area. We note that the Province has stated that it supports the agreement-in-principle but has yet to take action on the matter.

According to the Treaty and Aboriginal Rights Research Centre of Manitoba, the current outstanding treaty land entitlements are as follows:

LAND ENTITLEMENT (in Acres)

Band	1990 Population	1990 Entitlement	Lands Received To Date	Amount Outstanding
Barren Lands/Northlands	1,170	149,760	11,861	137,899
Brokenhead	949	30,368	12,903	17,465
Buffalo Point*	68	8,704	5,763	2,941
Fort Alexander *	3,781	120,992	22,148	98,844
Fort Churchill	517	16,544	524	16,020
Fox Lake	607	19,424	4,300	15,124
Gambler*	95	12,160	19,200	−7,040
God's Lake/God's River	1,941	62,112	9,832	52,280
Island Lake	5,767	184,544	18,084	166,460
Long Plain	1,511	48,352	10,880	37,472
Mathias Colomb	1,939	248,192	23,265	224,927
Nelson House	2,959	94,688	14,452	80,236
Norway House	3,937	125,984	18,559	107,425
Oxford House	1,532	49,024	12,049	36,975
Peguis*	4,620	147,840	37,915**	109,925
Rolling River	537	68,736	13,920	54,816
Roseau River	1,257	40,224	12,955	27,269
Sandy Bay*	2,886	92,352	16,495	75,857
Shamattawa	749	23,968	5,725	18,243
Shoal River/Indian Birch	1,203	153,984	5,377	148,607
Swan Lake	799	25,568	10,400	15,168
The Pas*	2,457	78,624	15,657	62,967
York Factory	624	19,968	2,391	17,578

Source: Treaty and Aboriginal Rights Research Centre, July 1991
* Claims of outstanding amounts have not yet been recognized by the federal government.
**Peguis does not include lands occupied prior to treaty (approx. 17,000 acres).

The effect of government inaction has been significant in many reserve communities where there is a shortage of land for housing, wildlife harvesting, economic and natural resource development, and for general needs. The absence of the land to which Indian people are entitled inhibits planning and community development.

We received very detailed information on the magnitude of this unsettled issue that unnecessarily damages the relationship between First Nations and the other two governments involved.

The government of Manitoba is in debt to the First Nations of this province. This debt is growing constantly and should be paid forthwith. The population at the time of the transfer of the land to reserve status is the legally proper basis for the calculation to be made. The outstanding treaty land entitlement now exceeds one million acres of Crown land.

The First Nations have been extraordinarily patient. One should not presume that this will continue indefinitely. They also have been very accommodating in their proposals for settlement. This, too, may not continue.

In our view, there is no real justification for a debate or an argument about a "formula." The treaties themselves establish the precise formula to be used. It is the governments which have delayed applying the formula and providing the remaining land as required by the treaties. The federal government has unilaterally increased the size of bands by enacting Bill C-31. The federal and Manitoba governments must take each band as they now find them. The Indian people of Manitoba are entitled to the full amount of land promised by the treaties in accordance with the population at the time the treaty obligations are finally fulfilled. The Manitoba and federal governments should not be permitted any further delays. If the matter is not settled expeditiously, the governments may have no choice but to obtain land from others whom they have allowed to acquire land contiguous to reserves in order to meet their constitutionally recognized obligations. In our opinion, the amount of land to which a band is entitled should be established in light of the band's population as of the day the land is transferred. Since the Indian population is continuing to grow rapidly through the twin impacts of Bill C-31 and a high birth rate, the size of the outstanding entitlements will continue to increase each year until the treaty commitments are properly honoured.

WE RECOMMEND THAT:

■ Current population figures be used for entitlement in conjunction with the formula set out in each treaty to determine the precise amount of land that is owed to each First Nation.

It is of critical importance that these obligations be fulfilled forthwith. Available Crown land is disappearing, and meeting these obligations will become progressively more difficult in the future. The treaty land entitlement First Nations are not to blame for the delays in fulfilling the Crown's obligations under the treaties, and they should not be forced into a position in which they must select Crown land that is unsatisfactory or accept financial compensation in lieu of land. It will become more expensive for the federal and provincial governments if they must purchase land on the open market. However, the likelihood of this option increases as Crown land is alienated.

WE RECOMMEND THAT:

- The government of Manitoba reinstitute a moratorium on the disposal of Crown land in the province and that no Crown land be made available to third parties by grant or lease until all First Nation land selection has been made or without the consent of the treaty land entitlement bands in the region.

It is also our opinion that the Manitoba and federal governments should pay compensation to those Indian bands with outstanding treaty land entitlements for breaching the treaties. They failed to make the necessary quantum of land available shortly after the treaties were signed. They have acted unconscionably in continuing to breach the treaty commitments. These First Nations have had their rights violated and have lost the benefits of possessing their full complement of reserve lands for almost a century, even though the treaty formulas were clear and should have been implemented readily, based upon the number of band members at the time. The delays have not resulted from any inaction or fault on the part of the First Nations concerned. They should be compensated, therefore, for the hardships they have suffered and the opportunities lost, in addition to finally receiving the reserve lands promised to them during the last century. The commitments in the treaties have been broken and damages should be paid, as would be the case if they were contracts between the government and private parties. The Province, in some cases, has been unjustly enriched by the profit from the sale of natural resources from lands that properly should have been conveyed to benefit the First Nations concerned many years ago. Immediate action to honour the treaty provisions and to compensate for lost enjoyment of the land is vital.

Both the Province and the Indian people can ill-afford any further delay in seeing justice done and solemn treaty commitments, now constitutionally protected, properly fulfilled.

We believe that the most appropriate method of resolving these disputes is to establish a Treaty Land Entitlement Commission.

WE RECOMMEND THAT:

- A Treaty Land Entitlement Commission be created for Manitoba, consisting of five members, namely, one provincial nominee, one federal nominee, two nominees from the Assembly of Manitoba Chiefs, and a neutral chairperson selected by the other members of the commission. This commission should be empowered to render binding decisions on any disputes that may arise over:

  - The exact population of an entitlement band.

  - The amount of land originally set aside for the reserve that is to be deducted from the current treaty entitlement.

  - The selection of Crown lands to fulfil the entitlement obligation.

  - The location of boundaries.

  - The amount of financial compensation for the delay.

In reaching its award of compensation, the commission should be authorized to consider resources that have been exploited by the federal or provincial governments over the years, as well as the cultural, social and economic significance to the individual First Nation of being deprived of rights to this land.

WE RECOMMEND THAT:

- The Treaty Land Entitlement Commission be created by complementary federal and provincial legislation with the endorsement of the Assembly of Manitoba Chiefs. We further recommend that this legislation be drafted jointly by both governments in conjunction with the treaty land entitlement First Nations.

We believe that disputes should be rare regarding the land entitlement issues, as the treaties establish a clear formula. All that is necessary is to determine the population as of the date the additional reserve land is to be set aside. Fulfilling this outstanding obligation should be done forthwith.

We believe that a commission with authority to render binding decisions is necessary, as governments have demonstrated through their delay and inaction, for over 100 years in many cases, that they are incapable or uninterested in meeting these solemn obligations. Furthermore, governments currently have the power to delay and this imbalance must be addressed.

The Most Recent Treaty—The Northern Flood Agreement

The Northern Flood Agreement (NFA), signed on December 16, 1977, came after more than a decade of heated public controversy in Manitoba. The controversy was protracted and it remains one of the most publicized modern disputes between Aboriginal people asserting their historical rights and a government committed to large-scale natural resource development.

Background

Hydro-electric projects in northern Manitoba have been undertaken for many years. In 1960 Manitoba Hydro built a dam at Grand Rapids, where the Saskatchewan River enters Lake Winnipeg. The project flooded the reserve community of Chemawawin, resulting in a relocation of its residents to Easterville. This move has proven to be socially and emotionally disruptive to the people of the band. The relocation was so ill-planned by government and Hydro officials that it caused serious social and economic problems in the community, from which it may never fully recover. The traditional economies of the Grand Rapids and Moose Lake First Nations also suffered from the effects of the flooding.

The Churchill River diversion project, which ultimately led to the Northern Flood Agreement, began to take shape in the latter part of the 1960s. The Nelson River is the major outlet of Lake Winnipeg, flowing northeast into Hudson Bay through a series of lakes. The plan was to divert the flow of the Churchill River into the Nelson River and construct power stations on the Nelson. The Churchill would be dammed at Missi Falls at the eastern end of Southern Indian Lake. The lake would then be used as a giant reservoir, ensuring an ample flow of water in the Nelson in the middle of winter, when demand for electricity is highest.

The project was huge. It was said that the completely harnessed Nelson would be the largest power development in Canada—bigger than Labrador's Churchill Falls and British Columbia's Peace and Columbia river developments. Early reports put the cost at one billion dollars; later reports said three billion. The project would provide power for use in Manitoba and for sale in the United States.

Large government-backed energy projects were characteristic of the period. There were many proposals to alter irrevocably the face of the northern landscape. These energy projects meant massive frontier development. All the initiatives helped to fuel the thinking that the Manitoba government should be cashing in on hydro-electric prospects in northern areas for the export market.

The Report of the Mackenzie Valley Pipeline Inquiry described such a conflict as essentially between those who viewed the land as a "frontier" and those who viewed it as a "homeland." The projects forced Aboriginal communities to defend their homelands, a fight that fundamentally altered Canadian legal and political views on Aboriginal rights. Aboriginal people began to turn to the courts for assistance and also to demand to negotiate land claims agreements to address the implications of these massive energy projects. This trend was also reflected by the response of Indian and Metis people in northern Manitoba to development proposals.

Early in 1973 the Supreme Court of Canada in the *Calder* case divided equally on the question of the survival of the Aboriginal title of the Nishga tribe in British Columbia. While technically indecisive, the judgment gave strong new legitimacy to Indian claims. Shortly after the Nishga judgment, the federal government announced it would negotiate a settlement of Indian and Inuit claims in limited parts of the country. The Cree of Quebec obtained an injunction in the Superior Court of Quebec against the James Bay hydro-electric project in September of 1973.[69] The Quebec Court of Appeal quickly lifted the injunction pending the full hearing of an appeal,[70] but the message was clear: the courts might side with Indians. The era of the energy megaprojects faded in the mid-1970s as a worldwide recession took hold. Some of the projects were built, but most were dropped or postponed.

Manitoba premier Ed Schreyer was unaffected by these developments elsewhere. He said that Indian people of northern Manitoba should not be able to veto development and suggested the federal government was facing that same issue in the Northwest Territories. He pointed to the James Bay project as demonstrating that the federal government would not interfere with provincial government hydro projects on environmental grounds. The federal Minister of Indian Affairs, Jean Chretien, said he was willing to fund an Indian lawsuit in Manitoba just as he had funded an Indian lawsuit in Quebec.

Pressure built on all sides. For the first time in a Canadian dispute involving Aboriginal people, a mediator was brought in to assist the parties to the negotiations. Although an agreement finally was reached, its implementation proved to be far more elusive.

The Terms of the Agreement

The Northern Flood Agreement was signed by Canada, Manitoba, Manitoba Hydro and the Northern Flood Committee representing the five First Nations (Nelson House, Norway House, Cross Lake, Split Lake and York Factory) whose reserve lands were to be flooded by the major hydro-electric projects planned. The agreement provided for an exchange of four acres for each acre flooded, the expansion and protection of wildlife harvesting rights, five million dollars to be paid over five years to support economic development projects on the reserves and promises of employment opportunities. The agreement was also to deal with any adverse effects to the "lands, pursuits, activities and lifestyles of reserve residents." The five First Nations were guaranteed a role in future resource development as well as in wildlife management and environmental protection. Certain water level guarantees were made and Manitoba Hydro generally accepted responsibility for any negative consequences that might emanate from the flooding. In return, Hydro obtained the right to flood reserve lands as part of the Churchill Diversion Project. Disputes over any adverse effects were to be settled by arbitration.

Breaches of the New Treaty

Manitoba Hydro obtained what it wanted as it proceeded with this massive project. The reaction from Aboriginal people has been far from positive. Only reserve residents were represented in the negotiations and were to receive any of the benefits. Many Metis and off-reserve Indians in the region still complain bitterly that their homes and traplines were destroyed and their hunting and fishing rights violated without any consultation or compensation.

Aboriginal people also argue that they were never told of the environmental destruction that would occur. They say that they were never told that graves would be washed away and fish habitats demolished, nor that an entire way of life for what previously had been strong communities would disappear. Over a decade later, they were still voicing their hurt and dissatisfaction to this Inquiry. Rosie Dumas, an elder from South Indian Lake, through an interpreter, told us:

> We used to make a good living out of our community ... [before] the flood. When you look into the future, there is really nothing there for us, for our children [and] grandchildren.

Another elder, Allison Kitchekeesik of Split Lake, through an interpreter, spoke of the future facing the community's young people:

> Their ways of life are shattered, Hydro has damaged many areas within our traplines.... Our fish are not safe to eat. I see how much damage Hydro has caused to our land and this is why I speak out.

Payments of $160 million have been made under the Northern Flood Agreement, including approximately $88 million from the federal government. Hydro has recently offered $243.5 million to bring the agreement to an end.[71] The majority of the First Nations affected have rejected this offer, saying that some aspects of this modern-day treaty have yet to be fully implemented. The promised partnership concerning future decision making in the area has not been implemented. Again, governments have failed to adhere to all the terms of the treaty.

We believe the Northern Flood Agreement is a "land claims agreement" within section 35(3) of the *Constitution Act, 1982* and that the rights within the NFA are treaty rights within section 35(1). As a treaty, the Northern Flood Agreement must be interpreted liberally from the Indian perspective so that its true spirit and intent are honoured.

WE RECOMMEND THAT:

- The governments of Manitoba and Canada recognize the Northern Flood Agreement as a treaty and honour and properly implement the NFA's terms.

- Appropriate measures be taken to ensure that equivalent rights are granted by agreement to the other Aboriginal people affected by the flooding.

There have been many negative consequences in northern Manitoba over the past 30 years resulting from large-scale hydro-electric and timber development. We believe that if future projects are likely to have significant impact upon reserve lands or the exercise of harvesting rights by Aboriginal people, they should not proceed unless or until consultation has occurred and agreement has been reached with the Aboriginal communities to be affected. Such agreements should address efforts to minimize or eliminate any negative environmental repercussions, promote Aboriginal economic opportunities, and provide suitable alternative lands and financial compensation.

WE RECOMMEND THAT:

- A moratorium be placed on major natural resource development projects unless, and until, agreements or treaties are reached with the Aboriginal people in the region who might be negatively affected by such projects in order to respect their Aboriginal or treaty rights in the territory concerned.

Land Claims

Aboriginal people have been distressed about violations of their rights to their traditional territory almost since the arrival of Europeans. The process of negotiating treaties was a necessary response to these complaints in the 19th and early 20th centuries. Treaties, however, were not negotiated regarding all territory in Canada or even in Manitoba. In addition, the reserves that were set aside under treaties have themselves become the basis of further grievances stemming from their maladministration by the Government of Canada. Not only was much of the treaty land entitlement to reserves never properly set aside, but thousands of acres of land which were dedicated as reserves were lost improperly, resulting in many years of petitions to the Crown for redress. Silence was usually the response from the federal government.

In 1969 the Government of Canada promised action on treaty violations and reserve land losses as part of its White Paper on Indian policy. Although the motivation was suspect, as this initiative was coupled with a plan to repeal the *Indian Act* and terminate special Indian status, it did reflect at least some understanding on the part of the federal government that these historic grievances had to be addressed if it hoped to obtain Indian support for the federal objectives.

The *Calder* decision, as mentioned earlier, caused a similar federal awakening to the reality of the continued existence of Aboriginal title in Canada. The government declared its new policy in August of 1973, through which it reiterated its willingness to settle treaty and reserve claims, and added a new openness regarding those claims related to unextinguished Aboriginal title. The government divided all these outstanding grievances into two basic categories: specific and comprehensive claims. However, many land claims, such as those of the Metis in Manitoba, are actually excluded from both categories—leaving them with no process by which they can be negotiated.

Specific Claims

There are several basic sub-categories within the broad purview of the federal specific claims policy that exist in Manitoba. Treaty land entitlement is one of these. It has required its own special initiative, due to the necessity to involve the government of Manitoba to transfer provincial Crown land to fulfil these outstanding obligations.

Another broad type of specific claim refers to "maladministration" of band assets. This covers instances of theft of band funds by Indian agents, failure to pay proper interest rates on band trust funds held in Ottawa, misdirection of treaty annuity payments and misapplication of band revenue from lease or sale of reserve land. Several First Nations in Manitoba, including Roseau River and The Pas, have this type of claim.

The last sub-category of claim relates to the illegal taking or damaging of reserve land. It covers a wide variety of circumstances, including instances of improper taking of reserve lands by the federal government and its agencies, as well as expropriations committed in accordance with the law but for which inadequate or no compensation was provided. There are also many claims relating to reserve lands that were sold without a surrender from the relevant band, or where the provisions of the *Indian Act* governing the surrender process were breached. There are a surprising number of claims that flow from a valid surrender of reserve land in which the sale proceeds were not allocated to the band. The lands were sold for far less than fair market value, or they were never actually sold but simply taken by the federal or provincial government. A number of Manitoba First Nations have claims of this nature, including Peguis, Keeseekoowenin, The Pas, Roseau River, Gambler and Rolling River.

The range of specific circumstances appears never-ending. One reason has been the particular attractiveness of reserve lands to governments for public and private purposes. Many reserves have been singled out for use as rights of way for pipelines, railways, hydro transmission lines, highways and bridges. Reserve lands have often been taken for government buildings and private developments of an industrial, commercial or recreational nature. As a result, significant quantities of reserve land have been removed from the beneficial use of First Nations, frequently in violation of the law.

First Nations complained about the limited scope of the initial federal policy on specific claims, which ultimately resulted in the release of a slightly modified policy in May of 1982, entitled *Outstanding Business*. It summarized a list of eligible claims and divided them into two categories: "lawful obligations" and "beyond lawful obligations." The latter label is completely inaccurate and misleading, as the policy's definition of these claims covers violations of the law for which the Government of Canada would be held responsible. As such, they are not "beyond" the lawful obligations of the Crown.

The rationale for having a specific claims policy has changed over time. In the White Paper of 1969 the purpose behind addressing these claims, and in appointing an Indian Claims Commissioner to study the matter, was that the "sense of grievance" of the Indian people "influences their relations with governments and the community and limits their participation in Canadian life." Therefore, it was felt that any claims which gave rise to "lawful obligations" should "be recognized ... and dealt with as soon as possible" to remove the sense of grievance. This would make it far easier to obtain Indian support for the transfer of title for reserves to the bands, for the repeal of the *Indian Act,* for having the provinces "take over the same responsibility for Indians that they have for other citizens," and for "equitably" ending the treaties so as to remove "the anomaly of treaties between groups within society and the government of that society." Although the White Paper and its philosophy have been abandoned, the desire to reduce this Indian "sense of grievance," with the problems it produces for normal political, social and economic processes in the country, is still a motivating factor underlying the continued existence of the specific claims policy.

In addition, there is a realization today that the honour of the Crown has been besmirched badly by the immoral and sometimes illegal actions of the federal government regarding reserve lands and band assets for over a century. Settling such claims would help to remove these stains and improve Canada's image abroad. That image has been severely tarnished by justifiable complaints of injustice from Indian organizations over the last two decades.

Claims agreements are also a means to provide First Nations with the resources to which they are entitled so as to promote their economic and social well-being.

The final rationale stems from the necessity to discharge proper and long-standing obligations of the Government of Canada. This is a matter of good public policy but also reflects, at least in many cases, a legal imperative. The federal government favours negotiation as a more fair and lower cost alternative to hundreds of court cases that could overwhelm our justice system. Many of these cases might result in compensation being ordered against the Crown in any event.

Specific Claims in Manitoba

According to the Treaty and Aboriginal Rights Research Centre, as of June 1991, 18 specific claims had been submitted to the federal government under this policy by Manitoba First Nations over the years.

Only one Manitoba claim has been completely settled under this policy: a claim by The Pas Band for reserve land lost to the Pasquia Reclamation Project. Lands were taken for irrigation works with the clear and stated expectation that a legal surrender or expropriation would be used and compensation paid. The obligation to compensate was put off and then forgotten. The obligation to settle this claim did not require a special land claims process because the only issue was the value of the land. The claim was submitted in August 1984 and settled on March 13, 1987, through the payment by the federal government of approximately $431,000 in compensation.

One other of the 18 claims in Manitoba was partially settled in May 1991. The Keeseekoowenin First Nation had 290 hectares of reserve land wrongfully included in the Riding Mountain National Park in 1930, without their consent and contrary to law. Band members were evicted forcibly in 1936 and relocated 28 kilometres to the southwest, and their homes were burned to the ground. Years of protest finally have met with success as the federal negotiator has recommended to the Minister of Indian Affairs that the land be restored to reserve status. Further negotiations will be necessary to reach agreement on the appropriate level of compensation for loss of use of the land for the last 61 years, as well as agreement over a second parcel also taken for the park.

Two other claims, involving the Peguis and Roseau River First Nations, were rejected by the federal government. Three more claims affecting four First Nations are currently in negotiation. The Brokenhead First Nation's claim reached the agreement-in-principle stage three years ago. The remaining 11 claims are at various stages in the specific claims process, but have not yet been accepted as valid claims by the federal government. Other possible claims are still being researched. Most of these 18 claims have to do with reserve lands that were taken by the Crown without a proper surrender, or for which adequate compensation was not provided.

The national figures point to the same picture: over 575 claims have been filed to date and less than 50 have been settled after two decades. The settlement rate has not even kept pace with the submission of new claims and has resulted in dozens of claims being pursued through litigation while others languish for years, awaiting official federal action. The federal specific claims policy has not been one that produces many settlements.

Criticisms of the Specific Claims Process

This policy has been criticized extensively on a number of grounds. There is a very restrictive federal interpretation of "acceptable" claims, with many alleged violations of law, justice and fair dealing excluded. Entrenching constitutional protection for Aboriginal and treaty rights has had no apparent impact upon how federal officials interpret the specific claims policy. Many treaty rights violations, such as those concerning hunting and fishing, cannot even be pursued within this process.

The Department of Justice is assigned contradictory roles as it defends the government position while serving as judge of the validity of the claim. The Department of Indian Affairs is also in a conflict of interest position, as it is the defendant while serving as the fiduciary and the funder of the claimants.

There is a lack of appreciation by the federal government that it is dealing with land claims within the context of a constitutional relationship between First Nations and the Crown. The federal fiduciary obligation to act in the best interests of Aboriginal people seems to be ignored both in the assessment of the validity of a claim and in determining what constitutes adequate compensation. First Nations also complain about the type of compensation. They are offered money, while what they want is the restoration of their original land, or at least comparable land nearby. The amount of cash compensation usually is insufficient to buy the land back in its developed state.

A major source of complaint is the absence of an appeal mechanism for First Nations when the Minister of Indian Affairs rejects a claim or the federal compensation offer is viewed as inadequate. This is particularly troublesome in a situation where the federal government is in a conflict of interest position in which it is the judge and jury as well as defendant and author of the laws that apply. The only option available to a First Nation at that point is to initiate litigation, with all the disadvantages this involves, including the federal government's ability to assert technical defences, such as asserting that a particular First Nation waited too long to sue. These criticisms, among others, have been voiced time and time again by First Nations all across Canada with almost no impact.

The Specific Claims Branch of the Department of Indian Affairs and the policy it is required to implement have not helped the federal government to achieve its professed goals. Not settling claims has exposed the government to criticism and is aggravating, rather than reducing, the Indian sense of grievance. It is in Canada's long-term interest, in our opinion, to settle claims. Governments which are resistant to the formulation of a workable and acceptable policy are doomed to encounter more and more vivid displays of Aboriginal discontent and to have settlements forced upon them by the courts.

The events of last summer, involving the Mohawks of Kanesatake and their dispute with the municipality of Oka over a pine forest that once was part of the community's territory, put the federal specific claims policy under a microscope. The Mohawks had submitted a specific claim in the late 1970s regarding this territory. It was rejected on the basis that the original owner of the land had been the Catholic Church, which was free to sell off the land as it wished. Denying the claim, however, had not caused it to go away, nor had the sense of grievance among the Mohawks been assuaged.

The Indian Commission of Ontario (ICO) undertook a review of the specific claims policy. The ICO tabled its 106-page report with 38 recommendations on September 24, 1990. The Minister of Indian Affairs then authorized a national chiefs' task force to investigate the matter, using the ICO report as its basis. The Assembly of First Nations also examined the policy and issued its report on December 16, 1990. This flurry of activity has had some effect as Prime Minister Mulroney announced several changes in a major address on April 23, 1991 to the First Nations Congress of British Columbia.

The prime minister stated that "a fast-track process" will be introduced for dealing with land claims of $500,000 or less. The human and financial resources assigned to specific claims will quadruple over the next five years. Pre-Confederation land claims will be accepted for the first time. A joint Indian-government working group is to be created to examine the many process and policy criticisms that remain unaddressed by these few changes. Finally, the prime minister declared that an "independent dispute resolution mechanism" would be established in the form of "a specific land claim commission."

While these promises are a positive sign, they fall far short of meeting Aboriginal demands or of resolving many of the criticisms we heard. The concept of the "fast track" is fraught with difficulties when it is tied to a maximum level of compensation. This suggests that many claims filed years ago now will again be put off if they involve more than $500,000 worth of land affected by illegal federal conduct. Federal attention will be given to small claims that can be settled relatively inexpensively. This policy, therefore, may encourage more injustice and frustrate some First Nations. It also provides a powerful club to federal negotiators who can tell poverty-stricken First Nations that they can obtain priority for a quick settlement if they will accept less then $500,000, regardless of what a fair agreement might entail, or else their claims will be deferred to some unspecified time in the future. This does not appear to reflect the fiduciary obligation on the Crown in right of Canada.

What Can Be Done?

At present, the parties have unequal bargaining power in a process that completely favours the federal government. Negotiations between unequals will rarely work. The stronger party will always be tempted to use its advantage. This inequality must be eliminated.

There is also a lack of commitment on the part of the government to settle claims. In practice there is little pressure on the federal government to move on specific claims. The lack of action on treaty land entitlement in Manitoba, and the disruption to the negotiations caused by each change in the minister or the party in power in the federal or provincial government, demonstrate this problem. With First Nations spread across the country, each having its own individual specific claim, it is difficult for them to sustain sufficient pressure through lobbying to achieve positive and speedy action on any of the particular claims. This fuels the belief that claims are only settled when there is a show of public anger or violence such as that witnessed in the summer of 1990 in Oka, or only settled for exceptionally well organized First Nations. Protests are not a preferred approach and will not result in a strong, ongoing federal commitment to settle all outstanding claims. Settlement of these claims should be made a high federal priority.

WE RECOMMEND THAT:

- The federal Specific Claims Branch and the federal claims policy be fundamentally changed by the Government of Canada to establish a claims negotiation office that is independent of existing ministries and has a clear mandate to negotiate and settle claims, and has senior officials who have been appointed from outside the government.

The establishment of a land claims commission or tribunal is long overdue. However, the prime minister's announcement is extremely vague. Bills were introduced in Parliament in 1963 and 1965 to establish a claims tribunal tailored on the model of the United States Indian Claims Commission. Both bills died on the order paper and they lacked Indian support, as the American experience was widely criticized by tribal leaders there. It is vital, therefore, that the new federal tribunal not displace the negotiation process, because it is the only vehicle through which the claimants possess any significant degree of direct involvement and control.

The proper role for such a commission, in our opinion, is to oversee the negotiations when requested to do so to ensure that good-faith bargaining occurs and to serve as an appeal mechanism when claims are rejected by the minister or when negotiations completely break down. Thus, we favour a situation in which the claimant can invoke the jurisdiction of the commission so as to avoid the undermining of good-faith bargaining. Furthermore, the commission should have authority to resolve the matters referred to it, rather than to act just in an investigatory and facilitating role. This has been the experience in Canada with the former Indian Claims Commission, created by the White

Paper in 1969, and the Manitoba Treaty Land Entitlement Commission, along with the Indian Commission of Ontario that has existed since 1978.

This new body needs to possess all the hallmarks of any administrative tribunal: to be fully independent, permanent, respected by all sides, judicial in its function and adequately funded to meet all the demands placed upon it. In addition, it should include a number of commissioners from across the country so that it can sit in smaller panels to handle the many claims that will probably come forward. Half its members should be Aboriginal people chosen from a broad range of backgrounds and experience. The very positive experience of the Waitangi Tribunal of New Zealand serves as a valuable guide on this matter. The tribunal should be authorized to establish its own rules of procedure and to impose deadlines on the federal government to respond to claims so that matters move forward expeditiously.

WE RECOMMEND THAT:

- An independent claims tribunal be created. The tribunal should have full authority to hear and adjudicate on the validity of claims and on compensation questions where the parties cannot reach agreement. The tribunal should be established by legislation with power to create its own rules of procedure, be free from the strict laws of evidence and be able to impose deadlines on the Crown for responding to claims submitted.

- The claims tribunal be a national board but with a sufficient number of members, half of whom should be nominees of First Nations, so that it can sit in panels of three to hear a variety of claims simultaneously, if necessary.

- Aboriginal people be participants in designing the tribunal's precise mandate, in drafting the necessary legislation and in selecting the members of the tribunal. The legislation should require that the tribunal, the federal claims policy and the process be subject to an independent review every five years with the evaluation report to be made to Parliament and Aboriginal groups.

- This tribunal be adequately funded and have its own research staff so as to be able to maintain sufficient distance from the federal government.

We believe that the mere existence of a tribunal with the mandate and power that we have proposed will assist in improving the negotiating process immensely. It will serve to prod federal negotiators to move quickly and to take more realistic positions.

While we believe that the proposed tribunal would have a great deal of work before it, as there are probably in excess of 2,000 claims across the country, many of which might end up before this board, we do not believe that it is necessary for it to become a permanent entity. We recommend that it be created by federal statute containing a clause requiring an independent review and evaluation to be conducted every five years. This report should be tabled in Parliament. This should foster a greater likelihood that necessary improvements will be made while ensuring that it does not outlive its usefulness.

Comprehensive Claims

The federal policy on comprehensive claims was released by Indian Affairs minister Jean Chretien on August 8, 1973 as a result of the *Calder* decision of the Supreme Court of Canada seven months earlier. The policy described its purpose and scope in these words:

> These claims come from groups of Indian people who have not entered into Treaty relationship with the Crown. They find their basis in what is variously described as "Indian Title," "Aboriginal Title," "Original Title," "Native Title," or "Usufructuary Rights". In essence, these claims relate to the loss of traditional use and occupancy of certain parts of Canada where Indian title was never extinguished by treaty or superseded by law.... The lands in question lie in British Columbia, Northern Quebec, the Yukon and Northwest Territories....
>
> The government has been fully aware that the claims are not only for money and land, but involve the loss of a way of life. Any settlement, therefore, must contribute positively to a lasting solution of cultural, social and economic problems....

This policy document has been demonstrated to contain inaccuracies. While the claims are founded on unextinguished Aboriginal title, they are not limited to the four regions identified. The federal government is also currently negotiating with the Labrador Inuit, and the Atikamekw and Montagnais in eastern Quebec. Claims are pending from the Algonquins of southwestern Quebec.

The Micmacs and Malecites of the Maritimes and Newfoundland also assert Aboriginal title, as do the Mohawks of the St. Lawrence Valley. Other comprehensive claims have been identified in Ontario and the Prairies. The Dakota and the Chipewyan argue that they possess comprehensive claims in southern and northern Manitoba, respectively, which have not yet been accepted by either the federal or provincial government.

It is also apparent that the claims do not necessarily relate to "loss of traditional use and occupancy" of certain lands, as many of the Aboriginal groups continue to occupy and use their historic territory.

The policy refers solely to the rights of Indian and Inuit people, thereby ignoring the Aboriginal title claims of the Metis. The Metis are involved, in fact, as a direct party along with the Dene to the comprehensive claim regarding the Mackenzie Valley of the Northwest Territories. Non-status Indians are also a party along with the 12 First Nations in the Yukon claim. The federal government, however, continues to refuse to accept Aboriginal title claims from the Metis and non-registered Indians outside the two territories.

As a result of Aboriginal complaints, the federal government issued a slightly revised version of its comprehensive claims policy in December of 1981, entitled *In All Fairness*. Although comprehensive claims were settled in the James Bay region in 1975 (later extended to the Naskapi Indians in northeastern Quebec in 1978) and the western Arctic in 1984, very vocal dissatisfaction with the terms of the policy continued. The Minister of Indian Affairs appointed a task force to investigate the matter and it issued a report in 1986, entitled *Living Treaties: Lasting Agreements*. Aspects of this report were adopted by the federal government in its Comprehensive Land Claims Policy, released in early 1987.

Aboriginal groups have continued to criticize this revamped policy, and progress toward reaching agreements has moved at a glacial pace. Even reaching an apparent final settlement is not a guarantee that the claim is resolved. Settlements in the Yukon and Mackenzie Valley came unglued in 1990. The complaints have sparked some further revisions, such as the prime minister's announcement in September 1990 that the federal government would lift its artificial limit of negotiating only six comprehensive claims at any one time. The British Columbia government's decision of August 1990 to participate in these claims negotiations is also a major breakthrough.

The federal government, however, still takes the position that there is no outstanding Aboriginal title in Manitoba. In view of the fact that the Dakota people of this province have never signed a treaty (despite the fact that the federal government was willing to do so in the 19th century) and of the assertion of Aboriginal title by the Metis and the Chipewyan, the resolution of comprehensive claims is likely to gain importance in Manitoba. The unresolved nature of Aboriginal title to water and beds of water may also constitute comprehensive claims.

WE RECOMMEND THAT:

- The provincial government develop a policy that respects the desire of Aboriginal people to retain a role in the management and conservation of their traditional territory.

- The federal government participate fully in the settlement of land claims through the tribunal we have recommended.

- The governments of Manitoba and Canada refrain from requiring Aboriginal groups to consent to extinguish Aboriginal rights when entering into land claims agreements.

We realize that if the experience of the federal policy elsewhere in Canada holds true, the resolution of land claims in Manitoba based on Aboriginal title will be a slow, arduous process. Therefore, we believe that the federal policy and process should be changed to facilitate the conclusion of agreements. One option to consider is a process of supervised negotiations. The presence of an independent party that can be called upon to intervene at appropriate moments is vital.

It is much better to resolve these issues by way of negotiated agreements, rather than imposed solutions. There are still, however, important matters that may not be susceptible to resolution through negotiation when the bargaining power of the parties is as unequal as it is at the present time. This is true particularly where a relevant government party refuses to negotiate at all or does so in a fashion that demonstrates bad faith.

WE RECOMMEND THAT:

- The independent claims tribunal have authority to resolve specific claims and comprehensive claims. The tribunal would have three basic functions:

  - To decide disputes concerning the validity of a claim or its precise boundaries.

  - To exercise supervisory authority over the negotiation process.

  - If negotiations break down, to hold hearings to resolve the matter and to make a binding decision.

If one party were to complain that another was refusing to bargain or was bargaining in bad faith, a complaint could be made to the tribunal. The tribunal should be given the authority to convene a hearing, to receive all relevant evidence and to render a decision on the complaint. Where the allegation is upheld, the tribunal would be empowered to issue a declaration that a party has been bargaining in bad faith and to give ancillary relief, such as requirements to provide critical information, to adhere to timelines, to attend negotiating sessions, to table an offer of settlement, to respond to an offer, or to declare that a subject is appropriate for negotiation.

At any time after negotiations have begun, any party should be able to refer the matter to the tribunal for a full hearing on the merits of the claim and the relief to be sought.

Natural Resources

There are a number of issues of considerable concern to the Aboriginal people of this province relating to the use of natural resources. There are three major aspects to these concerns: the infringement by federal and provincial policies and legislation of the exercise of Aboriginal and treaty rights by Aboriginal people; the negative repercussions for them produced by large-scale exploitation of renewable resources; and the ongoing disputes regarding the exact scope of constitutionally protected rights and their practical import for the decision-making process on the management of natural resources.

One of the major irritants between Aboriginal people and government has been the *Migratory Birds Convention Act*. The Act was passed by the federal government in 1917 to ratify an international convention between Canada, the United States and Mexico. The intention of the convention was to protect migratory birds and their nesting areas. The Act regulates seasons during which migratory birds may be hunted.

When the legislation was enacted, conservation officers in Manitoba believed that it did not apply to status Indians. Consequently, Indians were not prosecuted under the Act. In the 1970s, however, this policy changed and, subsequently, many status Indians were prosecuted and convicted for hunting migratory birds out of season. The Act became a symbol for Aboriginal people of government disregard for treaty and Aboriginal rights.

For example, Peter Sinclair of Pukatawagan said to us:

Despite these [treaty] promises Canada went ahead and agreed to the Migratory Birds Convention, without the consent of the Aboriginal First Nations. Today our First Nations members cannot exercise their treaty rights to hunt without facing criminal prosecution.

Given the importance of these issues and their potential for influencing the Aboriginal-Crown relationship in negative ways, we believe that it is important for us to make a few comments and observations.

Hunting, Fishing and Trapping Rights
Up to Sikyea

Modern Aboriginal and treaty rights litigation began in Canada in the 1960s with a series of hunting and fishing cases. The first major decision of the Supreme Court of Canada on these issues was in *R. v. Sikyea*, [1964] S.C.R. 642. While the greater part of this decision concentrated upon whether a mallard was a wild duck so as to be regulated by the *Migratory Birds Convention Act,* the court agreed with the decision of the Northwest Territories Court of Appeal that explicit treaty rights were subject to being overridden by federal statutes.

The results of the initial set of judgments can be generalized in three basic propositions:

1. Treaty promises are protected against provincial laws by section 88 of the *Indian Act* (and in the Prairies by provisions of the Natural Resources Transfer Agreements).

2. Any Aboriginal or treaty rights are subject to federal laws.

3. Aboriginal rights that are not confirmed by treaties are subject to provincial laws outside of reserves.

While the treaty rights to hunt or fish were protected against provincial game laws, they were held to be subject to limitations imposed by federal legislation such as the *Migratory Birds Convention Act* and the *Fisheries Act.*

Trying to Move Away from Sikyea

The application of the *Migratory Birds Convention Act* had serious effects on Aboriginal groups in Canada, who traditionally relied upon migratory birds as a plentiful and reliable source of food. This Act became a leading point of dispute between Aboriginal leaders and the federal government when conservation officers began to enforce it against Indian, Inuit and Metis peoples in the 1950s in the Northwest Territories and in the 1970s in Manitoba. In spite of repeated federal pledges to abide by the treaties, the *Migratory Birds Convention Act* still conflicted with Aboriginal and treaty rights. Repeated protests failed to change the law so as to bring federal legislation into line with federal promises.

In practice, the law itself was not acceptable even to governments, who sporadically followed a policy of limited and selective enforcement. A moratorium on charges against treaty Indians was in place in Manitoba for several years, although it was not binding on the Crown.[72]

There is also reason to think that the *Sikyea* line of cases no longer is acceptable to the Supreme Court of Canada. In various recent decisions, the Supreme Court has laid down three innovative rules:

- The biases and prejudices of another era are no longer acceptable in Canadian law; indeed, they are inconsistent with a growing sensitivity to Aboriginal and treaty rights in Canada.

- Legislation and treaties which contain provisions supportive of Aboriginal rights are to be interpreted liberally in favour of Aboriginal people.

- Aboriginal title can only be taken away by clear and unambiguous legislation. General legislation, enacted without consideration of these rights, is no longer considered capable of overriding Aboriginal title.

Using Section 35(1) to Reverse Sikyea

The *Constitution Act, 1982* has provided an opportunity for the courts to depart from the previous jurisprudence and to reconsider the status of Aboriginal and treaty rights in relation to the traditional activities of hunting, fishing and trapping, and their susceptibility to federal law.

As discussed earlier in this chapter in relation to Aboriginal and treaty rights generally, the primary conflict between individual Aboriginal persons and the federal or provincial governments has been concerning the harvesting of wildlife. Conservation officers seek to enforce the general fish and game legislation against people who firmly believe they have guarantees from the Crown that they can continue to hunt, fish and trap as their ancestors have done since time immemorial. This conflict in perspectives frequently results in the laying of charges against Aboriginal persons and the seizure not only of what they have harvested, but also of the tools of their trade (i.e., nets, rifles, boats, vehicles, etc).

The Supreme Court of Canada in the *Sparrow* case has made it clear that subsection 35(1) of the *Constitution Act, 1982* is to be given a broad, purposive interpretation in favour of Aboriginal people, and ensures a dramatically new level of legal importance to

Aboriginal and treaty rights. In the *Sparrow* case, the court established a detailed test that was to be applied to the federal *Fisheries Act* in individual cases to determine if the applicable provisions of that Act, or the regulations enacted for each province, were operative when they conflicted with Aboriginal and/or treaty rights. The Supreme Court lacked sufficient evidence in the *Sparrow* case to be able to decide if the charge could be sustained.

The court did conclude, however, that the test it outlined could be met in certain circumstances so that Aboriginal wildlife harvesting is not unregulated completely. The Crown has to demonstrate that a specific restraint on Aboriginal and treaty rights is justified by concerns that truly warrant the overriding of constitutionally protected rights. While the test imposes a high standard upon the party seeking to uphold the federal or provincial law, it is not a completely insurmountable one. The Supreme Court implies that legislative provisions which are essential to the preservation of a species, to the protection of public safety, or to the allocation of wildlife among competing Aboriginal groups probably would be sustained in the future. Simple assertions by the Crown that the legislation is in the "public interest" or is necessary to distribute harvesting rights fairly among all potential users are unacceptable.

Our courts in Manitoba have spoken clearly in relation to the *Migratory Birds Convention Act* in the *Flett* case. They have declared that this Act is of no force or effect to the extent that it conflicts with Aboriginal and treaty rights. They have ruled further that the Act did not extinguish any Aboriginal and treaty rights that are now entrenched in the Constitution.

It is important to mention, however, that these cases have dealt with instances of Indians hunting or fishing for food, social and ceremonial purposes. The law is not clear regarding commercial harvesting activities. The Ontario Court of Appeal has stated in *R. v. Agawa*, [1988] 3 C.N.L.R. 73, that the *Fisheries Act* still is valid to regulate commercial fishing, even where this is an activity encompassed within a treaty right. While the Supreme Court in *Sparrow* cited aspects of this decision with favour, it also developed a different and more stringent test. On the other hand, the Supreme Court did deny leave to appeal the *Agawa* decision on November 8, 1990. The same court earlier that year upheld a conviction for the sale of a bearskin by a treaty Indian in *R. v. Horseman*, [1990] 3 C.N.L.R. 95, ruling that the Natural Resources Transfer Agreement overrides treaty rights. While the treaty in question seemed to protect commercial hunting, this constitutional agreement from 1930 has been interpreted as exempting Indians from provincial laws only when harvesting food.

Hunting, fishing and trapping for commercial purposes are economic activities vital to the prosperity of many Aboriginal communities. There is extensive evidence available that a lively trade in fish and game existed prior to contact with Europeans, so as to constitute an Aboriginal right. Many treaties were negotiated between Indian nations and the Crown on the basis that commercial harvesting would be permitted to continue. Thus, we conclude, as a general proposition, that hunting, fishing and trapping for commercial purposes are "recognized and affirmed" as "existing aboriginal and treaty rights" within the meaning of subsection 35(1). At the same time, it is necessary to manage these activities to ensure that priority in the allocation of natural resources is granted to Aboriginal people who are hunting and fishing for social, ceremonial and food purposes.

It would be preferable for Aboriginal people and their representative organizations to be a partner with federal and provincial government departments in the establishment of appropriate regulations and standards. Co-management of natural resources is the only suitable method to ensure that the populations of animals, fish and birds not only are conserved, but also are encouraged to flourish. This clearly will benefit Aboriginal people, who are entitled to first priority in any allowable harvesting activities, and other Canadians, as well. It will promote wildlife habitat protection and enhancement of the existing stock of harvestable species.

A New Direction

Treaty and Aboriginal rights have continued to be denied on a daily basis by conservation officials when these rights appear to them to be in conflict with the federal *Migratory Birds Convention Act* and *Fisheries Act.* Even after the breaches of Aboriginal and treaty rights were described clearly in Supreme Court of Canada decisions in the 1960s, there was no legislative redress. Since the initial group of cases, the attitude of the Supreme Court of Canada to Aboriginal and treaty rights has shifted dramatically, although it has not yet expressly reversed its previous holdings and seems somewhat reluctant to do so in the area of hunting and fishing rights. Lower courts now are devising artful ways of distinguishing the earlier Supreme Court cases, and using section 35(1) of the *Constitution Act, 1982* to give legal force to treaty and Aboriginal rights to hunt and fish, subject only to reasonable restrictions for conservation and equitable management. The Supreme Court has given clear direction to federal and provincial governments, through the *Sparrow, Sioui* and *Simon* cases in particular, that the law has changed quite dramatically with the arrival of the Canadian Constitution. The former regime, which gave limited protection solely to treaty rights in relation to provincial law, is gone forever. The challenge now is for federal, provincial and Aboriginal leaders to work together as partners and good managers of fish and game in the best interests of all. Aboriginal people have had expertise as true conservationists for thousands of years that can be effectively applied in a way that meets their needs and respects the priority to be given to their rights, while also benefiting all other members of society.

WE RECOMMEND THAT:

- The federal government amend the *Fisheries Act* and the *Migratory Birds Convention Act* to clarify that Aboriginal and treaty rights prevail in cases of conflict.

The Special Issue of Wild Rice

Wild rice is a staple food for many Aboriginal people and its harvesting provides a significant commercial activity for many Manitobans. For most of Manitoba's history, the harvesting of wild rice was not regulated by the Province in any way. As a result,

Aboriginal people exercised their traditional harvesting activities free from any provincial restraints. Recent attempts at provincial regulation have led to charges of mismanagement by some harvesters, largely centred around questions of the Aboriginal role in relation to expansion, mechanization and capitalization of harvesting activities. The granting of licences to non-Aboriginal people resulted in protests from Aboriginal harvesters in Ontario, who claimed violation of their treaty rights. Conflicts between Aboriginal and non-Aboriginal harvesters have continued in both Manitoba and Ontario, while the positions taken by the respective provincial governments have, in some ways, exacerbated the tension.

Management Practices in Manitoba

Under the *Crown Lands Act*, and then the *Wild Rice Act* after 1984, Aboriginal people were protected by exclusive leasing of wild rice areas to Aboriginal co-ops in the Whiteshell region of the province, and by the block system for lakes traditionally harvested by five Indian reserves. In 1981, the Province cancelled leases in the Whiteshell, allowing only hand-harvesters in the area, thus effectively eliminating non-Aboriginal competition. Aboriginal people, except for those who had mechanical harvesters, generally saw this policy as favourable.

The block system set apart land and water traditionally used by five reserves for harvesting. A report commissioned by the Manitoba government noted that Indians wanted more control. The report was silent, however, on the appropriate extent of that Indian control.

The policy of granting a "leading role" to Aboriginal harvesters was instituted by the Province as an affirmative action program designed to ensure that all new licences would be granted solely to Aboriginal people. The program, however, did not recognize any basis in Aboriginal or treaty rights for granting preferred treatment to Aboriginal people over non-Aboriginal competitors.

The Wild Rice Act of 1984

This Act provided for regulation and management of the growing wild rice industry, designating some areas for exclusive hand-harvesting, and others for exclusive Aboriginal use. Aboriginal people were still permitted to harvest anywhere on Crown lands, providing it was for household purposes.

Following non-Aboriginal challenges to the leading role program, the Province sought and received approval from the Manitoba Human Rights Commission for an affirmative action program. That program was then challenged in Manitoba's Court of Queen's Bench by non-Aboriginal wild rice harvesters who complained that they were not being given a fair chance to compete for the licences. The Department of Natural Resources argued that development of wild rice was a new phenomenon in which the Aboriginal community would require assistance to achieve economic benefit. The judge noted that some non-Aboriginal applicants had been harvesting for two or three generations and no previous program had denied an existing right to those outside the target group. The affirmative action program was struck down as not being in compliance with the *Human Rights Act: Apsit v. Manitoba Human Rights Commission,* [1985] 37 Man. R. (2d) 50 (Q.B.). The decision was appealed to the Manitoba Court of Appeal, but leave was refused on the basis that the Act had been repealed and replaced with a new one: [1988] 55 Man. R. (2d) 263.

The Present Situation

The issue of wild rice harvesting has never been described by the government of Manitoba as an Aboriginal or a treaty right. Although the *Wild Rice Act* does refer to these rights, it does so only in the context of saying that the Act is not intended to derogate from those rights. This is not the same thing as accepting that such rights exist in relation to wild rice and that provincial jurisdiction is restrained.

Treaties explicitly promised that Aboriginal people were to retain their traditional economic pursuits in the form of hunting, fishing and trapping. According to some academics and Aboriginal groups, the Paypom Document, which contains a record of oral negotiations between a representative of the Crown and Chief Paypom, transcribed in 1873, sets out the "terms" of Treaty 3 as they were explained to the Indian signatories. The document is also seen as a narrative description of the treaty promises from the Indian perspective. Part of the document reads, "the Indians will be free as by the past for their hunting and rice harvest." Aboriginal people have argued that this document relates a treaty promise and has equal status to the written terms of the "official" version of Treaty 3. On this basis, the provisions would supersede provincial laws to the extent of any conflict. While the jurisprudence clearly supports such an interpretation in reference to treaties generally,[73] the exact status of the Paypom Document remains unresolved. As the legal force of the Paypom Document is a subject of litigation, we cannot comment on the strength of this argument.

Even where treaties are silent on the issue of wild rice, it is possible to demonstrate that the parties expected traditional economic pursuits to continue. It would be in keeping with recent court rulings to assume that references to hunting and fishing could extend to include other traditional economic pursuits such as the harvesting of wild rice.

Regardless of the status of wild rice as a treaty right, none of the treaties in force in Manitoba expressly extinguished the Aboriginal right to gather wild rice. The onus rests on the Crown to prove that this Aboriginal right was terminated lawfully. Failing such proof, the right to harvest wild rice continues to exist and now would have constitutional protection.

While not describing harvesting wild rice as an Aboriginal right, the Province has confirmed an Aboriginal role in the industry. It was made clear that provincial regulations are not to affect treaty and Aboriginal rights. The use of an affirmative action program targets Aboriginal people as impoverished, not as holders of special legal rights which are protected constitutionally. Affirmative action programs are also fundamentally transitional in nature, as they are designed to assist a targeted group temporarily until it is no longer disadvantaged, at which point the program will be withdrawn. Therefore, the use of a human rights orientation is inappropriate in this situation.

Aboriginal people see the harvesting of wild rice as a traditional occupation which their ancestors never would have given up intentionally at the signing of the treaties.

While the provincial legislation has recognized an Aboriginal role in the industry, the *Wild Rice Act* gives no assurance that this role will continue as a matter of right in the future.

In our opinion, based upon a review of the information before us, the right to harvest wild rice is, at least, an Aboriginal right. We believe that this Aboriginal right encompasses both personal consumption and commercial purposes. This right can be exercised on reserves and on Crown lands. As with other Aboriginal rights, it now has constitutional protection.

WE RECOMMEND THAT:

- The Province of Manitoba recognize the harvesting of wild rice as an Aboriginal right.

- The Province, if it wishes to exercise any influence over the regulation of this resource off-reserves, negotiate co-management agreements with the Aboriginal peoples concerned.

Timber Rights

An issue that has received almost no attention in Canadian courts or in government policy is the position of Aboriginal people regarding the harvesting of timber. It is clear, however, that large-scale forestry operations can have negative effects upon the exercise of Aboriginal and treaty rights in relation to land usage and wildlife harvesting.

There are really two facets to this issue. First, what historic rights do Aboriginal people possess as users of timber? Second, do their Aboriginal and treaty rights entitle Aboriginal people to oppose or regulate forestry operations in some way?

Beyond that, the precise parameters of Aboriginal and treaty rights to harvest timber are far from certain. It is clear, however, that First Nations do possess full rights to all timber on reserves, which are regulated in part by sections 58(4) and 93 of the *Indian Act.* The Supreme Court of Canada has accepted the right to cut trees for firewood for ceremonial purposes as a treaty right in *R. v. Sioui,* [1990] 1 S.C.R. 1025.

The other issue cannot be answered definitively by a review of the case law. While the British Columbia courts have granted to First Nations a number of interim injunctions to stop logging, these have all been in the context of preserving the status quo, pending a trial decision on Aboriginal title claims involving the land to be logged. Perhaps the closest case comes from the Court of Appeal in British Columbia in *Saanichton Marina Ltd. v. Claxton,* [1988] 1 W.W.R. 540 (B.C.S.C.); affirmed 36 B.C.L.R. (2d) 79. There, the court granted a permanent injunction to prevent the development of a tidal bay marina that would have destroyed a fish bed and impinged access across the foreshore to the bay. The court concluded that pre-Confederation treaty rights prevailed over private property rights exercised pursuant to a provincial licence.

In our view, Aboriginal people possess, at the very least, a right to harvest trees for ceremonial and personal purposes. In addition, Aboriginal and treaty rights to hunt, trap and fish must not be infringed or restricted by logging activities that disrupt the habitat of fish and game. Allowing such disruptions to occur unchecked would be tantamount to rendering the constitutionally protected Aboriginal and treaty rights meaningless. Aboriginal people have an interest in off-reserve forests that must be respected. Forestry management could best be realized, in our opinion, by co-management agreements between the Province and the Aboriginal groups affected.

WE RECOMMEND THAT:

- The Province of Manitoba recognize Aboriginal and treaty rights to harvest timber resources.

- The Province ensure that the exercise of wildlife harvesting rights is not infringed by timber management practices.

- The Province pursue the development of co-management agreements with the First Nations and Metis peoples regarding timber resources off-reserve in the Aboriginal people's traditional territory.

Water Rights

Like timber, the subject of rights to water for Aboriginal people is uncertain. It is similarly multifacetted in terms of both the rights to utilize this essential natural resource and to prevent others from exploiting it in a manner that harms the interests of Aboriginal people.

Once again, the position on Indian reserves is unique. Since reserve lands fall within exclusive federal jurisdiction, no provincial legislation can encroach upon any water rights attached to those lands. The determination of whether reserve boundaries include adjacent waters will depend upon precisely how and why each reserve was created, upon the survey that was conducted and upon the original description of each reserve. Since most reserves were situated next to bodies of water for fishing, transportation and domestic consumption purposes, it is logical to infer that the reserve included at least a portion of the surrounding waters as well as the land itself.

The United States Supreme Court has favoured this view for almost a century: *Winters v. United States*, 207 U.S. 564 (1908). The American jurisprudence recognizes that reservation users can pre-empt others from using the same water, even when those other parties have been using it for many years. The basic rationale stems from the fact that, while the Indian nations surrendered most of their territory by treaty, this did not include water rights unless the treaty expressly stated that effect. The American courts concluded that the Indian nations must have intended, as did the federal government, that the land base was to be viable economically so as to meet all their present and future needs. This entails the right to use water for agricultural and domestic purposes.

The U.S. government has been purchasing the Indian title to bodies of water since the late 1700s, as they have regarded Aboriginal title as applying to waterways as well as to land.

Recent Aboriginal title claims settlements in Canada also address the issue of water rights. The Aboriginal parties expressly surrender their interest in beds of waters within the territory in exchange for a wide variety of rights and benefits. The presence of these provisions demonstrates the necessity to recognize the existence of the Aboriginal title interest in the first place.

We believe that the legal principles established in the American case law, which recognize Aboriginal rights to lands under waters, applies equally in Manitoba. Therefore, Aboriginal title continues in force unless and until it can be demonstrated by the Crown that it has been surrendered validly by treaty. In addition, we have concluded that many of the reserves established pursuant to the treaties include adjacent waters.

First Nations also possess riparian rights. This means that First Nations and the Metis have the legal authority to protest any use of water that diminishes the quality or quantity of water available to them. The existence of these Aboriginal rights to water, of course, may have a significant impact on those hydro-electric projects throughout the province that dramatically affect water levels or water quality. All environmental management licences that permit companies to pollute waters should be subject to Aboriginal water rights.

Disputes over water rights in the U.S. have led to protracted litigation and negotiations between tribal and state governments. Clearly, it would be preferable if Manitoba and Canada could avoid endless lawsuits and conflict by recognizing the rights of Aboriginal people in this regard and resolving conflicting interests through amicable negotiations.

WE RECOMMEND THAT:

- Existing Aboriginal rights to water and beds of waters be recognized by the federal and provincial governments.

Subsurface Resources

The Province of Manitoba currently claims a 50% share in the "minerals" that are extracted from Indian reserve lands. The remaining one-half interest is received by Canada to hold for the benefit of the First Nation concerned. This is a result of section 12 of the Manitoba Natural Resources Transfer Agreement, which incorporated terms of the *Indian Reserve Lands Agreement* of 1924 between Canada and Ontario. The effect of the provision is that the Province can demand half the royalties, rent or sale proceeds that come from any minerals that are developed on a reserve by a third party. The term "minerals" is not defined, other than by way of reference to it including "precious minerals" in paragraph 2 of the Ontario agreement from 1924.

This arrangement was reached between the federal and Manitoba governments in 1929 without the consultation or consent of First Nations. This provision has inhibited the potential for mineral development on reserves and has been the subject of complaint by First Nations over the years.

We see no basis for the Province of Manitoba to claim any interest in minerals on Indian reserves. Accordingly, we believe that the Province should relinquish its interests in surface and subsurface minerals on all reserves. Any future reserve lands set aside from provincial Crown lands should be free from any continuing provincial interest, as well. Under the agreement-in-principle concerning treaty land entitlement reached in 1984, the government of Manitoba agreed to waive this right. The Province does not possess a right to share in mineral development in reference to Treaty 3 reserves.

We do not believe that the federal government ever had the authority to relinquish a 50% interest in these resources without compensation to First Nations in Manitoba. This was a violation of its fiduciary obligation to Aboriginal people.

WE RECOMMEND THAT:

■ In keeping with provincial fiduciary obligations and to assist in the economic advancement of First Nations, the Province of Manitoba formally renounce its half interest in minerals within Indian reserves.

■ First Nations have the right to use and control totally all mines and minerals on reserve lands and to receive 100% of the benefits and income therefrom.

■ The federal government begin a process of negotiations with the First Nations of Manitoba to transfer title to the reserve lands into the names of the various First Nations.

The Special Position of the Metis

The *Manitoba Act*, 1870 was negotiated by the Metis in part to protect their rights to land. Section 31 was included to guarantee that the Metis retained a sizeable portion of the land base they were occupying then in the Red River Valley. It stated:

31. And whereas, it is expedient, toward the extinguishment of the Indian Title to the lands in the Province, to appropriate a portion of such ungranted lands, to the extent of one million four hundred thousand acres thereof, for the benefit of the families of the half-breed residents, it is hereby enacted, that, under

regulations to be from time to time made by the Governor General in Council, the Lieutenant-Governor shall select such lots or tracts in such parts of the Province as he may deem expedient, to the extent aforesaid, and divide the same among the children of the half-breed heads of families residing in the Province at the time of the said transfer to Canada, and the same shall be granted to the said children respectively, in such mode and on such conditions as to settlement and otherwise, as the Governor General in Council may from time to time determine.

The constitutional commitment of 1.4 million acres for the Metis in the Manitoba Act did not, however, result in the establishment of a permanent land base.

Political Developments since 1870

During the Depression, Metis "locals" were organized in several Metis communities in Manitoba and elsewhere. A provincial commission of inquiry in Alberta recommended that land grants be issued to Metis communities rather than to individuals. Some land grants were made in Alberta and Saskatchewan, but none in Manitoba. In the 1970s, Metis political activity took a renewed form under the Native Council of Canada and the Manitoba Metis Federation, which were formed to represent the Metis and non-status Indians. Over the years, the identity of both groups became blurred. The Metis and non-status Indians often were lumped together by federal policy-makers for administrative convenience, since each group was of Aboriginal ancestry, but was unable to register as status Indians under the *Indian Act.*

Although the Metis were successful in obtaining program money for housing and other such issues, they refused to be content with government programs which failed to ascribe any special or unique rights to them. Consequently, they began focussing on asserting their rights and researching their historical claims.

Metis people regained a measure of their lost stature when they were included in section 35 of the *Constitution Act, 1982.* As one of the "aboriginal peoples" recognized as having "aboriginal and treaty rights" protected by the Constitution, Metis people have established a legal position hitherto denied to them since the 19th century. When the constitutional discussions of the 1980s began, the Native Council of Canada was included along with the representatives of First Nations and Inuit, primarily because they represented Metis and Indian people who had lost their status.

Only a few months after the Metis were included in the first draft of the section, the federal government responded to a Native Council of Canada document by rejecting any general formula of land claims for Metis and non-status Indians. Metis rights had been recognized in the Constitution, but the federal government was of the view that there were none to begin with.

During preliminary meetings leading up to the First Ministers' Conference of 1983, the Metis demanded separate recognition, apart from non-status Indians. They launched a lawsuit to back up their demand, which was settled by Prime Minister Trudeau's invitation to Metis representatives to participate in their own right at the First

Ministers' Conferences. At the second conference in 1984, Metis issues received considerable attention, with the main question being whose jurisdiction the Metis came under: the federal government's or the provinces'. Although the federal government accepted that there were Metis in the West and included in the constitutional family, it denied that it had legislative jurisdiction under section 91(24) of the *Constitution Act, 1867,* as it does in reference to the Indian and Inuit peoples.

The governments in Alberta and Saskatchewan met with provincial Metis leaders and stated a willingness to respond to Metis concerns. This led to an agreement between the Alberta Federation of Metis Settlements and the Alberta provincial government on a settlement package involving compensation for lost land and subsurface royalties, local self-government and constitutional protection for the remainder of the lands set aside for Metis in the Depression. The package was approved by referendum in the spring of 1989 and has been implemented. Two Metis farms in Saskatchewan have been turned over by the Saskatchewan government to special Metis corporate entities within the last few years.

There were no Metis land grants in a communal title sense in Manitoba. In 1985 the Manitoba government wrote to the Manitoba Metis Federation, agreeing to open negotiations. The federal government agreed to participate, while assigning the lead role to the Province. This willingness to have formal tripartite negotiations reflected the visibility Metis had achieved through the First Ministers' Conferences. Although initial agreement on a process occurred in 1985, serious negotiations have yet to achieve any tangible results.

The Conflict over Metis Rights

There are two fundamental issues that have plagued the Metis in their relationship with the federal and Manitoba governments. These issues centre upon jurisdiction and rights.

The federal government has a legislative and executive mandate under the *Constitution Act, 1867* in relation to "Indians, and Lands reserved for the Indians" under class 24 of section 91. Although the Supreme Court of Canada declared that the Inuit are within section 91(24) so as to be "Indians" for constitutional purposes,[74] our courts have never resolved definitively whether the Metis also come within this provision. Academic opinion is divided on this point. While the Metis initially thought that being expressly defined as "aboriginal people" through subsection 35(2) of the *Constitution Act, 1982* would settle this controversy, their view has not been borne out so far.

The Metis have argued consistently that they are "constitutional" Indians for the purposes of federal jurisdiction. The Government of Canada has disagreed consistently, asserting that it has no special authority or relationship with the Metis as it does with Indians and the Inuit. The federal government, therefore, states that the Metis are subject to provincial jurisdiction like all other Canadians. The government of Alberta agrees with the federal position and it has maintained special legislation for Metis lands and communities since the 1930s. All other provinces, including Manitoba, disagree with the position and support the Metis contention that they fall within federal jurisdiction by virtue of section 91(24). This is not entirely altruistic since this debate involves the question of primary financial responsibility for the advancement and well-being of a significant population, especially in Manitoba.

Related to this debate is the question as to whether the Metis are "Indians" within the meaning of paragraph 13 of the Manitoba Natural Resources Transfer Agreement. This agreement is contained in a schedule to the *Constitution Act, 1930* and protects "Indian" hunting, fishing and trapping for food from restriction by provincial law. This issue has not been the subject of scrutiny by the Supreme Court of Canada. However, courts in Saskatchewan have concluded that the Metis do not qualify for these rights as they are not Indians under the *Indian Act*. [75]

The other major source of conflict has revolved around whether the Metis possess Aboriginal and treaty rights. The federal and provincial governments take the same position on this issue. Both levels believe that the Metis have no such rights. The governments' view, therefore, interprets the inclusion of the Metis within section 35 as being largely meaningless, and asserts that the Metis have no "existing aboriginal and treaty rights" that could be recognized and affirmed in the Canadian Constitution.

Not surprisingly, the view of the Metis is completely contrary to this position. The Metis have vigorously asserted their special position in law and in politics since before the creation of Manitoba. The many arguments they have made over the years warrant particular attention.

Metis Arguments for Their Rights

While there is a general understanding of the foundation of Indian and Inuit claims to Aboriginal and treaty rights, the same cannot be said about either the basis or nature of Metis claims. The different arguments asserted in Manitoba for Metis rights are:

The Metis assert that they have Aboriginal rights by virtue of their share in Indian title.

The *Manitoba Act* and the *Dominion Lands Act* made provision for land grants or scrip for Metis as a response to the "Indian title" of the Metis. This grounds Metis claims on their descent from Indians.

The Metis assert that they have special rights under a treaty between their 1870 Provisional Government and Canada, given force in terms of the *Manitoba Act*.

Louis Riel often referred to the *Manitoba Act* as a treaty and called upon Canada to respect the treaty. Manitoba Metis Federation refers to the Act as The Manitoba Treaty and calls it a bargain between peoples—the Metis and the English-French Confederation.

The Metis argue that they have special rights as Aboriginal people because of the constitutional and statutory provisions applicable to them.

The Metis start with the position that the provisions in the *Manitoba Act* and the *Dominion Lands Act* expressly recognized special rights for them. So they argue that there is no need to go behind the documents to find any other source for the rights.

The Metis claim rights on the basis that they are a distinct people.

This claim is put in terms of natural law. The Metis claim status as a distinct people who were born and developed in the West. They assert that they had an economic base. Their claims to land vis-a-vis the Indians are explained in terms of Indians with traditional rights to the territory having vacated the Red River area, or, alternatively, that the Indians had acquiesced in the Metis presence and their use of the land. The Metis assert they were an "organized society" with established patterns of land use not contested by any other party. They argue, therefore, that they meet the common law tests for possession of Aboriginal title that have been outlined by Canadian courts.

The Metis assert that they are a "people" with a right of self-determination in international law.

The Manitoba Metis Federation has argued that provisions of the *Manitoba Act* recognized the Metis as a people. While the land grants appear to be to individuals or families, the MMF has argued that the fact that they are in recognition of "Indian title" means they are in response to a "collective interest."

The Metis assert that they are a founding people, having brought the West into Confederation.

The Metis assert rights as a founding people, who were the ones truly responsible for bringing Manitoba into Confederation. According to this line of reasoning, the *Manitoba Act* was more than an agreement that Canada was to recognize the particular right of the Metis to land. It was a Confederation pact. It was the basis upon which the Metis agreed to join the fledgling federal state when they held the upper hand in the balance of power in the Prairies.

The Metis argue that the reference to them in the *Constitution Act, 1982* requires that government negotiate with them to settle rights upon them.

The Manitoba Metis Federation has argued that the recognition of the Metis in the *Constitution Act, 1982* reflects a need to deal with the Metis. According to Yvon Dumont, the president of the MMF, Canada has an obligation to reach agreement with the Metis regarding their rightful place in the Constitution. This obligation is suggested to be a moral, political and legal one.

Despite these arguments and the apparent validity of the view that as Aboriginal people the Metis must have some type of Aboriginal rights, there is currently no agreement on the part of government that they have any. There is presently no land held in common by or for the Metis in Manitoba, nor is there any agreement on the part of government that there should be. Any titles that still exist in Metis hands that may have come from the "half-breed" provisions in the *Manitoba Act* are now held simply as regular, individual fee simple titles under general Manitoba land law. There may well be outstanding obligations under the early provisions or claims to damages, but, unlike Alberta and Saskatchewan, there are no lands in Manitoba today which are set aside as Metis lands in any special legal sense.

The legal system in Manitoba at the moment appears to recognize no rights peculiar to the Metis. Metis may own land, or hold registered traplines, domestic fishing licences or wild rice production licences, but they hold them as individual Manitobans, rather than as Metis.

Practice, however, is different. When the Grand Rapids Dam was constructed and the Chemawawin Indian reserve community was relocated to Easterville, Metis and non-status Indians living in the communities were included in the relocation and were provided with new homes. In the same way, Metis and non-status Indians have been included in the compensation arrangements for South Indian Lake and for the Northern Flood Agreement bands. But in all these cases, Metis and non-status Indians have not been included as a party to the negotiations and have been excluded from the community referendums that ratified the final agreement.

This represents a contradictory and inconsistent attitude towards Metis and non-status Indians. They do not have rights on their own, but they can have rights piggy-backed on the rights of status Indian communities. The same attitude can be seen in the James Bay Agreement, and in the Dene-Metis negotiations and agreement-in-principle in the Northwest Territories. The MMF has brought a lawsuit asserting that Metis land rights under the *Manitoba Act* were frustrated by various federal and provincial statutes. The action seeks a declaration that their rights were violated by statutes which are unconstitutional. As this matter is before the courts in Manitoba, we cannot comment on the merits of the legal arguments of the parties to the litigation.

The extent to which the Province has been prepared to become involved with Metis matters has been limited to making occasional financial grants to Metis organizations such as the Manitoba Metis Federation, some of which facilitate Metis involvement in social programs such as housing and child welfare. The Metis have spent a considerable amount of their time in developing the basis of their claims and very little on the matter of what an appropriate settlement would look like. The lack of a model for settlement is a major obstacle toward achieving a successful resolution. Ron Richard of the Manitoba Metis Federation told us:

> It is necessary that respective governments recognize the necessity of self-determination and the judicial control of Aboriginal peoples for Aboriginal peoples. It is equally imperative that governments negotiate in good faith with various Aboriginal peoples of Canada and Manitoba respectively to transfer necessary power and authority.

Non-status Indians are also in an uncertain position somewhat similar to the Metis in Manitoba. While the treaties did not envisage federal control of membership in Indian bands, such control came into play quickly after treaty in Manitoba. The *Indian*

Act provisions had the long-term effect of creating a population of non-status Indians, excluded from band membership by omission, by enfranchisement or by marriage to people who were not registered as Indians. The membership rules were changed in 1985 to restore the entitlement to registration as an Indian to women who had lost status by marriage and to grant some rights to their children. The result has been a significant increase in band membership, and a decrease in the most vocal and visible group of non-status Indians in the country. The remaining non-status Indians are without significant political influence and are virtually unknown in terms of the characteristics of the population. Non-status Indians will gain rights under the current legal regime only if:

1. they are taken into membership in a band under a band-controlled membership criteria; or

2. they are associated with a status Indian community in the assertion of land claims or in pursuing claims to damages to lands and habitat in use; or

3. they claim rights as Metis people.

Both the Metis and the non-status Indians are Aboriginal peoples according to section 35(2) of the *Constitution Act, 1982*. Nevertheless, this constitutional recognition has not been translated into respect for their Aboriginal or treaty rights in concrete ways. Instead, both the federal and Manitoba governments have denied that these Aboriginal groups have any such rights, while suggesting that the other level of government is responsible for and should address the social, economic, cultural and political objectives of the Metis and non-status Indians.

This principle is now being extended by the federal government to off-reserve status Indians. Although it is clear that they come within federal jurisdiction, the Department of Indian Affairs has adopted a policy that it will not provide or pay for services for off-reserve status Indians once they leave their home reserves. In other words, the federal government's position is to have off-reserve status Indians treated just like Metis and non-status Indians; i.e., similar to all other provincial residents.

These jurisdictional squabbles and efforts to deny responsibility should stop immediately. In our view, Metis people and non-status Indians fall within the constitutional definition of "Indians" for the purposes of section 91(24) of the *Constitution Act, 1867* and fall within primary federal jurisdiction.

Both the federal and provincial governments must demonstrate a sincere willingness to deal fairly with all off-reserve Aboriginal people, and must commence negotiations with a commitment to implementing meaningful measures to respect the Aboriginal and treaty rights of this population, in keeping with the spirit and intent of the fiduciary obligations of both levels of government. While the Government of Canada is empowered constitutionally to adopt the lead role and carry the primary financial burden, the Manitoba government has a critical role to play as well.

WE RECOMMEND THAT:

■ The federal and provincial governments, by resolution of their respective legislative assemblies, specifically acknowledge and recognize the Metis people as coming within the meaning of section 91(24) of the *Constitution Act, 1867* and that the Government of Canada accept that it has primary constitutional responsibility to seek to fulfil this mandate through devising appropriate initiatives in conjunction with the Metis people in Canada.

■ The Manitoba Aboriginal Justice Commission, which is proposed and discussed in detail elsewhere in this report, be mandated by the Manitoba Metis Federation and the provincial and federal governments to define and designate the boundaries for "Metis communities" for program delivery, local government and administration of justice purposes.

■ The issue of responsibility for off-reserve status Indian people be resolved by providing that, as a primary federal responsibility, financial services for them should come ultimately from the federal government, and that short-term interim measures recoverable from the federal government should be provided by the Province.

The *Indian Act*
Continuing Discrimination

The *Indian Act* was amended extensively in 1985 with the explicit objective of bringing it into line with the equality provision of the *Charter of Rights and Freedoms.* Section 15 of the *Charter*, which came into effect on April 17, 1985, declared that every person is "equal before and under the law and has the right to the equal protection and equal benefit of the law without discrimination and, in particular without discrimination based on race ... sex," and other enumerated grounds. The federal government was very concerned that the blatant sexual discrimination in the *Indian Act* was vulnerable to attack. Although the same discriminatory provisions had been upheld a decade earlier by the Supreme Court of Canada when challenged under the Canadian *Bill of Rights*,[76] it was felt that the constitutionalization of equality would lead to a different result. In addition, the United Nations Human Rights Committee had declared that Canada was in violation of the International Covenant on Civil and Political Rights for denying Indian women who had lost their status on marriage the right to reside in their own communities.[77] The *Indian Act* was amended, therefore, to change the rules regarding entitlement to registration and to empower Indian bands to enact their own membership codes if they so desired. This is how the amended act outlines the complex set of criteria which determine who the government considers to be an Indian:

6(1) Subject to section 7, a person is entitled to be registered if

(a) that person was registered or entitled to be registered immediately prior to April 17, 1985;

(b) that person is a member of a body of persons that has been declared by the Governor in council on or after April 17 1985 to be a Band for the purposes of this Act;

(c) the name of that person was omitted or deleted from the Indian Register, or from a Band list prior to September 4, 1951, under sub-paragraph 12(1)(a)(iv), paragraph 12(1)(b) or subsection 12(2) or under subparagraph 12(1)(a)(iii) pursuant to an order made under subsection 109(2), as each provision read immediately prior to April 17, 1985, or under any former provision of this Act relating to the same subject matter as any of those provisions;

(d) the name of that person was omitted or deleted from the Indian Register, or from a Band list prior to September 4, 1951, under subparagraph 12(1)(a)(iii) pursuant to an order made under subsection 109(1) as each provision read immediately prior to April 17, 1985 or under any former provision of this Act relating to the same subject matter as any of those provisions;

(e) the name of that person was omitted or deleted from the Indian Register or from a Band list prior to September 4, 1951,

(i) under section 13, as it read immediately prior to September 4, 1951, or under any former provision of this Act relating to the same subject matter as that section, or

(ii) under section 111, as it read immediately prior to July 1, 1920, or under any former provision of this Act relating to the same subject matter as that section; or

(f) that person is a person both of whose parents are or, if no longer living, were at the time of death entitled to be registered under this section.

(2) Subject to section 7, a person is entitled to be registered if that person is a person one of whose parents is or, if no longer living, was at the time of death entitled to be registered under subsection (1).

(3) For the purposes of paragraph (1)(f) and subsection (2),

    (a) a person who was no longer living immediately prior to April 17 1985, but who was at the time of death entitled to be registered shall be deemed to be entitled to be registered under paragraph (1)(a); and

    (b) a person described in paragraph (1)(c), (d), or (e) or (f) or in subsection (2) who is no longer living on April 17, 1985 shall be deemed to be entitled to be registered under that provision.

7(1) The following persons are not entitled to be registered:

    (a) a person who was registered under paragraph 11(1)(f), as it read immediately prior to April 17, 1985, or under any former provision of this Act relating to the same subject matter as that paragraph and whose name was subsequently omitted or deleted from the Indian Register under this Act; or

    (b) a person who is the child of a person who was registered or entitled to be registered under paragraph 11(1)(f), as it read immediately prior to April 17, 1985, or under any former provision of this Act relating to the same subject matter as that paragraph, and is also the child of a person who is not entitled to be registered.

(2) Paragraph (1)(a) does not apply in respect of a female person who was, at any time prior to being registered under paragraph 11(1)(f), entitled to be registered under any other provision of this Act.

(3) Paragraph 1(b) does not apply in respect of a child of a female person who was, at any time prior to being registered under paragraph 11(1)(f), entitled to be registered under any other provision of this Act.

Despite the amendments intended to remove discrimination, the *Indian Act* today still contains clear forms of sexual discrimination—as well as the seeds of eventual termination of Indian status altogether. The current provisions have the effect of "grandfathering" all people who were registered when the amendments took effect retroactively on April 17, 1985. That is, any person who "was registered or entitled to be registered" immediately prior to that date remains a status Indian or is entitled to obtain such status, based on the former provisions in the Act under section 6(1)(a). Women who had lost their status upon marriage now can regain it upon application under section 6(1)(c). Other individuals who voluntarily gave up their Indian status upon enfranchisement, or had it taken away from them for one of the many reasons that the Act has contained over the years (e.g., for acquiring a university education), are also eligible to apply for reinstatement under one of the provisions in subsection 6(1). Similarly, the children of those who lost their Indian status can be reinstated if one or both of their parents are entitled in their own right. (ss. 6(2) and 6(1)(f), respectively)

The continuing discrimination enters the picture in terms of the differential treatment between the sexes regarding the children of status Indians. This is an extremely convoluted registration scheme in which the discrimination is not readily apparent on the surface. It requires an examination of how the Act treats people to detect the fundamental unfairness. Examples are necessary to make this more obvious.

Joan and John, a brother and sister, were both registered Indians. Joan married a Metis man before 1985 so she lost her Indian status under section 12(1)(b) of the former Act. John married a white woman before 1985 and she automatically became a status Indian. Both John and Joan have had children over the years. Joan now is eligible to regain her status under section 6(1)(c) and her children will qualify under section 6(2). They are treated as having only one eligible parent, their mother, although both parents are Aboriginal. John's children gained status at birth as both parents were Indians legally, even though only one was an Aboriginal person.

Joan's children can pass on status to their offspring only if they also marry registered Indians. If they marry unregistered Aboriginal people or non-Aboriginal people, then no status will pass to their children. All John's grandchildren will be status Indians, regardless of who his children marry. Thus, entitlement to registration for the second generation has nothing to do with racial or cultural characteristics. The Act has eliminated the discrimination faced by those who lost status, but has passed it on to the next generation. Similar results flow from distinctions regarding how illegitimate children are treated under the amendments.

Not only does the *Indian Act* maintain improper and probably illegal forms of sexual discrimination, but it also threatens the long-term survival of Indians. The current regime has a *de facto* form of a "one-quarter blood" rule. As shown in the previous example, intermarriage between registered Indians and others over two successive generations results in descendants who are not entitled at law to be status Indians. This may threaten the very existence of First Nations in the not too distant future, especially small communities who have considerable interaction with neighbouring Metis or non-Aboriginal communities.

In our view, discriminating against Indian people by virtue of such provisions imposed by Parliament should cease.

WE RECOMMEND THAT:

■ The *Indian Act* be amended to eliminate all continuing forms of discrimination regarding the children of Indian women who regain their status under Bill C-31.

In addition, the Act must be changed so as to prevent the gradual elimination of First Nations and registered Indians. While the Act does permit bands to create their own membership rules, it does not permit them to extend federal recognition to those of their members who do not qualify for Indian status. The effect of the second generation cut-off rule is that many people of Indian ancestry who are raised as members of First Nations with full knowledge of their language, culture and history will be disenfranchised as Indians under the federal law in the not too distant future. Ultimately, some First Nations could be eliminated through this legislative provision.

WE RECOMMEND THAT:

- The *Indian Act* be amended to remove the two-generation rule.

- Any person designated as a full member of a recognized First Nation in Canada be accepted by the federal government as qualifying as a registered Indian for the purposes of federal legislation, funding formula and programs.

While the Act should be amended further to ensure that all forms of gender discrimination regarding the children of Indian women are removed, this does not mean that all Indian people will be band members. Instead, it is designed to entitle all persons of Indian ancestry to apply if they desire to be recognized in law as Indians. The category of so-called "non-status" or "unregistered" Indians should disappear. It is thoroughly inappropriate for the federal government to possess the authority or to legislate in such a way as to divide a people into those it will regard legally as being members of the group and those it will not, on grounds that violate the cultural, linguistic, spiritual, political and racial identity of these people.

The *Indian Act* should be amended to entitle any person to be registered who is descended from an Indian band member. This does not mean, however, that all such persons will acquire band membership, because such membership would be within the prerogative of the band membership codes of the individual First Nations.

Paternalism in Legislative Form

Indian people have attacked the *Indian Act* as paternalistic and colonialistic since its first passage. Presenters at our hearings were scathing in their condemnation of the Act. John Letandre of Winnipeg told us:

> The *Indian Act* [is] the most paternalistic piece of legislation that there is in our country. And I say to a lot of my white friends, you ought to get down on your knees every night and thank God that there is no such thing as a Department of White Affairs.

Chief Philip Michel of the Barren Lands Band made this comment about the Act:

> The *Indian Act* is out-dated and serves only to deter self-government. It gives the federal government control over every facet of our lives. It completely suppresses

our treaty right to jurisdiction over reserve lands and our human right to self-determination.

In recent years they have been gaining many non-Indian allies, such as the Canadian Human Rights Commission, several parliamentary committees and international organizations. It is long past the time that legislation that imposes almost complete federal control upon reserve life can be tolerated. Canada should begin to make appropriate changes immediately so as not to enter the 21st century with such patronizing and restrictive legislation in place.

The Government of Canada has repeated continuously since 1983 that it supports Aboriginal self-government, yet the pace of change within federal policies and legislative initiatives is grindingly slow. While recognizing that the right of Aboriginal people to self-determination in the Canadian Constitution may be made explicit in the very near future, we also recognize that there is a crying need for urgent legislative action. At the same time, the situation is far more complex than can be resolved by simply repealing the *Indian Act*. Eliminating the special legal position of individual Indians and First Nations is neither appropriate nor acceptable. We have moved forward irreversibly in recognizing the unique position of Aboriginal peoples in Canada, and a return to the White Paper proposals of 1969 would not be tolerated. The challenge is to enshrine federal promises and commitments which honour the special relationship between the Crown and Aboriginal people.

Change must also accommodate the wide diversity among First Nations. Some wish to remain under the Act largely as it now stands but with expanded administrative and law-making powers. This goal can be met by amending the *Indian Act* to increase the range of subjects over which by-laws may be enacted. The Penner Report, written by a unanimous Committee of the House of Commons in 1983, identifies a number of subject areas that could be included within the jurisdiction of band councils. While the committee concluded that the exact scope of this new jurisdiction should be resolved through direct negotiation, it also concluded that "a First Nation government should have authority to legislate in such areas as social and cultural development, including education and family relations, land and resource use, revenue raising, economic and commercial development, and justice and law enforcement, among others."[78]

A number of First Nations are currently seeking to negotiate their own special legislation to replace the *Indian Act*. The Sechelt Band of British Columbia and the Cree and Naskapi bands of Quebec already possess their own special federal legislation that almost completely replaces the *Indian Act* as the governing statute in their lives. The terms of these specific laws were negotiated between the federal government and the First Nations concerned.

Many First Nations call the approach taken in those instances inadequate, as it consists of the delegation of authority from Parliament, rather than the recognition of the right to self-government as being inherent and flowing from their sovereign status. It is true this special legislative route, which is being promoted actively by the Department of Indian Affairs, is subject to being repealed by Parliament at any time and does not provide constitutional protection of this Aboriginal authority. While it is not constitutionally entrenched in any way, it does reflect improvement over the *Indian Act*.

There is a pressing need for constitutional change. However, there is also a necessity for interim measures that can be used expeditiously. Parallel legislation to the *Indian Act* for specific First Nations would permit those First Nations who so desire to opt out of parts of the *Indian Act* while leaving the Act intact for those First Nations who still wish it. The prime minister recently has promised action on this front in relation to several aspects of the Act, such as land management and band election rules.

One critical component of these initiatives must be that First Nations not only consent to any future changes, but be involved actively in negotiating and drafting the terms of any new federal legislation or amendments to the *Indian Act.* Lip-service must not be paid to consultation, as has been the case too often in the past. Instead, a renewal of the Aboriginal-Crown relationship requires development of a partnership in this endeavour. At the same time, First Nations should not be penalized directly or indirectly if they do not wish to participate and prefer to proceed more gradually. Properly respecting the "honour of the Crown," as the Supreme Court of Canada emphasized in the *Sparrow* case, and the federal fiduciary obligation will permit a varied approach.

WE RECOMMEND THAT:

- ■ As a temporary measure, the *Indian Act* be amended to remove the authority of the minister to veto by-laws enacted by First Nations pursuant to the *Indian Act.*

- ■ That section 81 be amended to increase the law-making powers of band councils by expressly empowering them to replace provincial legislation that may apply on reserves currently as a result of section 88 of the Act. The revised law-making jurisdiction should expressly include the ability to enact a comprehensive civil and criminal code.

These amendments relating to the law-making powers under the *Indian Act* should be viewed as transitional until more complete intergovernmental arrangements are in place, which recognize the constitutionally protected rights of Aboriginal peoples to govern their own affairs.

WE RECOMMEND THAT:

- ■ Any amendments to the *Indian Act* be developed in accordance with certain key principles. They include recognition that:

  - • The Act is to be changed only in ways that enhance Indian self-determination.

- The amendments should have the support of First Nations.

- The legislation should be prepared in consultation with representatives selected by Indian people.

- The pace of change should be in accordance with the wishes of the people concerned.

We have reached the conclusion that the federal government has failed to meet its obligations to First Nations as a result of the dramatic increase in band membership brought about through the amendments to the *Indian Act* in 1985 by Bill C-31. While the removal of some discriminatory provisions was well intentioned and appropriate, the federal government has caused grave hardships for many First Nations who face significant added pressure for already scarce resources. This failure to respond to the increase in band size that the change has caused is, in our view, a breach of the federal fiduciary obligation.

WE RECOMMEND THAT:

■ The federal government accept its fiduciary obligations in relation to the increase in First Nations membership generated by Bill C-31 and assume the expenses for First Nations resulting from this increase.

Statutes in Conflict with Treaty and Aboriginal Rights

In our view, a number of federal and provincial statutes are in violation of Aboriginal and treaty rights. Given our conclusions regarding the current state of Canadian judicial decisions and our assessment of the effect of entrenching these rights constitutionally, we believe that certain federal and provincial laws are inoperative in relation to Indian, Inuit and Metis peoples when those laws conflict with the rights now protected by section 35 of the *Constitution Act, 1982*. The following laws are the ones that have been the source of most of the controversy and tension. They do not represent, however, a complete list of legislation that is now of doubtful validity.

Statutes of Canada

- The *Indian Act*
- The *Migratory Birds Convention Act*
- The *Fisheries Act*

Statutes of Manitoba

- The *Wild Rice Act*
- The *Wildlife Act*
- The *Provincial Parks Act*
- The *Crown Lands Act*

WE RECOMMEND THAT:

- The government of Manitoba invite the Assembly of Manitoba Chiefs and the Manitoba Metis Federation to designate representatives to work with senior provincial officials to review all relevant legislation that may conflict with Aboriginal and treaty rights. This review should identify specific areas of conflict and propose concrete solutions and statutory amendments. The Manitoba Aboriginal Justice Commission that we propose should be utilized to assist in this process if any of the parties wish.

One specific legislative change that could be implemented quickly, if Aboriginal organizations in this province agree, is in the area of the general *Interpretation Acts* of Manitoba and Canada. These acts deal with general principles of statutory interpretation and also provide rules and principles that apply unless a particular statute contains a provision that clearly has a different effect. Express recognition of Aboriginal and treaty rights within these laws would have a positive effect and assist in ensuring that all legislation is interpreted properly in light of these constitutionally protected rights.

WE RECOMMEND THAT:

- The federal and provincial governments establish a process to review all proposed legislation for its potential effect on the rights of Aboriginal peoples.

- The *Interpretation Acts* of Manitoba and Canada be amended to provide that all legislation be interpreted subject to Aboriginal and treaty rights.

Conclusion

We believe that Aboriginal people in Manitoba have been treated unfairly by federal and provincial governments, and by the legal system. There have been frequent violations of the letter and spirit of Indian treaties and Aboriginal rights over the years. Indians have been frustrated by the lack of movement on land entitlement issues. A long-awaited review of federal policy holds little promise of progress. The record on specific claims is just as dismal, with only one claim in Manitoba being settled thus far. Aboriginal people seem to have lost almost complete respect for and trust in both the federal and provincial governments. Dramatic change is required. We believe that the recommendations outlined in this chapter, if implemented by the governments of Manitoba and Canada, would go a long way in rectifying historic injustices.

THU

CHAPTER 6

———

MANITOBA COURTS

An Introduction to Manitoba's Justice System

At the centre of any justice system lie the courts. All accused individuals are entitled to their day in court, and all offenders are sentenced by a court. If there is to be any justice in our legal system, it includes the fair and equitable operation of the courts.

Jurisdiction

Manitoba courts deal with all manner of laws, whether passed by the federal, provincial, municipal or band authorities. Civil matters are dealt with by the Court of Queen's Bench. Criminal matters are dealt with by the Court of Queen's Bench and by the Provincial Court of Manitoba, depending on the nature of the charge and, in some cases, on the choice of the accused person. Family law is dealt with by both the Queen's Bench and the Provincial Court, depending on the type of case and the location of the dispute.

Criminal offences in Canada are defined by the federal *Criminal Code*, which creates three different kinds of offences, depending upon their seriousness: summary conviction offences, indictable offences and "hybrid" offences. Each type of offence is treated by the courts in a different manner.

Courts

There are three courts which play a crucial role in the daily administration of justice in Manitoba. These are the Provincial Court of Manitoba, the Court of Queen's Bench of Manitoba and the Court of Appeal.

Provincial Court

The Provincial Court has jurisdiction to deal with offences under federal criminal laws, provincial statutes and municipal by-laws. It also has jurisdiction to deal with *Child and Family Services Act* matters in certain parts of the province. The judges of the Provincial Court are appointed and paid by the Province of Manitoba.

Trials in Provincial Court are conducted by a judge sitting alone without a jury. With a few exceptions, this court has the jurisdiction to hear any criminal case. In serious cases where the charge has been designated as "indictable," an accused may have a choice to be tried by a Provincial Court judge, by a Queen's Bench judge sitting alone, or by a court composed of a Queen's Bench judge and a jury. In less serious cases, the accused may have no choice and the case is heard in the Provincial Court.

Where an accused chooses to have a trial in the Queen's Bench, either before a judge alone or with a judge and jury, a Provincial Court judge conducts a preliminary inquiry. The purpose of that hearing is to determine whether there is enough evidence to warrant a trial. If there is not sufficient evidence, the accused is discharged at that stage. If there is enough evidence, the accused is committed for trial, a transcript of the evidence is prepared and the case is transferred to the Queen's Bench for trial.

The Provincial Court is the designated Youth Court for Manitoba and it hears all matters under the *Young Offenders Act.* The Crown, however, may apply to have a case transferred for hearing in the Queen's Bench. The youth court judge may grant or deny that application. That decision, however, is subject to an appeal to a judge of the Queen's Bench.

In child protection matters, the Provincial Court has concurrent jurisdiction with the Family Division of the Queen's Bench, except in Winnipeg, Brandon, St. Boniface and Selkirk, where the Queen's Bench has exclusive jurisdiction in this field. The Provincial Court also deals with maintenance enforcement in locations where the Queen's Bench does not sit.

Where the Provincial Court has jurisdiction under the *Family Maintenance Act,* it may grant a separation, order custody of and access to children, and order child or spousal support. The Provincial Court does not have jurisdiction to grant a divorce, to divide marital property, to grant exclusive possession of a house, or to grant an order of prohibition or non-molestation in potentially abusive situations. It may grant, however, a non-molestation order if there is a charge under the *Criminal Code,* either as a condition of bail or as part of a probation order following a conviction.

Judges of the Provincial Court reside in Winnipeg, Portage la Prairie, Brandon, Dauphin, The Pas and Thompson. They also hold court in many small, rural communities and in the remote communities of northern Manitoba. The Provincial Court operates over 50 circuit courts out of six provincial judicial centres. The Winnipeg-based circuit of the Provincial Court sits in approximately 18 non-urban settings, while the Thompson circuit of the Provincial Court sits in approximately 20 remote communities, flying in to all but one of them. The frequency of these visits varies, depending on caseload and location, with some communities being visited twice a month and some only once a year.[1]

There are 39 full-time Provincial Court judges in Manitoba, one of whom is Aboriginal.

Court of Queen's Bench

The Court of Queen's Bench has wide civil and criminal jurisdiction, including jurisdiction accorded by federal and provincial legislation, as well as "inherent jurisdiction" to deal with other matters and procedures enshrined in the common law.

In criminal matters, depending on the charge or the choice of the accused, trials may be before a judge sitting alone or before a judge and jury. In each case there will have been a preliminary hearing in the Provincial Court and there will be a transcript of those proceedings. The Queen's Bench holds jury trials at Winnipeg, Portage la Prairie, Brandon, Dauphin, The Pas and Thompson.

Civil cases dealing with any legal dispute people wish to bring to court are dealt with by the Court of Queen's Bench. This court also deals with small claims, which are heard first by a hearing officer, but may be appealed to a judge of the court. Decisions of administrative tribunals are reviewed and declaratory orders may be made. Appeals from sentences or from decisions of the Youth Court dealing with raising a youth to adult court are heard.

The Family Division of the court has exclusive jurisdiction to deal with a number of family-related statutes, the most common of which are the *Divorce Act* of Canada and the provincial *Family Maintenance Act, Marital Property Act* and the *Child and Family Services Act*, in areas where there is a resident Family Division judge (Winnipeg, Brandon, St. Boniface and Selkirk). In other parts of the province, both the Family Division of the Queen's Bench and the Provincial Court have jurisdiction to deal with child protection cases. This division also deals with adoptions. The Family Division has attached to it a "social arm," Family Conciliation, which performs a mediation function in custody and access disputes and prepares reports for the court when requested. There are 15 counsellors resident in several locations throughout the province.

The Court of Queen's Bench, including the Family Division, holds regular sittings at Winnipeg, St. Boniface, Selkirk, Portage la Prairie, Morden, Brandon, Dauphin, Swan River, The Pas, Flin Flon and Thompson. Aside from occasional sittings in Minnedosa, these are the only communities in which the Court of Queen's Bench sits. The court does not sit in a single Aboriginal community. The court does not hold jury trials during July and August.

The judges of the Court of Queen's Bench are appointed and paid by the federal government. Judges are appointed either to the Court of Queen's Bench, without any other designation, or to the Family Division of the Court of Queen's Bench.

There are 33 Court of Queen's Bench judges in Manitoba, none of whom is Aboriginal.

Court of Appeal

The Court of Appeal hears appeals from the Provincial Court, from the Court of Queen's Bench, from administrative tribunals and, on occasion, a specific reference directly from the government on a constitutional issue. This court has seven judges, one of whom is the Chief Justice of Manitoba. None of the Court of Appeal judges is Aboriginal.

Witnesses seldom testify in this court. Appeals are invariably based on the record of the proceedings in the lower court and on the arguments of counsel. The record includes the documents that have been filed and, where evidence has been given, a transcript of that evidence. The court also hears appeals against the length of sentence imposed by a trial judge.

The Court of Appeal conducts all its hearings in Winnipeg. The court usually sits in panels of three, but for more serious matters five judges sit to hear an appeal. As the Supreme Court of Canada becomes busier, the Court of Appeal increasingly has become the court of last resort for Manitobans.

Supreme Court of Canada

This court hears appeals from the Manitoba Court of Appeal. Except in cases where the Court of Appeal is divided, no criminal appeal can be heard unless a preliminary application to appeal is made. In general, the Supreme Court limits appeals to matters of national, rather than local or personal, interest and to cases dealing with *Charter of Rights and Freedoms* and constitutional issues.

Personnel

Judges

Judges play a key role in the legal system. Not only do they make a determination of guilt or innocence at the end of a trial, but they have a large measure of control over the way a case proceeds from the time of the first appearance of the accused in court until the final disposition. In making decisions, judges are supposed to represent the community, since the judge applies the laws established by the community's representatives in the Legislature and Parliament. If they are to adequately fulfil this role of representing the community, judges must understand the community and must be aware of the cultural background and the circumstances of those who appear in court.

A judge should be seen as one who brings justice to the people and community he or she serves. Serving a community means not only the application of the law to cases, but also making dispositions that will be accepted and respected by those coming before the court and by the community at large. If the ultimate goal of the law is to regulate conduct and to maintain a safe environment in which individual and community rights are preserved, the judge must have an understanding of the individual before the court and of the community itself.

Lawyers

There are just over 1,600 lawyers in Manitoba. Approximately 880 of these lawyers practise at least some criminal law: approximately 800 of them as members of the private bar, 50 as Crown prosecutors and 30 as staff lawyers with Legal Aid Manitoba.

The duty of defence counsel is to represent a client to the best of his or her ability. In Manitoba an accused person, if he or she has sufficient resources, may hire a defence counsel from the private bar. If the accused meets the income qualifications, Legal Aid Manitoba will arrange to have the accused represented by a defence counsel of the accused's choice from the private bar who is willing to act, or by a Legal Aid staff attorney.

It is estimated that there are fewer than 200 Aboriginal lawyers in all of Canada— fewer than 10 of whom practise in Manitoba. There would be approximately 190 Aboriginal lawyers in Manitoba alone if Aboriginal people were to be represented in the legal profession proportionate to their share of the province's population.

Legal Aid Manitoba

Legal Aid Manitoba (LAM) provides a variety of legal services to low-income Manitobans. Although it keeps no records of the racial background of its clientele, Aboriginal people constitute a significant proportion. Legal Aid services are provided on a sliding scale, depending on an applicant's income and family size. According to guidelines presented to us, an individual with a family of four would have his or her legal costs fully covered if his or her family income is $25,000 a year or less. If this person's family income is between $25,000 and $27,000, he or she would have to repay a portion of the legal costs incurred by Legal Aid. If the family income is between $27,000 and $31,500, the individual would have to repay the full amount of the Legal Aid costs.

Legal Aid provides legal services for all indictable offences, for summary conviction cases where there is a likelihood of jail or loss of employment upon conviction, for civil cases where there is a reasonable likelihood of success, and for administrative tribunals where the merits of the case warrant. In 1987–88, 30,932 people applied for Legal Aid representation and 6,565 had their applications refused.[2]

There are Legal Aid offices in Winnipeg, Brandon, Dauphin, The Pas and Thompson. According to the Legal Aid brief presented to us, Legal Aid Manitoba employs 35 lawyers, seven articling students and six paralegals (two of whom are fluent in Aboriginal languages and service four Aboriginal communities from Thompson). Two lawyers are located in The Pas and four in Thompson. As of 1988, the agency had no Aboriginal lawyers on staff, although the agency has had a number of Aboriginal law students article with it over the years.

One of the most important services provided by Legal Aid is the provision of duty counsel. These lawyers are present in the courts to advise people who are appearing without a lawyer of their rights, to assist them in applying for bail or for Legal Aid assistance, and to speak to sentence if they wish to plead guilty. Duty counsel also can be appointed to act as defence counsel at a trial. Eligibility for duty counsel representation in criminal matters requires only that a person be charged with an offence. Legal Aid currently provides duty counsel on a routine basis at all provincial courts and at Youth Court at the Manitoba Youth Centre. In 1987–88 Legal Aid duty counsel served just over 28,000 persons, and provided information and advice to 17,200 more.[3]

People who qualify for Legal Aid are allowed to have their case handled by a member of the private bar, as long as that lawyer is on the LAM panel of private bar lawyers who have indicated their willingness to accept legal aid cases. In Saskatchewan private bar lawyers are allowed only for murder cases, while Alberta provides private bar lawyers on a strict rotation—allowing for no choice on the part of the accused. The private bar handles about 70% of the legal aid cases in Manitoba each year.[4]

There are two significant restrictions on the freedom of choice accorded to an accused person in Manitoba who qualifies for Legal Aid. First, Legal Aid Manitoba will not pay travel time or expenses for lawyers, unless there are no lawyers available, either in terms of resident lawyers or travelling duty counsel, in the community where the accused resides. For this reason very few private bar lawyers are willing to take cases in remote northern communities. Second, while an accused may choose to be represented by a prominent lawyer, he or she often finds that the case has been assigned to a junior lawyer working for the same firm as the requested lawyer.

Crown Attorneys

Crown attorneys are employees of the provincial Justice department. The Crown attorney may be consulted by the police on whether charges should be laid and, if so, what the appropriate charge should be. He or she will decide whether a hybrid offence will be pursued as an indictable offence or as a summary conviction, which witnesses are to be called, whether charges will be stayed at any point and whether there is going to be an appeal. The majority of the work of Crown attorneys involves consultation with the police, the prosecution of cases, and speaking to the sentencing of people who have entered a plea of guilty or have been convicted.

Magistrates and Justices of the Peace

These officers are appointed and paid by the provincial government. Some are full time and others act on a part-time basis. They have limited authority to hear minor offences under the *Criminal Code* of Canada or under a variety of provincial legislation. They also grant bail in some cases and issue subpoenas and warrants. While they may conduct some trials, they generally receive pleas of guilty and impose fines according to a schedule prepared by the Justice department. Most of their work involves offences under provincial laws. There are 20 Aboriginal magistrates in Manitoba.

Masters

Masters are officers of the Court of Queen's Bench, and are appointed and paid by the provincial government. They deal with all bankruptcy cases and with specific issues referred by judges. They deal with all manner of procedural disputes and are responsible for the Child Protection and Enforcement of Maintenance Orders dockets of the Queen's Bench in Winnipeg, Brandon, Selkirk and Dauphin. They have jurisdiction throughout the whole of the province, but, currently, only sit at the above locations. Hearing officers of the Court of Queen's Bench are responsible to the Senior Master. None is Aboriginal.

Hearing Officers

Hearing officers of the Court of Queen's Bench hear small claims civil cases involving less than $5,000. They also assist in the enforcement of maintenance orders. Hearing officers reside in Winnipeg and Brandon, and travel to other parts of the province from time to time. None is Aboriginal.

Court Reporters

Court reporters record the evidence and other proceedings of the Queen's Bench and Provincial courts. When requested, they provide transcripts of the evidence taken at a preliminary inquiry, a trial or sentencing hearing.

Aboriginal Court Workers

Since the early 1970s, Manitoba has had a program, run under the jurisdiction of the chief judge of the Provincial Court of Manitoba, to provide assistance to Aboriginal people who are charged with offences in Provincial Court. It originally was called the Court Communicators Program, but recently has been renamed the Aboriginal Court Worker Program. Aboriginal court workers help Aboriginal accused understand their rights and the court process. The court workers will help accused in obtaining a lawyer and applying for legal aid. They can attend court to provide information on the accused to the court. There are 10 full-time court workers, two part-time court workers and a chief court worker. They are located in Winnipeg, Fort Alexander, Brandon, Dauphin, The Pas, Thompson, Grand Rapids and Portage la Prairie. They are all Aboriginal persons.

The program has been recently evaluated by the Justice department and is currently undergoing a reorganization. A new advisory council, with representation from various Aboriginal organizations, has been created and the program was renamed. It is the only Aboriginal court worker program of its type in Canada which is not run by an Aboriginal agency.

Sheriffs

Sheriffs serve subpoenas to witnesses who are to appear in criminal cases, summon and assemble jury panels, maintain security and order in courts, and escort prisoners. There are approximately 80 sheriffs in Manitoba who operate under the supervision of a chief sheriff.[5]

Court Clerks / Court Monitors

Court clerks ready a court for a sitting. They prepare the docket or list for the day and make certain that the necessary files and documents are available. They mark and keep control over all exhibits that are filed and see that all orders are entered properly. Many act as court monitor as well, and record, and sometimes transcribe, court proceedings.

At present there are five Aboriginal court clerks in Manitoba. We understand that the Manitoba government, in conjunction with the Core Area Initiative program, is currently training 15 Aboriginal people to become court clerks.

In circuit courts, court clerks also function as magistrates with jurisdiction to hear guilty pleas, swear informations and issue court documents such as summonses or subpoenas.

Conclusion

A great many talented and dedicated people are involved in the operation of a very intricate and complex court system. Despite the best efforts of all involved, however, the court system is one which is becoming increasingly estranged from the general public and one which has never been accepted by Aboriginal communities. Justice in Manitoba is not being delivered in a manner which is sensitive to the concerns of local communities. There is not equal access to the services of courts across Manitoba, nor is there a swift resolution of cases. For Aboriginal people, the manner in which they are processed in the criminal court system is particularly unsettling.

The Criminal Court Process

Manitoba has two criminal trial courts and an appellate court. The Court of Queen's Bench hears the most serious of criminal cases and sits with a judge and jury or a judge alone. The Provincial Court hears 95% of all criminal matters and all youth court matters, and sits without a jury. There are numerous offences which start in one court and end up in the other, and there are numerous offences which can be tried entirely in either court, depending on choices made by either the Crown or the defence. Part of the problem, as we shall see, is that both courts are not equally accessible throughout the province.

This results in the provision of differing levels of service to different parts of the province. Northern Manitoba, where most Aboriginal communities are located, and where travel can be especially difficult and costly, suffers as a result of any matter having to be heard in both courts or solely in the Court of Queen's Bench. One can grasp the problems and delays that this creates for Aboriginal people only by following the route that offenders must travel through this system before they come to trial.

Summons or Arrest

In most cases a police officer sets the criminal court process in motion by presenting a justice of the peace or magistrate with a written allegation that a person has committed an offence. If the police officer swears that he or she believes there are reasonable and probable grounds for the charge, the justice can issue either a summons requiring the accused to attend a court hearing on a specific date, or a warrant for the arrest of the accused. In many cases the person may already have been apprehended by the police officer and be in custody. The *Charter of Rights and Freedoms* requires that, when an arrest takes place, the accused is to be informed of his or her legal rights. The formalities of the legal system can begin to frustrate the Aboriginal person even at this early stage in the proceedings. A Legal Aid paralegal in northern Manitoba told us of an Aboriginal accused who thought the police were telling him he must take counselling, when, in fact, they were advising him of his right to legal counsel.

Release from Custody

When a suspect is taken into custody, the first issue that must be resolved is whether the accused will be released by the police officer or granted judicial interim release or, as it is more commonly known, bail.

If an arrested person is charged with an offence that carries a maximum penalty of less than five years' imprisonment, he or she must be released by the police unless there are reasonable grounds to believe that he or she would not show up in court or that his or her release would not be in the public interest. This would include, for example, where the person presents a danger to himself or herself, to another individual or to society. In releasing the accused, the police may also require a promise to pay the Crown up to $500 should he or she fail to abide by the terms of the release. If the accused does not live within 200 kilometres of the community where he or she is being held in custody, the police can also require a cash deposit of up to $500 before releasing the individual.

If the police choose not to release him or her, the accused must be brought before a justice of the peace or a judge within 24 hours of arrest. Ordinarily, a person may be held in custody only if the prosecution satisfies the court that "his detention is necessary to ensure his attendance in court," or that detention "is necessary in the public interest or for the protection or safety of the public ... including the substantial likelihood that the accused will ... commit a criminal offence...."[6] Where the accused is already on bail, and in some other circumstances, the onus of proof is on the accused.

Where an accused is charged with murder or the other offences mentioned in section 469 of the *Criminal Code*, bail can be granted only by a Queen's Bench judge. In those cases the onus of proving he or she should not be detained also falls on the accused.[7]

Bail and Aboriginal People: Some Statistics

We examined the impact of the denial of bail on Aboriginal people. Our analysis of data collected in a study done on Provincial Court cases reveals that Aboriginal persons were 1.34 times more likely to be held in pre-trial detention. For Aboriginal women aged 18–34, the difference was 2.4 times. For adult males between the ages of 18 and 34, Aboriginal persons spent 1.5 times longer in pre-trial detention. Overall, we determined that Aboriginal detainees had a 21% chance of being granted bail, while non-Aboriginal detainees had a 56% chance. We discovered that in Winnipeg and Thompson, Aboriginal people spent considerably more time in pre-trial detention than did non-Aboriginal people.

In Winnipeg, the average length of detention for an Aboriginal detainee was more than twice as long as for non-Aboriginal detainees. In Thompson, the average length of detention was 6.5 times longer for Aboriginal detainees.

In Thompson, 28% of Aboriginal people who applied for bail had their applications denied, versus 10% of non-Aboriginal accused.

During the course of our Inquiry, we heard of cases where Aboriginal people were held in custody on remand for a year or longer.

The issue of pre-trial detention is particularly serious when one looks at the treatment of young offenders. According to our information, on average, Aboriginal youth in pre-trial detention were detained almost three times longer than non-Aboriginal youth.

The Consequences of Bail Denial

Persons who are denied bail face numerous difficulties. The most obvious is that they are denied their liberty until the court process has run its course, which can take over a year. This can seriously impair family life and can result in a loss of employment. Accused who are held in custody until trial also are less able to participate in the development of their legal defence.

Time spent in custody often is referred to as "dead time." An accused serving "dead time" languishes in jail, serving custodial time which may or may not be taken into account in the final disposition, and during which he or she quite literally has nothing to do. Many prisoners complained to us that they did not think they received credit for the time they spent in custody prior to sentencing, because a sentence only starts to run from the day it is imposed. They also complained that they could not take advantage of, or participate in, any of the institution's programs for sentenced inmates. Alcohol and drug counselling may have been offered to some of them, but even that was not always so.

Indeed, accused who serve their remand time in custody often serve this time in conditions which are more restrictive and punitive than those experienced by convicted criminals. The Winnipeg Remand Centre, which has been the scene of a number of suicides, is a prime example of this problem. The denial of bail also increases the pressure on an accused to plead guilty just to end the court process as quickly as possible and to obtain relief from the conditions of remand.

The denial of bail can have more sinister consequences. The strength of a case against an accused and the circumstances surrounding the commission of an offence are factors which the court can take into account when deciding whether to release an individual. If bail is denied, this sometimes can create an "aura" of guilt or suspicion. In the eyes of an Aboriginal accused and the general public, the fact that a person has been charged with a serious offence and has been denied bail is highly suggestive both of guilt and of the ultimate need to incarcerate. Studies have shown that individuals who have been denied bail are far more likely to be incarcerated upon conviction.[8] It is difficult to estimate the degree to which the trial or sentencing judge has been influenced in his or her decision, either to convict or to incarcerate, by the fact that the accused was denied bail. However, it is easy to imagine why the accused may feel he or she is at a disadvantage.

It is advisable for an accused to be represented by legal counsel at a bail hearing. However, an arrested person may not have acquired the services of a lawyer within 24 hours of arrest, and even if he or she has, the lawyer might need more time to become fully prepared for the hearing. As a result, the accused may have to ask for what is likely to be the first of many remands or delays in the court process.

Bail and Systemic Discrimination

It is worthwhile to note the number of ways the pre-trial detention system can discriminate against Aboriginal people, particularly those who reside in remote communities.

When police arrest an Aboriginal person in a remote community, they often remove the accused from the community immediately, on the grounds that there is no local facility in which to hold the individual, or there is no local person who can hear a bail application. From this point on, the Aboriginal accused begins to be shuttled about the province.

Because of the economic circumstances of many Aboriginal people in Manitoba, an Aboriginal offender is likely to need to have a lawyer appointed through Legal Aid Manitoba. Waiting for the Legal Aid appointment process to be completed can lead to delays in the bail hearing.

Once that hearing does take place, a number of bail requirements or conditions of release can discriminate against the Aboriginal accused. Factors such as mobility, family ties, whether the accused is employed, whether the accused has a fixed address and the accused's links with the community are all used by judges to determine whether a person is to be granted bail and how stringent the terms of release are to be. These factors militate against Aboriginal people and have a more adverse impact upon them than upon non-Aboriginal people. These factors also work against Aboriginal accused in urban areas.

Even if the accused is to be released, the court may impose a number of conditions that, while reasonable for many non-Aboriginal people, are out of reach and, therefore, unreasonable for Aboriginal persons. These might include a condition that another person undertake to ensure that the accused show up for trial and to provide a cash deposit, or a guarantee.

In 1986, for example, the unemployment rate for status Indians was four times the rate for non-Aboriginal people. In that year, 70% of Aboriginal Manitobans had incomes below $10,000.[9] Finding a relative or acquaintance with "sufficient means"—a precondition to qualifying as a surety or guarantor—can be more than simply problematic, it can border on the impossible. Aboriginal people, therefore, are discriminated against by conditions of bail which require that someone assume a significant debt if the accused fails to appear in court. A person may be fully eligible for release except that he or she does not know anyone who can come up with sufficient money to post a surety or who has sufficient property to act as a guarantor. Aboriginal people living in cities are unlikely to own their own homes.[10]

This clearly creates a situation where there appears to be one law for the rich and one for the poor. In one of its presentations to our Inquiry, the John Howard Society told us that it is regularly requested to sign sureties for inmates at the Winnipeg Remand Centre. The society must turn these requests away because it lacks the necessary financial resources.

Additionally, Aboriginal people are compelled by socio-economic circumstances to migrate frequently between reserve and city in search of employment. Provisions of the *Municipal Act* also state that status Indians are required to be free of public assistance for a year before being entitled to provincial or municipal assistance. This sometimes results in Indian people having to continue to rely on band assistance even if they move to the city to look for work, which in turn means that they have to return to their reserves once per month to obtain their assistance.

Aboriginal people who frequently move between urban centres and reserve communities are more likely to be said to lack fixed addresses—another factor which works against them when bail is considered. Our survey of Aboriginal inmates indicated that while most of them were arrested in urban areas, they still maintained strong links with their reserve communities. This high rate of Aboriginal mobility places especially adverse burdens on Aboriginal accused.

In the United States, bail criteria have been codified into a number of scoring systems. We applied one of these systems, the Minneapolis Scoring System, to inmates at the Winnipeg Remand Centre. The system poses a series of questions relating to employment, residence, family ties, substance abuse and previous criminal record— important factors which our own judges take into account when considering judicial interim release. The scoring system gives points for various answers. Individuals who receive five or more points are considered good risks for release. We found that 39.1% of the non-Aboriginal inmates were considered good risks under that system, compared to only 29.4% of the Aboriginal inmates. This suggests that the criteria that judges currently employ are likely to be biased against Aboriginal people.

Court Appearances and Remands

It should be noted that there is a difference between a trial and a court appearance. A trial takes place after an accused pleads not guilty to the charges. The Crown then must call witnesses to prove the case against the individual.

A court appearance is just that, an appearance of the accused in court. At various steps in the court process, the accused is required to appear in court, but the case often is remanded or adjourned at the request of either the Crown or the defence, or both. Remands may be granted because the accused does not yet have a lawyer, because the defence needs to receive information from the Crown, because the Crown has not finished preparing the case, or because the Crown and defence wish to negotiate a plea. Often the court appearance lasts just a few minutes as the lawyers and judge quickly agree to a remand and set the date for another court appearance. The accused is often required to attend each court hearing, even if it is apparent that the matter will not be dealt with on that day. Some cases are remanded without a word being spoken to the accused. To Aboriginal persons, who may have had great problems just getting to court, the system seems cold and uncaring when it takes their attendance for granted and does not even inquire about problems they may have in returning on another day chosen by the court party.

Elections

The next step in the court process is determined by the type of offence that is being tried and the type of trial the accused selects. Less serious offences, known as summary conviction offences, are tried in Provincial Court. Some indictable offences, such as mischief and theft under $1,000, are tried in Provincial Court, as well. Other indictable offences, such as murder, may be tried only in Queen's Bench.

For most indictable offences, except for those deemed to be in the absolute jurisdiction of the Provincial Court by virtue of section 553 of the *Criminal Code*, the accused may elect to be tried in the Provincial Court or the Queen's Bench. If the accused selects trial in the Court of Queen's Bench, he or she must also specify trial by a judge alone or by a judge and jury.

Before a person can be tried by the Court of Queen's Bench, a preliminary inquiry is almost always held. The Minister of Justice may issue a direct indictment, which by-passes the preliminary inquiry, but that is rarely done.

Preliminary Inquiry

If an accused elects to be tried by a Queen's Bench judge or jury, a preliminary inquiry will be held in the Provincial Court. If the person is committed to stand trial at the preliminary inquiry, there is an arraignment in the Queen's Bench when the indictment, or formal charge, is read and the plea of guilty or not guilty is entered. If the plea is "guilty," the case is adjourned for sentencing. If the plea is "not guilty," a trial date is set. The date will be determined to some extent by the date on which the transcript of the proceedings of the preliminary inquiry will be available.

A preliminary inquiry is a procedure in which there is a hearing to determine whether there is enough evidence to warrant the holding of a trial on charges that have been laid. The inquiry is held before a Provincial Court judge whose sole task is to determine whether there is sufficient evidence upon which a jury, properly instructed as to the law, might convict. The Provincial Court judge has very limited jurisdiction when presiding over this type of hearing. The judge may not determine guilt or innocence, but merely whether there should be a trial in another court. While the judge is permitted to make procedural rulings that might result in the dismissal of the charge, that jurisdiction is very limited. The judge may commit a person to stand trial on the original charge (e.g., murder), or may commit on a lesser charge (e.g., manslaughter), or may decline to commit the person to stand trial on any charge.

The preliminary inquiry is available only in cases where an accused has decided to have a trial in the Queen's Bench. If the accused has elected to be tried in the Provincial Court, there is no preliminary inquiry and the case proceeds directly to trial before a Provincial Court judge. In that situation the judge listens to the evidence presented by all the witnesses who are called to testify and makes a determination of whether the accused is guilty or not. If guilty, the judge sentences the accused.

Preliminary inquiries were established in England in the days when a Queen's Bench judge would go on circuit from London to other parts of the country to hear the more serious criminal cases. It was the responsibility of a local justice to hold a preliminary inquiry to weed out the weak cases in which there was insufficient evidence to warrant proceeding to trial.

Today, the responsibility for weeding out cases falls upon Crown attorneys. After reviewing statements taken by the police, and sometimes after interviewing witnesses, they are able to make a good assessment of the evidence available to them and the likelihood of a conviction. If they decide that the evidence will not support the charge, they either can reduce the charge to one the evidence will support, or apply their absolute discretion and stay the charge altogether.

The original need for the preliminary no longer exists. Cases seldom are dismissed at the preliminary inquiry stage. In a study conducted by our research staff, 208 preliminaries held in Winnipeg in 1989 were examined. Only three of the 208 cases, or 1.4%, were dismissed at the preliminary. The rest all went on to a trial or to a plea of guilty.

In its 1974 *Study Report: Discovery in Criminal Cases*,[11] the Law Reform Commission of Canada suggested that the preliminary inquiry be abolished. However, the defence bar strenuously objected and the proposal was dropped. Defence counsel who discussed the matter with us felt that the preliminary was important for a number of reasons. The Crown uses it to see how its witnesses stand up under questioning and to see if there are gaps in its case that should be filled. The defence uses the preliminary to see how strong the Crown's case is and to obtain evidence from witnesses that may be used in cross-examination at the trial. What the lawyers for both sides are doing is obtaining "discovery" of the case to help them determine how to proceed, or whether the Crown's case is so strong that a plea of guilty might be the wiser way to proceed.

We do not quarrel with the benefit to both the Crown and the defence of having a mechanism for learning more about the case. None of the reasons we heard in support of retaining the preliminary dealt with the likelihood of the case being dismissed. Rather, the call for its retention was based on the information that can be obtained during the hearing.

We believe that the preliminary, as it is now structured, is not the only way that information can be obtained. Nor is it the best way. It is also clear that the requirement for a preliminary inquiry causes several problems in the system. It causes delay in the processing of cases. It ties up judicial time that could be put to much better use. It involves two courts in bringing cases to trial.

In civil cases there is often an initial hearing, called an examination for discovery. We believe a procedure needs to be developed to replace the preliminary inquiry, one that combines the benefits of that type of hearing with the benefits of a pre-trial conference.

Re-elections

At the present time, if a person is committed to stand trial at a preliminary inquiry, the case is transferred from the Provincial Court to the Court of Queen's Bench, where the accused is arraigned. The formal charge is read to the accused and a plea is taken. A date for trial then is set for some time after it is anticipated that the transcript of the evidence taken at the preliminary will be ready.

The re-election procedure permitted by the *Criminal Code* still makes it possible for the accused, who had chosen originally to have a trial in Queen's Bench, to decide to have it in the Provincial Court. The accused has an absolute right to make that decision within 14 days of the preliminary inquiry, or even later with the consent of the Crown. There is also a provision in the Code that permits an accused to convert a preliminary inquiry into a trial before the Provincial Court judge, in certain cases with the consent of the Crown. These procedures are often employed where the accused, after hearing some of the Crown's evidence, decides it would be preferable to enter a plea of guilty before the Provincial Court judge.

There are also proceedings that permit an accused who has initially chosen to be tried in the Provincial Court to change that election and proceed to a preliminary inquiry and trial in the Court of Queen's Bench. The procedures clearly permit some judge-shopping.

The procedures in this area are complex and, in our opinion, outdated, unnecessary and inefficient. They contribute a great deal to delay in the processing of criminal cases.

Circuit Courts

There is no clearer example of the unequal and uneven manner in which the current justice system deals with Aboriginal people than in the circuit courts of northern Manitoba.

Three to four days a week, a Provincial Court judge, a Crown attorney, a Legal Aid lawyer, a court clerk, an Aboriginal court worker and a court reporter meet at the Thompson airport and board a small chartered aircraft. They comprise one of the two Thompson-based circuit court parties. During the course of a year, this party travels to approximately 20 communities; some are visited only once a year, but, in general, the court is scheduled to travel to most communities 10 to 12 times a year.

Almost all northern communities can be reached only by airplane, which creates the first problem for the circuit court. It is not uncommon for weather to delay, or even prevent, the court's departure or landing. In winter, flights can be delayed by storms, and in spring and fall, delays can be caused by problems with break-up and freeze-up on the lakes and rivers. Many runways are gravel-based and can be rendered unsafe by heavy rains. Circuit courts are tightly scheduled, so that a cancelled flight means that the court cannot visit for another month. This can create tremendous hardship for Aboriginal people.

While the circuit court travels to many remote communities, it does not reach all of them. The people of Lac Brochet, for example, must make a two-hour boat or snowmobile trip to appear in court in Brochet. They may well make this trip in dangerous weather conditions only to discover that court has been cancelled. The only comfort they can draw from the experience is to remind themselves that if they had not made the trip and if the court party had been able to arrive, they might have been charged with failing to appear in court. Similar problems exist in Red Sucker Lake, Wasagamack and St. Theresa Point, to name a few of the other communities which suffer from a lack of court service.

The residents of a remote community get their first sight of the circuit court when all its members, who are usually non-Aboriginal, with the exception of the Aboriginal court worker, descend from the plane at the local airport. The court party is then often driven from the airport in an RCMP vehicle to the building or hall where court is to be conducted.

CIRCUIT COURT SERVICE TO ABORIGINAL COMMUNITIES

Aboriginal Community	Nearest Court	Access to Court	Road Distance to Court
Aghaming	Pine Falls	road	80 km
Baden	Swan River	road	110 km
Barrows	Swan River	road	110 km
Berens River IR	local		
Birdtail Sioux IR	Minnedosa	road	50 km
Bissett	Pine Falls	road	80 km
Bloodvein IR	local		
Brochet IR	local		
Brokenhead IR	Selkirk	road	40 km
Buffalo Point IR	Steinbach	road	128 km
Camperville	Dauphin	road	106 km
Cormorant	The Pas	road	82 km
Crane River IR	Dauphin	road	130 km
Cross Lake IR	local		
Dakota Plains IR	Portage	road	30 km
Dakota Tipi IR	Portage	road	10 km
Dallas/Red Rose	Fisher Branch	road	34 km
Dauphin River	St. Martin	road	80 km
Dawson Bay	Swan River/The Pas	road	70 km
Duck Bay	Dauphin	road	128 km
Easterville IR	local		
Ebb & Flow IR	Dauphin	road	110 km
Fairford IR	St. Martin	road	13 km
Fisher Bay	Fisher Branch	road	65 km
Fisher River IR	Fisher Branch	road	53km
Fort Alexander IR	Pine Falls	road	18 km
Fox Lake IR	Gillam	rail	50 km
Gambler IR	Russell	road	25 km
Garden Hill IR	local		
God's Lake Narrows IR	local		

Aboriginal Community	Nearest Court	Access to Court	Road Distance to Court
God's River IR	local		
Grand Rapids IR	local		
Granville Lake	Leaf Rapids	air/boat/skidoo	
Hartwill	Fisher Branch	road	30 km
Herb Lake Landing	Snow Lake	road	42 km
Hollow Water IR	Pine Falls	road	75 km
Homebrook	Gypsumville	road	35 km
Ilford	Gillam	rail	65.5 km
Indian Birch IR	Swan River	road	55 km
Jackhead IR	Fisher Branch	road	146 km
Keeseekoowenin IR	Minnedosa	road	60 km
Lac Brochet IR	local		
Lake Manitoba IR	Ashern	road	50 km
Lake St. Martin IR	St. Martin	road	10 km
Little Black River IR	Pine Falls	road	40 km
Little Grand Rapids IR	local		
Little Saskatchewan IR	St. Martin	road	5 km
Long Body Creek (Bloodvein)	Bloodvein	boat/skidoo	
Long Plain IR	Portage	road	21 km
Loon Straits	Bloodvein	air	
Mallard	Dauphin	road	96 km
Manigotagen	Pine Falls	road	80 km
Matheson Island	Arborg	road	90 km
Meadow Portage	Dauphin	road	90 km
Moose Lake IR	local	road	
National Mills	Swan River	road	111 km
Nelson House IR	local		
Norway House IR	local		
Oak Lake Sioux IR	Virden	road	22 km
Oxford House IR	local		
Pauingassi IR	local		
Peguis IR	Fisher Branch	road	45 km
Pelican Rapids	Swan River	road	55 km
Pikwitonei	Thompson	rail	70 km

Aboriginal Community	Nearest Court	Access to Court	Road Distance to Court
Pine Creek IR	Dauphin	road	110 km
Pine Dock	Arborg	road	75 km
Poplar River IR	local		
Powell	Swan River	road	110 km
Pukatawagan IR	local		
Red Deer Lake	Swan River	road	115 km
Red Sucker Lake IR	Garden Hill	air/ boat/skidoo	
Rolling River	Minnedosa	road	30 km
Roseau River IR	local		
Salt Point	Dauphin	road	50 km
Sandy Bay IR	Amaranth	road	10 km
Seymourville	Pine Falls	road	80 km
Shamattawa IR	local		
Sherridon	Cranberry Ptge	road	46 km
Shoal River IR	Swan River	road	99 km
Sioux Valley IR	Virden	road	47 km
South Indian Lake	local		
Split Lake IR	local		
St. Theresa Pt. IR	Garden Hill	boat/skidoo	
Swan Lake IR	Morden	road	80 km
Tadoule Lake IR	Leaf Rapids	air	
The Pas IR	local		
Thicket Portage	Thompson	rail	80 km
Valley River IR	Roblin	road	35 km
Wabowden	Thompson	road	109 km
War Lake IR	Gillam	rail	65.5 km
Warrens Landing	Norway House	air	
Wasagamack IR	Garden Hill	boat	20 km
Waterhen IR	Dauphin	road	126 km
Waywayseecappo IR	Rossburn	road	11 km
Westgate	Swan River	road	130 km
York Landing	Gillam	road	165 km

Sources: Manitoba Department of Northern Affairs, Department of Justice, Department of Highways and Canada Department of Indian Affairs.

Plea Bargaining

Before the court session begins, the Crown and defence lawyers, as well as perhaps some of the police officers, may discuss the particulars of various cases and examine files. None of this is improper as it often is necessary for defence lawyers to acquire information about a case from the prosecutor, just as it is desirable for the prosecutor and defence to discuss the possibility of matters being resolved without having to go to trial.

In addition, members of circuit court parties work so closely together on a regular and intense basis that friendships often develop. This easygoing familiarity can leave the impression that cases have been decided before court opens. In particular, the sight of the judge being on friendly terms with lawyers on both sides of the case leads to a concern that all these people are in league together and that results are predetermined. The perception left with the Aboriginal community is not good.

Glen Smith, the mayor of Cross Lake, spoke to us on this issue:

It's not fair for the defence lawyer's clientele within this set-up. They can't get their full representation when everyone is making deals. The way the present system works, the outcome of cases are often settled before the court party has even arrived in the community.

Defence counsel and Crown attorneys do discuss cases and work out arrangements with each other before court commences, and sometimes before they arrive in the community. Such discussions often are called "plea bargaining." Plea bargaining is commonplace and occurs in urban centres, as well. Defence lawyers faced with a strong case against their client often speak to prosecutors in order to try to make a favourable arrangement. These "bargains" may involve pleading guilty to a lesser charge, pleading guilty to one charge if others are dropped, or pleading guilty if the Crown attorney agrees to recommend a lighter sentence.

It is an inevitable part of the criminal justice system and, in and of itself, is not to be discouraged or criticized. It can relieve the demand on victims to testify, can allow accused to have matters dealt with quickly, can save court time and can minimize the demand on public resources. While plea bargaining is a matter of some controversy, it is seen generally as a process which can and should benefit the accused.

In the case of circuit courts, however, plea bargaining can take on a more sinister appearance for Aboriginal accused. First of all, the adversarial system which gives rise to the propensity for "deal-making" or plea bargaining is at odds with Aboriginal cultures, where open discussion aimed at developing a consensus that resolves community (and private) matters is the hallmark.

Secondly, the plea bargaining process itself is almost always limited to the defence counsel and the prosecutor. The victim, the witnesses, the court and the community are never part of that process. The accused might be involved, but even his or her role is minimal, usually consisting of authorizing discussions or admissions, and agreeing to or rejecting the final outcome of the discussions.

Good counsel know that for a plea bargain to work best, he or she must have the full support and proper consent of his or her client, and the client, in turn, must have a full knowledge and appreciation of the evidence, the position to be taken by the Crown attorney, and the law as it affects his or her position. As well, good defence counsel ensure that the client understands that even if the Crown and defence agree on every-thing, including the sentence, the judge, who has no part in the discussions, has an over-riding discretion to accept or reject the deal and to impose whatever he or she thinks is an appropriate sentence.

In order for the client to fully appreciate all those factors, there must be appropri-ate and meaningful contact between defence counsel and the accused. Counsel and client must communicate well with each other. This is where the process breaks down for many Aboriginal accused.

When Aboriginal accused reside in remote communities and defence counsel reside and work in distant urban centres, the frequency and quality of communication between them are impaired. Additionally, if there are unresolved or unappreciated cul-tural or language barriers at play, whatever communication that does take place can be almost totally ineffective. Most often, Aboriginal accused never see or hear from their lawyers between court appearances. Usually, defence counsel only speak to their clients just before court starts or during one of the recesses in the proceedings. If counsel must speak to several clients as well as to the Crown attorney during those times, then matters can take on a sense of urgency not conducive to the ends of justice.

If one adds to that the noted tendency of all members of the court party to want to get court over with so that the plane carrying them can leave before dark or before antic-ipated bad weather sets in, then Aboriginal accused can justifiably feel that their inter-ests and rights are being ignored in favour of the desire of the court party to get finished and get out.

If, in fact, there are time pressures being brought to bear upon a lawyer because of a scheduled take-off time or impending bad weather, defence counsel may feel pres-sured to make a deal, or to get his or her client to accept a deal offered by the Crown. We believe that defence counsel, in fact, do press their clients to accept "deals" in situations that are not fair to them. Poor communication between non-Aboriginal defence counsel and Aboriginal accused and systemic pressures on counsel to "cooperate" contribute to this practice.

Ross Beardy (speaking through a translator) gave this example of the circuit court proceedings at Garden Hill, which are all too typical of those across the North.

> One of the most frustrating parts, as he sees it, I suppose, is that the timetable that the lawyers or Legal Aid has to work within, before 10:00 arrives, and that is for the purposes of consultation.

> There is hardly even time to get a character reference of that person that is being tried, for the purpose of timewise. Not only that, because there couldn't be any character references of an individual. Sometimes, quite often, it would

prove that the person would have to agree to plead guilty for the purposes of meeting the timetable.

Q   So, you think that people plead guilty just to ...

A   They're advised. Not think.

Q   They're advised to plead guilty by their lawyer because they've got to finish the day's work by a certain time?

A   They have to finish by that certain hour, so they're advised to plead guilty. Whether or not the truth is there. It's immaterial. But the timetable is the only weighing factor.

Q   Have you ever heard it said that court has to be completed by a certain time so people can get out of here?

A   No, they never state the time, not really, but there is always a plane standing by ready to take off whenever they're ready to go.

At the Portage Correctional Institution for women, inmates told us of how they were convinced to plead guilty when they either did not commit the offence, or did so under what they considered to be legitimate extenuating circumstances. Aboriginal women felt their lawyers had pressured them to plead guilty, and because of their ignorance of the legal system, the lack of alternative advice and a history of oppression, they agreed.

The following testimony of a group of four inmates at the Portage jail also was typical.

Q   You all pleaded guilty?

A   Yes.

Q   None of you had a trial or went through a trial.

A   It was easier to plead guilty because they don't really believe us.

We heard from another inmate that lawyers told their Aboriginal female clients to plead guilty and receive a lesser fine. This was true even if the client seemed to have a good defence.

I didn't understand court. I just thought I would listen to him because he knows more about law than I do. Maybe a white lady would have got acquitted.

My lawyer told me to plead guilty to the lesser offence. He said the Crown attorney and judge said, 'It doesn't matter what you are going to plead. You're still going to jail.' He said, 'They don't like you.'

Part of the problem appears to lie in the degree to which lawyers take over the conduct of the case from Aboriginal clients. It seems as though the client is sometimes taking direction from the lawyer, rather than the other way around. We believe that the court facilitates this process by allowing lawyers to waive the reading of charges to the accused and entering a plea on behalf of their clients. The most that clients are called upon to do in that circumstance is to nod their heads or say yes when asked by a lawyer whether they agree to a guilty plea.

Court Facilities

The facilities in which court is held in circuit points are rarely conducive to the administration of justice in a calm and dignified manner. Circuit court often sits in a community hall or school gymnasium. The court party is grouped at one end of the room and, as a result, court proceedings often cannot be heard by spectators.

Often, there are not enough seats, or room, to accommodate members of the public. While translation sometimes is available, it is for the benefit of the court party and the accused, not for the spectators. It is very rare indeed that words spoken by the court party are translated or explained to the people watching. There is little sense in calling it a public court if the public cannot hear or understand what is happening.

For some people, the court sitting may be the first chance to see a family member since his or her apprehension. As a result, the courtroom also serves as an often noisy visiting room. Most judges and litigants would refuse to proceed in the facilities provided in Aboriginal communities if those same facilities were offered in the city of Winnipeg. Indeed, circuit court judges have refused to hold court in some communities because of the poor condition of the facilities.

The Pressures on Duty Counsel

Many of the people who appeared before us said that court often commences well after the scheduled time. Even if court starts on time, it is not uncommon for the first significant order of business to be a request for an immediate recess. This often happens because the Crown attorney and defence counsel were unable to interview witnesses or clients prior to the hearing.

The Legal Aid lawyer on circuit generally provides service as duty counsel. Duty counsel is a lawyer designated by Legal Aid to provide assistance to accused appearing in court without counsel.

Duty counsel operating out of Thompson assisted over 2,600 people in the 1987–88 fiscal year. The Thompson Legal Aid office formally represented 894 persons on a more formal client-lawyer basis during the same period.[12] This means that counsel must conduct hurried conferences with as many clients as possible before the court convenes. As duty counsel, lawyers give an accused advice, help an accused apply for legal aid, assist an accused who is applying for bail and speak to the court about the appropriate sentence when the accused pleads guilty.

In cases where the individual wishes to plead not guilty and be represented by a lawyer through Legal Aid, the duty counsel will take his or her application and ask the judge to remand the case until the application can be approved, a certificate issued by Legal Aid and a lawyer appointed. If the accused qualifies for legal aid, it is likely that the Legal Aid staff lawyer who is scheduled to visit that community as duty counsel for the next sitting of circuit court will be assigned to handle the case. This may well be the same lawyer who originally took the accused's application for legal aid a month earlier. It should be noted that during the same visit, this lawyer will also be required to act as duty counsel for many other people and may not have more than a few minutes to speak with the persons they are going to be representing that day.

A study of Legal Aid conducted for the provincial government commented on this problem:

> Time and distance raise a different set of issues in the provision of duty counsel on some circuit courts. In some communities, the pressure of the docket and real possibility that defendants will not reappear at a later date force duty counsel to conclude as many matters as possible without the issuance of a certificate. Because of the nature of the circuits, remanding cases which might otherwise qualify for a certificate would add to future dockets, and increase the risk that some defendants might commit offences in the interim or fail to appear on the date set.[13]

For duty counsel to conclude matters without issuing a certificate encourages guilty pleas. Thus, there can be some pressure on duty counsel to allow an accused to plead guilty.

Although Legal Aid is prepared to pay for members of the private bar to represent accused, Legal Aid does not pay transportation time or costs to communities where alternative legal representation, either resident lawyers or travelling duty counsel, is available. As a result, Legal Aid only pays travel time and costs for private bar lawyers travelling to remote communities when the duty counsel is overbooked. Therefore, most of the defence work carried out in remote communities is conducted by Legal Aid staff lawyers.

We heard many complaints about the fact that duty counsel lawyers were not able to gain a full knowledge of their clients' situations under the circumstances that we have described. At our hearings in God's Lake Narrows, Doug Hastings told us that in his community:

> The defence lawyers or Legal Aids on an easy docket have 30 to 40 clients to interview before court commences usually by 11:00 or 11:30. It is humanly impossible for any lawyer to adequately prepare a defence for so many clients in such a short time. Plea bargaining is a normal routine.

In his presentation to our Inquiry, Thompson Legal Aid lawyer Michael Paluk told us that "the schedule of court sittings has meant that lawyers have not always been as accessible as they would like to be to their own clients in the communities served by the circuit court." Some presenters were more vigorous in their criticism, describing the system as a "kangaroo court" and a "make-work project for lawyers." In addition, not only do Aboriginal accused spend less time with their lawyers, and duty counsel have incentives to encourage guilty pleas, but Aboriginal accused are more likely than non-Aboriginal accused to appear without counsel at all.[14]

The lack of time with a lawyer can have significant consequences for how an accused is dealt with in the system. The lawyer will be less informed about the circumstances of the offence, the potential defences to the charge and the resources available as alternatives to pre-trial detention or harsh sentences. The accused will be less informed about the available options and less able to provide informed instructions to counsel. If the lawyer does not have time for the client in court, it is likely the lawyer will not have much time for pressing the prosecutor to reduce charges or to agree to reduced sentences outside court. These possibilities must not be overlooked when considering explanations for the treatment Aboriginal people receive in the justice system.

It is a matter of great concern to us that the Legal Aid duty counsel system gives an appearance of justice and fair legal representation to Aboriginal accused that is not borne out in reality.

The Mixing of Criminal and Family Matters

The dockets on the circuit court often are full—and varied. Provincial Court judges hear adult criminal cases, family cases and youth cases, and all these cases are often on the same docket. This is inappropriate. Heather York, a social worker in Norway House, told us:

> I felt that as a person employed to administer child welfare that if I was able to get parents to come to court with me in apprehension cases, that those parents were entitled to the respect that they would be entitled to in any other centre where family court is family court and is private.... We have a lot of juvenile offenders in Norway House. A lot of them. And, of course, as a worker who works with juveniles you attempt to have parents go to court with you. You can plan. It looks more positive if the judge sees the parents there, if the judge can ask parents questions, but again, all of these people are lumped together along with adult offenders.

It is clear that the present organization of circuit courts does not afford judges the necessary time to deal carefully, thoughtfully and separately with family matters and young offenders. These cases are regularly rushed through at the end of adult criminal dockets. The situation is so bad that in some communities family disputes are never taken to court at all. While it is good to encourage people to settle legal matters without going to court, it is another thing for the system to be unable to offer adequate court services to those who need them and who have the right to take their disputes to court if that is what they wish to do.

The Limited Jurisdiction of the Circuit Court

In addition to these problems, the Provincial Court does not have the power to deal with issues such as divorce and the division of marital property. Nor can Provincial Court grant restraining orders to people subjected to, or living in fear of, physical or sexual abuse. To have these matters attended to, families must travel to distant urban centres where the Court of Queen's Bench sits.

Residents of remote communities who have civil matters which they want dealt with by the court must also travel to urban centres to put their case before the Court of Queen's Bench. Unless they do this, they cannot resolve their private civil disputes legally. Nor is there any local way of challenging the decisions of local government in the courts.

Failure to Complete Dockets

Court parties rarely spend the night in the community they are serving. The feeling in the communities we visited was that the court party often operates with one eye on the clock so it can depart on time. There often is considerable pressure to get through the docket. This, in turn, creates pressure to make deals, pressure to limit discussions with the accused and witnesses, pressure to limit questioning during trials and, ultimately, pressure to simply get the process over with quickly by pleading guilty. We heard many complaints of cases on the docket not being reached and being adjourned for a month because the court party had to leave to board a waiting aircraft.

When people in the court party start looking at their watches and then speak of the need to hurry as the plane will be leaving at 4:00, the members of the community feel a lack of concern for their needs and their priorities. The feeling of Aboriginal people is, quite properly, "If you ask us to come to court today, then deal with our case. If you don't have time for our community, then don't come." The community feels insulted by the way it is treated.

Aboriginal people are also aware that they only receive one court hearing a month because decision-makers in Winnipeg have come to the conclusion that, for economic reasons, that is all the administrators of justice are willing to provide. They are left with the unfortunately correct assumption that they are on the short end of a cut-rate justice system.

During the course of our Inquiry, we heard countless stories of the hardships that Aboriginal people encounter as they deal with a system which metes out justice on a monthly basis. Percy and Irene Okimow told of the frustrations they experienced following their daughter's arrest for discharging a firearm, break and enter, and mischief. Upon her arrest in God's River, their daughter was taken first to God's Lake Narrows for court, where she was denied bail, and then sent to Thompson. Her parents followed her to both communities, attempting to arrange for her release. In the space of a week, the family spent $1,200 on transportation and accommodation. Another youth who had been arrested at the same time, whose parents had not been able to travel to Thompson, was denied bail.

Court location is not solely a northern problem. In his presentation to us, Chief Raymond Swan, on behalf of the Interlake Reserves Tribal Council, pointed out that 6,500 of the 10,353 people served by the Gypsumville and Ashern RCMP detachments are Aboriginal. Despite the fact that there are several Indian reserves in the area of the detachments, and that most of the accused charged by those detachments are Aboriginal, the circuit courts where the accused must appear are all held in non-Aboriginal communities.

We have begun our examination of the problems Aboriginal people experience with the court system by looking at northern circuit courts because the circuit courts throw the issues into their starkest relief. But it is in the area of delay that the circuit court presents special and seemingly insurmountable problems.

Delay

> To no man will we sell, or deny or delay right or justice.
>
> – The Magna Carta

The right to a trial within a reasonable time is guaranteed by section 11(b) of the *Charter of Rights and Freedoms*. This right was addressed most recently in the case of *R. v. Askov et al.*, [1990] 2 S.C.R. 1199, in which the Supreme Court of Canada upheld a stay of proceedings where a trial had been delayed unreasonably. In the majority decision, Mr. Justice Cory wrote that the courts should consider a number of factors in determining whether the delay in bringing an accused to trial has been unreasonable: the length of the delay, the explanation for the delay, waiver and prejudice to the accused.

He also noted that the right to a trial within a reasonable period of time is so important that "the lack of institutional resources cannot be employed to justify a continuing unreasonable postponement of trials."

The decision also underlines the point that it is the duty of the Crown to bring an accused to trial and that the Crown must bear the responsibility for delay.

> Where inordinate delays do occur, it is those who are responsible for the lack of facilities who should bear the public criticism that is bound to arise as a result of the stay of proceedings which must be the inevitable consequence of unreasonable delays. Members of the community will not and should not condone or accept a situation where those alleged to have committed serious crimes are never brought to trial solely as a result of long delays. It is a serious consequence with potentially dangerous overtones for the community.[15]

The importance of this decision is that it heightens the significance of the problem of delay in Manitoba courts. We believe that Aboriginal people in Manitoba are not having their cases disposed of within a reasonable time. People in almost every community we visited complained about the long delays in bringing cases to trial.

There are many reasons why the courts often work slowly. These include such things as resource limitations, judge-shopping by defence lawyers, undue accommodations for the personal schedules of lawyers, the requirement for preliminary hearings, delays in obtaining counsel and the structure of the court system. Even when the system works normally and at its most efficient, proceedings can take many months.

The Effect of Delay on Aboriginal People

Many presenters spoke to us of the pain and confusion created by a justice system which seemed to them to proceed at its own leisurely pace. The harmful effects of delay are felt not only by the victims and witnesses who may have to relive painful memories that can be several years old, and by the accused who must endure months, if not years, of anxiety and fear, but also by the justice system itself. Manitoba's justice system has lost the respect of the people it is meant to serve in Aboriginal communities. Leonard Mackay of Norway House concluded a list of complaints with the justice system by telling us that "The respect for the justice system diminishes every year."

Eddie Ross, a God's River band councillor and volunteer probation officer, spoke to us about his community's problems with having the nearest circuit court location at God's Lake Narrows, a community which is only 32 kilometres away, but which is only accessible to the residents of God's River by boat, snowmobile or plane.

> A round trip costs $240. If a person knows they are innocent and can prove it by having a witness present it means they have to pay for the witness to go to the Narrows to testify. If the witness is employed it sometimes means they have to pay for lost wages too. So it is often easier to just plead guilty and pay a fine if the charge isn't too serious....

> More often than not our people travel to the Narrows, wait all day and then are told their case is remanded. This means they have to go home, wait until the appointed time and try to save enough money to go back again. And when we go back we stand a good chance of being remanded again. This can happen many times to the same person.

Ross estimated that the community of God's River, which does not have a high crime rate, spent at least $2,000 a month on air fares to go to circuit court.

In God's River we were also presented with a brief from Wesley Okimow, which told of the 24 trips he had to take to attend circuit court in God's Lake Narrows because of charges pending against his son. At the time of our Inquiry, the family had spent $5,760 on air fare. In January 1988 Okimow took his son to court by snowmobile. If he did not show up at court there would be a warrant for his arrest.

> On the way back from this particular visit, by skidoo, back to God's River, my son suffered severe frostbite to his face. The following day we had to take him to Thompson for further treatment for the frostbite.

The court process ended when the boy pleaded guilty to charges of break, enter and theft, for which he was sentenced to six months at the Manitoba Youth Centre in Winnipeg.

Jemima Ross, the community health representative in God's River, told us of the problems she faced as a single parent whose children had been charged with various offences and whose cases were heard at the circuit court in God's Lake Narrows.

> So I would go to the Narrows with my child each time one of them was charged with something. When we got to the Narrows we would go to court. Then we would sit there and wait and wait and wait. Every time one of the children was charged and after sitting there waiting for a whole day somebody would come up to me and tell me they were the lawyer for my kid. Then I would be told the case was remanded.

Sometimes the remand would be until the next day. When that happened, I would have to find someplace for me and my kid to stay in the Narrows overnight. So I would stay overnight and come back to court the next morning. Then we would both wait again for the whole day. At the end of the day the lawyer would come up to me and say the case was remanded again. Sometimes it would be for a month or maybe two months.

She said that the only time her family had been given a reason for a remand was the one time she had not been able to go to court with her children and had their uncle accompany them. She said the court said at that time that "it wasn't good enough for the uncle to be there."

Following our hearings at God's River, the concerns of the community were brought to the attention of the Chief Judge of the Manitoba Provincial Court. Arrangements were made for court to sit at God's River on a regular basis. While this may have alleviated the problem of community members having to face difficult hurdles such as distance and cost to get to court, we are not satisfied that it solves the problems of delay.

Many Aboriginal people have low incomes and no vehicle, and are unable to hire transportation. In isolated communities, transportation to a court outside the community may not be readily available and is often prohibitively expensive for people on low incomes. If people are required to take a plane, bus or train to an outside community, they may have no way of getting home the same day and may have to pay accommodation costs. Incurring these expenses only to see a case remanded can be a very frustrating experience.

These problems exist in both northern and southern Manitoba. Low-income people simply cannot find the means to travel to distant communities. If people from the Sioux Valley reserve are charged with offences which occur on their reserve, they have to go to court in either Virden or Brandon, both of which are many kilometres away. Often, their lawyer will be in Brandon. If they do not own a car, they will have to pay someone to drive them to court. Hitchhiking is an unreliable alternative. If they cannot afford the cost, they don't go to court. This can lead to further problems for them.

The justice system and its operation have a very serious impact on the members of a community. Time and time again we heard Aboriginal elders tell us that they could not understand the decisions that the system was making, or why it took the system so long to reach those decisions. In Oxford House, elder Wesley Weenusk told us of the case of his grandson, who had pleaded guilty to a charge of break and enter. Despite the fact the young man entered a guilty plea on his first court appearance, the case took seven months to come to sentencing. Weenusk told us:

It is also the justice system as we know it ... it's more or less, like, just a game where people are sentenced and people laugh; the judge laughs, the police laugh, everybody laughs about a lot of these cases as if it's just one big joke.

Court cases often seem to develop a life of their own and are capable of wearing down all the involved parties. Bert Crocker, of the Sagkeeng Child and Family Services in

Fort Alexander, told us of a family case which had gone on for 10 months without resolution. The matter had started out as a contested case but, after nearly a year of court activity, the respondents had all but dropped out of the case. Crocker provided us with a brief summary of some of the delays the case had encountered:

> There was one adjournment because of weather.... There was one adjournment because someone neglected to lay on a court reporter and everybody had to get sent home. We are now wondering how many more adjournments this is all going to take.

> The respondents in question have come to an understanding with ourselves. This is not going to be a contested case. The respondents have, long ago, stopped coming to court. They are simply not prepared to deal with this frustration in a first hand way any more, and they send counsel to court.

> We find it difficult to explain to people why on the one hand, there are rigid time lines, such as four judicial days for the filing of information, when on the other hand a matter like this can drag on for nine or ten months and still be undealt with.

One inmate in Dauphin told of losing his job, due to repeated remands. It makes no sense to have an accused lose a job merely because a charge is delayed, yet this may be the result of having to attend court on a number of occasions. Even if time off work can be obtained, the accused probably will lose pay and suffer the frustration of having the process repeated.

In South Indian Lake, Janet Soulier asked, "How come the justice system cannot deal with cases when they come up?" She explained that people are inclined to get into more trouble when on remand. She said people "go through hell" while on remand.

Delays in the system may be intended to protect the interests of accused. Lawyers naturally should not want their clients to plead guilty to a charge until they have had the opportunity to review the particulars, satisfy themselves that the evidence supports the plea and prepare themselves to speak to sentence. The system, however, makes little effort to explain this to Aboriginal offenders. In Sandy Bay, Mervin Houle told us of seeing people repeatedly coming to court with the intention of pleading guilty, only to be told to come back to the next court hearing.

> A lot of times I have heard, when I have gone and observed in court, a man walking out of there cursing and swearing because he could not settle his case. Instead, he has had to spend the rest of whatever money he gets from social assistance to get back to court.

John Constant, a former RCMP special constable in The Pas, told us that many Aboriginal people view the court system as

> ... a puppet show, which means that when I had to travel to all the communities, such as Moose Lake, many of the accused snickered at the court, because

they knew they were going to get off or remanded or somebody would pro-
long the court cases, because in most cases the judge would not ask the
defence lawyers as to why their cases were not prepared.

Constant also felt defence lawyers were able to use remands to drag court proceedings out indefinitely. His years on the force left him with an image of a system where:

> ... the lawyers were manipulating the system and in many cases ... many of
> the accused got off very easy because of the fact that they were giving inno-
> cent people a hard time.

We heard from men and women who felt their lawyers continually were arranging
unnecessary remands. We heard of impaired driving charges taking over a year to be
dealt with and of people being remanded eight and 10 times.

Delays in completing cases may affect a whole community. We found the community of Lac Brochet in a state of shock when we visited. Several young men from that
community were awaiting trial on charges of sexual assault. Because of the number of
youth involved and the nature of the crime, the case deeply affected everyone in the
community. The community was aware that it had a serious problem, and leaders and
elders wanted to deal with it, but we were told that they could not begin to look at healing
the community until the trials were over.

The testimony we heard concerning the problem of court delay made a powerful
impression on us. It is clear that the system operates too slowly, and it is equally clear that
Aboriginal people suffer disproportionately from this delay.

Research on Court Delay in Manitoba

Two studies have recently examined the extent of delay in the Manitoba courts:
the Provincial Court study was conducted by the Attorney General's department in 1986
and our own research staff examined Court of Queen's Bench cases which had gone to a
preliminary inquiry in Winnipeg.

Provincial Court cases involving Aboriginal defendants which went to trial took
an average of 215 days between the date of arrest and the date of final disposition. This
means it took seven months for these cases to come to trial. In Provincial Court cases
which did not go to trial, the time between the date of arrest and final disposition averaged 125 days for Aboriginal defendants. In other words, cases involving guilty pleas, or
which culminated in stays of proceedings, took an average of four months.

The processing time for cases ending up in the Court of Queen's Bench was significantly longer. For jury trials, the process took an average of 354 days from arrest to final
disposition for Aboriginal people, while in the case of non-jury trials Aboriginal defendants spent an average of 340 days in the court process. The longest component of delay
in Court of Queen's Bench was the period between the date when a trial date was agreed
upon and the trial. The average time spent waiting for a trial, after the trial had been
scheduled, was 186 days for cases with jury trials and 154 days for cases where a jury was
not involved.

According to our analysis of the data from the Provincial Court study, the average time in Winnipeg between first appearance and date of disposition for Aboriginal defendants was 161 days. In the North, cases involving Aboriginal people were processed in 100 days. The Provincial Court study also looked at juvenile defendants and found that Aboriginal youth spent an average of 130 days from first appearance to disposition. While these data might suggest that trials are not taking inordinately long to schedule, one must take into account that the vast majority of cases in our courts are resolved by way of guilty plea. That length of time seems inordinate.

The study of court delay done by our research staff did not differentiate Aboriginal people because racial identification of defendants was not available in the data, but it did demonstrate that preliminary inquiries create extensive delays. Of 208 cases in which preliminary inquiries were held in Winnipeg, the average time from first appearance to first trial date was 400 days (13.3 months). The shortest time between the two dates was 101 days and the longest was 794 days. Half of the cases took over 389 days to complete.

In his submission to our Inquiry, Attorney General James McCrae addressed the question of backlog and delay, stating:

> In the Criminal Court area of the Winnipeg Provincial Court, the most serious backlog of cases is eight months for those trials of less than one day. This means there are approximately 3,200 cases pending.... Court delay in the Rural Courts is almost non-existent. Scheduling of court cases is running approximately 2.5 to six months, depending on the type of litigation and location. The increase in the court work load has been primarily in the Winnipeg offices and coincides with the population distribution in Manitoba.[16]

All of what the minister says may be accurate statistically, but we disagree with his conclusions.

To say there is no backlog because the courts can offer an early trial date when one is requested ignores the fact that there exists a considerable delay in the court system before a trial date can be set. During the course of our hearings, we were told that there were many cases on court lists that had not been given a trial date and yet had been in the system for longer than 180 days.

The research on court delay in Manitoba has shown clearly that court processing takes too long. A delay of one year on any matter is not acceptable, nor is it acceptable for simple matters to take six months or more to process. In our opinion, no matter should take more than 180 days from the date an individual is charged until the trial begins.

The General Impact of Court Delay

Lengthy delays have a number of potentially detrimental effects on those involved with the court process, including offenders, victims, witnesses and the general public. Delay makes the trial process more difficult as memories fade and witnesses become more difficult to find. The ability of both defence and prosecution to present their cases may suffer under such conditions. As the time between offence and trial becomes longer, the connection for the community between the offence and the penalty becomes less clear. While the impact of delay on persons held in custody is clear, the failure to resolve criminal charges promptly also can be disruptive to accused who have remained in the community. Victims also feel a great deal of anxiety about the eventual resolution of their cases. Repeated visits to court as remands are granted are very disruptive to the lives of all involved in the case.

In Winnipeg, Mary Roulette painted this vivid picture of the impact that the delays of the court system can have on Aboriginal people:

> The remand process further complicates the lack of justice. Sometimes remands are set up to six months to a year, with appearances in front of the judge periodically.
>
> A person cannot plan his or her life in that period of time, and I have seen one-year remands, where the pressure became so intense, that people became so demoralized, that they became suicidal.
>
> Many are ready to accept any sentence, or to make any plea to the courts. Remand can realistically be viewed as a more severe punishment than being incarcerated.

In *Mills v. The Queen*, [1986] 1 S.C.R. 863, Mr. Justice Lamer (now Chief Justice) noted that the *Charter of Rights and Freedoms* guarantee of a fair trial within a reasonable time is also a guarantee of "security of the person." He pointed out that a person accused of a crime is stigmatized, suffers from stress, anxiety and a loss of privacy, has his or her family life disrupted, and can lose his or her job. He also noted that outside the courts there is little respect for the concept of the presumption of innocence:

> Doubt will have been sown as to the accused's integrity and conduct in the eyes of the family, friends and colleagues. The repercussions and disruption will vary in intensity from case to case, but they inevitably arise and are part of the harsh reality of the criminal justice process.

The impact of delay is even more severe for Aboriginal people, many of whom live in remote communities where coming in from the trapline or travelling to another centre for a court appearance can cause a serious financial hardship. Also, according to our own studies, in Thompson courts Aboriginal defendants were more likely to have been denied bail than non-Aboriginal people, and thus were more likely to spend the duration of the delay in custody. According to the study, 10% of bail applications made by non-Aboriginal accused in Thompson were turned down, while 28% of the Aboriginal people who applied for bail were refused.

The tension, fears and concerns arising from a criminal charge may also have a devastating effect on family and friends close to an accused or to the victim. These feelings are compounded every time a matter is delayed. Delay may have the same effect on witnesses, who may not want to go to court and who may be anxious until the experience is over. The problem is intensified when the accused and the witnesses live in the same small community. Each of these people may have to rearrange his or her life to accommodate the scheduling and rescheduling of court sittings. While scheduling problems are not easy to deal with, we suggest in a later chapter that the problem of delay may be minimized if time limits and case management procedures designed to speed up the system are put into place. Changes must be made if Aboriginal people are to develop any faith in the justice system.

Delay clearly has brought the administration of justice and the reputation of lawyers into serious disrepute with Aboriginal people. Unfortunately, many lawyers see delay as a valid defence strategy. Some lawyers believe that the longer it takes a case to get through the system, the more likelihood there is of prosecution witnesses not appearing or of their memories of events fading. During the period of delay, the accused may find work or participate in a treatment program in order to look like a better risk at sentencing. Lawyers may seek adjournments in order to have a case heard by a particular judge, or to suit their own schedules. Some convicted people have told us that they were happy to have cases adjourned so they could go to court or go to jail at a time convenient to them.

It should be clear, and we emphasize this fact, that the court system does not operate to suit the pleasure of the accused or their counsel, but rather to see that justice is done with reasonable dispatch, to see that people who, in fact, are guilty of their charge are dealt with promptly, and to ensure that those who are not guilty can have the stigma attached to them removed and can get on with their lives as quickly as possible.

Causes of Delay

Systemic Causes of Delay

In studying the problem of delay, we canvassed many people working in the system in an attempt to determine the reason for the many remands and delays in processing cases. None of the key actors saw himself or herself as being responsible for court delay.

RCMP officers said that their investigation is usually completed by the time a charge is laid. In some cases of violence, the accused may be arrested and charged when there are initial grounds to justify a charge, and then the investigation continues. Generally, however, the RCMP representatives said they are ready to proceed to trial the first time the case appears on a court list.

Although others gave us a different impression, Legal Aid lawyers said they are generally ready to proceed quickly once they receive particulars from the Crown and have a chance to consult with their clients.

Crown attorneys said that once they make full disclosure to the defence, they are not responsible for any delay. They tended to blame defence counsel or the overburdened court calender. They also told us that there were not enough Crown attorneys to handle the workload, especially if extra time is to be devoted to each community.

Private defence counsel tended to blame the Legal Aid appointment system for much of the delay. They also felt that some delay was due to the lack of judges and Crown attorneys. Some delay, they said, is caused by their inability to get instructions and by the limited time they have to spend with clients in preparation for a hearing. They said there is delay in waiting for particulars from the Crown.

In short, all the parties involved in the court system claim that they are not responsible for delay, that others are, and that they are ready to proceed to trial quite quickly. Yet, this is not happening. It is clear that counsel and the judiciary must accept greater responsibility for the delays experienced by Aboriginal people in the court system.

It is likely that the problem of delay is a problem inherent to the circuit court system. While there are some efficiencies which various justice personnel can introduce which might ease the situation, major structural reforms are needed so that Manitoba's Aboriginal people will not continue to be subjected to the problems associated with court delay.

Efforts have been made to eliminate delays and to enable cases to be dealt with in a timely fashion. Improvements have been made in the Provincial Court in Winnipeg. The system there now operates more efficiently than it did at the time of our hearings. However, corresponding changes have not been made in the court system that serves rural and remote communities, and it is here that delay has its most serious impact on Manitoba's Aboriginal people. Delays still exist in the overall time it takes to resolve family disputes. Dramatic systemic changes will have to be made to address the needs and concerns expressed to us during our hearings.

Remands as a Cause of Delay on Circuit Courts

It will be very difficult to deal with cases more quickly as long as the circuit court system is based on monthly justice. Necessary remands take one month each and there are two or three necessary remands for every case.

- The first remand is for appointment of counsel.

- One month after first appearance, the accused appears for a second time, and a second remand for one month probably would be sought by counsel for receipt and review of particulars, including witness statements.

- Two months after first appearance, the accused appears again, at which time a third remand for another month probably would be sought for discussions between counsel leading to a guilty plea at the next date or a not guilty plea and the setting of a date.

- Three months after first appearance, the accused appears again to enter a plea. If he or she pleads guilty, then the matter could come to an end unless a pre-sentence report is sought and ordered. That can add two or three more months to the date of disposition, since probation services, which does not visit every Aboriginal community, must be contacted and arrange to see the accused. But if the accused pleads not guilty, a fourth remand is made directly to the hearing date. Hearing dates in most circuit points can be set within six months.

- Nine months after first appearance, the accused appears for his or her hearing. If the accused has chosen trial in Court of Queen's Bench, then a fifth remand (technically a committal) is made directly to the next assizes three to six months away.

- Twelve to 15 months later, the accused's trial might occur in Court of Queen's Bench. This also assumes that there have been no unusual requests for remands (which occur so frequently as not to be unusual), such as resetting trial dates because witnesses or accused fail to appear for trial, the accused fails to appear for a remand, court parties are weathered out, etc.

The Preliminary Inquiry as a Cause of Delay

We examined the impact of the preliminary inquiry on delay. Of 208 accused who had preliminary inquiries in 1989, the average length of time from first appearance to preliminary inquiry was 228 days (7.6 months). This figure included two cases with long delays—the longest was 1049 days—because of the failure of the accused to appear. Half the cases took longer than 205 days (6.5 months) between first appearance and preliminary inquiry. Clearly, the delays caused by the preliminary inquiry are substantial. Given the time needed to prepare and to hold a preliminary inquiry, the financial costs also are substantial.

We examined the length of time it took to prepare transcripts. We found that the average time between the date of the preliminary inquiry and the date that the Court of Queen's Bench received the transcript was 78 days. The shortest time in which a transcript was received was a mere five days, while the longest was 307 days (10.2 months). Twenty-five per cent of the transcripts were received in 48 days or less, 50% were received in 66 days or less, and 75% of the transcripts were received in 93 days or less after the preliminary inquiry. With the changes in the court reporting system currently being implemented, we are unable to say whether there will be any significant alteration in these time lines, although there is nothing to suggest that that will be the case.

The federal government's 1984 study, *Some Statistics on the Preliminary Inquiry in Canada*,[17] showed an average delay of five months caused by the preliminary inquiry. More Aboriginal than non-Aboriginal people are kept in custody until their preliminary inquiry, due to bail being refused or their inability to meet bail conditions, which means that delays caused by the preliminary inquiry have a more adverse affect on Aboriginal people.

What we heard at our community hearings leads us to believe that the impact of the preliminary inquiry in the North is even greater than that found by the Department of Justice.

The federal study described a typical case: [18]

- Charges are laid for an indictable offence, such as break and enter.

- The accused elects trial by judge and jury at the first court appearance.

- Two months pass.

- The preliminary inquiry is convened, at which the accused consents to trial or is committed as originally charged following the testimony of two or three Crown witnesses.

- The preliminary concludes on the same day it began, usually requiring less than a full day.

- Two or three months pass, during which the accused may re-elect down.

- The trial begins; the accused pleads guilty, and the verdict is rendered the same day, usually in a matter of hours.

The study found that an average of 61 days elapsed before the preliminary began, and an average of 82 days elapsed between its conclusion and the start of the trial. This led the report's authors to ask, "Is it really necessary for the non-exceptional [case] to take this long? Is a preliminary inquiry really necessary to resolve pleas?"

This is a question which we address further in Chapter 8.

Legal Aid Appointments and Delay

We have been informed by Legal Aid Manitoba that it generally processes an application on a criminal matter within 24 hours. This is not the impression we received from defence counsel. We believe that the Legal Aid appointment procedure contributes to delay, particularly on the circuit courts. In many cases, accused who live in communities served by the circuit courts are not able to apply for legal aid until the day the circuit court comes to the community. Their application is taken by the Legal Aid duty counsel—who may very well be appointed to represent those individuals when the circuit next visits the community. However, all that can be done during the individual's first court appearance is to request a remand pending appointment of counsel. That appointment may very well be authorized within the next 24 hours, but the process will have added another 30 days to the life of the case.

The Lack of Case Screening

Many cases remain in the legal system far longer than they should. This is because either the Crown persists in pursuing a prosecution, only to drop charges eventually, or an individual pleads not guilty through the early stages of the court process, only to plead guilty on the eve of a trial. Three years ago, 75% of cases scheduled for trial in the Provincial Court in Winnipeg collapsed on the eve of the trial with either a guilty plea or a staying of charges. The introduction of pre-trial screening procedures has brought this percentage down. Not only are these cases lingering too long in the court system, their collapse on the eve of trial creates a situation where there are judges with no cases to preside over and courtrooms that are not being used.

Conclusion

This chapter is far from exhaustive in outlining the problems experienced by Aboriginal people in their contacts with the justice system in Manitoba. In other chapters we deal with the appropriateness of the sentences handed down by our courts, the role of police, the future of correctional institutions in Manitoba, the problems faced by Aboriginal women, jury selection, child welfare and the youth court system, and the probation and parole system in Manitoba.

We do believe, however, that this chapter has demonstrated that the court system in Manitoba is not an equal system. As far as Aboriginal people are concerned, the inequality exists both in the services the system provides and the impact it has on their communities. It is foolish and naive for anyone to insist that the administration of justice in Manitoba provides a uniform standard of justice to all people in this province.

In examining the court system in Manitoba, we are struck by the fact that there clearly exists a distinguishable, separate justice system for Aboriginal people. Indeed, the rhetoric that surrounds the equality of the justice system evaporates as one examines the way the courts deal with Aboriginal people. It is a system administered by non-Aboriginal people. The laws which the courts apply are alien to Aboriginal people, the adversarial approach employed by the courts does not reflect Aboriginal values, and the sanctions these courts apply are ineffective in terms of deterring accused or others from further involvement.

The court system appears to view Aboriginal people and their communities with a mixture of disdain and disregard. The province's senior courts never hold hearings in their communities, while the courts that do travel there appear to want quite literally to "get out of town before the sun goes down." As a result, cases are either rushed through without due preparation and consideration, or are delayed from month to month.

In short, the current court system is inefficient, insensitive and, when compared to the service provided to non-Aboriginal people, decidedly unequal.

We now turn to an examination of alternatives to the current court system.

CHAPTER 7

ABORIGINAL JUSTICE SYSTEMS

With so much discrimination occurring against our people, it is often amazing how accepting we are of our situation. We know that without tolerance there can be no justice. Without understanding there can not be justice. Without equality there can be no justice. With justice we can begin to understand each other. With justice we can work and live with each other. With justice we can love and feel confident with each other. Aboriginal people want a judicial system that recognizes the native way of life, our own values and beliefs, and not the white man's way of life.

Elijah Harper
MLA Rupertsland

Introduction

We are convinced that acts of racism have been directed at Aboriginal people by personnel employed within the administration of justice. Without, in any way, belittling the impact which such acts have upon the lives of their Aboriginal victims, we believe, however, that that is not the essence of the problem which Aboriginal people face.

There are many reasons for the problems that Aboriginal people have with the justice system. Repeatedly, for example, we were told that one major problem which contributed to Aboriginal over-representation in the justice system was the socio-economic conditions faced by Aboriginal people throughout the province. It is clear, in fact, that Aboriginal people are "the poorest of the poor" and that that fact contributes to the over-representation of Aboriginal people in our courts.

However, we agree with Aboriginal people who told us that it is not enough simply to acknowledge the role that poverty and its accompanying social conditions play in the over-representation of the Aboriginal poor in the justice system. It is valid, in our view, to ask from where that poverty and those social conditions came. Ovide Mercredi, an Aboriginal lawyer and now Grand Chief of the Assembly of First Nations of Canada, told us on behalf of Southeast First Nations at Berens River, "It is our conviction that the denial of our collective rights have substantially contributed to the serious problems in our communities."

We have no hesitation in concluding that indeed many of the difficult socio-economic conditions which Aboriginal people face daily are attributable directly to past government practices and policies.

For Aboriginal people, the essential problem is that the Canadian system of justice is an imposed and foreign system. In order for a society to accept a justice system as part of its life and its community, it must see the system and experience it as being a positive influence working for that society. Aboriginal people do not.

Simply providing additional court services in Aboriginal communities or otherwise improving what is inherently a flawed approach to justice is not, in our view, the answer. Those have been the solutions preferred by governments in the past, but it would seem that that approach has been unproductive for government and unacceptable to Aboriginal people. Historically, Aboriginal people have not received justice from the government. Their experience at the hands of the current legal system has been only slightly more positive. Therefore, they need to achieve resolutions that recognize and do not perpetuate historical injustices.

The situation involving Aboriginal people and the justice system has deteriorated, rather than improved, in the recent past. The reason would seem to be that Aboriginal distance from Manitoba's justice system is not simply a geographical phenomenon, it is also a cultural one.

This is partly because the language of our courts is not clear, even to people for whom English is a first language. Many of its terms and concepts defy translation into Aboriginal languages. The conceptual difficulties are compounded by the fact that key figures in the justice system, such as judges and lawyers, do not have equivalents in Aboriginal society. Peace and harmony, the primary goals to which traditional Aboriginal concepts of justice were geared, have not been accommodated easily by an adversarial and adjudicative system.

Also, it is clear that while Aboriginal peoples have many of the same legal problems as non-Aboriginal people, and some unique ones as well, they do not turn to the legal system to resolve them. This is so even where Aboriginal peoples reside in communities where courts are readily accessible.

When they do engage the legal system, or become engaged by it, the manner in which their problems are dealt with often is out of tune with their unique position as Aboriginal people. As a result, they have come to mistrust the Canadian legal system and will avoid it when possible. Even when they do have to deal with it, we find that they simply minimize their exposure to it. This can take the form of inappropriate guilty pleas, failure to attend court appearances and a perpetual passivity that manifests itself in an apparent air of indifference about what happens to them in court.

There is significant over-representation of Aboriginal people as individuals charged with offences and incarcerated in our penal institutions. Yet, there is significant under-representation of Aboriginal people in the administration of justice as employees and managers of essential elements of the system, particularly in Aboriginal communities.

The delivery of justice to Aboriginal people in Aboriginal communities through the provincial circuit court system is inequitable and inadequate. It is a system characterized by delay and an air of colonialism. Its priorities are more often those of a society located far from the society of those appearing in the court, and few efforts to involve Aboriginal people from Aboriginal communities have met with any sustained success. Serious matters of greatest interest to the community are not even dealt with in the community where the offence occurs. It is not uncommon for people in Aboriginal communities to be completely uninformed about the fate of accused taken out of the community for prosecution.

There is evidence of systemic discrimination against Aboriginal people within the justice system. Aboriginal people are under-represented on juries, due to the manner in which potential jurors are selected and the manner in which they can be removed. Factors which case law has directed judges to take into account when deciding whether to deny or grant bail, or when considering the question of sentencing, often work against Aboriginal people.

Factors which judges are called upon to consider in the course of making dispositions generally are of importance to white society, but may not hold the same significance for Aboriginal people.

This has a number of implications. Not only is the accused judged by standards inappropriate to his or her community, but judicial dispositions may make little sense to an Aboriginal accused, because what judges take into account in sentencing may not have the same importance to the accused or to the community from which he or she comes.

The methods used by the Canadian legal system to resolve conflicts—particularly the adversarial system—are incompatible with traditional Aboriginal culture and methods of conflict resolution. Additionally, courts are not always a good forum for the resolution of many of the conflicts involving Aboriginal people and, indeed, can be counter-productive. This has to be considered along with the fact that there is an unwillingness by Aboriginal people to utilize the justice system to resolve personal legal problems as they arise, particularly those of a civil or family nature. Because there are few, if any, alternatives to the use of court in Aboriginal communities, many such conflicts go unresolved.

Aboriginal people are unfamiliar with the priorities and processes of the justice system and, more importantly, are unfamiliar with their rights within those processes. There is inadequate representation of Aboriginal people in the system among members of the judiciary and the legal profession.

Aboriginal accused lack proper legal representation for matters which bring them to court. Legal aid generally is unavailable if the matter is a summary conviction one or if treaty and Aboriginal rights issues are involved. When legal counsel is appointed for them by Legal Aid, they are unable to communicate with their lawyer except during breaks in the court proceedings on the day when circuit court arrives in their community.

Aboriginal people in Aboriginal communities face unreasonable delays within the justice system in resolving even simple matters. They become frustrated with the time it takes to finally resolve or determine a matter and often plead guilty to simply "get it over with."

We have found that past efforts at reforming the justice system, such as having more Aboriginal people in the system to serve as lawyers, court workers or interpreters, have not brought about significant improvements. This appears to be the case, in part, because the advocates of those changes have failed to take note of the importance of more fundamentally altering the approach being taken to the delivery of justice by the system and the individuals within it. The focus of past changes has been upon improving the manner of processing the Aboriginal people within it, rather than on understanding the inadequacies of the system itself. This is because there is a lack of understanding and appreciation of the cultural attributes of Aboriginal peoples by those within the administration of justice. From the perspective of Aboriginal people, there is a perception that the justice system, as it operates within their communities, is not accountable to their governments.

Aboriginal people are unable, because of socio-economic circumstances, to take advantage of available legal institutions and processes. For example, Aboriginal people in communities where court services are lacking have to expend large sums of money simply to make court appearances. People from Tadoule Lake, for example, when charged with an offence, must travel by plane to Leaf Rapids or Thompson for their court appearances, at a cost of several hundred dollars each time. If they have witnesses to call, they have to pay those costs, as well. This can result in innocent people having to face adverse conditions simply to protect their innocence. For civil matters, Aboriginal parties must travel into regional urban centres such as Thompson or The Pas simply to pursue or protect their rights.

Providing an appropriate response to these problems is becoming essential. Many of them are assuming critical proportions. Aboriginal youth represent a substantial presence in the Aboriginal population. Answers must be found quickly, therefore, which conform to clear and acceptable objectives.

If changes are to be made to the administration of justice in this province in order to resolve the issues we have identified, we believe that any such changes must be for the betterment of both Aboriginal and non-Aboriginal people alike. We believe that we should seek solutions that are acceptable to the people most affected, and stand the best chance of resolving those problems which Aboriginal people face within the justice system.

We conclude that the following principles must be followed:

- Solutions must be designed specifically to eliminate and not to perpetuate historical injustices.

- Solutions must ensure that the administration of justice to Aboriginal people is culturally appropriate.

- Solutions must overcome any misunderstandings about, and a general lack of appreciation of, the cultural attributes of Aboriginal peoples present within the administration of justice.

- Solutions must overcome the perception by Aboriginal people that the justice system as it operates within their communities is not accountable to them and their governments.

- Solutions must reduce the over-representation of Aboriginal people as individuals charged with offences and incarcerated in our penal institutions.

- Solutions must increase the presence of Aboriginal people in the administration of justice as employees, administrators and managers of essential elements of the system, particularly in Aboriginal communities.

- Solutions must ensure the delivery of equal and adequate justice to Aboriginal people in rural and remote communities.

- Solutions must provide essential legal services to Aboriginal people in culturally appropriate ways, in their communities.

- Solutions must establish a legal process which Aboriginal people can and will utilize to resolve private legal problems as they arise, particularly those of a civil or family nature.

- Solutions must provide culturally appropriate alternatives to the adversarial system as a legal process.

- Solutions must enable Aboriginal people to take advantage of available legal institutions and processes, despite their economic circumstances.

- Solutions must improve the image of the justice system in Manitoba as it affects Aboriginal people.

- Solutions must provide a better quality of justice for Aboriginal people.

- Solutions must identify and remove systemic discrimination and outright racism from the justice system.

We have come to the conclusion after much study and consideration that the best method of resolving the problems and following the principles which we have identified involves the establishment of Aboriginal justice systems in all Aboriginal communities, operated and controlled by Aboriginal people. Drawing upon the positive results of the American tribal court system, which we will discuss shortly, as well as on the failure of the *Indian Act* courts established by the Department of Indian Affairs and the failure of the established administration of justice to provide justice adequately to or for Aboriginal people, we conclude that the most appropriate course to follow is not simply to establish a system of Aboriginal courts in Manitoba, but to establish fully functional Aboriginal justice systems, complete with appropriate and related police and justice programs, support services and legal systems.

The Argument for Aboriginal Justice Systems

The call for separate, Aboriginally controlled justice systems was made repeatedly in our public hearings throughout Manitoba as one solution to all or most of the problems with the present system. We were quite impressed with the thoughtfulness and thoroughness of the commentary we received. The strength of those presentations was enhanced by the belief on the part of Aboriginal leaders that a great injustice has been perpetrated upon them.

Carl Roberts, former chief of the Roseau River Band, told us:

> The imposition of foreign laws as supreme is totally unjust. The notion that English Common Law and French Civil Law supersede First Nations Law was and is based on racist and colonist attitudes. To imagine inviting a person into your home and having that person dictate to you that your authority and your laws are of no value and that theirs is supreme is totally racist and borders on insanity.

Many people emphasized that past injustices must be corrected in a way that respects the right of Aboriginal people to take control of those institutions which most affect them. Ovide Mercredi said to us:

> We . . . believe that our own laws are important and need to be respected and applied in our daily lives. Unfortunately, neither parliament, the legislature, nor the judiciary fully understands our rights and laws.

He went on to add a factor that may have been an unarticulated premise underlying the concerns of other Aboriginal presenters, when he said:

> Unless we reaffirm our rights and rebuild our social and political institutions now, we are fearful that within decades, assimilation will be complete, and our civilization will disappear forever.

Mercredi's solution was one which we heard often:

It is ... our conviction that these problems can be resolved only through the full enjoyment of our collective rights to government and to our institutions of self-government.

In this context we believe that the foundation for change is self-determination. We need the support of all Manitobans for the recognition and establishment of ... Indian tribal courts in Manitoba as one of the basic units of Indian government and one of the practical measures for Indian self-determination.

Chief Larry Beardy of the Split Lake Band spoke to us on the same topic:

The underlying objective is to place the entire justice system, outside of serious crime, within the control of the Band and develop a system of justice consistent with our Cree heritage.

Chief Philip Michel of the Barren Lands Band made this comment on behalf of his people at the remote community of Brochet:

[Y]ou can see from our presentation the biggest injustice done to the Aboriginal people is the refusal and denial of the governments of Canada to recognize Indian self-government and Aboriginal rights.

If Aboriginal rights and Indian self-government were recognized, we wouldn't be here today, trying to rectify the existing problem. The injustices done to the Aboriginal people by the judicial system is only the tip of the iceberg. Living with injustice from the general public is part of our daily routine....

We have inherent rights that no one, no government, can ever take away. We do not ask for anything special. We are simply asking for recognition of what we have had through the centuries. We are nations within a nation and wish to be treated as such.

In order for the Aboriginal people to improve the appalling conditions of our lives and to have meaningful participation in the Canadian mosaic, we have to be treated as nations.

We can well understand those concerns. Aboriginal people feel a strong sense of injustice about the manner in which they have been treated by governments and the justice system over the years.

But for many non-Aboriginal people, it is difficult to understand the full dimension of this injustice. A large amount of cultural faith and assumption is at work in what Aboriginal people are saying. We imagine it would be equally difficult for a non-Aboriginal person to try to explain why "democracy" works, or how "capitalism" works. To a large extent, explanations of such phenomena require a high degree of conceptual background knowledge which is difficult to attain in as short a period of time as was available to the Inquiry.

It is clear that for Aboriginal people, their faith in the ability of their cultural institutions and their leaders to undertake the revival of ancient principles for modern institutions is quite high. They obviously, as well, place a high degree of importance on the matter. We heard from representatives of national Aboriginal organizations on the topic.

Christopher McCormick, national spokesperson for the Native Council of Canada, representing Metis and non-status Indians in Canada, said this:

> The first step is to recognize that tinkering won't work, and that what will work is empowerment. Until the justice system can accommodate the reality of our self-determination, it can hardly begin to deal with over-representation of natives in prisons, the lack of native jury members or judges, discrimination in policing and corrections.

Gordon Peters, Vice Chief of the Assembly of First Nations, a national organization representing status Indian people, stated:

> The one thing that we would like to express very clearly from the very beginning about where we stand and what we are looking for in our system, which makes it different from other systems throughout the world, is that we are talking about exclusive jurisdiction as a first and foremost avenue that we would be dealing with.

But Aboriginal justice systems were not being put forward as a total answer. Chief Peters pointed out that it would not solve all the problems between Aboriginal people and the justice system, but he clearly felt that it would provide a significant part of the solution:

> So, no, we didn't say, and we won't say that tribal courts are going to be the answer. We think it is part of the answer. We think it is one of the ways that we can deal with our own people.

There are, in our opinion, sound reasons to establish separate justice systems for Aboriginal people in Manitoba.

Taking Control

The term "self-government" causes some concern in the non-Aboriginal community. It should not. It means the right of Aboriginal people to run their own affairs. There is, or should be, agreement that the term, at the very least, means the right to establish rules of conduct in Aboriginal communities that are developed by the population of those communities and have their support, and to see to the enforcement of those rules.

When Aboriginal people seek the right to self-government, they mean the right to determine how matters such as health care, education and child welfare are provided to their people, in their own communities. It includes the right to establish their own court system with their own unique ways of adapting and applying long-established cultural mores. It includes the right to apply their own ways of resolving interpersonal and community problems.

The concept of Aboriginal self-government is no threat to the non-Aboriginal Canadian. Aboriginal people are simply saying, "Let us run our own affairs, in our own communities, in our own way."

Aboriginal self-government includes the right to create and maintain codes of civil and criminal law, and a system to enforce and apply those laws as well as any non-Aboriginal law that Aboriginal people choose to adopt. We believe that is doing no more than recognizing in Aboriginal people a right they had and exercised not so many decades ago. We do not see why that should be upsetting to Canadian society.

It is clear that Aboriginal people in Manitoba are content to be part of the Canadian mosaic. As part of Confederation, they simply wish to be able to live according to their own customs and traditions, and to apply their own decisions, within their own designated lands.

The manner in which the non-Aboriginal Canadian system has controlled the lives of Aboriginal people in recent times has led only to disaster. It is time Canadian society recognized that the "white man's" solutions have not worked. Courts and jails are filled with Aboriginal people. The situation is getting worse, not better. New solutions must be found. The obvious one is to allow Aboriginal self-government an opportunity to flourish to the fullest extent possible on Aboriginal lands, within the context of our Constitution.

It is not as if components of self-government are untested. Aboriginal people in this province, and elsewhere, have proven that they can run a better child welfare system for Aboriginal people than can non-Aboriginal agencies. Aboriginal children are no longer being shipped out of the province. They are being removed from parents when it is appropriate to do so, but the children are not being removed from their "larger" families or their people.

This is the Aboriginal tradition and it is seen by Aboriginal people as working well. The stigma of foster care that prevails in non-Aboriginal society does not apply in the Aboriginal system, where there is a family and community-wide responsibility for the children. The Aboriginal agencies have not yet been in existence for 10 years, but amazing improvements in the care of children already have been made. More are on the horizon.

Aboriginal people have applied their self-government to their own police forces, both local and regional. The Dakota Ojibway Tribal Police Force has been developing over the last 15 years. This is an example of a community taking responsibility for its own citizens and its own problems. It is also an example of self-government.

The schools in the North are increasingly receiving the benefits of Aboriginal teachers, educated in the South and returning to Aboriginal communities to help Aboriginal children and to manage the complexities of an educational system. The operating responsibility for many reserve schools has been transferred from the Department of Indian Affairs to the local First Nation government. The transfer of health services has been under discussion for some time. These too are components of self-government.

Aboriginal self-government is a reality. It exists. It benefits the Aboriginal person and his or her community, and takes nothing away from Canadian society. In fact, we believe that Aboriginal self-government adds to the overall positive growth and development of Canada.

It is time to apply similar advances to the administration of all aspects of the justice system. Aboriginal governments need to establish systems to deal appropriately with those people causing problems in their communities and to provide a means for other community members to resolve their legal problems. Aboriginal governments need to provide them with culturally appropriate ways to achieve the ultimate result of restoring and ensuring peace among individuals, and stability in the community.

To enable this to be done, Aboriginal communities must have the right, as part of self-government, to establish their own rules of conduct, to develop means of dealing with disputes (such as courts or peacemakers), appropriate sanctions (such as holding facilities or jails), and the full range of probation, parole, counselling and restorative mechanisms once applied by First Nations.

The Aboriginal right and opportunity to manage these matters themselves, within their own territory, is self-government. It stems from our history, from the existence of treaties, from the Aboriginal people's original title to the land and from the current provisions of the Canadian Constitution. As a distinct level of government, Aboriginal governments, either individually or collectively, may have to negotiate with federal and provincial authorities as to how these matters are to be managed, but those negotiations should be done on a government-to-government basis. That is what happened with respect to child welfare. It is in that context that we feel no hesitation to recommend the formal recognition of the principle of self-government for Aboriginal people and its extension to the administration of justice.

Section 35 of the Constitution recognizes and affirms the "existing aboriginal and treaty rights of the aboriginal peoples." From the material which we have reviewed, from the evidence provided to us by Aboriginal elders and from the evidence we heard during the course of our hearings, we conclude that the internal sovereignty which Aboriginal people always had exercised in controlling their daily lives has never been surrendered by them, or extinguished in any formal process involving Aboriginal consent or in any specific federal or provincial legislation. As we have noted, it continues to exist.

The existence of Aboriginal people and their unique rights is not derived from legislation. Aboriginal people had formed distinct self-governing societies long before Europeans arrived in this country. The treaty-making process was just one manner of recognizing that existence. Aboriginal governments, and the right of Aboriginal people to them, were an aspect of the original title which Aboriginal people had and, in one form or another, continue to hold.

Aboriginal people cannot be said to have surrendered that right by voluntarily entering into treaties with the Crown. We believe that the treaty-making process can be seen as a confirmation of their right to a collective existence into the future as a people. That right, we believe, has been captured and now finds protection in section 35 of the Constitution of Canada.

To the extent that Aboriginal rights of Aboriginal people have been confirmed in other Canadian or British laws, it has another form of recognition, but the state of the law in Canada, as we understand it, is that Aboriginal people and their rights did not depend upon non-Aboriginal recognition in order to exist.

The same principle applies, in our view, to both Indian and Metis people, the latter of whom derive Aboriginal rights under the Constitution from their Aboriginal ancestry. While Metis people may have no rights under the *Indian Act,* that is irrelevant, in our view, to the question of whether they have any right to self-determination.

The recent (in terms of Aboriginal history) enactment of Canada's *Indian Act,* with its reference to Indian bands, elections of chiefs and councils, and band by-law powers, is not the source of Aboriginal self-government. Despite the presumption in the legislation that nothing can happen on Indian lands without federal approval or compliance with the Act, the Act does not state that tribal authority pre-existing its passage is abolished. In fact, the Act seems to state very clearly that only when the minister declares that certain provisions apply to a First Nation does there occur a necessary interference with Aboriginal self-determination.

The fact that Indian bands have borne the burdens of the legislation over the years, or have tried to work with a federal bureaucracy itself dependent upon the legislation, should not be interpreted as acceptance or acquiescence by Aboriginal people to a derivative form of government dependent upon delegated powers from a federal authority.

The assertion of inherent political powers and jurisdiction by First Nations in Canada and more notably in Manitoba in such areas as child welfare, education and social services has resulted in governmental arrangements that increasingly support the perspective that Aboriginal people have a considerable role to play in governing themselves.

Aboriginal decisions to operate under the laws of the province, such as in the case of child welfare, and under federal laws, as in the case of the *Indian Act,* clearly resulted from processes whereby the opportunities to make other, more appropriate, arrangements were denied to them, and should not be misinterpreted as a willingness by Aboriginal people to forego any of their own rights.

Child welfare measures (which First Nations have classified as "interim") have been arranged to further the self-determination aspirations of First Nations, not to jeopardize or to undermine their inherent rights. These measures are regarded by them as practical steps necessary until such time as the federal and provincial governments finally agree to recognize explicitly, within the Canadian legal system, their inherent right as First Nations to govern themselves.

From that, we conclude that solutions that try to turn such interim arrangements into the norm for issues related to Aboriginal self-determination would be inappropriate.

As we understand it, the Aboriginal right of self-determination cannot be met through a federal/provincial commitment to delegate their current authority. It is a matter of recognizing that Aboriginal people have the legal right to exercise constitutionally protected powers, equivalent to those currently within the federal/provincial regime, on Aboriginal territories. Because of the manner in which their rights have been treated in the past and the impact that that treatment has had on their lives, we believe that to begin to move in the direction of establishing such a right in a variety of areas ultimately would provide Aboriginal people with "constitutional justice."

The power to establish and maintain institutions of government is an aspect of sovereignty. It is not within our mandate to attempt to define with any degree of fullness what Aboriginal self-government is. However, of this much we are satisfied: we believe that it includes the right to establish and maintain their own forms of justice systems in their own territories.

Social Cohesion

Aboriginal people in Manitoba have, in the past century, experienced a rapid decline in their systems of internal social cohesion, largely as a result of the imposition of laws, policies and new institutions based on different values prevalent in Canadian society.

For example, members of Aboriginal communities were traditionally educated by elders, who had the role of teaching and transmitting to children knowledge of their culture and their history as a people. Such knowledge of Aboriginal society and the Aboriginal way of survival taught Aboriginal children how to succeed and excel.

This method of teaching was displaced largely as a direct result of the intrusion of an alien educational system. New and non-indigenous teachers ignored the traditional teachings of Aboriginal people and proceeded to teach Aboriginal children the culture, the history and the knowledge of non-Aboriginal society, in ways which undermined the values and importance of Aboriginal traditions and cultures.

The impact of the educational system on the social institutions of Aboriginal communities, such as the traditional role of elders as teachers and spiritual leaders, was quite dramatic. How the new knowledge was transmitted and how it was taught in the schools not only affected the role of the traditional teachers, but also the role of the parents and the leaders of Aboriginal communities in their ability to transmit knowledge, culture and social norms.

Traditional methods of social control in the communities were redefined. The massive removal of Aboriginal children from parents, from their cultures and from their communities, in order that they could be trained in and made knowledgeable of the teachings of white society, virtually displaced the socialization institutions of Aboriginal people.

The new educational methods had the same effect whether education took place in a residential school or in a school situated within the Indian community. The effect was quite simply to question the culture of Aboriginal people and its continuing validity for Aboriginal youth. It was to teach Indian children to scorn their particular culture as being outdated, primitive, backwards and of no significance in the modern context.

It was to put into the minds of Indian children new notions that called into question the validity and authority of traditional Aboriginal institutions. It resulted in many Aboriginal children believing, for example, that the authority to teach or the authority to control the lives of Aboriginal people was the prerogative of non-Aboriginal people who did not live in the community. In the Cree and Ojibway languages, for example, the word used most commonly for "government," when translated, meant the "white man's government."

Practices such as child rearing, in which Indian people had readily helped one another, were very nearly destroyed by the introduction of a foreign child welfare system, a system that did not take into account the child development traditions and the child welfare practices of Aboriginal people.

The removal of authority and power from Aboriginal leaders has resulted in the near destruction of Aboriginal cultures, and has contributed to feelings of hopelessness, powerlessness and despair, which are exhibited in antisocial behaviour in Aboriginal communities.

The idea that other people have the power to determine the fate of Aboriginal people, whether they like it or not, we are told, explains the deep sense of mistrust that Aboriginal people feel toward the justice system.

There are very few examples where past Aboriginal contact with the governments of Canadian society has not resulted in some attempt to have their powers of self-determination stripped away from them, to be replaced by foreign or new ways of reorganizing their societies.

Despite the high incidence of crime in Aboriginal communities, it would not be fair, nor would it be accurate, to describe those communities as socially or politically dysfunctional. Clearly, there exists within all Aboriginal communities capable leadership well able to come to grips with difficult issues if they are supported properly and provided with appropriate resources.

Many elders within Aboriginal communities maintained an abiding faith that, eventually, matters would be restored to their rightful place. The result seems to be that there remains a very strong determination on the part of elders and leaders within Aboriginal communities to preserve what authority remains to them, and to take whatever steps are necessary to recapture and to reassert the right and jurisdiction to deal with their needs, problems and development in a manner that is consistent with their social values, historical traditions and cultures.

In the face of the current realities confronting Aboriginal people, we believe that it is important to recognize that the greatest potential for the resolution of significant Aboriginal social problems lies in Aboriginal people exercising greater control over their own lives.

The dependency on alcohol, the increasing rates of suicides, homicides and criminal charges, and the high rates of incarceration are problems that we believe can be dealt with best by Aboriginal people themselves.

These social conditions, we believe, are indeed the products of dependency and powerlessness, created by past government actions and felt deeply by the majority of Aboriginal people. This dependency will not disappear, we are convinced, until Aboriginal people are able to re-establish their own sense of identity and exercise a considerable degree of self-determination.

We are unable to define with certainty at this point how far that development needs to proceed in order to turn the tide of tragedy we see, but we are satisfied enough to state that we believe that the right of Aboriginal people to establish and maintain their own justice systems within their own communities, free from interference from federal and provincial governments, is of paramount importance to that development.

There must be a drastic shift in thinking about power and authority. The federal and provincial governments and their officials have to accept that Aboriginal people must have the necessary power and authority to govern themselves in this area. Impediments to the exercise of such power and jurisdiction must be removed.

The present judicial system has not done much to allay the concerns of Aboriginal people that the courts have little understanding of Aboriginal customs, traditions or laws. In fact, courts are perceived by Aboriginal people as being disinclined to apply or adopt Aboriginal customary law, even in areas where the culture of Aboriginal people should be a dominant consideration, such as in juvenile, family and child welfare law.

Aboriginal people have a right to their own cultures. They are entitled to apply traditional approaches to meeting the needs of Aboriginal children who, for whatever reason, are in need of help or protection.

Culture is more than the values, traditions or customary practices of Aboriginal people. Culture is also the laws, customary or contemporary, of the people who belong to a distinct society. Culture is the social and political organization of the people who constitute a distinct society. Culture also includes the administration of justice as a fundamental component of every organized society.

The right of Aboriginal people to control their own pace and direction of development must be retained. The use of Aboriginal social and cultural institutions, such as the Aboriginal family and the role of elders in maintaining peace and good order in their communities, and in transmitting knowledge about acceptable and unacceptable behaviour, is, we believe, the proper road to Aboriginal recovery and development.

Our Recommendation

It is wrong, in our view, simply to maintain the status quo on the assumption that eventually Aboriginal people will learn to accept the justice system as it presently exists. It is wrong to assume that if only Aboriginal people would accept the justice system, then there would be no more problems. It is wrong to assume that changes to the existing system will enable it to provide fully adequate services to Aboriginal people. To think in this manner is to ignore the impact of the past human experience of Aboriginal people. Their self-determination has been denied and suppressed, social disorganization has been the consequence, and they are unable to accept the "white man's solution" any longer.

The reality is that approaches taken by a non-Aboriginal justice system in Aboriginal communities will not address the social needs, development, culture, or the right to self-determination of those communities. A court system that is not seen as an institution that belongs to them, and that is unable to adapt to their indigenous concepts and mechanisms of justice, will not work in Aboriginal communities.

An important principle for change and for bringing about changes in Aboriginal communities is that Aboriginal people must be seen as having control. This principle, we discern, is gaining greater and greater acceptance in Canadian society.

Clearly, the maintenance of law and order on Aboriginal lands is an integral part of Aboriginal government jurisdiction. This means that in establishing a system of justice for Aboriginal people, the laws enacted by Aboriginal people themselves, or deliberately accepted by them for their purposes, must form the foundation for the system's existence.

This calls for systemic change and it is clear that systemic change is necessary. Efforts at reform over the last several years, such as through expanded legal aid services and the development of Aboriginal court worker programs, have been aimed at addressing issues that primarily arise in urban courts, as have attempts at "indigenizing" the justice system.

This has occurred, we believe, because the primary issue which was addressed in past efforts was not the fundamental issue of systemic bias within the justice system, but, rather, the perception that the over-representation of Aboriginal people in that system arose because Aboriginal people did not understand the processes in place to protect them and other accused, and that they simply required assistance to understand what was being done to them.

We believe that such a perception is inherently flawed, in that it represents a further bias: that there is nothing wrong with the system, only with Aboriginal people. We believe very strongly that cultural bias within the justice system represents the single greatest contributing factor among several that cause Aboriginal over-representation within the justice system. It is for that reason that we have concluded that Aboriginal aspirations for their own justice systems not only must be considered carefully, but that steps toward their implementation must be undertaken. To this point, all other efforts at reform have failed and are unacceptable to the people whom they are intended to benefit.

It is clear that there is widespread interest in and growing support for distinct Aboriginal justice systems.[1] Of particular significance is a recent position taken by the Canadian Bar Association. CBA, having established a special committee on imprisonment, issued a report entitled "Locking Up Natives in Canada" in August of 1988. This report contained several valuable recommendations, including one advocating the establishment of a parallel Aboriginal court system. This report was officially ratified as national policy of the CBA at its annual meeting in August 1989, as was another CBA report entitled "Aboriginal Rights: An Agenda for Action—The Report of the Special Committee on Aboriginal Justice."

These developments reflect, we believe, widespread general acceptance of the right of Aboriginal people to self-determination within their own communities, and a general appreciation that the extensive and negative experiences of Aboriginal people within the prevailing legal system are a tragedy that can be only corrected through major changes.

WE RECOMMEND THAT:

- The federal and provincial governments recognize the right of Aboriginal people to establish their own justice systems as part of their inherent right to self-government.

- The federal and provincial governments assist Aboriginal people in the establishment of Aboriginal justice systems in their communities in a manner that best conforms to the traditions, cultures and wishes of those communities, and the rights of their people.

- Federal, provincial and Aboriginal First Nations governments commit themselves to the establishment of tribal courts in the near future as a first step toward the establishment of a fully functioning, Aboriginally controlled justice system which includes (but need not necessarily be limited to):

  - A policing service.
  - A prosecution branch.
  - A legal aid system.
  - A court system that includes:
    1. a youth court system;
    2. a family court system;
    3. a criminal court system;
    4. a civil court system;
    5. an appellate court system.
  - A probation service including a system of monitoring community service orders.
  - A mediation/counselling service.
  - A fine collection and maintenance enforcement system.
  - A community-based correctional system.
  - A parole system.

- The federal and provincial governments begin the process of establishing Aboriginal justice systems by enacting appropriate legislation.

- At the same time as legislation to begin the process of establishing Aboriginal justice systems is enacted, the federal and provincial governments acknowledge, by resolution of their respective legislative bodies, that Aboriginal justice systems must be protected constitutionally from federal and provincial legislative incursions and that such systems will ultimately be recognized as an aspect of the right of

Aboriginal people to self-government and will not be dependent solely upon federal or provincial legislation for their existence.

■ Aboriginal governments enact their own constitutions setting out,
among other things, the principle of the separation of the judicial from
the executive and legislative arms of each Aboriginal government so as
to protect Aboriginal justice systems from interference and to provide
security for their independence.

In its closing statement to the Inquiry, the Assembly of Manitoba Chiefs stated
this priority:

Our most basic recommendation is that Aboriginal control of our justice systems is necessary. Furthermore, our commitment and expectation in the long
run is that the basis upon which Aboriginal justice will be premised and established is through the inherent authority of self-governing peoples.

We believe that what we propose is the restoration of two concepts:

• That the traditional system of Aboriginal justice served the needs of its
society based on the objects of healing, reconciliation and re-establish-
ment of the community in situations where the peace and harmony of
the community was disrupted.

• That the same object of peace and harmony was intended to serve the
needs of two societies when conflict arose.

The Department of Indian Affairs, in recent years, has stated repeatedly that it
maintains a policy of Indian self-determination. In his presentation to us on behalf of the
Department of Indian Affairs, Deputy Minister Harry Swain stated:

For the last several years the focus has been on moving from Indian administration to Indian management....

What we are interested in doing is moving along that scale to a stage where
Indian communities govern themselves within Canada....

The next stage is Indian jurisdiction—the challenge of the 1990s. The department
is working with Indian and provincial governments to draft laws that will create
room for Indian governments to legislate in fields of critical importance to them.

If there is to be peace and harmony between Aboriginal and non-Aboriginal people
in this country, it must be premised upon respect for each other's rights. The tenor of the
discussion, therefore, must shift from the "if" to the "how," regarding the establishment of
Aboriginal justice systems in Manitoba. The major issue, therefore, becomes how such a
system would relate to the existing system. In considering that question, we have carefully
looked at and considered the experience of the American tribal court systems. We believe
that analysing their experience will provide some useful information when determining
how to go about the establishment of Aboriginal justice systems in Manitoba.

American Indian Tribal Courts

The Indian tribal court systems in the United States have been, to a large extent, the inspiration for Aboriginal people in Canada. These systems provide a variety of examples of court systems operated by Indian tribal governments. We visited the Navajo Reservation, as well as tribal courts in other parts of the United States, in the spring of 1989.

One issue which struck us as significant was the fact that, although there was much that we could learn from large tribal systems such as the Navajo system, its sheer size clearly put it into a class by itself in terms of administration and resources. The Navajo Reservation covers many thousands of acres, with a resident population of close to 200,000 and a tribal justice budget in the millions of dollars. There are simply no Aboriginal communities of that size in Canada.

Nevertheless, we did learn a great deal from the Navajo operation, such as how to combine Anglo-American legal practices with traditional methods of dispute resolution when we looked at their peacemaker operation. But we decided that if we were to seriously consider whether Aboriginal communities in Canada could viably maintain an Aboriginal justice system, we had to look more closely at tribal court operations on reservations that were more similar in size, population and socio-economic status to those in Manitoba.

While it is difficult to make sound comparisons, we felt that viewing how tribal courts operated within the smaller Indian reservations and pueblos of New Mexico and Arizona would be beneficial, so we visited many of them.

In addition, we visited the state of Washington, where we met with Professor Ralph Johnson of the University of Washington in Seattle, who provided us with considerable information and insight into tribal court operations in the United States.

Professor Johnson introduced us to Judge (now Chief Judge) Elbridge Coochise of the Northwest Intertribal Court System, a court system established to provide circuit court services to 16 tribes in one region of the state of Washington. Judge Coochise, who is the president of the National American Indian Court Judges Association, discussed with us how his court system works.

We were impressed with the fact that the tribal communities serviced by the Northwest Intertribal Court System were remarkably similar in size, population, economy and socio-economic status to Aboriginal communities in Manitoba. Their populations range from 200 to 500 people. Their reservations are relatively small. The legal, jurisdictional and cultural conflicts extant in Canada, about which we heard so much in the course of our hearings, appeared to be very similar to those experienced by tribal authorities in the state of Washington.

We were sufficiently impressed with the systems we visited in the United States that we convened a special session of the Inquiry on the subject of tribal courts. We held a Tribal Courts Symposium at the University of Manitoba Faculty of Law in November 1989. At that symposium we heard from several American tribal court judges and court officials about the manner in which they go about their work and solve the myriad of jurisdictional, legal, administrative and political problems that continually affect them. Tribal court judges explained how they run their courts, and explained how they deal with the issues of cultural conflict and cultural adaptation both within and by their courts.

It is clear that the existence of fully functioning tribal court systems on a variety of Indian reservations in the United States, many of them similar in size and socio-economic status to Indian reserves in Manitoba, and the benefits which those communities derive from them, are strong evidence that separate Aboriginal justice systems are possible and practical.

Historical Background

Although the concept is not readily apparent today, Indian tribes of North America were recognized as being fully sovereign by all European nations including England, from which many of our legal principles come, for the first two and a half centuries following European arrival in America. This position did not begin to change until the mid-1700s when the British Crown began to assert a form of protectorate relationship with the still sovereign Indian nations.[2] In effect, a pattern highly prevalent in continental Europe was being transplanted to the New World—a pattern in which one nation claimed a right and a duty to protect smaller, subordinate sovereign states from the potentially dangerous actions of other European nations. In the case of England, the same claim of protectionism from other European nations, and even from its own colonies, was used to justify the Crown's assertion that Aboriginal nations were under its care and that no one else could deal with them. The *Royal Proclamation of 1763* articulated this position:

> And whereas it is just and reasonable, and essential to our interest, and the security of our Colonies, that the several Nations or tribes of Indians with whom We are connected, and who live under our protection, should not be molested or disturbed in the Possession of such Parts of Our Dominions and Territories as, not having been ceded to or purchased by Us, are reserved to them or any of them as their Hunting Grounds ...[3]

The terms of the *Royal Proclamation*, in reference to Indian nations, reflected the codification of a changed British policy, rather than a declaration of Aboriginal rights. In earlier 17th and 18th century treaties, as in the case of the Treaty of Fort Albany of 1664, full sovereign status on the part of Indians, including jurisdiction over all colonists within Indian territory, had been recognized by the British Crown.

Following the American Revolution of 1776, the newly independent United States of America claimed that it was the successor to the British position and acted accordingly in its early federal legislation.[4] American courts sustained this view and, in fact, expanded it somewhat in the early 1800s by articulating for the first time the doctrine of "domestic dependent nationhood" to describe the nature of the government-Indian relationship. Indians were not citizens, the doctrine held, nor were they "considered as subjects born under allegiance, and bound, in the common law sense of the term to all its duties," yet, they were "not aliens in every sense, because of their dependence as a tribe, and their rights to protection."

One court referred to the Oneida Tribe as a "distinct and independent tribe" of Indians who reside upon lands that they "hold and enjoy as the original proprietors of the soil."[5] As such, their political relation to the state is "peculiar, and sui generis."[6] At the same time, Indian nations were said to have lost "their rights to complete sovereignty, as independent nations," as this was "necessarily diminished and their power to dispose of the soil at their own will, to whomsoever they please, was denied by the original fundamental principle that discovery gave exclusive title to those who made it."[7]

Despite those latter words, however, it was clear that Indian nations had not lost all their sovereign status. The United States Supreme Court declared that as "domestic dependent nations," residing within the jurisdictional limits of the United States in law,[8] Indian nations retained many aspects of sovereignty:

> The Indian nations had always been considered as distinct, independent political communities, retaining their original natural rights, as the undisputed possessors of the soil, from time immemorial.... The very term "nation", so generally applied to them, means "a people distinct from others." The Constitution, by declaring treaties already made, as well as those to be made, to be the supreme law of the land, has adopted and sanctioned the previous treaties with Indian nations, and consequently admits their rank among those powers who are capable of making treaties. The words "treaty" and "nations", are words of our own language, selected in our diplomatic and legislative proceedings, by ourselves, having each a definite and well-understood meaning. We have applied them to Indians, as we have applied them to the other nations of the earth. They are applied to all in the same sense.[9]

U.S. Supreme Court Chief Justice John Marshall, who wrote the leading decisions of the time, crafted a legal decision that gave status to European nations to claim overriding rights through "discovery." The "discovering" European state obtained a monopoly on trading relations and the exclusive right to acquire title to the soil so as to locate settlements thereon. These rights accrued only to the country that was successful, through the imposition of "irresistible power," in being able to assert its authority effectively in relation to both the Indians resident in the area and the competing European states. In developing this argument, Chief Justice Marshall drew upon international law and the European experience:

> [T]he settled doctrine of the law of nations is, that a weaker power does not surrender its independence—its right to self-government, by associating with a stranger and taking its protection. A weak State, in order to provide for its safety, may place itself under the protection of one more powerful without stripping itself of the right of government, and ceasing to be a State. Examples of this kind are not wanting in Europe. "Tributary and feudatory states", says Vattel, "do not thereby cease to be sovereign and independent states so long as self-government and sovereign and independent authority are left in the administration of the state." At the present day, more than one state may be considered as holding its right of self government under the guaranty and protection of one or more allies.[10]

He then applied this result to the history of colonization to that time in the United States and concluded that the British Crown had obtained the status of being the paramount, discovering state. Its rights and responsibilities had passed after the American Revolution to the United States, whose constitution formally conveyed the powers relevant to Indian nations solely to federal jurisdiction. The practical effect was that state laws could have no force and effect upon Indian nations or their territory.

Thus, Indian nations were viewed as sovereign nations with continuing rights to govern their own affairs, to own their lands, and to enter into treaty relations with Europeans and successor governments, within certain limitations.

Chief Justice Marshall clearly wished to protect the territorial integrity of the new country and to nourish its imperial aspirations toward the West.[11] Therefore, Indian sovereignty was described in such a way as to be limited and internal in nature, operating within the overriding sovereignty of the United States while remaining inherent to the indigenous population.[12]

What is striking to us is the fact that there was nothing in American statute law or in the American Constitution which compelled Chief Justice Marshall to articulate the theory of "domestic dependent" nationhood. It is clear from his decision that he considered and applied principles of English common law and international law to come to his decision.

The result of his legal conclusion—which is now the law of the United States—was that Aboriginal tribes in the United States retained significant aspects of their sovereignty, subject to an overriding federal supervision and control. Tribes could exercise their sovereignty unless it was taken away from them by express federal action or law, or by necessary implication arising from a contrary intention as contained in another federal action or law.

In Canada, an opposite approach was taken. Aboriginal people in Canada, according to the law as it evolved in Canadian court decisions, only retained as much of their original sovereignty as the federal government specifically had recognized their having. Canadian courts have not acknowledged, as American courts have done, Aboriginal sovereignty to be inherent and a continuing legal fact. Part of the reason for this probably relates to the emphasis which Americans have placed on the doctrine of inherent rights. This concept played a significant role in the American moral and legal justification of its revolution against England several years earlier. A country premised upon what it perceived to be its own "inherent" right to self-government could not easily turn around and deny the existence of that right to others who had neither been conquered in battle, nor ever surrendered that right.

However, England, whose influence over Canada's legal system continues even to this day, had developed legal principles which emphasized the importance of the Crown and the doctrine of parliamentary supremacy. Those principles have played a large role in denying the existence or validity of any Aboriginal right which is inconsistent with full parliamentary supremacy and Crown title.

One of the implications of the American recognition of an inherent and continued Indian sovereign status was an acceptance of the right of Indian nations to retain control over their internal affairs. The principle of internal Indian sovereignty, however, was considered subject to the overriding power of Congress to intrude and regulate that jurisdiction through express legislation. This meant that Indian nations could develop new legal systems if they wished, or maintain their traditional laws and forms of dispute resolution. Similarly, they could develop new governmental institutions with Western overtones, or retain their traditional systems of government.

The Cherokee Tribe, for example, operated a tribal system based largely upon Anglo-American principles from 1808 to 1898, with written legal codes and constitution, trained lawyers and judges, as well as a full range of courts all operating in the Cherokee language. However, the overwhelming majority of Indian nations opted to ignore Anglo-American influences and continued to follow customary laws and governmental systems that had existed for centuries prior to European colonization.[13]

Indian sovereignty has long been recognized as being complete and exclusive in reference to matters affecting tribal members within Indian country. This position was confirmed by the Supreme Court of the United States in 1883 when it struck down a murder conviction by the U.S. District Court of the Dakota Territory of a member of the Oglala Sioux Tribe, as an improper assertion of state jurisdiction in a matter over which only the tribe had authority.

However, it is interesting to note that the relatively forceful recognition of Indian sovereignty in the Marshall decisions of the 1820s and 1830s had succumbed to a patronizing tone, in which members of First Nations were seen as inferior and needing to be introduced slowly to the "civilized" standards of the American government, as the justification for preventing state intrusion into tribal areas of sovereignty. Indians, it was said, were

> ... subject to the laws of the United States, not in the sense of citizens, but, as they had always been, as wards subject to a guardian; not as individuals, constituted members of the political community of the United States, with a voice in the selection of representatives and the framing of laws, but as a dependent community who were in a state of pupilage, advancing from the condition of a savage tribe to that of a people who, through the discipline of labor and by education, it was hoped might become a self-supporting and self-governed society.[14]

Therefore, the court concluded, it was "unfair" to hold Indians to the higher standard of white society, as it would be unfair to try them

> ... not by their peers, nor by the customs of their people, nor the law of their land, but by superiors of a different race, according to a law of a social state of which they have an imperfect conception, and which is opposed to the strongest prejudices of their savage nature.[15]

Despite the clearly racist tone of the decision, the ultimate result was that American Indians could not be prosecuted in American courts for crimes committed against other Indians in Indian territory. The federal government was not happy with a situation in which American courts (federal, state or territorial) had neither criminal nor civil jurisdiction over matters that arose on reservations. This displeasure was compounded by the fact that the Bureau of Indian Affairs (BIA) had no legal authority to interfere, since all laws and legal mechanisms on Indian reservations were under the control of the tribal governments. The bureau decided to take control of the situation by establishing Indian police forces responsible to and paid by the local Indian agents. Congress eventually sanctioned the program in 1878 through allocating funds, but these police never were given any legislative recognition.

The intent underlying the establishment of an Indian police force was articulated clearly by Hiram Price, Commissioner of Indian Affairs, in 1881 when he said:

> The police force is a perpetual educator. It is a power entirely independent of the chiefs. It weakens and will finally destroy, the power of tribes and bands.[16]

The agents of the Bureau of Indian Affairs directed and paid the Indian police officers to enforce "law and order" within the reservation, even though it was clear that any arrests they made were completely unlawful. The local Indian agent also often would act as a self-appointed judge and impose criminal sanctions, also without any legal authority.[17]

The next step was to create a formal court system with a greater semblance of legitimacy as a further civilizing force. A Court of Indian Offenses (or CIO) was established in 1883, again, initially without any legislative foundations from Congress. Indian judges were appointed to the court by local agents of the Bureau of Indian Affairs, and enforced a summary civil and criminal code drafted by the Commissioner of Indian Affairs in April of that year.

Courts of Indian Offenses still function today in various places. However, they now possess official legal status and authority under the *Code of Federal Regulations*. They are referred to sometimes as CFR courts. They can apply the customary law of the tribe on whose reservation they are located, to a limited degree.[18]

The final aspect to this evolution was the establishment of what has come to be called the tribal court system. Those Indian nations that wished to do so could exercise that option, which was made available as part of the Roosevelt New Deal via the federal *Indian Reorganization Act* of 1934 (the IRA).[19] Indian tribes were authorized by that legislation to enact their own tribal constitutions and law and order codes, under the supervision and ultimate control of the Bureau of Indian Affairs. Provisions creating tribal courts could be included as part of these constitutions or passed as a component of the regular tribal law and order codes. A large number of tribes seized upon this opportunity as a means to reduce the control of the Bureau of Indian Affairs operating directly within their reservations and to restore a greater degree of autonomy.

While the power of Indian agents was reduced somewhat and Courts of Indian Offenses were eliminated for those tribes which selected this option, it also meant that those tribes had to choose to function along the lines of American concepts of democracy and governmental structures by relinquishing their traditional system. Rather than recognizing tribal sovereignty, the *Indian Reorganization Act* reflected the exercise of further congressional power. It did not extend, however, solely "delegated powers." Choosing to incorporate under the *Indian Reorganization Act* did not involve formally renouncing tribal sovereignty. The tribal governments continued to retain their domestic, dependent nationhood status over internal affairs, but their governmental structure lost its traditional basis, and customary law was replaced by Indian statutory enactments, known as "tribal codes," as the basis under which daily life was regulated. This was the case, however, only for those Indian tribes who opted to come within the scope of the *Indian Reorganization Act*. Many Indian reservations still have no tribal court system whatsoever.

Public Law 280

In 1953 the United States Congress enacted *Public Law 280*.[20] It was a component of the prevailing congressional initiative to terminate federal responsibility for Indians by transferring that jurisdiction to state governments.

When first enacted, *Public Law 280* had transferred to state courts jurisdiction over "civil causes of action between Indians or to which Indians are parties" as well as "offenses committed by or against Indians in the areas of Indian country...." It went on to provide that "... the criminal laws of such State or Territory shall have the same force and effect within such Indian country as they have elsewhere...."[21] The statute listed the regions affected: all of California, Nebraska, Wisconsin, all of Minnesota except the Red Lake Indian Reservation, and all of Oregon except the Warm Springs Indian Reservation. The state of Alaska, except for the Metlakatla Indian community of the Annette Islands, was included in 1958 when it obtained statehood. The statute also allowed any other state to opt in by amending its own laws to assert jurisdiction. Ten states moved to exercise this option. Florida seized full jurisdiction on all reservations, while Utah and North Dakota required tribal consent first (none gave it). Arizona and Idaho only took jurisdiction over specified subjects, while Montana and Iowa did so in all spheres but only in reference to one reservation. South Dakota's assertion of jurisdiction was dependent upon the federal government paying all costs, a provision which was struck down later by the South Dakota Supreme Court. Washington assumed full jurisdiction over non-Indians on reservations, over Indians on non-trust lands and over Indians in eight subject areas on trust lands.[22]

The effect of the law was that in those states to which the law applied, most tribal courts have disappeared because of the prevailing and overriding jurisdiction given to state courts by the law. The recent rise in Indian desire for self-determination has reversed the trend toward such state usurpation of tribal jurisdiction. Reversing the growth of state jurisdiction over Indians and Indian lands was made possible by provisions in the *Indian Civil Rights Act* of 1968 that allowed the resumption of jurisdiction by tribal governments which had lost it. Nevada allowed its tribes to take back their original jurisdiction, if they so desired, from the very beginning of *Public Law 280*, and most have.

Tribal Court Systems Today

The net result of this historical development is that courts with three different origins, with radically different underlying jurisdictions and reflecting different philosophical orientations, exist simultaneously:

- **Traditional Courts.** These continue to exist with the original jurisdiction established by traditional tribal laws, restricted only by express federal legislation. Their orientation is to administer customary laws as supplemented by explicit tribal enactments.

- **Courts of Indian Offenses (CIOs).** These courts are regulated by the *Code of Federal Regulations* and their jurisdiction is limited by the terms of those regulations to minor crimes and a narrow range of civil matters. Most of the law applied and the structure of the court are established by the federal government.

- **Tribal Courts.** These courts are governed solely by tribal constitutions and tribal codes passed pursuant to the *Indian Reorganization Act* and any express federal legislation.

Approximately 145 American Indian tribes have some form of their own court system functioning.[23] In addition, there are an unknown number of tribes in the Midwest that operate "conservation courts," which deal only with hunting and fishing offences created by tribal law. Some of these courts are limited to on-reservation infractions, but a few also handle off-reservation offences involving tribal members harvesting within the tribe's treaty territory.

The number of Courts of Indian Offenses has declined dramatically over the years, with the result that there appear to be only 23 of them currently functioning. It is worth noting, however, that this structure still is chosen sometimes as a starting point for a court system for many tribes. For example, the Coushatta Tribe of Louisiana chose a Court of Indian Offenses in 1985 as their first effort at establishing a tribal court.

A further 14 tribes function in full or in part under a traditional or customary law system.

The remaining 108 tribes operate courts which derive their jurisdiction exclusively from tribal constitutions and/or tribal law codes as provided for in the *Indian Reorganization Act.*[24]

This reflects a significant change even since 1974, when the Bureau of Indian Affairs stated in different reports that between 91 and 111 courts existed on reservations.[25] Not only has the total number of courts increased substantially in recent years, but this increase has occurred largely among the IRA tribal courts, which have almost doubled in number. It is noteworthy that several communities have switched from traditional to tribal courts and a few have done the reverse, while most of the growth has arisen through the establishment of new courts that have retaken jurisdiction from the state court systems. These new systems usually have opted for the tribal court model.

It is ironic that, while traditional courts are being supplanted by tribal courts, some of the latter, such as those of the Navajo, have been developing more traditional methods of dispute resolution, such as peacemaker courts. While the precise reason for the former development is unclear, it may reflect the ease with which IRA tribal courts can be established when compared with the effort needed to determine tribal laws and traditions long unused or lost. There are clear policies concerning IRA tribal courts within the Bureau of Indian Affairs, while no policies exist for assisting in the establishment of traditional courts.

It is conceivable, as well, that a lessening of traditional religious influences within tribal communities has also contributed to the inclination toward establishing tribal courts under the *Indian Reorganization Act*, rather than traditional courts, which have more cultural roots.

The *Indian Civil Rights Act* of 1968,[26] with its due process requirements, appears to be compelling the development of a more Anglo-American legalistic format. One also might suspect that the legal experts available to assist tribes to establish tribal court systems are trained in Anglo-American jurisprudence to such an extent that their tendency is to recommend forms and legal processes taught at conventional law schools.

It is clear that the IRA tribal court system, operating under tribal law and order codes or constitutions, dominates the Indian justice picture in the United States, and that there is obvious preference on the part of American Indian governments for this model. In addition, it would appear that this version of "tribal courts" possesses the most promise for and attracts the most interest from Aboriginal people in Canada. As well, the tribal court models sanctioned under the *Indian Reorganization Act* have the flexibility to incorporate and implement traditional methods of dispute resolution. For that reason, it is our conclusion that they should be examined more closely in order to determine the utility of that model for Manitoba's Aboriginal people.

One of the noteworthy issues relating to the American tribal court system is its dependency on U.S. federal legislation, thereby rendering it subject to a non-Aboriginal institution. Congressional agendas, initiatives and enactments could easily override any Aboriginal interests. We were advised by several American observers that this jurisdictional superiority occasionally has been a sore point between Aboriginal people and the United States government. We have more to say about the implications of this later.

Tribal Court Jurisdiction

Tribal courts created pursuant to the *Indian Reorganization Act* are not considered as having inherent jurisdiction. The jurisdiction which they possess is determined by review of the legislative enactment which creates it, whether that is the tribe's constitution or its law and order code. Three issues of jurisdiction which are present with respect to all courts—i.e., jurisdiction over the territory, jurisdiction over the person and jurisdiction over the subject matter—are more complex when it comes to tribal courts, due to the fact that they function within a partially sovereign enclave, with different values, traditions and culture, all within a sovereign country with its own values, culture and traditions sometimes in conflict with those of the various tribes.

Territorial Jurisdiction

Most tribal courts are expressly limited to matters that arise within the boundaries of the reservation. This limitation emanates either from the provisions in the tribal constitution establishing the court or in the tribal legislation passed to flesh out the court's mandate. Despite this fact, a number of tribal courts actually exercise jurisdiction over off-reservation events. This can arise in one of several ways:

- Through an unofficial arrangement with local municipal authorities and their police to transfer minor criminal cases involving tribal accused where the offence occurred in town.

- In the enforcement of tribal hunting and fishing laws against tribal members harvesting outside their reservation lands but within their treaty territory with the approval of the state.

- In the retaining of jurisdiction over tribal children living off-reservation pursuant to the provisions of the *Indian Child Welfare Act* of 1978.[27]

Some tribal constitutions and codes, particularly those revised in recent years to move away from model codes prepared by the Bureau of Indian Affairs, do not contain any territorial limitation. These tribal courts are not excluded automatically from exercising jurisdiction over off-reservation activities. The ability of a tribal court to exercise such authority, however, is unclear in other than child welfare matters.

It is important to realize that although the term most commonly used is "Indian reservation," the relevant legal expression for identifying the geographical limits of tribal authority is "Indian Country." This latter phrase was defined legislatively by Congress in 1948:

> Except as otherwise provided in sections 1154 and 1156 of this title, the term "Indian Country", as used in this chapter, means
>
> (a) all land within the limits of any Indian reservation under the jurisdiction of the United States Government, notwithstanding the issuance of any patent, and, including rights-of-way running through the reservation,
>
> (b) all dependent Indian communities within the borders of the United States whether within the original or subsequently acquired territory thereof, and whether within or without the limits of a state, and
>
> (c) all Indian allotments, the Indian title to which have not been extinguished, including rights-of-way running through the same.[28]

The import of this definition is that it creates a presumption that "Indian Country" included all land, regardless of ownership, within the exterior boundaries of federally recognized Indian reservations. Lands allotted to individual tribal members, thereby rendering them legal owners of the land to the exclusion of the tribe and other tribal members, a common practice for many decades as a result of the *Dawes Act*,[29] as well as lands held for the tribe in common, fall within the jurisdiction of the tribal governments and its courts. In addition, lands that have been leased, alienated or subject to easements for the benefit of non-Indians, corporations and even public authorities will remain under tribal authority as long as they are inside the exterior borders of the reservation.

Determining the exact boundaries is not always an easy task, in light of extensive surrenders and congressional declarations of surplus Indian lands over the years.[30]

Although the definition of Indian Country was designed originally for criminal purposes, the courts have concluded that it also applies to tribal court and tribal civil jurisdiction.[31] As a result, tribal courts may possess territorial jurisdiction over lands that are not owned by or for the tribe or in the possession of the tribe, as long as they can be said to be part of Indian Country.

Personal Jurisdiction

The area of jurisdiction over the person is somewhat unsettled at the present time. Again, a number of tribal courts are limited by their tribal constitutions or codes either to tribal members only, or to a tribal member and another party where the latter voluntarily accedes to the jurisdiction of the tribal court. These limitations are self-imposed by the tribes, as they are not required by U.S. law, although the Bureau of Indian Affairs has fostered this form of restraint. Tribal courts not fettered in these ways still have limits on their personal jurisdiction that have been imposed by Congress or tribal court decisions.

Civil Cases

The jurisdiction over the person is largely unlimited in civil matters as long as the legal event, contract, etc. which forms the basis for the civil dispute was formed or occurred within the reservation. This jurisdiction clearly includes cases involving tribal members and Indians from other tribes.

The law is exceedingly complex when it comes to civil jurisdiction in relation to non-Indian litigants, however, as jurisdiction in the tribal court is affected by the precise nature of the land on which the event occurs, the degree to which there is a tribal interest involved in regulating that matter, who exactly are the parties and the impact of *Public Law 280* of 1953. Tribal courts make the initial determination as to whether tribal jurisdiction exists in the specific situations at hand. The federal courts, however, have asserted the power to exercise judicial review of such a decision.[32]

Numerous cases have been litigated over the last 40 years on this precise topic, since the United States Supreme Court opened the modern era of federal Indian law with its decision in *Williams v. Lee* 358 U.S. 217 (1959).[33] The court concluded that exclusive jurisdiction rested with the Navajo Tribal Court, rather than the Arizona Supreme Court, in an action brought by a non-Indian to enforce a debt under a contract entered into on the reservation with the Indian defendant. In reaching its decision, the court declared that this result was justified on the grounds that it was necessary to protect tribal self-government. The test to determine federal jurisdiction over a matter was whether the matter was an essential feature of the tribe's right to self-government.

The Supreme Court has since upheld a tribal cigarette tax on sales to non-Indians[34] and a mineral tax on companies operating on reservation lands even when they already were paying royalties under petroleum leases.[35] In the latter decision, the court declared that tribes retained inherent sovereign power as governments to exercise most forms of civil jurisdiction over non-Indians within their territory (i.e., to impose taxes), while also retaining their capacity as landowners (i.e., to collect royalties). The court went on to say:

To state that Indian sovereignty is different than that of Federal, State or local Governments, does not justify ignoring the principles announced by this Court for determining whether a sovereign has waived its taxing authority ... and we perceive no principled reason for holding that the different attributes of Indian sovereignty require different treatment in this regard.[36]

The court has also sustained business taxes on non-Indian corporations,[37] while striking down state taxes on tribal royalty interests in mineral leases to non-Indians[38] and state income taxes on an Indian in Indian Country.[39]

The rules are more convoluted in relation to non-Indians on non-Indian land within Indian Country. The primary standard outlined by the Supreme Court to support tribal jurisdiction is the "tribal interest test" as articulated in *Montana v. United States*. The question to be answered is whether "the conduct of non-Indians on fee lands within its reservation ... threatens or has some direct effect on the political integrity, the economic security, or the health and welfare of the tribe."[40] Applying this test has justified tribal zoning ordinances over non-Indians on non-Indian land,[41] tribal health and safety laws,[42] and tribal regulation of non-Indian lands bordering a reservation lake.[43] Nevertheless, the test can be applied only on a case-by-case basis. Thus it is hard to draw clear demarcations around tribal civil jurisdiction over non-Indians on non-Indian lands within Indian Country.

The Montana Test means that the tribe can effectively assert civil jurisdiction over non-Indians, including Bureau of Indian Affairs employees, if any of the four following factors is present in the case:

- A consensual relationship exists in which the non-Indian individual or corporation has chosen to work with the tribe, enter into contracts with the tribe, lease reservation land, acquire a tribal licence, or in some other way voluntarily enter into dealings with the tribal government or tribal members.

- The matter affects the political integrity of the tribe, making it vital for the tribe to assert this jurisdiction (e.g., in relation to conduct that disrupts tribal elections).

- The conduct challenged affects the economic security of the tribe.

- The activity affects the health or safety of the tribe.

It is possible to have a situation in which concurrent jurisdiction may exist between state and tribal courts in reference to non-Indians. This would occur on land that was once reservation land but is no longer, but is surrounded by reservation land. In this situation, state courts would have criminal jurisdiction and civil jurisdiction. The tribe has no criminal jurisdiction, but could have concurrent civil jurisdiction if the Montana Test is met.

Where there is no tribal jurisdiction present and the matter is civil in nature, the state courts clearly will have authority, although it is possible for limited federal court jurisdiction also to be present.

Criminal Matters

Criminal jurisdiction, by comparison, is less complicated. The state of the federal law is that tribal courts can handle cases involving offenders who are tribal members, no matter who the victim is. The Supreme Court has held, however, that tribal courts have no jurisdiction over non-member Indian offenders even where they commit crimes on the reservation.[44]

Jurisdiction over Indian offenders from other tribes who committed crimes within the territory of the tribal court had been assumed by tribal courts and tribal leaders since the beginning of the tribal court system. However, a conflict arose between the Eighth and Ninth Circuit Courts of Appeals of the United States. The U.S. Supreme Court resolved that conflict by deciding, in a 7–2 verdict, that tribal courts created by tribal constitution have no jurisdiction over Indians who are not tribal members.[45]

The tribe and various interveners, including the U.S. government, had argued that tribal courts always had exercised such jurisdiction. The majority in the court rejected that argument and decided that tribal courts lacked jurisdiction over such accused because non-member Indians had no voice in the tribal government or in the development of tribal law, and had no right to serve as a juror.

The Supreme Court reiterated the long-standing nature of tribal sovereignty and its importance, but limited its scope in criminal matters to tribal members on the basis that they "consent" to its authority. The decision contained a vigorous dissent by Justice Brennan, with Justice Marshall concurring.

The effect of this judgment is that a jurisdictional void has been created. Neither federal nor state courts have jurisdiction over minor criminal offences (i.e., those not committed on reservations), whether by tribal members or not. The majority of the court appear to doubt that a problem really will exist, but even if it does, then it simply leaves this difficulty for Congress to resolve.

The Bureau of Indian Affairs has responded with interim suggestions. Since this judgment does not apply to Courts of Indian Offenses, by virtue of the terms of the *Code of Federal Regulations*, the Bureau of Indian Affairs has offered to appoint all tribal judges as Court of Indian Offenses judges to vest them with this jurisdiction. Another possibility under consideration is for tribes to sign agreements with each other, extending jurisdiction over their own members to the other signatories. A number of tribes have already begun the process of lobbying for congressional action to overturn the judgment and expressly vest jurisdiction over non-member Indians in all Indian governments and courts.

The non-member Indian accused may not necessarily escape justice, as the federal Attorney General's department can initiate a prosecution in federal courts regarding federal felonies through the *General Crimes Act*.[46] Actions that constitute a felony under state law can also be prosecuted in federal courts by virtue of the *Assimilative Crimes Act*.[47]

The difficulty for tribes primarily stems from the reluctance of the Attorney General's department to prosecute. As there is no legal action available to compel prosecutions, tribes must rely upon their ability to entice prosecution through preparing overwhelming evidence in favour of conviction.

Non-Indians who commit misdemeanours on Indian reservations are also free of tribal jurisdiction. While the federal court will have jurisdiction under the *General Crimes Act* and the *Assimilative Crimes Act,* regarding federal and state crimes, respectively, there is an even greater difficulty in encouraging the U.S. district attorneys to prosecute such offences.

Special considerations apply as a result of *Public Law 280* as many tribes have lost criminal jurisdiction over Indian offenders in California, Alaska, Oklahoma, Washington, Nevada, Montana and Oregon. This does not apply, however, to all tribes in these states. In addition, it now is possible as a result of provisions within the *Indian Child Welfare Act* of 1978 for a state to retrocede its jurisdiction to the tribe, which has been done in reference to at least one Indian government in Nevada to date. Where the tribal court does not have jurisdiction, then the authorities must work with the local county prosecutor to pursue the charge in state courts.

Subject Matter Jurisdiction

In theory, tribal courts have full civil jurisdiction in all spheres of law. Some tribal codes have set maximums on the quantum of damages available from their courts, thereby encouraging litigants in major contract and tort lawsuits to opt for the state court system. Likewise, some tribal codes have not developed to encompass all relevant branches of law, while the tribal courts either have not crafted an "Indian common law" to fill the gap, or are precluded from acting by virtue of tribal provisions which establish the court's jurisdiction. Other tribes have met this problem of shortcomings in their codes through the device of "incorporation by reference." That is, when the tribal code is silent it directs the tribal court to apply external law as tribal law. The court then borrows the most appropriate concepts from the American common law, or applies the relevant state or federal statutory provision.

While Congress apparently has the constitutional authority to seize jurisdiction regarding any civil matter that it wishes, it has chosen so far not to do so in any field of non-criminal substantive law, insofar as tribal courts are concerned. Congress has imposed, however, significant restraints on tribal courts through the passage of the *Indian Civil Rights Act* of 1968 (ICRA). Although this statute is oriented primarily toward the criminal sphere, it does affect tribal civil jurisdiction in section 1302 by declaring:

No Indian tribe in exercising powers of self-government shall:

(1) make or enforce any law prohibiting the free exercise of religion, or abridging the freedom of speech, or of the press, or the right of the people peaceably to assemble and to petition for a redress of grievances;...

(5) take any private property for a public use without just compensation;...

(8) deny to any person within its jurisdiction the equal protection of its laws or deprive any person of liberty or property without due process of law;

(9) pass any bill of attainder or ex post facto law;...

These provisions impose guarantees of certain civil liberties in the passage and administration of tribal laws, but they do not remove the power to enact law on any particular subject.

Therefore, it would seem that the only limitations on substantive tribal civil law or on tribal courts in civil matters are those restrictions that are self-imposed by Indian tribes. As such, these restrictions can be removed whenever the tribes decide.

Criminal law jurisdiction is confused by congressional intervention and by tribal law. Only tribal courts have jurisdiction to enforce tribal offences, so flight by an offender can lead to successful avoidance of prosecution unless the state is prepared to return the offender.

The confusion began when the U.S. Congress removed certain designated "major crimes" in 1885 from tribal jurisdiction where the offender was an Indian. This was done to reverse the 1885 U.S. Supreme Court decision in *Ex parte Crow Dog*.[48] In that case the court had held that tribal law, with its non-incarceral penalties, governed in a case of murder by an Indian of another tribal member. The offences set out in the *Major Crimes Act* were to be tried in federal court and now include the following 16 offences:

> Any Indian who commits against the person or property of another Indian or other person any of the following offenses, namely, murder, manslaughter, kidnapping, maiming, rape, involuntary sodomy, carnal knowledge of any female, not his wife, who has not attained the age of sixteen years, assault with intent to commit rape, incest, assault with intent to commit murder, assault with a dangerous weapon, assault resulting in serious bodily injury, arson, burglary, robbery, and a felony under section 661 of this title within the Indian Country, shall be subject to the same law and penalties as all other persons committing any of the above offenses within the exclusive jurisdiction of the United States.

Tribal courts appear to have concurrent jurisdiction with federal courts in these areas, as long as there is no restraint present in the tribal code or constitution. In theory, this would mean that tribal courts could have full jurisdiction regarding criminal law subject matter, with practical limitations entering the picture only as a result of personal and territorial jurisdictional limitations. Many tribal codes and constitutions contain self-imposed limitations restricting the scope of tribal jurisdiction to minor crimes and misdemeanours.

The *Major Crimes Act* confers federal jurisdiction over only those crimes which are set out in that Act. State laws do not apply on Indian reservations except where *Public Law 280* applies and that law does not apply in every state. It is possible that in states where *Public Law 280* does not apply, or where tribes have regained their jurisdiction from the state, some criminal acts not on the Major Crimes list or not covered by a tribal code would fall into a legal vacuum. State criminal law would not apply of its own force on reservation land (except in a state where *Public Law 280* applies and the state has not relinquished its jurisdiction). This problem could be rectified by tribes amending their tribal laws so as to authorize full federal jurisdiction over any such gaps in the law by applying traditional law or Indian common law, or by referential incorporation of federal or state law. To date, apparently no tribes have felt the need to do so.

The *Indian Civil Rights Act* of 1968

The *Indian Civil Rights Act* [49] of 1968 imposes a variety of restraints on tribal law and requires tribal justice systems to comply with American concepts of due process and fairness. The Act applies to any group of Indians that is "subject to the jurisdiction of the United States and recognized as possessing powers of self-government"[50] and extends to "any Tribal Court or court of Indian offense."[51] It further governs any other tribal bodies and regulates not only legislative and judicial functions, but also the exercise of executive powers.[52]

In addition to the civil implications described earlier, the ICRA has specific provisions that alter criminal jurisdiction. The Act provides:

s.1302   No Indian tribe in exercising powers of self-government shall ...

(2) violate the right of the people to be secure in their persons, houses, papers, and effects against unreasonable search and seizures, nor issue warrants, but upon probable cause, supported by oath or affirmation, and particularly describing the place to be searched and the person or thing to be seized;

(3) subject any person for the same offense to be twice put in jeopardy;

(4) compel any person in any criminal case to be a witness against himself; ...

(6) deny to any person in a criminal proceeding the right to a speedy and public trial, to be informed of the nature and cause of the accusation, to be confronted with the witnesses against him, to have compulsory process for obtaining witnesses in his favor, and at his own expense to have the assistance of counsel for his defense;

(7) require excessive bail, impose excessive fines, inflict cruel and unusual punishments, and in no event impose for conviction of any one offense any penalty or punishment greater than imprisonment for a term of six months or a fine of $500, or both; ...

(10) deny to any person accused of an offense punishable by imprisonment the right, upon request, to a trial by jury of not less than six persons.

The Act was amended in 1986 to increase the scope of criminal penalties under tribal law to a maximum of one year's imprisonment, or $5,000 fine, or both, per offence.[53] While there does not appear to be an outcry by tribes for greater punitive authority, such limitations would appear to impose a restraint upon the efforts of tribal governments and their courts, should they wish to undertake to address serious criminal offences involving violence, narcotics, pollution and commercial crime, where a much larger fine or longer term of imprisonment might be more appropriate. The rationale for such limitations is difficult to perceive, but it is quite probable that the existence of federal authority to prosecute major crimes occurring on Indian reservations militates against the necessity of having greater penalties available for tribal courts to impose. From our visits to some of the tribal courts and after hearing from their representatives at the Tribal Court Symposium in Winnipeg organized by the Inquiry, it is apparent that, on occasion, the inability of tribal courts to impose more suitable penalties for a serious crime can have serious consequences.

In one instance, we were informed that a tribal police officer of the Navajo Tribal Police Force had been killed while pursuing an offender. The offender was caught and the matter was investigated by the FBI in accordance with the *Major Crimes Act*. Their conclusion was that they could not prosecute because they felt there was insufficient evidence to convict. Tribal authorities, not pleased with that decision, decided to prosecute the culprit anyway with a breach of their tribal code (which they were entitled to do), and a conviction was obtained. The court, however, was unable to impose anything other than the maximums set out above.

We also have been told that the presence of the maximums has resulted in the tribal courts circumventing the limitations in imaginative, although questionable, ways. We were told that tribal court judges impose consecutive sentences for multiple convictions arising out of a single transaction, a practice different from that followed in Manitoba courts. Generally, the established principle in our courts, when incarcerating an individual for separate offences arising from a single incident, is to sentence that person to concurrent terms of incarceration.

As a matter of principle, it would seem quite in order not to have unduly low maximum sentences apply only to tribal courts, provided that there are sufficient safeguards to protect the rights of an individual to a fair and thorough hearing before an impartial, adequately trained judge and a properly resourced tribunal, as well as a process of appeal to enable an accused to have his or her case reviewed.

The Act guarantees an accused in a tribal court proceeding the right of access to the federal courts by way of a writ of *habeas corpus* "to test the legality of his detention by order of an Indian tribe."[54] Although this provision appears limited in its scope, the very first case under the ICRA concluded that a U.S. district court had jurisdiction to invoke civil remedies to prevent the exclusion by the tribal council of a white lawyer who was director of the Navajo Legal Services from the reservation.[55] A number of subsequent cases expanded upon this interpretation of the ICRA to find an implied waiver of tribal sovereign immunity that permitted the remedies of injunction, declaratory relief, damages and mandamus. A wide variety of internal matters from elections to membership were deemed reviewable pursuant to the *Indian Civil Rights Act* by federal courts.[56] However, even this extension of federal judicial supervision was authorized only after all tribal remedies had been exhausted. As well, the similarity in language between the ICRA and the American *Bill of Rights* does not appear to have resulted in the incorporation of federal jurisprudence regarding the similarly worded constitutional provisions into tribal court decision making.

The intrusive nature of the *Indian Civil Rights Act* has been ameliorated somewhat by the decision of the United States Supreme Court in *Santa Clara Pueblo v.*

Martinez, 436 U.S. 49 (1978). The court was faced with the difficult choice of upholding tribal sovereignty or striking down a provision in a tribal ordinance somewhat similar to the former subsection 12(1)(b) of the *Indian Act* in Canada.

A provision of the Santa Clara membership code provided that children of a woman who married outside the tribe were denied membership, while membership was extended to children of a male member who married a non-Santa Claran. An action was brought by two women, one a member of the Santa Clara Pueblo who had married a Navajo, and the other, her daughter, who both argued that the membership rule was discriminatory on the basis of both sex and ancestry, contrary to the equal protection clause of the ICRA. The district court concluded that it had jurisdiction as the ICRA implicitly had waived sovereign immunity, but it rejected relief as it felt that membership rules were vital to the tribe's survival as a cultural and economic entity.

The Court of Appeals for the Tenth Circuit reversed, as it believed the tribe's interest was insufficient in the circumstances to support sexual discrimination. The Supreme Court overturned this latter decision. Justice Thurgood Marshall, speaking for the majority, stated:

> As separate sovereigns pre-existing the Constitution, tribes have historically been regarded as unconstrained by those constitutional provisions framed specifically as limitations on federal or state authority.

He went on to declare:

> Indian tribes have long been recognized as possessing the common law immunity from suit traditionally enjoyed by sovereign powers.... It is settled that a waiver of sovereign immunity "'Cannot be implied but must be unequivocally expressed.'"... Nothing on the face of Title I of the ICRA purports to subject tribes to the jurisdiction of the federal courts in civil actions for injunctive or declaratory relief.... In the absence here of any unequivocal expression of contrary legislative intent, we conclude that suits against the tribe under the ICRA are barred by its sovereign immunity from suit.

The court concluded that the governor of the tribe, as the petitioner, did not personally benefit from the tribe's immunity. Justice Marshall went on to consider the argument that civil remedies were authorized implicitly under the Act.

The judgment very clearly articulates the view that any infringements upon the authority of tribal courts, or the right of Indians to govern themselves, should not be imposed lightly without obvious expressions of legislative intent. This deference to tribal courts as "appropriate forums for the exclusive adjudication of disputes affecting important personal and property interests of both Indians and non-Indians" was supported by a footnote reference to the final report of the American Indian Policy Review Commission and its findings that in 1973 there were 117 operating tribal courts which handled approximately 70,000 cases. The majority reached the opinion that only express congressional intervention could or should be the basis for allowing any further intrusions on tribal sovereignty in the form of civil actions in a federal forum against a tribe or its officers.[57]

Congress has had occasion to reconsider the ICRA and has chosen not to expand the jurisdiction of the federal court system beyond the writ of *habeas corpus*.

The *Indian Civil Rights Act* has also had a number of other impacts upon tribes. The Act contained provisions to allow those states that had assumed jurisdiction over Indians and Indian reservations under *Public Law 280* to return it to the various tribes and to the federal government.

The civil rights guarantees, particularly equal protection and due process, have also had an obvious effect on tribal court procedures. While it was not uncommon for search warrants to be used by tribal and BIA police in the past, section 1302(2) of the ICRA clearly requires that tribal judges alone must authorize search warrants and that those warrants must be very precise in their terms. This has required tribal police and judges to be more careful and formal, and to reflect the general American approach in this area.

The Act also compels all criminal trials to be conducted in open court using an adversarial process.[58] While the accused has a right to counsel,[59] there is no obligation on the tribe to create a free legal aid or duty counsel scheme. Nevertheless, some tribes, such as the Yakima, have felt the need to provide legal services to indigent accused, at tribal expense. This is due, in part, to the standard practice of tribes using legally trained prosecutors to conduct all adult cases, but the presence of defence counsel further enhances the necessity for legally trained tribal prosecutors.

Furthermore, the Act extends a very broad right to the accused to demand a jury trial in any case in which imprisonment could result from conviction on that charge. Needless to say, this is a far more extensive right than that possessed by Canadians.

Tribal Court Administration

The normal elements of a Western judicial system are found in American Indian tribal courts.

Volume

Tribal court systems vary quite dramatically, depending upon the population of the reservations they service, the demand for services, the funding available, the extent of jurisdiction possessed by the courts and the philosophical orientation of the tribal governments. For example, the latest national figures available from 1983 indicate caseloads ranging from over 70,000 cases for the judicial system of the Navajo Tribe, to a low of three cases handled by the Jamestown Klallam Tribal Court.[60] The Yomba Shoshone Tribe, which is serviced by the Fallon Paiute Shoshone Court, had only one civil case in 1983.[61] Given such widespread disparity in workloads, it is not surprising to see significant differences in staffing. A similar range in population size also is apparent, with 1985 data from the Bureau of Indian Affairs indicating a high of 166,665 Navajos[62] to a low of 64 members of the Shoalwater Bay Indian Tribe.[63] Only five tribes had over 10,000 people in 1985. However, it is quite common for American Indian tribes to have several thousand members. On the other hand, there are a surprising number of quite small communities of less than 500. Some of these participate in regional justice systems, such as the Northwest Intertribal Court System of Washington (serving 13 tribes in 1985) and the Western Oklahoma Court of Indian Offenses (serving 18 tribes in 1985), while others enter into a contract with a larger neighbouring tribe to provide a judge that will enforce their own laws (e.g., the Havasupai Tribe uses the chief judge from Fort Apache on a part-time, case-by-case basis.)[64]

Nevertheless, there are a number of tribes with populations very similar to Indian First Nations in Canada who operate their own, fully functioning court system. The size of the land base also extends over a broad spectrum, with the Navajo again having the largest reservation with over 16 million acres (or some 25,000 square miles)[65] to a low of 2.12 acres.[66]

Judges

Numbers of Judges

There are approximately 360 tribal court judges in the United States. Nine tribal courts have more than four judges, 33 have four, 22 have three, 26 have two and 44 have one.

Some courts are very busy and their judges work full time. Other judges work on a part-time, as required, basis. Some are employed on a per-diem basis. This reflects the tremendous variations in workloads apparent from the information on volume of cases mentioned earlier. While the Navajo Tribe had several judges on staff, even the Yomba Shoshone Tribe, which had only one civil case in all of 1983, engaged its own judge to hear the matter. Such tribes do not have a judge of their own but they do have their own civil and criminal codes. They usually engage a judge from a neighbouring tribe to attend, to apply their law and to hear their cases when they arise. Some, however, engage a lawyer from a neighbouring community (not necessarily an Aboriginal one) to sit as a judge on a part-time basis.

Almost every tribe has its own tribal codes containing civil and criminal laws passed by the tribe's council. There may be other codes, as well, dealing with particular subject matters. The codes are similar to statutes passed by provincial and federal governments. They form the laws of the tribe that the judges interpret and apply. It was apparent to us that the fact that tribal court judges apply tribal law rendered their work considerably more meaningful to them and to those who appeared before them. Chief Judge Manuel, of the Pima-Papago Tribe on the Salt River Indian Reservation, told us that he regularly reminds those people from his tribe appearing before him that the law he is applying is their own law.

Selection of Judges

Judges of tribal courts are selected in a variety of ways, depending upon the mechanism preferred by each tribe or court district. The method usually is specified in the tribal code. Some methods of selection about which we were told included:

• **By Authority of Office**. Some Indians such as the Pueblo of New Mexico and Arizona extend judicial authority to the elected or traditionally recognized governor or lieutenant governor of their tribal council.

- **By Appointment**. In some tribes, judges are appointed by the tribal council or by a leading tribal official. On the Hopi and Navajo reservations, judges are appointed by the tribal chairman, although judicial appointments have to be approved by the tribal council. They are appointed for a probationary period usually of one year. If their appointment is confirmed they have indefinite tenure.

- **By Election**. Some tribal court judges are elected for a term of years. Although election to tribal council may take place more often, the judges usually all stand for election during tribal elections every three or four years.

- **By Engagement**. The Northwest Intertribal Court System in the state of Washington has a board of directors made up of delegates appointed by the 13 tribes served by its judges. That board advertises for candidates and hires its judges on a contract basis. As mentioned earlier, some tribes also hire local lawyers to act as tribal judges on a per-case or per-diem basis.

- **By Contract with Another Tribe**. Some smaller tribes, which do not have a judge of their own and which may not have sufficient resources or workload to employ or justify a full-time judge, contract with a neighbouring tribe to employ the latter's judge on a per-diem basis whenever the former has cases to be heard. For example, the Havasupai Tribe has an agreement with the Fort Apache Reservation whereby a Fort Apache judge will attend on the Havasupai Reservation from time to time to hear cases arising there. The Fort McDowell Indian Tribe, a small tribe near Phoenix, has a similar agreement with the Salt River Tribal Court.

- **By Government Appointment**. Where Courts of Indian Offenses still exist, judges are appointed by the Secretary of the Interior. In practice, the tribal council usually forwards the name of the person it wishes the secretary to appoint.

Qualification of Judges

Most tribes do not impose any academic requirements on those seeking judicial office. They usually require judicial candidates to be members of the tribe and to have lived on the reservation for a period of time prior to appointment or election, but this is not always the case.

Some tribal officials with whom we spoke strongly favour retaining non-legally trained judges. Others suggest that the time may come when judges will have to receive formal legal education before being appointed. The decision appears to be a matter left to the inclinations of each tribe, but, for the most part, it is safe to say that tribal judges generally are not trained as lawyers, although several are.

Tenure of Judges

Judges remain in office until their term expires. Once a tribal court judge's term expires, he or she then must be reappointed or again run for election. Of the 145 tribal courts for which there is information,[67] the single most popular term of office, as chosen by 65 tribes, is for a period of four years for the chief judges. A further 26 tribes give their chief judges only one-year terms, and 15 tribes have opted for two years. Ten tribes appoint their chief judges for three-year terms, while one tribe uses a five-year period, four use six years and another tribe makes a 10-year appointment. The remainder give open-ended or indefinite appointments (21 tribes), subject to continuing good behaviour, or lifetime appointments (two tribes).

There is some mechanism in each court for the removal of a judge for misconduct. In some cases, they may be removed by a vote of the members of the tribe. In other cases, they may be removed by a vote of the tribal council, or, as in the case of the Northwest Intertribal court, by a vote of the corporation's board of directors. It appears, therefore, that most tribes possess the authority to dismiss a judge from office. As with courts generally, the grounds for such removal are couched in vague language. There are, however, few reported instances of tribal court judges being discharged for dishonesty or malfeasance.[68]

One issue which we noted is that there appears to be a higher turnover of tribal court judges than is the case for the non-tribal judiciary. Many tribal court judges resign before completing their terms of office. A variety of factors, including low salaries, other, more attractive career opportunities, and the stresses and difficult nature of performing judicial functions in smaller, closely knit communities, results in this high turnover.

Courts of Appeal

Each tribe has its own appeal process to enable litigants to have a trial judge's decision, or the decision of a jury, reviewed. They each have their own court of appeal. We encountered different methods of selecting courts of appeal:

- Where there are more than three judges in a court, the three who did not sit on the case as the trial judge comprise the court of appeal. On occasion a judge from another tribal court may be asked to take one of the appeal positions.

- Where there are three or fewer judges, a judge or judges from another tribal court will be asked to attend to sit with the others who did not hear the case, and they will comprise the court of appeal.

- People from outside the community are appointed as members of an appellate branch to sit from time to time as needed. Sometimes they are tribal members, but this is not invariably the case. On occasion, local non-Aboriginal lawyers are members of the tribal court of appeal. In the Hopi system the court of appeal is made up of three legally trained tribal members who no longer live on the reservation. One is a judge in a state court, one is a practising lawyer and the other is a university professor. This court of appeal sits on the reservation from time to time.

- In the Navajo Court, a separate court of appeal with three full-time judges sits to hear all appeals.

Court Personnel

Attorneys

Both legally trained and lay attorneys appear in American tribal courts. The use of the tribal language or English is permitted during any court proceedings, so that those fluent in both have some advantage when they appear as advocates.

While some prosecuting attorneys are lawyers, others are not, but all have some legal training or related experience in other parts of the justice system, often as police officers or as counsellors. Where there were prosecutors without training as lawyers, it was generally the case that a lawyer was available for consultation on an as-needed basis to advise the prosecutor on legal issues as they arose.

Some tribal governments have extended rights of appearance as a courtesy to all attorneys who are licensed to practise in the state in which the reservation is located. Other tribes extend this privilege to all lawyers who are certified by any state. A number of tribes formally demand that a lawyer pass a bar examination created by them on tribal and federal Indian law before being able to appear in a tribal court.[69] An unknown number of tribes authorize the chief judge of the tribal court to control the admission process, which appears to result in an informal, oral interview system for admission.

Eligibility also can differ somewhat, as many tribes insist upon a degree from a law school approved by the American Bar Association, while many others do not. The apparent intent underlying the latter situation is to allow members of the tribes who are self-taught in their own law, or who have graduated from paralegal programs offered by community colleges, to have the opportunity to become "tribal advocates," which is the most commonly used term for defence lawyers and duty counsel. This can create a significant source of income for a number of people on larger reservations in criminal, family and minor civil matters.

The presence of a tribal bar exam helps to ensure that all counsel appearing in court will be fully knowledgeable in the substantive laws that govern life within the community, as well as tribal court procedure. This not only aids the judiciary in reaching proper decisions, but it also fosters respect for tribal law. Because any person appearing in the tribal court must be familiar with tribal law in order to pass the tribe's bar exam, this effectively eliminates the likelihood that state law will be argued blindly by attorneys who otherwise might assume that it applies automatically within the reservation.

The results of having a tribal bar exam process can be surprising. In one case we were told about, a retired judge of a state supreme court was denied the right to appear in a tribal court for having failed the tribal bar exam.

It also can lead to the creation of an active association of tribal practitioners. The Navajo Bar Association has over 250 dues-paying members, consisting of both Indians and non-Indians, many of whom do not have law degrees. The bar association prepares and administers the tribal bar exam, which is offered annually. It also conducts an annual conference on Navajo law, law reform proposals and developments in federal law as it affects American Indians. It further plays a role in seeking changes in the law and in court administration. The Navajo Bar Association clearly is atypical, due to the size of the Navajo population. Nevertheless, its experience is interesting in that its development may indicate future trends for other tribal courts.

Support Staff

In addition to employing over 360 judges, tribal courts employ over 800 other personnel, consisting of court clerks, administrators, bailiffs, prosecutors, secretaries, probation officers, juvenile counsellors, public defenders and detention officers. While few systems possess all these as separate job functions, the vast majority have a few key people who perform several tasks. The general pattern, for example, appears to be to have one or more employees who provide secretarial services to the judiciary, who also act as court reporters, process all dockets, distribute court forms, and deal with the public and the litigants. It also is common to have a tribal prosecutor who not only conducts criminal matters, but also acts for the tribe in legal affairs, advises the council on legal issues and provides legal direction to the tribal police. Some tribes cannot offer probation and counselling services, due to funding restrictions.

Tribal court clerks and administrators have formed a national association to represent their interests, and to organize and provide ongoing training for members. We attended one of the regular conferences and educational programs for court administrators organized by the Department of the Interior. The participants discussed matters ranging from the keeping of court records to the empanelling of a jury. Experienced educators, administrators and judges, mostly Aboriginal, presented and discussed the various topics. The delegates were encouraged to ask questions and to share their experiences in dealing with the various issues under discussion. The program was a very impressive indication of how tribal residents, with little formal training, can develop the skills needed to administer all aspects of a court system.

Continuing Education

Since many tribal court personnel do not have formal legal training before their appointment to the bench, before being hired as staff or before their admission to the bar, there is a need to obtain training on tribal law and court procedure. The influence of what is called in the United States "federal Indian law" on tribal life also requires that tribal judges be very conversant with the law that affects their court systems. The provisions of the *Indian Civil Rights Act* have compounded this need to have a sophisticated knowledge of the law to function effectively as a tribal court judge or lawyer. In addition, the rapid pace of change in the law, especially as a result of the high number of circuit courts of appeals and Supreme Court decisions on federal Indian law, necessitates the availability of continuing education for tribal judges, advocates and prosecutors.

Unfortunately, the relatively small size of most tribal court systems militates against operating local continuing education programs. Many tribal court judges are compelled to learn on the job, to seek advice from more experienced individuals and to teach themselves. Formal assistance, however, is available to some degree through several avenues.

The National American Indian Court Judges Association (NAICJA), which is based in Washington, D.C., offers occasional two-day conferences geared toward the needs of its members. These conferences tend to provide an overview of a large number of current issues affecting tribal judges, from recent legal developments to matters of stress or relations with tribal governments and outside agencies.

The National Indian Justice Center, near San Francisco, provides an extremely active and varied education program. In addition to conducting week-long intensive seminars on specific themes, it produces highly detailed manuals on several topics.

The seminars and the training manuals are available to anyone. Tribal court judges, clerks, advocates, police officers, social workers and others regularly take advantage of these opportunities. There usually is one seminar per month offered in different regional centres, with programs frequently repeated. This permits new members of tribal court systems to attend programs of interest relatively shortly after their selection, while experienced individuals can choose from more advanced or specialized offerings.

Both organizations have their own boards of directors, consisting of experienced tribal court judges. They rely primarily upon the Bureau of Indian Affairs for funding for their operations and to provide subsidies to judges to attend their programs. Both also make extensive use of judges as instructors.

Tribal Court Facilities

The facilities available for tribal courts vary dramatically. At one end of the scale are those tribes that have constructed buildings just to house courtrooms, judges' chambers and office space for other court staff. At the other end are tribes that have no permanent facilities, and court is held in the tribal council meeting room or a place used for other purposes. The judges and court staff usually then share offices with other tribal employees. Some tribal judges who work on a part-time basis have no chambers at all. There are, as well, tribal courts that have space dedicated for court personnel, but in buildings that house a variety of other users.

The quality of court facilities varies widely. A number of facilities are regarded by the Bureau of Indian Affairs as being inadequate. Few have court libraries, and the law books which do exist usually are located in judges' or attorneys' offices.

Access to the Law

The standard practice is for tribal law and order codes to be available for purchase from the tribal government. They are usually in a mimeographed or photocopied style. While a special project conducted by Professor Ralph Johnson of the University of Washington has made tribal codes from across the country available on microfiche, there is no official repository where revisions can be made available on a regular basis. Only the Navajo Tribal Code appears to be marketed by a commercial publisher.

There also is limited access to tribal court decisions. The written pronouncements of the Navajo Supreme Court, and many Navajo District Court decisions, are available in commercially produced volumes. A select number of other important tribal court decisions can be found in the *Indian Law Reporter*, produced by the American Indian Lawyer Training Program Inc. (AILTP) of Oakland, California. This system relies upon counsel or judges to send judgments to the AILTP for consideration for inclusion in this monthly service.

The National Indian Law Library in Boulder, Colorado also receives some tribal court decisions. Nevertheless, most tribal court judgments go unreported and are available solely from the court concerned. This has limited the development of a distinct Aboriginal jurisprudence and has hampered the cross-fertilization of legal thinking among tribal courts.

Financing

Every court system requires adequate financial resources to provide sufficient personnel and physical facilities. The Judicial Services Branch of the Bureau of Indian Affairs is mandated to negotiate annual agreements with federally recognized tribal governments to provide funding in relation to salaries, benefits, administration expenses, training and related matters.

A continual complaint from the tribes and tribal judges is that the BIA contributions are insufficient to meet the current costs of operating these unique courts, or to permit their expansion and improvement.

Salaries for court personnel, including judges, are low in comparison to state and federal court systems. The salary range for judges is generally $25,000 to $35,000 per year. Few tribes offer pension plans or other such employee benefits to tribal court personnel. The room for financial advancement for judges and other court staff is limited, which can produce discouragement and staff turnover as individuals leave for more lucrative employment.

The U.S. government has not extended funding yet for the construction of sufficient and appropriate court facilities on many reservations. While some court facilities compare well to any which we have in Manitoba, most tribal court facilities are inadequate and not conducive to the maintenance of respect for a court. Similarly, funding generally is not available to allow most tribal courts to develop library collections. Some critical staff positions cannot be created. Relatively few tribes have probation officers, juvenile counsellors, family mediators, public defenders and other important staff resources available to accused and litigants.

Tribal governments do have some flexibility in how they allocate the funding that they receive from the Bureau of Indian Affairs for judicial services. In addition, tribes are free to supplement federal assistance from their own resources. Many tribal governments do provide additional funds to allow an expansion of services beyond what the BIA funding will permit.

Tribal courts can be a source of revenue. It is very common for tribal court judges to impose court costs in criminal matters where there are guilty pleas or convictions. Furthermore, tribal courts often use small fines as a sanction in lieu of, or in addition to, other criminal penalties. Revenue can be raised through civil actions through the imposition of filing fees to begin and maintain litigation, from fees charged for the purchase of forms and from the imposition of court costs against the losing party if the lawsuit goes to trial. Highway traffic fines are a significant source of "income" for some tribes who have major thoroughfares within their reservations. In some systems the fines provide revenue directly to the court, whereas in others the fines are assessed and paid to the general fund of the tribe.

Conclusion

Concerns Expressed about Tribal Courts

Tribal courts in the United States are a relatively recent institution, arising as they have from the *Indian Reorganization Act* of 1934. The leading example of tribal courts, to which most observers point when talking of its potential, the Tribal Court of the Navajo Nation, has been in existence as such only since 1959.

Prior to the development of tribal courts, and continuing to some degree to the present, traditional courts existed in some areas where tribes had maintained strong ties with their cultures and their past. These were courts which had developed directly from within the cultures and sovereignty of those tribes without government direction or involvement. They have a strong cultural orientation. There are relatively few of them.

Despite the stronger ties to traditions and custom of traditional courts, however, it is apparent that the statutorily based tribal court system has taken a strong hold in Indian Country. It is likely that the growth of tribal justice systems in the United States will be in the area of tribal courts, rather than in the area of traditional courts.

The deference paid to tribal justice systems and the support for tribal courts, in particular, shown by state and federal courts over the last 30 years have increased dramatically the authority, importance and workload of tribal courts. This has led to expectations and demands upon tribal courts that are higher than ever before. Tribal courts now must respond to a broader range of legal issues, requiring the interpretation and application of tribal law to situations which more traditional means of resolving disputes might not be able to address as adequately.

Tribal court judges now must be constantly aware of developments in the jurisprudence regarding federal Indian law. They are being called upon more often by tribal members to review administrative decisions of tribal governments and their agencies. Non-Indians and corporations are becoming more aggressive in utilizing tribal courts for debt collection and other remedies. Family disputes increasingly demand court resolution. As the assets of tribal members increase, so does the need for judicial involvement in the administration of estates and the division of matrimonial property. Civil cases dealing with millions of dollars are beginning to appear in this unique system.

All these developments generate an increase in judicial business, warranting the allocation of more resources. In fact, there has been an increase in federal government expenditures on tribal courts over the years, but tribal authorities point out that it has not kept pace with their needs. Recent developments also suggest that the impact of tribal court decisions is greater than ever before.

Tribal courts have been criticized for a number of reasons. There is the problem of an inordinate level of judicial turnover. Some suggest that as many as one-quarter to one-third of all judges leave office each year. This may be induced, in part, by the rather short tenure granted by tribal codes and constitutions. However, many tribal court judges resign even before the expiration of their terms in office. This may be occasioned by the relatively low salaries and limited benefits that accompany the position.

There is clearly a significant problem with stress. Being a member of a small community and sitting in judgment over neighbours, friends and relatives is inevitably a thankless and personally arduous assignment. Having limited funds available can result in unattractive working conditions and frustration with the lack of creative dispositional alternatives.

Tribal courts have been accused of appearing to be susceptible to local political interference, a charge which many tribal court leaders whom we met are addressing through tribal constitutional provisions which guarantee the separation of the judiciary from the legislative and executive arms of tribal government, and which are intended to provide for an appointment and tenure process for judges which is secure and fair. Such developments, which tribal court officials are pursuing with their tribal councils, appear to be the most obvious and effective ways to deal with such criticisms.

The nature of the workload in tribal courts has also changed to such an extent that it requires judges to be more knowledgeable about the relevant law. On the one hand, this has meant that some judges lack the desired level of legal education or training necessary to address some of the more complicated legal questions coming before their courts.

On the other hand, there is a danger of over-professionalization facing tribal courts. It can result in the exclusion of members of First Nations, as happened through an increase in the Navajo Bar examination standards such that no Navajo candidate was able to pass the bar exams in 1988. Placing a premium on professional training also may result in advocates and judges who are not steeped in traditional values or knowledgeable about customary law. Adopting a Western legal style with formal educational requirements can lead to a loss of Aboriginal uniqueness and much of the strength that tribal courts possess, particularly their informality and acceptance within the community.

Tribal judges, surprisingly perhaps, appear to have been hesitant to rely upon tribal customary law as a basis for their decisions. They appear reluctant to supplement tribal codes where necessary through creating their own brands of Aboriginal common law. However, this may be a reflection of the degree to which tribal members are satisfied with the manner in which legal issues are dealt with in their codes, or the fact that tribal courts still, to a large extent, are finding their own way. We must not forget that tribal courts are a relatively recent development.

The number of civil cases has increased significantly in recent years, in part induced both directly and indirectly by the *Indian Child Welfare Act* of 1978, but civil matters still comprise a very small percentage of the total workload of tribal courts. The vast majority of the work of tribal courts appears to be in the field of criminal law.

Tribal courts have borrowed heavily from the Anglo-American legal system. While there are exceptions, such as the Peacemaker Court developed by the Navajo,[70] tribal courts generally have not widely developed or utilized traditional Aboriginal means of dispute resolution, or fostered Aboriginal-based alternatives to the adversarial approach through mediation, conciliation and peacemakers. Undoubtedly, this is due to the influence brought about by government officials and tribal legal advisers toward utilizing more recognizable Western legal concepts, processes and institutions. However, there does appear to be more thought being given to modifying the ways in which tribal courts go about their work, so as to include even more cultural aspects within tribal courtrooms.

Most tribal courts lack a sufficient range of effective sentencing options. While fines and incarceration commonly are used, the difficulty arises in relation to other, more creative strategies, such as fine option programs, community service orders, alcohol and drug abuse programs, detoxification centres, restitution, probation and victim-offender reconciliation. While tribal judges theoretically may be able to choose from this broader list, many cannot do so in reality because there are no such programs, due to a shortage of resources.

The danger, therefore, is that tribal courts may suffer the worst of both worlds. The common law adversarial model may be incompatible, in fact, with long-standing traditional values that promote harmony and reconciliation. Additionally, tribal courts may not be receiving sufficient resources to ensure that advocates are available for all indigent litigants so that they can benefit from the adversarial system, or to operate programs which provide alternatives to incarceration.

Advantages of Tribal Courts

There are many positive features of tribal courts. They provide a very efficient process in both civil and criminal matters. Cases deliberately are heard as quickly as possible so that the dispute does not fester, or an accused does not languish in jail on remand. As a result, punishment is meted out for criminal conduct while the evidence is fresh and the sanction still makes sense to the victim, the offender and the public at large. Similarly, child welfare and matrimonial disputes are settled with a minimum of the pain and hardship that often are created by delay.

Most reservations are located in rural areas. Often, they are far removed from state and federal courts, so that without tribal courts, cases might not come to court at all. Additionally, it is clear that state and federal courts in the United States are affected by systemic bias and discrimination against visible minorities,[71] including Indians, and that, at least insofar as Aboriginal people on Indian reservations are concerned, such discrimination is eliminated by using tribal courts.

Tribal courts, therefore, are not only more convenient to tribal members, they are perceived by them as being more understanding of their situation, more considerate of their customs, their values and their cultures, more respectful of their unique rights and status, and likely to be more fair to them than the non-Aboriginal justice system has been. In such a situation, where the court has the inherent respect of accused and the community, the impact and effect of its decisions will be that much greater.

Tribal courts obviously have the capacity to bridge the chasm that now exists between Anglo-American law and Indian cultures. They are not perceived as being alien to the values, traditions and beliefs of the Indian nations. Instead, they are seen by tribal members as representing the opportunity to protect their cultures and their central tenets by careful, sensitive application and utilization of the laws and customs developed by the tribe to govern the lives of its members.

Despite the high turnover among the tribal judiciary, it must be noted that the majority of tribal judges remain in their appointments for their complete terms. Tribal courts benefit greatly from their dedication, talent and hard work. Many of the tribal court judges with whom we met impressed us with their commitment to the ongoing improvement of "their" system and to the continual advancement of their communities.

Measuring the success of tribal courts is difficult. It would appear that no comparative analysis ever has been undertaken to determine if tribal courts function better or worse than non-Indian courts. One cannot "prove" that tribal courts are more effective than the general system in deterring crime. While it is obvious that they handle literally hundreds of thousands of cases each year, cases that otherwise would be processed in state or local courts if tribal courts did not exist, no studies have been found that indicate the financial and other benefits of tribal courts for their own communities or for non-Indian ones.

However, the tendency of federal and state courts to give at least comity, if not full faith and credit, to tribal court decisions in recent years gives a telling indication of the positive attitude that is growing among the American non-Indian judiciary toward the work the tribal courts do.[72]

In addition, some tribes have begun incorporating significant changes which indicate a high degree of institutional flexibility. Some tribes have developed modern versions of traditional justice systems. For example, at least one has created a formal Council of Elders to play a mediation role in minor criminal and civil matters. The Navajo have created an alternative to their district and supreme courts in the form of a Peacemaker Court.

Another strength is seen in the way that the Navajo Peacemaker Court operates. Where both parties agree, any dispute, including events that could be characterized as criminal misdemeanours (e.g., committing damage to property, trespass, etc.), can be diverted from the court to a peacemaker. Like an arbitrator, the peacemaker is mutually selected or drawn from a list approved by the court and paid by the parties. The peacemaker relies upon the consent and respect of the disputants to find a solution acceptable to both. The peacemaker's "decision" is then registered with the district court and is enforceable as a court order. If either party wishes, it can withdraw from this process and the dispute will be left unsettled, or will result in litigation before the tribal court.[73]

The Zuni, like a number of other tribes, have opted to revamp the tribal court itself so as to be less like the more formal common law system. The Zuni conduct a combination of mediation and pre-trial conferences shortly after criminal charges have been laid, in which the prosecutor, defence counsel, offender and victim appear before a tribal court judge to discuss the nature of the alleged crime and to determine if an acceptable resolution can be found. If no agreement can be reached, then the matter will proceed to trial before a different judge.

Many other tribal courts modify their official procedures by the judges adopting more of a mediative role between the disputants. This is more in keeping with the Indian approach of emphasizing informal discussion of problems with extensive consultation to achieve consensus. This suggests that the process of solving disputes often takes precedence over adherence to the dictates of substantive law.

Tribal courts are close to the people they serve. The vast majority of Indian reservations are small, so that people invariably know every resident. Therefore, tribal judges are likely to be familiar with the litigants and their backgrounds, and perhaps even aware of some of the details of the situation that gave rise to the trial. While this can be a problem in terms of the stress that it places on the judge, it also can be a source of strength when it comes to fashioning appropriate solutions to the issues that come before the judges. Many of the criticisms which we heard about our own circuit court system centred on its lack of connection with the Aboriginal communities where it sits.

American tribes are committed to the preservation and expansion of their court systems. This fact, perhaps more than anything, demonstrates a faith and belief in their ultimate value. The increasing level of federal financial support is a further sign of their importance, not only to the communities they serve, but to American society at large, as is the continuing commitment of tribal judges and commentators to encouraging their growth.

In addition, there is a growing respect shown by federal and state courts toward the importance and authority of this unique system. As one example, a joint annual judicial educational conference, entitled the Sovereignty Symposium, has been underway for the past few years involving the Oklahoma Supreme Court and the tribal courts of that state. This concept now is spreading to the state of Washington and is under consideration in Wisconsin.

All this leads us to conclude that tribal courts clearly have played a vital role in meeting the needs of American Indians for a fair, just and culturally acceptable legal system. That would be sufficient reason, in our view, to endorse their maintenance and expansion, but we also note that the existence of tribal courts undoubtedly provides a benefit to American society at large.

Relevant Australian and New Zealand Experience

There is no indigenous legal system functioning in either Australia or New Zealand that is remotely similar to the American Indian tribal courts. This is not to suggest, however, that their experience is without meaning or value to Canadians exploring these issues. In fact, the issue of developing a unique court for the Maori people is a topic of great interest and public debate at present in New Zealand. It already has been the subject of a study commissioned by the New Zealand Department of Justice and conducted by a Maori lawyer.[74] It is being examined currently by the New Zealand Law Reform Commission as part of its second phase of work on court reform and as an aspect of its investigation into possible changes in the criminal justice system.

The issue of establishing Aboriginal justice systems already has been reviewed in particular detail by the Australia Law Reform Commission as part of its report on Aboriginal customary law.[75] Therefore, both countries are in a position rather similar to Canada's in a number of ways.

All three nations suffer from a tragic over-representation of indigenous peoples in the adult and youth criminal justice system, including detention facilities. All three have few members of the indigenous population who work within the system as judges, lawyers, police or correctional officers. Aboriginal people in each country are making ever stronger demands upon the justice system to reform itself and to involve the indigenous community in its plans and operations.

Each country also is witnessing repeated charges from the Aboriginal community of unfair treatment and outright racism present within the justice system in its dealings with the indigenous population.

Perhaps the most graphic example of this has been in Australia, where intense lobbying by a broad sector of the public, led by the Aboriginal Deaths in Custody Committee, resulted in the appointment by the Commonwealth of the Royal Commission into Deaths of Aborigines in Custody. Its original mandate was to investigate the circumstances surrounding over 40 deaths of Aboriginals while in police custody or in a correctional institution. The size of the commission and the magnitude of its investigation had been expanded as approximately 100 suspicious deaths of Aboriginal persons in custody were uncovered.

Although Aboriginal customary law still operates in many parts of Australia, with and without official approval of the state,[76] dispute resolution conducted in the traditional manner has received little attention from the justice system, or from outside observers, other than as a factor that affects the selection of an appropriate sentence to be imposed by the general court.[77] Australia, however, has had some limited experience with the operation of separate court systems directed toward the Aboriginal and Torres Strait Islander peoples. In the Australian state of Queensland, the community council in each trust area (formerly called reserves) is empowered under state law to enact by-laws on matters including "the peace, order, discipline, comfort, health, moral safety, convenience, food supply, housing and welfare of the area for which it is established." Fines for violations of these by-laws may not exceed $500 or $50 per day. This is similar to the jurisdiction given to Indian bands under the Canadian *Indian Act*. The similarity with the *Indian Act* is also present in another aspect, in that there is a requirement in the Queensland legislation to have the by-law approved by the Governor in Council before it is effective (as section 82 of the *Indian Act* compels approval by the Minister of Indian Affairs).

The local Aboriginal and Torres Strait Islander communities can establish their own police forces to enforce these by-laws. In addition, the councils can create their own courts to hear and determine charges under any by-laws enacted. These courts consist of two residents who are appointed as justices of the peace by the council. Their jurisdiction is limited to the territory of the trust lands and the residents of the community, which can include non-Aboriginals and non-Islanders. The subject matter jurisdiction is also officially restricted to the by-laws and the "usages and customs" of the community. It is unclear how broad the latter source of jurisdiction really is, both in theory and in practice. It does appear that a few communities have made use of this provision to direct other disputes to this court system. At the very least, it seemingly would allow the justices to give due respect and life to traditional law. While appeals lie to the superior courts of Queensland, there do not appear to be any reported decisions or much use of this right of appeal.

The Western Australia government also has had legislation in force since 1979 authorizing the incorporation of Aboriginal communities whose local councils can pass by-laws, subject to approval by the state government, which apply to persons within the boundaries of the community. These by-laws relate to local matters and are similar in nature to section 81 of the *Indian Act,* with the penalty being a fine of up to $100, or imprisonment for less than three months, or both. This legislation was a substitute for an earlier statutory scheme, dating back to the Depression, which did not contain a local government structure but did include, at various points in time, a community court system comprised of a magistrate and Aboriginal justices of the peace sitting together in judgment on minor offences. There have also been a few Aboriginal justices of the peace appointed in the Northern Territory. While they serve within the general system, they are located primarily within Aboriginal communities.

Although Aboriginal customary law and criminal justice issues have received considerable attention from researchers and government policy analysts,[78] few changes have been implemented. The Australian Law Reform Commission has issued an extensive report on the subject but the implementation of its recommendations by the government of that country has yet to occur.

New Zealand makes extensive use of the justice of the peace model, following the British and New South Wales policy (the latter of which has reputedly over 30,000 justices of the peace). There are approximately 8,500 justices of the peace in New Zealand, appointed by the Minister of Justice after police scrutiny and nomination by the local member of Parliament. What makes the New Zealand experience so interesting is the degree to which the Maori have been involved, as there are currently over 500 Maori justices of the peace. The president of the Royal Federation of Justices of the Peace for 1990 also is Maori. There is, then, approximately one such judicial officer for every 400 people. They are all unpaid volunteers and cannot be lawyers, clergy or police officers. The presence of so many Maori justices has caused the production of many legal forms in the Maori language. Although their criminal jurisdiction is relatively limited, they do handle small claims cases and some apparently are involved unofficially as mediators in disputes between neighbours and family members.

New Zealand also has a special Aboriginal court system with exclusive jurisdiction in reference to the administration of Maori land-holdings and estates. Those lands which remain in the recognized hands of Maori people through their *iwi* (somewhat analogous to a tribe) or *whanau* (akin to a band or extended family) are not reserves or reservations as understood in North America. There are no recognized local or regional Maori governments who possess title to these lands, or who have regulatory authority over their usage.

On the other hand, Maori lands were not divided and allotted to individuals with fee simple title so as to be treated under the regular, imported British common law regime concerning real property. Instead, an unusual form of collective title was created, in which each person within the *whanau,* the extended family, was identified as having an interest in a particular parcel of land. The land could be used, leased or sold only by agreement among those who possessed a share. Over time, the number of people with interests in a specific plot can become rather sizeable as a person's share passes on to all his or her immediate descendants on death.

The function of the Maori Land Court is to identify who the stakeholders are regarding all Maori land, to determine the beneficial interests created through inheritance and to deal with real property transactions. One of the by-products of population growth, increased urbanization, greater intertribal marriages and the alteration in land use patterns is that it becomes exceedingly difficult to develop proposals for land use by the Maori people themselves. It is far easier to lease or sell the land, as money can be divided, than it is to agree that one beneficiary farm or build or log the land for his or her own needs. In many ways, the Maori Land Court and this entire regime were designed to encourage the transference of most Maori land to *pakeha* (settler) control.

In recent years, the Maori Land Court has earned considerable respect among the Maoris. This is in no small part a function of the fact that it now includes a number of Maori judges, including Chief Judge E. Durie, as well as several *pakeha* judges fluent in Maori. In addition, various members of this court are called upon to chair hearings of the Waitangi Tribunal, which conducts investigations into complaints of violations of the Treaty of Waitangi of 1840 (the sole treaty that has, through adhesions, come to encompass all of New Zealand and chart the broad parameters of the relationship between the Maori and the *pakeha*). The court's thrust has altered dramatically from its original orientation, as it now seeks ways to promote the retention of Maori land and its use by Maori people. One way has been through the creation of Maori Trusts, in which trustees are elected for a term of office by the beneficiaries to administer the land-holdings.

The Maori Land Court has no criminal or general civil authority. The judges proposed that they be granted family law and young offenders jurisdiction while the legislation in this area was being revamped. Their submission was rejected because the *Children, Young Persons and Their Families Act,* 1989 creates a new youth court to supplement a revised family court system, which applies to the population of New Zealand as a whole.

The New Zealand government has introduced initiatives to provide Maori people with a limited role in the criminal justice system. The *Maori Community Development Act,* 1975 allows Maori communities to deal with very minor offences of a quasi-criminal nature, such as public drunkenness and disorderly behaviour. The community committee can impose a fine of up to $20 or a prohibition order. It seems that this limited opportunity rarely has been used. A few district court judges have developed the occasional practice of not only holding court on *marae* (the Maori community lands on which spiritual and community centres are situated) but also of transferring selected cases to *marae* committees for determination of appropriate sentences. The latter usually occurs regarding young offenders as part of a diversion scheme, although it is done sometimes in relation to adult offenders.

The Te Atatu Maori Committee has functioned as a tribunal for a number of years to deal with cases diverted by youth aid officers prior to sentencing. It is based on a *marae* and seeks to ensure that the offender's extended family is involved actively in the disposition. The committee's sentencing philosophy is reflected by its emphasis upon imposing specific reparation orders to the benefit of the victim, and/or community service orders. The decision of the Te Atatu Maori Committee is referred back to the court for official ratification. The tribunal also is free to refuse to deal with a particular case when it feels that it is unable to have an effect on an offender.

A somewhat similar operation occurs in Rotorua through the Fordlands Scheme. Although it services an entire neighbourhood and not exclusively Maori people, most of the young offenders are Maori. It also attempts to involve the extended family and includes at least one Maori elder on any panel handling Maori cases.

The *Criminal Justice Act* of 1985 authorizes the establishment of Criminal Justice Advisory Councils to promote community initiatives. This has been little used to date by the Maori, perhaps, in part, due to the presence of from three to five justice system officials in each council's total membership of nine to 11 individuals. These officials typically are non-Maori, but, in theory, could be Maori people working within the system.

Proposals to develop a Maori court system currently are under active consideration by Maori people, and seem to have their active and general support. To date, there has been no formal endorsement of the idea by either the prime minister or the government of New Zealand.

The experience of the indigenous peoples in these two countries, with over-representation in the criminal justice system, prisons and child welfare agencies, parallels the experience in Canada for the Indian, Inuit and Metis peoples. The governments are responding by attempting to indigenize the general justice system and by creating mechanisms whereby the Maori, Aboriginal and Torres Strait Islander peoples can play a limited role through advisory bodies and community justice programs. There are a few examples of initiatives that go somewhat beyond the diversionary schemes. However, these developments are few and far between. Nevertheless, the debate regarding the wisdom and necessity of establishing separate justice systems under the control of the local indigenous populations is ongoing.

Relevant Canadian Experience

The History of the *Indian Act* Court

Although tribal courts as such never have been established in Canada, there has been a long-standing parallel development worthy of note. While the Courts of Indian Offenses were being imposed by the American Bureau of Indian Affairs in 1883, the Canadian government already had implemented a similar objective through an amendment to the *Indian Act* in 1881.[79] The effect of this provision was to appoint all Indian agents and their superiors as justices of the peace under the Act. A further amendment[80] the next year extended this authority by cloaking all Indian agents with the powers of a police or stipendiary magistrate.

Parliament obviously decided that Indian agents needed even more authority, as the Act was amended again in 1884.[81] This time the jurisdiction was extended to enable Indian agents to conduct trials wherever "it is considered by him conducive to the ends of justice." Trials could occur outside reserves.[82] The agent's mandate also included offences under the Act, regardless of where they were committed. These justices of the peace also had authority over "any other matter affecting Indians."[83] This presumably meant that Indian agents, as justices of the peace, could sit in judgment regarding all criminal offences then in existence, which included both statutory and common law offences because the *Criminal Code* had not yet been enacted.

As a result, this court should be considered more properly an "Indian Agent's Court," since it was a special court system created solely for lay judges who also were employees of the Department of Indian Affairs and, at least predominantly, people without any Aboriginal ancestry. These justices held appointments with no territorial limitations, either in terms of the court or of the event that gave rise to the proceedings. They also had full jurisdiction over the person in the sense that they could deal with charges laid against both Indians and non-Indians. The sole express restraint on their authority was that non-Indians could come before the court only for a violation of the *Indian Act*.

It was unclear initially if this was a criminal court only, or if the general language was intended to convey civil jurisdiction in addition. This doubt was removed by an amendment in 1886 that expressly limited the agents to violations under the *Indian Act* so as to exclude general civil and criminal jurisdiction.[84] Jurisdiction over all offenders breaching the *Indian Act,* regardless of race, was retained. Although the criminal scope was expanded once again in 1890 to include a number of sex offences under *An Act Respecting Offences against Public Morals and Public Convenience,*[85] this was limited to Indian offenders.[86] The passage for the first time of a comprehensive federal criminal statute in 1892 (the *Criminal Code*) and the repeal of the prior collection of criminal laws[87] meant the initial loss of jurisdiction over sex offences. *The Indian Act* was amended once again in 1894 to restore this jurisdiction.[88]

Indian agents also were given concurrent jurisdiction with other judges in reference to two *Criminal Code* provisions directed specifically toward Indian people. The first provision dealt with unenfranchised Indian women prostitutes and anyone who owned or occupied premises in which such prostitution occurred.[89] The second provision created the indictable offence of inciting "three or more Indians, non-treaty Indians, or halfbreeds" to breach the peace or make "riotous" or "threatening" demands on any civil servant.[90] The offence of vagrancy was added the next year.[91]

This subject matter jurisdiction remained untouched until the major overhaul of federal Indian legislation in 1951, so that for the first half of this century all Indian agents were justices of the peace with criminal jurisdiction over all violators of the *Indian Act,* in addition to having specific *Criminal Code* jurisdiction over Indians in relation to sex offences, prostitution, vagrancy, and aggressive political activity when conducted in groups of three or more Indians or Metis.

The Canadian government differed from its American counterpart in two critical ways. While the Bureau of Indian Affairs worked to develop an Indian police force to impose federal law under the watchful eye of the Bureau of Indian Affairs, the Canadian policy was to rely upon the RCMP whenever any policing was necessary.

The Americans also sought from the outset to use the court system as a "civilizing" tool to foster their values and beliefs in substitution for traditional law and governmental structures. It was felt that this was accomplished best through the hand-picking of individual tribal members to be appointed as judges under the supervision of the Bureau of Indian Affairs agents. The Canadian approach was much more oppressive. All Indian agents automatically were granted judicial authority to buttress their other powers, with the result that they not only could lodge a complaint with the police, but they could direct that a prosecution be conducted and then sit in judgment of it. Except as accused, Aboriginal people were excluded totally from the process.

The clear result of all this development was that Indian agents were armed with broad power over almost every aspect of Indian life. They presided at all Indian council meetings and virtually directed local decisions. As agents and as justices of the peace, they presided over the enforcement of laws in relation to:

- trespass to reserve lands;
- removal of renewable and non-renewable resources;
- sale or purchase of farm produce;
- logging;
- non-payment of rent;
- seizure of goods;
- band council by-laws;
- actions in debt, tort or contract;
- private purchase of Crown presents to Indians;
- intoxication offences;
- common bawdy houses;
- celebrating a Potlatch or Tamanawas;
- inciting Indians to make riotous demands or breach the peace;
- pursuing land claims or raising funds for that purpose;
- sale of ammunition to Indians when prohibited by the superintendent general; and
- regulating Indians in obtaining homesteads in Manitoba, the North-West Territories and the Keewatin District.

In addition, these justices had the normal authority to issue search warrants and notarize affidavits or other legal documents.

While their jurisdiction was concurrent with the regular provincial court system insofar as the *Indian Act* and the *Criminal Code* provisions applicable to Indians were concerned, the expectation on the part of the federal government was that Indian agents would serve for all intents and purposes as the only relevant justices in all matters within their jurisdiction, due to their intimate knowledge of reserve life, their awareness of the specific events and their presence within the community. The role they were expected to play was part of an overall federal policy of assimilation. Just as the provincial governments had little to do with bands and their needs due to financial, constitutional and other reasons, there was little incentive for the regular courts to get involved except when called upon to deal with more serious criminal offences.

One of the changes introduced in 1951 was that the Governor in Council was empowered to appoint "persons" to be justices of the peace.[92] All the Indian agents who previously had been appointed retained this status[93] and agents clearly were eligible to be appointed in the future. This should not be misinterpreted as being an attempt to follow the American approach of 70 years earlier, as Indians were not "persons" then under the Act. Instead, it merely gave added flexibility to the federal government to appoint people other than Indian agents if it so chose.

The Current Regime

A 1956 amendment to the *Indian Act* reflects a few further jurisdictional changes:

107. The Governor in Council may appoint persons to be, for the purposes of this Act, justices of the peace and those persons have and may exercise the powers and authority of two justices of the peace with regard to

(a) offences under this Act, and

(b) any offence against the provisions of the *Criminal Code* relating to cruelty to animals, common assault, breaking and entering and vagrancy, where the offence is committed by an Indian or relates to the person or property of an Indian.

Law reports normally do not record the decisions of justices of the peace, and the federal government also apparently has not documented the decisions of Indian agents as justices, with the result that we have no way of knowing how often this power was exercised. Only seven reported cases exist in the period from 1881 until the provision was overhauled in 1951. All these dealt with appeals or attacks on the validity of the agents' jurisdiction before the regular courts.[94] The subsequent jurisprudence on section 107 is even more sparse, consisting of a handful of decisions of the Quebec Superior Court and Court of Appeal, all but one of which are unreported, regarding challenges to the court functioning at the Kahnawake Indian Reserve near Montreal.[95]

Despite these challenges over the years, the overall integrity and validity of this unique court have been sustained repeatedly, as have the appointments of the justices. The subject matter jurisdiction set out has been interpreted liberally by courts called upon to review the jurisdiction of section 107 courts, as including not only the express provisions of the Act but also the regulations and by-laws enacted pursuant to the Act. It is also clear that jurisdiction over both Indians and non-Indians has been upheld in reference to violations of the Act. Jurisdiction extends beyond the boundaries of the reserve as long as the events constitute an offence under the Act, or involve Indians.

The courts also have assumed that all the normal elements of the general justice system apply, including due process, natural justice, right to counsel, etc. The appellate courts have not questioned their own jurisdiction to hear appeals or applications for judicial review.

With the elimination of Indian agents, starting with the Walpole Island First Nation in 1965, the policy basis for the section 107 court system seemingly has disappeared.

Nevertheless, the provision has continued to survive, despite several rounds of amendments to the Act over the intervening years. Furthermore, it is in active use today, albeit for a very different reason than its original intent. Three First Nations have been successful in being able to persuade the federal government to appoint people of their own choosing as justices of the peace for their communities. The Akwesasne Reserve has had a member appointed by the Governor General in Council as a justice of the peace since November 23, 1972. Other band members have subsequently received this status, and the first Mohawk justice of the peace appointed, Justice John Sharrow, conducted court at Kahnawake for many years, starting in 1974. There are now other Mohawks of that community who also have been appointed. The Pointe Bleu Reserve has also had a section 107 court functioning for some time.

Jurisdiction

The specific subject matter jurisdiction has been expanded by the changes introduced to the Indian Act in recent years and the greater use of the by-law-making powers of band councils under sections 81, 83 and 85.1. Therefore, the justices have full jurisdiction over offences created within the Act itself, as well as those enacted via federal regulations and band by-laws. In practical terms, the majority of the activity relates to offences regarding the following:

- Trespass to reserve land (s. 30).

- The sale of agricultural produce from reserves in the three Prairie provinces without departmental consent (ss. 32-33).

- Trading, removing or defacing certain cultural or burial objects (s. 91).

- Trading for profit without a licence by DIA employees, missionaries or school teachers (s. 92).

- Removal of renewable and non-renewable resources without ministerial consent (s. 93).

- Allowing a child between the ages of seven and 16 to refrain from attending school (s. 119(3)).

- Violating regulations regarding:

    - logging and mining (s. 57);

    - fur-bearing animals, fish and other game on reserves (s.73((1)(a), although no such regulations are in force);

    - highway traffic (s. 73(1)(c));

    - dog registration (s. 73(1)(d));

    - licensing of places of amusement, controlling behaviour at such places and outlawing gambling (s. 73(1)(e));

- controlling infectious diseases and requiring adherence to provincial health and sanitation standards (s. 73(1)(g));

- controlling garbage dumps, the disposal of waste and burning of rubbish (s. 7(1)(k)).

• Violating band by-laws enacted pursuant to ss. 81, 83 and 85.1.

The latter, of course, are specific to each reserve such that the justice of the peace could obtain broad or very narrow authority through this mechanism.

Some First Nations actively utilize this opportunity for delegated powers of local government by passing by-laws concerning health care, traffic, law and order, juvenile curfew, disorderly conduct and nuisances, building codes, water works, amusements, wildlife management, trespass, licensing of businesses, property taxes, the sale or manufacture of intoxicants, being intoxicated and possession of intoxicants. In addition, section 102 provides a general penalty where the Act or regulation is silent as to the consequences of committing an offence.

The justice also has a procedural role in relation to issuing search warrants (section 103(4) in relation to goods to be seized and section 119(2.2) in relation to entry of a dwelling-house in aid of finding a truant).

Paragraph 107(b) further extends authority to a justice concerning any provisions in the *Criminal Code* that could constitute the offences of cruelty to animals, common assault, breaking and entering, and vagrancy. The latter currently is not an offence under the Code, while the others are not tied to specific sections of the *Criminal Code* through section 107 of the Act.

While this subject matter limitation may appear to some to be rather narrow, it is important to realize that band by-laws are obtaining increasingly greater importance. Several recent decisions have held that band by-laws can take precedence over the federal *Fisheries Act* and its regulations.[96] The same reasoning could be extended logically to other areas in relation to federal legislation. In addition, section 88 of the *Indian Act* has the effect of rendering by-laws paramount over provincial laws of general application where they are inconsistent. It is unclear if the latter would apply only in relation to Indians, as section 88 expressly states, or if it also would extend to non-Indians within reserves.

Jurisdiction over the person varies between the two paragraphs of section 107. The latter is designed solely to apply to registered Indian offenders and other potential accused, as long as the alleged crime "relates to the person or property" of a status Indian. The broader range covered by the first paragraph makes no distinction based upon the race of the accused, or his or her entitlement to registration. As the Act does not tie registration to race explicitly, it is possible for individuals to have no Indian ancestry, yet have gained status under the Act so as to fall clearly within the jurisdiction of this unique court. The accused also does not have to be a member of the band or a resident of the reserve in relation to which the court is functioning. On the other hand, it is possible since Bill C-31 for someone to gain band membership under a First Nation's membership code passed pursuant to section 10 without qualifying for registration so as to be potentially outside the court's jurisdiction under section 107(b). To confuse matters somewhat further, a person is legally an "Indian" if he or she is "entitled to be registered" as such under section 6(1), even though that person may not, in fact, actually be registered.

Thus, all people can be brought before the court for offences committed under the Act, regulations or band by-laws.[97] Only Indians and those committing offences upon Indians or their property can be dealt with legally by a section 107 justice in relation to the *Criminal Code* offences.

The experience of the Kahnawake court is that a sizeable proportion of its offenders are non-Indian highway traffic violators. Section 107 does not refer directly to any territorial limitations upon the justices appointed. The long-standing tradition is that they carried a national appointment so that the Indian agents would not have to be reappointed every time they were transferred to another reserve. In addition, some agents were responsible for more than one band at a time. Therefore, the individuals received general appointments in their personal capacity after 1894, empowering them to serve as justices of the peace anywhere in the country. While the Act no longer explicitly states that these justices may conduct trials outside reserves, it also does not in any way restrict the location of the court. It is important to realize, however, that virtually all the offences under the Act relate to activities occurring solely on Indian reserves. The regulations are structured similarly and by-laws are presumed to be clearly limited to the boundaries of the reserve. It would be possible, though, for the offences delineated by section 107(b) to include incidents that occurred off-reserve, such that an urban case of common assault could be transferred from the provincial courts or initiated in the section 107 court.

The language of section 107 itself makes it clear that this separate court system is intended to operate in relation to criminal and quasi-criminal matters. For this purpose, the individual "may exercise the powers and authority of two justices of the peace" so as to match the language found in the *Criminal Code* over the years concerning the definition of a magistrate. The question remains, however, as to whether a section 107 justice of the peace has any civil jurisdiction. The Act is silent in this regard and the limited jurisprudence in the superior courts is of no guidance. At most, such civil jurisdiction would be limited to matters included within the Act, regulations and band by-laws, but even this is highly debatable in light of the use of the expression "offences" within paragraph 107(b).

The Creation of New Courts under Section 107

It has been the position of successive ministers of Indian Affairs for at least the last 10 years that no new courts will be created under section 107 of the *Indian Act*. Thus, the only appointments of recent vintage have been as replacements upon the death, resignation or incapacity of the sitting justices. The explanation for this unwillingness to utilize the legislation as it stands is that the *Indian Act* as a whole has been under review, and long-term initiatives that might prejudge or differ from the outcome of this consultation process should not be implemented for the time being. We question the validity of this explanation in view of the fact that other major changes have been instituted. Nonetheless, in view of the position we take with respect to the creation of Aboriginal justice systems, we do not want to be seen as suggesting that the use of section 107 of the *Indian Act* has any further validity. However, we do note that, as with the former Bill C-52 legislation on Indian self-government proposed by the Department of Indian Affairs in 1984, the existence of section 107 of the *Indian Act* and its latest usage shows some recognition by the federal government that the First Nations have a role to play in the administration of justice within their communities.

The section 107 court remains in the statute as a vestige of the ignominious past of federal colonization and domination of reserve life. It has been seized upon by three First Nations who wish to assert some level of control over the local justice system. The restrictions that exist in the Act are such that it offers little promise for the long-term future and is unlikely to satisfy current demands from First Nations to establish their own justice system. At most, it offers a short-term interim measure and an indication that a separate court system can function readily on Indian reserves without causing grave concerns within the rest of society or the legal community.

Unfortunately, over 100 years of experience with the *Indian Act* courts can provide little in the way of direction toward a new approach for the future. This helps explain the fact that the search for guidance generally has been directed toward the United States.

The other initiatives in Canada have been limited to appointing more Aboriginal people as provincial or territorial justices of the peace, or as advisers to presiding provincial or territorial court judges. Both these approaches have been used extensively in the Northwest Territories where a number of Dene, Metis and Inuit justices of the peace currently serve. In addition, some Inuit communities in the eastern Arctic use an elders' panel to advise the court on sentencing decisions and to help carry out behaviour change in offenders who receive non-custodial sentences.

The Ontario government also has had a special program for Aboriginal justices of the peace since the early 1980s, which has resulted in the selection of several full-time and part-time Indian and Metis JPs. The Ontario government recently has provided funding to the Sandy Lake and Attawapiskat First Nations to establish elders' panels to advise the court on sentencing in non-jury cases.[98] A similar system had been in operation in the 1970s on Christian Island regarding young offenders.

It is important to note that these types of initiatives still are based upon an application of existing federal and provincial laws, rather than incorporating the traditional and contemporary laws of Aboriginal communities. While they represent a positive step forward from the status quo, they do limit the involvement of Aboriginal people to a subordinate position within the general justice system in a way that is not in keeping with the professed desires of the Aboriginal peoples of Canada. As the Assembly of Manitoba Chiefs put it:

> This provision of the *Indian Act* has not been used to create a judicial system for Indians. Historically it was utilized to provide additional powers for Indian agents. As the officials of the Department of Indian Affairs, these agents applied and enforced federal Indian policy and the *Indian Act*. The provision of the *Indian Act* could be a legislative source for the establishment of a unique Indian justice system, however, it is not likely to be utilized considering the limited role and jurisdiction of such courts.

Indeed leaders of First Nations across Canada take the position that dealing with offences under the *Indian Act* or a few sections of the *Criminal Code* is not acceptable. An inferior court with limited jurisdiction is most definitely not an alternative to the establishment of an Indian court system. Paternalistic and patronizing alternatives are both insulting and degrading to our human dignity.[99]

We see no logic in having day-to-day decisions affecting the lives of members of First Nations being made by outsiders.

Creating Aboriginal Justice Systems

While more and more has been said in favour of the establishment of Aboriginal justice systems, few proponents have articulated in detail how such systems should be established legally or how they would function. The presentations which we received strongly emphasized the point of recognizing the right, but few addressed the surrounding issue in any significant manner.

Having already come to the conclusion that Aboriginal courts are an important aspect of solving the problems which we have identified, the focal point in this section will be on how Aboriginal justice systems could be created and how they could function in practical terms. This obviously will reflect the issues that are most pressing from the viewpoints of the administration of justice, which daily faces the problems, and of Aboriginal communities and organizations which wish to assume responsibility for these problems. The alternatives involved have to be confronted if they are to receive proper consideration.

At the outset, we wish to point out that we recognize that it is not appropriate for us to put forth a model that is intended to serve as a master plan or blueprint to be adopted by Aboriginal communities or to be pressed upon them. It is clearly up to the Aboriginal people themselves to debate the alternatives and make their own choices based upon what they believe will best fit their current needs and objectives for the future. It can be anticipated that this may produce different approaches throughout the province of Manitoba, just as there are different models in the United States.

We believe it is important to accept the principle that justice systems must not be imposed on Aboriginal people. To do so would be to perpetuate the policy of paternalism and imposition that has been the hallmark of Aboriginal affairs in this country for too long. Aboriginal people must have control over such major developments. Deputy Minister Harry Swain of the Department of Indian Affairs made the point when, in discussing with us the future of amendments to the *Indian Act*, he said:

> As noted, we are long past the day when Ottawa proposes to legislate without the consent of the governed. Instead the department is working in close collaboration with many Indian leaders and organizations across the country to see whether there exists a package of reforms that would command broad support among First Nations.

There undoubtedly will have to be negotiations involving federal and provincial governments and Aboriginal representatives if the establishment of Aboriginal justice systems is to become a reality. One of the purposes of this section of the report is to assist in those negotiations, if we can, by addressing those concerns that appear to be most obvious and by recommending how they might be addressed. We recognize that our views will have an impact upon the discussions concerning the content and form of future Aboriginal justice systems. Aboriginal-government negotiations are an inevitable outcome of our report. Aboriginal people must be seen as full and equal partners in Confederation and must be encouraged in their right to control the development of institutions that have an impact on the governance of their communities.

Discussions will be necessary to sort out the boundaries between the general legal system and the new one being forged, as well as to address conflicts of laws questions. Negotiations may be required to establish and clarify the legal basis for Aboriginal justice systems and the resolution of the potential for jurisdictional conflicts with existing courts.

The Legal Bases

There are several alternative means as to how Aboriginal justice systems could be established legally. They include:

- A constitutional amendment to section 35 of the *Constitution Act, 1982.*

- Federal legislation, enacted pursuant to the federal power to create courts under section 104 of the *Constitution Act, 1867.*

- Federal legislation enacted pursuant to the federal power over "Indians and lands reserved for the Indians" under section 91(24) of the *Constitution Act, 1867.*

- Provincial legislation enacted pursuant to the Province's power over the administration of justice.

- Federal-Indian negotiations leading to a recognition of the right of Aboriginal people to establish and maintain Aboriginal courts as an aspect of the "existing treaty and aboriginal rights of the aboriginal peoples," as recognized and affirmed by section 35 of the *Constitution Act, 1982.*

- A constitutional amendment applicable only to the Province of Manitoba through joint resolutions passed by the provincial Legislature and the federal Parliament.

- Aboriginal legislation enacted by virtue of Aboriginal powers to legislate either under new or existing legislation such as the *Indian Act,* or pursuant to Aboriginal powers of self-government as currently found in section 35 of the *Constitution Act, 1982.*

The preferred option put forward by the Assembly of Chiefs stems from what they refer to as the "treaty-based" approach. The essence of their position is that in their treaties with the Crown, they had undertaken to respect and obey the laws of Canada, and, in turn, they believed that the Crown had undertaken to respect and obey their right to self-government:

> It is our collective interest in this country to help each other, as neighbours, in seeking and finding treaty justice for the Indian people. Our understanding of the treaties is that they did not alter the sovereign authority of the Indian tribes on matters of self-government, but did, in fact, recognize and affirm our sovereignty.

In Manitoba all the treaties, except Treaty 1, contain a provision that Aboriginal people will maintain peace and good order and that they will obey and abide by the law. This provision, contained in Treaties 2, 3, 4, 5 and 6, has not been the subject of treaty litigation to date. It reads as follows:

> The undersigned Chiefs, on their own behalf and on behalf of all other Indians inhabiting the tract within ceded, do hereby solemnly promise and engage to strictly observe this treaty and also to conduct and behave themselves as good and loyal subjects of Her Majesty The Queen. They promise and engage that they will in all respects obey and abide by the law, *that they will maintain peace and good order between each other and also between themselves and other tribes of Indians, and between themselves and others of Her Majesty's subjects, whether Indians or whites, now inhabiting or hereafter to inhabit any part of the said ceded tract,* or that they will not molest a person or property of any inhabitants of such ceded tract or the property of Her Majesty The Queen, or interfere with or trouble any person passing or travelling through the said tract or any part thereof, and *that they will aid and assist the officers of Her Majesty in bringing to justice and punishment any Aboriginal offending against the stipulations of this treaty or infringing the laws in force in the country so ceded.* [Our emphasis]

In interpreting the meaning of peace and good order, the First Nations rely on the position that a treaty did not diminish, but confirmed, their right to govern themselves as separate and distinct peoples. In that context, this provision, when given practical meaning and application, according to the First Nations of Manitoba at least, entails full jurisdiction to establish and maintain peace and good order:

- Between the Indians of the Indian tribe.

- Between Indian tribes of the same Indian nation.

- Between Indian tribes of different Indian nations.

- Between Indian tribes and Her Majesty's subjects, white or Indians, who reside on ceded land.

The chiefs went on to say in their presentation to us:

This provision recognizes the jurisdiction of the Indian tribes to bring to justice and punishment any Indian offending against the stipulations of this treaty or infringing the laws enforced in the country so ceded.

In asserting such jurisdiction, the Indian tribes who signed the treaties containing this provision are to further aid and assist the officers of Her Majesty in bringing to justice and punishment such Indian offenders. Such aid and assistance provided by the Indian tribes goes beyond the policing of their people, but involves a role for the Indian tribe in the administration of justice and punishment even on lands that have been ceded under treaty.

In Manitoba the First Nations interpret this provision of the treaty as recognition that our tribal sovereignty extends to the exercise of jurisdiction over Indian persons who violate the treaty and the laws that apply on ceded lands.

We regard this provision as only one element of the treaties that merely confirms the pre-existing authority to administer and maintain justice. Under this provision of the treaties, in respect to the breaches of laws that are enforced in the lands ceded, the Indian tribes retain authority to enforce such laws and to bring to justice and punishment such Indians who offended treaty and non-Indian laws outside of reserved Indian lands.

Our analysis leads us to conclude that the manner of resolution that appears to provide the greatest potential for the successful establishment of Aboriginal justice systems for both First Nations, Metis and Inuit peoples involves a process of trilateral negotiations, leading to an agreement that contains within it an express provision that the right to establish and maintain Aboriginal justice systems is an "existing treaty or aboriginal right" within the meaning of section 35 of the *Constitution Act, 1982*. Whether that leads ultimately to a constitutional provision does not deter us from our conclusion that the establishment of Aboriginal justice systems can, with effort and cooperation, be accomplished.

It is conceivable that negotiations could occur only between Aboriginal people and the federal government. However, in view of the current significant provincial role in the administration of justice, we suggest that it would be in the best interests of Aboriginal organizations to ensure that as Aboriginal justice systems are established and developed, provincial institutions be involved to avoid jurisdictional conflicts.

It seems logical to us that one of the concerns which Aboriginal groups will want to address with the provincial government in particular is the question of having the provincial justice system withdraw from particular areas of jurisdiction at the same pace as they are being assumed by Aboriginal justice systems.

Ultimately, the greatest security for Aboriginal justice systems is as an aspect of the constitutionally protected rights of Aboriginal people contained within section 35 of the *Constitution Act, 1982*.

Therefore, the substance of the negotiations should lead to a constitutional amendment of section 35 to include either "self-government" or "Aboriginal justice systems" clearly within the meaning of "aboriginal rights." We note that a constitutional amendment can be accomplished through the constitutional amending formula set out in section 38 of the Constitution, or by joint resolutions of the Manitoba Legislature and the Canadian Parliament. Either process would appear suitable from a legal perspective, although we recognize the problems inherent in a constitutional amendment that applies only to one province.

Obviously, the issues surrounding the appropriate basis for the establishment of Aboriginal justice systems are complex. The manner in which this issue is resolved, we believe, must be left to a process of negotiation among the parties, and to a process of implementation involving a monitoring and public reporting mechanism. We discuss how such a sensitive matter can best be implemented later in this report.

For the purposes of this discussion, we conclude that there are sufficient mechanisms and viable options available within Canadian law for the establishment of Aboriginal justice systems to be accomplished.

Structure

We have spoken deliberately throughout this part of the report about "Aboriginal justice systems" rather than "Aboriginal courts." That is because we believe that it is important that it be recognized that the approach that must be taken is a systemic one, and not one which deals with elements of the administration of justice in an isolated way. It is not appropriate to believe that one can provide an answer to the problems we have identified merely by establishing Aboriginal police programs, for example. Aboriginal and non-Aboriginal accused, arrested and charged by Aboriginal police officers, should appear in front of Aboriginal judges, in an Aboriginal court system controlled by Aboriginal people.

The important issue is that every component of the justice system operational within an Aboriginal community be controlled by Aboriginal people. That would include everything from police, to prosecutor, to court, to probation, to jails. Only by approaching the matter in a systemic, holistic manner can one safely conclude that improvements will, in fact, take place. To proceed in a piecemeal manner not only is unfair to Aboriginal people, but also to Manitoba society, because that will not bear the kinds of results to which Manitoba's Aboriginal and non-Aboriginal people are entitled.

Although many of our comments in this part are directed toward the manner in which an Aboriginal court would function, in other parts of this report we discuss how other elements of the justice system should be incorporated into an overall approach to the delivery of justice to Aboriginal people in Aboriginal communities.

The issue of how to constitute Aboriginal justice systems is a major one in Canada, as it must reflect the reality that confronts us. Individual Aboriginal communities here are not as large in terms of acreage and population as some in the United States. Many Aboriginal communities are far apart and isolated from larger centres. Travel often is expensive and subject to the vagaries of the weather. Human and financial resources are likely to be limited somewhat.

Without belabouring the point, it is fair to say that these facts and many others impinge upon how an Aboriginal justice system should be constructed. Some of them tend to foster the attractiveness of a local system so as to minimize travel expenses and delays in dispensing justice. The lack of personnel available within small communities and the smaller caseloads bespeak the opposite, favouring a circuit court system. The many complaints voiced during the public hearings of the Inquiry about circuit courts, from Aboriginal and non-Aboriginal people alike, do not, however, provide a ringing endorsement of that approach, by any means.

Another concern relates to the formality of the court system. While some critics in the U.S. have criticized the American Indian tribal court system for paying too little attention to due process and the rights of the accused, others have chastised it for being too formal and too similar to the American courts. Some Indian people have been particularly critical of its tendency to mirror the general system, rather than acting in a way more in keeping with traditional Aboriginal approaches.

WE RECOMMEND THAT:

- Wherever possible, Aboriginal justice systems look toward the development of culturally appropriate rules and processes which have as their aim the establishment of a less formalistic approach to courtroom procedures so that Aboriginal litigants are able to gain a degree of comfort from the proceedings while not compromising the rights of an accused charged with a criminal offence.

One final aspect must be mentioned, as well. That has to do with the fact that Aboriginal communities with different legal bases but virtually identical cultures often are located side by side. Many Metis communities are located adjacent to Indian reserves. Residents of such Metis communities often are related closely to those on the reserve. Some of the residents of those communities are status Indians pursuant to Bill C-31 who have chosen to continue to reside on the Metis side.

We endorse the principle that each and every distinct Aboriginal community be entitled to its own justice system. We also encourage Aboriginal communities which are located side by side, as we have mentioned, to work out joint justice-management agreements so that one Aboriginal justice system can operate in both communities. We are aware that, historically and politically, jointly managed programs between Indian and Metis organizations have not been created frequently. However, we can see no reason for that to have to continue, particularly where the inability to develop such a joint approach may result in one or the other or both communities being unable to sustain or establish a local system.

WE RECOMMEND THAT:

- Where Indian and Metis communities are located side by side, the leaders of the two communities give serious consideration to establishing a jointly managed Aboriginal justice system which serves both communities.

A Regional Model

In recognizing the right of Aboriginal people to establish and maintain their own justice systems, we conclude that that right resides within each and every properly constituted Aboriginal community pursuant to section 35 of the *Constitution Act, 1982.* However, if we simply left the matter at that, the possibility would occur of several dozen separate Aboriginal courts arising without coordination or in ways that duplicated costs and effort. We would like to address that aspect.

Certain Aboriginal communities will be of sufficient size to justify a resident judge of their own. Others, we believe, should share their court system with neighbouring Aboriginal communities. It would be advisable, however, that this be restricted to the same linguistic group.

In addition, rather than creating a circuit court that functions out of regional centres like Thompson and The Pas, the result should truly be a court that is shared, in all senses of the word. There are a variety of American examples to consider on this point. Some small Indian reservations in the U.S. contract with larger tribes nearby to obtain the use of the latter's judge, court clerk and prosecutor to provide a full-fledged court system on an as-needed basis.

Another approach is the regional court model in use in parts of Oklahoma and the northwestern United States, where a number of tribes join together to operate a court system under the control of a representative board of directors. The board hires the necessary personnel to provide court services to each community. The law that is followed, however, in all these situations is the law of each tribe.

It would be possible in Manitoba to follow this concept of a regional approach, as has been done with Indian child and family services agencies throughout the province, with the DOTC Police Force, with the various tribal councils in existence, and with the regional offices of the Manitoba Metis Federation. The regional approach to administration and program delivery is one that appears well founded in Manitoba's Aboriginal community.

In doing so, particular care would have to be paid to structuring regions that are neither too large, nor too small. In addition, the earlier caveats regarding linguistic similarities should be kept in mind in delineating the regions.

One attractive aspect to the regional court model, especially when it is used in conjunction with peacemaker courts, is the element of critical mass, or economies of scale. This approach ensures that there is sufficient workload to justify all the personnel that a court requires. It also means that there can be more than one judge appointed to the court. The American experience again demonstrates that most modest-size tribes have appointed at least two judges. This allows for the accommodation of the human inevitability of vacations, illness, resignations and deaths. It further permits judges to attend conferences and training sessions in rotation. It also allows a judge to withdraw from specific cases, due to personal reasons or a conflict of interest. Finally, it allows judges to specialize to some degree. Judges could be appointed on a part-time basis to achieve these objectives.

WE RECOMMEND THAT:

- In establishing Aboriginal justice systems, the Aboriginal people of Manitoba consider using a regional model patterned on the Northwest Intertribal Court System in the state of Washington.

Appellate Courts

Where the regional court consists of four or more judges, it would be possible to appeal the decision of a trial court judge to three of the remaining members sitting as a panel. Although some may frown on this approach, due to the close working relationship in this situation between the trial and the "appellate" judges, it is done extensively in the American Indian tribal courts. Only the Navajo and the Hopi appear to have full-time courts of appeal, although Indian tribes in South Dakota collectively have created an intertribal appellate court.[100]

The common law courts in the United Kingdom utilized this system for centuries. This would allow any applications for court orders or judicial reviews to be kept within the Aboriginal court system. Having a number of judges would reduce the likelihood of backlogs being created in caseloads.

Sharing the burden of office with colleagues also would be important on a personal level for judges and other court personnel. The pressures that will accompany this work will be enormous and the support of others who are experiencing the same thing will be vital to avoid the "burn-out" syndrome. It may assist judges further to share their ideas, information and expertise with each other when they meet.

In addition, the force of their numbers may foster greater awareness and respect for Aboriginal courts within the broader legal community in the province.

WE RECOMMEND THAT:

- Regional Aboriginal justice systems establish an independent and separate appeal process which makes use of either separate appeal judges or other judges of the Aboriginal system as judges of appeal.

Jurisdiction

An important issue when it comes to the administration of justice is always the issue of jurisdiction. There are three constituent elements to jurisdiction: territorial jurisdiction, jurisdiction over the person, and subject matter jurisdiction.

Each will be dealt with separately, as they raise distinct problems even though they also interact closely.

Territory

We begin with the principle that an Aboriginal court system should function within each Aboriginal community in Manitoba, be it an Indian reserve or a Metis community. This suggests to us that where there is a community of Aboriginal people with a self-declared and recognizable collective identity distinct from that of the non-Aboriginal people surrounding them, then their "collective right" to govern themselves in accordance with their customs and traditions exists, as well. Their distinctiveness as a community assumes that they also have a distinctive geographical area dedicated or available to them for their use, not necessarily on an exclusive basis.

Many Aboriginal communities do not "own" or have a legal claim over the land they occupy. Again, that should not necessarily affect their status as an identifiable Aboriginal community. While territorial ownership would resolve many problematic issues surrounding jurisdiction, it is not necessary, in our opinion, for Aboriginal communities to "own" or have a valid legal claim to the land they occupy in order to be identified as Aboriginal communities for purposes of establishing Aboriginal justice systems.

Many examples of this principle arise in Manitoba. Almost no Metis community in the province has valid legal title to the land it occupies, yet its existence as a Metis community cannot be doubted. St. Laurent, Camperville and Duck Bay are Metis communities as distinctive culturally and geographically as any Indian reserve or municipality, yet without a legally defined title to their land. South Indian Lake, for example, is a distinct Aboriginal community although it has no legal title to the land which it occupies.

In fact, this principle points out, if anything, one of the fallacies which surrounds Aboriginal affairs in this country—that a land base is a prerequisite to the exercise of Aboriginal rights. One does not need to own land in order to assert jurisdiction over it. Legal ownership of the land is not to be equated with jurisdiction over it. Conversely, jurisdiction over land is not dependent upon first obtaining ownership of it. Section 35 of the *Constitution Act, 1982*, in its recognition of treaty and Aboriginal rights, does not limit those rights to geographically defined territories.

The government's policy of equating legal title over land with jurisdiction over it, particularly by the Department of Indian Affairs, has been a source of much confusion. The provisions of the *Indian Act* dealing with surrenders of reserve land presume that the Indian interest in the land is one of ownership and not one of governance. The band's surrender of its own legal interest in the land in favour of another party should not mean that it loses legal jurisdiction over the land, or that it cannot continue to exercise governmental powers over it, as would a provincial government who sold Crown land to an individual.

The legal system's failure to recognize the difference between the Aboriginal peoples' separate and distinct positions as land owners and as land governors has given rise to much misunderstanding in legal and political circles. It is also that failure which has given rise to the assertion that Aboriginal self-government is tied up inextricably with Aboriginal ownership of the land, and that the latter is a *sine qua non* of Aboriginal self-determination.

It is probable that the relationship between Aboriginal ownership and Aboriginal jurisdiction arose because of our legal system's inability to accept that any entity other than the Crown could or should have an underlying title to land, different from or greater than the land's owner. In fact, while our law asserts that the underlying title to all land in the country is vested in the Crown, it is clear that what is meant by this "underlying title" is jurisdiction, and not ownership in the real property law sense.

It is in that sense of the term, therefore, that we must approach the issue of jurisdiction of Aboriginal courts. We cannot allow the issue to be decided simply by a determination of the question of "who owns the land." What must be asked is whether the Aboriginal community in question enjoys, on the land where it resides, a collective Aboriginal right to self-determination within or over it. If so, then it is a matter of defining the area over which the community has jurisdiction.

For First Nations, the question of territory is relatively clear. They have and would continue to have jurisdiction over the land included within their reserve. For Metis communities, we believe that a process of Metis-provincial negotiations will have to take place to identify the area over which an Aboriginal justice system operational within a Metis community will have jurisdiction. If a First Nation and an adjacent Metis community establish a jointly managed Aboriginal justice system, then the territorial jurisdiction of that system will include the territories of both Aboriginal communities.

Clearly, an Aboriginal justice system should have jurisdiction over matters and people within the geographical territory of the Aboriginal community it serves. Examining the geographical scope of an Aboriginal justice system does raise the question of whether it should have jurisdiction outside the Aboriginal community's boundaries or agreed-upon territory.

We have a long history of circumscribing the jurisdiction of courts through geographical means, such as with municipal courts in Quebec and county or district courts across most of the country. The courts of Canada, at present, generally are limited in their jurisdiction to considering only events that occur within the legal borders of their respective provinces or territories. However, there are matters over which a Canadian court has jurisdiction even if they occur outside the geographical boundaries of the country.

The jurisdiction within the boundaries of the community should be exclusive to the Aboriginal system, and there may be occasions when an Aboriginal system should be able to exercise jurisdiction over events or its citizenry outside its geographical boundaries.

The trend of registered Indians of moving to cities in search of employment, educational opportunities and better services is continuing and appears to be increasing. It is worth noting, as well, that a sizeable percentage of the Aboriginal inmate population has been incarcerated for crimes committed outside Aboriginal communities such as Indian reserves and that approximately one-half of all inmates were raised off-reserve.[101]

Person

Since the primary purpose underlying the establishment of a separate court system is to empower Aboriginal people to administer justice for themselves, it is obvious that the court should have authority regarding, at the least, Aboriginal litigants and offenders. Stating this basic premise, however, does not address the entire matter fully. The first issue that arises is whether the jurisdiction should be exclusive or concurrent. Although allowing people to have the maximum possible freedom of choice is attractive in principle, the effect of permitting litigants in all cases to be able to choose between the Aboriginal court and the regular provincial courts would encourage forum-shopping.

One might argue that an element of choice is a net benefit, as it will encourage the new court system to function efficiently and in a way that will encourage individuals to choose it over the status quo. The disadvantage of this approach likely would occur in criminal matters, as some Aboriginal communities have expressed complaints about the existing courts being too lenient and not imposing a form of punishment that both penalized the offender as well as encouraged a change from antisocial behaviour. It is quite possible, therefore, that some Aboriginal courts may reflect this sentiment in longer periods of incarceration or non-incarceral sentences that may be seen as imposing unattractive burdens.

It is our conclusion, nevertheless, that the jurisdiction over litigants and offenders for events arising within the territory of the court should be exclusive so as to eliminate any possible forum-shopping. Aboriginal courts will need the respect that emanates from exclusive jurisdiction and Aboriginal communities will want the certainty that their court system will not be avoided or ignored. This certainty will assist all parties in knowing precisely where and in which court the charge will be heard, or the case will be tried.

The situation of non-Aboriginal residents of Aboriginal lands may be different somewhat, as they do not share common cultural, linguistic and racial characteristics. On the other hand, if they have chosen to live, pass through or do business in an Aboriginal community, it can be assumed they recognize and accept its jurisdiction. It would not be cost-effective, especially in remote communities, to have the provincial courts be called upon to be responsible for the small number of non-Aboriginal people who are resident on reserves, or who are temporarily present when incidents occur that give rise to legal repercussions.

Although the provincial courts could be called upon to enforce the prevailing Canadian law in reference to non-Aboriginal people, this would generate unnecessary confusion as to the law that applied within the reserve and who would enforce it.

Dividing jurisdiction on racial grounds alone would engender complex jurisdictional and conflicts of laws questions when the event that gave rise to the litigation or the criminal charge involved both Aboriginal and non-Aboriginal parties. One clear lesson that can be learned from the American Indian tribal court experience is that the interjurisdictional quagmire prevalent there should be minimized, or avoided if at all possible.

Therefore, it would appear to be most efficacious and justifiable for Aboriginal justice systems to have exclusive, original jurisdiction over all persons when the event arises within the territorial limits of the court, regardless of the background or ancestry of the individual.

Probably the soundest reason for concluding that Aboriginal courts should have total jurisdiction over all persons, matters and offences within the geographical boundaries of the Aboriginal community is the fact that Aboriginal courts should not be considered subordinate to provincial courts. Clearly, they should not be seen as being under the jurisdiction or as being controlled by the orders of those courts. Jurisdictional neatness and a sense of propriety demand that Aboriginal courts be seen as being on a par with provincial courts in all respects.

WE RECOMMEND THAT:

■ All people, Aboriginal and non-Aboriginal, within the geographical boundaries of a reserve or Aboriginal community, be subject to the jurisdiction of the Aboriginal justice system in place within that community.

Subject Matter

The third prong of the judiciary's authority also contains the recurring issues of the first two categories of jurisdiction: on and off Aboriginal lands, and Aboriginal and non-Aboriginal litigants. It is readily conceivable that the subject matter jurisdiction could differ, based on both the background of the litigant and the location of the incident. The section 107 *Indian Act* justice of the peace system makes both distinctions. All persons who violate that Act, regardless of race, are within its jurisdiction. However, violations of the *Indian Act* are restricted almost entirely to events that occur on reserves, thereby in practice largely limiting this court to band members in other than highway traffic offences. The limited *Criminal Code* jurisdiction is not tied to the borders of the reserve, but is restricted solely to incidents involving status Indians or those entitled to be registered.

The American Indian tribal courts also possess similar variations in the subject matters they can handle, as a result of legislation passed by Congress and the jurisprudence of the federal courts. The U.S. tribal courts have criminal jurisdiction only over Indians who are members of the tribe, rather than all persons, as they do in civil matters arising within Indian Country.

On the other hand, the *Indian Child Welfare Act* of 1978 extends extraterritorial jurisdiction to tribal courts over child welfare matters involving tribal members outside Indian reservations. This applies not only where the apprehension of children has occurred off the reservation, but even where it occurs in another state.

Interestingly, proposals were before Congress in 1988 to expand this directed transfer of jurisdiction so as to apply as well to Canadian Aboriginal children, which would have resulted in Canadian Indians in the United States being dealt with in an Aboriginal court in Canada. The absence of Aboriginal courts was envisaged and the bill proposed that the case then would be referred to the relevant Indian government or Aboriginal organization where no Aboriginal court existed to accept jurisdiction.[102]

A further issue which requires resolution relates not to the field of law, but to the lawmaker. That is, whose law would an Aboriginal justice system in Canada apply? One obvious option is for the court to apply the existing law of the dominant society. An Australian scholar and barrister active in Aboriginal legal issues for a number of years, Bryan Keon-Cohen, framed the crucial questions raised through the alternatives posed by legal pluralism in this way:

> In assessing social activity and the resolution of disputes, whose standards are to be applied, those of the Aboriginal community involved, or those of the majority community? When assessing what is right or wrong, condoned or condemned, humane or inhumane, legal or illegal, or just or unjust, should one be ethnocentric and apply Western notions; should one attempt to see things as Aboriginal people see them and judge accordingly; should one have "a bet each way" according to circumstances; or is the only realistic approach to accept that you have no choice in the matter? These are intransigent problems, but they are vital, for once a stance is adopted, all else follows.[103]

The last decade has witnessed a growing realization by Canadians generally, as well as by the federal, provincial and territorial governments, that Aboriginal people should regain their right to govern themselves. A unanimous report by a parliamentary committee[104] advocated acceptance of Indian self-government and called for its implementation through administrative, legislative and constitutional means. That report specifically recommended that Indian First Nations receive authority to enact laws in a number of important areas, as well as to control their own justice systems.

Implicit within our recommendations is that the subject matter of the Indian justice system would consist, at least to a significant degree, of laws passed by the Indian governments. Although the Aboriginal constitutional conference process from 1983 to 1987 did not succeed in achieving sufficient support for a specific amendment on self-government, the first ministers who participated joined with Aboriginal and territorial leaders in endorsing the concept of Aboriginal self-government.

It would be, therefore, a regressive step to assert that the substantive law to be applied within Aboriginal communities by Aboriginal justice systems would come only from "foreign" sources. This approach would have the effect of undermining the limited and delegated spheres of law-making that are already in the hands of band councils.

WE RECOMMEND THAT:

- Aboriginal communities be entitled to enact their own criminal, civil and family laws and to have those laws enforced by their own justice systems. If they wish they should also have the right to adopt any federal or provincial law and to apply or enforce that as well.

- Aboriginal traditions and customs be the basis upon which Aboriginal laws and Aboriginal justice systems are built.

This would reflect an appreciation for the unique nature of Aboriginal cultures, as well as the desire of Indian, Inuit and Metis peoples to restore to their communities a sense of harmony and respect for the teachings of elders.

Using customary law as the foundation for a legal system is not uncommon. Several African countries, along with Papua New Guinea, have constitutional provisions declaring that traditional law will have this status.[105] Furthermore, the Canadian courts have given recognition, albeit quite sparingly, to the validity of Indian and Inuit customary law for well over a century.[106] Our courts have done so, however, by incorporating aspects of traditional law into the common law, and giving it legal force and effect as part of the common law when not in conflict with federal or provincial legislation.

What we suggest is in keeping with the function served by the common law. Just as the English common law forms the backbone of the Canadian legal system, and is supplemented, modified or even overturned by express constitutionally valid legislation, the customary law of the particular Aboriginal nation or group could function in the same way.[107]

Aboriginal customary law has not been fixed in some static sense, but, instead, has continued to evolve slowly to meet the changing needs, values and circumstances present within Aboriginal communities. It has retained, however, a respect for the ways of the past, while being concerned about the interests of generations yet to be born. This philosophical orientation toward law and life has much to offer as the underpinnings for a system dedicated to the pursuit of justice.

Traditional law, then, would be subject to alteration by those express laws which are designed to preclude its operation through fully occupying the field or containing explicit provisions that contradict customary law. Aboriginal justice systems would also be free to foster the development of traditional law by further elaborating its terms in a fashion equivalent to the common law. In doing so, they would be reflecting the changes that have occurred within the communities, since the rules that govern daily life are the substance of customary law.

Declaring that customary law would form a foundation for the Aboriginal justice system does not determine the precise legal parameters of such a system. "Aboriginal customary law" is merely a label that describes a source of law, rather than a particular branch or field of law. Its status is similar to the "common law," except that the latter emanates from the jurisprudence pronounced by the courts, while traditional law flows from the customs of the people, practised over generations. Each tribe or Aboriginal community, if it chose to codify its traditional laws, would have to be satisfied that a particular custom or practice passed down from generation to generation is of sufficient import to become so enshrined, but we believe that each Aboriginal community is capable of reaching that decision on its own. If it chose not to codify its traditional laws, it would have to rely on each judge to apply traditional law (or, more properly perhaps, "Aboriginal common law") as he or she understood it.

The customary law regimes of all Aboriginal nations in Canada with which we are familiar commonly contained rules that determined what constituted criminal activity, as well as appropriate sanctions for its infraction. Likewise, traditional law regulated marriage, divorce, adoption, responsibility to children, care for the elderly and infirm, private ownership of personal property, obligations to share food and other vital goods, hunting and fishing practices, inheritance of personalty, the mechanism of selecting leaders of the nations or government, and citizenship. Traditional law also dictated what was suitable behaviour regarding Mother Earth and all living things, which we might characterize in legal jargon as environmental protection and real property laws. The thrust of customary law, then, was to regulate interpersonal conflict, and to determine each person's position within the clan, membership in the community, participation in governmental structure, and the relationship with the natural environment in which he or she lived.[108]

This approach requires that these courts have civil, family and criminal jurisdiction. The authority would include, but not necessarily be limited to, the following areas (when framed in Canadian legal terminology):

- Criminal law including procedure.
- Family law including child welfare, adoption, marriage solemnization, divorce, child custody, guardianship and matrimonial property distribution.
- Real property relating to interests in Aboriginal lands such as rights of occupancy, usage, easements, natural resource development, lease and sale.
- Personalty including the law regarding gifting, barter and sale.
- Estates in terms of inheritance by will or intestacy.
- Harvesting of fish, game, waterfowl, fur-bearing animals, wild rice and other foods as well as renewable natural resources.
- Membership within the community.
- The election or selection of government leaders in accordance with the procedure established by the community.
- The recognition and enforcement of the traditional laws and customs of the tribe or Aboriginal community.
- Environmental protection and management.

- Civil jurisdiction including civil suits and the enforcement of contracts between band members, and between band members and non-band members where the contract or matter occurred in Aboriginal lands.

- The enforcement and recognition of orders of courts from other jurisdictions.

The foregoing list would be limited most easily to territory that is exclusively in Aboriginal hands, such as reserves administered under the *Indian Act*. To do so, however, would be unduly restrictive for two reasons. First, some of these matters naturally extend beyond the boundaries of any one community. For example, the beneficiaries under a will may live throughout the province or further afield. While parents normally may be domiciled on a reserve, they could temporarily be present or resident in a town when their children are in need of protection. Drawing the territorial boundaries too tightly could preclude the Aboriginal courts from having authority in many cases in which there is a clear and pressing community interest. Likewise, it might encourage a flood of litigation centring on disputes between Aboriginal courts and the general system over who has jurisdiction, as has occurred in the United States. This would be a considerable waste of time, talent, energy and precious resources. Therefore, all possible efforts should be taken to avoid a similar result in Canada. As mentioned earlier, restricting the courts to Aboriginal territory also would exclude off-reserve Aboriginal people entirely.

Adopting the principle of following customary law to delineate subject jurisdiction as an initial step would mean that this court system should also have a mandate in the criminal law sphere. In some ways this reflects the history of the section 107 *Indian Act* justice of the peace experience. It also meets the particular needs of Aboriginal peoples to help reduce the level of conflict that exists between the original peoples and Canadian criminal law.

Another factor that must be considered is the capacity of the community to handle all forms of crime. Indian and Metis communities usually are small, with most containing less than 1,000 people. Acts of violence like murder and sexual assault are naturally very stressful for many people within the extended family constellation of these communities, and not just for the immediate families of the victim and the offender.

The responsibility to prosecute and judge the offence within these small groupings might impose a greater burden than the communities can or wish to bear. Although agreements can be reached for sentences of incarceration to be served in federal and/or provincial penitentiaries, some communities still may prefer to avoid the anguish of having to deal with the more serious crimes and the possibility of long sentences. If this proves to be true, then Aboriginal governments may wish to relinquish authority over violent crimes. We say, however, that this should be a decision for each Aboriginal community to make.

If they choose to do so, such a decision suggests that a division of jurisdiction be constructed in which some of the current indictable offences would remain within the existing court system. A further variation would be to develop a list of offences that could fall within the concurrent jurisdiction of Aboriginal and provincial courts. This would mean that the Aboriginal system could decline jurisdiction either in specific cases or with respect to certain offences for a period of time, leaving those offences to be prosecuted in the existing system.

The Aboriginal court then would have full authority over all other criminal matters, while having the opportunity to expand its mandate over time to assume jurisdiction over the entirety of the list of concurrent offences, if it so chose. The important point to keep in mind is that it would be up to the Aboriginal people and their governments to make those decisions.

We suggest that in the area of criminal law, Aboriginal justice systems begin with jurisdiction over summary conviction matters, and then acquire jurisdiction over some indictable matters and, ultimately, all matters. In our opinion, that is the most workable way to stage in jurisdiction and to enable the Aboriginal systems to become established.

Urban and Non-Aboriginal Communities

In considering the question of urban Aboriginal people, we recognize that the approach to Aboriginal justice inside and outside Aboriginal communities cannot be identical. That is, one must anticipate the creation of one type of Aboriginal justice approach in Aboriginal communities, and a different approach in urban and non-Aboriginal areas. On the other hand, as it is within the existing system, there likely will be situations where the court within an Aboriginal community should be able to have jurisdiction in a case involving a matter that occurs or arises elsewhere.

WE RECOMMEND THAT:

- The jurisdiction of Aboriginal courts within Aboriginal lands be clear and paramount, and that in appropriate cases Aboriginal courts be recognized as having jurisdiction over some matters arising in places other than the Aboriginal community, such as:

  - Child welfare cases in which the domicile of the child is the Aboriginal community over which the court has jurisdiction.

  - Cases in which a member of an Aboriginal community breaches the laws of his or her community, such as where a First Nation member hunts in a manner that is contrary to a First Nation law or regulation enacted by the government of that First Nation.

  - Cases in which an individual has breached a law of the Aboriginal community and has left the community to avoid detection or responsibility.

  - Civil matters in which the parties have agreed to submit the matter to an Aboriginal court for determination.

Within their borders, the Aboriginal courts must have exclusive, original jurisdiction so as to avoid forum-shopping by litigants, to reduce the potential impact of possibly contradictory rulings between the Aboriginal and provincial courts, and to give proper recognition to the stature and importance of the new system.

At the same time, different, alternative approaches must be established in non-Aboriginal communities where the numbers of Aboriginal residents are sufficiently large. In this situation, the approach can involve alternative dispute resolution mechanisms and alternative measures attached to the existing court system, which take into account, or are based upon, the cultures of Aboriginal people.

The development of an Aboriginal alternative measures component of an existing non-Aboriginal justice system could include the development of a peacemaker program supervised by judges of Manitoba's courts. In criminal, family and property disputes, where the parties are willing, they could agree to bring the complaint before a peacemaker, rather than initiating formal judicial proceedings. The peacemaker, who would have quasi-judicial status, would become seized of the case through the consent of the parties and would attempt to fashion a mutually acceptable resolution in accordance with provincial or federal law. Failure to reach agreement still would leave the parties able to pursue their civil remedies or proceed on the criminal charge in the existing system.

It also would be possible for the parties to agree to vest in the peacemaker the power to render binding decisions when mediation is unsuccessful. In this way, the peacemaker would change roles after the mediation stage and become an adjudicator, not unlike the very common way of resolving commercial and labour relations disputes. Drawing upon the employer-employee collective bargaining experience, the authority of the peacemaker, when acting as an adjudicator, could be clarified further through court rules or legislation.

Where the parties agree, the peacemaker could have the power to subpoena witnesses, to apply Aboriginal custom, and to render decisions that would be binding on the parties and that could be enforced as an order of the court. This variation could be especially attractive in the off-reserve context where the parties wish to avoid protracted and expensive litigation, yet are unable to reach consensus on an acceptable outcome through the intervention of the peacemaker as mediator.

The territorial jurisdiction for Aboriginal courts on lands declared to be for the use and benefit of individual First Nations, or for the Metis if that occurs in the future, is also not quite as clear-cut as it might appear on first impression. The *Indian Act* has allowed, and some might suggest it has fostered, the surrender of reserve lands to the Crown for alienation to non-Indians. It clearly is possible for this land to be considered as falling within the territorial jurisdiction of this special court system. On the other hand, non-Indian land users may assert that they would suffer a disadvantage if they were compelled to rely upon the Aboriginal justice system, rather than upon the provincial courts, as they would be a minority in the former, would not understand its underlying values or its substantive law, and would have no control over the government that operates the court. In other words, ironically, non-Indians might complain that this would put them in the same situation as Aboriginal people have been in relation to the Canadian legal system since the latter was imposed upon the original inhabitants of this land more than a century ago.

As is the case with those who move to another country, one could well assert that such people have emigrated to another legal regime to which they agree to be subject. That would appear to be the most logical and reasonable response to that issue.

Therefore, we conclude that all land totally surrounded by the external boundaries of an Indian reserve, whether included within the legal definition of the reserve or not, should be within the exclusive jurisdiction of the Aboriginal court in the following circumstances:

- Where surrendered land that was once part of an Indian reserve has been conditionally surrendered under the *Indian Act* for leasing purposes.[109]

- Where land within an Indian reserve has been leased or is subject to a certificate of possession or occupation without a surrender under the *Indian Act*.

- Where land within the external boundaries of an Indian reserve was unconditionally surrendered or conditionally surrendered for sale but never sold, such that it remains subject to an underlying Indian interest under the *Indian Act*.

- Where land within the external boundaries or contiguous to an Indian reserve was purchased in fee simple by the band, but has not received reserve status under the *Indian Act*.

- Where land within the external boundaries of an Indian reserve was formerly reserve land and remains surrounded by reserve land such that access is only possible through the reserve.[110]

- Where the land continues to be reserve land whether held for the benefit of the band as a whole or through allotments to individual band members.

WE RECOMMEND THAT:

- The Manitoba Metis Federation and the government of Manitoba establish a forum of elected and technical representatives with a mandate to identify those Metis communities in the province where Metis justice systems can be established.

- Metis communities that are identified as such by agreement of the Manitoba Metis Federation and the government of Manitoba be defined geographically through negotiations between the government of Manitoba and the Metis people of each community for the purpose of establishing a Metis justice system.

- The presence of non-Aboriginal people within a Metis community should not prevent the community from being declared a Metis community, and the legitimate concerns of that minority should be respected.

- If, and to the extent, that juries are a part of Aboriginal justice systems, jury selection processes be implemented which permit non-Aboriginal persons to sit on juries, provided they comply with appropriate residential criteria established by the community.

Court Facilities

Courts already function in remote areas of Canada in conditions that differ dramatically from the oak-panelled courthouses of the cities. The fact that court is conducted in legion halls, laundromats, schools, gymnasiums, restaurants, community centres and the like may make the dispensation of justice more uncomfortable but not less fair. However, a suitable courtroom should be created in each community, along with an office to serve as the judge's chambers and another to function as an interview room for clients with their counsel. In those communities with a resident court, there also will be a need for office space for the rest of the personnel (i.e., court clerk and prosecutor at a minimum as well as the staff defender if there is one). The accommodation does not have to be plush or immense to fulfil this need. As well, the possibility exists for the court or justice facility to be part of a larger complex, such as a band or community council office building. As a result, the capital cost does not have to be prohibitive and should be able to be readily met.

Personnel

Judges

The first issue that arises is eligibility for appointment to the bench. If a law degree and membership in the Law Society is a precondition, then very few Aboriginal people in the province would be eligible for selection. This would mean that most of the judges, in what is intended to be an Aboriginal justice system, would be non-Aboriginal lawyers. This is hardly a satisfactory result, even on a transitional basis.

Communities could develop the standards that they believe are appropriate. These include minimum age, literacy level, language fluency (e.g., English and the Aboriginal language of the region), familiarity with traditional law, as well as suitable personal characteristics. Operating a short, intensive training course for Aboriginal applicants could be utilized as a screening process so that only candidates who successfully complete the program would be eligible for appointment to the bench.

A different strategy is to require prior experience in the legal system as a constable, court communicator or paralegal. The Americans have largely opted for having no official eligibility criteria and many judges have to learn on the job after their appointment. It would seem to be preferable, particularly in the complete absence of any experienced judges available as mentors, to favour a somewhat more rigorous approach.

THE JUSTICE SYSTEM AND ABORIGINAL PEOPLE

There will still need to be a conscious effort devoted to developing training programs for the new judges. The Canadian Judicial Centre, the Centre for the Administration of Justice, the Western Judicial Education Centre and the provincial court judges' associations all operate their own training sessions in recognition that even senior judges are in need of refreshers and of exposure to recent developments in the law. The same will hold true for any Aboriginal court judges who do not have a full legal education and likely will be more isolated from law libraries and experienced counsel.

Therefore, a special intensive program tailored specifically for these judges, that includes an overview of the relevant legal system, as well as basic criminal and civil law programs, should be regularly available with videotaped materials provided to all judges for their own personal use, both before and after training sessions. Videotapes and written materials should be provided to all judges upon their appointment.

As the American Indian tribal court experience demonstrates, there will be a need for periodic training sessions of a more advanced nature so that Aboriginal judges are able to continue their education. This would also provide an opportunity for Aboriginal court judges to meet together to share their experiences. An independent body under Aboriginal control should offer this service in collaboration with existing judicial education programs. Aboriginal judges, we are sure, will want to draw upon each other's experience and expertise, as well. In another part of the report we recommend the establishment of an Aboriginal Justice College. That institution might deal best with Aboriginal judicial education.

A selection process will have to be determined. Many American tribes have opted for the electoral approach, which would be in keeping with the way a large number of First Nations choose their chiefs and councillors.

On the other hand, electing judges is neither the traditional Aboriginal nor Canadian way. It might leave judges vulnerable to local pressures from voters, or at least with a reasonable apprehension of such susceptibility. If an appointment is to be made, then one obvious choice is for it to emanate from a suitably representative Aboriginal organization. If our recommendation of an intertribal system is adopted, the system's board of directors could seek out and appoint judges.

Another factor to consider is tenure. American tribal courts are plagued continually by high turnover, induced, in part, by the relatively short terms in office that are common. This result should be avoided, and especially so in the early days of a new court system. On the other hand, it will be hard to predict how Aboriginal people in Canada will enjoy this position and how they will perform in office. Some American tribes have developed a probationary scheme in which the judges initially receive a short-term appointment of one or two years. If their performance is found to be satisfactory, then they are confirmed in office for a longer period (e.g., 10 years or life). We would suggest this approach be tried.

A further common problem with tribal courts in the United States has been the rather poor remuneration. While the inclination will be to establish a salary scale different from that associated with the general court system, every effort should be made to avoid that. Judicial independence and status demand that there be some consistent recognition of the importance that we place on the position of the judiciary in our society.

We recognize once again that the matter will have to be left to each Aboriginal community to resolve, but Aboriginal communities should be forewarned that judicial independence is essential to the operation of a court system and salaries should be paid which will allow judges to be free to devote their full time and effort to their judicial functions.

Therefore, the salary of a judge should be commensurate with the position. As well, a judge should be entitled to a full benefits package, including a pension plan, so that the position truly can become a career.

One aspect of this issue is civil liability. Aboriginal judges should be as free from liability as are other judicial officers within existing systems. This naturally follows upon the principle that members of the judiciary require freedom from liability so that they may exercise their authority without fear or favour. Judges require protection from unwarranted attacks by disgruntled litigants.

There must be, however, a *quid pro quo* to this exemption. That is, there will need to be a public complaint mechanism whereby allegations of improper judicial behaviour can be raised and pursued. The Aboriginal Judicial Council could be accorded the capacity and authority to meet this objective. As with the Canadian Judicial Council, it would be preferable that this council merely investigate and report with its recommendations, rather than be empowered to dismiss the offending judge itself. Therefore, the group making the initial appointment would receive a report and recommendation, and be free to adopt, alter or reject it.

WE RECOMMEND THAT:

- Aboriginal judges be exempt from all civil liability in reference to actions or omissions while in the exercise of their judicial capacity.

- Through appropriate Aboriginal legislation, an Aboriginal Judicial Council be established to which any person can complain of judicial misconduct on the part of an Aboriginal judicial officer.

- The same principles of judicial conduct be applied to Aboriginal judges as apply to other members of the judiciary.

Administrative Staff

Aboriginal courts will need staff in order to function. Court staff will be necessary to manage the court office, operate recording devices during proceedings, prepare case dockets, dispense court forms, keep court files and records, provide summary explanations of the court system, assist parties to complete court forms properly, prepare court orders for signature and generally manage the court. Police, probation and parole officers also will be required.

Lawyers

Aboriginal justice systems will require personnel to prosecute criminal charges. These could be either lawyers or paralegals. If the system depends upon paralegals to do this work, then lawyers will have to be engaged, we suspect, to assist them, or people with some legal experience will have to be sought.

There also will be a need for defence counsel. We suggest that as a general principle, Aboriginal courts permit any person with whom an accused feels comfortable to represent the accused. Appearing by agent is already permitted in summary conviction matters in our courts, but it could be expanded to permit such representation for all matters. Presumably, Aboriginal courts will also wish to permit non-Aboriginal lawyers to assist their citizens.

It is important to reduce the likelihood of Aboriginal courts becoming too similar to the general regime, both in terms of style as well as in the substance of the law, so as to become distant from the communities that they are created to serve. This can be minimized by fostering the development of Aboriginal paralegals with full rights of appearance akin to the tribal advocates in the United States. The experience in the American tribal court system has been that Aboriginal people who have worked in a variety of fields outside their reservations have been attracted to return to their home communities to seek judicial appointment, or to work in some capacity within the tribal court system. We believe that we would see a similar trend in Manitoba. We believe that there are a variety of well-qualified Aboriginal people who are available to fill the various personnel positions that will become available.

As to any alleged misconduct on the part of a prosecutor or a defender, judges of the Aboriginal courts could be authorized to discipline any prosecutor or defence counsel who appears in this system. The appropriate chief judge of an Aboriginal court could sanction counsel financially for improper or unprofessional conduct, or suspend the person's right to practise in that court.

Resources

Aboriginal courts will require financial resources in addition to human resources. A few may be able to become self-sufficient in a sense by providing enough revenue through the imposition of fines and court costs to cover the budgetary needs of the courts. Nevertheless, this is unlikely for the vast majority of Aboriginal communities. Furthermore, it is inappropriate to place this burden on a court system, as it creates the image that there is a personal incentive for the judge to make use of heavy fines as a sentencing option rather than other alternatives, so as to pay for his or her salary. This is not an image that should be fostered.

Therefore, a budget is required of sufficient magnitude to meet salaries, office costs, travel expenses and training needs. The overwhelming majority of First Nations and other Aboriginal groups simply do not at present have this capacity from internal revenue. Therefore, if Aboriginal courts are to become a reality, there will need to be a system of transfer payments between federal and provincial governments and Aboriginal systems.

The financial responsibility appears to be a joint one between those two levels of government, as we see it. The federal government has constitutional jurisdiction for Indian, Inuit and Metis people. The Province has constitutional responsibility for the administration of justice. Both have a fiduciary obligation to Aboriginal people.[111]

It is a fair assumption that creating Aboriginal courts will lead to significant reductions in caseloads within the provincial system which, when combined with the elimination of the need to continue providing court services in Aboriginal communities, should translate into noticeable cost savings to the Province, which it can pass along to the Aboriginal systems.

The *Charter of Rights and Freedoms*

One of the major challenges that will confront the establishment of an Aboriginal justice system in Canada is resolving the tension between individual and collective rights. The bias of the common law system in favour of the concept of due process and regard for the rights of the individual has been buttressed in recent decades by the Canadian *Bill of Rights* and the *Charter of Rights and Freedoms*. It is natural to ask whether the *Charter* would apply in an Aboriginal court.

The answer is unclear because it depends, in part, on how the Aboriginal courts are created. If they were to be established or recognized by federal or provincial legislation, or some combination thereof, then that legislation would be subject, of course, to the *Charter*. If the new court system is a function of the "existing aboriginal and treaty rights of the aboriginal peoples of Canada" within the meaning of subsection 35(1) of the *Constitution Act, 1982*, then the courts would be outside *Charter* scrutiny, as the foundation for the courts would emanate from Part II (i.e., section 35) of the Constitution rather than Part I (i.e., the *Charter of Rights and Freedoms*).

In addition, section 25 of the *Charter* is designed to serve as a shield for "aboriginal, treaty or other rights and freedoms of the aboriginal peoples" from any challenge based on the *Charter*. It should be noted, however, that the *Charter*'s concern with sexual discrimination is adhered to as an amendment to section 35 which came into force in 1984, guaranteeing all Aboriginal and treaty rights "equally to male and female persons." (35(4))

What may be more important than the application of the *Charter* to the court system itself is the relevance of the *Charter* to the law administered by these new courts. Here again, the current state of the jurisprudence is unclear. Where the law being applied is a by-law enacted pursuant to sections 81, 83 or 85.1 of the *Indian Act*, one would presume that the *Charter* would apply from the beginning, as this would represent the exercise of powers delegated by Parliament to a subordinate government. Not only does subsection 32(1) of the *Charter* make it clear that it applies to all federal legislation, thereby including the *Indian Act* and any regulations or by-laws passed pursuant to it, but the courts also have been interpreting this provision broadly so as to apply it to a wide range of entities exercising statutory powers, such as municipalities, school boards, universities and administrative tribunals. Section 25 might mean, however, that some of these laws cannot be challenged for certain reasons, such as distinguishing on the basis of race contrary to subsection 15(1).

The situation could well be different, however, where the law has been enacted by virtue of a sovereign power held by an Aboriginal government. This point reflects the debate vigorously raised by Aboriginal organizations since 1983 that they already possess a right of self-government, or self-determination, by virtue of their inherent sovereign status since time immemorial, and that this right now is protected by section 35. The so-called "full box" argument has received considerable support by the recent decision of the Supreme Court of Canada in the *Sparrow* case.[112]

One can reasonably expect the matter to continue to receive the attention of courts in the future. It is not possible at this time to predict the outcome of future cases. It can be said, though, that if the Canadian courts conclude that exercising legislative powers over internal matters is an Aboriginal or treaty right, creating a result analogous to the domestic dependent nationhood status of Indian tribes in the United States, then it would follow logically that the laws so enacted are outside the *Charter*, just as American Indian tribal law is unaffected by the American *Bill of Rights*.

A related issue is the position of the traditional or customary law of the Aboriginal nations that could be applied by this new court system. Aboriginal courts must be free to establish and develop their own rules and procedures in a way that is culturally compatible with their history and community. To do so they will have to draw upon their traditions and customs. Their situation is akin to the common law. What if there were a conflict between a particular customary law and the *Charter*?

For example, the *Charter* in paragraph 11(c) guarantees that an alleged offender is not a compellable witness in proceedings against himself or herself. This may conflict with some traditional laws that expect people to answer the complaints that have been lodged against them as part of the process of finding the truth and of healing the conflict within the community. Upholding the *Charter* principle of protecting the individual's rights could well be seen as violating the more accepted and long-standing primary law of that nation.

If traditional law is also viewed as part of Aboriginal and treaty rights, then it could gain the same exemption previously discussed regarding the import of sections 25 and 35 of the *Constitution Act, 1982*. Furthermore, if the Aboriginal court were to choose the *Charter* over the customary law of the people, the judiciary might find itself in the position of operating contrary to the spirit and rationale underlying the establishment of the court in the first place.

This issue is not a simple one, particularly as a growing number of Aboriginal people have come to accept the attractions of an emphasis on individual rights and liberties.

In addressing this issue before the Inquiry, the Assembly of Manitoba Chiefs stated:

> The *Charter of Rights and Freedoms* is a recent measure, but an old concept. Furthermore, it contains some universally recognized principles that should never be violated by any government.

> If we as First Nations espouse our self-determination, we realize and accept responsibilities and obligations that accompanies that maturity. We can assure

you that we are not displeased by the prospect that we have to accommodate basic and fundamental rights and freedoms within an Aboriginal justice system.

It is important to remember that traditional systems of justice have not been based on the adversarial approach to arrive at this position. We believe that the adversarial approach does put rights and freedoms at risk.

There is likely less danger of rights violations in a system that has a mediation orientation. The decision by individual communities as to the nature of our system of justice will determine how extensive and specific the elaboration and observation of rights shall be.

We started this particular discussion on the *Charter* by pointing out how recent it really is. No meaningful consideration has taken place of the significance of section 25 of the *Charter,* which many writers and interested observers have described as a shield against potential prejudice that may be visited upon the collective interest of Aboriginal people.

If indeed that was the intent, we would have to say that any attempt by federal or provincial authorities to extract a promise by Aboriginal peoples, that we would ensure full compliance by Aboriginal justice systems of the *Charter of Rights and Freedoms,* would amount to nothing less than blackmail and hypocrisy.

The reality is federal and provincial authorities have two important shields of their own against the prospect that the *Charter* will completely handcuff their power and procedures.

The very first section of the *Charter* subjects all of the rights and freedoms enumerated thereunder to reasonable limitations as may be determined in the interests of Canadian society. As well, the notwithstanding clause appearing as Section 33, is a complete and powerful tool for government to utilize as they so choose.

We would again close our commentary on this part by cautioning those concerned against presuming that accommodation with respect to the *Charter* would not be forthcoming from an Aboriginal justice system.

A preferable resolution would be to seriously examine the position raised by the national Aboriginal organizations from time to time during the Aboriginal constitutional reform process from 1982 to 1987, of developing an Aboriginal Charter of Rights and Freedoms. That is, to create a tailor-made Charter that incorporates only those fundamental freedoms and civil liberties that do not violate the beliefs and paramount collective rights of the Aboriginal peoples. We would suggest that there is a need to explore the American experience in this regard so as to avoid some of the difficulties that have been created by the imposition of the *Indian Civil Rights Act* and to realize that there would be significant resource implications for Aboriginal justice systems.

Aboriginal governments would be well advised to give this matter careful consideration as part of the exercise of establishing their own court system. They may wish to consider enacting their own bill of rights and human rights laws to forestall external intervention and to address the valid interests that may be voiced by their own constituents. This would be a strategy in keeping with the objective of Aboriginal self-determination, while also responding to the concerns that likely will be expressed by the broader Canadian population. This is an especially meaningful issue in those Aboriginal communities that contain a number of non-Aboriginal residents and employees who will be worried about how this system and its laws will affect them.

WE RECOMMEND THAT:

- First Nation governments draft a charter of rights and freedoms which reflects Aboriginal customs and values.

Conclusion

There is no question in our minds that jurisdiction to operate a court system should be accorded to Aboriginal people. The extent of jurisdiction initially should be a matter of decision by each community, and then should be a matter of negotiation and legislation with the federal and provincial governments. Most Aboriginal communities probably would wish to deal initially with a limited number of matters and to progress at their own pace. We encourage that thinking, particularly in light of the inexperience prevalent within Aboriginal communities.

We believe that incremental changes in the justice system cannot adequately address the problems that exist. We believe that the establishment of Aboriginal justice systems is the only appropriate response to the systemic problems inherent in the existing system that have given rise to extraordinarily high rates of Aboriginal people in the courts and in jail in recent years. It offers the logic of redressing in a significant way the wrongs inflicted on Aboriginal people by a foreign, unknowledgeable and insensitive system.

We believe an Aboriginal justice system will deal with legal matters affecting Aboriginal people in more appropriate ways. We are convinced the result will be of substantial benefit not only to Aboriginal people, but to all Manitobans.

PUBLIC INQUIRY INTO
THE ADMINISTRATION
OF JUSTICE AND
ABORIGINAL PEOPLE

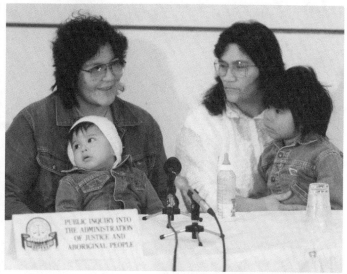

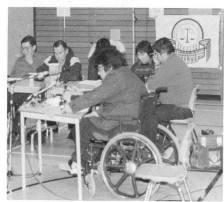

CHAPTER 8

———

COURT REFORM

Introduction

The previous chapters have outlined the problems Aboriginal people experience in their dealings with the court system in Manitoba and have recommended the creation of an Aboriginal justice system. This will be a major initiative and unless it goes forward, the problems of inequality and injustice will continue to plague our justice system.

However, the creation of such a system must be supplemented by other reforms, since many Aboriginal people do not live in communities that will have an Aboriginal justice system—the most obvious of these communities being the city of Winnipeg. As well, we recognize that there will be a period of transition before Aboriginal justice systems achieve the full jurisdiction that we anticipate they will assume.

We are recommending a series of reforms to the existing court system. In some cases, such as the improvement of circuit court services, these reforms should be seen as transitional steps to Aboriginal justice systems. As a result, all staff people hired to implement those steps should be selected with the involvement of the communities in which they will be working, and with the anticipation of an Aboriginal system.

Other reforms are more far-reaching and will have a more permanent impact on the courts. These include the amalgamation of the Court of Queen's Bench and Provincial Court of Manitoba, the elimination of preliminary inquiries and the adoption of time limits for case processing. These recommendations are intended to alleviate or eliminate a variety of problems facing Aboriginal people in their dealings with the court system.

These problems include a lack of access to the full range of court services in all parts of the province, delay in the court system and the excessive amount of pre-trial detention.

In making these recommendations for reform, we are guided by three over-arching goals:

- To create a court system which is fully responsive to the needs of the many different communities in Manitoba.

- To improve Aboriginal people's access to the full range of Manitoba court services.

- To reduce and eliminate delays that are present in Manitoba's court system.

We believe that the reforms we are recommending to fulfil these goals will benefit not only Aboriginal people, but all Manitobans. We believe too that a responsive, accessible and speedy court system will also be one which is less complex and easier for all Manitobans to understand.

We will discuss our vision of a reformed court system in terms of structure, services and personnel. Before it is possible to discuss these changes, it is necessary to review the existing court structure.

Changes to Court Structure and Administration

The Problems with the Current System

As we observed in our chapter on the current court system in Manitoba, the courts deliver their services to Aboriginal people in a complex and inadequate manner. This complexity and lack of equal accessibility arise from a number of causes: the fact that the courts are a product of a federal system that by its nature creates overlapping jurisdictions; the fact that there are three different classifications of criminal offences, with differing procedures for each; and the fact that a number of choices are available to people using the courts.

The existence of two levels of courts has created a number of problems, but none is more disturbing than the lack of equal access to judicial services throughout the province. As we noted earlier, there are a number of matters which can only be dealt with by the Court of Queen's Bench. These include, to name only a few, murder charges, civil actions, divorces and applications for injunctions to restrain abusers from entering another's property. Very few communities in Manitoba have enough of these matters requiring attention at any one time to justify the cost of a sitting of the Queen's Bench, which means that court never sits in most communities. Many people who appeared before us asked for civil law services in their communities. Others asked that the unified Family Court, with its specialized services, be made available to them. We believe that, however it be accomplished, all Manitobans, wherever they live, are entitled to better, more uniform and speedier court services. Some substantial changes will have to be made to bring that about.

The courts make crucial decisions about the lives of Manitobans. They deal with civil, criminal, family and youth matters. In civil law alone, suits involve everything from personal injury and contracts, to labour law, to landlord and tenant disputes, to the review of decisions of administrative tribunals. The fact is that these services are not available in Aboriginal communities. As a result of the limited services available to them, many Aboriginal people refrain from commencing legal proceedings they would initiate if the courts were more accessible.

Trials in serious criminal matters now take place in urban centres which are often a great distance from the community where the parties live and where the problem developed. Juries hearing such matters are often made up of people with no connection to the community where the offence took place. All this serves to further alienate Aboriginal people from the justice system. Members of those communities also feel particularly disadvantaged by what they consider to be a foreign system which has been imposed upon them.

At the present time, court services in remote communities are provided by the Provincial Court, and deal almost exclusively with a limited number of criminal and family matters. The Provincial Court is also the only court that attends in smaller rural centres, on a circuit basis. No jury or other Queen's Bench sittings are held in any Aboriginal community. No court services dealing with civil law matters are provided.

There is no question in our minds that people in remote and rural communities believe they now receive second-class court services. They are aware that there are matters the circuiting Provincial Court judge has no power to deal with. They are told that on a regular basis. The fact that the Court of Queen's Bench is known as a *superior* court and the Provincial Court as an *inferior* court reinforces the general impression among all Manitobans that there is a hierarchy of courts in the province and that one is more important than the other. Most people do not appreciate that the terms are technical ones, referring to the extent of jurisdiction. We, of course, do not share the belief that one court is more important than another, but the public perception remains. An unfortunate consequence of the present levels of service is that many Aboriginal people believe they are receiving an inferior level of justice. They are certainly receiving a lesser level of service than those who live in larger centres.

In the cities where the Court of Queen's Bench does hold regular sittings, the Provincial Court also sits, and the litigant must understand the rules and procedures of each to know where certain legal services are available. In criminal matters in these places, both courts are often involved. If an accused elects to have a trial in the Queen's Bench, a preliminary inquiry must first be held in the Provincial Court, a transcript of the evidence must be awaited and, if it is a jury trial, the date of the next assize must be awaited. Hearings in both courts may be necessary to determine where a young offender is to be tried.

The manner in which the courts now operate also separates different parts of the system that should be working more closely together. In other chapters we recommend that the Youth Court and child welfare systems should work more closely together. This cannot be done at the court level in places like Winnipeg and Brandon, where all child welfare cases are heard in the Queen's Bench and all prosecutions under the *Young Offenders Act* are heard in the Provincial Court. If the two services are to be better coordinated, it is essential that the same coordination apply at the court level.

Family law in the Winnipeg and Brandon areas is now handled solely by the Family Division of the Queen's Bench, but the service to families is incomplete. Although alleged abuse is an important factor in family cases dealing with the custody or guardianship of children, if there is a criminal charge laid against one party, that part of the family problem has to be heard by either the Provincial Court or the General Division of the Queen's Bench. In our opinion, all these matters should be in one court, with mediation, counselling and social services available to it.

The existence of two levels of courts makes it possible for accused individuals to transfer cases at various points in the court process, and creates what one observer has called a "natural mechanism for delay."[1] Indeed, a multicourt system almost invites manipulation on the part of some lawyers or parties who see some advantage in either bringing a trial on quickly or delaying it as long as possible. When a case is shifted from one court to another, there is a tremendous duplication of paperwork, as one set of files must be closed and another opened. More significantly, a switch of courts generally creates a three- or four-month delay in the case getting to trial.

At a time when there is obviously a demand and need for increased judicial service throughout the province, the present system continues antiquated practices that result in the under-utilization of the judiciary. Judges of the Provincial Court have to preside over preliminary inquiries that are little more than discovery procedures. Along with the elimination of the preliminary inquiry that we recommend elsewhere, a single court would release these judges for other duties. We believe there likely are sufficient judges now in Manitoba, if properly deployed, to provide the additional services that are required.

A New Trial Court

One possible solution to providing more equal court services throughout the province would be to have the Court of Queen's Bench sit in the same communities as the Provincial Court. While this would provide the needed court services, it would do so only by exacerbating the other problems of cost, complexity and inefficiency that we have identified. A unified criminal court has been called for in some circles. This measure, however, would not meet our concern to have a full range of civil and family services made available.

We have come to the conclusion that the only way in which a full range of civil, criminal and family services can be delivered to all residents of the province in an efficient manner is to have every judge able to deal with any kind of case.

One way to enable judges to deliver a full range of judicial service throughout the province would be to extend to the existing Provincial Court judges all the jurisdiction the judges of the Queen's Bench now have, and to extend to the existing Queen's Bench judges all the jurisdiction now held exclusively by the Provincial Court judges. The best way to bring this about is to create a new court by the amalgamation of the Provincial Court and the Court of Queen's Bench.

The concept of the amalgamation of courts is not new. In 1984 the county courts were amalgamated with the Court of Queen's Bench in Manitoba. The same process has now been completed in all but one of the provinces of Canada. Specialty courts also have been developed in Manitoba. The Provincial Court is designated as the Youth Court. It also has a special abuse section. In 1983 a Family Division was created within the Queen's Bench as a unified family court, and in 1989 it was expanded and now sits in those centres where the rest of the Queen's Bench regularly sits.

In 1989 the Attorney General of Ontario proposed the amalgamation of the courts in that province. The first stage of that proposal is now in place with the creation of the Ontario Court of Justice, which has replaced the former county and district courts and the High Court of the Supreme Court of Ontario. The second stage is to bring the provincial courts into the new court.

We suggest that a new court be created in Manitoba that might be called the Manitoba Trial Court, a new name which we think would give the public a clear indication of the work of the court. This court should be created as a superior court with full jurisdiction. The existing Court of Queen's Bench of Manitoba and the Provincial Court of Manitoba should cease to exist. The act creating the court could be an amalgamation of the court statutes that now exist. The court rules, as well, would have to be changed or amalgamated, on the recommendation of the new court.

The administrative structure of the courts now involves separate Queen's Bench and Provincial Court staff. Large, separate, administrative offices now exist in the city of Winnipeg. Although efforts to improve and coordinate staff have been made, particularly in rural areas, the creation of one court, either with one administration or at least one administration for each division of the new court, would further improve and simplify the process, and make better use of available resources. Making arrangements for court sittings and the assignment of the necessary support staff would be more efficient. The judges' coordination of dates when cases can be heard and the assignment of judges would be simplified.

The federal government will have to be asked, in consultation with the provincial government, to appoint the judges of the existing courts to the new court. Federal legislation, particularly the *Criminal Code*, should be amended to designate the Manitoba Trial Court as the one to have the criminal jurisdiction now held by the existing courts in Manitoba.

WE RECOMMEND THAT:

- The Manitoba Court of Queen's Bench and the Provincial Court of Manitoba be abolished and be replaced by a new court to be known as the Manitoba Trial Court. This court should have the combined jurisdiction of the courts it replaces.

Court Divisions

We suggest there might be two divisions of the Manitoba Trial Court: a General Division and a Family Division. It might have one chief justice and two associate chief justices, one in charge of each division. The chief justice should be responsible for the overall operation and supervision of the court, the coordination of the work of the divisions, and the performance and rotation of judges.

Each division should operate separately from the other and develop its own rules, practices and procedures, subject to any coordination the chief justice thinks necessary. The associate chief justices should be responsible for the day-to-day operation of the division to which they are appointed and, in conjunction with the chief justice, ensure that the services of the division are made available throughout the province.

Judges might be appointed to the court and then assigned by the chief justice to one division or the other, or they might be appointed to one of the divisions. We suggest they spend the majority of their time in the division to which they are assigned, but should spend a considerable amount of time working in the other division. While it is important for a judge to be particularly proficient in one area of work, it is equally important for all judges to be able to deal with any matter that comes before the court. This will be particularly important when judges preside in smaller communities where there is a wide variety of work to be attended to at each sitting. Where there is a case on a court list that would benefit from a judge with particular experience, such a judge should be assigned and then handle all other matters on the list, as well.

Another reason we consider it important for judges to have experience in both divisions is our assumption that judges of the Court of Appeal will be drawn from the Trial Court. In fact, we recommend that judges appointed to the Court of Appeal come only from the Trial Court. It is important that judges of the appeal court be familiar with the procedures and practices of a trial court and with the problems facing a trial judge. This is of particular importance with respect to Aboriginal people. As courts of appeal rarely hear witnesses, the judges of those courts must gain their court-related experience of Aboriginal people and their communities as trial judges.

The creation of one court will achieve one of our chief objectives, that child welfare and Youth Court matters be dealt with in the same division of the same court.

Another important change we recommend will not be achieved merely by the establishment of one court. It will require the assignment of one area now dealt with in the criminal courts to the Family Division. We recommend that all intrafamily abuse cases be dealt with in the Family Division. We conclude that the separation of abuse from other issues between spouses, or between spouses and their children, is not advisable. We believe that all family problems should be addressed at the same time.

If these cases are dealt with in the Family Division, several options would be open to the victim. The case could proceed as a criminal prosecution and the offender would be sentenced if found guilty. In cases where the victim was concerned about the family relationship, but did not wish to prosecute, counselling, mediation and other services should be provided. In some cases, both procedures might proceed at the same time. Even if a prosecution has started, it might be delayed while abuse counselling or mediation are attempted to put a halt to the unacceptable conduct. If the efforts to solve the problem are not proving effective, the prosecution could proceed.

The Family Conciliation branch, which is now attached to the Family Division of the Court of Queen's Bench, should be attached to the Family Division of the new court, as well. It might well be expanded to include counselling services for abused spouses, children and abusers. Existing programs of this nature might be transferred from other government agencies and attached to Family Conciliation.

All charges of abuse against a child or adult allegedly committed by anyone outside the family should be dealt with in the General Division.

We suggest that each division might have groupings of judges, or assignments of judges within it, to enable judges to specialize in a particular area, at least for a period of time. Some judges, because of their experience as lawyers or experience they have gained on the bench, are known to prefer and to be particularly effective in a certain area of work. We think these special abilities should be utilized and the preferences of judges accommodated, if that is at all possible. Merely by way of example, we suggest that judges might provide special services in fields such as the following:

General Division
- Contracts
- Judge-alone trials
- Labour
- Commercial
- Jury trials
- Small claims
- Estates
- Bail and procedural issues
- Torts
- Pre-trials
- Judicial review

Family Division
- Divorce
- Child welfare
- Family criminal
- Young offender
- Property division
- Reciprocal enforcement
- Custody of children
- Maintenance enforcement

In addition to providing all services in each community where it sits, the new court will enable the introduction of other changes. We believe that jury trials should be conducted in the community where the offence is alleged to have been committed. These trials, which deal with some of the most serious crimes, can result in the imposition of severe penalties and have a substantial impact upon the community. In addition to involving local people as jurors, these trials will offer an opportunity for the local residents to see the judicial system in operation. In our discussion of juries in Chapter 9 we deal with how the jurors should be selected.

WE RECOMMEND THAT:

■ Jury trials be held in the communities where the offence was committed.

■ The Manitoba Trial Court have a General Division and a Family Division.

■ The Family Division be responsible for young offender, child welfare and family matters as well as for cases involving intrafamily physical and sexual abuse; and that the General Division be responsible for all civil matters and those criminal matters not dealt with by the Family Division.

■ All judges appointed to the Manitoba Court of Appeal come from the Manitoba Trial Court.

We recognize that we have recommended some sweeping changes. We find them necessary as part of other changes needed to properly provide Aboriginal people, wherever they live, with a sensitive and accessible court system. While we acknowledge there may be other ways to bring the changes about, we have attempted to propose a model we think is workable and that will address the needs we have identified during this Inquiry.

Court Facilities in Remote Communities

As part of the creation of an Aboriginal justice system, court facilities in Aboriginal communities must be upgraded. As we noted earlier, the current facilities are simply unacceptable. Until Aboriginal justice systems assume full jurisdiction, the Manitoba Trial Court should hold trials (including jury trials) in Aboriginal communities that do not currently have formal courtrooms. We expect lawyers and court officials to spend more time in remote and rural communities, both to prepare and to hold trials. This will require improved facilities. Finally, and of greatest importance, we believe that the court system can gain the respect of Aboriginal communities only if the communities are able to see the court system treating their residents and concerns with the same respect accorded to the residents of urban communities.

We recognize that these recommendations will involve cost, but we believe the cost can be kept within reason if the court facilities are added to band or other community multipurpose facilities. We suggest that the court facilities be developed in such a way that they can be used for other purposes when not required for court sittings. In the end, however, rural and Aboriginal communities should be provided with services that meet the same standard as those available in other parts of the province. Extra resources required to deliver equal justice must be provided.

WE RECOMMEND THAT:

■ Proper court facilities be established in Aboriginal communities that will be available for court purposes as required.

Separation of Youth and Family Matters

Youth and family matters should not be heard as additions to a criminal docket. Greater sensitivity must be shown to the private nature of these highly personal matters and there should be separate family sittings wherever possible. Family abuse situations, child welfare problems and other matters of a personal nature should not be mixed with the adult criminal hearings. If there are not enough cases in a community to warrant sittings on separate days, arrangements must be made to deal with family matters at a separate sitting, either in the morning or afternoon, so the two sittings do not run into one another and force those involved in the family cases to mingle with those awaiting the hearing of adult criminal matters.

WE RECOMMEND THAT:

■ Hearings in the Family Division of the Manitoba Trial Court be held separately from criminal proceedings.

Travel Arrangements for Circuit Court Parties

Judges on circuit must be, and must appear to be, totally independent of the police and counsel. This is expected in all courts, but is particularly important in Aboriginal communities where the people start with a mistrust of what, to them, is just another foreign system.

We recommend that the practice of judges travelling with lawyers and police cease. Judges should not travel with the lawyers even if both prosecution and defence lawyers are present. The judge should fly in a separate aircraft. Even if there is additional cost, we consider this change essential if justice is to be seen to be done. Where the destination is served by commercial aircraft, the judge must take care not to travel with counsel to the hotel or to court.

The appearance of the judge being on friendly terms with lawyers on either side of the case reduces the respect the judge must have to administer justice impartially. The judge's conduct is carefully observed and judges should be aware of that close scrutiny. A judge's conduct and decorum must be, in all respects, beyond reproach.

To avoid members of the community associating the judge with the prosecution, the judge should not be driven around the community by police officers, because they may have been involved in the arrest of an accused over whose case the judge must preside. One of the tasks of the local court administrator should be to arrange for the necessary ground transportation for the court party.

WE RECOMMEND THAT:

- Unless they are travelling in commercial airplanes, circuit court judges not travel with lawyers or police to circuit court sittings.

Preventing Inappropriate Pleadings

On numerous occasions we were told by Aboriginal people that they were advised to plead guilty, even though they believed themselves to be innocent. It is apparent Aboriginal people are not receiving the full protection of their rights guaranteed by the law in such a proceeding.

WE RECOMMEND THAT:

- Judges insist that whenever an Aboriginal person is entering a guilty plea, the following procedure be followed:

  - The charge is read in full to the accused.

  - The judge confirms that the accused understands the charge by asking the accused to explain it.

  - The accused, and not counsel, enters a plea.

  - The judge confirms that the accused agrees with the guilty plea and that it is being given freely and voluntarily with a full appreciation of the nature and consequences of the plea.

Conclusion

We would like to stress our belief that the creation of a unified court system should in no way be seen as an acceptable substitute for the creation of an Aboriginal justice system. However, the unified court would create an efficient and simpler justice system for all Manitobans, and it would certainly address problems which weigh most heavily on Aboriginal people. It would also provide a needed improvement in the delivery of justice to remote communities as the transition is made to an Aboriginal justice system.

Eliminating Delay

Court Scheduling

As we noted in our discussion of the current court system, the Provincial Court of Manitoba has gone a long way toward reducing delay within the city of Winnipeg. Three years ago it was often the case that the courts were setting trial dates 13 months in advance. They now can give trial dates within a three-month period. It is instructive to examine the methods that have been employed to bring about this improvement.

Central to the process has been the fact that judges, with the cooperation of Crown and defence attorneys, have taken control over the court scheduling process. A number of administrative changes were required, but of greater importance was the judiciary's decision to assert its control over the flow of cases. In particular, judges became far less willing to grant motions that would contribute to the delay of a case. While the individual remands that were being granted in the past all may have been reasonable, the cumulative effect—the delaying of a trial for over a year—was seen to be extremely unreasonable. As a result, it is now uncommon for cases to go beyond three remands in the Provincial Court in Winnipeg.

The same approach, however, is not being applied outside Winnipeg. When trial dates or remands are being scheduled, the present system often limits its consideration to the schedules of the various professionals involved. If a case is not ready to proceed, the Crown attorney checks the calendar to see when the circuit court will return to the community. The Crown attorney indicates which date is suitable. If the police have a problem making witnesses available, the date is set to take that concern into account. If defence counsel has a heavy caseload, a date will be set when that lawyer is free. The date that is fixed for trial is then set, with these considerations. Throughout this process, the needs of the Aboriginal defendant, his or her family members, the victim and prospective witnesses are rarely taken into account.

The legal system appears to operate in the belief that the most important participants are those who are part of the legal establishment, yet, the legal system exists to serve the public. Many people are affected by every case that goes to court and it is important that the court ensure that it considers their needs, as well.

We believe that judges outside Winnipeg must make much greater use of their right to control the scheduling of cases. We do not think it is proper for the court to be adjourned so that the lawyers can speak with their clients. This should take place prior to court. Lawyers should be coming to circuit court points the day before court to meet with their clients. If lawyers knew in advance that adjournments would not be allowed, they would conduct the necessary consultations in advance of the court day. Judges should grant remands only for exceptional cause and they should bear in mind the burden that remands place on people in communities which have only one court hearing a month.

Dealing with Current Caseload

In 1989 the Provincial Court of Manitoba eliminated a tremendous backlog of cases in the city of Winnipeg. This was accomplished, in part, by a blitz which focussed on disposing of any cases which had been outstanding for several months. We believe it is necessary to conduct a similar blitz to clear up cases in the circuit courts. The blitz should focus on disposing of all cases which have been outstanding for six months or longer.

Such a blitz will require assigning additional judges, Crown attorneys and Legal Aid lawyers. We believe it should not take more than six months to eliminate the current backlog of cases.

Once the courts are current, the performance of each court location should be regularly monitored to see that no backlog develops. Should a trend in that direction be detected, additional sitting days should be made available.

WE RECOMMEND THAT:

- Special court sittings be organized to address all cases outside the city of Winnipeg which have been outstanding for more than six months. If necessary, additional staff should be hired until all these cases have been disposed of.

Improved Circuit Court Services

As they currently operate, circuit courts provide an unacceptable level of service to Aboriginal people. We believe the Aboriginal communities served by circuit courts will be among the first to develop their own justice systems. We believe such systems will be able to provide swift and appropriate justice at the community level. To aid in the transition to these new systems, circuit courts must be reformed immediately. We should make it clear that the reforms we are calling for will require additional resources—we need more court personnel in local communities, we need more lawyers providing defence, and we need to have these people spending more time in Aboriginal communities.

Justice cannot be delivered on a monthly fly-in, fly-out basis. Judges must be prepared to go into Aboriginal communities and stay until dockets are completed. This may mean that courts have to sit for more than one day, particularly if there are family and youth matters to be dealt with.

WE RECOMMEND THAT:

- Circuit court sittings be scheduled in such a manner as to allow all the matters on a docket to be dealt with in one court visit. This may entail scheduling two-day visits to many communities.

Changes to Legal Aid

We suggest a change in the way Legal Aid Manitoba provides representation to Aboriginal people in remote communities. We would like to see a switch made from the provision of representation by overburdened duty counsel to a system where Aboriginal people enjoy the same sort of lawyer-client relationship that characterizes legal representation in other parts of the province. At the present time, defence counsel, whether they be Legal Aid or private counsel, do not have adequate time to obtain all the information necessary to prepare a defence or to speak to sentence. There is virtually no time to discuss various options with an accused and members of the family. As far as we can determine, counsel do not discuss cases with the chief or other community representatives. Youth justice committees are not consulted.

This system can only be improved if Legal Aid lawyers travel to a community the day before court is scheduled and spend the day meeting with the people scheduled to appear in court the following day. Others in the community will also have to be seen if alternative measures are to be investigated and proposed to the court. This minimal step may require the hiring of more Legal Aid staff lawyers.

We also believe changes are necessary to the Legal Aid appointment process. Accused individuals in remote communities are often not able to apply for legal aid until the circuit court comes to town. We believe that this situation would be alleviated to some degree if Aboriginal court workers were resident in circuit points. These people should be authorized to accept Legal Aid applications. An application for the appointment of counsel should then be communicated to the appropriate Legal Aid office without delay. If a facsimile machine is available, the application should be forwarded by that means. If no facsimile machine is available, the application should be processed by telephone and the application form forwarded later.

Legal Aid duty counsel should be given the right to grant interim approval of an application and, as well, the power to appoint counsel to represent an accused at his or her first appearance. In many cases, this may result in duty counsel appointing themselves to represent an individual. If duty counsel arrive in the community a day before the court sitting, they will be able to meet with the individuals who would normally not make an application for Legal Aid until the day of the court sitting.

If this procedure is followed, it would eliminate at least one remand in the handling of many circuit court cases. It is particularly important to speed the appointment process for those in custody so that an application for bail can be made as soon as possible.

When Legal Aid makes an appointment, the Crown attorney's office should be notified immediately. Crown counsel then should take the responsibility for moving the case along. Particulars should be sent to the defence counsel without waiting for them to be requested.

WE RECOMMEND THAT:

- Lawyers attend in circuit court communities at least one day before court to ensure that cases can be properly prepared.

- Legal Aid duty counsel be authorized to grant interim approval of all Legal Aid applications. If, upon review, the applicant does not qualify for Legal Aid, the approval could be cancelled.

- Legal Aid application procedures be amended to allow accused individuals who live in communities where there is no Legal Aid office to apply by telephone. Where no Legal Aid staff are available, Aboriginal court workers be authorized to accept and forward Legal Aid applications.

Provision of Information to Defence

Before a plea is required of an accused, the Crown should have provided the defence with a statement of particulars setting out the Crown's case and copies of any statements from the accused and the complainant. As soon as a plea of not guilty is entered, the Crown should also provide the defence with the following:

- Statements from all witnesses intended to be called.

- Statements from others not intended to be called.

- Sketches and drawings.

- Experts' reports.

- Any other information relevant to the case.

If other information becomes available prior to trial, this should also be disclosed, otherwise the Crown should be precluded from introducing it at trial. If another witness later becomes available, or if it is determined that a witness may be able to deal with other issues, the same disclosure and notice should apply.

Pre-Trial Conferences

Compulsory pre-trial procedures are already in place in the Provincial Court and in the Court of Queen's Bench, and can easily be adapted to the changes we suggest. These pre-trial proceedings assist counsel in receiving an outline of the opposition's case. An efficient system of pre-trial proceedings will do a great deal to streamline the operation of the court and should lead to a significant reduction in court delay. We suggest there be a pre-trial conference in every case involving an indictable offence where a plea of not guilty has been entered. The length of the conference and the matters to be considered will vary, depending on the seriousness of the charge and the procedural and legal issues involved.

The pre-trial conference should be conducted by a judge who will not be the judge who presides at trial. The purposes of the conference are to ready the case for trial and to discuss the various options in an open and frank exchange. The main role of the judge is to see that the case is ready to proceed to trial. A secondary role may be to assist counsel in discussing alternatives that may arise from the evidence disclosed at the pre-trial conference. Everything said at a pre-trial conference should be confidential and no tentative agreements that are made should be binding on either the Crown or the defence. The conference should consider as many of the following issues as might apply to a particular case:

- Make certain that all documentary disclosure has been completed, or set the time within which that is to be done.

- Discuss the evidence with a view to ensuring that an appropriate charge has been laid.

- Determine what, if any, facts can be agreed upon to avoid calling certain witnesses.

- Determine whether there are any legal or technical issues to be present-ed and, if there are, to obtain lists of authorities that should be considered by the trial judge.

- Discuss the estimated length of trial.

- Determine the language of trial and whether interpreters will be required.

- Confirm the availability of all witnesses.

- Discuss the possibility of a change of plea or willingness to plead guilty to some lesser charge.

- Deal with any pre-trial motions that do not have to be dealt with by the trial judge.

- Set the trial date in consultation with all parties and the trial coordinator.

- Determine whether any pre-trial examination of witnesses is required by the defence and, if so, set the date for that to be done.

While the presence of an accused is probably unnecessary in most cases, we suggest that the accused have the option of being present at the pre-trial conference. The presence of the accused will enable defence counsel to keep the accused advised and to receive instructions. If the case is in a remote community, and counsel and the judge are not all present, the pre-trial conference could be conducted by a telephone conference call initiated by the court. The accused should have the option to participate in the call.

Elimination of the Preliminary Inquiry

As we noted in Chapter 6, the initial purpose of the preliminary inquiry has virtually disappeared. Instead of being a hearing to determine whether there is sufficient evidence to warrant a trial, it has become a discovery process.

If our proposal for the early delivery of information by the Crown to the defence is put in place, and if pre-trial conferences are held, the Crown will have determined the basis upon which it wishes to proceed and the defence will have most of the information it needs.

We recognize that the defence will still not have had an opportunity to question key witnesses and we believe that right should continue. We do not think that the preliminary inquiry is necessary to enable that to be done.

We suggest that if, at the pre-trial conference, the defence indicates a desire to question certain witnesses, a date be set for a "pre-trial examination of witnesses." We suggest that examination take place before a special examiner of the court. A special examiner is usually a court reporter who has been given that special designation. The special examiner can swear witnesses and make procedural rulings.

We recommend that the preliminary inquiry be abolished. We also strongly recommend that the pre-trial examination of witnesses *not* be conducted by a Provincial Court judge. The present use of judges to preside over preliminary inquiries is, we believe, an inappropriate and wasteful use of their time and talents.

We suggest that the elimination of the preliminary inquiry, along with the amalgamation of the courts and the imposition of some time restraints, will result in a much simplified and more efficient process.

WE RECOMMEND THAT:

___

- Preliminary inquiries be abolished and replaced with a discovery and pre-trial process.

___

Mandatory Time Limits

Another mechanism we recommend to eliminate the delay we have found with respect to the processing of young offender cases generally, and criminal cases in rural and remote Aboriginal communities in particular, is the imposition of time limits on the processing of cases.

The legal basis for controlling the processing of cases is found in the *Charter of Rights and Freedoms,* which is Part 1 of the *Constitution Act, 1982.* Section 11 provides:

> Any person charged with an offence has the right ... to be tried within a reasonable time.

In *Mills v. The Queen*, at page 941, Mr. Justice Lamer (now Chief Justice of the Supreme Court), spoke of the responsibility of those administering the system to accommodate it to the *Charter* and to change the system if necessary:

> Our legislators have, by the entrenchment of s. 11(b), established as a fundamental societal priority the maintenance of an effective and prompt system for the administration of criminal justice. There can be no assumption that the constitutional right to be tried within a reasonable time must conform to the status quo; rather, it is the system for the administration of criminal justice which must conform to the constitutional requirements of the Charter. We cannot shrink from our task of interpreting the Charter in a full and fair manner, even when, and perhaps especially when, we are confronted with the possibility of resulting significant institutional adjustment.

This topic has been the subject of comment by the Law Reform Commission of Canada, by bar associations and by the courts, but little has been done to establish actual guidelines.

The Law Reform Commission made proposals for having trials heard within a reasonable time in its 1978 report entitled *Criminal Procedure Part 1* and considered the matter again in a 1988 study paper on "Trial Within a Reasonable Time." In that document, it proposes a post-charge time limit of six months for summary conviction offences and one year in cases where there has been a preliminary inquiry.

The American Bar Association has agreed that at least 98% of all cases should be concluded within 180 days of arrest.[2] Time limits have been implemented in a number of jurisdictions in the United States. Again in *Mills*, Mr. Justice Lamer, at page 938, indicated some of the limitations being applied in the United States:

> *California Penal §1382* (West 1985) stipulates that when a person has been "held to answer" for an offence, an information must be filed within 15 days and that a defendant must be brought to trial within 60 days of the indictment or filing of the information; in misdemeanor cases, the defendant must be brought to trial within 30 days after arraignment if he is in custody, or 45 days in all other cases; *Colorado Criminal Code*, Colo. Rev. Stat. §18–1–405 (1973), states that a defendant must be brought to trial within 6 months; *Illinois Code of Criminal Procedure*, Ill. Ann. Stat. ch. 38, §103–5 (Smith-Hurd 1980), states that every person in custody shall be tried within 120 days from the date that he was taken into custody and that every person on bail or recognizance shall be tried within 160 days; *Michigan Code of Criminal Procedure*, Mich. Stat. Ann. § 28.978 (Callaghan 1985), provides that every person held in prison upon an indictment shall be tried at the next term of the court after the expiration of 6 months from the time when he was imprisoned; *South Carolina Code of Criminal Procedure*, , S. C. Code Ann. §17–23–90 (Law Co-op. 1985), provides that a person held in custody must be indicted and tried within two court terms after his confinement [see *State v. Fasket*, 5 Rich. (39 SCL) 255 (1851); 18 U.S.C. ch. 208 § 3161 (c)(1)(1982)] states that in any case in which a plea of not guilty is entered, the trial must commence within 70 days.[3]

In view of our recommendation that the preliminary inquiry be abolished, we believe that the target period, from the time of laying a charge to the commencement of all criminal trials, should be six months. There will be cases, of course, where an extension of time will have to be sought and granted, but we suggest those extensions be for unusual circumstances and be quite limited.

When time limits on criminal cases are being addressed, attention should also be directed to delay in bringing civil and family cases to trial. The new Ontario Court of Justice is experimenting with several models of case flow management. In Windsor, time limits for simple, standard and complex civil actions are set at six, 18 and 36 months. In family cases, the time from commencement of a proceeding to trial is set at 12 months, and a variation proceeding at six months. Similar time limits or guidelines should be established in Manitoba. The principle upon which case flow management is based is that once a case has started, the courts have an obligation to the litigants to see that it is dealt with in reasonable time.

WE RECOMMEND THAT:

- The judiciary establish timelines and procedures that will ensure that a case gets to trial within a reasonable time.

Case Flow Management Techniques

While time limits can be established relatively easily, their implementation does not automatically mean that the system will respond quickly. Along with time limits must come case flow management procedures which will enable the courts to meet their time limits. The study by the American Bar Association cited above examined procedures in a number of courts and identified a number of management techniques which enabled some courts to process their cases more quickly than others. It found that the caseload and the number of judges made little difference. Nor did one particular system appear to stand out above the others. Rather, the study found that it was the application of case flow management methods that made the difference.

WE RECOMMEND THAT:

- Manitoba courts implement a comprehensive case flow management program.

Such a management system should incorporate these principles:

- Once a court proceeding has been commenced, the court, and not counsel, should control its passage through the system.

- Case events should be scheduled at relatively short intervals.

- Once a trial date is set, every effort should be made to ensure it proceeds as scheduled.

- The trial of criminal cases should commence within six months of when the charge was laid.

- Efforts should be made by the Crown attorney to screen out of the court system cases which would be better resolved in some other way.

- A Crown attorney should review every charge that has been laid to see whether the available evidence supports it.

- Over-charging should be avoided. Where there is a difference of opinion between the police and the Crown attorney, the opinion of the Crown attorney should prevail.

- All murder charges should be reviewed and authorized by a senior Crown attorney.

- Judges should be assigned in such a way that if a trial does not proceed, the judge will be free to preside over other matters. It is important that enough judges be on standby for situations where a case continues longer than anticipated, where a court docket cannot be completed as quickly as anticipated, or where more trials proceed than were anticipated.

- We recommend that all matters scheduled for trial or set for guilty pleas on a court docket be disposed of at the sitting for which they are set. If remands are substantially reduced, the court should be able to deal with pleas of guilty first and then hear trials. The judge assigned to that sitting should remain as long as necessary to dispose of all matters on the list, even if that takes more than one day.

- Pre-sentence reports should not be ordered automatically. Where people who are present can provide the judge with the necessary information about the offence and the circumstances of the accused, a report should not be ordered.

- In order to ensure that backlogs do not grow and lead to delays, the court should continually monitor the processing of cases.

Delay and Court Appearances

Repeated remands and delays, and the regular court appearances they entail, create problems for Aboriginal accused who reside in remote and rural communities. They must often travel significant distances at great personal expense, only to have their court appearance last just a few minutes as a remand is granted. If they fail to appear, they risk having the charges against them multiply. We believe it is necessary to relax the requirements for court appearances.

For summary conviction matters, an accused can be represented in court by counsel or an agent properly instructed by the accused to appear for him or her. Such a person can act in the place of the accused, including agreeing to a remand or entering a plea if the court is satisfied that person has sufficient authority to do so. If there is any question in the judge's mind, he or she can still require the accused to be present and adjourn the matter for that purpose. If a counsel or agent appears without proper instructions, then the court can issue a warrant. We suggest that the same options apply with respect to all offences.

For indictable matters, it is not clear whether counsel or an agent can appear in place of an accused, even for a remand. The *Criminal Code*, which governs the procedure on indictable matters, is silent on the point. Some, including both the provincial and federal departments of Justice, have interpreted that silence to mean it cannot be done. They take the position that if an accused does not appear, the court loses jurisdiction, unless a warrant has been issued or the accused has consented to a remand in person. Therefore, where an accused charged with an indictable offence does not appear, the Crown attorney asks the court for a warrant of arrest, even if counsel for the accused has clear authority to agree to a remand. Most judges issue such warrants and order that they be "held" until the next remand date, an order of questionable validity. The warrants are usually held, but if the accused does not appear at his or her next remand, invariably the warrant is executed and the person is arrested. Sometimes, the warrant is acted upon on the day of the next hearing to make sure the accused is in court.

This can be a hardship for an Aboriginal accused charged with an offence in his or her home community, but who, for one reason or another, has to leave the community temporarily. We have already noted the high mobility of Aboriginal people between urban and reserve settings. If an accused cannot make it back to the community for court because of distance and cost, if he or she has counsel and if his or her matter is simply going to be remanded, we wonder why the court should have to issue a "jurisdictional warrant."

If, for reasons of health, weather or employment, an accused is unable to attend a court sitting to which he or she has been remanded, we believe counsel should be able to seek a further adjournment. If that were possible, an arrest warrant would not have to be issued.

Currently, the inability to appear, even for good reason, results in the accused being arrested. We believe that an accused should be able to appear by counsel or agent for all preliminary matters (summary conviction and indictable), provided that the counsel or agent has full authority to appear and the court is satisfied that the attendance of the accused is not necessary. Even a telephone call to the court administrator or Crown attorney should enable a remand to be made in an appropriate case, without the court losing jurisdiction.

WE RECOMMEND THAT:

- The *Criminal Code* be amended to allow accused to appear by counsel or agent for all preliminary purposes.

Where an accused does not have a counsel or an agent and is unable to attend court for good reason, and contact has been made with the RCMP, the Crown attorney, Legal Aid or court staff advising of the reason, we believe that the court should not have to issue a warrant for jurisdictional purposes. This is especially true in situations where the matter would have been remanded in any event. In fact, we do not understand why an accused's presence in court should ever be required, other than for bail or trial.

WE RECOMMEND THAT:

- The *Criminal Code* be amended to provide that once an information has been laid the court does not lose jurisdiction merely because the accused is not present.

We heard of cases in which Aboriginal people were arrested on a warrant because they failed to appear, and ended up in jail. Many said that they were then charged with failing to appear and, because they were in jail, they pleaded guilty to the original charge just to get the matter over with, since they then had two charges against them. It seems to us that some defence counsel are too willing to allow their clients to plead guilty to charges of failing to appear where the client has a reasonable excuse.

Conclusion

We believe that with the introduction of time limits, the elimination or reduction in remands, the elimination of procedures that now cause delay, such as the preliminary inquiry, and the application of case flow management techniques, a much higher quality of court services can be made available to all Manitobans. This is particularly the case for Aboriginal people who have trouble obtaining release on bail, or those who live in small rural locations or remote northern communities. We believe the justice system as a whole will also be a beneficiary.

Pre-Trial Detention

We believe that our justice system imprisons far too many people who have been found guilty of crimes. This is a serious problem and we deal with it in detail in Chapter 10. It is perhaps even more disturbing to discover the degree to which our system incarcerates individuals who have not been convicted of any crime. In some of the institutions we visited, many of the inmates, sometimes as many as 30%, were being held in custody pending consideration of their cases by the courts. Studies demonstrate that Manitoba makes excessive use of pre-trial detention and that this policy weighs adversely against Aboriginal people.

According to statistics in the 1988–89 *Annual Report* of the Manitoba Department of the Attorney General,[4] considerably more persons are taken into pre-trial detention than are sentenced to jail. This suggests that many of those pre-trial detentions were unnecessary, that either the court found the individuals to be not guilty or found that incarceration was not appropriate for them.

In 1988 there were 15,138 admissions at the Winnipeg Remand Centre and 2,658 temporary detentions at the Manitoba Youth Centre, for a total of 17,796 pre-trial detentions. The statistics do not reveal how many pre-trial detentions there were at the other jails in the province. There were less than 10,000 adults sentenced to jails in the province, including federal institutions. There were, at most, approximately 1,300 youth sentenced to jail in the province in 1988.

These figures suggest there were more than one and one-half times as many pre-trial admissions for adults as there were sentences to jail.

The figure of 1,300 for sentenced youth includes 600 youth admitted to institutions other than the Manitoba Youth Centre and Agassiz Youth Centre. It is not clear whether these youth were being held in pre-trial detention or were sentenced to those institutions. The figure also includes 460 youth sentenced to open custody, which is not supposed to be considered the same as jail, but, in practice, Manitoba open custody is very similar to closed custody (24-hour lockup). Even using the figure of 1,300, this suggests there were more than two times as many pre-trial detentions for youth as there were youth sentenced to jail.

For women, there were 1,819 admissions to the Winnipeg Remand Centre, but only 628 women admitted to the other jails in the province. This suggests there were three times as many pre-trial admissions for women as there were sentences to jail.

According to the Canadian Centre for Justice Statistics, in 1988–89 only 33% of the individuals in provincial custody in Manitoba had been sentenced to a term of imprisonment after being found guilty of a crime, while 66% were in custody awaiting further court appearances, trial or sentencing (these individuals are usually referred to as being held on remand). Quebec was the only other province in which the number of individuals being held on remand exceeded the number of individuals who had been sentenced to a term of imprisonment. In Saskatchewan 63% of the individuals in provincial custody were sentenced; in Alberta the figure is 68%.[5] The raw figures are equally disturbing. In 1988–89, 10,083 people were admitted to Manitoba's provincial correctional institutions on remand; the comparable figures for Saskatchewan, Alberta and British Columbia were, respectively, 4,464; 9,679; and 4,772.[6]

Some jurisdictions have dealt with these problems by establishing bail supervision programs. Under these programs, people who cannot find anyone to post bail for them, but otherwise qualify for release, are released on condition that they regularly report to designated officials. These programs are now available in Ontario, British Columbia and Saskatchewan. To date, the Manitoba government has shown little commitment to developing alternatives to pre-trial detention. We believe the time has come to do so. Such programs for Aboriginal accused should operate in remote communities and urban centres, and should come under the direction of Aboriginal people.

Local communities must be equipped with short-term custody facilities. Accused individuals should be held in these facilities and a bail hearing should be arranged in the community before a local judicial officer.

In remote communities and in urban centres, there is also a need to develop new criteria for determining whether an individual should be released. These must take into account, among other things, the strength of the Aboriginal community's network of extended families and this network's ability to provide pre-trial supervision.

The excessive use of pre-trial detention is another reason we recommend the establishment of time limits on prosecutions.

We believe an Aboriginal justice system will be able to deal effectively with many of the problems of pre-trial custody in remote communities. Such a system would be able to deal with the question of detention and supervision in the community where the offence took place.

WE RECOMMEND THAT:

- Bail hearings be conducted in the community where the offence was committed.

- The Manitoba government establish a bail supervision program to provide pre-trial supervision to accused persons as an alternative to detention.

- Inappropriate bail conditions, such as requiring cash deposits or financial guarantees from low-income people, that militate against Aboriginal people obtaining bail, no longer be applied.

Personnel

In our chapter describing the current court system, we noted that very few of the people employed by the Manitoba justice system are Aboriginal and that virtually none of the people in decision-making positions is Aboriginal. Elsewhere in this report, we recommend the adoption of an Employment Equity Act. We believe that the Justice department and its related agencies must make employment equity a priority.

WE RECOMMEND THAT:

- The provincial Justice department establish minimum and optimum targets for the employment of Aboriginal people at all levels. The minimum target must be no less than the percentage of Aboriginal people in Manitoba; the optimum target is to be equal to the percentage of Aboriginal people served by the department and its agencies.

- Legal Aid Manitoba establish minimum and optimum targets for the employment of Aboriginal people at all levels. The minimum target must be no less than the percentage of Aboriginal people in Manitoba; the optimum target is to be equal to the percentage of Aboriginal people served by Legal Aid Manitoba.

Judges

As we noted earlier, judges play a key role in the justice system. They exercise considerable control over the way a case will move through the court system, they preside over the courts, they must determine whether a person is guilty or innocent and they must pass sentence. In addition to this, the judge plays an important symbolic role in the judicial system. Manitobans have high expectations of their judiciary.

Some of the Aboriginal people who appeared before our Commission said their expectations are not being met. Presenters spoke of judges who treated Aboriginal people like children, of judges who comported themselves in an unprofessional manner, of judges who refused to hold court in Aboriginal communities because they were dissatisfied with the court facilities and of judges who did not respond to letters of complaint from community members.

We also believe that when it comes to sentencing, judges rely far too much on incarceration, do not pay enough attention to cultural factors, avoid, or are unaware of creative and available community sanctions, and impose unnecessary and inappropriate conditions on probation orders.

A survey conducted by our Inquiry revealed that some judges do not fully understand that Aboriginal people have unique legal and cultural rights; they appear to view Aboriginal people as being no different from Canada's other ethnic minorities. The survey also found that some judges believe that the present circuit court system provides adequate service and that there is no need for additional court sittings in Aboriginal communities.

It is not surprising, therefore, to discover that the system over which Manitoba's judges preside is not held in high esteem by Aboriginal people. There is little faith that it can resolve matters to the benefit of the Aboriginal accused, the victim, their families or the community. The system's most senior officials must bear no small measure of responsibility for this state of affairs.

The courts are seen as part of a foreign system applying a set of values established for the benefit of the non-Aboriginal community. They are seen as insensitive to individual and community needs. Instead of trying to resolve problems in a consultative manner and to restore harmonious relationships in the community, the adversarial system seeks to determine fault and to punish. This may not be the fault of the judge who is operating within the present rules, but judges often get the blame and are included when Aboriginal people speak of indifference and lack of understanding.

A judge must decide whether an accused should be released on bail and, if so, the conditions that should be imposed. The judge will determine whether there will be any delay at that point. Whether the case can be disposed of at an early appearance may depend upon whether the judge agrees to requests from lawyers for delays. The judge's knowledge of the effects of delay on the accused may determine his or her willingness to grant remands. A judge's decisions in all these matters may depend upon his or her knowledge of resources within the community. A judge should know if there are justice committees, elders, peacemakers or others to whom a matter might be referred, what counselling and supervision facilities exist, and what alternative measures might succeed in the circumstances of a particular case.

The decisions a judge makes on the movement of a case through the courts often have a substantial impact on those required to attend in court. Our investigations indicated that in some remote communities, judges may be unaware of the cost and disruption caused by a "simple" adjournment. Some seem to be unaware of the lack of transportation in southern Aboriginal communities, the problems of distance in the North and the economic impacts of return trips to court.

We believe that judges could do much to alleviate some of the problems resulting from current practices and procedures, if they were aware of the problems. The challenge is to provide judges with the necessary information and an understanding of how Aboriginal people are being affected by the current system. Ways of improving the delivery of judicial services should also be presented to or developed by the judiciary. For this reason, we recommend that Manitoba judges be provided with a cross-cultural training program. We discuss cultural awareness programs in more detail in the final chapter of this report.

Judicial Isolation

While a cross-cultural training program for judges will represent a positive step in improving the justice system for Aboriginal people in Manitoba, other problems must also be addressed. One of these is the isolation of judges from the communities they serve.

This isolation is a particular problem in cases involving Aboriginal people. Those working in the legal system who make decisions in cases involving Aboriginal people must be knowledgeable about them, their history and culture, the communities in which they live, their economy, their means of livelihood and their way of life. Most judges do not come from backgrounds which give them this knowledge.

This degree of knowledge about the customs and needs of Aboriginal communities cannot be obtained under the current circuit court system, where judges spend only a few hours each month in each of the communities they serve. Queen's Bench and Court of Appeal judges do not even have this exposure to Aboriginal communities. Judges are currently working within a structure which limits their contact with Aboriginal people.

Judges must be prepared to meet with the chief and council when they go to remote communities. They need not discuss particular cases, but should show that they are concerned about delivering good court services to the community. They should listen to suggestions as to how problems can be lessened and services improved.

It is clear that the best way to ensure that the judicial system has judges with knowledge of Aboriginal people is to establish a system of courts with Aboriginal judges. For the remaining judges in the province, while a cross-cultural program will address these issues, judges should also be meeting with community members to be properly aware of life in Aboriginal communities. They should be aware of the concerns of people living in different parts of the province. If individual judges feel it inappropriate to visit in the communities, at least the chief justice and associate chief justices should do so, and report and discuss their findings with all the judges of their court. Judges should also meet with Aboriginal community leaders in urban areas to ensure that the concerns of those leaders are also known.

Lawyers
Aboriginal Perceptions of Lawyers

The general role of lawyers in the criminal justice system is understood by Aboriginal people. The word "lawyer" is translated into some Aboriginal languages as "one who speaks for another." However, we learned from our hearings that many Aboriginal people are very disillusioned and dissatisfied with the services they receive from lawyers. In addition to specific complaints, there are general impressions of the legal profession that lawyers must address. The main criticism is that lawyers often do not tell their Aboriginal clients what they are doing or why. Lawyers are seen as a major cause of delay. Aboriginal people feel that many lawyers do not understand the people they represent, the situation in Aboriginal communities, or factors that should be raised in court. Legal Aid lawyers were particularly singled out for criticism by people who did not feel that they were as good as members of the private bar. As we discuss later, this is not an opinion that we share.

We heard numerous complaints about the treatment Aboriginal people received from lawyers who forced them to make decisions they did not understand, kept them in constant fear, pressed them to plead guilty when they felt they were innocent, did not act in their best interests and treated them as if they were guilty. On top of this, Aboriginal people believed that lawyers were enriching themselves on their misery.

Some complaints were directed specifically at Legal Aid lawyers, particularly the services provided by duty counsel in the circuit courts. People complained about having to stand in line to see their lawyer, that Legal Aid did not pursue bail with enough vigour and that, on occasion, it took several court appearances to have a Legal Aid lawyer appointed. On numerous occasions people wondered how it was possible for Legal Aid lawyers to defend people after only speaking to them for five or 10 minutes.

The suggestion that Legal Aid lawyers come to communities in advance of the day set for court was heard on many occasions. Aboriginal people, paralegals and Legal Aid lawyers all agree that there are not sufficient resources to devote enough time to the needs of Aboriginal clients.

Not all comments were unfavourable. Lawyers were credited with doing a good job in speaking to sentence in the southern courts. Many Aboriginal people who were convicted of an offence thought their lawyer presented a good defence and did all that was reasonably possible to obtain an acquittal. Some even expressed surprise with the extent of a lawyer's activity when the lawyer knew they were guilty of the offence with which they were charged.

Lawyers' Opinions Surveyed

Our Inquiry conducted a mail survey of 146 lawyers known to have extensive practices in criminal law in Manitoba. The survey confirms the perception of Aboriginal people that, with a few exceptions, lawyers often do not have a grasp of Aboriginal issues or concerns. While many lawyers recognized that Aboriginal people in remote communities did not receive a proper level of service, there does not appear to be an understanding of the Aboriginal community's desire for a greater degree of involvement in, and control over, the legal system. Where they do indicate some support for Aboriginal peoples' concerns, that support is less than unanimous.

Only 26% of all respondents indicated that they sometimes consulted with the chief or band council in the course of their duties. Even fewer reported consulting with mayors, local justice committees or elders. In all cases, Crown attorneys were less likely to consult with community leaders than were defence counsel. These findings support the view that the lawyers who work in the circuit court system are very isolated from the communities they serve.

This isolation from Aboriginal communities is particularly disturbing in light of the fact that Aboriginal people made up a substantial proportion of the caseloads of the lawyers who responded. Two-thirds of the Legal Aid and private defence counsel, and half of the Crown attorneys, reported that Aboriginal people represented more than one-half of their caseloads.

Many defence lawyers expressed concern about the availability of legal counsel in Aboriginal communities. Only 29% of the defence lawyers thought the availability of counsel in Aboriginal communities was adequate. As one commented, "Legal Aid does not have the resources to service remote communities adequately." Crown attorneys were more satisfied, with 56% reporting they felt availability of counsel was adequate.

Many lawyers expressed concern about the time available to them to do their work in circuit courts. One respondent noted, "Circuit lawyers have little time in circuit courts. Staff, defence and Crown lawyers on northern circuits handle far more cases than their southern counterparts." Virtually all the defence lawyers, as well as 72% of the Crown attorneys, agreed that at least some of the time there was not enough time to deal with all cases on the docket. The majority (70%) of respondents felt that more court sittings were required in Aboriginal circuit court locations.

Responses were more positive about the possibility of considering Aboriginal traditions when sentencing Aboriginal offenders. Seventy-four per cent of all respondents agreed that traditional Aboriginal ways of dealing with offences should be considered in sentencing, while only 12% felt they should never be used. Crown attorneys were the least likely to support this idea. The comments of two respondents illustrate both sides of this issue very effectively:

> • Use of native cultural conflict resolution tools (including reconciliation, elders, sweat lodges, etc.) can give Aboriginal communities control and ownership over the criminal justice process and could frequently replace prosecution. Ownership would give a sense of responsibility. Flying in a court party to 'solve' local problems keeps communities powerless and precludes problem-solving by the local community.

> • What should not be forgotten is that the law of the land is the Law of Canada, one law for one people. It cannot differ from jurisdiction to jurisdiction in the sense that substantive law and the applications of that substantive law must be the same (equality provisions demand it)....

While there was support for considering Aboriginal traditions in sentencing, other suggestions, such as altering the jury selection process, did not receive much support.

Generally, Crown attorneys appear to think that the present system is good and needs few, if any, changes. Legal Aid lawyers were at the opposite end of the spectrum, with many feeling that Aboriginal people are not well served by the present system. Members of the private bar seemed to be in the middle. We now turn to those different components of the bar.

Legal Aid Services

As we note above, Legal Aid Manitoba was often singled out for criticism by Aboriginal presenters in remote communities. Legal Aid lawyers appearing before us also acknowledged the problems that they experience in providing service to Aboriginal people in remote communities. We believe that there are, indeed, problems with the type of legal services provided by circuit courts, but we do not believe that this reflects any lack of commitment or ability on the part of Legal Aid lawyers. Legal Aid executive director Allan Fineblit said in his submission to us that "the current justice system is not serving Aboriginal people and must be dramatically changed." He reported that "it was the consensus of the Legal Aid staff that there is much to commend some form of Aboriginal justice system."

In 1987 a study of Legal Aid Manitoba commissioned by the federal government concluded that:

> [E]ven though conventional wisdom suggests that [Legal Aid] staff lawyers are less efficient and effective than the private Bar in the delivery of legal aid services, the analysis presented above indicates that this view is incorrect. [Legal Aid] Staff appear to be more efficient in time recorded per case than the private Bar; and, case outcomes for staff and private Bar cases do not present appreciable differences.[7]

We believe that concerns about the competency of Legal Aid staff lawyers are misplaced. Legal Aid staff lawyers are able to provide first-class legal service. Nevertheless, we recommend that Legal Aid lawyers visit circuit court communities the day before a court hearing. To accomplish this, it may be necessary to temporarily increase the size of the Legal Aid staff, particularly in northern Manitoba.

Legal Aid's Northern Paralegal program employs two Aboriginal paralegals who provide pre-trial legal advice in four communities served by circuit courts. This is an important initiative which has received positive assessments. During the course of our Inquiry, we heard from the paralegals on a number of occasions and were impressed with the services they provide. Their testimony indicates that this sort of program should be expanded. All communities should receive this type of service. We believe that, as good as the present program is, it should be integrated into the Aboriginal Court Worker program we recommend later.

One of the areas which we have identified as contributing to the over-representation of Aboriginal people in the justice system, particularly in our correctional institutions, centres on Legal Aid regulations which stipulate that even if an applicant meets the financial criteria, Legal Aid will not provide counsel in summary conviction cases, unless there is a likelihood of the accused either going to jail or losing his or her job upon conviction.

Many Aboriginal people appear to have developed a record of relatively minor offences prior to their first incarceration. We know that in considering what sentence is most appropriate for an accused, judges are often swayed by the existence of an accused's prior record. An accused with even a short history of arrests and convictions for minor offences runs a much greater risk of being incarcerated for another minor offence than one who lacks such a record.

Legal Aid's policy contributes, no doubt, to the compilation of a criminal record of minor offences for such accused. In effect, legal assistance is unavailable to otherwise eligible accused, assistance which would help prevent them from being improperly convicted, or from pleading guilty without legal advice. We know that duty counsel is available to assist such accused, but we also know that duty counsel can only provide the most superficial of assistance to unrepresented accused. For Aboriginal accused, who are the single largest group in court, Legal Aid's policy has an adverse impact upon them.

WE RECOMMEND THAT:

■ Legal Aid Manitoba provide representation in all criminal matters in which the accused meets the Legal Aid income criteria.

Private Counsel

We have focussed on Legal Aid staff lawyers in large part because the poverty of Aboriginal people means that they rely very heavily on Legal Aid services. However, private counsel who receive certificates, or who represent Aboriginal accused by private agreement, must also change their approach. They should be more accessible to their Aboriginal clients.

It is clear to us from our hearings that many Aboriginal people feel that the lawyers who represented them did not fully explain the process which was taking place, made deals their clients did not fully understand, and treated their clients in a patronizing and perfunctory fashion. Canadian law is complex and it is often practised under very difficult conditions; lawyers may not feel they have the time to explain how their actions are in the best interests of their client. But a lawyer who fails to do so is not properly representing his or her client, especially when that lawyer is supposed to be taking instructions from the clients, not telling them what to do.

Crown Attorneys

Crown attorneys play a large role in the administration of the criminal justice system. They review, or they should review, all charges that have been laid by police. They are responsible for making certain that the appropriate charge has been laid. They should only proceed with a charge which is supportable on the available evidence. Many defence counsel blame some of the problems with the system on over-charging by the Crown or the police, and the Crown attorney must make certain this does not occur.

If there are community support services, the Crown attorney must be aware of them and use them whenever possible. Some communities have justice committees in place that can be used to resolve problems without the need to apply the full force of the criminal justice system.

WE RECOMMEND THAT:

■ The Justice department provide regular workshops to Crown attorneys on the range and effectiveness of the various community services which are available in Manitoba.

In light of the crucial role Crown attorneys play in the justice system, we are disturbed by the fact that, according to our survey of provincial lawyers, Crown attorneys find little wrong with the status quo when it comes to the treatment afforded Aboriginal people by the justice system. We believe that many problems exist, that substantial changes should be made and that the cooperation of the Province's Crown attorneys will be essential in bringing these changes about. Any implementation strategy must include an orientation and training program for Crown attorneys.

Addition of Local Personnel to Circuit System

As we have noted earlier, we anticipate that many, if not all, Aboriginal communities served by circuit courts will move to establish Aboriginal justice systems. As a transitional measure, important court services should be provided by local personnel. The local community must have a role in the hiring and training of these individuals. This local involvement will also provide a continuing court presence in the community between visits of the court party and during the period when the Aboriginal justice system is being established. A variety of local personnel will be invaluable to the court and will significantly improve the delivery of services to the community.

It is possible for more than one of the required services to be provided by the same person. However, we see it as absolutely essential that the local community become involved in the current justice system, at least in these ways. When a more comprehensive Aboriginal court system is in place, some of these court officials will still be needed to serve that system.

Court Administrator

A resident court administrator is needed in every Aboriginal community served by the circuit court, to keep the records of the court, to provide information to litigants and witnesses and to make sure that facilities are readied for court hearings. That person might also have the authority of a magistrate to issue court processes and to deal with bail and other matters under the direction of the court. The court administrator should also have the authority of a hearing officer to deal with small claims, and maintenance and fine enforcement questions, in the same way hearing officers deal with them in urban centres.

At the present time, a court clerk is part of the fly-in court party. This practice should cease. We suggest that the local court administrator be trained to perform these duties. It should be the responsibility of the administrator to perform all the tasks of a registry officer, to make arrangements for the sittings of the court and to act as clerk when the court is in session.

There is an association of Aboriginal court clerks in the United States which offers ongoing training programs, in which clerks are instructed in such matters as office management, docket control, the conduct of civil and criminal trials and the empanelling of a jury. Similar training should be provided in Manitoba.

A court reporter also travels with the court party. We suggest that this is unnecessary. We recommend that each court facility have amplification and recording equipment. Amplification is needed to enable those present to hear what the judge, lawyers and witnesses are saying. As part of the installation of that equipment, we recommend that recording equipment be installed to record the court proceedings. The court administrator should be responsible for the operation of the equipment. If a transcript is required, the administrator should prepare it or engage another person in the community to prepare it.

Interpreter

Many Aboriginal people who come before the court do not understand what is happening or what is said to them. They are unable to fully express themselves in English. Section 14 of the *Charter of Rights and Freedoms* guarantees an interpreter to an accused who does not understand or speak the language. Even people who do speak English may not understand it well enough to understand the implications of court proceedings. Therefore, an interpreter who is familiar with the local language and dialect, and properly trained in court interpreting, must be available for all court proceedings, to interpret from English to the local language and from the local language to English. This would help eliminate many of the misunderstandings which exist at the present time, and would help educate community members on the role and function of the courts. The provision of interpretation services is essential as long as court officials do not speak the language of all those who come before the court. We understand that, at the present time, there are no interpreters in the employ of the government who are attached to any circuit court. Aboriginal court workers (formerly court communicators) often fulfil this function, but they and their clients feel that it creates a conflict to provide translation on behalf of the court while simultaneously attempting to represent the interests of an individual accused person.

An extreme example of the types of conflict that can arise was outlined during our Inquiry by Stanley Guiboche. He provided us with this account of what happened to him while he was a court communicator in The Pas:

> It was a corporal at the town detachment and this was quite some way back. I don't know where the officer is now, or whether he is still on the force. He asked if I could go see him, or said he needed to see me. So, I went to the detachment, where the town office is now, and on entering the office there I seen two young native kids sitting there. I asked them what was the matter. I asked them in Cree and they didn't say anything. I noticed they had no shoes on.

> When the corporal came out I asked him what did he want me to do. He said that they had picked up these two kids and they were 14, 15, maybe 16, and it seemed like they were quite scared. They wanted some assistance in taking statements off them, from them. I asked if any statements had been taken so far and they said that they took one from one of them. However, the other one didn't want to give a statement because he didn't understand.

> So, I said, "Well, what is it that you are investigating or why did you pick these fellows up." They said that they were suspects in murder. I informed the corporal then at the time, I said, well in that particular case I can only tell the boys not to say anything and that I should really get a lawyer for them. The corporal got very upset and wanted to know what the heck was my job.

> He said, "What the heck is your job anyway? You're an interpreter." I said, "I'm an interpreter in the sense that I communicate with lawyers and their clients, but not to the extent that I don't think my job includes assisting the police in taking statements."

Due to linguistic differences throughout Manitoba, interpreters should be selected from each community and be provided with proper training. During our public hearings, we occasionally asked Aboriginal people who travelled with us to act as interpreters. While that was satisfactory, we concluded that it was preferable to ask a resident of the community we were in to act as interpreter. That resident not only knew the linguistic distinctions, but he or she had the confidence of the other community members.

Interpreters should be trained in law and legal procedure through a formal, structured training course. In order to give this training, a dictionary of legal terminology should be developed, which would give Aboriginal people a means of expressing difficult legal concepts in Aboriginal languages.

A qualified interpreter should be in attendance at every sitting of the court in an Aboriginal community. It is important to allow the interpreter to discuss a question and answer with a witness, as it is often not possible to literally translate a question or answer from English to an Aboriginal language, or to give a simple "yes" or "no" answer.

WE RECOMMEND THAT:

- The position of court administrator with magistrate's powers be created in each Aboriginal community served by a circuit court.

- The Province of Manitoba establish a formal Court Interpreter's Program with staff trained in the interpretation of court proceedings, including legal terminology, from English into the Aboriginal languages of Manitoba. As part of this program, local court interpreters should be engaged in each Aboriginal community served by circuit courts.

- The Province of Manitoba, in consultation with the Manitoba Association for Native Languages, establish a Legal Interpretation Project to develop appropriate Aboriginal translations of English legal terms.

Aboriginal Court Worker

We believe that the Aboriginal Court Worker program should be significantly revamped. In particular, it should be placed under the administration of a separate Aboriginal board of directors and it should given responsibility to administer and expand the Legal Aid Manitoba Northern Paralegal program.

An Aboriginal court worker should be resident in Aboriginal communities served by circuit courts, in order to advise accused persons and other community members of the court procedures and of what is required of them. Currently, such services are provided by two paralegals employed by Legal Aid Manitoba, who serve four northern communities, and by the Aboriginal Court Worker program (formerly the Court Communicator program) which exists throughout the province and is run by the provincial Justice department.

The Court Communicator program in Manitoba has been a good beginning. In the areas where the worker is fluent in local languages, an important service is being provided to Aboriginal accused. Unfortunately, there are many courts not served by the present system. The Youth Court, for example, has none. The services court communicators have provided in the past were not well defined. As a result, their role has not been well understood. In many cases their existence has been unknown. A number of inmates told us they were unaware of the service. When it was described to them, they thought the service would be helpful. We are pleased to hear the program is undergoing a reorganization and is placing greater emphasis on outreach and education.

We have also examined the Legal Aid paralegal program. We congratulate Legal Aid Manitoba for taking this initiative, which has been positively evaluated. The two paralegals operating from Thompson are fluent in Cree and English, and work in Norway House, Cross Lake, God's Lake Narrows and Shamattawa. They operate drop-in clinics in these communities and assist Legal Aid lawyers in the preparation of cases. From what we know of the services they offer, we can say those services just scratch the surface of the type of services that are required in Aboriginal communities.

Alberta currently has a Native Court Workers program. That program is managed by an independent board accountable to, and appointed by, Aboriginal organizations, and offers services to Aboriginal people. The service we recommend for Manitoba is similar in structure to that in place in Alberta.

We recommend that this program and its workers assume the tasks now performed by Aboriginal court workers and by the northern paralegal officers employed by Legal Aid Manitoba. At the present time, both services concentrate on giving the accused some understanding of the situation, assisting them in obtaining a lawyer and facilitating communications between lawyer and client, if that is necessary. The additional duties we would like to see the worker undertake is to assist in communications and understanding between the accused and the judge, and vice versa. Court workers should be more actively involved in advising the court of any facts or local conditions the judge should be aware of before sentencing.

It is important that a judge not merely ask if an accused understands what is being said or explained. We have found that Aboriginal people may say they understand, when they do not. Some may think they understand, when they do not. Some may understand most of what they are told, but they may not understand the subtle details or the full implication of what has been said. One of the responsibilities of the court worker should be to make certain that the accused understands everything that is happening.

We suggest that the program be managed by an independent, Aboriginal board of directors. Such a board will be aware of the problems of those going to court and be able to adapt the service to the needs of the communities and of the Aboriginal accused.

WE RECOMMEND THAT:

- ■ The Aboriginal Court Worker program have an Aboriginal board of directors and take over the functions and staff of the existing court communicator and paralegal programs. Court workers should be available in every Aboriginal community serviced by the circuit courts.

Peacemaker

Alternate dispute resolution is a term that may include "diversion" but is generally equated with "mediation." Mediation is a process applied in the resolution of disputes between two people, organizations or public bodies that permits an individual ("mediator") to work with the parties in an effort to help them arrive at their own solution. In pure mediation, the mediator does not actively attempt to suggest his or her idea of how a dispute should be resolved, but acts as a facilitator to enable the parties to come together and to devise their own solution.

Other forms of alternate dispute resolution are similar to mediation, but may call upon the facilitator to take a more active role. Negotiators argue on behalf of one party to a dispute, and conciliators, or conciliation officers, carry messages and positions back and forth between disputing parties, making suggestions to each as to what concessions might result in an agreement.

In our discussion of Aboriginal justices systems, we examined the role that peacemakers play in American tribal courts. We believe that peacemakers can play a major role in helping those communities which choose to establish Aboriginal justice systems to make the transition from the current justice system. In addition, there is a role for peacemakers in the general justice system in non-Aboriginal communities with a large Aboriginal population.

A peacemaker, as that term is used, and as the practice in tribal courts in the United States demonstrates, may assume each of these roles from time to time, as he or she applies his or her art. The peacemaker's goal is to settle disputes between parties and to return them to a peaceful relationship with one another, and to restore stability to the community, without the need to involve the adversarial court system.

The goals of the peacemaker are to:

- Determine the cause of a problem that may result, or has resulted, in a dispute or a criminal charge.
- Determine the effect on the victim and his or her attitude towards the offence and the offender.
- Bring home to the offender that his or her conduct is unacceptable in the community.
- Counsel the offender.

- Attempt to ensure that there will be no repetition of the unacceptable conduct.

- Provide ongoing support to the offender and the family.

- Involve the families and place some continuing responsibility for the conduct of the offender upon his or her family.

- Restore peace in the community.

In order to achieve these goals, the peacemaker must be a person who has the respect of the community and is able to work with others to resolve interpersonal problems. A peacemaker, because of age, life experience and ability as a mediator and conciliator, can be effective in resolving problems that develop in a community. A peacemaker can deal with the parties on a personal basis in a way our formalized court system cannot. He or she may also be able to apply traditional ways to deal with Aboriginal offenders and families, which the court system is not equipped to do.

In the Navajo Tribal Court, a judge refers cases to a peacemaker whom the judge considers suitable for the particular case. The peacemaker meets with the parties, and often with their parents in the case of juveniles, to determine the cause of the trouble and to seek solutions. The peacemaker sends a written report to the court. The judge may accept the recommendation of the peacemaker or may deal with the case in some other way.

The role of the peacemaker is different from that of a judge, and the peacemaker's objective may be quite different. While a judge must listen to admissible evidence, convict or acquit, and impose sentences when there is a conviction, the peacemaker has as a goal the maintenance of stability in the community. Where there is an admission of fault (rather than a plea of guilty), the peacemaker can try to mend the harm that has been caused by determining the cause of the inappropriate action and finding a remedy. Family members and others can be involved in the solution.

Even at this stage, without having the benefit of an Aboriginal court system, we recommend that all courts have peacemakers attached to them. They should be Aboriginal people dealing with Aboriginal accused.

The role of the peacemaker should be to take referrals from the court in any case where the Crown attorney, the defence counsel, the accused or the victim can persuade the judge that the problem should be dealt with without using the full criminal court system. A judge should also be able to make such a reference, even if others do not agree.

If the recommendation of the peacemaker is accepted, the charge should be withdrawn or stayed by the Crown, or a conditional or unconditional discharge applied by the judge. If the peacemaker recommends a certain penalty and if the accused pleads guilty, that penalty should be given serious consideration by the presiding judge.

Several peacemakers may be attached to one court. The peacemakers we met in the Navajo court system were Aboriginal men and women with experience in teaching, in religious and community activity, and in dealing with young people and problems of substance abuse.

WE RECOMMEND THAT:

- Peacemakers be appointed in each Aboriginal community in Manitoba. They should be appointed through procedures which are agreed to by the community.

- Peacemakers, recommended by recognized local Aboriginal groups, be appointed in Winnipeg and in other urban centres throughout the province.

Conclusion

We believe that the reforms we have outlined above will remove much of the complexity and inequality that plague the current court system in Manitoba. A unified court system will provide full service at all court points. A streamlined court process will end the denial of justice that delay creates. The reform of the circuit courts and the hiring of additional Aboriginal staff in remote communities will provide for more complete local justice services and enable a smooth transition to an Aboriginal justice system.

CHAPTER 9

―――

JURIES

Introduction

The jury system has long been considered one of the most sacred institutions of the Anglo-Canadian legal system. It is the protection which people have against unjust laws and arbitrary decisions of government, the police, lawyers or judges, and it guarantees community scrutiny of the criminal justice system.

The jury is asked to listen to the evidence that is presented at a trial and to decide what happened. The jury members are then to take the judge's direction as to the law, to apply the law that fits with their findings of fact and to deliver a verdict.

In a criminal case the verdict will usually be one of guilty or not guilty. If there is more than one charge, or included and lesser counts, the jury will decide the particular offence of which the accused is guilty. In the case of murder, for example, a jury may find an accused guilty of murder, or of the lesser and included offence of manslaughter.

While the jury is instructed not to apply any personal knowledge of any fact related to the offence, it is expected that it will apply its general knowledge of the community, its understanding of human nature and its common sense.

In its 1982 *Report on the Jury*, the Law Reform Commission of Canada found that the jury system serves a number of vital functions in our criminal justice system:

> First, because the jury is composed of a number of people with a wide diversity of experience and because it reaches a collective decision only after

deliberating seriously and often robustly about the evidence, the jury is likely to be an excellent fact finder. Second, because it represents a cross-section of the community, the jury is able to act as the conscience of the community, ensuring that individual criminal cases are justly resolved. Third, the jury can act as the citizen's ultimate protection against oppressive laws and the oppressive enforcement of the law. When a properly instructed jury acting judicially acquits an accused, no judge or state official can reverse its decision. Fourth, because the jury involves the public in the central task of the criminal justice system, it provides a means whereby the public can learn about, and critically examine, the functioning of the criminal justice system. For the public, it acts as a window on the criminal justice system. Finally, by involving the public in judicial decision-making, the jury undoubtedly increases the public's trust in the system.[1]

These are very lofty and fine expressions of confidence in the jury system. Unfortunately, many of these principles do not apply to Aboriginal people who are excluded, in large measure, from participating in the system.

The Exclusion of Aboriginal People from Juries

Historical Exclusion

We believe that the jury system in Manitoba is a glaring example of systemic discrimination against Aboriginal people. Studies conducted for our Inquiry confirm that Aboriginal people are significantly under-represented on juries in northern Manitoba and are almost completely absent from juries in the city of Winnipeg.

Of all the ways that Aboriginal people are under-represented in the justice system, this is one of the most disturbing. Jurors, after all, require no special training or skills.

Juries represent the direct involvement of the lay public in the justice system. If a significant portion of that public is not properly represented on juries, it would not be surprising to discover that a portion of the public never comes to view the justice system as anything other than a foreign and imposed system.

The reasons for the under-representation of Aboriginal people on juries are numerous, but it is important to bear several facts in mind from the outset. From its inception, the legal system in Manitoba has systematically excluded Aboriginal people from juries. This discrimination has taken many forms. Jurors have traditionally been drawn from lists of voters. Since Indians or persons of Indian blood were denied the vote in Manitoba from 1886 until 1952, they were effectively denied the right to sit on juries. The situation did not significantly improve in 1952. For the following two decades, most Aboriginal people in Manitoba were effectively excluded from sitting on juries because reserve officials, unlike the mayors and reeves of municipalities, were not required to submit the names of potential jurors to the chief County Court judge. This policy was changed in 1971 and reserves were obliged to submit names drawn from their electoral lists. As was the case with lists from non-Aboriginal communities, these lists suffered from a lack of attention and were not regularly updated. It was only in 1983, when the

Province began using the computerized records of the Manitoba Health Services Commission, that Aboriginal people began to be properly represented on the lists of potential jurors. For a century the legal system made it clear that it did not want or need Aboriginal jurors. It is a message Aboriginal people have not forgotten.

While serving on juries can be seen to be a cornerstone of the Anglo-Canadian legal system, to an Aboriginal person it might well appear to be culturally irrelevant. As we have noted in earlier chapters, the determination of guilt, the primary function of a jury, does not play a large role in the traditional Aboriginal concepts of justice. The Aboriginal approach was to take the measures necessary to restore the community to a state of peaceful coexistence.

The legacy of past exclusions must be kept in mind as efforts are undertaken to make the jury system more truly representative. These efforts will only succeed by taking steps which bring local communities into close contact with the court and which involve more Aboriginal people in the jury system.

Contemporary Exclusion

Section 2 of the *Jury Act* of Manitoba, C.C.S.M. c. J30, states, "Every person has the right and duty to serve as a juror unless disqualified or exempted under the Act." This means that every citizen of the province has the right, and the obligation, to assist in the administration of the law when called upon to do so.

Our studies clearly show that Aboriginal people are not properly represented on juries, even on juries trying an Aboriginal person accused of committing an offence against another Aboriginal person in an Aboriginal community.

An illustration of the lack of Aboriginal involvement on juries was seen at the opening of the assizes in Winnipeg on September 28, 1988. Approximately 120 people appeared on the jury panel, from which juries for several cases were to be selected. Of these 120, only one appeared to be an Aboriginal person. A similar study was undertaken on January 30, 1989 at the Thompson assizes. Aboriginal people accounted for 36% of the jury panel members present, which means they were representative of the number of Aboriginal people in the Thompson Judicial Centre, but the three juries constituted from this panel contained only two Aboriginal persons each. This means Aboriginal people accounted for only 17% of each jury.

One of the reasons we have juries is to involve people from the community in the administration of justice. If one group is excluded from that jury service, that group is deprived of the opportunity to apply its scrutiny to cases and is deprived of the opportunity to improve its understanding of how the legal system operates. The fact that juries rarely include Aboriginal people means that the testimony of Aboriginal witnesses and accused are not understood by the jury, from the Aboriginal perspective. Also, it can be intimidating for Aboriginal people to testify before all-white judges and juries.

Aboriginal people are excluded from juries at the stage when people are summoned to form part of a jury panel. If they do appear on a panel, more are eliminated by stand-asides and challenges advanced by lawyers. It is the system that permits this to happen to which we direct our attention.

How Juries Are Selected

The Jurors' Roll

Jurors in Manitoba are selected according to the Manitoba *Jury Act*. Section 6(1) of the Act says a list of potential jurors, known as a jurors' roll, is to be prepared by random selection from "appropriate lists." These lists may be electors' rolls or other records of any department of government selected for the purpose. In Manitoba the jurors' roll is drawn from the list of Manitobans registered with the Manitoba Health Services Commission. Studies conducted by our Inquiry indicated jurors' rolls drawn from the lists provided from MHSC contain a properly representative number of Aboriginal people. The exception to this appears to be in the city of Winnipeg. Here, our study determined that Aboriginal people were under-represented on the Winnipeg Judicial Centre jurors' roll.

The Jury Panel

Prior to each assize sitting, the sheriff for each of Manitoba's six judicial centres creates a jury panel. Five weeks before any jury is to be selected, the sheriff sends out summonses by registered mail to those named on the jurors' roll. The summonses are accompanied by literature in French and English explaining the recipient's obligations. Upon receipt of a summons, people are obliged to contact the sheriff and are requested to do this by telephone. Those individuals who eventually respond to the summons and attend at court comprise the jury panel. The panel is the group of people required to be present at the beginning of a trial from which the 12-person jury is selected. The number of people to be summoned to form the panel is determined by the chief justice in consultation with the sheriff. The number required will depend upon the number of cases and the number of accused in each case to be heard at that assize (jury) sitting. More people than necessary are called, as some will be granted exemptions, some will fail to respond and many will be challenged.

The Jury

When a jury trial is to be held, all those who have been summoned must attend at the courthouse for jury duty. The names of all those on the panel are placed in a box and drawn at random. Those whose names are drawn are called forward in the courtroom. The judge asks those who have a specific knowledge of the accused or of the alleged crime, or who may, for any other reason, not be effective fact-finders in a specific case, to identify themselves. They may be excused by the judge. The Crown and defence lawyers then have the opportunity to accept or challenge other prospective jurors. There are three types of challenges to a juror, only two of which are available to the defence. These are: stand-asides, peremptory challenges and challenge for cause.

Stand-Asides

Without providing any reason, the Crown may ask a prospective juror who is called forward from the panel to be stood aside. The juror who has been stood aside returns to a seat with the rest of the panel. A person who has been stood aside cannot be called forward again until all others on the panel have been called. The Crown attorney is allowed to ask 48 jurors to stand aside.

The effect of this practice is to allow the Crown to reserve its decision as to whether to challenge a person. It also allows it to see the types of challenges advanced by the defence. If there are not too many defence challenges, the result is that those who were stood aside never sit on the jury. In practice, more than 48 persons are seldom called. The practice gives the Crown a considerable advantage in the choice of those who eventually make up the jury. If Aboriginal people are stood aside, they will not likely sit on the jury.

Peremptory Challenges

These challenges are made without cause or reasons having to be provided. A person who has been challenged peremptorily is automatically excluded from the jury. In first degree murder trials, the defence is allowed 20 peremptory challenges for each accused. In cases where the maximum penalty is greater than five years, the defence is allowed 12 peremptory challenges. In all other cases, the defence is allowed four peremptory challenges. The Crown is allowed four peremptory challenges in all cases.

As counsel do not have to give a reason for these challenges, there is no limitation on those who may be removed from consideration as jurors by this means. If either counsel decides it would be preferable not to have an Aboriginal person on the jury, that person can be eliminated by this means. The same would apply to women or to people of a particular occupation. No reason is given and none is demanded.

Challenge for Cause

Jurors can be objected to by either the Crown or the defence on the basis that the juror is not impartial. Both defence and Crown are allowed an unlimited number of these challenges. Challenges have to have some basis, and to determine whether there is any, both Crown and defence counsel are entitled, with the court's permission, to question prospective jurors. The judge may require that these questions be put in writing. In Manitoba the practice is to limit the extent of the questioning. If no particular facts are known that may show some relationship to a party or a witness, or some unusual knowledge of the case, the question is usually limited to whether the person believes that he or she can independently consider the evidence and give a verdict based on the evidence. Some "fishing" is permitted to test the juror's belief in his or her ability to render a just verdict in certain sensitive or emotionally charged situations. The validity of these challenges is ruled upon by two people who have been selected to sit on the jury, or, where none is yet selected, two other members of the jury panel, referred to as "triers."

If the triers decide the juror who has been challenged for cause is impartial, that person takes a seat on the jury unless one counsel or the other applies a peremptory challenge. If the triers decide the person will not be impartial, he or she may not sit on that jury. A jury is fully constituted once 12 people have been selected without challenge.

How Aboriginal People Are Excluded from Juries

On the face of it, the current system, which starts with a list that contains a representative number of Aboriginal people, should produce representative juries. But this is clearly not the case. For a variety of reasons, at a number of different points in the jury selection process, Aboriginal people either are excluded or are able to exclude themselves from the jury system.

Of particular concern to us is that:

- In many communities Aboriginal people are under-represented on jury panels.

- When Aboriginal people are present on jury panels, we believe that both prosecutors and defence attorneys have used their peremptory challenges and stand-asides to screen Aboriginal people out of the jury system.

We will examine these problems in turn.

Problems with Selection

Our studies indicate that while Aboriginal people are proportionately represented on the lists from which jurors' panels are summoned, they are often significantly under-represented on the panels themselves. We have concluded that the main reasons Aboriginal people are not properly represented on jury panels are that the manner in which they are summoned works against them, and the fact that the sheriff does not follow up on the summons. The summoning procedure works against Aboriginal people in a number of ways.

It may not appear that there is anything discriminatory about mailing summonses, or asking potential jurors to make a telephone call to indicate whether they are prepared to serve on a jury, but there are unique problems for Aboriginal people with both these practices. Non-Aboriginal communities are likely to have better mail service and better telephone service than Aboriginal communities. Aboriginal people in remote communities are far less able to check their mail every day. Because they are more likely to be renters, Aboriginal people in urban areas change addresses more frequently than non-Aboriginal people, as well. This means that Aboriginal people in both remote and urban centres are more difficult to reach by mail. In addition, there are many Aboriginal communities that do not have full telephone service. For that reason, and because of economic conditions, many Aboriginal families do not have personal telephone service. Aboriginal people, therefore, are less likely to receive their jury summonses and less able to respond to them quickly.

A person may be excused from jury duty by the sheriff for a number of reasons. Section 25 of the Act permits the sheriff to exempt a person on grounds of religion, serious hardship or, upon application, where a person has served on a jury during the previous two years or is over 75 years of age. In addition, a person can be excused for failing to meet the qualifications of a juror. Section 4 of the Act provides that where the language in which a trial is primarily to be conducted is one that a person is unable to understand, speak or read, that person is disqualified from serving as a juror in that trial. Thus, an Aboriginal person who tells the sheriff that he or she does not understand the English or the French language well enough to serve on a jury, or whom the sheriff believes cannot understand one of those languages well enough to serve on a jury, may be excused.

Finally, as noted above, the practice of sheriffs throughout the province is to send out more summonses to prospective jurors than the number of jurors actually needed. Once the number set for the panel has been reached, the sheriff stops pressing those who have failed to respond by that time and may also tell any further people who do respond by telephone that they are not needed.

Since sheriffs compile the jury panel from those who call in first, it is apparent that those people who get their mail first and call in first are going to be the first ones represented in such panels. The fact that the sheriff does not take any further names once his or her needs are met causes latecomers, often Aboriginal, to be excluded from jury panels.

While Aboriginal people are no longer legally barred from serving on juries, the law does not allow people who speak only Aboriginal languages to sit on juries. This requirement can regularly eliminate many of those Aboriginal people or allow them to eliminate themselves. Given that fact, Aboriginal people may well ask why they should make an effort to participate in a process which appears designed to eliminate them from participation.

Jury service not only may appear irrelevant, it can be quite costly. The travel costs associated with serving on juries are not paid in advance, but reimbursed after the fact. This is another factor which we believe causes many Aboriginal people to choose to disregard a summons or to ask the sheriff to be excused from service.

We appreciate that court sheriffs, like other officials in the judicial system, are struggling with high workloads and limited resources. To them, it is matter of simple expediency to summon considerably more people than they will need for an assize, and let many people simply ignore the summons. It is much easier to wait for travel claims than to make advance travel arrangements at government expense. Unfortunately, this concern for efficiency inadvertently serves to exclude Aboriginal people from juries.

WE RECOMMEND THAT:

- When a sheriff grants an exemption from jury duty, the person who is exempted be replaced with someone from the same community.

- Every person called for jury duty, who is not granted an exemption, be required to attend, and summonses be enforced even when sufficient jurors have responded.

Discriminatory Effect
of Peremptory Challenges and Stand-Asides

The purpose of the jury is to bring together 12 fair-minded representatives of the community to make a determination on the facts of a case. Counsel, however, see their role during jury selection as requiring them to try to select jurors likely to be supportive of their position. This attitude can distort the jury selection process. The ability, which both Crown and defence counsel have, to dismiss jurors without stating any reason makes this distortion of the process almost inevitable. We believe that any 12 people not otherwise disqualified by the Act, who direct their minds to the evidence and apply the law given to them by the judge, and have heard the arguments and submissions of the lawyers, will bring in a reasonable verdict.

We have concerns about the manner in which peremptory challenges and stand-asides are used. While some defence lawyers and Crown attorneys make no distinction on the basis of race, we believe it is common practice for some Crown attorneys and defence counsel to exclude Aboriginal jurors through the use of stand-asides and peremptory challenges.

One example of such exclusion is the Helen Betty Osborne case in The Pas. There, the jury had no Aboriginal members. The six Aboriginal people who were called forward were peremptorily challenged by counsel for the defence. The lack of Aboriginal people on a jury in a case of that kind, in an area of the province where Aboriginal people make up at least 50% of the population, raises valid concerns about the manner in which our jury selection process operates.

On one day of the Thompson assizes in January 1989, 35 of the 41 Aboriginal people who were called to serve on three juries were rejected. In one case, the Crown rejected 16 Aboriginal jurors; in another, the defence rejected two and the Crown rejected 10; in the third and final case, the defence accepted all the proposed Aboriginal jurors, while the Crown rejected nine. Two jurors were rejected twice.

A survey of lawyers' attitudes on a variety of topics was conducted for our Inquiry. Respondents were asked if they perceived discrimination in the system of jury selection. Eighty-three per cent of Legal Aid staff lawyers and 77% of private counsel thought the Crown challenged or stood aside Aboriginal persons more often than non-Aboriginal people. Only 17% of Crown attorneys thought so. By contrast, only 5% of Legal Aid staff lawyers and 12% of private counsel felt that defence lawyers challenged Aboriginal jurors more often than non-Aboriginal jurors, compared to 27% of Crown attorneys.

We are critical of a system that permits Aboriginal people to be so often and so easily excluded from sitting on a jury. Both the Crown and defence counsel have too many opportunities, through the use of peremptory challenges and stand-asides, to make decisions on the basis of racist or sexist stereotypes.

In its 1982 *Report on the Jury,* the Law Reform Commission of Canada recommended that the use of stand-asides be abolished and replaced by the same number of peremptory challenges available to the defence. While this would be an improvement over the current system, it does not go far enough, since the use of peremptory challenges by counsel for accused persons has also been abused.

While the practice of challenging people without having to give a reason is sanctioned by the *Criminal Code,* we question the logic and fairness of allowing the practice to continue when its application can prevent Aboriginal people from sitting on a jury solely because they are Aboriginal. We believe strongly that the use of stand-asides and peremptory challenges in such a manner must be brought to a halt.

The *Charter of Rights and Freedoms* and the Manitoba *Human Rights Code* prohibit discrimination on the basis of sex and race. Section 626 of the *Criminal Code* explicitly states that "no person may be disqualified, exempted or excused from serving as a juror in criminal proceedings on the grounds of his or her sex." The Manitoba *Jury Act* states that every person not "disqualified or exempted" has a "right" to serve on a jury. It would appear to us that peremptory challenges and stand-asides, which allow people to be deprived of their right to serve on juries without any reason, flies in the face of these guarantees. We believe no one should be deprived of his or her right to sit on a jury without reason being provided and without a judge making a ruling on the exemption.

Because we believe that both the prosecution and the defence should have the same right to exclude people for good reason, we do not wish to see challenges removed entirely. However, we do believe that only challenges for cause should be allowed.

WE RECOMMEND THAT:

■ The *Criminal Code* of Canada be amended so that the only challenges to prospective jurors be challenges for cause, and that both stand-asides and peremptory challenges be eliminated.

Initial information should be supplied by each member of the panel, after being told what the particular case is about and who is on trial, indicating whether the juror knows any of the people likely to testify, or if he or she has any personal knowledge about the occurrence itself. Armed with this information, counsel should then be permitted to question potential jurors to test their independence. The judge should be entitled to question the person and to determine if he or she will be able to listen to the evidence and to arrive at a verdict independently, based on the evidence he or she hears and on the law the judge will later describe.

Counsel should be able to make representations as to whether a certain person should become a juror, but the final decision should be made by the judge. We suggest that a judge is in a better position to make that determination than the triers, who are unfamiliar with the law applicable to the issue.

The judge should also have the authority to excuse jurors if it appears fair and just to do so, without going through the challenge procedure. Information may emerge that would warrant that action without having the person subjected to questioning. It should also be open to counsel to make a joint request that a certain person be excused, providing the reason in writing to the judge.

WE RECOMMEND THAT:

- The *Criminal Code* be amended so that rulings on challenges for cause be made by the presiding judge.

Local Jury Trials

We believe it is necessary to provide local communities with greater input into the legal system. Currently, the Manitoba Court of Queen's Bench is the only court in Manitoba with the authority to hold jury trials. That court only holds jury trials in six communities—none of which is Aboriginal. In our chapter on court reform, we recommend that jury trials be held in the community where the offence was alleged to have been committed. Recent changes in the Northwest Territories could serve as a model for what we are proposing.

The *Jury Act* of the Northwest Territories provides that no person who resides more than 20 miles from the place fixed for the sitting of the court shall be included in the jury list. The Act was amended in 1986 to add the following section:

> 5.2. An Aboriginal person who does not speak and understand either the French language or the English language, but who speaks and understands an Aboriginal language as defined in the *Official Languages Act* ... and is otherwise qualified under this Act, may serve as a juror in any action or proceeding that may be tried by a jury in the Territories.[2]

This has made it possible for an Aboriginal person to be tried by an all-Aboriginal jury and for all Aboriginal people to serve on juries. We are impressed by the Northwest Territories' method of limiting the area from which a jury is drawn. It has a number of advantages, the most important of which is that it involves the community in the trial of one of its members.

This sort of solution is attractive to us, since it seeks to return to the community involved a direct sense of involvement in, and control and understanding of, the justice system. Many of the problems we identify earlier, dealing with the problems of the mails, telephones and travel, would cease to be exclusionary factors if this sort of recommendation were put in place. It would be suited to an Aboriginal court system, but would also be important as long as the present system continues.

If there are not sufficient jurors able to sit on the case from the same community, the jury could include people from a similar community. In Aboriginal areas, those people would still be able to understand the nuances that might apply to the relationship between victim and accused, or local factors that might escape the attention of non-Aboriginal people.

These proposals could also be successfully adapted for use in urban communities, as well as in remote and rural communities. When jury panels are being created, it would be relatively easy to program a computer to use postal codes to draw potential jurors from the sections of the city where both the accused and the victim are resident. Given the fact that a large number of Aboriginal people brought before the courts are tried in Winnipeg, and the fact that Aboriginal people almost never serve on urban juries, we believe a measure of this sort is necessary. If a case arose in Thompson, for example, it should not be necessary to bring jurors all the way from Churchill. If the case arose in Steinbach, it should not be necessary to bring in people from St. Boniface.

WE RECOMMEND THAT:

- Jurors be drawn from within 40 kilometres of the community in which a trial is to be held.

- In the event that there is a need to look elsewhere for jurors, the jury be selected from a community as similar as possible demographically and culturally to the community where the offence took place.

- In urban areas, juries be drawn from specific neighbourhoods of the town or city in which victims and accused reside.

- The Manitoba *Jury Act* be amended to permit an Aboriginal person who does not speak and understand either French or English, but who speaks and understands an Aboriginal language, and is otherwise qualified, to serve as a juror in any action or proceeding that may be tried by a jury, and that, in such cases, translation services be provided.

Conclusion

It is apparent that in Manitoba even the jury system—a cornerstone of our justice system—is failing Aboriginal people. We do not doubt for a moment that its doing so arises as much through inadvertence as through wilfulness, but to Aboriginal people that difference is of no import. As well, there is an element of inertia at play, in that many of the concepts behind the jury process have their roots in the days of the Magna Carta and have seemingly developed a sanctity of their own. The American courts have recognized that a jury selection process that results in the systemic exclusion of blacks can amount to an infringement of their constitutional rights to due process. Some of the same considerations cause us to conclude that, despite the strengths of the jury system, changes to it are necessary in the interests of fairness and justice to Aboriginal people.

CHAPTER 10

ALTERNATIVES TO
INCARCERATION

Introduction

Sentencing is the final step of judicial involvement in the justice system and, in many respects, it is the most important and difficult one. Its importance lies in the obvious impact on the offender, the victim, families and the community. Its difficulty lies in the necessity of balancing many factors, including the human factors and the protection of society.

In order to accomplish these various aims Canadian criminal law accords the courts extremely wide latitude in sentencing. The *Criminal Code,* for example, does not prescribe specific sentences for most offences. Rather, it sets out a maximum penalty or a range of penalties—which includes not only incarceration, but a variety of community sanctions such as fines, community service and suspended sentences.

Given the range of options that judges have before them and the obvious importance of passing sentences which are appropriate to specific circumstances, one might expect to discover that Canadian judges are imposing a wide spectrum of creative sentences—sentences which serve to rehabilitate the offender, ease the pain or loss suffered by the victim of a crime, restore social harmony and demonstrate society's disapproval of criminal behaviour. Yet, the single most used sentence for those convicted of indictable offences is the one which is the most expensive, most punitive and least effective: incarceration.

During the course of our Inquiry, we had the opportunity to visit all the major correctional facilities in Manitoba. We heard from both the staff and the inmates. We also had an opportunity to consult with experts in the field of corrections and to consider a wide range of alternatives to the approaches currently adopted by our correctional system. Throughout our examination, one fact became abundantly clear: Manitoba relies too heavily on incarceration. As a direct result of Aboriginal people being over-represented in entering our court system, Aboriginal people are over-incarcerated, as well.

Large numbers of Aboriginal people are taken from their families and communities to be locked away in correctional institutions. In these institutions, which are costly to build, maintain and operate, there is little in the way of constructive programming. As a result, the institutions are not effective in rehabilitating or deterring offenders. Not surprisingly, the system is viewed by Aboriginal people as a foreign one, and there is much bitterness about the unfair way that Aboriginal people and Aboriginal communities are treated. The price that Aboriginal families pay, in terms of family breakdown, loss of income and educational opportunities, cannot be underestimated.

The emphasis on incarceration also ignores the needs of the victims of crimes, and the possibilities of reconciling offenders with victims and the broader community. Courts have the power to order restitution and community service, and we believe that for many people who are currently incarcerated these sorts of sentences would have been more appropriate. These sanctions are not only less expensive than incarceration, but they hold the promise of healing communities, rather than simply punishing offenders. They also provide a clearly visible sanction within the community.

We believe that current sentencing practices continue because the Canadian legal system has no clearly articulated philosophy of sentencing. Rather than taking into consideration the specifics of the case, the culture and background of the offender, and all the available sanctions, courts are inclined to impose sentences simply because they are in keeping with previously imposed sentences. To the extent that there is a philosophy of sentencing, it is one that denies the relevance of culture, insists on incarceration for certain offences, regardless of the particular circumstances, and discounts the effect of community sanctions.

As a result, court decisions seldom reflect the values, beliefs or traditions of Aboriginal communities. Sentencing is seen by Aboriginal people as an exercise conducted for the often mysterious purposes of the non-Aboriginal justice system.

What is needed is a philosophy of sentencing that would make less use of correctional facilities, strengthen the use of community sanctions, address the needs of victims and offenders, give proper consideration to cultural factors when formulating sentences and allow the community to play a meaningful role in the development and monitoring of sentences.

In this chapter we examine the reasons behind the current sentencing practices, and make proposals for a new approach to sentencing.

Current Sentencing Practice

Sentencing Theory

Canada inherits much of its legal tradition from Britain. This tradition, which still informs Canadian practices, calls for sentences to be crafted by the courts in order to achieve several purposes. Sentences in the Canadian legal tradition do not have, nor have they ever had, the punishment of the offender as their sole purpose. If this were the case, it would be quite simple to develop and use a range of harsh punishments reminiscent of centuries past. In the Canadian system of law, however, it is asserted that punishment must be balanced with other considerations that will contribute to the rehabilitation of the offender and the protection of the community in the long term.

Typical of the legal writings on the subject is the following quote from *Halsbury's Laws of England*:

> The aims of punishment are now considered to be retribution, justice, deterrence, reformation, and protection and modern sentencing policy reflects a combination of several or all of these aims. The retributive element is intended to show public revulsion to the offence and to punish the offender for his wrong conduct. The concept of justice as an aim of punishment means both that the punishment should fit the offence and also that like offences should receive similar punishments. An increasingly important aspect of punishment is deterrence and sentences are aimed at deterring not only the actual offender from further offences but also potential offenders from breaking the law. The importance of reformation of the offender is shown by the growing emphasis laid upon it by much modern legislation, but judicial opinion towards this particular aim is varied and rehabilitation will not usually be accorded precedence over deterrence. The main aim of punishment in judicial thought, however, is still the protection of society and the other objects frequently receive only secondary consideration when sentences are being decided.[1]

To achieve these aims, Canadian courts have at their disposal a wide variety of options. The *Criminal Code* provides for a maximum penalty or a range of penalties, and the sentencing judge is expected to take the particulars of each case into consideration before deciding on an appropriate sentence. The maximum sentence is, however, normally is reserved for the most serious offenders and the most serious offences. In most instances, the sentences prescribed by the courts are less than the maximums allowed by the statutes. The options available to a judge include:

- An absolute discharge.

- A conditional discharge or a suspended sentence.

- Probation, which can be supervised or unsupervised, and can include a variety of conditions, such as curfews, no contact with certain persons, residence at a particular address, counselling, community service orders and restitution orders.

- Restitution (separate from a probation order).
- A fine (from which the offender can enter a fine option program).
- A period of incarceration.

This list demonstrates that the concept of sentencing alternatives is well ingrained in Canadian legal traditions.

The Over-Use of Incarceration

Despite Canadian legal traditions, the discretion that is available to the courts and the availability of alternatives to incarceration, there appears to be remarkably little creativity in Canadian sentencing practices. The most prominent feature of Canadian sentencing practices is the over-reliance on jail. It often appears that judges do not feel they are confronted with a continuum of sentencing options, but, rather, a dichotomy: incarceration, which is viewed in some ways as a "real" sentence, or some form of community sanction, which is viewed as a form of "leniency."

In 1987–88 there were 44 federal correctional institutions in Canada. Over 10,000 inmates were incarcerated in these facilities at any one time. Provincial facilities held an additional 16,000 inmates.[2] Of those convicted of indictable offences in Canada, it is estimated that 43% to 55% receive a jail sentence.[3]

Offenders who are sentenced to two years or more in jail must serve their time in federal penitentiaries, while those who receive sentences of less than two years serve their time in provincial institutions. Stony Mountain Institution is the only federal penitentiary in Manitoba.

Our incarceration rates appear to be out of keeping with other countries. In Canada about 108 persons per 100,000 inhabitants are sent to jail each year. In Australia the comparable figure is 67.6 per 100,000 inhabitants, in Norway it is 44.9, and in the United Kingdom it is 96.5 (in the United States it is 286.8).[4] These disparities have led many others, including the Canadian Sentencing Commission, to conclude that incarceration is over-utilized in Canada.[5]

According to the Canadian Centre for Justice Statistics, in 1988–89 Manitoba sentenced more people to jail (15,341) than Saskatchewan (12,045), and more than British Columbia (14,635).[6] Not only are the number of jail admissions high in Manitoba, the sentences are also harsh. Manitoba had a lower proportion of intermittent sentences compared to total number of admissions than any other province in Canada (4%, compared to the national average of 12%).[7] Manitoba's median sentence length was the longest in Canada, two and a half times more than the national average, with half of all sentences being 75 days or more, compared to the national average of 30 days.[8]

When one looks at why people are being sent to jail, one discovers that, according to the 1988–89 *Annual Report* of the Manitoba Attorney General's department, only 20% of the 4,192 convicts held in Manitoba's provincial correctional institutions in 1988 were sentenced for major offences—homicide, sexual offences, assaults, dangerous substance/weapons offences and robbery. A further 33% were sentenced for driving offences, especially drunk driving.

Forty-five per cent of young offenders sent to jail in that year were there for offences against property. Another 7.6% were there for committing crimes against themselves such as drug possession, sexual immorality and intoxication in public, while 26.5% were there for victimless crimes such as failure to appear in court. Fully 79%, or 2,100 of the 2,658 young offenders in custody in 1988, had not committed a crime against the person.

Aboriginal people, in particular, are served poorly by the current practices. Aboriginal people comprise more than 55% of admissions to correctional institutions in Manitoba. A 1987–88 study prepared by the Canadian Centre for Justice Statistics revealed that Aboriginal offenders accounted for approximately 18% of all sentenced admissions to provincial correctional institutions. The percentage ranges from less than 10% in Newfoundland, Prince Edward Island, Nova Scotia, New Brunswick and Ontario, to over 50% in Manitoba, Saskatchewan, the Yukon and the Northwest Territories. In federal institutions, Aboriginal offenders made up 11% of all admissions.[9] Our own research indicates that the corresponding figure at Stony Mountain, the only federal penitentiary in Manitoba, was 42%.

ABORIGINAL AND NON-ABORIGINAL INMATES

Total Admissions to Correctional Institutions in Manitoba, 1989

Institution	Non-Aboriginal Inmates		Aboriginal Inmates		Total
	Number	Percent	Number	Percent	
1. Headingley	1468	59%	1019	41%	2487
2. Brandon	514	49%	527	51%	1041
3. Dauphin	111	30%	253	70%	364
4. Milner Ridge	6	67%	3	33%	9
5. Portage	79	33%	162	67%	241
6. The Pas	74	10%	650	90%	724
7. Stony Mountain	186	54%	156	46%	342
8. Rockwood	37	76%	12	24%	49
9. Manitoba Youth Centre	1163	38%	1882	62%	3045
10. Agassiz Youth Centre	64	37%	108	63%	172
Total	**3689**	**44%**	**4772**	**56%**	**8474**

Source: Manitoba Department of Justice and the Correctional Services of Canada.
1. Headingley figures include Bannock Point; The Pas figures include the Egg Lake Camp.
2. The figures for Milner Ridge, Stony Mountain, and Rockwood are lower than their actual populations because, in the case of Milner Ridge, many of its inmates are transferred from other institutions and only appear in the admission statistics of their former institutions, and in the cases of Stony Mountain and Rockwood, many of the inmates were admitted in years previous to 1989 but remain in population serving their sentences. A single day count on October 1, 1990 showed 44 Aboriginal and 74 non-Aboriginal inmates at Milner Ridge, 25 Aboriginal and 43 non-Aboriginal inmates at Rockwood, and 156 Aboriginal and 186 non-Aboriginal inmates at Stony Mountain.

Our own studies have revealed that the official statistics on Aboriginal admissions underestimate the true extent of Aboriginal over-representation. Most systems rely on self-identification at time of admission. Our staff, through interviews with inmates, concluded that Aboriginal inmates often do not identify themselves as being Aboriginal. As a result, the true rate of Aboriginal incarceration is higher than the official statistics indicate. The disproportionate incarceration of Aboriginal people is a growing phenomenon. In 1965, 22% of the prisoners at Stony Mountain were Aboriginal; in 1984 the figure was 33%. By 1989 the figure was up to 46%.

When one considers the high number of admissions relative to the size of the Aboriginal population, very serious concerns are raised. Indeed, one study done in Saskatchewan in the mid-1970s estimated that, compared to the general population, Indian men were 37 times more likely to be incarcerated, while Indian women were 131 times more likely to be incarcerated. [10]

The Problems of Incarceration

The over-use of incarceration for Aboriginal offenders concerns us for a number of reasons:

- Correctional institutions are not effective in deterring or rehabilitating offenders.

- Rather than rehabilitate, correctional institutions expose offenders to conditions in which they develop habits and attitudes that leave them less, rather than more, able to integrate into society after serving their sentences.

- Correctional institutions are costly to build, maintain and operate.

Effectiveness

The original philosophy was that a correctional institution would provide a sanctuary where offenders could contemplate their wrongdoing and reform their behaviour. Indeed, the term "penitentiary" is derived from the word "penitence." History has shown, however, that this objective has not been achieved.

Countless studies have shown that jails do not rehabilitate offenders.[11] Moreover, researchers have concluded that "there is no evidence that imprisonment works as either a specific or general deterrent."[12] While it is true that jails remove offenders from the community, this is a temporary reprieve, since the vast majority of offenders are released and return to the community. A Canadian parliamentary subcommittee concluded:

> Society has spent millions of dollars over the years to create and maintain the proven failure of prisons. Incarceration has failed in two essential purposes—correcting the offender and providing permanent protection to society. The recidivist rate of up to 80% is the evidence of both.[13]

High recidivism rates provide convincing evidence that correctional institutions are not effective. Between 1975 and 1985, for example, the Canadian Sentencing Commission found that 60% of those released from federal penitentiaries on mandatory supervision subsequently were readmitted to jail, while 49% of parolees were readmitted. Not surprisingly, on the basis of this and other data, the commission concluded that there was little evidence to suggest that incarceration was effective in reducing crime.[14] In fact, some studies have suggested that imprisonment actually can increase the likelihood of subsequent reoffending.[15] There is no doubt in our minds that this is the case.

Given the ineffectiveness of the current system, we believe that the apparent public demand for longer sentences requires a thoughtful response. While we can understand the anger at crime that motivates this reaction, we know that longer sentences will not reduce crime. We are firmly of the view that it is more important to determine what has caused a person to act in an inappropriate way, and to deal with the cause of the behaviour, than it is to sentence a person for longer periods to satisfy a public demand for punishment or retribution. As well, we fear that a response to public demands for longer sentences will have a more adverse impact upon Aboriginal people, who are charged and convicted at higher rates, but for less serious crimes, than upon non-Aboriginal people.

Developing Dependency in Offenders

Rather than encouraging reform and rehabilitation, the crowded, highly regimented and imposed nature of correctional institutions often creates bitterness, anger and a desire to "get even." In fact, research has shown that institutions "tend to be characterized by high levels of violence, punitiveness by correctional officers, strong anti-social sentiments among prisoners, tolerance of coercive homosexuality, and relatively poor social relations with both staff and peers."[16] Moreover, because correctional institutions bring together the novice and the career criminal, as well as offenders from a wide variety of backgrounds, they provide opportunities for antisocial values and skills to be learned and promoted.

Correctional institutions do not teach responsibility, but dependency. Those who have been institutionalized have had every aspect of their lives regulated. Therefore, they are ill-equipped to cope in society without a sustained period of reintegration, and some, it is argued, actually seek to return to the institution because it is the life they know.

Beyond the sociological and psychological effects of institutions, we found unacceptable physical conditions—overcrowding, deteriorating and unclean buildings, lack of sunlight, lack of exercise facilities, and heating and air-conditioning systems that did not function properly, thus exposing both inmates and staff to extreme conditions.

We consider the treatment of Aboriginal peoples in Manitoba prisons to be particularly inhumane. Not only do Aboriginal people suffer the same indignities as those applicable to other inmates, they also suffer from physical isolation and cultural deprivation. Because Aboriginal people are not afforded alternatives to imprisonment in their local communities, they are removed from their families and communities to be incarcerated in a distant institution that is completely insensitive to their culture and background.

Costs

In examining sentencing practices in Manitoba, and Canada generally, one is struck immediately by the focus on jails. The *Criminal Code* mentions jail as a penalty for virtually every offence. Sentences that do not involve jail are confined to their own small section in the back of the Code, with the clear reminders that these are not appropriate for serious offences.

From the emphasis in the Code, we go to the allocation of resources by governments. In Manitoba, according to the Department of the Attorney General 1988–89 *Annual Report*, there were 205.5 salaried staff in youth jails and 609 staff in adult jails. Federal correctional expenditures in Manitoba, from information supplied by the Correctional Services of Canada Regional Office in Saskatoon for 1990–91, include 392 salaries (not including members of the Parole Board, but including 60 Parole Board employees in Manitoba). A total of 1,206.5 staff are devoted to operating the jail system in Manitoba (not including court staff, lawyers or police).

By comparison, the Department of the Attorney General *Annual Report* shows only 165.5 salaries are devoted to other kinds of sentences—probation, community work orders, fine option program and special experimental projects. Of these positions, a significant amount of time is devoted to preparing pre-sentence reports. This means that there is seven times more jail staff than staff available for all other sentences combined—and this occurs despite the fact that jail is supposed to be limited to only the most serious offences, which are the minority of cases.

In terms of dollars, the Department of the Attorney General shows in its 1988–89 *Annual Report* that it spent $33,758,200 on jails in that year. The federal expenditure in Manitoba was $11,152,994 in 1990–91. This is a combined total of $44,911,194. The 1988–89 expenditures for non-jail sentences were $7,985,200. In other words, five and a half times more money is spent on jails than on other forms of sentences in Manitoba.

Indeed, while only $8,000,000 is spent on non-jail sentences, our research shows that fines create approximately $14,000,000 in revenue for the Province, not to mention the revenue from the victims of crime surcharge and from work provided through community service orders.

A similar picture emerges when one examines the number of people receiving each type of sentence. There were 287 young offenders held in custody on any given day in 1988, including 89 in temporary custody, 83 in secure custody and 115 in open custody.

There were approximately 800 adults in provincial jails on any given day in 1988, including 168 in the Remand Centre. There are approximately 550 inmates in federal institutions on a given day. This means there are approximately 1,655 persons in jail on any given day in Manitoba, and approximately one jail staff person for every 1.5 inmates. (This calculation does not include the 60 parole staff.)

For alternatives to incarceration, the 165.5 salary positions in Community and Youth Corrections have numerous tasks to accomplish. The most demanding of these is the supervision of offenders who have been placed on probation. In 1988 there were 3,200 probation supervisions, 3,000 youths admitted into alternative measures programs, 2,500 reports written, 9,000 new registrants for the fine option program, 1,600 new community service orders, 1,400 interim release supervisions and 600 persons sent to prison with periods of probation to follow their jail sentences.[17]

The staff responsible for overseeing these cases also must provide coordination and support for more than 40 community justice committees, involving 200 volunteers to supervise offenders, conduct crime prevention seminars and operate special programs for child sexual abuse, domestic violence and substance abuse.

Clearly, the extraordinary expenses involved in running a jail system take resources away from community programs. The Attorney General's 1988–89 *Annual Report* shows that courts have been taking increasing advantage of community sanctions over the past five years. We strongly encourage these developments. But these efforts are being jeopardized and inhibited by a lack of resources, and especially by an inappropriate allocation of resources between jails and community sanctions.

Reasons for Current Practices

Both in Canada and in other countries, the need to move away from the imprisonment of offenders to a more socially productive approach to sentencing has been well accepted at an official level for many years. Many organizations and government task forces have made this recommendation. Moreover, in Canada, the public appears to accept the idea that community programs are appropriate for many offenders who currently are being incarcerated.[18] It is also widely known that current practices adversely affect Aboriginal people. Yet, Canada continues to record high incarceration rates and Aboriginal people continue to be locked up in disproportionate numbers.

In order to account for the current practices, it is necessary to examine the factors that influence sentencing patterns in Canada. It is also necessary to examine the specific factors that affect the sentencing of Aboriginal people.

General Considerations

The reasons for the continued reliance on incarceration in Canada are varied and complex, but one conclusion we have reached is that despite all the political rhetoric about reform and rehabilitation, our justice system continues to lock people up for no better reason than the force of habit and the weight of tradition. There has been no deliberate and systematic attempt to change these practices. Anthony Doob, a member of the Canadian Sentencing Commission, summarized the problem this way:

> In order to implement a policy of reduced use of imprisonment, two of the necessary conditions appear to be an enactment by Parliament of a coherent sentencing policy that endorses the use of community sanctions and a method of providing authoritative and unambiguous guidance on sentencing to judges. These two conditions, combined with a program of well run community sanctions, are necessary to accomplish a goal that has been accepted in Canada for half a century.[19]

An examination of how courts make sentencing decisions illustrates how past practices continue, and how innovation and creativity in sentencing are discouraged.

The Lack of Pre-Sentence Information

Courts are provided with remarkably little information to assist them in making sentencing decisions. Ideally, there are Crown and defence attorneys who can speak knowledgeably to sentence, and police reports that describe the particulars of the offence in question. Ideally, the judge has gleaned much information about the offence and the offender from the trial. Ideally, the court receives a pre-sentence report that provides additional information about the offender's background and the available sentencing options. The reality, however, is far from the ideal.

The vast majority of people appearing before the courts do not have their cases proceed to trial; they simply plead guilty. According to the Department of Justice Hendrickson report on the Provincial Court study of 1,800 offenders appearing before the courts in Winnipeg and the North, trials occurred in only 3% of all cases. Whether or not there is a trial, there is usually no pre-sentence report.

Police reports typically are cursory and provide only the bare facts. Owing to high caseloads, neither the Crown nor defence attorneys have an opportunity to develop any more than a passing familiarity with the case, with the offender or with various community sanctions. In other words, very little information is available to the courts to assist them in making sentencing decisions. This is particularly true where accused plead guilty on first appearance or do not have a lawyer other than duty counsel.

The practice in recent years has been for courts to use probation officers to gather information to assist judges in making sentencing decisions. Without them, judges may not have all the information about the background of the accused, or the circumstances of the offence. Our Inquiry leads us to the conclusion that most reports are inadequate and still leave the judge without much vital information.

While the concept of a pre-sentence report certainly is sound, extremely high caseloads usually prevent the probation officer who prepared the report from attending court to discuss the findings or recommendations with the accused or with the judge. This alone has the effect of severely restricting the benefit to the court of the officer's investigations.

Lack of Knowledge of the Effectiveness of Various Sanctions

Judges require "case specific" information, but they also require other types of information for sentencing purposes. They need to receive feedback about the sentences they and their colleagues have imposed in the past. They need to know, for example, how particular individuals fared in particular programs and whether any went on to commit further crimes. More generally, they need information about the effectiveness of the various sentencing options. Regrettably, this information is not collected or made available. While judges receive reports from some probation officers, there is no formal system to provide them with feedback on the effectiveness of sentences they have imposed. In fact, the courts often do not receive adequate information about the sentencing options that are available to them.

How do judges make sentencing decisions in the absence of the important information they need? In our view, most sentences seem to be determined largely by judges' personal views, shaped by experience, or are dictated by the judge's knowledge of available community sanctions and sentences other judges have applied in similar circumstances.

Unfortunately, judges have no say as to the facilities to which a sentenced adult offender should go. Currently, judges impose sentences and it is up to the correctional authorities to decide where the offender will serve that sentence. During the course of our Inquiry, we came across individuals who were incarcerated in correctional institutions, but, we believe, should have been in psychiatric facilities. We suggest that judges should be entitled to designate the place of custody. There is little sense in a judge passing sentence, believing that the accused will be treated in a certain fashion, only to have the accused treated in a different fashion. We recognize that those who operate correctional facilities may later conclude that an offender should be moved or that it may not be possible to accommodate the offender in a particular institution. In those circumstances, it would be understandable if the judge's direction could not be followed. It would be reasonable to return the case to the judge for further consideration.

The Role of Appellate Courts in Standardizing Sentences

Provincial appellate courts frequently deal with "sentence appeals." These involve a review of the appropriateness of sentences imposed by trial judges. While we believe it is necessary for appellate courts to provide sentencing guidelines to ensure a certain degree of fairness and uniformity, we are concerned that the present system has gone too far in attempting to standardize what ought not to be, and cannot be, standardized. At the same time, too little attention is paid to the total picture of each case. Courts of appeal have the details of the offence and the criminal history of the offender, but may not know the support services available in specific communities and thus do not examine the full range of sentencing options.

One rather more disturbing aspect of appellate sentencing appears to occur frequently. That is the tendency of appellate courts simply to impose their own sentence in place of that of the lower court, instead of reviewing the lower court decision to ensure that it complies with established principles of sound sentencing practices.

The guidelines derived from appellate court judgments tend to limit the discretion of trial judges, particularly when it comes to the use of innovative sentences. As a consequence, a very traditional and conservative approach to sentencing has evolved. Past practices that rely on the use of incarceration are enshrined in appellate court judgments. In the absence of deliberate measures to change past practices, they continue unabated.

As the Canadian Sentencing Commission has pointed out:

Courts of Appeal are not ... adequately structured to make policy on sentencing. They are not organized nationally; hence there is no obvious way of creating a national policy. They do not have the means and resources required to gather all the necessary information to create policy on the appropriate levels of sanctions. They are structured to respond to individual cases that are brought before them rather than to create a comprehensive integrated policy for all criminal offences. Most importantly, Courts of Appeal do not represent the people of Canada as Parliament does; judges are understandably reluctant to transform their courts into legislative bodies making public policy with respect to sentencing decisions. They appear to prefer to do what they do best; to guide the interpretation of the will of Parliament in the determination of the appropriate sanction in an individual case.[20]

As a result, most trial judges impose sentences which are acceptable to their courts of appeal. This tends to standardize the severity of the punishment. That is, given the particular crime and the previous record of the offender, the courts deem a particular punishment to be appropriate. By their very nature, factors that should be taken into account in sentencing, such as culture, community wishes, the benefits of community-based sanctions and the accused's prospects for rehabilitation, are more difficult or impossible to standardize. Therefore, they tend to receive too little weight in sentencing.

A 1986 case from the Northwest Territories provides a good illustration of the way appeal courts can thwart judges who search for culturally appropriate sanctions.[21] A 21-year-old Aboriginal man in Arctic Bay pleaded guilty to a charge of sexually assaulting a minor. A distinctive feature of the sentencing hearing consisted of evidence about the traditional treatment of offenders that had been accorded by the Council of Elders in Arctic Bay.

The Council of Elders told the court that it wanted the accused to remain in the community to undergo his punishment. It expressed the view that he was already on the road to rehabilitation. Sending him to prison several hundred miles away would not only interfere with his future prospects in the community, it said, but any such sentence would be resented by the community. It also expressed concern about possible resentment against the victim.

Judge Bourassa of the Territorial Court of the Northwest Territories imposed a sentence of 90 days' imprisonment to be served intermittently at the local detachment of the RCMP at Arctic Bay, plus two years of probation and 100 hours of community service. In imposing sentence, Judge Bourassa stated:

> It is obvious to me from what has been said in evidence today that the community is willing to act, the Inumarit [Council of Elders] is willing to act and social services are willing to act in this case. It is not an empty promise. It is true. It is a fact. [The value of this type of involvement has been] proven in the past by the very absence of crime and disturbance. This special part of Arctic Bay is something I would be very sad to see in any way taken away or diminished. The very things the Inumarit are trying to do is what the court is trying to do: rehabilitating the offender; reconciling the offender, the victim and the community so that there is unity in the community and a program of education. Can any of us really say that jails do that? For the person that responds, the Inumarit, the social services committee and the whole community together can obviously heal; they can unite; they can reconcile and they can reform. I am

impressed with the Inumarit. They promise and appear in the past to have delivered more than what jails can do. I accept what they say without reservation because, as I say, for the last three years that I have been here we hardly ever come to Arctic Bay, because there is simply no trouble in this community.

So the issue is what do I do with this group of people in this community that is so eager to be involved and to take care of the problems within the community, and at the same time do what is right in the law. If the court can do something to help the community solve its own problems, to help those, whoever they are, and however they work to continue to keep Arctic Bay the good community that it is, then I think the court should do it. If whatever it is in Arctic Bay that keeps this community crime-free continues to function and work with respect to this man then everybody is served and the people in this community will be protected.[22]

Judge Bourassa's sentence was appealed by the Crown. The Alberta Court of Appeal, in its capacity as the Northwest Territories Court of Appeal, found Judge Bourassa's sentence "wholly inadequate" and they substituted a sentence of 18 months' imprisonment. In its judgment the appeal court argued that major sexual assault must be punished with a period of imprisonment. The justices also concluded that the Council of Elders was not a direct successor to the traditional Inuit government body and, therefore, would provide counselling "much as it would be done in any other Canadian community." This showed a lack of understanding that culture is dynamic, not static, and that for Aboriginal groups, whose self-government has been restricted for a considerable time, recreating and reviving dormant institutions is the only option.

The dissenting judge in the Court of Appeal, Mr. Justice Belzil, pointed out that the Aboriginal view of justice saw imprisonment as being destructive to the individual and as "containing the seed of disharmony and division and hence destructive of the community itself."[23] He continued:

The treatment is shown by the evidence to have achieved what must be the ultimate purpose in all punishment for crime, that is to say, protection of the community and rehabilitation of the offender. It has the added benefit of effecting reconciliation between victim and offender, a concept only now being advanced in our society by criminologists.[24]

In our opinion, this is an example of a court of appeal insisting on applying a standard non-Aboriginal sanction. In the process, the sentence developed by a judge who was familiar with the case and the community was rejected. The initiative shown by the community and the trial judge, and other communities (and, by implication, other trial judges), could only have been discouraged.

Implications of Current Practices for Aboriginal People

The over-reliance on incarceration and lack of judicial imagination weighs most heavily on Aboriginal people, who are convicted of crimes in numbers far out of proportion to their presence in society. Dr. Carol LaPrairie, in her study on the role of sentencing in the over-representation of Aboriginal people in correctional institutions, noted:

> Aboriginal people are treated differently than non-Aboriginal people by the justice system at discretionary decision making points such as charging, prosecuting, sentencing and releasing. Both deliberate racism and more subtle systemic discrimination are involved. In particular, Aboriginal people disproportionately reside in rural and northern areas and they have been relegated to a low socio-economic status. Therefore, when factors such as employment, education, place and stability of residence, the "standing" of the family or community resources are taken into account by the justice system, the result is systematic discrimination against Aboriginal people.[25]

The Need for a New Approach to Sentencing

The reform of current sentencing practices will not be easy. However, the present practices cannot continue. We believe reform must involve several elements:

- There must be less dependence on the use of incarceration and a strengthening of community sanctions and reconciliation programs.

- Parliament must adopt, and the courts must implement, a new philosophy based not on punishment, but, rather, on the needs of victims, communities and offenders.

- Cultural factors must be given greater consideration.

- The community must be allowed to play a more meaningful role.

Strengthening Community Sanctions

As we have pointed out, the current approach to sentencing relies too heavily on incarceration. This is a costly and ineffective approach. We believe that incarceration should be used as a last resort. For most offenders, including many who now are being incarcerated, community-based sentencing options should be employed.

The Canadian Sentencing Commission has pointed out that:

> The Criminal Code displays an apparent bias toward the use of incarceration since for most offences the penalty indicated is expressed in terms of a maximum term of imprisonment. A number of difficulties arise if imprisonment is perceived to be the preferred sanction for most offences. Perhaps most significant is that although we regularly impose this most onerous and expensive sanction, it accomplishes very little apart from separating offenders from society for a period of time. In the past few decades many groups and federally appointed committees and commissions given the responsibility for studying various aspects of the criminal justice system have argued that imprisonment

should be used only as a last resort and/or that it should be reserved for those convicted of only the most serious offences. However, although much has been said, little has been done to move us in this direction.[26]

The commission recommends that Parliament incorporate a statement of purpose and principles in the criminal law. Sentences, it contends, should reflect "the least onerous sanction appropriate to the circumstances." With respect to imprisonment, it states:

> A term of imprisonment should not be imposed, or its duration determined, solely for the purpose of rehabilitation.... A term of imprisonment should be imposed only: a) to protect the public from crimes of violence, b) where any other sanction would not sufficiently reflect the gravity of the offence or the repetitive nature of the criminal conduct of an offender, or adequately protect the public or the integrity of the administration of the justice, c) to penalize an offender from willful non-compliance with the terms of any other sentence that has been imposed on the offender where no other sanction appears adequate to compel compliance.[27]

We wish to reinforce the findings and recommendations of the Canadian Sentencing Commission.

WE RECOMMEND THAT:

- Incarceration be used only in instances where:
  - The offender poses a danger to another individual or to the community.
  - Any other sanction would not sufficiently reflect the gravity of the offence.
  - An offender wilfully refuses to comply with the terms of any other sentence that has been imposed.

- The provincial Justice department regularly and consistently collect, analyse and distribute information on the success rates of all sentences, and distribute that information to judges, Crown attorneys and the defence bar.

- Probation officers be available when courts sit in Aboriginal communities to explain the results of pre-sentence studies.

- The *Criminal Code* be amended to allow judges to designate the specific place of custody for offenders.

A New Sentencing Philosophy

Nowhere in Canada's criminal law are the purpose of the criminal law or the objectives to be accomplished in sentencing set out. While this is a gap that should be addressed by Parliament, at present it is the courts that articulate purpose and philosophy. If past practices are to be reformed, therefore, both Parliament and the courts will have an important role to play.

Trial judges must be more creative. Existing sentencing options must be utilized more fully, and the courts should encourage the establishment of other options and solutions that are tailored to particular offenders and particular communities.

There is a need to place less emphasis on the punishment factor in sentencing and greater emphasis on the needs of the individual and the community. By shifting the emphasis in this way, more socially productive and effective sanctions can be substituted for incarceration. While this shift is required generally in our justice system, it is particularly necessary in order to respond more effectively to Aboriginal offenders. As we have seen, at present their culture, with its values, beliefs and traditions, is largely ignored.

Trial judges are unlikely to engage in culturally appropriate sentencing unless appellate courts encourage more latitude and more creativity in sentencing, even within the existing legislative framework. It is a mistake for courts of appeal to apply the "same offence-same sentence" rule, and trial judges should be encouraged to depart from such a rigid approach.

An appellate court permits a dissatisfied party a review of a decision of a trial judge. Three to five judges review the transcript of the evidence given at trial, and counsel argue whether the trial judge's decision was correct in law and, in cases of sentences, whether accepted principles have been applied appropriately.

It is accepted in law that appeal court judges are not merely to substitute their opinions for those of the trial judge. There is obviously a temptation for a court of appeal judge to substitute his or her opinion—to say, in effect, "If I had been the trial judge, this is the sentence I would have imposed." The often minor alterations in sentences make it abundantly clear that this is what is happening.

When a court of appeal departs dramatically from an innovative approach developed by a trial judge, as in the *Naqitarvik* case, two things happen:

- The standardization of particular sentences for particular crimes, without much concern for unique circumstances, is perpetuated.

- Initiative on the part of trial judges is discouraged.

WE RECOMMEND THAT:

- The Manitoba Court of Appeal encourage more creativity in sentencing by trial court judges so that the use of incarceration is diminished and the use of sentencing alternatives is increased, particularly for Aboriginal peoples.

Cultural Factors in Sentencing

As we point out in greater detail in our discussion of Aboriginal culture, Aboriginal people traditionally have dealt with unacceptable conduct in a different manner from that of the Canadian penal and judicial system. In part, this helps to explain why conventional jails are a particularly inappropriate response to crime in Aboriginal communities, and why more culturally sensitive programs, operated by Aboriginal people, are required. During the course of our Inquiry, we met with numerous Aboriginal elders in Manitoba who helped provide us with an overview of traditional Aboriginal approaches to justice issues.

Instead of exacting vengeance and punishment, the intent in Aboriginal communities was to demonstrate the community's disapproval of the behaviour, to counsel the offender, and to return peace and order to the community without using imprisonment.

Traditional corrective measures involved a discussion with a parent, a grandparent, an elder or a chief. The offender usually admitted his or her wrongdoing. All efforts thereafter were directed to removing the cause of the unacceptable behaviour and to making sure that there was no repetition of the conduct. This principle was applied whether the offence was minor or serious.

If an accused person denied his or her wrongdoing, the elders would be called upon to determine the "truth." If they determined that an accusation was made falsely, then their efforts focussed on rehabilitating the accuser. Invariably, an accusation of misconduct was seen as evidence of disharmony within the tribe, and whatever the "truth" turned out to be—whether the accusation was true or false—the existence of a public accusation indicated a need for efforts to be undertaken to restore peace and harmony to the community. Most Aboriginal cultures strove to make sure that no one left this process feeling that he or she had suffered an injustice.

In cases where other forms of sanctions did not work, the person might receive the ultimate sanction: banishment from the community. That meant that while the person was not put to death, he or she had to survive the harshness of the land without the usual support of other members of the community.

A penalty that often worked in small communities was the simple act of making the conduct public. The embarrassment and public ridicule that followed such public disclosure were recognized as having the effect of preventing repetition of the unacceptable conduct. The Canadian legal system sometimes takes this into account as well, but too often it seems that it does so only for "prominent" persons.

Whatever the penalty and the adjudication process, it was effective. Members of bands lived in relative harmony over the centuries.

In our opinion, the principles of community control and community sanctions remain important. Aboriginal people should have been allowed to adapt and apply these principles many years ago. Instead, a completely foreign approach has been imposed on Aboriginal people. There is ample evidence that this approach is not very effective. We recognize that there can be no returning to the past and we do not advocate a simplistic turning back of the clock. But there are aspects of Aboriginal cultures that are as contemporary and beneficial as anything else society has to offer in our justice system.

Cultural factors should not be seen as extraordinary considerations for the court. Rather, they should be considered in the normal course of sentencing each and every Aboriginal defendant. Culture has, in fact, always been considered in the justice system. Unfortunately, it has been used too often in a racist and discriminatory manner. In 1916 a Crown prosecutor, who prosecuted two Inuit for murder, said:

> These remote savages, really cannibals, the Eskimo of the Arctic regions have got to be taught to recognize the authority of the British Crown ... just in the same way it was necessary to teach the Indians of the Indian Territories and of the North West Territories that they were under the law ... the great importance of this trial lies in this: that for the first time in history these people ... will be brought in contact with and will be taught what is the white man's justice.[28]

Here we can see how a foreign justice system was pressed upon Aboriginal people. And while contemporary court officials are not likely to give voice to such racist sentiments, the fact remains that the legal system has not developed a much more sophisticated understanding of Aboriginal culture.

There are probably several hundred cases in the law reports that mention that the accused was an "Indian." In most of these cases, there is no indication of how that fact was taken into consideration by the court. Yet, the mere fact that it was mentioned seems to suggest that some importance was attributed to it. There certainly are cases where the courts have explicitly used the accused's cultural background as a mitigating factor in sentencing.

In one of the earliest cases to address the subject comprehensively, the Ontario Court of Appeal in *R. vs. Fireman* dealt with an accused who had been convicted of manslaughter. The trial judge had rejected the contention that a lesser punishment would suffice to deter the accused and satisfy the community, and, instead, imposed a 10-year term of imprisonment. The appeal court, after considering the specifics of the accused and his community, decided that a much shorter period of incarceration would be appropriate. A term of two years was substituted.

The judgment of the appeal court is very instructive in pointing out the various ways that culture can be legitimately considered in the sentencing process:

One can only proceed to consider the fitness of the sentence meted out to this man upon a proper appreciation of his cultural background and of his character, as it is only then that the full effect of the sentence upon him will be clear.... When one considers these things, it is my opinion that even a short term of imprisonment in the penitentiary is substantial punishment to him ... the effect of his removal from his environment and his imprisonment would no doubt dull every sense by which he has lived in the north ... does this sentence of ten years take into consideration the desirability of his rehabilitation ... I think it is probable that such a term will greatly reduce the chance of this man assuming a normal tolerable role on returning to his society and may result in the creation of a social cripple.... To the rest of the community, the deterrent lies in the fact that this unsophisticated man of previous good character was sent to prison for his crime and surely, it is not dependent on the magnitude of the sentence for its value.... What is important in these circumstances is that to the whole community, justice appears to have been done.... This is best accomplished in the case of this first offender if he is returned to his society before time makes him a stranger and impairs his ability to live there with some dignity.[29]

Justice Tallis of the Supreme Court of the Northwest Territories has written:

In dealing with the question of sentencing, courts in the Northwest Territories cannot overlook the fact that society has the basic roots of ... three cultures. When the common law was transplanted into Canada, it proved to be very flexible, but native people, whether Inuit or Indian, had their own system of laws, tribunals, penalties, and in effect, their own justice system. Furthermore, such cultures did not have jails. This was a new concept introduced from the white man's world. It continues to be little understood by many of the elders in the Indian and Inuit communities. Consequently, a great deal of consideration is given to the possibility of imposing a non-custodial sentence with terms of probation, or community service orders. With approximately 50% of the population being 18 years or younger, this is particularly important. In the case of youthful first offenders, custodial sentences are generally avoided.[30]

Regrettably, this sort of sensitivity is the exception, rather than the rule, when it comes to sentencing. All too often Aboriginal offenders are given sentences based solely on the type of offence. Cultural and social relationships and informal community supports, especially from the extended family and elders, often are not brought adequately to the court's attention and, therefore, are not considered.

Probably one of the most difficult issues arises when the courts must sentence those for whom traditional Aboriginal culture is no longer a great influence. According to the 1986 census, only 25% of Aboriginal people under the age of 21 reported that an Aboriginal language was the primary language spoken in their home. This reflects the decline that has taken place in traditional Aboriginal cultures as a consequence of a broad array of pressures to assimilate. Many Aboriginal accused who appear before the courts, therefore, may appear to have lost identification with their Aboriginal heritage.

What are the courts to do in these instances? In *Sentencing in Canada*, one writer has stated:

> [A]s native populations become more culturally integrated, particularly in large urban areas, it is to be expected that cultural differences will recede in importance in the sentencing process.[31]

Simply put, it is suggested that if the accused has no connection to his or her Aboriginal culture, then it should no longer be a factor to take into consideration in sentencing.

Some experts have warned that the appearance of a lack of connection to past cultural practices or beliefs may be deceiving:

> Today's Indian cultures are not Aboriginal cultures. Many earlier sources of economic existence are gone. Much is being lost.... Some Indian languages are on the verge of extinction. Many Indians have adopted Christianity and no longer practice their sacred ways.... In dress, housing, employment and other external aspects of culture, Indian peoples are becoming almost indistinguishable from other Canadians.... But to conclude ... that Indians would eventually disappear as a distinctive cultural group would be a serious mistake. Indians have not assimilated.... Indians are engaged in a significant revitalization of their culture.[32]

Great care must be taken in these cases, because the influence of Aboriginal cultures is present, although difficult to detect. As we have noted earlier, it is important to distinguish between a person's lifestyle, which for some individuals may appear to be one of complete integration into the mainstream, and his or her culture, which is reflective of the values in which a person was raised and which continues to shape that person's behaviour. Thus, it is important for the courts to satisfy themselves as to the true influence of Aboriginal culture. The acceptance of outward appearances is not sufficient. In fact, where the influence of Aboriginal culture is difficult to detect, this itself may be a factor that the courts should take into consideration.

Courts have considered the difficulties experienced by the accused as a result of changes in cultural environment. In some cases, the accused moved from one cultural environment to another—perhaps from the reserve to the city. In other cases, changes affected the cultural environment of the accused's community. In both instances, the courts have held that "culture shock" may be considered as a mitigating factor in sentencing. We agree with that position.

Judges should ask themselves in each case how culture may be a factor, and whether it might explain:

- An apparently undue deference to authority.

- A reluctance to explain or defend one's actions.

- Any apparent lack of effect of the penalty (no apparent remorse or understanding of the seriousness, no deterrent rehabilitative effect).

- A willingness to admit guilt (poor understanding of English, deference to authority, belief the system cannot be impartial towards him or her, or that it cannot understand his or her motivations).

- The offender's anger or despair that led to the offence.

- Whether the sentence may be viewed by the victim, community or offender as ineffective.

Judges also must ask themselves if their own culture has biased their views of the offender, the offence, the victim or the penalty. Judges then must ask if a culturally specific sentence is available and would be more appropriate than incarceration. For apparently assimilated Aboriginal people, judges must ask also what the effect is on the offender of not belonging to, or not having a clear identity with, his or her culture.

WE RECOMMEND THAT:

- ■ The *Criminal Code* be amended to provide that cultural factors be taken into account in sentencing, and that in the meantime judges be encouraged to take this approach.

Community Involvement in Sentencing

If non-Aboriginal judges and courts are going to be able to formulate sentences which are appropriate to the needs of Aboriginal offenders, victims and communities, they will need direct input from those communities.

The need for community involvement and the need for cultural sensitivity are two of the most important reasons we have recommended the establishment of Aboriginal courts in Aboriginal communities throughout Manitoba. Where these courts are established, they will rely on the community, since this is a deeply ingrained tradition in Aboriginal cultures. Where these courts are not established, however, existing courts must take steps to ensure that communities develop greater ownership of the justice processes that affect them. In particular, communities need to be involved in the sentencing process, since sentences should, in part, reflect the needs and desires of the community.

We believe that a judge from a non-Aboriginal court should not sentence an Aboriginal offender without first receiving the advice of someone from the Aboriginal community. It is virtually impossible for a judge, particularly a non-Aboriginal judge who has never lived in an Aboriginal community, either in remote areas of Manitoba or downtown Winnipeg, to understand the circumstances of the accused, and the community factors that bear on the offence, which should be taken into consideration in sentencing.

The court communicator, a paralegal officer, the chief of the band, a respected elder, the peacemaker or some other appropriate individual should be asked to comment on the accused and the attitude of the community towards the particular offence.

This person also should be asked to provide advice to the court as to an appropriate sentence. The judge should accept these comments as evidence, but should retain the discretion to impose whatever penalty is appropriate. We would hope the judge, and any appellate court, would give considerable weight to community recommendations.

Sentencing Panels

Another option that some communities may wish to exercise would be to establish panels of community members to advise the courts on sentencing. Different communities might wish to structure their panels differently, but the approach of a panel of this sort should be to return the community and the victim to a relationship of security and harmony by attempting to resolve the matter in a manner acceptable to all. As we mention in our chapter on young offenders, this approach was used quite successfully by Provincial Court Judge Robert Kopstein at Roseau River in the 1970s.

The panel should meet with the accused, the victim and others to develop an understanding of what happened, the reasons for the behaviour, and the effects on the victim and the community. The attitude of the offender should be assessed. The panel should see if the accused accepts responsibility for the acts and apologizes for them. The panel should consider whether there is likely to be any repetition of the wrongdoing.

Where necessary, the panel also should discuss appropriate sanctions with the parties, relying as much as possible on traditional ways that would be acceptable to all. If the panel believes the dispute can be resolved by its intervention, it should so advise the court. If it thinks some type of penalty should be applied, whether by payment of compensation, the provision of some service to the victim, community service, a period of incarceration or some other sanction, it should recommend an appropriate penalty to the court.

On receipt of the panel's report, the judge would consider the panel's recommendations and pass sentence. If a judge does not accept the recommendations of the panel, the reasons should be given in open court.

Sentencing panels may be structured in a variety of ways, but we believe they would provide important benefits in instances where non-Aboriginal judges are sentencing Aboriginal people. At a bare minimum, courts must consult with representatives of the Aboriginal community before sentencing an Aboriginal offender to a term of incarceration.

WE RECOMMEND THAT:

- ■ Judges invite Aboriginal communities to express their views to the court on any case involving an offence or an offender from their community.

- ■ Aboriginal communities be encouraged to develop the best method of communicating their concerns to the court in a manner that is respectful of the rights of the accused, and of the dignity and importance of the proceedings.

Community Sanctions

While we believe that far too many Manitobans are currently being imprisoned by our court system, we recognize that the range of community sanctions available to the courts needs to be expanded and.strengthened. In proposing these changes we are guided by our concern that the justice system must become more responsive to the needs of Aboriginal victims, communities and offenders, and that it must give the same consideration to restitution and reconciliation that it gives to punishment. We now turn to the non-custodial sentences available to judges to see ways in which they can be integrated into this approach.

Discharges and Suspended Sentences

Unless there is a minimum sentence prescribed by law, the courts can give offenders an absolute or conditional discharge. The authority for these sanctions is set out in section 736(1) of the *Criminal Code*. When an absolute discharge is granted, a conviction is not registered and there is no criminal record. In the case of a conditional discharge, the offender will not acquire a criminal record if the conditions are adhered to.

Courts may also give an offender a suspended sentence with a term of probation. Failure to comply with the order may bring the offender back before the court. At this point a new sentence can be imposed. In addition, the offender can be charged with breaching a probation order.

We believe that the publicity, embarrassment, expense and trauma that result from a court appearance are underestimated in many cases. Just as we would prefer to see many cases not reach the courts, we believe that many more could be disposed of with suspended sentences or discharges.

Probation

A probation order allows courts to retain some control over an offender without incarceration. Probation orders are provided for in section 737(2) of the *Criminal Code,* and can be issued along with suspended sentences, conditional discharges and fines, and following terms of imprisonment of less than two years.

Probation is based on the belief that some offenders should have the opportunity to remain in the community under the supervision of a probation officer and the sentencing court. This disposition, which is imposed most frequently in the case of first offenders or in cases where the offence is relatively minor, allows the offender to maintain work, family and other responsibilities, while, at the same time, remaining under court supervision.

Offenders who fail to live up to the conditions of a probation order may be charged with breach of the order. Specifically, section 740 of the *Criminal Code* provides that a person who fails to comply with the terms of a probation order is guilty of a summary conviction offence and is subject to a maximum of six months' imprisonment, or a fine of $2,000.00, or both. However, this sentence can only be imposed by the court at a new court hearing.

We have noted that probation orders are imposed primarily to make an offender "keep his nose clean" for a period of time. That is, indeed, one of the purposes of a probation order: to require that the offender adopt a crime-free lifestyle for a period of time in the hope that living such a lifestyle will encourage her or him to continue, because the offender learns that she or he can do so. While this is, perhaps, a primitive way of modifying behaviour, we are not prepared to say it is an invalid consideration in some cases.

Yet, an accused's subsequent failure, after the probation period is over, to live a life free of crime is sometimes used to argue that future probation should not be available to the accused, even if he or she, in fact, remained uninvolved in crime while on the earlier probation. Rather than being used to show that probation *did* help the accused to remain uninvolved in criminal activity, subsequent offences are used to argue that the accused has *not* benefited from probation. We could understand that logic if the accused became reinvolved while on probation (thereby showing, perhaps, a disregard or disrespect for the order), but if he or she lived up to the conditions previously imposed, that should be seen as an encouraging sign.

Some caution is necessary, nevertheless. Judges often tack on a probation order almost as a matter of course. The danger in imposing probation in this manner is that if the conditions are not met, the subsequent penalty may become greater than the circumstances of the original offence warranted and greater than the judge intended.

Conditions of Probation

Every probation order requires that the offender keep the peace and be of good behaviour. The probationer is required to appear before the court if called upon to do so. Any number of additional conditions may also be imposed if, in the opinion of the judge, they are warranted in the circumstances. Common conditions include remaining under the supervision of a probation officer, supporting one's dependants, abstinence from drugs and alcohol, making restitution or reparation, remaining within the jurisdiction of the court, and making reasonable efforts to find and maintain employment.

Other conditions, intended either to assist in rehabilitation or to prevent a recurrence of the offence, might include a curfew or a prohibition against being with certain individuals or in certain places. Probationers also may be required to participate in treatment or education programs.

When it comes to the sentencing of Aboriginal people, many of these conditions are, in our opinion, inappropriate. As a result, matters which may have started as a minor infraction may escalate into something quite serious. We believe that, in too many cases, conditions of probation are not related directly to the offence at hand, and are included because the court believes they will "improve" the offender. This is particularly true in the case of orders which demand that the probationer refrain from the consumption of alcohol. Our survey of Aboriginal inmates revealed that Aboriginal inmates believe that the parole system holds the view that Aboriginal offenders have alcohol problems. We believe the courts also hold such stereotypical views and impose abstinence orders even when alcohol abuse is not a factor leading to the commission of the offence.

Such orders are problematic even when the individual does have a substance abuse problem. Simply telling a person who has a severe drinking problem not to drink, without providing him or her with the supports needed to break such an addiction, is to invite failure. If, on the other hand, the order required the offender to enrol in a culturally appropriate alcohol treatment program, the condition could be of benefit to the individual and to society.

During our Inquiry, Linda Buchanan, the director of the Rehabilitation Centre at The Pas Health Complex, told us that offenders are given orders to abstain from alcohol and then referred to her centre for counselling. She said the orders are out of step with the approach her counselling program takes, which recognizes that alcoholism is an addiction which must be treated if it is to be overcome. The probation order, on the other hand, tells "someone who possibly has no control over that particular disease that they have to abstain from it absolutely, which is an impossible thing to do."

Probation orders which require abstinence can, in fact, prevent a person from receiving treatment, since probation officers often are the only officials who can make referrals to alcohol rehabilitation centres. Buchanan outlined the dilemma this would create for an alcoholic who had been unable to live up to an order to abstain from alcohol, but wanted to be referred to a centre for treatment. To get a referral for alcohol abuse treatment, such a person would have to admit to the probation officer that she or he has been breaching the probation order by drinking. In this case, a person invites further punishment by seeking treatment.

Not only are many of the conditions of probation inappropriate, but the courts, we found, do not do a proper job of informing Aboriginal people of the purpose of a probation order and the consequences of violating it.

As a result, Aboriginal people are unaware of the fact that probation is a type of monitoring that follows, or is instead of, incarceration, and that it is intended for the benefit of the accused. Nor do they understand that a separate charge may result from a breach of the conditions of a probation order. As a result, people who have committed minor offences accumulate criminal records through confusion or misunderstanding. Aboriginal people throughout the province told us it is virtually impossible to find a translation for the concept of probation. Translator Angus Merrick told us, "There is no word in our language for that. I always told them that you have to wait for awhile. They have to wait for a while. That was [the] closest I could come to it."

In addition, probation officers usually are non-Aboriginal persons based in urban centres. This makes it difficult or impossible, when dealing with Aboriginal offenders from remote communities, to assist the offender or the court effectively, whether it is by way of explaining cultural or community factors to a judge, or by way of guiding an Aboriginal offender on probation. Urban non-Aboriginal probation workers also appear not to understand the problems experienced by urban Aboriginal people.

Community Service Orders

Although they are not referred to specifically in the *Criminal Code,* all provinces and territories make substantial use of community service orders (CSOs). A CSO is a condition of a probation order made pursuant to section 737, which gives judges discretion to impose such "reasonable conditions as the court considers desirable." A fact book of the Department of Justice defines a CSO as

> ... a sentence of the court whereby offenders are required to undertake unpaid work of value for a public or charitable recipient representing the community at large.[33]

Such orders usually specify the number of hours an offender is to work. In remote communities, this work can included flooding rinks, cutting grass, working in day care centres and schools as aides, cutting wood and hauling water, and setting up before and cleaning up after community bingos. In urban areas, it can include work at community centres, sorting clothing for the Salvation Army and working in senior citizens' residences.

These orders are intended to take the place of fines or incarceration. They differ from the fine option program in two important ways: the offender does not have the option of doing the work or simply paying a fine; and, offenders who breach community service orders are taken back to court, rather than being imprisoned automatically, as is the case with those who fail to do fine option work. While offenders can be incarcerated for violating a community service order, this is rarely done.

To administer CSOs the Department of Justice has entered into agreements with community-based organizations known as Community Resource Centres (CRCs). In 1989 there were over 140 CRCs in Manitoba which referred offenders to over 400 work centres. A listing of CRCs included over 45 band councils, as well as a variety of town and municipal governments, Lions Clubs, Friendship Centres and youth justice committees. These agencies register offenders, assign work and report on the performance of offenders to probation officers, Crown attorneys and the court. The centres also place offenders who have registered through the fine option program.

According to a report presented to us by the fine option program in 1989, 654 adults and 792 youths were registered through Community Service Orders; of this total 831 were in the city of Winnipeg, while 139 were in the Norman/Thompson region. In 1989 65% of offenders completed their community service orders and 107,795 hours of community service were ordered by courts.

Staffing

In Manitoba, probation orders are administered and supervised by the Department of Justice's Community and Youth Correctional Services. There are 100 probation officers employed in the provincial probation service. These officers are responsible for supervising over 5,000 people a year. Fifty-four per cent of the youth and 44% of the adults under probationary supervision are Aboriginal. Sixty probation officers are located in the Winnipeg area. Other communities with resident probation officers include: Portage, Morden, Beausejour, Steinbach, Selkirk, The Pas, Flin Flon, Dauphin, Swan River, Thompson, Norway House, God's Lake Narrows, Churchill, Brandon, Minnedosa and Hamiota. There are approximately 17 full-time Aboriginal probation officers and three half-time positions. Six Aboriginal probation officers are stationed in Winnipeg and 9.5 in northern Manitoba. In addition to the 100 full-time probation officers, there are 352 honorary probation officers who work in various communities on a fee-for-service basis. At least 45 of these officers identify themselves as Aboriginal. The average caseload per probation officer across the province is 68 cases, while the average caseload in northern Manitoba is 77.[34]

One probation officer who supported the use of alternative programs reminded us that "there are not a lot of staff should those programs increase drastically. Given the workload increases and the staff decreases over the last five years there is not a lot of manpower to meet those sorts of demands."

The same officer told us that while he believes there is less prejudice towards Aboriginal people in the probation service than when he started 18 years earlier, "it still exists to some degree and people still operate on the basis of stereotypes."

A number of Aboriginal and northern presenters said they had never seen a probation officer in their community. Bob McCleverty, the mayor of Thicket Portage, told us:

> There are not enough probation officers so, what happens is that an individual in the community is put on probation and it is like paying lip-service to a concern. The person goes through the court system, ends up back in the community and it is a matter of spending 60 days or six months on probation and they never report to an officer. We have never had a probation officer come into our community.

Presentations made at a number of reserves convince us that staffing problems lie behind the fact that the work ordered under both community service orders and the fine option program often may not be carried out properly. These programs often are viewed as being outside impositions and as being efforts by the justice system to off-load its responsibilities inexpensively. Chief Vera Mitchell of Poplar River told us:

> The Fine Option Program could be very beneficial to our community if we had a locally based probation officer. Matters such as these are shuffled to the Chief and Council. We have enough work to do without having to do the probation officer's work for them.... The Chief and Council are always given the undesired programs or the programs that are underfunded. So when there is a lack of services, the administration program with the local level looks unorganized, and services are inadequate.

Gordon Dumas, a volunteer probation worker in South Indian Lake, explained that he makes sure that offenders who have been given community service orders, or who are in the fine option program, register with the South Indian Lake Community Council. The council provides them with work. But from then on, he said, "Those people are on their own. Either they show up or they don't."

We were told bands receive $30 per offender to cover the cost of coordinating and supervising the work that is to be done. This appears to us to be inadequate. It also ensures that there is no regular, ongoing program.

Mr. Dumas also told us that he supervises five probationers, while up to 45 other probationers in the community are supervised by a probation officer based in

Thompson, who comes to the community every three months. Speaking of his ability to carry out his duties, Dumas said, "I am not trained to do that either. I think there should be a trained person in this community for that purpose."

Aboriginal presenters told us that non-Aboriginal probation officers had little understanding of the dynamics of life in an Aboriginal community. One person told us that his probation officer did not understand the pressures in an Aboriginal community that often caused a probation order to fail.

As they presently stand, we believe that probation services are unable to provide Aboriginal people with the level and type of service they need. This failure inevitably results in Aboriginal people being brought back before the courts for related or similar offences for which they had originally been placed on probation. When a judge is faced with an accused who is charged with an offence for which he or she had originally been placed on probation, or with a subsequent offence, the judge inevitably presumes that the individual failed to benefit from the earlier probation order and looks to a more punitive sanction to deter the offender. Judges may not stop to consider that perhaps the earlier probation order either was inappropriate or was not properly administered; that perhaps probation services failed and not the accused.

Section 737(a) of the *Criminal Code* permits the courts to require a person placed on probation to report to a "person designated by the court." This provision, unfortunately, is almost never used. We believe it is particularly suitable for Aboriginal communities. Such a person could be a family member, a band constable or band chief.

If probation services are to be effective, they must be provided by individuals who are familiar with the community and who understand the circumstances of the accused. We are satisfied that to serve those in an Aboriginal community properly, the probation officer must be Aboriginal, must reside in the community, and must have the resources and training needed to properly discharge his or her responsibilities. Community sanctions will not work unless the community truly believes it has ownership and control of the programs, and unless the people who are providing the service have an understanding of the community, have been properly trained and are being properly compensated for their efforts.

The Dakota Ojibway Probation Service

There is only one Aboriginally controlled probation agency in Manitoba: the Dakota Ojibway Probation Service (DOPS), with its head office in Brandon. This agency employs five staff: a director, a secretary and three probation officers. All staff are Aboriginal. DOPS took control of the probation services for seven of the eight member communities of the Dakota Ojibway Tribal Council in 1983. The service has jurisdiction over band members who live on DOTC reserves. Most observers agree that the jurisdiction was turned over too quickly and that the newly hired probation officers were not trained properly. In addition to this, there have been strained relations between the provincial probation services and DOPS.

The agency has struggled with the need to meet the standards of the provincial probation services and the courts, while trying to meet community expectations that it develop unique and culturally appropriate sanctions and policies. These strains have led to high staff turnover and, at times, criticism from the courts. However, it is clear that despite their concerns, the residents of the DOTC communities view the DOPS as a significant step in the communities' development.

We believe there is a need for a closer working relationship between the courts, the provincial corrections department and the DOPS, and for the development of a stable, long-term funding base for the agency.

Reforming Probation

We would like to see an improved probation policy that achieves a number of goals:

- That probation orders relate directly to the circumstances surrounding the offence for which a sentence is being passed and be culturally appropriate to the offender.

- That probation orders be used more often to reconcile communities, offenders and victims than is now done.

- That the number of Aboriginal persons employed in the provincial probation service be increased substantially.

- That those residing in rural, northern and Aboriginal communities have the services of a resident probation officer.

- That Aboriginal probation officers deal with Aboriginal offenders.

WE RECOMMEND THAT:

- Regional, Aboriginally controlled probation services be created to serve Aboriginal communities; and that Aboriginal people be employed by the Province as probation officers in numbers at least proportionate to their presence in the provincial population.

- All Aboriginal offenders be supervised by Aboriginal probation officers.

- Probation officers assigned to handle cases of Aboriginal persons be able to speak the language of the probationer.

- Conditions of probation orders be related directly to the circumstances of the offence and the offender, and be conditions that can be realistically adhered to by the probationer.

- There be a reorganization of the way community service orders are administered and supervised so that organizations are provided with the necessary resources to ensure that orders are fulfilled and that judges are provided with the necessary information to allow them to match offenders with programs.

- Cross-cultural training programs be mandatory for all non-Aboriginal probation staff, and that there be an ongoing series of refresher courses.

- When Aboriginal probation officers are not available to supervise Aboriginal offenders, judges make greater use of section 737(a) of the *Criminal Code*, which permits the court to place a person under the supervision of some "other person designated by the court."

- Courts seek out individuals in Aboriginal communities who are willing to accept the responsibility of supervising individuals placed on probation.

Restitution

Restitution is the return to a person of some money or goods taken by another. Presently, there are two different ways courts can address the issue. Compensation can be ordered under section 725(1) of the *Criminal Code*. If a compensation order is not complied with forthwith, the victim can file the compensation order with the Court of Queen's Bench and obtain a civil judgment. Additionally, section 737(2)(e) of the *Criminal Code* gives a judge the power to order that as a condition of probation the offender "make restitution or reparation to any person aggrieved or injured by the commission of the offence for the actual loss or damage sustained by that person as a result thereof."

Where the nature of the crime does not require the incarceration of the offender, we suggest that orders of restitution be considered as being preferable to a fine. The proceeds from an order of restitution benefit the victim, while the proceeds from a fine go to the state. Restitution is also in keeping with Aboriginal concepts of justice which, among other things, seek to determine the causes of wrongdoing, to correct them, and to return the parties to a state of peace and order. If, in an Aboriginal community, someone takes another's boat or snowmobile, the return of the item is the important thing, not sending the offender to jail. If some damage is done, work or payment is appropriate.

In Manitoba it is estimated that some 6% of adults sentenced by the provincial courts are ordered to pay restitution.[35] We believe this number can be increased significantly. Currently, restitution is not considered automatically by the courts and, when it is considered, there is no effective way of determining the amount of restitution that is warranted or the offender's ability to pay. When restitution is ordered, there is no proper way to monitor compliance, although court staff do play a bookkeeping role. While no statistics are available on completion rates, we have the impression that many orders are not supervised properly and that it is usually left to the victim to complain to the courts if restitution has not been made.

In Saskatchewan, which has had a formal restitution program since 1983, it was estimated after the first year of the program that restitution orders increased by 27%, and that, without the program, an additional 570 people would have been incarcerated for periods of one to 120 days.[36]

Under the Saskatchewan system, judges receive a restitution report which assesses the amount of damage done by the offender, the circumstances of the offence, the views of the victim, an assessment of the offender's ability to pay, and a recommendation whether restitution is appropriate and the amount that would be appropriate. The process ensures that the court considers restitution in lieu of short-term imprisonment or an alternate sentence.

In Saskatchewan restitution is paid to the courts and distributed to the victims. The program is administered by restitution coordinators, who work within the probation system. They do the restitution assessment reports, establish contact with the offender and monitor compliance, institute any needed enforcement measures, provide assistance to victims, and publicize the program within the court system and the community.

The Manitoba Maintenance Enforcement Program is another method of ensuring that court-ordered payments are indeed paid. The program provides computerized supervision of payments and administrative enforcement through garnishment of wages and close scrutiny of ability to pay. We believe the elements that make the Saskatchewan program successful—in particular, the contact that is made between restitution staff and offenders, and the assessment of ability to pay—and the collection provisions of the Maintenance Enforcement Program can be used to strengthen the effectiveness of orders of restitution in Manitoba.

WE RECOMMEND THAT:

- Judges make greater use of orders of restitution.

Fines and Fine Option

Fines

A wide range of *Criminal Code* offences, federal and provincial statutes, as well as numerous municipal by-laws, include fines as possible punishments. Fines are used extensively by courts, both alone and in conjunction with other sanctions.

Fines also are levied through Common Offence Notices (CONs). These were established to streamline the court process by allowing out-of-court settlement of minor offences through pre-set fines. They deal with violations of provincial statutes such as the *Highway Traffic Act*, the *Liquor Control Act* and the *Wildlife Act*. A peace officer serves the accused with an "offence notice." The notice imposes a deadline by which a person may contest the matter. If the accused does not take action to contest the charge, a guilty finding is entered and a fine is imposed automatically, without regard to the individual's ability to pay. A schedule of fines, including the amount of time a person will spend in jail if the fine is not paid, is determined by the Department of Justice, and applied by magistrates and justices of the peace.

The Department of Justice does not monitor the use of fines effectively. It does not know, for example, how many fines are assessed by the courts each year, or what the average fine is. We do know that in 1987, some $14 million in fine revenue was recovered in Manitoba. Our best estimate is that this resulted from some 160,000 fines.

In theory, fines simultaneously punish offenders and allow them to make a form of restitution to the community. Aboriginal communities do not necessarily share this view, since they see the fine money leaving the community and going to the provincial government.

The imposition of a fine, without any other penalty, indicates that the judge believes the offender does not present a threat to the community and, therefore, should not be jailed. However, under the provisions of sections 718(3) and 787(2) of the *Criminal Code*, a judge, when imposing a fine, can issue a default order. Under such an order, the offender may be imprisoned if the fine is not paid. When an offence proceeds by way of a common offence notice and the accused either fails to appear in court or to pay the fine, a default order is issued automatically and the offender is arrested. The amount of time the offender is required to serve is based on the size of the fine. Currently, fines are reduced at the rate of $10 for each day spent in custody. Fines differ significantly from probation orders in that fine defaulters are jailed without a formal hearing. While offenders who cannot pay fines may choose to enter the fine option program, many subsequently default. The police then are charged with the responsibility of arresting and imprisoning these people—an expensive task that the police feel takes them away from more important law enforcement activities. Unlike fine defaulters, offenders who breach probation are given a formal hearing to determine the reasons for the default before any new sanctions are imposed. The absence of this review process for fines has serious consequences.

Most Canadians would agree that there should not be one law for the rich and another for the poor, but it appears that this is the case when it comes to fines. In 1988, 754 of the 5,563 people admitted to provincial correctional institutions in Manitoba were fine defaulters. This means that 13% of the people admitted to Manitoba jails in that year were there, not because they were a danger to society, but because they could not, or would not, pay their fines. Research commissioned by our Inquiry indicates that in 1988, 60% of these imprisoned fine defaulters were Aboriginal.

Our research indicates that Aboriginal men who defaulted were twice as likely to be incarcerated as non-Aboriginal men, and Aboriginal women were three times more likely to be incarcerated than non-Aboriginal women. According to our study, the typical fine defaulter is an Aboriginal male between the ages of 22 to 29, who is single, unemployed, has less than grade 12 education and resides in rural Manitoba. Aboriginal offenders were twice as likely to be incarcerated for fine default for one outstanding fine than non-Aboriginal offenders. The average amount of the unpaid fines that led to the incarceration of Aboriginal people was $201.20. Aboriginal inmates incarcerated for defaulting on their fines served an average of 23 days in custody.

There are two aspects of the matter which concern us. First, Aboriginal people (and others) who have not committed serious crimes are still going to jail because they cannot afford to pay their fines. This is an intolerable state of affairs.

Second, it appears that judges are not adequately considering the question of an accused's ability to pay a fine when imposing one.

Judges are required by law to address their minds to the offender's ability to pay when determining whether to allow time to pay the fine (s. 718 (5) of the *Criminal Code*) and, additionally, when the accused is between 16 and 21 years of age, must order a special report on the accused's ability to pay before issuing a warrant of committal in default of paying a fine. (s. 718(10)) While it is possible that judges are addressing the issue of ability to pay when granting time to pay a fine, we are not certain that ability to pay is addressed when default orders are imposed.

It is not obligatory for judges to impose default orders, but it is common practice for judges to do so. The *Criminal Code* allows a judge to impose a fine and then, at a second hearing, to impose a default order if the fine has not been paid. The fact that this process is never used is a clear indication that imprisonment for non-payment of fines is viewed by those within the system as a means of enforcing the payment of fines—a practice long considered improper.

Nova Scotia Provincial Court Judge R. E. Kimball has stated that default orders are not always appropriate or necessary. He suggests that the order should not be imposed unless the Crown asks for it and provides reasons why the order should be granted.

> The decision to order imprisonment in default of payment is not to be lightly made. The determination of the question at all times must be free from any preconceived ideas or habits and with the realization that default orders are not mandatory. Provincial court judges must realize, after due consideration, that imprisonment in default of payment of the fine may not be ordered at all and when it is ordered the judge must do so with eyes open, fully responsible for the judicial act and fully aware of its consequences.[37]

We agree with these comments. We also believe that a major reason why judges in Manitoba impose default orders as a matter of course is because they believe offenders who cannot pay their fines will take advantage of the fine option program, rather than be incarcerated. That, of course, has not proven to be the case. For this reason it is important to review the operation of that program.

Fine Option

In 1983 Manitoba initiated a Fine Option Program. It was intended to reduce the number of offenders incarcerated for failure to pay a fine. It was a response to the fact that our jails traditionally have been "debtors' prisons," for those without the means to pay a fine. In 1982, for example, 24% (or 791 persons) of the people admitted to provincial correctional institutions were incarcerated for non-payment of fines.

The Manitoba *Summary Convictions Act*, section 21, allows offenders to perform unpaid community work in lieu of paying fines that have been assessed by the courts. The related regulation is entitled the "Fine Option Program Regulation." It enables offenders to register with Community Resource Centres. These centres perform the same function for those who register with the fine option program as they do for those offenders who are fulfilling community service orders; they arrange suitable work for program participants and then supervise the completion of the work. The number of hours to be spent performing community work is determined by dividing the fine by the hourly minimum wage.

In Manitoba offenders can enter the program in one of two ways. After the court has imposed a fine, they may sign up for fine option immediately. If they do not sign up at this stage and are unable to pay, or are subsequently incarcerated for defaulting on the fine, there is a further opportunity to enter the program at the correctional institution. In 1988, 245 of the 754 fine defaulters admitted to Manitoba jails entered the fine option program. In these cases, offenders were given temporary absences from the institutions in order to perform the required community work, unless they had already failed to perform work that was assigned previously under the fine option program.

In some cases, RCMP officers encourage the defaulters to enrol in the fine option program and, if that is done, the person does not have to be taken to jail. If the person defaults in a work program, however, he or she is arrested again and taken to jail.

As the program is presently structured, anyone can take advantage of it, regardless of his or her means. The court itself has no say in whether a person who is fined should, or plans to, enter the program. There also is no means test required for those who register with the program. Even those who are quite capable of paying the fine can register in the program. This, in fact, has been a criticism of the fine option program. Fine defaulters with the resources to pay a fine know that if they wait for the police to arrest them for non-payment, they can immediately register for the fine option program. If they default on the program, they cannot be re-arrested since the original warrant for non-payment of fine has been executed. A new warrant cannot be issued without a new hearing, a procedure not used now. Such defaulters, therefore, are shown in court records as having worked off their fine (by being shown as having registered) when, in fact, they have not. They are not pursued any further.

Even when the program does work, it is administratively inflexible and costly to deliver. When a fine is imposed, the offender has to make contact with the fine option system to enrol in the program. A program employee then will have to find suitable work for the offender. A contract is then entered into with the offender. The case has to be supervised to make sure the offender completes the work. If the offender does not keep to the work schedule, that fact has to be reported by the workplace supervisor to the fine option coordinator. Usually, no effort is expended to restore the work program. If, however, the work is not being carried out at all, a warrant is issued and the person is taken to jail to serve the time that has not been worked off.

In 1987 there were some 10,000 fine option program registrations. We estimate that approximately 6% of all fines are worked off through the program. There can be no doubt that the fine option program has managed to reduce the number of people who are being incarcerated for fine defaults; in 1980, 1,148 people were serving time in Manitoba jails for fine defaults, while in 1988 this number was 509 (excluding the 245 who registered with fine option upon admission to jail).

Despite the fact that the fine option program has been operating in Manitoba for eight years, hundreds of people, more than half of them Aboriginal, are going to jail every year for defaulting on their fines. We believe that for the vast majority this occurs simply because they lack the resources to pay. The archaic practice of putting people in jail because they cannot afford to pay a fine is being perpetuated. While the fine option program has succeeded in reducing somewhat the incarceration of fine defaulters, it has failed to bring this practice to an end.

Figures obtained by our research staff from the Saskatchewan program also seem to raise questions about the long-term effectiveness of fine options in reducing the incarceration of fine defaulters. In 1986–87, for example, 47.2% of female admissions and 35.9% of male admissions to provincial correctional institutions in Saskatchewan resulted from a fine default, notwithstanding the fact that a fine option program had been in existence in that province for well over a decade.[38]

There are several reasons for this. One lies in the fact that the program creates the illusion that people who are assessed fines will not go to jail. It appears to us that judges assume that offenders who are fined will pay or take advantage of the fine option program, rather than defaulting and going to jail. Unfortunately, this is not always the case. Had the fine option program not been available, we believe that, in many cases, judges would not have imposed a fine; instead, they would have used a less onerous sanction or made a community service order a condition of probation. In other words, the program entices the courts into imposing a penalty that results in jail when the judge had already decided that jail was inappropriate. The existence of the program seems to reduce a judge's need to assess an offender's ability to pay, or to take that into account when determining the amount of the fine.

As well, during our hearings, we found that many convicted Aboriginal people either were not aware of the existence of the program, or did not know how to enrol in it. There is no consistent way of notifying potential program participants about the options that are available to them. Moreover, we saw some written material about the program that was incorrect and out of date. We were told that some people who could benefit from the program never use the enrolment forms they are given. We believe the documents and the program are not being explained properly. John Sioux, a band councillor on the Sioux Valley Reserve with responsibility for the local fine option program, told us:

> I think that some of our people that go to court, that get fines or possibly incarceration, should be let known or more communication given to them about this Fine Option Program, so they could go on this program if they do the work.
>
> I think our court communicator or the judge, whoever, should let them know what the Fine Option is. Because I don't think it explains to them all the time what the Fine Option Program is. So I think they should get more information on the Fine Option Program, instead of being incarcerated or sometimes having a hard time to pay a fine.

A telephone survey of court offices by our Inquiry staff confirmed that there was a considerable lack of knowledge about the program, even among justice system officials. There were some very clearly mistaken beliefs as to who was entitled to use the program and, in particular, whether application could be made after a default had occurred. None of the court offices contacted had received any orientation or a policy manual on the program. All indicated they had never been approached by the administrators of the program for an orientation, nor had they received information relating to policy or procedures.

Persons employed to coordinate fine option programs are not present in many communities, including many Aboriginal communities. In some communities, this work is done by honorary coordinators and access to accurate information about the program is restricted. Where coordinators are present, they, like the court staff, often appear unsure of their responsibilities. The RCMP have offered some assistance to enable people to enrol in the program, even after they have defaulted. Unlike the RCMP, however, the Winnipeg and Brandon police forces do not advise people, as a matter of policy, of the existence of the fine option program, nor do they allow the offender time to register with the program before executing a warrant of arrest for defaulting on a fine.

It is not surprising that many offenders choose fine option once they have been incarcerated. For many, it is the first they have heard about the program. Others may have been hoping to avoid apprehension. Once an offender is incarcerated, his or her incentive to participate is considerable, since it results in immediate release from jail.

Female offenders do not participate in the fine option program to the same extent as men. Many with whom we spoke did not become aware of the program until they were incarcerated for fine default. Others, who told us they were aware of the program, were not able to take advantage of it owing to family demands, low self-esteem or a lack of assertiveness. Others have little or no work experience in an urban community and do not think the program is available to them.

On many reserves, there is a belief among Aboriginal men that women should not work outside the home. Such a belief certainly affects an Aboriginal woman's participation in the fine option program. In addition, single-parent families and families where the mother is the primary care-giver to the children predominate in Aboriginal communities. These situations make participation in a community work program problematic, if not impossible. In cities, the cost of transportation and the need to care for children are further factors that prevent women from participating. There does not appear to be any effort being made to encourage Aboriginal women to participate, or to provide them with viable options to defaulting on fines or breaching CSOs.

The fine option system is further complicated by common offence notices. Because there is no court hearing, there is no opportunity for a judge to consider the appropriateness of a fine or to substitute another sentence. Those who default on CONs can find themselves incarcerated without ever having had their case considered by a court.

We know that the fine option program was established with the best of intentions: to give offenders an option to stay out of jail if they cannot pay a fine. While there are certain administrative problems with the program, we believe the people responsible for it are doing their best to make sure it achieves its goals. However, we believe that it is necessary to make fundamental changes in the way we assess and recover fines.

A New Fine Enforcement System

The aim of sentencing is to find a sanction which is appropriate to the offence, to the individual offender and to the needs of the community. We believe that fines, restitution and community work are valuable sanctions, but they are not now being used properly or to their fullest potential. In particular, we would like to see an increase in the use of restitution orders and a decrease in the number of fines. We believe that CSOs and restitution can play an important role in restoring a sense of harmony to a community after a crime has been committed, and we also believe that an over-reliance on fines has led to the incarceration of far too many people.

The first step in reforming this process is to require judges to satisfy themselves that an offender is able to pay before any fine is imposed or before an order of restitution is made. Fines should not be imposed if the person is unable to pay the fine. The Manitoba *Summary Convictions Act* and the *Criminal Code* should be amended to eliminate the provision of incarceration for the non-payment of fines. In those cases where the judge determines that the offender does not possess the ability to pay a fine, the judge should impose probation or should make a community service order in place of the fine.

We are proposing changes to the way these three sanctions are imposed, monitored and enforced with these goals in mind:

- An elimination of the practice of incarcerating people for defaulting on fines.

- A reduction of fine defaults.

- A reduction of defaults on restitution orders.

These are ambitious goals. But we have the successful example of the Manitoba government's Maintenance Enforcement Program to draw upon. Because the province has been able to reduce welfare payments to dependent spouses since the program was introduced in 1980, the program, in effect, pays for itself. Millions of dollars have been collected from people ordered to pay child or spousal support. A similar fine recovery program would also increase the likelihood of fines being paid, while reducing expenses for incarceration and freeing police officers for other duties.

We recommend the establishment of a Fine and Restitution Recovery Program.

Once a fine is levied or an order of restitution is made, the Fine and Restitution Recovery Program should become responsible for its collection. All fines and restitution orders should automatically be registered with the enforcement program, whose officers would contact offenders when a default occurs. As a first step, financial advice and counselling might be offered. As a second step, the fine enforcement officers could accept a wage assignment or have the offender's salary or income tax refund garnisheed, or property attached.

Where the fine is related to the operation of a motor vehicle, authority should be conferred on the enforcement program to record the fine with the Motor Vehicle Branch. No further vehicle or driver's licence should be issued until the fine is paid.

If these efforts fail, the offender can be required to attend a hearing held by a master, judge or hearing officer. At this hearing, the offender would have explain why the fine or restitution payment is in default. After a thorough examination of assets and debts, the hearing officer would have the power to order the substitution of a period of community service for the original sentence, to extend the time to pay the fine, or to enter the default on the person's record. If the person is able to pay the fine, but wilfully refuses, only then would incarceration be appropriate, and even then this should only occur when ordered by a master or judge.

Changes are also required to the current practice with respect to common offence notices. As with parking tickets in the city of Winnipeg, the common offence notice might indicate a substantial fine which is subject to a discount if paid within a time limit. Defaulters would be dealt with by the enforcement practices we are recommending.

WE RECOMMEND THAT:

- The existing Fine Option Program be abolished and replaced with a Fine and Restitution Recovery Program which would follow these principles:

  - All fines and orders of restitution should be automatically registered with and enforced by the Fine and Restitution Recovery Program.

  - If the payment of a fine is not made, the program be empowered to collect the money by garnishment or attachment in the same manner as the way in which maintenance orders are now enforced, or to take other actions such as preventing licensing of vehicles by the Motor Vehicle Branch.

  - If these measures fail, the offender be brought to a show cause hearing presided over by a hearing officer.

  - If the hearing officer concludes that the offender does not have the ability to pay, the officer may order a period of community service or extend the time for payment of the fine.

  - If the hearing officer concludes that the offender has the ability to pay but is simply refusing to do so, the officer could refer the case to a master or a judge.

  - A judge or master would have the authority, after all other efforts at collection have failed, to incarcerate those who have the ability to pay but refuse to do so.

- The existing Maintenance Enforcement Program be expanded and adapted to administer the Fine and Restitution Recovery Program.

■ The automatic assessment of a term of imprisonment in default of payment of fines levied by Common Offence Notices be abolished, and that the Fine and Restitution Recovery Program apply.

■ The *Criminal Code* and other legislation allowing for the levying of fines be amended to require that, before levying any fine, judges be required to determine whether a person is able to pay a fine; and that fines not be imposed if the offender is unable to pay the fine at the time of sentence or within a reasonable time thereafter.

■ The *Criminal Code* of Canada, The Manitoba *Summary Convictions Act* and any other relevant legislation be amended to eliminate incarceration in default of fines.

■ Where a judge orders the performance of community service work of a specified number of hours, the judge have the option to specify the type and place of work, thus allowing the judge to fashion an appropriate sentence and eliminate the need for the offender to apply elsewhere to enter a program.

■ Where there is a default in the payment of a fine, the default be noted on the accused's record so that the default can be taken into account if the person comes before the court on a subsequent occasion.

Conclusion

Our justice system may claim to be fair and equitable, but it is largely a punishment system that makes insufficient use of its sentencing options. The needs of offenders, victims and communities, rather than sentencing precedents, should become the criteria when appropriate dispositions are being considered.

At present, our jails are filled to overcapacity. They are filled with large numbers of offenders who are not a danger to society. They are filled despite the fact that jail only punishes—it does not rehabilitate, deter or protect effectively. They are filled despite the fact that they are horrendously expensive to build and operate. They are filled despite the fact that more cost-effective alternatives are already in place, although under-utilized, and that others could easily be developed. They are filled even though they represent a particularly inappropriate response to the plight of Aboriginal people.

The challenge facing Canadian society is to find different means of dealing with unacceptable behaviour. Merely building more jails, or encouraging the judiciary to deal more severely with offenders, will not address the root causes of crime in our society. We believe that there are more effective ways of utilizing limited financial resources.

We believe our recommendations, if implemented, will go a long way to reduce incarceration, will improve the effectiveness of sentencing and will begin to develop the Aboriginal community's faith in the justice system. We would like to stress our belief that long-term solutions lie in the Aboriginal communities developing and controlling their own justice system, including correctional programs and facilities. Even with such developments, we recommend that the existing system be significantly reformed. Without a change in approach, the courts will continue to act on the basis of inadequate information, and Aboriginal people will continue to see the decisions of courts as foreign to them and as ones that do not meet their needs.

We believe the changes that we have recommended are mutually reinforcing. Canada must reduce its tendency to punish and incarcerate people. Courts must develop alternative sentences that more clearly identify the cause of inappropriate conduct and help to overcome any likelihood of repetition, and, at the same time, address the concerns of victims and the community.

The underlying problem with the programs we have reviewed in this chapter is no different than in the other justice programs we have reviewed. Aboriginal communities have to be given an opportunity to deal with their own problems and resolve them with their own institutions. Communication problems, discrimination, time delays, high costs, inappropriate decisions and many other problems that characterize the current system will be significantly reduced, we believe, when Aboriginal communities become more responsible for their own citizens.

CHAPTER 11

JAILS

Introduction

A trip to our legislatures and courthouses is enough to impress an observer with the majesty of Canada's legal system. But it is only by visiting our jails and prisons that a person can come to a full understanding of that system's power. Legislators pass laws and judges hand down sentences in awe-inspiring surroundings, but it is in prisons and jails that freedom finally is restrained. Because these institutions are so central to the current justice system, we made an effort to visit as many of them as possible.

We held hearings at the Stony Mountain Institution, the Headingley Correctional Institution, the Brandon Correctional Institution, the Portage Correctional Institution for women and The Pas Correctional Institution. We also visited the Rockwood Institution, the Dauphin Correctional Institution, the Egg Lake Rehabilitation Camp, the Milner Ridge Correctional Centre, the Manitoba Youth Centre and the Agassiz Youth Centre.

With few exceptions, what we encountered was not a correctional system but a punitive one. This was most apparent at Stony Mountain Institution. In the segregation area, when an inmate is taken out of his cell, two guards must be present. Inmates are not permitted to walk in the common area outside their cells, even though the common area appeared secure. Inmates are allowed only one hour of recreation a day in an adjacent outdoor enclosure.

The superintendent of Headingley Correctional Institution, Dennis Lemoine, ended his presentation to us with the sad conclusion that:

> Correctional institutions, or prisons if you wish, are harsh environments. I find the environment somewhat impersonal at times and stressful and that is not just for the native residents or white inmates or staff members, it applies to pretty well every staff member who works in this type of environment. It is difficult and sometimes makes for less human contact than more. It does not normally sensitize people to the better side of things.

Regrettably, the treatment that young people receive is not much different. At the Manitoba Youth Centre, each youth was intended to have a private or semi-private room. Yet, we saw that young women were required to sleep on the floor in one crowded sector of the centre that we went through. At the Agassiz Youth Centre, many of the residents are required to sleep on wooden bunks with thin mattresses. Heating is inadequate, the roofs leak and, in the summer, temperatures in some buildings rise to intolerable levels because there is no air conditioning.

The system even punishes those who have not been convicted of any crime. We were told, and we believe, that the poor conditions and long stays at the provincial Remand Centre have led some people to plead guilty in order to expedite their transfer from the centre. Even more tragically, there have been five suicides at the centre since 1985.

Most of the jails we visited reminded us of zoos where men and women were caged behind iron bars. For the most part, there is nothing to do as the months and years drag by. Even when modern facilities, such as the Milner Ridge Correctional Centre, are established, they quickly tend toward the usual patterns of older-style institutions.

Surely the inability to return home is punishment enough without locking people in small cells, counting them at every move, restricting their movement and otherwise dehumanizing them. Those treated as untrustworthy can hardly learn to trust. Those treated as subhuman can hardly be expected to develop good habits of human conduct.

We believe that incarceration in secure institutions should be used only as a last resort and only for individuals who pose a threat to some individual or the community. As we discussed in the previous chapter, we believe that alternative programs that do not involve custody can and should be used for most offenders. Yet, we recognize that even if our recommendations are accepted and implemented, jails will continue to be needed for some offenders. But those jails which continue to exist must be transformed. In the institutions that we are proposing, substantially less emphasis would be placed on security and substantially more emphasis would be placed on providing meaningful—and culturally appropriate—programs that will equip Aboriginal inmates to live in society on their release.

In this chapter we focus on the current state of Manitoba's jails and on some different approaches to custody that we believe would be far more effective than the existing institutions. We will deal with the specific problems of women inmates in greater detail in Chapter 13.

The Need for a New Correctional System

In subsequent sections we will touch on a number of improvements that would enhance the effectiveness of Manitoba's jails. However, we believe that specific program improvements are likely to have little overall effect. We feel that fundamental reforms, based on a new set of principles, are required. The reforms we recommend are designed with the Aboriginal offender in mind, but we believe that these reforms can be of benefit to all offenders.

We received many submissions that were highly critical of the correctional system and that called for its reform. One northern clergyman, John Thompson, correctly pointed out that there is little or no attempt at healing in our jails. A lawyer who has practised in the North for many years, Robert Mayer Q.C., recommended the use of alternate programs, such as restitution and community work. The publisher of the *Nickel Belt News*, Joan Wright, proposed the establishment of a large farm as an alternative to sending convicted persons to jail.

One Aboriginal inmate, who was serving a life sentence for murder in Stony Mountain, told us in a very thoughtful presentation that the government "should build penitentiaries or learning centres up north, staffed by inmates or native people instead of trying to meet the criteria of the training correctional officers—start from scratch." He made the point that unless people are given the opportunity to improve when in jail, the cycle of crime and jail will not be broken.

Other presenters called for greater access by Aboriginal inmates to self-improvement programs. Many said they would welcome meaningful work. Several called for specialized institutional programs for those convicted of child, spouse or sexual abuse.

As well, those who are responsible for the day-to-day running of Manitoba's jails told us on a number of occasions that high levels of security were not needed for most inmates.

These comments parallel many of our own observations and concerns. We are convinced that the prison system fails Aboriginal inmates. This failure involves:

- An over-use of high security institutions.

- A failure to meet the spiritual and personal needs of inmates through culturally appropriate programming.

- A failure to provide counselling, training and education to enable inmates to function in society on their release.

- A reliance on centralized institutions which isolate inmates from the community contacts which would be best suited to helping them prepare to rejoin society, and which reduces community responsibility for the conduct of its members.

- A corrections regime which establishes and flouts its own disciplinary rules and a corrections staff which is, at the very least, insensitive to the cultural concerns of Aboriginal people and, at its worst, is racist.

We believe that the incarceration of non-dangerous individuals on the basis that they will be reformed or deterred is foolish, since there is ample evidence that correctional institutions do not achieve these results.

It is clear that, at present, jails do little but keep some people out of society for a period of time. Once released, the majority of Aboriginal inmates are just dumped back into society. Many have nowhere to go. Most return to the community with no further education or training than that they went in with. They are no better equipped to deal with life.

We believe that meaningful reforms are possible. A strategy consisting of several major elements is required:

- Finding alternatives to custody for many of the Aboriginal offenders who are now incarcerated.

- Developing alternatives to the current secure jail system for Aboriginal offenders who require some form of custody.

- Making the current correctional system responsive to Aboriginal people. This will require extensive service delivery by Aboriginal organizations and a correctional policy that empowers communities to take responsibility for the antisocial behaviour of their members.

- Developing effective affirmative action and cross-cultural training programs, and independently adjudicated inmate complaint and disciplinary tribunals.

- Reducing the capacity of the province's high security jails with a simultaneous expansion of alternative services and facilities.

The first of these strategies is the subject of the previous chapter. The others are discussed in this section.

Aboriginal offenders requiring some form of institutional care should have available a number of alternatives that are matched to their needs. Specifically, we see the need for a program mix that contains the following elements:

- Secure facilities for Aboriginal offenders who present a physical threat to individuals or to the community, or who have repeatedly violated the regulations of lower security facilities. By "secure facilities" we mean those institutions that commonly spring to mind when one speaks of prisons; places where inmates are confined and which are sufficiently secure to prevent their departure. Stony Mountain and Headingley should be the only such institutions in Manitoba.

- Short-term, community-based holding facilities for Aboriginal offenders who require secure detention. Such facilities would be primarily for prisoners awaiting bail or trial.

- Camps, such as the one at Egg Lake, for many of the Aboriginal offenders who are now jailed but who are not dangerous.

- Open custody, community-based facilities for Aboriginal offenders requiring limited detention, with counselling, behaviour improvement, job training and other forms of assistance available.

- Policies that would make it possible for private individuals to take Aboriginal offenders and inmates into their homes, in a manner similar to that used in group homes for youths and halfway houses for released inmates.

Some elaboration on the types of programs we have in mind, and the ways in which they should be established, is required. Our correctional system should reinforce community involvement and responsibility. To this end, facilities ought to be smaller and closer to Aboriginal communities—not large institutions in some faraway place. Most Aboriginal offenders ought to be dealt with in their own community, and the programs that are offered to them should be designed and provided by Aboriginal people. This means that for any reforms to be meaningful, the Aboriginal communities affected must play a major role in designing and controlling a reformed corrections system. For this reason, we cannot provide a prescriptive blueprint of what sorts of correctional facilities should be available in each region or in each Aboriginal community. The Manitoba government must negotiate with Aboriginal groups to determine which institutions would suit their needs best. We fully expect that different communities will opt for different program elements.

Correctional institutions in and near Aboriginal communities must be administered by Aboriginal people. For those institutions within the provincial correctional system, this will mean the hiring of Aboriginal staff for senior positions in these facilities. As the Aboriginal justice systems that we recommend come into existence, the correctional institutions to which these systems send offenders should be placed under their administration and authority.

During the course of our Inquiry, we were presented with numerous creative proposals for the establishment of community-based corrections programming and facilities that provide us with a picture of what the Aboriginal community is seeking.

Chief Raymond Swan of the Interlake Reserves Tribal Council made a presentation to us in which he outlined his council's proposal for the creation of a Native Harmony and Restoration Centre at Pineimuta Place near Gypsumville:

> The goal of the Native Harmony and Restoration Centre is to create a program that will make it possible for those who have been in conflict with their community to return healed, reconciled, able to lead a productive life and to contribute to their society. The Centre will combine rehabilitation based on traditional tribal customs and values with upgrading and post-secondary education and work-related activities. All three components must be present in order for the program to work. A key element is that the offenders will not be separated from their families, who can reside at the Centre. Furthermore they will be reasonably close to their communities, enabling reconciliation to take place.

The Indigenous Women's Collective prepared a study for the Inquiry which spoke of the need for holistic treatment lodges, especially for cases of family violence:

> Qualified counsellors, who understand and practise traditional ways, would be involved in the treatment process. Their area of expertise would serve to help the people discuss their problems, feeling and attitudes, thereby relieving the elders, teachers and helpers of much of the stress and time required in the healing process.

> People involved in the holistic treatment could be paired up with another person as part of a "buddy" system. The buddy system would help one to focus on helping another, thereby giving one a great sense of responsibility and self-worth.

> The holistic treatment lodges would be set up in various regions throughout the province. Each lodge would take into account various factors such as language, accessibility, age groups, addictions, gender and spiritual beliefs. The holistic treatment lodges, as discussed in the foregoing text, would be established to help the individual and the whole family.[1]

Another option would be to establish facilities in Aboriginal communities from which open custody programs could be operated. Offenders would be required to be in residence every night, while during the day they would be free to pursue education, counselling or employment. The person also might be free to be at his or her own home.

During the time the offender is required to be in the facility, there should be counselling programs related to the most common causes of unacceptable conduct—substance abuse programs, anger management and abuse counselling, as well as specific skills training related to finding employment. Cultural or spiritual education might be a useful program for some. Those in charge of the facility, in addition to being responsible for the attendance of those under their charge, should have skills in counselling and family reparation.

In instances where it might not be practical to establish a separate secure holding facility, an open custody facility might also have a separate secure section so that Aboriginal people who are arrested could be held overnight until their release the next day. As we have already pointed out, many detentions result from alcohol or drug-related offences. When sober, these individuals can generally be released until their court appearance. We suggest that, rather than transporting accused persons a long distance, they be kept in the community. We believe it would also be possible to use these facilities as halfway houses for Aboriginal men and women leaving other, more secure correctional institutions.

A further option would be to make it possible for private individuals to bring Aboriginal offenders and inmates into their homes. A program of this sort would help offenders reintegrate into the community. This option could be made available to those serving sentences, as a condition of suspended sentence, or for those granted parole. We recognize that this sort of program, which we believe to be highly desirable, would be hobbled by the tremendous housing shortages which currently exist on many reserves. Nonetheless, the potential benefits of such a program and its community-based nature strongly commend its consideration.

While we recognize that these proposals are novel for Manitoba, some have been implemented successfully in other jurisdictions.[2] If precedent is required, we need look no further than the *Young Offenders Act*. In that Act, open custody is recognized as an appropriate type of custody for some individuals.

One advantage of this approach is that communities will become much more involved in dealing with the consequences of harmful conduct. We believe this will lead to more effective deterrence.

With these principles and strategies in mind, we turn to the specific problems of Manitoba's correctional system.

Security

Whether one is entering an ancient and imposing institution like Stony Mountain Institution or Headingley Correctional Institution, or a modern facility like the Brandon Correctional Institution or the Manitoba Youth Centre, one cannot help but be struck by the fact that our corrections system is obsessed with security. This was a common feature of most of the jails we visited. They function almost totally on a "worst case" basis, assuming that every inmate would try to escape or do something criminal if given an opportunity. The entire institutional focus appears to be aimed at guarding against these possibilities. No one seems prepared to assume that the individual might be interested in ways to escape, not from the jail, but from the circumstances that led to incarceration in the first place.

We realize that there are some who will try to escape if given the opportunity. For them, a more humane approach may be seen as lax security. Our system cannot operate on the assumption that these types of individuals do not exist. Our point is that they are in the minority. That is what we have observed and that is what the experts have told us.

At Stony Mountain, outer barred doors have to be unlocked to permit entrance to the cell blocks. Each cell block has a long, narrow corridor. The individual cells, also with bars, open into this area. The common area once had tables and chairs, but these were removed following a riot several years earlier and were replaced only after a number of years.

At Headingley, one sees a maze of bars and restrained humanity, here more tightly packed than at Stony Mountain. The Brandon Correctional Institution is a new facility, but the movement of inmates is strictly controlled and centrally monitored. Doors are opened only after a camera identifies the person to the operator of the central console. The Manitoba Youth Centre in south Winnipeg looks like a large, one-storey school from the outside, but entering the building for the first time is a shock. It too has a central security control. Although it is a youth facility, it quickly reminds one of an adult jail. The facility operates as a maximum security institution. Even the province's newest correctional institution at Milner Ridge, which in many respects has much to commend it, appears to have had the tight discipline and security approach of Headingley Correctional Institution transferred to it along with some of that jail's inmates.

Given the system's constant focus on security, it is interesting to note what many of the people charged with running the jails had to say. During his presentation, we asked Stony Mountain warden Art Majkut what percentage of inmates in the penitentiary he considered to be security risks or a danger to society. Here is his response:

> If you look at the records of the inmates who are at Stony Mountain Institution, you will find that probably in 80 per cent of those files there is an identified alcohol or drug problem.
>
> While an individual is not under the influence of drugs and alcohol certainly they are not dangerous. But when you see FPS [Fingerprint Sheet] reports that continually indicate an assault and you continually see the reference to alcohol and drugs, then, yes, under those conditions I would consider that the individual is dangerous and should not be in the community harming others.
>
> So, I can't give you a general picture. The inmates who are here today, the majority of them and the condition that they are in, would not be considered dangerous.

This assessment was reinforced by a presentation made to our Inquiry by Guy Tavener, the superintendent of The Pas Correctional Institution and the Egg Lake Rehabilitation Camp. In response to a question about the security requirements for inmates, he said:

> My personal opinion is that the majority of people don't really need to be locked up. Usually they're not normally security risks.... My guess is that the people that actually require secure custody are somewhere around five per cent of your population.

It appears to us that lower security institutions, close to or in the accused's community, would be adequate to house the other 95%.

The experience of the Dauphin Correctional Institution underscores this conclusion. It was once a medium security institution and is now operated as a minimum security one. Inmates may work in the community during the day, attend programs in the community, or work in or around the institution.

The superintendent of the institution stated that he is able to operate a minimum security institution due to the small size of the institution and to the fact that he can transfer inmates who might not be suitable for his program to Headingley. Generally, however, inmates are not a security risk.

Our visit to the camp at Egg Lake, which is administered by the jail at The Pas, showed another way that lower security sentenced offenders can be dealt with. The Egg Lake institution consists of low wooden buildings. At the time of our visit, some still were under construction. There is a kitchen, dining room and some activities rooms. The guards act as supervisors in the kitchen, in construction and in overseeing the inmate work crews. There are no bars on the windows and the doors are not locked at night.

The high level of security at the Manitoba Youth Centre, on the other hand, is extremely disturbing. While we could understand and accept the need for this level of security for a few offenders, all who reside in this facility are subjected to the same high level of security as soon as they are within the walls. Such an atmosphere of oppression and tension has to have a negative, if not devastating, effect on young people.

We believe over-use of custodial institutions is even more serious in the case of young offenders than it is in the case of adult offenders. We find the heavy and inappropriate reliance on custody for young people to be repugnant. Before trial, young offenders should be released on bail or kept in short-term facilities in their home community, except in exceptional circumstances. If they are convicted, incarceration should be a last resort. A full range of community-based alternatives to custody should be made available. The next option should be community or regional facilities.

Even where our existing jails have differing levels of security, such as the annexes at Headingley, the new facility at Milner Ridge, and Rockwood Institution, Aboriginal inmates do not have the same access to these facilities as do non-Aboriginal inmates. The 1988 *Report of the Task Force on Aboriginal People in Federal Corrections* had this to say:

> Access to programs varies according to security levels, and ... Aboriginal and non-Aboriginal offenders differed in terms of the security levels of the institutions in which they were placed.... Nearly twice as many Aboriginal inmates were placed in multi-level security institutions (24.6 per cent as compared to 12.6 per cent). Only 17.8 per cent of Aboriginal inmates as compared to 27.8 per cent of non-Aboriginal were in S4 institutions. Also 8.1 per cent of Aboriginal inmates compared to 15.6 per cent of non-Aboriginal were in minimum security (i.e., S1 and S2).[3]

According to the report, of the 235 Aboriginal persons placed in S5 institutions across Canada (S6 is the highest level of security), 150 of them were in Manitoba (63.8%). What the above shows is that Aboriginal inmates have less access to programs because they are kept in higher security facilities, and they are kept in higher security facilities, in Manitoba, in large part because the main federal institution is a higher security facility, not because of specific security requirements.

While some might suggest the solution is to build more federal jails with different levels of security in Manitoba, we reject any such direction, because the philosophy of the jail system would remain the same and Aboriginal inmates still would experience difficulty being placed in the lower security institutions. Also, the federal concept of "medium" or "minimum" security jails and our concept of that notion are quite different.

A final comment about our existing emphasis on high security jails, with their high technology monitoring and locking systems, and high guard-to-inmate ratios, is that they are extremely expensive for the dubious benefits they provide. In 1987–88, for example, the federal government alone expended some $800 million and employed about 11,000 staff to maintain the penitentiary system, while there are only 10,000 federal inmates at any one time.[4]

The cost of housing an inmate at Dauphin is $30,145 per year. This figure does not include the cost of the building or its maintenance. This is somewhat below the average cost of provincial institutions, which was $31,510 in 1988–89.[5] The cost of keeping an inmate at The Pas is $92.38 a day, or $33,700 per year. The cost at Egg Lake is $59.50 a day or $24,000 per year. Based on these figures, there is a difference in operating costs between the two institutions, based on 70 inmates, of about $680,000 per year. For 1988–89, $86.33 per day is the average inmate cost for provincial correctional institutions in Manitoba.[6] These figures do not include capital costs, which would be higher for higher security jails. It is clear that facilities like Egg Lake not only are more humane, but they are less costly to construct and administer. Of course, these arguments say nothing about the savings, both human and financial, to society if fewer persons are incarcerated and if programming assists in reducing recidivism. These effects would benefit potential victims, families of offenders, offenders themselves and taxpayers.

WE RECOMMEND THAT:

- Headingley Correctional Institution and Stony Mountain Institution be the only secure facilities for male offenders in Manitoba.

- Brandon and The Pas Correctional institutions be converted into minimum security, open-door institutions similar to Dauphin.

Jail Location and Capacity
Provincial Facilities

Imprisonment is a profoundly isolating experience. During the course of our Inquiry, we discovered that Manitoba's jails operate in a fashion that accentuates that isolation. Of particular concern is the loss of contact with family and relatives that many Aboriginal prisoners experience.

There are many problems associated with the current practice of transporting Aboriginal persons from their own communities to and from correctional institutions and holding facilities. This practice is very expensive and it is unfair to those from rural and northern communities. They must endure greater separation from their families than other inmates, and experience unnecessary hardships because of the distance and the absence of resources to assist them.

At Stony Mountain inmates are limited in the number of phone calls they are permitted to make and all long-distance phone calls must be made on a collect basis. This further discriminates against inmates from remote communities and families with little income. One Aboriginal inmate told us of the difficulty his family members had in coming to visit him from northwest Ontario. Because they had not made advance arrangements, and came at other than the prescribed time, they were not allowed to visit. Another Aboriginal inmate said his sister travelled 240 kilometres to visit him and was turned away at the gate because she did not have proper identification.

We are concerned to find few correctional programs in Aboriginal communities, either in rural areas or in the North. The problem persists even when jails are located in the North. Ninety per cent of the inmates of The Pas jail, almost all of whom are Aboriginal, came from northeastern Manitoba (from Nelson House and east of there). The identical situation exists at the Egg Lake Camp, also located at the western edge of the province. Here, all the residents were Aboriginal, most from communities in northeastern Manitoba. It is, for example, some 630 kilometres by air from Shamattawa to The Pas—and there is no connecting road between Thompson and Shamattawa, let alone The Pas and Shamattawa.

The nearest detention centre for youth is in Winnipeg. This means that many of the inmates are far from their homes and their families. Both the cost of transportation and the distance make it impossible for family members to visit. In addition, the system incurs inordinate transportation costs. Our visits to these institutions confirmed our belief that inmates should be housed closer to their home communities.

At the same time as we advocate the establishment of low security facilities in remote communities, we believe that those facilities should not be used to increase the overall capacity of the corrections system. The capacity of existing correctional institutions and custody system can and should be reduced substantially. Inmates who are not dangerous to individuals or the community should be transferred out of secure institutions to low security and open custody facilities. The vacated cells should be knocked down and the space converted to provide more room for programs, such as employment training and counselling, for the few who do require secure incarceration. Expenditures for upgrading and maintaining jails should be redirected to the creation of lower security facilities. The complete phasing out of some existing jails may be possible.

We do not favour the construction of a new provincial jail in Thompson, for which some people are calling. We believe that many of the Aboriginal people currently in jail could be housed in facilities in their home communities. We believe the needs of Aboriginal offenders from northeast Manitoba can be addressed best by the establishment of community correctional facilities and regional work camps, similar to the one at Egg Lake. This is not to suggest that a holding facility is not required in Thompson, but it must not be a holding facility designed to serve Aboriginal communities throughout northern Manitoba.

- Open custody programs for Aboriginal adult and young offenders requiring counselling, behaviour improvement, job training and other forms of assistance be established in Aboriginal communities.

- Work camps, such as the one at Egg Lake, be established near Aboriginal communities for non-dangerous Aboriginal offenders who require incarceration.

- As Aboriginal community-based facilities are opened, an equal number of units of capacity in existing correctional institutions be closed down and the space converted to vocational or academic programming.

- Financial assistance be provided for families of Aboriginal inmates to enable them to communicate with and travel to visit relatives.

Remand Cells

One of the problems we observed in many northern and rural communities was the unnecessary and expensive transportation of prisoners when they are arrested or pending their release on bail. They are now transported to Thompson, Winnipeg or elsewhere because there is no possibility of an early bail hearing in the community or in the circuit court system as it presently operates. There is no one present to make the bail decision, no possibility of meeting with a person able to give legal advice, due to a lack of lawyers, a lack of paralegals and restrictions on the advice existing paralegals are able to give. Prisoners are removed from the community simply because no holding cells exist, because there are no persons able to supervise RCMP holding cells (and provide meals, etc. for the accused), or because the cells are inappropriate.

In many communities, short-term holding facilities do exist in RCMP office trailers. We recommend elsewhere that there be better policing services, preferably provided by a regional force for Aboriginal communities, better court and legal services, with capacity to hold bail hearings in the communities within 24 hours of arrest, and local detention facilities. These recommendations, once implemented, will reduce the need to remove offenders from the communities while awaiting bail hearings. In those communities that do not have short-term remand cells, such cells must be installed.

Problems with the use of holding facilities are compounded by the current practice of transporting offenders to another location and then releasing them on bail without providing return transportation. This is unfair to the accused person. Persons who face such circumstances have no means of support in the community, no way home, and are often unaware and uninformed of the fact that the Department of Justice will provide financial assistance for their return home in such circumstances. This appears to be a policy which exists more on paper than in practice. It was not until close to the end of our hearings that we learned that such a policy existed.

WE RECOMMEND THAT:

- ■ Secure short-term holding facilities be established in Aboriginal communities.

- ■ Aboriginal accused be released on bail in their home communities whenever possible.

- ■ If Aboriginal accused are transported away from their home communities to be held in custody and are subsequently released on bail, the arresting authority be responsible to convey them back to their home communities.

We are satisfied that many services can be provided effectively in the accused's own community, and the development of such services will reduce reliance on the expensive and largely ineffective holding and bail programs now in common use. More expeditious trials will also reduce the numbers held on remand.

Responding to Aboriginal Needs

The personal needs of Aboriginal offenders—be it the need for spiritual fulfilment, for education and vocational training, or for counselling to help overcome personal problems—are not being met by the Manitoba correctional system. We base this very serious conclusion on the testimony of many inmates who appeared before the Commission, on our survey of the inmates and on the testimony of the people charged with administering our jails. The sheer weight of the numbers of Aboriginal inmates who reoffend underlines the fact that programming is not succeeding. We wish to stress that we believe this problem will not go away until Aboriginal people and Aboriginal organizations are directly involved in developing and providing spiritual, educational, vocational and counselling programs, within or outside correctional facilities.

Aboriginal Spirituality

It should be clear to even the most casual observer that in the case of Aboriginal inmates, spiritual needs must be met in a culturally appropriate manner. Yet, this is not being done. It is relatively easy to learn about Aboriginal worldviews, belief systems and spiritual practices. It is also relatively easy to discover who can provide spiritual leadership to Aboriginal people. If the jails cannot deliver these programs, then it is clear they have far to go in learning how to deliver other programs in culturally appropriate ways, which will require, among other things, learning subtle differences in manners of communication. Greater recognition of the importance of spiritual programming will be required on the part of correctional administrators if any progress is to be made.

According to a survey of 258 inmates (60 of whom were Aboriginal and 198 of whom were non-Aboriginal) conducted for our Inquiry, 81% of Aboriginal inmates reported they felt that Aboriginal spirituality was not respected in their institution. At present, Stony Mountain is the only institution which is served regularly by an Aboriginal elder. While Aboriginal spirituality is accorded greater status in federal institutions, unreasonable limitations are imposed even there, which arise primarily from ignorance of the importance of certain spiritual activities. One Aboriginal inmate at Stony Mountain, speaking in Ojibway, told us through our interpreter of the lack of cultural and religious activities available to Aboriginal inmates. While there are sweat lodges from time to time and a Sacred Circle every week, other important Aboriginal events, such as a shaking tent, ceremonies on the death of a relative, and religious feasts and fasts—which require a significant amount of ritual and must be held in spiritually significant locations—have not been accommodated. All these ceremonies are an important part of Aboriginal culture, and can contribute to the rectification of psychological and other problems that may be disturbing an inmate.

Headingley Correctional Institution has been inconsistent in meeting the spiritual needs of Aboriginal inmates. At the time of our visit to the institution, there was no Aboriginal elder regularly in attendance. We were told by Headingley superintendent Dennis Lemoine that elders do not work in his institution because they feel the environment is not conducive to cultural and spiritual practices and teachings. This is significant, since Headingley is the most highly populated provincial institution and has the second largest number of Aboriginal inmates in the province, exceeded only by Stony Mountain. That there is a strong desire for this sort of service is underscored by the fact that Headingley has a Native Brotherhood Organization which organizes sweat lodge ceremonies and other spiritual and cultural events. The president of that brotherhood told us that:

> To get myself ready for when I go back out into the free world, the elder could help me spiritually and mentally to be more strong on the outside. It would help me follow the right road in life.

Regrettably, Headingley is not alone in failing to meet the spiritual needs of its Aboriginal inmates. The Dauphin Correctional Institution has no Aboriginal programming whatsoever: no elder, no spiritual services, no culturally specific treatment program for drug or alcohol dependency, or counselling. The Egg Lake work camp also suffers from the same lack of programming that afflicts other correctional institutions.

The magnitude of this failure was reflected in our survey of inmates. According to it, 84% of Aboriginal inmates indicated that they would like to participate in a sweat lodge, while only 3% felt this sort of programming was regularly available; 61% wanted to participate in fasts, but only 1% felt they could on a regular basis. Similarly, only 1% of the Aboriginal inmates we surveyed felt they could participate in healing ceremonies or feasts—this despite the fact that over 70% of the respondents would have liked to participate in these ceremonies.

None of the provincial institutions we visited, whether for males, females or youth, paid appropriate attention to the importance of elders and Aboriginal spirituality. As a result, Aboriginal inmates suffer. The absence of elders stands in stark contrast to the availability of Christian chaplains. Chaplains, often from a variety of denominations, are present in every provincial institution. Simply making identical provisions for elders as is made for chaplains is, however, not enough. The forms of religious observance are different. Participating in natural, outdoor surroundings is integral to Aboriginal spirituality and correctional institutions must adapt to that; having Aboriginal staff who share the inmate's and elder's spirituality, be it Cree, Ojibway or other, to escort inmates to such observances is one solution. This, of course, will require more Aboriginal staff.

Our concern is not only that Aboriginal spirituality is not being encouraged. We believe these practices are being actively discouraged.

In particular, we believe elders and traditional persons should be afforded much greater respect. We were told that institutional practices, such as examining every article and package entering the institution and searching every individual, are objectionable to elders and traditional Aboriginal people. This practice is inconsistent with the treatment accorded Christian clergy and Christian religious articles. These can be brought into institutions uninspected if a priest or minister identifies them as religious articles. Sacramental wine, for example, is not tasted, and hosts are not opened and sent to a laboratory for examination. Yet, objects of equal importance to Aboriginal spirituality have not been shown the same respect. Aboriginal elders should be able to indicate the spiritual significance of special articles so that improper treatment of religious persons and articles is avoided. Traditional bundles, medicines and articles such as pipes should not be handled in the way currently called for by institutional policies. Correctional personnel who are unaware of the significance of these objects can easily offend elders and traditional persons, thereby discouraging them from returning.

We found some parts of the discipline at the Headingley Correctional Institution more restrictive than at Stony Mountain. One inmate wore a traditional headband when he appeared before us, although he knew this was contrary to institutional policy. In contrast, many headbands were seen at Stony Mountain. Personal jewellery is also prohibited at Headingley. This same inmate felt this to be an interference with cultural practices. He spoke of the need for religious programming and of the importance of having the assistance of an elder to discuss spiritual problems. Others spoke of the need for the help of an elder to enable them to accept their situation, and to deal with feelings of anger, hopelessness and frustration. No such services were being provided.

Correctional policy should include a clear and unambiguous principle that Aboriginal inmates, like other inmates, are entitled to the unhindered practise of their religions. Moreover, institutions should accept the responsibility for making the necessary spiritual services available. Aboriginal elders and Aboriginal traditional people should be allowed unhindered access to provincial institutions to provide spiritual services to Aboriginal inmates. Religious articles should be handled with respect.

The manner in which elders and other Aboriginal traditional healers are made known to, or are identified by, correctional authorities is an issue which has been raised on occasion. There appears to be some potential for problems in the fact that, in its policy governing the recognition of spiritual advisers and counsellors for inmates, the provincial corrections department specifically relies upon the qualifications for chaplains established by the Manitoba Interfaith Council, which represents faith groups in the province. The criteria require, "A candidate must be ordained, have pastoral experience, and receive institutional pastoral experience."[7]

Such a set of qualifications clearly was not written with the situation of Aboriginal elders in mind and, consequently, if applied rigorously, likely would prevent almost all traditional Aboriginal spiritual advisers from qualifying for consideration as "chaplains."

We do note that, recently, Headingley has had an Aboriginal elder service available for Aboriginal inmates, provided with the assistance of the Native Clan Organization. We are aware, as well, that the elder who participates with inmates in the institution on a regular basis is treated with respect by other chaplains, who invite him to attend the regular meetings of the chaplains whenever they are held. However, he is only one person from one particular tribe, and sometimes the assistance which he is called upon to provide requires knowledge specific to another tribe. The fact is, however, that without a process of "ordination," which is one of the premises of the qualifications established by the Manitoba Interfaith Council and which is a standard accepted by the Corrections Branch, Aboriginal elders cannot assert status as such without questions being raised. This can present problems since, as we mentioned earlier, Aboriginal elders are not necessarily healers, and vice versa. From time to time, therefore, other Aboriginal traditional people may be called upon to assist the "on-site" elder with a particular ceremony or to provide assistance with respect to an inmate of a different Aboriginal culture than that of the elder on staff.

Knowing whether a particular person who claims to be an elder or a traditional healer should be afforded credentials as such within an institution can be as problematic as knowing whether a particular person who claims to be a minister of a particular church or faith is so qualified. Correctional institutions do not, we are sure, accept every person who asserts that he or she is a minister of a church without some assurance that the denomination or church to which that person is affiliated has status as a religious organization, and that that person has status as a minister within it. In the same way, correctional institutions should develop a way of recognizing Aboriginal elders in cooperation with Aboriginal organizations.

We believe that, as with religious denominations, correctional officials should simply leave the designation or identification of Aboriginal elders, or traditional persons with authority to counsel or assist Aboriginal people in a traditional manner, to Aboriginal agencies who are more knowledgeable in this area.

For example, an Aboriginal organization recognized as having expertise in the area by Aboriginal people or organizations could be contracted to provide the service directly to provincial institutions. Alternatively, organizations such as the Assembly of Manitoba Chiefs could be asked to prepare a list of those persons whom they recognize as Aboriginal elders and forward that to correctional institutions. Indigenous women's groups also could be asked to identify Aboriginal women who could provide traditional healing to Aboriginal inmates at Portage. The same could be done for Manitoba's youth facilities: the Ma Mawi Chi Itata Centre has some involvement with Aboriginal youth and could be asked to help in this area. We do not believe that the problem should be a difficult one to resolve at all.

WE RECOMMEND THAT:

- Correctional institutions develop a policy whereby elders recognized by provincial Aboriginal organizations as capable of providing traditional assistance or spiritual advice and counselling to Aboriginal inmates in a culturally appropriate manner be granted status equivalent to chaplains under the Chaplaincy program of the Corrections Branch.

- The Correctional Services of Canada and the Corrections Branch of the Manitoba Department of Justice institute a policy on Aboriginal spirituality which:

  - Guarantees the right of Aboriginal people to spiritual services appropriate to their culture.

  - Recognizes appropriate Aboriginal organizations to provide Aboriginal spiritual services.

  - Provides training for correctional staff on Aboriginal spirituality, on the relative importance of such services to Aboriginal people, on the different practices and beliefs likely to be encountered, on how those practices and beliefs can and should be accommodated by correctional staff and on how to handle traditional items of spiritual significance to Aboriginal people.

  - Provides for the hiring of knowledgeable personnel within each institution who can advise corrections staff on how to deal with cultural issues arising within the institution's Aboriginal population.

  - Provides for the attendance of Aboriginal inmates at spiritual ceremonies outside jail.

Vocational and Counselling Programs

There are very few constructive programs for Aboriginal offenders offered in the correctional institutions we visited. Stony Mountain provides a range of educational, vocational and life skills programs, extending from literacy training to university courses, from building maintenance to life skills training, and many Aboriginal people enrol in these programs. During our hearings at Stony Mountain, however, Aboriginal inmates complained that the programs that do exist are not appropriate to their needs. Yet, if they do not participate in the programs that are offered, that fact appears on their record and harms their chances for parole.

Based on what we have observed and heard, it is apparent that Stony Mountain Institution is not an appropriate institution for most sentenced Aboriginal offenders. Most are not dangerous and should not be there. Few cultural programs are provided, and those that are provided suffer at the hands of institutional administrators primarily concerned about security issues—a factor which Warden Art Majkut (and others) indicated is not an issue for most Aboriginal inmates. Programs offered to inmates generally are not culturally appropriate or sensitive to Aboriginal inmates. The institution suffers, as well, from an under-representation of Aboriginal staff and from an over-emphasis on simply locking people up—a focus of little benefit to Aboriginal inmates who are not a danger to society and whose needs are more social than punitive. It is clear that federally sentenced Aboriginal inmates are in need of better alternatives than what Stony Mountain has to offer.

Rockwood generally offers the same type of Aboriginal programming as Stony Mountain. The difference is in the lack of emphasis on security. Inmates are permitted greater freedom than in Stony Mountain. Generally, inmates want to transfer from Stony Mountain and the administration uses the greater freedom at Rockwood as an inducement to encourage them to "work" toward being transferred there. Conversely, inmates who are uncooperative at Rockwood are threatened with being transferred (back) to Stony Mountain if their attitudes do not improve. There is a lower percentage of Aboriginal inmates in Rockwood than in Stony Mountain, confirming what the 1988 Task Force report said—that it is more difficult for Aboriginal people to be placed in lower security jails.

Aboriginal inmates at Stony Mountain said they had a hard time in the institution. They felt misunderstood and felt that the programs offered to them often had little or no relevance. Many Aboriginal inmates recognized that they had problems; however, requests for treatment or appropriate programs were ignored. One inmate said he asked when he would be ready for release and was told: "When you fit into our profile." It seemed to us that many Aboriginal inmates remained quiet and simply put in their time without any hope of benefits or early release.

If the programming at Stony Mountain is inadequate, it must be recognized that it is far superior to that offered in any provincial institution. The superintendent at Headingley Correctional Institution, Dennis Lemoine, told us that, "There has always been a fundamental problem with programming in a place like Headingley that was built in the 1930s first and foremost as a common jail." We were told that, partly due to the short sentences being served at Headingley, there are few educational or other programs aimed at improving the future opportunities of inmates. There is no trades training or job preparedness programming at Headingley, although inmates are allowed to attend training courses on temporary absences. At The Pas Correctional Institution, there is a part-time adult education instructor who visits the jail, and some inmates can take programs run by the Human Resources Centre and the Keewatin Community College. Other inmates work outside the institution, but, generally, we gained the impression that most of the inmates use their time very unproductively.

A representative of the Native Brotherhood Organization at Headingley Correctional Institution told us that Aboriginal inmates wanted to know why they "are always being dumped back into society."

I believe that we need the right equipment for inmates to use to rehabilitate themselves while being incarcerated. For one, a job training program here would help, woodwork shop, upholstery, sheet metal shop, as some of the inmates do not have the qualifications to do this type of work. But, some type of training program here would help a lot of the inmates in the long-run.

The programs that do exist are largely insensitive to Aboriginal culture and some border on being completely irrelevant to the needs or aspirations of Aboriginal people. An Aboriginal inmate at Headingley said the correspondence courses offered at that institution are "the least effective method of learning for any people."

The solution is that you teach people in small groups and you provide teachers. Not correspondence courses. Also, a great way for native people to learn is in a traditional way with sweats and pow-wows and to bring elders, wise, respected men and women who native people can listen to and learn from their experience.

Aboriginal inmates in all institutions are told to take programs in order to improve their chances of being granted parole. But these programs, which include Alcoholics Anonymous, anger management and counselling for sexual offenders, are designed by non-Aboriginal people. Often, they fail to consider the individuals' backgrounds, the reality of the situations to which they will be returning upon release or their aspirations. One Headingley inmate, for example, told us that he received no help in areas in which he had some qualifications but needed further training. Instead, he had spent 10 months simply pushing a broom.

Aboriginal inmates also require culturally appropriate assistance in readjusting to the community following a period of incarceration. We heard one story from a young man who entered school on his release from jail. Having no resources and no job, he wanted to improve his education so he could find employment. These opportunities had not been provided in jail.

There are other problems. A survey conducted by our Commission revealed that as many as 62% of Aboriginal inmates speak an Aboriginal language at home. There are, however, very few staff in the correctional institutions who speak an Aboriginal language and no programs are offered in an Aboriginal language. As a result, communication problems abound. Aboriginal inmates often do not understand institutional policies and programs. Many cannot read English and experience difficulty expressing themselves in a "foreign language."

We asked Aboriginal inmates what programs they would like to have offered. Most, 43%, wanted educational or vocational training. The next most-desired programming dealt with native culture and spirituality, which was requested by 29% of Aboriginal inmates. The next most-desired program was life skills training, identified by 14% of the inmates. Other programs suggested by inmates included those dealing with alcohol and drug dependency, stress management, crafts, parenting, marital counselling and native languages. Some specifically said they would like to see the Alcoholics Anonymous program delivered in a manner that was culturally appropriate to Aboriginal people.

By far the most common theme of the responses to our survey was that preparation for release is required and is not being offered. Clearly, inmates want to use programs, want to learn how to find employment and stay out of jail, want to learn how to deal with alcohol dependency, and want the programs to be relevant to them and to the conditions they will be encountering on release.

Whether it is vocational or religious programming in the institution, release planning or readjustment in the community, it is clear that Aboriginal inmates will be able to use existing or new programs effectively only if the programs are developed and directed by people from their own culture.

The programs will be particularly effective if the facilities and programs are offered close to the offender's community. If an inmate is serving a short sentence in a provincial jail, it is not possible for the inmate to enrol in a program that would terminate before the sentence is completed, or that would not require the inmate to return to the facility to complete. On the other hand, if programs were offered in open custody facilities in the home community, offenders sentenced to short terms could begin programs and complete them after their sentences were fully served.

WE RECOMMEND THAT:

■ Culturally appropriate education, trades training and counselling programs, particularly those having to do with the treatment of alcohol abuse, family violence, anger management and culturally appropriate ways for inmates to cope with their problems, be provided in every Manitoba correctional institution.

Separation of Pre-Trial and Sentenced Persons

Headingley Correctional Institution houses both sentenced offenders and those on remand who have been denied bail. Thirty per cent of the inmates of The Pas Correctional Institution were on remand at the time of our visit. Overcrowding at these and other facilities often prevents convicted offenders with outstanding charges from being transferred from the Provincial Remand Centre in a timely manner. Stays of a year or longer are not unheard of in that institution. We believe that sentenced inmates and those on remand are quite distinct in terms of their rights and their program needs, as well as in terms of security considerations. The presence of remanded inmates, we believe, interferes with the programs for sentenced inmates, while allowing people who have not been convicted of a crime to come under the influence of those who have been convicted of serious offences.

WE RECOMMEND THAT:

- Adults on remand be kept in physically separate institutions from those who have been convicted.

It is particularly disturbing to discover that this problem exists at the Manitoba Youth Centre, as well. While the justice system generally seems unconcerned about the separation of remanded and sentenced inmates, it goes to considerable expense to separate youths from adults. Instead of constructing appropriate youth facilities, the system engages in an extremely expensive and disruptive routine of transporting youth from all over the province back and forth to Winnipeg. Not only does the Youth Centre house those who have been sentenced to secure and open custody, but it also houses those on remand who are awaiting a court appearance somewhere in the province. While it is clear that a great deal of effort goes into the operation of the centre, we consider it totally inappropriate for this facility to try to meet this broad range of requirements. We believe that the MYC is unable to sufficiently separate convicted youth offenders and young people on remand, and we do not believe it should be used as an open custody facility. This one facility cannot properly serve the differing needs of these three categories of youth.

WE RECOMMEND THAT:

- The Manitoba Youth Centre and the Agassiz Youth Centre no longer be used as open custody facilities or as remand facilities, except for those youth who present a danger to themselves or others.
- Only home-type facilities or camps be used for open custody sentences.
- In the city of Winnipeg, the Corrections Branch seek out and develop alternatives to the use of the Manitoba Youth Centre as a remand facility. This should include the greater use of non-institutional settings such as group and foster homes.

We wish to emphasize that the long-term solution to this problem lies not with the construction of more remand centres, but in a reduction of the use of pre-trial custody, particularly for Aboriginal youths. Short-term custody provided at the community level, as well as pre-trial supervision in the community, will be more effective and less costly than traditional detention.

Staffing Issues and Discipline Procedures

We believe that most correctional officers are ill-equipped to deal with Aboriginal inmates. Dealing with inmates in a purely custodial fashion is the predominant, if not the only, method of dealing with inmates that occurs in Manitoba jails. Considering all the costs of custodial staffing, this is a considerable waste of human and financial resources. Furthermore, we found the custodial treatment to have significant problems.

Guard Behaviour, Affirmative Action and Cross-Cultural Training

Our survey of inmates revealed the extent to which Aboriginal inmates feel unfairly treated by the system and by some of the staff. Our survey indicated that 61% of Aboriginal inmates and 49% of non-Aboriginal inmates in provincial institutions believed that corrections staff treat Aboriginal inmates unfairly, and 70% of the Aboriginal inmates and 58% of the non-Aboriginal inmates in federal institutions whom we surveyed said they thought Aboriginal inmates were treated unfairly. The examples of unfair treatment include preferential treatment to non-Aboriginal inmates for phone calls and temporary absences, more accusations by guards about Aboriginal misconduct, greater tolerance of non-Aboriginal misbehaviour, more intimidation and assaults on Aboriginal inmates by the staff, non-Aboriginal inmates getting better jobs in the jails, and, at Headingley, non-Aboriginal inmates being kept in the lower security annexes while Aboriginal inmates are held primarily in the higher security main population. For some of the inmates who responded, there was no difference in treatment because, in their view, the guards treated everyone badly.

The interviewers who conducted our surveys found the same things as the Task Force on Aboriginal Peoples in Federal Corrections: Aboriginal inmates are held in higher security areas where there are fewer programs and privileges. They are not able to participate in some institutional programs and they have to serve a longer portion of their sentence before being released.

There is little cross-cultural training available for correctional staff. The superintendent of Headingley Correctional Institution explained that it was costly to send existing staff to training seminars, and, as a result, his institution focussed its efforts on providing cultural training for new recruits. This is another way of saying the jail cannot afford to be culturally sensitive. Society cannot afford jails that are *not* culturally sensitive.

Superintendent Dennis Lemoine described the cross-cultural training as "probably insufficient. Many of our staff who have been in the service here may have not gone back for retraining and in years previous there was virtually no native culture orientation." Aboriginal inmates cited numerous examples of correctional staff making racist comments and insulting people of Aboriginal background.

Aboriginal staff in our prison system are conspicuous by their absence. Only three of the 35 employees at the Rockwood Institution are Aboriginal, while at Egg Lake, where all the inmates are Aboriginal, there are no Aboriginal staff.

WE RECOMMEND THAT:

- The number of Aboriginal people employed in correctional facilities and correctional programs be at least proportionate to the population of Aboriginal people in the province of Manitoba.

- At least one-half of the Aboriginal staff of each institution be able to speak an Aboriginal language.

- Cross-cultural training programs and ongoing refresher courses be mandatory for all corrections staff.

Complaints and Disciplinary Matters

The truism that justice must not only be done, but must be seen to be done, is particularly applicable in prisons. Prisoners are not likely to emerge from prisons with an enhanced respect for society's laws and rules if, during their time in jail, they have been subjected to arbitrary rules and procedures, and have had no meaningful way to appeal their treatment, but in institution after institution, we found this to be the case.

The disciplinary hearing procedure at the Headingley Correctional Institution is largely a facade. The rules are often ignored and, when they are used, they are interpreted narrowly and against the interests of the inmate. In particular, they further dehumanize the inmate and make him feel like a pawn of the system, without any rights and without any respect.

In addressing the complaints that various inmates had about the Inmate Disciplinary Board at Headingley, Superintendent Lemoine said:

> Again, we are not bound by the system, we are not a judicial body, we are an administrative board. We try to follow the fundamental principles of justice but we are not bound by its technicalities or its complexities. We have an established policy and we also have consulted with our legal department and the Public Interest Branch of the Legal Aid Department to help us develop the policy.

> I believe that in the main it works reasonably well. Certainly there are inconsistencies and problems for some of the people who appear before the Board. I make no apologies for that.

According to the rules for disciplinary board hearings, the inmate is entitled to written notice of the hearing date and specific charges. We were told by the superintendent that the charge is read to the inmate only at the hearing. The rule, in other words, is not followed.

Another rule states the inmate is entitled to assistance from another person of the inmate's choice. We were told few have help. The superintendent told us inmates could not choose to get assistance from a lawyer, only from another inmate. And that inmate may not be allowed to attend the actual hearing. Another rule states the inmate has the opportunity to question and to call the complaining officer. In practice, the inmate is not permitted to question the complaining officer. When we asked Superintendent Lemoine if the effect of this system was to place the onus on the inmate to prove that he is innocent, he said, "It would appear that way."

Hearings are conducted by a senior staff member of the institution. This, we believe, creates a conflict of interest situation, both apparent and real. These disciplinary "trials," for that is what they are supposed to be, breach the rules of natural justice.

We note with interest the recent decision of Associate Chief Justice Oliphant of the Manitoba Court of Queen's Bench, in the case of an inmate who appealed the decision of a disciplinary hearing at the Brandon Correctional Institution. The inmate alleged that his rights under the *Charter of Rights and Freedoms* had not been respected. In quashing the disciplinary board's ruling, Associate Chief Justice Oliphant agreed with the plaintiff that basic rights to retain counsel and to cross-examine witnesses had been denied. He said, in part, that "From an administrative law point of view, inmates of correctional institutions are no less deserving of the right to procedural fairness than are other persons."[8]

The fact that the rules governing discipline hearings can be disregarded openly and routinely raises another problem. In both federal and provincial penal systems in Manitoba, there exists no satisfactory, culturally appropriate process for Aboriginal inmates to challenge or appeal their treatment. According to our survey of inmates, 64% of Aboriginal inmates had not made any complaints during their time in prison, compared with 40% of non-Aboriginal inmates. Thirty per cent of Aboriginal inmates felt there was no one they could go to with complaints about the way they were treated, and this figure rises to 41% when one looks only at provincial Aboriginal inmates. Sixty-nine per cent of those who did make their complaints known reported that their concerns were ignored.

Inmates at Stony Mountain and Rockwood can take their concerns to the Correctional Investigator. However, as the 1988–89 *Annual Report of the Correctional Investigator* notes:

> This office has long had concerns with the operation of the Correctional Service of Canada's internal grievance process specifically related to the thoroughness, objectivity and timeliness of the investigations and responses which in turn significantly influence the offender's perception of and willingness to use the process.[9]

Inmates of provincial institutions with complaints about either their individual or collective experiences are directed to the provincial Ombudsman. The backlog of cases at the Ombudsman office virtually guarantees that a provincial inmate will have been released from custody before his or her complaint is addressed. While the Ombudsman has carried out a number of important investigations of correctional facilities in Manitoba—including a sweeping indictment of the Agassiz Youth Centre—the fact that these institutions continue to exist largely unchanged underscores the fact that the Ombudsman office has limited effectiveness.

WE RECOMMEND THAT:

- ■ Rules for disciplinary hearings in correctional institutions be clarified and enforced to permit an inmate to have a friend or lawyer present to assist at the hearings and to guarantee the opportunity to make full answer and defence to a charge.

- ■ Disciplinary hearings in correctional institutions provide for fair adjudication by having an independent third party preside over the hearing and ensure the rules of natural justice are followed.

- ■ An independent tribunal be established to adjudicate inmate complaints about the treatment they receive within the correctional system; and that the tribunal have appropriate resources and authority to investigate complaints, mandate change and enforce compliance with its orders.

Work Programs

Jails in this province provide few vocational training programs, and none that is culturally appropriate for Aboriginal people, but a number of institutions allow inmates to work in the institution and in the general community. At the Brandon Correctional Institution, there are programs that permit inmates to work in parks and elsewhere. At the time of our hearing at the Dauphin Correctional Institution, six inmates were going out to work each day on temporary absences. They worked for minimum wage or more. When they have worked for 80 hours, they are required to start paying the institution for room and board at the rate of $8.70 per day. Some inmates at The Pas also work outside the institution. At the Egg Lake Rehabilitation Camp, inmates go out every day to work along the highways, to improve public campsites and, occasionally, to fight forest fires. At Milner Ridge, there are work details and some inmates attend trades training in Winnipeg. They receive credits for their work that are recognized by a community college.

There is much that is commendable in programs which develop a relationship between jails and communities, and helps prepare inmates for normal work experiences. But we are concerned about the fact that these programs often operate without any guidelines—and often become the institution's only focus—to the detriment of training, counselling and rehabilitation programs.

The debate about inmates working outside correctional institutions has gone on for many years. Inmates want to work to earn an income, to gain skills and to make connections that might lead to permanent employment after their release. When inmates earn money in this way, we believe they should be entitled to keep some of it, while they also should be required to pay some amount towards the public cost of housing them. Those who do not want to work outside the institution should have the option of working in and around the institution, thereby helping to defray institutional costs, or of participating in counselling or training programs that benefit themselves and society.

Work programs do have the potential to create some problems. Inmates presumably are incarcerated so that they can be rehabilitated and the public has a vested interest in ensuring this occurs. Inmates may serve as an all too convenient and ready source of labour to help institutional administrators defray the costs of running their institutions or to help local communities defray the cost of public works. A work program may or may not be consistent with the goal of rehabilitation for every inmate. Therefore, it is important that these types of programs take these considerations into account.

WE RECOMMEND THAT:

- Correctional officials develop work programs both inside and outside institutions which allow inmates to engage in meaningful activities and earn income.
- Corrections Branch develop written guidelines on the appropriate use of inmate work details.

Conclusion

As we have discussed elsewhere in this report, there is a need to institute fundamental reforms in order to overcome the deficiencies of the current approach to providing justice services to Aboriginal people. In particular, specific justice programs must be developed and administered by Aboriginal people.

It is recognized that the types of changes we are recommending will take time to implement. However, current policies and practices cannot be allowed to continue.

We have seen that far too much emphasis is placed on security, even though security is not an issue for 80% or more of the Aboriginal offenders who are incarcerated. Many opportunities exist to provide meaningful cultural, educational and training programs. These programs should become the focus of our institutions, not bars, headcounts and constant surveillance.

In cases where incarceration in secure jails is warranted, every effort should be made to ensure that the experience is socially productive and that the Aboriginal offender returns to society better equipped to take up a meaningful role in the community. We would like to see greater emphasis placed on culturally appropriate counselling to meet individual needs, on substance abuse programs, on anger management and abuse counselling, and on specific skills training related to employment.

During our visit to tribal courts in the United States, we saw that it is not always necessary to have long periods of incarceration to maintain peace and stability in Aboriginal communities.

We believe the changes we have recommended, if implemented, would substantially improve the effectiveness of the provincial corrections system for both Aboriginal and non-Aboriginal offenders. We also believe them to be cost-effective and, in some instances, cost-saving measures. Despite this, the compelling arguments for creating a new correctional system are not economical, but ethical and pragmatic.

Chapter 12

Parole

Introduction

Canada's parole system is based on the premise that most offenders should be returned to the community under a "conditional" release, prior to the end of their sentence. The intent is to support their reintegration into society on a gradual basis, with support from parole staff and from volunteers. We agree with this approach and believe that offenders do stand a better chance of being effectively reintegrated into the community if they are assisted following their release. However, of all the opportunities for discretionary decision making in the justice system, few are as controversial as the decision to grant or deny parole. The parole system has suffered from an inability to develop fair and effective release criteria, and to apply these criteria in a consistent fashion.

While the premise on which the parole system is based may well be sound, many of its policies and procedures do not serve Aboriginal people well. In 1988 the Task Force on Aboriginal Peoples in Federal Corrections, established by the Solicitor General of Canada, summed up the problem:

> We do know that fewer Aboriginal offenders are granted full parole by the National Parole Board; when granted some form of release, it is later in their sentence; and they are more likely to have their parole revoked.[1]

The failure of the parole system to serve Aboriginal persons adequately was confirmed in presentations made to our Inquiry. The Prairie regional manager of conditional release programs for the parole board told us that the approval rate for Aboriginal inmates applying for full parole was 15% to 18% lower than for non-Aboriginal inmates. We were also informed that 26.8% of Aboriginal inmates, as compared to 10.8% of non-Aboriginal inmates, have their conditional releases revoked. With respect to those released on mandatory supervision, the paroles of 22.1% of Aboriginal inmates and 11% of non-Aboriginal inmates were revoked. Forty-four per cent of Aboriginal inmates on full parole had their paroles revoked. The corresponding figure for non-Aboriginal inmates was 24.8%. In order to examine why these significant differences exist between Aboriginal and non-Aboriginal persons, we must first review the evolution and current state of Canada's parole system.

The Evolution of Canada's Parole System

A number of reports cite the complex and often contradictory objectives which have developed over the last 120 years within Canada's correctional system and, in particular, in the parole system.[2]

Under the *Penitentiary Act* of 1868, inmates were allowed up to five days per month of sentence "remission" (sentence reduction) for good behaviour. The only other way in which early release might occur was through the rarely used Royal Prerogative of Mercy, which could be exercised by the Governor General. With minor changes to the rate at which remission was earned, this practice remained in force until the introduction of mandatory supervision in 1970. Inmates who earned time off their sentence were released unconditionally without supervision when their accumulated earned remission equalled the balance of their remaining sentence.

The evolution towards our current parole system began in 1899, with the introduction of conditional release, or parole, through passage of the *Ticket of Leave Act*. At first, decisions to grant parole under this Act were made by the Minister of Justice, but by 1913 a "Remission Service" was developing in the Department of Justice. Initially, this service was administered by the RCMP and the Salvation Army. The Archambault Report of 1936 was harshly critical of the Remission Service, and recommended that parole officers be appointed to make the system more impartial and that efforts be more focussed towards rehabilitation.[3] This recommendation to appoint parole officers was not to be implemented for almost 30 years.

In the post-war period, a number of community-based agencies such as the John Howard and Elizabeth Fry societies began to assist traditional agencies such as the Salvation Army in the reintegration of offenders. The 1956 Fauteux Report led to the replacement of the *Ticket of Leave Act* with the *Parole Act* in 1958, bringing into existence the National Parole Board (NPB). This resulted in there being provisions in the *Parole Act* and the *Penitentiaries Act* which allowed inmates to be released prior to the end of their sentence. The two sets of provisions operated independently; release on parole did not affect previously earned remission entitlement. In 1961, also as a result of the Fauteux Report, the remission provisions of the *Penitentiary Act* were divided into two categories. The new provisions required that upon imprisonment, one-quarter of the sentence was to be credited to remission, but this could be lost for poor behaviour while in jail. A further amount of three days per month for good behaviour could be "earned" while in prison. Once earned, this time could not be revoked. Whether or not the prisoner applied for parole, he or she was released when accumulated remission was equal to the balance of the remaining sentence. There was no community supervision imposed on such releases.[4]

As the various supervised conditional release programs developed, they came into conflict with the concept of remission, where no supervision was provided after release into the community. Inmates who were well behaved, but considered poor parole risks, were being released without condition, while less well-behaved inmates who were good risks received supervision, serving their remaining sentences in the community. This set the stage for the introduction of what is now called mandatory supervision.

Beginning in 1964, the National Parole Board began to offer an incentive to prisoners who were approaching release under earned remission. The board offered to advance the date of release by one month for every year served, on condition that the inmate remain under supervision in the community for the balance of his or her sentence. By accepting this inducement, however, inmates lost their right to statutory remission.

The 1969 Ouimet Report noted that only 60% of prisoners were accepting this inducement and applying for parole, because they preferred to await their earned remission date, thereby eliminating the requirement for supervision.[5] Clearly, the incentive of earlier release, which meant giving up the right to earned remission, was not working.

The changes to the *Parole Act* in 1970 formalized the practice of mandatory supervision, even for those who had earned remission under the *Penitentiary Act.* All inmates now were to be released after two-thirds of their sentence had been served. However, they could be returned to prison immediately for any violation of parole conditions. All releases became conditional; those inmates with good behaviour no longer earned "time off" their sentence, but only the right to serve their remission time in the community. If they broke any condition of parole, no matter how minor, they stood to lose *all* their earned remission time.

With the passage of Bills C-67 and C-68 into law in 1986, further strictures were placed on the concept of remission. Under these revisions to the *Parole Act,* where the board feels that the release might result in serious harm to any person, the NPB can refuse a prisoner early release based upon either statutory remission or earned remission. For affected inmates, the correctional system has reverted to the practices in place in the mid-19th century. Once again, some prisoners are serving their full sentence in prison and are then being released without any access to social reintegration processes or programs, support or supervision. D.B. MacLean and R.S. Ratner state that:

> The logic of conditional release has come full circle, the outcome of which has been a more punitive and repressive carceral system, with prisoners being detained longer, and with good conduct remission essentially being negated.[6]

The incentive to earn remission has been diminished substantially by the ease with which mandatory parole can be revoked. The earning of remission is no longer time off a sentence, but only the permission to spend that time in the community, under supervision. In the case of offenders who are deemed violent or dangerous, there is no "earned remission," no matter what their behaviour has been while in prison. This is the overall context within which the parole system now deals with all offenders.

We believe that the issues raised by the confusion inherent in the current program, between earned remission and conditional release, must be addressed and resolved for the longer term, effective operation of the NPB. We also believe that Bills C-67 and C-68 make the system more punitive and repressive, and, therefore, less fair and effective. Our greatest concern is that Aboriginal people, because of their socio-economic status, are not treated in the same way as non-Aboriginal people.

WE RECOMMEND THAT:

- The National Parole Board accept as a governing principle that all inmates should be entitled to be released after having completed the same proportion of their sentence, except for those who are considered violent or dangerous.

- Any offence now giving rise to loss of earned remission be dealt with by loss of privileges or other penalty while in the institution.

An Overview of the Existing Parole Program

Canada's present parole system is administered by the National Parole Board, a federal government agency, and by provincial parole boards, where they exist. The national *Parole Act* has jurisdiction over any federal offence for which sentencing takes place. Although provincial boards have been established in British Columbia, Ontario and Quebec, there has never been a provincial parole board in Manitoba.

Parole is supervised by parole officers employed by the federal Correctional Services of Canada. There are 27 parole officers working in the province, located in Winnipeg, Thompson and Brandon. Two of the 27 are Aboriginal. Some parole supervision is contracted to outside organizations such as Native Clan and the Salvation Army. Service is also provided by volunteer parole officers in some northern communities.

The current objectives of conditional release orders are to assist offenders in fitting back into society and to protect society from the possibility of an offender getting into further trouble with the law. The board's mission statement indicates that:

> The National Parole Board, as part of the Criminal Justice System, makes independent, quality conditional release decisions and clemency recommendations. The Board, by facilitating the timely re-integration of offenders as law-abiding citizens, contributes to the protection of society.[7]

The board has 34 full-time members who may be appointed for up to 10 years. In addition, any number of temporary members may be appointed. These temporary members are appointed for one-year terms and sit at the direction of the board. According to the Act, those named are to be

> ... representatives of the police forces in any region of Canada, of the provincial government thereof, and of the municipal or other local authorities therein, or members of local professional, trade or community associations.[8]

The major responsibility of the board is to assess offenders' readiness for conditional release and to make release decisions. Section 16 of the Act allows the board to grant parole, subject to any terms or conditions it considers desirable. The board, however, is required by the Act (s. 16(1)) to be mindful of a number of release criteria. These may be summarized as follows:

- The inmate has derived the maximum benefit from imprisonment.
- The reform and rehabilitation of the inmate will be aided by the granting of parole.
- The release of the inmate on parole would not constitute an undue risk to society.

We agree with all these objectives. The problem, as will be seen, is in their application to Aboriginal inmates.

Types of Conditional Release

According to documentation issued by the National Parole Board, there are four types of conditional release: temporary absence, day parole, full parole and mandatory supervision.[9]

Temporary Absence

This type of absence may be escorted or unescorted. Temporary releases are granted for medical or humanitarian reasons, or to provide inmates with an opportunity to attend appropriate programs in the community. Unescorted temporary absences from federal maximum and medium security institutions are limited to 48 hours per month. The corresponding limit for minimum security institutions is 72 hours per month. Wardens have the right to grant temporary absences to inmates serving less than five years, while the board deals with those serving longer sentences. Provincial institutions have their own temporary absence policies and programs.

Day Parole

Day parole provides selected offenders with an opportunity to participate in approved community-based activities. It may be granted to complete education or training, to take part in community service projects or seasonal work such as forestry or harvesting, or to maintain or strengthen family ties. Day parole may be granted for a maximum of 12 months, but the usual term is four to six months. Offenders usually must return to the institution every night. Day parole decisions are made by the board.

Full Parole

Offenders may be eligible for full parole after serving as little as the first third of their sentence. Offenders sentenced to lengthy periods of incarceration, subject to certain exceptions, may be eligible for parole after serving seven years. If granted full parole, offenders will serve the balance of their sentence under supervision in the community. It is worth noting that persons serving lifetime sentences, if paroled, remain on parole for the remainder of their lives.

Mandatory Supervision

Time off for good behaviour, or earned remission, is credited to the offender when the offender is sentenced at the rate of one day of remission for every two days served. Remission time may be lost for unacceptable behaviour while in prison. The effect of this remission permits offenders to serve as much as the last third of their sentence under supervision in the community. Offenders are entitled to be released on mandatory supervision without going through the normal parole process. That is, they must be released when their earned remission time is equal to the balance of their outstanding sentence, unless they are deemed to be violent offenders under the provisions of the *Parole Act* which were passed in 1986.

The parole board is responsible for making conditional release decisions for over 12,900 federal inmates, as well as for provincial inmates in provinces like Manitoba, where there is no provincial parole board. Statistics supplied by the Prairie Regional Office of the Correctional Service indicate that at the end of March 1991, there were some 1,692 offenders participating in conditional release programs in the three prairie provinces. This number includes 535 on mandatory supervision, 303 on day parole and 692 on full parole. Temporary absences, while technically a form of conditional release, are not counted in this total, because most are under the discretionary control of penitentiary wardens. In addition, there are about 235 inmates from provincial institutions on full parole, and 27 inmates on day parole.

The prison term is deemed to continue while the offender is participating in any conditional release program in the community. Parole and temporary absences may be revoked at any time for the breach of a condition, to prevent the breach of a condition or to protect society. If parole is revoked, all earned remission time is lost and then is recalculated from the date of re-entering prison.

A study by the Canadian Centre for Justice Statistics indicates that the rate of utilization of these various conditional release programs in the Prairie region has been fairly stable, although early release appears to be in decline, over the past five years. During 1988–89 only 19% of the releases of federal inmates were on full parole (after completing one-third of their sentence), while 36% of provincial offender releases were on full parole. Compared to the figures for 1983–84, this represented a 5% decrease for federal inmates and an 8% decrease for provincial inmates.[10] This is a troubling trend, especially since the data suggest that in both cases, sentence expiry and mandatory parole have increased as a proportion of all parole.

The Decision to Grant Parole

Once a sentence has been imposed by the courts and the time for appeal has expired, the inmate's future is in the hands of the correctional authorities and the parole board. The parole board relies extensively on written documentation in making release decisions. Reports on the home and community environment are prepared. Reports also assess the conduct and training of the inmate while in the institution. Furthermore, consideration is given to the kind of accommodation, employment and treatment that will be available to the inmate upon release.

In the case of inmates of federal institutions, the parole board holds a hearing to assess the readiness of each inmate for parole after one-sixth of his or her sentence has been served, or, in the case of sentences of less than three years, after one year. Day parole or temporary absences may begin to be used after this time. Each case is again reviewed after one-third of a sentence has been served. Inmates do not have to apply to be heard, but may waive the hearing in writing if they choose to do so. Inmates serving longer sentences, who have been refused parole, may apply again for a hearing after six months. If they do not apply, the board must review their case within two years.

Inmates of provincial institutions must apply for parole and are eligible for consideration after one-sixth of their sentence has been served. However, there are no mandatory parole hearings at any stage for provincial inmates, as there are for federal inmates.

In preparation for a review, a case management team and the inmate meet to develop a release plan. When conditional release is approved, the inmate must sign a document that sets out the conditions of release, including supervision. Apart from extraordinary circumstances, virtually every inmate can expect to be released before completing the sentence imposed by the court.

The Parole System and Aboriginal Parole

Proportionately fewer Aboriginal people than non-Aboriginal are granted parole, and fewer successfully complete their parole without return to prison. Lisa Hobbs Birnie, a journalist and former member of the parole board, provides a number of important insights on these issues in her book *A Rock and a Hard Place*:

> When I found myself sitting opposite Samuel Grey Hawk, or Amos Morning Cloud, or Joseph Brave Bear, or when I caught the shy, uncertain eyes of a Cree-speaking teenager from the far North attempting to follow, through an interpreter, our ritualistic procedures and answer our thoroughly middle-class questions, I felt a little like a fraud. It seemed incalculably unfair that these men had the misfortune to have to depend on the decisions of people who might as well have come from another planet, as far as similarities in culture and lifestyle were concerned.[11]

> Sometimes the inmate was ready to go out, and if he was from a city, we would release him. Another inmate, just as ready, would be denied release

simply because he was from a community in the far North with no supports available to him—not only no work, but also no self-help group of former alcoholics, no local hospital with a mental health program, no drug counsellors, no sex-offender programs.[12]

Perhaps there only seemed to be no supports in northern native communities because the Parole Board and the Parole Service lacked sufficient knowledge of what was informally available in terms of community mechanisms for controlling, healing, or reconciling.[13]

I came to realize that the languages, the geography, and the culture of the North are so different from those of the South, that the solutions for the release of native offenders from the North lay in the North, under some form of `native justice' ... the creation of a separate native parole board seems essential if the current inequities are to be eliminated.[14]

We were told by Dorothy Betz, a former Aboriginal member of the National Parole Board, that many Aboriginal people do not apply for parole because parole and classification officers told them that it was unlikely to be granted. This was confirmed by inmates and former inmates who made presentations to us. This means that a disproportionate number of Aboriginal offenders are never properly considered for parole. We believe a number of factors help to explain why many Aboriginal inmates do not apply for parole, or agree in writing to waive their hearing:

- Many do not understand the prison and parole system.

- There are few Aboriginal people in the prison system to offer information and advice to those who might wish to apply for parole.

- They feel alienated by the way they are treated in the institution and have given up all hope of having any control over their own lives.

- They hear of Aboriginal people being returned to jail when their conduct out of jail has been found unsatisfactory by the parole officer or the police.

- They unnecessary or unrealistic parole conditions being imposed.

- Some are improperly encouraged to waive their right to apply for parole.

- Some may feel that they are not prepared for life in the community.

As an Aboriginal justice system develops, we believe that an Aboriginal parole board should take over a large part of the role now played by the National Parole Board. This new board would deal with parole applications from inmates sentenced to prison by Aboriginal courts. However, even when an Aboriginal parole board is fully functioning, the existing parole system still will have substantial control over the release from prison of Aboriginal people. In large measure, we believe that in order to resolve the critical problems which plague the present system, the membership, staffing and procedures of the National Parole Board must be amended.

WE RECOMMEND THAT:

- An Aboriginal Parole Board be established to deal with inmates incarcerated by Aboriginal courts.

- Every Aboriginal inmate be provided with a culturally appropriate information session upon admission to a correctional institution. Such a session should explain the parole eligibility rules. Further sessions should be given when the inmate becomes eligible to apply for parole.

- Parole be considered automatically and no inmate be allowed to waive his or her right to apply for parole.

The Composition of the Parole Board

At the time of our investigation, there were eight permanent board members and 18 temporary board members in the prairie region. Section 8 of the *Parole Act* provides for regional panels to be appointed by the Solicitor General on the recommendation of the chairperson of the board. When two or more members of the board are constituted in this way, they have all the powers of the full board to conduct application hearings and to deal with parole revocations. There are presently three permanent and five temporary members of the board from Manitoba. One permanent and one temporary member are Aboriginal. There are also two members from Manitoba who sit on all panels hearing applications from inmates serving life sentences, or inmates who are being held under the preventive detention provisions of the Act.

The parole board member profile, which outlines the desired qualifications of parole board members, provides an example of how systemic discrimination works against the involvement of Aboriginal people. While representation on the board of "bilingual," "female" and "minority" (specifically Aboriginal) people is encouraged, some of the conditions for membership on the board make it more difficult to attain adequate Aboriginal representation. For example, the educational requirements referred to in the profile are:

> High school graduation at a minimum. At least 50% of members should have graduate or post-graduate degrees in law, social sciences or psychiatry.[15]

These qualifications ensure that the parole board is unrepresentative of the community it serves, and that members of the dominant society will be asked to make critical judgments concerning groups with which they have little experience. Another of the "personal qualifications" referred to in the profile is "full security clearance." If that means that a member must never have been in trouble with the law, important experience and assistance may be excluded.

There is an obvious absence of Aboriginal people at every step of the parole process. The increased involvement of Aboriginal people needs to start in the institution where classification officers and other staff are involved in assessing inmates' suitability for parole. If classification officers who deal with Aboriginal inmates were Aboriginal, they would be better able to assess what the Aboriginal inmate is going through in prison, and what types of programs and services are required to help ensure success on parole. Aboriginal parole board members would be better able to make culturally appropriate parole decisions. Aboriginal parole officers would be better able to get to the bottom of any problems being experienced on parole.

There have been some attempts to hire Aboriginal staff, but these efforts have met with very limited success. The system continues to have major problems with limited resources and high caseloads. One Aboriginal parole officer who appeared at our hearings said his workload had doubled in the last five years. He told us that he did not have time to provide adequate supervision.

We are recommending the creation of an Aboriginally controlled parole system with an Aboriginal Parole Board, as well as regional, Aboriginally controlled probation services to serve Aboriginal communities. Whether the situation involves parole or probation, the community reintegration and support of persons who have been in conflict with the law is a similar process. In many cases it may be possible for the same individual to fulfil both roles.

WE RECOMMEND THAT:

- The federal parole service establish minimum and optimum targets for the employment of Aboriginal people. The minimum target must be no less than the percentage of Aboriginal people in Manitoba; the optimum target is the percentage of Aboriginal people served by the parole service.

- The National Parole Board, in conjunction with Aboriginal groups, establish release guidelines which take into account the cultural and social circumstances unique to Aboriginal people.

- There be Aboriginal parole officers in each Aboriginal community.

- The National Parole Board be given authority to transfer jurisdiction over a case to the Aboriginal Parole Board.

- The Solicitor General name an additional number of Aboriginal persons as National Parole Board members, in consultation with Aboriginal organizations.

- The National Parole Board ensure that all applications involving Aboriginal inmates, including applications for the revocation of parole, be heard by panels which have at least one Aboriginal member.

- The membership profile for National Parole Board members be changed to permit greater representation of Aboriginal people.

- A program of cross-cultural awareness be developed and implemented for all correctional and parole staff who are involved in making parole decisions about Aboriginal offenders; and that any such cross-cultural awareness program specifically take into account Aboriginal living conditions, Aboriginal values and customs, and the resources available in Aboriginal communities to support the reintegration of offenders.

- The separate roles of parole officer and probation officer be combined in Aboriginal communities.

Release Planning and Conditions of Parole for Aboriginal People

Even if Aboriginal inmates do apply for parole, they are less likely than non-Aboriginal inmates to be released. As we have already pointed out, many Aboriginal offenders do not understand the parole process and, usually, there is little assistance available to them. In addition, Aboriginal offenders may appear to be higher risks because, in the eyes of non-Aboriginal parole board members or parole officers, they are seen as lacking in formal education or employment experience. Furthermore, cultural and linguistic differences may prevent Aboriginal inmates from communicating effectively with parole officials.

Many Aboriginal inmates complained about the absence of effective release planning. They pointed to a lack of employment training, both within the institutions and as part of the parole program. Ironically, in assessing parole eligibility, much emphasis is placed on the availability of appropriate employment and educational programming in the community. Correctional institutions fail to provide these programs while the offender is incarcerated.

We were told that many assessments done of Aboriginal people by parole officers and others do not reflect the community or family situation, nor do they properly analyse the extent of the inmate's rehabilitation or readiness for release. In presentations to our Commission, parole officers were criticized for spending too little time with Aboriginal applicants, and for failing to take the time necessary to allow for full explanation and discussion of available options.

Many Aboriginal inmates felt that parole officers had made up their minds without talking to them. Several inmates complained to us about the attitude of counsellors, parole officers and the National Parole Board itself. They believed that "the system" had preconceived expectations about the actions and attitudes required to obtain parole, and that these expectations did not treat Aboriginal people fairly. One inmate, for example, told of a letter he received from the parole authorities. It said that when he learned to conform they would "look at him." Such a comment has racist overtones if conforming means meeting the non-Aboriginal standards of the system.

Many Aboriginal inmates feel that they have less opportunity for parole because they are Aboriginal. One inmate was told: "I suppose you're just a burden to society, living off welfare." Another told us: "Parole looks at your skin and your education." Still another inmate said he attended Alcoholics Anonymous meetings but the parole panel did not believe him when he was unable to recite Step Five of the A.A. program. He was denied parole.

We believe it is wrong to impose one culture's standards of performance on those from a different culture. This is true particularly when it comes to standards of "acceptable behaviour." The demand to conform is heard by the Aboriginal person as a demand to abandon traditional ways and to adapt to a foreign culture. Pride prevents some from conforming in order to please "the system." Some simply agree to conform to such expectations.

WE RECOMMEND THAT:

- Community assessments of parole applicants be done by Aboriginal parole officers who understand the applicant's community.

Parole Supervision

There are no full-time parole officers resident in remote communities, even though many inmates come from the North. While there are 16 northern communities and one southern one with volunteer parole officers, these staff are not involved in pre-release planning and do not receive significant training for their duties. They are given a brief orientation to the parole process, provide their reports by telephone to the nearest regional office and are paid on a per-case basis. We believe that volunteer parole officers serving Aboriginal communities should be replaced by properly trained, resident, Aboriginal parole officers.

WE RECOMMEND THAT:

- Aboriginal parole officers be hired in Aboriginal communities.

Income Security and Release Planning

Aboriginal inmates frequently do not have sufficient funds upon their release from prison to enable them to return to their home community, or even to provide basic necessities. These are matters of great concern to Aboriginal inmates, and matters that we believe influence the effectiveness of parole. These needs should be identified and dealt with prior to parole.

WE RECOMMEND THAT:

- The National Parole Board, working through its Aboriginal parole officers, make practical arrangements, including provision for financial assistance, to ensure the effective reintegration of Aboriginal inmates into their own communities.

- The National Parole Board, in consultation with Aboriginal organizations, develop and adopt more culturally sensitive release criteria and processes for reviewing conditional release applications from Aboriginal inmates.

Admission of Guilt as a Condition of Release

Some Aboriginal inmates are not released because the parole board's practice requires that they "show a good understanding of the offense, its gravity, effects and the factors surrounding its commission."[16] In effect, they must admit their guilt. Those who believe they are not guilty, or who have no recollection of the events in question, frequently are not prepared or are unable to make this admission. Some believe the system erred in convicting them, and many will not lie just to get parole. Those working within the legal system know that it is not infallible. The parole board should also accept that reality.

WE RECOMMEND THAT:

- The National Parole Board not require that guilt be admitted prior to an inmate obtaining parole.

Use of Inappropriate Conditions for Release

If they are successful in obtaining parole, Aboriginal offenders face further obstacles. In particular, the board seems bent on imposing special conditions, apparently thinking these will be of some benefit. We believe that these conditions often have the opposite effect and, in many instances, virtually guarantee failure.

Numerous commissions, including the Task Force on the Release of Inmates[17] and the federal working group on conditional release,[18] have concluded that parole conditions are too vague and general, that they are often misunderstood, and that they are sometimes so unrealistic that they are virtually impossible to respect. Yet, the use of such conditions by the board has continued unabated.

One frequently used condition that causes us particular concern involves prohibiting an inmate from a small community from returning to that community. One of the primary responsibilities of the parole board is to return inmates to society in a manner that permits them to readapt to their communities. Since it presumably would be unthinkable to prohibit a person from returning to live in Winnipeg or Selkirk or Melita, if that were his or her prior home, we believe an individual from God's River should also be allowed to return there.

Many Aboriginal persons on parole or probation are prohibited from consuming alcohol. It appears that this condition is applied whether or not alcohol was a factor in the original offence, leading us to believe that this prohibition may be as a result of the application of a stereotypical assumption that all Aboriginal offenders are alcoholics. Furthermore, applying an alcohol abstinence condition in effect criminalizes behaviour which is not in itself an offence under the *Criminal Code*.

It seems to us to be senseless to impose conditions to which it would be almost impossible to adhere. For example, a more reasonable condition in regard to alcohol would be to require the offender to undertake a program of alcohol treatment through such agencies as the Native Alcoholism Council.

Such excessive and unrealistic conditions clearly result in many Aboriginal people having their parole revoked. One of our Aboriginal researchers attended two hearings dealing with the revocation of parole. In both cases, Aboriginal parolees had breached conditions prohibiting the consumption of drugs or alcohol. In spite of the explanations as to how the infractions developed, and in spite of an otherwise good record while on parole, the parole board members believed they had no choice but to revoke parole. Despite the fact that neither board member involved had ever been on a reserve, they did not feel it was necessary to receive any evidence about reserve conditions before arriving at their decision.

WE RECOMMEND THAT:

- The practice of placing special parole conditions on Aboriginal inmates, such as abstention from the consumption of drugs or alcohol as a matter of course, cease.

- Where parole conditions are imposed, they be ones that, among other things, can reasonably be adhered to, that are in accord with the inmate's cultural standards, and that will positively benefit both the inmate and the community.

- The National Parole Board not prohibit the return of parolees to their home community. .

It appears to us that the board believes supervision is required in virtually all cases. Yet, we know that the majority of inmates are not dangerous. The requirement for supervision in all cases as now imposed has the effect of making it difficult to approve release plans which involve return to remote communities where there is no parole officer.

We believe the board should grant parole without formal supervision requirements in many more cases. Unless there is a specific need for constant supervision, we question why this requirement should be imposed.

WE RECOMMEND THAT:

- The practice of automatically requiring supervision of parolees by a parole officer be ended, and supervision only be required when necessary for the rehabilitation of the inmate and the protection of society.

Conclusion

Clearly, the present parole system is not working for Aboriginal peoples and systemically discriminates against them.

We regret that much of what we observed is not new. Many of the problems we discuss have been identified and analysed countless times before. Don McCaskill, for example, studied unrealistic parole rules and the lack of involvement of Aboriginal communities in the parole program over 20 years ago.[19] Gail Michalis and William T. Badcock analysed the inappropriate assessment criteria used to determine parole eligibility.[20] Carolyn Canfield and Linda Drinnan examined differential rates in the granting of parole.[21] Even the National Parole Board has studied and recognized many of the concerns.[22]

Even though we know that a fair, culturally sensitive parole process, with adequate services for Aboriginal offenders and their communities, holds the promise of reducing recidivism as well as lowering the Aboriginal jail population, reforms have not been implemented. A strong commitment for improvement is required and must come from the parole authorities and from the government. Without such a commitment, we fear that decades again may pass without the parole system being improved. This would be unfortunate not only for Aboriginal peoples, but for all Manitobans.

CHAPTER 13

———

ABORIGINAL WOMEN

Introduction

A boriginal women and their children suffer tremendously as victims in contemporary Canadian society. They are the victims of racism, of sexism and of unconscionable levels of domestic violence. The justice system has done little to protect them
from any of these assaults. At the same time, Aboriginal women have an even higher rate
of over-representation in the prison system than Aboriginal men. In community after
community, Aboriginal women brought these disturbing facts to our attention. We
believe the plight of Aboriginal women and their children must be a priority for any
changes in the justice system. In addition, we believe that changes must be based on the
proposals that Aboriginal women presented to us throughout our Inquiry.

Women in Traditional Aboriginal Society

Women traditionally played a central role within the Aboriginal family, within
Aboriginal government and in spiritual ceremonies. Men and women enjoyed considerable personal autonomy and both performed functions vital to the survival of Aboriginal
communities. The men were responsible for providing food, shelter and clothing.
Women were responsible for the domestic sphere and were viewed as both life-givers
and the caretakers of life. As a result, women were responsible for the early socialization
of children.

Traditional Aboriginal society experienced very little family breakdown. Husbands and wives were expected to respect and honour one another, and to care for one another with honesty and kindness. In matriarchal societies, such as of the Mohawk, women were honoured for their wisdom and vision. Aboriginal men also respected women for the sacred gifts which they believed the Creator had given to them.[1]

In Aboriginal teachings, passed on through the oral histories of the Aboriginal people of this province from generation to generation, Aboriginal men and women were equal in power and each had autonomy within their personal lives.

Women figured centrally in almost all Aboriginal creation legends. In Ojibway and Cree legends, it was a woman who came to earth through a hole in the sky to care for the earth. It was a woman, Nokomis (grandmother), who taught Original Man (Anishinabe, an Ojibway word meaning "human being") about the medicines of the earth and about technology. When a traditional Ojibway person prays, thanks is given and the pipe is raised in each of the four directions, then to Mother Earth as well as to Grandfather, Mishomis, in the sky.

To the Ojibway, the earth is woman, the Mother of the people, and her hair, the sweetgrass, is braided and used in ceremonies. The Dakota and Lakota (Sioux) people of Manitoba and the Dakotas tell how a woman—White Buffalo Calf Woman—brought the pipe to their people. It is through the pipe that prayer is carried by its smoke upwards to the Creator in their most sacred ceremonies.

The strength that Aboriginal peoples gain today from their traditional teachings and their cultures comes from centuries of oral tradition and Aboriginal teachings, which emphasized the equality of man and woman and the balanced roles of both in the continuation of life. Such teachings hold promise for the future of the Aboriginal community as a whole. We have been told that more and more young Aboriginal people are turning to the beliefs and values of Aboriginal traditions to find answers for the problems which they are facing in this day and age.

Aboriginal author Paula Gunn Allen points out:

> Since the coming of the Anglo-Europeans beginning in the fifteenth century, the fragile web of identity that long held tribal people secure has gradually been weakened and torn. But the oral tradition has prevented the complete destruction of the web, the ultimate disruption of tribal ways. The oral tradition is vital: it heals itself and the tribal web by adapting to the flow of the present while never relinquishing its connection to the past.[2]

This revival is necessitated, in large measure, by the assault that Aboriginal culture has experienced during the last century.

The Attack on Aboriginal Culture

Women were never considered inferior in Aboriginal society until Europeans arrived. Women had few rights in European society at the time of first contact with Aboriginal people. Men were considered their social, legal and political masters. Any rights which women had were those derived through their husbands. The law of England, for example, held that women did not have the right to vote, to own property or to enter into contracts. This attitude was ultimately reflected in the *Indian Act*, which blatantly discriminated against women.

This attitude toward women continued until relatively recently in Canada. Women had to fight battles in this century to win the right to vote and to be recognized as legal persons, and it was only within the past few decades that the final legal restrictions upon their right to contract and own property were lifted.

The imposition of new values and cultural standards brought about tremendous historical, social and economic changes which, for the most part, were destructive to Aboriginal communities. Dr. Sally Longstaffe of the Child Protection Centre has written:

> The razing of Indian societies and their traditions is well-documented. Symptoms of this dislocation are evident in high rates of unemployment, suicide, alcoholism, domestic violence, and other social problems. This loss of tradition has seriously damaged the oral means of preserving cultural norms, and the values which prohibit deviant behaviours have been obscured and often forgotten. Native peoples often appear reluctant to adopt "white" solutions to problems that stem from the latter's apparent destruction of their societies.[3]

Economic factors served as the initial catalyst for change within Aboriginal societies. Aboriginal people were first directed away from hunting into the economic order of the fur trade society. Gradually, more and more of them became removed from the land and went into settlements with a welfare economy. These changes to Aboriginal lifestyle distorted the traditional Aboriginal male and female roles.

> [W]ith the loss of Indian male roles and as a result of being reduced to a state of powerlessness and vulnerability which their own culture deemed highly inappropriate, Indian men came to experience severe role strain.[4]

Cultural changes resulting from the economic factors at play had their greatest impact on the role of Aboriginal women.

Cultural Changes—The Impact upon Aboriginal Women

For Aboriginal women, European economic and cultural expansion was especially destructive. Their value as equal partners in tribal society was undermined completely. The Aboriginal inmates in Kingston Prison for Women described the result this way:

> The critical difference is racism. We are born to it and spend our lives facing it. Racism lies at the root of our life experiences. The effect is violence, violence against us, and in turn our own violence.[5]

It is only in the past decade that writers have acknowledged the very important role Aboriginal women played in the first centuries of contact with Europeans and their descendants. Yet, while their role within Aboriginal society remained relatively stable for some time after contact, all that changed completely with the advent of the residential school system.

The victimization of Aboriginal women accelerated with the introduction after Confederation of residential schools for Aboriginal children. Children were removed from their families and homes at a young age, some to return eight to 10 years later, some never to return. The ability to speak Aboriginal languages and the motivation to do so were severely undermined. Aboriginal students were taught to devalue everything Aboriginal and value anything Euro-Canadian.

Many Aboriginal grandparents and parents today are products of the residential school system. The development of parenting skills, normally a significant aspect of their training as children within Aboriginal families, was denied to them by the fact that they were removed from their families and communities, and by the lack of attention paid to the issue by residential schools. Parenting skills neither were observed nor taught in those institutions. Aboriginal children traditionally learned their parenting skills from their parents through example and daily direction. That learning process was denied to several generations of Aboriginal parents. In addition to the physical and sexual abuse that Canadians are now hearing took place in residential schools, emotional abuse was the most prevalent and the most severe.

Not only did residential schools not support the development of traditional parental roles among the children, but they taught the children that they were "pagan"— an inferior state of being—and should never use their language or honour their religious beliefs. These messages were imparted to Aboriginal children in a sometimes brutal manner. Several presenters also pointed out that residential schools not only removed children from their families, but they also prevented any closeness, even contact, from occurring between siblings and relatives at the same school.

The damage done by residential schools is evident today as Aboriginal people, long deprived of parenting skills, struggle with family responsibilities and attempt to recapture cultural practices and beliefs so long denied.

Grand Chief Dave Courchene Sr. put the experience succinctly:

> Residential schools taught self-hate. That is child abuse.... Too many of our people got the message and passed it on. It is their younger generations that appear before you [in court].

We believe the breakdown of Aboriginal cultural values and the abuse suffered by Aboriginal children in the schools contributed to family breakdown. This began a cycle of abuse in Aboriginal communities, with women and children being the primary victims.

The Canadian government also undermined equality between Aboriginal men and women with the legalization of sexist and racist discrimination in successive pieces of legislation. In 1869 it introduced the concept of enfranchisement, whereby Indian people would lose their status as Indians and be treated the same as other Canadians. For Aboriginal women, this process of enfranchisement had particularly devastating consequences, because the role assigned to Canadian women was one of inferiority and subjugation to the male.

Upon becoming enfranchised, Aboriginal people lost their status under the *Indian Act.* An Indian woman lost her status automatically upon marrying a man who was not a status Indian. This was not true for Indian men, whose non-Indian wives gained status as Indians upon marriage. Under subsequent *Indian Act*s, Indian agents could enfranchise an Indian if he were deemed "progressive." In cases where a man became enfranchised, his wife and children automatically lost their status, as well.[6]

While Bill C-31 (1985) addressed many of these problems, it created new ones in terms of the differential treatment of male and female children of Aboriginal people. Under the new Act, anomalies can develop where the children of a status Indian woman can pass on status to their children only if they marry registered Indians, whereas the grandchildren of a status male will have full status, despite the fact that one of their parents does not have status. Chapter 5, on treaty and Aboriginal rights, discusses this problem in detail and outlines steps that must be taken to remedy it.

Aboriginal women traditionally played a prominent role in the consensual decision-making process of their communities. The *Indian Act* created the chief and council system of local government. The local Indian agent chaired the meetings of the chief and council, and had the power to remove the chief and council from office. Aboriginal women were denied any vote in the new system imposed by the Indian Affairs administration. As a result, they were stripped of any formal involvement in the political process.

The segregation of Aboriginal women, both from wider society and from their traditional role as equal and strong members of tribal society, continues to the present day. This is due partly to the fact that the effects of past discrimination have resulted in the poor socio-economic situation applicable to most Aboriginal women, but it is also attributable to the demeaning image of Aboriginal women that has developed over the years. North American society has adopted a destructive and stereotypical view of Aboriginal women.

The Changing Image of Aboriginal Women

The demeaning image of Aboriginal women is rampant in North American culture. School textbooks have portrayed Aboriginal woman as ill-treated at the hands of Aboriginal men, almost a "beast of burden." These images are more than symbolic—they have helped to facilitate the physical and sexual abuse of Aboriginal women in contemporary society. Emma LaRocque, a Metis woman and professor of Native Studies at the University of Manitoba, wrote to the Inquiry about such demeaning images.

> The portrayal of the squaw is one of the most degraded, most despised and most dehumanized anywhere in the world. The 'squaw' is the female counterpart to the Indian male 'savage' and as such she has no human face; she is lustful, immoral, unfeeling and dirty. Such grotesque dehumanization has rendered all Native women and girls vulnerable to gross physical, psychological and sexual violence.... I believe that there is a direct relationship between these horrible racist/sexist stereotypes and violence against Native women and girls. I believe, for example, that Helen Betty Osborne was murdered in 1972 by four young men from The Pas because these youths grew up with twisted notions of "Indian girls" as "squaws" ... Osborne's attempts to fight off these men's sexual advances challenged their racist expectations that an "Indian squaw" should show subservience ... [causing] the whites ... to go into a rage and proceed to brutalize the victim.[7]

Racist and sexist stereotypes not only hurt Aboriginal women and their sense of self-esteem, but actually encourage abuse—both by Aboriginal men and by others. The Ma Mawi Chi Itata Centre's Family Violence Program attempts to help both victims and offenders to see beyond the stereotypes. In a book used by the program, Paula Gunn Allen explains about "recovering the feminine in American Indian traditions":

> For the past 40 or 50 years, American popular media have depicted American Indian men as bloodthirsty savages devoted to treating women cruelly. While traditional Indian men seldom did any such thing—and in fact among most tribes abuse of women was simply unthinkable, as was abuse of children or the aged—the lie about "usual" male Indian behaviour seems to have taken root and now bears its brutal and bitter fruit.

> The colonizers' revisions of our lives, values, and histories have devastated us at the most critical level of all—that of our own minds, our own sense of who we are.

> Image casting and image control constitute the central process that American Indian women must come to terms with, for on that control rests our sense of self, our claim to a past and to a future that we define and that we build ... images must be changed before Indian women will see much relief from the violence that destroys so many lives....[8]

Our Inquiry was told by the Canadian Coalition for Equality and by the Manitoba Women's Directorate that the media today continue to employ stereotypical images of women. Both presentations compared lurid newspaper coverage of the Helen Betty Osborne murder in The Pas to the more straightforward and sympathetic coverage of the killing of a young non-Aboriginal woman in Winnipeg.

We consider societal attitudes to be an issue that this Inquiry must address. There is a perception among women's groups, both Aboriginal and non-Aboriginal, that abuse of Aboriginal women is more acceptable to the courts than abuse of non-Aboriginal women. While we do not subscribe to the view that there is differential treatment, we are disturbed enough by the perception to suggest that it needs to be addressed. At the heart of the problem is the belief that, fundamentally, justice authorities do not understand, and do not wish to understand, the unique issues facing Aboriginal women.

In order to address the underlying problems that give rise to this perception, the public generally, and those within the justice system specifically, need to be educated about those issues by Aboriginal women. Elsewhere in this report we have recommended that cross-cultural training be provided to a variety of individuals involved in the justice system. We would like to make it clear that Aboriginal women must play a central role in the development and delivery of those programs.

Unfortunately, Aboriginal men, over the centuries, have adopted the same attitude toward women as the European. As a result, the cultural and social degradation of Aboriginal women has been devastating.

According to the Manitoba Women's Directorate, the average annual income for Manitoba's Aboriginal women is less than 75% of that for other women. The labour force participation rate for Aboriginal women is 40%, while 72% of Aboriginal women do not have a high school diploma.

The status of Aboriginal women in the city of Winnipeg is particularly disturbing. Forty-three per cent of Aboriginal families are headed by single women, compared to 10% of non-Aboriginal families. In her presentation on behalf of the Women's Directorate, Janet Fontaine said:

> Poverty is an unmistakable factor in the lives of Manitoba Native women and children. Poverty has been shown to be positively correlated with conflict with the law, low levels of education, decreased opportunity for employment, and a low level of health.

While the "official" unemployment rate has been estimated at 16.5% for Aboriginal women, official statistics typically do not count those who are not actively looking for work.[9] Many Aboriginal women do not actively seek work because there is no employment available to them, or because it is impossible for them to work, due to their family circumstances or for other reasons. The actual employment rate for female status Indians age 15 or more has been estimated as low as 24%.[10] These numbers appear to be due, in part, to an absence of educational and employment opportunities for Aboriginal women.

This history of social, economic and cultural oppression should be seen as the backdrop for our discussion of Aboriginal women as both victims and offenders in the Manitoba justice system.

The Abuse of Women and Children

The presentations of Aboriginal women were blunt and direct. Violence and abuse in Aboriginal communities has reached epidemic proportions.

This violence takes a number of forms. Sometimes it involves physical assaults between adult males. More often—and more disturbingly—it involves the victimization of the least powerful members of the community: women and children.

The Manitoba Women's Directorate submitted to our Inquiry a document entitled "Native Perspective on Rape." According to one of the women interviewed for the study:

- Rape is a common and widespread experience.

- Rape extends back many generations.

- People treat rape as a personal, private pain and do not talk about it unless there is an unavoidable crisis.

- The individual who is raped comes to view violence as the norm.[11]

The Indigenous Women's Collective, and a joint presentation by the Native Women's Transition Centre, the Women's Post Treatment Centre, the North End Women's Centre and Ma Mawi Chi Itata Family Violence Program focussed on the question of the abuse which exists in Aboriginal communities. They wished to expose the level of sexual abuse and to end the silence that is leaving women and children unprotected. Aboriginal women saw sexual abuse as a tragedy. Josie Hill, the director of the Native Women's Transition Centre, told us:

> [I]t is no less than the absolute disrespect of a human being.... Our own ... grandmothers ... state that when a child is sexually abused, 'the spirit leaves; the spirit can hide; the spirit can die', as a result of the great shock ... the ultimate effect is that people become unable to function in home and community.

Professor LaRocque wrote:

> People violate persons and laws, not because of "cultural differences" but because of the human potential for evil which is perhaps influenced by socio-economic conditions. I believe sexual violence is best explained by sexism and misogyny which is nurtured and inherent in patriarchy. Rape in any culture and by any standards is warfare against women. [12]

Finally, she commented on the difficulty Aboriginal women experience in addressing this issue: "I know we have shied away from dealing with the [Native community abuse] issue partly because we had to fend off racism and stereotypes."

The victimization of Aboriginal women has not only been manifested in their abuse, but also in the manner in which Aboriginal female victims are treated. Women victims often suffer unsympathetic treatment from those who should be there to help them. We heard one example of such treatment from the Aboriginal mother of a 16-year-old rape victim. She told of how the police came to her home after her daughter had reported being raped and had undergone hospital examination and police questioning. The police told the mother that her daughter was lying and should be charged with public mischief. According to the mother, the officer added, "Didn't you want it when you were 16?"

In past times it was the abusers who were shunned; now it is the complainant who is shunned. The Manitoba Women's Directorate made the point that colonization has brought "many kinds and levels of abuse" to Aboriginal people. The directorate told us of one woman who

> ... had been abused by being deprived of her history, her family and her language. In her adult life, she had all the signs of an abused person although she had not been physically abused. She suffers from low self-esteem and being unable to believe she is loveable.

Spousal Abuse

One study presented to our Inquiry stated that while one in 10 women in Canada is abused by her partner, for Aboriginal women the figure is closer to one in three. [13]

The most recent study of Aboriginal women by Aboriginal women, a survey conducted by the Ontario Native Women's Association in 1989, found that 80% of Aboriginal women had personally experienced family violence.[14] Fifty-three per cent of Aboriginal women who responded to a survey conducted for us by the Indigenous Women's Collective indicated they had been physically abused. Seventy-four per cent of those women indicated they did not seek help.

The Thompson Crisis Centre stated that, generally, women are abused at least 20 times before seeking help.[15] A March 1991 study by the Manitoba Association of Women and the Law found that the statistics of a 1980 federal study, *Wife Battering in Canada: A Vicious Circle*, still held: women endure anywhere from 11 to 39 episodes of abuse before seeking help, and then they seek help more often from a shelter than from police.[16] The Manitoba government Family Disputes Services branch says that abuse occurs at least 35 times before any outside assistance is sought.

There are currently no statistics that indicate the number of complaints which result in a charge being laid. In 1983, before the current charging policy was established, only 9% resulted in arrest.

According to the 1991 report of the Manitoba Association of Women and the Law, some improvements have been made since 1983. Nevertheless, over 30% of domestic assault charges are stayed at some stage before trial. The percentage of those sentenced has increased from 48% in 1983 to 64% in 1986. However, only 7% of those sentenced in 1987 were sentenced to a term in jail.[17] While we agree that certain cases need to be prosecuted to the full extent of the law, it does not appear that that avenue has been very effective to date.

Aboriginal women surveyed by the Indigenous Women's Collective indicated that the police response received by others discouraged them from going to the police for help. They complained of the lack of understanding of the problem by officers, and their lack of sensitivity. They believe the police do not understand the situation of the abused woman and the needs of children.

More than one woman who spoke to us told of complaining to the police, only to become the one removed from the home. This happened in spite of the fact that young children were left in the care of an intoxicated father. Others told of situations where police attended in the home, saw the situation was calm when they were there and told the woman everything would be all right. When the police left, the violence became worse than before. With such lack of support from police authorities, it is not surprising that women suffer in silence.

From this information, it is clear that women in abusive situations, particularly in isolated communities in northern Manitoba, do not feel confident in turning to the justice system. We were told that many abused Aboriginal women did not feel safe enough even to bring their personal stories before the Inquiry.[18]

Testimony presented to us by the Manitoba Action Committee on the Status of Women in Thompson made it clear why this was the case:

> A man who beat his sister with a length of wood and who had a record of previous convictions for violent acts, was sentenced to seven months. A man who severely beat his common law wife, smashing her face against a fence,

kicking her in the face, and slamming her face against the wall, before dragging her into a house, was sentenced to five months in jail, to be followed by probation after his release.

Both these offenders were going to return to their home communities after serving their sentences. Offenders are returned to their community without notice to the victim—and without treatment—and, as a result, their victims were at risk upon their release. Reporting the crime to police authorities provides a temporary respite at best if the causes of abuse are not dealt with.

The experience of staff at the Thompson Crisis Centre in assisting women who finally do report abuse is that police officers do not consider spousal assault as a serious crime. This view is supported by a report from Statistics Canada entitled "Conjugal Violence Against Women":

> The primary reasons given by victims of wife assault who did not report the abuse to police were a belief that the incident was a personal matter and of no concern to the police (59%), a belief that the police would not be able to do anything about it (58%), and a fear of revenge by the offender (52%). Many also expressed a desire to protect the offender from the police (35%) or were concerned with the attitudes of the police or courts toward this incident (20%).... While almost half of all victims felt threatened enough by the violence to involve the police, half of those who did not report felt fearful of retaliation by the offender if they did involve the police. For some, the risk of having the abuser removed from the home, or involving the family in the justice system, would be worse than risking further violence. Some women seem to feel that the solution to the violence does not lie with the criminal justice system.[19]

In some cases, the Aboriginal woman making the complaint may be too frightened to testify. Should she decline to do so, she faces the risk of being charged with contempt of court. Aboriginal women said they would be more likely to lay charges and testify if someone were available to explain the court procedure to them, and if they were given emotional support throughout the proceedings.

Women's groups expressed concern about the whole criminal justice system, from police to Crown attorneys, judges and correctional institutions. Crisis shelter workers affirmed the experience Aboriginal women have in dealing with the justice system:

> ... indifference/arrogance of lawyers; long police response time; insensitive response of police to spousal abuse; humiliating questioning; failure of police to protect victims; failure of police to take spousal abuse as a serious crime; difficulties obtaining peace bonds; lack of supports to witnesses and treatment of witnesses as criminals; difficulties obtaining protection or getting away from abusive partners in small communities.[20]

In northern, isolated reserve communities, the abused woman is placed in a more difficult situation when the question of calling the police arises. If she calls the police, it may take a day or longer for them to arrive. If they arrive while a party is going on, they may refuse to remove the offender or may simply drive him down the road, from where he can return again, only angrier. There is a lack of housing for families in isolated communities and no "safe house" available for women and children trying to escape an abusive man. They may be forced to spend the night in the bush, or be forced to leave the reserve entirely.

Professor LaRocque points out that women move to urban centres to escape family or community problems. Men, on the other hand, cite employment as the reason for moving. In the new setting Aboriginal women experience personal, systemic, subtle and overt racial discrimination. What they are forced to run to is often as bad as what they had to run from. Why they feel they have to leave is a matter worthy of comment.

Most chiefs and council members are male and often exhibit bias in favour of the male partner in a domestic abuse situation. This can effectively chase the woman from her home and community.

The unwillingness of chiefs and councils to address the plight of women and children suffering abuse at the hands of husbands and fathers is quite alarming. We are concerned enough about it to state that we believe that the failure of Aboriginal government leaders to deal at all with the problem of domestic abuse is unconscionable. We believe that there is a heavy responsibility on Aboriginal leaders to recognize the significance of the problem within their own communities. They must begin to recognize, as well, how much their silence and failure to act actually contribute to the problem.

Aboriginal leaders must speak out against abuse within their communities to their own community members, and they must take steps within their own spheres of community influence to assist the true victims. Women and children who report abuse should never feel they have to leave their communities in order to feel safe. Aboriginal communities and their leaders must do what is possible to make the home communities of abused women and children havens from abuse. The problem of abuse is dealt with presently by women either staying on the reserves and putting up with the abuse, or leaving their communities to live elsewhere, just to escape from it. It is clear, however, that most would prefer to stay in their home communities if they could be protected.

Aboriginal women would like to see arbitration and community support systems in place in their communities. This is another area in which the development of local resources is badly needed. Aboriginal leadership must ensure that it is sought and governments must ensure that it is provided.

There is no equal division of property upon marriage breakdown recognized under the *Indian Act*. This has to be rectified. While we recognize that amending the *Indian Act* is not a high priority for either the federal government or the Aboriginal leadership of Canada, we do believe that this matter warrants immediate attention. The Act's failure to deal fairly and equitably with Aboriginal women is not only quite probably unconstitutional, but also appears to encourage administrative discrimination in the provision of housing and other services to Aboriginal women by the Department of Indian Affairs and local governments.

WE RECOMMEND THAT:

- The *Indian Act* be amended to provide for the equal division of property upon marriage breakdown.

At the provincial level, Aboriginal leaders must begin to support the types of programs which assist Aboriginal women and children to report abuse and to get help for its effects. The silence and inactivity of Aboriginal leadership on this issue cannot continue. It amounts to a denial of responsibility.

WE RECOMMEND THAT:

- Aboriginal leaders establish a local government portfolio for women and children, with responsibility to develop educational and support programs in the area of spousal and child abuse.

Police forces must join forces with social workers in developing a comprehensive response to domestic violence. In urban communities, we recommend the establishment of abuse teams made up of one or two police officers and a social worker trained in the area of family violence. When a complaint of a disturbance between partners is received, this team should be dispatched. It should be sufficiently expert to be able to assess the situation and to take the appropriate action.

A report of the team should be placed on computer. The report should explain the difficulty and should record any issues that should be considered or anticipated in any subsequent attendance. Before going out on a complaint, the team should examine the record to see if the family has had previous problems. This information might play a part in the steps taken by a team on a second attendance.

We heard of reports of repeated assaults, some leading to death. It is our belief that preventive policing by an abuse team may be able to catch volatile situations and deal with them before the violence escalates.

If there are peacemakers or other support groups in a community, the abuse team might be able to obtain the agreement of the parties to go to them for help. The abuse team should monitor the progress of the family.

WE RECOMMEND THAT:

■ Police forces establish family abuse teams which include police officers and social workers trained in dealing with domestic disputes.
Such teams should make extensive use of electronic record-keeping
and community resources.

Supports for Abused Aboriginal Women

There are now 10 shelters for abused women located in Manitoba, with the 11th
due to open in Dauphin in the fall of 1991. There is also a provincial toll-free crisis line
which provides immediate and culturally sensitive counselling and referral to women in
abusive situations. The provincial Family Disputes Services branch supports the crisis
line and provides each of the shelters with core funding and a per-diem overnight rate
per person.

Shelters are established to offer a secure environment where the abused are safe
from the abuser. Trained counsellors are available to assist the women and children. In
1989–90, 1,934 women and 2,804 children came into shelters in Manitoba, staying an
average of five days.

In some towns, local crisis committees operate safe homes where a woman and
her children may stay until space in an approved shelter is available. These homes may
either be the homes of volunteers or a motel. The Income Security Program of the
Department of Family Services pays a much lower per-diem rate per person than is allocated by the Family Disputes Services branch for shelters. The branch does not support
safe homes financially because it believes that it does not have a secure environment to
keep the abuser from the abused, nor any trained counsellors. We find such a policy to be
working adversely against Aboriginal communities where the need for a separate shelter
may not be sufficiently large to justify the establishment of one, but where having safe
houses to provide occasional relief would create a needed community-based resource.

Second-stage housing offers self-contained accommodation for women and children for a period of one year. This type of service is being made available in some Manitoba
communities: Women In Second-Stage Housing (WISH) in Winnipeg, Samaritan House in
Brandon, Thompson Crisis Centre, as well as accommodations in Steinbach, Portage,
Selkirk and Swan River. During this time, women benefit from individual and group sessions to enhance self-esteem, to heal from abuse, to begin family counselling, to learn new
parenting skills, and to undertake employment preparation training and assistance.

The contrast in services provided to Aboriginal women is shocking: there are no
Aboriginal shelters, other than one in Winnipeg, no Aboriginal safe homes and no Aboriginal second-stage housing anywhere. The only shelter established and directed by
Aboriginal people is Ikwe Widdjiitiwin in Winnipeg. It is designed to deal exclusively with
the unique cultural and social issues of Aboriginal women.

Ikwe Widdjiitiwin seeks to provide women with crisis support, supplemented with programs designed to empower Aboriginal women. Ikwe was established by Aboriginal women who believed that Aboriginal women have difficulty in benefiting from non-Aboriginal agencies, because their life experiences differ so significantly from the counsellors' and because the mandates of non-Aboriginal agencies are not appropriate to the cultural philosophies of Aboriginal people. In addition, the Native Women's Transition Centre provides full-time, long-term counselling, advocacy, child care, outreach and follow-up for women. The centre's philosophy stresses the right of Aboriginal women to self-sufficiency, dignity, self-respect, caring and self-determination.

As we were told numerous times, women who wish to escape an abusive home must leave the reserve community and go to the town or city. We consider this tragic and unacceptable. In situations where it is unsafe to leave the victim in the home, there should be shelters or safe houses in Aboriginal communities to which the victim can go.

WE RECOMMEND THAT:

- Shelters and safe homes for abused women and children be established in Aboriginal communities and in urban centres. These shelters should be controlled by Aboriginal women who can provide culturally appropriate services.

Counselling and support for the victims of abuse are essential. Of course, stopping the abuse is the best possible solution and may lead to a continuation of the family unit. If it appears that abuse is likely to continue, the victim should be assisted to terminate the relationship. This cannot be done without a great deal of local support.

We believe that if communities make it known that physical or sexual abuse will not be tolerated and that offenders will be dealt with harshly, there will be a significant reduction in abuse. Traditional Aboriginal means of punishment may be particularly helpful in these situations. Public ridicule and shunning, if applied with the support of the leadership in a community, may be as effective a deterrent as imprisonment.

The physical or sexual abuse of a family member, or of anyone else for that matter, must be treated as extremely serious. The community must support that attitude.

The support of chiefs and councillors is needed to provided the necessary feeling of security to women in Aboriginal communities. The local police, whether they be band constables or members of an Aboriginal police force, members of the City police forces or the RCMP, should be encouraged to remove offenders at the first sign of abuse.

We were told by a number of Aboriginal women that when a woman who has been abused calls the police, the police usually come to the home to investigate. If there are clear signs of abuse and the man is still in a foul humour, the man may be arrested and removed. Too often, however, the man is left in the home and the woman is encouraged to leave the home and seek refuge in a shelter, if there is one, or in the home of a friend or relative.

The emphasis in the past seems to have been to encourage an abused woman to go to a shelter. It is the abuser who should leave, if anyone has to. There should be support groups in every community that will assist the abused woman to stay in the home and to have the abuser removed. Orders of sole occupancy of a home and orders prohibiting an abuser from entering the premises where the spouse is living are obtainable in the Court of Queen's Bench, Family Division, and should be used to keep the abuser out of the home until something can be done to deal with the abuse.

Child Abuse

The most disturbing aspect of all this is child abuse. This abuse is both physical and sexual. All cultural groups have prohibitions against incest and sexual interference with children, but adherence to those rules appears to have broken down both in the broader Canadian society and in Aboriginal society in Manitoba. Dr. Sally Longstaffe, of the Child Advocacy Project with the Child Protection Centre, appeared before us and spoke of the problems society has had in coming to grips with sexual abuse. As part of her presentation, she submitted the project's report, entitled *A New Justice for Indian Children*, which states:

> The problem of child sexual assault is one that has reached epidemic proportions in recent years. Due to the rapid rise in reported instances of child sexual abuse, the demand for knowledge on the subject far exceeds supply. The knowledge that currently exists is rapidly changing as it undergoes examination and refinement by various professionals in the human service field.[21]

The Child Protection Centre of the Children's Hospital established a Child Advocacy Project to study and document the dynamics of sexual abuse involving children treated at the Children's Hospital of Winnipeg.

Longstaffe described the study that involved a detailed investigation into the cases of 147 Manitoba children (both Aboriginal and non-Aboriginal). Although there was medical evidence to support a belief that the children had been sexually abused, in 85 cases charges were never laid or were dismissed.

Dr. Longstaffe said that the situations facing Aboriginal children on reserves were particularly worrisome. The children often were the victims of multiple assaults from numerous, and often related, individuals, and often were threatened if they took their complaints to the authorities. In reserve communities, the lack of communication between social agencies, and the lack of connection between the community and the justice system, led to a number of disturbing consequences.

The report of the Child Advocacy Project stated:

> The need for bold action is apparent. Children are suffering from trauma, physical injury, and psychological devastation that result from sexual abuse. The injuries to self-esteem, trust, and emotional functioning last a lifetime. The incidence of sniffing, alcohol abuse, eating disorders, suicide, depression, and sexual acting out among Indian children suggest that the problem of child sexual abuse has reached epidemic proportions.[22]

The statistics examined by the project show that the court system is not the answer in all situations. Two-thirds of the children it looked at who were removed from unsafe homes were returned eventually to those homes by the courts, or were placed in a setting where the offender had direct or indirect access to them. In approximately 65% of what the project considered to be abuse cases, either no charges were laid or the charges were dismissed.

The project suggests the use of elders in responding to Aboriginal child sexual abuse. It suggests there are several merits to this approach:

> Elders command the respect necessary to mobilize reserve communities to deal with the problem. As well, their position in the community is well-suited to both confronting the offender and consulting ongoing treatment strategies for the offender with collaboration information and support from other treatment resources. Most importantly, elders are a source of expertise and credibility in performing the task of blending modern clinical expertise and theoretical knowledge with the traditional values of their people.[23]

The causes of sexual assault are complex and difficult to ascertain. Feelings of anger and frustration, and the need for a feeling of power or dominance over another, may partly explain this activity. Certainly, alcohol plays a major part, as many people do things under the influence of alcohol they would not normally do.

Children are easy targets for angry parents, and often verbal and then physical abuse are directed towards them. They are in a difficult position to resist physical attacks or sexual advances from a parent or an older relative. While some of the history we spoke of earlier may offer some explanations for such unacceptable conduct, and even if that conduct is part of the legacy of colonization, we wish to make it clear that we find none of the explanations an excuse for the manner in which Aboriginal women and children are treated. With eight out of 10 Aboriginal women reporting having been abused—many of them as young children—the question of child abuse must be addressed forcefully because, in our view, it represents the single greatest threat to the future of Aboriginal people and their societies.

The report of the Child Advocacy Project states:

> The social cost of child sexual abuse is higher than we can imagine. These child victims continue to be victimized throughout their lives. The burden of this victimization is preventing many Indian children from becoming the healthy, functioning adults they might otherwise be. The failure of the social, medical, and legal systems to provide a safe environment for the normal development of these children perpetuates the existence of future generations of victims. It is time to break the cycle of victimization. It is time to break the long standing pattern of non-action on reserve-based child sexual abuse. Quite simply, it is time for a new justice for Indian children.[24]

Specifically, the report recommends:

All rural detachments of the RCMP should receive additional training in child sexual abuse and the investigation of such cases. As well, RCMP training efforts in this area should be designed to include local tribal police for the dual purpose of maintaining a close relationship and providing these officers with proper information. Training should include the role of the peace officer in a multidisciplinary team....

That the Attorney General's office give serious consideration to developing a program that would address the coordination problems inherent in reserve-based child sexual abuse cases. Such a program would address the issue of consistency, (ie: having the same Crown attorney throughout the case), as well as developing a working relationship with local Justice Committees. One possible option would be to hire legal assistants or paralegals to be based on the reserves for the purpose of facilitating a logical and orderly collaboration on each case. The possibility of developing Tribal Courts should, in our view, be explored by examining the relative success of such in other jurisdictions....

That a program be initiated to promote the use of a multidisciplinary team approach on every reserve in Manitoba. The focus of such an approach would be tribal elders in conjunction with the local child-caring agency, the local Child Care Committee, and the local Justice and other pertinent Committees. By using such mechanisms as a foundation for a community-based approach, non-native institutions and methods can be adapted to use in reserve communities. If such teams demonstrate leadership and a willingness to act, legal and medical professionals from the white system can play a supportive rather than controlling role....

It is recommended that there be considerable new resources committed toward developing a treatment capacity in each reserve, for offenders and victims, such resources currently being negligible. The logical vehicle for providing treatment is the local child-care agency, with advice and support from community elders, or perhaps a larger council of elders. Much needed culturally based prevention (personal safety) programs could then be developed for use in reserve schools....

It is recommended that child-caring agencies with the responsibility for the protection of Indian children place a big priority on developing greater numbers of safe placement options for children. This includes the careful scrutiny of current placement options, as well as possible extended family placements. The development of innovative new safe places for child victims is an undertaking that would optimally be conducted in conjunction with Child Care Committees and multidisciplinary teams as they become operative.[25]

We accept the findings and echo the recommendations of the Child Advocacy Project. Provincial, federal and community governments must jointly develop and implement resources and programs to deal with this most serious of problems.

Longstaffe told us that there were also positive developments and that these generally occurred where community leaders and elders played a crucial role in enforcing community discipline.

> We had one situation in the course of this study where one of our elders had a sexual abuse situation that came to light in her own community during the course of the study and where, after some informal discussion, the community decided on its own to try to provide a ring of protection around potential victims. So, what happened was that the person in question who had been convicted of a very serious sexual assault on a small child in the past and was now living on this elder's reserve was told by other individuals of stature in the community that they knew what had happened; they knew that he was at risk for doing this again and they were going to warn the other children who lived around him; they were going to warn their parents and that if he committed any kind of offence or began drinking, that he would be asked to leave the community. And this process, although informal, seemed to be very effective and was carried out over many months with success, we thought.

WE RECOMMEND THAT:

- The provincial government implement the recommendations found in the report of the Child Advocacy Project entitled *A New Justice for Indian Children*.

Healing the Family and the Community

Women told us of painful experiences in seeking help to escape an abusive home, and of their wish for help to keep the family together. They emphasized that Aboriginally designed and directed programs were what they wanted to assist them; they believed that only Aboriginal services would emphasize healing within the family and keeping the family together within the home community. Aboriginal women did not feel comfortable with counselling that tended to exclude the abuser from any treatment process and appears to stressed the necessity of the woman leaving her husband.

Glennis Smith of the Zeebeequa Society, a group of Aboriginal women who seek to protect women and children at Roseau River, explained: "Abuse in general, and violence, it is a disease and it can be treated. We cannot forget, even our offenders have one time been victims of these types of abuses."

In their presentations to the Inquiry, Aboriginal women called for a healing of the people—women, men, children, families, communities. Aboriginal women, we are told, generally want to "fix" the problem and stay with their partner. They believe this can be done by programs that treat the whole family. Their philosophy is that strong, healthy families make strong, healthy communities. While they agree that some short-term crisis intervention often is needed, they want to go from that point to one where there is treatment provided for the family as a unit, including both the parents and the children.

Aboriginal women ask for treatment that will focus on the whole person and the whole family unit. They believe this approach must include traditional Aboriginal teachings and healing. To achieve that type of an approach, the leaders of programs must themselves be Aboriginal people with some skills or training.

We agree that, instead of sending all abusers to jail, there should be a careful screening process. Where jail does not appear to be the best answer to the situation, we suggest that abusers be required to attend a culturally appropriate treatment program with other members of the family. We believe this will be more effective than fines, restraining orders or community service orders.

The women who spoke to us called for Aboriginally designed and directed programs, similar to those at Alkali Lake, B.C. and at Hollow Water in eastern Manitoba. It is worthwhile to examine the history and success of these developments.

Alkali Lake, B.C.

In Alkali Lake, an Aboriginal community in British Columbia, one family turned from alcohol and began a change that affected the whole community. One by one, members of the community rejected the consumption of alcohol as an acceptable practice. Some alcohol abusers were even asked to leave the community. With the reduction in alcohol consumption abuse, crime declined, and energies were turned toward developing economic opportunities. Alkali Lake has developed an Aboriginal model of healing and self-actualization called "Flying on Your Own." This program of intensive group therapy has reached hundreds of Aboriginal people across Canada, and is often used by bands in Manitoba and by the Aboriginal social agency, Ma Mawi Chi Itata Centre.

In many ways, Aboriginal communities lead the rest of the province in addressing the consequences of sexual abuse and in devising imaginative ways, based on Aboriginal traditions, to deal with it. In Winnipeg, there are two Aboriginal women's agencies which attempt to provide holistic services to Aboriginal women.

The Hollow Water Resource Group

Hollow Water, Seymourville, Agaming and Manigotogan have taken a lead in dealing with sexual abuse cases in their communities by establishing the Hollow Water Resource Group. The emphasis in these communities is on healing and restitution, rather than on punishment. It uses the authority of the legal system when necessary, but concentrates on restoring harmony and balance to the family and the community by healing both the victim and the offender.

The Hollow Water Resource Group told us that their program began as a community workshop, organized by a few people who had survived lives of abuse. About 60 people met and were asked how many ever had been abused. Two-thirds said that they had been. A startling one-third admitted that they had victimized someone else. All agreed that something had to be done to help their communities. The courts were giving sentences considered by the communities to be both too lenient and inappropriate. At the same time, there was no treatment for an offender who was jailed. The group devised a plan of action.

When a person in the community is charged with abuse, whether the abuse is physical or sexual, the RCMP are notified and invited to attend a meeting of the Assessment Team. The team discusses the reported abuse and ensures the protection of the child. According to the resource group, the emphasis is on "protection, support and healing of the victim ... there can be no compromise made relative to the victim's healing process." At this point the RCMP may lay a charge. If so, the matter proceeds normally through the court system, and the group may become involved at the court level. It has found that even when a matter is resolved in the court system and proceeds to disposition, there is a role for it to play in assisting the court to determine the best manner of disposing of the case.

An example of the court's reaction to the community program, as applied to one offender, is found in the decision of Her Honour Judge Lea Duval in *R. v. Seymour*, a decision of the Provincial Court of Manitoba sitting at Pine Falls, dated May 24, 1989. In that case Judge Duval referred to the work done by the group, to the interest and involvement of the accused in rehabilitation and in reforming his conduct, and to the group's recommendation that incarceration not be applied. She accommodated that recommendation in her sentence.

The resource group meets separately with the offender, the victim and the family. In some instances, the victim and the offender will meet to discuss what harm has been caused to the family unit and what, if anything, can be done to restore harmony to the family. The resource group will also assess the likelihood of any repetition of the offence. This community involvement is intended to show the abuser that the community is on the side of the victim, to make him or her see that the offence is unacceptable, and to offer assistance if the offender will accept responsibility for the inappropriate conduct.

Following these meetings, the resource group representatives meet with the RCMP and the Crown attorney to indicate the plan they propose to undertake.

Depending on a number of factors, particularly on whether the victimizer accepts responsibility, the resource group may indicate its intention to continue to handle the case even if the offender is prosecuted, and it may ask to be allowed to make a recommendation to the court for appropriate punishment if the accused is convicted.

In the event that the Crown prosecutor does not proceed with a charge, for whatever reason, the resource group will continue to meet separately with the offender, the victim and the family of each to explain what will be expected in the healing process. A special gathering and ceremony then is held. The offender, victim, family members and resource group members gather and speak of how they feel about the offence, what responsibility the offender must take, and how each can help in the healing process of the victim and offender. This is the heart of the process and allows the community to show concern for all involved. The offender publicly apologizes and signs a Healing Contract, which usually commits the offender to some form of community service and treatment, and includes a promise by the offender against future victimization of the abused individual.

A special ceremony marks the conclusion of the contract. It recognizes the restoration of the offender to the community and marks a new beginning for all involved. The RCMP are kept advised of the progress of the group's efforts.

The advantage of the Hollow Water approach is that it offers options missing from other programs. Not only does it provide rehabilitation to the offender, and support and comfort to the victim, but it provides a mechanism to heal and restore harmony to the families and the community. This approach deals with the problem of abuse at its source. The Hollow Water model was created to protect people against repetition of the offence and to prevent any new incidents of abuse.

The Hollow Water model may be best suited to Indian and Metis communities with greater closeness to Aboriginal traditions of healing. However, we believe that such an approach could also be effective in an urban setting.

Other communities agree with the philosophy and method of seeking rehabilitation and restoration of relationships, rather than retribution. Glennis Smith of the Zeebeequa Society of Roseau River recommended treatment rather than incarceration of offenders, noting that many times offenders come out of jail with no treatment for, or understanding of, their behaviour. Janet Fontaine, a Cree woman and employee of the Manitoba Women's Directorate, agreed: "I don't choose to separate out the pain of women from the pain of men when it comes to the range of violence issues."

The role of Aboriginal women has been prominent in the design and implementation of Aboriginal models of healing the victim and abuser, and in developing community support for these programs.

It is clear to us that Aboriginal people must be allowed to develop culturally appropriate programs and institutions to deal with family violence issues. These institutions must come under Aboriginal control. The Indigenous Women's Collective and others recommended a healing lodge concept—a place where Aboriginal people can come together to learn the teachings of elders and to participate in healing ceremonies. The Interlake Reserves Tribal Council is working to develop their Harmony and Restoration Centre near Gypsumville to provide a more formalized program for offenders, while enabling their families and victims to join in the growing and healing process. The Assembly of Manitoba Chiefs has a research team investigating the development of the Healing Lodge to assist Aboriginal people and communities to recover from the ravages of residential school experiences.

We believe that the principles behind healing lodges can play a central role in addressing the issue of family violence in Aboriginal communities. These lodges can serve both as centres where women can address and overcome the experience of being abused, and as facilities or programs to which abusers could be sentenced on a non-custodial basis.

In Chapter 8, which discusses court reform, we propose that intrafamily abuse matters be dealt with in the Family Division of a new unified trial court where the counselling and mediation services of Family Conciliation would be available in appropriate abuse cases.

In our chapter on correctional institutions (Chapter 11), we recommend that "open custody programs for Aboriginal adult and young offenders requiring counselling, behaviour improvement, job training and other forms of assistance be established in Aboriginal communities." We believe it is important that, as Aboriginal people develop their own justice system, they play a central role in the design and administration of correctional institutions. For this reason, we are not providing details of open custody programs or facilities. We would like to stress, however, that the Manitoba government must work with Aboriginal communities to develop them.

WE RECOMMEND THAT:

- Community mediation programs such as the one operated by the Hollow Water Resource Group be expanded to Aboriginal communities throughout the province. Such programs must be designed and operated by Aboriginal people.

Dealing with the Abuser

In Aboriginal communities the abuser should have to meet with a peacemaker and efforts at reconciliation should then proceed. If these fail, then a charge should be proceeded with.

If the abuser is not going to be incarcerated, the courts still can be of assistance by requiring the abuser to make use of local community support systems. If local holding facilities are available, these should be used to house and counsel abusers.

If incarceration or a suspended sentence is imposed, a condition should be that the abuser obtain treatment and counselling for domestic violence, with a reference to an Aboriginally based program, if that is acceptable to the accused.

In spite of the need to use the criminal justice system to emphasize to an abuser the severity of abusive conduct, we believe that every effort should be made to save the family unit. If an offender is likely to return to the community and family after serving a sentence, it is better to try to cure the problem at an early stage. If the abuser can be stopped from a repetition of abusive conduct, that would be ideal. If it can be accomplished without the necessity of incarcerating the abuser, so much the better.

We know from experience that incarceration does not stop abuse, except for the months someone may be incarcerated. We know that incarceration of some abusers is not a deterrent to other abusers. The application of the criminal justice system is a band-aid or short-term solution at best.

Alcohol, Crime and Abuse

It was generally Aboriginal women who spoke to us of the effect of alcohol on crime in general and on family violence in particular. It is a fact established by a long line of studies that Aboriginal involvement in crime includes as a factor the abuse of alcohol. It is also the case that the consumption of alcohol contributes to the incidents of domestic violence and child abuse which occur on Indian reserves.

Women at God's Lake Narrows (a dry reserve) told us that, in their opinion, 95% of crime in their communities is related to the consumption of alcohol. Most of the many inmates and former inmates who spoke to us attribute their offence to the over-consumption of alcohol. A substantial number of those involved in causing the death of another did not even remember the event, due to alcohol consumption.

As is the case with the illegal use of drugs, we believe that attacking the illegal providers of the substance, rather than the addict, makes sense.

However, in one respect, alcoholism represents a problem that requires solutions which the justice system cannot adequately provide. It is not sufficient simply to lock up people for being intoxicated. The consumption of alcohol is not, on its own, illegal. Locking up people who have committed crimes while intoxicated also has questionable benefits. People must be held to account for their crimes and the principle of punishment is designed to accomplish that, but punishment has questionable benefits when the one being punished has no recollection of what he or she did.

Punishment is, as well, only one consideration in sentencing. Rehabilitation of the offender and deterrence from committing the offence in the future, either by the offender or by others, are equally important considerations. When an offender commits a crime while intoxicated—an act which many people might be prepared to assert is totally out of character for the accused—courts have to struggle with the issue of deterring someone who needs to be deterred more from the consumption of alcohol than from breaking the law.

Rehabilitation sometimes takes precedence as a factor in sentencing, but sending someone to jail simply so he or she can deal with a drinking problem seems an improper use of incarceration. However, incarceration for abusing alcohol appears to be happening with Aboriginal offenders. Frankly, as long as the justice system is saddled with the problem, we expect that it will continue to deal with the issue in this admittedly inadequate manner.

Efforts must be increased to deal with the alcohol abuser within Aboriginal communities. This requires resources to increase the availability of treatment programs that are culturally appropriate, Aboriginally run and community-based.

As is the case with other programs designed to "help" people, we believe that programs that are based upon the cultures and traditions of Aboriginal people, and that involve Aboriginal methods of healing and personal conflict resolution, have a much greater chance of succeeding than do programs developed and managed by non-Aboriginal institutions. This is true in both urban and Aboriginal communities, and, therefore, calls for the establishment of more Aboriginally based resources and treatment programs in both areas.

As well, correctional institutions must also enhance the availability of culturally appropriate treatment programs within their institutions on an ongoing and regular basis.

Ultimately, it must be recognized that the presence and influence of alcohol and substance abuse in Aboriginal communities and among Aboriginal people are a direct reflection of the nature and level of despair which permeates that population. We have spent a considerable amount of time and space in this report detailing the basis for that despair.

It is our view that beginning to address the causes of Aboriginal despair in an appropriate and adequate manner will have a fundamentally more significant impact on Aboriginal alcoholism than will the efforts of police, the judiciary or treatment programs.

The Sentencing of Aboriginal Women

As we noted at the beginning of this chapter, Aboriginal women are over-represented in federal and provincial correctional institutions at an even higher rate than Aboriginal males. An Elizabeth Fry Society study done in 1982[26] showed that 71% of Manitoba female inmates were Aboriginal. In 1988 the percentage of incarcerated Aboriginal females rose to 85%.

One of our early hearings, and the first one at a correctional institution, was at the Portage Correctional Institution. This women's jail has a capacity of 44 inmates. There were 43 residents when we were there. At the time of our visit, some 70% of them were Aboriginal.

Regrettably, the situation at Portage is not unique. In Saskatchewan it has been estimated that treaty Indian women are 131 times more likely to be incarcerated than non-Aboriginal women, while Metis women are 28 times more likely to be incarcerated.[27]

This over-representation can be traced, in part, to the victimization that Aboriginal women experience. A study of federally sentenced Aboriginal women, conducted for the Native Women's Association of Canada in 1990, found that 27 of the 39 women interviewed described experiences of childhood violence: rape, regular sexual assault, witnessing of murder, watching their mother repeatedly being beaten, beatings in juvenile detention homes at the hands of staff or other children. Twenty-seven of the 39 women experienced violence in adolescence and 34 of the 39 had been victims of assault as adults.[28]

> There is no accidental relationship between our convictions for violent offences, and our histories as victims. As victims we carry the burden of our memories: of pain inflicted on us, of violence done before our eyes to those we loved, of rape, of sexual assaults, of beatings, of death. For us, violence begets violence: our contained hatred and rage concentrated in an explosion that has left us with yet more memories to scar and mark us.[29]

Statistics collected by the Portage Correctional Institution for women show that at least 80% of the inmates had suffered either physical or sexual abuse; 40% reported both.

Our hearings at the Portage Correctional Institution underlined the devastating impact that poverty and cultural deprivation have had upon Aboriginal women. The women who were incarcerated there told us that they felt that they were discriminated against both as women and as Aboriginal persons. They felt they were unable to take advantage of programs such as fine option that are intended to keep people out of jail, and which are readily available to men, because those programs are designed from a male perspective. They believed that judges and other justice system officials treated them with a lack of respect and understanding.

Many of the women we spoke with admitted that the consumption of alcohol was a contributing factor to their criminal involvement. Statistics confirmed that fact. However, while alcohol was mentioned by Aboriginal women at Portage, it was not the most significant factor that caused them to be there. Most appeared to have been the victims of early childhood sexual abuse and ongoing domestic violence from their husbands or partners.

Many felt trapped in an impossible economic and social situation from which there was little chance of escape. They saw little hope for improvement in their lives. Their plight, although often couched in other terms, was economic. Their ability to cope with life was hampered by the abuse they had received and continued to receive, as well as their poor or nonexistent job skills.

None of the women we spoke to wanted to be involved in criminal activity, but often they believed it necessary to do so in order to obtain money to care for their children. In view of the earnestness with which those women expressed their concerns to us, we are satisfied that there is a much deeper issue at play in Aboriginal female crime than mere disrespect for the law. One inmate described her situation in this way:

> It all starts from welfare. It starts with the welfare system ... because I am a mother with kids and in order to do that, I had to do my crime. In order to barely live on welfare, I had to do my crime. You do get help from welfare, but it's just barely enough to live. From there, you get involved with your crime and after that then you get picked up, you go to jail and when they look at you they call you nothing but a thief or whatever you've done. Nobody's got no use for you, but like, you know, maybe that's how I was living, how I was keeping my kids together, my family, my home, whatever I had.

Many of the women were concerned particularly that their children had been taken away from them and that their criminal involvement had led to questions being raised about their competency as parents. Many of them stated that it was in order to feed and provide for their children that they had committed their crimes in the first place, and they felt particularly wronged for having had their love and concern for their children questioned because of what they had done.

In discussing the disproportionate crime rates among Aboriginal women compared to non-Aboriginal women, Carol LaPrairie notes:

> Native women may retaliate in kind against physically abusive Native men. Secondly, Native women may escape from a violent or otherwise abusive situation at home and migrate to an urban area where discrimination by a larger society combined by low level of skills and education, may relegate them to the ranks of the unemployed or unemployable. That in turn increases the probability of resorting to alcohol and drug abuse, or to prostitution, all of which

increases the probability of conflict with the law. Even without engaging in any of these activities, being in an urban area increases their exposure to police, some of whom may be biased in the way they exercise their discretionary judgment when deciding whether or not to arrest a Native person.[30]

We have recommended in Chapter 10 that judges make greater use of alternatives to incarceration within the justice system and that additional alternatives be developed. We are convinced that Aboriginal women must be fully involved in the design and delivery of these alternatives.

Recent statistics also reveal that Aboriginal women are being incarcerated for more violent offences than are non-Aboriginal women.

In P4W (the Kingston Penitentiary for Women), almost three quarters of Native women, have been committed for violent offences (i.e. murder, attempted murder, wounding, assault. and manslaughter) and less than one quarter for property offences (i.e. theft, break and entering), while for non-Native women the comparable figures are thirty-two percent and thirty-eight percent.[31]

A 1990 study examining women and crime found that while "the number of women committing violent crime is increasing, women continue to represent a small proportion of those charged with a violent crime."[32]

According to the Elizabeth Fry Society and the Ikwewak Justice Committee, Aboriginal women are often going to jail for unpaid fines, despite the existence of the fine option program. The Indigenous Women's Collective explained to us that it is often difficult for Aboriginal women to take advantage of community service orders and fine option programs. There is no support for child care or other arrangements that would enable a woman, often a single parent, to follow through with such an order. The collective stated that including restitution in fine option programs, "would ensure that the punishment fits the crime and would go further to lessen the indigenous persons incarcerated."[33]

Elsewhere in our report we have proposed major changes to the way fines are imposed and collected, and we have called for an end to the incarceration of offenders who default on fines. We propose improvements in the way that both restitution and community service orders are administered, and we believe these improvements will alleviate the problems that women offenders face in this area.

We also believe that Aboriginal women are over-represented in the Province's correctional system because of problems they experience with the courts. Aboriginal women told us that lawyers do not understand the problems of Aboriginal women, that the lawyers do not understand the Aboriginal community or how the forces within it affect women.

Aboriginal women at times lash out against continuing abuse, either in self-defence or as a delayed reaction to being violated. According to Professor LaRocque, few lawyers understand that fact well and seldom bring those extenuating circumstances to the attention of the court. Women who have experienced long-term abuse, leading up to the offence with which they are charged, feel they should be presented to the court as victims and not simply as offenders.

Members of the legal profession must become aware of their clients' life experience, particularly as it relates to domestic violence. We believe that defence counsel, Crown attorneys and members of the judiciary should receive in-depth training in the dynamics of domestic abuse.

Aboriginal women told us they found their court experience frustrating. They were particularly upset about the delays in the system and the length of time it takes to resolve a problem.

A number of women commented that they did not understand the court procedures. Some said they could not understand the language that was being used. Some knew nothing other than that they were told to plead guilty, so they did. Those who knew of it spoke highly of Legal Aid Manitoba's paralegal program, where Aboriginal women paralegals attend four reserves and provide some information and support to those required to attend court.

WE RECOMMEND THAT:

- Alternatives to incarceration appropriate to Aboriginal cultures be developed for Aboriginal women.

The Portage Correctional Institution

The Portage Correctional Institution is the province's only correctional institution for women. We believe the institution is an inappropriate facility for women and should be closed. In its place, we recommend the establishment of co-correctional facilities and community houses where female offenders can be required to live. These homes should exist in Aboriginal and in urban communities. Counselling and job-related training should be available in the home and in the community. The inmate should be able to attend school or work during the day, returning to the home for counselling and to stay at night.

We were told by the administrators of the Portage Correctional Institution that services provided at that institution include an adult basic education program and a life skills program provided by the Red River Community College. In addition, there are some employment-related opportunities. Inmates can work in food services, participate in a farm labour pool, or perform volunteer work on behalf of non-profit organizations. Services specific to Aboriginal women are provided mainly by the Ma Mawi Chi Itata Centre. A worker attends the institution once a week to counsel inmates and to assist in pre-release planning.

We were not convinced of the general application of these programs. We found existing programs to be inadequate. One woman indicated that she would have preferred to have been sentenced to the Prison for Women in Kingston:

There's more to do. Every month they have something happening and people come in and so on. They have music; they have pow wows; they have A.A. socials and so on.

Another inmate told us that school programs were available only to people serving a sentence of two months or longer. The president of the board of directors of the Elizabeth Fry Society told us, "Portage la Prairie is dealing with women usually who have much shorter sentences and therefore they do not have programs in place."

The inmates who spoke to us were not aware of any halfway houses for women, nor of any assistance available to them when they left the institution. There is a clear need for job-related training programs, personal employment counselling and an active program to place women in a job upon their release. This is not now being done.

The programming problems at Portage la Prairie highlight the problem with sending female offenders to large and distant correctional facilities to serve very short sentences. The sentence creates tremendous disruption in the offender's life, often leading to the break-up of families and loss of employment. The system's impact is almost exclusively punitive, and victimizes innocent children and communities as much as, or more than, it punishes offenders.

One of the complaints we heard about the women's jail in Portage la Prairie was its location. It is far from the homes of those from the North, making it impossible for family members, including children, to visit. The same problem exists for families in Winnipeg who find it difficult to visit and remain in contact with incarcerated women.

As an Aboriginal woman at the Portage Correctional Institution told us:

You come to jail and you sit here; your kids, your whole family is all split up. Child and Family Services ... have a way of getting involved.... They say you're not a good mother. They, too, don't listen to the person that has been through here. They haven't seen a mother look after her kids all those years. That's what they call you an unfit mother or you're not good enough to look after your own kids and who else can you turn to? If you go back to welfare, they tell you the same thing. It's all the same run around. Then, people like us, usually find ourselves back in the same circle, that we don't know how, or we can't, pull ourselves out of.

A parliamentary committee found that Aboriginal women were the most penalized by the prison experience:

Imprisoned women are triply disadvantaged: they suffer pains of incarceration common to all prisoners; in addition, they experience both the pains Native prisoners feel as a result of their cultural dislocation and those which women prisoners experience as a result of being incarcerated far from home and family.[34]

New programs must be devised to keep mothers who are incarcerated in close contact with their children, or the long-term consequences will be disastrous.

Studies have shown that women's prisons tend to increase women's dependency; stress women's domestic, rather than employment, role; aggravate women's emotional and physical isolation; destroy family and other relationships; and engender a sense of injustice.[35] In other words, they appear to accomplish the opposite of what is intended. What we saw at Portage confirms these conclusions.

While some of the people we heard from expressed a preference for the Prison for Women in Kingston, this preference was only expressed as an alternative to the Portage Correctional Institution. Other presenters spoke about the injustices that occur when women are required to serve a sentence in the country's only federal penitentiary for women. A number of presenters recommended that the Prison for Women in Kingston be abolished. The federal government recently has announced that there will be a regional centre for Aboriginal women, somewhere on the Prairies. While we support the intent to provide facilities closer to the homes of those sentenced in the West, the creation of a new institution in Saskatchewan or Alberta will not solve the problem. The facility will still be a "jail" and the problems of visiting still will remain.

In our opinion, more imaginative means of dealing with Aboriginal women offenders are required. It was clear to us that few, if any, of the inmates at Portage were security risks. Our research shows that the average sentence length at Portage is less than five months.

The report of the 1990 Task Force on women serving sentences in federal penitentiaries stated firmly that women offenders, even women convicted of violent crimes, are not a security risk or a threat to the safety of the community.[36] The report recommended replacing "risk/security management" by "risk/support," and recommends replacing "current 'security'" at the federal institution with "the provision of a healthy environment, supportive staff, and a good planning process."[37] Alternatives to incarceration would enhance opportunities for rehabilitation without endangering the wider community.

Many inmates at Portage had spent their early years as wards of children's aid societies and had been in conflict with the law since the age of 13 or 14. The despair of everyday living was too much for some of these Aboriginal women: a number of the women who testified before us in Portage la Prairie spoke of their attempts to commit suicide. All these facts lead us to the conclusion that existing facilities are not serving the needs of inmates or the best interests of society at large.

Co-Correctional Institutions

We believe that particular attention should be paid to the possibility of establishing co-correctional facilities. We believe that the conversion of existing programs to co-correctional programs might have many benefits, not the least of which could be making correctional services for Aboriginal women more readily available, either in their own communities or close to them.

Indian Ridge Corrections Centre, near Arlington in the state of Washington, was converted to a co-correctional facility in 1988. It houses 24 women and 86 men. Inmates engage in a full range of forestry work, including tree thinning, planting and forest fire fighting. Supplementing these forestry activities are in-camp work details, educational programs, counselling and social service programs. The rules of dress and conduct are strict. Fraternization of a sexual nature and sexual harassment by word, gesture or contact are forbidden. The more serious breaches result in the transfer of the inmate to unmixed medium security prisons. Common areas must be vacated by 10:00 p.m.

The administration and inmates are very positive about the program. As with other institutions of this type, there are limitations placed upon the extent of association between the sexes, but there is considerable freedom. The superintendent reported there are fewer disciplinary problems. A second co-correctional institution and possibly a third are now in the planning stage in Washington. Apparently 24 other American states now have co-correctional institutions.

We believe it to be a model that should be investigated carefully by the Manitoba government. As a first step in this direction, we believe that on the closure of the Portage Correctional Institution for women, the Milner Ridge Correctional Centre should be converted to a co-correctional facility. We understand that there are educational and employment training programs, as well as family violence and anger management courses, developed at Milner Ridge which could benefit both sexes. This transformation must be undertaken in consultation with women's groups throughout the province. In addition, men convicted of crimes of violence against women or children, or with a history of violence against women or children, should be excluded from any co-correctional institution. A more normal atmosphere, with opportunities for both sexes to learn new respect for one another, would exist. When almost every other institution in society accommodates both sexes, correctional and rehabilitation institutions should consider doing the same.

WE RECOMMEND THAT:

- The Portage Correctional Institution be closed.

- All women who are now sent to a federal penitentiary outside the province be permitted to serve their sentences in Manitoba.

- Culturally appropriate group homes be established in urban areas by Aboriginal women's organizations where urban Aboriginal women can serve any term of incarceration to which they may be sentenced, with access to programs of recovery from substance abuse, recovery from victimization and dependency, academic upgrading and training, and parenting skills.

- Aboriginal women living in isolated or rural communities be held in open custody facilities in their home communities. Such women would be free to attend to their families, to work or to obtain education during the day, to attend counselling sessions in the evenings, and remain in the facility each night until their sentence is served.

- The Milner Ridge Correctional Centre be converted to a co-correctional institution as a pilot project.

- When facilities for men and women are established near northern communities, Aboriginal women from the North be allowed to serve their sentence in the facility nearest to their home community.

- Arrangements be made for children to have frequent visits with their mother.

- Child and family service agencies provide necessary support to Aboriginal mothers in jail and their children to ensure that the family is kept together.

- Where children need to be taken into care following the incarceration of an Aboriginal mother, child and family service agencies make culturally appropriate foster arrangements for the children of such inmates.

Parole and Post-Release Issues

When a woman sentenced to prison has done her time and is released, in many cases she has no place to go, no job, and few if any qualifications for getting one.[38]

At the present time, there are virtually no facilities which provide housing specifically for female parolees, and no halfway houses designed solely for Aboriginal parolees. An official of the Ma Mawi Chi Itata Centre told us that the agency has great difficulty in maintaining contact with female parolees. She recommended that a suitable home be established to provide shelter and programs for between 10–12 female parolees and their children at any one time.

In her view, the program which best serves Aboriginal women is the Native Women's Transition Centre, a facility designed to provide long-term assistance for Aboriginal women relocating to the city and who experience problems in doing so. However, there is a great demand for this program and, consequently, space frequently is unavailable.

The Salvation Army, the St. Norbert Foundation and the United Church Half-Way Homes will accept applications from Aboriginal women parolees, but no beds are set aside for them, and these organizations are not Aboriginal. Because these facilities, as well as Native Clan's Regina House, primarily provide services to male parolees, it is frequently not appropriate to place a woman in them. This is especially true if, as is often the case, the woman has been in abusive relationships in the past.

In addition, little or no support is provided to assist female offenders to re-establish relationships with their families, and to establish a normal home life.

WE RECOMMEND THAT:

- Aboriginal women be appointed to the National Parole Board.

- Funding be provided to Aboriginal women to establish a halfway house for Aboriginal female inmates.

- The National Parole Board give direction that release plans for female inmates with children pay close attention to the need for family reintegration, and in particular to living and income security arrangements required for family reintegration. We further recommend that the federal and provincial governments ensure that income and housing support programs be developed for released female offenders with young children, designed to facilitate family reintegration.

Conclusion

Several themes were presented to us regarding Aboriginal women and the criminal justice system. There was an overall picture presented of racism, sexism and violence against Aboriginal women in Aboriginal communities, in wider society and in the justice system. There is a need to address the underlying causes of Aboriginal women coming into conflict with the law.

As the victims of childhood sexual abuse and adult domestic violence, they have borne the brunt of the breakdown of social controls within Aboriginal societies. There was substantial support for an entirely new system, to break the cycle of abuse and to restore Aboriginal methods of healing designed to return balance to the community, rather than punish the offender.

We have been impressed with the models of holistic healing that Aboriginal people are developing and putting into practice. The spiritual needs of the individual are considered foremost, with emotional, physical and intellectual support given as required. We were especially impressed with the Hollow Water Resource Group, where four communities work together to give support for victims and offenders of sexual abuse and family violence.

Aboriginal women come to the justice system with unique problems that arise from, or are related to, the fact that they face double discrimination in their lives. It is important that Aboriginal women be given positions of responsibility in the justice system. They should be involved as clerks, administrators, lawyers, judges, and so forth. They should be involved in the same way as men in law enforcement, in the administration of the courts, as probation officers and parole officers, and in the legal profession. Aboriginal women should be involved in substantial numbers in the RCMP and the City police forces, as well as in Aboriginal police forces. There is also a need for Aboriginal child welfare workers. Training programs will have to be developed and large numbers of Aboriginal women will have to be attracted to this important work.

We recommend elsewhere in this report that a number of positions in the legal system should be created in Aboriginal communities. We believe it is important that an equal number of men and women are hired to fill these positions. In the appointment of peacemakers and sentencing panels, it is important that both men and women be represented in each community. In order to accomplish this, we believe that enforceable employment equity plans will have to be developed and implemented.

We recommend that women be involved in the implementation of our recommendations, and that they be represented on the various administrative bodies that will become necessary.

While the role of Aboriginal women in Aboriginal society is not well understood in non-Aboriginal circles, we have been told, and accept, that a resumption of their traditional roles is the key to putting an end to Aboriginal female mistreatment.

The immediate need is for Aboriginal women to begin to heal from the decades of denigration they have experienced. But the ultimate objective is to encourage and assist Aboriginal women to regain and occupy their rightful place as equal partners in Aboriginal society.

We were moved by the situation of Aboriginal women. They suffer double discrimination: as women and as Aboriginal people; as victims and as offenders. We were convinced by arguments of Aboriginal women that a restoration of their traditional responsibility and position of equality in the family and community holds the key to resolving many of the problems we have identified.

CHAPTER 14

CHILD WELFARE

Introduction

Aboriginal people appearing before this Inquiry have repeatedly expressed their concern that any overhaul of the justice system in Manitoba must also include a re-examination of the child welfare system. They see the child welfare and justice systems as being interconnected and interwoven. To them, the child welfare system is but one more "outside" institution that disrupts their lives and societies.

The intrusion by child welfare authorities in the past has been paternalistic and colonial in nature, condescending and demeaning in fact, and often insensitive and brutal to Aboriginal people. Aboriginal children have been taken from their families, communities and societies, first by the residential school system and later by the child welfare system. Both systems have left Aboriginal people and their societies severely damaged.

If Aboriginal people are correct, and we believe they are, part of the reason for the high numbers of Aboriginal people in correctional facilities is the fact that Aboriginal people still do not fully control their own lives and destinies, or the lives of their own children. Aboriginal people must have more control over the ways in which their children are raised, taught and protected.

Failing this, we are convinced we will see more, not fewer, Aboriginal people in our correctional facilities in the future. We will see more young Aboriginal people falling into a pattern that is becoming all too familiar. It takes them from institution to institution, from foster home to young offender facility and, finally, on to adult jails. As Oscar Lathlin, the then chief of The Pas Band, asked our Inquiry, "Is the current system conditioning our young for lives in institutions and not in society?"

The implications of these patterns are most obvious to people in Aboriginal communities. People there worry because they know their young people make up a significant proportion of their populations today. The numbers of young people in these communities are increasing at a rate far higher than that of the general population. Aboriginal people worry about the future survival of their languages, cultures and societies if yet another generation is swept into institutions and away from their communities.

It is for these and many other reasons that we have made a careful examination of the child welfare system. We felt it necessary because:

- We feel many of the problems Aboriginal people face with the criminal justice system today have roots in the history of government-Aboriginal relations. No analysis of the justice system can be complete without understanding the devastating effect these relations, guided by government policies, have had on Aboriginal families. For many Aboriginal societies, existing child welfare practices have ranked as a major destructive force to their families, communities and cultures.

- Some people have suggested that the child welfare and criminal justice systems are distinct and should function completely independently of each other. We do not agree. We believe many of the reasons why the numbers of Aboriginal people are so disproportionately high in the child welfare system are the same as the reasons why they are so over-represented in the criminal justice system. "Clients" of one system frequently become "clients" of the other system. It would be impossible to present a complete picture of the criminal justice system, and the youth justice system, without also analysing the field of child and family services.

- The reforms we advocate, particularly in the youth justice area, involve the breaking down of artificial barriers between the criminal justice and child welfare systems. These systems, we believe, must work much more closely together. The needs and problems of Aboriginal families and communities are intertwined, and we feel we cannot separate them completely or relegate them to one system or the other.

- The available evidence indicates that the apprehension of Aboriginal children by the child welfare system tends to set a pattern of multiple foster home placements. The evidence also indicates this pattern often leads the children into young offender institutions and, ultimately, to "graduate" to the adult correctional system. Aboriginal families, communities and their leaders are rightly concerned about these patterns, and about their effects on the future of their children's lives and of their communities.

- There has been some remarkable progress in the child welfare system as Aboriginal people have assumed more control over the lives and well-being of their children in their communities. The criminal justice system must move in a similar direction if it hopes to achieve similar success.

- The numbers of Aboriginal children will continue to increase at a rate exceeding that of the general population. Therefore, there is every indication that child and family services will play an increasingly important role in Aboriginal communities in the future.

- Finally, we believe it is essential to review the child welfare system in urban centres, particularly in Winnipeg, where there continue to be significant problems for Aboriginal persons requiring services. We will identify some of these problems and offer suggestions to make this system more effective.

Child Welfare and Education:
An Historical Overview of Government-Aboriginal Relations

For some time, governments have undertaken to serve neglected children by taking them into their care or by helping the families of these children through what we now call child welfare services. Services may include family counselling, substance abuse counselling, assistance to an unmarried parent, or taking the child away from a disrupted home or family and placing the child in a foster home, a group home or with a new family, through adoption. In Canada, each province is responsible for developing and maintaining its own child welfare system. Each province gets financial help from the federal government under the Canada Assistance Plan, which pays approximately half the costs of these programs.

At first glance, this system appears to be one most people would support and encourage. It is certainly a far cry from the way Western or European societies have treated children in the past. Historically, the phrase "a man's home is his castle" meant just that. Society took a very dim view of interfering with the manner in which the head of a household treated his children. In ancient Rome, a father had "complete authority over his children, including the legal authority to sell them into slavery or even put them to death."[1]

Over time, a father's power over his children was tempered to a limited right of "reasonable chastisement," although this continued to mean a father could beat his children and even sell them into apprenticeship.[2] Eventually, there were laws that forbade parents from killing or maiming their children or failing to provide them with the necessities of life. Nevertheless, children were still subject to abuse and forced labour in mines and factories.

Society's attitudes toward children began to change when social reformers became increasingly concerned at the plight of the working poor and, in particular, with the way children were treated. In the latter part of the 1800s, they pressured governments to pass laws to make the lives of children better. Private children's aid societies formed with the intent of caring for abused, abandoned or neglected children. Governments passed child labour laws and provided for public school systems. For the first time, governments adopted a policy allowing for the intervention by child care workers to protect the life of a child in extreme situations.[3] These laws and policies make up the foundation of the modern child welfare system.

Most of these developments, however, passed by unnoticed in Aboriginal communities and reserves. The history of child welfare in these communities developed separately and much differently from the way it did in the rest of society.

Special Treatment for Aboriginal Children
The Residential School System

Since the time of earliest contact, Aboriginal people and European settlers have seen things from vastly divergent points of view, because their attitudes and philosophies differed. The interaction of the two groups has been characterized as one of "cooperation and conflict but, more importantly, by misconceptions and contradictions."[4] One of the first, and perhaps the most enduring, of these misconceptions was that:

> Europeans assumed the superiority of their culture over that of any Aboriginal peoples. Out of that misconception grew the European conviction that in order for the Indians to survive, they would have to be assimilated into the European social order.[5]

At first, these differences had minimal impact upon most Aboriginal people. The missionaries tried to convert Aboriginal people and to mould them into their religious ideal, often with mixed results.

> The Indians ... had no more idea of religious authority, as opposed to personal beliefs, than they had of a coercive political hierarchy. The individual freedom that was fundamental to Indian culture ruled out both the idea of heresy and of subordinating one's will to priestly guidance. The concept of authority and the respect for it that was inculcated into all civilized peoples provided the missionary and the civilized non-Christian with a common basis of understanding that was totally lacking between the missionary and the Indians of Eastern Canada. The fundamental problem that the Recollets saw impeding their work was that the Indians were too 'primitive' to be converted. From this they drew the devastatingly simple conclusion that if they were to convert the Indians they had first to find ways of 'civilizing' them.[6]

This was an impossible task as long as Aboriginal people continued to live in vibrant, self-sufficient communities often far removed from the missionaries' influence. However, this did not prevent the missionaries from forming opinions about the ways Aboriginal people raised and taught their children, or from laying the foundation for future misconceptions of Aboriginal child-rearing methods.

> In view of current ideas about child-rearing, it is interesting to reflect that no aspect of behavior shocked the French more than their refusal to use physical

punishment to discipline their children. On general principles, the Huron considered it wrong to coerce or humiliate an individual publicly. To their own way of thinking, a child was an individual with his or her own needs and rights rather than something amorphous that must be molded into shape. The Huron feared a child who was unduly humiliated, like an adult, might be driven to commit suicide.[7]

Aboriginal parents taught their children

... to assume adult roles in an atmosphere of warmth and affection. Learning emphasized such values as respect for all living things, sharing, self-reliance, individual responsibility, and proper conduct. Children also had to learn how to utilize the environment most effectively for economic survival. Integral to all aspects of the education of the young was the spiritual, and events in the life-cycle from birth to death were marked with ceremonies stressing the individual's link to the spiritual and sacred. Cultural continuity was thus ensured.[8]

The early missionaries also condemned Aboriginal child-rearing methods as being negligent, irresponsible and "uncivilized." This stereotype was to endure even after Aboriginal people had lost much of their independence and "in the point of view of the European, the Indian became irrelevant."[9] From then on, the relationship between Aboriginal people and Europeans became even more one-sided and paternalistic. Aboriginal people were reduced to being "wards of the state."[10] All relevant decision-making power on financial, social or political matters, and even education, came to rest in the hands of the federal government. Eventually, the cause of "civilizing" Aboriginal people to European cultures and values evolved into the government policy of "assimilation," and education became "the primary vehicle in the civilization and advancement of the Indian race."[11]

The federal government had little previous experience in "civilizing" Aboriginal people so it turned to the United States for an example. It sent Nicholas F. Davin to study the Americans' "aggressive civilization policy,"[12] based on sending Indian children to large, racially segregated, industrial schools. Davin was convinced the Americans were correct in their approach and the only way to "civilize" Aboriginal people was to remove them from the disruptive influences of the parents and the community. His final comment in the report to Ottawa was representative of attitudes of the time that "... if anything is to be done with the Indian, we must catch him very young."[13]

The federal government delegated the job of "civilizing" and "educating" Aboriginal people in Canada to religious organizations and churches. It encouraged the opening of large, industrial residential schools far from reserves and, later, of boarding schools for younger children nearer to their homes. There, every aspect of European life, from dress and behaviour to religion and language, was impressed upon the Aboriginal children. The belief was that Indians were a vanishing race and their only hope of surviving was to assimilate. Their uncivilized and pagan ways would be replaced by good Christian values.

The residential school system was a conscious, deliberate and often brutal attempt to force Aboriginal people to assimilate into mainstream society, mostly by forcing the children away from their languages, cultures and societies. In 1920, during debates in the House of Commons on planned changes to the *Indian Act*, Duncan Campbell Scott, the Deputy Superintendent of Indian Affairs, left no doubt about the federal government's aims:

> Our object is to continue until there is not a single Indian in Canada that has not been absorbed into the body politic and there is no Indian question, and no Indian department, that is the whole object of this Bill.[14]

The experience of residential schools is one shared by many Aboriginal people all across Canada. That experience was marked by emotional, physical and sexual abuse, social and spiritual deprivation, and substandard education. "Even as assimilation was stated as the goal of education for Native people," one researcher wrote, "the assimilation was to take place under conditions which would cause no threat to the surrounding business and farming community."[15] Few Aboriginal people achieved more than a grade five level of education.

The main goal of residential schools and the assimilation policy, however, was not further education, but, rather, to remove Aboriginal children from the influences of their parents and communities, and to rid them of their languages and cultures. The methods, as one former residential school student explained, often were brutally effective:

> The elimination of language has always been a primary stage in a process of cultural genocide. This was the primary function of the residential school. My father, who attended Alberni Indian Residential School for four years in the twenties, was physically tortured by his teachers for speaking Tseshaht: they pushed sewing needles through his tongue, a routine punishment for language offenders.... The needle tortures suffered by my father affected all my family (I have six brothers and six sisters). My Dad's attitude became 'why teach my children Indian if they are going to be punished for speaking it?' so he would not allow my mother to speak Indian to us in his presence. I never learned how to speak my own language. I am now, therefore, truly a 'dumb Indian'.[16]

After the Second World War, the federal government began to reconsider its assimilation policy. It wanted a more effective means of accomplishing the ultimate aims of the policy. This coincided with yet another revamping of the *Indian Act* and another set of hearings at the House of Commons. This also allowed another famous Canadian, noted anthropologist Diamond Jenness, to unveil his "Plan for Liquidating Canada's Indian Problems Within 25 Years." Jenness proposed abolishing Indian reserves, scrapping the treaties and integrating Indian students into the public school system. For the time being, the federal government shelved most of Jenness' proposals. It did, however, heed his suggestion to change the *Indian Act* to allow Indian children to be enrolled in public schools. This event signalled "the beginning of the end for many residential schools."[17]

The effects upon Aboriginal societies of the federal government's residential school system, and its policy of assimilation, have been astounding. Residential schools denigrated Aboriginal cultures, customs and religions, and disrupted the traditional practices of Aboriginal child-rearing and education. They tore apart families and extended families, leaving the children straddling two worlds, the European one and that of their own Aboriginal societies, but belonging to neither. These policies have caused a wound to fester in Aboriginal communities that has left them diminished to this day. In testimony to our Inquiry, Janet Ross said:

> I'd like to begin at the boarding school. The boarding school is where the alienation began. Children were placed there, plucked out of their homes. The bond between parents and children was fragmented severely—some lost forever. Some searched for the love between parent and child endlessly, searching for it in other ways, never to be restored. The boarding schools taught us violence. Violence was emphasized through physical, corporal punishment, strappings, beatings, bruising and control. We learned to understand that this was power and control.

> I remember being very confused when someone told me that my natural mother had died. Hence growing up for me not knowing whether my mother was really mine always created some more confusion. I searched for that love in [foster] parents, but that bond had been broken; you felt that it just wasn't there. The boarding schools were extremely influential towards our poor self-image and low self-esteem, because we were continuously put down by the use of text books portraying negative images of Indian people.

The loss of successive generations of children to residential schools, the destruction of Aboriginal economic bases, the decimation of their populations through diseases and the increasing dependence on government welfare have led to social chaos. This manifests itself in Aboriginal communities through staggering poverty rates, high unemployment rates, high suicide rates, lower education levels, high rates of alcoholism and high rates of crime. In individuals, the legacy of the residential schools has been lowered self-esteem, confusion of self-identity and cultural identity, and a distrust of, and antagonism toward, authority.

The residential school experience also resulted in a breakdown in traditional Aboriginal methods of teaching child-rearing and parenting. Entire families once took part in the raising of children. Young parents, like young parents everywhere, learned how to raise their children from their own parents, by example. Traditionally, they also drew upon the examples and advice of their extended families, their grandparents, uncles, aunts and siblings. The residential schools made this impossible. Without that example, many Aboriginal parents today feel that they have never learned how to raise their own children.

Aboriginal communities have not yet recovered from the damage caused by the residential schools. It is only in recent times that children are again being taught close to home. For the first time in over 100 years, many families are experiencing a generation of children who live with parents until their teens. The readjustment to this new situation has been difficult for both the parents and their children. The current generation of parents does not even have its own experiences as children growing up in a unified family upon which to draw.

The damage done by these schools is still evident today, as Aboriginal people struggle to recapture their cultural practices and beliefs. The return of self-identity and self-esteem is a slow process. Perhaps, if left alone, this social confusion might have corrected itself to some extent, once children returned to their communities. But, as we will see, there was another dramatic intrusion into their lives after the Second World War.

The Child Welfare System

The intrusion by state-run child welfare programs into the lives of Aboriginal children and families did not come about until quite recently, despite the devastating effects which colonization had wreaked on their communities and societies for more than a century. The modern child welfare system, for the most part, is a post-Second World War phenomenon. As one researcher has noted:

> Forty years ago, Native people were much more isolated from the mainstream of Canadian life than they now are. They were less likely to move from reserve and remote communities into urban areas and were consequently, less visible. Provincial child welfare departments and children's aid societies did not operate to any extent on reserves, and the number of Native children in the care of child welfare officials was minimal. As a result, the issue of child welfare and Native Peoples was of little concern or interest.

> That is not to suggest, however, that some Native children were not in need of alternative care. On reserves, such children would sometimes be taken in and looked after by members of their extended family, which included aunts, uncles and grandparents. In some cases, the Indian agent, an employee of the federal government who supervised the activities on reserves, would place a child with another family on the reserve. Often they were simply sent to live in Indian residential schools.[18]

However, the end of the Second World War brought about a number of new developments. There was a tremendous proliferation of government-operated and funded social services. These services, once concentrated in urban centres, were increasingly extended to more rural and northern communities, including Aboriginal communities.

This was mirrored by a corresponding proliferation in the new field of professional social work. This profession was anxious to carve a niche for itself. More importantly, the profession provided a means by which the standards of the dominant society could be used to judge traditional Aboriginal family and child care practices. At the same time,

Aboriginal peoples became much more visible because of increased mobility and, in particular, because of their massive migration to urban centres in search of jobs, an education or a better life. This increased the contacts between Aboriginal people and the dominant society, and led to heightened awareness of the dire social and economic conditions in Aboriginal communities.

One of the first alarms about living conditions on reserves was sounded in 1947 by the Canadian Welfare Council and the Canadian Association of Social Workers.[19] These groups presented a brief to a joint parliamentary committee examining possible changes to the federal *Indian Act*. The brief described living conditions as inadequate and the services delivered to Aboriginal communities as incompatible with similar services provided to non-Aboriginal communities.

In considering Indian adoptions and the role of the Indian agent, the brief stated that "the practice of adopting Indian children is loosely conceived and executed and is usually devoid of the careful legal and social protection afforded to white children."[20] As "wards" of the federal government, "Indian children who are neglected lack the protection afforded under social legislation available to white children in the community."[21] The council's submission also condemned the practice of sending Aboriginal children to residential schools.

In the minds of many experts of the day, the solution to these problems was obvious. They felt existing provincial child welfare programs should be extended to include federal Indian reserves, since the child welfare services provided by the Department of Indian Affairs were very limited or nonexistent. However, there were several problems with this apparently obvious solution.

The federal government had exclusive constitutional authority over "Indians and lands reserved for Indians" under s. 91(24) of the *British North America Act* of 1867. The *Indian Act* reinforced this exclusive federal jurisdiction. To complicate matters, at that time the federal government had no cost-sharing agreement with the provinces for social services, including child welfare programs, and it was reluctant to carry the costs of such programs itself.

Provincial governments, which were under pressure to extend their jurisdiction in certain areas such as education, policing and social services, including child welfare, were reluctant to extend their responsibilities without federal funding. In the end, neither level of government was prepared to provide child welfare to Indians living on- or off-reserve. This jurisdictional wrangling left Indians caught in a legal no-man's land, with devastating results for their children.

In 1951 the federal government amended s. 88 of the *Indian Act* to allow "all laws of general application ... in force in any province" to apply as well to Indians both on- and off-reserve.[22] This included child welfare programs. Unfortunately, while the federal government changed the law, it did not provide any additional money to help pay for these new provincial responsibilities. The result was a patchwork of provincial child welfare services to reserves: some agencies in some provinces extended some services to some reserves, some extended none, and some acted to apprehend children only when they considered them to be in a "life or death" situation.

During the 1960s, public and political attention was once again focussed on the living conditions endured by Aboriginal people on reserves and, specifically, on the welfare of Aboriginal children. In 1966 the federal Department of Indian Affairs and Northern Development completed an ambitious survey detailing all aspects of life for Canada's Aboriginal peoples living on reserves. It was called the Hawthorn Report, after its editor. In respect to child welfare services, the report found that "the situation varies from unsatisfactory to appalling."[23]

In the same year, the federal government, attempting once again to expand existing child welfare services to Aboriginal communities, signed an agreement with the provinces to share the costs of extending social services under the Canada Assistance Plan. No Aboriginal people or organizations were consulted about these changes, and there was no commitment to preserve Aboriginal culture or to provide for local Aboriginal control over child welfare services. These services were to be delivered by non-Aboriginal agencies employing non-Aboriginal social workers.

Aboriginal Peoples and the Child Welfare System in Manitoba

The history of Aboriginal child welfare in Manitoba closely parallels the situation across the country. During the late 1970s and 1980s, however, the Manitoba government made a number of changes to its child welfare system in order to provide Aboriginal communities with better and more humane services through greater local control.

Like other provinces, Manitoba had passed various laws over the years, dealing with child welfare matters. In 1887, for example, Manitoba passed the *Apprentices and Minors Act* (S.M. 1877, c. 40), and established a superintendent of neglected and dependent children. The next year, the *Act Respecting Infants* (S.M. 1878, c. 39) was passed. In 1895 the *Humane Societies Act* was amended to provide for the establishment of societies which served children, as well as animals. In 1898 *An Act for the Better Protection of Neglected and Dependent Children* (S.M. 1898, c. 6) was passed, in which provision for the formal establishment of a Children's Aid Society was made. In the same year, the Children's Aid Society of Winnipeg was established. In 1922 Manitoba introduced the *Child Welfare Act.* (S.M. 1922, c. 2). Following the introduction of this legislation, the first foster homes were established and, in the 1950s, the first group homes.

The child welfare system had only a limited impact on Aboriginal people before the 1950s and the accompanying government-sponsored boom in social service programs. However, as we have seen, this changed as two things occurred coincidentally. First, there was a massive migration by Aboriginal people into southern and urban areas. Second, there was an expansion into the North of better communication and transportation, and industrial development. With this expansion came southern bureaucracy. Aboriginal and non-Aboriginal people were no longer separated by vast distances or artificial barriers, such as reserve boundaries. To its astonishment and dismay, the latter group quickly learned of the appalling inequities which affected all aspects of the lives of Aboriginal people. Unfortunately, its responses only worsened the situation.

The "Sixties Scoop"

Before the mid-1960s, there was no organized way to provide child welfare services to Aboriginal peoples in Manitoba living on reserves. Then, in 1966 the federal government and the government of Manitoba entered into an agreement that provided for the existing Children's Aid Societies of Central, Eastern and Western Manitoba to deliver child welfare services to 14 bands in southern Manitoba. Three-quarters of the bands in Manitoba were not covered by this arrangement. As in the past, the northern bands continued to receive some services from the Department of Indian Affairs, but provincial child welfare authorities would intervene only in emergency or "life and death" situations.

This expansion of child welfare services to Aboriginal communities, which took place across Canada at this time, left a profound and negative impact on these communities. As the Canadian Council on Social Development documented:

In 1955, there were 3,433 children in the care of B.C.'s child welfare branch. Of that number it was estimated that 29 children, or less than 1 percent of the total, were of Indian ancestry. By 1964, however, 1,446 children in care in B.C. were of Indian extraction. That number represented 34.2 percent of all children in care. Within ten years, in other words, the representation of Native children in B.C.'s child welfare system had jumped from almost nil to a third. It was a pattern being repeated in other parts of Canada as well. [24]

In most provinces, these child welfare services were never provided in any kind of meaningful or culturally appropriate way. Instead of the counselling of families, or consultation with the community about alternatives to apprehending the child, the apprehension of Aboriginal children became the standard operating procedure with child welfare authorities in most provinces.

In Manitoba, the child welfare system "protected" many Aboriginal children by taking them away from their families and placing them for adoption with non-Aboriginal families. This came to be known as the "Sixties Scoop," but it continued into the 1980s. Although the flaws in this approach would only become evident to most of society later, Aboriginal people immediately condemned the practice. As Anthony Wood of God's River told our Inquiry:

There was no publicity for years and years about the brutalization of our families and children by the larger Canadian society. Kidnapping was called placement in foster homes. Exporting Aboriginal children to the U.S. was called preparing Indian children for the future. Parents who were heartbroken by the destruction of their families were written off as incompetent people.

The child welfare system was doing essentially the same thing with Aboriginal children that the residential schools had done. It removed Aboriginal children from their families, communities and cultures, and placed them in mainstream society. Child welfare workers removed Aboriginal children from their families and communities because they felt the best homes for the children were not Aboriginal homes. The ideal home would instil the values and lifestyles with which the child welfare workers themselves were familiar: white, middle-class homes in white, middle-class neighbourhoods. Aboriginal communities and Aboriginal parents and families were deemed to be "unfit." As a result, between 1971 and 1981 alone, over 3,400 Aboriginal children were shipped away to adoptive parents in other societies, and sometimes in other countries.[25]

> Gradually, as education ceased to function as the institutional agent of colonization, the child welfare system took its place. It could continue to remove Native children from their parents, devalue Native custom and traditions in the process, but still act "in the best interests of the child." Those who hold to this view argue that the Sixties Scoop was not coincidental; it was a consequence of fewer Indian children being sent to residential school and of the child welfare system emerging as the new method of colonization.[26]

As part of its comprehensive survey of Aboriginal child welfare policies and procedures, in 1983 the Canadian Council on Social Development compiled a statistical overview of Aboriginal children in the care of child welfare authorities across Canada. The director of the project, Patrick Johnston, found that Aboriginal children were highly over-represented in the child welfare system. They represented 40–50% of children in care in the province of Alberta, 60–70% of children in care in Saskatchewan and some 50–60% of children in care in Manitoba. Johnston estimated that, across Canada, Aboriginal children were 4.5 times more likely than non-Aboriginal children to be in the care of child welfare authorities. Similar findings have been reported by other experts.

What began in the 1960s, with very few exceptions, carried on through the 1970s and 1980s. Patrick Johnston, in examining the history of Aboriginal children's involvement with the child welfare system, wrote:

> In retrospect, the wholesale apprehension of Native children during the Sixties Scoop appears to have been a terrible mistake. While some individual children may have benefitted, many did not. Nor did their families. And Native culture suffered one more of many severe blows. Unfortunately, the damage is still being done. While attitudes may have changed to some extent since the Sixties, Native children continue to be represented in the child welfare system at a much greater rate than non-native children.[27]

These unprecedented levels of apprehensions led Aboriginal communities in the 1970s to put intense pressure on government to stop what, in their view, amounted to cultural genocide.

The Indian Child Welfare Sub-Committee

In 1977, in recognition of the serious problems that existed in delivering child welfare services to Aboriginal peoples, the federal and provincial governments established a tripartite working committee on Aboriginal child welfare. The committee was chaired by Caroll Hurd, from the provincial department of Intergovernmental Relations, with representatives from the Manitoba Indian Brotherhood, the provincial Department of Health and Social Development, and the federal departments of Indian Affairs and Health and Welfare. The Indian Child Welfare Sub-Committee, as it became known, completed its work in 1980. It called for sweeping reforms to the existing child welfare system to serve Aboriginal people better. In its final report, the subcommittee put the challenge this way:

> The movement toward the delivery of child welfare services to Indian people by Indian people graphically illustrates and establishes the principle *that Indian people must be involved at all levels and in all aspects of child welfare services.*[28] [Italics in original]

The subcommittee determined that the child welfare needs of Aboriginal people were a matter of urgent and immediate priority. The committee quoted the statement of Provincial Court Judge Garson, now the Deputy Minister of the Department of Justice, as typifying the disorganized state of services:

> The stark reality of the present situation ... is that the Treaty Indian is caught in a political, financial and legal limbo with both senior governments attempting to disclaim responsibility for the delivery of social and child welfare services, with the not unsurprising result that the Treaty Indian fails to get the services except in life threatening situations.... Such a denial of services, for whatever reasons, can only be termed discriminatory to the Treaty Indian.[29]

The Indian Child Welfare Sub-Committee soon learned it had to deal with certain realities and establish certain principles when dealing with Aboriginal people. It had to recognize that registered or status Indians have a unique status as laid out in the treaties, the *Indian Act* and the *British North America Act* of 1867. It had to realize that, in Aboriginal communities, the extended family is the first resource for the nurturing and the protection of children. It also determined some families would need support in their parenting role and that children, for a variety of reasons, might need substitute care.[30]

The subcommittee came quickly to the realization that, as a result of culture, geography and history, Indian people were in a unique situation, with needs peculiar to their special legal, political and social circumstances. One of the foremost issues identified by both Aboriginal people and the subcommittee was the need to preserve Indian identity, in terms of language and culture, within the framework of tribes, bands, communities, extended families and individuals.[31] Finally, the subcommittee determined that any child welfare service must include and involve Indian people.

The subcommittee examined the types of services that were required and recommended that a full range of community-based child welfare services be developed. It also recommended that these services include child care resources, services to single parents, adoption, and juvenile probation services.

The subcommittee considered different ways the governments and Aboriginal groups should deliver these programs. It decided that there needed to be a common legal base throughout the province, integrating the statutory provisions for all family-related services to registered Indians in Manitoba. It recommended the development of regional child welfare agencies for Indian reserves controlled by band chiefs and councils, with at least one Aboriginal staff member living in the community and supported by ongoing training, education, professional supervision, guidance and assistance. The report pointed out the need for clear management and administrative authority. There would be a local board or committee of residents that would function as an advisory, monitoring, evaluative and planning group, and which would be a liaison and communication channel between the chief and council and its staff. The board or committee might represent several communities. Some management functions might be included.[32]

The chief and council on a reserve were to play a unique role, which was to be recognized and respected through cooperative planning and action. A formal service was to be provided as soon as possible to all Aboriginal communities. Funding was to be based on such variables as population considerations, vulnerability of target populations, individual developmental needs, geographic considerations, degree of social and economic development of the local area, and the existing service structure, as well as accessibility to wider resources. The implementation of these programs needed to be flexible, and priority needed to be given to developing local or regional homes or facilities to ensure that children would be placed in their cultural or geographic area whenever possible.

These findings and recommendations proved to be important in laying the foundation for a series of tripartite agreements between Aboriginal groups and the Manitoba and federal governments.

Manitoba's Tripartite Agreements

Owing to the influences we have outlined already, Indian child welfare agencies began to develop at a rapid pace in the late 1970s and throughout the 1980s. By 1980, when the Indian Child Welfare Sub-Committee released its report, three bands and two area tribal councils were running their own child welfare services.

In 1976 the Fort Alexander Band signed an agreement with the Department of Indian Affairs and employed a director and three trainee social workers. That same year, The Pas Band hired a social worker for its new child and family service. The next year, 1977, the Peguis Band followed suit and set up a Child Care Committee. In 1979 the Island Lake Tribal Council, representing the bands of Garden Hill, St. Theresa Point, Wasagamack and Red Sucker Lake, hired a preventive services worker to serve those bands and to staff its Preventive Services Committee. Also in 1979, the Dakota Ojibway Tribal Council hired a social worker to work with existing child welfare agencies. For all these bands and tribal councils, the eventual aim was to take over complete control of all social services delivered to their communities, with child and family services as a first step. The 1980 report of the Indian Child Welfare Sub-Committee concluded that:

> The current state of affairs is unacceptable to both Indian people and to those professionals involved in the area of child welfare as it is fragmented, discriminatory and at the mercy of political and jurisdictional disputes.[33]

The report set the stage for negotiations between the federal and provincial governments and the Manitoba Indian Brotherhood, which represented the 49 Indian bands in the province.

The Manitoba Indian Brotherhood wanted 46 children's service workers at the band level and six resource support workers at the tribal council level. These would be in addition to the 15 child and family workers already working for the bands, and would be paid for by the Department of Indian Affairs. The agreement could be used to set up specific Aboriginal agencies that then could provide a full range of child welfare programs on reserves. Aboriginal communities could control these services and programs. The Aboriginal communities were unanimous in wanting some way of repatriating Aboriginal children already adopted by non-Aboriginal families, of helping families remain together, and of preventing further family breakdowns that could provoke an increase in the apprehension of their children.

Almost immediately, however, there were political problems with these negotiations. Most of the northern bands distrusted both the involvement of the provincial government and the willingness of the federal government to hand over jurisdictional responsibility for Indians on reserves to the Province. Their suspicion was that Ottawa would unload its legal responsibilities for Indians piecemeal, first with child welfare and later with some other areas of responsibility. As one researcher pointed out:

> The suspicion of Indian people may very well be justified.... Quite likely, the Manitoba agreement has been so strongly supported by the federal government because it supports the federal position of gradual transference of responsibility to the provinces.[34]

As well, Aboriginal people still bitterly remembered the 1969 White Paper, which clarified the federal government's preferred Indian policy in Canada. In effect, it advocated abolishing the legal rights of Indians, scrapping the reserves system, unilaterally abrogating the treaties with Indians, and removing any special rights Aboriginal people might have derived from specific legislation such as the *Indian Act.* Still, Aboriginal people faced tremendous problems in their home communities and there was great pressure to find some means of providing for the welfare of their children. However, the resulting tripartite agreement split the Manitoba Indian Brotherhood. The northern bands withdrew to form the Manitoba Keewatinowi Okimakinak, or MKO. The southern bands became the Four Nations Confederacy, or FNC.

The Kimelman Inquiry

Aboriginal people were particularly disturbed by the number of Aboriginal children who were being adopted by people who lived outside the country. By 1982 Manitoba was the only province that still allowed adoptions outside Canada. According to statistics for Manitoba, 38% of Indian adoptions and 17% of Metis adoptions in 1981 were placements in the United States.[35] Between 1971 and 1981, 70–80% of Manitoba's Aboriginal adoptions were in non-Aboriginal homes. Aboriginal leaders strenuously objected to these practices and accused the government of "selling babies" and committing "cultural genocide." In our hearings in Camperville, David Chartrand said:

You adopt a Metis child into a white community and you expect it to work? You take his total culture away from him, his heritage and you expect it to work? When I was going to school, an all white school, and this was a time that Indians didn't have respect in the States, and that is what they considered me, I really had a tough time in school.

They expected us all to work out, to come out beautiful. I was supposed to come out with a scholarship and become a lawyer or a doctor. This is what they thought. Well, I sure fooled them. I came back and I didn't have nothing to show for it. I have nothing but hate. Hate for the system, the welfare system, the child and family services system that has put me in this situation as well as other people.

As the scope of the export of children became more widely known, the reaction of Aboriginal people was one of anger and outrage. Aboriginal leaders linked the child welfare system to the residential school system and the policy of assimilation. They made no distinction between deliberate or unintentional adherence to these policies. To them, it was all part of one ongoing attack by outside authorities, first to destroy their culture and then to absorb them. Glenda Richards of Camperville told our Inquiry:

How can we expect an end to racism and discrimination while this country's school system continues to foster these types of negative images and stereotypes of Indian and Metis people? How can we expect to receive fair treatment and justice from police officers, lawyers and judges who were taught as children in grade school these same negative images and stereotypes.

The provincial government had been stung by the emotional nature of the charges from Aboriginal leaders and battered by an outraged public. In 1982 it ordered a stop to all out-of-province adoptions of Aboriginal children, and appointed Associate Chief Judge Edwin C. Kimelman of the Provincial Court, Family Division, to head an inquiry into the child welfare system and how it affected Aboriginal people. In his final report, *No Quiet Place*, Chief Judge Kimelman concluded that the Aboriginal leaders were right; the child welfare system was guilty of "cultural genocide."

In 1982, no one, except the Indian and Metis people, really believed the reality—that Native children were routinely being shipped to adoption homes in the United States and to other provinces in Canada. Every social worker, every administrator, and every agency or region viewed the situation from a narrow perspective and saw each individual case as an exception, as a case involving extenuating circumstances. No one fully comprehended that 25% of all children placed for adoption were placed outside of Manitoba. No one fully comprehended that virtually all those children were of Native descent. No one comprehended that Manitoba stood alone amongst all provinces in this abysmal practice.[36]

The "Sixties Scoop" stripped hundreds of Aboriginal children in Manitoba from their families and placed them in non-Aboriginal homes. Some reserves experienced extreme losses of children through the actions of child welfare authorities during this time. Aboriginal people complained that the child welfare agencies offered them "only one option—relinquish custody of the child."[37] The child care workers argued that these apprehensions were justified on the basis of "inadequate care," "improper supervision" or "unfit circumstances." Chief Judge Kimelman said the child welfare workers were "overzealous" in applying their authority. He called them "well-intentioned but misguided."

> It would be reassuring if blame could be laid to any single part of the system. The appalling reality is that everyone involved believed they were doing their best and stood firm in their belief that the system was working well. Some administrators took the ostrich approach to child welfare problems—they just did not exist. The miracle is that there were not more children lost in this system run by so many well-intentioned people. The road to hell was paved with good intentions, and the child welfare system was the paving contractor.[38]

There is a theme running through Chief Judge Kimelman's report. It refers constantly to the cultural misconceptions held by child care workers about Aboriginal people and about the way they raised their children. "Cultural bias in the child welfare system," Chief Judge Kimelman concluded, "is practiced at every level from the social worker who works directly with the family, through the lawyers who represent the various parties in a custody case, to the judges who make the final disposition in the case."[39]

However, they were not the only ones to blame.

> All parties have been at fault—federal and provincial governments who failed to resolve their jurisdictional dispute for the care of Treaty Indian children; former Directors of Child Welfare who neglected to build accountability into the system; the child care agencies, both public and private, who failed to examine the results of their policies and practices and who failed to keep accurate statistical data; the native organizations who remained too silent, too long before demanding control of their children.[40]

In the end, Chief Judge Kimelman recommended changes to Manitoba's child welfare legislation so that the determination of a child's "best interests" would include consideration of "the child's cultural and linguistic heritage." He also proposed that agencies increase the involvement of parents in child welfare programming, provide more counselling in the home to prevent children from being separated from their families and stress a more preventive approach to child abuse.[41]

Chief Judge Kimelman advocated a drastic overhaul of the child welfare system in Manitoba. Some of his recommendations included:

- That Aboriginal child and family services agencies be notified whenever an Aboriginal child came into care.

- That policies and standards be implemented that would improve repatriation of Aboriginal children to their own communities and reunify Aboriginal children with their own families.

- That more, and more appropriate, resources be devoted to allow for placement homes in Aboriginal communities.

- That greater support be given to Aboriginal agencies to help them provide services to their off-reserve populations.

- That greater use be made of the extended family.

- That adoption in a non-Aboriginal home be used only as a last resort.

- That cultural awareness training be provided to all those working in Aboriginal communities or with Aboriginal people.

- That there be a more vigorous and stringent court review of cases involving Aboriginal children in care.

- That a program of "affirmative action" hiring be instituted.[42]

Chief Judge Kimelman also recommended that the province hire more Aboriginal child care workers, have child care workers attend cultural awareness or Aboriginal studies programs, and recommend that the Province establish Aboriginal child care agencies. He also recommended a system of adoption subsidies, primarily to provide financial aid to people who otherwise could not consider taking care of an adoptive child. This recommendation was aimed at encouraging members of an extended family to take a child into their care. Most of the recommendations from that report have been implemented. Child welfare services on reserves have been taken out of the hands of non-Aboriginal child welfare workers, and now are provided by Aboriginal child and family agencies. However, Chief Judge Kimelman's major recommendation for the establishment of a Child Protector was not implemented.

A strong rationale for the Office of Child Protector was stated eloquently by the chairperson of another provincial inquiry into family and child welfare. In 1975 Justice Thomas R. Berger was chairperson of the British Columbia Royal Commission on Family and Children's Law. Writing 10 years later, Berger noted the vulnerability of children and families to massive child welfare systems:

> In reality the family is less protected than corporations or trade unions. The law does, of course, recognize, as a matter of public policy, the need for the maintenance and protection of the family. Yet the most profound questions of human rights arise with the family and within family law: questions relating to the custody of children, the obligations of the marriage partners, artificial insemination, and so on.

> Then there is the question of state intervention. When can the state take a child from its parents? When the law perceives people as dependent, it usually endows a guardian appointed by the state with substantial powers over their

lives. Women used to be treated this way. Native people are. And children are.... But children are the most helpless of such special interests....[43]

In cases such as these, there is no one to act as advocate for the parents or the child, to monitor the circumstances of apprehension, to monitor the actions of the child care agency, to ensure the prompt and appropriate disposition of the case or to do follow-up monitoring afterwards. Who is responsible for ensuring the adequate care of children in public and private agencies? Chief Judge Kimelman recommended the establishment of a Child Protector to provide some assurances of quality service. We believe a Child Protector is necessary to ensure the rights of the child and to ensure the proper administration of all child welfare agencies.

WE RECOMMEND THAT:

- The provincial government establish the Office of Child Protector, responsible to the Legislature, as recommended in the Kimelman Report. This office's responsibilities would be, among other things:

  - To ensure that children involved with the child welfare system have their interests and rights protected.

  - To receive and investigate complaints about the manner of treatment of children by child welfare agencies.

We recognize that in implementing this recommendation, the provincial government will have to amend the duties of the Director of Child and Family Services, under s. 4(2) of the *Child and Family Services Act*. We believe that the present legislative framework inappropriately combines the service delivery and administrative function of the director, with weak accountability for some of the appeal and supervisory functions outlined above for the Child Protector. A separation of these two roles is necessary.

Development of Aboriginal Child Welfare Services in Manitoba

There are two main types of child welfare services which agencies provide: mandated and non-mandated. Mandated agencies have the legal authority to apprehend children, while non-mandated agencies do not. Both types of agencies can offer a wide range of child and family support services. The actions taken to establish mandated Aboriginal child welfare agencies in Manitoba were preceded by the development of several local initiatives. The Sagkeeng Child and Family Services of the Fort Alexander Band started providing non-mandated services to the Fort Alexander Band in 1976, when it signed a funding agreement with the federal government. The band formed Sagkeeng in response to serious concerns of its residents about the delivery of social services to the reserve, including child welfare services. However, the reserve got caught in a jurisdictional battle between the federal and provincial governments. The Province did not want to extend its child welfare program to the reserve unless the federal government paid 100% of the costs, the band argued against such a provincial extension of service as an intrusion into its jurisdiction, and the federal government was unwilling to pay for statutory child welfare costs. In the end, Fort Alexander signed a separate agreement with only the federal government in order to deliver its own non-mandated child and family service programs. When Sagkeeng feels that, for the safety of the child, a child needs to be put into care, it calls on an outside agency to work with it. Sagkeeng has developed a fairly good relationship with other agencies, which usually heed its advice on placements. Often, this means a placement with someone in the child's extended family.

In 1981 the Dakota Ojibway Tribal Council signed separate agreements with both the federal and provincial governments, transferring child care from the non-Aboriginal agencies serving eight Indian bands within the Tribal Council's territory. The Dakota Ojibway Child and Family Services (DOCFS) became the first mandated Aboriginal child welfare agency in Canada. The transfer of authority was possible under a section of the former *Child Welfare Act*, which allowed a director of child welfare to empower a committee of "local citizens known to be interested in child welfare" to provide child welfare services. DOCFS now handles the full range of child and family welfare services as a mandated agency.

The completion of tripartite negotiations on child welfare between Aboriginal leaders of the Four Nations Confederacy and the federal and provincial governments, and the signing of a master agreement in 1982, were giant steps towards establishing Aboriginally controlled child and family service agencies serving status Indians living on reserves throughout Manitoba. This agreement has been called "perhaps the most comprehensive and significant development affecting child welfare services to Indian people" in Canada.[44]

The 1982 agreement has been referred to as the Master Agreement because it defines a broad relationship between the Aboriginal bands and their organizations and the governments. It allows for other subsidiary agreements authorizing the establishment of specific child and family service agencies. The Master Agreement outlines the obligations and responsibilities of the various parties, establishes guiding principles for the operation of Aboriginal child welfare services and specifies the way in which these agencies would be funded. Each government is responsible for funding services on behalf of children who are that government's responsibility. While the actual proportions vary from agency to agency, it appears that about three-quarters of the funding comes from the federal level and the remainder from the Province.

Agencies established through the tripartite agreement provide a full range of child welfare services to status Indians living on reserves. The mandated reserve-based agencies are funded by the federal government, but operate under provincial child welfare legislation, while the non-mandated services of Ma Mawi Chi Itata in Winnipeg are funded largely by the Province, with smaller amounts of funding from the federal government and the private sector.

In 1983 the Manitoba Keewatinowi Okimakinak (MKO) signed a similar tripartite agreement. The following year, the Brotherhood of Indian Nations signed the third such agreement. Today there are five mandated Aboriginal agencies in Manitoba: the Dakota Ojibway Child and Family Services, Southeast Child and Family Services, West Region Child and Family Services, Anishinaabe Child and Family Services, and Awasis Child and Family Services.

While the creation of regional Aboriginal child welfare agencies was authorized by the tripartite agreement and the subsidiary agreements with the tribal councils, it was left up to each band to consider whether to join an Aboriginal agency. Sixty of Manitoba's 61 bands have done so by 1991. The internal structure of each agency is determined by its board, which also does its own hiring and establishes operating policies. Most of the boards of directors are made up of the chiefs of the participating bands.

Each band has a volunteer child care committee or a resident child care worker appointed by the chief and council. One band councillor is responsible for child welfare and works with the committee or with the child care worker. In theory, the child care worker is not responsible to the local band child care committee, or to the chief and council. Rather, the worker reports to the agency supervisor and the agency's board. In practice, however, the worker receives considerable direction from local officials. This may present some problems for the local worker, since the lines of authority are not always clear. On the other hand, this system has the advantage of ensuring that the worker receives a lot of advice and assistance from the local community.

The non-mandated Ma Mawi Chi Itata Centre (Ma Mawi) was established in 1984 to serve Aboriginal families in Winnipeg as the result of a determined effort by Aboriginal people to remove services for Aboriginal families and children from the Children's Aid Society of Winnipeg. Aboriginal people were convinced that the C.A.S. of Winnipeg was more interested in apprehending children than in providing support to parents to help keep their families together. Ma Mawi was founded after a long series of negotiations between the provincial government and the Winnipeg Urban Indian Coalition. It did not replace the mandated services of other non-Aboriginal agencies in the city, but, rather, extended and complemented them. Most Aboriginal people tend to trust Ma Mawi more than the other agencies, perhaps because Ma Mawi is not mandated and, therefore, cannot apprehend their children. For this reason, we recommend that Ma Mawi remain a non-mandated agency. As we shall discuss more fully later, however, there is a need to improve the delivery of mandated services to Aboriginal people living in Winnipeg.

The philosophy of the Aboriginal agencies differs from that of non-Aboriginal child care agencies. The Aboriginal agencies are more sensitive to Aboriginal culture and the needs of the families. They are sometimes able to find solutions which those not familiar with the community might not even consider. While adhering to their understanding of the best interest of the child, they tend to view child and family situations and problems in a much more holistic fashion than do non-Aboriginal agencies, and treat the whole family, rather than intercede only when presented with a troubled or neglected child.

The Aboriginal view of the "best interests" of the child takes into account the needs of the family and of the community. The Aboriginal agencies believe they can serve the interests of the child best by ensuring a supportive family or, failing that, a supportive extended family. In many cases, the extended family encompasses the whole community. For Aboriginal agencies, the health of the community is an important factor in addressing the best interests of the child. Removing a child from one family in the community can have a negative impact on other children in that family, as well as on the wider community.

If removal of children occurs on a large scale, the ability of the community to function properly and to retain its cultural traditions with a sense of positive self-esteem are undermined, and social disorganization results. Taking measures on a child-by-child basis that undermine the long-term health of the community puts the entire culture at risk.

The child who is removed will always remain an Aboriginal person. Children have to deal with their heritage for their entire lives, must confront stereotypes about it and must learn how to accept it as part of themselves. If their communities and peoples are weakened and thrown into a state of social disorganization, the child will face the negative feelings and stereotypes created by those problems. If the child is placed in a non-Aboriginal home, the likelihood of even greater problems is increased.

Pursuing policies which foster conditions that lead to social disorganization and weaken families is not in the long-term best interests of the child. What is in the best interests of the child is a healthy community. Removing children, as was done in the past, cannot produce healthy communities. Solutions are needed that protect Aboriginal children, while sustaining the health of the communities. Aboriginal agencies believe it is not possible to "choose" between the best interests of the child and the best interests of the community; the one profoundly affects the other.

Secondly, Aboriginal agencies do not equate apprehension with removal from the family. Child apprehensions are done to remove a child from a particular situation, while still maintaining the maximum possible contact with the family, community and culture. The primary goal of planning for a child taken into care is to reunite the child with the parents, if and when the parents' situation improves. If the agencies conclude that the parents are unlikely to be able to reassume their role, then long-term planning involves placing the child with members of the extended family or, if that is not possible, with another family on the reserve. On the other hand, for many non-Aboriginal agencies, it seems that apprehension is both a first resort and a last step. Too often children, once apprehended, are kept removed from their parents or extended family.

A third difference seems to occur in the relative importance attached to economic, educational and other opportunities, compared to the importance of maintaining relationships with parents, extended families and community. Non-Aboriginal agencies give more emphasis to the former, and Aboriginal agencies place more emphasis on the latter.

In examining these differences, it becomes clear that interpretations of best interests of children are culturally bound, and not universal. Aboriginal views of the best interest of the child, or, for that matter, the views of any culture, can conflict with non-Aboriginal views. Such differences are legitimate and should be respected.

In summary, the pace of development and the success of Aboriginal child and family service agencies have been remarkable. In its presentation, the Department of Community Services informed our Inquiry that over 45,000 Indian people on reserves, and more than 28,000 off-reserve status Indian people, are now served by Aboriginal agencies. As a result, in 1987, 840 of the 1,200 Aboriginal children in care in Manitoba, or about 70%, were under the care of Aboriginal agencies. There are now more than 900 foster homes in Aboriginal communities and over 300 Aboriginal professionals who have been trained to deliver culturally appropriate child and family services.

Aboriginal Child and Family Service Agencies: An Evaluation

When the current state of Aboriginal child welfare in Manitoba is compared to the conditions that existed even 10 years ago, the changes cannot be characterized as anything less than remarkable. Prior to 1980, Aboriginal communities frequently were denied services and the few services they did receive were provided by non-Aboriginal agencies. These services often were disruptive and destructive to the very families and communities they were supposed to help. The federal and provincial government officials responsible for bringing about the positive changes that have occurred are to be commended for their efforts. However, it should not be overlooked or forgotten that it was Aboriginal people, particularly Aboriginal women, who refused to accept the status quo and pressed hard for most of the changes that have come about.

Tremendous advances have been made in Manitoba's approach to the delivery of Aboriginal child and family services, especially when compared to those of many other jurisdictions. The approach that has been adopted here is serving as a model for Aboriginal people in other provinces and countries, many of whose governments continue to operate as Manitoba did throughout the 1960s and 1970s. The numerous evaluations of the Manitoba approach that have been conducted to date, and the results in Aboriginal communities themselves, confirm our belief that Aboriginal communities benefit greatly when they gain more control of the services that affect them.

Limited space will not permit us to review the extensive documentation that has been prepared on the effectiveness of Aboriginal child and family service agencies. However, we would like to summarize some of the common findings and observations that have been reported in these studies. In particular, we will draw on the evaluation of the Canada-Manitoba-Brotherhood of Indian Nations Child Welfare Agreement that was conducted by Caroll P. Hurd and Jeanne M. Hurd,[45] the evaluation of the Northern Indian Child Welfare Agreement that was conducted by Peter Hudson and Sharon Taylor-Henley,[46] and the evaluation that was conducted of the West Region Child and Family Services and of the Southeast Child and Family Services by consultants Coopers and Lybrand.[47] These and other studies have found that:

- Aboriginal child and family service agencies have become remarkably effective in dealing with even the most difficult child welfare cases in a very short period of time.

- Services required by Aboriginal children and families that were being denied previously are now being provided.

- Attention has been drawn to the needs of Aboriginal children and families in a way that did not happen in the previous service system.

- A network of Aboriginal child and family services covering the province of Manitoba has been established.

- Aboriginal people living on reserves now receive services that are comparable to the services received by non-Aboriginal people.

- These agencies have been able to generate a level of community involvement and support that is far beyond what existed for non-Aboriginal agencies trying to do the same job in the same Aboriginal communities. This is evident in the number of self-referrals that Aboriginal agencies receive, in the extent of parental and community involvement in deciding where to place a child, and in the number of voluntary placement agreements into which parents have entered.

- Aboriginal agencies have been able to create culturally appropriate solutions to child welfare problems. This has resulted in better services being provided to children, families and Aboriginal communities. In particular, by relying extensively on extended families for providing substitute care, Aboriginal agencies have been able to drastically reduce the number of Aboriginal children who are removed from their community for placements. This, in turn, dramatically increases family involvement and the prospects of children being reunited with their families at some future point.

The relevant literature has also pointed to a number of problems:

- Aboriginal agencies have had to operate with inadequate financial resources even when compared to non-Aboriginal agencies. They have had to do more with less money. This has meant that essential services have consumed the bulk of available resources and that other areas such as prevention and public education have received a low priority. In addition, some Aboriginal agencies have experienced serious backlogs in key program areas such as foster and adoption placements.

- Aboriginal agencies have not received the type of support from either the federal or provincial governments that they need in order to attract and retain staff, and there has been inadequate support for the training of band and agency personnel.

- In some areas, Aboriginal agencies have had to operate in a policy vacuum because the agencies have not had the time or the resources to develop policies. In particular, the agencies need assistance to develop their own policies, standards and protocols in sensitive areas such as child abuse.

- There has been inadequate follow-up to the tripartite negotiation process by governments. While negotiations between the federal and provincial governments and the Aboriginal leadership were intended to be ongoing, for the most part they have not continued. In addition, time-limited agreements have been allowed to expire and the concerned parties, especially the Government of Canada, have not made concerted efforts to update and renew the agreements. This has created unnecessary uncertainty and confusion.

- A major problem exists with respect to the provision of services to treaty Indians living off the reserve. The responsibility for such services is often unclear. There is little coordination of the services between the various agencies that become involved. In some cases, Aboriginal agencies have tried to extend their services even though the government has given neither the funding nor the mandate to do so. This means agencies are trying to provide appropriate services to urban Aboriginal people with inadequate resources.

- The funding of Aboriginal child and family service agencies has tended to provide few financial incentives for preventive and educational services. Instead, the funding agreements have focussed on paying back the Aboriginal agencies after they have already dealt with family problems.

In 1980 there were no children in the care of mandated Aboriginal agencies. A review of the numbers of children in care in December 1984 and in March 1990 shows continuing progress in regard to the care of Aboriginal children by mandated Aboriginal agencies. In this latest five-year period, the proportion of Aboriginal children in the care of Aboriginal agencies has grown to almost 70%. When we take into account the fact that Aboriginal agencies are not mandated to provide service outside the reserve, this is a remarkable achievement.

CHILDREN IN CARE

	December 1984	March 1990	%Change
All Children in Care	2894	4167	+43%
Registered Indian Children	1030	1470	+42%
Reg. Ind. Children in Care of Aboriginal Agencies	629	1012	+61%
Proportion in Care of Aboriginal Agencies	61%	69%	

Source: Manitoba Child and Family Services Statistics

It must be remembered that the reforms we have been discussing have been aimed primarily at improving the services to status Indians living on reserves, many of which simply had little or no service prior to 1980. Considering the degree of poverty and stress on many reserves, it is remarkable that the rate of increase in the number of Aboriginal children in care has been no greater than that of non-Aboriginal children.

Manitoba's *Child and Family Services Act*

In 1987, Manitoba passed a new *Child and Family Services Act*. This Act incorporates many of the improvements that have been achieved in the delivery of Aboriginal child and family services in Manitoba. In particular, the declaration of principles provides that:

- Families are entitled to receive services in a manner that respects their cultural and linguistic heritage.

- Communities and families have a right to be involved in child welfare issues affecting them.

- Indian bands are entitled to the provision of child and family services in a manner that respects their unique status as Aboriginal peoples.

- The Act provides the legislative framework for the tripartite agreements and for the creation of Aboriginal child and family services agencies.

- The Act places restrictions on extraprovincial adoptions.

- Cultural and linguistic heritage is included within the concept of the "best interests" of the child, and agencies are compelled to respect the cultural and linguistic heritage of the families and children they serve.[48]

We believe that this Act is a very progressive piece of legislation and we commend the provincial government for recognizing the right of reserve communities to have control over the child and family services that affect them. We believe this step towards the Aboriginal administration of institutions and services is very significant. The success of these agencies points the way for a similar approach in the criminal justice system. However, Indians are the only Aboriginal community to which this recognition has been extended. Neither the Metis people, nor other Aboriginal people living off-reserve, can be served by mandated Aboriginal agencies. We believe this should change.

The reserve-based agencies demonstrate that Aboriginal communities, given the opportunity, can not only provide services, but can provide them better than the "outside" agencies or institutions they replace. Aboriginal agencies understand the people and the problems with which they are dealing. As a result, there is a greater degree of satisfaction among Aboriginal people with the Aboriginal agencies than with the non-Aboriginal ones.

At the same time, the existing child and family service system is not perfect. In particular, the improvement of the Aboriginal child and family service system in Manitoba requires the provincial government's attention on a number of issues. These include:

- Issues related to resources.

- Issues relating to the organizational structure of child and family services.

- Services to the Metis people.

- Services to off-reserve Indians.

- Services to Aboriginal people living in Winnipeg.

We will examine each of these issues and provide our recommendations as to how we think these challenges should be addressed.

Resources

There are a number of financial and other resource issues facing the child and family service system. Caseloads in all agencies have risen sharply, particularly cases related to abuse and serious neglect. Each worker is carrying more cases than workload studies suggest can be appropriately served. What is more striking is that available evidence suggests that on a per-case basis, real agency funding from provincial sources has actually fallen in the past three years.

While our focus is on services to Aboriginal peoples, we know that financial support for non-Aboriginal child and family service agencies is far from adequate. We are aware that there are no funding formulas related to caseloads or needs used to develop agency budgets, and that recent, severe funding constraints have resulted in reductions in prevention and early intervention services, particularly in Winnipeg. Among those most in need of child and family services in Winnipeg are Aboriginal residents. We are concerned that as services are reduced, these families will be among the hardest hit. It is false economy to reduce services to children and families in need, because the effects of such reductions inevitably will show up in other systems. Children will drop out of school, families will suffer higher levels of abuse and disintegration, and rates of involvement in the young offenders system will increase.

As with provincial funding, federal child and family service funding has developed over the years on an incremental basis, with annual adjustments related, but not necessarily equal, to inflation. Each agency negotiates its funding separately with the Department of Indian and Northern Affairs. Funding is not based upon population, remoteness, levels of need or any other criteria. Agencies' present funding levels restrict them to acting only when crises already have occurred. Inadequate funding has created deficits and prevented some families and children from receiving the services they require. This should not be allowed to continue.

Indian Affairs is proposing to introduce a formula funding approach which takes some of the above criteria into account. According to Indian Affairs staff, the formula will result in some increased support for all agencies, and substantial increases for those in the North. We believe that the new funding regime must recognize and support the full range of programs and services which are mandated under the Act. If this new funding will enable the agencies to be involved more extensively in community development, public education, support for family counselling and healing, and prevention, we welcome the development of the formula.

WE RECOMMEND THAT:

- Aboriginal and non-Aboriginal child and family service agencies be provided with sufficient resources to enable them to provide the communities they serve with the full range of direct service and preventive programs mandated by the *Child and Family Services Act.*

Aboriginal child and family service agencies need more than increased funding. They require other types of support and assistance, as well. There is a critical need to have more and better trained child care workers. Staff need better ongoing training and development plans after they are hired. Agencies should provide better working conditions, better advancement opportunities and improved benefits to attract and retain Aboriginal professionals in the field of child welfare. In short, human resources training and development are needed for the Aboriginal child welfare system.

There are already some examples upon which to draw. Distance education programs may be included in any long-term training and development plan for Aboriginal people in northern or remote communities. The Winnipeg Education Centre provides a range of degree programs for people seeking a career in social work. ACCESS programs have successfully demonstrated that Aboriginal people can complete higher education and training programs in a variety of professions.

The Brandon University Northern Teacher Education Program (BUNTEP) provides an example of an extremely effective program to increase the number of Aboriginal teachers, with over 200 graduates to date. This program provides training in northern communities, establishing "pods" to train people from a given settlement over a period of several years. The award-winning PENT (Project for the Education of Native Teachers) program which trains teacher aides as full teachers is a slightly different, but equally successful program. Students attend programs on Brandon campus during the summer, but are able to remain with their families during the remainder of the year, employed as school aides, gaining both theoretical and practical teaching experience. PENT has over 200 graduates, of whom 85% were employed as educators, according to a 1985 survey.[49]

All these examples make it clear that it is both practical and possible to develop successful programs to support substantial numbers of Aboriginal people to gain professional skills. All indications are that the graduates meet professional standards and remain employed in Aboriginal communities. Programs such as these should be taken into account when training and development plans for child and family service agencies are considered. Unfortunately, the recent provincial budget made severe reductions in the BUNTEP and ACCESS programs, and in other northern post-secondary education programs. We find these reductions to be regressive, in view of the continuing need and the high numbers of Aboriginal people who directly benefited from them.

Organizational Issues

Aboriginal Agency Accountability

We believe that the way in which the individual Aboriginal child and family service agencies are structured is appropriate, given the services they provide and the needs of the communities they serve. The agency board and administrative staff, the chief and council of a band, and the federal and provincial governments all are involved. However, we believe this can create a confusing mix of jurisdiction, responsibility and accountability. At present, there are multiple answers to the question of to whom the Aboriginal agencies are accountable. This issue will require continued attention as new forms of Aboriginal self-government evolve, expanding and clarifying the scope of agency mandates. We do not believe "outside" models or structures should be imposed upon the Aboriginal agencies by the funding agencies. Rather, we believe that the Aboriginal agencies and the Aboriginal communities must develop and clarify their own lines of authority. We must then be prepared to accept and to work with their structures.

Integrating Child Protection and Young Offenders Systems

We believe that a more holistic approach to the issues of young people is needed, whether they are involved in the child welfare system or in the youth justice system. Essentially, both systems are dealing with children, families and communities. There is a bewildering array of programs, services and jurisdictions involved. The Court of Queen's Bench, Family Division, has exclusive jurisdiction to hear child protection cases in Winnipeg, St. Boniface, Selkirk and Brandon. In the rest of the province, the Queen's Bench and the Provincial Court both have jurisdiction. At Provincial Court circuit points, only that court deals with these matters. Youth court matters are within the exclusive jurisdiction of the Provincial Court throughout the province. The youth court system is sometimes called upon to try to untangle the inevitable confusion when services or jurisdictions overlap. However, under the *Young Offenders Act*, there is no provision to refer cases to a child and family service agency.

Since both the youth court and child protection systems may be called upon to deal with the problems of the same young person and his or her family, we propose that these services be better coordinated. When two separate cases involving the same youth reach court, they should be dealt with by the same judge in the same division of one court. Judges should also have the authority to involve a child protection agency to assist a young person charged with an offence. We believe that the closer involvement of the youth courts and child and family service agencies, on an ongoing basis, would provide the opportunity for more informal and more productive resolutions when such entanglements occur. We deal at greater length with these issues and make specific recommendations in Chapter 8 on court reform and in Chapter 15 on young offenders.

We are anxious to see Aboriginal communities become more involved in justice services, and we believe that many of the barriers between the justice and child welfare systems are artificial ones that need to be broken down. There is also a need to change the philosophical focus of current justice services so that less emphasis is placed on punishment and more emphasis is placed on the needs of Aboriginal individuals and communities. Aboriginal child and family service agencies, we believe, are strategically placed to bring about these changes.

We see the opportunity for Aboriginal child and family service agencies to be a building block towards the development of more comprehensive social and justice services for Aboriginal communities. While more resources will obviously be required if the existing agencies are to take on an expanded role, there are significant opportunities to reallocate resources that are not now being used in a very effective manner.

Organizational and Management Support

Aboriginal child and family service agencies have not been receiving enough organizational support. In particular, these agencies need assistance to develop policies, standards, protocols and procedures in a wide array of areas. All child and family service agencies need modern information systems to enable them to communicate with other agencies, to track cases and to share information through some network. These are fundamental needs for any effective organization, and no less so for an Aboriginal child welfare agency. However, these needs of all agencies, including Aboriginal agencies, have largely been ignored.

WE RECOMMEND THAT:

- The federal and provincial governments provide resources to Aboriginal child and family service agencies for the purpose of developing policies, standards, protocols and procedures in various areas, but particularly for the purpose of developing computer systems that will permit them to communicate quickly and effectively with other agencies, to track cases and to share information.

Services for the Metis People

The current Aboriginal child and family service agencies we have referred to above are all Indian agencies. They do not include or serve non-band members or non-status Indians. They provide services to only a few Metis people who actually live on a reserve. As a consequence, most Metis people are served by non-Aboriginal agencies. Many of the problems that characterized child welfare services for Indians prior to the development of Aboriginal child and family service agencies continue to exist for Manitoba's Metis people.

"Metis" is a word historically used to describe a person of mixed Indian and French heritage in Manitoba and other western provinces. Today, it has become a term used to describe anyone in Canada of mixed Indian and white ancestry. A "non-status Indian" is an Indian person who had status or treaty rights, but has lost them or has had these rights taken away by government.

Both Metis and non-status Indians have been considered, for jurisdiction purposes, a part of the non-Aboriginal population by the federal and provincial governments. There have been few statistical studies to identify the numbers and social characteristics of either group. Metis and non-status Indians, therefore, have not been able to convince either government to fund specific services, except in conjunction with general "Aboriginal" programs which include status or treaty Indians and Inuit, as well.

A study commissioned by our Inquiry estimates that there are at least 47,000 Metis and 6,000 non-status Indians in the province. Neither of these groups, either jointly or separately, has been able to obtain the culturally appropriate child welfare services now considered absolutely rightful and necessary for status Indians.

In 1982, when the *Charter of Rights and Freedoms* was enacted, section 35 of the *Charter* recognized "aboriginal peoples" to include "Metis" and it "recognized and affirmed" their "existing aboriginal rights."[50] Unfortunately, unlike status Indians, for whom the legal sources of their rights are generally recognized, the sources of Metis rights and the meaning of "existing rights" remain unclear. Nor does there seem to be a government commitment to clarify these uncertainties.

There are no specific legislative references to Metis people in the *Child and Family Services Act* to regulate or improve child and family services in Metis communities. There do not appear to be "culturally appropriate" child welfare services for Metis communities, despite specific mention of this as a duty of an agency under s. 7(1)(m) of the Act. In terms of child and family welfare, Metis people face many of the same living conditions and social problems as Indian people. Metis organizations and communities also want control of the child and family services affecting their communities, because they feel their people have been as adversely affected by the intervention and policies of non-Aboriginal child welfare services as have Indians. We agree, and believe that the fundamental principles on which the Act is based should be revised.

WE RECOMMEND THAT:

- Principle 11 of the *Child and Family Services Act* be amended to read: "Aboriginal people are entitled to the provision of child and family services in a manner which respects their unique status, and their cultural and linguistic heritage."

The Indian and Metis have never considered themselves as part of the same culture. The Metis people have distinct problems and aspirations that require distinct solutions. The uniqueness of their culture and society should be recognized. Like the Indian people, the Metis people want and need to receive services from separate institutions— developed, administered and controlled by them. While Indian agencies do not oppose the provision of services to the Metis, they recommend that the Metis run their own separate agencies. That is certainly the wish of the Metis themselves.

WE RECOMMEND THAT:

- The Province of Manitoba in conjunction with the Manitoba Metis Federation develop a mandated Metis child and family service agency with jurisdiction over Metis and non-status children throughout Manitoba.

Services to Indians Living Off-Reserve

Band members frequently move to and from the reserve for both economic and social reasons. They retain a strong attachment to their home reserve for generations after they leave. Their extended families still live on the reserve and they may feel a stronger tie to their reserve than to the town or city in which they live. They still see the reserve government as theirs, representing their rights and continuing to care for them. It is appropriate, therefore, that the necessary arrangements be made to extend the authority of Aboriginal agencies to the members of their bands who live off-reserve.

Giving the reserve-based agencies a clear mandate to serve off-reserve members would also clarify the issues raised recently, in which the off-reserve authority of Aboriginal agencies has been challenged. Aboriginal agencies, with the apparent consent of government, have long provided services to band members living in Winnipeg. In a recent case, a judge of the Court of Queen's Bench, Family Division, was called upon to interpret the mandate of the agencies as set out in the Orders-in-Council creating them. She held that the authority of the Aboriginal agency did not extend beyond the reserve.[51] Our proposals would change that situation.

WE RECOMMEND THAT:

- The jurisdiction of the reserve-based Indian child and family service agencies be extended to include off-reserve band members.
- Indian agencies be provided with sufficient resources to ensure that this expanded mandate be effectively carried out.

Our recommendation is in line with the spirit, if not the letter, of the tripartite agreements and, we believe, would be the best way of delivering child and family services to off-reserve band members. If the present Aboriginal agencies can exercise jurisdiction off reserves, Aboriginal people living in non-Aboriginal communities throughout the province would be able to receive culturally appropriate services.

Aboriginal Child and Family Services in Winnipeg

It seems ironic that Aboriginal agencies are mandated to provide services on 60 reserves across Manitoba, but there is no mandated Aboriginal child care agency in Winnipeg, which has the greatest number of status, non-status and Metis people of any area in the province. Existing Aboriginal agencies have attempted to offer services to band members who have moved from their home reserves to other areas, or to urban areas such as Winnipeg, but they have neither the resources nor a clear legal mandate to do so. In total, there are over 40,000 Aboriginal people living in Winnipeg who are without access to a mandated Aboriginal agency.

In Winnipeg, at the time of writing, there were six non-Aboriginal child and family service agencies providing all mandated services to Winnipeg residents, including Aboriginal families.

Statistics indicate that two of these agencies had a particularly large volume of Aboriginal cases. Central Winnipeg Child and Family Services had an average Aboriginal caseload of 285 children in care at any one time, representing about 50% of their total cases. Thirty-eight per cent of their caseload (215 cases) were Metis or non-status Indians. This agency employed 11 Aboriginal people within its staff of 80. Northwest Child and Family Services reported that 45% or 490 of its caseload of 1,100 families were Aboriginal. Three hundred of these families, or more than two-thirds of the Aboriginal caseload, were Metis or non-status Indians. Northwest Child and Family Services employed 12 Aboriginal people within its staff of 82. Other child and family service agencies in Winnipeg reported that between 5% to 15% of their clients were Aboriginal. These agencies employed very few, if any, Aboriginal people.

The success of the Aboriginal agencies in rural Manitoba and in the North is in stark contrast to the lack of success with Aboriginal caseloads of the non-Aboriginal agencies in Winnipeg. They struggle to deal with people from a different culture who have a different language and who are in a foreign environment.

The many criticisms which we received concerning Child and Family Services in Winnipeg fell into four main categories:

- The inappropriateness of present services.
- The delays in the court system.
- The need for culturally appropriate services.
- The need for supportive services, rather than services that emphasize monitoring, controlling and the apprehension of children.

Many who spoke to us complained of the lack of Aboriginal workers in the Winnipeg agencies. Nevertheless, we acknowledge that the percentage of Aboriginal workers in Winnipeg Central and Northwest significantly exceeds that found in any other part of the justice system which we have examined, and more than meets the conventional tests of employment equity. This is a direct reflection of deliberate training strategies, coupled with a willingness on the part of agencies to hire Aboriginal staff members. We commend the agencies for their actions, and call for the continuance of this positive direction. Nevertheless, when agencies have Aboriginal caseloads of 50%, it is inevitable that many Aboriginal families will be served by non-Aboriginal workers. This points out a major problem whenever Aboriginal people use non-Aboriginal agencies. They will probably be served by non-Aboriginal staff.

Non-Aboriginal workers were accused of apprehending children without clearly communicating to the parents the reasons for the apprehension or the steps that would be followed in having their case reviewed. One mother said that she lost custody of her children because she did not understand what was being said in court. Another said she found the whole child welfare system to be strange because her worker was unable to understand the importance of the extended family. Still another person said that the existing non-Aboriginal agencies are not a "friendly open door to native people." Her children were held by an agency for seven months in a non-Aboriginal foster home. Her story is all too typical:

> It involves three children. The three children are my nieces. It involves an agency, NEW FACESS of Winnipeg. Northeast, I believe.... These children were apprehended in November of 1987 and I had made it known to the agency that I wanted to provide care, that I had been providing care up until the time I took the children back to their mother in Winnipeg, which was in October.
>
> What disturbs me about this case is that the children were apprehended in November and the case never went to court until May of this year. Like that is a long time. Like it was seven months before it was brought to a court of law. In the meantime, there was no real effort on the agency's part to try and establish if I was a good candidate or a potential candidate to provide care. I hired a lawyer so I could begin the proceedings as well, for an Application of Guardianship, in order to be heard, and to at least be considered. Well, today I have those kids living with me and they are temporary wards of NEW FACESS, but it was not until, like I said, I got a lawyer involved and began my own proceedings.

There is a common perception that the non-Aboriginal agencies apprehend first and offer assistance only afterwards to try to resolve the problems they, in part, have created. Thus, in spite of the fact that numbers of Aboriginal staff are employed by the mandated agencies in Winnipeg, many Aboriginal families voluntarily go to the non-mandated Ma Mawi Chi Itata Centre with their problems, rather than face a mandated non-Aboriginal agency. Most of the Aboriginal presenters to our Inquiry said that they trust Ma Mawi because they know it will not suggest apprehending their children as soon as it learns of a problem.

During our hearings we discussed the possibility of establishing an Aboriginal child care agency in Winnipeg. The consensus among the Aboriginal leadership and of the boards of Central and Northwest Child and Family Services agencies was that an Aboriginal agency was a worthwhile objective.

We believe there is considerable merit to having an Aboriginal agency operating in Winnipeg in the same way as Aboriginal agencies operate on reserves in Manitoba. We believe that many of the same positive results can be achieved. For example, Aboriginal agencies have very few contested cases proceeding to court. In addition, they are able to utilize the extended family more effectively than do the non-Aboriginal agencies. This is not surprising, because of their knowledge of the communities and because of the willingness of family members to communicate openly with Aboriginal workers in their own language.

As well, we were struck by the high numbers of Aboriginal people who continued to be involved with Northwest and Central Child and Family Services agencies. While we are certain that these agencies endeavoured to fulfil the mandate required of them in a manner consistent with the goals of the legislation, we believe that they were constrained by the fact that those in charge, both at the board and management levels, are non-Aboriginal. In their presentations to us, both agencies acknowledged these limitations and encouraged us to consider a mandated Aboriginal agency for Winnipeg.

We have also noted that the Ma Mawi Chi Itata Centre has enjoyed great success in its achievements with Aboriginal families. While this might be attributed in some part to its inability to apprehend children, and its resulting perception as a non-threatening resource, we believe Ma Mawi's success is more related to the agency's culturally appropriate approach to service provision.

Finally, we concur with the view that, for far too long, Aboriginal people have been clients of agencies and institutions which have failed miserably in their attempts to heal Aboriginal family problems. We believe that Aboriginal people should have the right and the means to control their own lives and to provide their own services to the fullest extent possible.

WE RECOMMEND THAT:

- A mandated Aboriginal child and family service agency be established in the city of Winnipeg.

The establishment of a mandated Aboriginal agency in Winnipeg, in conjunction with a Metis agency, and extended mandates for reserve agencies would raise a number of jurisdictional questions which would require resolution. For example, agencies would frequently come into contact with families of mixed heritage, with parents being status or non-status Indian, Metis or non-Aboriginal. A single, non-Aboriginal parent might be caring for an Aboriginal child. Which agency would have jurisdiction in such cases?

We suggest that relationships among mandated agencies be governed by the following protocols:

- Any mandated agency may provide any services, or take any action under the *Child and Family Services Act* which it deems proper.

- The mandated Winnipeg Aboriginal child and family service agency should have primacy in Winnipeg to provide service to all Aboriginal children and families.

- If a non-Aboriginal agency, or a reserve-based agency, or the proposed Metis agency apprehends an Aboriginal child in Winnipeg, or takes any action in Winnipeg which removes Aboriginal children from their family, that agency be required to contact the mandated Winnipeg Aboriginal agency, and indicate its willingness to transfer the case.

- The two agencies should then ascertain which agency is best suited to provide service, and make arrangements accordingly.

- In the event of continuing disputes, the Child Protector should determine and designate the appropriate agency.

This agency should be established in consultation with interested groups in the city of Winnipeg, including the existing child and family service agencies, representatives of the existing Aboriginal agencies in other parts of the province, the Manitoba Metis Federation and Ma Mawi Chi Itata Centre. Care should be taken to ensure that the agency is directed and controlled by Aboriginal people. While the agency should have a mandate to apprehend children in need of protection, we believe that its primary interest should be the needs of children and the maintenance of well-functioning families. We anticipate such an agency would offer extensive and flexible support services and that the removal of children from the extended family would be a last resort.

We expect that an Aboriginal agency in Winnipeg would also be able to work with the reserve-based Aboriginal agencies and with the proposed Metis agency with less conflict and greater understanding than is currently the case with the non-Aboriginal agencies. We believe that the result will be better service to children, to Aboriginal families and to Aboriginal communities.

To reflect some of the suggestions of the existing Aboriginal agencies, and some of our own thoughts and observations, we recommend that the proposed agency be established subject to the following guidelines:

- The agency be guided by the principles and philosophies contained in the Master Agreement concerning Indian child welfare.

- The board of directors be comprised solely of Aboriginal people.

- Most, if not all, of the employees be Aboriginal.

- The agency have jurisdiction throughout the city of Winnipeg.

- The agency be mandated to provide a full range of services, including the apprehension of children, if that becomes necessary.

- The agency be funded to serve all Aboriginal people in Winnipeg, including status or treaty Indians, non-status Indians, Metis and Inuit.

Conclusion

The interpretation of child welfare legislation is an area where cross-cultural misunderstanding frequently occurs. Terms such as "adequate care," "proper supervision" and "unfit circumstances," not to speak of "in the best interests" and "in need of protection," are vague and value-laden. For the past four decades, many problems have arisen because the interpretation of these phrases has been left to the discretion and understanding of social workers, police, lawyers and judges who possess little or no understanding of Aboriginal culture. Cultural differences between Aboriginal families and non-Aboriginal social workers have blinded many non-Aboriginal social workers to the fact that different Aboriginal child-rearing methods are not wrong or inadequate, but, rather, are acceptable alternatives.

In the past, non-Aboriginal individuals working within the child welfare system influenced policy and made decisions which directly affected the lives of Aboriginal children. The sad fact is that many of them were and continue to be ill-informed about Aboriginal cultures and about the alternatives available within Aboriginal communities to assist the child. Many were also incapable of working with Aboriginal people and their communities to assist those groups in coming to grips with their own role in the child welfare system.

Aboriginal communities in Manitoba have worked very hard to obtain a greater degree of control over the future of their children and communities. But they have yet to obtain full control, free from federal and provincial government interference. This becomes critical when one recognizes the continuing high levels of contact between Aboriginal families and the non-Aboriginal child welfare system in Manitoba. While many of the legal issues and practical problems have been addressed, to some extent, through the establishment of Indian child welfare agencies functioning on Indian reserves, many serious problems continue to exist in urban and non-Aboriginal communities.

We believe that the Aboriginal child care agencies have been an outstanding success and that they warrant further support and encouragement. They are dealing with Aboriginal families with sensitivity, commitment and ability. At the same time, it must be recognized that their programs and activities sometimes will become the subject of controversy and criticism. Every time an Aboriginal agency stumbles, some critics inevitably will cry out for its dismantling and a return to the old way. But, as we and other inquiries have concluded, the old way was neither the only way, nor the best way. The need for ongoing support and a commitment to Aboriginal child welfare agencies must be recognized and reaffirmed.

Aboriginal people have enjoyed little influence or control over many of the issues which affect them, often adversely. Manitoba's experience in the field of child welfare, however, suggests that when a consensus develops that something must be done, then positive changes can take place. The reform of the child welfare system is an example of that. It is proof that Aboriginal people are ready, willing and able to exercise greater control over aspects of their lives which some erroneously believe can only be dealt with by non-Aboriginal professionals.

We must now do more to support and extend the reforms that have taken place. Positive steps have been taken, but not all Aboriginal people have benefited. Existing agencies must be strengthened and those Aboriginal people not served by Aboriginal agencies must now be afforded this opportunity. Aboriginal peoples must continue to gain more responsibility for the child and family programs and services that affect them. By expanding the range and number of mandated Aboriginal agencies as we have recommended, all Aboriginal Manitobans will have the opportunity to receive culturally appropriate child and family services. We believe that the rapid and positive development of reserve-based agencies augers well for the future success of Aboriginally administered programs.

CHAPTER 15

YOUNG OFFENDERS

Introduction

We are failing to meet the needs of Aboriginal young people in the youth justice system just as surely as we are failing to meet the needs of adult Aboriginal people in the adult justice system. We know adult Aboriginal people are grossly over-represented in the adult justice system, but we find even higher proportions of young Aboriginal people in the youth justice system. We found that, in a count of inmates on October 1, 1990, Aboriginal youth accounted for 64% of the inmates at the Manitoba Youth Centre and 78% of the inmates of the Agassiz Youth Centre. This is particularly disturbing since many Aboriginal young people will "graduate" to more serious crimes later in their lives. These studies also show that Aboriginal youth, like Aboriginal adults, will be victimized by systemic discrimination at every stage in the justice system.

Particular concern has been expressed about the impact of the *Young Offenders Act* upon Aboriginal youth. In fact, some observers argue that the deficiencies of the Act are so significant that even the guiding principles should be modified to take into account the special needs and concerns of Aboriginal youth.[1]

Compared to non-Aboriginal youth, Aboriginal youth:

- Have more charges laid against them.

- Are less likely to benefit from legal representation.

- Are more often detained before trial.

- Are detained for longer periods.

- Are more likely to be denied bail.

- Experience longer delays before their cases are disposed of.

- Are required to appear in court more frequently before their cases are disposed of.

- Are more likely to be sentenced to custody.

- Serve longer sentences.

These problems are not new; it has long been known that these conditions are an everyday fact of life for too many young Aboriginal people. They testify to the fact that the justice system is not working fairly or effectively for Aboriginal youth.

The Canadian Research Institute for Law and the Family, for example, in a study commissioned by our Inquiry, summarized the current state of affairs as follows:

> Native youth are vastly over-represented in Canada's juvenile justice system. It is apparent that for these youths the extensive use of police, courts, and a corrections system operated and controlled by white society, has been a failure. It has failed to meet the special needs of native young offenders, many of whom continue to commit further offences after their involvement in the system. The system has also failed to meet the needs of native communities: first, by failing to give them responsibility for and involvement in helping their youth; and, second, by failing to rehabilitate young offenders, it has also failed to protect their communities from recurrent patterns of offences.[2]

In this chapter, we examine the youth justice system in detail, the historical approaches to the treatment of youth crime and the factors that gave rise to the current system. We provide an overview of the *Young Offenders Act*, [R.S.C. 1985, c. Y-1], and we discuss how the Act has been implemented in Manitoba. We examine the current inequities that characterize the treatment of Aboriginal youth and we propose reforms that we believe will reduce costs, improve effectiveness and, perhaps, even restore the tarnished reputation of the youth justice system in Aboriginal communities.

Historical Approaches to the Problem of Youth Crime

The late 19th and early 20th centuries were a period of rapid social change in Canada. The twin engines of immigration and industrialization gave birth to, among other things, city slums, homelessness, the breakdown of the extended family unit, increased juvenile delinquency and increased crime. It was no coincidence that many of the elements still seen in today's justice system first appeared during this period, as governments organized, established and expanded their police forces, courts and jails.

During the period of rapid development, particularly towards the end of the 19th century, the inability of the emerging social order to effectively accommodate young people became a matter of growing social concern. Disruptive behaviour, such as crime, sexual immorality and truancy, began to increase and commentators began to condemn what they called a "youth problem." Social reformers pressed governments to pass legislation that would ensure children received better treatment by society, both at home and in the workplace.

This reform movement in the late 1800s led to the establishment of privately operated children's aid societies with "the objective of helping orphaned, abandoned and neglected children."[3] This eventually led to new laws restricting the exploitation of children in the workplace, requiring children to attend school and giving the societies broad legal powers, "including the right to remove neglected or abused children from their homes and become legal guardians for such children."[4]

By the beginning of the 20th century, social reformers considered young people to be victims of their social environment, and their sometimes erratic or aberrant behaviour was seen as symptomatic of larger social ills. Young people were not seen to be completely responsible for their actions. And yet, young people who came into contact with the criminal justice system were often subjected to the same laws, the same adjudication process and the same penalties as were adults. In the years after Canada's first penitentiary was built at Kingston in the 1830s, for example, the institution housed both young people and adults of both sexes. As one author notes:

> Only in this century ... has juvenile delinquency existed in the legal sense of the term. Before the passage of the *Juvenile Delinquents Act* in 1908, legally there was no such thing as juvenile delinquency, but only crime by young persons, generally responded to in the same legislation as crime by adults.[5]

Reformers of the day pointed to the intolerable living conditions in the adult jails. They believed that young people should be treated differently, more humanely, by the law. They also felt that housing young offenders in the same institutions as adult criminals made rehabilitation less likely, since many of those adults had committed serious crimes. Furthermore, they felt the justice system should reflect the change in social attitudes towards youth, the justice system and rehabilitation.

These social reformers believed the state could correct wayward youth by enacting new criminal laws specifically for youth and by authorizing a separate youth justice system. The *Juvenile Delinquents Act,* [R.S.C. 1908], was the culmination of this reform process.

The *Juvenile Delinquents Act* (JDA) brought about a dramatic departure from earlier practices. The Act created a new legal status: a "delinquent." It defined a new category of acts: "delinquencies." It established separate courts and correctional programs for youth, and it articulated a new legal philosophy that differed in important respects from the philosophy of the adult criminal justice system.

The JDA defined a "delinquent" very broadly to include not only those who had committed criminal offences, but also those who exhibited a variety of other "vices." Specifically, the JDA defined a delinquent as

> ... any child who violates any provision of the Criminal Code or of any Dominion or provincial statute, or of any by-law or ordinance of any municipality, or who is guilty of sexual immorality or any similar form of vice, or who is liable by reason of any other act to be committed to an industrial school or juvenile reformatory under the provisions of any Dominion or provincial statute.[6]

Children who were seven years and older were believed to be sufficiently mature to come under the jurisdiction of the JDA. The upper age limit, however, was allowed to vary from 16 to 18, at the option of each province.

The JDA was based on a "child welfare philosophy" which held that the criminal justice system should act in the "best interests" of the child. It gave enormous discretionary powers to judges, the police and probation officers to do what they considered to be best for the child's welfare. In fact, the JDA was quite explicit:

> This act shall be liberally construed in order that its purpose may be carried out, namely, that the care and custody and discipline of a juvenile delinquent shall approximate as nearly as may be that which should be given by his parents, and that as far as practicable every juvenile delinquent shall be treated, not as a criminal, but as a misdirected and misguided child and one needing aid, encouragement, help and assistance.[7]

The JDA did not distinguish between "neglected" and "criminal" children because the "child welfare" philosophy of the time held, in effect, that children who broke the law did so because they were neglected. Delinquent youth who broke laws were simply showing the symptoms of their neglect and were products of desperate social conditions. Believers in this philosophy argued that the state could reform these wayward youth by meeting their underlying needs with discipline, guidance and education.

In order to accomplish this, the JDA gave the police, the courts and the child welfare authorities very wide latitude to do almost whatever they felt was in the child's best interests. There was, for example, no need to equate the seriousness of the child's acts with the court's disposition, since the purpose of the proceedings was "to help" and not "to punish." In addition, rights that normally would have been extended to adults, if charged with similar offences, were not felt to be necessary in proceedings dealing with youthful offenders.

The JDA remained in force with very few amendments for 76 years. During that time, society changed and so did people's attitudes towards youth, child welfare and the justice system. Increasingly, the JDA was criticized for a number of reasons.[8]

The most sweeping criticism of the JDA was that its philosophy was flawed. It presumed that the state always acted in the best interests of the child and that this approach had been effective. But critics of the JDA said the Act had not prevented delinquency and that it was time for other initiatives to be tried. One of the most vocal advocates for changing the JDA was Judge Omer Archambault, who wrote:

> The Juvenile Delinquents Act is believed to insufficiently emphasize the concepts of personal responsibility and protection of society, thereby failing to adequately reflect the interests and beliefs of contemporary society.[9]

By adopting the role of a caring parent, critics pointed out, the state was overlooking the basic rights of young people. Young people, they argued, were denied rights to due process, to be represented by a lawyer, to appeal, to cross-examine witnesses, to be informed about charges against them and to participate in legal proceedings. Moreover, they said, those in authority had too much discretionary power. Critics saw little connection between the dispositions handed out and the seriousness of the acts committed by young people. In fact, young people did not have to commit a criminal act to come under the jurisdiction of the juvenile court. Young people could run afoul of the JDA because of vague allegations relating to a variety of non-criminal behaviours.

The JDA was also considered to be out of date in terms of its categorization of offenders by age. Judge Archambault, one of the architects of the *Young Offenders Act,* argued that:

> [T]he simple dichotomy of child and adult, while innovative in 1908, is no longer considered adequate. Contemporary knowledge and cultural values now recognize a third crucial phase of maturation, namely adolescence. Whereas a child is perceived to be completely dependent and lacking the capacity for criminal responsibility and an adult is generally considered to be fully independent and responsible, the adolescent is in a state of transition and considered capable of independent thought and responsibility, although not to the same degree rightfully expected of adults.[10]

The JDA was also criticized for failing to provide a consistent legal framework for responding to youthful crime across Canada. For instance, the JDA allowed the maximum age to vary from province to province.

The *Young Offenders Act*

Provisions of the *Young Offenders Act*

After considerable discussion and consultation, the *Young Offenders Act* (YOA) was passed by Parliament in 1982 and came into effect in 1984. The *Juvenile Delinquents Act* was repealed that same year. The major features of the YOA are as follows:

Principles and Philosophy

The Act is based on four key principles:

- Young people are responsible for their behaviour and should be held accountable in a manner appropriate to their age and maturity.

- Society has a right to protection from illegal behaviour and a responsibility to prevent criminal conduct by young people.

- Young people have special needs because they are dependents at varying levels of development and maturity. In view of society's right to protection and these special needs, young people may require not only supervision, discipline and control but also guidance and assistance. In recognition of this, the *Act* declares that:

  - alternative measures to the formal court process, or no measures at all, should be considered for the young offender, as long as such a solution is consistent with the protection of society;

  - young offenders should be removed from their families only when continued parental supervision is inappropriate. The *Act* recognizes the responsibility of parents for the care and supervision of their children. Parents will be encouraged and, if necessary, required to take an active part in proceedings that involve their children.

- Young people have the same rights as adults to due process of law and fair and equal treatment, including all the rights stated in the *Canadian Charter of Rights and Freedoms* and in the 1960 *Bill of Rights*. To protect their rights and freedoms, and in view of their particular needs and circumstances, young people should have special rights and guarantees.[11]

The Declaration of Principles at the beginning of the Act mentions in particular that young people have the right to participate in deliberations that affect them, a right to the least interference with their freedom that is compatible with the protection of society, their own needs and their family's interests, and a right to be informed about their rights and freedoms.

Consistent with the principle of "least interference" is a scheme of "alternative measures," defined by the Act, that can be used to divert young offenders from formal court processing. In addition, it allows officials to do nothing in certain circumstances if the situation warrants.

Age Uniformity

The Act creates uniform maximum and minimum ages for determining those to be dealt with in the youth justice system. Only those who have attained the age of 12 can come under the jurisdiction of the Youth Court. Those under 12 are deemed to be incapable of fully forming the intent necessary to be held criminally responsible for their acts. Instead, they are to be dealt with pursuant to provincial child welfare legislation. In terms of the maximum age, the YOA stipulates that those under 18 years of age will be treated as young offenders. Those over 18 are subject to the provisions of the adult system.

Narrowed Jurisdiction

While the JDA dealt with violations of the *Criminal Code,* other federal and provincial statutes, municipal by-laws and other "vices," the YOA is more clearly concerned with criminal law. It covers only those young people charged with specific offences in the *Criminal Code* and certain other federal laws. The "catch all" offence of "delinquency" has been abolished. Rather, under the YOA, young people must be charged with a specific offence, and the same rules of evidence apply as in adult court. It is left to each province to decide how it will deal with offences involving provincial statutes and municipal by-laws. Manitoba allows such youth to be dealt with in the same manner as adults.

Range of Dispositions

The YOA stipulates and restricts the range of dispositions that are available to the Youth Court. These include: an absolute discharge; a fine of up to $1,000; compensation to the victim in terms of a monetary payment, an "in kind" payment, or the performance of personal services; a community service order; a treatment order; probation for up to two years; committal to intermittent or continuous detention in either "open" or "secure" custody for a period not exceeding three years; and any additional conditions that the judge considers to be in the best interests of society or the young offender. Each province is responsible for ensuring that the necessary programs are made available to the Youth Court.

"Custody" is a term meaning a situation where a person has some restraint placed upon his or her liberty or freedom of movement. "Open" custody is defined as "a community residential centre, group home, child care institution, or forest or wilderness camp," while "closed" or "secure" custody is "a place or facility designated by the Lieutenant Governor in Council of a province for the secure containment or restraint of young persons, and includes a place or facility within a class of such places or facilities so designated."[12]

The intent appears to be to have "open" custody in a place without bars or locks. "Secure" custody is custody in a jail. This distinction becomes more important to our discussion later in this chapter, since in Manitoba some facilities have been designated as both open and secure custody facilities.

Other Provisions

The Act addresses numerous aspects of the administration of the youth justice system that were not previously the subject of legislation. For example, the YOA deals with such matters as: the creation, retention and destruction of records; the identification of young offenders by the media; guidelines on the photographing and fingerprinting of young offenders by the police; and access by the public to youth court proceedings.

Despite the increased standardization that was brought about by the Act, provinces have been left with wide discretion to determine how the Act will be implemented and administered. Each province, including Manitoba, decides which court will hear young offenders' cases, which facilities will be designated for the purposes of providing pre-trial detention and custody, which facilities are "open" or "secure," which officials will perform the various duties that must be performed under the Act, and whether key programs, such as alternative measures and youth justice committees, will be established.

Because of the manner in which the *Young Offenders Act* has been implemented, it appears that the repeal of the *Juvenile Delinquents Act* merely replaced one set of problems with another. We believe that certain elements of the JDA's approach remain valid, and we will be calling for certain amendments to the YOA to reflect these concerns. At the same time, we believe that governments must also implement the YOA in the spirit in which it was intended.

Youth Involvement with the Justice System under the YOA

The most recent figures on the operations of the *Young Offenders Act* in Manitoba have been provided by the Canadian Centre for Justice Statistics. CCJS data[13] indicate that there were 10,476 *Criminal Code* charges laid against 3,834 youth in Manitoba during 1989–90. Although nearly half of the youth had only one charge, the average number of offences was 2.7 per person. More than half of the young people were 16 years of age or older at the time of their charge. Fewer than 20% were female.

In Manitoba, of the 10,476 charges heard by youth courts, four cases were transferred to adult court, 3,703 guilty decisions were registered, 27 not guilty decisions were registered, 80 charges were dismissed and 29 charges were withdrawn. Proceedings were stayed in 2,507 cases.

The CCJS also compiled statistics on the most serious crimes committed by these youth. About 20% had been charged with crimes against the person, usually assault. More than half had committed property crimes.

The CCJS also analysed the cases by most significant disposition. Of the 2,387 young persons who were found guilty (some young persons were found guilty of multiple charges), 242 young offenders, or about 10% of the total number of cases, were sentenced to secure custody. Two hundred and twenty-three young offenders, or about 9% of the cases, were sentenced to "open" custody. The most frequently imposed sanction was probation. Probation was used in 1,104 cases, or nearly half of all the dispositions. The court ordered 377 young offenders (16%) to pay fines. It ordered 235 young offenders (10%) to perform community service. An absolute discharge was issued in fewer than

120 cases, or less than 5% of the total dispositions. The average term of "open" custody was four months. The average term of "secure" custody was five and a half months. On average, young offenders were sentenced to 10 months of probation. The average fine was a little more than $200.

While the CCJS does not attempt to find out why nearly half of all these charges were stayed, a study completed for the Manitoba Attorney General's department in 1986[14] may provide some clues. In examining a sample of cases coming before the youth courts in Winnipeg, the study found that about 40% of stayed cases employed alternative measures, usually after some court work had been done. The other 60% involved cases that were either stayed absolutely or stayed while more serious charges were considered. Overall alternative measures were employed only in about one-fifth of the cases. The study concluded that "too many young people become too involved in the criminal justice system for relatively minor offences."[15]

Aboriginal Youth and the *Young Offenders Act*

The *Young Offenders Act* is a relatively new law and it remains controversial. It has already been the subject of amendments, and there is a significant and growing number of court challenges to the Act and to the way provincial governments have applied it. We believe the *Young Offenders Act*, as it is currently being implemented, is not serving Aboriginal young people well. There is little question that a more punitive approach has been adopted towards young offenders in Manitoba. As a result, more young Aboriginal people are being incarcerated.

For example, our analysis of Provincial Court study data concluded that Aboriginal young offenders received open custody sentences that were, on average, twice as long (242 days vs. 109 days) as those given to non-Aboriginal young offenders. In addition, 18% of Aboriginal offenders received closed custody sentences, compared to 11% of non-Aboriginal offenders.

Many observers and critics of the way the YOA is implemented have expressed concerns that the facilities and programs are inadequate, and that the Province is not devoting the resources needed to deal with young offenders. More young people are being put into custody in Manitoba. This has led some observers to conclude that provinces like Manitoba are adopting a punitive approach to young offenders, in part because the justice system demands more emphasis on "youth accountability."[16]

We consider the legal protections afforded to young people under the YOA as being positive developments. Any youth accused of breaking the law is entitled to have that allegation dealt with in accordance with criminal justice standards.

One important option that is no longer available to the courts is the ability to make a youth a ward of a child welfare agency, rather than incarcerating the youth. By taking this power away from the courts, we believe Parliament "threw out the baby with the bath water." When sentencing young offenders, judges should be able to include any solution that appears to be in the "best interest of the youth," providing that cultural concerns are taken into consideration when the best interests are being determined.

In Winnipeg, for example, a dramatic increase in the use of custody following the implementation of the YOA has been documented:

> The year-end statistics provided by the Winnipeg Youth Court show that 219 people were committed to custody in 1985; 114 to open custody; and 105 to secure custody. Similar year-end statistics for 1983 and 1984 demonstrate an increase in the number of custody committals for young people over the years. In 1983, 87 and in 1984, 98 people were committed to custody.[17]

In other words, the number of custody admissions in Winnipeg went up about 12% between 1983 and 1984, and more than doubled between 1984 and 1985, the year after the YOA was implemented.

We believe that the *Young Offenders Act* provides a chance for new opportunities and more effective and innovative programming. However, we are concerned that these new opportunities are not being pursued in Manitoba.

Failure to Implement the Principles of the YOA

Young Aboriginal people are not being dealt with according to the principles expressed in the *Young Offenders Act*. In particular, the statistics show the youth justice system does not deal with Aboriginal youth in a way that allows the "least possible interference"[18] with their freedom. On the contrary, it appears the Act has been used to bring about a more intrusive and punitive system than the one that existed under the old JDA. We are concerned that the police, Crown attorneys, lawyers and judges are not using alternative measures enough.[19] The Act gives officials the discretionary power to take no legal action whatsoever when the situation warrants, but they rarely exercise this discretion.

Section 3(1)(d) of the *Young Offenders Act* gives the police the discretion to lay charges, depending on the circumstances and the "best interests" of the young person. We are concerned that most police officers are not using this discretion and that they resort to charging Aboriginal young offenders in most instances. This has been confirmed in at least one study of the Manitoba youth justice system.[20]

It appears the police feel that a young offender's rights are more than adequately protected by the *Charter of Rights and Freedoms* and by the *Young Offenders Act*. Police also seem to believe that young people they charge will be "screened out" by the judicial process, through the use of alternative measures programs, after charges have been laid. As a result, the police lay charges in most cases, including many minor cases that could be dealt with more appropriately at a community level.

Although consultation with the Crown prosecutor may be warranted in some instances, we believe the law fully empowers the police and, in fact, encourages them to exercise pre-charge discretion. We believe it is essential that they exercise this discretion, where appropriate, in favour of not laying charges. Once Aboriginal young people are in the justice system, Aboriginal communities and parents are most frequently left out of the picture and Aboriginal youth are subjected to the discriminatory impact of the system. While we know that alternatives to charging are sometimes pursued, we believe these options are not given enough attention by the police.

Instead of arresting young people and automatically laying charges, we believe the police should consult with the community to see if there are alternatives to pressing charges. In some cases, a simple warning might suffice. In other cases, a parent or a knowledgeable community leader might be able to suggest a better approach. It also has been suggested the police might send warning letters explaining the behaviour of some young people to their parents. This system has been adopted in a number of jurisdictions, including British Columbia, apparently with some success.

Many police officers appear to be ill-equipped to deal with young offenders, particularly with Aboriginal youth. Part of the problem appears to be organizational. Larger police departments in urban areas have separate youth divisions. Smaller detachments, like the one in Norway House, should have one or more youth specialists. None does. Special training should be provided to all officers dealing with Aboriginal youth.

Reorganization and training, however, will not provide an adequate response to the problems we have observed. As we discuss more fully in Chapter 16, which deals with policing, there is also an urgent need to recruit more Aboriginal people to serve as police officers.

We believe a new philosophy of policing is required, particularly where young people are concerned. In our view, the police have abandoned their traditional role as peacekeepers in a community and, instead, have adopted a much narrower "law enforcement" role. In doing so, they have missed important opportunities to serve Aboriginal communities. All too often they have applied "the letter of the law," whether or not this is in keeping with the community's interests. An approach that attempts to discover and deal with the cause of unacceptable behaviour, and to restore harmony to the community, should be adopted.

Failure to Involve Aboriginal People in the Administration of the Youth Justice System

There has been little or no attempt to involve Aboriginal communities in the implementation of the *Young Offenders Act*, even though the Act provides many opportunities for community involvement. Further, as in the adult system, there are very few Aboriginal staff employed in the youth justice system. We are not aware of any Aboriginal staff in senior planning or administrative positions, and only very few full-time, paid staff, either Aboriginal or non-Aboriginal, work in Aboriginal communities.

We question whether the youth authorities are adhering to the principles ensuring parental involvement. Phillip Dorion of The Pas told our Inquiry this story:

Two years ago, in between Christmas and New Year's, there was an incident where the kids were joy riding. A couple of weeks later, the RCMP came to the house when I wasn't present. I was at work. The RCMP asked my boy if he could come up town, that there was a matter they needed to discuss with the boy.

The boy agreed. He went with the RCMP officer to the town detachment. The RCMP then began to question my boy on the incident between Christmas and

New Year's, apparently being friendly with him and encouraging him not to be afraid. He was under-age, a juvenile, still under my care.

I got home and my daughter said that the RCMP had arrived at the house and picked up my boy. I then proceeded to phone the RCMP town detachment. I enquired as to what the charge was. There was no charge, as yet.

I had a long conversation with the RCMP at that time as to what procedure he should take. Should he not have notified me that he was taking my boy, which was under my care first, prior to taking him out of the house? He did not read the rights to that boy until he got him to the station.

The parents or guardians of Aboriginal young offenders must be informed and involved at every step in the judicial process. It is not only police officers who overlook the parents. Lawyers, Crown attorneys, judges and probation officers should not only be consulting or informing parents or guardians, but they must be including the parents whenever decisions are made concerning their child.

Section 56 of the YOA allows young people to sign a document giving up their rights to have their parents or some other adult present when making a statement to the police. We believe this section allows for a dangerous intrusion into the rights of a young offender. It certainly violates the rights of parents. The parents of young offenders, or some other responsible adult, should be present at all times when their children make statements to the police. We recommend the waiver provision be removed from the Act.

In *R. v. James* in 1990, Chief Justice Dickson of the Supreme Court of Canada rejected the admissibility of a statement made to the police without parental or guardian supervision:

> By its enactment of s. 56 of the *Young Offenders Act,* Parliament has recognised the problems and difficulties that beset young people when confronted with authority. No matter what the bravado that young people may display, it is unlikely that they will have the same appreciation as adults to their legal rights or the consequences of oral statements made to persons in authority.[21]

We also believe that the questioning of a youth should take place at home, in the presence of the parents, rather than at a detachment.

WE RECOMMEND THAT:

- The police consider alternatives to the laying of charges in all cases involving Aboriginal youth and, when appropriate, exercise their discretion to take no legal measures or to take measures other than laying a charge.

■ Police departments designate youth specialists and provide special-ized training to all officers involved in the administration of the *Young Offenders Act.*

■ Section 56(4) of the *Young Offenders Act* be amended to remove the provision which allows young offenders to waive their right to have a parent or guardian present during questioning by the police.

Bail and Pre-Trial Detention

Aboriginal young offenders are not provided with the earliest possible opportuni-ty to obtain bail and are frequently denied bail. According to our analysis of Provincial Court study data, 59% of non-Aboriginal youth who spent time in pre-trial detention were released in less than three days, while the comparable figure for Aboriginal youth was 35%. Only 16% of non-Aboriginal youth spent more than 28 days in custody. For Aboriginal youth this figure was more than double: 34% of Aboriginal youth spend more than 28 days in pre-trial detention. It is shocking to learn that more than 90% of female young offenders held on remand were Aboriginal. Half of the male young offenders held on remand were Aboriginal.

These problems occur for a number of reasons:

• The lack of detention facilities in Aboriginal communities results in Abo-riginal youth being removed from their communities and their parents. Unless released quickly, youth from rural Manitoba who are taken into custody will end up at the Manitoba Youth Centre in Winnipeg. They are given the opportunity to obtain bail only after they arrive in Winnipeg or, alternatively, when they are returned to the community for their first court appearance.

• There are few officials resident in Aboriginal communities who are authorized to release young persons on bail; and even where there are such officials, the RCMP tendency is to transport the youth to an urban centre, rather than appear in front of a local judicial officer.

• Once Aboriginal young people have been charged, they often find it dif-ficult to get appropriate legal counsel. There are very few lawyers living in rural or northern Aboriginal communities. Even if there is a lawyer in the community where the youth lives, this may be of little value when the young person is put into custody and transferred to Winnipeg.

• Long distances may make provisions for parental involvement and supervision meaningless. Parents may not even know where their child is and there may be no one available to discuss the case with them.

• There is a general unwillingness on the part of youth court judges to grant bail to youth who "have nowhere to go," or who may be released into a situation with little or poor adult supervision. This applies to both Aboriginal and non-Aboriginal youth, but it is a more significant problem when youth from other parts of the province apply for bail in Winnipeg. It is also a serious problem in Aboriginal communities where there are no support programs to find a home or a responsible adult to supervise Aboriginal youth charged with offences.

- There are no Aboriginal youth court workers, or workers with community-based organizations, who can assure the court that work, a place to live or a responsible adult supervisor can be found for young persons charged with offences.

- There are few community-based programs to provide youth bail supervision.

We believe the present practice of detaining Aboriginal youth prior to trial is disgraceful. We believe it violates some of the rights of young offenders under the *Charter of Rights and Freedoms* and is contrary to the intention of the *Young Offenders Act.*

For example, section 515 of the *Criminal Code* requires a person to be released unless the Crown establishes that his or her detention is necessary.

Section 515(4) of the *Criminal Code* states that the judge must be satisfied, first, that the person's detention is necessary to "ensure his appearance in court." If the judge is satisfied that the person does not need to be detained for that reason, then the judge must consider whether the detention is in the public interest, "having regard to all the circumstances including any substantial likelihood that the accused will, if he is released from custody, commit a criminal offence or interfere with the administration of justice."

If a judge is not satisfied that the detention is necessary on one of these grounds, the youth must be released.

Section 7.1(1) of the *Young Offenders Act* provides that a young person may be placed in the care of a responsible person instead of being detained in custody if a youth court judge or a justice is satisfied that:

(a) a young person who has been arrested would, but for this subsection, be detained in custody,

(b) a responsible person is willing and able to take care of and exercise control over the young person, and

(c) the young person is willing to be placed in the care of that person.

While that section permits a judge to release a detained youth to a "responsible person," the only time a judge can consider doing so is once the decision has been made to deny bail. In other words, a youth who is denied bail for any reason can still be released to a responsible person. We question whether these sections are applied properly to Aboriginal young offenders.

We suggest that the vast majority of Aboriginal young offenders do not need to be detained while awaiting trial. Considering that the majority of Aboriginal youth are held in custody for property offences, it is hard to imagine that there is a social need to lock them up to protect society. We have noted the positive impact Aboriginal child welfare agencies have had upon the quality of care being provided to Aboriginal children caught in the child welfare system. We suspect that many youth now being incarcerated could be kept out of, or released from, custody.

These problems are illustrated best by the cases of Aboriginal youth from the North who are held at the Manitoba Youth Centre in Winnipeg while awaiting trial. They are held in custody with others who have committed crimes that range from the most trivial to the most serious. There is little doubt that the experience in both Agassiz and the Manitoba Youth Centre is not rehabilitative, but, instead, is destructive. In our view, early detention worsens the attitudes of Aboriginal young people.

Aboriginal youth are held in custody before trial for inexcusable periods of time, sometimes until bail assessment reports are prepared, or until it is convenient for lawyers and others operating within the system to bring their cases to trial. We have heard, for example, that youth court judges are sometimes reluctant to grant bail without the preparation of a bail assessment report. To use bail assessment reports as an excuse for a delaying a bail application is not acceptable. The youth who is held in custody is entitled to bail at his or her first appearance. At that time, it is up to the Crown to show why the young person should be detained. If the Crown cannot satisfy a judge that the youth should be detained in custody, then the youth should be released when the application for bail is made. If, however, there is a strong probability that the judge will deny a bail application by a young person based on the information available to him or her, and if defence counsel can persuade the judge that additional information might allow bail to be granted, only then should a bail assessment report be ordered. It should be recognized that the preparation of bail assessment reports can be the cause of inordinate delay, and their ordering should be done only in those situations where bail would likely have been denied in their absence. We question whether bail assessment reports are always necessary or of assistance to the court in the way they are presently being used.

While the YOA requires young offenders to be held in facilities separate and apart from adults, this does not, in our view, require sending youth hundreds of miles from their homes. Nor does it require a totally separate building. In The Pas, for example, young offenders can be kept in a separate part of the institution and have no contact with adult prisoners. In addition, we note that section 7 of the Act provides that adults and young persons do not have to be held in separate facilities if there is no place of detention for young people available within a reasonable distance. We suggest that a more innovative approach to the use of existing facilities could greatly reduce the current disruption in the lives of Aboriginal young people.

We suggest that holding young people and transporting them around the province like so much cargo is contrary to the intent and the principles of the *Young Offenders Act*, particularly subsections 3(1)(f),(g) and (h), which ostensibly protect young offenders from undue interference and restrictions. Presently, these young people must be transported by commercial or government aircraft, and they are accompanied by escorts at all times. Not only is the process expensive, insensitive and short-sighted, but it is probably unlawful.

The experiences of detention and release before trial are only marginally better for Aboriginal youth living in Winnipeg than for northern youth. They too are denied the right to a speedy bail hearing in disproportionate numbers and they too experience numerous delays in obtaining release.

Alternatives to detention can be provided by community-based Aboriginal organizations. The Ma Mawi Chi Itata Centre is a good example of such a program.

Ma Mawi Chi Itata Centre, as part of its youth program, operates a Judicial Release Supervision Program. It works with Aboriginal youth and court authorities to develop bail conditions. If bail is set, it monitors the youth. The bail supervision program has a staff of three Aboriginal workers whose objective is to have youth released from custody, rather than being kept on remand at the Manitoba Youth Centre. If the youth fails to abide by the conditions that are agreed upon, that youth's bail may be cancelled. In addition to making sure the youth respects the bail conditions, Ma Mawi Chi Itata tries to rehabilitate the young person by encouraging further education and training, and by helping that person find a job. Unfortunately, the centre is understaffed and underfunded.

We endorse the Ma Mawi Chi Itata Centre's program and recommend that it be expanded and adequately financed. We believe, as well, that this type of program should be expanded throughout the province, both as an aid to the granting and supervision of bail and for the additional assistance it provides to young people. This type of Aboriginal agency, in our opinion, can fill a need not met now by the traditional probation services. We also believe it could provide diversion and alternative measures programs.

In Chapter 8, which deals with court reform, we recommend that bail hearings be conducted in the community where the offence is committed, that communities be equipped to conduct assessments and to suggest alternatives to pre-trial detention before an accused person is removed from the community, and that community-based bail supervision programs be established.

In our chapter on correctional facilities (Chapter 11) we recommend that short-term holding facilities be established in remote and rural Aboriginal communities, that accused persons be released on bail in their home communities whenever possible and that the Manitoba Youth Centre and the Agassiz Youth Centre not be used as open custody facilities.

The adoption of these policies would end the current practice of transporting young people around the province and would also decrease the number of young Aboriginal people held in institutions.

The following recommendations further address problems of pre-trial detention in the case of young offenders.

WE RECOMMEND THAT:

■   When a youth court judge denies bail, the judge consider releasing the young offender into the custody of his or her parents, or another responsible person, as contemplated by section 7.1(1)(a) of the *Young Offenders Act.*

- The Ma Mawi Chi Itata Centre be given adequate funds and resources to expand its bail supervision program.

- Aboriginal communities be provided with resources to develop bail supervision and other programs that will serve as alternatives to detention.

- Accused youth who must be held in pre-trial detention be held in detention facilities in their own communities.

- Young offenders be removed from their community only as a last resort and only when the youth poses a danger to some individual or to the community.

Transfer to Adult Court

The YOA allows some youth who have been charged with more serious offences to be transferred to adult court. They are then dealt with in the adult court system in the same manner as adults. If incarcerated, they serve their sentence in an adult correctional facility. Many of these transfers appear to occur where the Crown attorney intends to ask for a greater penalty than the three-year maximum provided for by the YOA.

In our opinion, there is no need to transfer prosecutions under the *Young Offenders Act* to the adult courts. Judges of the Youth Court are perfectly capable of trying any type of charge. They have an advantage that other judges do not have. They deal regularly with the sentencing options available under the YOA and know how they can be applied in individual cases. They are familiar with the various youth correctional institutions and their services, and have experience in dealing with youth.

If Parliament is of the view that longer sentences should be applied to youth who are convicted of certain offences, we suggest that more options be made available to youth court judges. If a concern is that Youth Court is too private, we suggest that judges be given the authority to open a trial to the public and to permit the reporting of proceedings and the naming of names.

We consider these options preferable to transferring youths to trial in the adult criminal system and, when there is a conviction, incarceration in an adult institution. We believe it is in the interests of society and youth to have young people dealt with in the specialized Youth Court.

WE RECOMMEND THAT:

- The *Young Offenders Act* be amended to rescind those provisions which allow a youth to be transferred to adult court for trial.

- If Parliament considers it necessary, the *Young Offenders Act* be amended to give youth court judges the option of imposing lengthier sentences on youth convicted of serious offences.

- If Parliament considers it necessary, the *Young Offenders Act* be amended to allow judges to order that the trial of youth be open to the public and the media in appropriate cases.

Custody

As in the adult system, Manitoba youth courts place too much reliance on custodial sentences. Like their adult counterparts, Aboriginal youth are incarcerated disproportionately. Moreover, institutional programs for Aboriginal youth are insensitive to Aboriginal culture and discriminate against Aboriginal youth.

We believe that custody is not required in the vast majority of youth cases. Judges should make greater use of alternatives to incarceration. The Minister of Justice should ensure that alternative sentencing programs are made available to the courts. The present system of dealing with Aboriginal young offenders, by removing them from their communities, warehousing them and then returning them to their communities, is both ineffective and inconsistent with the principles of the YOA.

Young offenders should be left in their home communities, except in the most extreme situations. Efforts should be directed to determining the reason for their unacceptable conduct, and at helping the youth and the parents to deal with the reason for the offence and to avoid any repetition of it. The main objective should be to restore harmony in the community.

Most Aboriginal young offenders in Winnipeg who are detained in open custody end up at the Manitoba Youth Centre (MYC) in Winnipeg. The MYC is, we believe, a totally inappropriate place for the incarceration of youth on open custody sentences. Open custody should be in a facility without bars. At the MYC, however, there is little difference between open and secure custody.

MYC, without question, is unsuitable for youth in open custody. To be blunt, it is a jail. Section 24.1 of the *Young Offenders Act* clearly indicates that Parliament intended open custody to be different and distinct from secure custody. Open custody is defined as:

a) a community residential centre, group home, child care institution, or forest or wilderness camp; or

b) any other like place or facility designated by the Lieutenant Governor in Council of a province or his delegate as a place of open custody for the purposes of this Act, and includes a place or facility within a class of such places or facilities so designated.

It is hard to justify the use of the MYC, or of Agassiz for that matter, as an open custody facility, given the existing bars at the MYC and the nature of its staffing, policies, programs and thrust. It was suggested to us that the reason the MYC is used in place of regional facilities is purely economic. We find such reasoning abhorrent. The Province should never have designated the MYC or Agassiz as open custody facilities in the first place. The federal government should amend the law to prohibit provinces from mixing closed and open custody facilities.

Young people should not be mistreated by the justice system because of a lack of resources. There is a responsibility on the part of legislators to ensure that appropriate resources are provided to properly carry out the intent of the laws they enact. It is also the responsibility of those charged with implementing the Act to do so as the Act intended. While it is understandable, in hard economic times, that tough decisions have to be made about how to do many tasks with fewer dollars, we note that the MYC and Agassiz were designated as open custody facilities from the onset of the *Young Offenders Act*. We suggest that the MYC and Agassiz be limited to secure custody, and that young people be sent there only as a last resort and only when they pose a danger to society.

Unfortunately, judges have no say as to the facility to which a sentenced youth is to go. This is in the hands of the provincial government. We suggest, as we do for the adult system, that judges be entitled to designate the place of custody. When a judge is sentencing someone, the judge will want to have the youth receive appropriate treatment. The judge will have assessed the youth and the offence. Some youth may benefit from counselling; others, from a work preparation program. The judge will be familiar with the various programs available at different facilities and will be aware of the best facility for a particular youth. We recognize that those who operate a youth facility may conclude later that a youth should be moved, or the youth may not be able to be accommodated in a particular institution. In those circumstances, it would be understandable if the judge's direction could not be followed. We suggest, however, that much more attention be paid to the opinion of judges. Judges should also exercise more control over placement by using the provisions of the Act that allow the court to name an individual to take charge of a youth.

Aboriginal youth are not now receiving culturally relevant programs or training and assistance. MYC is making efforts in this direction but the atmosphere of the institution makes any chance of success unlikely.

In addition to the jail-like atmosphere of the MYC, we found the overcrowding to be deplorable. While the staff tried to make light of the situation, equating it to camping, we found many young women were forced to sleep on the floor in their overcrowded rooms. We would be surprised if health authorities would approve of this type of accommodation for anyone.

Recreation at the Manitoba Youth Centre, when we were there, was limited to one hour in the gymnasium every day. Admission to the weight room was limited and apparently depended on the youth's conduct. Skates that were once available in the winter have been removed. We believe there is a need for considerably more recreational programming.

The Agassiz Youth Centre at Portage la Prairie has good programs and deals with Aboriginal youth as well as might be expected in a non-Aboriginal institution. But the programs would function better if young offenders were counselled and directed by people from their own culture and their own communities. It too is another institution to which young people are sent from all over the province.

In spite of the old buildings, we found the programs at Agassiz far superior to those at the Manitoba Youth Centre. Agassiz operates on the peer pressure principle called "positive peer culture therapy." A great deal of time is spent in group discussions talking about personal problems and, in particular, the reason the youth got into trouble with the law. Residents receive lectures and view videos dealing with alcoholism, drug abuse and other issues. The residents are encouraged to work in the neighbouring community on a volunteer basis.

Neither institution takes Aboriginal culture into consideration. The educational programs are the standard fare offered in public schools, with their pro-European cultural bias. These types of educational programs have been shown recently to be the cause of much of the alienation among Aboriginal youth. At the time of our visits, there were no Aboriginal cultural programs for youth at either the MYC or Agassiz.

We believe that culturally appropriate programming for Aboriginal people must be an essential feature of any correctional facility. This is true especially for young Aboriginal people, since many of them have suffered from negative stereotyping or a lack of positive cultural models in non-Aboriginal school systems and other social institutions. We did not detect any awareness that such programs are needed, much less any commitment to their development in the future. Nor was there any appreciation of the rehabilitative potential of cultural programming.

The fact that existing correctional facilities are situated far from Aboriginal communities is a problem. Successive governments have refused to consider establishing appropriate facilities for youth who reside in northern Manitoba.

Most young people from the North have no contact with their family or friends during their incarceration. Because of distances and cost, these young people do not have the opportunity to visit their homes and to prepare for their eventual release. This creates a problem when Aboriginal young people try to reintegrate into their communities upon release. This is a lesser problem for Aboriginal families in the South, but even they have trouble visiting family members who are in custody.

The number of young people from the North who are incarcerated clearly shows the need for better programs and facilities in the North. We think it is absolutely essential that young people be dealt with in, or as close as possible to, their own communities. Many northern Aboriginal youth we saw at the Manitoba Youth Centre and the Agassiz Youth Centre could benefit more from supervision at home or in foster home settings in their own communities. Others could be housed in custodial facilities in their own communities so they might go to school or perform community service during the day. Even the more troublesome youth, who have to be removed from their communities, could live in a camp setting not too far from their homes.

We recommend the use of wilderness camps for Aboriginal youth. These camps should be staffed by Aboriginal people and should offer a combination of work, education, recreation and counselling. The education component should include Aboriginal culture and life skills courses. The work should be geared to providing skills to enable the youth to obtain employment upon their release. In our opinion, these camps would be less costly to establish and operate than traditional jails. Similar wilderness camps might be established in southern Manitoba.

In a brief to our Inquiry, the Ma Mawi Chi Itata Centre recommended that custody homes be established in Winnipeg to reduce the number of young people being held in secure custody before and after their trial. The custody homes would permit youth to find work or to continue their education during the day and to return to the homes at night. While we believe the use of any form of custody can be reduced substantially, the type of program advocated by Ma Mawi would be a significant improvement over the types of custody programs that are now being used.

Elsewhere in our report, we recommend that incarceration should only be used in instances where the offender poses a threat to an individual or the community, or where any other sanction would not sufficiently reflect the gravity of the offence or penalize an offender for wilful non-compliance with the terms of any other sentence that has been imposed. We also recommend that correctional institutions introduce policies which guarantee Aboriginal inmates the right and the opportunity to exercise their spiritual beliefs, and that institutions offer Aboriginal inmates culturally appropriate education, trades training and counselling programs. We believe these recommendations must be implemented in correctional institutions for young people, as well as in those for adults.

WE RECOMMEND THAT:

- The *Young Offenders Act* be amended to allow judges to designate the specific place of custody for young offenders.

- The *Young Offenders Act* be amended to prohibit the mixing of closed custody facilities with open custody.

- Open custody facilities and wilderness camps be established for Aboriginal youth throughout the province and, especially, in Aboriginal communities.

Finally, we are concerned about the youth older than 18 years who remain part of the youth justice system. Presently, the Act allows young people up to the age of 21 to serve their sentences in youth custody facilities. They may have committed their crime before the age of 18, or they may have had their sentence extended beyond their 18th birthday.

This creates two problems. First, the older youth do not have access to programs that are appropriate to their age and interests. In fact, they tend to stand out because they are much older than most of the other youth who are in custody. Secondly, some of these young adults appear to be a bad influence on the younger offenders. We strongly urge correctional administrators to use their discretion to bring such cases to the attention of the court. Consideration can then be given to transferring these older offenders to more appropriate adult facilities.

Section 24.5 of the *Young Offenders Act* already permits the transfer of young offenders to adult camps or correctional programs. Great care, of course, will have to be exercised in assessing the needs of those whose transfer is being considered.

Youth Justice and Child Welfare

Aboriginal young people have not been well served by the separation of the child welfare and the youth justice systems, a separation that has been accentuated by the *Young Offenders Act*. When family support systems fail, young Aboriginal people may resort to unacceptable conduct merely to call attention to their predicament. They may try to escape from their homes to find a more secure environment. We have heard of young people breaking the law so they could be sent to the Manitoba Youth Centre for that very reason. In these cases, we do not believe it is always appropriate for the criminal justice system to respond by treating them as criminals. Yet, that is what happens now.

As we discuss more fully in Chapter 14, which deals with the child welfare system, many Aboriginal youth who become involved in the justice system are products of a failed child welfare system. This failure is often signalled by a breach of the law, but it starts much earlier.

At present, if a youth in the care of an agency is charged, agencies appear to walk away from the youth, surrendering the child to the youth justice system. The agency may be relieved to lose a client, but the criminal justice system is ill-equipped to provide help for those young people with primarily social, cultural or family problems. Aboriginal young persons are often abandoned and left to their own resources, sometimes for years, while the criminal justice system tries to react in a narrow, legalistic fashion, resulting in social dysfunction.

There is an unfortunate lack of cohesion between family service agencies and the youth court system. Aboriginal youth involved in crime are often simply in need of additional and appropriate support services from social service agencies. In many cases, these types of services would be sufficient to keep the youth out of trouble with the law. Instead, because agencies refuse to get involved with a youth charged with an offence, the full and inappropriate force of the criminal justice system is often applied.

Many of the cases we are referring to could be diverted from the criminal justice system by the police, by the Crown prosecutor and by judges. When such cases must be dealt with in court, youth court judges should involve family service agencies where their services might be more appropriate than the correctional ones.

The *Juvenile Delinquents Act* had a provision that allowed judges to involve child welfare or family service agencies. It stated that "the court may, in its discretion ... commit the child to the charge of any children's aid society"[22] or to the superintendent of a municipality in cases where there was no such society. There is no similar provision in the *Young Offenders Act*.

WE RECOMMEND THAT:

- The *Young Offenders Act* be amended to allow a judge dealing with a criminal case to commit a youth to the care of a child and family service agency as an alternative to incarceration or custody.

We do not recommend a total return to the approach of the *Juvenile Delinquents Act*, but a better balance between the concerns of the JDA and the *Young Offenders Act*. It is disheartening to see a criminal justice system trying to deal with what are essentially problems of families and communities in crisis. Appropriate dispositions do not always flow from an adversarial criminal justice system, but can, we believe, flow better from a process which takes into account all options that serve the best interests of young people and their families. The "criminal justice" orientation of the dispositions now available under the YOA has proven to be inappropriate where the misdeeds of the youth stem from his or her response to a poor or negative family situation.

While we recognize that it is undesirable to have a youth justice system completely dominated by a child welfare philosophy, the current "criminal" approach is equally inappropriate. What is needed is to have the justice system and the child welfare system develop a coordinated and cooperative approach to the problems of young people. They should be working in unison, and not at arm's length, the way they have for many years. We leave others to consider whether there should be unification of certain parts of each system. Youth with problems should receive assistance from both services.

We also note that a more holistic approach, with family service agencies and youth courts working together for young people, was intended by the tripartite Indian Child Welfare agreements that were negotiated in the early 1980s. Article 4 of the Canada-Manitoba-Indian Child Welfare Agreement states, in part, that the agreement would be the basis for the integration of Indian child welfare, related family services and Indian juvenile probation services. These services would be transferred to the eventual control of Aboriginal communities and their institutions. The provincial position, however, was that probation should not be confused or integrated with a child welfare-oriented service. Therefore, the young offender component has not been transferred, except in the case of the programs provided by the Dakota Ojibway Tribal Council. We disagree with the opposition of the Province of Manitoba to the transfer of these services.

We are satisfied that Aboriginal communities suffer from a lack of probation services. This invariably results from the lack of commitment of adequate resources by provincial government departments, and a belief on the part of provincial officials that such programs, particularly in Indian communities, are the responsibility of the federal government. As a consequence, Aboriginal youth placed on probation suffer from lack of supervision. They do not see their probation officers often—if at all. Moreover, the probation worker is usually from a southern community, sometimes hundreds of miles away, and lacks important information about available resources, the community dynamics affecting the youth's behaviour, and many other important factors.

To overcome the problems we have identified will require a lot of work and cooperation on many fronts. In Aboriginal communities, Aboriginal child and family service agencies have been working for a number of years and are well accepted by Aboriginal communities. These agencies should have their mandates expanded so they can also deal with young offenders and their probation. They should be in a position to accept referrals from the courts and others. In addition to probation, they could establish bail supervision programs. They could provide the counselling and programs needed by young people. They will need additional resources, and these should be provided. These agencies, we believe, are in the best position to bring about the change in philosophy and approach that we think necessary.

While we hope and expect that many cases will be kept out of court if the recommendations we have proposed are adopted, we know that there will be some cases that will proceed to court. In Aboriginal communities, both child welfare and young offender cases should be dealt with by Aboriginal justice systems. We also deal with some alternative measures later in this chapter.

In non-Aboriginal communities, and in Aboriginal communities where Aboriginal courts are not yet developed, other changes will have to be made. We believe it will be necessary to unify the courts so that young offender and child welfare matters can be dealt with in one court with appropriate support services.

In Winnipeg, where separate courts hear these matters, delays can occur because a case handled by one court may have to wait while the other court deals with a related situation.

Elsewhere, we recommend the amalgamation of the Court of Queen's Bench and the Provincial Court of Manitoba. We believe the courts should have a range of options available to them in both the child welfare and youth justice systems dealing with young people. The unification of the courts would make this possible.

WE RECOMMEND THAT:

- Child and family service agencies be directed to continue to provide services to youth clients charged with an offence.

- Child welfare and youth justice services be more fully integrated and coordinated so that all their services are available to young people charged with offences.

- Youth probation for Aboriginal youth be made a part of the responsibility of Aboriginal child and family service agencies.

Diversion and Alternative Measures

As we have seen, the current youth justice system is neither effective nor fair as far as Aboriginal youth are concerned. While we have proposed a number of specific reforms throughout our discussion, it would be misleading to leave the impression that anything short of fundamental change is required. In particular, we believe that:

- Systemic discrimination must be eliminated.

- The principles of the YOA must be implemented.

- Aboriginal communities must be involved in the administration of the YOA in a meaningful way.

- More culturally sensitive programming must be provided.

- More Aboriginal staff must be retained and deployed in both rural and urban areas.

Perhaps most important of all, we believe that the administration of youth justice in Aboriginal communities should be vested in the governments of those communities. This should ultimately include the establishment of Aboriginal youth courts and the appointment of Aboriginal judges. We see the youth justice system as an important part of the Aboriginal court systems which we discuss in Chapter 7.

In non-Aboriginal communities, and in Aboriginal communities where Aboriginal courts are not established, it is our assessment that a significant expansion of diversion and alternative measures programs represents the best hope to achieve the fundamental restructuring of the youth justice system. These programs, we believe, offer the potential to radically alter the way we deal with youth. We see the opportunity for significant benefits, not only to young people, but also to their families and society as a whole. It is for this reason that we provide an extensive review of diversion and alternative measures programs in this section.

In Aboriginal communities where an Aboriginal justice system is established, formal alternative measures programs may not be needed. Aboriginal justice systems will undoubtedly incorporate traditional and customary Aboriginal practices. Provided that Aboriginal communities themselves manage and are accountable for those systems, we expect the philosophy will be based on their own customs and traditions that seek the restoration of peace and harmony in the community. In effect, "alternative measures" will be considered in just about every case.

The Purpose of Juvenile Diversion and Alternative Measures

The juvenile justice systems we discussed earlier were established first in the late 19th century to remove youth from the harshness of the adult system and to treat them in a manner which would more likely rehabilitate them. The creation of a juvenile justice system, distinct from the adult system, was an improvement over previous practices.

During the 1970s, in both Canada and the United States, there was a gradual move toward "diverting" some youth from the traditional justice system. The concept of "diversion" became very broad and was used to describe a wide array of distinct, but loosely related, types of programs and policies.

While there are some similarities between the terms "diversion" and "alternative measures," we will attempt to separate the two for the purposes of our discussion and to give each a distinct meaning.

We will speak of "diversion" to indicate any plan or program that is intended to keep a youth out of the court system altogether. Diversion programs can be used instead of laying a charge. As a result, the court would have no involvement with the youth. Whether a charge might have to be laid in the future might depend on the success or failure of the diversionary efforts.

"Alternative measures," on the other hand, will refer to programs or options for dealing with young offenders once they are charged with an offence and within the court system. The term "alternative measures" is dealt with in some detail in the *Young Offenders Act*. The court has some continuing involvement in that a charge hangs over the youth until the alternative measures prescribed by the court are complied with.

There are a number of related rationales for diversion and alternative measures, including: a concern that young people not be turned into or branded as criminals; a desire to rehabilitate rather than "warehouse" them; an interest in having greater community and victim involvement; and, ultimately, a reduction in youth criminal activity.

Young people who fall into the juvenile justice system come to see themselves, and to be seen, as offenders. They are labelled as "bad kids" and they come to think of themselves in that way. This greatly increases the risk of reinvolvement in the justice system. Their involvement in the justice system frequently exposes them to more serious offenders who may actually encourage their "graduation" into more serious crime. Once they have become involved in the system, the youth are likely to be responded to by authorities and others in a variety of ways that reinforce this negative self-image. Diversion may help reduce this labelling effect.

The traditional youth court setting is not as helpful as many hoped it would be, and often is harmful, particularly for Aboriginal youth. It is difficult to establish a meaningful dialogue with a young person in a formal court setting, where the judge is expected to be an impartial arbiter. Diversion offers a greater promise of overcoming this inherent problem within the legal system. It keeps the youth out of the courtroom altogether.

Diversion and alternative measures programs provide the opportunity for victims to play a more important role than that accorded to them by the criminal justice system. The role of the victim in our present system is still limited largely to being a witness in court proceedings. In Aboriginal communities, victims often can be close relatives or members of the extended family of the offender. They typically receive very little information about the cases in which they are involved, and often express bitterness about the lack of sensitivity of the criminal justice process toward them. Diversion and alternative measures programs have tended to be more sensitive to the needs of victims. Many programs employ victim-offender reconciliation and restitution. This type of reconciliation is preferable in Aboriginal communities where the restoration of harmony is the goal.

Diversion and alternative measures programs involve the community. They are designed to ensure that program decision makers and administrators are members of the same community as the offender. This allows community values and traditions to be accommodated. This is often difficult to achieve in the formal criminal justice system. Moreover, communities can be given a measure of responsibility for their own offenders.

Traditional adversarial models of juvenile justice have proven to be slow, expensive and cumbersome. Diversion and alternative measures programs can operate, we believe, in a more efficient and expeditious manner.

The *Young Offenders Act*, Alternative Measures and Diversion

The YOA's Declaration of Principles makes explicit reference to alternative measures, as well as to broader notions of minimal intervention. According to the Act, "alternative measures" includes "diversion." The Act says:

3(1) It is hereby recognized and declared that ...

(d) where it is not inconsistent with the protection of society, taking no measures or taking measures other than judicial proceedings under the Act should be considered for dealing with young persons who have committed offences;...

(f) in the application of this Act, the rights and freedoms of young persons include a right to the least possible interference that is consistent with the protection of society, having regard to the needs of young persons and the interests of their families.

Section 4 of the Act establishes a legal framework for the operation of alternative measures programs. Although this section gives substantial flexibility to governments and program operators, it is careful to protect the rights of young persons. For example, the young person must acknowledge responsibility for the act and consent to the specific alternative measures that are being proposed. In addition, the young person has the right to consult a lawyer and the right to have the case proceed to court.

The YOA has made possible a wide array of diversion and alternative measures programs across Canada. While, in theory, there is no limit on the types of offences or offenders which can be dealt with by diversion or alternative measures, most programs deal with first offenders or those charged with less serious offences.

Youth Justice Committees

One of the most promising delivery agencies for diversion and alternative measures programs are youth justice committees. In Manitoba, a number of community-based organizations operate diversion and alternative measures programs. Most of these organizations have developed as youth justice committees under section 69 of the YOA. The section states:

The Attorney General of a province ... may establish one or more committees of citizens, to be known as youth justice committees, to assist without remuneration in any aspect of the administration of this Act or in any programs or services for young offenders....

There are 10 Aboriginal youth justice committees currently operating in Manitoba. They become involved with youth in one of two ways. If a youth is causing trouble in the community, the band constable or another police officer, a member of the band council, the parents or any concerned person can ask the youth justice committee to become involved in the case before a charge has been laid. If a charge has been laid, the youth can still be referred to a youth justice committee by the Crown attorney or, later in the process, by a judge.

Once a young person agrees to participate, the youth justice committee meets with the youth to discuss the problem and the options that are available. These might include writing an essay, making restitution to the victim, performing community service work, participating in a recreation program, or seeking some form of counselling. The range of measures is limited only by the resources and imagination of program administrators and the consent of the youth.

Some youth justice committees provide bail supervision, others supervise probation orders, while still others are involved in victim-offender reconciliation and other forms of alternative dispute resolution. Some make representations to the court on behalf of young offenders. We believe these committees perform an important service and should be expanded, not only in urban centres, but also in rural and Aboriginal communities.

Aboriginal communities, which tend to be more remote, are not being encouraged to pursue or expand such programs at this time. Provincial guidelines and funding priorities must be adjusted to rectify this problem.

We do not understand why youth justice committees, some of which are becoming quite sophisticated, should be required to operate without the financial and administrative support that is accorded to other components of the justice system. Nor do we understand why section 69 of the YOA stipulates that members of youth justice committees must serve "without remuneration."

Some examples of successful youth justice committees include:

• **The Island Lake / St. Theresa Point Youth Justice Committee.** During the course of our hearings in the Island Lake area, residents of the St. Theresa Point Indian Band told us about the workings of their youth justice committee. Several parents lobbied for the establishment of the committee in hopes of dealing with a growing number of young people who appeared to be engaging in gas sniffing and truancy.

The committee was established by the community and is based on the traditions and customs of the tribe. The committee began calling young people who were sniffing gasoline and not attending school to appear at meetings where they were lectured by elders about their inappropriate behaviour. Generally, the rebuke took place in public meetings with others from the community in attendance. Soon, the parents were also called to account. In this way, the committee functioned as a true diversion program. Eventually, young people who faced criminal charges were being referred to the committee as an alternative to formal court processing.

The band council then took a further step by appointing a community "magistrate." While this position has no status under either provincial or federal laws, the individual is considered by the community to be acting upon authority stemming from known tribal customs. There does not appear to have been any instance where a person in the community has questioned the authority of the community magistrate.

The RCMP have been supportive of the program. They have found it so effective that they too refer young people to the program, rather than laying a charge, as they would likely have done before the program was instituted.

We were advised that the number of young offender crimes in the community has been reduced dramatically.

• **The Wi Chi Whey Wen Youth Justice Committee.** The Ma Mawi Chi Itata Centre, which provides voluntary services for Aboriginal families in Winnipeg under Manitoba's *Child and Family Services Act,* has established this youth justice committee under the YOA in conjunction with the Probation Service of the Province of Manitoba. The purpose of this committee is to provide diversion and alternative measures for Aboriginal youth. The close working relationship between a child and family service program and a youth justice committee is encouraging since, as we have noted elsewhere, there is often a direct link between Aboriginal youth in need of social services and Aboriginal youth crime. This sort of cooperation is rare and is to be encouraged.

While the program is beneficial, it needs more resources to deal with the large number of Aboriginal youth coming before the courts in Winnipeg.

• **The Roseau River Tribal Council Justice Committee.** In the 1970s, the Roseau River Indian Band had a reputation for rates of violence and crime that exceeded those of most other communities in Manitoba. In 1973, Judge Robert Kopstein of the Provincial Court, who had been hearing cases from Roseau in a nearby non-Aboriginal community, started to hold regular court sittings on the reserve. He and Milton Kotyk, a probation officer, met several times with the chief and council of the band to discuss the problems and what could be done about them. As a result of these meetings, the band established the Roseau River Justice Committee.

The committee was made up of several people from the band. At first, the committee members asked the judge if they could observe the court proceedings. He agreed. Later, the judge agreed to have a member of the committee sit beside him in the courtroom. From time to time, when sentencing a band member, the judge would ask the committee members for the opinion of the committee. The committee member often spoke about the community's concerns. In this way, the band had an effective voice in the proceedings.

The committee later instituted a youth diversion program, with the assistance of the local probation officer, the judge and the Crown attorney. Both the police and the

Crown attorney began referring cases to the committee. Sometimes, the committee would initiate meetings with youth and their parents to deal with complaints concerning a youth's conduct.

The committee could impose a variety of community sanctions, including requiring community service work, suspending a youth from involvement in recreational programs, suspending a youth from school, requiring a youth to apologize to the victim or the community, or even banishing a youth from the community. Anyone unhappy with the committee's disposition could appeal to the chief and council, although this rarely occurred.

At the time the committee was most active, the band was undergoing a cultural revival. This revival was partly responsible for the improved conditions on the reserve. But most residents feel that the efforts of the youth justice committee significantly helped to reduce the incidence of crime and violence.

The community committee continues to be active. It operates as a diversion and an alternative measures program, and deals with many of the cases where young people from the reserve get into trouble with the law.

Other Examples of Diversion and Alternative Measures

During the course of the Inquiry, we heard presentations from a number of organizations that either were operating diversion programs or were hoping to establish such programs. They included:

•**The Community Dispute Centre.** This service is a community-based organization in Winnipeg's North End and Inner City. The centre aims at providing people with the means to settle conflicts in a non-violent manner, without recourse to the legal system. The process relies on the use of face-to-face meetings between the parties to a dispute and third-party mediators. The centre's executive director, Robert Miller, said the centre "views mediation as a way of strengthening communities and empowering people to deal with conflict in their daily life." The centre deals with a variety of neighbourhood conflicts, such as landlord and tenant disputes, but it does not involve itself in matters where criminal charges have been laid.

• **Mediation Services.** This program, sponsored by the Mennonite Central Committee, works in cooperation with the Winnipeg Police Department and the Crown attorney's office to provide mediation as an alternative court process. According to Paul Redekop, the Mediation Services representative who appeared before our Inquiry, the service "is oriented to the principle of restorative justice. This principle sees justice to be done when relationships which were disrupted because of criminal acts are restored." The service makes use of face-to-face meetings of victims, accused individuals and trained volunteer mediators.

The mediation service is provided as an alternative to the court process in cases where criminal charges have been laid and a plea has not been entered. Cases from both adult court and Youth Court are diverted to Mediation Services. Both the victim and accused must agree to the process. The service subscribes to a model of restorative justice, as opposed to retributive justice. Mediation Services deals largely with assault cases, along with some property disputes and some abuse cases.

• **The Native Harmony and Restoration Centre.** This is a proposal of the Interlake Reserves Tribal Council. The council wishes to establish the centre at Pineimuta Place, a former federal radar base near Gypsumville now owned by the council, as a diversionary and alternative measures facility. The centre would combine traditional tribal customs and values with post-secondary education and vocational training. Its long-term goal is to allow those who have been in conflict with their community to return to it healed and reconciled. The centre would allow the offender's family members to reside at the centre and, because it is located in close proximity to a number of Aboriginal communities, would provide an opportunity for reconciliation between the victim and offender.

Diversion in Manitoba

Those involved in the justice system should give strong consideration to the use of diversion whenever an inappropriate act of a young person is brought to their attention.

• **The Police.** When an offence has been committed, the police are contacted and are usually the first representatives of the justice system to examine the circumstances. It is the police who decide if the youth should be charged and, if so, what charge is to be laid.

Police authorities should be directed by the Minister of Justice to consider whether some diversionary program is available and appropriate, rather than immediately laying a criminal charge. They should consider speaking to and, if necessary, lecturing the youth. A letter to the parents, warning of the youth's conduct, might be of value. A meeting with the youth, the parents and the band chief, or a member of a youth justice committee, might be all that is necessary to indicate the unacceptable nature of the conduct and to discourage repetition. If the police do not want to remain involved, referral to a justice committee might be appropriate. This is more likely to happen if community-based policing is being practised.

• **The Crown Attorney.** The Crown attorney should proceed in a manner similar to that which we propose for the police. If the police bring a matter to the Crown attorney and charges have been laid, or are being considered or recommended, the Crown should consider whether the case can be diverted from the court process. If the Crown attorney is not aware of any services available in a certain community, people from that community, such as the chief or the justice committee, should be consulted to see if they would be willing to try to deal with the problem.

It should be Department of Justice policy that diversion be carefully considered before a criminal charge is laid or proceeded with.

• **Youth Justice Committee.** These committees should do whatever is necessary to make sure that police, lawyers and the court are aware of their existence and the services they provide. They should also keep records to show the results of their efforts. It is important for others involved in the justice system to know which programs have been of value.

• **Chief and Council.** The chief and council, as representatives of their community, should support diversion programs and should encourage the establishment of youth justice committees and other support groups within their community. In this way, they can assume more control over what happens to youth from their community. A continuing and supportive dialogue should take place between the chief, the police, lawyers and judges serving their community.

Alternative Measures in Manitoba

The *Young Offenders Act* provides a number of suggestions and directions to the Youth Court and to others dealing with youth who come before the court. Unfortunately, not enough attention is given to exploring all these options in every case. There is too much use of traditional sentences, including probation. We would like to see alternative measures programs applied to take advantage of the options referred to in the Act. In this way, society and Aboriginal youth will benefit. If an alternative measures program has been complied with by a youth, section 4(4)(a) of the YOA says the court *shall* dismiss the charge.

The Act leaves it up the Attorney General of the province to develop guidelines for alternative measures programs. The current guidelines specify that young persons can only be referred to alternative measures if they have committed less serious offences and do not have a prior history of serious offences. Manitoba's alternative measures scheme excludes young persons charged with serious driving offences, crimes of violence or threatened violence, and crimes resulting in a total loss of over $1,000.

We consider it inappropriate that a provincial Attorney General can negate the principles of the YOA by establishing restrictive criteria for the use of alternative measures. We recommend that this power be removed from the Department of the Attorney General. We believe that youth court judges who deal with young offenders on a daily basis, and who continually search for ways to deal with them, are in a much better position to devise and apply alternative measures.

We recommend that new guidelines be established to provide that alternative measures programs are available to all offenders. The police, lawyers, Crown attorneys and judges should consider such measures in every case. This is particularly important if an offender has never been offered the opportunity to participate in an alternative measures program.

Some of the alternative measures we think should be considered are:

- Staying of proceedings. This might be appropriate where the youth has learned a lesson from his or her conduct and from what has happened to him or her in being apprehended and brought to court.

- Returning the youth to the parents with a reminder of the potential for problems and the direction to be responsible for the conduct of the youth.

- Placing the child with a person who is willing to have the youth in his or her residence and is prepared to give the youth needed support and guidance.

- Requiring the youth's attendance at counselling programs. These programs might be to develop life skills or to deal with a substance abuse problem.

- Requiring the youth's attendance at a particular school, either for academic or vocational training.

- Requiring the youth to apologize to the victim.

- Requiring the youth to make restitution or perform services for the victim.

- Requiring the youth to do general community work under the direction of some specified person or the administrator of community service orders.

- Referring the youth to a youth justice committee for its attention.

- Referring the youth to a peacemaker.

- Requiring the youth to appear before the chief and council and to make an apology to the whole community.

In our opinion, these types of measures will be much more effective in dealing with inappropriate conduct on the part of Aboriginal young people than would be a conviction and the imposition of a fine or incarceration. They certainly are more appropriate in Aboriginal communities. The person or group to whom a youth is referred can be asked to report to the court after a period of time. If the alternative measures program does not work, the youth can be brought back to court.

We recognize that all young offenders cannot be dealt with in this way. Many of those who have committed serious offences may require a more severe approach. Nevertheless, the court should keep alternative measures in mind in every case and should refrain from taking another step unless and until these alternatives have been discussed with the lawyers and the accused.

International Examples: The Scottish Experience

An example of the type of approach we believe should be examined is provided by the Scottish Children's Hearings System. Young offenders in Scotland benefit from having the court and social service systems work together to solve youth and family problems.

In 1964 the Secretary of State for Scotland appointed a committee under the chairmanship of Lord Kilbrandon to consider the manner in which truants, juvenile delinquents and children in need of protection were being dealt with. The committee made no distinction between children who were neglected and children who had committed offences. It took the position that all unacceptable behaviour was the result of abuse, neglect or deprivation on the part of care-giving adults, the community or the state. This was much like the philosophy of Canada's *Juvenile Delinquents Act*.

Because of the committee's philosophy, questions of guilt or innocence were seen as being largely irrelevant. In fact, the committee believed that most of the 95% of juveniles charged with an offence who plead guilty ought to be dealt with by social service agencies outside the court system. They argued that all troubled youth should receive treatment and education to assist them in becoming productive members of society.

The system recommended by the Kilbrandon committee to provide services to troubled youth was to be known as the Children's Hearings System. This program was intended to be distinct from the courts and to be a part of the social service system. It was to deal with all who would have been dealt with formerly by the juvenile court system or by the child welfare system.

Three basic assumptions and principles formed the basis for the new program:

1. Genuine concern on the part of parents for the well-being of their children was assumed.

2. Preventive and remedial measures, involving education away from deviant behaviour, were to be emphasized.

3. Wide discretionary powers to choose measures appropriate to individual cases were to be provided.

The position of "reporter" was key to the committee's proposals. A reporter, usually a professionally trained social worker, was given wide powers to receive and investigate complaints referred by the police, social welfare agencies, the schools or anyone in the community. Complaints could be dismissed by the reporter, the case could be monitored, or the complaint could be referred to a Children's Panel.

Under the Scottish system that now exists, a Children's Panel is appointed for a period of three years and members are expected to sit for at least three months a year. Members have experience in dealing with children and their problems, but they need not be trained professionally in social work or the law. Panel members undergo an intensive six-week training course. The only reason for referring a case to a panel is if "the child is in need of care."

When a reporter refers a case to the Children's Panel, both the youth and the parents are informed of the nature of the referral. A hearing date is set within a few days. Parents and child may be accompanied by a clergyman, doctor or any other person. Social workers, teachers, counsellors or psychologists may also be present. There are no particular rules of procedure. The hearing takes place, not in a courtroom, but in a room with those present seated around a table.

The intention of the hearing is for parents, children and panel members to assess the gravity of the problem and to reach agreement on how best to treat the situation. The system is designed specifically to avoid the formal adversarial procedures of a courtroom. Its decisions, nevertheless, are subject to appeal to a court.

If a dispute arises concerning the grounds of the referral, or if no agreement can be reached, the panel must inform the court. The court is then required to hold a hearing within seven days.

A panel may order the removal of children at risk, and young offenders may be sent to a residential school. Children removed from parents remain the responsibility of the panel, even if they are being looked after by foster parents or in a children's home. The panel may also order supervision of various kinds. For example, they may require a youth to go to an attendance centre, which is a day program, staffed by police officers, that provides programs on physical education, handicrafts, citizenship and the like. While there are aspects of the Scottish program that appeal to us, we do not support such extensive authority for an alternative measures or diversion program in Manitoba.

An important part of the Scottish system of dealing with youth is the role of the police and, in particular, the way they deal with young people who have committed offences that are not considered serious enough to warrant charges being laid. The police may require the youth and the parents to report to the police station to receive a warning. The Kilbrandon committee reported that about 90% of juveniles dealt with by the police in this way do not come into police hands again.

The Police Juvenile Liaison Scheme, which was introduced in Liverpool in 1949, continues, with local variations, in several parts of Scotland. The scheme is basically a program to follow up with the child, both at home and at school, after a warning has been issued. This usually involves visits by the police and sometimes by the clergy.

We believe the children's panels and Juvenile Liaison Scheme are examples of ways in which the justice system can employ "child welfare" principles in dealing with young people who have come into conflict with the law. As we mentioned earlier, however, such an approach works best in cases where the youth's responsibility for the breach of the law is either proven or admitted. As a way of disposing of such cases, we think the approach is commendable.

Application of Alternative Measures in Manitoba

There is a broad range of diversion and alternative measures programs, and most share, at least to some extent, the philosophy that rehabilitation, reconciliation and restitution should be emphasized over retribution, particularly with young offenders. Some programs focus on victim-offender mediation or reconciliation, while others are more broadly based alternatives to the formal court system.

It is apparent that the degree to which Aboriginal youth benefit from alternative measures programs, no matter how they are structured, will depend heavily upon the way such programs are delivered.

WE RECOMMEND THAT:

- Adequate administrative and financial support be provided to youth justice committees.

- The *Young Offenders Act* be amended to remove the provision prohibiting members of youth justice committees from being remunerated.

■ Manitoba's alternative measures guidelines be amended to allow any young offender to be referred to an alternative measures program. The police, lawyers, Crown attorneys and judges should consider such measures in every case.

■ The authority for the creation of alternative measures guidelines be shifted from the provincial government to the judiciary.

■ The provincial government establish Aboriginally focussed diversion and alternative measures programs which incorporate the following principles:

• Aboriginal culture must be integrated into the program. Diversion schemes which involve the use of Aboriginal elders, peacemakers and other aspects of Aboriginal culture appear to have the greatest potential for success. In the context of Manitoba's urban Aboriginal communities, the program decision-makers could be drawn from the Aboriginal community within the urban environment.

• Judges must allow the community to become involved in sentencing but they must retain ultimate responsibility for sentencing.

• The program should attempt to involve all those who have a direct interest in the case, including the victim and the community.

• Programs should be able to accept referrals at any stage of the criminal justice process. They should also be able to accept referrals from the community before any charges have been laid and, if possible, before the authorities become involved.

• The community's respect for the program is vital. This means that one primary goal of the program must be to seek reconciliation and the restoration of peace in the community.

• The establishment of a range of innovative options that can be used by the decision-makers will be critical to the success of alternative measures programs based in Aboriginal communities. An appropriate plan for an Aboriginal youth might, for example, involve participation in an Aboriginally operated wilderness program, an education program, an employment training program, or a treatment program.

• Aboriginal supervisors from the community must monitor the disposition. The community must see sanctions that originate from, and are enforced by, the community, and not some outside force.

• These programs should be formally designated and recognized as *Young Offenders Act* programs so that their role has official recognition and official support.

In our opinion, Aboriginal alternative measures programs, which provide culturally appropriate services and programs to Aboriginal youth, would go a long way towards reducing the over-representation of Aboriginal people in the youth justice system. These types of programs are needed not only in or near urban communities. Smaller Aboriginal and non-Aboriginal communities need them too.

Aboriginal Youth and the Justice System—General Issues

In addition to our criticisms of the *Young Offenders Act*, we believe that young Aboriginal people who are accused of crimes in Manitoba are victimized by the justice system in much the same manner as are adult Aboriginal people. Elsewhere in this report, we deal with the problems created by our court system, the method of providing legal representation, the provision of bail, pre-trial detention, sentencing, correctional institutions, the lack of culturally appropriate programming in the justice system and the problems created by the low numbers of Aboriginal people employed in the system. At the risk of repeating ourselves, we believe it is important to review the manner in which these issues affect Aboriginal young people.

Systemic Discrimination

Many Aboriginal people who testified before our Inquiry felt they were discriminated against by the justice system at nearly every step. They felt they were discriminated against by the police, lawyers, Crown attorneys, judges and probation officers for a variety of reasons. They felt they suffered discrimination because their cultures, societies and languages were different. They felt they suffered because of their low social standing and educational levels and their high unemployment. They felt they were discriminated against because of the poverty, living conditions and social problems in their communities. They felt discriminated against because of the remoteness of many of their communities, the lack of services and the absence of officials who might provide local alternatives to the incarceration of their youth in mainly southern institutions. Finally, they felt discriminated against and taken advantage of because they often did not understand either their legal rights or the legal process. They felt the steps taken to inform them of these rights were insufficient.

In their criticisms, many witnesses did not separate or distinguish between the youth and the adult justice systems. To them, the justice system was one monolithic entity. It was often symbolized by a plane that arrived in their communities perhaps once a month with the police, a Crown attorney, a Legal Aid lawyer and a judge. They often did not understand what was being said or what was being done in court proceedings, but they knew some of the results. Young people would be taken away and sentenced to custody in some faraway facility.

The problems begin even before any crime has been committed or any law has been broken. Aboriginal youth are frequently denied programs in their own communities that might help them steer themselves away from an encounter with the law. For example, there are few recreational facilities in Aboriginal communities. There are few, if any, crime prevention programs in Aboriginal communities. There are few, if any, public legal education programs that educate Aboriginal young people about the law. There are no programs to tell them their rights or what to do if they are arrested.[23]

If they are arrested, northern Aboriginal youth are more likely than non-Aboriginal youth to be taken from their families and communities to wait for a hearing in a correctional facility, usually hundreds of miles away. Since there are no open custody facilities in Aboriginal communities, few probation officers to speak on their behalf and few existing alternative measures, young Aboriginal people are more likely to be held in custody. They are more likely to be denied bail. They will probably not have much, if any, time to consult a lawyer before their hearings. They are more likely to have their hearings remanded, over and over again. They are more likely to be sentenced to custody after their hearings and to receive longer sentences than non-Aboriginal youth. They are less likely to be accepted for an early release program or to be able to take advantage of the appeal process. Time after time, people from Aboriginal communities repeated these complaints and observations to our Inquiry during its hearings around the province.

The justice system is much more likely to interfere with or to disrupt the lives of Aboriginal youth in ways that rarely happen to non-Aboriginal young people living in a southern city. For example, non-Aboriginal young people would not likely be "scooped up" from their homes and communities to be whisked away to pre-trial detention facilities hundreds of miles away. They would not likely have to appear for a hearing and have no one able to attend to vouch for their character or to suggest alternatives to incarceration. They would not be expected to endure undue hardship or expense in order to attend the court. They would have support programs and appropriate facilities available in their own communities.

It is well known that Aboriginal communities have long been isolated by culture, geography, poverty and deprivation, and so have been overlooked, ignored and excluded by the rest of society. This can be seen clearly in northern and remote Aboriginal communities. But what may not be well understood is the impact these conditions have had upon decisions made about their lives in the criminal justice system.

In deciding whether to grant bail, whether to consider a custody sentence or whether to release a young Aboriginal person from custody, criminal justice officials will frequently consider factors such as whether the young person has a job or is involved in an education program. The court considers whether the young person's parents are employed. It considers the perceived "stability" and resources of the family and the community, the presence of alcohol or drug problems, whether the youth or the youth's parents have a fixed address and, if so, how long they have lived at that address. Decisions made on the basis of these types of factors discriminate against Aboriginal people, because those factors are linked directly to the marginal social, cultural and economic place of Aboriginal people in society.

Crime Prevention

There is virtually no effort by the criminal justice system, or any other system, aimed at preventing youth crime in Aboriginal communities. However, the Province is allocating vast resources to respond to crime once it has occurred. We believe the priorities are misplaced.

Crime prevention must take into account the culture of the community, in addition to the severe social and economic realities of the community or area. This must include an understanding of the causes of family dysfunction, and the historical and contemporary situations facing young Aboriginal people. Crime prevention programs must take into account the poverty, deprivation and isolation faced by many Aboriginal communities and their youth. Crime cannot be prevented without addressing these problems. As LaPrairie explains:

> The available research clearly shows that in relation to mainstream society aboriginal society has been relegated to a status of socio-economic marginality. Aboriginal communities have weak or non-existent economies, poorly developed utility structures, large numbers of dependent children and single parents, few opportunities to work, limited recreational and social service resources and high rates of alcohol and drug abuse.[24]

Recreational activities for Aboriginal youth are nonexistent in many Aboriginal communities. Boredom is a common complaint of the young people and a serious concern of community leaders. Sadly, we heard that some youth commit offences just to enjoy the excitement of a trip out of their community. There is no question in our minds that the absence of constructive social and recreational opportunities is linked to the incidence of juvenile delinquency.

Some efforts have been made to improve recreational opportunities. In Berens River, for example, we were told of the tremendous drop in crime which accompanied the attendance by the community of the Northern Fly-In Sports Camp. This non-profit organization sets up sports camps in northern communities for several weeks each summer. This experience clearly shows that the problem of youth crime in northern Manitoba, and probably elsewhere, can be addressed to some significant degree by the provision of adequate and appropriate youth recreational programs. The government has reduced its support for this program. We recommend that support be reinstituted and expanded.

WE RECOMMEND THAT:

■ Aboriginal communities throughout Manitoba be encouraged and adequately funded to develop crime prevention programs for youth, based on the development of a full range of employment, cultural, social and recreational opportunities.

■ The funding for the Northern Fly-In Sports Camp be firmly established and that the camp be expanded to provide its services to all northern Aboriginal communities.

Youth Court Services

There is no court communicator in regular attendance at the Manitoba Youth Centre or in Youth Court. There is one Aboriginal judge. But there are no Aboriginal Crown attorneys in Youth Court or in any other court, for that matter.

Aboriginal young people have as great a need as adults for Aboriginal court workers. We see the functions as being similar to those of adult court workers. They should be available to explain procedures, identify options, and generally provide advice and assistance. When necessary, Aboriginal court workers should also advocate before the court on behalf of the Aboriginal young person. They can also assist in the identification of cases that may be suitable for alternative measures.

Aboriginal youth court workers would have a special interest in young Aboriginal people. These workers would understand the communities from which the youth come, the problems they are likely to confront and the resources that are available to assist them.

WE RECOMMEND THAT:

■ The Aboriginal Court Worker Program provide a court worker wherever Youth Court sits.

Staffing

If we are to begin restructuring the justice system, we have to begin with the people who plan and administer the system. According to the best information we have been able to obtain, there are no Aboriginal people involved in the planning or the administration of youth services at the senior or mid-management levels. This applies to the Manitoba Youth Centre, the Agassiz Youth Centre, probation services, and central office staffing in both the Community Services and Justice departments. In fact, there are too few Aboriginal staff members at all levels.

The staff at youth institutions do not speak an Aboriginal language. Many young Aboriginal people, particularly from remote areas, speak their own languages more fluently than English and they have difficulty comprehending English. This means non-Aboriginal workers cannot communicate well with Aboriginal youth. Aboriginal youth have been threatened with punishment for speaking their languages at institutions like Agassiz. That is unacceptable. The issue could be easily addressed by having supervisory staff who can speak the Aboriginal language of the youth, rather than coercing the youth to desist from its use. Because of their inability to speak Aboriginal languages, correctional staff are unable to fully appreciate the personal problems of Aboriginal youth, or the family or community dynamics, that might have contributed to the commission of offences or that may bear upon the youth's rehabilitation.

In our chapter on correctional institutions, we recommend that the number of Aboriginal people employed in correctional facilities and programs should at least represent the number of Aboriginal people in the province. At least one-half of these people should be able to speak an Aboriginal language. We also recommend that cross-cultural training programs should be mandatory for all corrections staff, and that there should be an ongoing series of refresher courses.

We believe that these recommendations must be implemented in both adult and youth correctional institutions.

Conclusion

The youth justice system fails Aboriginal youth in virtually every measurable way and there is no indication of plans to change the system. On the contrary, the plight of Aboriginal youth and the frustration and bitterness of Aboriginal communities are all but ignored.

Change will not come easily. But those in authority must commit themselves to massive reorganization and change. As with other criminal justice programs, we believe that fundamental changes in philosophy, policy and programs are needed in the youth justice system. In particular, we cannot imagine an effective youth justice system for Aboriginal youth without a substantial measure of control of this system being vested in Aboriginal communities. It is for this reason that we have recommended that youth justice be included within the responsibilities of the Aboriginal court system that we propose.

In both Aboriginal and non-Aboriginal communities, the intent and purpose of the *Young Offenders Act* are not being realized. This will continue as long as the system ignores the principles of the Act and, instead, blindly adopts the processes and procedures that have come to characterize the adult system. The youth justice system must be different. It must truly seek to provide minimal interference in the lives of youth by developing alternatives to criminal charges and to formal court processing. We believe much could be achieved with a strong determination to implement the YOA's philosophy.

We believe the answer to dealing with the problems of young offenders is to provide services that take into account the culture, background and needs of an Aboriginal young person. The services must be supportive, rather than punitive. Finally, they must be provided by Aboriginal people where possible and, if that is not possible, by individuals educated to work with Aboriginal people and to apply culturally appropriate solutions.

CHAPTER 16

POLICING

Introduction

In this chapter, we examine the central theme of policing in Aboriginal communities, and what should be done about it. We begin by stating seven strategies which we believe must undergird future policing policy, and then examine the need for new approaches to recruiting, training and supervision of police forces in Manitoba. Next, we examine the actual state of policing in Manitoba and make specific recommendations concerning each police force. A detailed examination of the current *Provincial Police Act* and the Law Enforcement Review Agency then provides a framework for recommendations which will affect the entire structure of policing in Manitoba.

The History of Police-Aboriginal Relations

During the Inquiry's hearings, we heard a large number of complaints about police services to Aboriginal people. It quickly became clear to us that Aboriginal-police relations in Manitoba are in a very poor state. We heard evidence that this was true in rural areas, cities, remote communities, and even in some communities served in part by an Aboriginal police force. Much of the suspicion and hostility which Aboriginal people feel toward the police is rooted in the history of this province and in the troubled relationship between Aboriginal people and the Royal Canadian Mounted Police.[1]

For the most part, the decision to create the forerunner of the RCMP, the North-West Mounted Police, came about because of the impending entry of the North-West

Territories into Confederation in the 1869–70 period. Prime Minister Sir John A. Macdonald foresaw the problems associated with having such a large territory, populated primarily by Aboriginal people, within the jurisdiction of the Dominion without a strong Dominion presence.

While Macdonald's first initiative was to enter into treaties with the Indians so as to be able to settle large numbers of new immigrants upon the land, part of his initial plan also included the establishment of a federally controlled police force. The establishment of the force did not proceed very quickly, however, until after the Cypress Hills Massacre of 1873 in what is now Saskatchewan, when American whisky traders murdered several Assiniboine Indians. At that time, the federal inability to monitor and control the relations between Aboriginal and non-Aboriginal people became apparent. At the same time, the need to prevent other, similar outbreaks was paramount if Indians were to willingly surrender their interest in the territory. There was no doubt that controlling the whisky trade required a police deterrent and the NWMP was selected to provide it.

The federal government, however, also had other objectives in mind for the Mounted Police. Lorne and Caroline Brown, in their study of the Mounted Police, state:

> Most people assume that the NWMP were founded in response to the Cypress Hills Massacre, when American whisky traders murdered several Assiniboine Indians in May, 1873. This is true only in the sense that the massacre hastened the organization of the Force. The establishment of the Force had been planned and officially authorized prior to this, and the primary reason for establishing it was to control the Indian and Metis population of the North-West....

> What the government feared most was an Indian war over the intrusion of whites from outside the area. Such a war would have been extremely costly to the authorities and could have delayed settlement, railway construction and economic development for many years. There was even the outside possibility of some form of American intervention should such a war continue for any length of time.[2]

After the formation of the NWMP the repressive government policies which we discussed in Chapter 3 began to take effect. Although the force did not make the policies, it was the main instrument employed to carry them out. The police were responsible for moving Indians to reserves and for keeping them there, and they were intimately involved in administering treaties and Indian affairs generally. Whenever an Indian agent felt the need for assistance in enforcing government policy regarding Indian people, he called upon the Mounted Police. Indian children who ran away from residential schools were sought and returned by NWMP officers. Indian adults who left their reserves without a pass from the Indian agent were apprehended by the Mounted Police.

It is difficult to obtain reliable documentary evidence of the Indian view of the Mounted Police, because the views of Indians on the matter were seldom recorded. Indian people do appear to have been grateful to the Mounted Police for suppressing the whisky trade and for helping to prevent a recurrence of outrages like the Cypress Hills massacre. However, the fact that the force represented the interests which were rapidly destroying the Indian economy and way of life, and that the force was frequently called upon to protect those same interests, led to a state of ongoing tension between the police and Indian nations across the West.

During and after the North-West Rebellion of 1885, any positive feeling that may have existed between the Mounted Police, the Metis and most of the Indian population in the Manitoba and Saskatchewan region came to an end. The police were not the cause of the rebellion, and, in fact, the evidence seems to be that they repeatedly warned the government that unrest and well-founded grievances might lead to open rebellion if concessions were not forthcoming. However, when the government did not respond and rebellion eventually did break out, the Mounted Police had little choice but to participate along with regular military forces in suppressing it.

They were also faced with the responsibility of apprehending and meting out punishment to the rebels. Eighteen Metis and 30 Indians were apprehended and convicted. Louis Riel and eight Indians were executed. Riel was hanged in Regina following his trial, but the Indians were executed publicly in the Mounted Police stockade at Battleford, Saskatchewan. The government "encouraged" Indians from nearby reserves to witness the execution, "as it was held that such a tragic spectacle would be an emphatic deterrent against a repetition of such offences."[3] The grim resolve of the government was reiterated to Aboriginal people throughout the West.

The consequences of Mounted Police actions were far-reaching:

> The authorities punished Metis and Indians suspected of having supported the rebellion regardless of whether they had been tried for specific offences. They virtually wiped out the Metis as a distinct national and political group. They burned and looted their homes and destroyed their property. They withheld annuities from those Indian bands that had participated in the rebellion and confiscated their horses and arms. From that time on they made greater efforts to restrict ammunition to them. Most of these punitive measures were carried out by the Mounted Police. The authorized strength of the Force was increased from 500 to 1,000 men in view of their increased activity and the fact that, since the Indians were now powerless, more settlers would migrate to the North West Territories.[4]

It seems clear that this early history has had an effect upon the relationship between Aboriginal people and the RCMP ever since. Memories of such treatment linger in many communities.

That history has also coloured the perceptions Aboriginal people hold of other police forces in the province. The impact of past wrongs has been reinforced by the negative experiences of today. We heard testimony that police-Aboriginal relations in the city of Winnipeg are not good. We heard complaints about the police refusing to follow up on allegations of assault. We heard of Aboriginal people being stopped on the street or in cars for no reason. Those arrested were afraid of the police and many reported being beaten by police officers. The large number of complaints which we received points to a problem of considerable magnitude concerning how Aboriginal people are treated by Winnipeg police.

There were notable exceptions to the pattern of mistrust. We heard of excellent relations between Aboriginal people and police officers in some Manitoba Aboriginal communities. These positive relationships seem to have developed when officers had remained in an area for some considerable time and where they had become involved with the community.

Policies and Strategies for Aboriginal Policing

There can be little question that the present arrangements satisfy few on either side, and frustrate many. From a positive perspective, there is general agreement among major police forces that they should be taking special initiatives to improve their relationship with Aboriginal people. However, what they should be doing is the issue; Aboriginal people and non-Aboriginal police forces generally do not agree on the most appropriate solutions to the problems.

Our recommendations are based upon seven strategies:

- The adoption of Aboriginal community-based policing as the favoured strategy for policing in all Aboriginal areas.

- The development of professional, fully trained, regional Aboriginal police forces, reporting to and serving Aboriginal communities, with a broad mandate for law enforcement and crime prevention.

- A significant strengthening of employment equity programs, particularly in the case of the Winnipeg and Brandon police forces, including targets and remedies.

- A significant expansion of the availability and quality of cross-cultural training and field experience, including processes for the orientation of new staff to the Aboriginal communities to which they are assigned.

- Major improvements in the *Provincial Police Act* and Regulations, and in the role and function of the Manitoba Police Commission, to properly support the development of standards and procedures to guide all aspects of policing in Manitoba.

- The development of Aboriginal police commissions to support the rapid recruitment, training and effective support of Aboriginal police forces.

- The development of an effective public complaints body to hear all complaints concerning policing.

We believe that the adoption of these strategies will improve the quality of policing for all Manitobans and, in particular, for Aboriginal people.

Simultaneous Realities: Over- and Under-Policing

Police services are provided to Manitoba communities under a variety of arrangements, which are detailed later in this chapter. The RCMP function as the provincial police force, providing services to rural areas, to Indian reserves and to all but eight smaller municipalities. RCMP services in Aboriginal communities may involve the employment of special RCMP constables hired under the now-discontinued Native Special Constable Program. The Dakota Ojibway Tribal Council Police Force provides policing services to eight reserves in southern Manitoba. Band constables hired directly by Indian bands, under a program of the Department of Indian Affairs and Northern Development, provide basic policing services to a number of reserves, while special constables serve 12 Metis communities. Brandon and Winnipeg have created their own police forces, using powers granted to those cities through their own acts of the Legislature.

Aboriginal Manitobans believe they are being provided with inappropriate levels and quality of policing. The most frequent complaints were that police force members are not in touch with the culture and needs of the Aboriginal communities they serve. Many communities feel that service is unavailable when needed. Aboriginal people see a large gap between the community and the police, a gap which cannot be bridged as long as the community is unable to exert some control or guidance over the police who are present in it. In effect, this is experienced as both over- and under-policing.

Over-policing generally results from the imposition of police control on individual or community activities at a level unlikely to occur in the dominant society. Under-policing usually results from a lack of preventive and supportive police services. While the possibility of simultaneously experiencing these two problems may appear unlikely at first, both arise because police forces are not under Aboriginal community direction, and likely do not know community priorities or cultural assumptions.

Over-Policing

Complaints of over-policing focus on the perception that Aboriginal people are singled out for enforcement action and subjected to stereotyping by police forces. Many who appeared before us complained about being stopped on the street or on a country road and questioned about their activities. We heard complaints that Aboriginal people are charged with offences more often than their white counterparts. They may also be charged with a multiplicity of offences arising out of the same incident. Many such charges are never proceeded with, and appear to be harassment. We believe that many Aboriginal people are arrested and held in custody when a white person in the same circumstances either might not be arrested at all, or might not be held.

We were given an example of such stereotyping by an Aboriginal girl in Winnipeg. She told us that her boyfriend had been stopped by police simply because he was running down a city street to meet her. The sight of an Aboriginal man running apparently provided the police officer with a cue for action. The police officer's attitude and reaction were stereotypical and discriminatory.

Under-Policing

Others who appeared before us complained of under-policing, with some people lamenting the fact that they saw the police only when they came to their community to make an arrest. The police were not present on a day-to-day basis to prevent crime or to provide other police services to the community.

Most modern policing is based upon patrol car responses, using a radio dispatch system. Many northern Aboriginal communities have limited telephone service and road access. A number have no resident police detachment. This means that police assistance can only be obtained during the daytime by contacting the nearest RCMP detachment and requesting assistance. At night, all phone calls from northern Manitoba are routed through Thompson, an even less direct process. This means that even the swiftest response time frequently must be measured in hours or, occasionally, days. This is not adequate and would not be tolerated in southern non-Aboriginal communities of a similar size. In short, Aboriginal people are expected to use nonexistent telephones to call non-resident police, who are unlikely to attend within a reasonable time. Just as important, the residents of many communities complained that the police did not enforce local by-laws against the importation of alcohol to the reserve, thereby contributing to the level of social disorder in the community.

Complaints of over- and under-policing are deep-rooted and stem from the police taking a narrow view of their role. This view emphasizes crime investigation to the exclusion of a broader approach, which might better address the underlying problems facing many Aboriginal communities and involve the community in the policing process. Appropriate corrective measures must be based upon a fresh understanding of the nature of the police function itself.

The Role of Police in Society

Aboriginal people view the police as representatives of a culture which is vastly different from their own. Their encounters with police are framed by a history of cultural oppression and economic domination, during which use of Aboriginal languages, governments, laws and customs was punished by laws developed by the same legal structures police now represent. While today's police cannot be blamed for the historical circumstances of Aboriginal people, they need to better understand the context which affects every encounter with them.

The word "police," like the related words "politics," "polity," "political" and "polite," lies at the heart of society's self-understanding, and is derived from the Greek words *polis* and *polites*, which mean "city" and "citizen." Our politics and political systems speak of how we govern ourselves. "Polity" tells us of the structures and processes of nations, provinces and communities. "Politeness" defines the ways in which we would wish to encounter each other, although, of course, we do not always do so. Hence, "police" can be understood as a social structure which a community puts in place and mandates to enforce the political decisions of society.

Philip Stenning, writing for the Law Reform Commission of Canada, suggests that even as late as 1860, this original understanding of "police" remained: the system of laws and regulations which bind a community together. A municipal manual of the day noted:

> The word "police" is generally applied to the internal regulations of Cities and Towns, whereby the individuals of any City or Town, like members of a well-governed family, are bound to conform their general behaviour to the rules of propriety, good neighbourhood, and good manners, and to be decent, industrious and inoffensive in their respective situations....[5]

For those of the dominant social, economic and cultural group, the need for such a "police" and the later development of police "forces" to enforce this framework of laws are welcomed as a source of support and security. Most citizens rarely encounter the police, and when they do, neither they nor the police perceive the encounter as particularly threatening. The law generally works for the dominant group, frequently to protect its interests and assets.

We heard a litany of complaints and examples indicating that many, if not most, Aboriginal people are afraid of the police. They consider the police force to be a foreign presence and do not feel understood by it. They certainly do not feel that the police are in any sense "their" force, that police operate on their behalf, or that the police are in any significant manner subject to a corresponding Aboriginal influence in their communities.

Encounters between Aboriginal peoples and police forces are not only cross-cultural in nature, but are made even more problematic by the economic underdevelopment and oppression of Aboriginal peoples, as our report has documented. It should come as no surprise, then, that these encounters frequently have adverse consequences for Aboriginal people.

We believe that the fundamental remedy to this problem is the creation of well-trained and well-equipped Aboriginal police forces, under Aboriginal direction, providing a full range of police services to Aboriginal communities. We also believe that a community policing approach is vital for the development of effective working relationships between communities and their police forces, and that Aboriginal police services will evolve naturally along the lines of what is becoming known as "community policing," because of the structure and values of Aboriginal communities themselves. Only in this way can the original concept of police, as a support structure for a community's system of laws and customs, be realized for Aboriginal communities.

Community-Based Policing

It is not widely known that the style of policing which has become dominant in North America in the latter part of this century was developed in response to problems of corruption and inefficiency which plagued many large American police departments. This new pattern was based upon two factors: the desire to remove the police from what were believed to be corrupting ties with the political leadership in the community; and the development of new police technology, including vehicles and radio dispatch systems. Control of the police was taken from local political organizations and central-ized in the hands of police administrators. Department-wide standards were established in areas such as recruiting, training and patrol methods. Tasks that had been carried out by patrol officers were now handled by specialized central units.

Activities of a community service nature were dropped and were replaced by a new emphasis on crime-fighting. The job of the patrol officer became one of driving around the streets in a car, isolated from the citizenry, waiting for a dispatcher to call. Officers' performances were judged, to a great extent, on the law enforcement statistics they generated. Activities which were not counted, such as citizen contacts, were not encouraged. Officers were frequently moved from one patrol area to another in order to keep them from developing ties with the community.

In the older system, citizens knew the police officers in their community. There was time to build relationships and networks, which could be of assistance in both pre-vention and resolution of crime. Under the new system, the citizens' role also changed. They were discouraged from participating in their own protection and had little say in the kinds of services they received from the police. All the citizen had to do was call the dispatcher, and the police would soon arrive to take care of the problem in their own way. This process was quite successful in alleviating many of the problems which had developed in the previous era, and it became the dominant model of policing in much of the world. Even though the police in Canada did not have all the same problems as their U.S. counterparts, our police soon patterned themselves after the American depart-ments. To a great extent, this is the way most departments are run today. The police are mainly reactive, responding to incidents as they are phoned in. While there is now some community input, this is typically limited to participation in crime prevention programs such as Neighbourhood Watch and Crime Stoppers, which are managed by the police.

This model of policing was not established on the basis of research showing its effectiveness, but, rather, as a response to problems with the earlier style of policing. It was not until the 1970s that research was done on the effectiveness of this new approach to policing. In general, this research was not encouraging. By the middle of the 1980s, a widespread movement toward "community-policing" had begun in most North American centres.

Community policing has six characteristics which give it a great deal of potential for improving the policing of Aboriginal people:

- Community policing is decentralized. Responsibility and resources are managed in local communities to the greatest degree possible. Thus, community policing can be responsive to local concerns.

- Community policing is prevention-oriented. The focus is on resolving underlying community problems proactively, rather than simply reacting to calls for service. The role of the police is expanded to a broad mandate to enhance the community's quality of life.

- Community policing involves a partnership between the police and the community. The police are responsive to community concerns and the community takes its share of responsibility for dealing with problems of crime and order. There are many ways in which links can be made with the community, including citizen advisory groups.

- Community policing is flexible enough to accommodate change, and the Aboriginal community is changing very quickly.

- Community policing is more easily adapted to Aboriginal cultural standards than are existing police methods.

- Community policing can accommodate the wide variation which exists in Aboriginal communities. It can be easily adapted to urban areas to enable forces such as in Winnipeg and Brandon to become more responsive to the needs of urban Aboriginal people.

As well as enhancing the capability of the police to enforce the law and to maintain order, community policing can play a role in community development by mobilizing the resources of the community itself. This may involve a diverse range of strategies and activities, including community-based prevention programs, as well as alternative means of resolving disputes and dealing with offenders, utilizing a broad array of community support mechanisms.

Because it focusses on community problems and provides community members with a real say in policing, community policing is much more effective than traditional public relations programs for strengthening relations between the community and the police. An example of the sorts of effects that even the beginning of a community approach to policing can have was seen in our visit to Shamattawa.

Shamattawa had long had a reputation for being a community out of control, where crime, particularly juvenile crime, was rampant. When we held our hearings in the community in 1989, we were informed that the RCMP presence and the methods of policing which they applied in the community were believed to be responsible for a 48% drop in juvenile crime and a smaller drop in adult crime. The officer in charge of the detachment felt that this success was not simply due to the presence of the RCMP, but also to the efforts of the officers to get to know the community and its people. He pointed to the fact that detachment members patrolled on all-terrain vehicles with a trailer in tow, in which property, suspects or witnesses could be carried. Whenever the trailer was not needed for transporting such persons or items, the detachment members allowed young people to ride along on their patrols. If they happened to pick up a young person for having committed an offence, the passengers would be allowed to ride along while the young person was taken home or to the detachment. In these cases, the young people would tease or deride the one who had been picked up.

This anecdote does not represent a fully developed community policing approach. However, it is an example of what can be accomplished by even modest efforts in this direction.

The adoption of a community policing approach in Aboriginal communities also implies the need for a different style of training for Aboriginal, as well as other, police officers. Research has shown that police officers from minority groups who are trained and supervised in a traditional manner may act in the same way as white police officers.[6] This should not be surprising, because minority police officers experience the same job socialization as their white peers. Providing different training to enable officers to adopt the new style of policing will be necessary if the goal of increasing sensitivity to Aboriginal concerns is to be met.

The RCMP have indicated that they believe that community policing should become the standard approach for all detachments. Chief Supt. L.J. Callens, in a paper delivered to a community meeting in Stonewall, noted that the force had instructed detachments "to form permanent community consultation groups, representing to the extent possible the many social elements of the community."[7]

This new structure is intended to provide a permanent forum for police-community discussion of issues which are of concern to either group, and to develop strategies which can be used by the police, or by the community, or jointly, for crime prevention and early detection. Chief Superintendent Callens describes this as the development of a functional partnership, based on clear and open communication and the development of trust. He goes on to describe the new partnership as "one of anticipation," based on the RCMP's view that change is so rapid that reactive policing approaches are insufficient.

In this new approach to policing, communities gain a longer term relationship with the officers upon whom they rely for police services and officers gain an intimate knowledge of the community they serve. However, in addition to regaining what may have been lost in the move to a reactive, patrol car style of policing, there are also new structures needed to ensure that consultation and communication become an integral part of the community-police partnership. Community policing places a high priority upon prevention and anticipation, rather than on reaction.

While we have stressed the desirability of Aboriginal control of forces policing Aboriginal communities, and later will emphasize the need for non-Aboriginal police departments to ensure that they have a greater proportion of Aboriginal members, neither of these important reforms will have a major impact if the police continue to follow their traditional patterns of community relationships. We believe that community policing is a vital strategy for enabling local residents to have a structured, open relationship with the police.

WE RECOMMEND THAT:

- ■ Police forces adopt a community policing approach, particularly in Aboriginal communities.

Employment Equity Programs

In addition to the adoption of community policing as an approach to the organization and delivery of services, we believe that any police force will be more effective if its members are representative of the community it serves. If the community is multicultural, the police force should have a similar multicultural mix of personnel. It is obvious that a force will be more effective if at least some of its members speak the language or languages of those with whom they have to deal. For example, it would be unthinkable to have only French-speaking police in an English-speaking community, or vice versa.

Employment equity (sometimes called affirmative action) programs are intended to correct imbalances that exist in the composition of employee groups. Aboriginal people are not represented on Manitoba police forces in proportion to their representation in the population, to say nothing of the proportion of persons of Aboriginal descent dealt with by the police. Neither the RCMP, nor municipal forces such as those in Winnipeg and Brandon, has sufficient numbers of Aboriginal members, or of any other visible minority, for that matter.

One way in which the police may begin to convince Aboriginal people of the sincerity of their efforts to improve relations with them is to ensure that Aboriginal people are substantially represented among the members of the force. In a paper prepared for the Inquiry, researchers Douglas Skoog and Irwin Barker say:

> Ideally, the police force should mirror the ethnic composition of the community it serves. That is, the target number should be based on the proportion of the Aboriginal people in the community. The hiring of a small number of Aboriginal officers would be misinterpreted as a transparent gesture designed to pacify relations with police among Aboriginals without allowing Aboriginal officers to make a meaningful impact on the force or on the community it serves.[8]

Advantages of Having Aboriginal Officers

While employment equity programs should primarily be viewed as supporting the rights of minority group members to employment, there are also other sound reasons for adopting such a policy. Among these are:

- Aboriginal people will have more confidence that the police force is interested in them.

- Aboriginal youth will see such officers as excellent role models.

- The general population will benefit from seeing Aboriginal people in positions of responsibility, protecting the public peace.

- Aboriginal officers will be able to assist other officers in a better understanding of Aboriginal culture and behaviour.

- If an Aboriginal person is being arrested and needs family or community support of some kind, an Aboriginal officer will likely have a better idea of where that support might be available. The same will be true of recommending services for victims of crime.

- Within the force, there will be officers who speak Aboriginal languages. For example, while most younger Aboriginal people do speak English, they may not fully understand everything said to them by non-Aboriginal police. The need for police who know the language is particularly acute in isolated communities where Aboriginal languages are commonly used and where knowledge of English is minimal.

- Aboriginal officers will be able to do preventive policing more effectively among Aboriginal community members.

- Because Aboriginal officers will have a better understanding of Aboriginal culture, they will be better able to determine whether a situation they encounter requires an arrest or can be settled in an alternative way.

- When making an arrest, Aboriginal police will be better able to make certain that Aboriginal people understand their rights and what is happening.

- Aboriginal officers will be better able to assist those wishing to give statements in ensuring that their true intent is reflected.

Hiring sufficient numbers of Aboriginal officers will require a massive recruiting and training effort by Manitoba police forces. Later in the chapter, we will discuss specific hiring targets which Manitoba police forces should adopt.

WE RECOMMEND THAT:

- Police forces immediately institute employment equity programs to achieve Aboriginal representation equivalent to the Aboriginal proportion of the Manitoba population.

In making this recommendation, we know that the increased numbers will not ensure, by any means, that a significant percentage of police contacts with Aboriginal persons will be handled by Aboriginal officers. Given the realities of shift-scheduling and the numbers of contacts with the public, Aboriginal people will still frequently encounter non-Aboriginal officers. However, the benefits will be significant. An employment equity policy should be pursued.

Cross-Cultural Training

Imagine a situation in which the police of Manitoba were members of the Cree Nation, spoke the Cree language as a mother tongue, and were born into and formed by that culture. Further, imagine that they represented the power to enforce the economic and social customs of that nation, including laws of property, marriage and criminal offence. Imagine the bewilderment of the townspeople of a typical, southern Manitoba town, as they encounter these police officers going about their duties, speaking their own language. Imagine the bewilderment of the officers as they seek to understand the strange ways of the townsfolk. And imagine the possibilities for confusion, misunderstanding and misapplication of Cree laws and police procedures.

This imaginary world is, in fact, quite similar to the experience of many Aboriginal communities and of many Aboriginal individuals when they encounter non-Aboriginal police. The police function to enforce the norms, actions and wishes of the citizens from the dominant culture, which is alien to Aboriginal people. The resulting confusion on the part of Aboriginal people is frequently matched by the confusion and misunderstanding of the police. While neither group intends to confuse, misunderstand or offend, these are natural consequences of policing from a foreign culture.

Throughout our hearings, we heard many complaints about racist comments made by the police to members of the public and to Aboriginal police officers. We do not believe that most police officers intend to make racist or stereotypical remarks, but some do. The testimony of Dr. Neil McDonald in this regard was most revealing. Dr. McDonald is a consultant involved in the research, development and delivery of cross-cultural training materials for public and private agencies across Canada, including the RCMP Depot Training Centre in Regina and the Winnipeg Police Department. McDonald testified that:

> I think racist and prejudiced attitudes are fairly prevalent in society at large. And in my view, at least from my experience, the prejudice towards Aboriginal peoples is probably the strongest, and certainly they are the peoples that are the most widely and wildly stereotyped in our society....
>
> Police officers ... are as likely to hold as negative attitudes as anyone else. And ... I would say that the only difference that I would find in my training with police officers,... is that they're more inclined to be up front about their expressions.... I find this helpful in the sense that it allows me to deal with the attitudes and the views that are in the room ... prejudice and racism is certainly an issue.

Dr. McDonald testified about the negative racial attitudes exhibited in the Winnipeg Police Department recruit class of 1988, in which a number of recruits made very strong racist statements about Aboriginal people. He stated that recruits made statements such as:

> "The whites will soon be the minorities."

> "[Aboriginal people] are always getting something for nothing."

> "You find them on Main Street and that's what they do with what they get."

Such negative and racist attitudes cannot help but affect the quality of police service. Officers must come to understand the devastating effects their remarks can have.

Therefore, we believe that cross-cultural educational courses should be given to every member of each force. Cross-cultural courses for recruits should be enhanced and regular refresher courses should also be given to all officers, from the police chief down. Entrance tests should attempt to determine the presence of racial prejudice or intolerance within each recruit or officer and how those recruits and officers are likely to react to people with whom they deal. Any applicants displaying racist tendencies should be rejected.

Racist conduct can be addressed, to some extent, by a combination of carefully thought out, cross-cultural educational programs given to recruits and older officers alike, use of clear and consistent police procedures, and strong and unequivocal leadership. However, the strongest method of combatting racism is through a clear and unequivocal policy on the part of senior officers of not tolerating such behaviour and of formally disciplining those whose conduct implies overtly or covertly racist approaches to their duties.

WE RECOMMEND THAT:

- Cross-cultural education components of all police training courses be reviewed and strengthened, and this process actively involve members of the Aboriginal community, resource persons and recognized experts.

- All police officers be rotated through cross-cultural education programs, and periodic refresher programs be provided as part of the regular professional development programs of all police departments.

- Any police recruits displaying racist attitudes be screened out of training, and police officers who display such conduct after joining the force be required to take further training or, if necessary, be formally disciplined or dismissed.

Culture and Language

Even very good cross-cultural education programs cannot overcome the significant barriers between Aboriginal and non-Aboriginal cultures which are frequently produced by language differences. Probably one of the more perplexing issues which will arise in the course of dealing with Aboriginal accused concerns the admissibility of confessions. The rules relating to the admissibility of statements by accused persons have been developed to provide protection to an accused. Only those statements which are given freely and voluntarily, and with the full knowledge and appreciation of one's legal rights (including a full appreciation of the right not to give a statement), are admissible.

Despite these general safeguards, however, Aboriginal people, particularly those in remote communities and those whose primary language is not English, appear to have special problems in exercising their rights to remain silent and to refrain from incriminating themselves. Their statements appear to be particularly open to being misunderstood by police interrogators and, as a result, may convey inaccurate information when read out in court. Their vulnerability arises from the legal system's inability to break down the barriers to effective communication between Aboriginal people and legal personnel, and to differences of language, etiquette, concepts of time and distance, and so on. This matter has been considered in a number of courts, but perhaps the fullest explanation was given in an Australian court. This issue is so central to the role of the police in questioning suspects and taking statements that we quote in full the explanation given by Justice Forster in setting forth what are now called the Anunga Rules.

> [A]boriginal people often do not understand English very well and even if they do understand the words, they may not understand the concepts which English phrases and sentences express. Even with the use of interpreters this problem is by no means solved. Police (terminology) and legal English sometimes is not translatable into the Aboriginal languages at all and there are no separate Aboriginal words for some simple words like "in", "at", "on", "by", "with", or "over", these being suffixes added to the word they qualify. Some words may translate literally into Aboriginal language but mean something different. "Did you go into his house?" means to an English speaking person "Did you go into the building?" But to an Aboriginal it may also mean, "Did you go within the fence surrounding the house?" English concepts of time, number and distance are imperfectly understood, if at all, by Aboriginal people, many of the more primitive of whom can not tell the time by a clock. One frequently hears the answer, "long time", which depending on the context may be minutes, hours, days, weeks or years. In case I may be misunderstood, I should also emphasize that I am not expressing the view that Aboriginal people are any less intelligent than white people but simply that their concepts of certain things and the terms in which they are expressed may only be different to those of white people.
>
> Another matter which needs to be understood is that most Aboriginal people are basically courteous and polite and will answer questions by white people in the way in which they think the questioner wants. Even if they are not courteous and polite there is the same reaction when they are dealing with an authority figure such as a policeman. Indeed, their action is probably a combination of natural politeness and their attitude to someone in authority. Some Aboriginal people find a standard caution quite bewildering, even if they understand that they do not have to answer questions, because, if they do not have to answer questions, then why are the questions being asked? Bearing in mind these preliminary observations which are based partly upon my own knowledge and observations and partly by evidence I have heard in numerous cases, I lay down the following guidelines. They apply, of course, to persons who are being questioned as suspects:

1. When an Aboriginal person is being interrogated as a suspect, unless he is as fluent in English as the average white man of English descent, an interpreter able to interpret in and from the Aboriginal person's language should be present, and his assistance should be utilized whenever necessary to ensure complete and mutual understanding.

2. When an Aboriginal person is being interrogated it is desirable where practicable that a "prisoner's friend" (who may also be the interpreter) be present. The "prisoner's friend" should be someone in whom the Aboriginal has apparent confidence. He may be a mission or settlement superintendent, or a member of the staff of one of these institutions who knows and is known by the Aboriginal. He may be a station owner, manager or overseer or an officer from the Department of Aboriginal Affairs. Combinations of persons in situations are variable and the categories of persons I have mentioned are not exclusive. The important thing is that the "prisoner's friend" be someone in whom the Aboriginal has confidence, by whom he will feel supported.

3. Great care should be taken in administering the caution when it is appropriate to do so. It is simply not adequate to administer it in the usual terms.... Police officers, having explained the caution in simple terms, should ask the Aboriginal person to tell them what is meant by the caution, phrase by phrase, and should not proceed with the interrogation until it is clear the Aboriginal has apparent understanding of his right to remain silent. Most experienced police officers in the territory already do this. The problem of the caution is a difficult one but the presence of a "prisoner's friend" or interpreter and adequate and simple questioning about the caution should go a long way towards solving it.

4. Great care should be taken in formulating questions so that, so far as possible, the answer which is wanted or expected is not suggested in any way. Anything in the nature of cross-examination should be scrupulously avoided as answers to it have no probative value. It should be borne in mind that it is not only the wording of the question which may suggest the answer but also the manner and tone of voice which are used.

5. Even when an apparently frank and free confession has been obtained relating to the commission of an offence, police should continue to investigate the matter and endeavour to obtain proof of the commission of the offence from other sources.

6. Because Aboriginal people are often nervous and ill at ease in the presence of white authority figures like policemen, it is particularly important that they be offered a meal, if they are being interviewed in the police station, or in the company of police or in custody when a meal time

arrives. They should also be offered tea or coffee if the facilities exist for preparation of it. They should always be offered a drink of water. They should be asked if they wish to use the lavatory, if they are in the company of police or are under arrest.

7. It is particularly important that Aboriginal and other people are not interrogated when they are disabled by illness, drunkenness or tiredness. Admissions so gained will probably be rejected by a court. Interrogation should not continue for an unreasonably long time.

8. Should an Aboriginal person seek legal assistance, reasonable steps should be taken to obtain such assistance. If an Aboriginal person states he does not wish to answer further questions or any questions the interrogation should not continue.

9. When it is necessary to remove clothing for forensic examination or for the purposes of medical examination, steps must be taken forthwith to supply substitute clothing.

It may be thought by some that these guidelines are unduly paternal and therefore offensive to Aboriginal people. It may be thought by others that they are unduly favourable to Aboriginal people. The truth of the matter is that they are designed simply to remove or obviate some of the disadvantages from which Aboriginal people suffer in their dealings with police. These guidelines are not absolute rules departure from which will necessarily lead to statements being excluded, but police officers who depart from them without reason may find statements are excluded.

The judges of this court do not consider the effectiveness of police investigation will be set back by compliance with these recommendations. It is basic that persons in custody should be treated with courtesy and patience.[9]

The Anunga Rules have now become almost universally applied throughout Australia in one form or another and have become part of the training manuals for police departments in that country. Much controversy arose, particularly from police authorities, when this decision was made, but the existence of the rules was strongly endorsed by the Australian Law Reform Commission in their report on the recognition of Aboriginal customary law in 1986.[10]

It is interesting that in Australia, where the treatment of Aboriginal people by police authorities has been the focus of international research and comment, and where the over-representation of Aboriginal people in the justice system probably exceeds the level in Canada, such an approach to the reception of statements by Aboriginal accused has been judicially mandated. We believe that it would be appropriate for Manitoba courts to adopt and apply the Anunga Rules, keeping in mind the differences between Canada and Australia.

WE RECOMMEND THAT:

- The courts adopt the Anunga Rules of Australia, as rules of the court governing the reception into evidence of statements to police made by Aboriginal persons.

  In addition to these rules on interrogation procedures, there are other procedures police should adopt. In our report on the death of J.J. Harper, we discuss and make recommendations concerning the recording of interrogations. Those recommendations are:

- All statements taken by police officers be either audio- or video-recorded. If the contents of a transcribed statement are challenged, or some tribunal wishes to hear how certain words were expressed, the tape or video can be played.

- Video equipment be used to record the statements of all suspects in cases involving deaths and other serious cases. We suggest that the taping record the totality of each interview, including all introductory comments and explanations and warnings given by the police, and including any formal statement or other comments that result.

  The videotape will be of great value. The impact would be reduced if accused persons could allege that promises or inducements were offered or pressure was applied to them before the taping began.

- Where video equipment is not available, all statements be audio-recorded. The RCMP has tape-recorded some statements for years. We recommend that all police make that practice mandatory in all cases, with the use of video where statements are taken in an office with that equipment.

The recording of interrogations will give better protection to all parties, as well as be of assistance to the courts. By adopting these procedures and employing more culturally sensitive interrogation techniques, Manitoba's police forces should be able to break down many of the barriers which exist in their dealings with Aboriginal people.

Police Forces in Manitoba

Aboriginal people in Manitoba live in three types of settings: Aboriginal communities (either on reserves or in non-reserve areas), in communities with mixed populations and in the major urban areas. In a minority of reserves, Aboriginal police forces, such as the Dakota Ojibway Tribal Council Police Force, or "special" RCMP constables provide limited police services. In these communities, major crimes are investigated by the RCMP. Northern community constables provide services to Metis areas, with the

RCMP also providing back-up services for major crimes. Eight smaller communities and Brandon and Winnipeg have their own municipal forces. The RCMP provides police services to the remainder of the province in their contracted role as the "provincial" police force. In this section, we will review and examine the police forces which serve Aboriginal people in these three settings.

Policing in Aboriginal Communities

A variety of Aboriginal policing programs have developed across Canada, usually with the primary purpose of involving more Aboriginal people as constables. This has been done either through trying to enlist Aboriginal people in existing forces, or through the development of what are essentially new police forces or auxiliary forces. Efforts have also been directed toward giving Aboriginal people some limited measure of control over policing functions within their communities. These programs have ranged from shared control with pre-existing agencies to complete control over a limited range of police functions in reserve and Metis communities. In no case does an Aboriginal community have full control over policing and provide a complete range of police functions to its community members.

There has been a clear policy within government departments in favour of using existing "white" police forces to police Aboriginal communities, rather than empowering and funding Aboriginal people to do the job themselves. The preferred solution of non-Aboriginal forces policing Aboriginal communities, such as the RCMP and the Ontario Provincial Police, has been to recruit Aboriginal officers and make other internal changes, rather than to encourage the development of police forces controlled and staffed by Aboriginal people. Even though such programs have been in operation for many years, they have not been successful in changing the reality that most Aboriginal communities are still policed by white officers.

WE RECOMMEND THAT:

- As soon as possible, Aboriginal police forces take over from the RCMP the responsibility for providing all police services in Aboriginal communities.

- The RCMP support the establishment of Aboriginal police forces and develop a policy of cooperation with such forces.

The difficulties encountered by Aboriginal people who come into contact with non-Aboriginal police forces frequently persist even with some Aboriginal special police programs. Some reasons for this will become clear as we review the Aboriginal policing programs now in place in Manitoba.

RCMP On-Reserve Policing

Our hearings indicated that, unfortunately, in many cases, the relationships between Aboriginal communities and the RCMP are seriously deficient. There are strong feelings of mistrust, if not hatred, directed towards RCMP members in some areas. Many police officers are seen as being arbitrary and antagonistic toward Aboriginal people.

In one Aboriginal community we visited, the hall was almost empty when we arrived. We were told that people from the community would not come as long as the police were in attendance. We asked the police representatives to leave and as soon as they had gone, the hall filled with local residents. This was a sad commentary on RCMP-community relations in that area. We were told that this obvious distrust had developed as a result of what was viewed as police harassment. There, and in other communities which we visited, actions taken by the police have resulted in diminished respect.

We were told, and we believe, that RCMP officers have taken advantage of Aboriginal people when questioning them. Some accused will say almost anything to get out and away from a frightening situation they do not understand. Many do not understand the cautions given by police, because of their difficulty with English. Such stories make obvious the need for the interrogation safeguards we discussed earlier in this chapter. RCMP members have told some people that they will be held in custody until they give a statement. Some are reported to have then given false statements, as that was seen as the only way to end police questioning.

We heard complaints in a great many of the communities we visited that accidents involving injury or death to Aboriginal people either were not investigated at all, or were investigated with less vigour than similar incidents involving white people. We heard of difficulties in contacting officers at all. Given these perceptions, it is not surprising that the police are held in low regard by Aboriginal people.

Each complaint heard by our Inquiry was examined and investigated by the RCMP. We received detailed reports of each investigation from Asst. Commissioner Dale Henry, Commanding Officer of "D" Division. In many, if not all, cases, Assistant Commissioner Henry also sent a copy of the report to the person who had complained to us. We believe that it was appropriate for him to have used the Inquiry and the complaints as an opportunity to attempt to improve communications with the Aboriginal communities. We commend him for taking that initiative.

In discussing their relations with the Aboriginal community, RCMP officers were open to suggestions as to how those relations might be further improved. The force appeared anxious to have more Aboriginal members and efforts have been made to recruit Aboriginal people, either as special constables or as regular constables. Officers saw the greater involvement of Aboriginal officers as necessary and as important to the force. Increasing the numbers of Aboriginal officers as full constables and in senior ranks is, perhaps, the most essential action which could be taken by the force in the immediate future. However, we also noted that while the policy of the force appeared to be to encourage more Aboriginal representation, there was no RCMP support for the establishment of independent Aboriginal police forces.

Our fundamental recommendation is that Aboriginal police forces take over the present RCMP responsibility for all police services in Aboriginal communities as soon as possible. The quality of RCMP services must also be improved. At the same time, it is essential to repair the damaged relationship between the Aboriginal community and the RCMP in order that mutual respect may develop once again.

While the RCMP receive the most extensive cross-cultural training of any Canadian police force, many Aboriginal people who are working in the system feel that this training does not properly prepare officers for service in the Aboriginal communities to which they are assigned. The same presenters believe that RCMP constables frequently bring their own cultural concepts with them and expect Aboriginal people to behave according to those concepts. They said that RCMP Aboriginal constables are often placed in the awkward situation of having to meet "white" police expectations and are not being given the flexibility to adapt their RCMP training to their knowledge of Aboriginal culture. We believe that additional training in cross-cultural issues, particularly relating to Aboriginal culture, is required, both for new constables and in the form of regular in-service training for all officers.

Those who appeared before us made many suggestions which would improve relations between the RCMP and the Aboriginal communities they police. For example, where there has been a death in a road accident or in some way other than by natural causes, the family and often the elected leadership in the community, acting on behalf of the whole community, are anxious to know that the matter has been fully investigated and what conclusions were reached. It was suggested that, in the future, reports with respect to this type of death be forwarded to the head of the family and to the chief and council. Where criminal charges have been laid, that information should also be made known, as should the eventual outcome of any trial.

When a crime is being investigated in an Aboriginal community, particularly by officers who do not live there, the elected leadership in the community should be made as aware as possible of the investigation. We can understand that there may be situations where that is not possible, due to the sensitivity of an investigation. Nevertheless, a greater effort to keep elected representatives informed should be made. Due to the limited nature of information that is provided, the statistical reports that are now provided to councils are of little value.

Providing complete information about problems in the community will go a long way toward improving relations, and also will create opportunities for ongoing contact and discussions between members of the local detachment and the community.

Detachment commanders and officers should meet with Aboriginal community leaders on a regular basis. One purpose of these meetings should be to have the officers become known to Aboriginal leaders. Another purpose should be to exchange information and concerns with respect to community problems and law enforcement. Improved communication and community involvement should be seen as key strategies to improving the Aboriginal communities' relationships with the RCMP.

On a broader level, regular meetings should be held between the assistant commissioner and his or her staff, the Assembly of Manitoba Chiefs and the Manitoba Metis

Federation. These meetings should provide a forum in which the chiefs and Metis leaders can express their concerns about law enforcement and hear from the assistant commissioner about his or her concerns.

We believe that the RCMP wishes to improve their relationships with the Aboriginal community, and that they have taken appropriate action in ending the Native Special Constable Program (which we discuss later), in developing initial standards for cross-cultural training and in setting national employment equity goals. We reiterate our belief that the first strategy in improving Aboriginal policing services is the development of Aboriginally controlled police forces. Such forces will need the support of the RCMP, as do many small, municipal non-Aboriginal forces in Canada.

WE RECOMMEND THAT:

- While they continue to police Aboriginal communities, the RCMP and all other Manitoba police forces develop and make public an integrated strategy to strengthen their capacity to provide culturally appropriate policing services, and the strategy include the development of a process of regular communication with Aboriginal organizations and communities, and the annual publication of reports which indicate progress in meeting the goals of the strategy.

The RCMP Native Special Constable Program

To date, the largest Aboriginal policing program in Canada has been the RCMP Native Special Constable Program. The program was established by the RCMP in 1973 and is frequently referred to as "option 3(b)." While the program has now been ended, it provided some important experience to guide the future development of Aboriginal policing policy.

A major goal of the special constable program was to recruit more Aboriginal members at a time when a sufficient number of Aboriginal people could not be attracted through the regular recruiting and training process. Native special constables were to help regular RCMP members serve Aboriginal communities.

By 1989 there were 189 native special constables, 30 of whom worked in Manitoba. The program was funded by the Department of Indian and Northern Affairs and by the participating provincial governments. Special constables worked in RCMP detachments and were responsible to the detachment commander, not to the local band.

Recruits in this program had varied educational backgrounds and did not have to meet the same entrance requirements as regular members. Training took place at the RCMP Depot over a period of 16 weeks, compared to the 25 weeks for regular RCMP members. Recruit training was followed by six months of field training. Native special constables were given full peace officer status on and off reserves. However, the salaries they received were lower than those paid to regular constables and they were supposed to be assigned different duties from regular members.

We received some positive comments about the program during our visit to Little Grand Rapids. Tony Bittern, who was a member of the RCMP for 11 years and now works for the band, told of his experiences. He became the only special constable to be placed in charge of an RCMP detachment (God's Lake). He was obviously very proud of his years in the RCMP and said the special constable program was a good one. He pointed out that the force did not have to introduce it and he commended it for adjusting its entrance qualifications so Aboriginal people could become officers.

In large measure, the strengths of the special constable program derived from the fact that it operated under the RCMP. As in most civil service jobs, there was considerable job security, and health and welfare benefits were similar to those of regular RCMP members. As part of a larger force, there were some opportunities for advancement, particularly as the special constables became regular members. However, there were also a number of problems with the special constable program, including the fact that the program was not controlled by local bands. The Aboriginal police officers were clearly under a great deal of stress and many left the force. Because special constables did not receive the full training program available to other recruits, they were not seen as full-fledged Mounties by other officers, or by those in the communities they served. The RCMP policy was to assign these constables to their home reserves, often leading to extreme local pressure on the individual. This method of assignment of special constables was severely criticized.

Former native special constables have also complained about the conduct of some other members of the force. Careless comments can suggest that the Aboriginal person is not considered an equal, or is not wanted in the force. Chief Enil Keeper of Little Grand Rapids was a special constable at one time. He spoke of being called names and being given the dirty jobs to do. He said he did not have the same privileges as the white officers. He was called "Blood" and his partner used to say things like, "Come on, let's go and shoot another Indian." He was accused of being a "faggot" by one officer. He was also concerned about being part of a force where other officers abused Aboriginal people.

In 1990 the RCMP eliminated the Native Special Constable Program. In order to ensure that Aboriginal constables have the same status and opportunities as other members of the force, all newly enrolled Aboriginal recruits will now train to be full constables. Those who are currently special constables will undergo training to upgrade their status to full constable. As part of this new program, those who lack the minimum educational qualifications will be taken on the force and given up to two years' additional training to enable them to achieve grade 12 equivalency. They may also spend some time working with the RCMP in their home communities to familiarize themselves with police work prior to attending the training depot. We commend the RCMP for recognizing some of the shortcomings of the former Native Special Constable Program and for taking steps to address these problems. However, as we discuss more fully in our report on the death of J.J. Harper, the grade 12 criterion for recruitment is an unnecessary impediment to the employment of Aboriginal people on police forces. We believe recruitment should be based on competency and job-related skills, rather than on educational attainment.

The Band Constable Program

The initial model for locally controlled policing on reserves was a program which was created in 1968 by the Department of Indian and Northern Affairs under Circular 34, and amended in 1971 under Circular 55. Indian bands on reserves are permitted to apply to the Department of Indian Affairs for funding to establish positions for constables, to be hired and supervised by band councils. Band constables report to council, typically through one of the council members who has police as his or her responsibility. The Department of Indian and Northern Affairs sponsors a two-week training program, but many constables have not received even this minimal level of training. Approximately 200 band constables are employed primarily in the Prairies and in Ontario, with about 65 in Manitoba.

The program was intended to provide limited local law enforcement services. The terms of Circular 55 allow band constables "to supplement locally the senior police forces but not to supplant them." On direction from the Justice department, the RCMP performs security checks on names submitted by bands. The Minister of Justice can approve the carrying of firearms, if adequate training is provided. No such approvals have been given to date in Manitoba, although this matter is under discussion at the present time. In practice, then, band constables have limited independent authority, including responsibility for such issues as band by-law enforcement.

When working with the RCMP, band constables are used for their local knowledge of people and situations, to interpret and to assist in arrests. Those we spoke to or heard about had a good working relationship with the RCMP, which provides some on-the-job training.

Many band constables feel that they are not accepted and that their work is not appreciated by the communities they serve. During a visit to one remote community, we heard from a band constable in private. He was afraid to appear and speak in public for fear of losing his job. Nevertheless, he spoke well of his relationship with the chief and council, and spoke highly of RCMP officers with whom he worked. However, he should not be placed in a position where his employment is so tenuous that he is afraid to speak in public.

The band constable program is popular, in part, because of the combination of local control and steady funding through the Department of Indian and Northern Affairs. However, there are many problems with the program because of its inadequate training, poor pay and high turnover rates, which may be due to the fact that band constables have very low status in their communities and among other law enforcement personnel.

Despite the apparently good working relationships, we believe that a much greater degree of cooperation with the RCMP must be developed. Organized, on-the-job training should be given by the RCMP to the band constables, who also need better access to RCMP facilities and services. For example, they need to be able to use the local RCMP lockup facilities for arrests they make when no RCMP officer is in the community. Most importantly, they need both the training and authority to provide a fuller range of police services to their communities.

The Dakota Ojibway Tribal Council Police Force

The Dakota Ojibway Tribal Council (DOTC) Police Force was established in Manitoba in 1978 to deliver locally controlled police services to eight Dakota and Ojibway reserves. Establishing the force was seen as part of a move toward greater self-governance in other areas. The program is cost-shared between the Department of Indian and Northern Affairs and the Province of Manitoba on an 85% –15% basis.

The force of 25 constables is administered by a chief of police who reports to a police commission, which is recognized under section 26(1) of the *Provincial Police Act.* Members of the commission include chiefs of the participating reserves, as well as representatives of the provincial Justice department, the Department of Indian and Northern Affairs, the Solicitor General of Canada, the RCMP and the Manitoba Police Commission.

Detachments are located on the various reserves, each having a senior officer who reports to the deputy police chief located in Brandon. Recruits are trained in Regina at the RCMP Depot, in the same program which formerly trained special constables.

While DOTC constables have authority to enforce all legislation and statutes, their jurisdiction is limited to the DOTC reserves. DOTC police have primary responsibility for policing their communities, but call upon the RCMP for assistance in some situations, using a written protocol under which DOTC constables handle less serious offences, while major *Criminal Code* violations are reported to the RCMP.

The DOTC policing program has had mixed success. DOTC Police Chief Frank McKay said that:

> It is a well known fact that white people who work for natives bring their own ideas. They don't give Indian people a chance to express their needs. This time we decided we weren't going to accept that. We put our own ideas forward and got financial assistance from the government to put them into action.

Chief McKay felt that Aboriginal constables' skills are much better in defusing a crisis in family conflict situations, handling them calmly, even-handedly and non-aggressively. An evaluation supported this view that DOTC officers were more successful at crisis intervention. It concluded that:

> [B]y sharing the same or a similar culture and knowing the disputants personally, the DOTC officers are better able than regular members of the RCMP to deal with conflict situations by finding alternative remedies to maintain order.[11]

The evaluation also found tentative evidence that the presence of DOTC police led to a decrease in the numbers of reserve residents who became involved in the criminal justice system.

The national evaluation of 1983 concluded that the program should continue and that it is preferred to regular RCMP policing.[12]

Despite these positive evaluation findings, the program has had some difficulties. There have been serious concerns expressed regarding service administration, operations and funding. There has been high staff turnover. Community support has not always been strong and some dissatisfaction with the service appears to continue. Citizens expressed concerns about inconsistent or lenient enforcement practices of the police, especially with respect to driving and liquor offences. Difficulties have also been created when constables are posted to their home reserves.

A considerable amount of work remains to be done in the area of public education. Aboriginal police officers should be going into the schools to talk to young people about the law and the role of the police. If young people come to appreciate that the police are there to protect them and to enforce the laws agreed to by the community, not only will there be an eventual acceptance of the police, but young people may see the police as good role models and aspire to become police officers themselves.

In short, DOTC officers face similar problems to those of any smaller local police force. Aboriginal communities are not yet used to Aboriginal people being police officers. Constables based in their own community face pressures because they may be perceived to have "joined the opposition," while those who work on other than their home reserves are criticized for being insensitive to local conditions.

Like all smaller forces, DOTC police need better training, support for their professional independence, and clear local accountability and understanding. We believe that the DOTC Police Force will also grow in effectiveness as it moves more and more towards a community policing model of service delivery.

WE RECOMMEND THAT:

- The Dakota Ojibway Tribal Council Police Force be provided with sufficient resources so that it can increase staff training and development in modern police methods, and gradually assume full responsibility for all law enforcement duties within its geographic jurisdiction.

- Aboriginal communities be encouraged to form regional police forces and regional police commissions following the model of the Dakota Ojibway Tribal Council Police Force. These should be established under Aboriginal control and management.

Metis Policing

Many Aboriginal communities in the province have both Indian and Metis components. There is often an Indian reserve next to, or surrounded by, a community of non-status or Metis people. Neither group is now policed by the police force of the other.

Twelve Metis or non-status communities now have one or more police constables appointed by local community police committees under the *Northern Affairs Act*. These constables then apply for, and are usually granted, status under the *Provincial Police Act* as special constables, thereby attaining peace officer status under section 2 of the *Criminal Code*. Like band constables, these officers also suffer from a severe lack of training opportunities.

While we think it is ultimately preferable to have one force able to police a whole Aboriginal community, encompassing reserve and off-reserve land, we recognize that this may be difficult to achieve in the short term. Therefore, as long as municipal and northern constables continue, we believe it is vital to ensure that they are properly trained, equipped and supervised. These constables, once properly trained, should have wide jurisdiction and take over much of the work now being done by the RCMP.

WE RECOMMEND THAT:

■ Metis and non-status communities consider the development of a regional police force, with a police commission.

Our recommendations concerning the Aboriginal and Manitoba Police commissions apply also to non-status and Metis police forces.

The Police and Bootlegging

The illegal bootlegging of alcohol presents a particular problem in some communities. Aboriginal women pointed out to us how justice authorities have failed to deal adequately with the bootlegging taking place in their supposedly "dry" communties. They feel let down when the police fail to lay charges against a known bootlegging operator, or when a judge fails to deal severely with offenders. When police refuse to do spot checks of people coming off aircraft and walking or driving onto a reserve, Aboriginal people find this refusal difficult to understand and accept, especially when they hear of frequent roadside checks occurring in southern Manitoba. The bootleggers, they believe, are well known, yet nothing is done to stop them. The fines which judges impose, they say, can be made up in a few illegal sales.

If violence in Aboriginal communities is to be overcome, we believe that the problem of alcohol abuse must be vigorously attacked. Governments must begin to turn their attention and energies to the effects which the consumption of alcohol is having on Aboriginal communities and, in particular, on Aboriginal crime. There is a tremendous cost to society, due to alcohol abuse. Many Aboriginal deaths and suicides are alcohol-related, and hundreds of Aboriginal inmates would not be in jail now if it were not for the abuse of alcohol.

To begin with, the government, which has a direct financial interest in the income derived from alcohol, due to its role as the sole supplier, has an obligation, in our view, to deal more strongly with bootlegging in Aboriginal communities. As a first step, we suggest that limits be placed upon the amount of alcohol which an individual can purchase at any one time from a liquor or beer outlet. Any purchases in excess of that limit should require a special permit, obtainable only by persons who do not have a prior conviction for a bootlegging offence. Any applicant for such a permit must declare the purpose for the purchase, the ultimate destination, the place where the alcohol is to be consumed and the method of transportation.

The actual transportation of large amounts of liquor should also require a special permit from the Manitoba Liquor Control Commission. Common carriers who transport liquor without such a permit should be liable to penalties against their carrier licences.

Air transport authorities should also take action against the licences of air carrier licensees and pilots who transport large amounts of alcohol without special permit from the commission.

The RCMP should develop, in conjunction with local Aboriginal authorities, roadside checks designed to catch those engaged in the wholesale transportation of large amounts of alcohol. Obtaining information of such purchases from the Manitoba Liquor Control Commission by local detachments is possible, and should make those efforts both reasonable and feasible.

In the case of dry reserves, automatic checks of incoming cargo should occur to ensure that alcohol is not being brought in. Houses of known bootleggers should be made known to police by local officials, and surveillance operations instituted. If sufficient information exists upon which a warrant to search the premises can be obtained, then one should be sought.

WE RECOMMEND THAT:

- The *Liquor Control Act* be amended to place limits on the amount of alcohol an individual can purchase at any one time without a permit.

- The transport of large quantities of alcohol without a permit be made illegal. Transporters of illegal shipments should not only be subject to fines, but should also face the loss of their licences and vehicles.

- Police forces, in conjunction with local Aboriginal governments that have prohibited the importation of alcohol to their reserves, undertake special enforcement programs designed to halt any illegal importation.

Policing in Non-Aboriginal Communities

The RCMP, acting as provincial police, provide services in all parts of Manitoba. Much of what we have said about their role in Aboriginal communities applies equally to their role in serving Aboriginal people in non-Aboriginal communities. The RCMP are making efforts to attract a wider range of officers who reflect the ethnic composition of the communities they serve. As Aboriginal police forces develop, and the RCMP withdraw from regular policing in Aboriginal communities, regular liaison with Aboriginal leaders will become even more vital. Cross-cultural training will continue to be important, as will the development of effective and professional working relationships with Aboriginal police forces. These issues are addressed in other recommendations in this chapter.

The RCMP recognize the need for more Aboriginal officers. They have made some efforts at recruitment but, apparently, the problems encountered by some Aboriginal officers to date have deterred many Aboriginal people from applying. Even though the force has set targets to increase its Aboriginal representation, it has been unable to fill those quotas. We believe that if new targets are set to recruit substantial numbers of Aboriginal officers, some success will result, particularly now that the Native Special Constable Program has been eliminated in favour of full officer status for all Aboriginal recruits.

WE RECOMMEND THAT:

- New targets be set by the RCMP to bring appropriate numbers of Aboriginal men and women into the force as full officers more quickly than is currently contemplated.

- The RCMP employ Aboriginal police and civilian staff in their detachments in proportion to at least the Aboriginal population of the province and preferably in proportion to the Aboriginal population being served.

It may be necessary to commence recruiting programs in schools so that more Aboriginal youth will consider a career in the RCMP and pursue their education with that option in mind. Students often lose interest in their education if they cannot see employment opportunities upon graduation. If pre-training upgrading programs are needed to bring older recruits to an acceptable entrance level, these can be provided under the new Aboriginal policing program.

Eight Manitoba municipalities now have their own police forces, formed under the *Municipal Act*. Constables in these forces have full peace officer status and carry weapons. We expect that as funding pressures mount on all municipal areas of Manitoba, the pressure to abandon RCMP contracts will grow. This will lead to the development of more local, small and, under current conditions, totally unregulated forces.

There are no standards regulating any aspect of activities of these forces. Not only are they not required to have cross-cultural training, they are not required to have training of any description. We view this as a serious matter, which could easily give rise to what is frequently disparaged as "small town sheriff" policing. We will discuss the need for a speedy resolution to these problems in our section on the *Provincial Police Act.*

Policing in Urban Areas
Winnipeg Police Department

Aboriginal people are greatly under-represented in the Winnipeg Police Department. In December 1990 there were 18 Aboriginal officers on the force, out of a total of 1,125 officers. Despite extensive public criticism about the lack of participation of Aboriginal people on the force, the department has been unable to increase Aboriginal recruitment. This was evident during Police Chief Herb Stephen's testimony before us. He stated that the current test for acceptance is that if two applicants are considered to be equally qualified, preference may be given to an Aboriginal applicant. From what we heard about the selection criteria, we doubt that the present system will allow any Aboriginal applicants to be considered equal in every category.

A major impediment to the recruitment of Aboriginal police officers has been the department's requirement that recruits must have completed grade 12 in order to be accepted. Although this criterion has put Aboriginal people at a serious disadvantage, the Chief has been firm in his insistence that it must be retained to ensure a high standard of policing. Even when special initiatives have been taken to help recruits meet the department's criteria, increased Aboriginal recruitment does not result. The Core Area Initiative, a joint project of the federal, provincial and city governments, offered a Human Justice Training Program to assist members of minority groups to develop the skills necessary to find employment in police forces and other branches of the justice system. During the three years of the training program, only one of the 16 Aboriginal students who completed the course was accepted into the Winnipeg Police Department.

The department's present recruitment methods will not find many Aboriginal applicants. Because of the attitudes perceived to exist in the force, not many Aboriginal people are interested in applying for a position. Radical steps will have to be taken to engage the necessary numbers of Aboriginal police officers and to make them feel welcome in the force. It has been clearly demonstrated elsewhere that without hiring targets, employment equity programs are usually ineffective. We feel such targets are an absolute necessity in the Winnipeg Police Department. We strongly recommend that a substantial target number be set and that those numbers be filled without delay. Since Aboriginal people make up 11.8% of Manitoba's population, the force must hire an additional 115 Aboriginal officers in order to reach a representative number of 133.

We believe too that the grade 12 criterion for recruitment should be eliminated. In its place, the department should adopt tests which better assess whether an applicant has the skills required to be a police officer. This matter is discussed more fully in our report on the death of J.J. Harper.

We have already noted the testimony of Dr. Neil McDonald in regard to the need for particular attention to be paid to cross-cultural education for recruits. His experience with recruit classes in Winnipeg shows the need to expand the provision of such training for the entire Winnipeg Police Department, and for the department to give leadership from the Chief on down in regard to cross-cultural policing issues.

Because of the involvement of the Winnipeg Police Department in the Harper case, we have dealt at length with recruitment issues affecting the department in that volume of this report. In that volume we make the following recommendations about the measures necessary to employ more Aboriginal people in the department.

WE RECOMMEND THAT:

- The Winnipeg Police Department prepare and table with the city council and the Minister of Justice, no later than December 31, 1991, an employment equity plan which has clear targets, target dates and remedies should targets not be achieved.

- The City of Winnipeg Police Department set an initial target of 133 Aboriginal police officers. The first step in reaching that goal should be to designate the next recruiting class as entirely Aboriginal. Thereafter, 50% of each recruit class be dedicated to Aboriginal recruits until the target has been met.

- The Winnipeg Police Department be required to report publicly the progress of its employment equity program to the Minister of Justice.

- A portion of the funding provided by the Province to the City of Winnipeg for police salaries be conditional on the Winnipeg Police Department's using that funding only for the hiring of Aboriginal police officers.

- The assignment of Aboriginal police officers not be restricted to the core area or other Aboriginal areas of the city of Winnipeg

- The Winnipeg Police Department no longer rely on the grade 12 educational criterion for police recruitment and develop approaches which more appropriately test recruits' ability to perform the functions required of police officers.

Brandon Police Department

Brandon is Manitoba's second largest city and for Aboriginal people it is a key centre for services, education and employment. A substantial percentage of the work of the Brandon Police Department involves Aboriginal people who either live in the city or visit there from Aboriginal communities in southwestern Manitoba. Relationships between the Brandon police and Aboriginal people have been a matter of concern since at least 1971, when the Toal Commission examined complaints against the force brought by Aboriginal people. Those who spoke to us indicated significant continuing concerns about Aboriginal-police relations.

We believe that it is important that the City of Brandon play a leadership role in enabling Aboriginal people to receive appropriate police services in the city, and to support them in making the transition to living in an urban environment.

The Brandon Police Department, like others in Manitoba, has not achieved employment equity with regard to Aboriginal officers. Brandon has an additional problem in that it serves many Aboriginal people who are transient residents of the city and region, as well as its resident Aboriginal population. Because Brandon is a relatively small force of 72 members, proportional representation of 11.8% would require about nine Aboriginal officers. At present, there are three Aboriginal officers on the force. We believe that to achieve adequate coverage and availability of Aboriginal officers, a somewhat higher target should be set which is more representative of the actual work of the force.

Since our hearings were held, the Brandon Police Department has introduced an innovative cross-cultural training program with the support of the Secretary of State. Following a cross-cultural training session similar to those conducted by other departments, the Brandon police sent seven of their officers to reserves policed by the Dakota Ojibway Tribal Council Police Force. Each of the officers spent two days on patrol with a DOTC officer. During this period, they were encouraged to familiarize themselves with life on reserves and to speak with as many members of the community as possible.

The officers who participated in this program felt that this contact with Aboriginal life and culture would help them police Brandon's Aboriginal community more effectively. The second part of the exchange involved DOTC officers patrolling in the city with members of the Brandon Police Department. We encourage this type of exchange program as an effective way of providing the positive contacts between Aboriginal and non-Aboriginal people which are necessary if the barriers between police and the Aboriginal community are to be reduced. In addition, we believe that the department should undertake a public relations program directed towards the Aboriginal people living in or visiting Brandon. This could be done in cooperation with the Brandon Friendship Centre.

WE RECOMMEND THAT:

- The City of Brandon Police Department prepare and table with Brandon City Council and the Minister of Justice an employment equity plan no later than December 31, 1991, which will increase the numbers of Aboriginal people on the City of Brandon Police Department to a level equal to their proportion of the Manitoba population. The plan should include target dates by which to achieve that proportion and remedies should those targets not be met.

- The City of Brandon Police Department set an initial target of nine Aboriginal police officers and that the Brandon City Police dedicate that number of positions for Aboriginal recruits in its next recruit class.

- Both the City of Winnipeg Police Department and the City of Brandon Police Department consider hiring Aboriginal police officers who already have policing experience with an Aboriginal force or with the RCMP.

- Aboriginal people be represented among the civilian members of both the City of Winnipeg Police Department and the City of Brandon Police Department in the same proportion as their presence in the province's population.

- The City of Brandon Police Department, in cooperation with the Brandon Friendship Centre, develop a program to reach out to and inform Aboriginal people living in Brandon about policing issues.

The *Provincial Police Act* and the Manitoba Police Commission

Policing in Manitoba is regulated by the *Provincial Police Act*. This Act is extremely brief, containing only 29 sections, the first 14 of which contemplate a provincial police force which does not exist. Responsibility for provincial policing has been contracted to the RCMP under section 15(1). Sections 22–25 of the Act provide for the appointment and duties of the Manitoba Police Commission, including a very lengthy description of the role of the commission. Matters covered include:

- Providing advice to municipal police authorities.

- Examining and advising on lockup facilities.

- Evaluating police forces.

- Recommending standards for training at all levels of policing, including post-secondary education programs.

- Making recommendations on communications systems, equipment and on any other matters pertaining to police activities.

The commission, which has only two staff at present, has never had sufficient resources to carry out the range of duties specified in the Act. Hence, some delegation of duties to staff of the Justice department has occurred. The Law Enforcement Services Branch provides staffing to carry out some of the commission's duties in relation to crime prevention and supervision of local police forces, and provides support for the RCMP-Manitoba policing agreements. However, the commission remains formally responsible for these activities.

It is notable that no regulations exist under the Act to cover training or equipment standards. Some draft regulations are now being examined by government in the area of equipment. At present, a municipal constable can carry any weapon and can use equipment of any sort. A municipality may appoint a person without any training as a constable. Even if the appointed person has had some policing experience, there are neither provisions for, nor policies covering, periodic retraining. Manitoba has no police college, nor does it require constables to undergo training elsewhere. Apart from the RCMP, standards exist only in the larger municipalities such as Brandon and Winnipeg, which have developed their own training programs.

During our review, we became aware of the severe fragmentation of the authority to appoint constables through the various statutes which govern policing in Manitoba. The power to appoint police officers is found in at least five statutes, including the *Provincial Police Act*, the *Municipal Act*, the *Brandon City Charter*, the *City of Winnipeg Act* and, by implication, under the *Northern Affairs Act*.

The Manitoba *Provincial Police Act* broadly regulates the provision of policing services which are covered under the other Acts mentioned above, and provides the authority for contractual arrangements with the RCMP. However, RCMP regular and special constables derive their individual policing authority from the federal *RCMP Act*, and are not subject to any of the appeal or regulatory provisions of the *Provincial Police Act*. Eight municipalities have created police forces under the *Municipal Act*. Band constables derive their mandate from the *Indian Act*. Band constables of the Dakota Ojibway Tribal Council have authority as police officers because section 26(1) of the *Provincial Police Act* recognizes the DOTC Police Commission. Northern Community Special Constables provide limited services to about 12 Metis communities, and are appointed under very vague provisions of the *Northern Affairs Act*. It is doubtful whether, under that Act, they have any status as police constables.

Under an Order-in-Council, constables appointed by bands and municipalities under their respective statutes may be granted authority as "special constables" through section 9(1) of the Manitoba *Provincial Police Act*. Through this appointment, they are designated as peace officers and, thereby, have authority to enforce the *Criminal Code* and provincial statutes. This authority may be granted with some territorial limitations, such as the radius within which their authority extends.

Contrary to generally held perceptions, having the status of peace officer means that "special" and "northern" and "band" constables have identical authority to that held by a regular RCMP constable, or an officer of the City of Winnipeg or Brandon police departments. By administrative regulation, they may or may not carry firearms and they may call upon RCMP services for assistance with serious crimes, but their status as peace officers is the same as that of RCMP constables.

Manitoba compares poorly with other western provinces in its regulation of police activities. Each of these other jurisdictions has an Act which provides, among other things, clear definitions of relevant terms, limitations on the terms of appointment of police commissioners, powers to make regulations, powers to set and enforce wide-ranging standards for the selection and training of constables and the equipping of police forces, the establishment of a disciplinary code and ethical conduct codes, and the establishment of a police training facility. Manitoba's Act provides few of the specific details of similar acts in those provinces, and no regulations currently exist to actually enforce the standards which the Act implies, but does not define.

The present lack of a clear mandate and the absence of relevant regulations in regard to police appointment, training and supervision create a potential danger to the security of Manitobans, particularly in areas not served locally by the RCMP. Three different Acts may be involved in the empowerment of any one officer. The confusion in regard to the source, scope and validity of the police powers of band and municipal constables is unacceptable.

We believe that it is vital to make major amendments to the *Provincial Police Act*, to provide a framework for the Manitoba Police Commission and for Aboriginal police forces and commissions formed by bands and tribal councils. We have reviewed a study of the Manitoba Police Commission by sociologist Rick Linden, which notes a wide range of concerns similar to our own,[13] and we have also examined the policing statutes of Ontario, Saskatchewan, Alberta and British Columbia. We view the Manitoba Police Commission and the Law Enforcement Services Branch as essentially administrative support services, similar to those provided by a number of government departments. We believe that they should be given sufficient resources to allow them to carry out their responsibilities in regard to regulating and supporting police forces in Manitoba.

We further believe that the use of the terms "special" or "band" to designate some constables is inappropriate. All constables who are recognized under the *Provincial Police Act* become peace officers by virtue of section 2 of the *Criminal Code*. They have the same status as any other constable. Good practice may require that any force, including large, urban police systems, may sometimes wish to call upon the greater resources or experience of another force.

WE RECOMMEND THAT:

- The *Provincial Police Act* make explicit provision for the recognition of any police commission or committee which is established to provide police services in any municipality, unorganized territory, or Aboriginal community in Manitoba.

- The Manitoba Police Commission prepare and enforce a wide range of regulations covering recruitment, training, equipment, procedures, supervision of, and support for, police forces in Manitoba.

Aboriginal Systems of Policing

Creating Aboriginal Police Forces

We believe that the first priority for reform of policing of Aboriginal communities is to enable those communities to take full responsibility for police services. We believe that the legal mechanisms to enable this to happen immediately are already in place: the present *Provincial Police Act* provides for the recognition of police committees or commissions as they are formed. There was a specific amendment made to ensure that the Dakota Ojibway Tribal Council Police Commission is recognized. (s. 26(1)(d)) What is missing are the administrative will and funding from governments to make possible the creation of such forces in other Aboriginal communities. In this regard, we note that when Aboriginal forces take over from the RCMP, expenditures for RCMP services will decrease. Therefore, in the medium term, we would expect that turning over policing to Aboriginal communities will not be more costly than the present RCMP services.

Creating an Aboriginal Police Commission

As Aboriginally controlled police departments and regional or local police commissions become more prevalent in Manitoba, it will be desirable to establish a provincial Aboriginal Police Commission to support and coordinate Aboriginal policing. It is our hope that this structure will not lessen the interest and support required from each community, or reduce the sense of ownership that communities should have concerning their police forces. Functions of the commission might include the following:

- Supporting the establishment of Aboriginal police forces throughout the province.

- Establishing a training facility, standards, curriculum and continuing education for Aboriginal police officers.

- Cooperating with the RCMP, the City of Winnipeg and other police forces in regard to officer training and the delivery of police services.

- Overseeing the operation of Aboriginal police forces, receiving and hearing complaints, and offering assistance.

- Helping other police forces recruit Aboriginal police officers.

- Receiving submissions and recommendations from Aboriginal communities, their chiefs and councils.

Aboriginal police forces should adhere to appropriate province-wide standards and be subject to culturally appropriate province-wide regulations. The commission will also require a chief executive officer who might be called the Aboriginal Police Commissioner.

WE RECOMMEND THAT:

- The *Provincial Police Act* be amended to provide for the establishment of a provincial Aboriginal Police Commission with authority to prepare and enforce a wide range of regulations covering recruitment, training, equipment, procedures, supervision of, and support for, Aboriginal police forces in Manitoba.

- Final decisions concerning the size, composition and manner of appointment to the Aboriginal Police Commission be made by Aboriginal people.

- The *Provincial Police Act* be amended to provide for the appointment of an Aboriginal Police Commissioner, to serve the Aboriginal Police Commission, with any such person being selected by Aboriginal organizations responsible for Aboriginal police forces.

- Agreements be developed between the provincial Aboriginal Police Commission, local police commissions, the RCMP and the provincial Justice department for Aboriginal police forces to provide full police services to Aboriginal communities, with a firm timetable for achieving this goal, including training, equipping and supporting the local forces with appropriate back-up services as required.

There will be many other details to be considered and negotiated between Aboriginal communities and the provincial and federal governments concerning the operation of such a commission.

An Aboriginal Justice College

Throughout this report, we recommend a much greater level of involvement of Aboriginal people in the criminal justice system. We suggest that the present training for Aboriginal police officers be substantially expanded, through a division of the proposed Aboriginal Justice College. In addition to increased numbers of Aboriginal police, there will need to be training programs for court clerks, court administrators, court communicators or peacemakers, fine option clerks, probation officers, parole officers, custodial staff for local holding facilities and for jails, justices of the peace and Aboriginal judges. It may be possible, by agreement, to access basic police training through the RCMP Depot facility in Regina. However, it will also be appropriate to provide in-service and other training or pre-training of Aboriginal police through an Aboriginal Justice College in Manitoba.

We believe that such a college would be unique in Canada, and could well develop as a national resource for the training of Aboriginal justice system staff from other parts of the country. It could also develop the capacity to provide cross-cultural training to a wide range of non-Aboriginal staff from the justice systems of Manitoba, as well as other provinces. This matter will be more fully detailed in the final chapter.

Public Complaints and Policing in Manitoba

In our report on the death of J.J. Harper, we make recommendations concerning the need for independent investigations of serious incidents involving the police, especially those where possible criminal acts are alleged against the police, or where a person dies or suffers serious injury in an incident involving the police. The problems of actual and perceived conflict of interest are just too great to expect a police force to be seen as effectively and objectively investigating its own members. We made the following recommendations:

WE RECOMMEND THAT:

- The Minister of Justice establish a plan of action to deal with any incident where possible criminal acts are alleged against the police, or where a person dies or suffers serious injury in an incident involving a police officer.

- This plan of action include either the creation of a standing special investigations unit, or a plan to quickly assemble a special investigations team for a particular incident, able to take control of the investigation immediately following report of the incident. The unit or team should not include officers from the police department under investigation. The plan should include independent counsel to give advice concerning the laying of criminal charges. This counsel should not be a Crown attorney. The unit or team should report directly to the Minister of Justice.

- The police forces in the province be required to provide all available assistance and cooperation to the special investigations team.

We now turn our attention more generally to public complaints. These complaints can include any number of "disciplinary defaults," including discrimination on the basis of race, failing to exercise restraint with a firearm, altering an official document, use of excessive force, use of abusive language, being discourteous or uncivil, and so forth. Whether the complaint is related to excessive use of force, death, or any other matter arising in the course of police-citizen relations, the complainant and the officer both want to know that they will have a chance to be heard, to be dealt with fairly by an independent adjudicator and to have effective remedies available. The nature of the complaint does not change this need.

During our hearings, we received numerous complaints about police conduct. In many of these cases, the person bringing the complaint to our attention either had not brought the complaint to the attention of existing complaint agencies at all, or had found the process completely unsatisfactory. In addition, during the course of the Inquiry, it became clear that many people are not aware of how to file a complaint against the police, because our office received numerous telephone calls from individuals wishing to know how they could have their complaints addressed.

In Manitoba, there are two main processes for dealing with police complaints: the RCMP Public Complaints Commission and the Law Enforcement Review Agency (LERA), which deals with complaints against all municipal police forces in Manitoba.

There is a different process for the Dakota Ojibway Tribal Council Police Force and for special constables appointed under section 9 of the *Provincial Police Act,* cap. P150, C.C.S.M. In these cases, the Manitoba Police Commission is involved.

The Law Enforcement Review Agency

LERA was created in February 1985 and is governed by the *Law Enforcement Review Act,* cap. L75, C.C.S.M., which provides that any person "who feels aggrieved by a disciplinary default allegedly committed by any member of a police department may file a complaint." A disciplinary default is defined in section 29 of the Act and includes such matters as assault, being discourteous and a variety of other improper acts. Section 30 prescribes penalties ranging from admonition to dismissal. Under the LERA Act, the commissioner of LERA is an officer of the Manitoba Police Commission.

The Law Enforcement Review Agency includes a commissioner and a Law Enforcement Review Board. The board decides upon the validity of complaints against police officers and, within certain limits, the penalties to be imposed against them. The board is composed of a presiding officer and a deputy presiding officer, both of whom are to be lawyers, at least two other persons who are or have been police officers and at least three laypersons. All members are selected by the government. Three persons sit at each hearing. Those to sit at a given hearing are to be chosen "sequentially" as their names appear on a list prepared by the presiding officer at the beginning of each year. A board member who is a present or former police officer may not sit at a hearing into the conduct of a member from his or her own present or former police force.

LERA is assisted by two investigators employed by the Law Enforcement Services Branch of the Manitoba Department of Justice and by a lawyer from the Justice department. Every complaint goes through a number of stages before it gets to a hearing and most cases are resolved in one way or another before reaching the board.

When a complaint is filed, it is investigated by the commissioner, who then decides whether the complaint falls within the jurisdiction of LERA. The commissioner has the authority to dismiss the complaint if he or she is "satisfied" the complaint is frivolous or vexatious, or does not fall within the range of misconduct in section 29. If a complainant disagrees with dismissal of a complaint by the commissioner, the complainant can appeal to the Manitoba Police Commission.

Once the commissioner has decided not to dismiss the complaint, it proceeds to the next step: informal resolution. Under the Act, the commissioner is required to seek informal resolution. When a complaint is informally resolved, no record of the complaint is placed on the officer's file and there are no consequences to the officer. Between 1985 and 1989, 119 complaints were informally resolved. In addition, complaints are frequently withdrawn, including 126 cases between 1985 and 1989.

Cases do not proceed to formal consideration if the officer admits a disciplinary default. In such an event, the LERA commissioner asks the police chief's opinion about the severity of the incident and the service record of the officer. The commissioner then recommends a penalty. If the officer agrees with the penalty, it is imposed. According to LERA annual reports, it is rare that an officer admits wrongdoing.

If a complaint proceeds past these preliminary steps, it goes to the board for hearing. The complainant has the burden of proof and must present the case personally, or with the assistance of his or her own lawyer. The case must be proved beyond a reasonable doubt, while in Ontario the test is "clear and convincing evidence." The Act prohibits the name of the officer from being made public until the board has made a decision, or the officer admits committing a disciplinary default.

Even if a case is proved by the complainant, the maximum penalty to be imposed is decided upon in advance of the hearing by the commissioner after consulting with the officer's chief of police. The complainant, the officer and the board are excluded from this process.

If a complainant wishes to appeal a decision of the board, the complainant can appeal to the Court of Queen's Bench for a review, but only on a question involving the jurisdiction of the board or a question of law.

The annual reports of LERA list the complaints it has received and how they were dealt with.

Complaints Received and Dealt with between 1985–1989

- Received (may have been verbal or written) 882
- Not proceeded with (no jurisdiction/too minor) 376
- Files opened... 518
- Files subsequently closed on later evidence (either not fitting LERA's jurisdiction, or "frivolous and vexatious").......... 194
- Resolved informally 119
- Cases withdrawn by complainant... 126
- Cases remaining in formal consideration................................. 79
- Cases not responded to or still in process................................ 42

Hearings Held 37

Obviously, the vast majority of complaints received by LERA do not proceed to a hearing. Between 1985 and 1989, only 7.1% of all files which were opened were ultimately heard by the Law Enforcement Review Board.

There are a number of problems with the way LERA is currently operating. We believe the LERA process is not as independent as it should be, because the commissioner and police chief have too much influence in resolving complaints and in selecting the penalty to be applied, while the board has too little. The board should have the discretion to determine the appropriate penalty.

The process is not as open as it should be. The board has discretion to keep proceedings private, but there are no statutory guidelines as to how that discretion is to be exercised, other than as "the maintenance of order or the proper administration of justice requires." (s. 24(11)) Further, we are concerned that LERA's annual reports do not provide enough information about its activities. In particular, the annual reports do not say how many board hearings find in favour of the complainant, how many penalties have been imposed or the nature of the penalties. LERA does not describe the process of informal resolution (the nature of complaints informally resolved, or how the matters were "resolved"), comment on the number of withdrawn complaints, or comment on the number or nature of dismissed complaints.

The LERA process is not as effective as it could be, primarily because the authority of the board is too restricted and the authority of the commissioner too broad. The standard of proof is too stringent and the penalty procedures are too limited. As well, there is concern that it does not have sufficient resources for investigations, quick decisions and resolutions of complaints. According to LERA annual reports, the majority of complaints take more than three months to complete and many take more than nine months.

The process does not provide complainants with sufficient assistance in presenting their complaint. Complainants often appear without counsel and are ill-prepared to lead evidence at a formal hearing. This is all the more difficult when the police officer is represented by counsel at no cost to the officer. Once LERA has decided a case should be presented to the board, it should have its own counsel present the case.

In light of the above problems, we believe that this public complaints process should be significantly changed. Before we proceed to making recommendations, we will consider the RCMP complaints process.

RCMP Public Complaints Commission

The 1976 Commission of Inquiry Relating to Public Complaints, Internal Discipline and Grievance Procedure within the RCMP, which recommended appointment of a police ombudsman, noted that:

> [T]he concern has been expressed at some hearings that an external reviewing authority for public complaints would be an "outsider" who would lack understanding of the particular problems the Force has to face. We are of the opinion, however, that it is precisely because he is an "outsider" that he will bring to the position the independence in judgement that is so necessary. Furthermore, although initially an "outsider", a police ombudsman will soon acquire a detailed and intimate knowledge of the Force and its members.[14]

Instead of the appointment of an ombudsman, the RCMP Public Complaints Commission was established in 1988. We regret to say that we are not impressed with the new procedures of the RCMP for dealing with public complaints. If the ultimate goal is to provide an effective mechanism whereby a person may complain about police conduct, the procedures now in place are neither realistic nor appropriate.

The RCMP Public Complaints Commission was established in response to two separate public inquiries into the conduct of the RCMP: the Marin Commission of 1976, which examined the issue of public complaints, and the Macdonald Commission of 1981, which examined certain RCMP activities.

The Public Complaints Commission is established under Part 6 of the *Royal Canadian Mounted Police Act*. The commission is composed of a chairperson, a vice-chairperson, one member from each jurisdiction in Canada that uses the RCMP for provincial policing, and not more than three others. Members are chosen by the federal government, after consulting with each provincial government. Members may not be current RCMP officers. The commission is based in Ottawa.

A person wishing to lodge a complaint about the conduct of an RCMP officer can notify any member of the force, a local detachment or the new commission. If the complaint is received by the commission, its first step is to refer the complaint to the RCMP. At that point, the complaint will likely be referred to the local detachment of which the officer whose conduct is called into question is a member. The detachment then does an investigation by having an officer visit the complainant to discuss the complaint. When he appeared before us, the chairperson of the Public Complaints Commission, Dr. Richard Gosse, confirmed that it might be the very officer complained against who is sent to speak to the complainant.

We find this first step in the process to be totally inappropriate. Certainly, if a member of the public complains about the services or conduct of a lawyer or doctor, the professional society does not dispatch the lawyer or doctor in question to speak to the person, nor do they send someone else from the same office to investigate.

During our Inquiry, we heard from a woman who, several years ago, wanted to complain about the improper conduct of an officer towards her. She was shocked to find that in order to lay the complaint she had to attend at the officer's detachment to fill out a form. This left the impression with her that the process would find in favour of the officer at every step. She gave up and did not pursue what sounded to us like a valid complaint.

The new complaints process does not get any better at the next stage. To carry the complaint further than the local RCMP investigation, the person has to write the commission again. If that is done, the commissioner looks at the complaint and can do one of a number of things. He or she can decide that the RCMP investigation was satisfactory and do nothing further, or ask the RCMP to investigate further. He or she can write a report on the matter to the minister, have staff do a further investigation, or institute a hearing to consider the complaint. Even though we are critical of the RCMP complaints process, it does have at least one positive feature. During hearings, officers against whom complaints have been brought can be compelled to testify.

A report will then be prepared and sent to all parties, including the minister and the commissioner of the RCMP, making findings and recommendations. The commissioner of the RCMP can choose not to follow the recommendations. All he or she has to do is notify the Solicitor General and the chairperson of the complaints commission of his or her decision. There is no appeal. There is no mechanism whereby an aggrieved citizen can require a hearing. The system is not independent, because the RCMP have such an overwhelming influence over the entire process, including power to dismiss the complaint, control of the conduct of the investigation and power to disregard the findings of the commission.

We find the process not to be in the public interest. Rather, it appears to be a process designed to protect the RCMP and to leave all its decisions to its own officers, at one level or another.

Obviously, the RCMP public complaint process is seriously flawed. Its officers are remote from Manitoba, and particularly from Aboriginal communities for whom even Winnipeg seems distant. It promises to be a slow, private process. We are not aware of how many complaints have reached an actual hearing. We recommend that the present RCMP public complaints process be replaced by a public (non-police) agency which has its own investigative staff capable of investigating public complaints in an independent manner.

New Approaches to Hearing Public Complaints

We recommend that the Law Enforcement Review Board be reconstituted as an independent civilian agency to review complaints against all police. The recent report, *Police-Challenge 2000, A Vision of the Future of Policing in Canada,* from the federal Department of the Solicitor General, 1990, stresses the importance of public account-ability and effective handling of public complaints.

> Public complaints mechanisms can play an educative and preventive role, sen-sitizing police personnel about minorities and stepping in when tensions between police and a segment of the community are running high. Ultimately, such bodies can enhance the standing of the police in the community.[15]

The report discusses opposition by police forces to public complaint mecha-nisms, citing the example of the Metropolitan Toronto Police Association's "wholeheart-ed effort to undermine the position of the Public Complaints Commissioner."[16] The report mentions "the historical failure of the police to vigorously and openly investigate allegations of misconduct" as the reason for the establishment of formal mechanisms to deal with complaints.

Britain has its own Independent Police Complaints Authority. Their 1987 annual report states the importance of such mechanisms.

> We believe we are in a pre-eminent position to communicate to the police the feelings of the general public about their work and its reaction to specific inci-dents. Conversely we are now fitted to convey to the public the difficulties which the police encounter in doing what society requires of them. We thus hope to form a civilian bridge between society and its police forces across which there may pass a better mutual understanding and tolerance.[17]

Ontario's response to the problem of complaints against the Toronto police during the 1970s was to create the Office of the Public Complaints Commissioner in 1981. This office was established so that a civilian agency would conduct investigations.

If the commission is satisfied a complaint has merit, it then assumes the responsibility of taking conduct of the case and presenting it before an independent civilian board of inquiry.

Like Manitoba, Ontario has had its own recent controversies with police-related shootings, particularly the shooting of black persons. These shootings gave rise to the Ontario Race Relations and Policing Task Force of 1989. The task force said:

> The Task Force does wish to state that its public hearings throughout the province suggest a considerable need for a consistent approach by govern-ment to the issue. It is patently obvious that a publicly credible, accountable and independent civilian mechanism for public complaints is basic to respond-ing to allegations of racial intolerance or other misconduct by all police.[18]

In July 1990 another Ontario task force, this time the Osnaburgh-Windigo Tribal Council Justice Review Committee, also reported. This committee had the mandate of reviewing and making recommendations about the state of the administration of justice in a tribal council area in northwestern Ontario. Recommendation 32.6 calls for the "development of a system of investigating citizen complaints against the police which would ensure the independence and objectivity of the investigator."[19]

On December 31, 1990 Ontario proclaimed its new *Police Services Act*. This Act makes wide-ranging recommendations concerning policing principles, organization, monitoring and public complaints, and, among other things, applies the Toronto complaints system to the whole province. Throughout the Act, the importance of public input and public accountability is stressed.

Before the new Act came into effect, outside police forces were brought in to con-duct investigations in some cases. This was found to be an inadequate solution. It is true that the appearance of independence is enhanced when an outside police force is asked to investigate particular situations, but the appearance of independence is still compro-mised when police investigate police, especially when police forces must work so closely together on a day-to-day basis to provide good policing.

The Ontario commission has a staff of investigators, half of whom are civilians and half of whom are former police officers. Former police officers are not allowed to investigate complaints against their former police forces. The Act also creates new procedures to ensure that investigations are conducted in a fair and independent manner, with review and monitoring by the commission.

If the commission takes the view that the complaint is justified, it presents the case to a board of inquiry and does not require the complainant to carry the financial burden of legal costs. (s. 95) The commission has engaged a number of lawyers to act for it, but now has its own staff lawyers.

A board of inquiry consists of three persons to hear each case, one lawyer and two laypersons. One of the laypersons is selected from a list of names provided by the Ontario Police Association, while the other is from a list provided by the Ontario Association of Municipalities. The lawyer is from a list provided by the Attorney General.

Ontario used to require that complaints be proved beyond a reasonable doubt, but this has been changed to proof that is "clear and convincing," which is thought to be a standard somewhat less stringent than the criminal standard. (s. 97) The board has full powers to impose penalties, including dismissals.

During the period since 1981, during which the board dealt only with cases concerning the Toronto police, there have been 65 hearings, with 23 cases resulting in findings of misconduct against police officers, and two police officers have been dismissed from their jobs. The Toronto Police Association chose, as a matter of policy, to appeal every decision against a police officer to the Ontario Divisional Court. Only two decisions were modified on appeal.

We believe a process similar to the one now in place in Ontario should be implemented in Manitoba. The process should strive for independence, openness, fairness, effectiveness and accountability. The government should also consider whether a process similar to the one for the police would be appropriate to deal with complaints in other parts of the justice system, including complaints about prison treatment, lawyers, judges, social workers and civil servants. We heard many complaints during our hearings in all these areas. It is clear there needs to be a greater effort by all concerned to demonstrate to the public, and especially Aboriginal people, that their complaints will be fully and fairly dealt with, no matter what component of the justice system is involved.

WE RECOMMEND THAT:

- The Law Enforcement Review Board be reconstituted and the *Law Enforcement Review Act* be amended to approximate the Ontario model.

- The board appoint independent counsel to have conduct of each case and be responsible for presenting the evidence.

- Where the complaint is from an Aboriginal person, at least one member of a panel be Aboriginal.

- The test to be applied by the board be proof by clear and convincing evidence, rather than beyond a reasonable doubt.

- If the board decides that the complaint is proven, it have full power to impose whatever penalties it deems appropriate.

- In addition to what is now in Law Enforcement Review Agency reports, the agency report annually on the nature of complaints, how many were found to have merit, how many were dismissed and the type of penalty applied.

- Police officers, including the officer against whom the complaint is made, be compellable witnesses.

- Aboriginal justice systems establish and maintain an agency to receive, investigate and resolve complaints against Aboriginal police officers similar to what we recommend for provincial police forces.

- Complaints against the RCMP in Manitoba, when acting as a provincial police force, be investigated and heard by the Law Enforcement Review Board.

Conclusion

It is both appropriate and desirable that wherever possible, Aboriginal communities receive police services from Aboriginal police forces. We believe that Aboriginal police forces, properly trained and with full jurisdiction, would substantially relieve the RCMP of the need to serve remote communities.

Good working relationships and close cooperation between Aboriginal police forces and the RCMP are vital. There will be cases where, for a variety of reasons, the local police will find it appropriate to call upon the RCMP. The RCMP should make their forensic and technical services available to Aboriginal forces.

We believe it is important to establish a good relationship between police forces and Aboriginal people. The objectives of our recommendations are to foster the establishment of effective Aboriginal police forces, staffed with officers who will be sensitive to Aboriginal people, and to improve the manner in which non-Aboriginal forces serve Aboriginal people. Such forces, using a community policing approach, will provide services which are culturally appropriate and support the deep commitment to justice which was frequently raised with us by Aboriginal presenters.

CHAPTER 17

A STRATEGY FOR ACTION

Introduction

From time to time throughout the Inquiry's public hearings, presenters—especially Aboriginal presenters—expressed concern about the effectiveness of the process and particularly about the likelihood of any changes resulting from it.

Rufus Prince, an elder of the Long Plain First Nation at the time of his presentation, who has since passed away, said:

> There is one last point I want to raise, and that deals with the repercussions which are going to happen, and I think that was mentioned here this morning as a result of this Commission of Inquiry. You exposed a lot of injustices. You have lifted up the rock and the worms are scurrying for cover. But as soon as this Commission is over and all the spotlights and flash bulbs are over, the rogues will come out from the dark and be twice as bad, determined to put the system of injustice back into full swing.

> It's like poking a stick into a hornet's nest. If you are going to do that, the hornets are going to get mad.

> We ask that the Province extend the power to this Commission to monitor the implementation of its recommendation and to see no retaliation is taken by rogue officials against those who have spoken out in the Commission.

You've got to do this or we're going to suffer repercussions, and the bureaucrats are going to find a nice high shelf for your report and recommendation,
and a generation later, if they have another Commission on the same subject,
they'll find it there covered with dust.

All the time and effort and sacrifice you have devoted to this Commission will
go to nothing and be all in vain. We will only have dug the ruts a little deeper.

Ron Richard of the Manitoba Metis Federation said:

[A]lthough we are encouraged by the establishment of the judicial inquiry, we
still harbour reservations about the outcome of this exercise, remembering that
in the past there have been inquiries and recommendations with regard to the
problems which plague the Metis community.

Billyjo De La Ronde, also of the Manitoba Metis Federation, echoed his remarks:

The Federation also feels and would like to see that this Inquiry is not put aside
to collect dust, and that the recommendations, whatever you may have, will be
acted upon.

Chief Louis Stevenson, on behalf of the Assembly of Manitoba Chiefs, stated:

It must be abundantly clear that any recommendations that flow from this
Inquiry and stated in unequivocal terms, that these recommendations have to
be actioned, otherwise this Inquiry will result only in an exercise that builds up
the hope of Indian people only to devastate whatever little faith that remains.

Chief Oscar Lathlin of The Pas Band stated, "This is the biggest fear that we have
of this Inquiry, that nothing will be done once the Inquiry is over."

Aboriginal people are tired of being studied and are concerned that reports on
Aboriginal issues have a history of being placed on a shelf to gather dust.

There was a recurring request that we provide for a process by which our recommendations could be implemented and long-term change facilitated. Given the problems that have arisen in the past where the implementation of reforms for Aboriginal
issues are concerned, and the loss of momentum that has occurred in some areas, we
have decided that it is appropriate for us to make suggestions in this area.

We cannot, of course, offer any assurance that any of our recommendations will
be accepted or acted upon. The decision to implement our recommendations is, we recognize, a matter for both federal and provincial governments. Whether they do so will
depend upon the overall persuasiveness of the report, the degree to which there is support among Aboriginal and non-Aboriginal people for the initiatives, the governments'
ability and inclination to make the changes recommended, and their overall responsibility to govern in a manner that takes into account the interests of all members of society.

However, we do believe that a special process is called for, by which the issues we have concluded need to be resolved are dealt with. We have found that the nature of government decision making in the past, where Aboriginal people and their interests were concerned, has been cumbersome and inappropriate. In addition, Aboriginal people are in a unique position insofar as their right to self-determination is concerned. It appears to us, therefore, that in future, Aboriginal issues will be approached and resolved on a more government-to-government basis.

We begin by addressing what needs to be done by various agencies and by each level of government to put our recommendations into place. We then discuss the matter of an implementation commission with Aboriginal and government representation, and a proposed mandate for it. We also discuss the question of how Aboriginal people can be trained to take over many of the functions necessary to the operation of the justice system within their own communities. Finally, we address the question of an overall approach to cross-cultural training for those within the justice system, and how the numbers of Aboriginal people within the existing justice system can be increased.

The Recommendations

During the course of this report, we have made a large number of recommendations. Some have been addressed to the provincial or federal governments, while others have been addressed to Aboriginal people and their communities or agencies, or to other government agencies or programs. We do not intend to re-list all those recommendations.

Rather, it is our intention in this part to summarize the major recommendations we have made throughout the report, and to make broad statements as to the nature of the responsibilities which flow from them to specific entities. We view it as essential that all our recommendations be implemented. We do not wish it to be thought that in preparing the following section, we intend to suggest that any recommendations not specifically referred to should be ignored.

In this section we set forth the action which each government or institution will have to take to enable our recommendations to be put into place.

Aboriginal Self-Government

Aboriginal self-government means the right of Aboriginal communities to run their own affairs within their own territory. In recent years, Aboriginal people have developed a capacity to control a wide range of services, including child and family services, band housing programs, educational programs and local services. While Aboriginal self-government has been recognized in a *de facto* manner by all governments, it needs official recognition so that no further questions need arise as to its existence, or as to the right of Aboriginal people to their enjoyment of it. Additionally, the matter of the perceived ability of the federal government to unilaterally determine its parameters remains a constant threat to the very existence of Aboriginal self-government.

Action to be Taken by the Federal Government:

- Recognize the reality of Aboriginal self-government through parliamentary resolution.

- Propose a specific amendment to the Constitution recognizing Aboriginal self-government and pursue its passage with all provincial governments.

- Amend the *Indian Act* to remove restrictions on Aboriginal self-determination and recognize specifically the right of Aboriginal governments to establish their own constitutions, civil and criminal laws, and institutions of government.

Action to be Taken by the Provincial Government:

- Recognize the reality of Aboriginal self-government through a legislative resolution and work with the federal and other provincial governments toward a constitutional amendment recognizing it.

- Recognize the right of Aboriginal communities to establish an Aboriginal justice system and work toward its implementation.

Aboriginal Justice Systems

Aboriginal justice systems should be established in Aboriginal communities, beginning with the establishment of Aboriginal courts. We recommend that Aboriginal communities consider doing so on a regional basis, patterned on such systems as the Northwest Intertribal Court System in the state of Washington.

We suggest that Aboriginal courts assume jurisdiction on a gradual basis, starting with summary conviction criminal cases, small claims and child welfare matters. Ultimately, there is no reason why Aboriginal courts and their justice systems cannot assume full jurisdiction over all matters at their own pace.

The law to be applied in such systems would ultimately be the criminal and civil codes of each Aboriginal community, and such part of federal and provincial laws as each community selects.

Action to be Taken by Aboriginal Communities:

- Meet to consider the establishment of either local or regional justice systems, including trial and appeal courts.

- Prepare to enact civil and criminal laws.

- Prepare to establish Aboriginal police forces.

- Prepare to select and appoint judges and administrative personnel.

Action to be Taken by the Provincial Government:

- Enact legislation that recognizes the right of Aboriginal people to establish their own justice systems and recognizes their jurisdiction and authority to enact their own laws.

Action to be Taken by the Federal Government:

- Amend the *Criminal Code* to recognize Aboriginal courts and their jurisdiction.

- Amend the *Indian Act* and enact other appropriate federal legislation to recognize the right of Aboriginal communities to establish and maintain their own justice systems, and to recognize their jurisdiction and authority to enact their own laws without requiring the approval of any other level of government.

Aboriginal Peoples' Rights

Aboriginal people have a variety of rights arising from their treaties, from Aboriginal title, from specific statutes and from the Constitution of Canada. Federal and provincial governments, and Canadian society generally, by and large have not well understood the Aboriginal perspective of the importance which these rights hold for them. As weil, Aboriginal people have largely been unable to enforce their rights legally or politically in a manner which reflects their own understandings.

Many Aboriginal, treaty and constitutional rights pertaining to Aboriginal people require clarification. While the process of clarifying those issues undoubtedly will be one of negotiation between Aboriginal people and government, we recognize that governments have a number of advantages in the negotiations, including a considerable incentive to delay the process. Therefore, we recommend mechanisms that are intended to see that outstanding issues are resolved in a fair manner within a reasonable period of time.

One such entity which we recommend is a Treaty Land Entitlement Commission, consisting of Aboriginal and government representatives, with a mandate to hear submissions and make binding decisions on reserve populations, boundaries and the dedication of reserve land.

We have concluded that the population of a reserve at the time the matter is finally resolved should be the number used to determine the amount of land to which a First Nation is entitled.

The Treaty Land Entitlement Commission should also have authority to award compensation to Indian bands for losses suffered by the delay in settling lands.

We also recommend the establishment of an Aboriginal Claims Tribunal to deal with other sorts of claims against the government. Issues involving resource development, water rights, hunting and fishing, wild rice, timber management, membership codes, Metis claims, the financial implications of Bill C-31, and others which need to be resolved could be referred to this tribunal.

Because Aboriginal people have shown a preference for negotiation over litigation in the area of resolving these claims, we believe that the claims tribunal should have a role to play in monitoring the negotiations to ensure that they occur in as fair a manner as possible. The tribunal should be given sufficient authority to monitor the negotiations that occur between Aboriginal people and governments, as experience has shown that Aboriginal-government negotiations are marked by an imbalance of power in favour of government.

As well, the claims tribunal should be given sufficient authority to resolve any matter referred to it, including allegations that one party or the other is not bargaining in good faith, as well as authority to determine the best manner of resolving the entire claim. Aboriginal people must have equal representation in the process.

Conflicts—sometimes inadvertently created—between the rights of Aboriginal people and laws passed by provincial or federal governments have created confusion as to the state of enforceability of the rights of Aboriginal people. We recommend that the Aboriginal Justice Commission which we propose undertake a study of those laws.

We believe that the confusion can be remedied most easily by rendering specific federal and provincial laws subject to the rights of Aboriginal people, and amending the federal and provincial *Interpretation Acts* to provide that federal and provincial laws are to be interpreted in such a manner as not to derogate or adversely affect those rights.

Action to be Taken by the Federal Government:

- Work with the provincial government and with Aboriginal people to legislatively establish a Treaty Land Entitlement Commission.

- Establish a separate Aboriginal Claims Tribunal to deal with all outstanding and future specific and comprehensive claims between Aboriginal people and the federal or provincial governments.

- Review all federal legislation including regulations to remove any provisions which conflict with the rights of Aboriginal people, or amend the legislation to render those regulations subject to the rights of Aboriginal people, including their treaty and Aboriginal rights. The *Fisheries Act,* the *Migratory Birds Convention Act* and the convention itself, for example, will need to be amended to achieve this purpose.

- Amend the federal *Interpretation Act* to require that all legislation must be interpreted in a manner that does not derogate or adversely affect the rights of Aboriginal people.

Action to be Taken by the Provincial Government:

- Amend specific provincial legislation that is in direct conflict with the rights of Aboriginal people so as to make those laws subject to their rights.

- Amend the provincial *Interpretation Act* to require that all legislation must be interpreted in a manner that does not derogate or adversely affect the rights of Aboriginal people.

- Remove provisions that purport to require Aboriginal people to obtain licences to exercise their rights.

Action to be Taken by Aboriginal Communities:

- Establish conservation laws to protect the natural resources which fall within their jurisdiction and to regulate their development and use.

Police

We believe that the future of Aboriginal policing in Manitoba lies in the creation of Aboriginally controlled police forces for Aboriginal communities, and in increasing the numbers of Aboriginal police officers on existing forces. Increasing the level of awareness of the cultural uniqueness of Aboriginal people is also important. Each Aboriginal police force should ultimately assume responsibility for all law enforcement in their communities. Metis communities also should develop regional Metis police forces, with their own police commissions.

All police forces within the province should increase the numbers of Aboriginal officers, strengthen cross-cultural education, improve relations with Aboriginal communities and change some of their practices.

Government should take responsibility for improving the manner in which complaints of police misconduct are investigated and handled. This will necessitate amendments to the *Law Enforcement Review Act* so as to increase Aboriginal representation on the board and hearing panels of the Law Enforcement Review Agency. The authority of the board needs to be altered so that it can make its own determination as to the penalty that should be imposed on any officer found to have been at fault. At present, the authority of the board is restricted to the maximum penalty the commissioner has determined in advance.

Government will also have to be responsible for overseeing the implementation of employment equity programs within police forces. Eventually, an Employment Equity Commission should take responsibility for that area. Other statutes will require amendment.

Action to be Taken by Municipal Police Forces:

- Prepare and table with their governing bodies and with the Minister of Justice an employment equity plan, no later than December 31, 1991, that will result in there being more Aboriginal male and female officers on their police forces, and more Aboriginal civilian employees on their staff, in numbers proportionate to the percentage of Aboriginal people in the province.

- Review departmental hiring practices to eliminate criteria or processes that have adverse impacts upon Aboriginal people and replace those practices or criteria with more appropriate ones.

- Review and strengthen cross-cultural and public education programs and involve Aboriginal people in their development and presentation.

Action to be Taken by the RCMP:

- Support the establishment of Aboriginal police forces and cooperate with them.

- Increase the numbers of Aboriginal men and women on the force and engage Aboriginal civilian staff in numbers proportionate to the Aboriginal population of the province.

Action to be Taken by Aboriginal Communities:

- Establish regional police forces with Aboriginal members and their own regional police commissions, following the model of the Dakota Ojibway Tribal Council Police Force.

Action to be Taken by the Provincial Government:

- Make provincial grants to the City of Winnipeg for police services conditional upon the development and implementation of employment equity programs and targets for the hiring of Aboriginal personnel.

- In conjunction with Aboriginal communities, create a provincial Aboriginal Police Commission and a commissioner to develop standards for all aspects of Aboriginal policing in Manitoba, and ensure that Aboriginal police forces and their officers attain and maintain appropriate standards of recruitment, training, professional development and comportment.

- Through the Manitoba Police Commission, develop standards for all aspects of policing in non-Aboriginal communities in Manitoba, and ensure that non-Aboriginal police forces and their officers attain and maintain appropriate standards of recruitment, training, professional development and comportment.

- Amend the *Law Enforcement Review Act* to ensure Aboriginal representation on the board and on any panel hearing a complaint from an Aboriginal person.

- Ensure that proper and independent procedures for the investigation and resolution of allegations of police misconduct are put into place.

- Take such steps as are necessary to ensure that, in cases where the RCMP is performing duties as a provincial police force, RCMP officers are subject to the same complaint mechanisms as other police officers under provincial jurisdiction.

- Establish a special investigations unit through special legislation, responsible directly to the Minister of Justice, to take control of the investigation of any incident involving a police officer where possible criminal conduct arises or where a person dies or suffers serious injury. The unit should consist of experienced criminal investigators, but must not include officers from the police department under investigation. The unit should have access to legal counsel independent of the police force involved and of the Attorney General's department to consider whether criminal charges should be laid.

Sentencing

Incarceration should be used only as a last resort and only where a person poses a threat to another individual or to the community, or where other sanctions would not sufficiently reflect the gravity of the offence, or where the offender refuses to comply with the terms of another sentence that has been imposed upon him or her. Incarceration for non-payment of a fine should rarely occur. Other procedures for the collection of fines should be considered. If an individual wilfully refuses to pay a fine, and is able to do so, then incarceration can be considered after a show cause hearing.

Where incarceration is required for an Aboriginal person, it should be in a community-based facility in his or her home community, if one exists, or in a more culturally appropriate facility as close to that individual's home as possible.

Action to be Taken by the Judiciary:

- Make greater use of restitution, community service orders, placing the adult under the supervision of someone in the community, open custody and other options, in place of fines or incarceration.

- Impose fines only if the individual is able to pay.

- Refrain from imposing incarceration in default of payment of fines.

- Meet with leaders of the Aboriginal communities served by circuit court and assist in the development (where the community wishes to do so) of local Aboriginal sentencing panels. They should then seek the advice of those panels, in open court, when attempting to determine an appropriate sentence.

- Look for innovative sentences that will not only have the offender recognize the impropriety of his or her actions, but will prevent any repetition and will return the accused, the victim and the community to a state of harmony, all without having to send the offender to jail.

- (In the case of Court of Appeal judges) attempt to be more supportive of innovative sentences imposed by trial judges.

Action to be Taken by the Federal Government:

- Amend the *Criminal Code* to remove the authority of a judge or magistrate to impose incarceration for failing to pay a fine, except where the individual wilfully refuses to do so after a show cause hearing.

- Amend the *Criminal Code* to authorize judges to stipulate the type of community service or the place of incarceration of an offender.

- Amend the *Criminal Code* to allow for the imposition of open custody sentences on adults in community residential centres, group homes, or forest or wilderness camps, as is the case with young offenders.

Action to be Taken by the Provincial Government:

- Amend the *Summary Convictions Act* to remove the authority of judges or magistrates to impose incarceration for failure to pay a fine, except where the individual wilfully refuses to do so after a show cause hearing.

- Abolish the Fine Option Program and in its place establish a Fine and Restitution Recovery Program, patterned after the Maintenance Enforcement Program.

- Appoint resident Aboriginal probation officers in each Aboriginal community and in urban centres, proportionate to the presence of Aboriginal people in the provincial population at a minimum, but closer to the proportion of Aboriginal people receiving probation services. The probation officer should be in court when Aboriginal people are being sentenced to assist the court's understanding of the accused, of any programs available in the community, and of sentencing options.

- Assist Aboriginal communities in the establishment of regional Aboriginal probation services.

- Gather statistical information on an ongoing basis on the impacts of particular sentences so that a judge can be provided with a report on the results of a particular sentence, and the judiciary at large can see the effectiveness of various types of sentences.

Aboriginal Women

The abuse to which Aboriginal women and children have been subjected is criminal and culturally unacceptable. On reserves, in particular, chiefs and councillors must accept the protection of women and children as one of their most pressing responsibilities. Greater numbers of safe houses and shelters need to be provided. More appropriate treatment programs for Aboriginal abusers need to be made available. New initiatives within the justice system are a necessity. Abusers should be removed from the home, and the victim and children returned to it with the support of local government, the police and the courts.

Action to be Taken by the Provincial Government:

- Provide more safe homes or shelters in each Aboriginal community.

- Prosecute those suspected of domestic abuse where the evidence is available and that is the wish of the victim.

- Provide mediation, counselling and other support services where the victim wishes to see the abuser treated and the family held together.

- Encourage and provide sufficient resources to expand to other Aboriginal communities throughout the province the method of dealing with abusers that has been developed and is used by the Hollow Water Resource Group.

- Close the Portage Correctional Institution for women.

- Consider the use of co-correctional institutions for those women who must be incarcerated.

- Establish local open custody facilities where the offender can work and attend school, counselling or other programs during the day.

- Establish programs to deal with alcoholism, drug abuse, emotional or other personal problems, and provide that programs are available to prepare any inmate who wishes to seek an occupation upon release.

- Ensure that Aboriginal women are involved in all aspects of the provincial justice system, from local court administrators to program developers and directors.

Action to be Taken by the Federal Government:

- Ensure that all sentenced women who live in Manitoba serve their sentence in Manitoba.

- Ensure that Aboriginal women are involved in all aspects of the justice system, from parole board members to correctional officers.

Action to be Taken by Aboriginal Communities:

- Establish a local government portfolio and other support mechanisms to protect women and children from abuse.

Jails

The whole jail system should be reformed. Local community-based facilities in Aboriginal communities, staffed by Aboriginal correctional officers and designed to provide culturally appropriate programs for Aboriginal inmates, should be established.

Aboriginal people charged with an offence should be released on bail in their own communities. Many who are incarcerated should spend their time in open custody institutions in their own communities where they can work, take education or job training or counselling in the community during the day, and return to the facility at night.

Aboriginal youth should be held in their own communities before their trials, and either in their own communities or in wilderness youth camps not far from their homes if they are sentenced to incarceration.

Aboriginal inmates prefer to work and should be given that opportunity unless they are enrolled in training, educational or counselling programs.

The nature of institutions generally should change from purely custodial "prisons" to places where personal problems can be addressed and where work, education, job training and personal development programs are available. The number of Aboriginal people in jail should be substantially reduced. The overall capacity of the jail system should also be reduced.

Action to be Taken by the Provincial Government:

- Ensure that Headingley Correctional Institution is the only secure provincial institution.

- Convert the provincial correctional institutions in Brandon and The Pas to open custody facilities similar to the one in Dauphin.

- Establish throughout the province more wilderness camps, similar to Egg Lake, which are administered by Aboriginal people.

- Ensure that each Aboriginal community has its own secure temporary holding facilities so people will no longer have to be transported around the province prior to their trial.

- Discontinue using the Manitoba Youth Centre as an open custody facility.

- Ensure that the rules for disciplinary hearings, which are now not honoured, are revised, and that an independent process is established.

- Engage Aboriginal staff in correctional institutions in numbers at least proportionate to the percentage of Aboriginal people in the province, and perhaps as high as the proportion of Aboriginal inmates in each institution.

- Ensure that at least 50% of Aboriginal people on staff in correctional institutions speak an Aboriginal language.

- Ensure that recognized elders and other traditional Aboriginal people attending correctional institutions for ceremonial or spiritual purposes have access to those institutions, and be permitted to bring with them items of spiritual significance on the same basis as chaplains who are recognized under the Corrections department's chaplaincy program.

Action to be Taken by the Federal Government:

- Engage Aboriginal staff in correctional institutions in numbers at least proportionate to the percentage of Aboriginal people in the province, with the optimum number being equal to the proportion of Aboriginal inmates in each institution.

- Ensure that at least 50% of Aboriginal people on staff in correctional institutions speak an Aboriginal language.

- Ensure that recognized elders and other traditional Aboriginal people attending federal institutions for ceremonial or spiritual purposes have access to those institutions, and be permitted to bring with them items of spiritual significance on the same basis as chaplains who are recognized under the federal chaplaincy program.

Parole

All inmates should be released after the same percentage of their sentence has been served, unless there are unusual circumstances making it inappropriate to release a person on parole, such as his or her being violent or a clear danger to another person. Aboriginal parole officers should be increased in number, and the manner in which the National Parole Board considers Aboriginal parole applicants should be more culturally sensitive. Rather than merely supervising Aboriginal parolees, parole officers should be assisting them with obtaining employment and financial assistance, and providing appropriate counselling. Parole assessments should be done by Aboriginal people in the accused's community.

Action to be Taken by the Federal Government:

- Change the National Parole Board regulations to ensure that Aboriginal people are well represented on the parole board and to ensure that a majority of Aboriginal members sit on any panel considering an Aboriginal inmate's eligibility for parole, parole conditions or alleged breach of conditions of parole.

- Ensure that presently inappropriate parole conditions are no longer imposed. The condition that an inmate must admit guilt before being considered for parole should be abolished.

- Appoint Aboriginal parole officers in every community and ensure that Aboriginal parole officers deal with Aboriginal people on parole. Ensure that parole assessments are done by Aboriginal people in the accused's community.

- Give consideration to having the same person fulfil the roles of a probation and a parole officer in Aboriginal communities.

Action to be Taken by Aboriginal Communities:

- Take steps to establish an Aboriginal Parole Board in Manitoba to deal with those people sentenced by Aboriginal courts.

Child Welfare

Aboriginal people are not being well served by non-Aboriginal child and family service agencies. Their staff and policies are seen as insensitive to Aboriginal people and their child care traditions. The authority of Aboriginal child welfare agencies, which are well received, should be expanded.

Action to be Taken by the Provincial Government:

- Establish the office of Child Protector, as recommended by Judge Kimelman, to protect the interests of children, to investigate any complaint into the practices of any child welfare agency and to be responsible to the Legislature.

- Establish an Aboriginal child and family service agency in the city of Winnipeg, to handle all Aboriginal cases.

- Expand the authority of existing Indian agencies to enable them to offer services to band members living off-reserve.

- Establish a mandated province-wide Metis agency.

- Ensure that child welfare agencies work more closely with youth justice personnel and with Youth Court.

Action to be Taken by the Federal Government:

- Renew the tripartite child welfare agreements with the provincial government and First Nations of Manitoba and provide increased funding to cover services for new band members resulting from the government's Bill C-31.

Young Offenders

Aboriginal young offenders are now transported from all parts of Manitoba to the Manitoba Youth Centre upon their arrest, while awaiting bail, while awaiting trial and then while awaiting sentence. In addition to the tremendous financial and emotional cost, the system is adding to jail populations and hardening young people.

Action to be Taken by the Provincial Government:

- Ensure that diversion and alternative measures are applied by the police, Crown attorneys, judges and others to keep young people out of the courts.

- Take steps to substantially reduce pre-trial detention, and address the unacceptable delays in bringing young offender cases to a conclusion.

- Expand bail supervision programs, such as the one operated by Ma Mawi Chi Itata Centre, throughout the province.

- Establish short-term youth detention facilities in each Aboriginal community, and longer term facilities which focus on the use of wilderness camps at which youth can further their education, receive job training and counselling to deal with any problems they may have, to provide them with a meaningful role upon their return to their community.

- Ensure that child and family service agencies are instructed to continue their involvement with youth who are under their care when charged with an offence.

- Expand the number of youth justice committees throughout the province and ensure that they are used by police, Crown attorneys and judges when dealing with youth-related problems.

- Transfer the responsibility to establish alternative measures guidelines to the judiciary.

- Ensure that alternative measures are based upon Aboriginal culture, that they include the use of Aboriginal peacemakers, that these measures are available to all youth, not just first-time offenders, and that their use be expanded in consultation with Aboriginal youth justice committees.

- Ensure that the Aboriginal Court Worker Program is available to young offenders wherever Youth Court sits.

- Ensure that child welfare and youth justice services are integrated and coordinated.

Action to be Taken by Aboriginal Communities:

- Establish youth justice committees in their communities.

Action to be Taken by the Federal Government:

- Amend the *Young Offenders Act* to remove provisions permitting cases to be transferred from Youth Court to adult court. If harsher penalties are considered desirable, or if a more open court process is sought, enable the youth court judge to impose more substantial sentences in some cases, to hear cases with a jury and to permit the more complete reporting of proceedings.

- Amend the *Young Offenders Act* to permit judges to commit a youth to the care of a child care agency as a disposition under the Act.

- Amend the *Young Offenders Act* to provide that judges, rather than the Attorney General, have the authority to devise alternative measures guidelines.

- Amend the *Young Offenders Act* to remove the provision permitting youth to waive the right to have a parent or guardian present during police questioning.

Courts

The Court of Queen's Bench and the Provincial Court should be replaced with a new court to be known as the Manitoba Trial Court. Judges sitting in Aboriginal and other communities throughout the province would then have the jurisdiction to deal with any type of case. Various court practices should be altered to ensure the disposition of all types of cases within a reasonable time.

Action to be Taken by the Provincial Government:

- Enact legislation to establish the Manitoba Trial Court with the jurisdiction now attached to existing courts. A General Division should deal with all civil and most criminal cases. A Family Division should deal with young offender, child welfare and all family cases, including all intrafamily physical and sexual abuse criminal cases.

- Cooperate with the federal government in the appointment of all existing Queen's Bench and Provincial Court judges to the new Manitoba Trial Court.

- Provide proper facilities in every community where court is to sit that will be available for court purposes as required. Ensure that all trials, including jury trials, are held in the community where the offence was alleged to have been committed.

- Hire local staff for courts that sit in Aboriginal communities. These would include a court administrator, a court interpreter, and an Aboriginal court worker.

- In conjunction with the judiciary, undertake a blitz to dispose of all outstanding cases in remote and rural Aboriginal communities.

- Appoint Aboriginal peacemakers as officers of the court who would take referrals of cases involving Aboriginal accused and attempt to arrive at a reconciliation between the victim and the offender through the use of more traditional Aboriginal dispute resolution techniques.

Action to be Taken by the Federal Government:

- In cooperation with the provincial government, appoint the judges of the Queen's Bench and Provincial Court to the Manitoba Trial Court.

- Appoint judges to the Court of Appeal only from judges of the Trial Court.

- Abolish the preliminary inquiry.

- Amend the *Criminal Code* to permit an accused to appear by counsel, agent or by telephone for purposes of adjournment or other procedural or pre-trial matters, and to provide that a judge does not lose jurisdiction over a case due to the failure of an accused to appear.

Action to be Taken by the Judiciary:

- Establish court schedules to deal with all matters on a court docket on the day they are set to proceed, whether the sitting takes one or more days.

- Establish and enforce guidelines for the expeditious completion of all cases.

- In conjunction with the provincial government, undertake a blitz to dispose of all outstanding cases in remote and rural Aboriginal communities.

- Establish appropriate pre-trial procedures in each division of the court, particularly to accommodate disclosure when the preliminary inquiry is abolished.

- Refrain from flying or driving to circuit court with counsel or the police.

Action to be Taken by Legal Aid Manitoba:

- Ensure the appointment of counsel in all cases where the applicant meets the income criteria. In criminal matters, counsel should be appointed, at least on an interim basis, by telephone or by duty counsel.

- Ensure that Legal Aid staff arrive in a community the day before court to have adequate time to interview clients and witnesses.

Fatality Inquiries

Unlike other proceedings, those who are not happy with any decision made by a judge during the course of an inquiry have limited recourse to have that decision overturned. As well, the appearance of a conflict of interest can arise where one of the parties involved works closely with Crown attorneys, who normally have conduct of the fatality inquiry.

Action to be Taken by the Provincial Government:

- Amend the *Fatality Inquiries Act* to permit greater participation by interested persons, and to make inquest reports and records available to the public, to relatives, and to band or community councils.

- Amend the Act to provide that where a police officer or a government agency is involved, a non-government lawyer be retained to conduct the inquest.

- Amend the Act to provide that an appeal (rather than a judicial review) of an inquest, or of the decision not to hold one, is permitted. Any citizen should be entitled to ask that an inquest be held or that one already held be reopened. Judges should be permitted to direct that to be done if they are persuaded that it is in the public interest to do so.

Juries

Systemic discrimination is clearly seen in the jury selection process. The right and responsibility of Aboriginal citizens to sit on a jury should be ensured by legislative and administrative change. The ease with which Aboriginal people can be excluded from the jury selection process should be stopped.

Action to be Taken by the Federal Government:

- Amend the *Criminal Code* to do away with stand-asides and peremptory challenges, to provide that only challenges for cause, dealing with the impartiality of the juror, be permitted, and that the trial judge be the one to rule on any challenge.

Action to be Taken by the Provincial Government:

- Amend the *Jury Act*:

    - To require that jury trials be held in each place where the court sits.

    - To provide that juries be chosen from people who reside within 40 kilometres of the place of trial. Where sufficient jurors cannot be obtained from within that area, jurors should then be selected from the closest similar community.

- To provide that every person called for jury duty is required to attend.

- To provide that translation services are available for those jurors who speak an Aboriginal language.

Action to be Taken by Aboriginal Communities:

- Develop programs in conjunction with public legal education authorities to acquaint community members with the law and the jury system, and encourage Aboriginal participation as jurors.

Aboriginal Justice Commission

We believe that an Aboriginal Justice Commission of Manitoba should be established by federal and provincial legislation and by appropriate processes of the Aboriginal people of Manitoba. We suggest that the commission have a board of directors made up of equal numbers of Aboriginal and governmental representatives, with an independent person, acceptable to all parties, as chairperson. Aboriginal representatives should include status Indians, Metis, non-status Indians, and representatives of Aboriginal women and urban Aboriginal people.

The board of directors of the commission should appoint an Aboriginal Justice Commissioner acceptable to Aboriginal people, with authority to take action in the name of the commission as its chief executive officer, and appoint sufficient permanent staff to deal with its various responsibilities. In our view, the Aboriginal Justice Commission is key to the implementation process.

It is apparent to us that there will be considerable work involving both levels of government and Aboriginal people in the implementation of the recommendations which we make. We believe that the implementation of those recommendations and any consequent negotiations should be overseen by the Office of the Aboriginal Justice Commissioner, whose primary role would be to ensure that Aboriginal-government negotiations occur in as fair and productive a manner as possible and that any assistance necessary to overcome areas or points of disagreement is provided.

In addition, while we believe that the Aboriginal Justice Commission should have the support of both levels of government and of Aboriginal people, it should have a degree of independence. The commissioner should be responsible to, and take direction from, the commission and report to it on his or her activities.

The commission's primary responsibility, we believe, would be to monitor the degree to which governments are proceeding toward the implementation of the recommendations in this report, and to report publicly on its progress from time to time.

As well, the office of the commissioner could facilitate any negotiations which need to occur between governments and Aboriginal people, and assist in resolving points of disagreement. That could be done in whatever way the parties agree, but we believe that utilizing mediation or other dispute resolution techniques, including arbitration, should be considered.

The tasks of the commission should be to:

- Enter into discussions with Aboriginal people to determine their wishes with respect to the various recommendations.

- Recommend the form and method of the implementation of recommendations.

- Monitor the implementation of the changes we suggest.

- Report to governments, Aboriginal people and the general public on the progress of implementation.

- Assist in the establishment of Aboriginal justice systems.

- Take steps to establish an Aboriginal Justice College.

- Monitor the progress of affirmative action programs.

- Initiate discussions between Aboriginal people and governments to establish mechanisms to deal with Aboriginal self-government and the settlement of outstanding claims.

- Receive concerns and complaints of any nature from Aboriginal people and forward them to the appropriate department or agency for attention, and monitor the results.

- Mediate Aboriginal concerns or complaints with governments or agencies.

- Become involved in any issue involving Aboriginal people.

- Advise government on Aboriginal concerns and recommend appropriate action.

- Propose legislation or legislative change.

WE RECOMMEND THAT:

- An Aboriginal Justice Commission of Manitoba be established by legislation and by appropriate processes of the Aboriginal people of Manitoba, with a board of directors made up of equal numbers of Aboriginal and government representatives, and an independent chairperson. The commission should be provided with all necessary staff and resources.

- The position of Aboriginal Justice Commissioner be established as the chief executive officer of the Aboriginal Justice Commission. The commissioner's tasks will include monitoring and assisting government implementation of the recommendations of this Inquiry.

Aboriginal Justice College

An Aboriginal Justice College will be needed to provide training and continuing education for the Aboriginal people required to assume positions of responsibility within both the existing justice system and Aboriginal justice systems. In almost every chapter of this report, we discuss the need for Aboriginal people in Aboriginal communities to perform all the tasks within the system.

Training will be required for Aboriginal judges, attorneys, police, correctional officers, court clerks, administrators, interpreters, court workers, peacemakers, youth justice committee directors, social workers, probation and parole officers, and others.

The Brandon University Northern Teacher Training Program (BUNTEP) has been successful in attracting and educating Aboriginal teachers. The concentration of large numbers of Aboriginal students in the course and the resulting peer group support have been described as the single most important factor in the success of the program. The corrections officers program at Assiniboine Community College had similar success. The experience of both programs should be examined when programs for the college are being developed.

While we recommend that the Aboriginal Justice Commission undertake the establishment of the Aboriginal Justice College, we suggest that once it is established it be an independent body with its own board of directors and staff, most of whom should be Aboriginal people.

The college might also organize the courses in cultural understanding for non-Aboriginal judges, lawyers, court staff, police, correctional and classification officers, educators, and others that we recommend in this report.

WE RECOMMEND THAT:

- The Aboriginal Justice Commission establish an Aboriginal Justice College with its own Aboriginal board of directors, and staffed by Aboriginal people, to provide training and continuing education for Aboriginal people who wish to assume positions of employment within both the existing justice system and Aboriginal justice systems.

- Training provided by the Aboriginal Justice College include preparation for such positions as judges, attorneys, police officers, correctional officers, court clerks, administrators, interpreters, court workers, peacemakers, youth justice committee directors, social workers, probation and parole officers, and others, as exist within the present justice system and as are needed to establish and maintain Aboriginal justice systems.

- The Aboriginal Justice College organize courses in cross-cultural understanding for non-Aboriginal personnel.

Cross-Cultural Issues

Purpose

Most people in the justice system have little understanding of Aboriginal people, their history, culture, or way of life. Our study has convinced us that there are widespread misconceptions about Aboriginal people and about their perception of the law and the legal system.

We are convinced that those administering the system have no idea of some of the hardships they cause by automatically applying practices and procedures that work in other communities. They do not do this intentionally, but lack sufficient knowledge of the impact on Aboriginal people to foresee the results.

Problems of distance, time and lack of resources have to be appreciated. The impact of procedures, such as a simple adjournment or the imposition of inappropriate conditions of probation or parole, have to be understood.

If those who operate the justice system are supposed to be doing so on behalf of society, they require a better understanding of Aboriginal society. The cultural differences, such as the non-confrontational, non-adversarial approach of Aboriginal people, should be appreciated. The Aboriginal desire to return people and communities to a state of harmony should be understood. Those operating the present system should hear why Aboriginal people consider the existing system to be a foreign one that is not serving their needs.

We believe that many of the problems resulting from current practices cannot begin to be alleviated until those who work in the system understand those problems. We also believe that those working within the system would appreciate an opportunity to expand their knowledge of this sector of their clientele.

While courses have been made available to some police departments and to civil servants, these programs have not been extensive. Little, if any, cross-cultural education has been provided to the judiciary and lawyers. Cross-cultural educational courses are urgently required.

We accept the opinion of experts that cross-cultural training courses should ideally last for several days. However, given the nature of the demands within the justice system, we believe that more than one training course, lasting at least three days each, is the best way to cover the necessary materials and to provide time for questions and discussion. Once the first training session is held, there should be follow-up programs and the sessions should be regularly evaluated.

We suggest that separate programs be provided for different professionals working in the system so the program can then be adapted to their particular tasks. The programs could nevertheless be similar.

WE RECOMMEND THAT:

■ Federal, provincial and municipal governments, individually or in concert, with the assistance and involvement of Aboriginal people, establish formal cross-cultural educational programs for all those working in any part of the justice system who have even occasional contact with Aboriginal people.

Contents

The curriculum of the cross-cultural training course should include the following matters:

•**The History of Aboriginal Peoples.** This should include a review of the early pre-contact history of Aboriginal peoples, the number and variety of Aboriginal cultures and tribes in Canada, the Aboriginal use of land and traditional tribal forms of organization.

Early contact with the Europeans, their relationship with Aboriginal peoples up to Confederation, and the circumstances leading up to and including the negotiation of the treaties should be reviewed. It is particularly important to ensure that non-Aboriginal people understand and appreciate how Aboriginal people feel about their historical rights and why.

The history of residential schools and the child welfare policies of the 1950s, 1960s, 1970s and 1980s, and how these affect today's parents and children, are important to understand.

•**Aboriginal Culture.** The role of men and women, the role of chiefs, elders, the family and extended family, and the role of children in Aboriginal society should be explained. Ethical principles, such as non-interference, acceptance, truthfulness, silence, emotional restraint and sharing, are important to understand.

The philosophy, spirituality and "religious" beliefs of the various Aboriginal cultures of Manitoba should be explained. An explanation of the significance of Aboriginal sacred objects, such as the sweat lodge, the shaking tent, the Sundance, pow wows, the use of the pipe, eagle feathers, sacred medicines such as sweetgrass and so forth, should be given.

The questions of "law" and wrongdoing, and how they are dealt with, are important for those in another system to understand. The traditional methods of dispute resolution and their level of acceptance are relevant.

•**Discrimination.** Identifying racism, discrimination and prejudice is an important part of cross-cultural awareness. The existence of racism, prejudice, stereotyping and discrimination as experienced by Aboriginal people should be discussed. The tendency to make assumptions and to generalize when dealing with Aboriginal people, and the affect of this, should be explored.

How systemic discrimination works and what to do about it is an equally important part of cross-cultural awareness.

• **Statistics.** Demographic material outlining the situation of Aboriginal people should be presented. The numbers of Aboriginal people in the courts and jails, and the reasons for this, should be discussed. The reasons for unacceptable conduct should also be considered.

•**Aboriginal Community Life Today.** The current political, social and economic realities of life in Aboriginal communities should be explained. The efforts being made by Aboriginal people to improve life in their communities, and the services that are available to people and to the justice system, should be understood. Advances made in the fields of education, health and welfare, child welfare, budgetary control, alcohol reduction and abuse programs should be described.

•**Urban Living.** The realities of life for Aboriginal people in urban areas should be presented. Aboriginal-police, Aboriginal-jail and Aboriginal-court relationships should be explained from the Aboriginal perspective. The knowledge, or lack of knowledge, on the part of Aboriginal people concerning the law and the legal system should be made known.

•**Aboriginal Concepts.** Those working in the justice system need to be made aware of the problems which arise for Aboriginal people as a result of their different concepts. That information would help justice officials to understand the reasons for Aboriginal reactions to the legal process, such as an unwillingness to testify, apparently conflicting or changing testimony, delays in answering questions and misapprehensions of the consequences of testifying. The extent to which Aboriginal people understand English, and their reaction to the police, to parole boards and to the courts, also need to be understood.

•**Impact of Existing Systems.** The effect on Aboriginal people of incarceration and of delays in getting a case disposed of should be explained. The cost of repeated attendances should become known.

Presentation

Those presenting the programs should be familiar with the historical and current situation of Aboriginal people, and have a good working knowledge of the legal system. We consider it essential that numerous Aboriginal people of both sexes be involved in the presentation, including men and women who have been incarcerated.

There should be an opportunity for conversation, apart from formal sessions, between justice system personnel and Aboriginal people. Those participating in the program should visit an Aboriginal community such as an Indian reserve to observe the way of life and amenities available to Aboriginal people. Similar visits to Aboriginal neighbourhoods in Winnipeg would be of value. Some cultural event might be included in the three-day program.

In our opinion, these courses should be provided to all new personnel, as well as to judges, lawyers, and service providers now working within the justice system.

Affirmative Action

Employment Equity

Throughout this report, we have stressed the need to have more Aboriginal people involved in every part of the existing justice system. Because of their almost complete absence other than as accused, the system is now considered to be a foreign and uncaring one by Aboriginal people. It must become, and it must appear to Aboriginal people to be, more relevant to them and their issues. This can be accomplished, we believe, only if the numbers of Aboriginal people within the justice system at all levels are increased.

Many Aboriginal accused do not understand the law. They do not understand, for example, how they can be convicted of wildlife offences when hunting and fishing rights are enshrined in their treaties, and they do not appreciate the role of those in authority within the system. Many do not understand the purposes of various procedures and are unable to follow court proceedings. This can and does lead to their making uninformed and inappropriate decisions at very crucial times in the process, including, we believe, guilty pleas.

One of the problems is that there are almost no Aboriginal people in the system to whom they can turn for assistance or advice. Other than some police officers or band constables, there are few, if any, Aboriginal people employed by the legal system resident in Aboriginal communities. Police are generally associated with authority and prosecution, and are not the appropriate resource to turn to for help once a charge has been laid. Even in towns and cities, there are few Aboriginal people within the system with whom the Aboriginal person can enter into a meaningful discussion about his or her charge and from whom he or she can receive advice and information.

We are satisfied that if there were Aboriginal people working in the legal system, there would be a greater understanding of the problems faced by Aboriginal accused, victims, witnesses and their families, and higher levels of assistance and advice. Aboriginal communities would benefit economically and socially from having people within their community who hold positions of importance within the justice system.

Aboriginal justice systems, which will deal almost exclusively with Aboriginal people, will additionally require Aboriginal staff. The existing system can provide a training ground for those eventually hired by those systems.

We are not alone in our belief in the necessity of having Aboriginal people in all parts of the legal system. During our hearings, whenever the question was raised, police officials, government agencies and others agreed that there was a need to involve more Aboriginal people in the justice system. The problem is that there is no agreement as to how this is to be accomplished, nor has much attention been given to the breadth of representation that is required.

We are aware that government and public sector employers have, on occasion, established "affirmative action" guidelines for the hiring of minorities. We are unimpressed with their results to date. It is clear that voluntary initiatives have had little impact and that a lack of public accountability for such poor results contributes to their continuance.

A recent report prepared for the Department of Labour about recruitment, selection and classification processes in the government reveals that much is wrong with how the government utilizes affirmative action:

> There are no real consequences for managers, including Deputy Ministers, who fail to effectively manage the Affirmative Action process.... Affirmative Action does not have a high profile in departmental affairs.[1]

Therefore, despite all the good will that was expressed to us during the hearings by police, government and other agency officials, we do not believe that increasing the numbers of Aboriginal people within the justice system can be brought about without strong and assertive action and, in some cases, without the direct intervention of an enforcement agency.

We believe that the continuing under-representation of Aboriginal people at all levels of the public service demands that all components of the government and, in particular, the justice system, formally adopt legally enforceable, target driven, equity employment programs. We include all levels of the system in that conclusion, from police officers and prison guards to members of the judiciary and bureaucracy. We believe that the progress of those programs should be reported annually to an appropriate entity with powers to enforce compliance. Such an entity should have access to specific and appropriate remedies.

We recommend that the Province enact an Employment Equity Act. Such legislation would provide for an Employment Equity Commission with adequate professional and investigatory staff. The commission should report directly to the Legislature. The commission would have wide powers to support, to monitor and to require the development and implementation of employment equity programs in all government services, and in those areas over which the Province has legal jurisdiction, particularly those whose services are purchased or funded, in whole or in part, by government.

The government should freely and openly utilize the principle of contract compliance by making its grants and contracts subject to the fulfilment by the recipient of employment targets for identified minorities and particularly for women and Aboriginal people. Grants or payments to cities and municipalities that include support for police services should be conditional upon the implementation of an acceptable employment equity plan and targets that have been set by the commission. The same rules should apply to the government's own employment practices. The implementation of approved programs should be carefully monitored by the commission.

We believe that it is particularly important that the commission have the capacity to enforce compliance by government contractors and to apply remedial action when such compliance has failed to occur.

While we suggest no limit on the authority of the Employment Equity Commission, we would like to see its initial efforts directed towards the justice system and the employment within it of greater numbers of Aboriginal people.

Employment Targets

A key question is the appropriate level of Aboriginal representation within various components of the system. Appropriate employment levels for Aboriginal people within the justice system should depend upon where the services are to be delivered and the extent of the Aboriginal population being served. While setting targets which reflect the overall percentage of Aboriginal people within the provincial population would represent significant progress, a higher standard is appropriate in many cases.

As a minimum, therefore, the target for Aboriginal people should be the percentage of Aboriginal people in the Manitoba population. As an optimum target, the numbers of Aboriginal people in a particular service should equal the percentage of the population of the clientele being served. If, for example, the Headingley Correctional Institution population is 55% Aboriginal, the percentage of Aboriginal staff should be between 12% (the Aboriginal percentage of the Manitoba population) and 55% (the Aboriginal population of the institution). For the staff at Egg Lake, where all the inmates are Aboriginal, the Aboriginal people on staff should be between 12% and 100%.

WE RECOMMEND THAT:

- The Province of Manitoba legislate the establishment of an Employment Equity Commission with appropriate Aboriginal representation on its governing body.

- The Employment Equity Commission have two arms: an investigative arm responsible for examining any matter covered by the legislation, and an adjudicative arm responsible for hearing any complaint made under the legislation. Those on the adjudicative side who sit as hearing panels to determine a complaint should include an Aboriginal person if the complaint involves an Aboriginal issue or complainant.

- The mandate of the commission be:
  - To develop employment equity targets for employers within the legislative jurisdiction of the Province of Manitoba, including any department of the government of Manitoba and any municipality, town or city within the province.

  - To ensure that employers set policies and programs for the advancement and promotion of Aboriginal people.

  - To monitor compliance with established employment equity targets.

  - To require employers in receipt of government grants or contracts to establish an acceptable employment equity plan with appropriate time frames, within which Aboriginal people will be hired.

- To hear and determine complaints against any person or employer who fails to comply with an established employment equity plan.

■ Hearing panels called upon to determine complaints be entitled to make orders requiring compliance with an employment equity plan acceptable to the commission, or make such other order as may appear appropriate to it, such as financial compensation either to an individual or to a group of individuals.

Although our focus is upon the Province's responsibilities in this area, we also suggest that the federal government take similar measures.

WE RECOMMEND THAT:

■ The federal government strengthen its employment equity legislation to establish an Employment Equity Commission similar to that which we recommend for the Province of Manitoba.

Removing Barriers to Equitable Employment

Equality has a number of dimensions. Equality in employment requires that an individual not only have equal opportunity to be considered for employment, but also have equal opportunity to gain skills needed for employment, equal opportunity to information about the availability of employment, and equal consideration of his or her actual skills which are relevant to the employment in question.

One of the greatest barriers to employment opportunities lies in the formal qualifications which are used in hiring. The problems for Aboriginal people are obvious; if university degrees are a major criterion for hiring, then few Aboriginal people will be considered. The best alternative appears to be to ensure that all jobs are described in terms of the specific skills and knowledge required to do the job and to identify those related experiences which may be substituted for any formal requirement. Some jobs, we believe, could just as easily specify a proven ability to learn, as opposed to a specified level of educational attainment. As the report looking at government affirmative action and its own hiring process stated:

> [T]here has been an unwarranted increase in the level of credentials required for positions being filled in recent years. This increase in qualification requirements is viewed as not being the result of bona fide job requirements and therefore, as a means of discriminating on the basis of education.[2]

We comment elsewhere upon the consequences which this has for Aboriginal people.

We believe that jobs which require or will inevitably result in high contact with Aboriginal people should place greater emphasis upon the applicant's knowledge and skills in the area of Aboriginal culture and languages. Such positions could be designated as "Aboriginal bilingual positions" within government, much as the government now designates some positions as "bilingual" for purposes of its French language policy.

WE RECOMMEND THAT:

- Federal and provincial government positions which require or will inevitably result in high contact with Aboriginal people be designated as "Aboriginal bilingual positions."

We are convinced that the effectiveness of the justice system will be immeasurably improved, and Aboriginal people served much more appropriately, if the approaches we have recommended are taken.

Affirmative Action for Aboriginal Lawyers

The number of Aboriginal lawyers in Manitoba and in Canada is disproportionately low. According to information provided by Statistics Canada, there were approximately 43,000 lawyers in Canada in 1988. Of that number, fewer than 200 were Aboriginal. If the national Aboriginal presence in the population of 3% is considered, then there should be nearly 1,300 Aboriginal lawyers in Canada.

In Manitoba there are approximately 1,600 lawyers. There should be approximately 190 Aboriginal lawyers in Manitoba alone if Aboriginal people were to be proportionately represented in the legal profession. In fact, less than 10 Aboriginal lawyers are actually engaged in the practice of law in this province.

If we are ever to increase the number of Aboriginal judges within the existing system, the pool of Aboriginal lawyers available from which to select must first be enlarged.

One of the reasons for the low numbers of Aboriginal lawyers is the low level of Aboriginal students in post-secondary institutions. However, it would appear that even among those Aboriginal students who do go on to post-secondary education, law school has not been an option often considered.

Increasing the number of Aboriginal students should be a priority for the University of Manitoba Law School. Once Aboriginal law students are enrolled in law school, additional supports are required to ensure they go on to graduate. Don Purich, the director of the Native Law Centre at the University of Saskatchewan, told us:

In our review of what happens in law schools, we have determined that there are three things that very much influence the success that [Aboriginal] students have in a law faculty and those are the availability of supports services; the existence of a peer group at the law school which we find to be a very important factor; and the number of faculty members researching and teaching in the Aboriginal law area.

The University of Manitoba Law School does not have on its faculty an Aboriginal person with the responsibility of providing support services to Aboriginal students. We believe that it should do so. In addition, we believe that the Law School should immediately undertake the development of a full credit course or courses in Aboriginal people and their legal issues, as well as ensuring that Aboriginal issues are taught as part of various law courses.

As is the case with educational criteria generally, a concern arises about an over-reliance upon law school selection criteria shown to be culturally and ethnically biased. The University of Manitoba Law School, as is the case generally across Canada, relies heavily upon the student's previous university marks, as well as the student's score in the Law Schools Admissions Test (LSAT). The manual which accompanies the LSAT states:

> Scores on the LSAT, as in other tests of its kind, never completely represent the potential of any student. This is especially true for American Indian, Black, Mexican American, Puerto Rican or other minority students whose educational experience in and out of school may have differed significantly from that of the great majority of students.

LSAT scores are becoming more and more widely used as a method of eliminating applicants from consideration, rather than as an indication of the student's potential ability to successfully complete law school. Generally, those students with the highest grade point averages and the highest LSAT scores are admitted first. Over the years, the average LSAT score for successful first-year law school applicants has risen dramatically, and the tendency has been to eliminate those with lower scores, even though those eliminated can probably successfully complete the law school program. According to Purich, the average LSAT score at the time of his presentation to us was approximately 33, whereas he believed that students with an LSAT score over 20 could succeed at law school:

> Roughly ten people apply for every one position in our Canadian law schools. In order to be considered or gain admission through [the] general admission category, one would probably need [a] minimum of a 75 percent grade point average and a Law School Admission Test score of probably at least 35 out of 48.

> Our studies at the Native Law Centre have shown that people with a Law School Admission Test score of 20 have a reasonably good chance of succeeding in law school and I think we should bear in mind that at one time, getting into law school, and I will confess when I got into law school all one needed was a 65 percent grade point average.

So, I think the criteria used in the general category do in fact work to the disadvantage . . . of many qualified applicants . . . who have faced some educational disadvantages or other problems in terms of gaining entry.

In recognition of the fact that the general admission category may, in fact, work to
the prejudice of minority students, all Canadian law schools have set up "special admissions" categories. The people who are considered in that category vary somewhat from
law school to law school.

The University of Manitoba does have a special admissions category for Aboriginal (and other) law students. As with other special admissions categories across Canada,
there are certain minimum standards which each applicant must meet, but such applicants are not required to compete with other students in the general admissions category. Their applications are considered on the basis of their LSAT score, their grade point
average, their life and work experiences, and their maturity level.

But even with a special admissions category, it is hard to imagine that the number
of Aboriginal lawyers in Manitoba will reach the level we believe to be necessary. With a
first-year class of approximately 100 students, the University of Manitoba will have to
ensure that 12 students of each class are Aboriginal simply to maintain an adequate Aboriginal presence in the profession into the future. However, an additional number will
need to be admitted in order to eliminate historical imbalances. If that were attacked at
the rate of 20 lawyers per year (additional to the 12 per year needed to maintain parity), it
would still take almost nine years to overcome the imbalance. Clearly, this has implications for the limiting of Aboriginal students to a special admissions category. Some will
have to be admitted in the general admissions category, as well. This raises questions
about how the Law Faculty considers all law school applicants generally.

We believe it is important that Aboriginal law school applicants be required to
meet those standards which are essential determinants of the students' ability to perform the work necessary in law school and thereafter as lawyers. As with police recruits,
we believe that it is improper to develop what are perceived as "lower" standards for
Aboriginal students. However, we also believe that the use of educational criteria which
do not primarily indicate the individual's ability to perform the tasks required for the
intended position should be eliminated, or the manner of their use altered.

Because the use of a special admissions category does have the potential to stig-
matize qualified Aboriginal students, we encourage the Faculty of Law to review its
entrance processes so as to ensure that minimum eligibility criteria for all students are
identified and applied, and that all students are thereafter selected in a process which is
not more favourable to non-Aboriginal students than to Aboriginal ones.

Law schools generally have an obligation to address this issue and we believe that
they should be coordinating efforts to do so as soon as possible.

One of the options which we recommend is the establishment of a one-year, pre-
law program, where Aboriginal students could attend and study legal and other courses
designed to assist them in entering and graduating from law schools in more significant
numbers than current law school initiatives are able to generate. Their successful completion of such a program should be a factor to be considered on their application for

admission into the Faculty of Law. We note that a similar program has been utilized with some success for Aboriginal medical students. Such a pre-law program could be offered at the Aboriginal Justice College.

WE RECOMMEND THAT:

- The University of Manitoba Faculty of Law establish a recruitment program whereby Aboriginal students (including those in high schools) throughout Manitoba and Northwestern Ontario are encouraged to attend law school.

- The Faculty of Law review the manner in which it makes use of the Law School Admission Test scores and grade point averages of law school applicants to ensure that Aboriginal students capable of successfully completing law school are not thereby unfairly eliminated.

- The Faculty of Law increase the number of Aboriginal law students it accepts into first-year law. The minimum number of students it should be accepting would be 12% of each class, the same proportion as the proportion of Aboriginal people in the general population. Entrance levels should also include an additional number to overcome historical imbalances.

- The Faculty of Law engage an Aboriginal person as a member of its faculty with the primary responsibility of providing support services to Aboriginal students and with the secondary role of developing materials on, and teaching, Aboriginal law.

- The Faculty of Law undertake the development of a full credit course or courses in Aboriginal legal issues, and ensure that Aboriginal issues are included as part of the core courses taught to each law student.

- The Faculty of Law organize and sponsor a conference of law schools from across Canada, to be held for the purpose of addressing the issue of increasing the numbers of Aboriginal law graduates in Canada so as to accomplish two objectives:

  - To overcome historical imbalances in Aboriginal under-representation in the legal profession.

  - To establish entry levels of Aboriginal law students that will ensure that the Aboriginal presence in the legal profession reflects the Aboriginal presence in the population generally.

- The Faculty of Law and the Aboriginal Justice College establish a pre-law program for Aboriginal students wishing to enter law school.

Information-Gathering and Statistics

It is clear that our justice system has been sorely tested and found wanting in the course of this Inquiry. Inquiries in other provinces which have looked at Aboriginal people and the justice system have concluded, much as we have, that Aboriginal people are being treated unfairly, and that major reforms to the manner in which justice is delivered to them need to be brought about.

One of the problems which became apparent to us from the outset is the fact that the justice system is largely unaware of the nature and the magnitude of the problem with which Aboriginal people are confronted. This arises, in part, because there is an insufficient collection of data. For the most part, administrators simply are not aware of what the justice system is doing, insofar as Aboriginal people are concerned. We believe that is not compatible with sound planning or proper administration. Therefore, we believe that data-gathering to determine the impact of the justice system on Aboriginal people should be done systematically.

While it may be argued that improved record-keeping would be expensive, cost has not prevented the establishment of elaborate data collection of criminal records and fingerprints. We also understand the concerns of those who suggest that keeping records based on ethnic background could lead to other problems. Aboriginal people have been subjected for too long to intrusive scrutiny.

We believe, however, that justice system data can play an important role in the future, although waiting for that data should not be used as an excuse for inaction. Record-keeping that simply identifies offenders by ethnic background also would not achieve much. Instead, records should be kept that focus on different processes within the justice system. Support for this was expressed to us by Ken Filkow, chairperson of the Manitoba Human Rights Commission, in his presentation to us.

> There has been some newspaper accounts reporting that the City of Winnipeg Police Force has taken the position that the human rights legislation has precluded the department from collecting data regarding the participation of Aboriginal people in the system. This is a very serious misunderstanding which the Commission wants to correct. The collection of such data is clearly an important element in the planning and delivery of affirmative action programs.

Aboriginal people themselves need to be able to assess the manner in which they are affected by the justice system. We believe that Aboriginal organizations see the wisdom and the validity of the need to gather such information. If the Canadian Centre for Justice Statistics or the provincial Department of Justice were to consult with Aboriginal groups on the kinds of data that should be gathered, we are sure any objections could be overcome.

WE RECOMMEND THAT:

- Governments consult with Aboriginal groups to design and implement a data collection system that will provide detailed information to compare the impact on, and treatment of, Aboriginal and non-Aboriginal persons by the justice system, to evaluate the success of programs dealing with Aboriginal offenders and to provide information to help identify needed reforms.

Resources

There are two aspects to the matter of resources which we wish to address. One has to do with the issue of the extent to which our recommendations call for the expenditure of additional resources on the administration of justice in Canada. Secondly, there is the related question of how best to provide resources for the increased responsibilities and jurisdiction which we call upon Aboriginal communities to accept and exercise in the future.

It is clear that the delivery of justice to Manitoba's Aboriginal people is costly. Tens of millions of dollars are spent every year by the federal and provincial governments to pay for justice services involving Aboriginal people. Simply redeploying those resources in a manner that is less reactive to crime and more preventive would be a substantial improvement.

We are mindful of the fact that the end result of our recommendations likely will be that additional resources will have to be found. We have refrained from costing out the recommendations, because we do not believe that a cost-benefit analysis is the way to approach the question of justice for Aboriginal people.

It should also be clear that we view some of our recommendations ultimately as cost-saving measures. Many of them address ways to avoid the continued incarceration of Aboriginal people, a practice which constitutes the single greatest drain on the already limited resources of the justice system.

From time to time, we have addressed the necessity for Aboriginal leaders and their governments to accept their responsibilities and to take action. We do so on the clear understanding that Aboriginal governments, to a large extent, are dependent on other governments for their funding. We note that raising revenues from the limited sources available to them is next to impossible. The land included in most Indian reserves and other Aboriginal communities in Manitoba has limited economic potential.

Therefore, Aboriginal governments will need to obtain additional resources from government to implement change. However, improvement in the delivery of justice to Manitoba's Aboriginal people is an urgent matter. We cannot continue to deliver justice to Aboriginal people as it has been delivered in the past.

Providing ongoing and consistent levels of resources to Aboriginal governments is a fundamental issue, and is one which cries out for solution. We believe the Aboriginal Justice Commission should address this question as a matter of first importance, but we encourage government and the residents of Manitoba to rethink their approach to funding.

Requiring Aboriginal governments to go on bended knee to other governments each year for a financial contribution so that they can fulfil their own governmental responsibilities is not only demeaning to Aboriginal people, but is an inappropriate way to treat such an issue over the long term. A satisfactory solution needs to be found that takes into account not only the ongoing needs and responsibilities of each level of government involved (including Aboriginal), but also the fact that access to adequate resources to accomplish valid governmental objectives is part of the Aboriginal right to self-government.

We encourage the development of a firmer funding arrangement for Aboriginal government. We suggest that the matter be approached on several fronts:

- That a formula be worked out between federal, provincial and Aboriginal governments whereby a base level of funding would be provided to Aboriginal governments at a level equivalent to a proportionate share of government revenue.

- That, as descendants of the original owners of the land and as an aspect of their treaty rights, Aboriginal people, through their governments, be entitled to a share of resource revenue from each level of government.

- That a system of transfer payments be worked out whereby Aboriginal people can benefit from the greater access to the revenue-producing powers available to other levels of government—particularly the federal powers.

We believe that as long as the question of funding to Aboriginal government is approached as a question of government discretion, the evolution of the relationship between Aboriginal people and non-Aboriginal people will be impaired. It is a matter that needs to be resolved fairly, equitably and with dignity.

WE RECOMMEND THAT:

- As a matter of urgent importance, governments and Aboriginal people, with the assistance of the Aboriginal Justice Commission, negotiate an acceptable process to provide ongoing funding for Aboriginal governments to undertake the initiatives we suggest, in a manner consistent with:

  - The need of Aboriginal people for an ongoing, consistent revenue base.

- The right of Aboriginal people, as original owners of the land, to a fair share of revenue resources from both levels of government.

- The greater access to the revenue-generating powers and sources available to federal and provincial governments.

Conclusion

We now conclude our report.

We have investigated the administration of justice in Manitoba and have come to the conclusion that it does not deliver justice to Manitoba's Aboriginal people. In almost every aspect of our legal system, the treatment of Aboriginal people is tragic. We marvel at the degree to which Aboriginal people have endured, and continue to endure, what the justice system is doing to them. However, they have paid the price of high rates of alcoholism, crime and family abuse.

The time to act is at hand. Aboriginal people will be able to find their way out of the destructive labyrinth to which they have been consigned, but only if federal and provincial governments take positive action to fulfil their historic responsibilities and obligations. In this manner, government can begin to build a new relationship with Aboriginal people based upon respect, understanding and good will.

With greater self-determination in their own territories, Aboriginal people can begin to feel they are being dealt with fairly. With their own justice system, they can assume responsibility and once again deal with their own problems in their own culturally appropriate manner.

For those Aboriginal people not living in an Aboriginal community, a restructuring of the existing justice system will enable them to be dealt with in a humane and positive manner. With Aboriginal people working in every aspect of that system, a sensitive, informed and positive approach to Aboriginal people will become possible.

We have suggested what we believe has to be done and we have indicated how governments and agencies can bring about the necessary changes. We have completed our assignment. Government and others must now accept the responsibility to make the changes that cry out for action.

Canada's treatment of its first citizens has been an international disgrace. To fail to take every needed step to redress this lingering injustice will continue to bring tragedy and suffering to Aboriginal people, and to blacken our country's name throughout the world. By acting now, governments can give positive expression to the public support and good will we have encountered from Manitobans during the past three years.

ENDNOTES

Chapter 1 – The Inquiry and the Issues

1. Dansys Consultants, "Aboriginal People in Manitoba: Population Estimates for 1986 and 1991," research paper prepared for the Aboriginal Justice Inquiry, Ottawa, November, 1990.

2. Jeremy Hull, *An Overview of Registered Indian Conditions in Manitoba* (Ottawa: Department of Indian and Northern Affairs, 1987), p. 20.

3. *Ibid.*

4. Canada, Statistics Canada, Census Canada 1986, *A Data Book on Canada's Aboriginal Population from the 1986 Census of Canada* (Ottawa, March 1989), pp. 173–74.

5. Hull, *Registered Indian Conditions*, p. 48.

6. *Ibid.*, p. 30.

7. *Ibid.*, pp. 77–78, 81.

8. *Ibid.*, p. 97.

9. *Ibid.*, p. 137.

10. *Ibid.*, pp. 68–69.

11. Michael Jackson, "Locking Up Natives in Canada," *University of British Columbia Law Review*, 23, 2 (1989): 215–300, at 215.

12. Presentation to Aboriginal Justice Inquiry hearings, 12 April 1989.

13. Don McCaskill, *Patterns of Criminality and Correction among Native Offenders in Manitoba: A Longitudinal Analysis* (Ottawa: Correctional Service of Canada, 1985), p. 2.

14. Presentation to Aboriginal Justice Inquiry hearings, 25 April 1989.

15. Hull, *Registered Indian Conditions*, p. 25.

16. *Ibid.*, p. 30.

17. This estimate is based on public estimates for 1990–91 for the Manitoba departments of Justice, Family Services and Natural Resources; 1991–92 estimates for the federal departments of Indian and Northern Affairs, Justice and Solicitor General; and the 1990 current estimates for the City of Winnipeg and the Brandon City Police budget.

Chapter 2 – Aboriginal Concepts of Justice

1. New English Bible, Genesis 1:28–30.

2. Freda Ahenakew, Cecil King and Catherine I. Littlejohn, "Indigenous Languages in the Delivery of Justice in Manitoba," research paper prepared for the Aboriginal Justice Inquiry, Winnipeg, March 1990, p. 23.

3. James Dumont, "Justice and Aboriginal People," research paper prepared for the Aboriginal Justice Inquiry, Sudbury, September 1990.

4. Edward Benton Banai, *The Mishomis Book* (St. Paul, Minnesota: Indian Country Press, 1979), p. 64, cited in Dumont, "Justice and Aboriginal People," p. 4.

5. John R. Bryde, *Modern Indian Psychology* (Vermillion, South Dakota: Institute of Indian Studies, University of South Dakota, 1971), cited in Dumont, "Justice and Aboriginal People," pp. 6–7.

6. James R. Walker, "The Sun Dance and Other Ceremonies of the Oglala Division of the Teton Dakota," *American Museum of Natural History, Anthropological Papers*, 16 (1917): 62, cited in Dumont, "Justice and Aboriginal People," p. 7.

7. K. Basso, "To Give Up on Words: Silence in Western Apache Culture," *Southwestern Journal of Anthropology*, 26, 2 (1970): 213–30; James S. Chisholm, *Navaho Infancy: An Ethnological Study of Child Development* (New York: Aldine Publishing Co., 1983), cited in Dumont, "Justice and Aboriginal People," p. 7.

8. E. Adamson Hoebel, *The Cheyennes: Indians of the Great Plains* (New York: Holt, Rinehart and Winston, 1960), quoted in Dumont, "Justice and Aboriginal People," p. 10.

9. Dumont, "Justice and Aboriginal People," p. 32.

10. Diamond Jenness, *Indians of Canada*, 7th ed. (Toronto: University of Toronto Press, National Museums of Canada, 1989), p. 125.

11. Francis Jennings, *The Invasion of America: Indians, Colonialism and the Cant of Conquest* (New York: W. W. Norton, 1976), pp. 111–12.

12. *Ibid.*, pp. 147–49.

13. Menno Wiebe, *Native Culture and Canadian Law: A Cultural Look at Native People and the Canadian Justice System* (Kingston: Queen's Theological College, 1984), p. 8.

14. Bruce G. Trigger, *The Children of Aataentsic: A History of the Huron People to 1660* (Montreal and Kingston: McGill-Queen's University Press, 1976), pp. 59–62.

15. *Ibid.*, p. 60.

16. Jennings, *Invasion of America*, pp. 147–49.

17. Rupert Ross, "Dancing with a Ghost: Exploring Indian Reality," unpublished manuscript, Kenora, 1987, pp. 5–6; see also his "Leaving Our White Eyes Behind: The Sentencing of Native Accused," [1989] 3 C.N.L.R. 1.

18. Clare Brant, "Native Ethics and Rules of Behaviour," *Canadian Journal of Psychiatry*, 35 (August 1990): 534.

19. *Ibid.*

20. Ross, "Dancing with a Ghost," p. 6.

21. Ahenakew, King and Littlejohn, "Indigenous Languages," p. 22.

22. Brant, "Native Ethics," pp. 534–35.

23. *Ibid.*, p. 535.

24. *Ibid.*

25. *Ibid.*

26. *Ibid.*

27. *Ibid.*

28. *Ibid.*, p. 536.

29. *Ibid.*

30. Bernard Francis, presentation to the Royal Commission on the Donald Marshall, Jr., Prosecution, 2 November 1987, quoted in Ahenakew, King and Littlejohn, "Indigenous Languages," p. 27.

31. Brant, "Native Ethics," p. 537.

32. *Ibid.*, p. 538.

33. Ross, "Dancing with a Ghost," p. 16.

34. *Ibid.*, p. 5.

35. Francis, 2 November 1987, presentation quoted in Ahenakew, King and Littlejohn, "Indigenous Languages," p. 30.

36. Ahenakew, King and Littlejohn, "Indigenous Languages," p. 25.

37. *Native Court Interpreter's Manual* (Winnipeg: Department of the Attorney General, 1987), p. i.

38. *Ibid.*

39. Ahenakew, King and Littlejohn, "Indigenous Languages," p. 4.

40. *Ibid.*, p. 25.

41. Basil Johnston, Ojibway writer, in correspondence with Cecil King, 10 January 1990, quoted in Ahenakew, King and Littlejohn, "Indigenous Languages," p. 25.

42. Francis, 2 November 1987 presentation quoted in Ahenakew, King and Littlejohn, "Indigenous Languages," p. 26.

43. Ahenakew, King and Littlejohn, "Indigenous Languages," p. 29.

44. *Ibid.*, p. 81.

45. *Ibid.*

46. *Ibid.*, p. 83.

47. *Ibid.*, p. 23.

Chapter 3 – An Historical Overview

1.   James W. S. Walker, "The Indian in Canadian Historical Writing," *Canadian Historical Association Historical Papers* (1971), pp. 21–51.

2.   Simon Roberts, *Order and Dispute: An Introduction to Legal Anthropology* (Harmondsworth, England: Penguin Books, 1979), p. 185.

3.   Michael Coyle, "Traditional Indian Justice in Ontario: A Role for the Present?" *Osgoode Hall Law Journal*, 24, 3 (1986): 605–33.

4.   E.E. Rich, ed., *Cumberland House Journals and Inland Journal, 1775–82 (First Series, 1775–79),* (London: Hudson's Bay Record Society, 1951), p. 36.

5.   W. Kaye Lamb, ed., *Sixteen Years in the Indian Country: The Journal of Daniel William Harmon, 1800–1816* (Toronto: Macmillan, 1957), p. 87.

6.   Quoted in H.M. Chittenden and A.T. Richardson, eds., *Life, Letters and Travels of Father Pierre-Jean de Smet*, vol. 3, p. 1028; cited in Diamond Jenness, *The Indians of Canada*, 7th ed. (Toronto: University of Toronto Press, 1977), p. 129; also see H.E. Driver, *Indians of North America*, 2d ed. (Chicago: University of Chicago Press, 1969), pp. 312–15.

7.   Alexander Ross, *The Red River Settlement: Its Rise, Progress, and Present State* (Minneapolis: Ross and Haines, 1957), pp. 249–50.

8.   E. Adamson Hoebel, *The Law of Primitive Man: A Study in Comparative Legal Dynamics* (Cambridge, Massachusetts: Harvard University Press, 1954), p. 28.

9. Peter R. Grant, "Recognition of Traditional Laws in State Courts and the Formulation of State Legislation," in *Indigenous Law and the State*, edited by Bradford W. Morse and Gordon R. Woodman (Dordrecht, Netherlands: Foris Publications, 1988), p. 260.

10. Scott Clark, "Aboriginal Customary Law: Literature Review," research paper prepared for the Aboriginal Justice Inquiry, 1990, p. 8.

11. Gisday Wa and Delgam Uukw, *The Spirit in the Land: The Opening Statement of the Gitksan and Wet'suwet'en Hereditary Chiefs in the Supreme Court of British Columbia* (Gabriola, British Columbia: Reflections, 1989), p. 8.

12. Robert Gordon and Mervyn Meggitt, "The Customary Law Option," in their *Law and Order in the New Guinea Highlands* (Hanover, New Hampshire: University Press of New England, 1985), pp. 202–4.

13. John West, *The Substance of a Journal during a Residence at the Red River Colony, British North America in the Years 1820–1823* (Vancouver: Alcuin Society, 1967), p. 140.

14. Meriwether Lewis and William Clark, *History of the Expedition under the Command of Captains Lewis and Clark to the Sources of the Missouri*, vol. 2 (Toronto: Morang, n.d.), p. 108.

15. Alexandre-Antonin Taché, *Sketch of the North-West of America* (Montreal: John Lovell, 1870), p. 110.

16. An isolated and unconvincing critic of this conclusion is L.C. Green in Green and O.P. Dickason, *The Law of Nations and the New World* (Edmonton: University of Alberta Press, 1989). James Crawford, "The Original Status of Aboriginal Peoples in North America: A Critique of L.C. Green and O.P. Dickason, *The Law of Nations and the New World* (1989)," research paper prepared for the Aboriginal Justice Inquiry (Sydney, Australia, January 1991).

17. This interpretation is presented most clearly in the writings of James Crawford, including his "Aboriginal Self-Government in Canada," research report for the Committee on Native Justice, Canadian Bar Association (Ottawa: Canadian Bar Association, 1988). The above quotation comes from page 22 of this document. See also Crawford's *The Creation of States in International Law* (Oxford: Clarendon Press, 1979).

18. *Guerin v. R.*, [1984] 2 S.C.R. 335.

19. Sylvia Van Kirk, *"Many Tender Ties": Women in Fur-Trade Society in Western Canada, 1670–1870* (Winnipeg: Watson and Dwyer, 1980), p. 4.

20. Cited in J. Lagasse, "The Metis in Manitoba," in *The Other Natives: The Metis*, vol. 2, edited by A.S. Lussier and D.B. Sealey (Winnipeg: Manitoba Metis Federation Press, 1978), p. 110.

21. Paul C. Thistle, *Indian-European Trade Relations in the Lower Saskatchewan River Region to 1840*, Manitoba Studies in Native History No. 2 (Winnipeg: University of Manitoba Press, 1986), pp. 67, 73–74.

22. *Ibid.*, pp. 67, 77.

23. *Ibid.*, p. 86.

24. S.C. 1765, 6 Geo. 3, c. 18.

25. Dale Gibson and Lee Gibson, *Substantial Justice: Law and Lawyers in Manitoba, 1670–1970* (Winnipeg: Peguis, 1972), pp. 1–5.

26. See Desmond H. Brown, "Unpredictable and Uncertain: Criminal Law in the Canadian North West before 1886," *Alberta Law Review*, 17, 3 (1979): 497–512, for a summary of these issues.

27. Gibson and Gibson, *Substantial Justice*, p. 27.

28. *An Act providing for the organization of the Department of the Secretary of State of Canada, and for the management of Indian and Ordinance Lands*, S.C. 1868, c. 42.

29. W.L. Morton, *Manitoba: A History* (lst ed., 1957; reprint ed., Toronto: University of Toronto Press, 1967); W.L. Morton, "Introduction" to *Alexander Begg's Red River Journal and Other Papers Relative to the Red River Resistance of 1869–70* (Toronto: Champlain Society, 1956).

30. *Manitoba Act*, 1870, R.S.C. 1985, App. II, No. 8.

31. The legislative record includes *Rupert's Land Act, 1868*, 31–32 Vict., c. 105 (U.K.), reprinted in R.S.C. 1985, App. II, No. 6; *Act for the Temporary Government of Rupert's Land and the North-Western Territory*, S.C. 1869, c. 3; "Order of Her Majesty in Council Admitting Rupert's Land and the North-Western Territory into the Union, 23 June 1870," a sequence of 1868–69 documents contained in E.H. Oliver, *The Canadian North-West: Its Early Development and Legislative Records* (Ottawa: Government Printing Bureau, 1914–15), pp. 939–63; other documents appear in W.L. Morton, ed., *Manitoba: The Birth of a Province*, vol. 1 (Altona, Manitoba: Manitoba Record Society Publications, 1965). The 1871 British legislation was entitled *Act Respecting the Establishment of Provinces in the Dominion of Canada, 1871*, 34 & 35 Vict. c. 28 (U.K.).

32. D. Thorburn to R. Pennefather, 13 October 1858, PAC, RG 10, v. 245, part I, cited in John S. Milloy, "The Early Indian Acts: Developmental Strategy and Constitutional Change," in *As Long as the Sun Shines and Water Flows: A Reader in Canadian Native Studies*, edited by Ian A.L. Getty and A.S. Lussier (Vancouver: Nakoda Institute and University of British Columbia Press, 1983).

33. S.C. 1869, 32–33 Vict., c. 6, s. 10.

34. S.C. 1876, 39 Vict., c. 18, s. 63.

35. Jean Usher, *William Duncan of Metlakatla: A Victorian Missionary in British Columbia* (Ottawa: National Museum of Man, 1974), p. 63.

36. *Regina Leader*, 9 October 1888, cited in Jacqueline Kennedy Gresko, "Qu'Appelle Industrial School: White 'Rites' for the Indians of the Old North West," M.A. thesis, Carleton University, Ottawa, 1970, p. 116.

37. George T. Denison, cited in Peter B. Waite, *Canada, 1874–1896: Arduous Destiny* (Toronto: McClelland and Stewart, 1971), p. 162, and in Sandra Estlin Bingaman, "The Trials of the 'White Rebels,' 1885," *Saskatchewan History*, 25, 2 (1972): 41–54.

38. Hugh A. Dempsey, *Big Bear: The End of Freedom* (Vancouver: Douglas and McIntyre, 1984), p. 192; Sandra Estlin Bingaman, "The Trials of Poundmaker and Big Bear, 1885," *Saskatchewan History*, 28, 3 (1975): 81–94.

39. Joseph F. Dion, *My Tribe the Crees* (Calgary: Glenbow Museum, 1979), p. 113, cited in Dempsey, *Big Bear*, pp. 193–94.

40. Dan Kennedy, *Recollections of an Assiniboine Chief*, edited by James R. Stephens (Toronto and Montreal: McClelland and Stewart, 1972), pp. 54–55, cited in J.R. Miller, *Skyscrapers Hide the Heavens: A History of Indian-White Relations in Canada* (Toronto: University of Toronto Press, 1989), p. 196.

41. Cited in Miller, *Skyscrapers Hide the Heavens*, p. 196.

42. F. Laurie Barron, "A Summary of Federal Indian Policy in the Canadian West, 1867–1984," *Native Studies Review*, 1, 1 (1984): 28–39.

43. K.A. Pettipas, "Severing the Ties That Bind: The Canadian Indian Act and the Repression of Indigenous Religious Systems in the Prairie Region, 1896–1951," PhD dissertation, University of Manitoba, Winnipeg, 1988 (Winnipeg: University of Manitoba Press, forthcoming); Douglas Cole and Ira Chaikin, *An Iron Hand upon the People: The Law Against the Potlatch on the Northwest Coast* (Vancouver: Douglas and McIntyre, 1990).

44. Department of Indian Affairs, J.M. to Secretary, 19 September 1908, PAC, RG 10, v. 3825, file 60, 511–2, cited in Pettipas, "Severing the Ties," p. 268.

45. Edward Ahenakew, *Voices of the Plains Cree*, edited by Ruth Buck (Toronto: McClelland and Stewart, 1973), pp. 69, 72.

46. Vankoughnet to Macdonald, 14 August 1885, PAC, RG 10, v. 3710, file 19, 550–3, cited in F. Laurie Barron, "The Indian Pass System in the Canadian West, 1882–1935," *Prairie Forum*, 13, 1 (1988): 28.

47. Sarah Carter, *Lost Harvests: Prairie Indian Reserve Farmers and Government Policy* (Montreal and Kingston: McGill-Queen's University Press, 1990).

48. S.C. 1876, 39 Vict., c. 18, s. 70.

49. Canada, Sessional Papers, 14, 1896, *Report of the Deputy Superintendent-General of Indian Affairs*, cited in Sarah Carter, "Agriculture and Agitation on the Oak River Reserve, 1875–1895," *Manitoba History*, 6 (Fall 1983): 5.

50. Stuart Raby, "Indian Land Surrenders in Southern Saskatchewan," *Canadian Geographer*, 17, 1 (1973): 36–52.

51. Cited in Tyler, Wright and Daniel Ltd., "The Illegal Surrender of St. Peter's Reserve," manuscript report prepared for the Treaty and Aboriginal Rights Research Centre of Manitoba (Winnipeg, 1983), p. 534.

52. S.C. 1916, 6–7 Geo. 5, c. 24.

53. Treaty and Aboriginal Rights Research Program, *Treaty Land Entitlement in Manitoba, 1970–1981* (Winnipeg: Treaty and Aboriginal Rights Research Centre, 1982).

54. Peter Douglas Elias, *The Dakota of the Canadian Northwest: Lessons for Survival*, Manitoba Studies in Native History No. 5 (Winnipeg: University of Manitoba Press, 1988), p. 146.

55. Cited in John S. Milloy, "A Partnership of Races: Indian and White, Cross-Cultural Relations and Criminal Justice in Manitoba, 1670–1949," research paper prepared for the Aboriginal Justice Inquiry, Peterborough, June 1990, p. 67.

56. Miller, *Skyscrapers Hide the Heavens*, pp. 206–7.

57. Canada, Parliament, Special Joint Committee of the Senate and House of Commons on the *Indian Act*, "Minutes and Proceedings of Evidence," No. 30, pp. 1563–1600, cited in Milloy, "Partnership of Races," pp. 81–94.

58. *Ibid.*, p. 1585.

59. A wide sample of the literature on this theme is presented in Jacqueline Peterson and Jennifer S.H. Brown, eds., *The New Peoples: Being and Becoming Metis in North America* (Winnipeg: University of Manitoba Press, 1985), and in F. Laurie Barron and James B. Waldram, eds., *1885 and After: Native Society in Transition*, proceedings of a conference held at the University of Saskatchewan, Saskatoon, May 1985 (Regina: Canadian Plains Research Centre, University of Regina, 1986). A survey is presented in Jennifer S.H. Brown, "Metis," *Canadian Encyclopedia*, 2d ed. (Edmonton: Hurtig Publishers, 1988), pp. 1343–46.

60. Auguste-Henri de Tremaudan, *Histoire de la nation metisse dans l'ouest canadien*, reprint ed. (St. Boniface: Les Editions du Ble, 1979), published in English as *Hold High Your Heads: History of the Metis Nation in Western Canada*, translated by E. Maguet (Winnipeg: Pemmican Publications, 1982).

61. de Tremaudan, *Hold High Your Heads*, p. xvi.

62. Allen Edgar Ronaghan, "The Archibald Administration in Manitoba, 1870–72," PhD dissertation, University of Manitoba, Winnipeg, 1987.

63. Archibald to J.A. Macdonald, 9 October 1871, in *Journals of the House of Commons of the Dominion of Canada 1874*, 8, appx. 6.

64. Jean H. Lagasse, *A Study of the Population of Indian Ancestry Living in Manitoba* (Winnipeg: Department of Agriculture and Immigration, 1959), pp. 54–57.

65. Lagasse, "The Metis in Manitoba," p. 78.

66. *Ibid.*, p. 3.

67. S.C. 1916, 7–8 Geo. 5, c. 24; S.C. 1919, 9–10 Geo. 5, c. 71.

68. S.C. 1942, c. 33.

69. *An Act to amend the Indian Act*, S.C. 1919, 9–10 Geo. 5, c. 56.

70. R.S.C. 1906, c. 81, ss. 21–23.

71. R.S.C. 1906, c. 81, s. 164.

72. P.C. 2122.

73. See James Dempsey, "The Indians and World War One," *Alberta History*, 31, 3 (1983): 1–8; RES Policy Research, *Indian Veterans and Veterans' Benefits in New Brunswick and Prince Edward Island* (Ottawa: National Indian Veterans Association, 1984); Bruce D. Sealey and Peter Van De Vyvere, *Thomas George Prince* (Winnipeg: Peguis, 1981); Alastair Sweeney, *Government Policy and Saskatchewan Indian Veterans* (Saskatchewan Indian Veterans Association, 1979); *Indian Act*, S.C. 1952, c. 149; *Soldier Settlement Act*, S.C. 1917, c. 21; *Veterans Land Act*, S.C. 1952, c. 280; *Indian Veterans' Rights*, Report No. 3 (Saskatoon: Native Law Centre, 1979).

74. Canada, Sessional Papers, *Annual Reports of the Superintendent of Penitentiaries*; figures from 1900–1960 can be extracted from tables published in the annual reports of the Superintendent, latterly Commissioner, of Penitentiaries. After 1960, statistical data concerning correctional facilities is published in various Statistics Canada reports under the rubric of the "85" series. Ethnicity was not used again as a description of prisoners until 1975.

75. M.S. Donnelly, *The Government of Manitoba* (Toronto: University of Toronto Press, 1963), p. 72.

76. *An Act respecting the Electoral Franchise*, S.C. 1885, 47–49 Vict., c. 40, ss. 2 and 11(c).

77. *Election Act*, S.M. 1886, 49 Vict., c. 29, s. 130(5).

78. *Election Act*, S.M. 1931, c. 10, s. 16(5); also R.S.M. 1940, c. 57, ss. 15(1)(b) and 16(5); similar Ontario legislation was *The Elections Act*, R.S.O. 1927, c. 8, s. 18(s); in 1945 the Manitoba legislation *The Active Service Election and Representation Act*, S.M. 1945 (2nd. Sess.), c. 1, s. 3, extended the right to Indians who had served in the Second World War.

79. *An Act to amend The Manitoba Elections Act*, S.M. 1952 (1st Sess.), c. 18, ss. 5 and 6.

80. 8–9 Eliz. II, c. 39 repealed R.S.C. 1952, c. 23, the relevant clauses of which were s. 14(2)(e) and 14(4).

81. Patrick Johnston, *Native Children and the Child Welfare System* (Toronto: James Lorimer, 1983).

82. *Calder v. Attorney General of British Columbia*, [1973] S.C.R. 313.

83. Canada, House of Commons, Special Committee on Indian Self-Government, *Indian Self-Government in Canada* (Penner Report), (Ottawa, 1983).

Chapter 4 – Aboriginal Over-Representation

1. "Indians Policing Reserves," background information for Department of Indian Affairs and Northern Development news release 1–9157, "Federal Government Funds Plan to Improve Policing Services for Indian Reserves," 27 June 1991.

2. Correspondence to Aboriginal Justice Inquiry from Insp. L.R. Chipperfield, Planning Branch, "D" Division, Manitoba, 29 April 1991.

3. The Provincial Court study conducted by the Manitoba Department of Justice in 1986 is one of the most ambitious justice-related data collection projects ever undertaken in Canada and one of the few that compares Aboriginal and non-Aboriginal experiences in the justice system. The study involved a random sample of Aboriginal and non-Aboriginal cases in Winnipeg, Thompson, The Pas and nine reserves in northern Manitoba. Our Inquiry engaged Dansys Consultants, a firm that specializes in statistical analysis of the justice system, to conduct an independent review of the data generated by the Provincial Court study. Our figures on the Provincial Courts are based on this analysis. Dansys Consultants, "Manitoba Aboriginal Justice Study," research paper prepared for the Aboriginal Justice Inquiry, Ottawa, May 1991.

4. Mary Hyde and Carol LaPrairie, "Amerindian Police Crime Prevention," working paper prepared for the Solicitor General of Canada, Ottawa, 1987, pp. 55–56.

5. *Ibid.*, p. 38.

6. Paul Havemann, Keith Couse, Lori Foster, and Rae Matonovich, *Law and Order for Canada's Indigenous People: A Review of Recent Research Literature Relating to the Operation of the Criminal Justice System and Canada's Indigenous People* (Regina: Prairie Justice Research, 1985), pp. 112–17.

7. K.D. Harries, *Crime and the Environment* (Springfield, Illinois: Charles C. Thomas, 1980), pp. 4–5.

8. Emile Durkheim, "The Normal and the Pathological" (1938), and Robert A. Dentler and Kai T. Erikson, "The Functions of Deviance in Groups" (1959), in *Theories of Deviance*, edited by Stuart H. Traub and Craig B. Little (Itasca, Illinois: F.E. Peacock Publishers, 1975).

9. Alfred Adler, referred to in John Braithwaite, *Inequality, Crime and Public Policy* (London: Routledge and Kegan Paul, 1979).

10. Theodore N. Ferdinand, "The Methods of Delinquency Theory," *Criminology*, 25, 4 (1987): 841–62, at 849.

11. Thorsten Sellin, "Culture Conflict and Crime" (1938), in Traub and Little, *Theories of Deviance*, pp. 49–58.

12. W.I. Thomas and Florian Znaniecki, "The Concept of Social Disorganization" (1920), and Robert E. Park, "Social Change and Social Disorganization" (1967), in Traub and Little, *Theories of Deviance*.

13. Rodney Stark, "Deviant Places: A Theory of the Ecology of Crime," *Criminology*, 25, 4 (1987): 893–909.

14. Walter Gover, Michael Hughes and Omer Galle, "Overcrowding in the Home: An Empirical Investigation of Its Possible Pathological Consequences," *American Sociological Review*, 44 (1979): 59–82.

15. Edwin H. Sutherland, "The Theory of Differential Association" (1947), in Traub and Little, *Theories of Deviance*.

16. Daniel Glaser, "Criminality Theories and Behavioural Images" (1956), in Traub and Little, *Theories of Deviance.*

17. Michael Lynch and W. Byron Groves, *A Primer in Radical Criminology*, 2d ed. (Albany, New York: Harrow and Heston, 1989).

18. Jeffrey Fagan and Sandra Wexler, "Family Origins of Violent Delinquents," *Criminology*, 25, 3 (1987): 643–69.

19. Donald West, *Delinquency: Its Roots, Careers, and Prospects* (Cambridge, Massachusetts: Harvard University Press, 1982), pp. 28, 37, 117.

20. Tavs Fulmer Anderson, "Persistence of Social and Health Problems in the Welfare State: A Danish Cohort Experience from 1948 to 1979," *Social Science and Medicine*, 18, 7 (1984): 555–60.

21. Marvin Wolfgang, Marvin Figlio and Thorsten Sellin, *Delinquency in a Birth Cohort* (Chicago: University of Chicago Press, 1972), pp. 245–49.

22. Elliott Currie, *Confronting Crime* (New York: Pantheon Books, 1985), p. 162, discussing a study by Judith and Peter Blau.

23. *Ibid.*, p. 174.

24. *Ibid.*, p. 178.

25. Hyde and LaPrairie, "Amerindian Police Crime Prevention," pp. 8–10, 25–27.

26. Canada, Statistics Canada, Census Canada 1986, *A Data Book on Canada's Aboriginal Population from the 1986 Census of Canada* (Ottawa, March 1989), p. 191.

27. Winnipeg, Social Planning Council of Winnipeg, *Selected Profile of Winnipeg's Aboriginal Population* (Winnipeg, 1989), p. 9.

28. Canada, Department of Indian and Northern Affairs, *Highlights of Aboriginal Conditions, 1981–2001, Part III: Economic Conditions* (Ottawa, 1989), p. 13.

29. *Ibid.*, p. 184.

30. Jeremy Hull, *An Overview of Registered Indian Conditions in Manitoba* (Ottawa: Department of Indian and Northern Affairs, 1987), p. 116.

31. *Ibid.*, p. 25.

32. *Ibid.*, p. 30.

33. *Ibid.*, p. 46.

34. *Ibid.*, p. 37.

35. *Ibid.*, pp. 68–69.

36. Indian and Northern Affairs, *Highlights of Aboriginal Conditions, Part III*, p. 5.

37. Hull, *Registered Indian Conditions*, p. 48.

38. *Ibid.*, p. 47.

39. *Ibid.*, p. 125.

40. *Ibid.*, pp. 123, 131.

41. Statistics Canada, *A Data Book*, p. 81.

42. M. Harvey Brenner, *Estimating the Social Costs of National Economic Policy*, report prepared for the Joint Economic Committee of the U.S. Congress (Washington, D.C.: U.S. Government Printing Office, 1976).

43. Michael Rutter, "Protective Factors in Children's Responses to Stress and Disadvantage," in *Promoting Social Competence and Coping in Children*, vol. 3 of *Primary Prevention and Cycle Pathology*, edited by M.W. Kent and J.E. Rolf (Hanover, New Hampshire: University Press of New England, 1979), pp. 49–74.

44. Lisa Hobbs Birnie, *A Rock and a Hard Place: Inside Canada's Parole Board* (Toronto: Macmillan, 1990), p. 205.

45. Among the many sources on this topic is W.S. Tarnopolsky, "Discrimination in Canada: Our History and Our Legacy," paper delivered to the Canadian Institute of Administration of Justice seminar on discrimination in the law, Kananaskis, Alberta, 12 October 1989.

46. J.E. Hodgetts, *Pioneer Public Service*, quoted in Kahn-Tineta Miller and George Lerchs, *The Historical Development of the Indian Act* (Ottawa: Treaties and Historical Research Branch, Department of Indian and Northern Affairs, 1978), p. 191.

47. *Andrews v. Law Society of British Columbia*, [1989] 2 W.W.R. 289 (S.C.C.), at 308, per Mr. Justice McIntyre.

48. *Ibid.*, at 307.

49. Michael Jackson, "Locking Up Natives in Canada," *University of British Columbia Law Review*, 23, 2 (1989): 215–300, at 215.

50. Don McCaskill, *Patterns of Criminality and Correction among Native Offenders in Manitoba: A Longitudinal Analysis* (Ottawa: Correctional Service of Canada, 1985), p. 2.

51. Canada, Department of the Solicitor General, *Report of the Task Force on Aboriginal Peoples in Federal Corrections* (Ottawa, 1988), p. 5.

52. Statistics Canada, *A Data Book*, pp. 173–74.

53. Hull, *Registered Indian Conditions*, p. 59.

54. Dansys Consultants, "Aboriginal People in Manitoba: Population Estimates for 1986 and 1991," research paper prepared for the Aboriginal Justice Inquiry, Ottawa, November 1990.

55. Birnie, *A Rock and a Hard Place*, p. 197.

56. W.K. Greenaway, "Crime and Class: Unequal before the Law," in *Structural Inequality in Canada*, edited by John Harp and John R. Hofley (Scarborough: Prentice-Hall, 1980), p. 257; Traub and Little, *Theories of Deviance*, p. 181.

57. See Curtis T. Griffiths and Simon N. Verdun-Jones, *Canadian Criminal Justice* (Toronto: Butterworths, 1989), p. 191.

58. Written presentation of Manitoba Department of Justice to the Aboriginal Justice Inquiry, 25 April 1989, Appendix E.

59. Elliott Johnston, Commissioner, Royal Commission into Aboriginal Deaths in Custody, *National Report*, vol. 1 (Canberra: Australian Government Publishing Service, 1991), pp. 8–9.

60. Sheilah Martin and Kathleen Mahoney, eds., *Equality and Judicial Neutrality* (Toronto: Carswell, 1987), p. 4.

61. Rosalie S. Abella, "Limitations on the Right to Equality before the Law," in *The Limitation of Human Rights in Comparative Constitutional Law*, edited by Armand de Mestral et al. (Montreal: Editions Yvon Blais, 1986), p. 226.

62. *R. v. Big M Drug Mart* (1985), 18 D.L.R. (4th) 321, at 362.

63. Abella, "Limitations," p. 229.

64. *Ibid.*, p. 235.

65. *Preliminary Report*, p. 99, translation, quoted in Dale Gibson, *The Law of the Charter: Equality Rights* (Toronto: Carswell, 1990), p. vii.

66. Martin and Mahoney, *Equality and Judicial Neutrality*, pp. 50–58.

67. *Report of the Task Force on Aboriginal Peoples in Federal Corrections*, pp. 13–14.

Chapter 5 – Aboriginal and Treaty Rights

1. *Doe d. Sheldon v. Ramsay* (1852), 9 U.C.Q.B. 105, at 123.

2. *Sikyea v. R.*, [1964] S.C.R. 642.

3. *Calder v. Attorney General of British Columbia*, [1973] S.C.R. 313.

4. *Guerin v. R.*, [1984] 2 S.C.R. 335.

5. *R. v. Simon*, [1985] 2 S.C.R. 387; *Nowegijick v. R.*, [1983] 1 S.C.R. 29.

6. R.S.C. 1985, App. II, No. 1, at 4–5.

7. *Re Paulette*, [1973] 6 W.W.R. 97 (N.W.T.S.C.) and 115; reversed on other grounds [1976] 2 W.W.R. 193 (N.W.T.C.A.); affirmed on other grounds [1977] 2 S.C.R. 628.

8. *Kanatewat v. James Bay Development Corp.*, [1974] R.P. 38; reversed [1975] (C.A.) 166; leave to appeal dismissed [1975] 1 S.C.R. 48.

9. *Hamlet of Baker Lake v. Minister of Indian Affairs and Northern Development*, [1980] 1 F.C. 518 (T.D.).

10. *U.S. ex rel. Hualpai Indians v. Santa Fe Pacific Railroad*, 314 U.S. 339 (1941), at 347.

11. *Island of Palmas* (1928), 2 R.I.A.A. 829; *Western Sahara Advisory Opinion*, I.C.J. Reports (1975), at 12; *Legal Consequences for States of the Continued Presence of South Africa in Namibia (South West Africa) notwithstanding Security Council Resolution 276 (1970), Advisory Opinion*, I.C.J. Reports (1971), at 16.

12. See, e.g., L.C. Green and O.P. Dickason, *The Law of Nations and the New World* (Edmonton: University of Alberta Press, 1989).

13. Felix S. Cohen, *Handbook of Federal Indian Law* (Washinton, D.C.: U.S. Government Printing Office, 1942; reprint ed., Albuquerque: University of New Mexico Press, 1972); G. Bennet, *Aboriginal Rights in International Law*, Occasional Working Paper No. 37 (London: Royal Anthropological Institute, 1978); J. Crawford, *The Creation of States in International Law* (Oxford: Clarendon Press, 1979).

14. *Re Southern Rhodesia*, [1919] A.C. 211 (P.C.).

15. *Re Southern Rhodesia; Hamlet of Baker Lake v. Minister of Indian Affairs and Northern Development*, [1980], 1 F.C. 518 (T.D.); *Attorney General of Ontario v. Bear Island Foundation*, [1989] 2 C.N.L.R. 73 (Ont. C.A.), affirming (1982), 138 D.L.R. (3d) 683 (Ont. H.C.); *Calder v. Attorney General of British Columbia*, [1973] S.C.R. 313; *R. v. Sparrow* [1990] 1 S.C.R. 1075; *R. v. Sioui*, [1990] 1 S.C.R. 1025; *Milirrum v. Nabalco Pty. Ltd.* (1971), 17 F.L.R. 141 (N.T.S.C.).

16. *Delgamuukw et al. v. Attorney General of British Columbia*, [1991] 3 W.W.R. 97, at 389 (B.C.S.C.).

17. M.F. Lindley, *The Acquisition and Government of Backward Territory in International Law* (London: Longman, Green & Co., 1926), pp. 22–23.

18. See *R. v. Simon*, [1985] 2 S.C.R. 387.

19. *Johnson v. M'Intosh*, 21 U.S. (8 Wheat.) 543 (1823).

20. *Vienna Convention on the Law of Treaties*, 1969, U.N. Doc. 81, I.M., quoted in Maureen Davies, "Aspects of Aboriginal Rights in International Law," in *Aboriginal People and the Law: Indian, Metis, and Inuit Rights in Canada*, edited by Bradford W. Morse (Ottawa: Carleton University Press, 1989), p. 29.

21. *Mohegan Indians v. Connecticut*, a series of three decisions by the Board of Trade, the precursor to the Judicial Committee of the Privy Council. The first decision was in 1706. The cases can be found in Joseph Henry Smith, *Appeals to the Privy Council from the American Plantations* (New York: Columbia University Press, 1950), p. 422.

22. *St. Catherine's Milling & Lumber Co. v. R.* (1888), 14 A.C. 46 (P.C.), at 54.

23. *Order of Her Majesty in Council Admitting Rupert's Land and the North-Western Territory into the Union*, S.C. 1869, c. 3.

24. See, e.g., *Doe d. Sheldon v. Ramsay* (1852), 9 U.C.Q.B. 105.

25. See, e.g., *Pawis v. R.*, [1980] 2 F.C. (18 T.D.).

26. *R. v. Simon*, [1985] 2 S.C.R. 387, at 404.

27. *Dreaver v. R.* (1935), 5 C.N.L.C. 92.

28. *R. v. Johnston* (1966), 56 W.W.R. 565.

29. *Calder v. Attorney General of British Columbia*, [1973] S.C.R. 313; *Hamlet of Baker Lake v. Minister of Indian Affairs and Northern Development*, [1980] 1 F.C. 518 (T.D.).

30. See, e.g., *Sikyea v. R.*, [1964] S.C.R. 642, and *Kruger and Manuel v. R.*, [1978] 1 S.C.R. 104, respectively.

31. *R. v. Laprise*, [1978] 6 W.W.R. 85 (Sask. C.A.).

32. *R. v. White and Bob* (1965), 52 D.L.R. (2d) 481 (S.C.C.); *R. v. Sutherland*, [1980] 2 S.C.R. 451.

33. *R. v. Kootenay* (1978), 6 Alta. L.R. (2d) 220 (Prov. Ct.).

34. *Myran v. R.*, [1976] 2 S.C.R. 137.

35. *R. v. George*, [1966] S.C.R. 267.

36. *R. v. Taylor and Williams* (1981), 34 O.R. (2d) 360 (C.A.).

37. *R. v. Simon*, [1985] 2 S.C.R. 387.

38. *R. v. Wesley*, [1932] 4 D.L.R. 774 (Alta. C.A.); *R. v. White and Bob* (1965), 52 D.L.R. (2d) 481 (S.C.C.); *R. v. Taylor and Williams*.

39. *R. v. Batisse* (1978), 19 O.R. (2d) 145 (Dist. Ct.).

40. *Nowegijick v. R.*, [1983] 1 S.C.R. 29.

41. *Frank v. R.* (1978), 75 D.L.R. (3d) 481, at 484.

42. *R. v. Horseman*, [1990] 3 C.N.L.R. 95 (S.C.C.).

43. *R. v. Horseman*.

44. *R. v. Eninew; R. v. Bear* (1984), 10 D.L.R. (4th) 137 (Sask. C.A.).

45. *R. v. Horse*, [1985] 1 W.W.R. 1 (Sask C.A.); affirmed on other grounds [1988] 1 S.C.R. 187.

46. See, e.g., *Eastmain Band v. Gilpin*, [1987] 3 C.N.L.R. 54 (Que. Prov. Ct.).

47. *R. v. Sparrow*, [1990] 1 S.C.R. 1075.

48. See, e.g., *R. v. Eninew; R. v. Bear* (1984), 10 D.L.R. (4th) 137 (Sask. C.A.), affirming *R. v. Eninew*, [1984] 2 C.N.L.R. 122 (Sask. Q.B.); and *R. v. Bear*, [1983] 3 C.N.L.R. 57 (Q.B.); *R. v. Martin* (1985), 65 N.B.R. (2d) 21 (Q.B.).

49. *R. v. Hare and Debassige*, [1985] 3 C.N.L.R. 139 (Ont. C.A.).

50. See, e.g., *MacMillan Bloedel v. Mullin; Martin v. The Queen in right of British Columbia,* [1985] 3 W.W.R. 577 (B.C.C.A.) leave to appeal to S.C.C. refused [1985] 5 W.W.R. lxiv.

51. *Guerin v. R.,* [1984] 2 S.C.R. 335, at 379.

52. *R. v. Sparrow,* [1990] 1 S.C.R. 1075, at 1109.

53. See *R. v. Sparrow,* [1987] 2 W.W.R. 577 (B.C.C.A.); *R. v. Agawa,* [1988] 3 C.N.L.R. 73; *R. v. Denny et al.* (1990), 94 N.S.R. (2d) 253 (C.A.), respectively.

54. *R. v. Eninew; R. v. Bear* (1984), 10 D.L.R. (4th) 137 (Sask. C.A.).

55. *R. v. Derriksan,* [1976] 6 W.W.R. 480.

56. *R. v. Sparrow,* [1990] 1 S.C.R. 1075, at 1091.

57. *Ibid.,* at 1093, per C.J.C. Dickson and J. La Forest.

58. *Ibid.,* at 1093, quoting from Brian Slattery, "Understanding Aboriginal Rights," *Canadian Bar Review,* 66 (1987): 727, at 782.

59. *R. v. Sparrow,* [1990] 1 S.C.R. 1075, at 1112.

60. *Ibid.,* at 1105.

61. *Ibid.,* at 1109.

62. *Ibid.,* at 1114.

63. *R. v. Joseph,* [1990] 4 C.N.L.R. 59 (B.C.S.C.).

64. *R. v. Bones,* [1990] 4 C.N.L.R. 37 (B.C. Prov. Ct.).

65. See, e.g., *R. v. George,* [1966] S.C.R. 267.

66. *R. v. Flett,* [1987] 5 W.W.R. 115 (Prov. Ct.), at 121.

67. *R. v. Arcand,* [1989] 2 C.N.L.R. 110 (the federal government filed an appeal but subsequently withdrew it).

68. *R. v. Weremy,* [1943] Ex. C.R. 44.

69. *Kanatewat v. James Bay Development Corp.,* [1974] Que. R.P. 38.

70. (1974–75) 8 C.N.L.R. 414.

71. Information provided by Ken Young, lawyer for the Northern Flood Committee, 21 June 1991.

72. *R. v. Catagas* (1977), 81 D.L.R. (3d) 396 (Man. C.A.); reversing [1977] 3 W.W.R. 282 (Co. Ct.).

73. *R. v. Taylor and Williams* (1981), 34 O.R. (2d) 360 (C.A.).

74. *Reference re Eskimos,* [1939] S.C.R. 104.

75. *R. v. Laprise,* [1978] 6 W.W.R. 85 (Sask. C.A.); *R. v. Budd; R. v. Crane,* [1979] 6 W.W.R. 450 (Sask. Q.B.); *Attorney General of Canada v. Lavell; Isaac v. Bedard,* [1974] S.C.R. 1349.

76. *Attorney General of Canada v. Lavell; Isaac v. Bedard.*

77. *Lovelace v. Canada,* [1981] 2 H.R.L.J. 158.

78. Canada, House of Commons, Special Committee on Indian Self-Government, *Indian Self-Government in Canada* (Penner Report), (Ottawa: Queen's Printer, 1983), p. 64.

Chapter 6 – Manitoba Courts

1. Presentation to Aboriginal Justice Inquiry hearings, 25 April 1989, and Appendix D: Sample Schedule of Court Sittings in Manitoba.

2. Manitoba, Department of the Attorney General, Research and Planning Branch, *Justice in Manitoba: Key Indicators* (Winnipeg, 1988), p. 35.

3. *Ibid.*

4. *Ibid.*

5. *Ibid.*, p. 76.

6. *Criminal Code*, R.S.C. 1985, c. C.-46, subsections 515(10)(a) and 515(10)(b).

7. *Criminal Code*, R.S.C. 1985, c. C.-46, subsection 522(2).

8. Curtis T. Griffiths and Simon N. Verdun-Jones, *Canadian Criminal Justice* (Toronto: Butterworths, 1989), p. 195.

9. Canada, Statistics Canada, Census Canada 1986, *Aboriginal Peoples Output* (Ottawa, 1981), p. 191.

10. Jeremy Hull, *An Overview of Registered Indian Conditions in Manitoba* (Ottawa: Department of Indian and Northern Affairs, 1987), p. xi.

11. Canada, Law Reform Commission, *Study Report: Discovery in Criminal Cases* (Ottawa, 1974).

12. Michael D. Paluk, written presentation to the Aboriginal Justice Inquiry, 14 March 1989.

13. Rick Sloan, *Legal Aid in Manitoba: An Evaluation Report* (Winnipeg: Department of Justice Canada, September 1987), p. 49.

14. Barbara Hendrickson, *A Study of the Operation of the Manitoba Provincial Court in Winnipeg and Selected Northern Communities with Reference to the Treatment of Aboriginal Offenders* (Winnipeg: Manitoba Department of Justice, 1989), p. 103.

15. *R. v. Askov,* [1990] 2 S.C.R. 1199, at 1225–26.

16. Attorney General James McCrae, presentation to Aboriginal Justice Inquiry hearings, 25 April 1989.

17. Canada, Department of Justice, *Some Statistics on the Preliminary Inquiry in Canada,* prepared by David G. Alford, Paul Chumak, Lise Cloutier, David Johnson, and David McKercher (Ottawa, 1984).

18. *Ibid.*, p. 81.

Chapter 7 – Aboriginal Justice Systems

1. See, e.g., Bradford W. Morse, "Native People and Legal Services in Canada," *McGill Law Journal,* 22 (1976): 504–40, at 536; Bradford W. Morse, *Indian Tribal Courts in the United States: A Model for Canada?* (Saskatoon: Native Law Centre, 1980); Rick H. Hemmingson, "Jurisdiction of Future Trial Courts in Canada: Learning from the American Experience," [1988] 2 C.N.L.R. 1; and Paul Havemann, "The Indigenization of Social Control in Canada," in *Indigenous Law and the State,* edited by Bradford W. Morse and Gordon R. Woodman, pp. 71–100 (Dordrecht, Netherlands: Foris Publications, 1988).

2. See, e.g., Paul Williams, "The Covenant Chain," LL.M. thesis, Osgoode Hall Law School, York University, 1982.

3. *Royal Proclamation of 1763*, R.S.C. 1985, App. II, No. l.

4. See, e.g., the *Northwest Ordinance* of 1786 and the *Trade and Intercourse Act* of 1790 (often referred to as the *Nonintercourse Act*), 25 U.S.C. s. 177.

5. *Jackson ex dem Gilbert v. Wood*, 7 Johns. 290 (1810), at 295 (N.Y.S.C.), per Chief Justice Kent.

6. *Ibid.*

7. *Johnson v. M'Intosh*, 21 U.S. (8 Wheat.) 543 (1823), at 574, per Chief Justice Marshall.

8. *Cherokee Nation v. Georgia*, 30 U.S. (5 Pet.) 1 (1831), at 18, per Chief Justice Marshall.

9. *Worcester v. Georgia*, 31 U.S. (6 Pet.) 515 (1832), at 559–60.

10. *Worcester v. Georgia*, at 560–61. This decision has been criticized in recent years for interpreting the congressional plenary power too broadly so as to leave Indian sovereignty improperly open to interference. See, e.g., Steven Paul McSloy, "American Indians and the Constitution: An Argument for Nationhood," *American Indian Law Review*, 17 (1989): 139.

11. J. Youngblood Henderson and Russel L. Barsh, "Oyate kin haye keyuga u pe, Part II: The Courts and the Indian Tribes," *Harvard Law School Bulletin*, 25, 10 (1974).

12. For a more detailed review of these issues, see, e.g., Felix S. Cohen, *Handbook of Federal Indian Law* (Washington, D.C.: U.S. Government Printing Office, 1942; reprint ed., Albuquerque: University of New Mexico Press, 1972); Kirke Kickingbird et al., *Indian Sovereignty* (Washington, D.C.: Institute for the Development of Indian Law, 1977); *Indian Tribes as Sovereign Governments* (Oakland, California: American Indian Resources Institute Press, 1988); and Charles F. Wilkinson, *American Indians, Time, and the Law* (New Haven, Connecticut: Yale University Press, 1987).

13. For examples of studies of specific Indian nations, see E. Adamson Hoebel, *The Cheyennes: Indians of the Great Plains* (New York: Holt, Rinehart and Winston, 1960); Karl N. Llewellyn and E. Adamson Hoebel, *The Cheyenne Way: Conflict and Case Law in Primitive Jurisprudence* (Norman, Oklahoma: University of Oklahoma Press, 1961); Robert H. Lowie, "Property Rights and Coercive Powers of Plains Indian Military Societies," *Journal of Law and Political Science*, 1 (1943): 59; William B. Newell, *Crime and Justice among the Iroquois Nations* (Montreal: Caughnawaga Historical Society, 1965); John A. Noon, *Law and Government of the Grand River Iroquois* (New York: Johnson Reprint Corp., 1964); John Phillip Reid, *A Law of Blood: The Primitive Law of the Cherokee Nation* (New York: New York University Press, 1970); Jane Richardson, *Law and Status among the Kiowa Indians* (Seattle: University of Washington Press, 1966); Rennard Strickland, *Fire and the Spirits: Cherokee Law from Clan to Court* (Norman, Oklahoma: University of Oklahoma Press, 1975); and Elias Johnson, *Legends, Traditions, and Laws of the Iroquois or Six Nations, and History of the Tuscarora Indians* (Lockport, New York: Union Printing and Publishing Co., 1881; reprint ed., New York: AMS Press, 1978).

14. *Ex parte Crow Dog*, 109 U.S. 556 (1883), at 568–69.

15. *Ibid.*, at 571. For an exhaustive review of the historical background of this case, see Sidney L. Harring, "Crow Dog's Case: A Chapter in the Legal History of Tribal Sovereignty," *American Indian Law Review*, 17 (1989): 191–239.

16. Quoted in J.E. Chamberlin, *The Harrowing of Eden: White Attitudes Towards North American Natives* (Toronto: Fitzhenry and Whiteside, 1975), p. 217.

17. For a thorough review of this initiative, see William T. Hagan, *Indian Police and Judges: Experiments in Acculturation and Control* (New Haven, Connecticut: Yale University Press, 1966). A major rationale for their creation was to serve as a "civilizing force." Even the policeman's appearance was to reflect this purpose as he was "supposed to give up his long braids, cease painting his face, trade moccasins for boots, and eschew any other outward manifestation of the blanketed Indian" (Hagan, p. 70). See also Robert Young, *Historical Backgrounds for Modern Indian Law and Order* (Washington, D.C.: Bureau of Indian Affairs, 1969), and *Indian Law Enforcement History* (Washington, D.C.: Bureau of Indian Affairs, 1975).

18. The jurisdiction is set out in 25 C.F.R. ss. 11.1 et seq.

19. *Act of June 18, 1934,* Pub. L. No. 73–383, c. 576, 48 Stat. 984.

20. *Act of August 15, 1953,* c. 505, 67 Stat. 588, as amended 18 U.S.C. s. 1162 and U.S.C. s. 1360.

21. *Ibid.*

22. *Indian Tribes as Sovereign Governments,* pp. 41–43.

23. *Native American Tribal Court Profiles* (Washington, D.C.: Judicial Services Branch, Bureau of Indian Affairs, 1985). These totals do not include the peacemaker courts that function under New York state law or most of the purely "conservation courts" functioning in parts of the United States.

24. *Ibid.*

25. The Bureau of Indian Affairs figures varied from 91 courts (17 CFR courts, 58 tribal courts and 16 traditional courts) in *Indian Reservation Criminal Justice Task Force Analysis, 1974–75* (Washington, D.C.: Bureau of Indian Affairs, 1975) to 111 courts in *Indian Criminal Justice Program Display* (Washington, D.C.: Bureau of Indian Affairs, 1974). The number had jumped to 140 by 1982, with 24 CFR courts, 13 traditional courts and 103 tribal courts including several intertribal courts. See *Native American Tribal Court Profiles* (Washington, D.C.: Judicial Services Branch, Bureau of Indian Affairs, 1982).

26. 25 U.S.C. ss. 1301–1341 as amended Pub. L. 99–570, Title IV, ss. 4217, 27 October 1986, 100 Stat. 3207–146.

27. 25 U.S.C. ss. 1901–1963.

28. 18 U.S.C. s. 1151.

29. *The General Allotment Act* of 1887, 25 U.S.C. ss. 331–334, 339, 341–342, 348–349, 354 and 381.

30. See, e.g., *Solem v. Barlett,* 465 U.S. 463 (1984), and *DeCoteau v. District County Court,* 420 U.S. 425 (1975).

31. *DeCoteau v. District County Court,* 420 U.S. 425 (1975); *Moe v. Confederated Salish and Kootenai Tribes,* 425 U.S. 463 (1976).

32. *National Farmers Union Insurance Co. v. Crow Tribe of Indians,* 471 U.S. 845 (1985).

33. See also *Kennerly v. District Court,* 400 U.S. 423 (1971).

34. *Washington v. Confederated Tribes of the Colville Indian Reservation,* 447 U.S. 134 (1980).

35. *Merrion v. Jicarilla Apache Tribe,* 455 U.S. 130 (1982).

36. *Ibid.,* at 148.

37. *Kerr-McGee Corp. v. Navajo Tribe,* 105 S. Ct. 1900 (1985).

38. *Montana v. Blackfeet Tribe of Indians,* 105 S. Ct. 2399 (1985).

39. *McClanahan v. Arizona State Tax Commission,* 411 U.S. 164 (1973).

40. *Montana v. United States,* 450 U.S. 544 (1981).

41. *Knight v. Shoshone and Arapahoe Indian Tribes*, 670 F. (2d) 900 (10th Circ.) (1982).

42. *Cardin v. De La Cruz*, 671 F. (2d) 363 (9th Circ.) (1982); cert. denied 459 U.S. 967 (1982).

43. *Confederated Salish and Kootenai Tribes v. Namen*, 665 F. (2d) 951 (9th Circ.) (1982); cert. denied 459 U.S. 977 (1982).

44. *Oliphant v. Suquamish Indian Tribe*, 435 U.S. 191 (1978). For a discussion of the significance of this case, see John A. Vaskov, "Indians Rights—What's Left? Oliphant Tribal Courts and Non-Indians," *University of Pittsburgh Law Review*, 41 (1979-80): 75–88; Catherine Baker-Stetson, "Decriminalizing Tribal Codes: A Response to Oliphant," *American Indian Law Review*, 9 (1981): 51–81; and Russel L. Barsh and James Youngblood Henderson, "The Betrayal: *Oliphant v. Suquamish Indian Tribe* and the Hunting of the Shark," *Minnesota Law Review*, 63 (1979): 609–40.

45. *Duro v. Reina et al.* (U.S.S.C., unreported, 29 May 1990) reversing 821 F. (2d) 1358 (9th Circ.) (1987) and 851 F. (2d) 1136 (9th Circ.) (1988). This result agrees with *Greywater et al. v. Joshua et al.*, 846 F. (2d) 486 (8th Circ.) (1988).

46. 18 U.S.C. s. 1152 (also referred to as the *Indian Country Crimes Act*, the *Interracial Crime Provision* and the *Federal Enclave Statute*).

47. 18 U.S.C.A. s. 13.

48. *Ex parte Crow Dog*, 109 U.S. 556 (1883), at 568–69.

49. Title WE of the *Indian Civil Rights Act* is codified at 25 U.S.C.A. ss. 1301–1303.

50. *Ibid.*, s. 1301(1).

51. *Ibid.*, s. 1301(3).

52. *Ibid.*, s. 1301(2).

53. Pub. L. 99–570, Title IV, s. 4217, 27 October 1986, 100 Stat. 3207–146.

54. *Indian Civil Rights Act*, s. 1303.

55. *Dodge v. Nakai*, 298 F. Supp. 26 (D. Ariz.) (1969).

56. For further information on this body of case law, see "Note: Implication of Civil Remedies under the Indian Civil Rights Act," *Michigan Law Review*, 75 (1970): 210–35.

57. This case has sparked a considerable level of commentary within the legal literature as well as among Indian people. For further analysis of the judgment and its implications, see Michael N. Deegan, "Closing the Door to Federal Court," *Land and Water Law Review*, 14 (1979): 625–34. Gregory Schultz, "The Federal Due Process and Equal Protection Rights of Non-Indian Civil Litigants in Tribal Courts after *Santa Clara Pueblo v. Martinez*," *Denver University Law Review*, 62 (1985): 761–87; and Richard B. Collins, "Implied Limitations on the Jurisdiction of Indian Tribes," *Washington Law Review*, 54 (1979): 479–529.

58. *Indian Civil Rights Act*, s. 1302(6).

59. *Ibid.*

60. *Native American Tribal Court Profiles*, 1985, at 144.

61. *Ibid.*, at 139.

62. *Ibid.*, at 62.

63. *Ibid.*, at 108.

64. *Ibid.*, at 34.

65. David E. Wilkins, *Dine Bibeehaz'acnii—A Handbook of Navajo Government* (Tsaile, Arizona: Navajo Community College Press, 1987), p. xv.

66. See *Native American Tribal Court Profiles*, 1985, at 144, regarding the Jamestown Klallam Tribe in Sequim, Washington.

67. *Ibid.*

68. David Getches, ed., *Indian Courts and the Future* (Washington, D.C.: National American Indian Court Judges Association, 1978).

69. For further information on this matter, see Frank Pommersheim, "The Contextual Legitimacy of Adjudication in Tribal Courts and the Role of the Tribal Bar as an Interpretive Community: An Essay," *New Mexico Law Review*, 18 (1988): 49.

70. See James W. Zion, "The Navajo Peacemaker Court: Deference to the Old and Accommodation to the New," *American Indian Law Review*, 11 (1984–85): 89–109.

71. See "Developments in the Law—Race and the Criminal Process," *Harvard Law Review*, 101 (1988): 1472–1641.

72. See, e.g., K. Bliss Adams, "Order in the Courts: Resolution of Tribal/State Criminal Jurisdictional Disputes," *Tulsa Law Journal*, 24 (1988): 89; Gordon K. Wright, "Recognition of Tribal Decisions in the State Courts," *Stanford Law Review*, 37 (1984–85): 1397–1424; and William V. Vetter, "Of Tribal Courts and 'Territories': Is Full Faith and Credit Required?" *California and Western Law Review*, 23 (1987): 219–72.

73. See Zion, "Navajo Peacemaker Court," p. 89.

74. Moana Jackson, *The Maori and the Criminal Justice System: A New Perspective: He Whaipaanga Hou, Part 2* (Wellington, New Zealand: Department of Justice, 1988).

75. Australian Law Reform Commission, *The Recognition of Aboriginal Customary Laws*, Report No. 31, 2 vols. (Canberra: Australian Government Publishing Service, 1986).

76. *Ibid.*

77. For a rare study of traditional Aboriginal justice in operation at the community level in Australia, see Nancy M. Williams, *Two Laws: Managing Disputes in a Contemporary Aboriginal Community* (Canberra: Australian Institute of Aboriginal Studies, 1987).

78. For further information on this general subject, see Kayleen M. Hazlehurst, ed., *Justice Programs for Aboriginal and Other Indigenous Communities* (Canberra: Australian Institute of Criminology, 1985), for an excellent collection of essays, including Annie Hoddinot, "Aboriginal Justices of the Peace and Public Law," p. 171, and H.C. Coombs, "The Yirrkala Proposals for the Control of Law and Order," p. 201; Bruce Swanton, ed., *Aborigines and Criminal Justice* (Canberra: Australian Institute of Criminology, 1984); Peter K. Hennessy, *Aboriginal Customary Law and Local Justice Mechanisms: Principles, Options and Proposals*, Research Paper No. 11/12 (Canberra: Australian Law Reform Commission, 1984); and Kayleen M. Hazlehurst, ed., *Ivory Scales: Black Australia and the Law* (Kensington, N.S.W.: New South Wales University Press, 1987).

79. *An Act to amend "The Indian Act, 1880,"* S.C. 1881, c. 17, s. 12.

80. *An Act to further amend "The Indian Act, 1880,"* S.C. 1882, c. 30, s. 3.

81. *An Act to further amend "The Indian Act, 1880,"* S.C. 1884, c. 27, ss. 22 and 23.

82. *Ibid.*, s. 23.

83. *Ibid.*

84. *Indian Act*, R.S.C. 1886, c. 43, s. 177.

85. R.S.C. 1886, c. 157.

86. *An Act to further amend "The Indian Act, Chapter Forty-three of the Revised Statutes,"* S.C. 1890, c. 29, s. 9.

87. *Criminal Code, 1892,* S.C. 1892, c. 29.

88. *An Act to further amend "The Indian Act,"* S.C. 1894, c. 32, s. 8.

89. *Criminal Code, 1892,* s. 190.

90. *Ibid.,* s. 98.

91. *Ibid.*

92. *Indian Act,* S.C. 1951, c. 29, s. 105.

93. *Ibid.,* s. 106.

94. For a review of this jurisprudence and the subject generally, see Bradford W. Morse, "A Unique Court: S. 107 Indian Act Justices of the Peace," *Canadian Legal Aid Bulletin,* 5, 2–3 (1982): 139–43.

95. *Ibid.,* at 143–44.

96. See, e.g., *R. v. Jimmy,* [1987] 5 W.W.R. 755 (B.C.C.A.); and *R. v. Sacobie* (1987), 182 A.P.R. 430 (N.B.C.A.).

97. It is possible, of course, for a by-law or regulation to limit its application to certain classes of people, such as band members only. For an example of a limitation to Indian and non-Indian residents of a reserve, see *Indian Health Regulations,* C.R.C. 1987, c. 955, s. 3.

98. "Natives enjoy taste of tribal justice," *Toronto Star,* 8 July 1990.

99. Presentation to Aboriginal Justice Inquiry hearings by the Assembly of Manitoba Chiefs, 22 November 1989.

100. *Native American Tribal Court Profiles,* 1985.

101. Bradford Morse and Linda Lock, *Native Offenders' Perceptions of the Criminal Justice System* (Ottawa: Policy, Programs and Research Branch, Department of Justice, 1988), p. 22.

102. At the time of writing, this bill was not passed into law.

103. Bryan A. Keon-Cohen, "Native Justice in Australia, Canada, and the U.S.A.: A Comparative Analysis," *Canadian Legal Aid Bulletin,* 5, 1 (1982): 187-258, at 189; an earlier version of this article also appeared in *Monash Law Review,* 7 (1981): 250.

104. Canada, House of Commons, Special Committee on Indian Self-Government, *Indian Self-Government in Canada* (Penner Report), (Ottawa: Queen's Printer, 1983). At least one Canadian judge has recognized a right of self-government in reference to the Cree of James Bay in *Eastmain Band v. Gilpin,* [1987] 3 C.N.L.R. 54 (Que. Prov. Ct.).

105. For further information on this point, see, e.g., Bradford W. Morse and Gordon Woodman, eds. *Indigenous Law and the State* (Dordrecht, Netherlands: Foris Publications, 1988); M.B. Hooker, *Legal Pluralism: An Introduction to Colonial and Neo-Colonial Laws* (Oxford: Clarendon Press, 1975); and Australian Law Reform Commission, *The Recognition of Aboriginal Customary Laws.*

106. Bradford W. Morse, "Indian and Inuit Family Law and the Canadian Legal System," *American Indian Law Review,* 8 (1980): 199–257.

107. James Zion, "Searching for Indian Common Law," in Morse and Woodman, *Indigenous Law,* p. 121, and "Harmony among the People: Torts and Indian Courts," *Montana Law Review,* 45 (1984): 265–79.

108. See, e.g., Morse, "Indian and Inuit," and Michael Coyle, "Traditional Indian Justice in Ontario: A Role for the Present?" *Osgoode Hall Law Journal,* 24 (1986): 605–33.

109. In this situation the courts have held the land to be part of the reserve and exempt from provincial and municipal land-related legislation. See, e.g., *Corporation of Surrey et al. v. Peace Arch Enterprises* (1970), 74 W.W.R. 380 (B.C.C.A.), which has been cited with approval by the Supreme Court of Canada on several occasions.

110. There are many such enclaves in reserves across the country that were created as a result of enfranchisement of band members; of dedication as church or government lands; because they were once railway lines, public roads or right-of-ways that have since been closed; or because they were lands expropriated by the Crown in right of Canada, the provincial government or a public authority with the power to expropriate (see, e.g., s. 35 of the current *Indian Act*).

111. See, e.g, *Guerin v. R.*, [1984] 2 S.C.R. 335; and *R. v. Sparrow*, [1990] 1 S.C.R. 1075.

112. *Ibid.*

Chapter 8 – Court Reform

1. *Report of the Provincial Criminal Court Judges' Special Committee on Criminal Justice in Ontario* (Vanek Report), 1987, pp. 30–31, in *Toward a Unified Criminal Court*, Law Reform Commission of Canada (Ottawa, 1989), p. 12.

2. *American Bar Association Standards Relating to Trial Courts*, approved by the American Bar Association House of Delegates, August 1984.

3. *Mills v. The Queen*, [1986] 1 S.C.R. 938–39.

4. Manitoba, Department of the Attorney General, *Annual Report of the Manitoba Department of the Attorney General, 1988–89* (Winnipeg, 1989), Tables 9, 13, 14, 15 on pp. 67–69. Federal information provided by telephone by Audrey MacDonnell of the Correctional Services of Canada, April 1991.

5. Canada, Statistics Canada, Canadian Centre for Justice Statistics, *Adult Correctional Services in Canada: 1988–89* (Ottawa: Supply and Services Canada, 1989), p. 58.

6. *Ibid.*, p. 68.

7. Rick Sloan, *Legal Aid in Manitoba: A Evaluation Report* (Winnipeg: Department of Justice Canada, September 1987), p. 191.

Chapter 9 – Juries

1. *Report on the Jury*, Canada, Law Reform Commission, (Ottawa: Supply and Services Canada, 1982), p. 5.

2. *An Act to Amend the Jury Act*, S.N.W.T. 1986 (1), c. 7.

3. In the Northwest Territories *An Ordinance to Recognize and Provide for the Use of the Aboriginal Languages and to Establish the Official Languages of the Northwest Territories*, O.N.W.T. 1984 (2), c. 2, s. 5, recognizes a number of Aboriginal languages as official languages of the NWT. The federal *Official Languages Act*, R.S.C. 1985, c. O-3, s. 2, of course, makes French and English the official languages of Canada. The territorial law supplements the federal law.

Chapter 10 – Alternatives to Incarceration

1. Lord Hailsham, *Halsbury's Laws of England*, 4th ed. (London: Butterworths, 1976), p. 288.

2. Curtis T. Griffiths and Simon N. Verdun-Jones, *Canadian Criminal Justice* (Toronto: Butterworths, 1989).

3. R.G. Hann et al., *Sentencing Practices and Trends in Canada: A Summary of Statistical Information* (Ottawa: Department of Justice Canada, 1983).

4. Canada, Correctional Service of Canada, *Basic Facts about Corrections in Canada* (Ottawa: Supply and Services Canada, 1986), pp. 9–10.

5. *Ibid.*

6. Canada, Statistics Canada, Canadian Centre for Justice Statistics, *Adult Correctional Services in Canada, 1988–89* (Ottawa: Supply and Services Canada, 1989), p. 59.

7. *Ibid.*, p. 67.

8. *Ibid.*, p. 66.

9. Canada, Statistics Canada, Canadian Centre for Justice Statistics, *Adult Correctional Services in Canada, 1987–88* (Ottawa: Supply and Services Canada, 1988) pp. 63 and 96.

10. John H. Hylton, "Locking Up Indians in Saskatchewan: Some Recent Findings," *Canadian Ethnic Studies*, 13, 3 (1981): 145.

11. R.M. Martinson, "What Works? Questions and Answers about Prison Reform," *The Public Interest*, 35 (1974): 22–54.

12. Griffiths and Verdun-Jones, *Criminal Justice*, p. 401.

13. Canada, Parliamentary Sub-Committee on the Penitentiary System in Canada (Mark MacGuigan, Chair), *Report to Parliament by the Sub-Committee on the Penitentiary System in Canada* (Ottawa: Supply and Services Canada, 1977), p. 35.

14. Canada, Canadian Sentencing Commission, *Sentencing Reform: A Canadian Approach* (Ottawa: Supply and Services Canada, 1987).

15. G.S. Bridges and J.A. Stone, "Effects of Criminal Punishment on Perceived Threat of Punishment: Toward an Understanding of Specific Deterrence," *Journal of Research on Crime and Delinquency*, 23 (1986): 207–39.

16. L.H. Bowker, *Corrections—The Science and the Art* (New York: Macmillan, 1982), p. 155.

17. Canada, Correctional Services of Canada, Regional Office in Saskatoon, *Annual Report of the Manitoba Department of the Attorney General, 1988–89* (Winnipeg, 1989), pp. 58–68.

18. Canadian Sentencing Commission, *Sentencing Reform*.

19. Anthony M. Doob, "Community Sanctions and Imprisonment: Hoping for a Miracle But Not Bothering to Even Pray for It," *Canadian Journal of Criminology*, 32, 3 (July 1990): 415–28.

20. Canadian Sentencing Commission, *Sentencing Reform*, p. xxiv.

21. *R. v. Naqitarvik* (1986), 26 C.C.C. (3d) 193 (N.W.T.C.A.).

22. *Ibid.*, at 205.

23. *Ibid.*, at 200.

24. *Ibid.*

25. Carol LaPrairie, "The Role of Sentencing in the Over-representation of Aboriginal People in Correctional Institutions," *Canadian Journal of Criminology*, 32, 3 (July 1990): 429–40.

26. Canadian Sentencing Commission, *Sentencing Reform*, p. xxiv.

27. *Ibid.*, p. 154.

28. R.G. Moyles, *British Law and Arctic Men* (Saskatoon: Western Producer Prairie Books, 1979), p. 38.

29. *R. v. Fireman*, [1971] 3 O.R. 380 (C.A.).

30. In B.A. Grossman, ed., *New Directions in Sentencing* (Toronto: Butterworths, 1980), p. 305.

31. P. Nadin-Davis, *Sentencing in Canada* (Ottawa: Carswell, 1982), p. 125.

32. Jean Barman, Yvonne Hebert and Don McCaskill, eds., *Indian Education in Canada, Vol. 2: The Challenge* (Vancouver: University of British Columbia Press, 1986), p. 156.

33. Canada, Department of Justice, *Fact Book on Community Service Order Programs in Canada* (Ottawa: 1986), p. 2.

34. Information in this paragraph is based on a memorandum to the Aboriginal Justice Inquiry from Ron Robinson, Coordinator of Information Systems, Corrections, Winnipeg, 19 March 1991.

35. Barbara Hendrickson, *A Study of the Operation of the Manitoba Provincial Court in Winnipeg and Selected Northern Communities with Reference to the Treatment of Aboriginal Offenders* (Winnipeg: Manitoba Department of Justice, 1989).

36. J.W. Ekstedt and M.A. Jackson, *A Profile of Canadian Alternative Sentencing Programmes: A National Review of Policy Issues* (Burnaby, B.C.: School of Criminology, Simon Fraser University, 1986); J. Bonta et al., "Restitution in Correctional Halfway Houses: Victim Satisfaction, Attitudes and Recidivism," *Canadian Journal of Criminology*, 25 (1983): 277–93.

37. R.E. Kimball, "In the Matter of Judicial Discretion and the Imposition of Default Orders," *Criminal Law Quarterly*, 32 (September 1990): 467–77.

38. Statistics received from telephone conversation with the Saskatchewan Department of Justice, 21 July 1991.

Chapter 11 – Jails

1. Indigenous Women's Collective, "Aboriginal Women's Perspective of the Justice System in Manitoba," research paper prepared for the Aboriginal Justice Inquiry, Winnipeg, June 1990, pp. 48–49.

2. See, e.g., S.E. Doeren and M.J. Hageman, *Community Corrections* (Cincinnati, Ohio: Anderson Publishing, 1982).

3. Canada, Department of the Solicitor General, *Report of the Task Force on Aboriginal Peoples in Federal Corrections* (Ottawa, 1988), pp. 23–24.

4. Curtis T. Griffiths and Simon N. Verdun-Jones, *Canadian Criminal Justice* (Toronto: Butterworths, 1989).

5. Canada, Statistics Canada, Canadian Centre for Justice Statistics, *Adult Correctional Services in Canada: 1988–1989* (Ottawa: Supply and Services Canada, 1989), p. 54.

6. *Ibid.*, p. 55.

7. "Chaplains Contribute to Total Well-Being," *Corrections Community* (Newsletter of the Corrections Branch of the Department of Justice), 7, 1 (December 1990–February 1991).

8. *Brown and Hunter v. R.* (29 November 1990, unreported), p. 5.

9. Canada, Correctional Investigator, *Annual Report of the Correctional Investigator 1988–1989* (Ottawa: Supply and Services Canada, 1990), p. 27.

Chapter 12 – Parole

1. Canada, Department of the Solicitor General, *Report of the Task Force on Aboriginal Peoples in Federal Corrections* (Ottawa, 1988), p. 5.

2. See, e.g., D.P. Cole and A. Manson, *Release from Imprisonment: The Law of Sentencing, Parole and Judicial Review* (Toronto: Carswell, 1990); L. Newby, *Native Peoples of Canada and the Federal Corrections System: Development of a National Policy—A Preliminary Issues Report* (Ottawa: Correctional Services of Canada, 1981); Brian D. MacLean and R.S. Ratner, "An Historical Analysis of Bills C-67 and C-68: Implications for the Native Offender," *Native Studies Review*, 3 (1987): 31–58.

3. Canada, Royal Commission to Investigate the Penal System of Canada, *Report* (Archambault Report), (Ottawa: King's Printer, 1938).

4. Canada, Committee Appointed to Enquire into the Principles and Procedures Followed in the Remission Service of the Department of Justice, *Report* (Fauteux Report), (Ottawa: Queen's Printer, 1956).

5. Canada, Canadian Committee on Corrections, *Toward Unity: Criminal Justice and Corrections* (Ouimet Report), (Ottawa: Queen's Printer, 1969), pp. 348–51.

6. MacLean and Ratner, "Historical Analysis," p. 43.

7. Canada, National Parole Board, *Mission Statement* (Ottawa: Department of the Solicitor General, 1987), p. 1.

8. *Parole Act*, R.S.C. 1985, c. P-2, s. 8(1).

9. Canada, National Parole Board, *A Guide to the Parole Act and Regulations*, revised and updated edition of the *National Parole Board Handbook for Judges and Crown Attorneys* (Ottawa, 1988), pp. 11–15.

10. Canada, Statistics Canada, Canadian Centre for Justice Statistics, *Adult Correctional Services in Canada: 1988–89* (Ottawa, 1989), p. 132.

11. Lisa Hobbs Birnie, *A Rock and a Hard Place: Inside Canada's Parole Board* (Toronto: Macmillan, 1990) p. 197.

12. *Ibid.*, p. 196.

13. *Ibid.*, p. 197.

14. *Ibid.*

15. Canada, National Parole Board, *Briefing Book for Members of the Standing Committee on Justice and Solicitor General*, vol.1 (Ottawa,1987), p.18.

16. Canada, National Parole Board, *Pre- and Post-Release Decision Policies*, interim ed. (Ottawa, December 1988), p.13.

17. Canada, Department of the Solicitor General, *Report of the Task Force on the Release of Inmates* (Hugesson Report), (Ottawa, 1972).

18. Canada, Department of the Solicitor General, *Solicitor General's Study of Conditional Release: Report of the Working Group* (Ottawa: Supply and Services Canada, 1981).

19. Don McCaskill, *Studies of Needs and Resources Related to Offenders of Native Origin in Manitoba* (Ottawa: Department of the Solicitor General, 1971).

20. Gail Michalis and William T. Badcock, *Native People and Canada's Justice System* (Ottawa: Department of Indian and Northern Affairs, 1979).

21. Carolyn Canfield and Linda Drinnan, *Comparative Statistics on Native and Non-Native Inmates—A Five Year History* (Ottawa: Correctional Service of Canada, 1981).

22. *Report of the Task Force on Aboriginal People in Federal Corrections.*

Chapter 13 – Aboriginal Women

1. Indigenous Women's Collective, "Aboriginal Women's Perspective of the Justice System in Manitoba," research paper prepared for the Aboriginal Justice Inquiry, Winnipeg, June, 1990, pp. 18–22.

2. Paula Gunn Allen, *Sacred Hoop: Restoring the Feminine to Native American Tradition* (Boston: Beacon Press, 1986), p. 45.

3. Children's Hospital Child Protection Centre, *A New Justice for Indian Children* (Final Report of the Child Advocacy Project, prepared by S. Longstaffe and B. Hamilton), (Winnipeg: Department of the Solicitor General of Canada, 1987), p. 8.

4. Carol LaPrairie, "Native Women and Crime in Canada: A Theoretical Model," in *Too Few to Count: Canadian Women in Conflict with the Law,* edited by Ellen Adelberg and Claudia Currie (Vancouver: Press Gang Publishers, 1987), p. 107.

5. Fran Sugar and Lana Fox, *Survey of Federally Sentenced Aboriginal Women in the Community* (Ottawa: Native Women's Association of Canada, 1990), p. 18.

6. Kathleen Jamieson, *Indian Women and the Law in Canada: Citizens Minus*, Canadian Action Committee on the Status of Women (Ottawa: Supply and Services Canada, 1978).

7. Emma LaRocque, written presentation to Aboriginal Justice Inquiry hearings, 5 February 1990.

8. Allen, *Sacred Hoop*, pp. 192–93.

9. P.M. White, *Native Women: A Statistical Overview* (Ottawa: Supply and Services Canada, 1985), p. 15.

10. Jeremy Hull, *An Overview of Registered Indian Conditions in Manitoba* (Ottawa: Department of Indian and Northern Affairs, 1987), p. 98.

11. Janet Spence Fontaine, "Native Perspective on Rape," presentation to the Northern Conference on Sexual Assault, Thompson, Manitoba, 23 October 1987, p. 3.

12. LaRocque, 5 February 1990 presentation.

13. Thompson Crisis Centre, presentation to Aboriginal Justice Inquiry hearings, Thompson, Manitoba, 21 September 1988.

14. Ontario Native Women's Association, *Breaking Free: A Proposal for Change to Aboriginal Family Violence* (Thunder Bay, December 1989), p. 19.

15. Thompson Crisis Centre, 21 September 1988 presentation.

16. Mona Brown et al., *Gender Equality in the Courts—Criminal Law: A Study by the Manitoba Association of Women and the Law* (Ottawa: National Association of Women and the Law, March 1991), pp. 2–4.

17. *Ibid.*, pp. 3–11.

18. Thompson Crisis Centre, 21 September 1988 presentation.

19. "Conjugal Violence Against Women," *Juristat* (Statistics Canada), 10, 7 (May 1990): 1–2, at 2.

20. Thompson Crisis Centre, 21 September 1988 presentation.

21. Children's Hospital Child Protection Centre, *New Justice*, p. 1.

22. *Ibid.*, p. 27.

23. *Ibid.*, p. 23.

24. *Ibid.*, p. 27.

25. *Ibid.*, pp. 25–26.

26. Elizabeth Fry Society, presentation to Aboriginal Justice Inquiry hearings, Winnipeg, 16 November 1988.

27. John H. Hylton, "Locking Up Indians in Saskatchewan: Some Recent Findings," *Canadian Ethnic Studies*, 13, 3 (1981): 144–51, at 145.

28. Sugar and Fox, *Federally Sentenced Aboriginal Women*, pp. 6–7.

29. *Ibid.*, p. 8.

30. LaPrairie, "Native Women," p. 109.

31. *Ibid.*, p. 104.

32. Gayle Campbell, "Women and Crime," *Juristat* (Statistics Canada), 10, 20 (December 1990): 1–9, at 4.

33. Presentation to Aboriginal Justice Inquiry hearings, Winnipeg, 22 November 1989.

34. Canada, House of Commons, Standing Committee on Justice and Solicitor General (David Daubney, Chair), *Taking Responsibility* (Report on Its Review of Sentencing, Conditional Release and Related Aspects of Corrections), (Ottawa: Queen's Printer, 1988), p. 237.

35. Allison Morris, *Women, Crime and Criminal Justice* (New York: Basil Blackwell, 1987).

36. Canada, Correctional Service of Canada, *Creating Choices, The Report of the Task Force on Federally Sentenced Women* (Ottawa, 1990).

37. *Ibid.*, p. 110.

38. Ikwewak Justice Committee, presentation to the Aboriginal Justice Inquiry hearings, Winnipeg, 14 September 1988.

Chapter 14 – Child Welfare

1. Nicholas Bala, "The History of Child Protection in Canada," in *Canadian Child Welfare Law: Children, Families and the State*, edited by Nicholas Bala, Joseph P. Hornick and Robin Vogl (Toronto: Thompson Educational Publishing, 1991), p. 2.

2. *Ibid.*

3. *Ibid.*, pp. 2–3.

4. Jean Barman, Yvonne Hebert and Don McCaskill, eds., *Indian Education in Canada, Vol. I: The Legacy* (Vancouver: University of British Columbia Press, 1986), p. 2.

5. *Ibid.*

6. Bruce G. Trigger, *The Children of Aataentsic: A History of the Huron People to 1660* (Montreal and Kingston: McGill-Queen's University Press, 1976), p. 378.

7. *Ibid.*, p. 47.

8. Barman, Hebert and McCaskill, *Indian Education in Canada*, p. 3.

9. E.P. Patterson, *The Canadian Indian: A History since 1500* (Don Mills: Collier-Macmillan, 1972), p. 72.

10. Kahn-Tineta Miller and George Lerchs, *The Historical Development of the Indian Act* (Ottawa: Treaties and Historical Research Branch, Department of Indian Affairs and Northern Development, 1978), p. 114.

11. Canada, Department of Indian Affairs and Northern Development, *Annual Report* (Ottawa, 1976), p. 6.

12. N.F. Davin, "Report on Industrial Schools for Indians and Halfbreeds" (Ottawa: Public Archives, 14 March 1879), PAC RG 10, Vol. 6001, File 1-1-1, Part 1.

13. *Ibid.*

14. Cited in J.R. Miller, *Skyscrapers Hide the Heavens: A History of Indian-White Relations in Canada* (Toronto: University of Toronto Press, 1989), pp. 206–7.

15. Celia Haig-Brown, *Resistance and Renewal: Surviving the Indian Residential School* (Vancouver: Tillacum Library, 1988), p. 67.

16. Randy Fred, "Introduction," in *Ibid.*, pp. 1–2.

17. Haig-Brown, *Resistance and Renewal*, p. 28.

18. Patrick Johnston, *Native Children and the Child Welfare System* (Toronto: Lorimer, 1983), p. 2.

19. *Ibid.*, pp. 2–3.

20. Canadian Welfare Council and Canadian Association of Social Workers, *Joint Submission to the Special Joint Committee of the Senate and the House of Commons Appointed to Examine and Consider the Indian Act* (Ottawa: Canadian Welfare Council, 1947), p. 3.

21. *Ibid.*, p. 6.

22. *Indian Act*, R.S.C. 1970, c. 1–6, s. 88.

23. H.B. Hawthorn, ed., *A Survey of the Contemporary Indians of Canada: A Report on Economic, Political, Educational Needs and Policies*, vols. 1 and 2 (Ottawa: Canada Department of Indian Affairs and Northern Development, 1966), p. 327.

24. Johnston, *Native Children*, p. 23.

25. *Ibid.*, p. 57.

26. *Ibid.*, p. 24.

27. *Ibid.*, p. 62.

28. Manitoba, Department of Health and Social Development, *Report of the Indian Child Welfare Sub-Committee, Manitoba, to the Tripartite Committee* (Winnipeg, 1980), p. 1.

29. *Director of Child Welfare for Manitoba v. B*, [1979] 6 W.W.R. 229 (Man. Prov. Ct.), at 237.

30. Department of Health and Social Development, *Indian Child Welfare*, pp. 11–13.

31. *Ibid.*

32. *Ibid.*, pp. 15–29.

33. *Ibid.*, p. 13.

34. Johnston, *Native Children*, p. 111.

35. *Ibid.*, p. 23.

36. Edwin C. Kimelman et al., *No Quiet Place*, Review Committee on Indian and Metis Adoptions and Placements (Winnipeg: Manitoba Department of Community Services, 1985), pp. 272–73.

37. *Ibid.*, p. 196.

38. *Ibid.*, pp. 275–76.

39. *Ibid.*, p. 185.

40. *Ibid.*, p. 361.

41. *Ibid.*, pp. 277–78.

42. *Ibid.*, pp. iii–xxxviii.

43. Thomas R. Berger, "Introduction," in *The Challenge of Child Welfare* by Kenneth L. Levitt and Brian Wharf (Vancouver: University of British Columbia Press, 1985), p. vii.

44. Johnston, *Native Children*, p. 109.

45. Carroll P. Hurd and Jeanne M. Hurd, *Evaluation: Implementation of the Canada-Manitoba-Brotherhood of Indian Nations Child Welfare Agreement* (Edmonton: MacKay-Hurd Associates International, 1986).

46. Peter Hudson and Sharon Taylor-Henley, *Agreement and Disagreement: An Evaluation of the Canada-Manitoba Northern Indian Child Welfare Agreement* (Winnipeg: School of Social Work, University of Manitoba, 1987).

47. Coopers and Lybrand Consulting Group, *An Assessment of Services Delivered under the Canada-Manitoba Northern Indian Child Welfare Agreement"* (Winnipeg, 1986).

48. *Child and Family Services Act*, R.S.M. 1987, c. C80, ss. 1–82.

49. Salasan Associates, "Evaluation of the Project for the Education of Native Teachers," Brandon, 1986.

50. *Charter of Rights and Freedoms*, Part 1 of *Constitution Act, 1982*, being Schedule B of the *Canada Act, 1982* (U.K.), c. 11, s. 35(1).

51. *Northwest Child and Family Services Agency v. T. (S.J.)*, [1991] 1 C.N.L.R. 82 (Man. Q.B.)

Chapter 15 – Young Offenders

1. Carol LaPrairie, "The Young Offenders Act and Aboriginal Youth," in *Justice and the Young Offender in Canada*, edited by J. Hudson et al. (Toronto: Wall & Thompson, 1988), pp. 159–68.

2. Canadian Research Institute for Law and the Family, *Alternative Measures Programs for Native Youth* (Alberta, 1990), p. 1.

3. Nicholas Bala, "An Introduction to Child Protection Problems: The History of Child Protection in Canada," in *Canadian Child Welfare Law: Children, Families and the State*, edited by Nicholas Bala, Joseph P. Hornick and Robin Vogl (Toronto: Thompson Educational Publishing, 1991), pp. 2–3.

4. *Ibid.*

5. Gordon West, *Young Offenders and the State* (Toronto: Butterworths, 1988).

6. *Juvenile Delinquents Act*, R.S.C. 1970, c. J-3, s. 2(1)(h).

7. *Ibid.*, s. 38.

8. For a full discussion of the *Juvenile Delinquents Act*, see Graham E. Parker, "Some Historical Observations on the Juvenile Court," *Criminal Law Quarterly*, 9, 4 (1967): 467–502; Kechin Wang, "The Continuing Turbulence Surrounding the Parens Patriae Concept in Juvenile Courts," *McGill Law Journal* 18, 2 (1972): 219–45; Jeffrey S. Leon, "The Development of Canadian Juvenile Justice: A Backgound for Reform," *Osgoode Hall Law Journal*, 15, 1 (1977): 71–106; Richard G. Fox and Maureen J. Spencer, "The Young Offenders Bill: Destigmatizing Juvenile Delinquency?" *Criminal Law Quarterly*, 14 (1972): 172–219; B.A. Grosman, "Young Offenders before the Courts," *Canadian Bar Journal* (Nova Scotia), 2, 2 (May 1971): 6–7; P.B. Chapman, "The Lawyer in Juvenile Court: 'A Gulliver among Lilliputians,'" *University of Western Ontario Law Review*, 10 (1971): 88–107; and C.H. McNairn, "Juvenile Delinquent Act Characterized as Criminal Law Legislation," *Canadian Bar Review*, 46 (1968): 473–82.

9. Omer Archambault, "Young Offenders Act: Philosophy and Principles," in *Crime in Canadian Society*, 3d ed., edited by Robert Silverman and James Teevan, pp. 473–82 (Toronto: Butterworths, 1986).

10. *Ibid.*

11. Canada, Department of Justice, *Highlights: The Young Offenders Act* (Ottawa, 1988), pp. 2–3.

12. *Young Offenders Act*, R.S.C. 1985, c. 4-1, s. 24(1)(1).

13. Canada, Statistics Canada, Centre for Justice Statistics, *Youth Court Statistics* (Ottawa, 1990).

14. C.A. Latimer, "Winnipeg Youth Courts and the Young Offenders Act" (Winnipeg: Research, Planning and Evaluation Branch, Manitoba Department of the Attorney General, 1986).

15. *Ibid.*

16. Nicholas Bala, "The Young Offenders Act: The Legal Structure,'" in *Juvenile Justice in Canada*, edited by Ray Corrado et al. (Toronto: Butterworths, forthcoming).

17. Latimer, "Winnipeg Youth Courts."

18. S. 3(1)(f).

19. Hendrickson, *Manitoba Provincial Courts.*

20. Latimer, "Winnipeg Youth Courts."

21. *R. v. James*, [1990] 6 W.R.R., 152 (S.C.C.).

22. *Juvenile Delinquents Act*, R.S.C. 1970, c. J-3, s. 2(1)(h).

23. R. Kueneman, Rick Linden and Rick Kosmick, *A Study of Manitoba's Northern and Rural Juvenile Courts* (Ottawa: Department of the Solicitor General of Canada, 1986).

24. LaPrairie, "Young Offenders Act," p. 164.

Chapter 16 – Policing

1. See W.P. Ward, "The Administration of Justice in the North West Territories, 1870–1887," M.A. thesis, University of Alberta, Edmonton, 1966; Lorne Brown and Caroline Brown, *An Unauthorized History of the RCMP* (Toronto: Lewis and Samuel, 1973; reprint ed., James Lorimer, 1978); S.W. Horrall, "Sir John A. Macdonald and the Mounted Police Force for the North West Territories," *Canadian Historical Review*, 53, 2 (June 1972): 179–200; E.C. Morgan, "The North West Mounted Police, 1873–1883," M.A. thesis, University of Saskatchewan, Regina, 1970; W.L. Morton, "Canada and the Canadian Indians: What Went Wrong?" *Quarterly of Canadian Studies for the Secondary School*, 2, 1 (Spring 1972): 3–12; John Peter Turner, *The North West Mounted Police, 1873 to 1893*, vol. 2 (Ottawa: King's Printer, 1950); Hugh A. Dempsey, ed., *Men in Scarlet* (Calgary: Historical Society of Alberta, McClelland and Stewart West, 1974).

2. Brown and Brown, *Unauthorized History of the RCMP* pp. 10, 14; see also Horrall, "Sir John A. Macdonald," and Morgan, "North West Mounted Police."

3. See Turner, *North West Mounted Police*, pp. 518–21.

4. Brown and Brown, *Unauthorized History of the RCMP* p. 22.

5. Robert A. Harrison, ed., *The New Municipal Manual for Upper Canada* (Toronto: Maclear & Co., 1859), p. 158, quoted in Philip C. Stenning, *Legal Status of the Police* (Ottawa: Supply and Services Canada, 1982), p. 10.

6. Alex Nicholas, *Black in Blue: A Study of the Negro Policeman* (New York: Appleton-Century-Crofts, 1969).

7. L.J. Callens, "Community Based Policing," paper delivered in Stonewall, Manitoba, February 1991, p. 5.

8. Angus Reid Group, "Effects of Contact with Police among Aboriginals in Manitoba," research paper prepared for the Aboriginal Justice Inquiry, Winnipeg, 1989, p. 76.

9. *R. v. Anunga and Others* (1976), 11 A.L.R. 412 (N.T.S.C.).

10. Australian Law Reform Commission, *The Recognition of Aboriginal Customary Laws*, Report No. 31, 2 vols. (Canberra: Australian Government Publishing Service, 1986).

11. Charles Singer and Sharon Moyer, *The Dakota-Ojibway Tribal Council Police Program: An Evaluation, 1979–1981* (Ottawa: Department of the Solicitor General of Canada, 1981), p. 34.

12. Social Policy Research Associates/The Evaluation Group Inc., *National Evaluation Overview of Indian Policing: Executive Summary and Main Report* (Ottawa: Department of Indian and Northern Affairs, 1983).

13. Rick Linden, *An Assessment of the Role of the Manitoba Police Commission* (Winnipeg: Department of the Attorney General, 1986).

14. Canada, Commission of Inquiry Relating to Public Complaints, Internal Discipline and Grievance Procedure within the Royal Canadian Mounted Police, *Report* (Ottawa: Department of the Solicitor General of Canada, 1976).

15. Canada, Department of the Solicitor General, *Police-Challenge 2000: A Vision of the Future of Policing in Canada* (Ottawa, 1990), Background Document, p. ix.

16. *Ibid.*, p. 73.

17. *Annual Report of the Police Complaints Authority, 1 January 1987–31 December 1987* (London: Her Majesty's Stationery Office, 1988), p. 5.

18. Ontario, Race Relations and Policing Task Force, *The Report of the Race Relations and Policing Task Force* (Toronto, 1989), p. 184.

19. Osnaburgh-Windigo Tribal Council Justice Review Committee, *Report* (Ontario: Attorney General, 1990).

Chapter 17 – A Strategy for Action

1. Hay Management Consultants, *Report-Review of the Recruitment, Selection, and Classification Processes within the Manitoba Civil Service* (Winnipeg,1991), p. 47. While the report finds that "native representation is approaching parity with the availability statistics" (p. 15), it is also clear that the report did not examine Aboriginal issues closely. Most particularly, given the under-estimation of Aboriginal persons in the census, and in unemployment figures, we doubt that Aboriginal people are adequately reflected in "availability statistics."

2. Hay Management Consultants, *Report*, p. 35.

BIBLIOGRAPHY

This bibliography represents primarily those works cited in our report. It represents only a small portion of works reviewed in the preparation of this report, and only a fraction of works written on the subject matters discussed. There are a number of more complete bibliographies on the various subjects. Three bibliographies in particular that we refer the researcher to are *Law and Order for Canada's Indigenous People, A Review of Recent Research Literature Relating to the Operation of the Criminal Justice System and Canada's Indigenous People*, Prairie Justice Research, School of Human Justice, University of Regina, 1985; *Native Law Bibliography*, 2d ed., Linda Fritz, University of Saskatchewan Native Law Centre, 1990; and *Native Northern Americans: Crime, Conflict and Criminal Justice, A Research Bibliography*, 4th ed., Charles Horn and Curt Taylor Griffiths, the Northern Justice Society Resource Centre, Simon Fraser University.

Journal Articles

Adams, K. Bliss. "Order in the Courts: Resolution of Tribal/State Criminal Jurisdictional Disputes." *Tulsa Law Journal*, 24 (1988): 89.

Anderson, Tavs Fulmer. "Persistence of Social and Health Problems in the Welfare State: A Danish Cohort Experience from 1948 to 1979." *Social Science and Medicine*, 18, 7 (1984): 555-60.

Baker-Stetson, Catherine. "Decriminalizing Tribal Codes: A Response to Oliphant." *American Indian Law Review*, 9 (1981): 51-81.

Barron, F. Laurie. "A Summary of Federal Indian Policy in the Canadian West, 1867-1984." *Native Studies Review*, 1, 1 (1984): 28-39.

_____. "The Indian Pass System in the Canadian West, 1882-1935." *Prairie Forum*, 13, 1 (1988): 25-42.

Barsh, Russel L., and James Youngblood Henderson. "The Betrayal: *Oliphant v. Suquamish Indian Tribe* and the Hunting of the Shark." *Minnesota Law Review*, 63 (1979): 609-40.

Basso, K. "To Give Up on Words: Silence in Western Apache Culture." *Southwestern Journal of Anthropology*, 26, 2 (1970): 213-30.

Bingaman, Sandra Estlin. "The Trials of Poundmaker and Big Bear, 1885." *Saskatchewan History*, 28, 1 (1975): 81-94.

_____. "The Trials of the 'White Rebels,' 1885." *Saskatchewan History*, 25, 2 (1972): 41-54.

Bonta, J., et al. "Restitution in Correctional Halfway Houses: Victim Satisfaction, Attitudes and Recidivism." *Canadian Journal of Criminology*, 25 (1983): 277-93.

Brant, Clare. "Native Ethics and Rules of Behaviour." *Canadian Journal of Psychiatry*, 35 (August 1990): 534-39.

Bridges, G.S., and J.A. Stone. "Effects of Criminal Punishment on Perceived Threat of Punishment: Toward an Understanding of Specific Deterrence." *Journal of Research on Crime and Delinquency*, 23 (1986): 207-39.

Brown, Desmond H. "Unpredictable and Uncertain: Criminal Law in the Canadian North West before 1886." *Alberta Law Review*, 17, 3 (1979): 497-512.

Campbell, Gayle. "Women and Crime." *Juristat* (Statistics Canada), 10, 20 (December 1990): 1-9.

Carter, Sarah. "Agriculture and Agitation on the Oak River Reserve, 1875-1895." *Manitoba History,* 6 (Fall 1983): 2-9.

Chapman, P.B. "The Lawyer in Juvenile Court: 'A Gulliver among Lilliputians.'" *Western Ontario Law Review,* 10 (1971): 88-107.

Collins, Richard B. "Implied Limitations on the Jurisdiction of Indian Tribes." *Washington Law Review,* 54 (1979): 479-529.

"Conjugal Violence Against Women." *Juristat* (Statistics Canada), 10, 7 (May 1990): 1-2.

Coyle, Michael. "Traditional Indian Justice in Ontario: A Role for the Present?" *Osgoode Hall Law Journal,* 24 (1986): 605-33.

Deegan, Michael N. "Closing the Door to Federal Court." *Land and Water Law Review,* 14 (1979): 625-34.

Dempsey, James. "The Indians and World War One." *Alberta History,* 31, 3 (1983): 1-8.

"Developments in the Law—Race and the Criminal Process." *Harvard Law Review,* 101 (1988): 1472-1641.

Fagan, Jeffrey, and Sandra Wexler. "Family Origins of Violent Delinquents." *Criminology,* 25, 3 (1987): 643-69.

Ferdinand, Theodore N. "The Methods of Delinquency Theory." *Criminology,* 25, 4 (1987): 841-62.

Fox, Richard G., and Maureen J. Spencer. "The Young Offenders Bill: Destigmatizing Juvenile Delinquency?" *Criminal Law Quarterly,* 14 (1972): 172-219.

Gover, Walter, Michael Hughes and Omer Galle. "Overcrowding in the Home: An Empirical Investigation of Its Possible Pathological Consequences." *American Sociological Review,* 44 (1979): 59-82.

Grosman, B.A. "Young Offenders before the Courts." *Canadian Bar Journal* (Nova Scotia), 13 (1971): 6-7.

Harring, Sidney L. "Crow Dog's Case: A Chapter in the Legal History of Tribal Sovereignty." *American Indian Law Review,* 17 (1989): 191-239.

Hemmingson, Rick H. "Jurisdiction of Future Tribal Courts in Canada: Learning from the American Experience," [1989] 3 C.N.L.R. 1.

Henderson, J. Youngblood, and Russel L. Barsh. "Oyate kin haye keyuga u pe, Part II: The Courts and the Indian Tribes." *Harvard Law School Bulletin,* 25, 10 (1974).

Horrall, S.W.. "Sir John A. Macdonald and the Mounted Police Force for the North West Territories." *Canadian Historical Review,* 53, 2 (June 1972): 179-200.

Hylton, John H. "Locking Up Indians in Saskatchewan: Some Recent Findings." *Canadian Ethnic Studies,* 13, 3 (1981): 144-51.

_____. "The Native Offender in Saskatchewan: Implications for Crime Prevention Programming." *Canadian Journal of Criminology,* 24, 2 (1982): 121-31.

Jackson, Michael. "Locking Up Natives in Canada." *University of British Columbia Law Review,* 23, 2 (1989): 215-300.

Keon-Cohen, Bryan A. "Native Justice in Australia, Canada, and the U.S.A.: A Comparative Analysis." *Canadian Legal Aid Bulletin,* 5, 2-3 (1982): 187-258. (An earlier version of this article also appeared in *Monash Law Review,* 7 [1981]: 250.)

Kimball, R.E. "In the Matter of Judicial Discretion and the Imposition of Default Orders." *Criminal Law Quarterly,* 32 (September 1990): 467-77.

LaPrairie, Carol. "The Role of Sentencing in the Over-representation of Aboriginal People in Correctional Institutions." *Canadian Journal of Criminology*, 32, 3 (July 1990): 429-440.

Leon, J. "The Development of Canadian Juvenile Justice: A Background for Reform." *Osgoode Hall Law Journal*, 15 (1977): 71-106.

Lowie, Robert H. "Property Rights and Coercive Powers of Plains Indian Military Societies." *Journal of Law and Politics*, 1 (1943): 59.

MacLean, Brian D., and R.S. Ratner. "An Historical Analysis of Bills C-67 and C-68: Implications for the Native Offender." *Native Studies Review*, 3 (1987): 31-58.

Martinson, R.M. "What Works? Questions and Answers about Prison Reform." *The Public Interest*, 35 (1974): 22-54.

McNairn, C.H. "Juvenile Delinquent Act Characterized as Criminal Law Legislation." *Canadian Bar Review*, 46 (1968): 473-82.

McSloy, Steven Paul. "American Indians and the Constitution: An Argument for Nationhood." *American Indian Law Review*, 17 (1989): 139.

Morse, Bradford W. "Indian and Inuit Family Law and the Canadian Legal System." *American Indian Law Review*, 8 (1980): 199-257.

_____. *Indian Tribal Courts in the United States: A Model for Canada?* Saskatoon: Native Law Centre, 1980.

_____. "Native People and Legal Services in Canada." *McGill Law Journal*, 22 (1976): 504-40.

_____. "A Unique Court: S. 107 Indian Act Justices of the Peace." *Canadian Legal Aid Bulletin*, 5, 2-3 (1982): 139-43.

Morton, W.L. "Canada and the Canadian Indians: What Went Wrong?" *Quarterly of Canadian Studies in the Secondary School*, 2, 1 (Spring 1972): 3-12.

"Note: Implication of Civil Remedies under the Indian Civil Rights Act." *Michigan Law Review*, 75 (1970): 210-35.

Parker, Graham E. "Some Historical Observations on the Juvenile Court. *Criminal Law Quarterly*, 9 (1967): 467-502.

Pommersheim, Frank. "The Contextual Legitimacy of Adjudication in Tribal Courts and the Role of the Tribal Bar as an Interpretive Community: An Essay." *New Mexico Law Review*, 18 (1988): 49.

Raby, Stuart. "Indian Land Surrenders in Southern Saskatchewan." *Canadian Geographer*, 17, 1 (1973): 36-52.

Ross, Rupert. "Leaving Our White Eyes Behind: The Sentencing of Native Accused," [1989] 3 C.N.L.R.1.

Schultz, Gregory. "The Federal Due Process and Equal Protection Rights of Non-Indian Civil Litigants in Tribal Courts after *Santa Clara Pueblo v. Martinez.*" *Denver University Law Review*, 62 (1985): 761-87.

Stark, Rodney. "Deviant Places: A Theory of the Ecology of Crime." *Canadian Journal of Criminology*, 25, 4 (1987): 893-909.

Vaskov, John A. "Note: Indians Rights— What's Left? Oliphant, Tribal Courts, and Non-Indians." *University of Pittsburgh Law Review*, 41 (1979-80): 75-88.

Vetter, William V. "Of Tribal Courts and 'Territories': Is Full Faith and Credit Required?" *California Western Law Review,* 23 (1987): 219-72.

Wang, Kechin. "The Continuing Turbulence Surrounding the Parens Patriae Concept in Juvenile Courts." *McGill Law Journal,* 18 (1972): 219-45.

Wright, Gordon K. "Recognition of Tribal Decisions in State Courts." *Stanford Law Review,* 37 (1984-85): 1397-1424.

Zion, James W. "Harmony among the People: Torts and Indian Courts." *Montana Law Review,* 45 (1984): 265-79.

_____. "The Navajo Peacemaker Court: Deference to the Old and Accommodation to the New." *American Indian Law Review,* 11 (1984-85): 89-109.

Books and Chapters in Books

Abella, Rosalie S. "Limitations on the Right to Equality before the Law." In *The Limitation of Human Rights in Comparative Constitutional Law.* Edited by Armand de Mestral et al. Montreal: Les Editions Yvon Blais, 1986.

Adelberg, Ellen, and Claudia Currie, eds. *Too Few to Count: Canadian Women in Conflict with the Law.* Vancouver: Press Gang Publishers, 1987.

Ahenakew, Edward. *Voices of the Plains Cree.* Edited by Ruth Buck. Toronto: McClelland and Stewart, 1973.

Allen, Paula Gunn. *Sacred Hoop: Restoring the Feminine to Native American Tradition.* Boston: Beacon Press, 1986.

Archambault, Omer. "Young Offenders Act: Philosophy and Principles." In *Crime in Canadian Society*, 3d ed. Edited by Robert Silverman and James Teevan. Toronto: Butterworths, 1986.

Bala, Nicholas. "The History of Child Protection in Canada." In *Canadian Child Welfare Law: Children, Families and the State.* Edited by Nicholas Bala, Joseph P. Hornick and Robin Vogl. Toronto: Thompson Educational Publishing, 1991.

_____. "An Introduction to Child Protection Problems: The History of Child Protection in Canada." In *Canadian Child Welfare Law: Children, Families and the State.* Edited by Nicholas Bala, Joseph P. Hornick and Robin Vogl. Toronto: Thompson Educational Publishing, 1991.

_____. "The Young Offenders Act: The Legal Structure." In *Juvenile Justice in Canada.* Edited by Ray Corrado et al. Toronto: Butterworths, forthcoming.

Bala, Nicholas, Joseph P. Hornick and Robin Vogl, eds. *Canadian Child Welfare Law: Children, Families and the State.* Toronto: Thompson Educational Publishing, 1991.

Barman, Jean, Yvonne Hebert and Don McCaskill, eds. *Indian Education in Canada. Vol. 1: The Legacy. Vol. 2: The Challenge.* Vancouver: University of British Columbia Press, 1986.

Barron, F. Laurie and James Waldram, eds. *1885 and After: Native Society in Transition.* Proceedings of a conference held at the University of Saskatchewan, Saskatoon, May 1985. Regina: Canadian Plains Research Centre, University of Regina, 1986.

Berger, Thomas R. "Introduction" to *The Challenge of Child Welfare.* By Kenneth L. Levitt and Brian Wharf. Vancouver: University of British Columbia Press, 1985.

Birnie, Lisa Hobbs. *A Rock and a Hard Place: Inside Canada's Parole Board.* Toronto: Macmillan, 1990.

Bowker, L.H. *Corrections—The Science and the Art.* New York: Macmillan, 1982.

Braithwaite, John. *Inequality, Crime and Public Policy.* London: Routledge and Kegan Paul, 1979.

Brown, Lorne, and Caroline Brown. *An Unauthorized History of the RCMP.* Toronto: Lewis and Samuel, 1973; reprint ed., James Lorimer, 1978.

Carter, Sarah. *Lost Harvests: Prairie Indian Reserve Farmers and Government Policy.* Montreal and Kingston: McGill-Queen's University Press, 1990.

Chamberlin, J.E. *The Harrowing of Eden: White Attitudes Towards North American Natives.* Toronto: Fitzhenry and Whiteside, 1975.

Chartrand, Paul L.A.H. *Manitoba's Metis Settlement Scheme of 1870.* Saskatoon: Native Law Centre, University of Saskatchewan, 1991.

Cohen, Felix S. *Handbook of Federal Indian Law.* Washington, D.C.: U.S. Government Printing Office, 1942. Reprint ed., Albuquerque: University of New Mexico Press, 1972.

Cole, D.P., and A. Manson. *Release from Imprisonment: The Law of Sentencing, Parole and Judicial Review.* Toronto: Carswell, 1990.

Cole, Douglas, and Ira Chaikin. *An Iron Hand upon the People: The Law Against the Potlatch on the Northwest Coast.* Vancouver: Douglas and McIntyre, 1990.

Coombs, H.C. "The Yirrkala Proposals for the Control of Law and Order." In *Justice Programs for Aboriginal and Other Indigenous Communities.* Edited by Kayleen M. Hazlehurst. Canberra: Australian Institute of Criminogy, 1985.

Crawford, James. *The Creation of States in International Law.* Oxford: Clarendon Press, 1979.

Currie, Elliott. *Confronting Crime.* New York: Pantheon Books, 1985.

Davies, Maureen. "Aspects of Aboriginal Rights in International Law." In *Aboriginal People and the Law: Indian, Metis, and Inuit Rights in Canada.* Edited by Bradford W. Morse. Ottawa: Carleton University Press, 1989.

Dempsey, Hugh A. *Big Bear: The End of Freedom.* Vancouver: Douglas and McIntyre, 1984.

Dempsey, Hugh A., ed. *Men in Scarlet.* Calgary: Historical Society of Alberta, McClelland and Stewart West, 1974.

Dentler, Robert A., and Kai T. Erikson. "The Functions of Deviance in Groups" (1959). In *Theories of Deviance.* Edited by Stuart H. Traub and Craig B. Little. Itasca, Illinois: F.E. Peacock, 1975.

Doeren, S.E., and M.J. Hageman. *Community Corrections.* Cincinnati, Ohio: Anderson Publishing, 1982.

Donnelly, M.S. *The Government of Manitoba.* Toronto: University of Toronto Press, 1963.

Driver, H.E. *Indians of North America,* 2d ed. Chicago: University of Chicago Press, 1969.

Durkheim, Emile. "The Normal and the Pathological" (1938). In *Theories of Deviance.* Edited by Stuart H. Traub and Craig B. Little. Itasca, Illinois: F.E. Peacock, 1975.

Ekstedt, J.W., and M.A. Jackson. *A Profile of Canadian Alternative Sentencing Programmes: A National Review of Policy Issues.* Burnaby, B.C.: School of Criminology, Simon Fraser University, 1986.

Elias, Peter Douglas. *The Dakota of the Canadian Northwest: Lessons for Survival.* Manitoba Studies in Native History No. 5. Winnipeg: University of Manitoba Press, 1988.

Friesen, Gerald. *The Canadian Prairies: A History.* Toronto: University of Toronto Press, 1987.

Getches, David, ed. *Indian Courts and the Future.* Washington, D.C.: National American Indian Court Judges Association, 1978.

Getty, Ian A.L., and A.S. Lussier, eds. *As Long as the Sun Shines and Water Flows: A Reader in Canadian Native Studies.* Vancouver: Nakoda Institute and University of British Columbia Press, 1983.

Gibson, Dale. *The Law of the Charter: Equality Rights.* Toronto: Carswell, 1990.

Gibson, Dale, and Lee Gibson. *Substantial Justice: Law and Lawyers in Manitoba, 1670-1970.* Winnipeg: Peguis, 1972.

Glaser, Daniel. "Criminality Theories and Behavioural Images" (1956). In *Theories of Deviance.* Edited by Stuart H. Traub and Craig B. Little. Itasca, Illinois: F.E. Peacock, 1975.

Gordon, Robert, and Mervyn Meggitt. "The Customary Law Option." In their *Law and Order in the New Guinea Highlands.* Hanover, New Hampshire: University Press of New England, 1985.

Grant, Peter R. "Recognition of Traditional Laws in State Courts and the Formulation of State Legislation." In *Indigenous Law and the State.* Edited by Bradford W. Morse and Gordon R. Woodman. Dordrecht, Netherlands: Foris Publications, 1988.

Green, L.C., and O.P. Dickason. *The Law of Nations and the New World.* Edmonton: University of Alberta Press, 1989.

Greenaway, W.K. "Crime and Class: Unequal before the Law." In *Structured Inequality in Canada.* Edited by John Harp and John R. Hofley. Scarborough: Prentice-Hall, 1980.

Griffiths, Curtis T., and Simon N. Verdun-Jones. *Canadian Criminal Justice.* Toronto: Butterworths, 1989.

Grossman, B.A., ed. *New Directions in Sentencing.* Toronto: Butterworths, 1980.

Hagan, William T. *Indian Police and Judges: Experiments in Acculturation and Control.* New Haven, Connecticut: Yale University Press, 1966.

Haig-Brown, Celia. *Resistance and Renewal: Surviving the Indian Residential School.* Vancouver: Tillacum Library, 1988.

Lord Hailsham. *Laws of England,* 4th ed. London: Butterworths, 1976.

Hann, R.G., et al. *Sentencing Practices and Trends in Canada: A Summary of Statistical Information.* Ottawa: Department of Justice, 1983.

Harp, John, and John R. Hofley, eds. *Structured Inequality in Canada.* Scarborough: Prentice-Hall, 1980.

Harries, K.D. *Crime and the Environment.* Springfield, Illinois: Charles C. Thomas, 1980.

Havemann, Paul. "The Indigenization of Social Control in Canada." In *Indigenous Law and the State,* pp. 71-100. Edited by Bradford W. Morse and Gordon R. Woodman. Dordrecht, Netherlands: Foris Publications, 1988.

Havemann, Paul, Keith Couse, Lori Foster, and Rae Matonovich. *Law and Order for Canada's Indigenous People: A Review of Recent Research Literature Relating to the Operation of the Criminal Justice System and Canada's Indigenous People.* Regina: Prairie Justice Research, 1985.

Hazlehurst, Kayleen M., ed. *Ivory Scales: Black Australia and the Law.* Kensington, New South Wales: New South Wales University Press, 1987.

_____. *Justice Programs for Aboriginal and Other Indigenous Communities.* Canberra: Australian Institute of Criminology, 1985.

Hoddinot, Annie. "Aboriginal Justices of the Peace and Public Law." In *Justice Programs for Aboriginals and Other Indigenous Communities.* Edited by Kayleen M. Hazlehurst. Canberra: Australian Institute of Criminology, 1985.

Hoebel, E. Adamson. *The Cheyennes: Indians of the Great Plains.* New York: Holt, Rinehart and Winston, 1960.

_____. *The Law of Primitive Man: A Study in Comparative Legal Dynamics.* Cambridge, Massachusetts: Harvard University Press, 1954.

Hooker, M.B. *Legal Pluralism: An Introduction to Colonial and Neo-Colonial Laws.* Oxford: Clarendon Press, 1975.

Hudson, J., et al., eds. *Justice and the Young Offender in Canada.* Toronto: Wall and Thompson, 1988.

Indian Tribes as Sovereign Governments. Oakland, California: American Indian Resources Institute Press, 1988.

Jackson, Moana. *The Maori and the Criminal Justice System: New Perspective: He Whaipaanga Hou, Part 2.* Wellington, New Zealand: Department of Justice, 1988.

Jenness, Diamond. *Indians of Canada,* 7th ed. Toronto: University of Toronto Press, National Museums of Canada, 1989.

Jennings, Francis. *The Invasion of America: Indians, Colonialism and the Cant of Conquest.* New York: W. W. Norton, 1976.

Johnson, Elias. *Legends, Traditions, and Laws of the Iroquois or Six Nations, and History of the Tuscarora Indians.* Lockport, New York: Union Printing and Publishing Co., 1881; reprint ed., New York: AMS Press, 1978.

Johnston, Patrick. *Native Children and the Child Welfare System.* Toronto: James Lorimer, 1983.

Kent, M.W., and J.E. Rolf, eds. *Promoting Social Competence and Coping in Children,* vol. 3 of *Primary Prevention and Cycle Pathology.* Hanover, New Hampshire: University Press of New England, 1979.

Kickingbird, Kirke, et al. *Indian Sovereignty.* Washington, D.C.: Institute for the Development of Indian Law, 1977.

Lagasse, J. "The Metis in Manitoba." In *The Other Natives: The Metis,* vol. 2. Edited by A.S. Lussier and D.B. Sealey. Winnipeg: Manitoba Metis Federation Press, 1978.

Lamb, Kaye, ed. *Sixteen Years in the Indian Country: The Journal of Daniel William Harmon, 1800-1816.* Toronto: Macmillan, 1957.

LaPrairie, Carol. "Native Women and Crime in Canada: A Theoretical Model." In *Too Few to Count: Canadian Women in Conflict with the Law.* Edited by Ellen Adelberg and Claudia Currie. Vancouver: Press Gang Publishers, 1987.

_____. "The Young Offenders Act and Aboriginal Youth." In *Justice and the Young Offender in Canada.* Edited by J. Hudson et al. Toronto: Wall and Thompson, 1988.

Levitt, Kenneth L., and Brian Wharf. *The Challenge of Child Welfare.* Vancouver: University of British Columbia Press, 1985.

Lewis, Meriwether, and William Clark. *History of the Expedition under the Command of Captains Lewis and Clark to the Sources of the Missouri,* vol. 2. Toronto: Morang, n.d.

Lindley, M.F. *The Acquisition and Government of Backward Territory in International Law.* London: Longman, Green & Co., 1926.

Llewellyn, Karl N., and E. Adamson Hoebel. *The Cheyenne Way: Conflict and Case Law in Primitive Jurisprudence.* Norman, Oklahoma: University of Oklahoma Press, 1961.

Lussier, A.S., and D.B. Sealey, eds. *The Other Natives: The Metis,* vol. 2. Winnipeg: Manitoba Metis Federation Press, 1978.

Lynch, Michael, and W. Byron Groves. *A Primer in Radical Criminology*, 2d ed. Albany, New York: Harrow and Heston, 1989.

Martin, Sheilah, and Kathleen Mahoney, eds. *Equality and Judicial Neutrality*. Toronto: Carswell, 1987.

de Mestral, Armand, et al., eds. *The Limitation of Human Rights in Comparative Constitutional Law*. Montreal: Les Editions Yvon Blais, 1986.

Miller, J.R. *Skyscrapers Hide the Heavens: A History of Indian-White Relations in Canada*. Toronto: University of Toronto Press, 1989.

Milloy, John S. "The Early Indian Acts: Developmental Strategy and Constitutional Change." In *As Long as the Sun Shines and Water Flows: A Reader in Canadian Native Studies*. Edited by Ian A.L. Getty and A.S. Lussier. Vancouver: Nakoda Institute and University of British Columbia Press, 1983.

_____. *The Plains Cree: Trade, Diplomacy and War, 1790 to 1870*. Manitoba Studies in History No. 4. Winnipeg: University of Manitoba Press, 1988.

Morris, Alexander. *The Treaties of Canada with The Indians of Manitoba, The North-West Territories, including the Negotiations on which they were based, and other information relating thereto*. Originally published in 1880 by Belfords, Clarke & Co., Toronto. Facsimilie edition Toronto: Coles Publishing Co., 1971.

Morris, Allison. *Women, Crime and Criminal Justice*. New York: Basil Blackwell, 1987.

Morse, Bradford W., ed. *Aboriginal People and the Law: Indian, Metis, and Inuit Rights in Canada*. Ottawa: Carleton University Press, 1989.

Morse, Bradford W., and Gordon Woodman, eds. *Indigenous Law and the State*. Dordrecht, Netherlands: Foris Publications, 1988.

Morton, W.L. "Introduction" to *Alexander Begg's Red River Journal and Other Papers Relative to the Red River Resistance of 1869-70*. Toronto: Champlain Society, 1956.

_____. *Manitoba: A History*. 1st ed., 1957. Rev. ed., Toronto: University of Toronto Press, 1967.

Morton, W.L., ed. *Manitoba: The Birth of a Province*, vol. 1. Altona, Manitoba: Record Society Publications, 1965.

Moyles, R.G. *British Law and Arctic Men*. Saskatoon: Western Producer Prairie Books, 1979.

Nadin-Davis, P. *Sentencing in Canada*. Ottawa: Carswell, 1982.

Newell, William B. *Crime and Justice among the Iroquois Nations*. Montreal: Caughnawaga Historical Society, 1965.

Nicholas, Alex. *Black in Blue: A Study of the Negro Policeman*. New York: Appleton-Century-Crofts, 1969.

Noon, John A. *Law and Government of the Grand River Iroquois*. New York: Johnson Reprint Corp., 1964.

Oliver, E.H. *The Canadian North-West: Its Early Development and Legislative Records*. Ottawa: Government Printing Office, 1915.

Park, Robert E. "Social Change and Social Disorganization" (1967). In *Theories of Deviance*. Edited by Stuart H. Traub and Craig B. Little. Itasca, Illinois: F.E. Peacock, 1975.

Patterson, E.P. *The Canadian Indian: A History since 1500*. Don Mills: Collier-Macmillan, 1972.

Peterson, Jacqueline, and Jennifer S.H. Brown, eds. *The New Peoples: Being and Becoming Metis in North America.* Winnipeg: University of Manitoba Press, 1985.

Pettipas, K.A. "Severing the Ties That Bind: The Canadian Indian Act and the Repression of Indigenous Religious Systems in the Prairie Region, 1896-1951." PhD dissertation, University of Manitoba, Winnipeg, 1988. Winnipeg: University of Manitoba Press (forthcoming).

Reid, John Phillip. *A Law of Blood: The Primitive Law of the Cherokee Nation.* New York: New York University Press, 1970.

Rich, E.E., ed. *Cumberland House Journals and Inland Journal, 1775-82 (First Series, 1775-79).* London: Hudson's Bay Record Society, 1951.

Richardson, Jane. *Law and Status among the Kiowa Indians.* Seattle: University of Washington Press, 1966.

Roberts, Simon. *Order and Dispute: An Introduction to Legal Anthropology.* Harmondsworth, England: Penguin Books, 1979.

Ross, Alexander. *The Red River Settlement: Its Rise, Progress, and Present State.* Minneapolis: Ross and Haines, 1957.

Rutter, Michael. "Protective Factors in Children's Responses to Stress and Disadvantage." In *Promoting Social Competence and Coping in Children,* vol. 3 of *Primary Prevention and Cycle Pathology.* Edited by M.W. Kent and J.E. Rolf. Hanover, New Hampshire: University Press of New England, 1979.

Sealey, Bruce D., and Peter Van De Vyvere. *Thomas George Prince.* Winnipeg: Peguis, 1981.

Sellin, Thorsten. "Culture Conflict and Crime" (1938). In *Theories of Deviance.* Edited by Stuart H. Traub and Craig B. Little. Itasca, Illinois: F.E. Peacock, 1975.

Silverman, Robert, and James Teevan, eds. *Crime in Canadian Society,* 3d ed. Toronto: Butterworths, 1986.

Smith, Joseph Henry. *Appeals to the Privy Council from the American Plantations.* New York: Columbia University Press, 1950.

Strickland, Rennard. *Fire and the Spirits: Cherokee Law from Clan to Court.* Norman, Oklahoma: University of Oklahoma Press, 1975.

Sutherland, Edwin H. "The Theory of Differential Association" (1947). In *Theories of Deviance.* Edited by Stuart H. Traub and Craig B. Little. Itasca, Illinois: F.E. Peacock, 1975.

Swanton, Bruce, ed. *Aborigines and Criminal Justice.* Canberra: Australian Institute of Criminology, 1984.

Taché, Alexandre-Antonin. *Sketch of the North-West of America.* Montreal: John Lovell, 1870.

Thistle, Paul C. *Indian-European Trade Relations in the Lower Saskatchewan River Region to 1840.* Manitoba Studies in Native History No. 2. Winnipeg: University of Manitoba Press, 1986.

Thomas, W.I., and Florian Znaniecki. "The Concept of Social Disorganization" (1920). In *Theories of Deviance.* Edited by Stuart H. Traub and Craig B. Little. Itasca, Ill.: F.E. Peacock, 1975.

Traub, Stuart H., and Craig B. Little, eds. *Theories of Deviance.* Itasca, Illinois: F.E. Peacock Publishers, 1975.

de Tremaudan, Auguste-Henri. *Histoire de la nation metisse dans l'ouest canadien.* Reprint ed. St. Boniface: Les Editions du Ble, 1979. Published in English as *Hold High Your Heads: History of the Metis Nation in Western Canada.* Translated by E. Maguet. Winnipeg: Pemmican Publications, 1982.

Trigger, Bruce G. *The Children of Aataentsic: A History of the Huron People to 1660.* Montreal and Kingston: McGill-Queen's University Press, 1976.

Usher, Jean. *William Duncan of Metlakatla: A Victorian Missionary in British Columbia.* Ottawa: National Museum of Man, 1974.

Van Kirk, Sylvia. *"Many Tender Ties": Women in Fur-Trade Society in Western Canada, 1670-1870.* Winnipeg: Watson and Dwyer, 1980.

Vizkelety, Béatrice. *Proving Discrimination in Canada.* Toronto: Carswell, 1987.

Wa, Gisday, and Delgam Uukw. *The Spirit in the Land: The Opening Statement of the Gitksan and Wet'suwet'en Hereditary Chiefs in the Supreme Court of British Columbia.* Gabriola, British Columbia: Reflections, 1989.

Waite, Peter B. *Canada, 1874-1896: Arduous Destiny.* Toronto: McClelland and Stewart, 1971.

Walker, James W.S. "The Indian in Canadian Historical Writing." *Canadian Historical Association Papers* (1971): 21-51.

West, Donald. *Delinquency: Its Roots, Careers, and Prospects.* Cambridge, Massachusetts: Harvard University Press, 1982.

West, Gordon. *Young Offenders and the State.* Toronto: Butterworths, 1988.

West, John. *The Substance of a Journal during a Residence at the Red River Colony, British North America in the Years 1820-1823.* Vancouver: Alcuin Society, 1967.

Wilkins, David E. *Dine Bibeehaz'acnii—A Handbook of Navajo Government.* Tsaile, Arizona: Navajo Community College Press, 1987.

Wilkinson, Charles F. *American Indians, Time, and the Law.* New Haven, Connecticut: Yale University Press, 1987.

Williams, Nancy M. *Two Laws: Managing Disputes in a Contemporary Aboriginal Community.* Canberra: Australian Institute of Aboriginal Studies, 1987.

Wolfgang, Marvin, Marvin Figlio, and Thorsten Sellin. *Delinquency in a Birth Cohort.* Chicago: University of Chicago Press, 1972.

Zion, James. "Searching for Indian Common Law." In *Indigenous Law and the State.* Edited by Bradford W. Morse and Gordon Woodman. Dordrecht, Netherlands: Foris Publications, 1988.

Government Publications

Alberta

Alberta. Commission of Inquiry on Policing in Relation to the Blood Tribe(C.H. Rolf, Commissioner). *Report.* Edmonton, February 1991.

Alberta. Task Force on the Criminal Justice System and Its Impact on the Indian and Metis People of Alberta. *Justice on Trial.* Edmonton, March 1991.

Australia

Australian Law Reform Commission. *The Recognition of Aboriginal Customary Laws.* Report No. 31, 2 vols. Canberra: Australian Government Publishing Service, 1986.

Hennessy, Peter K. *Aboriginal Customary Law and Local Justice Mechanisms: Principles, Options and Proposals.* Research Paper No. 11/12. Canberra: Australian Law Reform Commission, 1984.

Canada

Canada. Canadian Sentencing Commission. *Sentencing Reform: A Canadian Approach.* Ottawa: Supply and Services Canada, 1987.

Canada. Commission of Inquiry Relating to Public Complaints, Internal Discipline and Grievance Procedure within the Royal Canadian Mounted Police. *Report* (Marin Report). Ottawa: Department of the Solicitor General of Canada, 1976.

Canada. Committee Appointed to Enquire into the Principles and Procedures Followed in the Remission Service of the Department of Justice. *Report* (Fauteux Report). Ottawa: Queen's Printer, 1956.

Canada. Committee on Corrections. *Toward Unity: Criminal Justice and Corrections* (Ouimet Report). Ottawa: Queen's Printer, 1969.

Canada. Correctional Officer. *Annual Report of the Correctional Officer, 1988-1989.* Ottawa: Supply and Services Canada, 1990.

Canada. Correctional Service of Canada. *Basic Facts about Corrections in Canada.* Ottawa: Supply and Services Canada, 1986.

Canada. Correctional Service of Canada. *Creating Choices, The Report of the Task Force on Federally Sentenced Women.* Ottawa, 1990.

Canada. Department of Indian Affairs and Northern Development. *Annual Report.* Ottawa, 1976.

Canada. Department of Indian and Northern Affairs. *Highlights of Aboriginal Conditions, 1981-2001, Part III: Economic Conditions.* Ottawa, 1989.

Canada. Department of Indian and Northern Affairs. *Indian Policing Policy Review: Task Force Report.* Ottawa, January 1990.

Canada. Department of Justice. *Fact Book on Community Service Order Programs in Canada.* Ottawa, 1986.

Canada. Department of Justice. *Highlights: The Young Offenders Act, 1982.* Ottawa, 1982.

Canada. Department of Justice. *Some Statistics on the Preliminary Inquiry in Canada.* Prepared by David G. Alford, Paul Chumak, Lise Cloutier, David Johnson, and David McKercher. Ottawa, 1984.

Canada. Department of the Solicitor General. "Correctional Issues Affecting Native Peoples." Correctional Law Review Working Paper No. 7. Ottawa, February 1988.

Canada. Department of the Solicitor General. *Police-Challenge 2000: A Vision of the Future of Policing in Canada.* Ottawa, 1990.

Canada. Department of the Solicitor General. *Report of the Task Force on Aboriginal Peoples in Federal Corrections.* Ottawa, 1988.

Canada. Department of Solicitor General. *Report of the Task Force on the Release of Inmates* (Hugessen Report). Ottawa, 1972.

Canada. Department of the Solicitor General. *Solicitor General's Study of Conditional Release: Report of the Working Group.* Ottawa: Supply and Services Canada, 1981.

Canada. House of Commons. Special Committee on Indian Self-Government. *Indian Self-Government in Canada* (Penner Report). Ottawa: Queen's Printer, 1983.

Canada. House of Commons. Standing Committee on Justice and Solicitor General (David Daubney, Chair). *Taking Responsibility* (Report on Its Review of Sentencing, Conditional Release and Related Aspects of Corrections). Ottawa: Queen's Printer, 1988.

Canada. Law Reform Commission. *Study Report: Discovery in Criminal Cases.* Ottawa, 1974.

Canada. Law Reform Commission. *Toward a Unified Criminal Court.* Ottawa, 1989.

Canada. Mackenzie Valley Pipeline Inquiry (Thomas Berger, Chair). *Northern Frontier, Northern Homeland: The Report of the Mackenzie Valley Pipeline Inquiry,* vol. 1. Ottawa: Supply and Services Canada, 1977.

Canada. National Parole Board. *Briefing Book for Members of the Standing committee on Justice and Solicitor General,* vol. 1. Ottawa, 1987.

Canada. National Parole Board. *A Guide to the Parole Act and Regulations.* Revised and updated edition of the *National Parole Board Handbook for Judges and Crown Attorneys.* Ottawa, 1988.

Canada. National Parole Board. *Mission Statement.* Ottawa: Department of the Solicitor General of Canada, 1987.

Canada. National Parole Board. *Pre- and Post-Release Decision Policies.* Interim report.

Canada. Parliamentary Sub-Committee on the Penitentiary System in Canada (Mark MacGuigan, Chair). *Report to Parliament by the Sub-Committee on the Penitentiary System in Canada.* Ottawa: Supply and Services Canada, 1977.

Canada. Royal Commission to Investigate the Penal System of Canada. *Report* (Archambault Report). Ottawa: King's Printer, 1938.

Canada. Sessional Papers. *Annual Reports of the Superintendent of Penitentiaries.* Ottawa, 1900-1960.

Canada. Statistics Canada. Canadian Centre for Justice Statistics. *Adult Correctional Services in Canada: 1988-89.* Ottawa: Supply and Services Canada, 1989.

Canada. Statistics Canada. Canadian Centre for Justice Statistics. *Youth Court Statistics.* Ottawa, 1990.

Canada. Statistics Canada. Census Canada 1986. *Aboriginal Peoples Output*. Ottawa, 1981.

Canada. Statistics Canada. Census Canada 1986. *A Data Book on Canada's Aboriginal Population from the 1986 Census of Canada*. Ottawa, March 1989.

Canfield, Carolyn, and Linda Drinnan. *Comparative Statistics on Native and Non-Native Inmates—A Five Year History*. Ottawa: Correctional Service of Canada, 1981.

Children's Hospital Child Protection Centre. *A New Justice for Indian Children* (Final report of the Child Advocacy Project, prepared by S. Longstaffe and B. Hamilton). Winnipeg: Department of the Solicitor General of Canada, 1987.

Hann, R.G., et al. *Sentencing Practices and Trends in Canada: A Summary of Statistical Information*. Ottawa: Department of Justice, 1983.

Hawthorn, H.B., ed. *A Survey of the Contemporary Indians of Canada: A Report on Economic, Political, Educational Needs and Policies*, vols. 1 and 2. Ottawa: Department of Indian Affairs and Northern Development, 1966.

Hull, Jeremy. *An Overview of Registered Indian Conditions in Manitoba*. Ottawa: Department of Indian and Northern Affairs, 1987.

Hyde, Mary, and Carol LaPrairie. "Amerindian Police Crime Prevention." Working paper prepared for the Solicitor General of Canada, 1987.

"Indians Policing Reserves." Background information for Department of Indian and Northern Affairs news release 1-9157, "Federal Government Funds Plan to Improve Policing Services for Indian Reserves," 27 June 1991.

Jamieson, Kathleen. *Indian Women and the Law in Canada: Citizens Minus*. Canadian Action Committee on the Status of Women. Ottawa: Supply and Services Canada, 1978.

Kueneman, R., Rick Linden, and Rick Kosmick. *A Study of Manitoba's Northern and Rural Juvenile Courts*. Ottawa: Department of the Solicitor General of Canada, 1986.

McCaskill, Don. *Patterns of Criminality and Correction among Native Offenders in Manitoba: A Longitudinal Analysis*. Ottawa: Correctional Service of Canada, 1985.

_____. *Studies of Needs and Resources Related to Offenders of Native Origin in Manitoba*. Ottawa: Department of the Solicitor General of Canada, 1971.

Michalis, Gail, and William T. Badcock. *Native People and Canada's Justice System*. Ottawa: Department of Indian and Northern Affairs, 1979.

Miller, Kahn-Tineta, and George Lerchs. *The Historical Development of the Indian Act*. Ottawa: Treaties and Historical Research Branch, Department of Indian and Northern Affairs, 1978.

Morse, Bradford, and Linda Lock. "Native Offenders' Perceptions of the Criminal Justice System." Research paper prepared for the Canadian Sentencing Commission. Ottawa: Policy, Programs and Research Branch, Department of Justice, 1988.

Newby, L. *Native Peoples of Canada and the Federal Corrections System: Development of a National Policy—A Preliminary Issues Report*. Ottawa: Correctional Services of Canada, 1981.

Singer, Charles, and Sharon Moyer. *The Dakota-Ojibway Tribal Council Police Program: An Evaluation, 1979-1981*. Ottawa: Department of the Solicitor General of Canada, 1981.

Sloan, Rick. *Legal Aid in Manitoba: An Evaluation Report*. Winnipeg: Department of Justice Canada, September 1987.

Social Policy Research Associates/The Evaluation Group Inc. *National Evaluation Overview of Indian Policing: Executive Summary and Main Report*. Ottawa: Department of Indian and Northern Affairs, 1983.

Stenning, Philip C. *Legal Status of the Police*. Ottawa: Supply and Services Canada, 1982.

Turner, John Peter. *The North West Mounted Police, 1873 to 1893*, vol. 2. Ottawa: King's Printer, 1950.

White, P.M. *Native Women: A Statistical Overview*. Ottawa: Supply and Services Canada, 1985.

Great Britain

Annual Report of the Police Complaints Authority, 1 January 1987 - 31 December 1987. London: Her Majesty's Stationery Office, 1988.

Manitoba

"Chaplains Contribute to Total Well-Being." *Corrections Community* (Newsletter of the Corrections Branch of the Department of Justice), 7, 1 (December 1990-February 1991).

Hay Management Consultants. *Report-Review of the Recruitment, Selection, and Classification Processes within the Manitoba Civil Service*. Winnipeg, 1991.

Hendrickson, Barbara. *A Study of the Operation of the Manitoba Provincial Court in Winnipeg and Selected Northern Communities with Reference to the Treatment of Aboriginal Offenders*. Winnipeg: Department of Justice, 1989.

Kimelman, Edwin C., et al. *No Quiet Place*. Report of the Review Committee on Indian and Metis Adoptions and Placements. Winnipeg: Department of Community Services, 1985.

Lagasse, Jean H. *A Study of the Population of Indian Ancestry Living in Manitoba*. Winnipeg: Department of Agriculture and Immigration, 1959.

Latimer, C.A. "Winnipeg Youth Courts and the Young Offenders Act." Winnipeg: Research, Planning and Evaluation Branch, Department of the Attorney General, 1986.

Linden, Rick. *An Assessment of the Role of the Manitoba Police Commission*. Winnipeg: Department of the Attorney General, 1986.

Manitoba. Department of Health and Social Development. *Report of the Indian Child Welfare Sub-Committee, Manitoba, to the Tripartite Committee*. Winnipeg, 1980.

Manitoba. Department of the Attorney General. *Annual Report of the Manitoba Department of the Attorney General, 1988-89*. Winnipeg, 1989.

Manitoba. Department of the Attorney General. *Native Court Interpreter's Manual*. Winnipeg, 1987.

Manitoba. Department of the Attorney General. Research and Planning Branch. *Justice in Manitoba: Key Indicators, 1988*. Winnipeg, 1988.

Nova Scotia

Nova Scotia. Royal Commission on the Donald Marshall, Jr., Prosecution (T. Alexander Hickman, Chair). *Report.* Halifax, December 1989.

Ontario

Ontario. Race Relations and Policing Task Force (Clare Lewis, Chair). *The Report of the Race Relations and Policing Task Force.* Toronto, 1989.

Osnaburgh-Windigo Tribal Council Review Committee. *Report.* Toronto: Department of the Attorney General, 1990.

United States

Brenner, M. Harvey. *Estimating the Social Costs of National Economic Policy.* Report prepared for the Joint Economic Committee of the U.S. Congress. Washington, D.C.: U.S. Government Printing Office, 1976.

Indian Criminal Justice Program Display. Washington, D.C.: Bureau of Indian Affairs, 1974.

Indian Reservation Criminal Justice Task Force Analysis, 1974-75. Washington, D.C.: Bureau of Indian Affairs, 1975.

Native American Tribal Court Profiles. Washington, D.C.: Branch of Judicial Services, Bureau of Indian Affairs, 1982.

Native American Tribal Court Profiles. Washington, D.C.: Branch of Judicial Services, Bureau of Indian Affairs, 1985.

Young, Robert. *Historical Backgrounds for Modern Indian Law and Order.* Washington, D.C.: Bureau of Indian Affairs, 1969.

_____. *Indian Law Enforcement History.* Washington, D.C.: Bureau of Indian Affairs, 1975.

A.J.I. Research Papers

Ahenakew, Freda, Cecil King, and Catherine I. Littlejohn. "Indigenous Languages in the Delivery of Justice in Manitoba." Winnipeg, March 1990.

Angus Reid Group. "Effects of Contact with Police among Aboriginals in Manitoba." Winnipeg, 1989.

Animus Research Consultants. "Manitoba Child and Family Services: Report on Services to Aboriginal Children and Families." Ottawa, March 1991.

_____. "The Manitoba Justice System and Aboriginal Young Offenders." Ottawa, July 1991.

A.R.A. Consultants. "Feasibility Study of Alternate Dispute Mechanisms for Aboriginal People in Manitoba." Toronto, February, 1990.

Canadian Research Institute for Law and the Family. " Alternative Measures Programs for Native Youth." Calgary, January 1990.

Chartrand, Paul. "Metis People and the Justice System." Winnipeg, October 1989.

Clark, Scott. "Aboriginal Customary Law: Literature Review." Ottawa, 1990.

Crawford, James. "The Original Status of Aboriginal Peoples in North America: A Critique of L.C. Green and O.P. Dickason, *The Law of Nations and the New World* (1989)." Sydney, Australia, January 1991.

Cross-Cultural Consulting, Inc. "Cross-Cultural Orientation: A Model for the Justice System." Winnipeg, March 1990.

Dansys Consultants. "Aboriginal People in Manitoba: Population Estimates for 1986 and 1991." Ottawa, November 1990.

_____. "Manitoba Aboriginal Justice Study." Ottawa, May 1991.

_____. "The Utility of Data Collected by the Manitoba Provincial Court Study." Ottawa, June 1990.

Dumont, James. "Justice and Aboriginal People." Sudbury, September 1990.

Fossett, Renée. "Aboriginal Child Welfare in Canada: Literature Review and Selected Bibliography." Winnipeg, April 1990.

_____. "Alternatives to Incarceration: Literature Review and Selected Annotated Bibliography." Winnipeg, February 1990.

_____. "Conflict with the Law: Literature Survey of Criminal Causation Theory." Winnipeg, March, 1990.

_____. "Education of Aboriginal Peoples in Manitoba: Literature Review and Selected Annotated Bibliography." Winnipeg, January 1990.

_____. "Juvenile Offenders and Children at Risk in the Children's Hearings System of Scotland: Interviews and Brief Literature Survey." Winnipeg, June 1990.

_____. "Nature, Causes, Effects and Remedies of Systemic Discrimination: Literature Survey and Selected Bibliography." Winnipeg, February 1990.

Hackett, Christopher. "Media Treatment of Aboriginal People: An Annotated Bibliography and Report." Winnipeg, January 1990.

Indigenous Women's Collective. "Aboriginal Women's Perspective of the Justice System in Manitoba." Winnipeg, June 1990.

King, Jack A.. "Criminal Appeals in England." Winnipeg, 1990.

_____. "Justices of the Peace in England." Winnipeg, 1990.

"Manitoba Inmate Survey." Survey designed, data collected or analyzed by Doris Young, Eric Robinson, Jennifer Yarnell, Jeannie Daniels, Harry Daniels, Laurie Messer, Maryanne Boulton, Tom McMahon, Brad Morse. Winnipeg, 1991.

Messer, Laurie. "Manitoba Fine Option Program: A Survey of Fine Defaulters." Winnipeg, April 1990.

_____. "Manitoba Jury Study." Winnipeg, April 1990.

_____. "A Survey of Manitoba Judges." Winnipeg, March 1990.

_____. (with the assistance of Maryanne Boulton). "A Survey of Manitoba Lawyers." Winnipeg, February 1990.

Milloy, John S. "A Partnership of Races: Indian and White, Cross-Cultural Relations and Criminal Justice in Manitoba, 1670-1949." Peterborough, 1990.

Peat, Marwick, Stevenson and Kellogg Consultants. "An Analysis of Costs of the Justice System Attributable to Aboriginal People." Winnipeg, May 1990.

Sanders, Douglas. "Aboriginal and Treaty Rights in Manitoba." Vancouver, July 1990.

Sawatzky, Peter D.B. "Winnipeg Remand Study: A Re-Analysis, Comparing Aboriginal and Non-Aboriginal Inmates." Winnipeg, March 1990.

Shewchuk, Eileen A. "National Survey of Police Forces." Winnipeg, December 1989.

_____. "Report on Affirmative Action/Employment Equity." Winnipeg, December 1989.

_____. "Report on Courtworkers in Canada." Winnipeg, December 1989.

Stevens, Samuel. "Cross-Cultural Training for Justice Personnel on Aboriginal Cultures and Their Unique Legal Status." Vancouver, June 1990.

van der Put, Daphne. "Literature Review on Aboriginal Victims of Crime." St. Boniface, 1990.

Westarc Group Inc. "Provincial Court - Criminal Division and Court of Queen's Bench: Time Study." Brandon, May 1990.

Yarnell, Jennifer. "Urban Aboriginal Issues: A Literature Review." Winnipeg, February 1990.

Zimmerman, Susan. "The Revolving Door of Despair: Native Involvement in the Criminal Justice System." Ottawa, Aboriginal Justice Inquiry and Law Reform Commission of Canada, 1991.

Other

*American Bar Association Standards Relating to Trial Courts.*Chicago, Illinoois: American Bar Association, August 1984.

Archibald to J.A. Macdonald, 9 October 1871. *Journals of the House of Commons of the Dominion of Canada 1874*, 8, appx. 6.

Bennet, G. *Aboriginal Rights in International Law.* Occasional Working Paper No. 37. London: Royal Anthropological Institute, 1978.

Brown, Jennifer S.H. "Metis." *Canadian Encyclopedia*, 2d ed. Edmonton: Hurtig Publishers, 1988.

Brown, Mona G., et al. *Gender Equality in the Courts–Criminal Law: A Study by the Manitoba Association of Women and the Law.* Ottawa: National Association of Women and the Law, March 1991.

Callens, L.J., Chief Superintendent, RCMP. "Community Based Policing." Paper delivered in Stonewall, Manitoba, February 1991.

Canadian Welfare Council and Canadian Association of Social Workers. *Joint Submission to the Special Joint Committee of the Senate and the House of Commons Appointed to Examine and Consider the Indian Act.* Ottawa: Canadian Welfare Council, 1947.

Coopers and Lybrand Consulting Group. *An Assessment of Services Delivered under the Canada-Manitoba Northern Indian Child Welfare Agreement.* Winnipeg, 1986.

Crawford, James. *Aboriginal Self-Government in Canada.* Research Report for the Canadian Bar Association, Committee on Native Justice. Ottawa: Committee on Native Justice, Canadian Bar Association, 1988.

Davin, N.F. "Report on Industrial Schools for Indians and Halfbreeds." Ottawa: Public Archives, 14 March 1879 (PAC RG 10, Vol. 6001, File 1-1-1, Part 1).

Hudson, Peter, and Sharon Taylor-Henley. *Agreement and Disagreement: An Evaluation of the Canada-Manitoba Northern Indian Child Welfare Agreement.* Winnipeg: School of Social Work, University of Manitoba, 1987.

Hurd, Carroll P., and Jeanne M. Hurd. *Evaluation: Implementation of the Canada-Manitoba Brotherhood of Indian Nations Child Welfare Agreement.* Edmonton: MacKay-Hurd Associates International, 1986.

Morgan, E.C. "The North West Mounted Police, 1873-1883." M.A. thesis, University of Saskatchewan, Regina, 1970.

Ontario Native Women's Association. *Breaking Free: A Proposal for Change to Aboriginal Family Violence.* Thunder Bay, December 1989.

RES Policy Research. *Indian Veterans and Veterans' Benefits in New Brunswick and Prince Edward Island.* Ottawa: National Indian Veterans Association, 1984.

Ronaghan, Allen Edgar. "The Archibald Administration in Manitoba, 1870-72." PhD dissertation, University of Manitoba, Winnipeg, 1987.

Salasan Associates. "Evaluation of the Project for the Education of Native Teachers." Brandon, 1986.

Ross, Rupert. "Dancing with a Ghost: Exploring Indian Reality." Unpublished manuscript, Kenora, 1987.

Social Planning Council of Winnipeg. *Selected Profile of Winnipeg's Aboriginal Population.* Winnipeg, 1989.

Sugar, Fran, and Lana Fox. *Survey of Federally Sentenced Aboriginal Women in the Community.* Ottawa: Native Women's Association of Canada, 1990.

Sweeney, Alastair. *Government Policy and Saskatchewan Indian Veterans.* Saskatchewan Indian Veterans Association, 1979.

Tarnopolsky, W.S. "Discrimination in Canada: Our History and Our Legacy." Paper delivered at the Canadian Institute of Administration of Justice seminar on discrimination in the law, Kananaskis, Alberta, 12 October 1989.

Treaty and Aboriginal Rights Research Program. *Treaty Land Entitlement in Manitoba, 1970-1981.* Winnipeg: Treaty and Aboriginal Rights Research Centre, 1982.

Tyler, Wright and Daniel Ltd. "The Illegal Surrender of St. Peter's Reserve." Research paper prepared for the Treaty and Aboriginal Rights Research Centre. Winnipeg, 1983.

Ward, W.P. "The Administration of Justice in the North West Territories, 1870-1887." M.A. thesis, University of Alberta, Edmonton, 1966.

Wiebe, Menno. *Native Culture and Canadian Law: A Cultural Look at Native People and the Canadian Justice System.* Kingston: Queen's Theological College, 1984.

Williams, Paul, "The Covenant Chain." LL.M. thesis, Osgoode Hall Law School, York University, 1982.

CASE LIST

Andrews v. Law Society of British
Columbia, [1989] 2 W.W.R. 289 (S.C.C.)

Apsit v. Manitoba Human Rights Commission (1985), 37 Man. R. (2d) 50
(Q.B.)

Attorney General of Canada v. Lavell;
Isaac v. Bedard, [1974] S.C.R. 1349

Attorney General of Ontario v. Bear
Island Foundation, [1989] 2 C.N.L.R.
73 (Ont. C.A.); affirming (1982), 138
D.L.R. (3d) 683 (Ont. H.C.)

Boucher v. R., [1955] S.C.R. 16

Brown and Hunter v. R. (29 November
1990, unreported).

Calder v. Attorney General of British
Columbia, [1973] S.C.R. 313

Cardin v. De La Cruz, 671 F. 2d 363 (9th
Circ.) (1982), cert. denied, 459 U.S. 967

Cayuga Indians Case (1926), 6 R.I.A.A. 173

Cherokee Nation v. Georgia, 30 U.S. (5
Pet.) 1 (1831)

Confederated Salish and Kootenai Tribes v.
Namen, 665 F. 2d 951 (9th Circ.) (1982),
cert. denied, 459 U.S. 977 (1982)

Corporation of Surrey et al. v. Peace Arch
Enterprises (1970), 74 W.W.R. 380
(B.C.C.A.)

DeCoteau v. District County Court, 420
U.S. 425 (1975)

Dedman v. The Queen, [1985] 2 S.C.R. 2

Delgamuukw et al. v. Attorney General of
British Columbia, [1991] 3 W.W.R. 97
(B.C.S.C.)

Director of Child Welfare for Manitoba v.
B, [1979] 6 W.W.R. 229 (Man. Prov.
Ct.), at 237.

Dodge v. Nakai, 298 F. Supp. 26 (D. Ariz.)
(1969)

Doe d. Sheldon v. Ramsay (1852), 9
U.C.Q.B. 105

Dreaver v. R. (1935), 5 C.N.L.C. 92 (Ex. Ct.)

Duro v. Reina et al. (U.S.S.C. unreported, May 29, 1990); reversing 821 F. 2d
1358 (9th Circ.) (1987) and 851 F. 2d
1136 (9th Circ.) (1988)

Eastmain Band v. Gilpin, [1987] 3
C.N.L.R. 54 (Que. Prov. Ct)

Eccles v. Bourque (1974), 19 C.C.C. (2d)
129 (S.C.C.)

Ex parte Crow Dog, 109 U.S. 556 (1883)

Frank v. R. (1978), 75 D.L.R. (3d) 481 (S.C.C.)

Gilbert v. Wood, 7 Johns. 290 (N.Y.S.C.) (1810)

Greywater et al. v. Joshua et al., 846 F. 2d
486 (8th Circ.) (1988)

Griggs v. Duke Power Co. 91 S.Ct. 849 (1971)

Guerin v. R., [1984] 2 S.C.R. 335

Hamlet of Baker Lake v. Minister of
Indian Affairs and Northern
Development, [1980] 1 F.C. 518 (T.D.)

Island of Palmas Case (1928), 2 R.I.A.A. 829

Johnson v. M'Intosh, 21 U.S. (Wheat. 8)
543 (1823)

Kanatewat v. James Bay Dev. Corp.,
[1974] Que. R.P. 38; reversed [1975]
(C.A.) 166; leave to appeal dismissed
[1975] 1 S.C.R. 48

Kennerly v. District Court, 400 U.S. 423 (1971)

Kerr-McGee Corp. v. Navajo Tribe, 105
S.Ct. 1900 (1985)

Knight v. Shoshone and Arapahoe Indian Tribes, 670 F. 2d 900 (10th Circ.) (1982)

Kruger and Manuel v. R., [1978] 1 S.C.R. 104

Legal Consequences for States of the Continued Presence of South Africa in Namibia (South West Africa) notwithstanding Security Council Resolution 276 (1970), Adivisory Opinion, I.C.J. Reports (1971), p. 16

Lovelace v. Canada, [1981] 2 H.R.L.J. 158

MacMillan Bloedel v. Mullin; Martin v. The Queen in right of British Columbia, [1985] 3 W.W.R. 577 (B.C.C.A.); leave to appeal to S.C.C. refused [1985] 5 W.W.R. lxiv

McClanahan v. Arizona State Tax Commission, 411 U.S. 164 (1973)

Merrion v. Jicarilla Apache Tribe, 455 U.S. 130 (1982)

Milirrum v. Nabalco Pty. Ltd. (1971), 17 F.L.R. 141 (N.T.S.C.)

Mills v. R., [1986] 1 S.C.R. 863

Moe v. Confederated Salish and Kootenai Tribes, 425 U.S. 463 (1976)

Mohegan Indians v. Connecticut, a series of three decisions by the Board of Trade, the precursor to the Judicial Committee of the Privy Council. The first decision was in 1706. The cases can be found in Joseph Henry Smith, *Appeals to the Privy Council from the American Plantations* (New York: Columbia University Press, 1950), p. 422. *Myran v. R.*, [1976] 2 S.C.R. 137

Montana v. Blackfeet Tribe of Indians, 105 S.Ct. 2399 (1985)

Montana v. United States, 450 U.S. 544 (1985)

Moore v. The Queen (1979), 43 C.C.C. (2d) 83 (S.C.C)

National Farmers Union Insurance Co. v. Crow Tribe of Indians, 471 U.S. 845 (1985)

Natural Parents v. Superintendent of Child Welfare, [1976] 1 W.W.R. 699 (S.C.C.)

Northwest Child and Family Services Agency v. T (S.J.) and D. (C.), [1990] Winnipeg Centre 88-01-02570 (Man. Q.B.-Family Division)

Nowegijick v. R., [1983] 1 S.C.R. 29

O'Hara v. British Columbia, [1987] 2 S.C.R. 591

Oliphant v. Suquamish Indian Tribe, 435 U.S. 191 (1978)

Pawis v. R., [1980] 2 F.C. 18 (T. D.)

R. v. Agawa, [1988] 3 C.N.L.R. 73 (Ont. C.A.)

R. v. Anunga and Others (1976), 11 A.L.R. 412 (N.T.S.C.)

R. v. Arcand, [1989] 2 C.N.L.R. 110 (Alta. C.A.)

R. v. Askov et al., [1990] 2 S.C.R. 1199

R. v. Batisse (1978), 19 O.R. (2d) 145 (Dist. Ct.)

R. v. Big M Drug Mart (1985), 18 D.L.R. (4th) 321

R. v. Biron (1975), 23 C.C.C. (2d) 513 (S.C.C.)

R. v. Bones, [1990] 4 C.N.L.R. 37 (B.C. Prov. Ct.)

R. v. Bouchard (1982), 66 C.C.C. (2d) 338 (Man C.A.)

R. v. Budd; R. v. Crane, [1979] 6 W.W.R. 450 (Sask. Q.B.)

R. v. Catagas (1977), 81 D.L.R. (3d) 396 (Man. C.A.); reversing [1977] 3 W.W.R. 282 (Co. Ct.)

R. v. Colpitts, [1966] 47 C.R. 175 (S.C.C.)

R. v. Conway, [1989] 1 S.C.R. 1659

R. v. Denny et al. (1990), 94 N.S.R. (2d) 253 (C.A.)

R. v. Derriksan, [1976] 6 W.W.R. 480 (S.C.C.)

R. v. Duguay (1989), 46 C.C.C. (3d) 1 (S.C.C.)

R. v. Eninew; R. v. Bear (1984), 10 D.L.R. (4th) 137 (Sask. C.A.) affirming *R. vs. Eninew* [1984] 2 C.N.L.R. 122 and *R. v. Bear,* [1983] 3 C.N.L.R. 57 (Q.B.)

R. v. Fireman, [1971] 3 O.R. 380 (C.A.)

R. v. Flett, [1991] 1 C.N.L.R. 140 (Man. C.A.); affirming [1989] 4 C.N.L.R. 128 (Q.B.); affirming [1987] 5 W.W.R. 115 (Prov. Ct.)

R. v. George, [1966] S.C.R. 267

R. v. Guthrie (1982), 69 C.C.C. (2d) 216 (Alta. C.A.)

R. v. Hare and Debassige, [1985] 3 C.N.L.R. 139 (Ont. C.A.)

R. v. Horse, [1985] 1 W.W.R. 1 (Sask. C.A.); affirmed on other grounds [1988] 1 S.C.R. 187

R. v. Horseman, [1990] 3 C.N.L.R. 95 (S.C.C.)

R. v. James, [1990] 6 W.R.R., 152 (S.C.C.).

R. v. Jimmy, [1987] 5 W.W.R. 755 (B.C.C.A.)

R. v. Johnston (1966), 56 W.W.R. 565 (Sask. C.A.)

R. v. Kirkness (1989), 58 Man. R. (2d) 131 (Q.B.)

R. v. Kootenay (1978), 6 Alta. L.R. (2d) 220 (Prov. Ct.)

R. v. Laprise, [1978] 6 W.W.R. 85 (Sask. C.A.)

R. v. Martin (1985), 65 N.B.R. (2d) 21 (Q.B.)

R. v. Naqitarvik (1986), 26 C.C.C. (3d) 193 (N.W.T.C.A.)

R. v. O'Donnelly; R. v. Cluett (1982), 3 C.C.C. (3d) 333 (N.S.S.C.); reversed on other grounds *Cluett v. R.* (1985), 21 C.C.C. (3d) 318 (S.C.C.)

R. v. Sacobie (1987), 182 A.P.R. 430 (N.B.C.A.)

R. v. Seymour, a decision of the Provincial Court of Manitoba sitting at Pine Falls, dated May 24, 1989

R. v. Sikyea, [1964] S.C.R. 642

R. v. Sikyea (1964), 43 D.L.R. (2d) 150 (N.W.T.C.A.)

R. v. Simon, [1985] 2 S.C.R. 387

R. v. Sioui, [1990] 1 S.C.R. 1025

R. v. Sparrow, [1987] 2 W.W.R. 577 (B.C.C.A.)

R. v. Sutherland, [1980] 2 S.C.R. 451

R. v. Syliboy, [1929] 1 D.L.R. 307 (N.S. Co. Ct.)

R. v. Taylor and Williams (1981), 34 O.R. (2d) 360 (C.A.)

R. v. The Secretary of State for Foreign and Commonwealth Affairs, Ex parte: The Indian Association of Alberta, Union of New Brunswick Indians, Union of Nova Scotia Indians, [1981] 4 C.L.N.R. 86 (Eng. C.A.)

R. v. Trineer, [1970] 3 C.C.C. 289 (S.C.C.)

R. v. Turpin et al. (1989), 69 C.R. (3d) 97

R. v. Vaillancourt, [1987] 2 S.C.R. 636

R. v. Weremy, [1943] Ex. C.R. 44

R. v. Wesley, [1932] 4 D.L.R. 774 (Alta. C.A.)

R. v. White and Bob (1965), 52 D.L.R. (2d) 481 (S.C.C.)

R. v. Whitfield [1970] 1 C.C.C. 129 (S.C.C)

Re Paulette, [1973] 6 W.W.R. 97 (N.W.T.S.C.) and 115; reversed on other grounds [1976] 2 W.W.R. 193 (N.W.T.C.A.); affirmed on other grounds [1977] 2 S.C.R. 628

Re Southern Rhodesia, [1919] A.C. 211 (P.C.)

Reference re Eskimos, [1939] S.C.R. 104

Saanichton Marina Ltd. v. Claxton, [1988] 1 W.W.R. 540 (B.C.S.C.); affirmed 36 B.C.L.R. (2d) 79 (C.A.)

Santa Clara Pueblo v. Martinez, 436 U.S. 49 (1978)

Solem v. Bartlett, 465 U.S. 463 (1984)

Sparrow v. The Queen, [1990] 1 S.C.R. 1075

St. Catherine's Milling & Lumber Co. v. R. (1888), 14 A.C. 46 (P.C.)

Starr v. Houlden, [1990] S.C.R. 1366

State v. Fasket, 5 Rich. (39 S.C.L.) 255 (1851); 18 U.S.C. ch. 208 § 3161 (c) (1) (1982)

Status of Eastern Greenland Case (1933), 3 W.C.R. 148 (P.C.I.J.)

United States ex rel. Hualpai Indians v. Santa Fe Pacific Railroad, 314 U.S. 339 (1941)

Washington v. Confederated Tribes of the Colville Indian Reservation, 447 U.S. 134 (1980)

Western Sahara, Advisory Opinion, I.C.J. Reports (1975), p. 12

Williams v. Lee, 358 U.S. 217 (1959)

Winters v. United States, 207 U.S. 564 (1908)

Worcester v. Georgia, 31 U.S. (6 Pet.) 515 (1832)

Appendix I

Recommendations

Aboriginal and Treaty Rights

The Evolving Law on Aboriginal and Treaty Rights

■ The federal and provincial governments each issue a public statement within 180 days of the release of our findings describing how each government intends to meet its fiduciary obligation to the Aboriginal people of this province.

Land Rights

■ Current population figures be used for entitlement in conjunction with the formula set out in each treaty to determine the precise amount of land that is owed to each First Nation.

■ The government of Manitoba reinstitute a moratorium on the disposal of Crown land in the Province and that no Crown land be made available to third parties by grant or lease until all First Nation land selection has been made or without the consent of the treaty land entitlement bands in the region.

■ A Treaty Land Entitlement Commission be created for Manitoba consisting of five members, namely, one provincial nominee, one federal nominee, two nominees from the Assembly of Manitoba Chiefs, and a neutral chairperson selected by the other members of the Commission. This Commission should be empowered to render binding decisions on any disputes that may arise over:

  • The exact population of an entitlement band.

  • The amount of land originally set aside for the reserve that is to be deducted from the current treaty entitlement.

  • The selection of Crown lands to fulfil the entitlement obligation.

  • The location of boundaries.

  • The amount of financial compensation for the delay.

■ The Treaty Land Entitlement Commission be created by complementary federal and provincial legislation with the endorsement of the Assembly of Manitoba Chiefs. We further recommend that this legislation be drafted jointly by both governments in conjunction with the treaty land entitlement First Nations

■ The governments of Manitoba and Canada recognize the Northern Flood Agreement as a treaty. The two governments should honour and properly implement the NFA's terms.

Appropriate measures be taken to ensure that equivalent rights are granted by agreement to the other Aboriginal people affected by the flooding.

■ A moratorium be placed on major natural resource development projects unless, and until, agreements or treaties are reached with the Aboriginal people in the region who might be negatively affected by such projects in order to respect their Aboriginal or treaty rights in the territory concerned.

■ The Federal Specific Claims Branch and the federal claims policy be fundamentally changed so that the Government of Canada establish a claims negotiation office that is independent of existing ministries and has a clear mandate to negotiate and settle claims, and has senior officials who have been appointed from outside the government.

■ An independent claims tribunal be created. The tribunal should have full authority to hear and adjudicate on the validity of claims and on compensation questions where the parties cannot reach agreement. The tribunal should be established by legislation with power to create its own rules of procedure, be free from the strict laws of evidence and be able to impose deadlines on the Crown for responding to claims submitted.

The claims tribunal be a national board but with a sufficient number of members, half of whom should be nominees of First Nations, so that it can sit in panels of three to hear a variety of claims simultaneously, if necessary.

Aboriginal people be participants in the designing of the tribunal's precise mandate, drafting the necessary legislation and in selecting the members of the tribunal. The legislation should require that the tribunal, the federal claims policy and the process, be subject to an independent review every five years with the evaluation report to be made to Parliament and Aboriginal groups.

This tribunal be adequately funded and have its own research staff so as to be able to maintain sufficient distance from the federal government.

■ The provincial government develop a policy that respects the desire of Aboriginal people to retain a role in the management and conservation of their traditional territory.

The federal government participate fully in the settlement of land claims through the tribunal we have recommended.

The governments of Manitoba and Canada refrain from requiring Aboriginal groups to consent to extinguish Aboriginal rights when entering into land claims agreements.

■ The independent claims tribunal have authority to resolve specific claims and comprehensive claims. The tribunal would have three basic functions:

- To decide disputes concerning the validity of a claim or its precise boundaries.

- To exercise supervisory authority over the negotiation process.

- If negotiations break down, to hold hearings to resolve the matter and to make a binding decision.

Natural Resources

■ The federal government amend the *Fisheries Act* and the *Migratory Birds Convention Act* to clarify that Aboriginal and treaty rights prevail in cases of conflict.

■ The Province of Manitoba recognize the harvesting of wild rice as an Aboriginal right.

The Province, if it wishes to exercise any influence over the regulation of this resource off-reserves, negotiate co-management agreements with the Aboriginal peoples concerned.

■ The Province of Manitoba recognize Aboriginal and treaty rights to harvest timber resources.

The Province ensure that the exercise of wildlife harvesting rights is not infringed by timber management practices.

The provincial government pursue the development of co-management agreements with the First Nations and Metis peoples regarding timber resources off-reserve in the Aboriginal people's traditional territory.

■ Existing Aboriginal rights to water and beds of waters be recognized by the federal and provincial governments.

■ In keeping with provincial fiduciary obligations and to assist in the economic advancement of First Nations, the Province of Manitoba formally renounce its half interest in minerals within Indian reserves.

First Nations have the right to use and control totally all mines and minerals on reserve lands and to receive 100% of the benefits and income therefrom.

The federal government begin a process of negotiations with the First Nations of Manitoba to transfer title to the reserve lands into the names of the various First Nations.

The Special Position of the Metis

■ The federal and provincial governments, by resolution of their respective legislative assemblies, specifically acknowledge and recognize the Metis people as coming within the meaning of section 91(24) of the *Constitution Act, 1867* and that the Government of Canada accept that it has primary constitutional responsibility to seek to fulfil this mandate through devising appropriate initiatives in conjunction with the Metis people in Canada.

The Manitoba Aboriginal Justice Commission, which is proposed and discussed in detail elsewhere in this report, be mandated by the Manitoba Metis Federation, and the provincial and federal governments to define and designate the boundaries for "Metis communities" for program delivery, local government and administration of justice purposes.

The issue of responsibility for off-reserve status Indian people be resolved by providing that, as a primary federal responsibility, financial services for them should come ultimately from the federal government, and that short term interim measures recoverable from the federal government should be provided by the Province.

The Indian Act

■ The *Indian Act* be amended to eliminate all continuing forms of discrimination, regarding the children of Indian women who regain their status under Bill C-31.

■ The Indian Act be amended to remove the two generation rule.

Any person designated as a full member of a recognized First Nation in Canada be accepted by the federal government as qualifying as a registered Indian for the purposes of federal legislation, funding formula and programs.

■ As a temporary measure, the *Indian Act* be amended to remove the authority of the Minister to veto by-laws enacted by First Nations pursuant to the *Indian Act.*

That section 81 be amended to increase the lawmaking powers of band councils by expressly empowering them to replace provincial legislation that may apply on reserves currently as a result of section 88 of the Act. The revised law-making jurisdiction should expressly include the ability to enact a comprehensive civil and criminal code.

■ Any amendments to the *Indian Act* be developed in accordance with certain key principles. They include recognition that:

• The Act is to be changed only in ways that enhance Indian self-determination.

• The amendments should have the support of First Nations.

• The legislation should be prepared in consultation with representatives selected by Indian people.

• The pace of change should be in accordance with the wishes of the people concerned.

■ The federal government accept its fiduciary obligations in relation to the increase in First Nations membership generated by Bill C-31 and assume the expenses for First Nations resulting from this increase.

Statutes in Conflict with Treaty and Aboriginal Rights

■ The government of Manitoba invite the Assembly of Manitoba Chiefs and the Manitoba Metis Federation to designate representatives to work with senior provincial officials to review all relevant legislation that may conflict with Aboriginal and treaty rights. This review should identify specific areas of conflict and propose concrete solutions and statutory amendments. The Manitoba Aboriginal Justice Commission that we propose should be utilized to assist in this process if any of the parties wish.

■ The federal and provincial governments establish a process to review all proposed legislation for its potential effect on the rights of Aboriginal peoples.

■ The *Interpretation Acts* of Manitoba and Canada be amended to provide that all legislation be interpreted subject to Aboriginal and treaty rights.

Aboriginal Justice Systems

The Argument for Aboriginal Justice Systems

■ The federal and provincial governments recognize the right of Aboriginal people to establish their own justice systems as part of their inherent right to self-government.

The federal and provincial governments assist Aboriginal people in the establishment of Aboriginal justice systems in their communities in a manner that best conforms to the traditions, cultures and wishes of those communities, and the rights of their people.

■ Federal, provincial and Aboriginal First Nations governments commit themselves to the establishment of tribal courts in the near future as a first step toward the establishment of a fully functioning, Aboriginally controlled justice system which includes (but need not necessarily be limited to):

  • A policing service.

  • A prosecution branch.

  • A legal aid system.

  • A court system that includes:

    1. a youth court system;

    2. a family court system;

    3. a criminal court system;

    4. a civil court system;

    5. an appellate court system.

  • A probation service including a system of monitoring community service orders.

  • A mediation/counselling service.

  • A fine collection and maintenance enforcement system.

  • A community-based correctional system.

  • A parole system.

The federal and provincial governments begin the process of establishing Aboriginal justice systems by enacting appropriate legislation.

At the same time as legislation to begin the process of establishing Aboriginal justice systems is enacted, the federal and provincial governments acknowledge, by resolution of their respective legislative bodies, that Aboriginal justice systems must be protected constitutionally from federal and provincial legislative incursions and that such systems will ultimately be recognized as an aspect of the right of Aboriginal people to self-government and will not be dependent solely upon federal or provincial legislation for their existence.

Aboriginal governments enact their own constitutions setting out, among other things, the principle of the separation of the judicial from the executive and legislative arms of each Aboriginal government so as to protect Aboriginal justice systems from interference and to provide security for their independence.

Creating Aboriginal Justice Systems

■ Wherever possible, Aboriginal justice systems look toward the development of culturally appropriate rules and processes which have as their aim the establishment of a less formalistic approach to courtroom procedures so that Aboriginal litigants are able to gain a degree of comfort from the proceedings while not compromising the rights of an accused charged with a criminal offence.

■ Where Indian and Metis communities are located side by side, the leaders of the two communities give serious consideration to establishing a jointly managed Aboriginal justice system which serves both communities.

■ In establishing Aboriginal justice systems, the Aboriginal people of Manitoba consider using a regional model patterned on the Northwest Intertribal Court System in the state of Washington.

■ Regional Aboriginal justice systems establish an independent and separate appeal process which makes use of either separate appeal judges or other judges of the Aboriginal system as judges of appeal.

■ All people, Aboriginal and non-Aboriginal, within the geographical boundaries of a reserve or Aboriginal community, be subject to the jurisdiction of the Aboriginal justice system in place within that community.

■ Aboriginal communities be entitled to enact their own criminal, civil and family laws and to have those laws enforced by their own justice systems. If they wish they should also have the right to adopt any federal or provincial law and to apply or enforce that as well.

Aboriginal traditions and customs be the basis upon which Aboriginal laws and Aboriginal justice systems are built.

■ The jurisdiction of Aboriginal courts within Aboriginal lands be clear and paramount, and that in appropriate cases Aboriginal courts be recognized as having jurisdiction over some matters arising in places other than the Aboriginal community, such as:

- Child welfare cases in which the domicile of the child is the Aboriginal community over which the court has jurisdiction.

- Cases in which a member of an Aboriginal community breaches the laws of his or her community, such as where a First Nation member hunts in a manner that is contrary to a First Nation law or regulation enacted by the government of that First Nation.

- Cases in which an individual has breached a law of the Aboriginal community and has left the community to avoid detection or responsibility.

- Civil matters in which the parties have agreed to submit the matter to an Aboriginal court for determination.

■ The Manitoba Metis Federation and the government of Manitoba establish a forum of elected and technical representatives with a mandate to identify those Metis communities in the province where Metis justice systems can be established.

Metis communities that are identified as such by agreement of the Manitoba Metis Federation and the government of Manitoba be defined geographically through negotiations between the government of Manitoba and the Metis people of each community for the purpose of establishing a Metis justice system.

The presence of non-Aboriginal people within a Metis community should not prevent the community from being declared a Metis community, and the legitimate concerns of that minority should be respected.

If, and to the extent, that juries are a part of Aboriginal justice systems, jury selection processes be implemented which permit non-Aboriginal persons to sit on juries, provided they comply with appropriate residential criteria established by the community.

■ Aboriginal judges be exempt from all civil liability in reference to actions or omissions while in the exercise of their judicial capacity.

Through appropriate Aboriginal legislation an Aboriginal Judicial Council be established to which any person can complain of judicial misconduct on the part of an Aboriginal judicial officer.

The same principles of judicial conduct be applied to Aboriginal judges as apply to other members of the judiciary

The Charter of Rights and Freedoms

■ First Nation governments draft a charter of rights and freedoms which reflects Aboriginal customs and values.

Court Reform

Changes to Court Structure and Administration

■ The Manitoba Court of Queen's Bench and the Provincial Court of Manitoba be abolished and be replaced by a new court to be known as the Manitoba Trial Court. This court should have the combined jurisdiction of the courts it replaces.

■ Jury trials be held in the communities where the offence was committed.

The Manitoba Trial Court have a General Division and a Family Division.

The Family Division be responsible for young offender, child welfare and family matters as well as for cases involving intrafamily physical and sexual abuse; and that the General Division be responsible for all civil matters and those criminal matters not dealt with by the Family Division.

All judges appointed to the Manitoba Court of Appeal come from the Manitoba Trial Court.

■ Proper court facilities be established in Aboriginal communities that will be available for court purposes as required.

■ Hearings in the Family Division of the Manitoba Trial Court be held separately from criminal proceedings.

■ Unless they are travelling in commercial airplanes, circuit court judges not travel with lawyers or police to circuit court sittings.

■ Judges insist that whenever an Aboriginal person is entering a guilty plea, the following procedure be followed:

• The charge is read in full to the accused.

• The judge confirms that the accused understands the charge by asking the accused to explain it.

• The accused, and not counsel, enters a plea.

• The judge confirms that the accused agrees with the guilty plea and that it is being given freely and voluntarily with a full appreciation of the nature and consequences of the plea.

Eliminating Delay

■ Special court sittings be organized to address all cases outside the city of Winnipeg which have been outstanding for more than six months. If necessary, additional staff should be hired until all these cases have been disposed of.

■ Circuit court sittings be scheduled in such a manner as to allow all the matters on a docket to be dealt with in one court visit. This may entail scheduling two-day visits to many communities.

■ Lawyers attend in circuit court communities at least one day before court to ensure that cases can be properly prepared.

Legal Aid duty counsel be authorized to grant interim approval of all Legal Aid applications. If, upon review, the applicant does not qualify for Legal Aid, the approval could be cancelled.

Legal Aid application procedures be amended to allow accused individuals who live in communities where there is no Legal Aid office to apply by telephone. Where no Legal Aid staff are available, Aboriginal court workers be authorized to accept and forward Legal Aid applications.

■ Preliminary inquiries be abolished and replaced with a discovery and pre-trial process.

■ The judiciary establish timelines and procedures that will ensure that a case gets to trial within a reasonable time.

■ Manitoba courts implement a comprehensive case flow management program.

■ The *Criminal Code* be amended to allow accused to appear by counsel or agent for all preliminary purposes.

■ The *Criminal Code* be amended to provide that once an information has been laid the court does not lose jurisdiction merely because the accused is not present.

Pre-Trial Detention

■ Bail hearings be conducted in the community where the offence was committed.

The Manitoba government establish a bail supervision program to provide pre-trial supervision to accused persons as an alternative to detention.

Inappropriate bail conditions, such as requiring cash deposits or financial guarantees from low-income people, that militate against Aboriginal people obtaining bail no longer be applied.

Personnel

■ The provincial Justice department establish minimum and optimum targets for the employment of Aboriginal people at all levels. The minimum target must be no less than the percentage of Aboriginal people in Manitoba; the optimum target is to be equal to the percentage of Aboriginal people served by the department and its agencies.

Legal Aid Manitoba establish minimum and optimum targets for the employment of Aboriginal people at all levels. The minimum target must be no less than the percentage of Aboriginal people in Manitoba; the optimum target is to be equal to the percentage of Aboriginal people served by Legal Aid Manitoba.

■ Legal Aid Manitoba provide representation in all criminal matters in which the accused meets the Legal Aid income criteria.

■ The Justice department provide regular workshops to Crown attorneys on the range and effectiveness of the various community services which are available in Manitoba.

■ The position of court administrator with magistrate's powers be created in each Aboriginal community served by a circuit court.

The Province of Manitoba establish a formal Court Interpreter's Program with staff trained in the interpretation of court proceedings, including legal terminology, from English into the Aboriginal languages of Manitoba. As part of this program, local court interpreters should be engaged in each Aboriginal community served by circuit courts.

The Province of Manitoba, in consultation with the Manitoba Association for Native Languages, establish a Legal Interpretation Project to develop appropriate Aboriginal translations of English legal terms.

■ The Aboriginal Court Worker program have an Aboriginal board of directors and take over the functions and staff of the existing court communicator and paralegal programs. Court workers should be available in every Aboriginal community serviced by the circuit courts.

■ Peacemakers be appointed in each Aboriginal community in Manitoba. They should be appointed through procedures which are agreed to by the community.

Peacemakers, recommended by recognized local Aboriginal groups, be appointed in Winnipeg and in other urban centres throughout the province.

Juries

How Aboriginal People Are Excluded from Juries

■ When a sheriff grants an exemption from jury duty, the person who is exempted be replaced with someone from the same community.

Every person called for jury duty, who is not granted an exemption, be required to attend, and that summonses be enforced even when sufficient jurors have responded.

■ The *Criminal Code* of Canada be amended so that the only challenges to prospective jurors be challenges for cause, and that both stand-asides and peremptory challenges be eliminated.

■ The *Criminal Code* be amended so that rulings on challenges for cause be made by the presiding judge

Local Jury Trials

■ Jurors be drawn from within 40 kilometres of the community in which a trial is to be held.

In the event that there is a need to look elsewhere for jurors, the jury be selected from a community as similar as possible demographically and culturally to the community where the offence took place.

In urban areas, juries be drawn from specific neighbourhoods of the town or city in which victims and accused reside.

The Manitoba *Jury Act* be amended to permit an Aboriginal person who does not speak and understand either French or English but who speaks and understands an Aboriginal language, and is otherwise qualified, to serve as a juror in any action or proceeding that may be tried by a jury, and that, in such cases, translation services be provided.

Alternatives to Incarceration

The Need for a New Approach to Sentencing

- Incarceration be used only in instances where:
  - The offender poses a danger to another individual or to the community.
  - Any other sanction would not sufficiently reflect the gravity of the offence.
  - An offender wilfully refuses to comply with the terms of any other sentence that has been imposed.

The provincial Justice department regularly and consistently collect, analyse and distribute information on the success rates of all sentences, and distribute that information to judges, Crown attorneys and the defence bar.

Probation officers be available when courts sit in Aboriginal communities to explain the results of pre-sentence studies.

The *Criminal Code* be amended to allow judges to designate the specific place of custody for offenders.

- The Manitoba Court of Appeal encourage more creativity in sentencing by trial court judges so that the use of incarceration is diminished and the use of sentencing alternatives is increased, particularly for Aboriginal peoples.

- The *Criminal Code* be amended to provide that cultural factors be taken into account in sentencing, and that in the meantime judges be encouraged to take this approach.

- Judges invite Aboriginal communities to express their views to the court on any case involving an offence or an offender from their community.

Aboriginal communities be encouraged to develop the best method of communicating their concerns to the court in a manner that is respectful of the rights of the accused, and of the dignity and importance of the proceedings.

Community Sanctions

■ Regional, Aboriginally controlled probation services be created to serve Aboriginal communities; and that Aboriginal people be employed by the Province as probation officers in numbers at least proportionate to their presence in the provincial population.

All Aboriginal offenders be supervised by Aboriginal probation officers.

Probation officers assigned to handle cases of Aboriginal persons be able to speak the language of the probationer.

Conditions of probation orders be related directly to the circumstances of the offence and the offender, and be conditions that can be realistically adhered to by the probationer.

There be a reorganization of the way community service orders are administered and supervised so that organizations are provided with the necessary resources to ensure that orders are fulfilled and that judges are provided with the necessary information to allow them to match offenders with programs.

Cross-cultural training programs be mandatory for all non-Aboriginal probation staff, and that there be an ongoing series of refresher courses.

When Aboriginal probation officers are not available to supervise Aboriginal offenders, judges make greater use of section 737(a) of the *Criminal Code,* which permits the court to place a person under the supervision of some "other person designated by the court."

Courts seek out individuals in Aboriginal communities who are willing to accept the responsibility of supervising individuals placed on probation.

■ Judges make greater use of orders of restitution.

■ The existing Fine Option Program be abolished and replaced with a Fine and Restitution Recovery Program which would follow these principles:

• All fines and orders of restitution should be automatically registered with and enforced by the Fine and Restitution Recovery Program.

• If the payment of a fine is not made, the program be empowered to collect the money by garnishment or attachment in the same manner as the way in which maintenance orders are now enforced, or to take other actions such as preventing licensing of vehicles by the Motor Vehicle Branch.

• If these measures fail, the offender be brought to a show cause hearing presided over by a hearing officer.

• If the hearing officer concludes that the offender does not have the ability to pay, the officer may order a period of community service or extend the time for payment of the fine.

- • If the hearing officer concludes that the offender has the ability to pay but is simply refusing to do so, the officer could refer the case to a master or a judge.

- • A judge or master would have the authority, after all other efforts at collection have failed, to incarcerate those who have the ability to pay but refuse to do so.

The existing Maintenance Enforcement Program be expanded and adapted to administer the Fine and Restitution Recovery Program.

The automatic assessment of a term of imprisonment in default of payment of fines levied by Common Offence Notices be abolished, and that the Fine and Restitution Recovery Program apply.

The *Criminal Code* and other legislation allowing for the levying of fines be amended to require that, before levying any fine, judges be required to determine whether a person is able to pay a fine; and that fines not be imposed if the offender is unable to pay the fine at the time of sentence or within a reasonable time thereafter.

The *Criminal Code* of Canada, The *Manitoba Summary Convictions Act* and any other relevant legislation be amended to eliminate incarceration in default of fines.

Where a judge orders the performance of community service work of a specified number of hours, the judge have the option to specify the type and place of work, thus allowing the judge to fashion an appropriate sentence and eliminate the need for the offender to apply elsewhere to enter a program.

Where there is a default in the payment of a fine, the default be noted on the accused's record so that the default can be taken into account if the person comes before the court on a subsequent occasion.

Jails

Security

■ Headingley Correctional Institution and Stony Mountain Institution be the only secure facilities for male offenders in Manitoba.

Brandon and The Pas Correctional institutions be converted into minimum security, open-door institutions similar to Dauphin.

Jail Location and Capacity

■ Open custody programs for Aboriginal adult and young offenders requiring counselling, behaviour improvement, job training and other forms of assistance be established in Aboriginal communities.

Work camps, such as the one at Egg Lake, be established near Aboriginal communities for non-dangerous Aboriginal offenders who require incarceration.

As Aboriginal community-based facilities are opened, an equal number of units of capacity in existing correctional institutions be closed down and the space converted to vocational or academic programming.

Financial assistance be provided for families of Aboriginal inmates to enable them to communicate with and travel to visit relatives.

■ Secure short-term holding facilities be established in Aboriginal communities.

Aboriginal accused be released on bail in their home communities whenever possible.

If Aboriginal accused are transported away from their home communities to be held in custody and are subsequently released on bail, the arresting authority be responsible to convey them back to their home communities.

Responding to Aboriginal Needs

■ Correctional institutions develop a policy whereby elders recognized by provincial Aboriginal organizations as capable of providing traditional assistance or spiritual advice and counselling to Aboriginal inmates in a culturally appropriate manner, be granted status equivalent to chaplains under the Chaplaincy program of the Corrections Branch.

■ The Correctional Services of Canada and the Corrections Branch of the Manitoba Department of Justice institute a policy on Aboriginal spirituality which:

- • Guarantees the right of Aboriginal people to spiritual services appropriate to their culture.

- • Recognizes appropriate Aboriginal organizations to provide Aboriginal spiritual services.

- • Provides training for correctional staff on Aboriginal spirituality, on the relative importance of such services to Aboriginal people, on the different practices and beliefs likely to be encountered, on how those practices and beliefs can and should be accommodated by correctional staff and on how to handle traditional items of spiritual significance to Aboriginal people.

- • Provides for the hiring of knowledgeable personnel within each institution who can advise corrections staff on how to deal with cultural issues arising within the institution's Aboriginal population.

- • Provides for the attendance of Aboriginal inmates at spiritual ceremonies outside jail.

■ Culturally appropriate education, trades training and counselling programs, particularly those having to do with the treatment of alcohol abuse, family violence, anger management and culturally appropriate ways for inmates to cope with their problems, be provided in every Manitoba correctional institution.

Separation of Pre-Trial and Sentenced Persons

■ Adults on remand be kept in physically separate institutions from those who have been convicted.

■ The Manitoba Youth Centre and the Agassiz Youth Centre no longer be used as open custody facilities or as remand facilities, except for those youth who present a danger to themselves or others.

Only home-type facilities or camps be used for open custody sentences.

In the city of Winnipeg, the Corrections Branch seek out and develop alternatives to the use of the Manitoba Youth Centre as a remand facility. This should include the greater use of non-institutional settings such as group and foster homes.

Staffing Issues and Discipline Procedures

■ The number of Aboriginal people employed in correctional facilities and correctional programs be at least proportionate to the population of Aboriginal people in the province of Manitoba.

At least one-half of the Aboriginal staff of each institution be able to speak an Aboriginal language.

Cross-cultural training programs and ongoing refresher courses be mandatory for all corrections staff.

■ Rules for disciplinary hearings in correctional institutions be clarified and enforced to permit an inmate to have a friend or lawyer present to assist at the hearings and to guarantee the opportunity to make full answer and defence to a charge.

Disciplinary hearings in correctional institutions provide for fair adjudication by having an independent third party preside over the hearing and ensure the rules of natural justice are followed.

An independent tribunal be established to adjudicate inmate complaints about the treatment they receive within a correctional system; and that the tribunal have appropriate resources and authority to investigate complaints, mandate change and enforce compliance with its orders.

Work Programs

■ Correctional officials develop work programs both inside and outside institutions which allow inmates to engage in meaningful activities and earn income.

Corrections Branch develop written guidelines on the appropriate use of inmate work details.

Parole

The Evolution of Canada's Parole System

■ The National Parole Board accept as a governing principle that all inmates should be entitled to be released after having completed the same proportion of their sentence, except for those who are considered violent or dangerous.

Any offence now giving rise to loss of earned remission be dealt with by loss of privileges or other penalty while in the institution.

The Parole System and Aboriginal Parole

■ An Aboriginal Parole Board be established to deal with inmates incarcerated by Aboriginal courts.

Every Aboriginal inmate be provided with a culturally appropriate information session upon admission to a correctional institution. Such a session should explain the parole eligibility rules. Further sessions should be given when the inmate becomes eligible to apply for parole.

Parole be considered automatically and no inmate be allowed to waive his or her right to apply for parole.

The Composition of the Parole Board

■ The federal parole service establish minimum and optimum targets for the employment of Aboriginal people. The minimum target must be no less than the percentage of Aboriginal people in Manitoba; the optimum target is the percentage of Aboriginal people served by the parole service.

The National Parole Board, in conjunction with Aboriginal groups, establish release guidelines which take into account the cultural and social circumstances unique to Aboriginal people.

There be Aboriginal parole officers in each Aboriginal community.

The National Parole Board be given authority to transfer jurisdiction over a case to the Aboriginal Parole Board.

The Solicitor General name an additional number of Aboriginal persons as National Parole Board members, in consultation with Aboriginal organizations.

The National Parole Board ensure that all applications involving Aboriginal inmates, including applications for the revocation of parole, be heard by panels which have at least one Aboriginal member.

The membership profile for National Parole Board members be changed to permit greater representation of Aboriginal people.

A program of cross-cultural awareness be developed and implemented for all correctional and parole staff who are involved in making parole decisions about Aboriginal offenders; and that any such cross-cultural awareness program specifically take into account Aboriginal living conditions, Aboriginal values and customs, and the resources available in Aboriginal communities to support the reintegration of offenders.

The separate roles of parole officer and probation officer be combined in Aboriginal communities.

Release Planning and Conditions of Parole for Aboriginal People

■ Community assessments of parole applicants be done by Aboriginal parole officers who understand the applicant's community.

■ Aboriginal parole officers be hired in Aboriginal communities.

■ The National Parole Board, working through its Aboriginal parole officers, make practical arrangements, including provision for financial assistance, to ensure the effective reintegration of Aboriginal inmates into their own communities.

The National Parole Board, in consultation with Aboriginal organizations, develop and adopt more culturally sensitive release criteria and processes for reviewing conditional release applications from Aboriginal inmates.

■ The National Parole Board not require that guilt be admitted prior to an inmate's obtaining parole.

■ The practice of placing special parole conditions on Aboriginal inmates, such as abstention from the consumption of drugs or alcohol as a matter of course, cease.

Where parole conditions are imposed, they be ones that, among other things, can reasonably be adhered to, that are in accord with the inmate's cultural standards, and that will positively benefit both the inmate and the community.

The National Parole Board not prohibit the return of parolees to their home community.

■ The practice of automatically requiring supervision of parolees by a parole officer be ended, and supervision only be required when necessary for the rehabilitation of the inmate and the protection of society.

Aboriginal Women

The Abuse of Women and Children

■ The Indian Act be amended to provide for the equal division of property upon marriage breakdown.

■ Aboriginal leaders establish a local government portfolio for women and children, with responsibility to develop educational and support programs in the area of spousal and child abuse.

■ Police forces establish family abuse teams which include police officers and social workers trained in dealing with domestic disputes. Such teams should make extensive use of electronic record-keeping and community resources.

■ Shelters and safe homes for abused women and children be established in Aboriginal communities and in urban centres. These shelters should be controlled by Aboriginal women who can provide culturally appropriate services.

■ The provincial government implement the recommendations found in the report of the Child Advocacy Project entitled *A New Justice for Indian Children.*

■ Community mediation programs such as the one operated by the Hollow Water Resource Group be expanded to Aboriginal communities throughout the province. Such programs must be designed and operated by Aboriginal people.

The Sentencing of Aboriginal Women

■ Alternatives to incarceration appropriate to Aboriginal cultures be developed for Aboriginal women.

■ The Portage Correctional Institution be closed.

All women who are now sent to a federal penitentiary outside the province be permitted to serve their sentences in Manitoba.

Culturally appropriate group homes be established in urban areas by Aboriginal women's organizations where urban Aboriginal women can serve any term of incarceration to which they may be sentenced, with access to programs of recovery from substance abuse, recovery from victimization and dependency, academic upgrading and training, and parenting skills.

Aboriginal women living in isolated or rural communities be held in open custody facilities in their home communities. Such women would be free to attend to their families, to work or to obtain education during the day, to attend counselling sessions in the evenings, and remain in the facility each night until their sentence is served.

The Milner Ridge Correctional Centre be converted to a co-correctional institution as a pilot project.

When facilities for men and women are established near northern communities, Aboriginal women from the North be allowed to serve their sentences in the facility nearest to their home community.

Arrangements be made for children to have frequent visits with their mother.

Child and family service agencies provide necessary support to Aboriginal mothers in jail and their children to ensure that the family is kept together. Where children need to be taken into care following the incarceration of an Aboriginal mother, child and family service agencies make culturally appropriate foster arrangements for the children of such inmates.

Parole and Post-Release Issues

■ Aboriginal women be appointed to the National Parole Board.

Funding be provided to Aboriginal women to establish a halfway house for Aboriginal female inmates.

The National Parole Board give direction that release plans for female inmates with children pay close attention to the need for family reintegration, and in particular to living and income security arrangements required for family reintegration. We further recommend that the federal and provincial governments ensure that income and housing support programs be developed for released female offenders with young children, designed to facilitate family reintegration.

Child Welfare

Aboriginal Peoples and the Child Welfare System in Manitoba

■ The provincial government establish the Office of Child Protector, responsible to the Legislature, as recommended in the Kimelman Report. This office's responsibilities would be, among other things:

  • To ensure that children involved with the child welfare system have their interests and rights protected.

  • To receive and investigate complaints about the manner of treatment of children by child welfare agencies.

Manitoba's Child and Family Services Act

■ Aboriginal and non-Aboriginal child and family service agencies be provided with sufficient resources to enable them to provide the communities they serve with the full range of direct service and preventive programs mandated by the *Child and Family Services Act.*

■ The federal and provincial governments provide resources to Aboriginal child and family service agencies for the purpose of developing policies, standards, protocols and procedures in various areas, but particularly for the purpose of developing computer systems that will permit them to communicate quickly and effectively with other agencies, to track cases and to share information.

■ Principle 11 of the *Child and Family Services Act* be amended to read: "Aboriginal people are entitled to the provision of child and family services in a manner which respects their unique status, and their cultural and linguistic heritage.

- The Province of Manitoba in conjunction with the Manitoba Metis Federation develop a mandated Metis child and family service agency with jurisdiction over Metis and non-status children throughout Manitoba.

- The jurisdiction of the reserve-based Indian child and family service agencies be extended to include off-reserve band members.

  Indian agencies be provided with sufficient resources to ensure that this expanded mandate be effectively carried out.

- A mandated Aboriginal child and family service agency be established in the city of Winnipeg.

Young Offenders

Aboriginal Youth and the Young Offenders Act

- The police consider alternatives to the laying of charges in all cases involving Aboriginal youth and, when appropriate, exercise their discretion to take no legal measures or to take measures other than laying a charge.

  Police departments designate youth specialists and provide specialized training to all officers involved in the administration of the *Young Offenders Act.*

  Section 56(4) of the *Young Offenders Act* be amended to remove the provision which allows young offenders to waive their right to have a parent or guardian present during questioning by the police.

- When a youth court judge denies bail, the judge consider releasing the young offender into the custody of his or her parents, or another responsible person, as contemplated by section 7.1(1)(a) of the *Young Offenders Act.*

  The Ma Mawi Chi Itata Centre be given adequate funds and resources to expand its bail supervision program.

  Aboriginal communities be provided with resources to develop bail supervision and other programs that will serve as alternatives to detention.

  Accused youth who must be held in pre-trial detention be held in detention facilities in their own communities.

  Young offenders be removed from their community only as a last resort and only when the youth poses a danger to some individual or to the community.

- The *Young Offenders Act* be amended to rescind those provisions which allow a youth to be transferred to adult court for trial.

  If Parliament considers it necessary, the *Young Offenders Act* be amended to give youth court judges the option of imposing lengthier sentences on youth convicted of serious offences.

If Parliament considers it necessary, the *Young Offenders Act* be amended to allow judges to order that the trial of youth be open to the public and the media in appropriate cases.

■ The *Young Offenders Act* be amended to allow judges to designate the specific place of custody for young offenders.

The *Young Offenders Act* be amended to prohibit the mixing of closed custody facilities with open custody.

Open custody facilities and wilderness camps be established for Aboriginal youth throughout the province and, especially, in Aboriginal communities.

■ The *Young Offenders Act* be amended to allow a judge dealing with a criminal case to commit a youth to the care of a child and family service agency as an alternative to incarceration or custody.

■ Child and family service agencies be directed to continue to provide services to youth clients charged with an offence.

Child welfare and youth justice services be more fully integrated and coordinated so that all their services are available to young people charged with offences.

Youth probation for Aboriginal youth be made a part of the responsibility of Aboriginal child and family service agencies.

Diversion and Alternative Measures

■ Adequate administrative and financial support be provided to youth justice committees.

The *Young Offenders Act* be amended to remove the provision prohibiting members of youth justice committees from being remunerated.

Manitoba's alternative measures guidelines be amended to allow any young offender to be referred to an alternative measures program. The police, lawyers, Crown attorneys and judges should consider such measures in every case.

The authority for the creation of alternative measures guidelines be shifted from the provincial government to the judiciary.

The provincial government establish Aboriginally focussed diversion and alternative measure programs which incorporate the following principles:

- Aboriginal culture must be integrated into the program. Diversion schemes which involve the use of Aboriginal elders, peacemakers and other aspects of Aboriginal culture appear to have the greatest potential for success. In the context of Manitoba's urban Aboriginal communities, the program decision-makers could be drawn from the Aboriginal community within the urban environment.

- Judges must allow the community to become involved in sentencing but they must retain ultimate responsibility for sentencing.

- The program should attempt to involve all those who have a direct interest in the case, including the victim and the community.

- Programs should be able to accept referrals at any stage of the criminal justice process. They should also be able to accept referrals from the community before any charges have been laid and, if possible, before the authorities become involved.

- The community's respect for the program is vital. This means that one primary goal of the program must be to seek reconciliation and the restoration of peace in the community.

- The establishment of a range of innovative options that can be used by the decision-makers will be critical to the success of alternative measures programs based in Aboriginal communities. An appropriate plan for an Aboriginal youth might, for example, involve participation in an Aboriginally operated wilderness program, an education program, an employment training program, or a treatment program.

- Aboriginal supervisors from the community must monitor the disposition. The community must see sanctions that originate from, and are enforced by, the community, and not some outside force.

- These programs should be formally designated and recognized as Young Offenders Act programs so that their role has official recognition and official support.

Aboriginal Youth and the Justice System — General Issues

■ Aboriginal communities throughout Manitoba be encouraged and adequately funded to develop crime prevention programs for youth, based on the development of a full range of employment, cultural, social and recreational opportunities.

The funding for the Northern Fly-In Sports Camp be firmly established and that the camp be expanded to provide its services to all northern Aboriginal communities.

■ The Aboriginal Court Worker Program provide a court worker wherever Youth Court sits.

Policing

The Role of Police in Society

■ Police forces adopt a community policing approach, particularly in Aboriginal communities.

Employment Equity Programs

■ Police forces immediately institute employment equity programs to achieve Aboriginal representation equivalent to the Aboriginal proportion of the Manitoba population

Cross-Cultural Training

- Cross-cultural education components of all police training courses be reviewed and strengthened, and this process actively involve members of the Aboriginal community, resource persons and recognized experts.

  All police officers be rotated through cross-cultural education programs, and periodic refresher programs be provided as part of the regular professional development programs of all police departments.

  Any police recruits displaying racist attitudes be screened out of training, and police officers who display such conduct after joining the force be required to take further training or, if necessary, be formally disciplined or dismissed.

- The courts adopt the Anunga Rules of Australia, as rules of the court governing the reception into evidence of statements to police made by Aboriginal persons.

- All statements taken by police officers be either audio- or video-recorded. If the contents of a transcribed statement are challenged, or some tribunal wishes to hear how certain words were expressed, the tape or video can be played.

  Video equipment be used to record the statements of all suspects in cases involving deaths and other serious cases. We suggest that the taping record the totality of each interview, including all introductory comments and explanations and warnings given by the police, and including any formal statement or other comments that result.

  The videotape will be of great value. The impact would be reduced if accused persons could allege that promises or inducements were offered or pressure was applied to them before the taping began.

  Where video equipment is not available, all statements be audio-recorded. The RCMP has tape-recorded some statements for years. We recommend that all police make that practice mandatory in all cases, with the use of video where statements are taken in an office with that equipment.

Police Forces in Manitoba

- As soon as possible, Aboriginal police forces take over from the RCMP the responsibility for providing all police services in Aboriginal communities.

  The RCMP support the establishment of Aboriginal police forces and develop a policy of cooperation with such forces.

- While they continue to police Aboriginal communities, the RCMP and all other Manitoba police forces develop and make public an integrated strategy to strengthen their capacity to provide culturally appropriate policing services, and the strategy include the development of a process of regular communication with Aboriginal organizations and communities, and the annual publication of reports which indicate progress in meeting the goals of the strategy.

- ■ The Dakota Ojibway Tribal Council Police Force be provided with sufficient resources so that it can increase staff training and development in modern police methods, and gradually assume full responsibility for all law enforcement duties within its geographic jurisdiction.

  Aboriginal communities be encouraged to form regional police forces and regional police commissions following the model of the Dakota Ojibway Tribal Council Police Force. These should be established under Aboriginal control and management.

- ■ Metis and non-status communities consider the development of a regional police force, with a police commission

- ■ The *Liquor Control Act* be amended to place limits on the amount of alcohol an individual can purchase at any one time without a permit.

  The transport of large quantities of alcohol without a permit be made illegal. Transporters of illegal shipments should not only be subject to fines, but should also face the loss of their licences and vehicles.

  Police forces, in conjunction with local Aboriginal governments that have prohibited the importation of alcohol to their reserves, undertake special enforcement programs designed to halt any illegal importation.

- ■ New targets be set by the RCMP to bring appropriate numbers of Aboriginal men and women into the force as full officers more quickly than is currently contemplated.

  The RCMP employ Aboriginal police and civilian staff in their detachments in proportion to at least the Aboriginal population of the province and preferably in proportion to the Aboriginal population being served.

- ■ The Winnipeg Police Department prepare and table with the city council and the Minister of Justice, no later than December 31, 1991, an employment equity plan which has clear targets, target dates and remedies should targets not be achieved.

  The City of Winnipeg Police Department set an initial target of 133 Aboriginal police officers. The first step in reaching that goal should be to designate the next recruiting class as entirely Aboriginal. Thereafter, 50% of each recruit class be dedicated to Aboriginal recruits until the target has been met.

  The Winnipeg Police Department be required to report publicly the progress of its employment equity program to the Minister of Justice.

  A portion of the funding provided by the Province to the City of Winnipeg for police salaries be conditional on the Winnipeg Police Department's using that funding only for the hiring of Aboriginal police officers.

  The assignment of Aboriginal police officers not be restricted to the core area or other Aboriginal areas of the city of Winnipeg

The Winnipeg Police Department no longer rely on the grade 12 educational criterion for police recruitment and develop approaches which more appropriately test recruits' ability to perform the functions required of police officers.

■ The City of Brandon Police Department prepare and table with Brandon City Council and the Minister of Justice an employment equity plan no later than December 31, 1991, which will increase the numbers of Aboriginal people on the City of Brandon Police Department to a level equal to their proportion of the Manitoba population. The plan should include target dates by which to achieve that proportion and remedies should those targets not be met.

The Brandon Police Department set an initial target of nine Aboriginal police officers and that the City of Brandon Police Department dedicate that number of positions for Aboriginal recruits in its next recruit class.

Both the City of Winnipeg Police Department and the City of Brandon Police Department consider hiring Aboriginal police officers who already have policing experience with an Aboriginal force or with the RCMP.

Aboriginal people be represented among the civilian members of both the City of Winnipeg Police Department and the City of Brandon Police Department in the same proportion as their presence in the province's population.

The City of Brandon Police Department, in cooperation with the Brandon Friendship Centre, develop a program to reach out to and inform Aboriginal people living in Brandon about policing issues.

The Provincial Police Act *and the Manitoba Police Commission*

■ The *Provincial Police Act* make explicit provision for the recognition of any police commission or committee which is established to provide police services in any municipality, unorganized territory, or Aboriginal community in Manitoba.

The Manitoba Police Commission prepare and enforce a wide range of regulations covering recruitment, training, equipment, procedures, supervision of, and support for, police forces in Manitoba.

Aboriginal Systems of Policing

■ The *Provincial Police Act* be amended to provide for the establishment of a provincial Aboriginal Police Commission with authority to prepare and enforce a wide range of regulations covering recruitment, training, equipment, procedures, supervision of, and support for, Aboriginal police forces in Manitoba.

Final decisions concerning the size, composition and manner of appointment to the Aboriginal Police Commission be made by Aboriginal people.

The *Provincial Police Act* be amended to provide for the appointment of an Aboriginal Police Commissioner, to serve the Aboriginal Police Commission, with any such person being selected by Aboriginal organizations responsible for Aboriginal police forces.

Agreements be developed between the provincial Aboriginal Police Commission, local police commissions, the RCMP and the provincial Justice department for Aboriginal police forces to provide full police services to Aboriginal communities, with a firm timetable for achieving this goal, including training, equipping and supporting the local forces with appropriate back-up services as required.

Public Complaints and Policing in Manitoba

■ The Minister of Justice establish a plan of action to deal with any incident where possible criminal acts are alleged against the police, or where a person dies or suffers serious injury in an incident involving a police officer.

This plan of action include either the creation of a standing special investigations unit, or a plan to quickly assemble a special investigations team for a particular incident, able to take control of the investigation immediately following report of the incident. The unit or team should not include officers from the police department under investigation. The plan should include independent counsel to give advice concerning the laying of criminal charges. This counsel should not be a Crown attorney. The unit or team should report directly to the Minister of Justice.

The police forces in the province be required to provide all available assistance and cooperation to the special investigations team.

■ The Law Enforcement Review Board be reconstituted and the *Law Enforcement Review Act* be amended to approximate the Ontario model.

The board appoint independent counsel to have conduct of each case and be responsible for presenting the evidence.

Where the complaint is from an Aboriginal person, one member of a panel be Aboriginal.

The test to be applied by the board be proof by clear and convincing evidence, rather than beyond a reasonable doubt.

If the board decides that the complaint is proven, it have full power to impose whatever penalties it deems appropriate.

In addition to what is now in the Law Enforcement Review Agency reports, the agency report annually on the nature of complaints, how many were found to have merit, how many were dismissed and the type of penalty applied.

Police officers, including the officer against whom the complaint is made, be compellable witnesses.

Aboriginal justice systems establish and maintain an agency to receive, investigate and resolve complaints against Aboriginal police officers similar to what we recommend for provincial police forces.

Complaints against the RCMP in Manitoba, when acting as a provincial police force, be investigated and heard by the Law Enforcement Review Board.

A Strategy For Action

Aboriginal Justice Commission

■ An Aboriginal Justice Commission of Manitoba be established by legislation and by appropriate processes of the Aboriginal people of Manitoba, with a board of directors made up of equal numbers of Aboriginal and government representatives, and an independent chairperson. The commission should be provided with all necessary staff and resources.

The position of Aboriginal Justice Commissioner be established as the chief executive officer of the Aboriginal Justice Commission. The commissioner's tasks will include monitoring and assisting government implementation of the recommendations of this Inquiry.

Aboriginal Justice College

■ The Aboriginal Justice Commission establish an Aboriginal Justice College with its own Aboriginal board of directors, and staffed by Aboriginal people, to provide training and continuing education for Aboriginal people who wish to assume positions of employment within both the existing justice system and Aboriginal justice systems.

Training provided by the Aboriginal Justice College include preparation for such positions as judges, attorneys, police officers, correctional officers, court clerks, administrators, interpreters, court workers, peacemakers, youth justice committee directors, social workers, probation and parole officers, and others, as exist within the present justice system and as are needed to establish and maintain Aboriginal justice systems.

The Aboriginal Justice College organize courses in cross-cultural understanding for non-Aboriginal personnel.

Cross-Cultural Issues

■ Federal, provincial and municipal governments, individually or in concert, with the assistance and involvement of Aboriginal people, establish formal cross-cultural educational programs for all those working in any part of the justice system who have even occasional contact with Aboriginal people.

Affirmative Action

■ The Province of Manitoba legislate the establishment of an Employment Equity Commission with appropriate Aboriginal representation on its governing body.

The Employment Equity Commission have two arms: an investigative arm responsible for examining any matter covered by the legislation, and an adjudicative arm responsible for hearing any complaint made under the legislation. Those on the adjudicative side who sit as hearing panels to determine a complaint should include an Aboriginal person if the complaint involves an Aboriginal issue or complainant.

The mandate of the commission be:

- To develop employment equity targets for employers within the legislative jurisdiction of the Province of Manitoba, including any department of the government of Manitoba and any municipality, town or city within the province.

- To ensure that employers set policies and programs for the advancement and promotion of Aboriginal people.

- To monitor compliance with established employment equity targets.

- To require employers in receipt of government grants or contracts to establish an acceptable employment equity plan with appropriate time frames, within which Aboriginal people will be hired.

- To hear and determine complaints against any person or employer who fails to comply with an established employment equity plan.

Hearing panels called upon to determine complaints be entitled to make orders requiring compliance with an employment equity plan acceptable to the commission, or make such other order as may appear appropriate to it, such as financial compensation either to an individual or to a group of individuals.

■ The federal government strengthen its employment equity legislation to establish an Employment Equity Commission similar to that which we recommend for the Province of Manitoba.

■ Federal and provincial government positions which require or will inevitably result in high contact with Aboriginal people be designated as "Aboriginal bilingual positions."

■ The University of Manitoba Faculty of Law establish a recruitment program whereby Aboriginal students (including those in high schools) throughout Manitoba and Northwestern Ontario are encouraged to attend law school.

The Faculty of Law review the manner in which it makes use of the Law School Admission Test scores and grade point averages of law school applicants to ensure that Aboriginal students capable of successfully completing law school are not thereby unfairly eliminated.

The Faculty of Law increase the number of Aboriginal law students it accepts into first-year law. The minimum number of students it should be accepting would be 12% of each class, the same proportion as the proportion of Aboriginal people in the general population. Entrance levels should also include an additional number to overcome historical imbalances.

The Faculty of Law engage an Aboriginal person as a member of its faculty with the primary responsibility of providing support services to Aboriginal students and with the secondary role of developing materials on, and teaching, Aboriginal law.

The Faculty of Law undertake the development of a full credit course or courses in Aboriginal legal issues, and ensure that Aboriginal issues are included as part of the core courses taught to each law student.

The Faculty of Law organize and sponsor a conference of law schools from across Canada, to be held for the purpose of addressing the issue of increasing the numbers of Aboriginal law graduates in Canada so as to accomplish two objectives:

- To overcome historical imbalances in Aboriginal under-representation in the legal profession.

- To establish entry levels of Aboriginal law students that will ensure that the Aboriginal presence in the legal profession reflects the Aboriginal presence in the population generally.

The Faculty of Law and the Aboriginal Justice College establish a pre-law program for Aboriginal students wishing to enter law school.

Information Gathering and Statistics

■ Governments consult with Aboriginal groups to design and implement a data collection system that will provide detailed information to compare the impact on, and treatment of, Aboriginal and non-Aboriginal persons by the justice system, to evaluate the success of programs dealing with Aboriginal offenders and to provide information to help identify needed reforms.

Resources

■ As a matter of urgent importance, governments and Aboriginal people, with the assistance of the Aboriginal Justice Commission, negotiate an acceptable process to provide ongoing funding for Aboriginal governments to undertake the intiatives we suggest, in a manner consistent with:

- The need of Aboriginal people for an ongoing, consistent revenue base.

- The right of Aboriginal people, as original owners of the land, to a fair share of revenue resources from both levels of government.

- The greater access to the revenue-generating powers and sources available to federal and provincial governments.

Appendix II

Bill 28
AN ACT TO ESTABLISH AND VALIDATE
THE PUBLIC INQUIRY
INTO THE ADMINISTRATION
OF JUSTICE AND ABORIGINAL PEOPLE

WHEREAS aboriginal peoples are a valued and integral part of the Manitoba community;

AND WHEREAS the Province of Manitoba is committed to ensuring the fair and equitable administration of justice to all Manitobans, as guaranteed by the Canadian Charter of Rights and Freedoms;

AND WHEREAS aboriginal peoples have unique problems with and concerns about the administration of justice in Manitoba;

AND WHEREAS there may be reasons for these problems and concerns, including the cultural differences between aboriginal people and the established legal and social structure, the existence of many aboriginal communities in remote and isolated areas of Manitoba, the separation of constitutional responsibilities of provincial and federal governments towards aboriginal peoples, the over-representation of aboriginal peoples in conflict with the criminal law, and the under-representation of aboriginal peoples employed in the administration of justice;

AND WHEREAS leaders of aboriginal peoples in Manitoba have been increasingly concerned about the relationship between the administration of justice in Manitoba and the legitimate aspirations of aboriginal peoples for greater self-government;

AND WHEREAS recent events, including the death of J.J. Harper and the conduct of the Helen Betty Osborne case, have raised additional concerns about systemic discrimination against aboriginal peoples in the administration of justice in Manitoba;

AND WHEREAS the Lieutenant Governor in Council, by Order in Council No. 468/88 dated April 13, 1988 appointed The Public Inquiry into the Administration of Justice and Aboriginal People as a committee under section 4 of The Attorney General's Act;

AND WHEREAS the Lieutenant Governor in Council, by Order in Council No. 1308/88 dated November 2, 1988, established and continued The Public Inquiry into the Administration of Justice and Aboriginal People as a commission under Part V of The Manitoba Evidence Act and revoked Order in Council No. 468/88;

AND WHEREAS it is considered advisable to validate the establishment and continuation of The Public Inquiry into the Administration of Justice and Aboriginal People, its actions and the actions of the commissioners appointed to it from the date of its first establishment;

THEREFORE HER MAJESTY, by and with the advice and consent of the Legislative Assembly of Manitoba, enacts as follows:

Definition
1   In this Act, "commission" means The Public Inquiry into the Administration of Justice and Aboriginal People established in subsection 2(1).

Commission established
2(1)   A commission known as The Public Inquiry into the Administration of Justice and Aboriginal people is hereby established.

Members appointed
2(2)   The members of the commission are the Honourable Associate Chief Justice A.C. Hamilton of the Court of Queen's Bench of Manitoba and His Honour, Associate Chief Judge C.M. Sinclair of the Provincial Court of Manitoba.

Scope of inquiry
3(1)   The commissioners shall investigate, report and make recommendations to the Minister of Justice on the relationship between the administration of justice and Aboriginal peoples of Manitoba, guided by but not limited to the terms of reference set out in the Schedule.

Report to minister
3(2)   The report of the commission shall be delivered to the Minister of Justice on or before March 31, 1990 or a later date prescribed by the Lieutenant Governor in Council.

Powers
4   Without restricting the powers granted to the commissioners under this Act, the commissioners may

(a) adopt procedures and methods that they consider necessary or advisable for the full and proper conduct of the inquiry, including the exclusion of the public, or any member of the public, from the hearing;

(b) hold public hearings at the places and times that they consider desirable and necessary; and

(c) engage the services of counsel and investigators to aid and assist in the inquiry as the commissioners consider necessary or advisable.

Access to records
5   The commissioners, or persons that they designate, are hereby authorized to have complete access to personnel and all relevant papers, documents, vouchers, records and books of any kind in the possession of departments and agencies of the Government of Manitoba.

Costs

6 On the certification of the Clerk of the Executive Council, the Minister of Finance shall pay out of the Consolidated Fund, travelling and other incidental expenses incurred in carrying out the inquiry, and fees and salaries of advisors and assistants employed or retained for the purposes of the commission unless the Lieutenant Governor in Council makes further or other provisions respecting the payment of those incidental expenses or fees and salaries.

Powers of inquiry

7 For greater certainty, The Public Inquiry into the Administration of Justice and Aboriginal People and the commissioners appointed to it, without limiting the powers of the commission or the commissioners,

(a) is and are declared to have the right to investigate all aspects of the events leading up to the death of J.J. Harper, the investigation which was conducted by the City of Winnipeg Police Department after the death of J.J. Harper, announcements made by the City of Winnipeg Police Department and the appropriateness of those announcements, the training and regulations of the City of Winnipeg Police Department relating to stopping persons on the street, the arrest of persons, the use and protection of firearms and the manner of dealing with aboriginal people, whether there exists any evidence of racial prejudice with respect to any of the events which led to the death of J.J. Harper or the investigation of his death, the adequacy of procedures for inquiry into the death of persons whose deaths occurred while in contact with the police and all matters on which evidence was led and findings made at the inquest which was conducted into the death of J.J. Harper pursuant to the provisions of The Fatality Inquiries Act;

(b) is and are declared to have the right to investigate all aspects of the police investigation into the death of Helen Betty Osborne and all aspects of the laying and prosecution of charges which followed, including whether the right persons were charged, whether the appropriate charges were laid, whether charges should have been laid earlier, whether immunity from prosecution should have been granted to Lee Colgan, whether there exists any evidence of racial prejudice with respect to the investigation of the death of Helen Betty Osborne, whether the acts or omissions of any persons outside the police department impaired the investigation and whether the prosecution was properly conducted;

(c) is and are declared to have the right upon completion of the inquiry and the making of its report to make such findings of fact as it deems appropriate, and, where it deems proper, to name the names of persons whose conduct ought, in the opinion of the commissioners, to be called into question; and

(d) may convene a special hearing or hearings to compel the production of documents which, in the opinion of the commissioners, are deemed relevant directly or indirectly to matters before the commission or to the credibility of any person.

Validation of actions of Inquiry

8   All orders, decisions, legal process, proceedings, actions and expenditures of The Public Inquiry into the Administration of Justice and Aboriginal People before this Act receives royal assent are hereby declared to be valid as though done pursuant to this Act and shall not be called into question in any court of law.

Part V of C.C.S.M. c. E150

9(1)   Except as provided by subsection (2), Part V of The Manitoba Evidence Act does not apply to this Act.

Application of Part V of C.C.SM. c. E150

9(2)   Subsection 83(4), sections 84, 87, 88, 89, 90, 91, 92, 93 and 94 and subsections 95(1), (2) and (4) of Part V of The Manitoba Evidence Act apply to this Act with appropriate changes as the circumstances required.

Act prevails

10   In the event of an inconsistency between this Act and another Act of the Legislature, the provisions of this Act prevail to the extent of the inconsistency.

Powers of the L.G. in C.

11   The Lieutenant Governor in Council may

(a) wind up the commission;

(b) appoint, or revoke the appointment of, a member of the commission;

(c) modify, enlarge or clarify the scope of the commission;

(d) make further or other provisions for the payment of travelling and other incidental expenses and fees and salaries of advisors and assistances employed or retained for purposes of the commission;

(e) prescribe a later date for the delivery of the report of the commission to the Minister of Justice; and

(f) provide for matters and circumstances for which no provision or no adequate provision is made in this Act.

Coming into force

12   This Act is retroactive and deemed to have come into force on April 13, 1988.

SCHEDULE
TERMS OF REFERENCE

Purpose of commission

The purpose of the commission is to inquire into, and make findings about, the state of conditions with respect to aboriginal people in the justice system in Manitoba and produce a final report for the Minister of Justice with conclusions, options and recommendations.

The commission's deliberations are to include consideration of all aspects of the cases of J.J. Harper and Helen Betty Osborne, and the commission may make any additional recommendations that it deems appropriate with respect to those cases, including a recommendation that there be further consideration of particular matters or further inquiry into any aspect of either case.

Scope of inquiry

The scope of the commission is to include all components of the justice system, that is, policing, courts and correctional services. The commission is to consider whether and to what extent aboriginal and non-aboriginal persons are treated differently by the justice system and whether there are specific adverse effects, including possible systemic discrimination against aboriginal people, in the justice system. The commission is to consider the manner in which the justice system now operates and whether there are alternative methods of dealing with aboriginal persons involved with the law. For example, the commission may review the following issues:

Policing:
- policing issues in relation to aboriginal people;
- deployment of personnel and accessibility of policing services;
- arrest and charging procedures;
- cultural sensitization for police officers and affirmative action programs;
- the conduct and training of wildlife officers relating to aboriginal people.

Access to and adequacy of legal counsel:
- eligibility and access to Legal Aid;
- access in remote communities.

Court processes:
- use of bail and custody;
- prosecutorial discretion and plea bargaining;
- role of court communicators;
- effect of time delays from arrest to trial;
- family proceedings;
- Youth Court;
- child welfare proceedings.

Court dispositions:
- comparative types of dispositions among aboriginal and non-aboriginal people;
- use of custodial sentences;
- availability of sentencing alternatives.

Post sentencing:
- differential success of aboriginal and non-aboriginal groups on probation;
- availability and use of fine option program;
- prison experiences, such as temporary absences and parole;
- use of half-way houses;
- re-integration to communities and reserves.

Other:
- awareness and knowledge of justice system by aboriginal people;
- communication between justice system personnel and aboriginal people;
- employment of aboriginal people in justice system.

Appendix III

Hearing Dates and Locations

Date	Community
September 13, 1988	Winnipeg
September 14, 1988	Winnipeg
September 20, 1988	Thompson
September 21, 1988	Thompson
September 29, 1988	Portage Correctional Institution
September 29, 1988	Portage La Prairie
October 11, 1988	The Town of The Pas
October 12, 1988	The Town of The Pas
October 13, 1988	The Pas Correctional Institution
October 18, 1988	Winnipeg
October 19, 1988	Winnipeg
October 20, 1988	Winnipeg
November 1, 1988	God's Lake Narrows
November 2, 1988	God's River
November 3, 1988	Oxford House
November 8, 1988	Cross Lake
November 9, 1988	Grand Rapids
November 10, 1988	Norway House
November 15, 1988	Winnipeg
November 16, 1988	Winnipeg
November 17, 1988	Winnipeg
December 5, 1988	Red Sucker Lake
December 6, 1988	Wasagamack
December 7, 1988	Garden Hill
December 8, 1988	St. Theresa Point
December 13, 1988	Brokenhead Reserve
December 13, 1988	Selkirk
December 14, 1988	Winnipeg

December 15, 1988	Winnipeg
January 3, 1989	Brandon Correctional Institution
January 4, 1989	Brandon
January 10, 1989	Brochet - Barren Lands
January 11, 1989	Lac Brochet - North Lands
January 12, 1989	Tadoule Lake
January 17, 1989	The Pas Reserve
January 18, 1989	Pukatawagan
January 19, 1989	Moose Lake
January 24, 1989	Dakota Tipi Reserve
January 25, 1989	Winnipeg
January 26, 1989	Winnipeg
January 31, 1989	Fort Alexander
February 1, 1989	Hollow Water
February 2, 1989	Peguis
February 8, 1989	Pineimuta Place
February 9, 1989	Easterville
February 28, 1989	Roseau River
March 1, 1989	Long Plain
March 2, 1989	Sandy Bay
March 3, 1989	St. Laurent
March 9, 1989	Sioux Valley
March 14, 1989	Winnipeg
March 15, 1989	Winnipeg
March 16, 1989	Winnipeg
March 21, 1989	Split Lake
March 22, 1989	South Indian Lake
March 23, 1989	Shamattawa
March 28, 1989	Little Grand Rapids
March 29, 1989	Poplar River
March 30, 1989	Berens River
March 31, 1989	Bloodvein
April 4, 1989	Winnipeg
April 12, 1989	Stony Mountain Institution

April 13, 1989	Headingley Correctional Institution
April 18, 1989	Dauphin
April 19, 1989	Camperville
April 25, 1989	Winnipeg
April 26, 1989	Winnipeg
April 26, 1989	Stony Mountain Institution
April 27, 1989	Winnipeg
April 28, 1989	Winnipeg
November 21, 1989	Winnipeg
November 22, 1989	Winnipeg

APPENDIX IV

Presenters at the Community Hearings

Abbors, John
Abdilla, Leonard
Abigosis, Joyce
Abraham, Gilbert
Abramson, Ralph
  (Treaty Land Entitlement Committee)
Anderson, Caroline
Anderson, Chief Ed
  (Fairford Indian Band)
  (Anishinaabe Child and
  Family Services)
Anderson, Eva
Andrews, Adelade
Andrews, Rhoda
Antoine, Elvis
Antoine, Richard
Antoine, Russell
Antsanen, Abel
Armstrong, Carolyn
  (Project Opikihiwawin)
Arnold, Abraham
  (Manitoba Association for
  Rights and Liberties)
Baker, Cecilia
Baker, Irene
Baker, Lee
Bakken, Jim
  (Manitoba Family Services,
  Child and Family Services)
Balfour, Charlie
Ball, Barbara
  (Women's Post-Treatment Centre)
Ballantyne, Adolph
Ballantyne, Clifford
  (Manitoba Metis Federation,
  Moose Lake Local)
Ballantyne, Edna
  (Opasquia Women's Association)
Ballantyne, Greg
  (Manitoba Metis Federation,
  Fine Option Program)

Ballantyne, Percy
Balmer, Sergeant Greg
  (RCMP, Lynn Lake)
Barkwell, Lawrence
Barrie, Sergeant
  (RCMP, Virden)
Batenchuk, Virginia
Bear, Eugene
Bear, Marie Elizabeth
Bear, Rose
Beardy, Charles
  (Winnipeg Council of Treaty
  and Status Indians)
Beardy, Doreen
  (Opasquia Women's Association)
Beardy, Eliza
Beardy, Joe
Beardy, Chief Larry
  (Split Lake Indian Band)
Beardy, Rodney
Beardy, Ross
  (NADAP)
Beardy, Ruby
Beardy, Sandy
Beardy, Sheila
Beardy, Tania
Beaulieu, Diana
  (Dakota Ojibway Probation Services)
Beaulieu, Isaac
  (Assembly of Manitoba Chiefs)
Beaulieu, Noah
Belanger, Father Noel
  (Oblates of Mary Immaculate)
Bell, Albert
Bell, Lee Marie
Bender, Clarence
Betz, Dorothy
Bighead, King
Bighetty, Chief Pascal
  (Mathias Colomb Indian Band)
Bighetty, Cornelius
Bighetty, Gabe
Bighetty, Stanley

Bignell, Eric
(The Pas Indian Band,
Youth Council)
Bigus, Barry
(Project Opikihiwawin)
Bird, Chief Henry
(Southeast Child and Family Services)
Bissett, John
(National Parole Board,
Conditional Release Program)
Bittern, Albert
Bittern, Chief Andrew
(Berens River Indian Band)
Bittern, Marcel
Bittern, Norway
Bittern, Tony
Bjornson, Jeri
(Charter of Rights Coalition)
Bjornsson, Don
Black, Debra
(Winnipeg Native Probation Caucus)
Blacksmith, Grace
(Dakota Rehabilitation Centre,
NADAP)
Blacksmith, Harold
Blacksmith, Harvey
(Cross Lake Justice Committee)
Bland, Earlen
Bland, Madeline
Blaquiere, Jerry
(Lynn Lake Friendship Centre)
Bone, Chief Robert
(Sioux Valley Indian Band)
Bone, John
Bonner, John
Boubard, Larry
(Dakota Ojibway Tribal Council,
Social Services)
Bouchie, Bill
Bouchie, Charlie
Boudreau, Linda
(Dauphin Friendship Centre)
Boyes, Ken
Bradburn, Johnny
Bradburn, Stanley
Brass, Chief Alpheus
(Chemawawin Indian Band)

Braun, Theresa
Breed, Dennis
Brightnose, Jeff
Brown, Corporal Dave
(RCMP, Lac du Bonnet)
Bruce, Ernest
Bruce, Marvin
(Manitoba Attorney General)
Bruyere, Caroline
(Indigenous Women's Collective)
Buchanan, Linda
(Rosaire House)
Budd, Jean
Budd, Ken
Bunn, Cynthia
Bunn, John
Bushie, Burma
(Hollow Water Resource Group)
Bushie, Ezra
Bushie, Garf
Bushie, Chief Rod
(Assembly of Manitoba Chiefs)
(Hollow Water Indian Band)
Bushie, Violet
Bussidor, Ernie
Cameron, Barbara
(Dakota Ojibway Tribal Council)
Cameron, Lloyd
(Dakota Ojibway Tribal Council
Police)
Campbell, Clayton
Campbell, Dave
Campbell, Ed
(Northern Association of
Community Councils)
Campbell, Murray
Caribou, Ralph
Castel, Flora
Castel, Lloyd
Castel, Shirley
Castel, Sidney
Chapman Smyth, Erma
(Knowles Centre)
Charles, Philip
Chartrand, Al
(Court Communicators Program)
(Native Clan Organization)

Chartrand, Darin
Chartrand, David
Chartrand, Dennis
Chartrand, Garnet
Chartrand, Lionel
  (Manitoba Metis Federation)
Chartrand, Lorraine
Chartrand, Ted
Chartrand, Thomas
Chaske, David
Chaske, Harold
Chaske, Lou
Cherry, Albert
Chief, Howard
  (Native Brotherhood Organization,
  Headingley Correctional Institution)
Chippeway, Bev
  (Aboriginal Peoples Brotherhood)
Christianson, Susan
  (Dauphin Friendship Centre)
Chubb, Rita
Chubb, Thomas
Church, Mary
Clarkson, Mayor Jack
Clifford, Gil
  (Legal Aid Services Society)
Clipping, Suzanne
Colomb, Celestine
Colomb, Eliase
Colomb, Elie
Colomb, Jimmy
Colomb, John
Colonval, Victor
Constant, John
Cook, Cecil
Cook, Dave
Cook, Emma
  (Opasquia Women's Association)
Cook, Jackie
Couillonneur, Darcy
Courchene, Grand Chief Dave
Courchene, Joyce
  (Indigenous Women's Collective)
Courchene, Chief Ken
  (Fort Alexander Indian Band)
Courchene, Norman
Courchene, Patricia
Courchene, Victor

Coyle, Debbie
Crane, George
Crane, Thomas
Crate, Ginger
  (Anishinaabe Child and
  Family Services)
Creighton, Sergeant Douglas
  (RCMP, Emerson)
Crocker, Bert
  (Sagkeeng Child and Family Services)
Cromarty, Brian
  (Norway House Youth Council)
Cunningham, Chester
  (Native Counselling Services
  of Alberta)
Cutlip, Maggie
Daniels, Patrick
Daniels, Robert
  (Urban Indian Association)
Daniels, Rose
Danyluk, Audrey
  (Thompson Crisis Centre)
Debrecen, Fred
DeLaRonde, Billyjo
  (Manitoba Metis Federation)
Delaronde, Donna
Delaronde, Sandra
  (Manitoba Advisory Council
  on the Status of Women)
  (Manitoba Metis Federation, The Pas)
Delorme, Debbie
Demers, Don
  (Manitoba Attorney General)
Denechezhe, Alfred
Denechezhe, Alphonse
Denechezhe, Chief Jerome
  (Northlands Indian Band)
Denechezhe, Constable Paul
Denechezhe, Virginia
Desjarlais, Cecil
  (Dakota Ojibway Tribal Council
  Police)
Desjarlais, Chief Harry
  (Sandy Bay Indian Band)
Desjarlais, Joe
Desjarlais, Lance
Desjarlais, Michael
Detteniekazie, Ceceila

Devine, Cynthia
(Child Abuse Videotaping Project)
Dione, Dale
(Kahnawake Nation)
Dojack, Robert
(Fine Option Program)
Donkey, Florence
Dorion, Philip
Dowan, Roy
(Dakota Rehab Centre, NADAP)
Duck, John
Duck, Thomas
Dueck, Anna
(Mennonite Central Committee)
Dumas, Genevieve
Dumas, Gordon
Dumas, Jack
Dumas, Mary Ann
Dumas, Rosie
Dumont, Guy
(Manitoba Metis Federation,
St. Laurent Local)
Dumont, Yvon
(Manitoba Metis Federation)
Duncan, Alex
Dunham, Ken
Durocher, Robert
Dyck, David
Dysart, Hilda
Dysart, Mayor Jack
Dysart, Pat
Eagle, Noella
Easter, Clarence
Easter, Dennis
(Urban Indian Association)
Eastman, Angela
Eastman, Chief Clarence
(Oak Lake Indian Band)
Ehinger, John
Elias, Henry
Elliott, Brenda
(Elizabeth Fry Society)
Ellis, Brian
Emberly, Kenneth
Erickson, Stan
Esquega, Elizabeth
Essie, Wally

Eyolfson, Connie
Faurschou, Bruce
(Manitoba Correctional
Chaplains Association)
Ferland, Zerlina
Fiddler, Josias
Filkow, Ken
(Manitoba Human Rights
Commission)
Fineblit, Allan
(Legal Aid Services Society)
Finnigan, Brian
Fisher, Emma
Fisher, James
Fisher, Martina
Flett, Bryan
Flett, Elsie
(West Region Child and
Family Services)
Flett, Gabby
Flett, Hilda
Flett, John Arthur
Flett, Jonathan
Flett, Lloyd
Flett, Maria
(Opasquia Women's Association)
Flett, Moyer
Flett, Percy
Flett, Philip
(Native United Church)
Flett, Rita
(Native United Church)
Flett, Simon
Flett, William
Fobister, Cindy
Fontaine, Ann
Fontaine, Carl
(Sagkeeng Education
Foundation Inc.)
Fontaine, Curtis
(Native Clan Organization)
Fontaine, Janet
(Manitoba Women's Directorate)
Fontaine, Jody
Fontaine, Marilyn
(Ma Mawi Chi Itata Centre Inc.)
Fontaine, Melvin

Fontaine, Phil
  (Grand Chief, Provincial Leader,
  Assembly of Manitoba Chiefs)
Fontaine, Vincent
  (George Guimond Care Centre Inc.)
Fosseneuve, Henry
Foster, Hubert
Fouad, Mark
  (Yellowquill College)
Francoise, Moise
Franklin, Russell
Freeman, Staff Sergeant
  (RCMP)
Funk, Catherine
Funk, Sandi
  (Ikwewak Justice Society)
Funk-Unrau, Neil
  (Conference of Mennonites of
  Canada, Native Ministries)
Garson, Ann
Garson, Joe
Geddes, Staff Sergeant
  (RCMP)
Genaille, Hubert
George, Ralph
Germschied, Darlene
  (Manitoba Human Rights
  Commission)
Giesbrecht, Lorne
Gilholme, Superintendent
  (RCMP, Thompson Subdivision)
Goaden, Lottie
Godwin, Don
Goosehead, James
Gordon, Ellen
  (Manitoba Bar Association,
  Criminal Justice Subsection)
Gosling, Noela
Gosse, Dr. Richard
  (RCMP Public Complaints
  Commission)
Gowryluk, Melinda
Graveline, Jean
  (Manitoba Action Committee
  on the Status of Women)
Green, Donna
  (Child and Family Services of
  Central Winnipeg)

Green, Philip
Greenwood, Irene
  (United Church of Canada)
Grieger, Waltraud
  (Nova House)
Grier, Sylvia
  (Legal Aid Services Society,
  Northern Paralegal Project)
Grieves, Dennis
Grieves, Douglas
  (NADAP)
Grieves, Jack
Grieves, Lena
Grieves, Linda
  (Southeast Resource Tribal Council)
Grieves, Sheila
Guiboche, Bill
Guiboche, Fortunat
Guiboche, Stanley
Guimond, Lloyd
  (George Guimond Care Centre Inc.)
Guy, John
  (Manitoba Attorney General)
Hagel, Lorne
  (Hollow Water Resource Group)
Haig, Graeme
  (RCMP Public Complaints
  Commission)
Halcrow, Lillian
Hall, Mary
Halliwell, Gayle
  (Lord Selkirk School Division,
  Continuing Education Divison)
Halpin, Janet
  (Manitoba Coalition
  Against Apartheid)
Hanska, Wilma
Harabi, Asan
Hardisty, Marcel
  (Hollow Water Resource Group)
Hardisty, Norbert
Haroun, Ellen
Harper, Allan
Harper, Andrew
Harper, Chief Billy
  (Red Sucker Lake Indian Band)
Harper, Carol
  (NADAP)

Jessens, Ieva
Johnson, Damon
  (Indian Council of First Nations)
Johnson, Doreen
Johnston, Eunadie
  (Thompson Crisis Centre)
Joseph, Allan
  (Ma Mawi Chi Itata Centre Inc.,
  Bail Supervision Program)
Joynson, Cliff
  (Ma Mawi Chi Itata Centre)
Kahkeeway, Doug
Kakegamik, Solly
  (Native United Church)
Kanabee, Henry
Kasto, Jack
  (Dakota Ojibway Tribal Council)
Keeper, Chief Enil
  (Little Grand Rapids Indian Band)
Keeper, John
Keeper, Nelson
Kelly-Kinew, Peter
Kematch, Gilbert
Kenney, Richard
Kent, Hazel
Kent, Ralph
Killeen, Tim
Kirkness, Lawrence
Kitchekeesik, Allison
Kitchekeesik, George
Klassen, Ron
  (Legal Aid Services Society, Winnipeg)
Klyne, Joseph Sonny
  (Mayor, Camperville)
Knight, Phil
  (Community Legal
  Education Association)
Knott, Chief Elijah
  (Wasagamack Indian Band)
Korchinski, Emil
  (Indian Affairs and Northern
  Development, Canada)
Kotyk, Ted
  (Inmate Welfare Committee, Stony
  Mountain Correctional Institution)
Krenn, Ingrid

Krouchuk, Albert
Labrador, Louie
LaFond, Superintendent Dennis
  (Dauphin Correctional Institution)
Laforte, Sylvia
Lafreniere, Claire
  (Ma Mawi Chi Itata Centre Inc.,
  Bail Supervision Program)
Lagidmodiere, Julyda
Lamirande, Brian
  (Court Communicators Program)
Langevin, Ed
  (Child Abuse Videotaping Project)
Langin, Doug
Larocque, Alphonse
Larocque, Martha
Larsen, Sergeant
  (RCMP, The Pas)
Lathlin, Chief Oscar
  (Justice Committee,
  Assembly of Manitoba Chiefs)
  (The Pas Indian Band)
Laugher, Ila
Lavallee, Jules
  (Anishinaabe Respect)
Lavallee, Mark
Lavallee, Maureen
Leach, Linda
  (Southeast Child and Family Services)
Leclair, Ted
Ledoux, Blaine
LeDrew, Sharon
  (Legal Aid Services Society,
  Thompson, Northern Paralegal
  Project)
Lemoine, Superintendent Dennis
  (Headingley Correctional Institution)
Leonoff, Heather S.
Letandre, John
Levine, Naomi
  (Manitoba Defence Lawyers
  Association)
Lilly, Helen
Linden, Bill
Linklater, Solomon
Linklater, Tina
Little, Cornelius
Little, Edward

Little, John
Little, Ron
Littlechief, Judy
Littlejohn, John
Longstaffe, Dr. Sally
  (Child Advocacy Project)
Ludwig, Israel
  (League for Human Rights of
  B'nai Brith of Canada)
Lund, Terry
  (Manitoba Association for
  Continuing Education)
MacFarlane, John
MacKenzie, John
  (Manitoba Association for
  Continuing Education)
Majkut, Art
  (Stony Mountain
  Correctional Institution)
Malcolm, Cindy
Malcolm, Dennis
Mallett, Kathy
  (Canadian Alliance in
  Solidarity with Native Peoples)
Maloney, Tim
  (Northwest Child and
  Family Services)
Mann, Lorna
  (Journeys Education Association)
Martin, Amy
Martindale, Rev. Doug
Maskiw, Ken
  (Manitoba Family Services,
  Child and Family Services)
Mason, Jack
Mason, James
Mason, Tekaquita
Massan, Horace
Massey, James
Matas, David
  (Manitoba Association for
  Rights and Liberties)
Mayer, Bob
Mazawasicuna, Nelson
McCleverty, Bob
  (Mayor, Thicket Portage)
McCormick, Christopher
  (Native Council of Canada)

McCrae, Hon. James C.
  (Attorney General of Manitoba)
McDonald, Jim
McDougall, Alfred
McDougall, Angus
McDougall, David
McDougall, Simon
McDougall, Wilfred
McEvoy, Catherine
McFall, A.G.
McFarlane, John
  (Native United Church)
McGillivary, Malcolm
McIvor, Don
McIvor, Jacqueline
  (Cross Lake Justice Committee)
McIvor, Randy
McKay, Chief Clifford
  (Assembly of Manitoba Chiefs)
McKay, Ed
McKay, Eva
McKay, Frank
  (Dakota Ojibway Probation Services)
McKay, John
McKay, Kenny
  (Outreach Program, Sioux Valley)
McKay, Leonard
McKay, Lorraine
McKay, Professor Raoul
McKay, Sophia
McKay, Reverend Stan
  (Native United Church)
McKay, Sue
McKay, Thomas
McKay, Verna
  (Project Opikihiwawin)
McKillop, Ginny
  (Cross Cultural Consulting Inc.)
McLean, Gary
  (City of Winnipeg Community Race
  Relations Committee)
McLean, Howard
McLeod, Chris
McPherson, Abraham
McPherson, Doreen
  (Peguis Justice Committee)

McPherson, Rosemary
  (Court Communicators Program)
McVicar, Superintendent Brian,
  (Brandon Correctional Institution)
Meconse, Grace
Meeches, Chief John
  (Long Plain Indian Band)
Meikle, Wava
Mentuk, Gabe
Merasty, Gerry
Merasty, Seonaid
Mercredi, Ovide
  (Southeast Resource
  Development Council)
Merrick, Angus
Merrick, Lawrence
  (Dakota Ojibway Tribal Council)
Michel, Chief Philip
  (Manitoba Keewatinowi Okimakanak)
  (Treaty Land Entitlement Committee)
Miles, Chief Sam
  (Shamattawa Indian Band)
Milgaard, David
Miller, Constable Allen
  (Dakota Ojibway Tribal Council
  Police, Sioux Valley)
Miller, Craig
  (Dakota Oyate Lodge)
Miller, Robert
  (Community Dispute Centre)
Mink, Hazel
Mink, Walter
Missyabit, Dale
  (Rossbrook House Inc.)
Mitchell, Chief Vera
  (Poplar River Indian Band)
Moar, Melvin
  (Manitoba Metis Federation,
  Child and Family Services)
Monias, Eli
Monias, Michael
Moore, Maria
Moose, Freida
Moose, Gilbert
Moose, Ronald
Moose, Virginia
Moose, Wellington

Morris, Joseph
Morrison, David
Morrisseau, Donna
Morrisseau, Stanford
Morrissette, Larry
  (Ma Mawi Chi Itata Centre)
Morrissette, Pat
  (Child and Family Services of
  Central Winnipeg)
Mowatt, John
Munroe, Dorothy
Munroe, Waylon
Murphy, Sergeant Don
  (Hollow Water Resource Group)
  (RCMP, Powerview)
Murray, Debra
  (United Church of Canada)
Muskego, Violet
Mutcheson, Heather
  (Manitoba Adolescent
  Treatment Centre)
Myerion, Calvin
Myers, Cecil
Myran, Calvin
Myran, Lawrence
Napoakeesick, Robinson
Neepin, George
  (Manitoba Keewatinowi Okimakanak)
Nelson, Charles
  (Pembina Anishinaabe)
Nelson, Leonard
Nelson, Marjorie
Nelson, Rose
Nelson, Stan
  (Pembina Anishinaabe)
Nelson, Terrance
  (Pembina Anishinaabe)
Nepetaybo, Tom
  (Keewatin Tribal Council)
Nepinak, Terrilene
Nepitabo, Mary
Newton, Dr. Jim
  (Manitoba Adolescent
  Treatment Centre)
Nicholas, Rudy
Noel, Carole
  (Agassiz Youth Centre)

Norquay, Gordon
   (Dakota Ojibway Tribal Council,
   NADAP)
Norrie, Mayor William
   (City of Winnipeg Community Race
   Relations Committee)
Norris, Eileen
Novedale, Ernie
Okemow, Harold
Okemow, Oliver
Okemow, Thomas
Okimaw, Andrew
Okimaw, Cecilia
Okimaw, Chief Alex
   (God's Lake Narrows Indian Band)
Okimaw, Ellice
Okimaw, Esola
Okimaw, Irene
Okimaw, Chief Marcel
   (God's River Indian Band)
Okimaw, Percy
Okimaw, Thomas
Okimaw, Wesley
Olson, Carl
   (Brokenhead Mental Health
   Steering Committee)
Olson, George
O'Reilly, Sergeant
   (RCMP, Gypsumville)
Osinksi, Mary Ann
   (Women's Post-Treatment Centre)
Ouskan, Chief Alex
   (War Lake Indian Band)
Owen, George Thomas
Packo, Bobbi
Packo, Richard
Paluk, Mike
   (Legal Aid Services Society, Northern
   Paralegal Project)
Parisien, Peter
Parrott, Jim
Parsons, Sergeant Doug
   (RCMP, Thompson)
Pashe, Barry
Pashe, Chief Dennis
   (Dakota Tipi Indian Band)

Pashe, Delores
Paul, Benjamin
Paul, Harry
Paul, Peter
   (Urban Indian Association)
Paul, Wilfred
Paxton, Janet
Peltz, Arnie
   (Legal Aid Services Society)
Penny, Inspector Bob
   (RCMP, Thompson)
Perreault, Sharon
   (Ma Mawi Chi Itata Centre Inc.)
Personius, Irene
Peters, Barry
Peters, Chief Gordon
   (Assembly of First Nations)
Phaneuf, Louise
   (Assiniboine Community College,
   Native Correctional
   Officer Training Program)
Philips, Henry
Pierre, Chief Vincent
   (Dakota Ojibway Tribal Council)
Pinet, Father Bernard
   (Oblates of Mary Immaculate)
Pompana, Calvin
   (Urban Indian Association)
Potts, Inspector Jim
   (RCMP)
Powderhorn, Moses
Powderhorn, Roger
Pranteau, Dave
   (Awasis Child and Family Services)
Pratt, Dorothy
Prince, Adrianne
Prince, Cecil
Prince, Rufus
   (Dakota Ojibway Tribal Council
   Police)
Pritchard, Dawna
   (Concerned Citizens for Equality)
Purdy, Chris
Purich, Don
   (Native Law Centre,
   University of Saskatchewan)
Quill, Roger

Rampersad, Harold
  (City of Winnipeg Community Race
  Relations Committee)
Rankowski, Inspector
  (RCMP)
Ranville, Stirling
  (Indian and Metis Friendship Centre
  of Winnipeg)
Raven, Gary
Razor, Billy
Redekop, Paul
  (Mediation Services)
Redhead, Alex
Redhead, Eric
Rempel, Melita
Richard, Glenda
Richard, Mary
  (Indigenous Women's Collective)
Richard, Ron
  (Manitoba Metis Federation,
  Northwest Region)
Roberts, Carl
  (Dakota Ojibway Tribal Council)
Roberts, Mary
  (Dakota Ojibway Tribal Council)
Robertson, Irene
Robinson, Jack
  (Ma-Mow-We-Tak Centre)
Robinson, Mary
Robinson, Ray
Robinson, Russell
Rodgers, John
Rodin, Greg
  (League for Human Rights of
  B'nai Brith of Canada)
Ross, Chief Alan
  (Norway House Indian Band)
Ross, Albert
Ross, Eddie
Ross, Ellice
Ross, George
Ross, Gordon
Ross, Janett
Ross, Jemima
Ross, Leonard
Ross, Lillian
Ross, Louis
Ross, Lydia

Ross, Rebecca
Ross, Rex
Ross, Staff Sergeant
  (RCMP)
Roulette, Allan
Roulette, Arthur
Roulette, Mary
Routledge, Susan
Rundle, Dave
  (Southeast Child and Family Services)
Rupp, Irene
Sanderson, Ella
Sanderson, Marguerite
Saunders, Maggie
Saunders, Mary
Sawatsky, Len
  (John Howard Society)
Sayese, Eileen
Sayese, Irving
Schellenberg, Dave
  (Child and Family Services of
  Central Winnipeg)
Scott, Edwin
Scott, Ernest
Scott, Grace
Scott, Lindsey
Scott, Marianne
Scott, Reverend Sandy
  (United Church of Canada)
Seaton, Marie
  (Ma-Mow-We-Tak Centre)
Semple, Gerald
Settee, Frank
Severight, Dolores
Severight, Vimy
Seymour, Thelma
  (Hollow Water Resource Group)
Seymour, Valdie
  (Hollow Water Resource Group)
Shingoose, Cindy
Shorting, Chief Dennis
  (Little Saskatchewan Indian Band)
Simpson, Geraldine
Simpson, Victor
Sinclair, Reverend Allen
  (United Church of Canada)
Sinclair, Clifford
Sinclair, Daniel

Tetlock, Chriss
  (North End Women's Centre)
Thomas, Bill
Thomas, Carson
Thomas, Cleo
Thomas, Doug
Thomas, Olga
  (Peguis Justice Committee)
Thomas, William John
Thompson, Caroline
Thompson, Fern
Thompson, John
Thompson, Lori Ann
Thorassie, Albert
  (Churchill Indian Band)
Thorassie, Joe
Tobacco, Chief Jim
  (Moose Lake Indian Band)
Tobacco, Joe
Tomczack, Mila
Topey, Adrian
Toupin, Rene
  (Interlake Tribal Council)
Traverse, Chief Bill
  (Jackhead Indian Band)
Trottier, Clyde
Trout, Mayor Raymond
Tumak, Donna
Turenne, Barbara
  (Sioux Valley Indian Band)
Turner, Chief Esau
  (Swampy Cree Tribal Council)
Unfried, Bruce
  (Mayor, The Pas)
Van Mill, Rene
Versteeg, Jerry
Vincent, Barry
Wachniak, Terry
Walker, Elizabeth
Walker, Grace
Walker, Harvey
Wambidee, Art
Wand, Dr. R.R.
  (Manitoba Adolescent
  Treatment Centre)
Wastasecoot, Nancy
Wasteste, Wilfred
Wavey, Robert

Weenusk, Paul
Weenusk, Chief Tommy
  (Oxford House Indian Band)
Weenusk, Wesley
Weiss, Laurie
Weitman, Harold
Wescoupe, Marie
White, Maggie
White, Marty
White, Rolanda
Whitebird, Chief Dennis
  (Treaty and Aboriginal Rights
  Research Centre)
  (West Region
  Child and Family Services)
Whitecloud, Kathy
Whiteway, Dominic
Whitford, Barbara
Whitney, Gene
  (Environment Canada,
  Canadian Wildlife Services)
Widmeyer, Denise
Wiebe, Menno
  (Mennonite Central Committee)
Wikstrom, Janet
  (Manitoba Family Services,
  Child and Family Services)
Wilkie, Dr. Clarke
Williams, Stan
Williamson, Norman
Wilson, Gail
Witchard, Evelyn
  (POWER [Prostitutes and Other
  Women for Equal Rights])
Wolch, E. Hersh
Wood, Aime
Wood, Ambrose
Wood, Anthony
  (Awasis Child and Family Services)
Wood, Bernard
Wood, Cathy
Wood, Daniel
Wood, Reverend Ellen
  (Parkland Crisis Centre)
Wood, Harry
Wood, Jack
Wood, Jeremiah

Wood, Jerry
Wood, Joe Guy
   (Island Lake Tribal Council)
Wood, John
Wood, Chief Ken
   (Assembly of Manitoba Chiefs)
   (Island Lake Tribal Council)
   (St. Theresa Point Indian Band)
Wood, Lillian
Wood, Martin
Wood, Morris
Wood, Moses
Wood, Philip
Wood, Robert
Wood, Sandra
Wood, William
Woodhouse, Allan
   (Native Brotherhood Organization,
   Stony Mountain Correctional
   Institution)
Wright, Joan
   (Nickel Belt News)
Yalden, Max
   (Canadian Human Rights
   Commission)
Yard, Doug
   (Legal Aid Services Society)
Yassie, Ivan
Yassie, Peter
Yellowback, Thelma
Yellowquill, Peter
Yellowquill, Sheila
York, Heather
Young, Chief Frank
   (Bloodvein Indian Band)
Young, Gloria
Young, Harvey
Young, Isabel
Young, John
Young, Ken
   (Canadian Bar Association)
Young, Leonard
Young, Louis
Young, Mary
Young, Thomas
Zoldy, Grace

Written Presentations from Persons Who Did Not Appear at The Hearings

Alexander, Carl Ingram
Armstrong, Jack and Glenda
Arsenault, Lillian
Beaulieu, Leo
Bennett, Charles
Borovoy, Alan
Braid, Arthur E.
Brass, Elizabeth
Burmaster Ellie
Burrows, Christine
Burrows, Teresa
Bushman, The
Christianson, Bjorn
Clarke, Mary Anne
Concerned Citizens Committee of
   Winnipeg
Culhane, Claire
Daniels, Ernie
   (Dakota Ojibway Tribal Council)
Dawson, Roy W.
   (Dauphin Bar Association)
Dillabaugh, Vern
Duncan, Jean
Dychko, Stan
Eaglehunt, Brenda
Grant, Agnes
Green, Mary
Greyeyes, Robert
Keam, Charles
Kennedy, Anita
King, Carol
Krocker, Fred
Langen-Jones, Rhys Wm.
LaRocque, Emma
Lavosseur, William
Lewis, Errol
Lofters, Peter
Mallea, Paula
Marchand, Barry
Martin, A.
Maytwayashing, M. A.
McCue, H. A.
McKay, Ralph
Michelle, Roderick

Miller, James
O'Berten, William
Penner, Harry
Philips, Glen
Randeree, Dr. S.A.
Saunders, Fred
Schwartz, Bryan
Shillington, Mary
  (Child and Family Services of
  Western Manitoba)
Spence, Zelda
Stevens, Richard
Swan, Lawrence
Volek, Ed
Webster, William
Whyte, Helen
Wiklund, Ray
Wilson, Bob
Winther, Neil
Yerex, Roy

Organizations That Presented at Community Hearings

Aboriginal Peoples Brotherhood
Agassiz Youth Centre
Anishinaabe Child and Family Services
Anishinaabe Respect
Assembly of First Nations
Assembly of Manitoba Chiefs
Awasis Child and Family Services
Berens River Indian Band
Bloodvein Indian Band
Brokenhead Indian Band
Brokenhead Mental Health
  Steering Committee
Canada, Government of
  Canadian Human Rights Commission
  Environment Canada,
    Canadian Wildlife Services
  Indian Affairs and Northern
    Development Canada
  Justice Canada
  Solicitor-General Canada,
    National Parole Board
  Solicitor-General Canada,
    Stony Mountain
    Correctional Institution

Canadian Alliance in Solidarity
  with Native Peoples
Canadian Bar Association,
  Aboriginal Law Section
Charter of Rights Coalition
Chemawawin Indian Band
Child Advocacy Project
Child and Family Services of
  Central Winnipeg
Churchill Indian Band
City of Winnipeg Police Department
City of Winnipeg Race Relations
  Committee
Community Dispute Centre
Community Legal Education
  Association
Concerned Citizens for Equality
Conference of Mennonites of Canada,
  Native Ministries
Cross Cultural Consulting Services
Cross Lake Indian Band
Cross Lake Justice Committee
Dakota Ojibway Child and
  Family Services
Dakota Ojibway Probation Services
Dakota Ojibway Tribal Council
Dakota Ojibway Tribal Council, NADAP
Dakota Ojibway Tribal Council,
  Social Services
Dakota Ojibway Tribal Council Police
Dakota Ojibway Tribal Council Police,
  Sioux Valley
Dakota Oyate Lodge
Dakota Rehab Centre, NADAP
Dakota Tipi Indian Band
Dauphin Friendship Centre
Dauphin River Indian Band
Elizabeth Fry Society
Fairford Indian Band
Fort Alexander Indian Band
Garden Hill Indian Band
George Guimond Care Centre Inc.
God's Lake Narrows Indian Band
God's River Indian Band
Grand Rapids Indian Band
Hollow Water Indian Band
Hollow Water Resource Group

Ikwewak Justice Society
Indian and Metis Friendship Centre
of Winnipeg
Indian Council of First Nations
of Manitoba
Indigenous Women's Collective
Inmate Welfare Committee, Stony
Mountain Correctional Institution
Interlake Tribal Council
Island Lake Tribal Council
Jackhead Indian Band
John Howard Society
Journey Education Association
Kahnawake Nation
Keewatin Tribal Council
KLINC Inc.
Knowles Centre
Lake Manitoba Indian Band
League for Human Rights of B'nai Brith
of Canada
Little Grand Rapids Indian Band
Little Saskatchewan Indian Band
Long Plain Indian Band
Lord Selkirk School Division,
Continuing Education Divison
Lynn Lake Friendship Centre
Ma Mawi Chi Itata Centre Inc.
Ma Mawi Chi Itata Centre Inc.,
Bail Supervision Program
Ma-Wow-We-Tok Centre
Manitoba Action Committee on
the Status of Women
Manitoba Adolescent Treatment Centre
Manitoba Association for
Continuing Education
Manitoba Association for Rights
and Liberties
Manitoba Bar Association,
Criminal Justice Subsection
Manitoba Coalition Against Apartheid
Manitoba Correctional
Chaplains Association
Manitoba Defence Lawyers Association
Manitoba Keewatinowi Okimakanak
Manitoba Metis Federation
Child and Family Services
Moose Lake Local

Northwest Region
Saint Laurent Local
The Pas
The Pas, Fine Option Program
Manitoba, Government of
Legal Aid Services Society
Manitoba Advisory Council on
the Status of Women
Manitoba Family Services
Manitoba Human Rights
Commission
Manitoba Justice
Manitoba Natural Resources
Manitoba Women's Directorate
Mathias Colomb Indian Band
Mathias Colomb Indian Band,
Treaty Land Entitlement Committee
Mediation Services
Mennonite Central Committee
Mennonite Central Committee,
Open Circle Program
Moose Lake Indian Band
Native Brotherhood Organization,
Headingley Correctional Institution
Native Brotherhood Organization,
Stony Mountain Correctional
Institution
Native Clan Organization
Native Council of Canada
Native Counselling Services of Alberta
Native Women's Transition Centre
North End Women's Centre
Northern Association of
Community Councils
Northlands Indian Band
Northwest Child and Family Services
Northwest Metis Council
Norway House Indian Band
Norway House Youth Council
Nova House
Oak Lake Indian Band
Oblates of Mary Immaculate
Opasquia Women's Association
Outreach Program, Sioux Valley Reserve
Oxford House Indian Band
Parkland Crisis Centre
Peguis Indian Band
Peguis Justice Committee

Pembina Anishinaabe
Poplar River Indian Band
POWER
(Prostitutes and Other Women
for Equal Rights)
Project Opikihiwawin
RCMP
Aboriginal Policing Directorate
Emerson
Gypsumville
Lac du Bonnet
Lynn Lake
Planning Branch
Powerview
Shamattawa
Staffing and Personnel
The Pas
Thompson Subdivision
Virden
Winnipeg
RCMP Public Complaints Commission
Red Sucker Lake Indian Band
Rosaire House
Roseau River Indian Band
Rossbrook House Inc.
Sagkeeng Child and Family Services
Sagkeeng Education Foundation Inc.
St. Theresa Point Indian Band
Sandy Bay Indian Band
Shamattawa Indian Band
Sioux Valley Indian Band
Southeast Child and Family Services
Southeast Resource Development
Council
Southeast Resource Tribal Council,
NADAP
Split Lake Indian Band
Swampy Cree Tribal Council
The Pas Indian Band
The Pas Indian Band, Youth Council
Thompson Crisis Centre
Treaty and Aboriginal Rights
Research Centre
Treaty Land Entitlement Committee
United Church of Canada
United Church of Canada,
Native United Church

University of Manitoba,
School of Social Work
University of Saskatchewan,
Native Law Centre
Urban Indian Association
War Lake Indian Band
Wasagamack Indian Band
West Region Child and Family Services
Winnipeg Council of Treaty and
Status Indians
Winnipeg Native Probation Caucus
Women's Post-Treatment Centre
Yellowquill College
Zeebeequa Society of
Roseau River Women

Appendix V

Staff and Consultants

Executive Secretary
Tom McMahon

Co-ordinating Editor
Ed Reed

Commission Counsel
Perry Schulman, Q. C.
Randy McNicol, Q. C.

*Special Assistant to
Commissioner Sinclair*
Diane Gielis

*Special Assistant to
Commissioner Hamilton*
Phil Lancaster

Hearings Coordinators
Jeannie Daniels
Eric Robinson

Editorial Staff
Kathi Avery
Jane Curran
Dan David
Professor Gerald Friesen
John Hylton
Professor Rick Linden
Tim Sale
Pat Sanders
Doug Smith

Director of Research
Brad Morse
  Professor of Law,
  University of Ottawa

Senior Research Officer
Doris Young

Researchers
Harry Daniels
Renée Fossett
Laurie Messer
Peter Sawatzky
Eileen Shewchuk

Law Students
Loretta Kocsis
Sean Kocsis

Summer Students
Anita Bedard
Myles Courchene
Trisha Delormier
Chris Hackett
Paul Hackett
Deborah Hanly
Don Langford
Daphne van der Put
Jennifer Yarnell

Transcript Summaries
Michele Fitzgerald

Office Managers
Darlene Black
Maryanne Boulton

Support Staff
Louise Bombay
Della Cummer
Marie Lands
Michele Nabozniak
Laura Pompana
Glenna Redsky

Librarians
Wanda Chandler
Lynn Innerst
Dennis Stoesz

*Staff at Osborne and
Harper Hearings*
Nick Blanchard
Bill Miscavish
Ben Moroz
Allan Rouse

Photographs
Jeff Thomas

Poster Design
Joe Mercredi

Consultants

Professors Freda
Ahenakew, Cecil
King,Catherine Littlejohn

Animus Research
Associates

Angus Reid and Associates

Canadian Institute for Law
and the Family

Professor Paul Chartrand

Scott Clark

Professor James Crawford

Cross-Cultural
Consulting Inc.

Dansys Consultants

Professor Jim Dumont

Indigenous Women's
Collective

Jack King

Professor John Milloy

A.R.A. Consultants

Peat Marwick Stevenson &
Kellogg

Professor Doug Sanders

Professor Sam Stevens

Touche Ross

Westarc Group

Other Research Assistance

Professor Dennis Bracken

Stan Cohen

Barb Hendrickson

Professor Peter Hudson

Professor Michael Jackson

Professor Len Kaminski

Professor Rod Kueneman

Melanie Lautt

Law Reform Commission
of Canada

Prairie Research Associates

Rick Sloan

Joy Waters

Tribal Court Symposium

Ralph Johnson,
Professor of Law, University of Washington

James Zion,
General Counsel, Navajo Housing Authority

Chief Judge Hilda Manuel,
Tohono O'odham Nation, Arizona

Chief Justice Don Dupuis,
Confederated Salish-Kootenai Tribal Court, Montana

Judge William A. Thorne Jr.,
3rd Circuit Court, Utah

Joe Myers, Executive Director,
National Indian Justice Centre

Senior Judge James Delaney,
Colorado Judicial District

Chief Judge William Johnson,
Umatilla Tribal Court, Oregon

Judge Wayne Cadman,
Navajo District Court

Chief Judge Elbridge Coochise,
Northwest Intertribal Court, Washington

Ed Martin, Court Administrator,
Judicial Branch of the Navajo Nation

Evelyn Stevenson,
Tribal Attorney, Confederated Salish-Kootenai Tribal
Court, Montana

Elders Conference

Jim Dumont

Jean Folster

Robin Green

Paul Huntinghawk

Eva McKay

Joe Roan

Mary Roberts

Edna Manitowabe

Art Solomon

Myrtle Thomas

Photo Credits